core
WEB
PROGRAMMING

MARTY HALL
LARRY BROWN

PH
PTR

Prentice Hall PTR, Upper Saddle River, NJ 07458
www.phptr.com

Sun Microsystems Press
A Prentice Hall Title

Library of Congress Cataloging-in-Publication Data

Hall, Marty.
   Core web programming / Marty Hall, Larry Brown.
      p. cm.
   Only Marty Hall's name appears on previous edition.
   Includes index.
   ISBN 0-13-089793-0
      1. Internet programming. 2. HTML (Document markup language) 3. Java (Computer
   program language) 4. CGI (Computer network protocol) 5. World Wide Web. I. Hall,
   Marty. II. Title.

   QA76.625 .B757 2001
   005.2'76--dc21

                                                                    2001021692

The publisher offers discounts on this book when ordered in bulk quantities.
For more information, contact Corporate Sales Department, Prentice Hall PTR ,
One Lake Street, Upper Saddle River, NJ 07458. Phone: 800-382-3419; FAX: 201- 236-7141.
E-mail: corpsales@prenhall.com.

Production Editor and Compositor: *Vanessa Moore*
Project Coordinator: *Anne Trowbridge*
Acquisitions Editor: *Gregory G. Doench*
Editorial Assistant: *Brandt Kenna*
Cover Design Director: *Jerry Votta*
Cover Designer: *Nina Scuderi*
Cover Illustration: *Karen Strelecki*
Art Director: *Gail Cocker-Bogusz*
Manufacturing Manager: *Alexis R. Heydt*
Marketing Manager: *Debby vanDijk*

Sun Microsystems Press:
Marketing manager: *Michael Llwyd Alread*
Publisher: *Rachel Borden*

10   9   8   7   6   5   4   3   2

ISBN 0-13-089793-0

Sun Microsystems Press
A Prentice Hall Title

Contents

CHAPTER 2
BLOCK-LEVEL ELEMENTS IN HTML 4.0   28

CHAPTER 3
TEXT-LEVEL ELEMENTS IN HTML 4.0   58

CHAPTER 4
FRAMES   88

CHAPTER 5
CASCADING STYLE SHEETS   114

PART 2
JAVA PROGRAMMING 158

CHAPTER 6
GETTING STARTED WITH JAVA 160

CHAPTER 7

OBJECT-ORIENTED PROGRAMMING IN JAVA   190

CHAPTER 8

BASIC JAVA SYNTAX   242

CHAPTER 9
APPLETS AND BASIC GRAPHICS   304

CHAPTER 10

JAVA 2D: GRAPHICS IN JAVA 2   358

CHAPTER 11

HANDLING MOUSE AND KEYBOARD EVENTS   398

CHAPTER 12
LAYOUT MANAGERS 426

CHAPTER 13
AWT COMPONENTS   466

CHAPTER 14
BASIC SWING   562

CHAPTER 15

ADVANCED SWING 628

CHAPTER 16
CONCURRENT PROGRAMMING WITH JAVA THREADS   698

CHAPTER 17
NETWORK PROGRAMMING   760

PART 3
SERVER-SIDE PROGRAMMING   830

CHAPTER 18
HTML FORMS   832

CHAPTER 19
SERVER-SIDE JAVA: SERVLETS   872

CHAPTER 21
USING APPLETS AS FRONT ENDS TO SERVER-SIDE PROGRAMS   1064

CHAPTER 22

JDBC 1092

CHAPTER 23
XML PROCESSING WITH JAVA 1132

PART 4
JAVASCRIPT 1188

CHAPTER 24
JAVASCRIPT: ADDING DYNAMIC CONTENT TO WEB PAGES 1190

CHAPTER 25
JAVASCRIPT QUICK REFERENCE   1274

Introduction

In late 1995, Marty Hall proposed a new course for the part-time graduate program in Computer Science at the Johns Hopkins University. The idea was to bring together the major Web-related topics in a single course dubbed "Distributed Development on the World Wide Web," with Java technology as a unifying theme. Students would look at HTML, Java, HTTP, CGI programming, and JavaScript, with lots of hands-on projects and no exams. Little did Marty know what he was getting himself into. By the time the first section was offered in the summer of 1996, the Java tidal wave had swept through the university and the companies that the students represented. Shortly after enrollment opened, the class was filled. There were more students on the waiting list than in the course. Marty got frantic phone calls from students insisting that they absolutely *had* to be in the course. Several local companies called, asking for on-site courses. What fun!

However, when Marty went shopping for texts over the next semester or two, he got a rude surprise. Despite the availability of good books in most of the individual areas he wanted to cover, Marty found that he needed three, four, or even five separate books to get good coverage of the overall material. Similarly, for his day job, Marty was constantly switching back and forth among the best of the huge stack of books he had accumulated and various on-line references. Surely there was a better way. Shouldn't it be possible to fit 85 percent of what professional programmers use in about 35 percent of the space, and get it all in one book?

That was the genesis of the first edition of *Core Web Programming*. The book was very popular, but the industry has been rapidly moving since the book's release. Browsers moved from HTML 3.2 to 4.0. The Java 2 platform was released, providing greatly improved performance and graphics libraries suitable for commercial-quality applications. JSP 1.0 came along, resulting in an explosion of interest in both servlets and JSP as an alternative to CGI and to proprietary solutions like ASP and Cold-Fusion. XML burst upon the scene. The server equalled or even surpassed the desktop as the biggest application area for the Java programming language.

Wow. And demand has only been growing since then. Although readers were clamoring for a new edition of the book, it was just too much for Marty to handle alone. Enter Larry Brown, with broad development and teaching experience in Java and Web technologies, and with particular expertise in the Java Foundation Classes, multithreaded programming, RMI, and XML processing with Java. Larry teamed up with Marty to totally update the existing material to HTML 4, CSS/1, HTTP 1.1, and the Java 2 platform; to replace the CGI sections with chapters on servlets 2.2 and JSP 1.1; and to add completely new sections on Swing, Java 2D, and XML processing with JAXP, DOM Level 2, SAX 2.0, and XSLT. They even got a little bit of sleep along the way.

We—Marty and Larry—hope you find the result enjoyable and useful!

Real Code for Real Programmers

This book is aimed at serious software developers. If you are looking for a book that shows you how to use a browser, lists the current hottest Web sites, and pontificates about how Web-enabled applications will revolutionize your business, you've come to the wrong place. If you're already a programmer of some sort and want to get started with HTML, XML, Java applets, desktop applications in Java, servlets, JavaServer Pages, and JavaScript as quickly as possible, this is the book for you. We illustrate the most important approaches and warn you of the most common pitfalls. To do so, we include plenty of working code: over 250 complete Java classes, for instance. We try to give detailed examples of the most important and frequently used features, summarize the lesser-used ones, and refer you to the API (available on-line) for a few of the rarely used ones.

DILBERT © UFS. Reprinted by permission.

A word of caution, however. Nobody becomes a great developer just by reading. *You* have to write some real code too. The more, the better. In each chapter, we suggest that you start by making a simple program or a small variation of one of the examples given, then strike off on your own with a more significant project. Skim the sections you don't plan on using right away, then come back when you are ready to try them out.

If you do this, you should quickly develop the confidence to handle the real-world problems that brought you here in the first place. You should be able to balance the demand for the latest features in Web pages with the need for multiplatform support. You should be comfortable with frames, style sheets, and layered HTML. You should be able to make portable stand-alone graphical applications. You should have no qualms about developing Web interfaces to your corporate database through JDBC. You should be able to connect these applications to remote systems over the network. You should understand how to easily distribute computation among multiple threads, or even spin it off to separate systems by using RMI. You should be able to decide where servlets apply well, where JSP is better, and where a combination is best. You should understand HTTP 1.1 well enough to use its capabilities to enhance the effectiveness of your pages. You should be able to spin off complex server-side behaviors into JavaBeans components or custom JSP tag libraries. You should be able to use JavaScript to validate HTML forms or to animate Web pages. You should get a raise. A big one, preferably.

How This Book Is Organized

This book is divided into four parts: HTML, Java programming, server-side programming, and JavaScript.

Part 1: The HyperText Markup Language

Web pages are created with HTML, the HyperText Markup Language. HTML lets you mix regular text with special tags that describe the content, layout, or appearance of the text. These tags are then used by Web browsers like Netscape Navigator or Microsoft Internet Explorer to format the page. This first part of the book covers the following topics in HTML.

- **HTML 4.01.** Full coverage of all the elements in the latest official HTML standard. Hypertext links, fonts, images, tables, client-side image maps, and more.

- **Major Netscape and Internet Explorer extensions.** Forwarding pages, using custom colors and font faces, embedding audio, video, and ActiveX components.

- **Frames.** Dividing the screen into rectangular regions, each associated with a separate HTML document. Borderless frames. Floating frames. Targeting frame cells from hypertext links.
- **Cascading style sheets.** Level-one style sheets for customizing fonts, colors, images, text formatting, indentation, lists, and more.

Part 2: Java Programming

Java is a powerful general-purpose programming language that can be used to create stand-alone programs as well as ones that are embedded in Web pages. The following Java topics are covered.

- **Unique features of Java.** What's different about Java? The truth about Java myths and hype.
- **Object-oriented programming in Java.** Variables, methods, constructors, overloading, and interfaces. Modifiers in class declarations. Packages, the CLASSPATH, and JAR files.
- **Java syntax.** Primitive types, operators, strings, vectors, arrays, input/output and the Math class.
- **Graphics.** Applets. Applications. Drawing, color, font, and clipping area operations. Loading and drawing images. Java Plug-In.
- **Java 2D.** Creating professional, high-quality 2D graphics. Creating custom shapes, tiling images, using local fonts, creating transparent shapes, and transforming coordinates.
- **Mouse and keyboard events.** Processing events. Event types, event listeners, and low-level event handlers. Inner classes. Anonymous classes.
- **Layout managers.** FlowLayout, BorderLayout, GridLayout, CardLayout, GridBagLayout, and BoxLayout. Positioning components by hand. Strategies for using layout managers effectively.
- **AWT components.** Canvas, Panel, Applet, ScrollPane, Frame, Dialog, FileDialog, and Window. Component and Container. Buttons, check boxes, radio buttons, combo boxes, list boxes, textfields, text areas, labels, scrollbars, and pop-up menus. Saving and loading windows with object serialization.
- **Basic Swing components.** Building Swing applets and applications. Changing the GUI look and feel. Adding custom borders to components. Using HTML in labels and buttons. Sending dialog alerts for user input. Adding child frames to applications. Building custom toolbars. Implementing a Web browser in Swing.
- **Advanced Swing.** JList, JTree, and JTable. Using custom data models and renderers. Printing Swing components. Updating Swing components in a thread-safe manner.

- **Multithreaded programming.** Threads in separate or existing objects. Synchronizing access to shared resources. Grouping threads. Multithreaded graphics and double buffering. Animating images. Controlling timers.
- **Network programming.** Clients and servers using sockets. The URL class. Implementing a generic network server. Creating a simple HTTP server. Invoking distributed objects with RMI.

Part 3: Server-Side Programming

Programs that run on a Web server can generate dynamic content based on client data. Servlets are Java technology's answer to CGI programming and JSP is Java's answer to Active Server Pages or ColdFusion. The following server-side topics are discussed.

- **HTML forms.** Sending data from forms. Text controls. Push buttons. Check boxes and radio buttons. Combo boxes and list boxes. File upload controls. Server-side image maps. Hidden fields. Tab ordering.
- **Java servlets.** The advantages of servlets over competing technologies. Servlet life cycle. Servlet initialization parameters. Accessing form data. Using HTTP 1.1 request headers, response headers, and status codes. Using cookies in servlets. Session tracking.
- **JavaServer Pages (JSP).** The benefits of JSP. JSP expressions, scriptlets, and declarations. Using JavaBeans components with JSP. Creating custom JSP tag libraries. Combining servlets and JSP.
- **Using applets as servlet front ends.** Sending GET and POST data. HTTP tunneling. Using object serialization to exchange high-level data structures between applets and servlets. Bypassing the HTTP server altogether.
- **Java Database Connectivity (JDBC).** The seven basic steps in connecting to databases. Some utilities that simplify JDBC usage. Formatting a database result as plain text or HTML. An interactive graphical query viewer. Precompiled queries.
- **XML processing with Java.** Representing an entire XML document by using the Document Object Model (DOM) Level 2. Responding to individual XML parsing events with the Simple API for XML Parsing (SAX) 2.0. Transforming XML with XSLT. Hiding vendor-specific details with the Java API for XML Processing (JAXP).

Part 4: JavaScript

JavaScript is a scripting language that can be embedded in Web pages and interpreted as the pages are loaded. The final part covers the following Java-Script topics.

- **JavaScript syntax.** Fields, methods, functions, strings, objects, arrays, and regular expressions.
- **Customizing Web pages.** Adapting to different browsers, JavaScript releases, and screen sizes.
- **Making pages dynamic.** Animating images. Manipulating layers. Responding to user events.
- **Validating HTML forms.** Checking form entries as they are changed. Checking data when form is submitted.
- **Handling cookies.** Reading and setting values. The `Cookie` object.
- **Controlling frames.** Sending results to specific frames. Preventing documents from being framed. Updating multiple frame cells. Giving frame cells the focus automatically.
- **Integrating Java and JavaScript.** `LiveConnect` and the `JSObject` class.
- **JavaScript quick reference.** Major classes in JavaScript 1.2. All fields, methods, and event handlers. `Document`, `Window`, `Form`, `Element`, `String`, `Math`, `RegExp`, and so forth.

Conventions

Throughout the book, concrete programming constructs or program output is presented in a monospaced font. For example, when abstractly describing Java programs that can be embedded in Web pages, we refer to "applets," but when we refer to `Applet` we are talking about the specific Java class from which all applets are derived.

User input is indicated in boldface, and command-line prompts are either generic (`Prompt>`) or indicate the operating system to which they apply (`Unix>`). For instance, the following indicates that "`Some  Output`" is the result when "`java SomeProgram`" is executed.

```
Prompt> java SomeProgram
Some Output
```

Important standard techniques are indicated by specially marked entries, as in the following example.

Core Approach

Pay particular attention to items in "Core Approach" sections. They indicate techniques that should always or almost always be used.

Notes and warnings are called out in a similar manner.

About the Web Site

The book has a companion Web site at

> `http://www.corewebprogramming.com/`

This free site includes:

- Documented source code for all examples shown in the book; this code can be downloaded for unrestricted use.
- On-line versions of all HTML pages, Java applets, and JavaScript examples.
- Links to all URLs mentioned in the text of the book.
- Information on book discounts.
- Reports on Java short courses.
- Book additions, updates, and news.
- A free Ronco combination paring knife and e-commerce tool. OK, maybe not.

About the Authors

Marty Hall is a Senior Computer Scientist in the Research and Technology Development Center at the Johns Hopkins University Applied Physics Lab, where he specializes in the application of Java and Web technology to customer problems. He also teaches Java and Web programming in the Johns Hopkins part-time graduate program in Computer Science, where he directs the Distributed Computing and Web Technology concentration areas. When he gets a chance, he also teaches industry short courses on servlets, JavaServer Pages, and other Java technology areas. He is the author of *Core Servlets and JavaServer Pages* and the first edition of *Core Web Programming*. Marty can be reached at the following address:

> *Research and Technology Development Center*
> *The Johns Hopkins University Applied Physics Laboratory*
> *11100 Johns Hopkins Road*
> *Laurel, MD 20723*
> *hall@corewebprogramming.com*

Larry Brown is a Senior Network Engineer at the Naval Surface Warfare Center, Carderock Division, where he specializes in developing and deploying network and Web solutions in an enterprise environment. He is also a Computer Science faculty member at the Johns Hopkins University, where he teaches server-side programming, distributed Web programming, and Java user interface development for the part-time graduate program in Computer Science. Larry can be reached at the following address:

Naval Surface Warfare Center, Carderock Division
9500 MacArthur Boulevard
West Bethesda, MD 20817
brown@corewebprogramming.com

Acknowledgments

Many people have helped us out with this book. Without their assistance, we would still be on the fourth chapter. Those that provided valuable technical feedback, pointed out errors, and gave useful suggestions include Don Aldridge, Chris Bennett, Camille Bell, Pete Clark, Maria Dimalanta, Nguyen-Khoa Duy, Denise Evans, Amy Karlson, Paul McNamee, Toddi Norum, Walter Pasquinni, Rich Slywczak, Bob Tinker, and Kim Topley. This book would not be a success without their contributions. Mary Lou "Eagle Eye" Nohr spotted our errant commas, awkward sentences, typographical errors, and grammatical inconsistencies. She improved the result immensely. We hope that we learned from her advice. Vanessa Moore produced the final version; she did a great job despite our last-minute changes and crazy travel schedules. Ralph Semmel and Julie Wessel both provided supportive work environments and flexible schedules. Greg Doench of Prentice Hall believed in a second edition and encouraged us to write the book. Thanks to all.

Most of all, I–Marty–thank B.J., Lindsay, and Nathan for their patience with my long hours and funny schedule. I–Larry–thank Lee for her loving support and patience while I disappeared to the computer room every weekend.

God has blessed us both with great families.

Part **1**

THE HYPERTEXT
MARKUP LANGUAGE

DESIGNING WEB PAGES WITH HTML 4.0

Topics in This Chapter

- An overview of the HyperText Markup Language

- Comparison of HTML 4.0 with other HTML specifications

- Validation of HTML documents

- The process of creating and publishing a Web page

- The fundamental structure of HTML documents

- Common elements in the header of an HTML document

- Inclusion of keyword information for search engines

- Use of the BODY tag to set up the basic look of the page

Chapter

T his is the first of five chapters that cover the HyperText Markup Language (HTML). Together, they teach you the techniques for creating professional Web pages. This first chapter examines the underlying structure of an HTML document, and the remaining four chapters cover additional topics for building quality Web pages, including block-level elements, text-level elements, frames, and cascading style sheets. Once you've learned these basics, the remainder of *Core Web Programming* covers advanced topics like Java applets, sockets, database connectivity, Java servlets, JavaServer Pages (JSP), and processing XML. All of these technologies are critical in developing quality Web sites.

The history of the HyperText Markup Language is briefly covered in this chapter, followed by the steps necessary to create and publish a WWW page. We then focus on the general structure of Web pages, describe which HTML elements are required in all documents, and explain how to specify settings that affect the document as a whole. In addition, we show you how to validate your Web page as legal HTML and how to record information in your Web page for use by search engines.

1.1   The HyperText Markup Language

Web pages are created with the HyperText Markup Language, which lets you mix regular text with "markup" tags describing the text. These tags can describe the *appearance* (display this in red) or *layout* (arrange the following in a 3-row, 4-column table) of the text, but the majority simply describe the *content* (this is a main heading) and leave many of the appearance and layout decisions to the browser. For example, Listing 1.1 shows the HTML document used to create the Web page shown in Figure 1–1. For now, don't worry about the details of each of the HTML elements; they are discussed in detail in the rest of Part 1 of this book. However, even at first glance you can pick out some basic features, such as the mix of regular text and elements enclosed in angle brackets and that some but not all the elements come in pairs of the form <NAME> and </NAME>.

The Web page shown in Figure 1–1 is the result for a particular browser (Internet Explorer 5.0) on a particular operating system (Windows 2000 Professional) with the browser and desktop preferences (font face, size, and color) set by the user. In addition to honoring user customizations, browsers usually have wide latitude in how they implement the various types of elements, and authors who try to enforce an exact appearance for pages that will be viewed by multiple browsers often end up frustrated. In Chapter 5 (Cascading Style Sheets), you will see a new standard that gives authors a high degree of control over the final look of their pages. But even with style sheets, authors of general Web pages should realize that they cannot control all aspects of the final appearance of their page.

Listing 1.1   An HTML document for a simple home page

```
<!DOCTYPE HTML PUBLIC "-//W3C//DTD HTML 4.0 Transitional//EN">
<HTML>
<HEAD>
  <Title>Home Page for Lawrence M. Brown</Title>
</HEAD>
<BODY BGCOLOR="WHITE">
<H1 ALIGN="CENTER">Home Page for Lawrence M. Brown</H1>
<HR>
<IMG SRC="images/navsea-nswc.gif" WIDTH=300 HEIGHT=117
     HSPACE=10 VSPACE=5 ALIGN="LEFT" ALT="NSWC Logo">
Senior Network Engineer<BR>
<A HREF="http://www.dt.navy.mil/">
Naval Surface Warfare Center</A><BR>
9500 MacArthor Boulevard<BR>
West Bethesda, Maryland, MD 20817-5700<BR>
<I>email:</I> <A HREF="mailto:larry@corewebprogramming.com">
larry@corewebprogramming.com</A><BR>
<I>Phone:</I> (301) 277-4648<BR CLEAR="ALL">
<P>
This is my personal home page. For more specific
programming-related resources pages, please see:
<!-- Rest of Sample Page Deleted -->
</BODY>
</HTML>
```

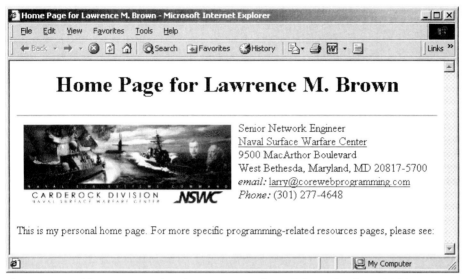

Figure 1–1 This page, rendered in Internet Explorer 5.0 on Windows 2000 Professional, is the result of the document in Listing 1.1.

Core Note

Trying to enforce an exact look for pages that will be viewed by people using a variety of browsers will only lead to frustration.

The page design issue is further complicated because Web browsers are not the only type of programs that use HTML documents. A variety of applications can display, print, index, or even synthesize speech based on an HTML document. In this book, however, we concentrate on how HTML documents are used by WWW browsers.

1.2 HTML 4.0 and Other HTML Standards

Along with browser issues, to a lesser degree, authors must also contend with changes in the HTML specification. Until January 1997, HTML 2.0, introduced by the World Wide Web Consortium (W3C), was the most up-to-date standard available. The HTML 2.0 specification describes the capabilities supported by most browsers as of mid-1994. Even before the HTML 2.0 was published, work was under way to define the next-generation specification, known first as HTML+ and later as HTML 3.0. Unfortunately, the vendors that emerged as the dominant players in the Web browser world could not agree on supporting HTML 3.0, and the effort was dropped. Instead, HTML 3.2 (originally code-named "Wilbur"), an intermediate specification, was drafted. Perhaps the specification should have been called "HTML 2.3," because it actually supports fewer features than HTML 3.0. Soon afterwards, in December of 1997, HTML 4.0 became the standard of choice.

Technically, no current browsers completely support the HTML 4.0 specification. However, Netscape 4.0 and later, as well as Internet Explorer 4.0 and later, are mostly compliant with HTML 4.0 specification (release 3.x of those browsers supports only HTML 3.2). Compared to HTML 3.2, the major changes in HTML 4.0 include:

- Addition of document frames
- A preference for style sheets instead of formatting elements and attributes
- Improved cell alignment and row/column grouping in tables
- Mouse and keyboard events for nearly *all* elements
- Internationalization features
- Improved support for nonvisual browsers

Since the HTML 4.0 standard was accepted in 1997, the W3C introduced HTML 4.01, which fixes a few typographical errors and adds a couple of omitted attributes. The HTML 4.01 specification was accepted by the W3C on December 24, 1999. More importantly, the new XHTML 1.0 specification, designed to support XML in Web pages, heavily relies on the HTML 4.01 specification for the meaning of the HTML tags. XML allows you to identify unique structures in your document and to define your own markup formats for the identified structures. XML is beneficial to rich data formats common to e-commerce transactions, vector graphics, and application servers. XML is discussed in Chapter 23 (XML Processing with Java). The XHTML 1.0 specification became official on January 26, 2000.

The official HTML on-line specifications are available from the following locations:

HTML 4.01
```
http://www.w3.org/TR/html401/
```

HTML 4.0
```
http://www.w3.org/TR/1998/REC-html40-19980424/
```

HTML 3.2
```
http://www.w3.org/TR/REC-html32.html
```

XHTML 1.0
```
http://www.w3.org/TR/xhtml1/
```

HTML supported by Netscape
```
http://developer.netscape.com/library/documentation/htmlguid/
index.htm
```

HTML supported by Internet Explorer
```
http://msdn.microsoft.com/workshop/author/html/reference/
elements.asp
```

1.3 Steps to Publish a Document on the Web

Three main steps are involved in posting a document to the WWW:

1. Create an HTML document.
2. Place the document in a Web-accessible location.
3. Verify that the HTML is legal and results in the presentation you had in mind.

These steps are explained more thoroughly in the following sections.

Create the Document

Since HTML is formed with normal ASCII text, you can create an HTML document with a text editor, such as Notepad, UltraEdit, emacs, or BBEdit. You can also create documents with an HTML editor, such as HomeSite, FrontPage, or Dreamweaver, or by using a utility that converts an existing word processor document to HTML, such as Microsoft Word or WordPerfect. Since HTML is primarily a logical markup language, not a page layout language, automatically converting a word processor document to HTML often results in a Web page that differs somewhat from the original and requires some hand tuning.

Similarly, because browsers are allowed significant flexibility in how they display many HTML elements and because users can select their preferred fonts and colors, a "WYSIWYG" (What You See Is What You Get) HTML editor is not strictly possible, at least in the absence of cascading style sheets (Chapter 5). Of course, an author could always tailor the display to the default look of a particular browser. Nevertheless, HTML editors are a big timesaver: many let you visually lay out tables and frames; most even support style sheets. If you do use an HTML editor, you will want one that allows you to directly edit the HTML if desired, because you will inevitably want to use some capability not supported by a purely graphical HTML editor. In all cases, once the Web page is created, you will want to check the syntax and appearance before posting on a Web server.

Put the Document on the Web

To be accessible to other Internet users, your document needs to be on a computer that is connected to the Internet and running an HTTP server. If you don't already have Internet access through a work or school system or through a commercial Internet Service Provider (ISP), "The List" (`http://thelist.internet.com/`) gives information on thousands of ISPs throughout the world. Some authors create their Web pages on the same machine from which the pages will be accessed. This approach is common for work and university computers. Frequently, however, authors create the pages on a home or office PC and then upload the page to the server machine. In this latter case, authors need to be sure that they upload to an accessible location. This process is discussed in the following subsections.

Create a Directory for the File

The computer hosting your Web page will be running an HTTP server. HTTP, the HyperText Transfer Protocol, is discussed in more detail in Chapter 19 (Server-Side Java: Servlets). For now, you only need to know that HTTP is the protocol by which WWW *clients* (browsers) talk to systems that are hosting Web pages. The program that answers the client's request for files is the HTTP *server*. This server takes the URL (Uniform Resource Locator, which is the Web "address") specified by the client and translates the URL into a specific filename on the server's system. Typically, when a client requests a file from a user's directory, the server looks in a subdirectory such as `public_html` or www that is not listed in the URL but is part of the real location of the file. The webmaster or system administrator on the machine or ISP you are using can give the definitive name.

Often, Web sites are leased through an ISP and authors use FTP to access the ISP's server to post their Web pages. Typically, the ISP administrator sets up the initial directory structure for your Web site before giving you an account and password. Other users, especially in a corporate or academic setting, may already have an account on a Web server. For a Unix-based Web server, the user must first create a Web-accessible directory (often `public_html` or www) with the `mkdir` command and then post the Web pages to the directory created.

For instance, suppose that user `janedoe` wants to publish a page named `test.html` on the system `www.some-isp.com`. In such a case, she would put the document in `/home/janedoe/public_html/test.html`, assuming that her home directory is `/home/janedoe` and that `public_html` is the "hidden" directory name used by her Web server. Outsiders could access the page by designating a URL of `http://www.some-isp.com/~janedoe/test.html`.

The symbol "~" is generally interpreted as "the home directory of." Some programs encode characters by their ASCII or ISO Latin-1 numbers, so you sometimes see "%7E" instead of "~". So, don't be confused if you see `http://some.host/%7Euser/path/`.

Put the File in That Directory

If you are working on the same system that is running the HTTP server, you will probably create your HTML documents directly in the target directory (e.g., `public_html`). If you create the document on a remote system that is on the Internet (e.g., via PPP or a direct connection), you can upload the file by using an FTP client such as `Fetch` on a Mac, `ftp.exe` from the main `Windows` directory on a Windows 95/98/2000/NT system, or `/usr/bin/ftp` on a Unix system. Remember that filenames are case sensitive on many operating systems.

In addition to a default hidden directory name, most HTTP servers also have a default filename that will be used if the URL specifies a directory but no filename. Some common defaults are `index.html`, `Welcome.html`, `default.html`, and variations ending in `.htm` instead of `.html`. For instance, Jane's home page might be `/home/janedoe/public_html/index.html` but could be accessed remotely simply by `http://www.some-isp.com/~janedoe/`. The URL listing the filename explicitly is also legal, for example, `http://www.some-isp.com/~janedoe/index.html`.

Set File and Directory Permissions

For the file to be accessible on the Web, the file and directory must be readable by the process running the HTTP server. This often means that they must be world readable because the HTTP server is typically run in an unprivileged mode. Many ISPs that use Unix set the proper permissions by default, so this step might not be necessary if you use a commercial service provider. Unix users can look at their `umask` to determine this setting. If it *is* necessary to set the permissions, the Unix incantation would be:

```
Unix> cd
Unix> chmod a+x .
Unix> cd public_html
Unix> chmod a+x .
Unix> chmod a+r file
```

Because Web browsers can display plain-text documents as well as HTML documents, a good first step is to create a simple file called `test.txt` that contains a single line like "`Hello`," put the file in the Web subdirectory of your account, and try to access the file with `http://your.isp.com/~your-account/test.txt`. If that works, you don't have to mess around with the cryptic file permission settings.

Validate the Document

Once you place a document on the Web, you want to check that the document has no syntax errors. Checking how the page looks in your Web browser is a good first step but is not sufficient. Browsers try to "guess" what to do when they see incorrect HTML, but different browsers may guess differently. So, if your HTML document contains errors, your browser might guess well and the page might still look fine. But the page might look completely different or have portions not display *at all* on other browsers. Because HTML is defined by the Standard Generalized Markup Language (SGML), a program can use the official SGML specification for HTML to verify that your document is conforming. Some HTML editors do this automatically, or you can submit the URL to a free on-line validator. The most popular validator is the W3C HTML Validation Service. In addition, several free or commercial validators can be installed on your local machine. See the following URLs for details:

The W3C HTML Validation Service
`http://validator.w3.org/`

The Web Design Group Validation Service
`http://www.htmlhelp.com/tools/validator/`

The W3C CSS Validation Service
`http://jigsaw.w3.org/css-validator/`

Core Approach

Trust, but verify: check the syntax of your Web pages with a formal HTML validator.

1.4   The Basic Structure of HTML Documents

HTML *elements* are indicated by markup *tags*, which are enclosed by angle brackets. For instance, `<TITLE>` is the starting tag for the `TITLE` element. The tags are not displayed in the resultant Web page but rather provide descriptive information to the browser. HTML elements can also have *attributes*, which supply additional information in the form *attribute=value*. For instance, in the tag `<IMG SRC="images/sample.gif">`, `images/sample.gif` is the *value* of the `SRC` *attribute* of the `IMG` *element*. Most nonalphanumeric characters in attribute values require you to have double quotes around the value, so a wise convention is to always enclose values in double quotes unless the value is a simple integer. All HTML element and attribute names are case insensitive, unlike the attribute values. Extra white space is ignored inside most parts of the document and around element names and attributes but may be significant inside attribute values. Interestingly, in the XHTML 1.0 specification, lowercase is required for elements, and all attributes, including numbers, must be enclosed in quotes. This follows the XML rules; see Chapter 23 (XML Processing with Java).

Some elements are *containers*, which have a start tag (e.g., `<BODY>`) and a corresponding end tag beginning with "`</`" (e.g., `</BODY>`). Other elements are stand-alone and only have a single tag (e.g., `<HR>`). If a browser does not recognize a given HTML element or attribute, then the browser simply ignores it. The browser does not ignore the regular text between unrecognized start and end tags; the browser ignores only the tags themselves. HTML comments are enclosed between `<!--` and `-->`, can span multiple lines, and should not contain a double hyphen (i.e., `--`) in the body of the comment.

HTML Document Template

HTML documents start with a `DOCTYPE` declaration that identifies the version of the HTML page to the browser or validation service. After the `DOCTYPE` statement is an HTML element that contains a HEAD element and a BODY element. The HEAD element must contain a TITLE element. The BODY element, immediately following the HEAD element, often starts with the largest-sized heading (H1), followed by the body of the Web page.

Strictly speaking, only the `DOCTYPE` and TITLE are required because HTML, HEAD, and BODY can be inferred by the parser. But in practice, the template shown is a recommended starting point for HTML documents, and a good idea is to keep a copy around to insert into new HTML documents if your text editor or HTML editor cannot be configured to insert the tags automatically.

Figure 1–2 shows a standard browser display of the HTML document template in Listing 1.2. The template is a good starting point for all HTML 4.0 documents (except those that use frames; see Chapter 4).

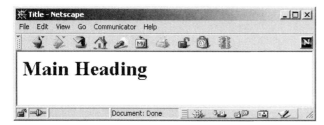

Figure 1–2 A standard HTML 4.0 template, as rendered in Netscape 4.7 on Windows 2000 Professional.

Listing 1.2 `HTML4.0-Template.html`

```
<!DOCTYPE HTML PUBLIC "-//W3C//DTD HTML 4.0 Transitional//EN">
<HTML>
<HEAD>
  <TITLE>Title</TITLE>
</HEAD>

<BODY>
<H1>Main Heading</H1>

<!-- Rest of page goes here -->

</BODY>
</HTML>
```

DOCTYPE Declarations

Depending on the content of the HTML document, one of three DOCTYPE declarations is possible:

Strict HTML 4.01 DOCTYPE

```
<!DOCTYPE HTML PUBLIC "-//W3C//DTD HTML 4.01//EN">
```

Transitional HTML 4.01 DOCTYPE

```
<!DOCTYPE HTML PUBLIC "-//W3C//DTD HTML 4.01
          Transitional//EN">
```

Frameset HTML 4.01 DOCTYPE

```
<!DOCTYPE HTML PUBLIC "-//W3C//DTD HTML 4.01 Frameset//EN">
```

If the document strictly conforms to the HTML 4.01 specification without the use of any deprecated or loosely defined elements and attributes, then add the *strict* DOCTYPE statement to the beginning of the HTML document. However, if the document uses deprecated elements (such as fonts and alignments defined outside of a style sheet) or links that target a FRAME, then the *transitional* DOCTYPE is appropriate. Elements that are deprecated are ones for which a better alternative now exists but are supported for backward compatibility with previous HTML versions. To determine which elements or attributes are deprecated in the HTML 4.01 standard, see the following two URLs:

Index of HTML 4.01 Elements

```
http://www.w3.org/TR/html4/index/elements.html
```

Index of HTML 4.01 Attributes

`http://www.w3.org/TR/html4/index/attributes.html`

If the HTML document defines a set of FRAMEs, then use the *Frameset* DOCTYPE.

Following is a detailed description of the HTML element and associated attributes. Throughout this book each HTML element is presented in a reference format clearly stating the syntax for the element, followed by a listing of the legal attributes. The start tag is shown first with all *required* attributes explicitly listed. Ellipses (. . .) expressed in the start tag indicate that additional material or optional attributes can also be present. The start tag is followed either by the end tag or a statement that no end tag is required for the element. The attributes listed after the element are presented in the order of their usage frequency in documents. Attributes not part of the HTML 4.0 specification but supported by Netscape or Internet Explorer are indicated as "nonstandard." Unless otherwise stated, each HTML element and attribute was tested in English versions of Netscape versions 4.08–4.7 and Internet Explorer versions 4.01–5.5.

HTML Element: <HTML ...> ... </HTML>
Attributes: LANG, DIR, VERSION

The HTML element immediately follows the DOCTYPE and represents a container holding the HEAD and BODY of the document. The HTML tag can optionally contain attributes stating the language of the document, the direction of the text, and the HTML version for the source. Technically, the HTML tags are optional because browsers can determine from the source text that the document is HTML. However, including the HTML tags is a good, standard practice.

LANG

LANG defines a language abbreviation to specify the base language of the text. Currently, browsers simply treat the LANG attributes as informational and do not change how the text is rendered. However, search engines and spell checkers can take advantage of the language code when examining the document. See RFC 1766 for a listing of language codes. You can access the official RFCs from one of the archieve sites listed at `http://www.rfc-editor.org/`.

DIR

DIR specifies the base direction of the text: LTR (left-to-right) or RTL (right-to-left). Internet Explorer supports the DIR attribute; however, depending on the underlying charset encoding, the displayed direction of ASCII characters will vary. Since this new attribute is not supported in Netscape, at least as of Netscape version 4.7, you should reserve DIR for intranets that use Internet Explorer exclusively.

Core Warning

Netscape does not support the DIR *attribute of the HTML element.*

VERSION

The VERSION attribute simply states the HTML version of the document. This information is redundant and rarely provided because the browser can determine the HTML version from the DOCTYPE statement. The VERSION attribute is technically deprecated in the HTML 4.0 standard.

The HTML specification adds LANG and DIR attributes to *all* HTML elements except APPLET, BASE, BASEFONT, BR, FRAME, FRAMESET, IFRAME, NOFRAMES, PARAM, and SCRIPT. The LANG and DIR attributes are not discussed separately for each HTML element.

1.5   HEAD—High-Level Information About the Page

HTML Element: <HEAD> ... </HEAD>
Attributes: PROFILE

The HEAD section is the first main section of an HTML document, coming immediately after the DOCTYPE declaration and the <HTML> start tag and just before the BODY section. The TITLE element is required and is often the only element inside the HEAD. The PROFILE attribute does not impact the browser presentation but does provide information for search engines and other user-agents (nonvisual browsers, index servers, development software). The PROFILE attribute specifies the URL of a file that provides additional information to search engines for parsing optional META data in the HEAD section (the META element is discussed later in this section). The HTML specification also defines LANG and DIR attributes for the HEAD element. These two attributes are discussed earlier in Section 1.4 on the HTML element.

Required HEAD Element

HTML Element: `<TITLE>` ... `</TITLE>`
Attributes: None

The `TITLE` element is required in all HTML 4.0 documents and consists of plain text with no other HTML tags. The title can, however, contain character or entity references such as `&copy;` to display © (see Table 2.1). This title normally appears on the bar on the top of the browser window and is typically used in the bookmarks (favorites) and browsing history lists. In addition, Netscape and Internet Explorer add the title of the document in the top banner of printed pages. However, the title does not appear in the main document itself, so should not be confused with the first main heading of the document, often informally viewed by readers as the "title." The HTML 4.0 specification adds `LANG` and `DIR` attributes to the `TITLE` element, but these attributes are not currently supported by Netscape or Internet Explorer. Any use of non-ASCII characters in the title simply results in the document filename being displayed as the title.

Optional HEAD Elements

In addition to the required `TITLE` element, a number of optional elements—`BASE`, `META`, `BGSOUND`, and `LINK`—are occasionally employed by advanced HTML authors. If you're just starting HTML, you're probably better off skipping this part until you have a handle on the more important and more frequently used elements.

HTML Element: `<BASE HREF="..."  ...>` (No End Tag)
Attributes: HREF (required), TARGET

The `BASE` element specifies the starting location for *relative URLs*, that is, incompletely specified URLs that give the filename without hostname or protocol. The default location is the directory from which the current document was loaded. If a document is copied to a different site but its supporting documents are not, the `BASE` entry can be used to make sure that relative URLs will still refer to correct locations. The `HREF` attribute explicitly states the location for all relative URLs. For example, suppose that `http://www.microsoft.com/windows2000/Buy-Win2000.html` is a document that the authors know will be mirrored at `www.apple.com` and `www.sun.com`. In such a case, authors could use a `HEAD` such as the following:

```
<HEAD>
  <TITLE>Why You Should Buy Windows 2000</TITLE>
  <BASE HREF="http://www.microsoft.com/windows2000/">
</HEAD>
```

You can also supply a `TARGET` attribute to display the selected link in a new browser window or, when you are using frames, the `TARGET` attribute can specify the default frame cell in which to display selected links. Authors commonly use `<BASE TARGET="..." >` (without the required `HREF` attribute) to direct all links on a page to the targeted frame cell. See the discussion of frames in Chapter 4 for more details.

HTML Element: `<META ...>` (No End Tag)

Attributes: NAME, CONTENT (required), HTTP-EQUIV, SCHEME

`META` elements can record document information, forward and refresh pages, and include sound files. The exact way in which `META` tags are used to record document information varies from system to system. However, most information in a `META` tag is defined by a `NAME-CONTENT` property pair, where the `NAME` identifies the property name and the `CONTENT` identifies the property value. Common entries used with `NAME` are `author` (person who wrote the document), `description` (brief summary), `keywords` (comma-separated descriptive words to be used by search engines), and `generator` (program that generated the document). Search engines such as Google, Infoseek, and Lycos use the `keywords` entry for their internal indexing (but ignore the entire entry if a word appears more than seven times) and use the `description` entry in lieu of the first part of the document itself when describing the document to the search engine user. The `META` tag is illustrated in Listing 1.3.

Listing 1.3   A sample HEAD section using META

```
<HEAD>
  <TITLE>Why You Should Buy Windows 2000</TITLE>
  <BASE HREF="http://www.microsoft.com/windows2000/">
  <META NAME="author" CONTENT="Bill Gates">
  <META NAME="keywords"
      CONTENT="Windows,Advocacy,OS,Operating Systems">
  <META NAME="description"
      CONTENT="A summary of the advantages of Windows 2000.">
</HEAD>
```

One use of `HTTP-EQUIV` is to set automatic refreshing or forwarding of pages by supplying the `Refresh` header. For instance, an on-line newspaper or magazine might have headlines that change periodically and should automatically update every 30 minutes (1800 seconds). Consider a fictional page located at `http://www.microsoft.com/windows2000/Buy-Win2000.html`. The third line of Listing 1.5 shows how `META` could automatically reload the same document by specifying `HTTP-EQUIV="Refresh"` and a `CONTENT` attribute that gives a time of 1800 seconds to reload the page (assuming that the reader remains on the same page for 30 minutes).

Listing 1.4   A Web page with automatic reloading every 30 minutes

```
<HEAD>
  <TITLE>Why You Should Buy Windows 2000</TITLE>
  <META HTTP-EQUIV="Refresh" CONTENT="1800">
</HEAD>
. . .
```

Instead of reloading the same page, an author might want a document to automatically send readers to a new location (see Listing 1.5). This could happen when the URL of a page has changed and the author wants to leave a forwarding address so that people connecting to the old URL get the new page after five seconds. To do this, use the `Refresh` value but specify a different URL than that of the current page. Be aware however, that on some browsers this breaks the Back button; clicking Back returns to the original page containing the `META` tag, which reforwards to where the users were before they clicked Back.

Listing 1.5   Forwarding to a new destination

```
<HEAD>
  <TITLE>Why You Should Buy Windows 2000 (New Address)</TITLE>
  <META HTTP-EQUIV="Refresh"
        CONTENT="5;
                 URL=http://www.apple.com/Buy-Win2000.html">
</HEAD>
. . .
```

Note: if the specified URL is a sound file in a format supported by the browser, this method will play the sound file on some browsers. Several browser-specific methods are also available for playing sound files. For instance, Internet Explorer supports the `BGSOUND` element (discussed next) and both Netscape and Internet Explorer support `EMBED` (Section 3.6, "Embedding Other Objects in Documents") for some types of sound files. But be cautious; many users consider it to be a bug, not a feature, when sound files begin playing automatically when users visit a site.

Core Approach

Rather than playing sound files automatically, inform users that a given link will play a sound file or give them a choice of using or not using sound.

HTTP-EQUIV can also define the encoding CHARSET to use when presenting the text in the browser or user-agent. For example, the following META tag indicates that all text should be resolved by the GB2312 Chinese charset (byte-sequence to character mapping):

```
<META HTTP-EQUIV="Content-type"
      CONTENT="text/html; CHARSET=GB2312">
```

ISO standards define character mappings for many languages. Interestingly, nearly all available charsets include the standard ASCII characters; thus, English text can be added to any document written in another language. However, if the document contains *multiple* languages, then the text should be expressed as 16-bit Unicode characters. A popular encoding of Unicode is UTF-8, where the encoding scheme transforms each 16-bit Unicode character into a variable byte sequence, with the ASCII characters requiring a single 8-bit byte. For additional information on Unicode for expressing multiple languages, see http://www.unicode.org/.

Note that you can assign any HTTP response header to HTTP-EQUIV where the CONTENT is the corresponding value for the HTTP header. HTTP-EQUIV is simply an HTML extension (that Netscape and Internet Explorer support) that effectively "sets" the response header without formal generation of the particular header as with servlets or CGI. See Chapter 19 (Server-Side Java: Servlets) for further details on HTTP headers.

The SCHEME attribute defines the format of a property value associated with a NAME-CONTENT pair in the META element. Again, the NAME identifies the property name, and the CONTENT identifies the property value. For example in

```
<META SCHEME="Month-Day-Year"
      NAME="Date"
      VALUE="05-01-2000">
```

the SCHEME attribute can clarify the format of a date property as SCHEME="Month-Day-Year" to distinguish the date from a European format of "Day-Month-Year".

Finally, aside from the use by search engines or other user-agents, the LANG and DIR attributes in a META element are ignored.

HTML Element: <BGSOUND SRC="..." ...> (No End Tag)
Attributes: SRC (required), LOOP

This is a nonstandard element supported by Internet Explorer for playing sound files. The BGSOUND element can appear in the BODY as well as the HEAD.

SRC
SRC specifies the URL of the sound file, which should be in .wav, .au, or MIDI format.

LOOP

`LOOP` specifies how many times the sound file will be repeated. The default is 1. Specifying a value of –1 or `INFINITE` will result in the sound file playing continuously while the page is open.

HTML Element: `<SCRIPT TYPE="..." ...> ... </SCRIPT>`
Attributes: LANGUAGE, SRC, TYPE (required), CHARSET, DEFER

`SCRIPT` is used for embedded programs, usually in JavaScript. See Chapter 24 (Java-Script: Adding Dynamic Content to Web Pages) for details.

HTML Element: `<STYLE TYPE="..." ...> ... </STYLE>`
Attributes: TYPE (required), TITLE, MEDIA

`STYLE` specifies cascading style sheets, an extremely useful and flexible capability that allows you to specify details about the fonts, colors, backgrounds, margins, and other features used for various elements in the document. See Chapter 5 for a discussion of style sheets.

HTML Element: `<LINK ...>` (No End Tag)
Attributes: HREF, REL, REV, TYPE, CHARSET, HREFLANG, MEDIA,
ONCLICK, ONDBLCLICK, ONMOUSEDOWN, ONMOUSEUP,
ONMOUSEOVER, ONMOUSEMOVE, ONMOUSEOUT,
ONKEYPRESS, ONKEYDOWN, ONKEYUP, TARGET, TITLE, ID,
CLASS, STYLE

The `LINK` element provides information on how the current document fits into a larger set of documents by specifying a table of contents location, the previous and next document in the series, an advisory title, and so forth. A `HEAD` section can contain more than one `LINK` element.

HREF, REL, REV

`HREF` defines the URL to the linked document. `REL` gives the relationship of the linked document to the current one; `REV` gives the reverse relationship, that of the current document to the specified one. The most common types of relationships are `CONTENTS`, `INDEX`, `GLOSSARY`, `HELP`, `NEXT`, and `PREVIOUS` for navigation, `MADE` for the document author, and `STYLESHEET` for links to cascading style sheets. For example:

```
<LINK REL=STYLESHEET
      HREF="My-Styles.css"
      TYPE="text/css">
```

TYPE, CHARSET, HREFLANG, MEDIA

TYPE defines the MIME type associated with the resource referenced by the link, as in TYPE="text/html". MIME types are described in RFC 1521 (see http://www.rfc-editor.org/ for an up-to-date list of RFC archive sites) and define the format for specific types of files, for example, text, pdf, and gif. The CHARSET attribute indicates the character encoding of the referenced link, for example, CHARSET="ISO-8859-6". The HREFLANG attribute indicates the base language of the link; for example, the syntax HREFLANG="pt" would indicate that the referenced link is written in Portuguese. MEDIA specifies the medium type of the referenced link. Legal values include ALL, AURAL, BRAILLE, HANDHELD, PRINT, PROJECTION, SCREEN (default), SPEECH, TTY, and TV.

The remaining LINK attributes are not supported by current browsers and are not further discussed.

1.6   BODY—Creating the Main Document

HTML documents should have exactly one BODY section defining the main contents of the page. The only exception is a document that uses frames. In such a case, the top-level document simply defines the general layout and specifies which documents go in which frames, omitting the BODY altogether. See Chapter 4 (Frames) for more detail. In nonframes documents, the BODY element contains the text and HTML markup constituting the main document. Because the TITLE portion of the HEAD element appears on the title bar of the window, not in the page itself, and because that title does not always appear on printouts of the document, the BODY normally starts with a "title," often using the largest heading size (H1). The BODY "title" is frequently the exact same text as in the TITLE element. Thus, many HTML documents look like Listing 1.6.

The BODY section uses two major classes of HTML elements, block-level and text-level. The block-level elements normally break the flow of the document and start at the beginning of a new line; block-level elements cause paragraph breaks. Examples of block-level elements include headings, basic text sections, lists, tables, horizontal lines used as dividers, and input forms. Block-level elements can contain text-level elements almost anywhere and nested block-level elements in many places (e.g., list elements and table cells): they are discussed in Chapter 2 (Block-Level Elements in HTML 4.0).

Listing 1.6   HTML 4.0 template with first heading matching title

```
<!DOCTYPE HTML PUBLIC "-//W3C//DTD HTML 4.0 Transitional//EN">
<HTML>
<HEAD>
  <TITLE>My First Web Page</TITLE>
</HEAD>
<BODY>
<H1>My First Web Page</H1>
<!-- Remainder of HTML Document Here -->
</BODY>
</HTML>
```

The text-level elements don't cause paragraph breaks. Examples of text-level elements include tags for fonts, hypertext links, embedded images, applets, plug-ins, ActiveX components, and image maps. Text-level elements can be embedded inside block-level elements and often nested in other text-level elements but cannot contain block-level elements. They are discussed in Chapter 3 (Text-Level Elements in HTML 4.0).

HTML Element: `<BODY ...> ... </BODY>`
Attributes: BACKGROUND, BGCOLOR, TEXT, LINK, VLINK, ALINK, TITLE, ONCLICK, ONDBLCLICK, ONMOUSEDOWN, ONMOUSEUP, ONMOUSEMOVE, ONMOUSEOUT, ONKEYPRESS, ONKEYDOWN, ONLOAD, ONUNLOAD, ONFOCUS (nonstandard), ONBLUR (nonstandard), ONERROR (nonstandard), ONMOVE (nonstandard), ONRESIZE (nonstandard), ONDRAGDROP (nonstandard), BGPROPERTIES (nonstandard), CLASS, ID, STYLE

The BODY tag is often used without attributes, (e.g., simply `<BODY>` as the start tag), but can optionally contain attributes designating the background image, the background color, and the foreground colors of normal text, unvisited hypertext links, visited hypertext links, and links that are being selected. JavaScript-enabled browsers also support attributes that specify code to be executed under various conditions.

BACKGROUND and BGCOLOR
The BACKGROUND attribute specifies the URL of an image file that is to be tiled across the background of the page. Image repetition (tiling) minimizes download time of a repetitive background pattern. For instance, a page with colors that fade left-to-right across the page would use a BACKGROUND image with fading colors that is very wide but only one pixel high. A good idea is to supply a background color (BGCOLOR) as insurance when specifying a background image (BACKGROUND) in case the reader has image loading disabled.

Most browsers use white (WHITE or #FFFFFF) or light gray (SILVER or #C0C0C0) as the default BGCOLOR. Although widely used, both the BACK-GROUND and BGCOLOR attributes are technically deprecated, with the recommendation that style sheets be used instead.

TEXT, LINK, VLINK, and ALINK

These attributes specify the foreground color of normal text, of unvisited hypertext links (based on the browser's current history), of visited links, and of links currently being selected. This last category is a temporary color to show when the user has pressed the mouse down over a link but not yet released the mouse. Colors can be specified either by a symbolic name taken from the original Windows VGA palette or by the hexidecimal equivalent, that is, a # sign followed by six hexadecimal digits, two each for red, green, and blue. Table 1.1 lists color names and their hex equivalents. For systems that can only support 256 colors, the Color-Safe palette defines the subset of 216 colors that will not dither on the monitor. An example of the Color-Safe palette is located at http://www.docnprof.com/safecolorA.html. Both Netscape and Internet Explorer also allow the use of the X11 window system color names. An example of each of the X11 colors is provided at http://www.zdnet.com/devhead/resources/tag_library/misc/x11names.html. Again, these attributes are deprecated in favor of style sheets.

Table 1.1 Predefined color names in HTML 4.0

Color Name	Hex Equivalent	Color Name	Hex Equivalent
AQUA	#00FFFF	NAVY	#000080
BLACK	#000000	OLIVE	#808000
BLUE	#0000FF	PURPLE	#800080
FUCHSIA	#FF00FF	RED	#FF0000
GRAY	#808080	SILVER	#C0C0C0
GREEN	#008000	TEAL	#008080
LIME	#00FF00	WHITE	#FFFFFF
MAROON	#800000	YELLOW	#FFFF00

Most browsers use black (BLACK or #000000) as the default TEXT color, blue (BLUE or, in the case of Netscape, a slightly darker #0000EE) as the default LINK color, dark purple/blue (#551A8B in Netscape) as the default VLINK color, and red (RED or #FF0000) as the default color for ALINK.

TITLE

TITLE displays a tool-tip when the mouse is paused over the document. TITLE is supported by Internet Explorer 4.0 and above. However, this attribute is not supported by Netscape, at least as of Netscape version 4.7.

Core Warning

Netscape does not support the TITLE attribute.

ONCLICK, ONDBLCLICK, ONMOUSEDOWN, ONMOUSEUP, ONMOUSEMOVE, ONMOUSEOUT, ONKEYPRESS, ONKEY-DOWN, ONLOAD, ONUNLOAD, ONFOCUS, ONBLUR, ONERROR, ONMOVE, ONRESIZE, and ONDRAGDROP

These attributes specify JavaScript code that should be executed when the page receives a mouse event or keyboard event or when the focus of the page changes. For further details on JavaScript, see Chapter 24 (JavaScript: Adding Dynamic Content to Web Pages).

BGPROPERTIES

In Internet Explorer, supplying BGPROPERTIES="FIXED" signifies that the background image specified by the BACKGROUND attribute should not scroll with the rest of the page. This property is sometimes described as a watermark.

Finally, the cascading style sheet specification also adds CLASS, ID, and STYLE attributes to *all* HTML elements except for BASE, BASEFONT (ID allowed), HEAD, HTML, META, PARAM (ID allowed), SCRIPT, STYLE, and TITLE. These style sheet attributes are not discussed separately for each HTML element. See Chapter 5 (Cascading Style Sheets) for details.

1.7 Summary

HTML is the foundation for creating a professional Web site. Whether providing on-line technical support, stock market quotes, international news, or e-commerce shopping, the information viewed by the user is contained in an HTML document.

Today, most browsers support the HTML 4.0 specification. This chapter covered the basic structure of an HTML document and showed you how to create, validate, and post your first Web page on the Internet.

Every HTML 4.0 document should contain a DOCTYPE declaration followed by an element containing a HEAD and a BODY. The HEAD should always contain a TITLE and can also contain STYLE, META, or other high-level information that specifies the author, gives a forwarding location, or otherwise describes the overall document. The META data is often used by search engines to populate databases with information about the document. The BODY tag itself is often empty, but attributes can be used to specify page colors or images or to designate JavaScript actions that take place in various circumstances.

Once you have the outline of the HTML document in place, you will want to actually put something into the document. The following chapters describe how to add more content to your document. Chapter 2 (Block-Level Elements in HTML 4.0) describes the major text blocks that make up your documents, and Chapter 3 (Text-Level Elements in HTML 4.0) covers the smaller elements that can go inside the various text sections. Then Chapter 4 discusses frames, which allow you to divide your Web page into cells and place a different HTML document in each cell. Finally, users who want to customize the way certain browsers display various HTML elements can use cascading style sheets, as described in Chapter 5.

BLOCK-LEVEL ELEMENTS IN HTML 4.0

Topics in This Chapter

- Section headings
- Basic paragraph types
- Bulleted and numbered lists
- Tables
- Horizontal separator lines
- Options for setting default paragraph alignment

Chapter 2

T his chapter describes how to specify the major paragraph types or text blocks that appear in the BODY portion of an HTML document. These "block-level" elements define how blocks of text are formatted and displayed by the Web browser. They are in contrast to text-level elements that only affect the appearance of the text. Block-level elements can contain text, text-level elements, and other block-level elements, whereas, text-level elements can only contain text and other text-level elements.

The HTML 4.0 specification adds JavaScript event-handling attributes (ONCLICK, ONDBLCLICK, ONKEYDOWN, ONKEYPRESS, ONKEYUP, ONMOUSEDOWN, ONMOUSEMOVE, ONMOUSEOUT, ONMOUSEOVER, and ONMOUSEUP) to *all* elements except APPLET, BASE, BASEFONT, BDO, BR, FRAME, FRAMESET, HEAD, HTML, IFRAME, META, PARAM, SCRIPT, STYLE, and TITLE. These attributes are discussed only where commonly used in HTML documents. See Chapter 24 (JavaScript: Adding Dynamic Content to Web Pages) for details on event handling with Java-Script.

In addition, the cascading style sheet specification adds CLASS, ID, and STYLE attributes to *all* elements except BASE, BASEFONT (ID allowed), HEAD, HTML, META, PARAM (ID allowed), SCRIPT, STYLE, and TITLE. These three style sheet attributes are covered in Chapter 5 (Cascading Style Sheets) and are not discussed for each HTML element.

Furthermore, the HTML 4.0 specification adds DIR, and LANG attributes for *all* elements except for APPLET, BASE, BASEFONT, BR, FRAME, FRAMESET, IFRAME, PARAM, and SCRIPT. These two attributes are covered in Section 1.4 (The Basic Structure of HTML Documents) and are not discussed separately for each HTML element.

Lastly, the TITLE attribute, also covered in Section 1.6 (BODY—Creating the Main Document) is allowed for *all* elements except BASE, BASEFONT, HEAD, HTML, META, PARAM, SCRIPT, and TITLE. The TITLE attribute is not covered individually for each element.

2.1   Headings

HTML Element: `<H1 ...> ... </H1>`
`<H2 ...> ... </H2>`
`<H3 ...> ... </H3>`
`<H4 ...> ... </H4>`
`<H5 ...> ... </H5>`
`<H6 ...> ... </H6>`

Attributes: ALIGN

H1 through H6 are used for document headings, with H1 being the first or top-level section headings, H2 second-level headings, H3 third-level headings, and so forth. However, a common style is to start the BODY with a level-one heading containing the same text as the TITLE element, treating H1 as a document title. In the remainder of the document, level-two headings (H2) are used for the major section headings, H3 for section subheadings, and so forth.

Most browsers render headings in boldface, with H1 the largest size and H6 the smallest size. The smaller headings should be used with caution because, depending on the browser being used and the user's selection of font sizes, the minor headings may be rendered smaller than the default paragraph text. A paragraph break is placed directly beneath the heading. Unlike many other block-level elements, headings cannot contain or be contained in most other block-level items except for TABLE cells and input FORMs. They can, however, contain text-level elements. Thus, the two headings of Listing 2.1 are legal because the text-level elements that italicize the text and create an anchor for a hypertext link are completely contained within the heading element.

Listing 2.1   Properly formatted headings containing text-level elements

---

```
<H2><I>An Italic Heading</I></H2>

<H2><A NAME="Section5">Section Five</A></H2>
```

On the other hand, the two headings of Listing 2.2 are illegal because they are embedded in text-level elements.

Listing 2.2   Illegally formatted headings contained inside text-level elements

```
<I><H2>An Italic Heading</H2></I>

<A NAME="Section5"><H2>Section Five</H2></A>
```

This example also illustrates the benefits of a formal HTML validator. Because most, but not necessarily all, browsers display both sets of headings identically, authors could conclude that both formats are fine, leaving a heading that displays poorly on more rigid browsers.

ALIGN

Headings are left-aligned by default, but centered or right-aligned headings can be created with the ALIGN attribute (legal values LEFT, RIGHT, CENTER, JUSTIFY). For headings greater than the width of the browser window, JUSTIFY aligns the text to both the left and right margin. The default alignment can be changed with the DIV tag (Section 2.6). The ALIGN attribute for headings is deprecated in HTML 4.0 in favor of style sheets. See Chapter 5 (Cascading Style Sheets) for details.

A sample of the six heading types with various alignment options is shown in Listing 2.3. The third heading is underlined. Figure 2–1 shows a typical result in Internet Explorer 5.0 on Windows 2000 Professional.

Listing 2.3   Document-Headings.html

```
<!DOCTYPE HTML PUBLIC "-//W3C//DTD HTML 4.0 Transitional//EN">
<HTML>
<HEAD>
  <TITLE>Document Headings</TITLE>
</HEAD>
<BODY>
Samples of the six heading types:
<H1>Level-1 (H1)</H1>
<H2 ALIGN="CENTER">Level-2 (H2)</H2>
<H3><U>Level-3 (H3)</U></H3>
<H4 ALIGN="RIGHT">Level-4 (H4)</H4>
<H5>Level-5 (H5)</H5>
<H6>Level-6 (H6)</H6>
</BODY>
</HTML>
```

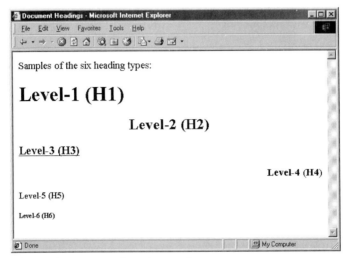

Figure 2-1   Typical rendering of `Document-Headings.html`.

2.2   Basic Text Elements

The basic text section elements include P (basic paragraph), PRE (preformatted text where white space is preserved), ADDRESS (for listing contact information), and BLOCKQUOTE (for large quotations or for regular paragraphs with indented left and right margins).

Basic Paragraphs

HTML Element: `<P ...> ... </P>` (End Tag Optional)
Attributes: `ALIGN`

The P element designates basic paragraphs, resulting in a section of text with blank space above and below. Although P is a container, the end tag is optional and most other block-level elements imply an end to the previous paragraph. Furthermore, body text not appearing inside any other block-level element is assumed to be inside a P element. Thus, many authors treat P as though it was a paragraph *separator*, even though it is really a paragraph *container*. Listing 2.4 illustrates the use of the paragraph tag, where in example (a) the ending tag is explicitly listed, and in (b) the ending tag is implied.

Extra white space inside a basic paragraph is ignored, with the text filled to fit the space currently available. Multiple consecutive P tags do not result in extra blank space. Cascading style sheets (Chapter 5) enable you to specify the size of the top and bottom paragraph margins. In the absence of style sheets, you can use the BR element (see Section 3.7, "Controlling Line Breaks") or a PRE element (discussed next) to put blank lines in a Web page.

Listing 2.4   (a) Explicit and (b) implied ending paragraph tags

```
<BODY>                          <BODY>
<P>                             Paragraph 1
Paragraph 1                     <P>
</P>                            Paragraph 2
<P>                             <P>
Paragraph 2                     Paragraph 3
</P>                            </BODY>
<P>
Paragraph 3
</P>
</BODY>
            (a)                             (b)
```

Core Warning

Multiple consecutive <P> entries generally do not result in multiple blank lines.

ALIGN

The ALIGN attribute of P is used just like ALIGN in headings. Like headings, basic paragraphs are aligned flush left with a ragged right margin by default, but can be centered or right-aligned by use of the ALIGN attribute (legal values are LEFT, RIGHT, CENTER, JUSTIFY). For a multiple-line paragraph, JUSTIFY aligns the text to both the left and right margin. The default alignment can be changed with the DIV tag (Section 2.6) or style sheets (Chapter 5). Again, ALIGN is deprecated in HTML 4.0 in favor of style sheets.

Paragraphs with White Space Preserved

HTML Element: `<PRE>` ... `</PRE>`
Attributes: `WIDTH`

Normally, extra white space (such as carriage returns and multiple spaces) in an HTML document is not displayed by the browser. The `PRE` element specifies a pre-formatted paragraph that maintains the white space from the source document and uses a fixed-width font. The `PRE` element is often used to display sections of code from sample programs. HTML elements that do change the font size are not allowed within the `PRE` declaration. As a result, sample code containing `<` or `&` can also be interpreted as HTML markup. For example, `if (a < b && c < d)` will likely cause formatting errors within a preformatted paragraph, since the `< b` will be interpreted as the beginning of a `<B>` tag. Correct such text by replacing `<` with `&lt;` and `&` with `&amp;`.

In general, any ISO 8859-1 (Latin-1) character can be inserted by `&#xxx;`, where xxx is the decimal value of the character in the ISO Latin-1 character set. For instance, `&#169;` results in ©. In addition, most characters have a mnemonic entity reference, such as `&copy;` in the case of the copyright symbol. A full list of the Latin-1 character set, with mnemonic character entities, can be found at `http://www.htmlhelp.com/reference/html40/entities/latin1.html`.

Table 2.1 lists popular entity references supported by all HTML 4.0 browsers. These characters are considered plain-text and thus can be used in the `TITLE` element, as labels of `SUBMIT` buttons and in other places that prohibit HTML markup.

Table 2.1   Special characters in HTML

Desired Character	HTML Required
<	`&lt;`
>	`&gt;`
&	`&amp;`
"	`&quot;`
Nonbreaking space	` `

WIDTH

The `WIDTH` attribute is deprecated and not widely supported. The intent is to specify the expected width in *characters* so that the browser can choose an appropriate font and indentation.

Indented Quotations

HTML Element: `<BLOCKQUOTE> ... </BLOCKQUOTE>`
Attributes: `CITE`

The `BLOCKQUOTE` element is intended for long quotations. The majority of browsers display `BLOCKQUOTE` sections with indented left and right margins. However, because this indentation is technically not required, authors should be wary of using `BLOCKQUOTE` purely for indentation unless it is for an internal application where they can be confident of the browsers that are used to read the pages. Style sheets are the preferred way to control indentation, but in a few circumstances, `BLOCK-QUOTE` or a borderless `TABLE` can be used instead. The `CITE` attribute, not rendered by the browser, allows specification of a URL from which the quotation originated.

Core Approach

> *HTML 4.0 does not define an element to give indented left and right margins. Some authors use* `BLOCKQUOTE` *or a centered, borderless* `TABLE` *as a way to implement indentation. Both approaches have drawbacks, so use style sheets instead.*

Addresses

HTML Element: `<ADDRESS> ... </ADDRESS>`
Attributes: None

The `ADDRESS` element supplies author and contact information for the current document and usually appears at the top or bottom of the document. Most browsers display the address in italics. With `ADDRESS`, just as with most section types other than `PRE`, the browser wraps the resulting text. If you want line breaks in specific places, you must explicitly insert `BR`.

2.3   Numbered, Bulleted, and Indented Lists

HTML enables you to create numbered or ordered lists (`OL`), bulleted or unordered lists (`UL`), and definition lists (`DL`) with left-indented sections but without a number or bullet. Lists can be nested and can appear inside table cells. The older `MENU` and `DIR` lists are still supported by browsers, but because these lists have been superseded by newer constructs, we do not discuss them here.

Numbered Lists

HTML Element: `<OL ...> ... </OL>`

Attributes: `TYPE, START, COMPACT`

The `OL` element creates numbered (ordered) lists. The `LI` (list item) element specifies individual entries within a list and can contain most other block-level elements (including tables and other lists) except for heading (`H1` through `H6`) and `ADDRESS` elements. For instance, Listing 2.5 shows a simple ordered list. Figure 2–2 shows the result in Netscape 4.0 on a Sun/Solaris workstation.

Listing 2.5   A simple numbered list

```
A sample list:
<OL>
  <LI>List Item One
  <LI>List Item Two
  <LI>List Item Three
</OL>
```

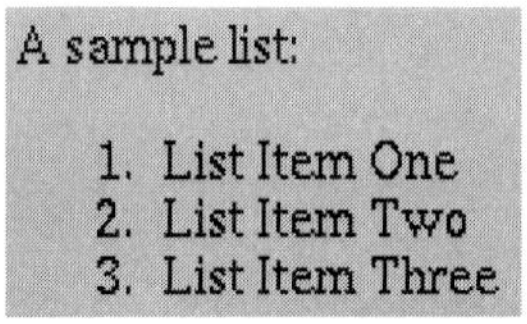

A sample list:

1. List Item One
2. List Item Two
3. List Item Three

Figure 2–2   Numbers in `OL` lists, like this one from Listing 2.5, are generated automatically.

The `OL` tag has three optional attributes: `TYPE`, `START`, and `COMPACT`.

TYPE

The `TYPE` attribute specifies the style of numbering to use. Legal values for `TYPE` are summarized in Table 2.2. Officially, `TYPE` is deprecated in favor of style sheets, but many authors find its use convenient.

START

`START`, also technically deprecated, is an integer specifying where numbering should start. It can be used with any value of `TYPE`. There is no option to specify a prefix to appear before each number.

Table 2.2 Values for the `TYPE` attribute of numbered lists	
Value	*Meaning*
`1`	Arabic: 1, 2, 3, etc. Default.
`A`	Alphabetic uppercase: A, B, C, etc.
`a`	Alphabetic lowercase: a, b, c, etc.
`I`	Roman numeral uppercase: I, II, III, IV, etc.
`i`	Roman numeral lowercase: i, ii, iii, iv, etc.

COMPACT

`COMPACT` specifies that the list should be rendered more compactly (i.e., in less space) than usual but is deprecated and not widely supported.

Listing 2.6 gives a more complex use of numbered lists; Figure 2–3 shows a typical result. Note that nested lists are indented and are numbered starting at 1, not at the last value of the outer list.

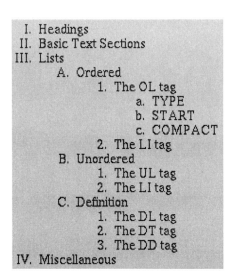

Figure 2–3 Nested lists, like this one from Listing 2.6, are automatically indented.

Listing 2.6   Nested ordered lists

```
<OL TYPE="I">
<LI>Headings
  <LI>Basic Text Sections
  <LI>Lists
      <OL TYPE="A">
        <LI>Ordered
            <OL TYPE="1">
              <LI>The OL tag
                  <OL TYPE="a">
                    <LI>TYPE
                    <LI>START
                    <LI>COMPACT
                  </OL>
              <LI>The LI tag
            </OL>
        <LI>Unordered
            <OL TYPE="1">
              <LI>The UL tag
              <LI>The LI tag
            </OL>
        <LI>Definition
            <OL TYPE="1">
              <LI>The DL tag
              <LI>The DT tag
              <LI>The DD tag
            </OL>
      </OL>
  <LI>Miscellaneous
</OL>
```

HTML Element: `<LI ...> ... </LI>` (End Tag Optional)
Attributes: (When inside OL) VALUE, TYPE

LI entries support different attributes depending on what type of list they are in. Numbered lists support the VALUE and TYPE attributes in list items. Strictly speaking, LI is a container element, but in many cases the end tag is omitted.

VALUE

The VALUE attribute, technically deprecated in favor of style sheets, specifies a specific number for an entry in a list. the VALUE attribute affects not just the current LI, but all the subsequent LI elements in the list.

TYPE

List items can also have a TYPE attribute with the same potential values as in the OL element, used in the rare case when you want to switch numbering styles within a list.

Bulleted Lists

HTML Element: <UL ...> ... </UL>
Attributes: TYPE, COMPACT

The UL element creates bulleted (unordered) lists. The LI (*list item*) tag specifies individual entries within a list. For instance, Listing 2.7 shows a simple bulleted list; Figure 2–4 shows the result in Netscape 4.0 on Sun/Solaris workstation.

Listing 2.7   A simple bulleted list

```
A sample list:
<UL>
   <LI>List Item One
   <LI>List Item Two
   <LI>List Item Three
</UL>
```

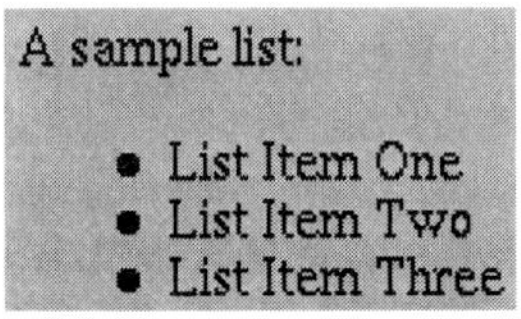

Figure 2–4   The UL element generates bullets for each LI item.

The UL tag has two optional attributes: TYPE and COMPACT.

TYPE

The TYPE attribute, officially deprecated in favor of style sheets, specifies which bullet style to use. Legal values for TYPE are summarized in Table 2.3.

COMPACT

COMPACT, also deprecated, signifies that the list should take up less space than usual. COMPACT is not widely supported.

Table 2.3 Values for the TYPE attribute of bulleted lists	
Value	*Meaning*
DISC	A solid circle. Often the default for nonnested lists.
CIRCLE	A hollow circle. Often the default for nested lists.
SQUARE	A solid or hollow square, depending on the browser.

HTML Element: `<LI ...> ... </LI>` (End Tag Optional)

Attributes: (When inside UL) TYPE

Depending on the type of list, different attributes are supported by the LI element. In bulleted lists, only the TYPE attribute is supported in list elements. LI is a container element, but the end tag is omitted in many cases.

TYPE

The TYPE attribute, deprecated in favor of style sheets, specifies the bullet type of the particular list element. It has the same allowable values as the TYPE attribute for UL itself (legal values are DISC, CIRCLE, or SQUARE).

Definition Lists

HTML Element: `<DL ...> ... </DL>`

Attributes: COMPACT

HTML Element: `<DT> ... </DT>` (End Tag Optional)

Attributes: None

HTML Element: `<DD> ... </DD>` (End Tag Optional)

Attributes: None

The DL element creates lists containing both indented and nonindented items. Items are not numbered or bulleted. The standard use is for definition terms (DT) to have normal margins and the definition descriptions (DD) to have indented left margins. For instance, Listing 2.8 shows a simple definition list, with the result shown in Figure 2–5. DL has an optional COMPACT attribute, but it is deprecated and not widely supported. Strictly, DT and DD are container elements, but the end tags are optional.

Listing 2.8   A simple definition list

```
<DL>
  <DT>Term One
  <DD>The definition of term number one.
  <DT>Term Two
  <DD>The definition of term number two.
</DL>
```

Term One
       The definition of term
       number one.
Term Two
       The definition of term   ***Figure 2–5***   This rendering of Listing 2.8
       number two.   illustrates the typical indentation of the DD element.

DD elements are allowed to contain other block-level elements except for headings and addresses. A DD element can appear in a DL list without an associated DT; it is the only HTML block-level element that is normally rendered with an indented left margin but a standard right margin. In previous HTML releases, DD elements (and borderless tables with empty, fixed-width, left columns) were used to implement left-indented paragraphs. In HTML 4.0, style sheets are a more flexible and reliable alternative.

2.4   Tables

HTML tables are widely used not only for traditional tables (data presented in tabular format) but also to control layout and group related items. The majority of the most popular Web sites use tables to control the overall layout of the main page. Table entries can contain images, multiple paragraph types including lists, and even other tables. The border around the table and between cells can be suppressed so that the reader is unaware that a table is being used. Creating complex tables by hand can be tedious and error prone, especially if there are nested tables or entries that span rows and columns. HTML editors that let you lay out tables visually can be a big help, especially if they let you go back to the "raw" HTML to add features (such as BGCOLOR) that they might not support.

The Basic Table Structure

A basic HTML table consists of the TABLE element containing an optional CAPTION element, followed by table rows specified by TR. The rows can contain either TH (table heading) elements or TD (table data) elements. TH uses centered, bold text by default, and TD uses normal, left-aligned text. This structure is exemplified in Listing 2.9, with a typical result shown in Figure 2–6. Note that the </TR>, </TH>, and </TD> end tags are optional but help to organize the HTML.

In addition to the basic structure of individual rows in a table, the HTML 4.0 specification adds new elements for grouping table rows (THEAD, TBODY, and TFOOT), and new elements for grouping table columns (COLGROUP and COL). These new elements, provide formatting control of individual or grouped columns. We talk about table grouping elements after our discussion of the basic TABLE structure.

Listing 2.9   A simple HTML table

```
<TABLE BORDER=1>
<CAPTION>Table Caption</CAPTION>
   <TR><TH>Heading1</TH>        <TH>Heading2</TH></TR>
   <TR><TD>Row1 Col1 Data</TD><TD>Row1 Col2 Data</TD></TR>
   <TR><TD>Row2 Col1 Data</TD><TD>Row2 Col2 Data</TD></TR>
   <TR><TD>Row3 Col1 Data</TD><TD>Row3 Col2 Data</TD></TR>
</TABLE>
```

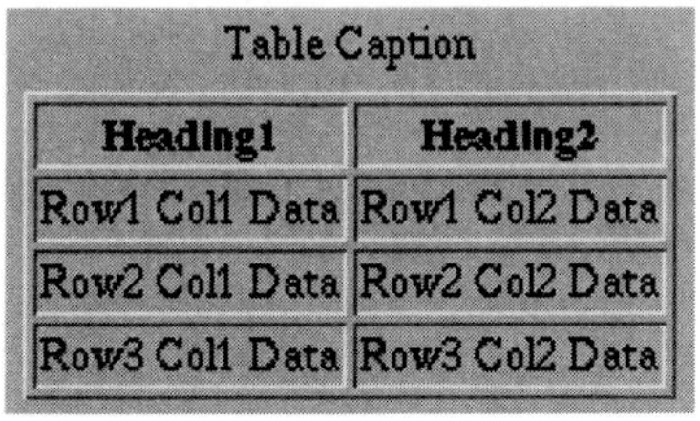

Table Caption	
Heading1	**Heading2**
Row1 Col1 Data	Row1 Col2 Data
Row2 Col1 Data	Row2 Col2 Data
Row3 Col1 Data	Row3 Col2 Data

Figure 2–6   This is a typical rendering of the simple table given in Listing 2.9.

HTML Element: `<TABLE...>` ... `</TABLE>`

Attributes: BORDER, ALIGN, WIDTH, CELLSPACING, CELLPADDING, FRAME, RULES, SUMMARY, BGCOLOR, BORDERCOLOR (nonstandard), BORDERCOLORDARK (nonstandard), BORDERCOLORLIGHT (nonstandard), BACKGROUND (nonstandard)

The `<TABLE>` tag can be used with no attributes, yielding a borderless left-aligned table. For more control, the following attributes can be specified.

ALIGN

The ALIGN attribute, deprecated in favor of style sheets, gives the horizontal alignment of the table as a whole. Legal values are LEFT, RIGHT, and CENTER, with LEFT being the default. Note that text immediately after a right-aligned table is displayed on the left side of the table in the browser. To force the text to appear below the table use <BR CLEAR="ALL">. See Section 3.7 (Controlling Line Breaks) for discussion of the BR element.

BORDER

The main purpose of the BORDER attribute is to control the width in pixels of the the visible border around the table. However, if set to zero (the default), BORDER also turns off the dividing lines between table cells. This width is *in addition to* the border around each cell (CELLSPACING). Some browsers allow <TABLE BORDER> to mean the same as <TABLE BORDER=1>. The latter should be avoided because it prevents validation by the formal HTML validators.

Core Note

The thickness of the outside border is the <u>sum</u> of BORDER and CELLSPACING, assuming BORDER is not zero.

CELLSPACING

CELLSPACING gives the space in pixels between adjacent table cells. The space is drawn as a 3D line if BORDER is nonzero; otherwise, the space is simply drawn in the background color. The default space size is usually three pixels.

CELLPADDING

CELLPADDING determines the empty space, in pixels, between the cell's border and the cell data. The default is usually one pixel.

FRAME

The FRAME attribute is new in HTML 4.0 and specifies which outer borders are drawn. All four borders are drawn if this attribute is omitted. Legal values are BORDER or BOX (all), VOID (none), ABOVE (top), BELOW (bottom), HSIDES (top and bottom, despite the somewhat confusing name), VSIDES (left and right), LHS (left), and RHS (right). Listing 2.10 gives a simple example, with the result shown in Figure 2–7. The FRAME attribute is not supported in Netscape, at least as of Netscape version 4.7.

Listing 2.10 `TicTacToe.html`

```
<!DOCTYPE HTML PUBLIC "-//W3C//DTD HTML 4.0 Transitional//EN">
<HTML>
<HEAD>
  <TITLE>2000 World Championship</TITLE>
</HEAD>
<BODY>
<H2 ALIGN="CENTER">2000 World Championship</H2>
Final result in the 2000 world tic-tac-toe championship.
Deep Green is "X", Barry Kasparov is "O".
<TABLE ALIGN="CENTER" BORDER=1 FRAME="VOID">
  <TR><TH>X<TH>O<TH>X
  <TR><TH>X<TH>O<TH>X
  <TR><TH>O<TH>X<TH>O
</TABLE>
</BODY>
</HTML>
```

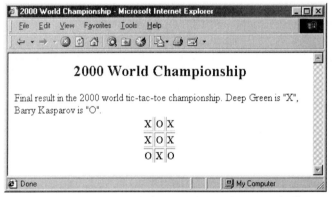

Figure 2-7   A table with the outside borders turned off.

Core Warning

Netscape does not support the `FRAME` *attribute of the* `TABLE` *element.*

RULES

This new HTML 4.0 attribute, supported by Internet Explorer, but not
Netscape, specifies which inner dividing lines are drawn. All are drawn if this
attribute is omitted. Legal values are NONE, ROWS, COLS, ALL, and GROUPS.

Core Warning

Netscape does not support the RULES attribute of the TABLE element.

SUMMARY

The SUMMARY attribute, new in HTML 4.0, provides a description of the table for user agents rendering the document in nonvisual media such as speech or Braille.

WIDTH

The WIDTH attribute specifies the width of the table, either in pixels (<TABLE WIDTH=250>) or as a percentage of the current browser window width (<TABLE WIDTH="75%">). Specify absolute sizes with caution—in most cases you know little about the window sizes used by visitors to your page. If you specify a percentage, be sure to enclose the value in double quotes. The default size is derived from the size of table elements.

BGCOLOR

Specifying colors for tables (or individual table rows or cells) adds greatly to the appearance of Web pages. You can use the BGCOLOR attribute of TABLE to specify the color of the whole table (alternatively, you can use style sheets as discussed in Chapter 5). The advantage of style sheets is that if you change your mind about the specific colors, you only have to make a single modification to effect changes on all pages that use the same style sheet.

BORDERCOLOR, BORDERCOLORDARK, BORDERCOLORLIGHT

These nonstandard attributes, supported only by Internet Explorer 4.0 and above, specify the colors to use for the borders of the table. BORDERCOLOR defines the main color, and BORDERCOLORDARK and BORDERCOLORLIGHT define the colors to use for the 3D shading. They are applicable only when the BORDER attribute is nonzero.

BACKGROUND

This attribute is an Internet Explorer-specific method to specify an image file that will be tiled as the background of the table. With borders turned off, this attribute provides a way to overlay images with text, but it is not portable to other browsers. Style sheets provide the same capability in a manner supported by many new browsers, so avoid the BACKGROUND attribute even for internal applications that primarily use Internet Explorer.

HTML Element: <CAPTION ...> ... </CAPTION>
Attributes: ALIGN

The CAPTION element, placed between the TABLE tags, adds a title above (ALIGN="TOP") or below (ALIGN="BOTTOM") the table. The default placement is TOP. Many developers forego the use of CAPTION and create captions using HTML elements that give them more control over the caption format.

Defining Table Rows

HTML Element: <TR ...> ... </TR> (End Tag Optional)
Attributes: ALIGN, VALIGN, BGCOLOR, BORDERCOLOR (nonstandard),
            BORDERCOLORDARK (nonstandard), BORDERCOLORLIGHT
            (nonstandard), CHAR, CHAROFF

TR defines each row in the table. Each row will then contain TH or TD entries.

ALIGN
ALIGN (legal values are LEFT, RIGHT, CENTER, JUSTIFY, or CHAR) sets the horizontal alignment for the content of the table cells. LEFT is the default. Neither Netscape nor Internet Explorer support JUSTIFY or CHAR cell alignments.

VALIGN
VALIGN (legal values are TOP, MIDDLE, BOTTOM, or BASELINE) sets the vertical alignment for the content of the table cells. BASELINE positions the *first* line of text in each cell to a common baseline. MIDDLE is the default.

BGCOLOR
BGCOLOR sets the color for the table row, overriding any values set for the table as a whole by the BGCOLOR attribute of TABLE. It, in turn, can be overridden by a BGCOLOR attribute in a TD or TH entry in the row. This feature is useful for making tables in which the header row is shaded differently from the remaining rows. For instance, Listing 2.11 defines a table with the headers presented with white text on a black background, and the other rows presented with black text on a light gray background. The result shown in Figure 2–8 is a common table format that is preferred by a number of users.

BORDERCOLOR, BORDERCOLORDARK, BORDERCOLORLIGHT

Supported only by Internet Explorer, these attributes specify the color to use for the borders of the row. BORDERCOLOR define the main color,

BORDERCOLORDARK and BORDERCOLORLIGHT defines the colors to use for 3D shading. The attributes are only applicable when the BORDER attribute of the TABLE is nonzero.

Lastly, the HTML 4.0 specification defines CHAR and CHAROFF attributes for TR, TH, TD, THEAD, TBODY, and TFOOT elements. For the CHAR attribute, the browser will align each cell in a a row so that the given character, for example, a decimal point, always appears in the same relative location. The CHAROFF attribute specifies an offset to the first alignment character. Neither Netscape nor Internet Explorer support these two attributes, and we do not discuss them for each of the table elements.

Listing 2.11 `BG-Colors.html`

```
<!DOCTYPE HTML PUBLIC "-//W3C//DTD HTML 4.0 Transitional//EN">
<HTML>
<HEAD>
  <TITLE>WWW Standards</TITLE>
</HEAD>
<BODY BGCOLOR="WHITE">
<H1 ALIGN="CENTER">WWW Standards</H1>

<TABLE BORDER=1 BGCOLOR="#EEEEEE">
  <TR BGCOLOR="BLACK">
    <TH><FONT COLOR="WHITE">Standard</FONT>
    <TH><FONT COLOR="WHITE">Obsolete Version</FONT>
    <TH><FONT COLOR="WHITE">Most Widely Supported
        Version</FONT>
    <TH><FONT COLOR="WHITE">Upcoming Version</FONT>
  <TR><TD>HTML
      <TD>3.2
      <TD>4.0
      <TD>XHTML
  <TR><TD>HTTP
      <TD>1.0
      <TD>1.1
      <TD>1.2
</TABLE>

</BODY>
</HTML>
```

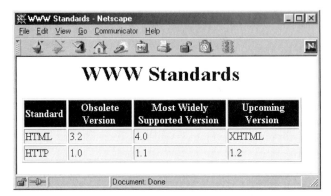

Figure 2–8   The BGCOLOR attribute makes some tables look nicer.

Table Headings and Data Cells

HTML Element: **<TH ...> ... </TH>** **(End Tag Optional)**
                  <TD ...> ... </TD> **(End Tag Optional)**

Attributes: COLSPAN, ROWSPAN, ALIGN, VALIGN, WIDTH, HEIGHT,
                   NOWRAP, BGCOLOR, BACKGROUND (nonstandard),
                   BORDERCOLOR (nonstandard), BORDERCOLORDARK
                   (nonstandard), BORDERCOLORLIGHT (nonstandard), ABBR,
                   AXIS, HEADERS, SCOPE

COLSPAN

COLSPAN defines a heading or cell data entry that spans multiple columns.
Listing 2.12 gives a simple example, and Figure 2-9(a) shows a typical result.

Listing 2.12 A heading that spans two columns

```
<TABLE BORDER=1>
  <TR><TH COLSPAN=2>Col 1&2 Heading
      <TH>Col3 Heading
  <TR><TD>Col1 Data
      <TD>Col2 Data
      <TD>Col3 Data
</TABLE>
```

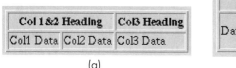

(a)   (b)

Figure 2-9   (a) This is a typical result from the column-spanning example of Listing 2.12. (b) This is a typical result from the row-spanning example of Listing 2.13.

ROWSPAN

ROWSPAN defines a heading or cell data entry that spans multiple rows. Listing 2.13 gives a simple example, and Figure 2–9(b) shows a typical result.

Listing 2.13 A data cell that spans two rows

```
<TABLE BORDER=1>
<TR><TH>Heading1<TH>Heading2
    <TR><TD ROWSPAN=2>Data for Row 1&2, Col1
        <TD>Row1 Col2 Data
    <TR><TD>Row2 Col2 Data
</TABLE>
```

ALIGN and VALIGN

The ALIGN attribute (legal values are LEFT, RIGHT, CENTER, JUSTIFY, or CHAR) specifies the horizontal alignment of items in a table cell. The default is LEFT for TD and CENTER for TH, unless overridden by the ALIGN attribute of TR. The VALIGN attribute (legal values are TOP, MIDDLE, BOTTOM, or BASELINE) specifies the vertical alignment of the table cell items. See the TR element for definitions of CHAR and BASELINE. The default is MIDDLE.

WIDTH and HEIGHT

In the absence of WIDTH and HEIGHT attributes, cell sizes are set by the browser, based on the window size and the data contained in the cell. The WIDTH and HEIGHT attributes enable you to specify an exact size in pixels. Use absolute sizes with caution because they may prevent reasonable formatting if the browser window is not the size the document author expected. HTML authors sometimes use fixed-size cells when implementing toolbars with images, since the image size is known and at least one other column or row in the table is specified with a variable size. According to the HTML 4.0 specification, percent values are not allowed. However, both Netscape and Internet Explorer support using the value as a percentage of the *table* width or height (not of the *browser* window width or height). Both WIDTH and HEIGHT are deprecated in favor of style sheets.

NOWRAP

The NOWRAP attribute, deprecated in favor of style sheets, suppresses word wrapping within a cell. A similar effect can be achieved with nonbreaking spaces ( ) between words or with a PRE paragraph inside a cell (this also results in a fixed-width font and an unwanted carriage return in some browsers). NOWRAP should be used with caution because it can result in text extending beyond the browser limits if the browser window is not sized appropriately.

BGCOLOR and BACKGROUND

The BGCOLOR attribute, officially deprecated in HTML 4.0, sets a background color for the particular table cell. The BACKGROUND attribute, supported by Internet Explorer 3.0 and later, specifies an image file that will be tiled as the background of the cell.

BORDERCOLOR, BORDERCOLORDARK, BORDERCOLORLIGHT

Supported only by Internet Explorer, these attributes specify the color to use for the borders of the cell. BORDERCOLOR defines the main color; BORDER-COLORDARK and BORDERCOLORLIGHT define the colors to use for 3D shading. The attributes are applicable only when the BORDER attribute of the TABLE is nonzero.

Finally, the new HTML 4.0 attributes, ABBR, HEADERS, SCOPE, and AXIS, are not yet widely supported. ABBR, HEADERS, and SCOPE provide simplified information for nonvisual browsers. The AXIS attribute (unsupported) can assign a category to one or more table cells for selection by a browser query.

Grouping Table Contents

HTML Element:
```
<THEAD ...> ... </THEAD> (End Tag Optional)
<TBODY ...> ... </TBODY> (End Tag Optional)
<TFOOT ...> ... </TFOOT> (End Tag Optional)
```
Attributes: ALIGN, VALIGN

The elements THEAD, TBODY, and TFOOT group parts of a table into logical sections that, when used in conjunction with the TABLE attribute RULES="GROUPS", are displayed separated by a horizontal rule. Technically, only one header and footer section is allowed in the table; however, multiple body sections are permitted. Each section group can contain one or more table rows, TR, with formatting applied to *all* rows in a group simultaneously. This approach is more advantageous than setting the format for *each* row separately. Interestingly, these grouping elements originated as Internet Explorer extensions and were later adopted as standard in HTML 4.0. However, Netscape 4.x does not support these elements.

Core Alert

Netscape 4.x does not support the table grouping elements THEAD, TBODY, and TFOOT.

ALIGN and VALIGN

The ALIGN attribute (legal values are LEFT, RIGHT, CENTER, JUSTIFY, or CHAR) specifies the horizontal alignment of all cells in the section group. The default is CENTER for THEAD, and LEFT for TBODY and TFOOT. See the TR element for a definition of the CHAR alignment. The VALIGN attribute (TOP, MIDDLE, BOTTOM, or BASELINE) specifies the vertical alignment. See the ALIGN attribute of TR for a definition of BASELINE. The default is MIDDLE.

Listing 2.14 gives a simple example of a table divided into a header, a footer, and two body sections. The result, as displayed by Internet Explorer 5.0 on Windows 2000 Professional, is shown in Figure 2–10. Specifying GROUPS for the table RULES causes a horizontal line to be displayed to separate each of the four defined table sections.

Listing 2.14 A table divided into group sections

```
<TABLE BORDER=1 CELLPADDING=4 RULES="GROUPS">
  <CAPTION>Table Groups
  <THEAD>
    <TR><TH>Table Head<TH>Table Head
  <TBODY>
    <TR><TD>Group 1<TD>Group 1
    <TR><TD>Group 1<TD>Group 1
  <TBODY ALIGN="RIGHT">
    <TR><TD>Group 2<TD>Group 2
    <TR><TD>Group 2<TD>Group 2
  <TFOOT ALIGN="CENTER">
    <TR><TD COLSPAN=2>Footer
</TABLE>
```

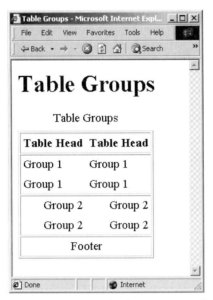

Figure 2-10 Result of Listing 2.14; the table borders are delimited by groups.

HTML Element:
  `<COLGROUP ...> ... </COLGROUP>` **(End Tag Optional)**
  `<COL ...> ... </COL>` **(End Tag Optional)**
Attributes: `ALIGN, VALIGN, SPAN, WIDTH`

Originally an Internet Explorer extension, the `COLGROUP` element establishes a common group of columns in the table. The `COLGROUP` element provides a big advantage for controlling the format of different columns. Without this element, formatting of cells in a table is only accessible on a row-by-row basis using `TR` and `TD`. The most common application of `COLGROUP` is to control the horizontal alignment of text in one or more columns. When displayed by the browser, the boundary of each `COLGROUP` is delimited by a vertical line (when used in conjunction with the `TABLE` attribute `RULES="GROUPS"`). If individual columns *within* a `COLGROUP` require different formatting attributes, then provide individual control through the `COL` element. Note that the `COL` element must appear immediately after a `COLGROUP` element; note also that the `COLGROUP` element must appear before the `THEAD` or `TBODY` element.

ALIGN and VALIGN
The `ALIGN` attribute (legal values `LEFT`, `RIGHT`, `CENTER`, `JUSTIFY`, or `CHAR`) specifies the horizontal alignment of all cells in the `COLGROUP` or `COL`. The default is `LEFT`, unless the cells are in the `THEAD`, in which case the default

horizontal alignment is CENTER. Unfortunately, specifying an alignment for a column overrides the default alignment for the header cell, which is CENTER. By adding an ALIGN attribute for the individual TH cell or by using style sheets, you can easily resolve this side effect. The CHAR alignment is defined by the TR element. The VALIGN attribute (TOP, MIDDLE, BOTTOM, or BASELINE) specifies the vertical alignment of all cells in the column group. The default is MIDDLE. A definition of BASELINE is provided by the TR ALIGN attribute. Not all browsers support JUSTIFY, CHAR, or BASELINE attribute values.

SPAN and WIDTH

The SPAN attribute specifies how many consecutive columns are governed by the corresponding COLGROUP or COL element. The WIDTH attributes defines what percentage of the total table width the COLGROUP or COL should occupy.

Listing 2.15 gives a simple example of grouping the columns in a table and controlling the alignment of individual columns. Prior to the THEAD element, one COLGROUP is associated with the first three columns, and a second COLGROUP is associated with the remaining column. The alignment of each column in the first group is individually controlled through the COL element. The result, as displayed by Internet Explorer 5.0 on Windows 2000 Professional, is shown in Figure 2–11. Specifying GROUPS for the table RULES causes the two column groups to be separated by a horizontal line.

Listing 2.15 Controlling column alignment and borders

```
<TABLE CELLPADDING=3 RULES="GROUPS">
  <CAPTION>Stout Medal Award</CAPTION>
  <COLGROUP>
    <COL ALIGN="CENTER">
    <COL ALIGN="LEFT">
    <COL ALIGN="CENTER">
  <COLGROUP ALIGN="RIGHT">
  <THEAD>
    <TR><TH>Year<TH>Cultivar<TH>Bloom Season<TH>Cost
  <TBODY>
    <TR><TD>1965<TD>Luxury Lace   <TD>M   <TD>11.75
    <TR><TD>1976<TD>Green Flutter<TD>M   <TD> 7.50
    <TR><TD>1984<TD>My Belle      <TD>E   <TD>12.00
    <TR><TD>1985<TD>Stella De Oro<TD>E-L<TD> 5.00
    <TR><TD>1989<TD>Brocaded Gown<TD>E   <TD>14.50
  <TFOOT>
    <TR><TD COLSPAN=4>E-early M-midseason L-late
</TABLE>
```

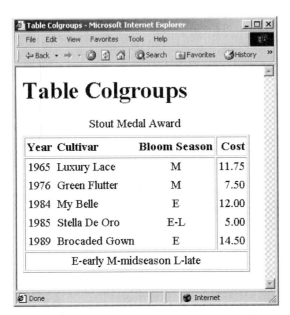

Figure 2–11 Result of Listing 2.15; COLSPAN and COL control column borders and alignment.

2.5   Fill-Out Forms

HTML FORM elements enable you to create data-entry documents that can be filled out by the reader and to send data to programs on a server for processing. Common FORM elements include textfields, text areas, password fields, check boxes, radio buttons, combo boxes, list boxes, image maps, and button controls. These HTML form elements are discussed in detail in Chapter 18 (HTML Forms).

2.6   Miscellaneous Block-Level Elements

The remaining block-level elements include HR for a horizontal rule used as a divider, DIV for setting up default alignments for other block-level elements, and CENTER for centering a section of text.

HTML Element: `<HR ...>` (No End Tag)
Attributes: `ALIGN, WIDTH, SIZE, NOSHADE, COLOR` (nonstandard)

Horizontal rules, indicated by the `HR` element, divide sections by drawing a horizontal "etched" line all or partway across the browser window. The following paragraphs summarize the five optional attributes, all of which are deprecated in favor of style sheets.

ALIGN
`ALIGN` specifies the horizontal alignment. Legal options are `LEFT`, `RIGHT`, and `CENTER`, with `CENTER` being the default.

WIDTH
This attribute gives the width in pixels (`<HR WIDTH=75>`) or as a percentage of current window width (`<HR WIDTH="50%">`). The default is 100%.

SIZE
`SIZE` is the thickness of the line in pixels. This thickness is in addition to any shadowing used to make the line etched. The default is about one pixel.

NOSHADE
If present, `NOSHADE` tells the browser to use a solid color instead of the default etched line.

COLOR
`COLOR` is a nonstandard attribute supported by Internet Explorer that changes the color of the line. Color names and RGB values are legal (see Table 1.1 for values).

HTML Element: `<DIV ...>` ... `</DIV>`
Attributes: `ALIGN`

The `DIV` element divides a document into distinct sections. Through use of the `ALIGN` attribute or style sheets, the alignment of large sections of the document can be independently controlled. Acceptable values for the `ALIGN` attribute are `LEFT`, `RIGHT`, `CENTER`, or `JUSTIFY`. Style sheets are preferred for aligning divisions because the `ALIGN` attribute is deprecated in HTML 4.0.

HTML Element: `<CENTER>` ... `</CENTER>`
Attributes: None

Officially deprecated in the HTML 4.0 specification, `<CENTER>` is shorthand for `<DIV ALIGN="CENTER">` and is still widely used to accommodate earlier browser versions.

HTML Element: `<SCRIPT TYPE="..." ...>...</SCRIPT>`
Attributes: TYPE (required), LANGUAGE, SRC, DEFER, CHARSET

SCRIPT is used for embedded programs, usually JavaScript. See Chapter 24 (Java-Script: Adding Dynamic Content to Web Pages) for details.

HTML Element: `<NOSCRIPT>...</NOSCRIPT>`
Attributes: None

The intention of NOSCRIPT is that the contents be ignored by browsers that support JavaScript, and thus, NOSCRIPT provides alternative text for browsers that do not support JavaScript. See Chapter 24 (JavaScript: Adding Dynamic Content to Web Pages) for details.

HTML Element:
`<MULTICOL COLS=xxx ...>` ... `</MULTICOL>` (Nonstandard)
Attributes: COLS (required), GUTTER, WIDTH

MULTICOL is a Netscape-specific extension introduced in Navigator 3.0 to support multicolumn text, as in a newspaper or magazine. Creating multicolumn text with MULTICOL differs from standard HTML tables (Section 2.4) in that MULTICOL lets text flow from one column to another but requires that all the columns be the same width. Tables, on the other hand, require you to assign sections of text to table cells in advance but let the columns be of varying sizes. Tables in Netscape and Internet Explorer also let you assign different background colors to different cells, something that MULTICOL does not support.

COLS
This required attribute specifies the number of columns of text, which should be two or greater.

GUTTER
This optional attribute specifies the number of pixels between the columns. The default is 10.

WIDTH
This optional attribute specifies the width in pixels of each of the columns. If WIDTH is omitted, then Netscape divides the space available, after the gutters, evenly among all the columns.

2.7 Summary

Block-level elements enable you to define the major sections of your Web page. You can define headings, several different paragraph types, lists, tables, data-input forms, and a few miscellaneous elements. However, in order to specify formatting changes within a text section, you must use the text-level elements discussed in the next chapter.

Finally, remember that many of the HTML 3.2 elements and attributes are deprecated in the newer HTML 4.0 specification, as indicated throughout the chapter. Though still supported by Netscape and Internet Explorer, deprecated elements or attributes in a document require the *transitional* DOCTYPE statement to validate as legal HTML 4.0. Furthermore, a lot of the newer constructs (like THEAD, COLGROUP, and MULTICOL) are not supported by all browsers, and authors should use them with care.

TEXT-LEVEL ELEMENTS IN HTML 4.0

Topics in This Chapter

- Using explicit character styles
- Using logical character styles
- Specifying hypertext links
- Embedding images
- Setting clickable regions in images
- Embedding applets, audio, video, and ActiveX controls
- Controlling line breaks

Chapter 3

This chapter describes how to change character styles, create hypertext links, set line breaks, and embed objects in paragraphs. The text-level elements used to accomplish these tasks specify the appearance of text within existing text blocks and do not cause paragraph breaks as do block-level elements. Text-level elements can contain other text-level elements, but not block-level elements.

Note that the general HTML attributes derived from style sheets (Chapter 5) and JavaScript event handling (Chapter 24) are not discussed for each element. Furthermore, the DIR and LANG attributes (covered in Section 1.6, "BODY—Creating the Main Document"), as well as the TITLE attribute (also covered in Section 1.6) are not discussed separately for each HTML element.

3.1 Physical Character Styles

These elements specify the type of font or character style that should be applied to the enclosed text. They can be used almost anywhere, with a few exceptions such as the TITLE and labels of SUBMIT. Character styles can be nested to compose styles for bold-italic, an underlined fixed-width font, a large, green, bold, italic, strike-through font, and so forth.

HTML Element: `<B> ... </B>`

Attributes: None

The B element instructs the browser to use a bold version of the current font for the enclosed text. This rendering can be overridden by the use of style sheets (see Chapter 5 for details).

HTML Element: `<I> ... </I>`

Attributes: None

The I element instructs the browser to use italics for the enclosed text.

HTML Element: `<TT> ... </TT>`

Attributes: None

The TT element instructs the browser to use a monospaced (fixed-width or "teletype") font for the enclosed text.

HTML Element: `<U> ... </U>`

Attributes: None

The U element, technically deprecated in HTML 4.0, specifies that the enclosed text be underlined.

HTML Element: `<SUB> ... </SUB>`

Attributes: None

The SUB element instructs the browser to use subscripts for the enclosed text.

HTML Element: `<SUP> ... </SUP>`

Attributes: None

The SUP element instructs the browser to use superscripts for the enclosed text.

HTML Element: `<BIG> ... </BIG>`

Attributes: None

The BIG element instructs the browser to use text one size bigger than the current size, on a scale of seven possible sizes. The actual point sizes available are determined by the browser. For more details, see the FONT element later in this section.

HTML Element: <SMALL> ... </SMALL>
Attributes: None

The SMALL element instructs the browser to use text one size smaller than the current size, on a scale of seven possible sizes. Again, the actual point sizes are determined by the browser. For details, see the FONT element later in this section.

HTML Element: <DEL> ... </DEL>
Attributes: CITE, DATETIME

The DEL element is for marking deleted content from an earlier version of the document. In Internet Explorer 5.0, deleted text is presented with a strike-through line. Netscape does not change the appearance of the deleted text. The optional CITE attribute specifies a URI whose corresponding document clarifies why the content was deleted. The DATETIME attribute specifies the date and time when the material was marked for deletion in the document. The format for the DATETIME stamp is YYYY-MM-DDThh:mm:ssTZD. Please see http://www.w3.org/TR/html40/ types.html#type-datetime for clarification of this DATETIME format.

HTML Element: <INS> ... </INS>
Attributes: CITE, DATETIME

The INS element is complementary to DEL; INS indicates newly added material since an earlier version of the document. Internet Explorer 5.0 displays the inserted text with an underline, whereas Netscape does not change the presentation of the text. The CITE and DATETIME attributes are the same as for the DEL element.

HTML Element: <Q> ... </Q>
Attributes: CITE

The Q element is suitable for a short, in-line quoted text. The CITE attribute specifies a URI from which the quotation originated. Neither Netscape nor Internet Explorer supports this new element.

HTML Element: <BDO DIR="..." ...> ... </BDO>
Attributes: DIR, LANG

Characters in Unicode and ISO character sets have a specific direction, left to right (LTR) or right to left (RTL). The BDO element overrides the bidirectional algorithm of the charset for the enclosed characters. The DIR attribute specifically defines the override direction as either LTR or RTL. The case-sensitive LANG attribute defines the language code of the text. See Section 1.6 (BODY—Creating the Main Document) for further details.

Listing 3.1 gives a sampling of various character styles, with Figure 3–1 showing a typical result.

Listing 3.1   A sample of physical character styles

```
<!DOCTYPE HTML PUBLIC "-//W3C//DTD HTML 4.0 Transitional//EN">
<HTML>
<HEAD>
  <TITLE>Physical Character Styles</TITLE>
</HEAD>
<BODY BGCOLOR="WHITE">
<H1>Physical Character Styles</H1>
<B>Bold</B><BR>
<I>Italic</I><BR>
<TT>Teletype (Monospaced)</TT><BR>
<U>Underlined</U><BR>
Subscripts: f<SUB>0</SUB> + f<SUB>1</SUB><BR>
Superscripts: x<SUP>2</SUP> + y<SUP>2</SUP><BR>
<SMALL>Smaller</SMALL><BR>
<BIG>Bigger</BIG><BR>
<STRIKE>Strike Through</STRIKE><BR>
<B><I>Bold Italic</I></B><BR>
<BIG><TT>Big Monospaced</TT></BIG><BR>
<SMALL><I>Small Italic</I></SMALL><BR>
<FONT COLOR="GRAY">Gray</FONT><BR>
<DEL>Delete</DEL><BR>
<INS>Insert</INS><BR>
</BODY>
</HTML>
```

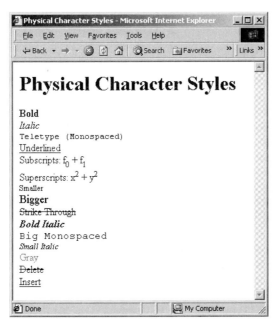

Figure 3–1   Rendering of physical character styles in Internet Explorer 5.0 on Windows 2000 Professional.

HTML Element: `<FONT ...> ... </FONT>`
Attributes: `SIZE, COLOR, FACE` (nonstandard)

The `FONT` tag defines the size or color to use for the enclosed text. The `SIZE` attribute gives the author control over font size, and the `COLOR` attribute lets the user assign text colors to individual text, that is, other than globally. Remember that text-level elements cannot enclose paragraphs. This means that if you have several consecutive paragraphs, lists, or tables for which you want to specify a particular color or size, you need to repeat the `FONT` entry in each. However, global colors can be set in the `BODY` element (Section 1.6), and global sizes can be set with `BASEFONT` (discussed later in this section). The `FONT` element is technically deprecated in HTML 4.0. Cascading style sheets also provide a flexible alternative of specifying font size, color, and face information for paragraphs or sections of text. See Chapter 5 for details.

SIZE

The `SIZE` attribute can be an absolute value from 1 (smallest) to 7 (largest) or a relative value (`SIZE="+1"`, `SIZE="-1"`, `SIZE="+2"`, and so forth) indicating the change with respect to the current font. The actual point sizes to which these numbers correspond to are determined by the browser. Be careful with absolute sizes; they can be annoying to users who have customized their browser to use a particular font size.

Core Approach

Whenever possible, use relative font sizes, not absolute ones.

COLOR

As with the colors in the `BODY` element, these colors can be a logical color name (Table 1.1 in Section 1.6) or an explicit RGB value, and you should take care to avoid the likelihood of text in the same color as the background, which would appear to be blank to the reader.

FACE

Netscape and Internet Explorer allow a `FACE` attribute containing a list of preferred font names, separated by commas. The first font in the list should be used if available on the client machine; otherwise, the second should be used, and so on. If no font in the list is available, a default should be used, just as if the `FACE` attribute was omitted.

HTML Element: `<BASEFONT SIZE=xxx>` (No End Tag)
Attributes: `SIZE` (required)

BASEFONT sets the default font size for nonheading text for the remainder of document, using absolute values from 1 (smallest) to 7 (largest). The default is 3. As with FONT, BIG, and SMALL, the mapping from these seven values to actual pixel sizes is determined by the browser.

    BASEFONT doesn't affect colors; to set the default color, use the TEXT attribute of BODY for global values, or FONT for local color changes, or cascading style sheets. BASEFONT is technically deprecated in the HTML 4.0 specification. Use BASE-FONT with caution because many users set the default text size for their browser to suit their own tastes.

3.2   Logical Character Styles

Rather than specifying the specific font to be used, some authors prefer to describe the type of text being rendered and let the browser decide the details of the resultant look. That is the purpose of logical character style elements. These elements can also provide additional information to automatic document indexers, but in the absence of style sheets, they give the author less explicit control over the look of the document. All of these elements require start and end tags, can be nested to compose styles, and can be combined with the physical character style tags.

HTML Element: `<EM>` ... `</EM>`
Attributes: None

EM specifies that the browser emphasize the enclosed text. EM is rendered in italics by most browsers.

HTML Element: `<STRONG>` ... `</STRONG>`
Attributes: None

The STRONG element tells the browser to strongly emphasize the enclosed text. STRONG is usually rendered in boldface.

HTML Element: `<CODE>` ... `</CODE>`
Attributes: None

The CODE element is used for excerpts from computer code and is rendered in a fixed-width font. Don't forget that certain characters such as < and & get interpreted as HTML markup and need to be replaced with <, &, and so forth. See Table 2.1 for a list of these characters.

Core Alert

You can't put arbitrary program excerpts inside a CODE, SAMP, or KBD block without first checking for special characters such as <, &, and the like.

HTML Element: `<SAMP> ... </SAMP>`
Attributes: None

The SAMP element is used for sample program output. SAMP is typically rendered in fixed-width font just like CODE.

HTML Element: `<KBD> ... </KBD>`
Attributes: None

The KBD element indicates keyboard input to be entered by the user. Text enclosed in the KBD element is typically rendered in fixed-width font similar to CODE.

HTML Element: `<DFN> ... </DFN>`
Attributes: None

The DFN element is used for the defining occurrence of a term. Internet Explorer uses italics to present the enclosed text. Netscape uses the current character style and does not change the rendering of the text contained in a DFN element.

HTML Element: `<VAR> ... </VAR>`
Attributes: None

VAR represents a variable or argument to a function or procedure and is usually rendered in italics.

HTML Element: `<CITE> ... </CITE>`
Attributes: None

CITE indicates that the enclosed text is a citation or reference and is usually rendered in italics.

HTML Element: `<ACRONYM> ... </ACRONYM>`
Attributes: TITLE

The ACRONYM element is often used in conjunction with the TITLE attribute to define an acronym. For example,

```
<ACRONYM TITLE="Java Development Kit">JDK</ACRONYM>
```

In Internet Explorer 5.x, the TITLE is displayed as a pop-up when the mouse is over the element. Netscape does not display the TITLE attribute.

Listing 3.2 gives a sample of each of these character styles, with a typical result shown in Figure 3–2.

Listing 3.2   A sample of logical character styles

```
<!DOCTYPE HTML PUBLIC "-//W3C//DTD HTML 4.0 Transitional//EN">
<HTML>
<HEAD>
  <TITLE>Logical Character Styles</TITLE>
</HEAD>
<BODY BGCOLOR="WHITE">
<H1>Logical Character Styles</H1>
<EM>Emphasized</EM><BR>
<STRONG>Strongly Emphasized</STRONG><BR>
<CODE>Code</CODE><BR>
<SAMP>Sample Output</SAMP><BR>
<KBD>Keyboard Text</KBD><BR>
<DFN>Definition</DFN><BR>
<VAR>Variable</VAR><BR>
<CITE>Citation</CITE><BR>
<EM><CODE>Emphasized Code</CODE></EM><BR>
<FONT COLOR="GRAY"><CITE>Gray Citation</CITE></FONT><BR>
<ACRONYM TITLE="Java Development Kit">JDK Acronym</ACRONYM>
</BODY>
</HTML>
```

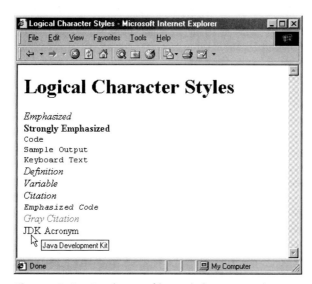

Figure 3–2   Rendering of logical character styles in Internet Explorer 5.0 on Windows 2000 Professional.

HTML Element: `<ABBR ...> ... </ABBR>`
Attributes: `TITLE`

The `ABBR` element indicates an abbreviation, as in

```
<ABBR TITLE="cubic inches">cu. in.</ABBR>.
```

Neither Netscape nor Internet Explorer supports this element.

HTML Element: `<SPAN ...> ... </SPAN>`
Attributes: `CLASS, ID, STYLE`

`SPAN` is a text-level element added to support cascading style sheets. The default behavior is to leave the enclosed text unchanged, but `SPAN` delimits user-defined character styles. `SPAN` is discussed in Chapter 5 (Cascading Style Sheets).

3.3 Specifying Hypertext Links

One of the central ideas of HTML is that documents do not have to be read from top to bottom in a linear fashion. Instead, authors can create documents or sets of documents with links to other sections or documents, thus allowing readers to proceed in directions according to their interests. The anchor element `A` allows the author to specify sections of text or images that, when selected by the reader, will transfer the browser to a specific section of a designated document. The `A` element also allows the author to name a section of the document so that other links can refer to the section.

HTML Element: `<A ...> ... </A>`
Attributes: `HREF, NAME, TARGET, REL, REV, TITLE, ONFOCUS, ONBLUR, COORDS, SHAPE, TYPE, HREFLANG, CHARSET, ACCESSKEY, TABINDEX`

The anchor element is a container with a required end tag. With `HREF`, the section enclosed becomes the clickable region in the resultant page. This region is often underlined and highlighted in the default link color (often blue), or in the color specified by the `LINK` attribute of the `BODY` element, or in the color specified by the style sheet. Links that have been visited in the current session are generally underlined and highlighted in the `VLINK` color. Depending on how the browser's history mechanism is configured, links visited in previous sessions can be indicated this way as well.

HREF
The `HREF` attribute specifies the address that the browser should visit when the user clicks upon the designated region. The value can be an absolute URL, a

relative URL, a pound sign followed by a section name (see the NAME attribute), or a URL followed by a pound sign followed by a section name. If a specific section is supplied, the browser transfers to that section of the designated document when the active region is selected. Otherwise, the browser transfers to the top of the given document.

As explained in Chapter 19 (Server-Side Java: Servlets), URLs that specify directories but omit the trailing slash result in the browser making two connections to the HTTP server: the first to request the original URL and the second to request the one with the trailing slash included, based on a `Location` response header from the HTTP server. This double trip can waste time if the network connection to the referenced site is slow. So, use `http://some.host.com/some/directory/`, not `http://some.host.com/some/directory`.

Core Performance Tip

If a URL specifies a directory, be sure to include the trailing slash.

For instance, Listing 3.3 shows four types of hypertext links: to an absolute URL, to a relative URL, to a section within the current document, and to a section within a specific URL. In addition to `http:` links, most browsers also support `mailto:` links (for e-mail addresses), `file:` links (for local files on the client machine, usually used for testing), and `ftp:` links (for FTP sites).

Listing 3.3   Hypertext links

```
The official HTML specifications are available from
<A HREF="http://www.w3.org/MarkUp/"> the World Wide Web
Consortium (W3C)</A>, with some examples given in
<A HREF="HTML-Examples.html">my example page</A>.

The Java programming language is discussed in
<A HREF="#Section-3">Section 3</A>. For a discussion of COBOL, see
<A HREF="johndoe.html#COBOL">my husband's home page</A>.
```

Finally, a stylistic note on the use of hypertext links: the document is more readable when the linked text is descriptive, rather than when the description is before or after the link with the linked text simply a filler such as "click here." For instance, a better approach is to say

```
Recent Dilbert strips are available on-line at
<A HREF="http://www.unitedmedia.com/comics/dilbert/">
The Dilbert Zone</A>.
```

rather than to say

```
<A HREF="http://www.unitedmedia.com/comics/dilbert/">
Click here</A> to see recent Dilbert strips that are
available on-line at The Dilbert Zone.
```

Core Approach

Avoid "click here" links. Instead, make the linked text descriptive enough so users know where it goes.

NAME

The NAME attribute gives a section a name so that other links can reference it through HREFs containing a # sign. For instance:

```
<A NAME="COBOL">COBOL: A Programming Language for the Future</A>
```

Note that this name is case sensitive.

TARGET

The TARGET attribute specifies that the referenced document be placed in a particular frame, or even in a new browser window. TARGET is discussed in Chapter 4 (Frames).

TITLE

TITLE can be used to supply a title for documents that wouldn't already have one (e.g., an FTP directory). TITLE is used by some browsers to suggest an e-mail subject line in mailto: links and could be used by indexing programs to build a menu of links.

REL and REV

The REL and REV attributes are used much less frequently than the other attributes. They can be used to describe the relationship of the current document to the linked document (REL) or the linked document to the current one (REV).

ONFOCUS and ONBLUR

These attributes are used by JavaScript-capable browsers to designate JavaScript code to be executed when the link receives focus and loses focus, respectively. An element focus event can occur either through the mouse or the keyboard. See Chapter 24 (JavaScript: Adding Dynamic Content to Web Pages) for more details.

COORDS and SHAPE

If the hyperlink represents a server-side image map connected to a CGI program, then COORDS specifies the (x,y) coordinate region of the image. The SHAPE attribute determines how the (x,y) pairs are interpreted. See Section 3.5 (Client-Side Image Maps) for further clarification of these two attributes.

TYPE, CHARSET, and HREFLANG

TYPE defines the MIME type associated with the resource indicated by the link, as in TYPE="text/html". The CHARSET attribute indicates the character encoding of the referenced link, for example, CHARSET="ISO-8859-6". The HREFLANG attribute indicates the base language of the link, for example, the syntax HREFLANG="pt" would mean that the referenced link is written in Portuguese.

ACCESSKEY and TABINDEX

ACCESSKEY is a single character (from the charset of the document) that acts as a hot key when used in conjunction with the Alt key on MS-Window systems or the Cmd key on Apple systems. When the key sequence is invoked, the document focus is set to the corresponding A element. TABINDEX is an integer between 0 and 32,767 that defines the tabbing order of the element in the document. When users navigate the document via the keyboard, the TABINDEX determines in which order the elements receive focus. By default, all elements that do not support the TABINDEX attributes have a value of 0. Elements with the same value receive focus in the order in which they appear in the document. Internet Explorer 5.x supports both of these attributes; Netscape 4.x supports neither.

3.4   Embedded Images

DILBERT © UFS. Reprinted by permission.

The `IMG` element enables you to insert images into the document. Most browsers support GIF (Graphics Interchange Format), JPEG (Joint Photographic Experts Group), and PNG (Portable Network Graphic) formats, but some browsers support others such as xbm, xpm, or bmp either directly or through plug-ins. In most cases, GIF images are more compact than JPEGs for images that have few color changes, such as drawings generated by graphics packages. JPEGs tend to be smaller for images with many changes, such as scanned photographs. Because image loading time can dominate the total Web page loading time, trying images both ways and checking the resulting sizes and quality is highly recommended.

Animated GIFs

Many browsers include support for the GIF89A standard, which allows multiple frames to be incorporated into an image file. The frames are overlaid on top of each other in a predefined cycle, resulting in a simple animation. Browsers that only support the GIF87 format but that are given an animated GIF in GIF89A format will still correctly display the first frame. An animated GIF is a good alternative to Java-based animations when the requirements are simple. Many commercial packages support the creation of animated GIFs from multiple GIF, TIFF, or other single-image formats, or by converting AVI or QuickTime movies.

The IMG Element

HTML Element:
    `<IMG SRC="..." ALT="..." ...>` **(No End Tag)**

Attributes: `SRC` (required), `ALT` (required), `ALIGN`, `WIDTH`, `HEIGHT`,
               `HSPACE`, `VSPACE`, `BORDER`, `USEMAP`, `ISMAP`, `NAME`,
               `LONGDESC`, `ONLOAD` (nonstandard), `ONERROR` (nonstandard),
               `ONABORT` (nonstandard)

`IMG` inserts an image at the current location of this document. Note that `IMG` is a text-level element and thus does not cause a paragraph break. `IMG` is not a container and has no end tag.

SRC

`SRC` is a required attribute that specifies the location of the image file to be inserted. The URL can be either an absolute or a relative one. For instance:

```
<IMG SRC="http://www.some-isp.com/~jane/portrait.jpg"
    ALT="Jane Doe">
<IMG SRC="images/spot.gif" WIDTH=150 HEIGHT=120
    ALT="My dog Spot">
```

ALT

ALT designates a string to display to text-only browsers, browsers with graphics temporarily disabled, or temporarily in regular browsers if text is loaded before images. In HTML 4.0, the ALT attribute is required.

WIDTH and HEIGHT

These two attributes specify the intended size of the image in pixels. Providing a WIDTH and HEIGHT allows many browsers to load the text first, then come back and insert the image without rearranging any of the rest of the page, giving a much more pleasing result to the reader. If you load an image file directly in Netscape, choosing Page Info from the View menu will show you the dimensions of the image. The size of the image is also displayed in the title of the Netscape window. In Internet Explorer 5.x, the task is a little easier; simply place the mouse pointer over the image, click the right mouse button, and select Properties. Note: if you supply dimensions different from the original image dimensions, then the image will be stretched or shrunk to fit the specified width and height. In this situation, Internet Explorer yields the displayed image dimensions, not the original image dimensions, when you select the Properties option.

Core Approach

Always supply ALT, WIDTH, and HEIGHT attributes for images.

ALIGN

The ALIGN attribute, technically deprecated in HTML 4.0, specifies the position of the image with respect to the line of text in which it occurs. Possible values are LEFT, RIGHT, TOP, BOTTOM, and MIDDLE, with BOTTOM being the default. The LEFT and RIGHT values allow the text to flow around the image and are generally used when the image is being used as an illustration. If you use LEFT or RIGHT alignment and do not want text to appear beside the image, use <BR CLEAR="ALL">. See Section 3.7 (Controlling Line Breaks). MIDDLE is useful when a small image is being used as a bullet. Listing 3.4 gives an example of each of the alignment options, with the result shown in Figure 3–3.

Listing 3.4 `Image-Alignment.html`

```
<!DOCTYPE HTML PUBLIC "-//W3C//DTD HTML 4.0 Transitional//EN">
<HTML>
<HEAD>
  <TITLE>Image Alignment</TITLE>
</HEAD>
<BODY>
<H1 ALIGN="CENTER">Image Alignment</H1>

<TABLE BORDER=1>
  <TR><TH>Alignment
      <TH>Result
  <TR><TH><CODE>LEFT</CODE>
      <TD><IMG SRC="rude-pc.gif" ALIGN="LEFT"
           ALT="Rude PC" WIDTH=54 HEIGHT=77>
          This positions the image at the left side,
          with text flowing around it on the right.
  <TR><TH><CODE>RIGHT</CODE>
      <TD><IMG SRC="rude-pc.gif" ALIGN="RIGHT"
           ALT="Rude PC" WIDTH=54 HEIGHT=77>
          This positions the image at the right side,
          with text flowing around it on the left.
  <TR><TH><CODE>TOP</CODE>
      <TD><IMG SRC="rude-pc.gif" ALIGN="TOP"
           ALT="Rude PC" WIDTH=54 HEIGHT=77>
          Here, the image runs into the paragraph
          and the line containing the image is
          aligned with the image top.
  <TR><TH><CODE>BOTTOM</CODE>
      <TD><IMG SRC="rude-pc.gif" ALIGN="BOTTOM"
           ALT="Rude PC" WIDTH=54 HEIGHT=77>
          Here, the image runs into the paragraph
          and the line containing the image is aligned
          with the image bottom.
  <TR><TH><CODE>MIDDLE</CODE>
      <TD><IMG SRC="rude-pc.gif" ALIGN="MIDDLE"
           ALT="Rude PC" WIDTH=54 HEIGHT=77>
          Here, the image runs into the paragraph
          and the line containing the image is aligned
          with the image center.
</TABLE>

</BODY>
</HTML>
```

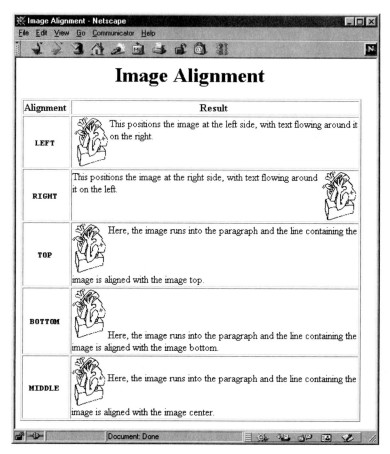

Figure 3–3   Five ways to align images.

HSPACE and VSPACE

These attributes stipulate the number of empty pixels to leave on the left and right (HSPACE) or top and bottom (VSPACE) of the image. The default is usually about 2. HTML 4.0 does not directly support methods for overlapping images or overlaying them with text, but such image layout can be done by use of negative margins with cascading style sheets. Because HSPACE and VSPACE are both officially deprecated, we recommend a style sheet approach for controlling margins. See Chapter 5 for details.

BORDER

The BORDER attribute, also officially deprecated in the HTML 4.0 specification, designates the width of the border to draw around the image when it is part of a hypertext link. The default is usually 2.

USEMAP

USEMAP supplies the name of a MAP entry, specified as "#name" or
"URL#name". See Section 3.5 (Client-Side Image Maps) for explanation and
an example.

ISMAP

ISMAP causes the image to be used as a server-side image map connected to a
CGI program. The use of ISMAP is only legal when the image is part of a
hypertext link. See Chapter 18 (HTML Forms).

NAME

The NAME attribute gives the image a name. JavaScript-enabled browsers can
refer to the image in JavaScript through the name.

LONGDESC

The LONGDESC attribute simply provides a URI to a detailed description of the
image. This attribute is useful for users of nongraphic browsers.

ONLOAD, ONERROR, and ONABORT

These attributes are extensions for JavaScript-enabled browsers and specify
code to be executed when the image is loaded, when an error occurs in loading
the image, and when the user terminates image loading before completion,
respectively.

3.5   Client-Side Image Maps

HTML Element: `<MAP NAME="...">  ...  </MAP>`
Attributes: NAME (required)

The MAP element enables the author to designate client-side image maps. This element enables the author to associate URLs with different regions of an image, a useful capability for creating toolbars and navigation images as well as for more
traditional maps. These image maps are processed entirely in the user's browser, as
opposed to server-side image maps provided by ISMAP or the image INPUT type
(both are described in Chapter 18, "HTML Forms"), both of which require communication with the server to determine the action. The NAME attribute is required and
provides a target for the USEMAP attribute of the IMG element. Each of the clickable
regions is described by an AREA element appearing inside between the start and end
MAP tags.

Listing 3.5 gives an example that divides an image into four quadrants with an HTML document associated with each. Results before and after clicking in the southwest corner for Internet Explorer 5.0 on Mac OS 9 are shown in Figure 3–4 and Figure 3–5, respectively.

Listing 3.5 An image map

```
<!DOCTYPE HTML PUBLIC "-//W3C//DTD HTML 4.0 Transitional//EN">
<HTML>
<HEAD>
  <TITLE>Kansas Topography</TITLE>
</HEAD>
<BODY>
<H1 ALIGN="CENTER">Kansas Topography</H1>
Click on a region of Kansas to get information on
the terrain in that area.
<P>
<IMG SRC="kansas.gif" ALT="Kansas" WIDTH=385 HEIGHT=170
     USEMAP="#Kansas" BORDER=0>
<MAP NAME="Kansas">
  <AREA HREF="nw.html"
        SHAPE="RECT"
        COORDS="0,0,192,85"
        ALT="North West">
  <AREA HREF="ne.html"
        SHAPE="RECT"
        COORDS="193,0,385,85"
        ALT="North East">
  <AREA HREF="sw.html"
        SHAPE="RECT"
        COORDS="0,86,192,170"
        ALT="South West">
  <AREA HREF="se.html"
        SHAPE="RECT"
        COORDS="193,86,385,170"
        ALT="South East">
</MAP>
</BODY>
</HTML>
```

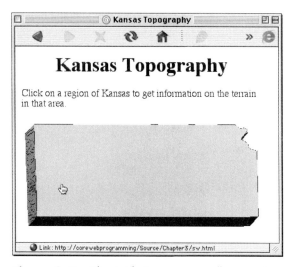

Figure 3–4 Client-side image maps allow you to associate Web pages with various parts of an image.

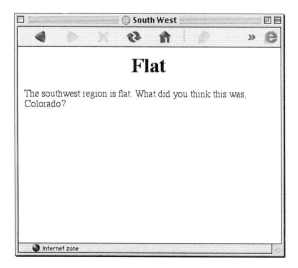

Figure 3–5 Results of clicking in the lower-left quadrant of the map in Figure 3–4.

HTML Element: `<AREA ALT="..." ...>` (No End Tag)
Attributes: HREF, COORDS, SHAPE, ALT (required), NOHREF, TARGET, ONFOCUS, ONBLUR, ACCESSKEY, TABINDEX

The AREA element can only appear inside a MAP element and describes a clickable region in an image map. One AREA entry is used for each region and describes the location of the hot zone, the destination URL, and a textual description normally displayed by the browser in the status line when the mouse or cursor moves over the designated region. If regions overlap, the first region specified takes precedence.

HREF
The HREF attribute specifies the target document and, as is typical with URLs, can be absolute or relative and can include a section name following a #.

COORDS
COORDS supplies a comma-separated list of the coordinates of the particular region. The number and interpretation of the coordinates depends on the SHAPE attribute (see examples in following section). The coordinates should be integers and are interpreted as pixels relative to the top-left corner of the image.

SHAPE
The SHAPE attribute should be one of RECT (the default shape), CIRCLE, POLY, or DEFAULT. Except for the DEFAULT value, SHAPE should be followed by a COORDS entry supplying coordinates appropriate to that type of region. The RECT entry should have associated coordinates in a comma-separated string of the form "left, top, right, bottom." For instance, the following associates `region3.html` with a 200 x 200 area whose top-left corner is at (20,40).

```
<AREA HREF="region3.html"
      SHAPE="RECT"
      COORDS="20,40,220,240">
```

The CIRCLE entry takes a COORDS string of the form "x, y, radius," and the POLY entry takes a string of the form "$x_1, y_1, x_2, y_2, ... , x_n, y_n$" giving the vertices of the bounding polygon. The DEFAULT entry has no associated COORDS and indicates the entire image. The URL belonging to overlapping regions is determined by the first AREA element enclosing the region. Thus, the default entry should always come last, whether or not the AREA element explicitly uses DEFAULT.

ALT
The ALT attribute supplies a string describing the destination URL. ALT is often shown by the browser in the status line when the mouse moves over the associated hot zone.

NOHREF

The NOHREF attribute designates a region with no associated URL. NOHREF is only needed if you want to turn off part of a region that would otherwise be active owing to some other AREA entry. Because the action associated with more than one AREA is determined by the first AREA entry, NOHREF entries should always come first.

Core Approach

Because the URL of areas in multiple regions is determined by the first applicable AREA element, NOHREF entries should come first in a MAP element and the entry for the default URL should come last.

TARGET

The TARGET attribute designates the target frame in which to show the results. Frames are particularly prevalent for documents that use image maps; see the discussion of frames in Chapter 4 for details.

ONFOCUS, ONBLUR, ACCESSKEY, and TABINDEX

These attributes are defined exactly the same as for the IMG element in Section 3.4 (Embedded Images).

3.6   Embedding Other Objects in Documents

Although there are a few text-only browsers, almost all browsers support embedded image files. But images are not the only kind of objects that can be placed in Web pages. Java applets are also supported by most major browsers. Other audio, video, VRML, and ActiveX objects typically either depend on the user having a specific plug-in or are browser specific.

Embedded Applets

HTML Element: `<APPLET CODE="..." WIDTH=xxx`
`HEIGHT=xxx ...> ... </APPLET>`

Attributes: `CODE`, `WIDTH` (required), `HEIGHT` (required), `CODEBASE`, `ALT`, `ALIGN`, `HSPACE`, `VSPACE`, `NAME`, `OBJECT`, `ARCHIVE` (nonstandard), `MAYSCRIPT` (nonstandard)

The `APPLET` tag enables you to embed an applet into a page and is discussed in detail in Chapter 9 (Applets and Basic Graphics).

CODE

`CODE` designates the filename of the Java class file to load and is required unless the `OBJECT` attribute is present. This attribute does not define an absolute URL; the filename is interpreted with respect to the current document's default directory unless `CODEBASE` is supplied.

Core Note

`CODE` cannot be used to give an absolute URL. Use `CODEBASE` if you want to load applets from someplace other than the current document's location.

WIDTH and HEIGHT

These attributes specify the size of the area the applet will occupy. They can be specified in pixels or as a percentage of the browser window width. However, Sun's "appletviewer" (a lightweight pseudobrowser that ignores all the HTML except for the `APPLET` part) cannot handle percentages because no preexisting window for the percentage to refer to is present. `WIDTH` and `HEIGHT` are required in all applets.

Core Alert

Sun's appletviewer cannot handle `WIDTH` and `HEIGHT` attributes as percentages.

CODEBASE

`CODEBASE` designates the base URL. The entry in `CODE` is taken with respect to this base directory. See Section 9.9 (The Java Plug-In) for an example.

ALT

Java-enabled browsers ignore markup between `<APPLET ...>` and `</APPLET>`, so alternative text for these browsers is normally displayed at the location of the applet. The `ALT` attribute was intended for browsers that support Java but have disabled this capability. `ALT` is not widely supported; thus, we recommend avoiding it.

ALIGN

The `ALIGN` attribute specifies alignment options and has the same possible values and interpretation of values as the `IMG` element (Section 3.4).

HSPACE

`HSPACE` specifies the empty space at the left and right of the applet in pixels.

VSPACE

`VSPACE` specifies the empty space at the top and bottom of the applet in pixels.

NAME

`NAME` gives a name to the applet. Used in Java for interapplet communication and by JavaScript to reference an applet by name.

OBJECT

The `OBJECT` attribute can be used to supply a serialized applet that was saved by the object serialization facility of Java.

ARCHIVE

`ARCHIVE` specifies an archive of class files to be preloaded. The archive should be Java Archive (`.jar`) format, but Netscape allows *uncompressed* Zip (`.zip`) archives.

MAYSCRIPT

Netscape and Internet Explorer use this attribute to determine if the applet can be controlled from JavaScript. For details, see Chapter 24 (JavaScript: Adding Dynamic Content to Web Pages).

Technically, the `APPLET` element, along with all the corresponding attributes, is deprecated in the HTML 4.0 specification. The recommended alternative is the `OBJECT` element. However, many authors still prefer the simpler `APPLET` element. See Sections 9.6 and 9.8 for additional information on the `APPLET` and `OBJECT` element.

HTML Element:
<PARAM NAME="..." VALUE="..."> (No End Tag)

Attributes: NAME (required), VALUE (required)

The PARAM element supplies customization values to the applet, which can read them by using getParameter. See Section 9.7 (Reading Applet Parameters) for details. A PARAM name of WIDTH or HEIGHT overrides the WIDTH and HEIGHT values in the APPLET tag, so you should avoid <PARAM NAME="WIDTH" ...> and <PARAM NAME="HEIGHT" ...>. Note: PARAM elements can also customize an HTML OBJECT, as discussed later in this section.

Core Alert

Never use WIDTH or HEIGHT as PARAM names.

Embedded Video, Audio, and Other Formats with Plug-ins

HTML Element: <EMBED SRC="..." ...> ... </EMBED>

Attributes: SRC, WIDTH, HEIGHT, *Plug-in-Specific Attributes*

The EMBED element is not part of the HTML 4.0 specification but can be used to create in-line objects of types supported by plug-ins for a particular browser. Text inside the element is ignored by browsers that support plug ins. In addition to the standard SRC, WIDTH, and HEIGHT attributes, other attributes particular to a specific plug-in are possible. For instance, both Netscape and Internet Explorer have standard plug-ins such as LiveVideo that support the playing of video clips in AVI format. These plug-ins support an additional attribute of AUTOSTART with values of TRUE or FALSE that determine if the video should begin playing automatically when the page is loaded or wait until the user clicks on the video (the default). For instance, the following would embed a video file in browsers with an appropriate plug-in that would begin playing only when the user clicks on the video object,

```
<EMBED SRC="martian-invasion.avi" WIDTH=120 HEIGHT=90>
```

A large list of free and for-fee plug-ins, along with usage descriptions and EMBED attributes supported, can be found at:

```
http://home.netscape.com/plugins/
```

Highlights include support for VRML, QuickTime, streaming audio, Adobe Acrobat files, PNG images, and more.

Embedded ActiveX Controls

HTML Element: `<OBJECT ...> ... </OBJECT>`
Attributes: CLASSID, CODETYPE, CODEBASE, ALIGN, BORDER, WIDTH,
HEIGHT, HSPACE, VSPACE, STANDBY, ARCHIVE, DATA,
TYPE, NAME, TABINDEX, DECLARE, USEMAP

Internet Explorer allows authors to embed any ActiveX control in a Web page. Customization parameters are supplied by PARAM elements, just as with Java applets. Because ActiveX controls, unlike Java applets, can perform arbitrary actions on the client system (including, in principle, deleting files, running arbitrary programs, and so forth), readers shouldn't allow arbitrary controls to be downloaded, but certain controls are bundled with Internet Explorer, and third-party controls can be digitally signed to verify their source. Many users are reluctant to allow any ActiveX controls to be downloaded to their machine, and Web pages with such controls shouldn't be considered portable even to readers using Internet Explorer. However, ActiveX controls can be *very* useful for trusted intranet environments. The most important attributes are as follows.

CLASSID

CLASSID specifies the URL. For registered controls, CLASSID is of the form
`clsid:class-identifier`.

CODETYPE

CODETYPE defines the content type of the object. The form for applets is
`CODETYPE="application/java"`. See Section 9.8 (HTML OBJECT
Element) for details.

CODEBASE

CODEBASE specifies the directory from which to load, just like the CODEBASE
attribute of APPLET.

ALIGN, BORDER, WIDTH, HEIGHT, HSPACE, and VSPACE

These attributes are used exactly the same way as they are for the IMG element.
See Section 3.4 (Embedded Images).

STANDBY

STANDBY supplies a string to be displayed while the object is loading.

ARCHIVE

The ARCHIVE attribute defines a space-separated list of URIs to preload before rendering of the object. The URIs are interpreted relative to the CODEBASE attribute. For applets, the standard archive is JAR format, which can be generated through the JDK jar utility.

DATA and TYPE

The DATA attribute is a URI specifying a data file to be processed by the object, where the TYPE attribute specifies the MIME type of the DATA.

NAME

The NAME attribute is used by browsers that support JavaScript to give a name that can be used by JavaScript to refer to the image.

TABINDEX

When users navigate the document via the keyboard, TABINDEX determines in which order the elements receive focus. Values between 0 and 32,767 are legal for the TABINDEX. By default, all elements that do not support the TABINDEX attributes have a value of 0. Furthermore, elements with the same value receive focus in the same order in which they appear in the document. Internet Explorer 5.x supports both of these attributes; Netscape 4.x supports neither.

The HTML 4.0 specification adds a DECLARE attribute that is currently unsupported by Netscape and Internet Explorer. DECLARE restrains the browser from initially loading the OBJECT, permitting loading later though a link, another OBJECT, or a button.

In addition, the HTML specification includes a USEMAP attribute for the OBJECT element to specify a client-side image map. USEMAP is not supported by Internet Explorer 5.x and earlier, or Netscape 4.7 and earlier. However, USEMAP is supported by Netscape 6.

A wide variety of third-party ActiveX controls can be found at CNET's ActiveX Download Gallery at http://www.activex.com/.

Embedded Scrolling Text Banners

HTML Element: `<MARQUEE ...> ... </MARQUEE>`
Attributes: `WIDTH, HEIGHT, ALIGN, BEHAVIOR, BGCOLOR, DIRECTION, HSPACE, VSPACE, LOOP, SCROLLAMOUNT, SCROLLDELAY`

The `MARQUEE` element is an Internet Explorer extension that displays the text enclosed between the start (`<MARQUEE ...>`) and end (`</MARQUEE>`) tags in a scrolling banner, or "marquee." Text-level markup is not allowed inside `MARQUEE`, but a `MARQUEE` element can be embedded inside markup such as a `FONT` element to give, for instance, large, scrolling, blue text. Browsers other than Internet Explorer ignore the `MARQUEE` tags and treat the enclosed text as part of the current paragraph. You can simply use `<MARQUEE>` as the start tag, or you can supply one of the following attributes to customize the behavior. Many end users consider `MARQUEE` to be an annoying distraction, so use it with caution.

WIDTH and HEIGHT

These attributes define the width and height for the marquee region, either in pixels or as a percentage of the Internet Explorer window's size. The default width is 100%, and the default height is based on the current font.

ALIGN

The `ALIGN` attribute specifies how the marquee should be aligned with respect to the surrounding text. Legal values are `LEFT`, `RIGHT`, `CENTER`, `TOP`, `BOTTOM`, and `MIDDLE`. These values are used in exactly the same way as in the `IMG` element covered in Section 3.4 (Embedded Images).

BEHAVIOR

The `BEHAVIOR` attribute describes how the text should move. `SCROLL`, the default, means that the text should scroll in one direction until off the screen, then repeat. `SLIDE` means that the text should scroll until reaching one side, then stop. `BOUNCE` means that the text should alternate back and forth within the defined region.

BGCOLOR

`BGCOLOR` defines the background color of the region.

DIRECTION

The `DIRECTION` attribute specifies the direction in which the text scrolls (or first scrolls, in the case of `BEHAVIOR="BOUNCE"`). Legal values are `LEFT` (from right to left) and `RIGHT` (from left to right). `LEFT` is the default.

HSPACE and VSPACE

HSPACE and VSPACE give the amount of horizontal and vertical space (in pixels) around the region, respectively.

LOOP

The LOOP attributes specifies how many times the scrolling will repeat. A value of -1 or INFINITE means that the scrolling text will repeat indefinitely; -1 is the default.

SCROLLAMOUNT

SCROLLAMOUNT specifies the number of pixels between each successive drawing of the text.

SCROLLDELAY

SCROLLDELAY specifies the number of milliseconds between each successive drawing.

3.7   Controlling Line Breaks

When displaying most types of text, the browser inserts line breaks to fit the available space. In Section 2.2 (Basic Text Elements), you saw the PRE tag that set a fixed-width font and turned off word wrapping for an entire paragraph. In addition to PRE, HTML lets you insert explicit line breaks with the BR tag and prevent line breaks by the use of either nonbreaking spaces or the nonstandard, but widely supported, NOBR tag.

HTML Element: <BR ...> (No End Tag)
Attributes: CLEAR

BR inserts a line break without ending the current paragraph. Because carriage returns in the HTML source are ignored except within a few special elements such as PRE or TEXTAREA, BR is necessary to guarantee a line break in the resultant page. The CLEAR attribute, with possible values of NONE (default), LEFT, RIGHT, and ALL, enables you to skip down past floating images at the left or right margins. On most browsers, including Netscape and Internet Explorer, multiple consecutive <BR> tags result in extra blank lines (unlike consecutive empty <P> tags).

HTML Element: <NOBR> ... </NOBR>
Attributes: None

The NOBR element is not part of HTML 4.0 but is supported by Netscape and Internet Explorer. NOBR suppresses word-wrapping for the enclosed text, except possibly at places indicated by WBR. The same effect can be obtained in standard HTML 4.0 by use of nonbreaking spaces ( ) between each word in the region of interest.

HTML Element: <WBR> (No End Tag)
Attributes: None

The WBR element, which should be used only inside a NOBR element, indicates that a line break can be placed at the tag if necessary. WBR is not part of HTML 4.0 but is typically supported by browsers that support NOBR.

3.8   Summary

Text-level elements let you specify character styles, line breaks, and hypertext links in paragraphs in a Web page. You can also embed images, either purely as static graphics, as a hypertext link, or with multiple hypertext links associated with different regions of the image. Finally, depending on your browser, you can embed Java applets, audio, video, Adobe Acrobat files, VRML, or ActiveX components.

The following two chapters build on this material, adding considerable functionality and control to a document. In Chapter 4 we look at frames, a capability that enables you to divide the Web page into rectangular regions and load a separate HTML document in each region. In Chapter 5 we discuss cascading style sheets, which give you much more control over the fonts, indentation, and style used for the various block-level and text-level elements.

FRAMES

Topics in This Chapter

- The basic structure of framed documents
- Specifying how the main browser window is divided
- Supplying the content of each of the frame cells
- Specifying that certain hypertext links be displayed in particular frames
- Using the preassigned frame names
- Solving common frame problems
- Using inline (floating) frames

Chapter 4

With frames, you can divide the current window into various rectangular cells, each associated with a separate HTML document. Frames were first developed by Netscape Corporation for use in Navigator 2.0 and were later adopted by Microsoft Corporation in Internet Explorer 3.0. Although not part of the earlier HTML 3.2 standard, frames, due to their significant capability and popularity in modern Web pages, became an integral part of HTML 4.0. Even though frames provide capabilities not obtainable with other HTML constructs, frames still remain slightly controversial because of some minor drawbacks. A few advantages of frames include the following:

- The author can guarantee that certain parts of the interface (e.g., a table of contents) are always on the screen.
- The author can avoid retyping common sections of multiple Web pages. Instead, the same document can be included in a frame in each of the Web pages.
- Users can navigate large Web sites more easily.
- Frames are a convenient way to mix text-oriented HTML with Java applets.
- Image maps are more convenient if the map image remains on screen and only the results section changes.

As a result, some users *love* frames and prefer pages that use them. However, frames have a few disadvantages as well:

- The meaning of the Back and Forward buttons can be confusing to users.
- Poorly designed frames can get the user lost.
- Because the address bar at the top of the document shows the URL of the *top-level document*, finding the URL of a particular *frame cell* when the user wants to remember or bookmark it may be difficult.
- Because a bookmark (favorite) can only specify a particular URL, users cannot save a particular frame *configuration* (i.e., the way the document looks after several selections).
- When you select Print, many browsers print the active frame cell, which, in most cases, is the Table of Contents cell that you just clicked in, not the new content cell.

As a result, some users *hate* frames and strongly prefer pages that do not use them. Although this chapter will help you avoid many of the disadvantages of frames, a good rule of thumb is to reserve frames for situations where the advantages are significant enough that you are willing to risk losing the readers that dislike frames.

In the HTML 4.0 specification, the TITLE attribute, covered in Chapter 1 (Designing Web Pages with HTML 4.0), is allowed for *all* elements in this chapter and is not covered individually for each element. Furthermore, the cascading style sheet specification also adds CLASS, ID, and STYLE attributes to *all* elements in this chapter. These three style sheet attributes are covered in Chapter 5 (Cascading Style Sheets) and are not covered separately here.

4.1   Frame Document Template

In a normal HTML document, the BODY section immediately follows the HEAD and contains the body of the Web page that the user sees. In a frame document, the BODY is omitted or relegated to a NOFRAMES section only seen by browsers that do not support frames. In lieu of BODY, a FRAMESET elements defines the basic row and column structure of the document. Listing 4.1 gives a basic template illustrating this structure. A FRAMESET can contain nested FRAMESETs that further subdivide the window, or it can contain FRAME elements that reference the URLs of the actual documents that will be displayed in the frame cells. A frame document should include the *Frameset* DOCTYPE,

```
<!DOCTYPE HTML PUBLIC "-//W3C//DTD HTML 4.0 Frameset//EN">
```

to be validated as legal HTML 4.0.

Listing 4.1   Template for frame documents

```
<!DOCTYPE HTML PUBLIC "-//W3C//DTD HTML 4.0 Frameset//EN">
<HTML>
<HEAD>
  <TITLE>Document Title</TITLE>
</HEAD>
<FRAMESET ...>
  <!-- FRAME and Nested FRAMESET Entries -->
  <NOFRAMES>
    <BODY>
      <!-- Stuff for non-frames browsers -->
    </BODY>
  </NOFRAMES>
</FRAMESET>
</HTML>
```

4.2   Specifying Frame Layout

The FRAMESET element defines the number and size of frame cells in a page.

HTML Element: <FRAMESET ...> ... </FRAMESET>
Attributes: ROWS, COLS, FRAMEBORDER (nonstandard), BORDER
(nonstandard), FRAMESPACING (nonstandard),
BORDERCOLOR (nonstandard), ONFOCUS (nonstandard),
ONBLUR (nonstandard), ONLOAD, ONUNLOAD

FRAMESET divides the current window or frame cell into rows or columns. Entries can be nested, so you can divide the window into complex rectangular regions. ROWS and COLS are basic to frames. FRAMEBORDER, BORDER, BORDERCOLOR, ONFOCUS, and ONBLUR are nonstandard attributes supported by both Netscape and Internet Explorer in versions 4.0 and later. FRAMESPACING is also a nonstandard attribute, supported only by Internet Explorer. ONLOAD and ONUNLOAD specify JavaScript code to execute when the frameset is loaded and unloaded, respectively.

ROWS

The ROWS attribute divides the browser window (or current cell, in the case of nested frames) horizontally, as used below.

```
<FRAMESET ROWS="Row1-Size, ... , RowN-Size">
  ...
</FRAMESET>
```

This code divides the current window or frame cell into *N* rows. Each size entry can be an integer (representing absolute pixels), an integer followed by % (indicating percentage of total available space), or an entry containing *. The * indicates "whatever space is left" and can be weighted by an integer placed in front if there is more than one such entry. For instance:

```
<FRAMESET ROWS="50,10%,*,2*">
   . . .
</FRAMESET>
```

This code specifies four rows. The first will be 50 pixels high, the second will be 10 percent of the total height, and the remaining space will be allocated to the last two rows, with the third row getting one-third of that remaining space and the fourth getting two-thirds (see Figure 4–1).

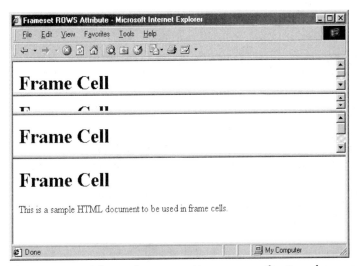

Figure 4–1   A frame document with a row specification of `"50,10%,*,2*"`.

As can be seen in Figure 4–1, small frame cells can result in sections that are hard or impossible to read, and you should keep in mind the possibility that the reader might use different-sized windows or fonts different from the ones you normally use. One of either ROWS or COLS is required. Finally, note that the ROWS values should always have at least two entries or the rows will not display properly in Netscape. For example,

```
<FRAMESET ROWS="*">
   <FRAME SRC="CoreWebProgramming.html">
</FRAMESET>
```

results in an empty frame cell (Netscape only).

Core Alert

FRAMESET entries should always specify at least two rows or columns.

COLS

The COLS attribute divides the current window or frame cell vertically; the syntax is the same as for the ROWS attribute. Like the ROWS attribute, COLS can appear at the top level or within another cell that was specified by FRAMESET. The COL values should always have at least two entries; wrapping FRAMESET around a single FRAME entry is unnecessary, and, in fact, doing so can cause incorrect results in Netscape. One of either ROWS or COLS is required.

FRAMEBORDER

The FRAMEBORDER attribute indicates whether borders will be drawn between frame cells. The default is to use borders. FRAMEBORDER=0 is often used in conjunction with BORDER=0 and FRAMESPACING=0 to produce a frame completely without inner and outer borders. The FRAMEBORDER setting for the overall FRAMESET can be overridden by FRAMEBORDER settings in individual FRAME entries or in nested FRAMESETs. Netscape 3.0 and later and Internet Explorer 4.0 and later accept YES or 1 to specify that borders should be shown and NO or 0 to specify that no borders should be used. As an example, Listings 4.2 and 4.3 show the source for two framed documents that are identical except for the FRAMEBORDER value. Figures 4–2 and 4–3 show the results.

Listing 4.2   Frame-Borders.html

```
<!DOCTYPE HTML PUBLIC "-//W3C//DTD HTML 4.0 Frameset//EN">
<HTML>
<HEAD>
  <TITLE>Frames with Borders</TITLE>
</HEAD>
<FRAMESET ROWS="40%,60%">
  <FRAME SRC="Frame-Cell.html">
  <FRAMESET COLS="*,*">
    <FRAME SRC="Frame-Cell.html">
    <FRAME SRC="Frame-Cell.html">
  </FRAMESET>
  <NOFRAMES>
    <BODY>
      Your browser does not support frames. Please see
      <A HREF="Frame-Cell.html">nonframes version</A>.
    </BODY>
  </NOFRAMES>
</FRAMESET>
</HTML>
```

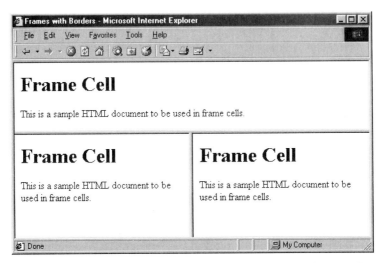

Figure 4–2   By default, 3D borders are drawn between frame cells.

Listing 4.3   `Frame-Borderless.html`

```
<!DOCTYPE HTML PUBLIC "-//W3C//DTD HTML 4.0 Frameset//EN">
<HTML>
<HEAD>
  <TITLE>Borderless Frames</TITLE>
</HEAD>

<FRAMESET ROWS="40%,60%" FRAMEBORDER=0
                         BORDER=0 FRAMESPACING=0>
  <FRAME SRC="Frame-Cell.html">

  <FRAMESET COLS="*,*">
    <FRAME SRC="Frame-Cell.html">
    <FRAME SRC="Frame-Cell.html">
  </FRAMESET>

  <NOFRAMES>
    <BODY>
      Your browser does not support frames. Please see
      <A HREF="Frame-Cell.html">nonframes version</A>.
    </BODY>
  </NOFRAMES>
</FRAMESET>

</HTML>
```

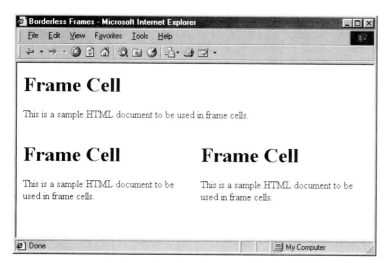

Figure 4–3 The 3D border between frame cells can be suppressed by the FRAMEBORDER attribute.

BORDER and FRAMESPACING (Internet Explorer)

These Internet Explorer-specific attributes specify the thickness of the border between cells and apply to the outermost FRAMESET only. The default is 5.

BORDERCOLOR

This nonstandard attribute, supported by both Netscape and Internet Explorer, sets the color of the border between cells, using either a hex RGB value or color name. The default is to use a 3D shadowed version of the background color. The border color can be overridden by BORDERCOLOR in FRAME entries or in a nested FRAMESET.

ONFOCUS and ONBLUR

These attributes designate JavaScript code to be executed when the frame gains/loses the input focus. Although attribute names are always case insensitive in HTML, traditional JavaScript calls them onFocus and onBlur rather than ONFOCUS and ONBLUR.

ONLOAD and ONUNLOAD

These attributes specify JavaScript code to be executed when the frameset is loaded and unloaded (i.e., when the user enters and exits the page). These attributes are usually called onLoad and onUnload in JavaScript.

4.3 Specifying the Content of Frame Cells

HTML Element: <FRAME SRC="..." ...> (No End Tag)
Attributes: SRC, NAME, FRAMEBORDER, BORDERCOLOR (nonstandard), MARGINWIDTH, MARGINHEIGHT, SCROLLING, NORESIZE, LONGDESC

The FRAME element designates the HTML document that will be placed in a particular frame cell. FRAME entries are legal only inside FRAMESET containers. BORDER-COLOR is a nonstandard attribute supported by both Netscape and Internet Explorer.

SRC

SRC specifies the URL of the document to be placed in the current cell. SRC is not strictly required because the HTML 4.0 specification permits empty frames. However, to avoid unexpected results, treat SRC as required in Netscape. See Section 4.5 (Solving Common Frame Problems) for more details.

Core Alert

FRAME entries with NAME but no SRC give unexpected results in Netscape.

NAME

The NAME attribute gives a name to the current cell. The TARGET attribute of A, AREA, BASE, and FORM can then be used to display new documents in the cell. See Section 4.4 (Targeting Frame Cells) for details. Similarly, a show-Document call in Java can supply a second argument with the cell name. The name must be begin with an alphanumeric character, but four predefined cell names that begin with an underscore are available. See Table 4.1 for more details on these predefined names.

FRAMEBORDER

FRAMEBORDER specifies whether or not the 3D border between cells is drawn. A FRAMEBORDER entry in an individual FRAME overrides that of the enclosing FRAMESET, with the proviso that a border is omitted only if adjacent cells also have FRAMEBORDER turned off. Netscape 3.0 and later and Internet Explorer 4.0 and later accepts YES or 1 to specify that borders should be shown and NO or 0 to specify that no borders should be used.

BORDERCOLOR

The BORDERCOLOR attribute determines the color of the frame's borders and can be a color name or a hex RGB value (see Table 1.1 in Section 1.6). When colors conflict at shared borders, the innermost definition wins, with Netscape resolving ties in an unspecified fashion.

MARGINWIDTH

MARGINWIDTH specifies the left and right cell margins.

MARGINHEIGHT

MARGINHEIGHT specifies the top and bottom cell margins.

SCROLLING

SCROLLING specifies whether cells should have scrollbars. In Netscape, YES results in a cell always having scrollbars, and AUTO (the default) means that a cell should have scrollbars only if the associated HTML document doesn't fit in the allocated space. In Internet Explorer, YES (the default) means the same as AUTO in Netscape. NO disables scrollbars in both cases.

NORESIZE

By default, the user can resize frame cells by dragging the border between cells. NORESIZE disables this capability.

LONGDESC

LONGDESC specifies a URI that provides a detailed description of the frame and is most suitable for nonvisual browsers.

HTML Element: `<NOFRAMES> ... </NOFRAMES>`
Attributes: None

A browser that supports frames ignores text inside the NOFRAMES container. However, the text will be shown by other browsers, which simply ignore the `<NOFRAMES>` and `</NOFRAMES>` tags, just like all other unrecognized tags. The text and markup inside a NOFRAMES element can be used to give a nonframe version of the page or to supply links to a separate nonframe version or the "main" cell of the document. Inflammatory alternate text like

```
<NOFRAMES>
Your browser doesn't support frames.
Get a <B>real</B> browser.
</NOFRAMES>
```

may be amusing (we hackers are easily amused), but not particularly helpful.

The HTML 4.0 specification adds event handling attributes (ONCLICK, ONDBLCLICK, ONKEYDOWN, ONKEYPRESS, ONKEYUP, ONMOUSEDOWN, ONMOUSE-MOVE, ONMOUSEOUT, ONMOUSEOVER, ONMOUSEUP) to the NOFRAMES element. See Chapter 24 (JavaScript: Adding Dynamic Content to Web Pages) for complete details on event handling in JavaScript. Furthermore, the HTML 4.0 specification also adds DIR and LANG attributes to the NOFRAMES element. These two attributes are covered in Section 1.6 (BODY—Creating the Main Document).

Examples

Listing 4.4 divides the top-level window into two rows, the first with three columns, and the second with two columns. The result is shown in Figure 4–4.

Listing 4.4   `Frame-Example1.html`

```
<!DOCTYPE HTML PUBLIC "-//W3C//DTD HTML 4.0 Frameset//EN">
<HTML>
<HEAD>
  <TITLE>Frame Example 1</TITLE>
</HEAD>
<FRAMESET ROWS="55%,45%">
  <FRAMESET COLS="*,*,*">
    <FRAME SRC="Frame-Cell.html">
    <FRAME SRC="Frame-Cell.html">
    <FRAME SRC="Frame-Cell.html">
  </FRAMESET>
  <FRAMESET COLS="*,*">
    <FRAME SRC="Frame-Cell.html">
    <FRAME SRC="Frame-Cell.html">
  </FRAMESET>
  <NOFRAMES>
    <BODY>
      Your browser does not support frames. Please see
      <A HREF="Frame-Cell.html">nonframes version</A>.
    </BODY>
  </NOFRAMES>
</FRAMESET>
</HTML>
```

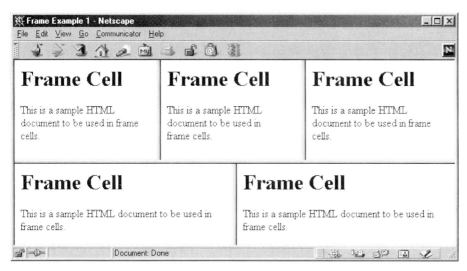

Figure 4–4 A document divided into two rows: the first with three columns, the second with two.

Listing 4.5 divides the top-level window into two columns, the first with three rows, and the second with two rows. The result is shown in Figure 4–5.

Listing 4.5 `Frame-Example2.html`

```
<!DOCTYPE HTML PUBLIC "-//W3C//DTD HTML 4.0 Frameset//EN">
<HTML>
<HEAD>
  <TITLE>Frame Example 2</TITLE>
</HEAD>
<FRAMESET COLS="55%,45%">
  <FRAMESET ROWS="*,*,*">
    <FRAME SRC="Frame-Cell.html">
    <FRAME SRC="Frame-Cell.html">
    <FRAME SRC="Frame-Cell.html">
  </FRAMESET>
  <FRAMESET ROWS="*,*">
    <FRAME SRC="Frame-Cell.html">
    <FRAME SRC="Frame-Cell.html">
  </FRAMESET>
  <NOFRAMES>
    <BODY>
      Your browser does not support frames. Please see
      <A HREF="Frame-Cell.html">nonframes version</A>.
    </BODY>
  </NOFRAMES>
</FRAMESET>
</HTML>
```

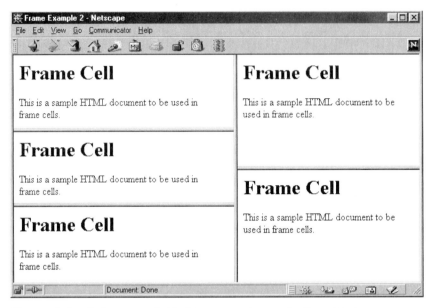

Figure 4–5   A document divided into two columns: the first with three rows, the second with two.

4.4   Targeting Frame Cells

A document can specify that pages referenced by hypertext links be placed in certain frames when selected. To target a particular frame, name the frame cell with the NAME attribute of FRAME; then, the hypertext reference gives a TARGET using that name. Be aware that user-defined names (see Table 4.1 in Section 4.4, "Targeting Frame Cells") that begin with an underscore are illegal. In the absence of a TARGET attribute, the new document will appear in whatever cell the selected cross-reference is located. If you supply a TARGET that does not yet exist, the designated document is placed in a new browser window and assigned the given name for future reference. Elements that allow a TARGET attribute include A, AREA, BASE (for giving a default target), and FORM. Java applets can target named frame cells by supplying a second argument to getAppletContext().showDocument.

Core Approach

Avoid beginning underscores when specifying user-defined frame names.

One common use of frames is to supply a small toolbar or table of contents frame at the top or left of the document, with a larger region reserved for the main document. Clicking on entries in the table of contents displays the designated link in the main document area. For instance, consider the example layout shown in Figure 4–6.

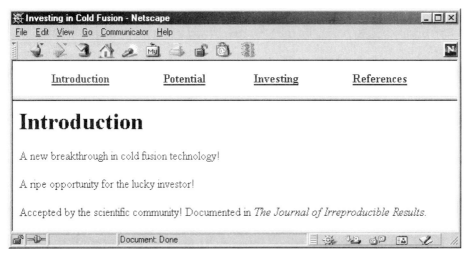

Figure 4–6 A document containing two frames: a table of contents frame and a second frame displaying one of the content sections.

The overall page is laid out to give the table of contents a fixed amount of space, with the remaining space devoted to the main document (named `Main`). Listing 4.6 gives the HTML used for the top-level layout.

Listing 4.6 `Cold-Fusion.html`

```
<!DOCTYPE HTML PUBLIC "-//W3C//DTD HTML 4.0 Frameset//EN">
<HTML>
<HEAD>
  <TITLE>Investing in Cold Fusion</TITLE>
</HEAD>
<FRAMESET ROWS="75,*">
  <FRAME SRC="TOC.html" NAME="TOC">
  <FRAME SRC="Introduction.html" NAME="Main">
  <NOFRAMES>
    <BODY>
      This page requires Frames. For a non-Frames version,
      <A HREF="Introduction.html">the introduction</A>.
    </BODY>
  </NOFRAMES>
</FRAMESET>
</HTML>
```

Next, links in the TOC.html document supply a TARGET attribute of Main, so that links selected in the upper frame are displayed in the lower frame. The table of contents document would have targeted anchor links, as shown in Listing 4.7.

Listing 4.7   TOC.html

```
<!DOCTYPE HTML PUBLIC "-//W3C//DTD HTML 4.0 Transitional//EN">
<HTML>
<HEAD>
  <TITLE>Table of Contents</TITLE>
</HEAD>
<BODY>
<TABLE WIDTH="100%">
  <TR><TH><A HREF="Introduction.html" TARGET="Main">
        Introduction</A></TH>
      <TH><A HREF="Potential.html" TARGET="Main">
        Potential</A></TH>
      <TH><A HREF="Investing.html" TARGET="Main">
        Investing</A></TH>
      <TH><A HREF="References.html" TARGET="Main">
        References</A></TH></TR>
</TABLE>
</BODY>
</HTML>
```

The idea is that if one of the entries in the table of contents is selected, the designated page gets shown in the lower frame, with the table of contents remaining unchanged. Note: you could have achieved the same effect by omitting the TARGET attributes in the links and supplying <BASE TARGET="Main"> in the HEAD. Figure 4–7 shows the result after the "Investing" link was selected. Any document with a TARGET attribute is not *strict* HTML 4.0 and requires a *Transitional* DOCTYPE at the beginning of the document. Of course, the four documents referenced by TOC.html can be standard HTML 4.0 with no TARGET attributes because untargeted links automatically display in the current frame cell.

Core Approach

If all links in the document target the same frame cell, then use
<BASE TARGET="..."> in the HEAD section to set the target for
all the links.

Predefined Frame Names

Four built-in frame names can be used when you specify TARGET attributes: _blank, _top, _parent, and _self. Since user-defined frame names cannot begin with an underscore, these names have the same interpretation in all framed documents. Table 4.1 summarizes the hyperlink action associated with the four reserved target names.

Table 4.1 Predefined Frame Names

Target	Redirection Action
_blank	Using a link target of _blank causes the linked document to be loaded into a new unnamed window.
_top	Using _top as a link target causes the linked document to take up the whole browser window. That is, the document referenced by the link will not be contained *in* a frame cell, although the document can still *contain* frames.
_parent	Using a target of _parent causes the linked document to be placed in the cell occupied by the immediate FRAMESET parent of the document. This use gives the same result as _top if there are no nested frames.
_self	Using a target of _self causes the linked document to be placed in the current cell. Explicitly specifying _self is only necessary to override a BASE entry. In the absence of <BASE TARGET="*frameName*">, the default behavior is to place the linked document in the cell containing the link.

4.5 Solving Common Frame Problems

Frames can cause difficulties for users and developers. Some of these problems are due to misconceptions that people have about the "page" stemming from a single HTML document. This section describes the most common difficulties and provides suggestions for avoiding them or minimizing their impact.

Bookmarking Frames

Suppose you are visiting a page that uses frames. Call this page `Url1`. You browse around for a while and find a document that is of particular interest to you. Call this `Url2`. So, you try to save a reference to `Url2` by adding it to your bookmarks list (also called "favorites" or "hotlist," depending on the browser). Later, you select that bookmark, but the browser brings you to the *original* frames-based page (`Url1`), not the *second* page you found (`Url2`). What's going on? The problem is that selecting Add from the Bookmarks or Favorites menu saves the URL of the top-level document (as shown on the address/location field at the top of the browser), not the one displayed in the frame cell you were interested in saving. This problem can be particularly unexpected when you visit a page that has frame borders turned off, because if you are not watching the address bar, you might not even realize that frames are being used.

In Netscape and Internet Explorer on Windows, clicking with the secondary (right) mouse button in a frame cell brings up a menu that allows you to save a bookmark to the URL of that particular cell. Now, selecting that entry later doesn't return you to the original frameset page, but rather to the individual frame cell.

Knowing how to save bookmarks to individual frame cells is important to Web users, but a realization that many users have trouble with this is also important to developers of frame-based sites. First of all, you should provide navigation aids so that users who bookmark your top-level page can quickly find the subpage of interest. Second, pages that are likely to be commonly referenced should contain their URL in plain-text in the body of the document. Third, you should consider maintaining a nonframes version of the site that contains links to all the documents in your main site. Although a full nonframes version can be difficult to maintain for sites that change frequently, a simple option that also satisfies the goal of putting the URL in the document is to make the reference to the current URL be part of a link that places the document in an unframed window, as below.

```
The original of this page can be found at
<A HREF="http://some-site.com/some-page.html TARGET="_top">
http://some-site.com/some-page.html</A>.
```

Printing Frames

Because each part of a frame is a separate HTML document, some browsers cannot print an entire framed document formatted in the same general layout as on-screen. Instead, they print a single frame cell. The question is: Which cell do they print? Many users assume that the answer is the cell that was most recently updated, but in fact the one printed is the cell with the current input focus. Selecting a hypertext link that displays a document in a particular frame cell does *not* change the input focus to the new frame. It can be extremely annoying to click on a link in the table of contents frame, get the result you want, select Print, and get a printout of the table of contents instead of the newly displayed frame! The solution is to explicitly click on the frame cell of interest before printing.

Core Tip

Before attempting to print part of a framed document, always click on the frame cell you want printed.

In Internet Explorer 5.x, frame printing is significantly easier. After selecting Print from the main File menu, you have three frame printing options:

- As laid out on the screen
- Only the selected frame
- All frames individually

These three options enable you to print the frame page exactly as desired. In addition, Internet Explorer 5.x supports a couple of additional printing options when an individual frame cell has focus: Print all linked documents (use with caution) and Print table of links.

As a developer, you can minimize the difficulties users will have in printing your pages. First, you can attach JavaScript code to the OnClick attribute of targeted hypertext links, specifying that the designated frame automatically gets the input focus whenever the link is selected. For details, see Chapter 24 (JavaScript: Adding Dynamic Content to Web Pages). Second, you can provide the users with a composite document to use for printing. This option is particularly convenient when you are making a reference page that is broken down into many separate documents, which would otherwise be tedious for users to print.

Updating Multiple Frame Cells Simultaneously

HTML does not have a method that allows a single hypertext link to update the contents of more than one frame cell. However, there are two potential solutions:

- Combine the cells into a single FRAME
- Use JavaScript

Each of these solutions is detailed in the following sections.

Combine the Cells into a Single Frame

Suppose that the initial FRAMESET looked like this:

```
<FRAMESET ROWS="*,*,*">
  <FRAME SRC="Top.html">
  <FRAME SRC="Middle.html" NAME="MIDDLE">
  <FRAME SRC="Bottom.html" NAME="BOTTOM">
</FRAMESET>
```

In such a case, no purely HTML method for a link in the Top.html document to replace the contents of *both* Middle.html and Bottom.html is available. However, the initial design could be replaced by:

```
<FRAMESET ROWS="*,2*">
  <FRAME SRC="Top.html">
  <FRAME SRC="Middle+Bottom.html" NAME="LOWER">
</FRAMESET>
```

Then, Middle+Bottom.html can itself contain a FRAMESET entry:

```
<FRAMESET ROWS="*,*">
  <FRAME SRC="Middle.html" NAME="MIDDLE">
  <FRAME SRC="Bottom.html" NAME="BOTTOM">
</FRAMESET>
```

Now, links can target the frame named LOWER, supplying the URL of a file that also contains two FRAME entries. This solution is not completely satisfactory, because it requires that the cells of interest be next to each other, and that all of the HTML documents in question be under the control of the author of the main layout and be modifiable to fit the new design. On the other hand, this approach works even for users who have disabled JavaScript or whose browsers do not support it, unlike the JavaScript alternative described next.

Using JavaScript

With JavaScript, authors can to attach code to the OnClick attribute of a hypertext link. This code can call any number of JavaScript statements, including top.*frameName*.location = *someURL*, which assigns new documents to particular frame cells. Any number of cells can be updated, and there is no requirement that the top-level framed document change structure nor that the updated cells be next to each other. Of course, this solution only works for browsers that support JavaScript. JavaScript is described in more detail in Chapter 24 (JavaScript: Adding Dynamic Content to Web Pages), but we'll look at a quick example here. Consider Listing 4.8, which creates one cell in the top row and three named cells in the bottom row.

Listing 4.8 `Multiple-Updates.html`

```
<!DOCTYPE HTML PUBLIC "-//W3C//DTD HTML 4.0 Frameset//EN">
<HTML>
<HEAD>
  <TITLE>Updating Multiple Frames Simultaneously</TITLE>
</HEAD>
<FRAMESET ROWS="75,*">
  <FRAME SRC="Top-Frame.html">
  <FRAMESET COLS="*,*,*">
    <FRAME SRC="Bottom1.html" NAME="Bottom1">
    <FRAME SRC="Bottom2.html" NAME="Bottom2">
    <FRAME SRC="Bottom3.html" NAME="Bottom3">
  </FRAMESET>
</FRAMESET>
</HTML>
```

Now, to have a link in the top frame send results to bottom cell 1 and 3, the top frame can contain JavaScript code that references the names `Bottom1` and `Bottom3`. This approach is shown in Listing 4.9, which defines the `updateCells` function and then attaches the function to the hypertext link's `OnClick` attribute. Figures 4–7 and 4–8 show the results before and after the link is selected.

Listing 4.9 `Top-Frame.html`

```
<!DOCTYPE HTML PUBLIC "-//W3C//DTD HTML 4.0 Transitional//EN">
<HTML>
<HEAD>
  <TITLE>Table of Contents</TITLE>
<SCRIPT TYPE="text/javascript">
<!--
function updateCells() {
  top.Bottom1.location = "Result1.html";
  top.Bottom3.location = "Result3.html";
}
// -->
</SCRIPT>
</HEAD>
<BODY BGCOLOR="WHITE" TEXT="BLACK">
When selected on JavaScript-capable browsers,
<A HREF="Result1.html" TARGET="Bottom1" OnClick="updateCells()">
this link</A> will update cell one and three below.
</BODY>
</HTML>
```

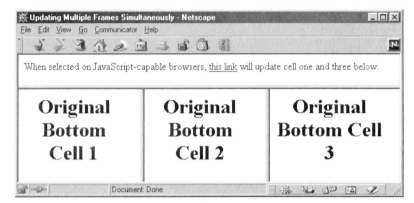

Figure 4–7   Framed document before hypertext link is selected.

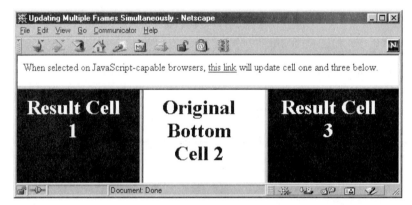

Figure 4–8   Framed document showing two updated cells after hypertext link is selected.

Preventing Your Documents from Being Framed

Some authors don't want their pages to appear in frame cells in other people's documents. One solution is to specify `<BASE TARGET="_top">` in the HEAD of the document. Although this doesn't prevent the initial appearance of your page, it prevents the page from remaining part of a frame after a link has been selected. JavaScript can also be used to prevent a page from appearing in a frame at all. Simply insert the following in the HEAD of the document:

```
<SCRIPT TYPE="text/javascript">
<!--
if (top.frames.length > 0)
  top.location = document.location;
// -->
</SCRIPT>
```

See Chapter 24 (JavaScript: Adding Dynamic Content to Web Pages) for more details on JavaScript. Since some users may have JavaScript disabled, you might want to use *both* techniques if you really want to prevent framing.

Creating Empty Frame Cells

In Internet Explorer version 3.0 and later, a FRAME can have a NAME but no SRC. In such a case, space is allocated for that cell as specified in the enclosing FRAMESET. Hypertext links that have a TARGET that designates the empty cell will behave as expected, with the associated file appearing in that cell. In Netscape, space is also allocated for frame cells, based on the enclosing FRAMESET. However, hypertext links that have a TARGET designating the initially empty cell behave as though no such frame exists. That is, the linked page appears in an entirely new browser window. This behavior is a bit inconvenient, because it is quite reasonable to want to populate certain frame cells in advance but fill in others only when the user makes a selection. The solution is to treat SRC as a required attribute, supplying the URL of an HTML document that has an empty BODY in situations where you want an "empty" cell.

Core Warning

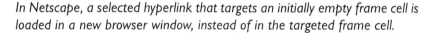

In Netscape, a selected hyperlink that targets an initially empty frame cell is loaded in a new browser window, instead of in the targeted frame cell.

4.6 Inline Frames

Internet Explorer and Netscape 6 have a nice feature whereby a frame can be defined in a manner similar to the definition of an image. You specify a width, height, source URL, and alignment, and the inline frame occupies a fixed position *in the HTML document*. This behavior is in contrast to normal frames, which occupy a fixed position *in the browser window*. Inline frames are very convenient for sidebars, contact information, and other things that you want to include in multiple documents. Unfortunately, however, although floating frames are part of the HTML 4.0 specification, they are supported only by Internet Explorer and Netscape 6. Earlier versions of Netscape do not support inline frames but do support *layers*, which provide a more general mechanism for this type of application. See Section 5.12 (Layers) for a complete discussion on layers. However, be aware that to be compliant with the HTML 4.0 specification, Netscape 6 no longer supports layers. The Web site, `http://sites.netscape.net/ekrock/standards.html`, provides information on how to support inline frames and layers for cross-browser support and backward compatibility.

To illustrate floating frames: Suppose that Professor Ithim teaches a variety of Computer Science courses. Being at a modern university, he naturally publishes the syllabus and other class information on Web pages. He wants to put his name, campus mailing address, and e-mail address on every page, but like all good programmers, hates to repeat himself and risk inconsistent versions. To avoid this, he can create a simple contact information file first, as in Listing 4.10.

Listing 4.10   `Contact-Info.html`

```
<!DOCTYPE HTML PUBLIC "-//W3C//DTD HTML 4.0//EN">
<HTML>
<HEAD>
  <TITLE>Prof. Al Gore Ithim</TITLE>
</HEAD>
<BODY>
Prof. Al Gore Ithim<BR>
Computer Science Department<BR>
Podunk University<BR>
<A HREF="mailto:algy@podunk.edu"> algy@podunk.edu</A>
</BODY>
</HTML>
```

Once Ithim has the contact file, he can use an `IFRAME` element to include the file at the bottom of each Web page that he creates. For instance, Listing 4.11   shows a simplified version of a page for Computer Science 401.

Listing 4.11   `CS-401.html`

```
<!DOCTYPE HTML PUBLIC "-//W3C//DTD HTML 4.0//EN">
<HTML>
<HEAD>
  <TITLE>Design and Analysis of Algorithms</TITLE>
</HEAD>
<BODY>
<H1>Design and Analysis of Algorithms</H1>
This course covers the techniques required to design and
analyze computer algorithms. The textbook is <I>Introduction
to Algorithms</I> by Cormen, Leiserson, and Rivest
(McGraw Hill, 1990, ISBN 0-07-013143-0).
```

(continued)

Listing 4.11 `CS-401.html` *(continued)*

```
<P>
Blah, blah, blah, algorithms. Yada, yada, yada, time. Blah,
blah, blah, space. Yada, yada, yada, iterative. Blah, blah,
blah, recurrences. Yada, yada, yard, data structures. Blah,
blah, blah, sorting. Yada, yada, yada, dynamic programming.
Blah, blah, blah, graph algorithms. Yada, yada, yada,
NP-Completeness.
<P>
<IFRAME SRC="Contact-Info.html" FRAMEBORDER=0></IFRAME>
</BODY>
</HTML>
```

Now, when this page is displayed in Internet Explorer, the contact information is placed at the bottom of the Web page, as illustrated in Figures 4–9 and 4–10.

Figure 4–9 Top part of `CS-401.html`: floating frame does not appear.

As can be seen, floating frames, unlike normal frames, do not occupy a fixed part of the Web browser window, but rather scroll with the rest of the document.

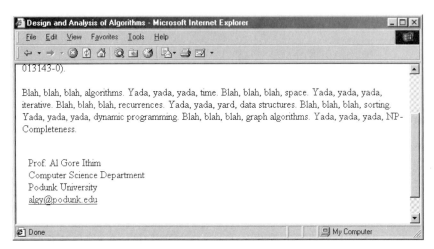

Figure 4-10 Bottom part of `CS-401.html`: floating frame scrolls into view.

HTML Element: `<IFRAME SRC="..." ...> ... </IFRAME>`

Attributes: SRC, WIDTH, HEIGHT, ALIGN, NAME, FRAMEBORDER, MARGINWIDTH, MARGINHEIGHT, SCROLLING, LONGDESC

`IFRAME` specifies a floating or inline frame. It is available only in Internet Explorer in version 3.0 and later. Text for incompatible browsers can be placed between the start and end tags and will be ignored by compatible browsers.

SRC

`SRC` specifies the URL of the document to be displayed in the floating frame.

WIDTH and HEIGHT

These attributes give the size of the floating frame in pixels. A percentage value is not permitted. An author can omit these values and let the browser size the frame appropriately.

ALIGN

`ALIGN` specifies the alignment of the frame with respect to the surrounding text, in a manner similar to alignment of embedded images. Legal values are `LEFT`, `RIGHT`, `CENTER`, `TOP`, `BOTTOM`, and `MIDDLE`.

NAME

Floating frames can be the end points of targeted links, just like normal frames. The `NAME` attribute gives the name for this purpose.

FRAMEBORDER

The FRAMEBORDER attribute determines whether (FRAMEBORDER=1) or not (FRAMEBORDER=0) borders should be drawn around the floating frame. The default is to use borders.

MARGINWIDTH

MARGINWIDTH gives the width of the left and right margins, in pixels.

MARGINHEIGHT

MARGINHEIGHT gives height of the top and bottom margins, in pixels.

SCROLLING

The SCROLLING attribute determines whether scrollbars should be used (SCROLLING="YES") or not (SCROLLING="NO").

LONGDESC

LONGDESC specifies a URI that provides a detailed description of the frame and is most suitable for nonvisual browsers.

4.7　Summary

Frames are an important addition to HTML 4.0 and are widely supported by current browsers. The FRAMESET element divides window or current cell into rectangular regions, and HTML documents are associated with the regions by the FRAME element. Hypertext links, forms, and Java applets can target user-defined or standard frame names, specifying that certain documents be displayed in particular frames. The most common frame problems can be avoided by careful design or use of Java-Script. Finally, floating frames provide a logical next step from fixed frames.

Cascading style sheets are another important addition to HTML 4.0. They enable you to customize the appearance and layout of standard and custom HTML elements, providing you with much more control over the final layout and look of Web pages you create. An extension to cascading style sheets lets you define "layers," which allow Web pages to define separate markup for various absolute or relative regions of the page. Layers go two steps beyond frames, since these regions can be overlapping and since their size and position can be dynamically changed through the use of JavaScript functions. Style sheets are discussed in the next chapter.

CASCADING STYLE SHEETS

Topics in This Chapter

- Defining style sheet rules
- Associating style rules with an HTML document
- Determining which elements support style rules
- Understanding the precedence rules of conflicting styles
- Controlling font characteristics
- Applying color and image characteristics
- Formatting text with styles
- Controlling the bounding box around HTML elements
- Adding image and floating text properties
- Improving lists through styles
- Using size units and color properties
- Adding multiple layers to a document

Chapter 5

C ascading style sheets are a powerful and flexible way of specifying formatting information for Web pages. They let you define the font, size, background and foreground color, background image, margin, and other characteristics for each of the standard HTML elements. In addition to specifying how standard elements should be displayed, style sheets let you define your own classes, effectively letting authors define new HTML elements, albeit with some constraints on the characteristics these new elements can have. Formatting rules are applied in a hierarchical or "cascading" manner, letting default rules from the browser combine with explicit rules from both the reader and the author. Style sheets can be loaded from external sites, permitting sharing of style sheets and letting authors change the look and feel of entire Web sites by changing only a single file. The current standard for style sheets is "Cascading Style Sheets, Level 1," known as "CSS1." Style sheets are supported by Netscape and Internet Explorer, versions 4.0x and above. Internet Explorer, version 3.0, supports most, but not all, of CSS1.

In addition to CSS1, the World Wide Web Consortium introduced CSS2, which adds support for media-specific style sheets so that authors can tailor the presentation of their documents to visual browsers, aural devices, printers, braille devices, and handheld devices. In addition, CSS2 supports content positioning, downloadable fonts, table layout, features for internationalization, automatic counters, and numbering. Extensive work is underway to extend style sheets in numerous areas. See the following links for additional information on the upcoming standards.

Cascading Style Sheets, Level 1

```
http://www.w3.org/TR/REC-CSS1
```

Cascading Style Sheets, Level 2

```
http://www.w3.org/TR/REC-CSS2
```

Extensible Stylesheet Language

```
http://www.w3.org/Style/XSL/
```

Style Sheet News and Proposed Extensions

```
http://www.w3.org/Style/
```

Only Cascading Style Sheets, Level 1 are covered in this chapter.

5.1   Specifying Style Rules

HTML elements are customized by the use of *style rules*. The most common practice is to place the style rules in a separate text file and refer to the text file through a LINK element located in the HEAD section of the document. However, style rules can also be placed directly in the HEAD section of an HTML document or in the body of the document. Style rules are of the form

```
selector { property: value }
```

or

```
selector { property1: value1;
           property2: value2;
           ...
           propertyN: valueN }
```

Note that multiple properties for a single selector should end in a semicolon; the last property of a selector does not require a semicolon.

The types of selectors that can be used are discussed in Section 5.3, but the most basic type is simply the name of an HTML element, signifying that the properties listed inside the braces should apply to all occurrences of that element in the document. The available properties and their possible values are described in Sections 5.5 through 5.10. For instance, consider the small HTML document shown in Listing 5.1.

When displayed in Internet Explorer, the result looks like Figure 5–1.

Listing 5.1   Fizzics1.html

```
<!DOCTYPE HTML PUBLIC "-//W3C//DTD HTML 4.0 Transitional//EN">
<HTML>
<HEAD>
  <TITLE>New Advances in Physics</TITLE>
</HEAD>
<BODY>
<H1>New Advances in Physics</H1>

<H2>Turning Gold into Lead</H2>
In a startling breakthrough, scientist B.O. "Gus" Fizzics
has invented a <STRONG>practical</STRONG> technique for
transmutation! For more details, please see
<A HREF="give-us-your-gold.html">our transmutation thesis</A>.

<H2>Perpetual Inactivity Machine</H2>
In a radical approach that turned traditional attempts to
develop perpetual motion machines on their heads, Prof.
Fizzics has developed a verified, bona-fide perpetual
<STRONG>inaction</STRONG> machine. To purchase your own for
only $99.00 (plus $43.29 shipping and handling), please see
<A HREF="rock.html">our order form</A>.
</BODY>
</HTML>
```

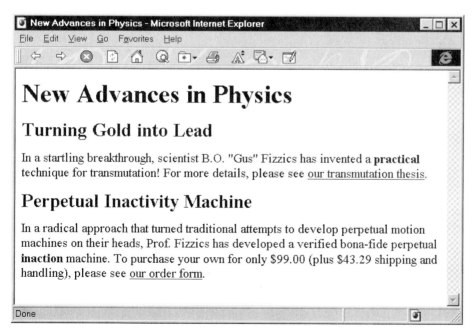

Figure 5-1   Fizzics1.html without style information.

However, when the style information shown in the following snippet is added to the document HEAD, the result changes to that of Figure 5–2. Note the use of HTML comments to prevent non-CSS-capable browsers from seeing the text between `<STYLE>` and `</STYLE>`.

```
<STYLE TYPE="text/css">
<!--
BODY { background: URL(images/confetti-background.jpg) }
H1 { text-align: center;
     font-family: Blackout }
H2 { font-family: MeppDisplayShadow }
STRONG { text-decoration: underline }
-->
</STYLE>
```

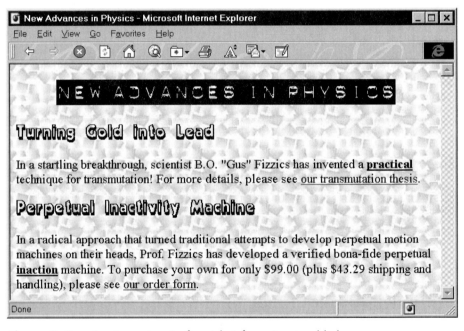

Figure 5–2   `Fizzics1.html` after style information is added.

5.2   Using External and Local Style Sheets

Style rules are most commonly placed in a separate text file on the Web site and referred to through a link in the HTML document. By creating an external file, you greatly simplify the application of the same set of style rules to multiple HTML files on the Web site. Alternatively, you can place the style rules locally in the document HEAD or directly in the body of the document.

External Style Sheets

If you plan to use the same formatting styles in several documents, you can create a separate style sheet in a WWW-accessible file. You can then link this file to HTML documents by using a LINK element in the document HEAD with a REL value of STYLESHEET, an HREF giving the location, and a TYPE of text/css. For instance, if the external style sheet is called Site-style.css and is located in the css directory, the file could be associated with the current document by a LINK element that looked like:

```
<LINK REL=STYLESHEET
      HREF="http://www.oursite.com/css/Site-style.css"
      TYPE="text/css">
```

The style sheet file should include the style rules for each selector, as shown in Listing 5.2. Including the STYLE tags in linked external file is optional—the style sheet is implied through the TYPE attribute in the LINK element. Many authors still include the STYLE tags and comment deliminators in the external style sheet, even though doing so is not required.

Core Approach

Simplify maintenance of your Web site and HTML files by placing your style sheets in external text files.

Listing 5.2   `Sitestyle.css`

```
/* Example of an external style sheet */

H1 { text-align: center;
     font-family: Arial
}
H2 { color: #440000;
     text-align: center;
     font-family: Arial Black, Arial, Helvetica, sans-serif
}

...
```

Styles rules placed in the HEAD section of the HTML document must be enclosed in the STYLE element.

HTML Element: `<STYLE TYPE="..." ...> ... </STYLE>`
Attributes: TYPE (required), MEDIA

The STYLE element defines a container for style sheet rules and can only appear within the HEAD section of a document. The standard syntax is:

```
<STYLE TYPE="text/css">
<!--
/* optional comment */
Style Rules
-->
</STYLE>
```

Typically, the style rules are enclosed in HTML comments to accommodate older browsers that do not support style sheets and would normally see the rules in between the `<STYLE>` and `</STYLE>` tags.

Core Approach

Enclose your STYLE rules in HTML comments.

TYPE
The TYPE attribute is required and defines the format of the style sheet rules. For a cascading style sheet the type is `"text/css"`. The type for a JavaScript style sheet is `"text/javascript"`.

MEDIA

The MEDIA attribute is currently unsupported by Netscape and Internet Explorer but is intended to indicate the required media device before the rules are applied, the idea being that a document could have multiple style sheets, depend on a particular media type. Legal values include ALL, AURAL, BRAILLE, HANDHELD, HELD, PRINT, PROJECTION, SCREEN (default), SPEECH, TTY, and TV.

The STYLE Element and JavaScript Style Sheets

In addition to a style TYPE of `"text/css"`, Netscape 4.x also supports a value of `"text/javascript"`. JavaScript style sheets use the `tags` object, use normal JavaScript syntax, and change property names of the form `property-name` to `propertyName`. For instance,

```
<STYLE TYPE="text/css">
<!--
H1 { text-align: center;
     font-family: Arial }
-->
</STYLE>
```

is equivalent to

```
<STYLE TYPE="text/javascript">
<!--
tags.H1.textAlign="center";
tags.H1.fontFamily="Arial";
//-->
</STYLE>
```

The standard syntax is more portable, but for Netscape-specific applications, Java-Script allows you to *calculate* values, rather than just specify them statically. Java-Script is discussed in more detail in Chapter 24.

Inline Style Specification

The CSS1 specification allows you to specify formatting information directly in an HTML element by use of the STYLE *attribute* added to all elements in the HTML 4.0 specification. Inline rules look just like normal rules except that the braces and HTML element name are omitted. For instance:

```
<H1>New Advances in Physics</H1>
<P STYLE="margin-left: 0.5in;
          margin-right: 0.5in;
          font-style: italic">
This paper gives the solution to three
previously unsolved problems: turning lead into gold,
antigravity, and a practical perpetual motion machine.
```

Inline rules override separate styles declared in the HEAD section. Separate style rules are easier to extend and maintain than inline styles and should generally be used when you are defining complex rules.

5.3   Selectors

You usually define style rules by placing an entry of the following form in the STYLE element:

```
selector { property1: value1; ... ; propertyN: valueN }
```

Up to this point, we have only given examples where the selector was an HTML element name, indicating that the rule should be applied to all elements of that type unless overridden in the element declaration itself. For instance, to specify that strongly emphasized text be rendered in bold with a 50% increased font size, you could use:

```
STRONG { font-weight: bold; font-size: 150% }
```

Although HTML elements are a common selector type, they are not the only option. The cascading style sheet standard allows a variety of selector types to define formatting rules that apply only in certain situations. The four most common categories of selectors are:

- HTML elements
- User-defined classes
- User-defined IDs
- Anchor pseudoclasses

To support style rules that apply only in certain conditions, use the attributes CLASS, ID, and STYLE, which are allowed for *all* HTML elements except for BASE, BASEFONT (ID allowed), HEAD, HTML, META, PARAM (ID allowed), SCRIPT, STYLE, and TITLE. In addition, the HTML 4.0 specification supports a SPAN element to apply a style to any arbitrary section of a document.

HTML Elements

Any HTML element can be used as a selector, although BR has no associated text, so rules would be meaningless. Property settings are inherited, for example, background colors for BODY apply to paragraphs within the body by default, font sizes for P apply to CODE sections within the paragraph unless overridden, and so forth. For instance, to make blue the default color for all text except first-level headings, with top-level headings in red, you could use:

```
BODY { color: blue }
H1 { color: red }
```

Elements can be grouped in comma-separated lists to allow common styles to be set for multiple HTML elements. For instance, you could use

```
H1, H2, H3, H4, H5, H6 { text-align: center;
                         font-family: sans-serif }
```

rather than setting each of H1 through H6 separately.

Most property settings are inherited. Elements contained within stylized elements receive the styles of the outer elements. Consider the following styles:

```
BODY { color: blue }
H1 { color: red }
EM { color: red }
```

In this example, setting the style of color: blue at the BODY element is also inherited by all elements in the HTML document, for example, P, UL, OL, and TABLE elements; basically, all text in the document will be blue, except for any overriding styles, as is the case with the H1 and EM style declarations.

One problem with the preceding example is that emphasized text *inside* a level-one heading would not be distinguishable from the rest of the heading. So, you could add a rule specifying that emphasized text be green *only* when inside a main heading, as follows:

```
H1 EM { color: green }
```

Contexts can be arbitrarily nested. The CSS specification clarifies which styles are inherited by child containers. However, be advised that Netscape 4.x suffers from numerous style sheet bugs. As a result, styles are not inherited by containers as expected. A workaround is to explicitly state the style for every nested container or to apply a user-defined class to problem containers.

Core Warning

In Netscape 4.x, not all styles are properly inherited by child containers, so thoroughly test your HTML document before posting on a Web site.

User-Defined Classes

You can also define your own classes of selectors, separated by a period from the associated HTML element. For instance, to define an "abstract" paragraph type, `<P>`, with indented left and right margins and italic text, you could use the following:

```
P.abstract { margin-left: 0.5in;
             margin-right: 0.5in;
             font-style: italic }
```

To use this class, you would supply the name of the class inside the CLASS attribute of the HTML element in the body of the document. For example, given the preceding abstract class, you could use the defined style as follows:

```
<H1>New Advances in Physics</H1>
<P CLASS="abstract">
This paper gives the solution to three previously unsolved
problems: turning lead into gold, antigravity, and a
practical perpetual motion machine.
```

You can also define classes that apply to any HTML element by omitting the HTML element that normally precedes the class name in the definition. For instance, the following defines a class that sets the foreground color to blue and uses a bold font:

```
.blue { color: blue; font-weight: bold }
```

This style could be used in an existing paragraph:

```
This text is in the default color, but
<SPAN CLASS="blue">this text is blue.</SPAN>
```

or could be applied to an entire block:

```
<H2 CLASS="blue">A Blue Heading</H2>
```

Be aware that Netscape does not recognize user-defined class names that contain an underscore. For example, Netscape would not recognize .blue_font as a style.

Core Warning

Class names that contain an underscore (_) are not recognized by Netscape.

User-Defined IDs

An ID is like a class but can be applied only once in a document. You define an ID by preceding the name with a #, then you reference the definition with the ID attribute, as follows:

```
<HEAD>
<TITLE>...</TITLE>
<STYLE TYPE="text/css">
<!--
#foo { color: red }
-->
</STYLE>
</HEAD>
<BODY>
...
<P ID="foo">
...
</BODY>
```

In most cases, classes are better choices than IDs.

Anchor Pseudoclasses

Although HTML has a single element to indicate a hypertext link (the anchor element A), browsers typically treat links in one of four different ways, depending on whether the links are new, visited, or active. The CSS1 standard lets you specify separate properties for each link type. To indicate the type of link, use one of the following selectors:

A:link or :link

This selector matches anchor elements only if they have *not* been visited, as determined from the browser's history log.

A:visited or :visited

This selector matches anchor elements only if they *have* been visited, as determined from the browser's history log.

A:active or :active

This selector indicates how links should be displayed as the user clicks on them (but before releasing the mouse).

A:hover or :hover

This selector, supported only in Internet Explorer, applies when the mouse is over the link.

These pseudoclasses can be combined with other selectors. For instance, in the following, the first style rule applies only to visited links inside text sections in a particular class, and the second style rule applies only to images that are inside hypertext links that have not been visited.

```
.bizarre :active { font-size: 300% }
A:link IMG { border: solid green }
```

5.4   Cascading: Style Sheet Precedence Rules

Multiple style rules may apply to a particular section of text; thus, the browser needs to know the order in which to apply the rules. The highest-precedence rules are applied last so that they replace conflicting values from lower-priority rules. The rules for determining the precedence (or "cascading") order are as outlined below.

1. Rules marked "important" have the highest priority.

A style rule can have the tag `!important` appended. For instance, in the following example, the foreground color property is marked as important.

```
H1 { color: black !important;
     font-family: sans-serif }
```

These declarations are normally used sparingly, if at all.

2. Author's rules have precedence over reader's rules.

Browsers may permit readers to create style sheets to override the system defaults. In such a case, explicit settings by the Web page author have higher priority over the browser settings.

3. More specific rules have precedence over less specific rules.

In specificity determination, ID attributes in the selector have the highest priority. Ties based on ID selectors are broken by counting the number of class attributes in the selector. Finally, if a rule is still tied, the number of HTML element (tag) names determines specificity. For instance, the following rules are sorted in order of specificity. The first is most specific because it has an ID selector. The other three are tied according to this measure, but the second rule has a class selector (big) and so has precedence over rules three and four, which don't. Finally, the third style rule is more specific than the fourth style rule because of the presence of two tags rather than one.

```
#foo { ... }
P.big H1 { ... }
P STRONG { ... }
STRONG { ... }
```

4. In case of a tie, the last rule specified has priority.

If two or more rules have the same priority after the previous three rules are applied, then later rules are given priority over earlier rules.

5.5 Font Properties

CSS1 gives the author control over several aspects of the font: whether the font is bold, italic, or normal, what size to use, what font families are preferred, and whether a small-cap variation should be used. Netscape also supports *dynamic fonts*, which let you attach a font definition file to a document rather than depending on certain fonts already being on the client system. Underlined text, subscripts, and superscripts are not set by these font properties but rather by the text-decoration and vertical-align properties, covered in Section 5.7 (Text Properties). In Sections 5.5 through 5.10, the style values are listed immediately after the style declaration, with the default value indicated in bold.

font-weight
normal | lighter | bold | bolder | 100 | 200 | ... | 900
This style specifies the weight of the font and has legal values of 100 (lightest) through 900 (heaviest) in units of 100, plus the relative values normal, lighter, bold, and bolder. For instance,

```
H1 { font-weight : 200 }
H2 { font-weight : bolder }
```

Netscape does not support the `bolder` font weight.

font-style
normal | italic | oblique
This property selects the font face type within a family. Legal values are `normal`, `italic`, and `oblique`.

```
P  { font-style : normal }
TH { font-sytle : italic }
```

Netscape does not support `oblique`.

font-size
pt, pc, in, cm, mm | em, ex, px, % |
xx-large | x-large | large | **medium** | small | x-small | xx-small |
smaller | larger
This style specifies the font size. A value can be in standard length units (see Table 5.1 in Section 5.11), a symbolic value, or a percentage. Symbolic values can be absolute (`xx-large`, `x-large`, `large`, `medium`, `small`, `x-small`, and `xx-small`) or relative (`smaller` or `larger`). A percentage is interpreted with respect to the font size of the container. For instance,

```
STRONG { font-size: 150% }
```

should mean that text in a `STRONG` element should be 50% larger than the current font size. Additional examples:

```
P { font-size: 14pt }
P { font-size: 1cm }
P { font-size: xx-large }
```

Note that Netscape will not recognize the style if you place a space between the numerical declaration and unit declaration, as in "14 pt" versus "14pt".

font-family
family name

This style specifies the typeface. For instance, Listing 5.3 shows a rather dry page describing "Camp Bear Claw," with the standard look in Internet Explorer shown in Figure 5–3.

Listing 5.3   A boring summer camp

```
<!DOCTYPE HTML PUBLIC "-//W3C//DTD HTML 4.0 Transitional//EN">
<HTML>
<HEAD>
  <TITLE>Camp Bear Claw</TITLE>
</HEAD>
<BODY>
<H1>Camp Bear Claw</H1>
We have the following activities:
<H2>Archery</H2>
<H2>Arts and Crafts</H2>
<H2>Horseback Riding</H2>
<H2>Hiking</H2>
<H2>Campfire Song Times</H2>
<H2>C++ Programming</H2>
</BODY>
</HTML>
```

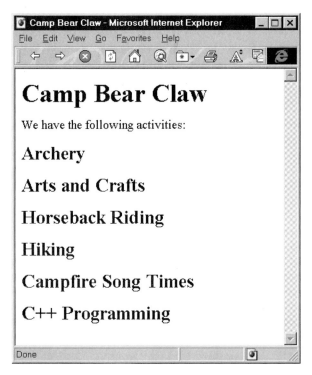

Figure 5–3   Bear Claw page with standard fonts.

However, by adding `font-family` entries (Listing 5.4 and Listing 5.5), we obtain a much more pleasing result (Figure 5–4).

Listing 5.4   An exciting summer camp

```
<!DOCTYPE HTML PUBLIC "-//W3C//DTD HTML 4.0 Transitional//EN">
<HTML>
<HEAD>
  <TITLE>Camp Bear Claw</TITLE>
  <LINK REL=STYLESHEET HREF="CampBearClaw.css" TYPE="text/css">
</HEAD>
<BODY>
<H1>Camp Bear Claw</H1>
We have the following activities:
<H2 CLASS="archery">Archery</H2>
<H2 CLASS="arts">Arts and Crafts</H2>
<H2 CLASS="horseback">Horseback Riding</H2>
<H2 CLASS="hiking">Hiking</H2>
<H2 CLASS="campfire">Campfire Song Times</H2>
<H2 CLASS="java">Java Programming</H2>
</BODY>
</HTML>
```

Listing 5.5   `CampBearClaw.css`

```
H1 { text-align: center;
     font-family: Funstuff }
H2.archery { font-family: ArcheryDisplay }
H2.arts { font-family: ClampettsDisplay }
H2.horseback { font-family: Rodeo }
H2.hiking { font-family: SnowtopCaps }
H2.campfire { font-family: Music Hall }
H2.java { font-family: Digiface }
```

Note that if `font-family` is used inside a `STYLE` attribute and enclosed in double quotes (e.g., `<P STYLE="font-family: SomeFont">`), the multi-word font names can be enclosed in single quotes as per the CSS1 specification. In addition, instead of a single font name, you can use a comma-separated list indicating the preferred order. The system will choose the first font available. You can put a generic typeface name such as "sansserif" at the end, or let the system choose a default font if none of the preferred choices are available.

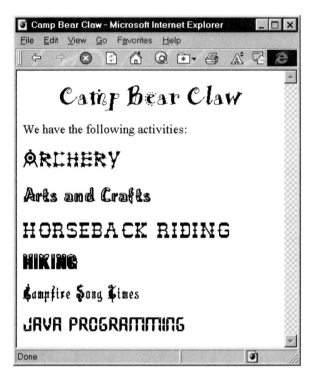

Figure 5–4   Bear Claw page with custom fonts.

Choosing font faces appropriately can make pages significantly more attractive, especially for intranet applications where a standard set of fonts can be assumed. On the Web, however, finding a font that is likely to be installed on all of the different systems that access your page is not easy. If you use a graphical or foreign-language font to present icons or cyrillic text in your page and that particular font is not installed on the user's machine, your page will appear as a jumbled mess. Your best bet is to create GIF files in such a case, but they can result in much longer download times and prevent users and Web indexing robots from correctly searching your page. Cascading Style Sheets, Level 2, offers an extremely useful extension: dynamic fonts. See `fontdef` later in this section for implementing dynamic fonts in Netscape, and see `font-face` for implementing dynamic fonts in Internet Explorer.

font-variant
normal | small-caps

This property is intended to be applied to text to make a variation in small caps. Legal values are `normal` and `small-caps`. Internet Explorer displays `small-caps` in capital letters, not *small* capital letters. Netscape does not support this font property.

font

The font property lets you group font-weight, font-variant, font-style, font-size, line-height, and font-family in a single entry. Items can be omitted, but if included, they should appear in that order, with spaces, between all except font-size and line-height, which should be separated by a slash (/). For instance,

```
P { font-weight: demi-bold;
    font-style: italic;
    font-size: 14pt;
    line-height: 150%;
    font-family: Times, serif }
```

could be replaced by

```
P { font: demi-bold italic 14pt/150% Times, serif }
```

fontdef

Dynamic fonts, an extension to CSS1, let you supply a font definition file for use in your HTML document. Netscape supports *dynamic fonts both through the* fontdef *style,*

```
<STYLE TYPE="text/css">
<!--
@fontdef URL(http://.../font-file.pfr);
...
-->
</STYLE>
```

and through the LINK *element placed in the* HEAD *section of the document,*

```
<LINK REL="fontdef"
      SRC="http://.../font-file.pfr">
```

After providing the link to the pfr file, you simply use the dynamic font as any normal font. Internet Explorer does not support the pfr file format directly. However, Bitstream, Inc., provides an ActiveX control to enable pfr font files in Internet Explorer. For more information on dynamic fonts and for several free font-definition files, see the following sites:

```
http://www.truedoc.com/webpages/intro/
http://www.bitstream.com/
```

font-face

Internet Explorer supports dynamic fonts through the font-face style defined in Cascading Style Sheets, Level 2 (see http://www.w3.org/TR/REC-CSS2/fonts.html#font-descriptions). To specify a dynamic font in Internet Explorer, use

```
<STYLE TYPE="text/css">
<!--
@font-face {
```

```
      font-family: fontname;
      font-style: normal;
      font-weight: normal;
      src: url(http://.../font-file.eot)
    }
    </STYLE>
```

Note that the font file format differs between Internet Explorer (`eot`) and Netscape (`pfr`). Microsoft provides Web Embedding Fonts Tools (WEFT) for creating `eot` object files. For examples of Microsoft dynamic fonts see,

```
    http://www.microsoft.com/typography/
```

The site also provides a free download of WEFT Version 2.

5.6   Foreground and Background Properties

Style sheets support a powerful and convenient way of changing foreground colors, background colors, and background images for regions of text. Style sheets don't suffer from the problem of a color becoming invisible if the user overrides the author's settings on the `BODY`'s `BGCOLOR`. Setting the `BGCOLOR` through a style sheet overrides the browser setting.

color
color-name | #RRGGBB | #RGB | rgb(rrr, ggg, bbb) | rgb(rrr%, ggg%, bbb%)
This property specifies the color of text or the foreground color of the associated section, using any of the standard color designators (Table 5.2 in Section 5.11). For example,

```
    P  { color : blue }
    H1 { color : #00AABB }
    H2 { color : #0AB }
    H3 { color : rgb(255, 0, 0 ) } /* red */
    H4 { color : rgb(0, 0, 255 ) } /* blue */
```

background-color
transparent |
color-name | #RRGGBB | #RGB | rgb(rrr, ggg, bbb) | rgb(rrr%, ggg%, bbb%)
This property specifies the background color of the associated section by using any of the standard color designators. Alternatively, the keyword `transparent` can be used to let an inherited color show through.

background-image
none | url(*filename*)

This property specifies an image to be used as the background of the specified region only. Authors should supply a background color to use if the image is unavailable or if the user has disabled image loading. For example,

```
H2 { background-image: url(Bluedrop.gif);}
```

background-repeat
repeat | repeat-x | repeat-y | norepeat

This property takes values of repeat, repeat-x, repeat-y, or no-repeat and means, respectively, that the image should be tiled in both directions, just in the x direction, just in the y direction, or displayed once in the background but not tiled. For instance,

```
BODY {
   background-image: url(Bluedot.gif);
   background-repeat: repeat-x;
}
```

background-attachment
scroll | fixed

This property determines whether the background image scrolls with the content (value: scroll) or is fixed (value: fixed). Netscape does not support this background property.

background-position
[top | center | bottom] [left | center | right] |
[pt, pc, in, cm, mm][pt, pc, in, cm, mm] |
[em, ex, px, %][em, ex, px, %]

The background-position property specifies the position of the background image with respect to the upper-left corner of the region You normally specify a pair of values (separated by a space), specified with the keywords left/center/right, top/middle/bottom, percentages, or distances in the standard units (see Table 5.1 in Section 5.11). For instance, a value of 50% means to put the center of the image at the center of the region. Similarly, a horizontal value of 25px means to position the left side of the image 25 pixels from the left side of the region. If you supply a single value instead of a pair, the value applies just to the horizontal position; the vertical position is set to 50%. The default position is 0% 0%. Negative positions are permitted, allowing images to hang into margins or previous text sections. For example,

```
BODY { background-image: url(Marty.jpg);
       background-position: 10% 10%; }
H1 { background-image: Bluedrop.gif;
     background-position: center; } /* 50% 50% */
```

Netscape does not support the `background-position` property.

background

The background property lets you combine `background-color`, `background-image`, `background-repeat`, `background-attachment`, and `background-position` in a single entry.

As an example, consider Listing 5.6 and Listing 5.7, which defines a page for Joe's Carpenter Shop and uses "wooden" boards repeated horizontally as the background image of the title banner. Figure 5–5 shows the result in Netscape Communicator 4.7.

Listing 5.6   `Cabinets.html`

```
<!DOCTYPE HTML PUBLIC "-//W3C//DTD HTML 4.0 Transitional//EN">
<HTML>
<HEAD>
  <TITLE>Joe's Cabinets</TITLE>
  <LINK REL=STYLESHEET HREF="Cabinets.css" TYPE="text/css">
</HEAD>
<BODY>
<CENTER>
<TABLE WIDTH=360 HEIGHT=199>
  <TR><TD ALIGN="CENTER" CLASS="banner">Joe's Cabinets
</TABLE>
</CENTER>
<P>
Welcome to Joe's Cabinets. We specialize in
<UL>
  <LI>Custom Cabinets
  <LI>Kitchen Remodeling
  <!-- Etc -->
</UL>
<!-- Etc -->
</BODY>
</HTML>
```

Listing 5.7   `Cabinets.css`

```
.banner { background: url(images/boards.jpg) repeat-x;
        font-size: 50pt;
        font-family: Arial Rounded MT Bold }
```

Figure 5-5   Background images can be used for individual text sections.

5.7   Text Properties

The text properties control the way text in a paragraph is laid out. Options let the user customize characteristics like interword spacing, paragraph justification, and indentation of leading lines in paragraphs.

word-spacing, letter-spacing
normal | +/– pt, pc, in, cm, mm | +/– em, ex, px

These properties specify a change to the default spacing between words or characters. Values are expressed in the standard length units (see Table 5.1 in Section 5.11) or by the keyword normal. Numeric values can be positive (add the space to the default word spacing) or negative (subtract the space from the default). Neither Netscape nor Internet Explorer supports word-spacing. Netscape does not support letter-spacing.

text-decoration
none | underline | overline | line-through | blink

The text-decoration property describes text additions, or "decorations" that are added to the text of an element. Legal values are none, underline, overline, line-through, and blink. For instance, to make hypertext links blue but not underlined and to underline text in paragraphs, use:

```
A:link { color:blue; text-decoration: none }
P { text-decoration: underline }
```

Note that Internet Explorer does not support the `blink` value. Netscape does not support the `overline` value.

vertical-align
top | bottom | **baseline** | middle | sub | super | text-top | text-bottom | %
This property determines how elements are positioned vertically. The value can be a percentage (positive or negative), indicating how far to raise the baseline of the element above the baseline of the parent element, or can be a symbolic value. Legal symbolic values are `top` (align the top with the tallest element in the line), `bottom` (align the bottom with the lowest element in the line), `baseline` (align the baseline of the element with the baseline of the parent element), `middle` (align the middle of the element with a point halfway up from the parent element's baseline), `sub` (make the element a subscript), `super` (make the element a superscript), `text-top` (align the top with the top of the parent element's font), and `text-bottom` (align the bottom of the element with the bottom of the parent element's font).

text-transform
none | uppercase | lowercase | capitalize
This property determines whether the text should be changed to all uppercase (`uppercase`), changed to all lowercase (`lowercase`), have the first letter of each word uppercase (`capitalize`), or have inherited text transformations suppressed (`none`).

text-align
left | right | center | justify
This property creates left-aligned, center-aligned, and right-aligned paragraphs or paragraphs aligned on both sides (i.e., justified).

text-indent
+/– pt, pc, in, cm, mm | +/– em, ex, px, %
This property specifies the indentation of the *first* line of the paragraph and is calculated with respect to the existing left margin as specified by `margin- left`. Values can be in standard length units or can be a percentage interpreted with respect to the width of the parent element. The default value is 0. Negative values indicate that the first line should hang out into the left margin. For example,

```
P { text-indent: -25px } /* Hanging indent */
```

line-height
normal | *number* | pt, pc, in, cm, mm | em, ex, px, %

This property specifies the height of each line—the distance between two consecutive baselines in a paragraph (sometimes known as *leading*, pronounced "ledding"). In addition to the standard length units (see Table 5.1 in Section 5.11), a percent value can be supplied, interpreted with respect to the font size. For instance,

```
.double { line-height: 200% }
.triple { line-height: 3 } /* 3x the font size */
DIV { line-height: 1.5em }
```

white-space
normal | pre | nowrap

The `white-space` property specifies how spaces, tabs, carriage returns, and new lines should be treated within the element. Legal values are `normal` (collapse white space to a single space), `pre` (maintain whites space as in the `PRE` element), and `nowrap` (only wrap at `BR` elements). Internet Explorer does not support the `white-space` style. Netscape does not recognize the `nowrap` option.

By way of example, consider a Web page that is intended to look like a business letter. Listing 5.8 gives the HTML source. First, the default spacing between all paragraphs is reduced by

```
P { margin-top: 5px }
```

Next, right-aligned (`rhead`) and left-aligned (`lhead`) paragraph classes are created for the date, return address, and receiver's address. The main body of the letter (`body`) uses indented lines and justified text, and the footer used for the signature (`foot`) is indented 60% and has a large interline spacing. Figure 5–6 shows the result in Internet Explorer 5.0 on Windows 2000.

Listing 5.8   `Bates.html`

```
<!DOCTYPE HTML PUBLIC "-//W3C//DTD HTML 4.0 Transitional//EN">
<HTML>
<HEAD>
  <TITLE>An Open Letter to the IRS</TITLE>
  <LINK REL=STYLESHEET HREF="Bates.css" TYPE="text/css">
</HEAD>
```

(continued)

Listing 5.8 `Bates.html` *(continued)*

```
<BODY BACKGROUND="images/bond-paper.jpg">
<P CLASS="rhead">
April 1, 2001
<HR>
<P CLASS="rhead">
William A. Bates<BR>
Macrosoft Corporation<BR>
Blumond, WA 12345
<P CLASS="lhead">
Internal Revenue Service<BR>
Philadelphia, PA 67890
<P>
<BR>
Dear Sirs,
<P CLASS="body">
I am writing to inform you that, due to financial difficulties,
I will be unable to pay my taxes this year.
<P CLASS="body">
You see, my company has had reduced profits this year. In fact
gross revenues have now dropped below the GDP of <B>twelve</B>
foreign countries! Given this intolerable situation, I am sure
you will understand.
<P CLASS="foot">
Sincerely,<BR>
William A. Bates
</BODY>
</HTML>
```

Listing 5.9 `Bates.css`

```
P { margin-top: 5px }
P.rhead { text-align: right;
        margin-right: 0.5in;
        font-family: sans-serif }
P.lhead { font-family: sans-serif }
P.body { text-align: justify;
        text-indent: 0.5in }
P.foot { margin-left: 60%;
        line-height: 300% }
```

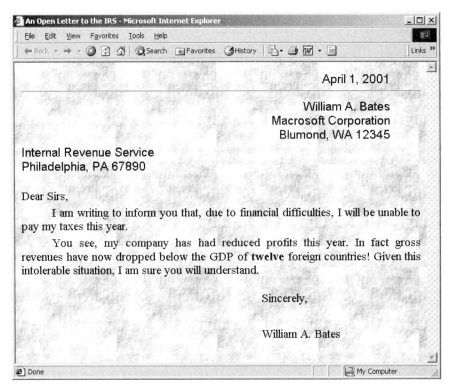

Figure 5–6   Using text properties enables customized text formatting.

5.8   Properties of the Bounding Box

Cascading style sheets assume that all elements will result in one or more *rectangular* regions. Such a region is known as the "bounding box" (or simply "box") and contains a margin, border, padding area, and main element, each nested within the other. The width and height of the total box is the sum of the width and height of the main element, the padding area that surrounds the main element, the border surrounding the padding, and the margins surrounding the border. Margins are always transparent, letting the color or image underneath show through. The padding always takes on the background color or image of the main element. The border, which is in between, can have a separate background. For instance, you could set margins, border, and padding to a quarter of an inch each (but using different colors/patterns) by the following:

```
P { margin: 0.25in;
    border: 0.25in solid black;
    padding: 0.25in;
    background: URL(images/bond-paper.jpg) }
BODY { background: URL(images/bricks.jpg) }
```

Figure 5–7 shows a page created with these settings. The details of the property specifications are explained later, but for now the important point is that the margin is outside the border, which is outside the padding, which is outside the main element area.

Figure 5–7   The differences between margin, border, and padding.

Margins

An element's margins are the reserved areas around the element where the background colors or images show through. Margins can be negative to allow paragraphs to overlap.

margin-left, margin-right, margin-top, margin-bottom
auto | +/– pt, pc, in, cm, mm | +/– em, ex, px, %
These properties set the left, right, top, and bottom margins, using normal length units (see Table 5.1 in Section 5.11), percentages, or the keyword auto. The default value is 0. Negative values are permitted; they allow text or graphics to hang into the left margin or overlap previous paragraphs. For instance,

```
P  { margin-right: 5ex }
H1 { margin-top: 200% }
```

margin

This property lets you set the top, right, bottom, and left margins (in that order) in one property. If only one value is supplied, then the value applies to all four margins. If two or three values are supplied, then values for any unspecified margin are taken from the opposite margin. Negative values are permitted and are sometimes used to implement layered text effects.

Borders

An element's borders are the reserved areas around the element where a specific color or background image is displayed. The borders are inside the margins. Borders can have zero thicknesses but cannot be negative.

border-left-width, border-right-width, border-top-width, border-bottom-width

none | thin | **medium** | thick |

pt, pc, in, cm, mm | em, ex, px

These properties set the left, right, top, and bottom border sizes, using normal length units (see Table 5.1 in Section 5.11) or the symbolic names thin, medium, thick, or none. Negative values are prohibited.

border-width

none | thin | **medium** | thick |

pt, pc, in, cm, mm | em, ex, px

This property is a shorthand method for setting border-width-top, border-width-right, border-width-bottom, and border-width-left (in that order) in one fell swoop. If only one value is supplied, the value applies to all four borders. If two or three values are supplied, values for any missing border are taken from the opposite border. For example,

```
DIV { border-width: medium thin }
```

produces a division with a medium border for the top and bottom sides, and a thin border for the left and right sides.

border-color

color-name | #RRGGBB | #RGB | rgb(rrr, ggg, bbb) | rgb(rrr%, ggg%, bbb%)

This property sets the border colors. One to four values can be supplied, specifying characteristics for the top, right, bottom, and left borders in the same manner as with border-width. Each value can be a color specified in the normal way (see Table 5.2 in Section 5.11). For example,

```
P { border-style: solid;
    border-color: black gray gray black;
}
```

Netscape does not properly support specification of more than one color value.

border-style
none | dotted | dashed | solid | double | groove | ridge | inset | outset
This property specifies the way in which the borders will be drawn. One to four values can be supplied, specifying characteristics for the top, right, bottom, and left borders in the same manner as with `border-width`. Each value can be one of `none`, `dotted`, `dashed`, `solid`, `double`, `groove`, `ridge`, `inset`, or `outset`. The main element's background shows through for the nonforeground part of `double`. Neither Netscape nor Internet Explorer supports the `dashed` or `dotted` values. In addition, Netscape does not supports the values for this style directly. These values can be stated in the `border` style. For example,

```
P { border-sytle: ridge }
```

is not recognized by Netscape, but the following is properly recognized,

```
P { border: ridge }
```

Internet Explorer properly supports both approaches.

border-left, border-right, border-top, border-bottom
This property lets you set the width, style, and color for each of the four borders. For instance, to display major headings in red with a solid blue line above and below, you could use:

```
H1 { color: red;
     border-top: 10px solid blue;
     border-bottom: 10px solid blue }
```

border
This property sets the width, style, and color for all four borders at once. For instance, the quarter-inch solid black border of Figure 5–7 was specified by:

```
border: 0.25in solid black
```

Padding

An element's padding area is the reserved space around an element and inside its borders where the background color or image of the element itself shows through. Padding area sizes cannot be negative.

padding-left, padding-right, padding-top, padding-bottom
pt, pc, in, cm, mm | em, ex, px, %
These properties let you set the left, right, top, and bottom sizes of the padding area. Recall that the padding area is inside the margin and the border. The

margin lets the background of the parent element (often the BODY) show through, the border can have an independent background, and the padding area has the same background as the main element it is associated with. Values can be lengths (see Table 5.1 in Section 5.11) or percentages, where percentages are interpreted with respect to the parent element's width and height. The default value is 0. Negative values are not allowed.

padding

This property lets you set the sizes of the top, right, bottom, and left sides of the padding area in one location. If only one value is supplied, the value applies to all four sides. Otherwise, if fewer than four values are supplied, then the value for any missing side is taken from the opposite side. For instance, the quarter-inch padding area used in Figure 5–7 was specified with

```
padding: 0.25in
```

Bounding Box Display Types

Most HTML elements can have margins, borders, and padding areas. However, the way these box components are interpreted depends on whether an element is embedded in another paragraph (i.e., an inline, text-level element), is a separate block-level element, or is part of a list. The display property can be used to change how the box is interpreted.

display
block | inline | list-item | none

This property determines whether the element should be considered to have a separate bounding box, as would a paragraph such as P or PRE, or have inline bounding boxes on each line inside an existing box, as would the various character-style elements (B, I, CODE, and so forth). Legal values are block, inline, list-item, and none. The list-item value is treated just like block except that a list item marker is added (see Section 5.10).

5.9   Images and Floating Elements

Most style rules apply to elements at fixed locations. Images and text items that "float" to the margins are in a special category, however.

width, height

auto | pt, pc, in, cm, mm | em, ex, px

These properties specify a fixed size for the element and are usually applied to images. Values can be in normal length units (see Table 5.1 in Section 5.11) or can be the keyword auto. For instance, a "bullet" type might be created as follows:

```
IMG.bullet { width: 50px; height: 50px }
```

The auto keyword applies to images where only one of width or height is specified as a length; it means that the image should be scaled, maintaining the original aspect ratio.

float

none | left | right

This property lets elements float into the left or right margins with text wrapping around. The legal values are left, right, and none. This style property can be used to implement drop caps, floating images, and the like. For instance, Listing 5.10 implements a 75 point drop capital to lead off Psalm 23. The result is shown in Figure 5–8.

Listing 5.10 `Psalm23.html`

```
<!DOCTYPE HTML PUBLIC "-//W3C//DTD HTML 4.0 Transitional//EN">
<HTML>
<HEAD>
  <TITLE>The 23rd Psalm</TITLE>
<STYLE>
<!--
SPAN { float: left;
       font-family: "Cushing Book";
       font-size: 75pt }
-->
</STYLE>
</HEAD>
<BODY>
<H2 ALIGN="CENTER">
The 23rd Psalm (King James Version)</H2>
<SPAN>T</SPAN>he LORD is my shepherd; I shall not want.
He maketh me to lie down in green pastures: he leadeth me
beside the still waters. He restoreth my soul: he leadeth me
in the paths of righteousness for his name's sake. Yea,
though I walk through the valley of the shadow of death, I
will fear no evil: for thou art with me; thy rod and thy
staff they comfort me. Thou preparest a table before me in
the presence of mine enemies: thou anointest my head with oil;
my cup runneth over. Surely goodness and mercy shall follow me
all the days of my life: and I will dwell in the house of the
LORD forever.
</BODY>
</HTML>
```

Figure 5-8 The `float` property can be used to implement "drop caps."

clear
none | left | right | both

This property specifies whether the element permits floating elements on its sides. Legal values are `left` (skip below any floating elements on the left), `right` (skip past floating elements on the right), `both` (skip past all floating elements), and `none` (permit floating elements). For instance, in the 23rd Psalm shown in Listing 5.10 and Figure 5–8, suppose a new paragraph was inserted after the first sentence. If the paragraph break were simply `<P>`, the result would be as shown in Figure 5–9 (a), with the second sentence beginning before the bottom of the drop cap T.

(a) 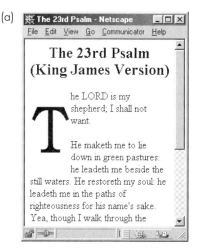 (b)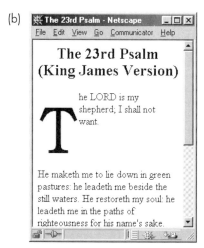

Figure 5-9 (a) When a paragraph break is added, the default behavior is to permit the floating element and continue the flow, instead of skipping past the floating element. (b) Paragraphs can skip past floating elements from previous paragraphs.

However, if the paragraph was <P STYLE="clear: left">, then the result would be as shown in Figure 5–9 (b), with the second sentence beginning below the bottom of the initial T.

5.10 List Properties

Cascading style sheets allow you to customize the way list items are formatted in ordered lists (OL), unordered lists (UL), and definition lists (DL). These properties are not supported by Internet Explorer version 3, and Netscape 4 supports only the list-style-type property.

list-style-image
none | url(*filename*)

This property allows you to set your own "bullets" for lists. However, this property is only supported by Internet Explorer. The value should be a URL or the keyword none. For instance, the following would set the default bullet for unordered lists to be a diamond, plus set up a "star" class that can be used in unordered lists to get a star as a bullet.

```
UL { list-style-image: url(diamond.gif) }
UL.star { list-style-image: url(star.gif) }
```

If a browser supports animated GIFs, they should be permitted as bullets. Netscape does not support the list-style-image style.

list-style-type
none | **disc** | circle | square | decimal | upper-alpha | lower-alpha | upper-roman | lower-roman

This property sets the list item marker in the cases when the list-style image is none (the default for OL and DL). Legal values are disc (solid circle), circle (hollow circle), square, decimal (1, 2, 3, and so forth), upper-alpha (A, B, C, and so forth), lower-alpha (a, b, c, and so forth), upper-roman (I, II, III, and so forth), lower-roman (i, ii, iii, and so forth), and none.

list-style-position
outside | inside

This property, with legal values of outside (default) and inside, determines whether the list item marker runs into the paragraph (inside) or hangs out to the left (outside). Neither Netscape nor Internet Explorer supports list-style-position.

list-style

The `list-style` property permits you to set the list's image, style type, and position in a single property.

5.11 Standard Property Units

Cascading style sheets allow you to specify sizes and colors in a variety of different formats. You can specify lengths in either absolute or relative units, using either integers or decimal floating-point numbers. Some properties allow negative lengths, which are indicated by a leading minus sign ("–") before a length otherwise specified in the normal manner.

Lengths

Cascading style sheets permit authors to use any of the following formats in Table 5.1 for properties that describe lengths (sizes).

Table 5.1 Absolute and Relative Length Units

cm	Centimeters (absolute unit)
em	The height of the current font (relative unit)
ex	The height of the letter "x" in the current font (relative unit)
in	Inches (absolute unit)
mm	Millimeters (absolute unit)
pc	Picas; 6 picas per inch; 12 points per pica (absolute unit)
pt	Points; 72 points per inch (absolute unit)
px	Pixels (relative unit)

Colors

Cascading style sheets allow you to specify colors in any of the ways listed.

Table 5.2 Color Formats in CSS 1

color-name	This color should be one of the standard HTML colors listed in Table 1.1 (Section 1.6). Netscape and Internet Explorer also support the X11 window system color names.
#RRGGBB	Each of RR, GG, and BB should be hexadecimal numbers ranging from 00 to FF, as with standard HTML colors.
#RGB	This format is a shorthand notation for #RRGGBB. For instance, #0AF is equivalent to #00AAFF.
rgb(rrr, ggg, bbb)	In this format, each of rrr, ggg, and bbb should be decimal numbers ranging from 0 to 255.
rgb(rrr%, ggg%, bbb%)	In this format, each of rrr, ggg, and bbb should be decimal numbers ranging from 0 to 100.

5.12 Layers

Netscape 4 supports a capability known as *layers* which allows you to place HTML markup in separate rectangular regions, then to position the regions at particular absolute or relative positions on the page. Regions can overlap, and upper regions can be transparent to let lower regions show through. Layers let you create overlapping banners and sidebars, make multicolumn text, annotate diagrams and other pictures, and create composite images by placing transparent GIFs on top of other images. Furthermore, you can use JavaScript to dynamically make regions visible or invisible, to change the stacking order, or to shrink, expand, or move regions on the screen. The specifics of how to change layers dynamically is covered in Chapter 24 (JavaScript: Adding Dynamic Content to Web Pages), but it is worthwhile to keep this capability in mind when evaluating the benefits of layers. Layers can be defined in the BODY of the document with the LAYER and ILAYER elements. To be compliant with the HTML 4.0 specification, Netscape 6 no longer supports the LAYER and ILAYER elements. Internet Explorer only supports layers through cascading style sheets.

Core Note

Internet Explorer and Netscape 6 do not support the LAYER and ILAYER element, but do support layers through the use of style sheets.

Specifying Layers with the LAYER and ILAYER Elements

HTML Element: `<LAYER ...> ... </LAYER>`
`<ILAYER ...> ... </ILAYER>`

Attributes: ABOVE, BACKGROUND, BELOW, BGCOLOR, CLIP, HEIGHT, ID, LEFT, ONBLUR, ONFOCUS, ONLOAD, ONMOUSEOVER, ONMOUSEOUT, PAGEX, PAGEY, SRC, TOP, VISIBILITY, WIDTH, Z-INDEX

The LAYER element creates regions that have an absolute position with respect to the window or parent layer. ILAYER creates inline layers: regions that are embedded in the flow of the text. Alternate text for browsers that do not support layers can be placed in a NOLAYER element. Contents of NOLAYER are ignored by browsers that support LAYER.

ABOVE, BELOW, Z-INDEX

Normally, layers are stacked in the order in which they appear in the document, with the first being on the bottom and later ones stacking above. You can use these attributes to override this behavior. Only one of ABOVE, BELOW, or Z-INDEX should be used for a given layer. Z-INDEX takes a positive integer, where layers with higher numbers are stacked on lower-numbered layers. ABOVE and BELOW give the ID of a layer that should be immediately above or below the current layer. This definition is a bit counterintuitive to some people; `<LAYER ID="Foo" ABOVE="Bar">` means that Bar is above Foo, not that Foo is above Bar.

Core Warning

ABOVE and *BELOW* specify whether the referenced layer is above or below the current layer, not whether the current layer is above or below the referenced one. Thus, `<LAYER ID="currentLayer" ABOVE="referencedLayer">` means that `currentLayer` is **below** `referencedLayer`.

Listing 5.11 gives a simple example, with the result shown in Figure 5–10.

Listing 5.11 Using ABOVE and BELOW

```
<!DOCTYPE HTML PUBLIC "-//W3C//DTD HTML 4.0 Transitional//EN">
<HTML>
<HEAD>
  <TITLE>Using ABOVE and BELOW</TITLE>
</HEAD>
<BODY>
<H1>Using <CODE>ABOVE</CODE> and <CODE>BELOW</CODE></H1>

<LAYER ID="Top" LEFT=60 TOP=120
       WIDTH=500 HEIGHT=100 BGCOLOR="#F5DEB3">
This layer is on top, even though it appears
first in the HTML document.
</LAYER>

<LAYER ID="Bottom" ABOVE="Top" LEFT=10 TOP=70
       WIDTH=500 HEIGHT=100 BGCOLOR="gray">
This layer is on the bottom, even though it appears
second in the HTML document.
</LAYER>

</BODY>
</HTML>
```

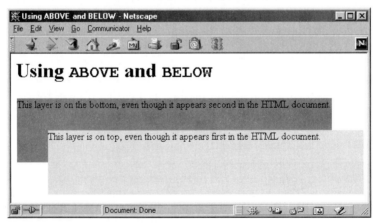

Figure 5–10   ABOVE, BELOW, and Z-INDEX can override layer stacking order.

BACKGROUND, BGCOLOR

By default, layers are transparent. However, you can use a background image or color to make the layer opaque. BACKGROUND and BGCOLOR are used for this purpose. For instance, the two layers shown in the ABOVE and BELOW example (Listing 5.11, Figure 5–10) use BGCOLOR to assign colors to each layer. Although BGCOLOR always creates an opaque background, BACKGROUND can make a partially transparent background if a transparent GIF is specified.

CLIP

This attribute takes comma-separated integers as a value, specifying the boundaries of the visible area of the layer. The HTML is rendered in the full size of the region, but part of the layer may be chopped off when displayed. Boundaries are specified either by "left, top, right, bottom" or "right, bottom". The latter form is equivalent to "0, 0, right, bottom".

These attributes specify a minimum width and height for the layer. Otherwise, the browser uses the smallest possible width and height that encloses the layer's content. These values give minimums, not maximums; the width and height will be expanded if necessary to fit the content of layer. For example, the two layers shown in the ABOVE and BELOW example (Listing 5.11, Figure 5–10) use WIDTH and HEIGHT to specify sizes for the layers.

ID

This attribute gives a name to the layer. The name can be used by the ABOVE or BELOW attributes or by JavaScript code.

LEFT, TOP, PAGEX, PAGEY

For positioned layers (LAYER), these attributes specify the position of the layer in pixels relative to the position of the enclosing layer (LEFT, TOP) or with respect to the entire page (PAGEX, PAGEY). In the absence of these attributes, the layer starts at the current location in the Web page. For instance, the two layers shown in the ABOVE and BELOW example (Listing 5.11, Figure 5–10) use LEFT and TOP to specify locations for the layers.

For in-line layers (ILAYER), the LEFT and TOP attributes are interpreted with respect to the current location in the Web page. For instance, Listing 5.12 uses TOP to move each of the words in the line "Gently down the stream" 10 pixels down from the previous word. The result is shown in Figure 5–11.

Listing 5.12 Using TOP in ILAYER

```
<!DOCTYPE HTML PUBLIC "-//W3C//DTD HTML 4.0 Transitional//EN">
<HTML>
<HEAD>
  <TITLE>Row, Row, Row Your Boat</TITLE>
</HEAD>
<BODY>
<IMG SRC="images/Rowboat.gif" ALIGN="RIGHT">
<HR>
<B>Row, Row, Row Your Boat</B><BR>
Row, row, row your boat<BR>
Gently
<ILAYER TOP=10>down</ILAYER>
<ILAYER TOP=20>the</ILAYER>
<ILAYER TOP=30>stream<BR>
Merrily, merrily, merrily, merrily<BR>
Life is but a dream<BR>
<HR>
</ILAYER>
</BODY>
</HTML>
```

Figure 5–11   Using TOP in ILAYER can move text up or down in the current paragraph.

SRC

This attribute gives the URL of an HTML document to be placed inside the specified layer. Any layers in the designated file are treated as child layers of the current layer. This behavior is particularly useful when you include components that you want to put in multiple documents or when you have a frequently changing part of an otherwise static page. For instance, you could include contact information at the bottom of every Web page in a site by specifying `<LAYER SRC="Contact-Info.html></LAYER>` just before the `</BODY>` tag of each document. Alternatively, you could specify a dynamic piece of an otherwise fixed document as follows:

```
<H1>Menu for Joe's Diner</H1>
<ILAYER SRC="Blue-Plate-Special.html"></ILAYER>
<H2>Appetizers</H2> ...
<H2>Main Dishes</H2> ...
<H2>Vegetables</H2> ...
```

VISIBILITY

This attribute determines whether the layer will be displayed or not. Legal values are `SHOW`, `INHERIT`, and `HIDDEN`, specifying that the layer should be shown, should inherit the parent layer's visibility, or be hidden, respectively. Hidden frames are not particularly useful for static pages but can be used with JavaScript to hide and display regions interactively.

ONBLUR, ONFOCUS, ONLOAD, ONMOUSEOVER, ONMOUSEOUT

These attributes can be used to supply JavaScript code to be executed in various situations. For details, see Chapter 24 (JavaScript: Adding Dynamic Content to Web Pages).

Specifying Layers with Style Sheets

Style sheets let you do most, but not all, of the things that can be done with the `LAYER` and `ILAYER` elements. Style sheets don't let you specify an external file for the content of a layer through the `SRC` attribute, and there are no attributes equivalent to `PAGEX` and `PAGEY` for positioning nested layers independently of the parent layer's location. Furthermore, Netscape 4's support for layers is more complete and reliable when the `LAYER` or `ILAYER` element is used. For instance, when style sheets are used to specify a background color for a layer, the background of the underlying layer or page shows through in the margins between paragraphs. Background images work as expected. However, Netscape 6 does not support the `LAYER` and `ILAYER` element. Thus, use of style sheets for layers fits more cleanly with the general way in which style sheets are used and supports positioning of content using standard CSS length units (rather than just pixels). More importantly, both Internet Explorer and Netscape support layers through style sheets and are an excellent approach for creating layers that run on both browsers.

Layer declarations should use either the ID tag format (#tag) in the header, or be declared inline through <DIV   STYLE="..."> (block-level) or <SPAN STYLE="..."> (text-level). Layer declarations should contain a position property. For instance, combining the style rule

```
#layer1 { position: absolute;
          left: 50px; top: 75px;
          ... }
```

with

```
<SPAN ID="layer1">
...
</SPAN>
```

is roughly equivalent to

```
<LAYER ID="layer1" LEFT=50 TOP=75 ...>
...
</LAYER>
```

Similarly, combining

```
#layer2 { position: relative;
          top: 10px;
          ... }
```

with

```
<SPAN ID="layer2">
...
</SPAN>
```

is roughly equivalent to

```
<ILAYER ID="layer2" TOP=10 ...>
...
</ILAYER>
```

In addition to the standard attributes available in CSS1, layers support the following attributes:

clip
Clipping is specified by rect(top right bottom left) or by the keyword auto (the default). The clip property is equivalent to the CLIP attribute of LAYER and ILAYER. Note that the clipping region, like each of the other layer positions, can be specified by normal CSS length units (Section 5.11). These included pixels, points, inches, and centimeters, not just pixels like LAYER and ILAYER.

left, top
These properties specify the left and top sides of the layer, in normal CSS length units. They are equivalent to the LEFT and TOP attributes of LAYER and ILAYER.

overflow

This property determines what happens when an element's contents exceed the height or width of the layer. A value of `none` (the default) means the contents should be drawn normally, obscuring any underlying layers. A value of `clip` indicates that clipping should occur; `scroll` means the browser should scroll to accommodate the overflow.

position

This property can have the value `absolute`, `relative`, or `static`. These correspond to LAYER elements, ILAYER elements, and normal, unlayered CSS elements, respectively. The default is `static`.

visibility

This property determines whether a layer is visible or hidden. Legal values are `visible`, `hidden`, or `inherit`, signifying that the layer should be shown normally, hidden, or that the parent layer's visibility be used, respectively. This property is useful when you use JavaScript to change visibility values dynamically. JavaScript is discussed at more length in Chapter 24 (JavaScript: Adding Dynamic Content to Web Pages), but Listing 5.13 gives a simple example. A two-button input form is created with two invisible layers sharing the region below the buttons. The result of Listing 5.13 is shown in Figure 5–12. Clicking on the first button displays the first hidden layer (Figure 5–13), hiding the second if necessary. The document model is different in Internet Explorer and Netscape, so a helper JavaScript function, `display`, is added to provide cross-platform capability for dynamically changing the layers.

Listing 5.13 Dynamically changing a layer's visibility

```
<!DOCTYPE HTML PUBLIC "-//W3C//DTD HTML 4.0 Transitional//EN">
<HTML>
<HEAD>
  <TITLE>Changing Visibility Dynamically</TITLE>
<STYLE>
<!--
#layer1 { position: absolute; left: 0.25in; top: 1.5in;
          color: black; background-color: #F5DEB3;
          visibility: hidden }
#layer2 { position: absolute; left: 0.25in; top: 1.5in;
          color: #F5DEB3; background-color: black;
          visibility: hidden }
H1 { text-align: center;
     font-family: Arial }
FORM { text-align: center }
```

(continued)

> **Listing 5.13 Dynamically changing a layer's visibility** *(continued)*

```
-->
</STYLE>
<SCRIPT TYPE="text/javascript">
<!--
function display(value1,value2){
  if(document.layers) { //Test for Netscape.
    document.layers.layer1.visibility = value1;
    document.layers.layer2.visibility = value2;
  } else {
    document.all.layer1.style.visibility = value1;
    document.all.layer2.style.visibility = value2;
  }
}
//-->
</SCRIPT>
</HEAD>
<BODY BGCOLOR="WHITE">
<H1>Changing Visibility Dynamically</H1>
<FORM>
  <INPUT TYPE="BUTTON" VALUE="Show Layer1"
         onClick="display('visible','hidden')">
  <INPUT TYPE="BUTTON" VALUE="Show Layer2"
         onClick="display('hidden','visible')">
</FORM>
<DIV ID="layer1">
<H1>This is layer1.</H1>
</DIV>
<DIV ID="layer2">
<H1>This is layer2.</H1>
</DIV>
</BODY>
</HTML>
```

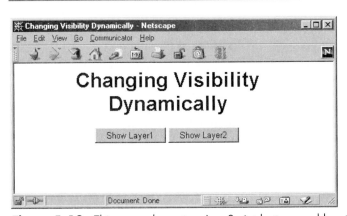

Figure 5-12 This page shows two JavaScript buttons and has two hidden layers.

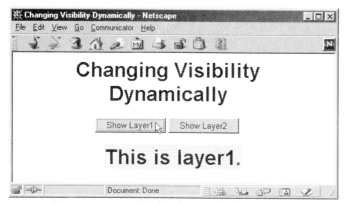

Figure 5–13 Clicking the first button displays the first hidden layer.

width, height

These properties specify the size of the layer; they are equivalent to the WIDTH and HEIGHT attributes of LAYER and ILAYER.

z-index

Normally, layers are stacked from the bottom to the top according to their order in the HTML source. The z-index property overrides this behavior. Values are integers; lower numbers are stacked below higher numbers. This property is equivalent to the Z-INDEX attribute of LAYER and ILAYER.

5.13 Summary

Cascading style sheets provide a powerful capability for customizing the look of Web pages and are now the preferred approach for specifying page formatting in HTML 4.0 documents. Style sheets let you specify fonts, background colors, and images for individual sections of text, floating elements, margins and indentation, and list styles. In addition to the new effects that style sheets enable, they also allow you to give pages a much more consistent look across browsers. Through style sheets, layers are supported on both Netscape and Internet Explorer.

Even with this capability, however, HTML is still a markup language, not a programming language, so the types of applications you can create are limited. The Java programming language, however, lets you create general programs that can be attached to Web pages and run in the browser when the page is loaded. Java is also widely used as a general-purpose programming language, independent of any association with an HTML document or Web browser. Onward! Java technology is the topic of Part 2.

Part 2

JAVA PROGRAMMING

GETTING STARTED WITH JAVA

Topics in This Chapter

- Unique features of Java: What's so unusual, and why everyone is so excited about it
- Java myths: Separating hype from reality
- The evolution of Java: Past and current Java versions
- Ready, set: The Java software and documentation you'll need
- Go: How to compile and run a Java program
- Appetizers: Some simple Java programs
- Java in the real world: Some sample Java applications

Chapter 6

J ava is a programming language that looks a lot like C++ and can be used for general-purpose applications, for embedding programs in WWW pages, and for enterprise programs on e-commerce sites. Programmers think it's cool; software managers think it's hot. In fact, two companies in particular, IBM and Oracle, love Java so much that the first step in their Enterprise Developer program is to become certified in Java (see `http://www-4.ibm.com/software/ad/certify/adedserv.html` and `http://education.oracle.com/certification/javatrack.html`).

Why is Java so hot? Here are a few reasons that we'll discuss in Section 6.1.

- Java is Web-enabled and network savvy
- Java is cross-platform
- Java is simple
- Java is object oriented
- Java is rich with powerful standard libraries

Although Java can do Windows and take out the garbage, some Java advocates would have us believe that Java is the One True Programming Language to which all hitherto unenlightened programmers will convert for all applications. On the other hand, some of the supposed drawbacks to Java are imagined or exaggerated as well. In Section 6.2 we debunk these common myths:

- Java is only for the Web
- Java is cross-platform

- Java is simple
- Java is object oriented (the one true way of programming)
- Java is the programming language for all software development

If you're not sure which version of Java is for you, Section 6.3 summarizes the differences among the available releases. Now, if somehow you've been in a time capsule and don't already have Java on your computer, we show you in Section 6.4 where to get all the software and documentation you need. Finally, Section 6.5 shows some simple, ready-to-run programs to get you started.

If you are wondering what Java stands for, it is not an acronym at all; the word was chosen because of the use of "java" as American slang for "coffee." This choice came about after Sun had to change the original name (Oak) because of a conflict with an existing name. The name Java is meant to imply something exciting and hip. Digging a little deeper: coffee became known as "java" because of coffee imports from Indonesia, where the main population lives on the island of Java. But where did the island get its name? Turns out that Java came from Yava, which meant "rice" in a dialect of the eighth century, at which time Java was known as Yava Dwipa, or Rice Island.

6.1   Unique Features of Java

Actually, many of the capabilities described in this section are *not* truly one of a kind, just unique in the experience of most developers. Java is an excellent language, but not, as some proponents claim, a brilliant breakthrough packed with ideas that have never been seen before. The vast majority of Java language features are already available in other languages. So why all the excitement about Java? What Java has done that few other languages have been able to do is to combine standard capabilities (C/C++ syntax), powerful features of niche-market languages (automatic memory management, bytecode interpreters), and key APIs for enterprise development. The following sections highlight some of the most important characteristics of Java.

Java Is Web-Enabled and Network Savvy

The World Wide Web helped catapult Java to its current prominent position as an Internet programming language. If you're writing applications that need to run on the Web, access Internet resources, or simply talk to other programs on the network, Java has numerous facilities to make your life easier.

Java Enforces Safety
Because Java checks array bounds, forbids direct manipulation of memory addresses, and enforces datatypes, Java programs cannot access arbitrary mem-

ory locations. Thus, before execution of any line of code, a security manager can reliably analyze what operations the program can legally perform. This analysis permits a restricted class of Java programs known as "applets" to be run in your Web browser without danger of introducing viruses, finding and reporting on private information about your system, erasing your disk, snooping behind your corporate firewall, or starting up programs like Doom just when your boss is entering your office.

DILBERT © UFS. Reprinted with permission.

The Web Can Deliver Software

Java applets are supported in most versions of Netscape and Internet Explorer, and, therefore, applets run on nearly every operating system on the market and are available to virtually anyone on the Internet. This capability opens up a whole new way of viewing the WWW and a browser: as a medium for software delivery and execution, not just as a medium for document delivery and display. If you have an application that you update frequently, you no longer need your users to reinstall the latest version every time you make a change. In fact, your users don't need to install anything at all; all they have to do is keep a bookmark to your applet in the Web browser they already have on their system. This shifts the burden of software installation and maintenance from the user to the developer, who can control versions at a single centralized location. For example, the Hubble Control Center System, shown in Figure 6–1, is accessed in a variety of locations over the Web, providing up-to-the-minute status on the Hubble Space Telescope.

Java's Network Library Is Easy to Use

Java's networking library is used exactly the same way on all operating systems. Ordinary mortals can actually use the network library, a welcome change from other languages where you leave such magic to the local wizards who are probably on another project just when you need them the most. Compared to, for instance, Berkeley sockets or the POSIX Transport Layer Interface, creating

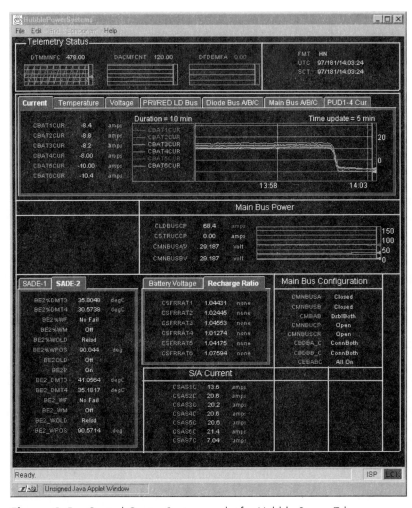

Figure 6–1   Control Center System applet for Hubble Space Telescope, developed at NASA.

clients or servers is positively a joy in Java. Furthermore, Java already understands the HTTP protocol, letting you retrieve files on the Web and communicate with HTTP servers without even dealing directly with sockets. For example, Figure 6–2 shows a Web-based interface (applet) for configuring ports on a Cisco Catalyst 6000 (Ethernet switch). The HTTP service running on the Catalyst switch permits configuration through a browser instead of entering command-line changes over a telnet session.

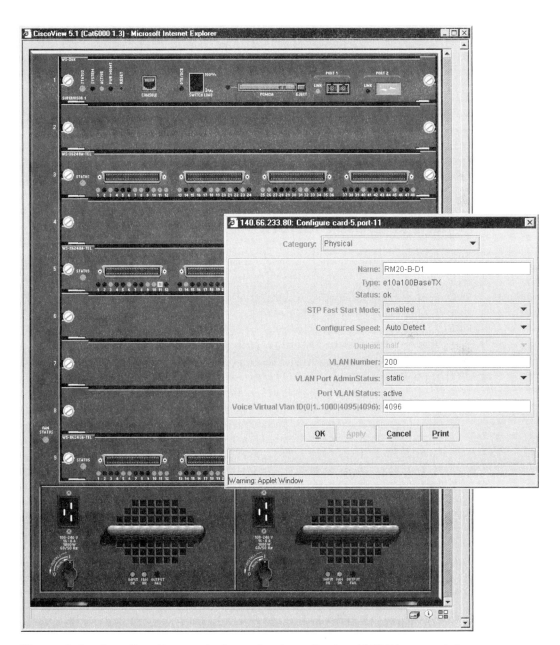

Figure 6–2   Cisco OpenView applet for configuring a Catalyst 6000 Ethernet switch. [This material has been reproduced by Prentice Hall with the permission of Cisco Systems, Inc. © 2001 Cisco Systems, Inc. All rights reserved.]

Java Provides Complete Enterprise Development

Since 1995, Sun has introduced numerous libraries and extensions to Java in support of enterprise solutions. Java supports Remote Method Invocation (RMI) that lets you invoke methods in objects on remote platforms, allowing you to pass arbitrary Java objects back and forth across the network. Java servlets let you write server-side applications and create session objects to track users across multiple Web pages. JDBC lets your applications interface with multiple database vendors in a standard manner and lets your applets or servlets bypass older CGI interfaces and talk directly to a database. Enterprise JavaBeans components, accessible from servlets or JavaServer pages, allow you to store business rules in a multi-tier architecture.

Java Is Cross-Platform

Java is designed to be portable, and Java programs developed on one platform can often run unchanged on many other computer systems. Why? Well, a number of reasons exist, but the three most important characteristics that make Java portable are outlined here.

Java Compiles to Machine-Independent Bytecode

Java is typically compiled and executed in a two-step process. In the first step, Java source code is compiled to "bytecode"—assembly language for an idealized Java Virtual Machine (JVM). In the second step, this bytecode is executed by a run-time system. This run-time system can either be an interpreter (an emulator for the JVM) or a Just In Time (JIT) compiler that first compiles the bytecode to native code, then executes the result. The beauty of this process is that the two steps can be performed on totally separate platforms. The source can be compiled on a Windows 2000 machine with Borland's compiler, then the result can be executed on a Macintosh through Apple's run-time system, or on Solaris with Sun's software. For example, Figure 6–3 presents StarOffice™, a cross-platform, document processing suite that runs on Windows, Solaris, and Linux. In addition, most modern Web browsers include a JVM, letting Web page developers compile applets and attach the resultant bytecode to Web pages for execution on a variety of platforms.

Java Offers a Portable Graphics Library

In many software systems, the biggest hindrance to portability was the user interface. Interfaces were typically developed with the native windowing system rather than a cross-platform graphics toolkit because this was the most convenient and widely available option. However, this approach often meant that distribution on a different operating system required a complete rewrite of the GUI. The Java developers realized that a truly portable language would require a standard graphics library and, in the original release of Java, Sun

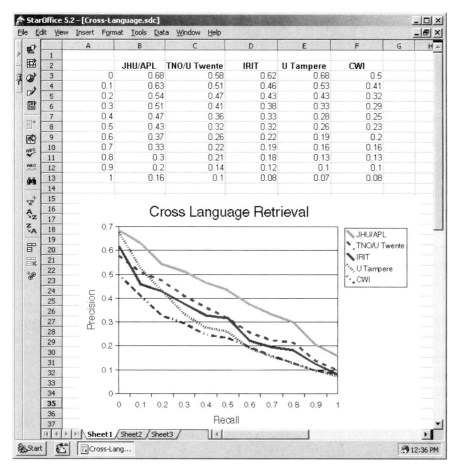

Figure 6–3 StarOffice 5.2, a cross-platform suite for document processing written completely in Java. StarOffice™ is a registered trademark of Sun Microsystems, Inc.

Microsystems introduced the Abstract Window Toolkit (AWT) for platform-independent GUI development. The AWT provides a standard set of graphical controls (buttons, lists, combo boxes, check boxes, textfields, etc.) for development of stand-alone application and applet-based GUIs that are supported in nearly all browsers.

Later, in the Java 2 Platform release, Sun introduced Swing—a richer, more robust, graphical package for creating professional user interfaces. Swing is the preferred library for developing graphical programs, unless you are writing applets for Web pages. Among the various versions of Netscape and Internet Explorer, Netscape 6 is the only browser that currently supports Swing without a plug-in.

Figure 6–4 shows the applet-based GUI created when NASA was faced with the problem of making Pathfinder data available to a huge number of users on different platforms.

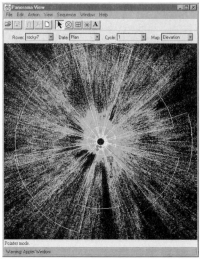

Figure 6–4   Jet Propulsion Lab's Web Interface for Telescience, used for worldwide viewing of Mars Pathfinder data.

Java Avoids Hard-to-Port Constructs

The Java specification defines the size of primitive datatypes such as `ints`, `booleans`, and `doubles`, unlike other languages that allow the size to vary among implementations. For objects, Java programs can't imprudently depend on implementation-specific details such as the amount of memory an object consumes (Java has no need for the equivalent to the C/C++ `sizeof` operator), the internals of how fields or functions are laid out within an object, or the like. Java even avoids reference to the local file system when specifying which classes your program requires, using operating-system-neutral class and package names instead.

Java Is Simple

Java started with familiar C++ syntax but cleaned up many of the complicated syntactic features. In addition, header files are never needed, makefiles are usually not necessary, and the networking process is easier, not to mention numerous other improvements. In addition to a long list of similar minor features, Java has two major features that simplify life for the programmer: automatic memory management and simplified pointer handling.

Java Automatically Manages Memory

The Java programmer is freed from the time-consuming and error-prone process of manually allocating and deallocating memory for objects. Instead, an automatic system, known as a *garbage collector*, doles out memory when it is needed and reclaims memory from objects that can no longer be accessed. Poof! In one fell swoop, Java has eliminated dangling pointers (references to memory that has been recycled) and memory leaks (inaccessible memory that is never reclaimed)—two problems that often account for half of the development time in large systems programmed in languages with manual memory management.

Java Simplifies Pointer Handling

When you pass an object (i.e., any nonprimitive data type) to a function in Java, the system actually passes a pointer or "reference" to the object. That is, the entire object is not copied onto the run-time stack, only the reference is copied. All the details are hidden from the user, who can simply view "the object" as being passed to the function. You do not need to explicitly reference or dereference the pointer; pointer arithmetic is unnecessary (banned, in fact), and the whole process is considerably simpler. Automated memory management lets the programmer stop thinking in terms of pointers altogether if desired, while still making it easy to implement data structures that depend on pointers, such as linked lists and trees. Although at first this seems strange to the C or C++ programmer, it is the way things have worked for decades in languages like Smalltalk and Lisp.

Java Is Object Oriented

Java is pervasively and consistently object oriented. "Object obsessed," some people would say.

All Functions Are Associated with Objects

In many other object-oriented languages, there are "normal" functions that are independent of objects, as well as "methods" or "member functions" that are associated with objects. Java, however, is like Smalltalk in this regard, where methods are the *only* type of allowable function.

Almost All Datatypes Are Objects

In some object-oriented languages, a distinction exists between regular datatypes and classes. Strings, arrays, structures, files, sockets, and other types might not be objects that can be processed in the same way as user-defined objects. In contrast, in Java all complex types are true objects, and every object has a common ancestor, the `Object` class, thus simplifying the creation of arrays or other collections of heterogeneous object types. Although a few "primitive" datatypes (int, double, boolean, char, among others) are kept distinct from objects for efficiency, there is a corresponding wrapper object for each of them (Integer, Double, Boolean, Character, and so forth). These wrapper objects can be obtained from the primitive type through simple conversion methods.

Java Is Rich with Powerful Standard Libraries

In addition to the graphics and client/server libraries already mentioned, Java has standard libraries for, to name a few, the following tasks:

- Building and using data structures
- Manipulating and parsing strings and streams
- Saving objects (even graphical ones) to disk and reassembling them later
- Using arbitrary-precision, fixed-point numbers
- Accessing files over the Internet
- Granting security privileges based on digital signatures
- Invoking remote Java objects
- Interfacing with relational databases
- Distributing computation among multiple threads of execution

As a result, you can write large applications completely in Java without recourse to libraries specific to a particular operating system. Figure 6–5 illustrates one such system.

Now, such a wide array of built-in capabilities is a mixed blessing. On the one hand, it provides a large set of standard, portable tools that you can pick through for your particular application. On the other hand, Java as a whole is so large that learning it seems intimidating. Fortunately, you don't have to learn Java all at once. Everyone will need to know how to construct and use objects (Chapter 7) and understand the core syntax (Chapter 8). Other than that, the pieces are fairly independent. Because Java loads classes dynamically, the size of the Java run-time environment and compiled classes is independent of the total language size. And you don't have to get a handle on everything before making good progress. If you're going to be writing a server that doesn't require a user interface, you can skip learning about the AWT (Chapter 13) and Swing (Chapters 14 and 15) until you actually need them. Similarly, you need not know anything about the networking library when writing a typical applet. Even so, no doubt you'll occasionally write some utility, only to discover later that it is already available in one of Java APIs. Okay, we admit that seems frustrating. But it's still better than using a bare-bones language where you *always* have to write every utility you need.

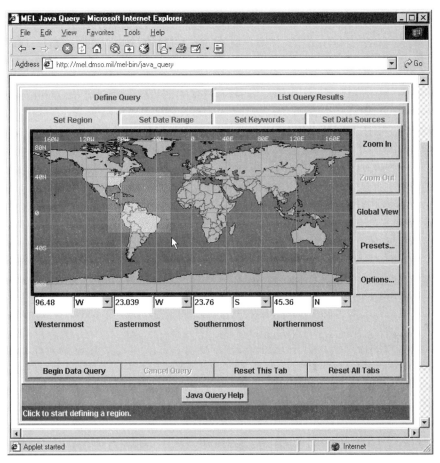

Figure 6–5   The Java query interface to the Master Environmental Library (MEL) for geospatial data discovery and retrieval. A Java applet provides an interactive graphical specification of the region of interest. From Naim Alper and the MEL Project.

6.2   Myths About Java

When Java burst on the software scene in 1995, many misconceptions popped up. Because some of these misconceptions still persist, we'll try to refute the most prevalent ones here.

Java Is Only for the Web

When Java was first introduced, the majority of hype revolved around creating Java applets. Certainly, Java applets can run in Web pages; however, Java is a general-purpose programming language and does not require applets or the Internet. You could use Java to write a new driver for a color printer or even to write a numerical integration library. Java is not limited to the Internet. That's not to say that Java isn't the language of choice for Internet programming. With support for database connectivity, Java Servlets, Enterprise JavaBeans, and JavaMessaging, Java is the Internet language of choice! As more applications become distributed and more companies enter the e-commerce and business-to-business marketplace, Java will dominate Web programming. But don't get locked into thinking that Java is strictly for the Web.

Java Is Cross-Platform

Yes, Java was designed with portability in mind and has succeeded in many ways. Many Java programs run unchanged on multiple operating systems. Nevertheless, some things can make some Java programs difficult or even impossible to port to other platforms. We describe the three most important ones here.

Java Programs Can Execute Local, Nonportable Programs

The exec method of the Runtime class lets Java applications call local programs. The "native method" interface supports linking Java and C programs together. The first can make Java programs completely nonportable, and the second makes them only as portable as the associated C code. Now, it is hardly fair to say that Java is nonportable just because it connects to something that is nonportable. After all, that is not "pure" Java. True, but it is still worth remembering that not all "Java" programs are completely written in Java and that many do indeed connect to other components. Many programs, of course, can avoid accessing native code. But some programs need to format a disk, get a list of users currently logged in, or link with legacy C or C++ code, even if the programs need to sacrifice portability to do so. This behavior is not necessarily a bad thing; accessing local applications is sometimes more important than portability. The important thing is not to sacrifice portability *without knowing it*, and Java has done a good job of avoiding nasty surprises in this regard. Be wary of third-party libraries that don't make it clear which part is pure Java and which part is nonportable.

The Behavior of the Thread Scheduler Is Loosely Defined

Java has one of the best threading libraries around. It lets you execute independent parts of your program in separate processes. However, to allow a compiler to use efficient mechanisms on a particular OS, some of the interactions among threads are only loosely specified. For instance, how long a given thread will run before being replaced by another is almost certain to vary from machine to machine and even from run to run on the same machine. In some sense, this nondeterminism is an advantage of using threads, but it can lead beginning programmers to inappropriately depend on certain behavior by the scheduler in order to operate correctly. If your program depends on thread priorities or the time interval in which threads are swapped in and out of the CPU, your program may not run the same on all platforms. Solaris, Windows NT, and Macintosh all use different priorities and algorithms for scheduling threads. So, when writing multithreaded programs using Java, you should be careful not to deliver your product before you thoroughly test the software on all platforms.

The Graphics Library Behaves Differently on Different Systems

In the first release of Java, the development team decided that the graphic elements should adopt the look and feel of the local windowing system, rather than trying to have a consistent look and feel across platforms. In some sense, this was a wise approach, since experience has shown that some Macintosh users would rather die than use an application that looks like Windows 2000, no matter how much you preach that they should. But supporting a native look in the Abstract Window Toolkit came at a price: scrollbars, buttons, textfields, and the like can have slightly different sizes and behave slightly differently on different platforms. Some of these problems associated with component sizes on different operating systems can be minimized through the proper selection of layout managers. But, as Sun quickly realized, for Java to be accepted as a true cross-platform language for GUI development, the platform dependence of the component behavior would need to be resolved.

DILBERT © UFS. Reprinted by permission.

In the Java 2 Platform, Sun introduced Swing, a new and complete graphical package that does not rely on the underlying operating system for rendering the components. In essence, a GUI written in Swing is truly platform independent. Unfortunately, if you intend to deliver your Swing GUI through a web-based applet, most browsers do not directly support the Swing components without a plug-in. In contrast, an applet written with AWT components is supported in nearly all available browsers.

Java Is Simple

Simple? Ha. Who said it was simple? Oh, we did? Hmm.

The problem is that simplicity is a relative concept. Compared to some of the intricacies of C and C++, Java syntax seems positively streamlined. People who have fought with memory leaks and dangling pointers are relieved to let the Java garbage collector take over the battle. But Java is a full-blown programming language, and programming is anything but simple. So, for instance, the HTML developer will find Java programming a huge leap up in complexity. And given the ever-increasing number of standard and third-party libraries, it is becoming harder and harder to be knowledgeable in all of them.

Not only is programming hard, but programmers tend to continually push the envelope of what can reasonably be done. In many other languages, only the guru would attempt client-server or multithreaded applications, but Java makes these techniques accessible to "ordinary" programmers. This is a double-edged sword. On the one hand, developers can do useful things they couldn't do before. On the other hand, programs using these techniques can be very tricky to develop and debug.

So, Java programming is certainly not simple. Far from it. But Java is designed so that the various libraries and approaches can be learned in bite-sized pieces, and the relatively clean syntax and design make the learning process more palatable than in most other languages.

DILBERT © UFS. Reprinted by permission.

Java Is Object Oriented (the One True Way of Programming)

"It's not?" Blasphemy! you say. There are various ways to view programming. Some people take the religious view, where technical evangelists argue fervently to convert disciples of one software dogma to another. In some arenas, there *is* a single right answer. But we think the carpenter's model fits the software world better. Under this analogy, the various technical approaches are tools in the software developer's toolbox. Clearly, some tools are more broadly applicable than others, and certain tools are well suited to certain jobs. OOP is a useful and broadly applicable tool, and it should occupy a central place in the developer's toolkit. But functional programming, structured programming, rule-based programming, divide-and-conquer approaches, greedy algorithms, and the like are also useful tools, and the expert craftsman should be skilled with them as well. OOP is complementary to some of them, independent of others, and occasionally in conflict with some.

Choosing OOP as the underlying structure for Java was a wise choice, but once in a while the object-oriented viewpoint will get in the way. Rejecting a useful technique in Java simply because it "doesn't fit with the object-oriented philosophy" is, well, heresy.

Java Is the Programming Language for All Software Development

Java is a good general-purpose programming language. It is an excellent tool, perhaps even the best, for a number of jobs. But it's not the best tool for *every* job. Sometimes it will be more convenient to write a Unix utility in C, a Windows utility in Visual Basic, or a quick Web application in JavaScript or VBScript. To return to the carpenter analogy, the expert practitioner will be more successful knowing the strengths and weaknesses of various tools instead of using the same tool in all circumstances. On the other hand, portability and interoperability are important considerations, and heterogeneous systems tend to be less portable and interoperable than homogeneous ones. So sticking to Java even when a small piece of the system is easier in another language is sometimes preferable. Knowing where the balance lies requires experience.

6.3   Java Versions

Java 1.0 was first released by Sun Microsystems in 1995 and took off in early 1996 when Netscape released Navigator version 2.0, the first widely used browser that supported Java applets. After a couple of bug fixes, Java 1.02 was released and is what most people mean when they say "Java 1.0." Later, in early 1997, Sun released Java 1.1, which contained a wide variety of enhancements and new features, including:

- A new event-handling model based on listeners
- Remote method invocation (RMI) and object serialization
- Support for inner and anonymous classes
- Arbitrary precision integers and floating-point numbers
- Java DataBase Connectivity (JDBC) API for connecting relations databases
- JavaBeans component architecture (Java's answer to ActiveX)

- Digitally signed applets to extended security privileges without resorting to the "all or nothing" model of browser plug-ins or ActiveX

Your best strategy when writing applets is to write code specific to the Java 1.1 API, since this version of Java is supported by Netscape 4.06 and later and Internet Explorer 4.0 and later. By choosing to use capabilities from later versions of Java, you run the risk of your applet not being supported by all customers that download your applet to their browser.

The Java 2 Platform, often identified by users as JDK 1.2 (Java Development Kit 1.2), was released in December of 1998. Significant changes introduced in JDK 1.2 include:

- Swing GUI components based on 100% Pure Java
- Java 2D for professional, high-quality, two-dimensional graphics and imaging
- The Collections Framework supporting advanced data structures like linked lists, trees, and sets
- Audio enhancements to support `.wav`, `.aiff`, `.au`, `.midi`, and `.rmf` file formats
- Printing of graphic objects
- Java IDL API, which adds CORBA capability to Java

In the Spring of 2000, Sun released JDK 1.3. In this version, minor fixes and enhancements were introduced throughout the API. The two most significant enhancements were:

- Java Naming and Directory Interface (JNDI)—a directory service for registering and looking up resources (objects)
- RMI-IIOP—a protocol to communicate with distributed clients that are written in CORBA-compliant language

Now, if those lists aren't daunting enough, JDK 1.2 and JDK 1.3 are really part of the Java 2 Platform, *Standard Edition*. At the same time the Standard Edition was released, Sun also introduced the Java 2 Platform, *Enterprise Edition*, for e-commerce solutions. The Enterprise Edition adds:

- Java Servlets and JavaServer Pages—Sun's answer to Microsoft Active Server Pages and ColdFusion
- Enterprise JavaBeans for bundling business logic in server-side components
- JDBC data access for scrollable database queries (result sets)
- JavaMail to send and receive mail with SMTP, POP3, or IMAP4 protocols
- JAXP for parsing XML documents
- Java Message Service for asynchronous communication between enterprise applications

Which Version Should You Use?

Well, of course, you want the latest and greatest version of Java! But, depending on where your Java programs are executing, choosing the latest Java version may not be possible in all situations. In short, consider the following when choosing a Java version:

- **Applets**—For applets, you'll want to go with Java Development Kit, Version 1.1 (JDK 1.1; last version is JDK 1.1.8_005). Netscape 4.06 and later and Internet Explorer 4.01 and later do not support Java versions later than 1.1 without a plug-in. Note that the latest release of Netscape, Version 6, is an exception to this rule and does support JDK 1.3. Regardless, for applets delivered over the Internet you shouldn't make assumptions about which browser the client is using, so you should write applets specific to the JDK 1.1 API.
- **Applications**—For stand-alone applications, you'll want to go with JDK 1.3, marketed as Java SDK, Standard Edition, Version 3.0. If you're writing server-side programs that rely on other vendor products, check which version of the JDK the vendor product supports.

Your best approach is to go with the JDK 1.3 but to bookmark the JDK 1.1 API when writing applets so that you can make sure that you are using methods and classes that are supported by the majority of client browsers.

Whichever Version You Use

Certainly, the Java 2 Platform provides a lot of capability. Our intent is to present material essential to developing distributed programs using Java.

Chapters 7 and 8 cover the basic syntax of Java. Then, we focus on Java applets (Chapter 9) and teach you how to use layout mangers (Chapter 12) to improve graphical user interfaces developed with the AWT (Chapter 13) or Swing components (Chapters 14 and 15).

Once we've covered the basics, we move to distributed programs by first examining sockets to open TCP connections to other computers on the Internet (Chapter 17). Distributed programs are often multithreaded for efficient handling of client requests, so integrated throughout this material are examples of multithreading programming. We cover multithread and synchronization of data (to eliminate race conditions that can occur between shared resources) in Chapter 16.

We next head over to server-side and enterprise programming, teaching you about Java servlets (Chapter 19) and JavaServer Pages (Chapter 20). This material covers cookies, sessions, and JavaBeans. Afterwards, we introduce you to database queries with JDBC (Chapter 22). Finally, we wrap up enterprise Java programming with XML and JAXP (Chapter 23) for processing platform-independent, business transactions (order requests).

After you've tackled this material, you'll have a firm background for developing distributed applications with Java and for diving into advanced topics like Enterprise JavaBeans, JNDI, and JavaMessaging.

6.4   Getting Started: Nuts and Bolts

Okay, okay, enough talk. Let's get on with it.

If you're wise, you won't sit down and read these Java chapters straight through, engrossing though they may be to you. <SARCASTIC>No doubt it will be difficult to tear yourself away, but you've got to do it.</SARCASTIC> Seriously though, we suggest installing Java as soon as possible, reading a little, practicing a little, reading a bit more, trying a more complex application, and so on. Write some real programs as *soon* as possible, and experiment with as many techniques as possible. There's no substitute for experience. Here's how to start:

- Install Java.
- Install a Java-enabled browser.
- Bookmark or install the on-line Java API.
- Optional: Get an integrated development environment.
- Create and run a Java program.

Install Java

Java is already bundled with some operating systems (e.g., OS/2, MacOS 10, Solaris 2.6), so you may have Java on your system already. If not, there are *free* versions of Java for Windows, MacOS, OS/2, Novell IntranetWare, Solaris, Irix, HP-UX, AIX, SCO Unixware, Linux, Amiga, BeOS, and most other major operating systems. Following is a list of a few of the most important download sites and versions available. For other operating systems and for-fee systems, check out Sun's list of Java ports at

```
http://java.sun.com/cgi-bin/java-ports.cgi
```

Note that each of these URLs, like every URL listed in the book, is available on-line at `http://www.corewebprogramming.com/`.

Java SDK, Standard Edition, Version 1.3 (JDK 1.3)

Microsoft Windows
```
http://java.sun.com/j2se/1.3/download-windows.html
```

Solaris SPARC/x86
```
http://java.sun.com/j2se/1.3/download-solaris.html
```

Linux x86

```
http://java.sun.com/j2se/1.3/download-linux.html
```

Java SDK, Standard Edition, Version 1.2 (JDK 1.2)

Microsoft Windows

```
http://java.sun.com/products/jdk/1.2/download-windows.html
```

Solaris SPARC/x86

```
http://java.sun.com/products/jdk/1.2/download-solaris.html
```

Linux x86

```
http://java.sun.com/products/jdk/1.2/download-linux.html
```

Java Development Kit, Version 1.1 (JDK 1.1)

Microsoft Windows

```
http://java.sun.com/products/jdk/1.1/download-windows.html
```

Solaris SPARC/x86

```
http://java.sun.com/products/jdk/1.2/download-jdk-solaris.html
```

Install a Java-Enabled Browser

This step will let you run Java programs embedded in Web pages (applets). Many IDEs and free versions of Java include "appletviewer," a mini-browser that ignores all of the HTML except for the applets. This is a quick way to test applets. For a fuller test, you'll want Netscape Navigator or Communicator, Microsoft Internet Explorer, Sun's HotJava, or another Java-enabled browser. This is a bit of a chicken-and-egg problem, since many of the download sites are accessible only by HTTP, which won't help you much if you don't have a browser already. For other platforms, presumably *some* browser came with your system or was provided by your ISP. If not, try using Netscape's anonymous FTP site.

Netscape Navigator

```
http://home.netscape.com/download/
```

Microsoft Internet Explorer

```
http://www.microsoft.com/ie/download/
```

Sun's HotJava

```
http://java.sun.com/products/hotjava/
```

Bookmark or Install the On-Line Java API

The official Application Programmer's Interface (API) describes *every* nonprivate variable and method in *every* standard library, something neither this nor any other single book can do. HTML versions for JDK 1.1, 1.2, and 1.3 are available at Sun and are bundled with many IDEs. The API can be accessed on-line directly from Sun's site, but the serious developer with plenty (5–10 MB) of extra disk space will want to install a local version for faster access.

Java 2 SDK, Version 1.3 (JDK 1.3)

API Specification
```
http://java.sun.com/j2se/1.3/docs/api/
```

API Download
```
http://java.sun.com/j2se/1.3/docs.html
```

Java 2 SDK, Version 1.2 (JDK 1.2)

API Specification
```
http://java.sun.com/products/jdk/1.2/docs/api/
```

API Download
```
http://java.sun.com/products/jdk/1.2/download-docs.html
```

Java 1.1 (JDK 1.1)

API Specification
```
http://java.sun.com/products/jdk/1.1/docs/api/packages.html
```

API Download
```
http://java.sun.com/products/jdk/1.1/#docs
```

Note that you can find a list of all Java products available through Sun at `http://java.sun.com/products/`.

Optional: Get an Integrated Development Environment

In addition to a Java compiler and run-time system, you may want an integrated environment with a graphical debugger, class browser, drag-and-drop GUI builder, templates/wizards for database connectivity, and so on. A wide variety of IDEs are available on the market. You may want to look at John Zukowski's collection of IDE reviews and download sites at `http://java.miningco.com/msub9.htm`. A couple of popular IDEs are listed below.

Borland JBuilder
`http://www.borland.com/jbuilder/`

IBM VisualAge
`http://www-4.ibm.com/software/ad/vajava/`

Oracle JDeveloper
`http://www.oracle.com/ip/develop/ids/jdeveloper.html`

WebGain Visual Café
`http://www.visualcafe.com/Products/VisualCafe_Overview.html`

Sun Forte Developer
`http://www.sun.com/forte/ffj/`

Create and Run a Java Program

Create the File
Write and save a file (say, `Test.java`) that defines the public class `Test`. Note that the filename and classname are case sensitive and must match exactly. If you are not using a Java development environment, use the text editor of your choice. Section 6.5 gives some simple examples.

Compile It
If you are using the standard `javac` compiler from the Sun JDK on Windows or Unix, compile `Test.java` using `javac Test.java`. On a Mac, drag the source file onto the Java compiler. If you are using an Integrated Development Environment, refer to the vendor's instructions. The compilation creates a file called `Test.class`.

Run It
For a stand-alone Java application with a command-line interface, run it by `java Test`. Note that this is `java`, not `javac` and that you refer to `Test`, not `Test.class`. On a Mac, drag the class file onto the Java runner. For an applet that will run in a browser, run it by loading the Web page that refers to it. For example, if you want the file `Test.html` to run the applet, then `Test.html` needs to refer to the URL of `Test.class` in an `<APPLET>` tag. We give details of this later.

6.5   Some Simple Java Programs

Following are some very basic programs to give a flavor of the language. Don't worry about understanding every detail; we'll go over things step by step later on. But it *is* a good idea to run these programs. Try making a few changes after successfully executing the original versions.

The Basic Hello World Application

"Application" is Java lingo for a stand-alone Java program. An application *must* contain a class whose name exactly matches the filename (including case) and that contains a main method declared public static void with an a single string array as an argument. A string array can be declared String[] *argName*, or String *argName*[]. Listing 6.1 presents a simple application that prints "Hello, world." when run. Additional application examples are given in Chapter 7 (Object-Oriented Programming in Java). Also, Java applications frequently use a graphical user interface. Section 9.10 (Graphical Applications) gives an overview, with more details given in Chapter 13 (AWT Components).

Core Approach

A public class named SomeClass *must be defined in* SomeClass.java. *Case matters even on Windows 98/NT/2000;* SOMECLASS.java *or* someclass.java *will not work.*

Listing 6.1   HelloWorld.java

```
public class HelloWorld {
  public static void main(String[] args) {
    System.out.println("Hello, world.");
  }
}
```

Compiling:
```
javac HelloWorld.java
```

Running:
```
java HelloWorld
```

Output:
```
Hello, world.
```

Command-Line Arguments

Listing 6.2 shows a program that reports on user input. This example looks a lot like C but illustrates a couple of important differences: String is a real type in Java, Java arrays have length associated with them, and the filename is not part of the command-line arguments. If you've never seen C or C++ before, you'll want to read the description of basic loops and conditionals given in Chapter 8 (Basic Java Syntax). Note that you *can* read command-line input on Macintosh systems even though there is no "command line"; in most implementations a small window pops up when the program starts to collect that input.

Listing 6.2   ShowArgs.java

```java
public class ShowArgs {
  public static void main(String[] args) {
    for(int i=0; i<args.length; i++) {
      System.out.println("Arg " + i + " is " + args[i]);
    }
  }
}
```

Compiling:
```
javac ShowArgs.java
```

Running:
```
java ShowArgs fee fie foe fum
```

Output:
```
Arg 0 is fee
Arg 1 is fie
Arg 2 is foe
Arg 3 is fum
```

The Basic Hello World (Wide Web) Applet

"Applet" is Java lingo for a Java program that runs as part of a WWW page in a browser. Like an application, an applet must contain a class matching the filename, but applets don't use the main method. Instead, initialization is typically performed in the init method and drawing is done in paint. Listing 6.3 shows a simple Java applet that draws "Hello, World Wide Web." in a small window. Listing 6.4 shows the HTML document that loads it. Note that the name of the HTML file need not match the name of the Java file, but it is sometimes a useful convention. For more information on creating applets and drawing in windows, see Chapter 9 (Applets and Basic Graphics).

Listing 6.3 `HelloWWW.java`

```java
import java.applet.Applet;
import java.awt.*;

public class HelloWWW extends Applet {
  private int fontSize = 40;

  public void init() {
    setBackground(Color.black);
    setForeground(Color.white);
    setFont(new Font("SansSerif", Font.BOLD, fontSize));
  }

  public void paint(Graphics g) {
    g.drawString("Hello, World Wide Web.", 5, fontSize+5);
  }
}
```

Listing 6.4 `HelloWWW.html`

```html
<!DOCTYPE HTML PUBLIC "-//W3C//DTD HTML 4.0 Transitional//EN">
<HTML>
<HEAD>
  <TITLE>HelloWWW: Simple Applet Test.</TITLE>
</HEAD>
<BODY BGCOLOR="WHITE">

<H1>HelloWWW: Simple Applet Test.</H1>
<P>
<APPLET CODE="HelloWWW.class" WIDTH=460 HEIGHT=50>
  <B>Error! You must use a Java enabled browser.</B>
</APPLET>

</BODY>
</HTML>
```

Compiling:

```
javac HelloWWW.java
```

Running:

Load `HelloWWW.html` in a Java-enabled browser.

Output:

Figure 6–6 shows a typical result.

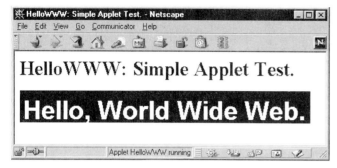

Figure 6-6   A simple applet, shown in Netscape Navigator 4.7 on Windows 98.

Applet Customization Parameters

Applets don't get command-line arguments because they are started by the browser. However, you can supply parameters to the applet by putting them inside PARAM elements between the <APPLET ...> and </APPLET> tags. The applet reads the values by calling getParameter. Listing 6.5 shows a variation of the HelloWWW applet that bases message text on PARAM values supplied. Listing 6.6 shows an HTML document that loads this applet four times with various messages. The use of PARAM is explained in detail in Section 9.7 (Reading Applet Parameters).

Listing 6.5   Message.java

```java
import java.applet.Applet;
import java.awt.*;

public class Message extends Applet {
  private int fontSize;
  private String message;

  public void init() {
    setBackground(Color.black);
    setForeground(Color.white);

    // Base font size on window height.
    fontSize = getSize().height - 10;

    setFont(new Font("SansSerif", Font.BOLD, fontSize));
```

(continued)

Listing 6.5 `Message.java` *(continued)*

```java
    // Read heading message from PARAM entry in HTML.
    message = getParameter("MESSAGE");
  }

  public void paint(Graphics g) {
    if (message != null) {
      g.drawString(message, 5, fontSize+5);
    }
  }
}
```

Listing 6.6 `Message.html`

```html
<!DOCTYPE HTML PUBLIC "-//W3C//DTD HTML 4.0 Transitional//EN">
<HTML>
<HEAD>
  <TITLE>The Message Applet</TITLE>
</HEAD>
<BODY BGCOLOR="WHITE">

<H1>The <CODE>Message</CODE> Applet</H1>
<P>
<APPLET CODE="Message.class" WIDTH=325 HEIGHT=25>
  <PARAM NAME="MESSAGE" VALUE="Tiny">
  <B>Sorry, these examples require Java</B>
</APPLET>
<P>
<APPLET CODE="Message.class" WIDTH=325 HEIGHT=50>
  <PARAM NAME="MESSAGE" VALUE="Small">
  <B>Sorry, these examples require Java</B>
</APPLET>
<P>
<APPLET CODE="Message.class" WIDTH=325 HEIGHT=75>
  <PARAM NAME="MESSAGE" VALUE="Medium">
  <B>Sorry, these examples require Java</B>
</APPLET>
<P>
<APPLET CODE="Message.class" WIDTH=325 HEIGHT=100>
  <PARAM NAME="MESSAGE" VALUE="Giant">
  <B>Sorry, these examples require Java</B>
</APPLET>

</BODY>
</HTML>
```

Compiling:

```
javac Message.java
```

Running:

Load `Message.html` in a browser that supports Java.

Output:

Figure 6–7 shows the result of a Web page that loads the same applet four different times, supplying various PARAM values and differing HEIGHTs.

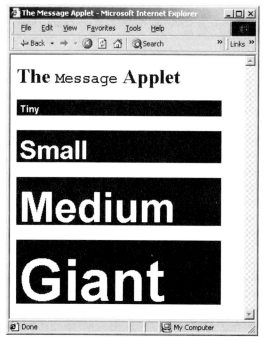

Figure 6–7 Four versions of the same applet, shown in Internet Explorer 5.5 on Windows 2000.

6.6   Summary

Java burst on the scene a few years ago and has been growing rapidly ever since. A number of features of Java will be new to most developers, even though many of the ideas were taken from existing languages, not invented just for Java. We hope this chapter helped you understand these and you now recognize the common misconceptions about Java as well. After installing Java, a Java-capable browser, and the Java API, you're ready to really get hacking.

Where you go next depends on your experience. If you've never used an object-oriented language before, you should carefully read Chapter 7 (Object-Oriented Programming in Java). If you're an OOP expert already, you can just skim the chapter to pick up on Java differences. Similarly, if you've never seen C or C++, you'll need to read through Chapter 8 (Basic Java Syntax) and try writing a number of programs. The experienced C/C++ hacker can quickly browse that chapter and move on. After that, the subsequent chapters cover graphics, windows, event-handling, threading, network programming, Java servlets, JavaServer Pages, and similar advanced Java topics.

OBJECT-ORIENTED PROGRAMMING IN JAVA

Topics in This Chapter

- Instance variables: Creating classes with named fields
- Methods: Adding functions to classes
- Constructors: Defining functions that help build classes
- Destructors: Understanding why Java doesn't need functions to destroy objects
- Overloading: Creating more than one method with the same name
- Javadoc: Making hypertext documentation for your classes
- Inheritance: Reusing and augmenting capabilities from other classes
- Interfaces: Describing the behavior of multiple different classes
- Packages: Organizing classes
- Classpath: Telling Java where to look for classes
- Modifiers: Specifying which parts of your class are exposed

Chapter 7

Objects are central to the Java programming language. Understanding how they are created and used is the first task for a beginning Java programmer. Understanding objects in Java is even more fundamental than the basic syntax summarized in Chapter 8. If you've never seen object-oriented programming, you'll want to take your time with this chapter. As usual, trying things out is more important than reading; be sure to write several of your own classes along the way. The time spent will more than pay for itself in increased productivity later. If you have worked with objects in other languages, you can skim most of these sections. But pay close attention to Sections 7.7 (Javadoc), 7.9 (Interfaces and Abstract Classes), and 7.10 (Packages, Classpath, and JAR Archives).

7.1 Instance Variables

In the simplest case, a class is like a structure or a record. An object (an instance of a class) is normally created by new before a call to a class constructor. The constructor looks like a method with the same name as the class being created. For example:

```
Point p1 = new Point(2, 4);
Color red = new Color(255, 0, 0);
```

Sometimes, however, the call to new can be hidden. For instance, method calls often return an object; the methods might call new internally or might return an object that already exists. For instance:

```
OutputStream out = someSocket.getOutputStream();
Point p1 = someWindow.location();
```

In a very few cases, such as for strings and arrays, Java has shorthand syntax for creating an object. For instance, the following are equivalent ways of creating a `String` object:

```
String string1 = new String("A String");
String string2 = "Another String";
```

The "fields" or "data members" of a class are often called "instance variables" in Java nomenclature. They are accessed through

```
objectReference.variableName
```

that is, by supplying the name of the instance variable separated by a dot from the reference to the actual object.

To illustrate, Listing 7.1 shows a class named `Ship1` used to represent a boat, perhaps for a simple simulation system. The test routine creates two `Ship1` instances with `new Ship1()`, then initializes the various instance variables. These fields are then updated to represent one "move" of the ship, and the new values for the speed and location of the ships are printed out.

Listing 7.1   `Test1.java`

```
// Create a class with five instance variables (fields):
// x, y, speed, direction, and name. Note that Ship1 is
// not declared "public", so it can be in the same file as
// Test1. A Java file can only contain one "public" class
// definition.

class Ship1 {
  public double x, y, speed, direction;
  public String name;
}

// The "driver" class containing "main".

public class Test1 {
  public static void main(String[] args) {
    Ship1 s1 = new Ship1();
    s1.x = 0.0;
    s1.y = 0.0;
    s1.speed = 1.0;
    s1.direction = 0.0;    // East
  s1.name = "Ship1";
    Ship1 s2 = new Ship1();
```

(continued)

Listing 7.1   `Test1.java` *(continued)*

```
    s2.x = 0.0;
    s2.y = 0.0;
    s2.speed = 2.0;
    s2.direction = 135.0; // Northwest
    s2.name = "Ship2";
    s1.x = s1.x + s1.speed
           * Math.cos(s1.direction * Math.PI / 180.0);
    s1.y = s1.y + s1.speed
           * Math.sin(s1.direction * Math.PI / 180.0);
    s2.x = s2.x + s2.speed
           * Math.cos(s2.direction * Math.PI / 180.0);
    s2.y = s2.y + s2.speed
           * Math.sin(s2.direction * Math.PI / 180.0);
    System.out.println(s1.name + " is at ("
                       + s1.x + "," + s1.y + ").");
    System.out.println(s2.name + " is at ("
                       + s2.x + "," + s2.y + ").");
  }
}
```

Compiling and Running:

```
javac Test1.java
java Test1
```

Output:

```
Ship1 is at (1,0).
Ship2 is at (-1.41421,1.41421).
```

You may have noticed a pattern in the variable names and classnames used in this example. A standard convention in Java is to name local variables and instance variables with the initial letter in lowercase (e.g., `someString`, `window`, `outputStream1`) and to name classes with a leading uppercase letter (e.g., `String`, `Window`, `OutputStream`). Subsequent "words" in the variable or class name typically have leading uppercase letters (e.g., `someInstanceVariable`, `SomeClass`), although that notation is not quite as universal a convention, since some people prefer underscores (`some_instance_variable`, `Some_Class`). Constants typically are all uppercase (`PI`). These conventions help people reading your code, and we suggest that you adopt them.

Core Approach

Name variables with an initial lowercase letter (myVar). For class names, use an initial uppercase letter (MyClass).

Now, the astute reader may observe that the example of Listing 7.1 appears to violate this naming convention. For instance, if Math is some global variable containing an object with a PI constant, why is it named Math instead of math? It turns out that this is not a global variable (Java has no such thing, in fact!) but is indeed the name of the Java Math class. Furthermore, in addition to instance variables, Java allows class variables: variables that are shared by all members of the class. These variables are indicated by the static keyword in their declaration and can be accessed either through an object reference or through the class name. So, the naming convention actually makes things clearer here; a reader who has never seen the Math class can tell that PI is a static final (constant) variable in the Math class simply by seeing the reference to Math.PI.

7.2   Methods

In the previous example, virtually identical code was repeated several times to update the x and y instance variables of the two ships. This approach represents poor coding style, not only because the initial repetition takes time, but, more importantly, because updates require changing code in multiple places. To solve this problem, classes can have functions associated with them, not just data, as in Listing 7.2. Java calls them "methods" as in Lisp/CLOS rather than "member functions" as in C++. Notice that, unlike the case with C++, instance variables can be directly initialized in the declaration, as with

```
public double x=0.0;
```

Note also the use of public and private. These modifiers are discussed in more detail in Section 7.11, but the basic point is that you use public for functionality that you are deliberately making available to users of your class. You use private for functionality that you use internally to implement your class but do not want exposed to users of your class.

Listing 7.2 `Test2.java`

```java
// Give the ship public move and printLocation methods.

class Ship2 {
  public double x=0.0, y=0.0, speed=1.0, direction=0.0;
  public String name = "UnnamedShip";

  private double degreesToRadians(double degrees) {
    return(degrees * Math.PI / 180.0);
  }

  public void move() {
    double angle = degreesToRadians(direction);
    x = x + speed * Math.cos(angle);
    y = y + speed * Math.sin(angle);
  }

  public void printLocation() {
    System.out.println(name + " is at " +
                       "(" + x + "," + y + ").");
  }
}

public class Test2 {
  public static void main(String[] args) {
    Ship2 s1 = new Ship2();
    s1.name = "Ship1";
    Ship2 s2 = new Ship2();
    s2.direction = 135.0; // Northwest
    s2.speed = 2.0;
    s2.name = "Ship2";
    s1.move();
    s2.move();
    s1.printLocation();
    s2.printLocation();
  }
}
```

Compiling and Running:

```
javac Test2.java
java Test2
```

Output:

```
Ship1 is at (1,0).
Ship2 is at (-1.41421,1.41421).
```

7.3   Constructors and the "this" Reference

A class constructor is a special routine used to build an object. A constructor is called when you use `new ClassName(...)` to build an instance of a class. Constructors are defined similarly to an ordinary public method, except that the name must match the class name and no return type is given. Note that if you include a return type (e.g., `public` **void** `Ship2(...)` `{...}`), the class will compile without warning on most Java systems, but your constructor will not be called when you try to invoke it.

Core Warning

Be sure your constructor does not specify a return type.

You can define constructors with any number of arguments to let the user supply parameters at the time the object is instantiated. If you fail to define a constructor in the class, the Java compiler automatically provides the class an empty, zero-argument constructor, as in

```
public SomeClass() { }
```

However, if you define *any* constructors for the class, then the default zero-argument constructor is not added by the compiler. Therefore, if you provide any constructors in your class that contain arguments and you would still like a zero-argument constructor, then you will need to explicitly type in a zero-argument constructor.

Core Note

If you do not define constructors in your class, then the Java compiler will provide a default, zero-argument constructor. However, if you define any constructors in your class, then the compiler does not automatically provide the zero-argument constructor if one is missing.

A drawback to `Ship2` is that changing multiple fields takes multiple steps. A more convenient approach is to specify all of the fields when the ship is created. Furthermore, some people feel that relying on default values makes the code more difficult to read, since someone looking only at the code that creates a ship would not know what default values the various fields are assigned. So, we could make an improved `Ship3` with a constructor like the following:

```
public Ship3(double x, double y, ...) {
  // Initialize fields
}
```

However, this presents a problem: the local variable named x "shadows" (hides) the instance variable of the same name. So,

```
public Ship3(double x, double y, ...) {
  x = x;
  y = y;
  ...
}
```

is perfectly legal, but not too useful. All you'd be doing is reassigning the local variables of the method back to their current values. One alternative is to simply use different names, as follows:

```
public Ship3(double inputX, double inputY, ...) {
  x = inputX;
  y = inputY;
  ...
}
```

A second alternative is to use the this reference, as in Listing 7.3. Inside any class you can always use this to refer to the current instance of the class. In addition, this is often used to pass to external routines a reference to themselves. You can legally use this to refer to internal fields or methods, so that the move method could be implemented as:

```
public void move() {
  double angle = this.degreesToRadians(this.direction);
  this.x = this.x + this.speed * Math.cos(this.angle);
  this.y = this.y + this.speed * Math.sin(this.angle);
}
```

instead of the much simpler

```
public void move() {
  double angle = degreesToRadians(direction);
  x = x + speed * Math.cos(angle);
  y = y + speed * Math.sin(angle);
}
```

However, the former is quite cumbersome and tedious, so we recommend that you save this for situations that require it: namely, passing references to the current object to external routines and differentiating local variables from fields with the same names.

Listing 7.3   `Test3.java`

```java
// Give Ship3 a constructor to let the instance variables
// be specified when the object is created.

class Ship3 {
  public double x, y, speed, direction;
  public String name;

  public Ship3(double x, double y, double speed,
               double direction, String name) {
    this.x = x; // "this" differentiates instance vars
    this.y = y; //  from local vars.
    this.speed = speed;
    this.direction = direction;
    this.name = name;
  }

  private double degreesToRadians(double degrees) {
    return(degrees * Math.PI / 180.0);
  }

  public void move() {
    double angle = degreesToRadians(direction);
    x = x + speed * Math.cos(angle);
    y = y + speed * Math.sin(angle);
  }

  public void printLocation() {
    System.out.println(name + " is at " +
                       "(" + x + "," + y + ").");
  }
}

public class Test3 {
  public static void main(String[] args) {
    Ship3 s1 = new Ship3(0.0, 0.0, 1.0,   0.0, "Ship1");
    Ship3 s2 = new Ship3(0.0, 0.0, 2.0, 135.0, "Ship2");
    s1.move();
    s2.move();
    s1.printLocation();
    s2.printLocation();
  }
}
```

Compiling and Running:

```
javac Test3.java

java Test3
```

Output:
```
Ship1 is at (1,0).
Ship2 is at (-1.41421,1.41421).
```

Static Initialization Blocks

If you need something a little more complex than default variable values but a little less complicated than constructors, you can use a `static` initialization block, which is executed when the *class* is loaded (a class is loaded the first time an instance of the class is instantiated or when a `static` variable or method of the class is accessed). Here's an example:

```
public class SomeClass {
   int[] values = new int[12];

   static {
     for(int i=0; i<values.length; i++) {
       values[i] = 2 * i + 5;
     }
   }

   int lastValue = values[11];


   ...
}
```

In most cases, such behavior is placed in the class constructor. You probably won't want `static` initializers very often either.

7.4   Destructors

This section is intentionally left blank.

Just kidding, but destructors (functions to destroy objects) aren't needed in Java. If no reference to an object exists, then the garbage collector frees up the memory for you automatically. If the only reference to an object is a local variable, the object is available for collection when the method exits, or earlier if the variable is reassigned. If an instance variable has the only reference to an object, the object can be collected whenever the variable is reassigned. Not having destructors seems amazing to C++ programmers, but it really works. No dangling pointers: Java will *not* collect an object if a forgotten reference to it is still hanging around somewhere. No memory leaks: Java *will* collect any object that can't be reached from another live object, even if it has nonzero references (as with objects in a circularly linked structure disconnected from everything else). You still have to worry about "leaklets" (stashing a reference in an array or variable and forgetting to reassign it to `null` or some other value), but they are a relatively minor problem.

Although Java will collect all unused objects automatically, you sometimes want to do some bookkeeping when an object is destroyed. For instance, you might want to decrement a count, write a log to disk, or some such. For this kind of situation, you can use the `finalize` method of an object:

```
protected void finalize() throws Throwable {
  doSomeBookkeeping();
  super.finalize(); // Use parent's finalizer
}
```

Don't worry about the `throws` business or how Java knows which methods have `finalize` methods; the details will become clear later. For now, just declare the method exactly as written but do whatever you want for the `doSomeBookkeeping` part.

7.5 Overloading

As in C++ and other object-oriented languages, Java allows more than one method with the same name but with different behaviors, depending on the type or number of its arguments. For instance, you could define two `isBig` methods: one that determines if a `String` is "big" (by some arbitrary measure) and another that determines if an `int` is "big," as follows:

```
public boolean isBig(String s) {
  return(s.length() > 10);
}

public boolean isBig(int n) {
  return(n > 1000);
}
```

Note that

```
return(n > 1000);
```

is a more compact way of accomplishing the same thing as

```
if (n > 1000) {
  return(true);
} else {
  return(false);
}
```

In Listing 7.4, the `Ship4` constructor and the move method are overloaded. One constructor can call another constructor in the class by using `this(args)`, but the call has to be the first line of the constructor. Also, don't confuse the `this` constructor call with the `this` reference. For example:

```
public class SomeClass {
  public SomeClass() {
    this(12); // Invoke other constructor
    doSomething();
  }

  public SomeClass(int num) {
    doSomethingWith(num);
    doSomeOtherStuff();
  }

  ...
}
```

We also want to define a new version of move that lets you specify the number of "steps" the ship should move. If you assume that you will create a new method but leave the original one unchanged, the question is whether the new move should use the old version, as follows:

```
public void move() {
  double angle = degreesToRadians(direction);
  x = x + speed * Math.cos(angle);
  y = y + speed * Math.sin(angle);
}

public void move(int steps) {
  for(int i=0; i<steps; i++) {
    move();
  }
}
```

or if it should repeat the code, as in the following version:

```
public void move() {
  double angle = degreesToRadians(direction);
  x = x + speed * Math.cos(angle);
  y = y + speed * Math.sin(angle);
}

public void move2(int steps) {
  double angle = degreesToRadians(direction);
  x = x + (double)steps * speed * Math.cos(angle);
  y = y + (double)steps * speed * Math.sin(angle);
}
```

The first approach has the advantage that changes to the way in which movement is calculated only have to be implemented in one location but has the disadvantage that significant extra calculations are performed. This example illustrates a common dilemma: the tension between reusability and efficiency. In some instances, reuse can be achieved with no performance reduction. In others, performance has to be traded off against extensibility and reuse, and the appropriate balance depends on the situation. In this particular case, it is possible to get the best of both worlds by modifying the original move method, as follows:

```java
public void move() {
  move(1);
}

public void move(int steps) {
  double angle = degreesToRadians(direction);
  x = x + (double)steps * speed * Math.cos(angle);
  y = y + (double)steps * speed * Math.sin(angle);
}
```

You can find this type of solution more often than you might think, so you should look for such an approach whenever you are faced with a similar problem. However, this approach is not possible if the original move was located in a class that we could not modify.

Listing 7.4 gives the full class definition.

Listing 7.4   Test4.java

```java
class Ship4 {
  public double x=0.0, y=0.0, speed=1.0, direction=0.0;
  public String name;

  // This constructor takes the parameters explicitly.

  public Ship4(double x, double y, double speed,
               double direction, String name) {
    this.x = x;
    this.y = y;
    this.speed = speed;
    this.direction = direction;
    this.name = name;
  }

  // This constructor requires a name but lets you accept
  // the default values for x, y, speed, and direction.
```

(continued)

Listing 7.4 `Test4.java` *(continued)*

```java
public Ship4(String name) {
  this.name = name;
}

private double degreesToRadians(double degrees) {
  return(degrees * Math.PI / 180.0);
}

// Move one step.

public void move() {
  move(1);
}

// Move N steps.

public void move(int steps) {
  double angle = degreesToRadians(direction);
  x = x + (double)steps * speed * Math.cos(angle);
  y = y + (double)steps * speed * Math.sin(angle);
}

public void printLocation() {
  System.out.println(name + " is at (" + x + "," + y + ").");
}
}

public class Test4 {
  public static void main(String[] args) {
    Ship4 s1 = new Ship4("Ship1");
    Ship4 s2 = new Ship4(0.0, 0.0, 2.0, 135.0, "Ship2");
    s1.move();
    s2.move(3);
    s1.printLocation();
    s2.printLocation();
  }
}
```

Compiling and Running:

```
javac Test4.java
java Test4
```

Output:

```
Ship1 is at (1,0).
Ship2 is at (-4.24264,4.24264).
```

7.6   Public Version in Separate File

Classes used in a single place are often combined in the same file as in the previous examples. Often, however, classes are designed to be reused and are placed in separate files where multiple other classes can have public access to them. For instance, Listing 7.5 defines the `Ship` class, and Listing 7.6 defines a driver routine that tests the class. When a developer is building reusable classes, there is a much greater burden to be sure the code is documented and extensible. Two particular strategies help in this regard.

Replace public instance variables with accessor methods.

Instead of direct access to the variables, a common practice is to create a pair of helping methods to set and retrieve the values. For instance, in the ship example, instead of the `x` and `y` fields being `public`, they are made `private`, and `getX`, `getY`, `setX`, and `setY` methods (accessor methods) are created to enable users to look up and modify the fields. Although this strategy appears to be considerable extra work, the time is well invested for classes that are widely used.

First of all, accessor methods provide a placeholder for later functionality. For instance, suppose that the developer decides to provide error checking to ensure that directions are nonnegative or that the ship's maximum speed wasn't exceeded. If users explicitly manipulated the variables directly, then there would be no mechanism for performing this check without having all the users change their code. But if `setX` and `setY` methods were already in place, checking legal values could be performed without any changes in user code. Similarly, suppose that the ship becomes part of a simulation and a graphical representation needs to be updated every time the `x` and `y` locations change. The `setX` and `setY` methods provide a perfect place for changing the values.

Second, using accessor methods shields users of the class from implementation changes. Suppose that the developer decides to use a `Point` data structure to store `x` and `y` instead of storing them individually. If the `x` and `y` variables are referenced directly, users of the class would have to change their code. But if the variables can only be modified through accessor methods, the definitions of `getX` and `getY` could be updated with no required changes by users of the class.

Use javadoc to create on-line documentation.

Documentation enclosed between `/**` and `*/` can be used by the `javadoc` program to create hypertext documentation for all the nonprivate methods and variables (if any). The `javadoc` command-line program is described in Section

7.7. Again, this approach is likely to require considerable extra effort but is well worth that effort for classes that are frequently used by multiple developers. For instance, Figure 7–1 was generated directly from the documentation of `Ship.java` (Listing 7.5).

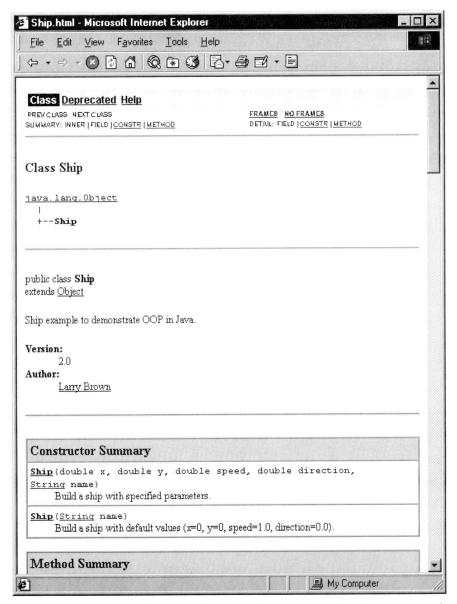

Figure 7–1 Javadoc will generate hypertext documentation from Java source code.

Listing 7.5   `Ship.java`

```java
/** Ship example to demonstrate OOP in Java.
 *
 * @author <A HREF="mailto:larry@corewebprogramming.com">
 *         Larry Brown</A>
 * @version 2.0
 */

public class Ship {
  // Instance variables

  private double x=0.0, y=0.0, speed=1.0, direction=0.0;
  private String name;

  // Constructors

  /** Build a ship with specified parameters. */

  public Ship(double x, double y, double speed,
              double direction, String name) {
    setX(x);
    setY(y);
    setSpeed(speed);
    setDirection(direction);
    setName(name);
  }

  /** Build a ship with default values
   *  (x=0, y=0, speed=1.0, direction=0.0).
   */

  public Ship(String name) {
    setName(name);
  }

  /** Move ship one step at current speed/direction. */

  public void move() {
    moveInternal(1);
  }

  /** Move N steps. */

  public void move(int steps) {
    moveInternal(steps);
  }
```

(continued)

Listing 7.5 `Ship.java` *(continued)*

```java
private void moveInternal(int steps) {
  double angle = degreesToRadians(direction);
  x = x + (double)steps * speed * Math.cos(angle);
  y = y + (double)steps * speed * Math.sin(angle);
}

private double degreesToRadians(double degrees) {
  return(degrees * Math.PI / 180.0);
}

/** Report location to standard output. */

public void printLocation() {
  System.out.println(getName() + " is at (" + getX() +
                     "," + getY() + ").");
}

/** Get current X location. */

public double getX() {
  return(x);
}

/** Set current X location. */

public void setX(double x) {
  this.x = x;
}

/** Get current Y location. */

public double getY() {
  return(y);
}

/** Set current Y location. */

public void setY(double y) {
  this.y = y;
}
```

(continued)

Listing 7.5   `Ship.java` *(continued)*

```java
/** Get current speed. */

public double getSpeed() {
  return(speed);
}

/** Set current speed. */

public void setSpeed(double speed) {
  this.speed = speed;
}

/** Get current heading (0=East, 90=North, 180=West,
 *  270=South).  I.e., uses standard math angles, <B>not</B>
 *  nautical system where 0=North, 90=East, etc.
 */

public double getDirection() {
  return(direction);
}

/** Set current direction (0=East, 90=North, 180=West,
 *  270=South). I.e., uses standard math angles,<B>not</B>
 *  nautical system where 0=North,90=East, etc.
 */

public void setDirection(double direction) {
  this.direction = direction;
}

/** Get Ship's name. Can't be modified by user. */

public String getName() {
  return(name);
}

private void setName(String name) {
  this.name = name;
}
}
```

Listing 7.6 `ShipTest.java`

```
public class ShipTest {
  public static void main(String[] args) {
    Ship s1 = new Ship("Ship1");
    Ship s2 = new Ship(0.0, 0.0, 2.0, 135.0, "Ship2");
    s1.move();
    s2.move(3);
    s1.printLocation();
    s2.printLocation();
  }
}
```

Compiling and Running:

```
javac ShipTest.java
java ShipTest
```

The first line calls `javac` on `Ship.java` automatically. The Java compiler automatically checks the file creation date of each `.class` file used by the class it compiles, compares it to the creation date of the source file (if available), and recompiles if necessary. Java does not require makefiles as in C/C++; all classes *directly* used are recompiled if out of date. If you want to keep a given `.class` file in use even while you are updating the `.java` source, simply keep the source in a separate directory.

Core Note

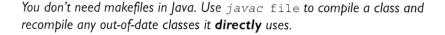

*You don't need makefiles in Java. Use `javac file` to compile a class and recompile any out-of-date classes it **directly** uses.*

Output:

```
Ship1 is at (1,0).
Ship2 is at (-4.24264,4.24264).
```

7.7 Javadoc

The `javadoc` program is distributed with Sun's JDK and by most third-party vendors. The command-line program uses comments enclosed between `/**` and `*/` to generate on-line documentation that includes hypertext links to other user-defined and system classes. You generally place `javadoc` comments above the class definition and before every nonprivate method and class. The first sentence of the variable or method description is placed in the alphabetized index at the top of the resultant page, with the full description available in the detailed sections at the bottom. To create the documentation, supply one or more file or package names to javadoc, as follows:

```
javadoc Foo.java
javadoc Foo.java Bar.java
javadoc graphics.newWidgets
javadoc graphics.newWidgets math.geometry
```

You can also supply various options to javadoc. These options are described later in this section, but here are some simple examples:

```
javadoc -author -version SomeClass.java
javadoc -noindex -notree somePackage
```

Packages are described in Section 7.10.

By default, the javadoc program uses a standard doclet template to generate HTML-formatted API output. The doclet template recognizes HTML markup, not just standard text, inside your comments. Thus, you can use <A HREF="..."> to create hypertext links to your organization's home page, use the IMG element to include a screen dump of your program in action, and even use the APPLET element to load an interactive demonstration that illustrates some of the most important uses of your class. You probably want to avoid headings, however, since they are likely to break up the outline javadoc generates. Extra white space is ignored inside these comments unless they occur inside a space-preserving element such as PRE.

If you would like a different overall HTML format for the generated API, you can write your own custom doclets, since doclets are simply Java programs that use the doclet API to specify the content and format of the output from the javadoc tool. The following URLs provide complete documentation for the javadoc tool and doclets.

Javadoc 1.3 Home Page
```
http://java.sun.com/j2se/1.3/docs/tooldocs/javadoc/
```

Javadoc Tool Reference Page
```
http://java.sun.com/j2se/1.3/docs/tooldocs/solaris/javadoc.html
http://java.sun.com/j2se/1.3/docs/tooldocs/win32/javadoc.html
```

Doclet Overview and Doclet API
```
http://java.sun.com/j2se/1.3/docs/tooldocs/javadoc/overview.html
http://java.sun.com/j2se/1.3/docs/tooldocs/javadoc/doclet/
```

Javadoc Tags

In addition to HTML markup and text, there are some special tags that you can insert in the documentation to get certain effects. For instance, you can use @param to describe individual parameters that a method expects, @return to describe the return value, and @see to reference related classes or methods. Here's an example:

```
/** Converts an angle in degrees to one in radians.
 *
 * @param degrees The input angle in degrees.
 * @return The equivalent of the input, in radians.
 * @see #radiansToDegrees.
 */

public double degreesToRadians(double degrees) {
  return(degrees * Math.PI / 180.0);
}
```

These special tags must occur at the beginning of a line, and all text following the tag and before the next tag or the end of the comment is considered part of the tagged paragraph.

The legal tags are described below. Unless otherwise noted, the tag is supported in JDK 1.1 and later.

@author

This tag is used in the class documentation to specify the author. You must use "javadoc -author ..." for this specification to take effect. HTML markup is allowed here; for example:

```
/** Description for SomeClass
 *   ...
 * @author <A HREF="mailto:ellison@microsoft.com">
 *         Larry Ellison</A>
 */
```

@deprecated

This tag indicates classes, fields, or methods that should no longer be used, that is, ones that are currently supported for backward compatibility but that might be dropped in future releases.

{@docRoot} [Java 1.3]

This tag represents a relative path from the generated document to the root document page in a package hierarchy. This tag is useful when you are generating documentation for a large package that has numerous subdirectories and you would like to refer to a common page, for example, a copyright or license page, located in the root directory. For example, if a link to licensing information is needed in the documentation for `corewebprogramming/Ship.java`, then

```
<a href="{@docRoot}/license.html">
```

would resolve to

```
<a href="../license.html">
```

assuming here that `license.html` is located in the `corewebprogramming` directory.

@exception

This tag documents methods and constructors and should be followed by an exception classname, a space, and a description.

{@link} [Java 1.2]

This tag is similar to the `@see` tag; however, instead of a See Also section being created in the document, an inline hyperlink is created. This approach is useful in a descriptive paragraph for creating links to other methods. For example, in `Ship.java`, a descriptive paragraph could contain

```
To change the location of a ship use
{@link #move(int) move}.
```

which is translated to

```
To change the location of a ship use
<a href="Ship.html#move(int)">move</a>.
```

@param

The `@param` tag documents the arguments that a method (or constructor) takes. The tag should be followed by the parameter name, a space, and the description of the parameter.

@return

This tag documents the return value of a method.

@see

This tag creates hypertext links to the `javadoc` documentation for other methods or classes. Methods should normally be prefaced by the classname and a #, but the classname can be omitted for methods in the current class. For instance:

```
/**
 * ...
 * @see #getWidget
 * @see Widget
 * @see Frob#setWidget
 */

public void setWidget(Widget w) { ... }
```

@serial [Java 1.2]
@serialData [Java 1.2]
@serialField [Java 1.2]
These three tags provide a way to document the form for a `Serializable` class. The first tag describes a default field that is serializable in the class. The second tag describes any `ObjectStreamFields`, and the third tag describes the sequence and types of any data that is `Externalizable`. For detailed information on these tags, see `http://java.sun.com/j2se/1.3/docs/guide/serialization/spec/serial-arch.doc6.html`.

@since
This tag creates a "Since" section used to document when the class, field, or method was added. It is typically used for classes or packages undergoing revisions to distinguish new features from preexisting ones.

@throws [Java 1.2]
This tag defines an `Exception` that the method or class may throw. The tag is immediately followed by the exception classname, a space, and then a description of the exception.

@version
This tag is used in the class documentation to list a version number. You must use "`javadoc -version ...`" for this specification to take effect.

Javadoc Command-Line Arguments

The `javadoc` tool lets you supply a number of options to customize its behavior. For instance, authors often use

```
javadoc -author -version -noindex -notree Class.java
```

to honor the `@author` and `@version` tags and to suppress generation of the index and class hierarchy. As of JDK 1.3, over 40 options flags are available for `javadoc` when the standard doclet template is used. Below we summarize only the most frequently used option flags.

-author
This flags tells `javadoc` to include the author information, which is omitted by default.

-bottom [Java 1.2]
The `bottom` flag specifies text to be placed at the bottom of each output file below the lower navigation bar. If the text contains white space, then enclose the text in quotes.

-classpath
-sourcepath

These flags tell `javadoc` where to look for the specified `.java` files. Multiple directories should be separated by a colon on Solaris and a semicolon on Windows. Directories specified in the `CLASSPATH` variable are searched automatically.

-d

This flag supplies a destination directory for the HTML files. An absolute or relative directory can be used. If the flag is omitted, the HTML files are placed in the same directory as the source file. You often use `-d` to specify a directory that already contains the `images` subdirectory holding the GIF files used by documentation files.

-encoding
-docencoding

These flags allow you to specify the character encoding used for the source file (`-encoding`) or that should be used for the documentation (`-docencoding`).

-link [Java 1.2]
-linkoffline [Java 1.2]

The `link` flag tells `javadoc` where to look to resolve links to other packages when generating the documentation. For example, if you would like to resolve the links to the on-line documentation at `java.sun.com` for Java classes found in your documentation, you would use

```
-link http://java.sun.com/j2se/1.3/docs/api
```

The `javadoc` program actually uses the `package-list` file located at the above URL to correctly resolve the links for the external packages. If Internet access is not available, you can use the `linkoffline` to point to a local copy of the `package-list` file. If you've locally installed the JDK 1.3 documentation, then the list for the Java packages is located at `/root/jdk1.3/docs/api`. Thus, to resolve the external links locally on a Windows platform, you might use

```
-linkoffline http://java.sun.com/j2se/1.3/docs/api
            c:\jdk1.3\docs\api
```

-J

The `javadoc` tool is itself a Java program. The `-J` flag lets you pass parameters directly to the Java runtime. For instance, if the documentation set will be very large, you might want to specify a large (24 megabyte) startup size through

```
javadoc -J-ms24m ...
```

-nodeprecated
-nodeprecatedlist [Java 1.2]

The first flag tells javadoc to omit all deprecated entries. The second flag omits the deprecated-list.html page and the deprecation link in the navigation bar but still generates deprecated information throughout the documentation.

-noindex

This tells javadoc not to generate the AllNames.html index. The index is useful for packages, but you often want to omit it when building documentation for a single class.

-nonavbar [Java 1.2]

This tag suppresses the generation of the navigation bar found at the top and bottom of pages.

-notree

This tells javadoc not to generate the tree.html class hierarchy.

-public
-protected
-package
-private

These flag options let you specify which classes and members get documented. They are ordered here from the most restrictive to the most inclusive, and each option automatically includes all of the ones above it in the list. The default is protected, which generates documentation only for public and protected members. This documentation is what users of your class normally want, but developers that are changing the class might want to know about private data as well.

-splitindex [Java 1.2]

This flag specifies a separate index file for each letter in the index, instead of a single alphabetical index file. In addition, a single, separate file is generated for index entries that do not start with an alphabetical character.

-verbose

This flag tells javadoc to print information about the time taken to parse each file.

-version

The -version flag tells javadoc to include version numbers (as specified through @version). They are omitted by default.

-windowtitle [Java 1.2]

This flag defines the title used when generating the HTML document and appears in the browser window title. The text, preceding the flag and enclosed in quotes, is placed in the <title> ... </title> container within the HTML document. The title cannot contain any HTML markup tags.

For example, the following javadoc command was used on Windows 98 with JDK 1.3 to generate the HTML documentation shown in Figure 7–1.

```
>javadoc -author -version -noindex -notree
        -linkoffline
        http://java.sun.com/j2se/1.3/docs/api
        c:\jdk1.3\docs\api Ship.java
```

For a large list of command options, you can exceed the character limit for some shells. In such cases, you need to create a makefile to use with javadoc. For example makefiles on Windows, see http://java.sun.com/products/jdk/java-doc/makefiles. Makefiles for other platforms are given in the Javadoc Tool Reference Page for the various platforms at http://java.sun.com/j2se/1.3/docstooldocs/javadoc/index.html.

7.8 Inheritance

Inheritance is the process by which a new class is built on top of a previously written class without the existing class's functionality needing to be rewritten. The extends keyword is used to indicate that one class inherits from another. The original class is usually referred to as the *parent class* or *superclass* (called base class in C++ lingo). The new class is known as the *child class* or *subclass* (called derived class in C++ lingo). The new child class inherits the nonprivate instance variables and methods but *not* the constructors of the parent class. However, a constructor in a child class can explicitly call the constructor in the parent class by using super on the first line of the new constructor. Here is a simplified example:

```
// ParentClass.java: original parent/base/superclass.
// Has fields a and b and methods foo and bar.
// Has two constructors.
```

```java
public class ParentClass {
  public int a;
  private int b;

  public ParentClass() { ... }
  public ParentClass(double z) { ... }

  public String foo(int x, String s) { ... }

  private void bar() { ... }
}

// ChildClass.java: the new child/derived/subclass.
// Has fields a (by inheritance) and c, and methods
// foo (by inheritance) and baz. Has one constructor
// which uses ParentClass's constructor.

public class ChildClass extends ParentClass {
  public int c;

  public ChildClass(double z) {
    super(z); // call ParentClass's constructor
    ...
  }

  public void baz(boolean isReady) { ... }
}
```

Be aware that if the subclass constructor does not explicitly call a constructor in the superclass through the keyword `super`, then the zero-argument constructor in the superclass is implicitly called before any code is executed in the subclass constructor. Furthermore, if the superclass does not have a zero-argument constructor, then a compile error is produced when the subclass is compiled. Remember that the compiler will add a default, zero-argument constructor to any class that does not define constructors. Also, remember that if any constructors are explicitly defined in a class, then the compiler does not automatically add a default constructor.

Core Note

When calling a constructor in the superclass, you must make the `super` call the first line in the subclass constructor. If no constructor in the superclass is explicitly called, then the zero-argument constructor in the superclass is implicitly called.

One benefit of inheritance is the ability to "override" a method inherited from the parent class and provide a new implementation of the method in the child class. The overridden method in the child class must have the same signature: method name, parameter list, and return type. If needed, the new method can access the previous version by calling

```
super.overriddenMethodName(...)
```

You cannot invoke `super.super` to access overridden methods higher up in the inheritance hierarchy, though. Also, if desired, you can relax the visibility of an overridden method to provide greater access; a method declared `protected` in the parent class can be redeclared `public` in the child class.

An initial misconception about inheritance is that the keyword `super` is necessary to access any of the methods in the parent class. The keyword `super` is really only necessary when both the parent class and the child class have a method with the same name—the child class has overridden the method in the parent class—and you would like to access the method in the parent class from the child class. Otherwise, the inherited methods (non-overridden methods) are immediately available in the child class directly through the method name and the keyword `super` is not required.

Core Note

Inherited methods are immediately available to the child class through the method name. The keyword `super` is only necessary when you want to access the parent version of an inherited method that has been overridden in child class.

Technically, you can override variables inherited from the parent class. However, overriding a variable is *never* done in practice, since an instance of the child class would have two variables with the same name—one variable is exposed when a method is executed in the child class and the other variable is exposed when an inherited method is executed in the parent class. Because the two variables have the same name, this behavior is very difficult to debug, so, for good practice, do not override variables.

Following, we illustrate an example that uses inheritance and overrides a method. Listing 7.7 presents a `Speedboat` class that adds color methods and variables and overrides the `printLocation` method. A driver for the class is given in Listing 7.8.

Listing 7.7   Speedboat.java

```java
/** A fast Ship. Red and going 20 knots by default. */

public class Speedboat extends Ship {
  private String color = "red";

  /** Builds a red Speedboat going N at 20 knots. */

  public Speedboat(String name) {
    super(name);
    setSpeed(20);
  }

  /** Builds a speedboat with specified parameters. */

  public Speedboat(double x, double y, double speed,
                   double direction, String name,
                   String color) {
    super(x, y, speed, direction, name);
    setColor(color);
  }

  /** Report location. Override version from Ship. */

  public void printLocation() {
    System.out.print(getColor().toUpperCase() + " ");
    super.printLocation();
  }

  /** Gets the Speedboat's color. */

  public String getColor() {
    return(color);
  }

  /** Sets the Speedboat's color. */

  public void setColor(String colorName) {
    color = colorName;
  }
}
```

Listing 7.8   `SpeedboatTest.java`

```java
/** Try a couple of Speedboats and a regular Ship. */

public class SpeedboatTest {
  public static void main(String[] args) {
    Speedboat s1 = new Speedboat("Speedboat1");
    Speedboat s2 = new Speedboat(0.0, 0.0, 2.0, 135.0,
                                 "Speedboat2", "blue");
    Ship s3 = new Ship(0.0, 0.0, 2.0, 135.0, "Ship1");
    s1.move();
    s2.move();
    s3.move();
    s1.printLocation();
    s2.printLocation();
    s3.printLocation();
  }
}
```

Compiling and Running:

```
javac -depend SpeedboatTest.java
java SpeedboatTest
```

The first line above calls `javac` on `Speedboat.java` and `Ship.java` automatically.

Output:

```
RED Speedboat1 is at (20,0).
BLUE Speedboat2 is at (-1.41421,1.41421).
Ship1 is at (-1.41421,1.41421).
```

Java, unlike C++ and Lisp/CLOS but like Smalltalk, supports single inheritance only. This means that although your class can have many ancestor classes, it can have only one *immediate* parent. This behavior is normally what you want; in some situations, though, multiple inheritance is useful, but Java doesn't support it. However, many of the benefits of multiple inheritance can be attained with less complexity by the use of *interfaces*, which is discussed in the next section.

7.9   Interfaces and Abstract Classes

Suppose that you want to define a class to act as a parent of other classes, but you don't want to let people directly instantiate the class. For instance, you might want to provide some common behavior in the class, but the class will not have enough information to be used by itself. In this case, Java lets you declare a class abstract, and the compiler will not let you build an instance of the class. For instance, Listing 7.9 shows an abstract Shape class. The example says that all Shape subclasses will have methods to look up and set locations (getX, getY, and so forth) but that you are prohibited from directly building a Shape object.

Listing 7.9   `Shape.java`

```
/** The parent class for all closed, open, curved, and
 *  straight-edged shapes.
 */

public abstract class Shape {
  protected int x, y;

  public int getX() {
    return(x);
  }

  public void setX(int x) {
    this.x = x;
  }

  public int getY() {
    return(y);
  }

  public void setY(int y) {
    this.y = y;
  }
}
```

Java also lets you define abstract methods—methods that define the return type and parameters but don't provide a method body—as follows:

```
public ReturnType methodName(Type1 arg1, Type2 arg2);
```

Classes that contain an abstract method *must* be declared abstract. Their subclasses must also be abstract *unless* they implement all of the abstract methods in the superclass. Abstract methods are useful when you want to require all members of a class to have certain general categories of behavior but where each member of the class will implement the behavior slightly differently.

Since the `Shape` class does not define abstract methods, its subclasses can be abstract or concrete. In this particular case, we create two further abstract subclasses for curved shapes and for those with straight edges. See Listings 7.10 and 7.11.

Listing 7.10 `Curve.java`

```
/** A curved shape (open or closed). Subclasses will include
 *  arcs and circles.
 */

public abstract class Curve extends Shape {}
```

Listing 7.11 `StraightEdgedShape.java`

```
/** A Shape with straight edges (open or closed). Subclasses
 *  will include Line, LineSegment, LinkedLineSegments,
 *  and Polygon.
 */

public abstract class StraightEdgedShape extends Shape {}
```

Now, suppose that we want to extend the `Curve` class to create a `Circle` and we want the `Circle` to have a method to calculate its area. We could simply have `Circle` extend `Curve` (*without* including the `abstract` declaration) and include a `getArea` method. This approach works fine if circles are the only shapes whose area can be measured. But if we planned ahead for a `Rectangle` class descended from `StraightEdgedShape`, we might be dissatisfied with this approach, since the areas of rectangles can be measured as well. Creating general routines that deal with areas will now be difficult because `Rectangle` and `Circle` have no common ancestor containing `getArea`. For instance, how would we easily make an array of shapes whose areas can be summed? A `Circle[]` wouldn't allow rectangles, and a `Rectangle[]` also would be too restrictive, since it would exclude circles. But a `Shape[]` would not be restrictive enough, since it would permit shapes that didn't have a `getArea` method. Similarly, if we wanted to return the larger area from two shapes, what argument types should such a `maxArea` method take? Not `Shape`, since some shapes lack `getArea`. Putting an abstract `getArea` method into `Shape` doesn't make sense since some shapes (line segments, arcs, and such) won't have measurable areas. In fact, there *is* no clean approach if we use regular classes.

Fortunately, Java has a solution for just this type of dilemma: interfaces. Interfaces look like abstract classes where all of the methods are abstract. The big difference is that a class can directly implement *multiple* interfaces, whereas it can only directly

extend a single class. A class that implements an interface must either provide definitions for all methods or declare itself abstract. To illustrate, Listing 7.12 shows a simple interface.

Listing 7.12 `Interface1.java`

```
public interface Interface1 {
  ReturnType1 method1(ArgType1 arg);
  ReturnType2 method2(ArgType2 arg);
}
```

Note that the `interface` keyword is used instead of `class` and that the method
declarations end in a semicolon with no method body (just like abstract methods).
Also note that the `public` declarations before methods in an interface are optional;
the methods are implicitly public, so the explicit declarations are normally omitted.
Listing 7.13 shows a class that uses the interface.

Listing 7.13 `Class1.java`

```
// This class is not abstract, so it must provide
// implementations of method1 and method2.

public class Class1 extends SomeClass
                    implements Interface1 {
  public ReturnType1 method1(ArgType1 arg) {
    someCodeHere();
    ...
  }

  public ReturnType2 method2(ArgType2 arg) {
    someCodeHere();
    ...
  }

  ...
}
```

Listing 7.14 presents another interface.

Listing 7.14 `Interface2.java`

```
public interface Interface2 {
  ReturnType3 method3(ArgType3 arg);
}
```

Next, Listing 7.15 outlines a class that uses *both* interfaces. It is abstract, so does not have to provide implementations of the methods of the interfaces.

Listing 7.15 `Class2.java`

```
// This class is abstract, so does not have to provide
// implementations of the methods of Interface 1 and 2.

public abstract class Class2 extends SomeOtherClass
                           implements Interface1,
                                      Interface2 {
  ...
}
```

Finally, Listing 7.16 shows a concrete subclass of `Class2`.

Listing 7.16 `Class3.java`

```
// This class is not abstract, so it must provide
// implementations of method1, method2, and method3.

public class Class3 extends Class2 {
  public ReturnType1 method1(ArgType1 arg) {
    someCodeHere();
    ...
  }

  public ReturnType2 method2(ArgType2 arg) {
    someCodeHere();
    ...
  }

  public ReturnType3 method3(ArgType3 arg) {
    someCodeHere();
    ...
  }

  ...
}
```

Since interfaces do not contain method definitions, they cannot be directly instantiated. However, an interface can `extend` (not `implement`) one or more other interfaces (use commas if you extend more than one), so that interface definitions can be built up hierarchically just like class definitions can. Interfaces cannot include normal instance variables but can include constants. The `public`, `static`, and `final` declarations for the constants are implicit, so are normally omitted. Listing 7.17 gives an example.

Listing 7.17 `Interface3.java`

```
// This interface has three methods (by inheritance) and
// two constants.

public interface Interface3 extends Interface1,
                                     Interface2 {
  int MIN_VALUE = 0;
  int MAX_VALUE = 1000;
}
```

Now, how does all this help us with the `Shape` class hierarchy? Well, the key point is that methods can refer to an interface as though it were a regular class. So, we first define a `Measurable` interface, as shown in Listing 7.18. Note that it is common to end interface names with "able" (`Runnable`, `Serializable`, `Sortable`, `Drawable`, and so on).

Listing 7.18 `Measurable.java`

```
/** Used in classes with measurable areas. */

public interface Measurable {
  double getArea();
}
```

Next, we define a `Circle` class that implements this interface, as shown in Listing 7.19.

Listing 7.19 `Circle.java`

```
/** A circle. Since you can calculate the area of
 *  circles, class implements the Measurable interface.
 */

public class Circle extends Curve implements Measurable {
  private double radius;
```

(continued)

Listing 7.19 `Circle.java` *(continued)*

```java
public Circle(int x, int y, double radius) {
  setX(x);
  setY(y);
  setRadius(radius);
}

public double getRadius() {
  return(radius);
}

public void setRadius(double radius) {
  this.radius = radius;
}

/** Required for Measurable interface. */

public double getArea() {
  return(Math.PI * radius * radius);
}
}
```

Having Measurable as an interface lets us define a class that uses Measurable without having to know which specific classes actually implement it. Listing 7.20 gives an example.

Listing 7.20 `MeasureUtil.java`

```java
/** Some operations on Measurable instances. */

public class MeasureUtil {
  public static double maxArea(Measurable m1,
                               Measurable m2) {
    return(Math.max(m1.getArea(), m2.getArea()));
  }

  public static double totalArea(Measurable[] mArray) {
    double total = 0;
    for(int i=0; i<mArray.length; i++) {
      total = total + mArray[i].getArea();
    }
    return(total);
  }
}
```

Because of this design, other classes can implement the Measurable interface and automatically become available to the MeasureUtil methods. For instance, Listings 7.21 and 7.22 show an abstract Polygon class and one of its concrete subclasses. All polygons should have measurable areas but will be calculated differently.

Listing 7.21 `Polygon.java`

```
/** A closed Shape with straight edges. */

public abstract class Polygon extends StraightEdgedShape
                            implements Measurable {
  private int numSides;

  public int getNumSides() {
    return(numSides);
  }

  protected void setNumSides(int numSides) {
    this.numSides = numSides;
  }
}
```

Listing 7.22 `Rectangle.java`

```
/** A rectangle implements the getArea method. This satisfies
 *  the Measurable interface, so rectangles can be instantiated.
 */

public class Rectangle extends Polygon {
  private double width, height;

  public Rectangle(int x, int y,
                   double width, double height) {
    setNumSides(2);
    setX(x);
    setY(y);
    setWidth(width);
    setHeight(height);
  }

  public double getWidth() {
    return(width);
  }
```

(continued)

Listing 7.22 `Rectangle.java` *(continued)*

```
public void setWidth(double width) {
  this.width = width;
}

public double getHeight() {
  return(height);
}

public void setHeight(double height) {
  this.height = height;
}

/** Required to implement Measurable interface. */

public double getArea() {
  return(width * height);
}
}
```

Although *we* took a long time explaining what was going on, using interfaces did not substantially increase the *code* required in the Shape hierarchy. The Measurable interface took three lines, and the only other thing needed was the "implements Measurable" declaration. However, the interface saved a large amount of work in the MeasureUtil class and made it immune to changes in which classes actually have getArea methods. Listing 7.23 shows a simple test of the MeasureUtil class.

It has been widely claimed in the Java community that interfaces provide all of the good features of *multiple inheritance* (the ability of a class to have more than one immediate parent class) with little of the complexity. We suspect that these claims are mostly made by people without significant experience with multiple inheritance. It is absolutely true that interfaces are a convenient and useful construct, and you'll see them used in several places in the rest of the book. However, if you come from a language that supports multiple inheritance (e.g., C++, Eiffel, Lisp/CLOS, among others), you will find that they do not provide everything that you are accustomed to in other languages.

Listing 7.23 `MeasureTest.java`

```
/** Test of MeasureUtil. Note that we could change the
 *  actual classes of elements in the measurables array (as
 *  long as they implemented Measurable) without changing
 *  the rest of the code.
 */

public class MeasureTest {
  public static void main(String[] args) {
    Measurable[] measurables =
      { new Rectangle(0, 0, 5.0, 10.0),
        new Rectangle(0, 0, 4.0, 9.0),
        new Circle(0, 0, 4.0),
        new Circle(0, 0, 5.0) };
    System.out.print("Areas:");
    for(int i=0; i<measurables.length; i++)
      System.out.print(" " + measurables[i].getArea());
    System.out.println();
    System.out.println("Larger of 1st, 3rd: " +
      MeasureUtil.maxArea(measurables[0],
                    measurables[2]) +
                    "\nTotal area: " +
                    MeasureUtil.totalArea(measurables));
  }
}
```

From the viewpoint of someone who will be *using* a class (e.g., the person writing `MeasureUtil`), interfaces are better; they let you treat classes in different hierarchies as though they were part of a common class, but without all the confusion multiple inheritance can cause. However, from the viewpoint of the person *writing* the classes themselves (e.g., the person writing the `Shape` hierarchy), they may save little. In particular, interfaces do not let you inherit the implementation of methods, although such inheritance can sometimes be a timesaver. For example, suppose that you have a variety of custom buttons, windows, and textfields, each of which has a private `name` field used for debugging, and each of which should have a `debug` method that prints out the location, parent window, and name of the graphical component. In Java, you would have to repeat this code in each subclass, whereas multiple inheritance would let you place it in a single parent class (`Debuggable`) and have each graphical object simply extend this class.

The use of multiple inheritance to provide characteristics shared by classes at varying locations in the class hierarchy is sometimes known as a "mix in" style, and Java provides nothing equivalent. Whether the simplicity benefit gained by leaving out this capability is worth the cost in the relatively small number of cases where mix-ins would have been valuable is open to debate.

7.10 Packages, Classpath, and JAR Archives

Java lets you group class libraries into separate modules or "packages" to avoid naming conflicts and to simplify their handling. For instance, in a real project, the `Ship` and `Shape` class hierarchies would have been easier to create and use if placed in separate packages. To create a package called `packagename`, first make a subdirectory with the same name and place all source files there. Each of these files should contain

```
package packagename;
```

as the first noncomment line. Files that lack a package declaration are automatically placed in an unnamed package. Files in the main directory that want to use the package should include

```
import packagename.ClassName;
```

or

```
import packagename.*;
```

before the class definitions (but after the `package` declaration, if any). This statement tells the compiler that all the specified classes ("`*`" means "all") should be available for use if they are needed. Otherwise, the compiler only looks for classes it needs in the current directory or, as we will see shortly, in directories specified through the `CLASSPATH` variable.

Package names can contain dots ("."); these correspond to subdirectories. For example, assume that your application is being developed on Windows 2000 or NT in `C:\Java\classes`. Now suppose that the classes shown in Listings 7.24 through 7.27 are created. They include the following:

- `package1` package (in `C:\Java\classes\package1`) containing `Class1`
- `package2` package (in `C:\Java\classes\package2`) containing `Class2`
- `package2.package3` package (in `C:\Java\classes\package2\package3`) containing `Class3`
- `package4` package (in `C:\Java\classes\package4`) containing `Class1`

Note the name conflict between `package1` and `package4`: they both contain a class named `Class1`. If a single program needs to use both, it simply omits the `import` statement for one of them and uses `packagename.Class1` instead. This is known as the "fully qualified classname" and can be used in lieu of `import` any time.

For instance, an applet could explicitly extend java.applet.Applet and not import java.applet.Applet or java.applet.*.

Also notice that the printInfo methods of the test classes are declared static. You can invoke static methods by using the name of the class (like Math.cos) without creating an object instance.

Listing 7.24 C:\Java\classes\package1\Class1.java

```
package package1;

public class Class1 {
  public static void printInfo() {
    System.out.println("This is Class1 in package1.");
  }
}
```

Listing 7.25 C:\Java\classes\package2\Class2.java

```
package package2;

public class Class2 {
  public static void printInfo() {
    System.out.println("This is Class2 in package2.");
  }
}
```

Listing 7.26 C:\Java\classes\package2\package3\
Class3.java

```
package package2.package3;

public class Class3 {
  public static void printInfo() {
    System.out.println("This is Class3 in " +
                       "package2.package3.");
  }
}
```

Listing 7.27 `C:\Java\classes\package4\Class1.java`

```
package package4;

public class Class1 {
  public static void printInfo() {
    System.out.println("This is Class1 in package4.");
  }
}
```

Now, let's make a test program that uses these classes (Listing 7.28). This file will be placed back in the root directory, not in the package-specific subclasses.

Listing 7.28 `C:\Java\classes\PackageExample.java`

```
import package1.*;
import package2.Class2;
import package2.package3.*;

public class PackageExample {
  public static void main(String[] args) {
    Class1.printInfo();
    Class2.printInfo();
    Class3.printInfo();
    package4.Class1.printInfo();
  }
}
```

Compiling and Running:

```
javac PackageExample.java
java PackageExample
```

The first line above compiles all four other classes automatically.

Output:

```
This is Class1 in package1.
This is Class2 in package2.
This is Class3 in package2.package3.
This is Class1 in package4.
```

In the above example, compiling `PackageExample.java` automatically compiled the other source files located in the four packages, since `PackageExample` uses these classes directly (they are automatically compiled if out of date). If you would like to compile the four source files individually, you would need to specify the full subdirectory path in the command line, as in

```
javac package1/Class1.java
javac package2/Class2.java
javac package2/package3/Class3.java
javac package4/Class1.java
```

In general, when compiling files in packages you have two choices:

1. Compile the files from the directory just above the package directory (the package directory is below the working directory). For example, you would compile the file `C:\Java\classes\package2\Class2.java` located in the `package2` directory from `C:\Java\classes\`, specifying `javac package2/Class2.java`.

2. Include the root package directory in the `CLASSPATH` and compile the file from the same directory in which the source is located. For this example, you would include `C:\Java\classes` on your `CLASSPATH`.

We describe how to set the `CLASSPATH` in the next section.

The CLASSPATH

Up to now, we've been acting as though you must have a single root directory for all your Java files. This approach would be inconvenient if you develop a large number of applications. Rather than just looking in the current directory, Java lets you supply a list of directories in which it should look for classes. This mechanism complements packages; it doesn't replace them. In particular, the directory list should contain the *roots* of package hierarchies, not the subdirectories corresponding to the individual packages. The classpath defines the starting points for the search; the `import` statements specify which subdirectories should be examined. Most Java systems also allow entries in the classpath to be compressed JAR files; this is a convenient mechanism for moving large package hierarchies around.

You can specify the classpath in two ways. The first is to supply a `-classpath` argument to `javac` and `java`. The second, and more common, approach is to use the `CLASSPATH` environment variable. If this variable is not set, Java looks for class files and package subdirectories relative to the current directory. In many cases, looking in subdirectories of the working directory is usually what you want, so if you set the `CLASSPATH` variable, be sure to include "." if you want the current directory to be examined. Directories are separated by semicolons or colons, depending on the operating system. For instance, on Unix (`csh`, `tcsh`), you could set the environment variables through:

```
setenv CLASSPATH .:~/classes:/home/mcnealy/classes
```

On Windows 98/2000/NT, you could set the environment variables through

```
set CLASSPATH=.;C:\BillGates\classes;D:\Java\classes
```

MacOS doesn't have the concept of environment variables, but you can set the classpath on an application-by-application basis by changing the 'STR ' (0) resource. Fortunately, most Mac-based Java IDEs have easier ways of doing this. It is not necessary to include the location of the standard Java classes in the CLASSPATH; it is included automatically. Furthermore, java.lang.* is automatically imported, so there is no need to do this yourself.

Many browsers, including Netscape and appletviewer, look for classes in the classpath before trying to load them from the network. These classes are then granted special privileges. If someone knew your classpath and could look at the classes in it (e.g., on a multiuser system), that person could make an applet that uses these classes to perform privileged or destructive operations from your account. to avoid this situation, you want to make sure CLASSPATH is not set when you start the browser.

Core Security Warning

Unset *CLASSPATH* before starting your Web browser.

Using JAR Files

The CLASSPATH is a nice, convenient place to specify a list of directories in which to look for class files. However, if you are using a lot of large package hierarchies, eventually your CLASSPATH will exceed the number of characters allowed for your environment variable. To solve this problem, Java also lets you place classes in Java ARchive (JAR) files and include the JAR files in your classpath. Included with the JDK is a jar tool that compresses multiple class files into a single JAR file, using a compression algorithm based on the common ZIP format.

The most common command options for the jar tool are summarized below.

c
This option specifies creation of a new JAR file.

f
The f option specifies which file to process or the target JAR file.

m, M
The first option, lowercase m, means that a manifest file is provided for advanced capabilities (signed JAR files, executable JAR files). If both the m and f option are used, then the order of the manifest and JAR file must be the same order of the command options. The second option, uppercase M, specifies that a manifest file not be created. By default, a manifest is included in the JAR file; you can then examine the manifest by decompressing the JAR file. For additional information of manifests, see http://java.sun.com/docs/books/tutorial/jar/basics/manifest.html.

t

This option lists the contents of the JAR file.

u

This option updates a JAR file, for example, adding additional files or changing the manifest.

v

This option generates verbose output.

x *file*

This option decompresses the *file* located in the JAR file. If no file is specified, then all files in the achieve are decompressed.

0

This option (numerical 0) creates an uncompressed JAR file.

As an example, to place the `ClassX.class` files in the previous example in a single JAR file, you would use

```
C:\Java\classes>jar cfv example.jar package1 package2 package4
```

Output
```
added manifest
adding: package1/(in = 0) (out= 0)(stored 0%)
adding: package1/Class1.class(in = 468)
       (out= 326)(deflated 30%)
adding: package2/(in = 0) (out= 0)(stored 0%)
adding: package2/Class2.class(in = 468)
       (out= 327)(deflated 30%)
adding: package2/package3/(in = 0) (out= 0)
       (stored 0%)
adding: package2/package3/Class3.class(in = 486)
       (out= 338)(deflated 30%)
adding: package4/(in = 0) (out= 0)(stored 0%)
adding: package4/Class1.class(in = 431)
       (out= 298)(deflated 30%)
```

Here, we assumed that the package directories contained only the class files; otherwise, all files, including source files, would be compressed into `example.jar`. To avoid adding all directory files, you would need to individually specify the `class` files on the command line. If necessary, you can place a list of `jar` commands in a separate file and then refer to the file on the command line through `@filename`.

Once you've created a `jar` file, you can add the file to your classpath; or if your classpath is still too long, you can place the file in the `/root/jdk1.3/jre/lib/ext/` directory. Java automatically examines the JAR files located in this directory for class files as if they were listed in your classpath.

Core Note

If your classpath is too long, you can place your JAR files in the `/root/jdk1.3/jre/lib/ext/` directory for automatic inclusion by `javac` and `java`.

7.11 Modifiers in Declarations

We've used a variety of class, method, and instance variable modifiers in this chapter: `public`, `private`, `protected`, and `static`. These were relatively obvious from context or from the brief explanation provided when they were used, but it is worth reviewing all the possible modifiers and explicitly stating their purpose.

Visibility Modifiers

These modifiers designate the other classes that are allowed to see the data inside an object you write. Table 7.1 summarizes them, with more details given below. If you are not familiar with object-oriented programming already, just look at `public` and `private` and forget the other options for now. For people with a C++ background, consider classes within the same package to be friendly to each other.

Table 7.1 Summary of Visibility Modifiers

Variables or Methods with This Modifier Can Be Accessed by Methods in:	Variable or Method Modifier			
	public	private	protected	no modifier (default)
Same Class	Y	Y	Y	Y
Classes in Same Package	Y	N	Y	Y
Subclasses	Y	N	Y	N
Classes in Different Packages	Y	N	N	N

public

This visibility modifier indicates that the variable or method can be accessed by anyone who can access an instance of the class. You normally use this modifier for the functionality you are deliberately providing to the outside world, and you should generally document it with `javadoc`.

Many people feel that instance variables should *never* be public and should be accessed *only* by methods. See Section 7.6 for some of the reasons. This is the approach used in the `Ship` example (Listing 7.5) and a convention necessary for JavaBeans, Java's component architecture. However, some practitioners believe that "never" is too strong and that public fields are acceptable for small classes that act simply as records (C-style structs). They think that for such classes, if the get and set methods only set and read the variables without any modification, side effects, or error checking, then the methods are an unnecessary level of abstraction and the variables should be public instead. For instance, the `java.awt.Point` class contains public x and y variables, since the whole idea of a `Point` is to wrap up two integers into a single object. At the very least, we recommend that you avoid public instance variables for all complex classes.

Core Approach

Avoid public instance variables.

A *class* can also have the designation `public`, which means that any other class can load and use the class definition. The name of a public class must match the filename.

private

This visibility modifier specifies that the variable or method can only be accessed by methods within the same class. This modifier is what you normally use for internal data and methods that are needed to implement your public interface but which users need not or should not (because of potential changes) access.

protected

This visibility modifier specifies that the variable or method can be accessed by methods within the class and within classes in the same package. It is inherited by subclasses. Variables and methods that are protected can cross package boundaries through inheritance. This modifier is what you use for data that is normally considered private but might be of interest to people extending your class.

no modifier (default)

Omitting a visibility modifier specifies that the variable or method can be accessed by methods within the class and within classes in the same package but is not inherited by subclasses. Variables and methods with default visibility cannot cross package boundaries through inheritance. Although no modifier is the default, the other modifiers represent more common intentions.

Other Modifiers

static

This modifier indicates that the variable or method is shared by the entire class. Variables or methods that are `static` can be accessed through the classname instead of just by an instance. So, if a class `Foo` had a static variable `bar` and there were two instances, `foo1` and `foo2`, `bar` could be accessed by `foo1.bar`, `foo2.bar`, or `Foo.bar`. All three would access the same, shared, data. In a similar example of `Math.cos`, `cos` is a static method of the class `Math`.

Static methods can only refer to static variables or other static methods unless they create an instance. For example, in Listing 7.29, code in `main` can refer directly to `staticMethod` but requires an instance of the class to refer to `regularMethod`.

Listing 7.29 `Statics.java`

```java
public class Statics {
  public static void main(String[] args) {
    staticMethod();
    Statics s1 = new Statics();
    s1.regularMethod();
  }

  public static void staticMethod() {
    System.out.println("This is a static method.");
  }

  public void regularMethod() {
    System.out.println("This is a regular method.");
  }
}
```

---

final

For a class, the `final` modifier indicates that it cannot be subclassed. This declaration may let the compiler optimize to method calls on variables of this type. For a variable or method, `final` indicates that it cannot be changed at runtime or overridden in subclasses. Think of `final` as the final representation (constant).

abstract

This declaration can apply to classes or methods and indicates that the class cannot be directly instantiated. See Section 7.9 (Interfaces and Abstract Classes) for some examples.

synchronized

The `synchronized` declaration is used to set locks for methods in multithreaded programming. Only one thread can access a synchronized method at any given time. For more details, see Chapter 16 (Concurrent Programming with Java Threads).

volatile

For multithreaded efficiency, Java permits methods to keep local copies of instance variables, reconciling changes only at lock and unlock points. For some data types (e.g., `long`), multithreaded code that does not use locking risks having one thread partially update a field before another accesses it. The `volatile` declaration prevents this situation.

transient

Variables can be marked `transient` to stipulate that they should not be saved by the object serialization system when writing an object to disk or network.

native

This modifier signifies that a method is implemented using C or C++ code that is linked to the Java image.

7.12 Summary

The Java programming language is pervasively and consistently object oriented. You cannot go anywhere in Java without a good grasp of how to use objects. This chapter summarized how to create objects, give them state (instance variables), and assign them behavior (methods). Using inheritance, you can build hierarchies of classes without repeating code that is shared by subclasses. Although Java lacks multiple inheritance, interfaces are a convenient mechanism for letting one method handle objects from different hierarchies in a uniform manner. Class hierarchies that are intended to be reused should be documented with `javadoc` and can be organized into packages for convenience.

Getting comfortable with objects takes a bit of a conceptual leap and may take awhile if you've never seen objects before. Chapter 8 requires no such leap; it is a laundry list of basic constructs supported by Java. It should be quick going. In fact, if you know C or C++, you can just skim through, looking for the differences.

BASIC JAVA
SYNTAX

Chapter

Now that you have a handle on object-oriented programming (Chapter 7), you are ready for a whirlwind tour of the basic syntax of the Java programming language. If you are a C++ programmer, you can skim much of the material: primitive types, operators, and loops are pretty similar to the C++ versions. However, you'll want to look more closely at later sections, including input and output (Section 8.5), execution of non-Java programs (Section 8.6), reference types (Section 8.7), vectors (Section 8.10), and exceptions (Section 8.12); they may be new to you.

8.1 Rules of Syntax

As you start writing real-world programs and try to decipher cryptic error messages from your compiler, it is nice to know the rules of the game. This short section describes some of the lexical and grammatical rules in Java.

Careful use of descriptive comments, white space, and indentation can make your source code easier to read. Two types of comments are permitted: block style and line style. Block-style comments are contained between /* (slash-star) and */ (star-slash) tokens; they can span multiple lines and are sometimes used to quickly comment-out a large block of code during testing. Line-style comments begin with two slashes, //; these comments extend just until the end of the line of code.

White space refers to a sequence of nondisplaying characters, for example, space, tab, and newline characters, which are used to separate pieces of code. White space is used principally for clarity, for example, to separate individual statements into different lines, to distinguish arguments in a function call, or to make expressions using mathematical operators easier to read. Another major use of white space is to provide indentation that helps to offset a section of code, typically sections of code in looping or if-else structures. Here is an example using comments, white space, and indentation:

```java
/* Block style comments. These may span multiple
   lines. They may not be nested. */

// Single-line comment

while (int i=1; i<=5; i++) {
  if (i==2)
    System.out.println("Tea for two.");
  else
    System.out.println("Not two.");
}
```

All of the comments and most of the spaces in this example are optional. The following code snippet would be treated identically to the example above by a Java compiler. In fact, this code could be expressed on a single line and the compiler would still not complain.

```java
while(int i=1;i<=5;i++){if(i==2)
System.out.println("Tea for two.");else
System.out.println("Not two.");}
```

You might ask, "Why is the space in the fragment 'int i' required?" The answer is that this space separates two tokens, the Java keyword int and the variable i. In the same way that English sentences are made up of words, Java programs consist of tokens such as numbers, variable names, punctuation characters, and special keywords. Just as we use rules of grammar to properly construct sentences when we speak or write in human languages, computers use grammatical rules to make programs clear and unambiguous. Two of the key grammatical rules regarding tokenization are:

1. Tokens are case sensitive. For example, While or WHILE are not considered the same as the token while.
2. Identifiers (i.e., the names of variables and methods), must start with an alphabetical character or an underscore (_) and may contain letters, numbers, and underscores. Technically, dollar signs and other currency symbols are also allowed where underscores are permitted; however, such use is not recommended since some compilers use dollar signs as special symbols internally.

Finally, separators are special symbols used to delimit parts of code. Semicolons, periods, commas, parentheses, and braces all act as separators: semicolons indicate the end of an expression, periods qualify variable and method identifiers, commas separate arguments in a method call, parentheses clarify arithmetic expressions and enclose argument lists, curly braces denote the start and end of control blocks, and square brackets indicate the use of arrays.

For additional details about Java syntax, refer to *The Java Language Specification*, which you can view on-line at: `http://java.sun.com/docs/books/jls/`.

8.2   Primitive Types

Java has two fundamental kinds of data types: *primitive* and *reference*. Primitive types are those simple types that are not "objects" (described in the previous chapter)—integers, characters, floating-point numbers, and the like. There are eight primitive types: `boolean`, `char`, `byte`, `short`, `int`, `long`, `float`, and `double`. A ninth type, `void`, is used only to indicate when a method does not return a value.

boolean

This is a type with only two possible values: `true` and `false`. A boolean is an actual type, *not* merely a disguised `int`. For example:

```
boolean flag1 = false;
boolean flag2 = (6 < 7); // true
boolean flag3 = !true;   // false
boolean flag4 = 0;       // compiler error!
```

char

This is a 16-bit unsigned integer value representing a Unicode character. You can specify values numerically or with a character enclosed inside single quotes. These characters can be keyboard chars, unicode escape chars (\u*xxxx* with *x* in hex), or one of the special escape sequences \b (backspace), \t (tab), \n (newline), \f (form feed), \r (carriage return), \" (double quote), \' (single quote), or \\ (backslash). For instance:

```
char c0= 3;
char c1 = 'Q';
char c2 = '\u0000'; // Smallest value
char c3 = '\uFFFF'; // Biggest value
char c4 = '\b';     // Backspace
```

Learn more about the Unicode standard at `http://www.unicode.org/`.

byte

This is an 8-bit, signed, two's-complement integer. See the description of int for ways to represent integral values. Bytes can range in value from −128 to +127.

short

This is a 16-bit, signed, two's-complement integer. See the description of int for ways to represent integral values. Shorts range in value from -32768 to +32767.

int

This is a 32-bit, signed, two's-complement integer. You can specify integer constants in base 10 (1, 10, and 100 for 1, 10, and 100, respectively), octal with a prefix of 0 (01, 012, 0144 for 1, 10, and 100), or hex by using a prefix of 0x (0x1, 0xA, 0x64 for 1, 10, and 100). For hexadecimal numbers, you can use uppercase or lowercase for x, A, B, C, D, E, and F. Ints range from Integer.MIN_VALUE (-2^{31}) to Integer.MAX_VALUE ($2^{31} - 1$). For example:

```
int i0 = 0;
int i1 = -12345;
int i2 = 0xCafeBabe; // Magic number of .class files
int i3 = 0777;       // Octal number, 511 in decimal
```

long

This is a 64-bit, signed, two's-complement integer. Use a trailing L for literals. A lowercase l is also legal to designate a long literal, but discouraged. Depending on the display font, the lowercase l can be confused with a numerical 1 (one). You can use base 10, 8, or 16 for values. Longs range from Long.MIN_VALUE (-2^{63}) to Long.MAX_VALUE ($2^{63} - 1$). Some examples:

```
long a0 = 0L;
long a1 = -12345l;
long a2 = 0xBabeL; // Tower of Babel?
long a3 = -067671;
```

Except for char, the integral types (byte, char, short, int, and long) are signed values. There is no built-in support for unsigned integer values in Java as in the C or C++ programming languages. When using integral types, especially smaller types such as byte or short, you should ensure that the numbers you wish to represent do not exceed the representable range of the primitive type. For example, if you want to represent the day of the year, you cannot use a byte, because it can only store a number as large as 127. Instead, you need to use a short, int, or long. An int is probably sufficient for most applications.

float

This is a 32-bit, IEEE 754 floating-point number. You must use a trailing f or F to distinguish single precision floating-point literals. In the example below, the f is required or else the compiler interprets the constant as a double precision floating-point number that needs a cast before being assigned to a float:

```
float f0 = -1.23f;
```

You can also use an e or E to indicate an exponent (power of 10). For instance, the first expression below assigns the value 6.02×10^{23} to the variable f1 while the second gives the value 4.5×10^{-17} to f2.

```
float f1 = 6.02E23F;
float f2 = 4.5e-17f;
```

Floats range from Float.MIN_VALUE (1.4×10^{-45}) to Float.MAX_VALUE (3.4×10^{38}). Floating-point arithmetic never generates an exception, even in divide-by-zero cases. The Float class defines the constants POSITIVE_INFINITY, NEGATIVE_INFINITY, and NaN (not-a-number) to use for some of these special cases. Use Float.isNaN to compare to NaN because (Float.NaN == Float.NaN) returns false, in conformance with the IEEE specification, which states that all comparisons to NaNs should fail.

double

This is a 64-bit, IEEE 754 floating-point number. You are allowed to append a trailing d or D, but it is normally omitted. Some examples:

```
double d0 = 1.23;
double d2 = -4.56d;
double d3 = 6.02214E+23;
double d4 = 1e-99;
```

Doubles range from Double.MIN_VALUE (4.9×10^{-324}) to Double.MAX_VALUE (1.7×10^{308}). As with float, double-precision arithmetic never generates an exception. To handle unusual situations, the Double class also defines fields named POSITIVE_INFINITY, NEGATIVE_INFINITY, and NaN. Use Double.isNaN to compare a double to Double.NaN.

Primitive-Type Conversion

The Java programming language requires explicit *typecasts* to convert a value stored in a larger primitive type into a type with a smaller range or different domain. For example:

```
Type2 type2Var = (Type2)type1Var;
```

Truncation or loss of some significant digits may result from these casts, but even so, an exception is not thrown. For instance:

```
int i = 3;
byte b = (byte)i; // Cast i to a byte; no effect
long x = 123456L;
short s = (short)x; // Cast x to a short; lossy
```

Note that in the last example s does not contain an equivalent value to x because 123456 is not representable as a 16-bit integer quantity. In addition to downward conversions, those from larger to smaller types, conversions from floating-point to integer types also require a cast:

```
double d = 3.1416;
float f = (float)d; // Cast from 64 to 32 bits
short s = (short)f; // Cast a float to a short
int i = s; // Upward conversion, no cast is required
```

To perform rounding instead of truncation when performing cast conversions, use the rounding methods in the Math class; see Section 8.4 for more information. Note that numeric types may not be cast to boolean, or vice versa. The Java Language Specification, http://java.sun.com/docs/books/jls/, explains in detail the cases when casts are required between types.

8.3   Operators, Conditionals, Iteration

This section describes the basic arithmetic operators (+, -, *, and so forth), conditionals (if, and switch), and looping constructs (while, do, and for). Some languages such as C++ permit programmers to adopt built-in operators as a syntactic shorthand for user-defined classes. For example, a C++ programmer might write the following code to add two geometric points together:

```
Point p1(3,4), p2(1,3); // C++ constructor syntax
p1 += p2; // To translate point p1 by p2
```

The Java programming language does not allow programmers to overload operators, a technique which some programmers find confusing when they try it with user-defined types. In such cases, method calls are used in the Java programming language instead, for example:

```
p1.translate(p2);
```

Arithmetic Operators

Table 8.1 summarizes the basic numerical operators. You might notice the lack of an exponentiation operator. Don't panic; exponentiation is possible through methods in the Math class (Section 8.4). Also, note that + can be used for String concatenation; see Section 8.8 for details.

Table 8.1 Numerical Operators

Operators	Meaning	Example
+, -	addition, subtraction	`x = y + 5;`

*, /, %	multiplication, division, remainder	`int x = 3, y = 2;`
		`int z = x / y; // 1`
		(integer division truncates)

++, --	prefix/postfix increment/decrement	`int i = 1, j = 1;`
		`int x = i++; // x=1, i=2`
		`int y = ++j; // y=2, j=2`

<<, >>, >>>	signed and unsigned shifts	`int x = 3;` `int y = x << 2; // 12`
~	bitwise complement	`int x = ~127; // -128`

&, |, ^	bitwise AND, OR, XOR	`int x = 127 & 2; // 2`
		`int y = 127 | 2; // 127`
		`int z = 127 ^ 2; // 125`

Java, like C and C++, lets you write

```
var op= val;
```

as a shorthand for

```
var = var op val;
```

For example, instead of

```
i = i + 5;
x = x * 3;
```

you can write

```
i += 5;
x *= 3;
```

Conditionals

The Java programming language has three conditional constructs: `if`, `switch`, and "? :". They are summarized in Table 8.2, with more details given in the following section. If you are familiar with C or C++, you can skip this section because these operators are virtually identical to their C and C++ counterparts, except that conditions must be `boolean` valued. Table 8.3 summarizes the `boolean` operators that are frequently used in conjunction with these three conditionals.

Table 8.2 Conditionals

Operator	Standard Forms

if	```if (boolean-expression) {```
	`    statement;`
	`}`
	`if (boolean-expression) {`
	`    statement1;`
	`} else {`
	`    statement2;`
	`}`

? :	`boolean-expression ? val1 : val2;`

switch	`switch(someInt) {`
	`    case val1: statement1;`
	`                break;`
	`    case val2: statement2a;`
	`               statement2b;`
	`               break;`
	`    ...`
	`    default: statementN;`
	`}`

Table 8.3 Boolean Operators

Operator	Meaning
==, !=	Equality, inequality. In addition to comparing primitive types, == tests if two objects are identical (the same object), not just if they appear equal (have the same fields).
<, <=, >, >=	Numeric less than, less than or equal to, greater than, greater than or equal to.
&&, ||	Logical AND, OR. Both use short-circuit evaluation to more efficiently compute the results of complicated expressions.
!	Logical negation.

if (boolean-expression) statement
if (boolean-expression) statement1 else statement2

The if keyword expects a boolean expression in parentheses. If the expression evaluates to true, the subsequent statement is executed. If the expression is `false`, the `else` statement (if present) is executed. Supplying a non-`bool-ean` expression results in a compile-time error, unlike the case with C and C++, which treat anything not equal to zero as `true`. Here is an example that returns the larger of two integers:

```
// See Math.max
public static int max2(int n1, int n2) {
  if (n1 >= n2)
    return(n1);
  else
    return(n2);
}
```

You can combine multiple statements in the if-else clause by enclosing them in curly braces. For instance:

```
public static int max2Verbose(int n1, int n2) {
  if (n1 >= n2) {
    System.out.println(n1 + " is larger.");
    return(n1);
  } else {
    System.out.println(n2 + " is larger.");
    return(n2);
  }
}
```

Next, note that an `else` always goes with the most recent preceding `if` that does not already have a matching `else`. For example:

```
public static int max3(int n1, int n2, int n3) {
  if (n1 >= n2)
    if (n1 >= n3)
      return(n1);
    else
      return(n3);
  else
    if (n2 >= n3)
      return(n2);
    else
      return(n3);
}
```

Two more points should be made here. First of all, note that the nested (indented) `if` statements are considered single statements; thus, curly braces are not required even though the statements flow over several lines. More importantly, see how indentation makes the association of the `else` clauses clearer.

Several different indentation styles are consistent with this approach. Following are a few of the most popular; we use the first style throughout most of the book.

```java
// Indentation Style 1
public SomeType someMethod(...) {
  if {
    statement1;
    ....
    statementN
  } else {
    statementA;
    ...
    statementZ;
  }
}

// Indentation Style 2
public SomeType someMethod(...)
{ if
  { statement1;
    ...
    statementN;
  } else
  { statementA;
    ...
    statementZ;
  }
}

// Indentation Style 3
public SomeType someMethod(...)
{
  if
  {
    statement1;
    ...
    statementN;
  }
  else
  {
    statementA;
    ...
    statementZ;
  }
}
```

In certain cases, you can simplify multiple comparisons by combining them using logical operators && (logical AND) or || (logical OR). As in C and C++, these operators perform "short circuit" evaluation, which means that they return an answer as soon as they have enough information to do so (even if all the subexpressions have not been evaluated). In particular, a comparison with

`&&` evaluates to `false` whenever the leftmost conjunct is `false`; the right side is not then evaluated. Likewise, an expression with `||` immediately evaluates as `true` if the leftmost disjunct is `true`. Here's an example:

```
public static int max3(int n1, int n2, int n3) {
  if ((n1 >= n2) && (n1 >= n3))
    return(n1);
  else if ((n2 >= n1) && (n2 >= n3))
    return(n2);
  else
    return(n3);
}
```

There are single character forms of the logical operators, `&` and `|`, that do evaluate all of their operands. However, they are rarely used and may be confused with the bitwise arithmetic operators.

boolean-expression ? thenValue : elseValue

Since `if` statements do not return a value, Java provides a shortcut when the purpose of the `if` is to assign to a single variable. For example, you can express the following four lines

```
if (someCondition)
  someVar = value1;
else
  someVar = value2;
```

more simply as

```
someVar = (someCondition ? value1 : value2);
```

In fact, you can use this form whenever you need to return a value, although overuse can make code difficult to read. Here is a variation of `max2` that uses it:

```
public static int max2Short(int n1, int n2) {
  return((n1 >= n2) ? n1 : n2);
}
```

switch(integralExpression) { switchBody }

The `switch` construct provides a compact way to compare an expression to a variety of integer types (`char`, `byte`, `short`, or `int`, but not `long`). The idea is to supply an integer expression and then provide, inside the `switch` body, one or more `case` statements that designate different possible values of the expression. When one matches, it *and all subsequent cases* are executed. Here is an example that uses `switch` to generate the string representation of a single-digit integer:

```
public static String number(int digit) {
  switch(digit) {
    case 0: return("zero");
    case 1: return("one");
```

```
    case 2:  return("two");
    case 3:  return("three");
    case 4:  return("four");
    case 5:  return("five");
    case 6:  return("six");
    case 7:  return("seven");
    case 8:  return("eight");
    case 9:  return("nine");
    default: return("Not a single digit");
  }
}
```

Section 8.9 (Arrays) describes a simpler way to perform this integer-to-string conversion by using arrays. The most confusing thing about switch statements is that code "falls through" cases; *all* statements after the first matching case are executed. This is handy in some situations because it lets you combine cases, as follows:

```
switch(val) {
  case test1:
  case test2:
    actionForTest1and2();
  ...
}
```

However, it can catch you by surprise if the case statements do not contain an explicit return or break. For example, consider the following verbose variation of the number method:

```
// Incorrect version that forgets about case
// fall-through.

public static String numberVerbose(int digit) {
  String result;
  switch(digit) {
    case 0:  System.out.println("zero");
             result = "zero";
    case 1:  System.out.println("one");
             result = "one";
    case 2:  System.out.println("two");
             result = "two";
    case 3:  System.out.println("three");
             result = "three";
    case 4:  System.out.println("four");
             result = "four";
    case 5:  System.out.println("five");
             result = "five";
    case 6:  System.out.println("six");
             result = "six";
    case 7:  System.out.println("seven");
             result = "seven";
```

```
    case 8:  System.out.println("eight");
             result = "eight";
    case 9:  System.out.println("nine");
             result = "nine";
    default: System.out.println(
                "Not a single digit");
             result = "Not a single digit";
  }
  return(result);
}
```

Because there is no explicit direction to exit the switch after the first match, multiple cases are executed. For instance, here is the output when number-Verbose(5) is called:

```
five
six
seven
eight
nine
Not a single digit
```

The standard solution is to use the break statement to exit the switch after the first match, as in the following corrected version:

```
public static String numberVerboseFixed(int digit) {
  String result;
  switch(digit) {
    case 0: System.out.println("zero");
            result = "zero";
            break;
    case 1: System.out.println("one");
            result = "one";
            break;
    ...
    default: System.out.println("Not a single digit");
             result = "Not a single digit";
  }
  return(result);
}
```

Loops

The Java programming language supports the same basic looping constructs as do C and C++: while, do, and for. These constructs are summarized in Table 8.4 and described in more detail following the table. In addition, Java supports the break and continue keywords, which are used to exit the loop or to interrupt the body and restart at the beginning, respectively.

Table 8.4 Looping Constructs

Construct	Standard Form

while	```while (continueTest) {```
	 ``` body;```
	 ```}```

do	```do {```
	 ``` body;```
	 ```} while (continueTest);```

for	```for(init; continueTest; updateOp) {```
	 ``` body;```
	 ```}```

while loops

The while construct tests the supplied boolean continuation test, executing the body as long as the test returns true. For example, the following method prints out the numbers in the range from 0 to max.

```java
public static void listNums1(int max) {
  int i = 0;
  while (i <= max) {
    System.out.println("Number: " + i);
    i++;
  }
}
```

Executing listNums1(5) results in the following output:

```
0: zero
1: one
2: two
3: three
4: four
```

do loops

The do construct differs from while in that the test is evaluated after the loop body rather than before. This means that the body will always be executed at least once, regardless of the test's value. Following is a variation of the list-Nums method, using do. The result of listNums2(5) is identical to that shown for listNums1(5); however, listNums2(-5) would print "Number: 0", while listNums1(-5) would print nothing. The reason is that with a do loop the test is performed after the loop body, whereas a while loop tests before the loop body. In listNums1(-5), the loop body is never entered.

```
public static void listNums2(int max) {
   int i = 0;
   do {
     System.out.println("Number: " + i);
     i++;
   } while (i <= max); // Don't forget the semicolon
}
```

Forgetting the final semicolon in a do loop is a common syntax error.

for loops

The for construct is by far the most common way to create loops with numbered counters. First, the init part is executed once. Then, as long as the continuation test evaluates to true, the statement is executed and then the update operation is performed. Here's an example that gives the same result as the previous two versions when passed a positive argument.

```
public static void listNums3(int max) {
   for(int i=0; i<max; i++) {
     System.out.println("Number: " + i);
   }
}
```

It is also legal to omit any (or all) of the three for clauses. A missing continueTest is treated as true. Thus,

```
for(;;) { body }
```

and

```
while(true) { body }
```

are equivalent. These forms are occasionally used when the termination test cannot be easily placed in the initial for or while clause. Instead, the body contains a conditional return or break.

The various forms of loops, while, do, and for, are all equally expressive, and any loop that can be written with one can be rewritten with another instead. Individual programmers usually adopt a style for using each. Some programmers tend to use for loops predominantly, especially when looping over arrays or ranges of numbers. Some prefer while loops in cases where the number of times the loop will be executed is not generally known in advance, for example, based on the number of lines in an input file.

Listing 8.1 contains an example of using a while loop to determine how long it takes a ball to fall from the top of the Washington Monument. The body of the loop is executed seven times. The loop is terminated when the ball has dropped a distance greater than the height of the monument; thus, the ball falls for slightly less than 6 seconds. The output for DropBall is shown in Listing 8.2.

Listing 8.1   `DropBall.java`

```java
/** Simulating dropping a ball from the top of the Washington
 *  Monument. The program outputs the height of the ball each
 *  second until the ball hits the ground.
 */

public class DropBall {
  public static void main(String[] args) {
    int time = 0;
    double start = 550.0, drop = 0.0;
    double height = start;
    while (height > 0) {
      System.out.println("After " + time +
                (time==1 ? " second, " : " seconds,") +
                "the ball is at " + height + " feet.");
      time++;
      drop = freeFall(time);
      height = start - drop;
    }
    System.out.println("Before " + time + " seconds could " +
                "expire, the ball hit the ground!");
  }

  /** Calculate the distance in feet for an object in
   *  free fall.
   */

  public static double freeFall (float time) {
    // Gravitational constant is 32 feet per second squared
    return(16.0 * time * time); // 1/2 gt^2
  }
}
```

Listing 8.2   **Output from** `DropBall`

```
Prompt> java DropBall
After 0 seconds,the ball is at 550.0 feet.
After 1 second, the ball is at 534.0 feet.
After 2 seconds,the ball is at 486.0 feet.
After 3 seconds,the ball is at 406.0 feet.
After 4 seconds,the ball is at 294.0 feet.
After 5 seconds,the ball is at 150.0 feet.
Before 6 seconds could expire, the ball hit the ground!
```

8.4   The Math Class

Math provides a range of arithmetic methods not available as built-in operators. All of these methods are static, so there would never be any reason to create an instance of the Math class.

Constants

public static final double E
This constant is e, the base for natural logarithms, 2.7182818284590452354.

public static final double PI
This constant is π, 3.14159265358979323846.

General-Purpose Methods

public static int abs(int num)
public static long abs(long num)
public static float abs(float num)
public static double abs(double num)
These methods return the absolute value of the specified number.

public static double ceil(double num)
public static double floor(double num)
The ceil method returns a double corresponding to the smallest integer greater than or equal to the specified number; floor returns a double corresponding to the largest integer less than or equal to the number.

public static exp(double num)
This method returns e^{num}.

public static double IEEEremainder(double f1, double f2)
This method returns the remainder of f1 divided by f2, as specified in the IEEE 754 standard.

public static double log(double num)
This method returns the natural logarithm of the specified number. Java does not provide a method for calculating logs in other common bases (e.g., 10 or 2), but following is a method that does this computation, using the relationship:

$$\log_{b1}(n) = \frac{\log_{b2}(n)}{\log_{b2}(b1)}$$

```
public static double log(double num, double base) {
  return(Math.log(num) / Math.log(base));
}
```

public static int max(int num1, int num2)
public static long max(long num1, long num2)
public static float max(float num1, float num2)
public static double max(double num1, double num2)
public static int min(int num1, int num2)
public static long min(long num1, long num2)
public static float min(float num1, float num2)
public static double min(double num1, double num2)

These methods return the bigger (`max`) or smaller (`min`) of the two numbers.

public static double pow(double base, double exponent)

The `pow` method returns $base^{exponent}$.

public static double random()

This method returns a random number from `0.0` (inclusive) to `1.0` (exclusive). For more control over random numbers, use the `java.util.Random` class.

public static double rint(double num)
public static int round(float num)
public static long round(double num)

These methods round the number toward the nearest integer. They differ in their return types and what they do for a number of the form `xxx.5`. The `round` methods round up in such a case; `rint` rounds to the nearest even number, as specified in the IEEE 754 standard. Although less intuitive, the behavior of `rint` avoids skewing sums of rounded numbers upwards.

public static double sqrt(double num)

This method returns $\sqrt{num}$ for nonnegative numbers and returns `Double.NaN` if the input is `NaN` or is negative.

Trigonometric Methods

public static double sin(double radians)
public static double cos(double radians)
public static double tan(double radians)

These methods return the sine, cosine, and tangent of the specified number, interpreted as an angle *in radians*.

public static double toDegrees(double radians)
public static double toRadians(double degrees)

These methods perform conversions between angles expressed in radians and degrees. For example, the following computes the sine of 60 degrees:

```
Math.sin(Math.toRadians(60.0))
```

public static double acos(double val)
public static double asin(double val)
public static double atan(double val)

These methods return the arc cosine, arc sine, and arc tangent of the specified value. The result is expressed *in radians*.

public static double atan2(double y, double x)

This method returns the θ part of the polar coordinate (r, θ) that corresponds to the cartesian coordinate (x, y). This is the atan of y/x that is in the range $-\pi$ to π.

BigInteger and BigDecimal

The Java programming language supports two arbitrary-precision number formats: java.math.BigInteger and java.math.BigDecimal. These classes contain methods for addition, multiplication, division, exponentiation, primality testing, greatest common divisors, and more. See the API for details, but the key point is that these classes can be used to obtain any desired level of accuracy. For instance, *every* digit in a BigInteger is significant, and it cannot overflow. To illustrate this, Listing 8.3 uses BigInteger to represent the exact value of $N!$ (the factorial of N, i.e., $(N)(N-1)(N-2) \ldots (1)$) for large values of N. Listing 8.4 shows the result.

Listing 8.3   `Factorial.java`

```
import java.math.BigInteger;

/** Computes an exact factorial, using a BigInteger. */

public class Factorial {
  public static void main(String[] args) {
    for(int i=1; i<=256; i*=2) {
      System.out.println(i + "!=" + factorial(i));
    }
  }

  public static BigInteger factorial(int n) {
    if (n <= 1) {
      return(new BigInteger("1"));
    } else {
      BigInteger bigN = new BigInteger(String.valueOf(n));
      return(bigN.multiply(factorial(n - 1)));
    }
  }
}
```

Listing 8.4   `Factorial` Output

```
Prompt> java Factorial
1!=1
2!=2
4!=24
8!=40320
16!=20922789888000
32!=263130836933693530167218012160000000
64!=12688693218588416410343338933516148080286551617454519219880189
43752147042304000000000000000
128!=385620482362580421735677065923463640617493109590223590278828
40327637340257516554356068616858850736153403005183305891634759217
29322624988577661149552450393577600346447092792476924955852800000
0000000000000000000000000000
256!=857817775342842654119082271681232625157781520279485619859655
65037726945255314758937744029136045140845037588534233658430615719
68346936964753222892884974260256796373325633687864426752076267945
60187968867971521143307702077526664645146470918732610083287632570
28189807736717814541702505230186084953190681382574810702528175594
59476987034665712738139286205234756808218860701203611083152093501
94743710910172696826286160626366243502284094419140842461593600000
0000000000000000000000000000000000000000000000000000000000000000
```

Core Warning

Do not confuse the `java.math` *package, where classes* `BigInteger` *and* `BigDecimal` *are found, with the* `java.lang.Math` *class. The* `Math` *class is more commonly used; it provides all of the methods in the standard mathematical library.*

8.5 Input and Output

The simplest forms of I/O are discussed in this section: printing to standard output and reading from standard input.

Printing to Standard Output

You've already seen examples of printing with `System.out.println`. As you probably guessed from the Java naming conventions, `out` is a `static` variable in the `System` class, and `println` is a method in the class that belongs to `out`. That class is `PrintStream`; it also contains a `print` method that works just like `println` except that it omits the trailing newline. Both `println` and `print` take a single argument of any type. Primitive types are converted to strings by the `String.valueOf` method, and non-`String` objects are converted to strings by their `toString` method. Longer strings can be formed from components joined through the + concatenation operator. For example:

```
System.out.println(
    2 + 'B' + " || ! " + new Integer(2) + "B");
```

In addition to `println` and `print`, the `PrintStream` class also contains a `flush` method. This method is useful when you want to be sure that output has not been cached (e.g., when reading from standard input just after writing a prompt). For full details, see the on-line API for `java.io.PrintStream`.

Surprisingly, Java's way of controlling the spacing and formatting of numbers is not as simple as C's `printf` or `sprintf` functions. The `java.text.DecimalFormat` class provides this sort of functionality indirectly. `DecimalFormat` works by creating an object that describes the desired formatting of your number(s). You then use this object's `format` method as needed to convert numbers into formatted strings. Listing 8.5 gives a simple example with results shown in Listing 8.6.

Listing 8.5   `NumFormat.java`

```java
import java.text.*;

/** Formatting real numbers with DecimalFormat. */

public class NumFormat {
  public static void main (String[] args) {
    DecimalFormat science = new DecimalFormat("0.000E0");
    DecimalFormat plain = new DecimalFormat("0.0000");

    for(double d=100.0; d<140.0; d*=1.10) {
      System.out.println("Scientific: " + science.format(d) +
                          " and Plain: " + plain.format(d));
    }
  }
}
```

Listing 8.6   `NumFormat` Output

```
Prompt> java NumFormat
Scientific: 1.000E2 and Plain: 100.0000
Scientific: 1.100E2 and Plain: 110.0000
Scientific: 1.210E2 and Plain: 121.0000
Scientific: 1.331E2 and Plain: 133.1000
```

In the previous example, the `DecimalFormat` constructor used expects a `String` defining the pattern in which to display the number when converting to a `String` by the format method. The pattern can indicate the number of digits to display and possible separators. Table 8.5 summarizes some of the available characters for creating the formatting pattern. For example, `,###.0` would format a number with a single digit after the decimal point and would display a comma separator if the number is in the thousands: the number `23767.82` would format as `23,767.8`, the number `0.43` would format as `.4` (no leading zero).

`DecimalFormat` provides only coarse control when printing numbers. If you find `DecimalFormat` too cumbersome, you can use one of the public domain `printf` substitutes. One of the best ones is from Jef Poskanzer; see `http://www.acme.com/java/software/Acme.Fmt.html`.

Finally, output sent to `System.out` can be redirected to a different stream instead. One situation where redirection is useful occurs when you want to produce a log file instead of sending messages to the console window. To accomplish this, you simply call `System.setOut` once with the `PrintStream` to which you want to send output.

Table 8.5 Formatting Characters

Symbol	Meaning
0	Placeholder for a digit.
#	Placeholder for a digit. If the digit is leading or trailing zero, then don't display.
.	Location of decimal point.
,	Display comma at this location.
-	Minus sign.
E	Scientific notation. Indications the location to separate the mantissa from the exponent.
%	Multiply the value by 100 and display as a percent.

Printing to Standard Error

In addition to the System.out variable, the System.err variable can be used on operating systems that maintain a distinction between normal output and error output. It, too, is a PrintStream and can be used in exactly the same way as System.out. It also can be redirected; you use System.setErr for this purpose.

Reading from Standard Input

It is relatively uncommon to read from standard input in the Java programming language. Nongraphical applications typically use the command-line arguments for the data they need, and graphical programs use a textfield, button, slider, or other GUI control. If you *do* need to read input this way, the standard approach is first to turn System.in into a BufferedReader as follows:

```
BufferedReader keyboard =
  new BufferedReader(
    new InputStreamReader(System.in));
```

Then, you can use keyboard.readLine to retrieve a line of input:

```
String line = keyboard.readLine();
```

8.6   Execution of Non-Java Programs

Because of default security restrictions, applets (Java programs embedded in Web pages) cannot execute system programs; however, applications (stand-alone Java programs) can execute system programs. Starting a local program involves the following four steps:

1. **Get the special Runtime object.** Use the static `getRuntime` method of the `Runtime` class for this, as follows:

   ```
   Runtime rt = Runtime.getRuntime();
   ```

2. **Execute the program.** Use the `exec` method, which returns a `Process` object, as illustrated below:

   ```
   Process proc = rt.exec("someProgram");
   ```

   This starts the program but does *not* wait for the program to terminate or print the program results. Note that the `exec` method does not make use of your `PATH` environment variable (used on Windows 98/NT and Unix to identify where to look for programs), so you need to specify the full pathname. Also, `exec` does not start a shell, so special shell characters (such as > or | in Unix) will not be recognized. Finally, note that the `Runtime` class provides versions of `exec` that take an array of strings and pass the strings as command-line arguments to a program. For example,

   ```
   String[] args = { "-l", "*.java" };
   rt.exec("ls", args); // Directory listing.
   ```

3. **Optional: wait for the program to exit.** The `exec` method returns immediately, regardless of how long it takes the program to run. This behavior enables you to start long-running programs such as Netscape and still continue processing; however, this behavior catches many users off guard. If you want the program to wait until the program exits before returning, use the `waitFor` method after you start the process:

   ```
   proc.waitFor();
   ```

   While you might simply use `exec` to start Netscape, you would add `waitFor` if one program needs to terminate before another can begin. For example, you might call `javac` on a source file and use `java` to execute the result, but the compilation must finish before the program can invoke a new instance of the JVM to execute the complied class file. Note that `waitFor` does not print the program results; it simply waits for the program to finish before returning.

4. **Optional: process the results.** Rather than simply waiting for the program to terminate, you might want to capture its output. For example, telling the system to do a directory listing is not too useful unless you access the results. You can print the results by attaching a `BufferedReader` to the process, then reading from it, as in the following example:

```
try {
  BufferedReader buffer =
   new BufferedReader(
     new InputStreamReader(proc.getInputStream()));
  String s = null;
  while ((s = buffer.readLine()) != null) {
    System.out.println("Output: " + s);
  }
  buffer.close();
} catch(Exception e) {
  /* Ignore read errors */
}
```

Listing 8.7 shows the entire process, wrapping all four steps into an easy-to-use Exec class containing `exec`, `execPrint`, and `execWait` methods. Listing 8.8 illustrates its use.

Finally, because starting processes and then communicating with them requires native operating system support, some risk is associated with their use. In particular, there are situations where the virtual machine can hang due to a deadlocked process.

Core Warning

Be judicious when starting system processes. In situations where input or output streams are not processed efficiently, deadlock can occur.

Listing 8.7 `Exec.java`

```
import java.io.*;

/** A class that eases the pain of running external processes
 *  from applications. Lets you run a program three ways:
```

 (continued)

Listing 8.7   `Exec.java` *(continued)*

```
 *   <OL>
 *     <LI><B>exec</B>: Execute the command, returning
 *         immediately even if the command is still running.
 *         This would be appropriate for printing a file.
 *     <LI><B>execWait</B>: Execute the command, but don't
 *         return until the command finishes. This would be
 *         appropriate for sequential commands where the first
 *         depends on the second having finished (e.g.,
 *         <CODE>javac</CODE> followed by <CODE>java</CODE>).
 *     <LI><B>execPrint</B>: Execute the command and print the
 *         output. This would be appropriate for the Unix
 *         command <CODE>ls</CODE>.
 *   </OL>
 *   Note that the PATH is not taken into account, so you must
 *   specify the <B>full</B> pathname to the command, and shell
 *   built-in commands will not work. For instance, on Unix the
 *   above three examples might look like:
 *   <OL>
 *     <LI><PRE>Exec.exec("/usr/ucb/lpr Some-File");</PRE>
 *     <LI><PRE>Exec.execWait("/usr/local/bin/javac Foo.java");
 *         Exec.execWait("/usr/local/bin/java Foo");</PRE>
 *     <LI><PRE>Exec.execPrint("/usr/bin/ls -al");</PRE>
 *   </OL>
 */
public class Exec {

  private static boolean verbose = true;

  /** Determines if the Exec class should print which commands
   * are being executed, and prints error messages if a problem
   * is found. Default is true.
   *
   * @param verboseFlag true: print messages, false: don't.
   */

  public static void setVerbose(boolean verboseFlag) {
    verbose = verboseFlag;
  }

  /** Will Exec print status messages? */

  public static boolean getVerbose() {
    return(verbose);
  }
```

(continued)

Listing 8.7 `Exec.java` *(continued)*

```
/** Starts a process to execute the command. Returns
 * immediately, even if the new process is still running.
 *
 * @param command The <B>full</B> pathname of the command to
 * be executed. No shell built-ins (e.g., "cd") or shell
 * meta-chars (e.g. ">") are allowed.
 * @return false if a problem is known to occur, but since
 * this returns immediately, problems aren't usually found
 * in time. Returns true otherwise.
 */

public static boolean exec(String command) {
  return(exec(command, false, false));
}

/** Starts a process to execute the command. Waits for the
 * process to finish before returning.
 *
 * @param command The <B>full</B> pathname of the command to
 * be executed. No shell built-ins or shell metachars are
 * allowed.
 * @return false if a problem is known to occur, either due
 * to an exception or from the subprocess returning a
 * nonzero value. Returns true otherwise.
 */

public static boolean execWait(String command) {
  return(exec(command, false, true));
}

/** Starts a process to execute the command. Prints any output
 * the command produces.
 *
 * @param command The <B>full</B> pathname of the command to
 * be executed. No shell built-ins or shell meta-chars are
 * allowed.
 * @return false if a problem is known to occur, either due
 * to an exception or from the subprocess returning a
 * nonzero value. Returns true otherwise.
 */

public static boolean execPrint(String command) {
  return(exec(command, true, false));
}
```

(continued)

Listing 8.7   `Exec.java` *(continued)*

```java
/** This creates a Process object via Runtime.getRuntime.exec()
 * Depending on the flags, it may call waitFor on the process
 * to avoid continuing until the process terminates, and open
 * an input stream from the process to read the results.
 */

private static boolean exec(String command,
                           boolean printResults,
                           boolean wait) {
  if (verbose) {
    printSeparator();
    System.out.println("Executing '" + command + "'.");
  }
  try {
    // Start running command, returning immediately.
    Process p  = Runtime.getRuntime().exec(command);

    // Print the output. Since we read until there is no more
    // input, this causes us to wait until the process is
    // completed.
    if(printResults) {
      BufferedReader buffer = new BufferedReader(
        new InputStreamReader(p.getInputStream()));
      String s = null;
      try {
        while ((s = buffer.readLine()) != null) {
          System.out.println("Output: " + s);
        }
        buffer.close();
        if (p.exitValue() != 0) {
          if (verbose) {
            printError(command + " -- p.exitValue() != 0");
          }
          return(false);
        }
      } catch (Exception e) {
        // Ignore read errors; they mean the process is done.
      }

    // If not printing the results, then we should call waitFor
    // to stop until the process is completed.
```

(continued)

Listing 8.7   `Exec.java` *(continued)*

```
      } else if (wait) {
        try {
          System.out.println(" ");
          int returnVal = p.waitFor();
          if (returnVal != 0) {
            if (verbose) {
              printError(command);
            }
            return(false);
          }
        } catch (Exception e) {
          if (verbose) {
            printError(command, e);
          }
          return(false);
        }
      }
    } catch (Exception e) {
      if (verbose) {
        printError(command, e);
      }
      return(false);
    }
    return(true);
  }

  private static void printError(String command,
                                 Exception e) {
    System.out.println("Error doing exec(" + command + "): " +
                       e.getMessage());
    System.out.println("Did you specify the full " +
                       "pathname?");
  }

  private static void printError(String command) {
    System.out.println("Error executing '" + command + "'.");
  }

  private static void printSeparator() {
    System.out.println
      ("=============================================");
  }
}
```

Listing 8.8 illustrates the `Exec` class in action on a Unix system, with the result shown in Listing 8.9.

Listing 8.8   `ExecTest.java`

```
/** A test of the Exec class. */

public class ExecTest {
  public static void main(String[] args) {
    // Note: no trailing "&" -- special shell chars not
    // understood, since no shell started. Besides, exec
    // doesn't wait, so the program continues along even
    // before Netscape pops up.
    Exec.exec("/usr/local/bin/netscape");

    // Run commands, printing results.
    Exec.execPrint("/usr/bin/ls");
    Exec.execPrint("/usr/bin/cat Test.java");

    // Don't print results, but wait until this finishes.
    Exec.execWait("/usr/java1.3/bin/javac Test.java");

    // Now Test.class should exist.
    Exec.execPrint("/usr/bin/ls");
  }
}
```

Listing 8.9   `ExecTest` Output

```
Unix> java ExecTest
================================================
Executing '/usr/local/bin/netscape'.
================================================
Executing '/usr/bin/ls'.
Output: Exec.class
Output: Exec.java
Output: ExecTest.class
Output: ExecTest.java
Output: Test.java
================================================
Executing '/usr/bin/cat Test.java'.
Output: public class Test {
Output:   boolean flag;
Output: }
================================================
Executing '/usr/java1.3/bin/javac Test.java'.
================================================
Executing '/usr/bin/ls'.
Output: Exec.class
Output: Exec.java
Output: ExecTest.class
Output: ExecTest.java
Output: Test.class
Output: Test.java
```

8.7   Reference Types

Values that are objects (i.e., class instances or arrays; anything nonprimitive) are known as *reference values* or simply *references*. In the Java world, we normally say that the value of such and such a variable "is" an object. Because the Java programming language has no explicit referencing or dereferencing of pointers or pointer arithmetic, it is commonly but erroneously stated that Java does not have pointers. Wrong! In fact, *all* nonprimitive variables in Java are pointers. So, a C programmer might find it clearer to say that such and such a nonprimitive variable "points to" an object. This is the only kind of nonprimitive type in Java; there is no distinction between variables that *are* objects and variables that *point to* objects as in some languages.

If you are not already familiar with pointers, the basic idea is that you can pass big complicated objects around efficiently; Java doesn't copy them every time you pass them from one method to another. If you've used pointers extensively in other languages, be aware that Java forbids dereferencing pointers; given a referenced object, a method cannot modify a reference so that it refers to a different object.

Listing 8.10 gives an example, with the result shown in Listing 8.11.

Listing 8.10 `ReferenceTest.java`

```java
import java.awt.Point;

public class ReferenceTest {
  public static void main(String[] args) {
    Point p1 = new Point(1, 2); // Assign Point to p1
    Point p2 = p1; // p2 is new reference to *same* Point
    print("p1", p1); // (1, 2)
    print("p2", p2); // (1, 2)
    triple(p2); // Doesn't change p2
    print("p2", p2); // (1, 2)
    p2 = triple(p2); // Have p2 point to *new* Point
    print("p2", p2); // (3, 6)
    print("p1", p1); // p1 unchanged: (1, 2)
  }

  public static Point triple(Point p) {
    p = new Point(p.x * 3, p.y * 3); // Redirect p
    return(p);
  }

  public static void print(String name, Point p) {
    System.out.println("Point " + name + "= (" +
                       p.x + ", " + p.y + ").");
  }
}
```

Listing 8.11 ReferenceTest Output

```
Prompt> java ReferenceTest
Point p1= (1, 2).
Point p2= (1, 2).
Point p2= (1, 2).
Point p2= (3, 6).
Point p1= (1, 2).
```

Notice that changing the local variable p in the `triple` method didn't change the variable passed in (p2); it merely made p point someplace new, leaving p2 referring to the original place. To change p2 to a new object, we assigned it to the return value of `triple`. Although it is not possible for a method to change where an external variable points (i.e., the *object* to which it refers), it is possible for a method to change the *fields* of an object, assuming that the field's access permissions are appropriate. This is illustrated in Listing 8.12, with the result shown in Listing 8.13.

Listing 8.12 ModificationTest.java

```java
import java.awt.Point;

public class ModificationTest extends ReferenceTest {
  public static void main(String[] args) {
    Point p1 = new Point(1, 2); // Assign Point to p1
    Point p2 = p1; // p2 is new reference to *same* Point
    print("p1", p1); // (1, 2)
    print("p2", p2); // (1, 2)
    munge(p2); // Changes fields of the *single* Point
    print("p1", p1); // (5, 10)
    print("p2", p2); // (5, 10)
  }

  public static void munge(Point p) {
    p.x = 5;
    p.y = 10;
  }
}
```

Listing 8.13 ModificationTest **Output**

```
Prompt> java ModificationTest
Point p1= (1, 2).
Point p2= (1, 2).
Point p1= (5, 10).
Point p2= (5, 10).
```

Java Argument-Passing Conventions

Now, if you are already familiar with the terms "call by value" and "call by reference," you may be puzzled as to which scheme Java uses. It cannot be call by reference, because the change to p in triple didn't change the external value. But the convention doesn't look like call by value either, because the munge method showed that methods don't get copies of objects. Don't worry about the definitions—simply remember the following rule.

Core Note

---

*If you pass a variable to a method in Java, the method cannot change which **object** the variable references but might be able to change the **fields** of that object.*

If you are absolutely determined to pin the definition down, then you can say that Java uses call by value, but that the values themselves are references (restricted pointers).

The instanceof Operator

The instanceof operator returns true only if the left-hand argument is a direct or indirect instance of the class or interface named by the right-hand argument. For example:

```
if (item instanceof Breakable) {
   add(item, chinaCabinet);
}
```

Use this operator with caution; instanceof can often be replaced with polymorphism, yielding a faster, simpler, and more maintainable result. One problem with instanceof is that you need to know the name of the class or interface when you write your code. To provide a general solution that will work in all situations, a dynamic version of this test was added in Java 1.1. This second approach involves calling the isInstance method of an instance of java.lang.Class with the object you want to examine. See the example in Listing 8.14 and its output in Listing 8.15.

Listing 8.14 `InstanceOf.java`

```java
interface Barking {}

class Mammal {}

class Canine extends Mammal {}

class Dog extends Canine implements Barking {}

class Retriever extends Dog {}

public class InstanceOf {
  public static void main(String[] args) {
    Canine wolf = new Canine();
    Retriever rover = new Retriever();

    System.out.println("Testing instanceof:");
    report(wolf, "wolf");
    System.out.println();
    report(rover, "rover");

    System.out.println("\nTesting isInstance:");
    Class barkingClass = Barking.class;
    Class dogClass = Dog.class;
    Class retrieverClass = Retriever.class;
    System.out.println("  Does a retriever bark? " +
                       barkingClass.isInstance(rover));
    System.out.println("  Is a retriever a dog? " +
                       dogClass.isInstance(rover));
    System.out.println("  Is a dog necessarily a retriever? " +
                       retrieverClass.isInstance(new Dog()));
  }

  public static void report(Object object, String name) {
    System.out.println("  " + name + " is a mammal: " +
                       (object instanceof Mammal));
    System.out.println("  " + name + " is a canine: " +
                       (object instanceof Canine));
    System.out.println("  " + name + " is a dog: " +
                       (object instanceof Dog));
    System.out.println("  " + name + " is a retriever: " +
                       (object instanceof Retriever));
  }
}
```

Listing 8.15 `InstanceOf` **Output**

```
prompt> java InstanceOf
Testing instanceof:
  wolf is a mammal: true
  wolf is a canine: true
  wolf is a dog: false
  wolf is a retriever: false

  rover is a mammal: true
  rover is a canine: true
  rover is a dog: true
  rover is a retriever: true

Testing isInstance:
  Does a retriever bark? true
  Is a retriever a dog? true
  Is a dog necessarily a retriever? false
```

8.8 Strings

In Java, strings are real objects, members of the `java.lang.String` class. However, because they are so frequently used, you are allowed to create them simply by using double quotes, as follows:

```
String s1 = "This is a String";
```

The normal object-creation approach of using new is legal also, for example,

```
String s2 = new String("This is a String too");
```

but is rarely used.

The most unusual thing about the `String` class is that strings are immutable; once created they cannot be changed. "Hold on," you say, "I know there is no `set-CharacterAt` method, but I've seen string concatenation used lots of places." That's a good point; the + character can be used to concatenate strings, as follows:

```
String test = "foo" + "bar"; // "foobar"
```

However, in this example *three* strings are created: `foo`, `bar`, and a new third string `foobar`. This distinction doesn't seem important in the previous example but is very significant in the following code:

```
String foo = "foo";
String bar = "bar";
String test = foo + bar;
```

The key point here is that neither `foo` nor `bar` is modified by the concatenation performed on the third line. This is a convenient feature; it means that it is safe to pass strings to arbitrary methods without worrying about them being modified. On the other hand, to implement this unchangeable nature, Java has to copy the strings when concatenation is performed. This can be expensive, so Java supplies a `StringBuffer` class that is mutable.

Note that + is the only overloaded operators in Java; it has a totally different meaning for strings than it has for numbers. You cannot define your own operators or overload existing ones. One other thing you should know about `String` is that it is a final class and therefore you cannot create a subclass of `String`.

String Methods

The Java programming language provides a number of useful methods for working with strings. They are summarized below.

public char charAt(int index)

This method returns the character at the specified location.

public int compareTo(String comparison)
public int compareTo(Object object)

The `compareTo` method compares the current string to the supplied string, character by character, checking Unicode ordering. It returns 0 if the strings are equal (have the same characters), a negative number if the current string is lexicographically less than the comparison, and a positive number otherwise. This method is generally used for determining if strings are in order. The actual number is the difference in Unicode values between the first nonmatching characters, or the difference in lengths if the shorter string is a prefix of the longer one. To satisfy the `Comparable` interface, the method for objects was added in Java 1.2. It acts like the string `compareTo` method but throws a `ClassCastException` if the input is not a string.

public String concat(String suffix)

The `concat` method concatenates two strings, forming a new `String`. The following two forms are identical:

```
String result = someString.concat(someOtherString);
String result = someString + someOtherString;
```

Neither `someString` nor `someOtherString` is modified in these examples; instead a new `String` is created.

public static String copyValueOf(char[ ] characters)
public static String copyValueOf(char[ ] data, int startIndex, int count)

These static methods convert character arrays to strings.

public boolean endsWith(String suffix)

This method checks for a suffix of a string.

public boolean equals(Object comparison)

If the comparison object is not a `String`, `equals` returns `false`. Otherwise, it compares character by character. Thus, two different strings with the same characters will be `equals` but not `==`. For example, Listing 8.16 compares the first input argument to a fixed string, using `equals` and `==`. As Listing 8.17 shows, the `==` test fails but the `equals` test succeeds. Also note that different occurrences of literal strings may or may not be `==` since the compiler may collapse such constants.

Core Warning

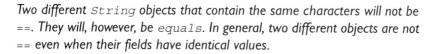

Two different `String` objects that contain the same characters will not be `==`. They will, however, be `equals`. In general, two different objects are not `==` even when their fields have identical values.

public boolean equalsIgnoreCase(String comparison)

This method performs a case-insensitive, character-by-character comparison.

public byte[ ] getBytes()
public byte[ ] getBytes(String encoding)

These methods convert a string to a byte array.

public void getChars(int sourceStart, int sourceEnd, char[ ] destination, int destinationStart)

This method copies the characters from `sourceStart` (inclusive) to `sourceEnd` (exclusive) into the specified part of the destination array.

public int indexOf(int character)
public int indexOf(int character, int startIndex)
public int indexOf(String subString)
public int indexOf(String subString, int startIndex)

These methods return the index of the first occurrence of the specified target.

public native String intern()

The `intern` method returns a canonical `String` containing the same characters as the supplied string. The interned result of two strings is `==` if and only if the strings themselves are `equals`.

public int lastIndexOf(int character)
public int lastIndexOf(int character, int startIndex)
public int lastIndexOf(String subString)
public int lastIndexOf(String subString, int startIndex)
These methods return the index of the last occurrence of the specified target.

public int length()
This method gives the length of the string. Note that this is a method call, not
an instance variable. So, don't forget that for strings you have to do

```
int len = someString.length(); // length()
```

and for arrays you do

```
int len = someArray.length; // No parens
```

public boolean regionMatches(int startIndex1, String string2,
                              int startIndex2, int count)
public boolean regionMatches(boolean ignoreCase,
                              int startIndex1, String string2,
                              int startIndex2, int count)
These methods perform a case-sensitive or -insensitive comparison of two
substrings.

public String replace(char oldChar, char newChar)
The replace method returns a *new* String that is the result of replacing all
occurrences of oldChar by newChar. The original string is not modified.

public boolean startsWith(String prefix)
public boolean startsWith(String prefix, int startIndex)
These methods check for string prefixes.

public String substring(int startIndex, int endIndex)
public String substring(int startIndex)
These methods return substrings in the specified range. If no ending index is
supplied, the substring goes to the end of the original string.

public char[ ] toCharArray()
Use this method to generate a character array.

public String toLowerCase()
public String toLowerCase(Locale locale)
public String toUpperCase()
public String toUpperCase(Locale locale)

These methods convert the entire string to lower case or upper case, optionally using the rules of the specified locale.

public String trim()

This method returns a *new* String with leading and trailing white space and control characters removed. The original String is not modified.

public static String valueOf(boolean b)
public static String valueOf(char c)
public static String valueOf(char[ ] data)
public static String valueOf(char[ ] data, int startIndex,
                                        int count)
public static String valueOf(double d)
public static String valueOf(float f)
public static String valueOf(int i)
public static String valueOf(long l)

These static methods convert the specified primitive values to strings.

public static String valueOf(Object o)

This static method uses the object's toString method to generate a string.

Listing 8.16 is an example that demonstrates the use of many String methods. The results are shown in Listing 8.17.

Listing 8.16 `stringTest.java`

```java
public class StringTest {
  public static void main (String[] args) {
    String str = "";
    if (args.length > 0) {
        str = args[0];
    }
    if (str.length()>8) {
      System.out.println("String is \"" + str + "\"\n");
      System.out.println("  charAt(3) ------------------ " +
                    str.charAt(3));
```

(continued)

Listing 8.16 `stringTest.java` *(continued)*

```
System.out.println("  compareTo(Moscow) ---------- " +
                    str.compareTo("Moscow"));
System.out.println("  concat(SuFFiX) ------------- " +
                    str.concat("SuFFiX"));
System.out.println("  endsWith(hic) ------------- " +
                    str.endsWith("hic"));
System.out.println("  == Geographic ------------- " +
                    (str == "Geographic"));
System.out.println("  equals(geographic) --------- " +
                    str.equals("geographic"));
System.out.println("  equalsIgnoreCase(geographic) " +
                    str.equalsIgnoreCase("geographic"));
System.out.println("  indexOf('o') -------------- " +
                    str.indexOf('o'));
System.out.println("  indexOf('i',5) ------------ " +
                    str.indexOf('i',5));
System.out.println("  indexOf('o',5) ------------ " +
                    str.indexOf('o',5));
System.out.println("  indexOf(rap) -------------- " +
                    str.indexOf("rap"));
System.out.println("  indexOf(rap, 5) ----------- " +
                    str.indexOf("rap", 5));
System.out.println("  lastIndexOf('o') ---------- " +
                    str.lastIndexOf('o'));
System.out.println("  lastIndexOf('i',5) --------- " +
                    str.lastIndexOf('i',5));
System.out.println("  lastIndexOf('o',5) --------- " +
                    str.lastIndexOf('o',5));
System.out.println("  lastIndexOf(rap) ---------- " +
                    str.lastIndexOf("rap"));
System.out.println("  lastIndexOf(rap, 5) -------- " +
                    str.lastIndexOf("rap", 5));
System.out.println("  length() ------------------ " +
                    str.length());
System.out.println("  replace('c','k') ---------- " +
                    str.replace('c','k'));
System.out.println("  startsWith(eog,1) ---------- " +
                    str.startsWith("eog",1));
System.out.println("  startsWith(eog) ----------- " +
                    str.startsWith("eog"));
System.out.println("  substring(3) -------------- " +
                    str.substring(3));
System.out.println("  substring(3,8) ------------ " +
                    str.substring(3,8));
```

(continued)

Listing 8.16 `stringTest.java` *(continued)*

```
        System.out.println("  toLowerCase() -------------- " +
                           str.toLowerCase());
        System.out.println("  toUpperCase() -------------- " +
                           str.toUpperCase());
        System.out.println("  trim() -------------------- " +
                           str.trim());
        System.out.println("\nString is still \"" + str + "\"\n");
    }
  }
}
```

Listing 8.17 `StringTest` Output

```
Prompt> java StringTest Geographic
String is "Geographic"
charAt(3) ------------------ g
compareTo(Moscow) ---------- -6
concat(SuFFiX) ------------- GeographicSuFFiX
endsWith(hic) ------------- true
== Geographic ------------- false
equals(geographic) -------- false
equalsIgnoreCase(geographic) true
indexOf('o') -------------- 2
indexOf('i',5) ------------ 8
indexOf('o',5) ------------ -1
indexOf(rap) -------------- 4
indexOf(rap, 5) ----------- -1
lastIndexOf('o') ---------- 2
lastIndexOf('i',5) -------- -1
lastIndexOf('o',5) -------- 2
lastIndexOf(rap) ---------- 4
lastIndexOf(rap, 5) ------- 4
length() ------------------ 10
replace('c','k') ---------- Geographik
startsWith(eog,1) --------- true
startsWith(eog) ----------- false
substring(3) -------------- graphic
substring(3,8) ------------ graph
toLowerCase() ------------- geographic
toUpperCase() ------------- GEOGRAPHIC
trim() -------------------- Geographic

String is still "Geographic"
```

Constructors

public String()
This constructor builds a zero-length but non-null string.

public String(byte[ ] bytes)
public String(byte[ ] bytes, String encoding)
public String(byte[ ] bytes, int startIndex, int count)
public String(byte[ ] bytes, int startIndex, int count,
               String encoding)
These constructors build a string from byte arrays.

public String(char[ ] chars)
public String(char[ ] chars, int startIndex, int count)
These constructors build a string from character arrays.

public String(String string)
This constructor copies the string. The result is equals but not == to the input.

public String(StringBuffer stringBuffer)
This constructor converts a StringBuffer to a String.

8.9   Arrays

An array is a simple and efficient data structure used in virtually all programming languages. Arrays are used principally to provide constant-time access to a fixed-size collection of primitive datatypes or objects and are a way of referring to many distinct values by a single identifier. Arrays are implemented as real objects with the following properties:

- Their length can be determined through the length field.
- They can be assigned to variables of type Object as well as to variables of their specific type.
- Arrays are efficiently passed to methods by reference just like any other Object.

Array indexing is zero-based, so elements in an array of 10 values can be referred to with subscripts from 0 through 9. Arrays are normally created in two steps: allocation and assignment of values. For an array of primitive datatypes, each element of the array is initialized to the default value for the primitive datatype. For an array of objects, each element of the array is initialized to `null`. When accessing array elements, you should be careful to avoid referring to an array location larger than the size of the array.

Following we present two approaches for allocating an array. The first approach allocates an array in two steps, first declaring the size of the array and then assigning values. The second approach allocates the array in one stop, assigning the values at the same time the array is declared.

Two-Step Array Allocation

In the first step, an array of the proper size and desired type is allocated:

```
int[] values = new int[2]; // a 2-element array
Point[] points = new Point[5]; // a 5-element array
int numNames = askHowManyNames(); // Set at runtime
String[] names = new String[numNames];
```

This step does not build any of the objects that actually go into the array. That building is done in a separate step by means of the `arrayReference[index]` notation to access array locations. For example:

```
values[0] = 10;
values[1] = 100;
for(int i=0; i<points.length; i++) {
  points[i] = new Point(i*2, i*4);
}
for(int j=0; j<names.length; j++) {
  names[j] = "Name " + j;
}
```

A common error is to forget the second step. If you get a `NullPointer-Exception` whenever you access an array element, check for this problem first.

Core Warning

*The following allocates n **references** to* `SomeObject`; *it doesn't actually build any **instances** of* `SomeObject`:
```
SomeObject[] objArray = new SomeObject[n];
```

By the way, you are allowed to assign values in an array over time; that is, the array does not have to be completely initialized immediately after it is created, though it is considered good form to do so. Also, if you are a die-hard C hacker, you are permitted to declare arrays with the syntax

```
Type someVar[] = ...
```

instead of

```
Type[] someVar = ...
```

Just be aware that this reduces your JHF (Java Hipness Factor) by 2.5 units.

One-Step Array Allocation

You can also allocate arrays and assign to them in one fell swoop by specifying comma-separated elements inside curly braces in the initialization portion of a variable declaration. For instance:

```
int[] values = { 10, 100 };
Point[] points = { new Point(0, 0),
                   new Point(2, 4),
                   new Point(4, 8),
                   ... };
```

The Java Virtual Machine will count the number of elements you are placing in the array initially and determine the length of the array accordingly. Listing 8.18 is an example that uses one-step initialization of arrays and passes arrays to other methods. Listing 8.19 shows the result of Golf.java.

Listing 8.18 Golf.java

```
/** Report on a round of golf at St. Andy's. */

public class Golf {
  public static void main(String[] args) {
    int[] pars   = { 4,5,3,4,5,4,4,3,4 };
    int[] scores = { 5,6,3,4,5,3,2,4,3 };
    report(pars, scores);
  }

  /** Reports on a short round of golf. */
```

(continued)

```java
public static void report(int[] pars, int[] scores) {
  for(int i=0; i<scores.length; i++) {
    int hole = i+1;
    int difference = scores[i] - pars[i];
    System.out.println("Hole " + hole + ": " +
                       diffToString(difference));
  }
}

/** Convert to English. */

public static String diffToString(int diff) {
  String[] names = {"Eagle", "Birdie", "Par", "Bogey",
                    "Double Bogey", "Triple Bogey", "Bad"};
  // If diff is -2, return names[0], or "Eagle".
  int offset = 2;
  return(names[offset + diff]);
}
}
```

```
Prompt> java Golf
Hole 1: Bogey
Hole 2: Bogey
Hole 3: Par
Hole 4: Par
Hole 5: Par
Hole 6: Birdie
Hole 7: Eagle
Hole 8: Bogey
Hole 9: Birdie
```

Multidimensional Arrays

In the Java programming language, multidimensional arrays are implemented by arrays-of-arrays, just as in C and C++. For instance, the following allocates and fills a 12 × 14 array.

```java
int[][] values = new int[12][14];
for(int i=0; i<12; i++) {
  for(int j=0; j<14; j++) {
    values[i][j] = someFunctionOf(i, j);
  }
}
```

You can access individual elements as follows:

```
int someVal = values[i][j]; // i<12, j<14
values[i][j] = someInt;
```

You can also access entire rows by omitting the second subscript:

```
int[] someArray = values[i]; // 0<=i<=11
values[i] = someOtherArray;
```

You can generalize this process to dimensions higher than 2. Also, the internal arrays need not be of the same length. To implement nonrectangular arrays, omit the rightmost size declarations. Here is an example:

```
String[][] names = new String[3][];
String[] name0 = { "John", "Q.", "Public" };
String[] name1 = { "Jane", "Doe" };
String[] name2 = { "Pele" };
names[0] = name0; // 3 elements
names[1] = name1; // 2 elements
names[2] = name2; // 1 element
```

The "shorthand" array declaration is legal with multidimensional arrays also:

```
String[][] altNames = { { "John", "Q.", "Public" },
                        { "Jane", "Doe" },
                        { "Pele" }
                      };
```

8.10 Vectors

Arrays are extremely useful, but they are limited by the fact that they cannot grow or change in size over time. To address this limitation, Java provides a "stretchable" array class: `java.util.Vector`. It is used for many of the same purposes as linked lists because you can insert or remove elements at any location. Arrays are used for the underlying implementation of `Vector`. Therefore, it only takes constant time to access a specified location, but takes time proportional to the number of elements contained to insert elements at the beginning or in the middle of the `Vector`.

Following is a summary of the `Vector` methods; see Section 8.11 for an example. Notice that the insertion and retrieval methods return elements of type `Object`. This choice makes it difficult, but not impossible, to make vectors that can hold objects only of a particular type and that let you retrieve values without typecasting the return value.

Constructors

public Vector()
public Vector(int initialCapacity)
public Vector(int initialCapacity, int capacityIncrement)
These constructors build an empty Vector. The initial capacity (size of the underlying array) is 10 if not specified, but Java automatically copies the data into a bigger array if more elements are added than the current vector size allows.

Methods

public void addElement(Object object)
public void insertElementAt(Object object, int index)
public void setElementAt(Object object, int index)
These synchronized methods add elements to the Vector. The addElement method inserts at the end; the other two methods use the location specified. With insertElementAt, the objects at and to the right of the specified location are shifted one location to the right. With setElementAt, the object at the specified location is replaced.

public int capacity()
This method returns the size of the underlying array, that is, the number of elements the Vector can hold before it will be resized.

public boolean contains(Object object)
The contains method determines whether the Vector contains an object that equals the one specified.

public void copyInto(Object[ ] newArray)
This synchronized method copies the object references into the specified array, in order.

public Object elementAt(int index)
The synchronized elementAt method returns the element at the specified location.

public Enumeration elements()
The java.util.Enumeration class defines an interface used by several enumerable classes. You can use elements to get an Enumeration object corresponding to the Vector.

public void ensureCapacity(int minimum)

This synchronized method guarantees that the underlying array has at least the specified number of elements.

public Object firstElement()
public Object lastElement()

These synchronized methods return the first and last entry in the `Vector`, respectively.

public int indexOf(Object object)
public int indexOf(Object object, int startIndex)
public int lastIndexOf(Object object)
public int lastIndexOf(Object object, int startIndex)

These synchronized methods return the leftmost or rightmost index of the element that `equals` the object specified.

public boolean isEmpty()

This method returns `false` if the `Vector` has any elements; `true` otherwise.

public boolean removeElement(Object object)
public void removeElementAt(int index)
public void removeAllElements()

These synchronized methods let you remove entries from the `Vector`.

public void setSize(int newSize)

This synchronized method sets a specific size for the `Vector`. It differs from `ensureCapacity` in that it will truncate the `Vector` if the `Vector` is larger than the specified size.

public int size()

The `size` method returns the number of elements in the `Vector` (not the size of the underlying array, which might be larger).

public void trimToSize()

This synchronized method sets the underlying array to be exactly the same size as the current number of elements. You should avoid this method while elements are being added and removed, but it might save memory if the method is used once the `Vector` elements are fixed.

Many of the `Vector` methods are synchronized to prevent potential race conditionals as a result of multiple threads accessing the same data. Synchronization does incur a performance hit. Therefore, Java 2 added two unsynchronized classes, similar in function to `Vector` class: `ArrayList` and `LinkedList`. However, these two new classes are only available in JDK 1.2 and later and are not available in most browsers supporting applets. For additional information on synchronization and multithreaded programs, see Chapter 16 (Concurrent Programming with Java Threads).

8.11 Example: A Simple Binary Tree

This section shows how references and the `Vector` class can be used to create a binary tree class. This data structure includes a `depthFirstSearch` method, which traverses the tree in depth-first order (staying to the left and going as deep as possible until having to backtrack). Notice that this method is recursive; recursion is natural for depth-first search. The `depthFirstSearch` method also uses the `NodeOperator` interface (see Listing 8.21) to generalize the operation that will be performed on each node. This interface lets you change what to do with a tree without modifying the `Node` class, which is shown in Listing 8.20. `Leaf` nodes are implemented as a subclass of `Node`, see Listing 8.22. The data structure also includes a `breadthFirstSearch` method that uses a `Vector` to build a queue that traverses the tree in breadth-first order (visiting all nodes on a given level before moving on to the next).

Note that many data structures like this have been added as a core part of the language in Java 2. For details, see `http://java.sun.com/j2se/1.3/docs/guide/collections/`. The Java Collections Framework comes with an extensible API for building, manipulating, and iterating over data structures. Implementations of hash tables, growing arrays, doubly linked lists, and balanced binary trees are provided. Although existing classes like `Vector` and `Hashtable` provide some of the same functionality, the older classes are explicitly synchronized and therefore possibly slower in certain situations. Collections also provides standard methods for sorting, filling arrays, and binary search that were missing in earlier Java releases.

Listing 8.20 `Node.java`

```
import java.util.Vector;

/** A data structure representing a node in a binary tree.
 *  It contains a node value and a reference (pointer) to
 *  the left and right subtrees.
 */
```

(continued)

Listing 8.20 Node.java *(continued)*

```java
public class Node {
  private Object nodeValue;
  private Node leftChild, rightChild;

 /** Build Node with specified value and subtrees. */

  public Node(Object nodeValue, Node leftChild,
              Node rightChild) {
    this.nodeValue = nodeValue;
    this.leftChild = leftChild;
    this.rightChild = rightChild;
  }

  /** Build Node with specified value and L subtree. R child
   *  will be null. If you want both children to be null, use
   *  the Leaf constructor.
   */

  public Node(Object nodeValue, Node leftChild) {
    this(nodeValue, leftChild, null);
  }

  /** Return the value of this node. */

  public Object getNodeValue() {
    return(nodeValue);
  }

  /** Specify the value of this node. */

  public void setNodeValue(Object nodeValue) {
    this.nodeValue = nodeValue;
  }

 /** Return the L subtree. */

  public Node getLeftChild() {
    return(leftChild);
  }

  /** Specify the L subtree. */

  public void setLeftChild(Node leftChild) {
    this.leftChild = leftChild;
  }
```

(continued)

Listing 8.20 Node.java *(continued)*

```java
/** Return the R subtree. */

public Node getRightChild() {
  return(rightChild);
}

/** Specify the R subtree. */

public void setRightChild(Node rightChild) {
  this.rightChild = rightChild;
}

/** Traverse the tree in depth-first order, applying
 *  the specified operation to each node along the way.
 */

public void depthFirstSearch(NodeOperator op) {
  op.operateOn(this);
  if (leftChild != null) {
    leftChild.depthFirstSearch(op);
  }
  if (rightChild != null) {
    rightChild.depthFirstSearch(op);
  }
}

/** Traverse the tree in breadth-first order, applying the
 *  specified operation to each node along the way.
 */

public void breadthFirstSearch(NodeOperator op) {
  Vector nodeQueue = new Vector();
  nodeQueue.addElement(this);
  Node node;
  while (!nodeQueue.isEmpty()) {
    node = (Node)nodeQueue.elementAt(0);
    nodeQueue.removeElementAt(0);
    op.operateOn(node);
    if (node.getLeftChild() != null) {
      nodeQueue.addElement(node.getLeftChild());
    }
    if (node.getRightChild() != null) {
      nodeQueue.addElement(node.getRightChild());
    }
  }
}
}
```

Listing 8.21 `NodeOperator.java`

```
/** An interface used in the Node class to ensure that
 *  an object has an operateOn method.
 */

public interface NodeOperator {
  void operateOn(Node node);
}
```

Listing 8.22 `Leaf.java`

```
/** Leaf node: a node with no subtrees. */

public class Leaf extends Node {
  public Leaf(Object value) {
    super(value, null, null);
  }
}
```

Now that we have a general data structure, let's build a specific test case. Figure 8–1 shows a simple tree; Listing 8.23 represents the tree by using the `Node` and `Leaf` classes just shown and makes a `NodeOperator` that does nothing but print the value of each node it visits. Listing 8.24 shows the results.

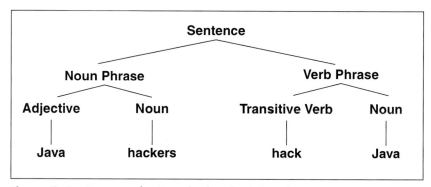

Figure 8–1   Parse tree for "Java hackers hack Java."

Listing 8.23 `TreeTest.java`

```
/** A NodeOperator that prints each node. */

class PrintOperator implements NodeOperator {
  public void operateOn(Node node) {
    System.out.println(node.getNodeValue());
  }
}

/** A sample tree representing a parse tree of
 *  the sentence "Java hackers hack Java", using
 *  some simple context-free grammar.
 */

public class TreeTest {
  public static void main(String[] args) {
    Node adjective =
      new Node("  Adjective", new Leaf("    Java"));
    Node noun1 =
      new Node("  Noun", new Leaf("    hackers"));
    Node verb =
      new Node("  TransitiveVerb", new Leaf("    hack"));
    Node noun2 =
      new Node("  Noun", new Leaf("    Java"));
    Node np = new Node(" NounPhrase", adjective, noun1);
    Node vp = new Node(" VerbPhrase", verb, noun2);
    Node sentence = new Node("Sentence", np, vp);
    PrintOperator printOp = new PrintOperator();
    System.out.println("Depth first traversal:");
    sentence.depthFirstSearch(printOp);
    System.out.println("\nBreadth first traversal:");
    sentence.breadthFirstSearch(printOp);
  }
}
```

Listing 8.24 `TreeTest` Output

```
Prompt> java TreeTest
Depth first traversal:
Sentence
 NounPhrase
  Adjective
   Java
```

(continued)

Listing 8.24 `TreeTest` Output *(continued)*

```
 Noun
  hackers
VerbPhrase
 TransitiveVerb
  hack
 Noun
  Java

Breadth first traversal:
Sentence
 NounPhrase
 VerbPhrase
  Adjective
  Noun
  TransitiveVerb
  Noun
   Java
   hackers
   hack
   Java
```

8.12 Exceptions

The Java programming language has a very nice error-handling system: *exceptions*. Exceptions can be "thrown" (generated) in one block of code and "caught" (handled) in an outer block or in a method that called the current one. Java exceptions differ from C++ exceptions in two major ways. The first major difference is that the exception-handling construct (`try/catch`) has a `finally` clause that always gets executed, regardless of whether or not an exception was thrown. The second significant difference is that you can *require* users of your methods to handle exceptions your methods generate; if they fail to do that, their code will not compile.

Basic Form

The simplest form of exception handling is a block of the following form:

```
try {
  statement1;
  statement2;
  ...
} catch(SomeException someVar) {
  handleTheException(someVar);
}
```

For example, the constructor for `java.net.URL` potentially generates a `java.net.MalformedURLException`, and the `readLine` method of `java.io.BufferedReader` potentially generates a `java.io.IOException`. Listing 8.25 uses both the URL constructor and the readLine method to read a URL from the user and print descriptive information about it, so it needs to catch both possible exceptions. As Listing 8.26 shows, `MalformedURLException` verifies that the URL is in legal format; it doesn't retrieve the referenced file or even check that it exists. You can see plenty of examples of reading the contents of such files in Chapter 17 (Network Programming).

Listing 8.25 `URLTest.java`

```
import java.net.*; // For URL, MalformedURLException
import java.io.*;  // For BufferedReader

/** A small class to demonstrate try/catch blocks. */

public class URLTest {
  public static void main(String[] args) {
    URLTest test = new URLTest();
    test.getURL();
    test.printURL();
  }

  private URL url = null;

  /** Read a string from user and create a URL from it. If
   *  reading fails, give up and report error. If reading
   *  succeeds but URL is illegal, try again.
   */

  public URL getURL() {
    if (url != null) {
      return(url);
    }
    System.out.print("Enter URL: ");
    System.out.flush();
    BufferedReader in = new BufferedReader(
                          new InputStreamReader(System.in));
    String urlString;
    try {
      urlString = in.readLine();
    } catch(IOException ioe) {
      System.out.println("IOError when reading input: " + ioe);
      ioe.printStackTrace(); // Show stack dump.
```

(continued)

Listing 8.25 URLTest.java *(continued)*

```
      return(null);
    }
    try {
      url = new URL(urlString);
    } catch(MalformedURLException mue) {
      System.out.println(urlString + " is not valid.\n" +
                         "Try again.");
      getURL();
    }
    return(url);
  }

  /** Print info on URL. */

  public void printURL() {
    if (url == null) {
      System.out.println("No URL.");
    } else {
      String protocol = url.getProtocol();
      String host = url.getHost();
      int port = url.getPort();
      if (protocol.equals("http") && (port == -1)) {
        port = 80;
      }
      String file = url.getFile();
      System.out.println("Protocol: " + protocol +
                         "\nHost: " + host +
                         "\nPort: " + port +
                         "\nFile: " + file);
    }
  }
}
```

Listing 8.26 URLTest Output

```
> java URLTest
> Enter URL: http://java.sun.com/ConvertingToActiveX.html
Protocol: http
Host: java.sun.com
Port: 80
File: /ConvertingToActiveX.html
```

Note the use of the `printStackTrace` method in `getURL`. This shows the method call stack at the point the exception occurred. In many implementations, it even includes line numbers in the source files. This is such a useful debugging tool that it is sometimes used even when no exceptions are generated. For instance, the following simply prints a stack dump:

```
new Throwable().printStackTrace();
```

Multiple Catch Clauses

A single `try` can have more than one `catch`. If an exception is generated, Java executes the first `catch` clause that matches the type of exception thrown. Since exceptions can be created hierarchically like other Java classes, you must catch a more specific exception before a more general one. For instance, although the `getURL` method could be simplified to use a single `try` block with two `catch` clauses (Listing 8.27), the order of the `catch` clauses needs to be reversed since a `Malformed-URLException` is actually a subclass of `IOException`.

Core Approach

If you have multiple `catch` *clauses, you must order them from the most specific to the most general.*

Listing 8.27 Simplified `getURL` Method

```
public URL getURL() {
  if (url != null) {
    return(url);
  }
  System.out.print("Enter URL: ");
  System.out.flush();
  BufferedReader in = new BufferedReader(
                    new InputStreamReader(System.in));
  String urlString = null;
  try {
    urlString = in.readLine();
    url = new URL(urlString);
  } catch(MalformedURLException mue) {
    System.out.println(urlString + " is not valid.\n" +
                      "Try again.");
    getURL();
  } catch(IOException ioe) {
    System.out.println("IOError when reading input: " + ioe);
    ioe.printStackTrace(); // Show stack dump
    return(null);
  }
  return(url);
}
```

The Finally Clause

After the last `catch` clause, you are permitted a `finally` clause that *always* gets executed, regardless of whether or not exceptions are thrown. It is executed even if `break`, `continue`, or `return` is used within the `try` or `catch` clauses. Listing 8.28 shows a third version of `getURL` that uses this approach.

Listing 8.28 Further Simplified `getURL` Method

```
public URL getURL() {
   if (url != null) {
      return(url);
   }
   System.out.print("Enter URL: ");
   System.out.flush();
   BufferedReader in = new BufferedReader(
                       new InputStreamReader(System.in));
   String urlString = null;
   try {
     urlString = in.readLine();
     url = new URL(urlString);
   } catch(MalformedURLException mue) {
     System.out.println(urlString + " is not valid.\n" +
                        "Try again.");
     getURL();
   } catch(IOException ioe) {
     System.out.println("IOError when reading input: " + ioe);
     ioe.printStackTrace(); // Can skip return(null) now
   } finally {
     return(url);
   }
}
```

Thrown Exceptions

If you write a method that potentially generates one or more exceptions and you don't handle them explicitly, you need to declare them with the `throws` construct, as follows:

```
public SomeType someMethod(...) throws SomeException {
```

or

```
public SomeType someMethod(...)
      throws ExceptionType1, ExceptionType2 {
```

This declaration lets you do two things. First, it permits you to write methods that have enforced safety checking; users are required to handle the exception when calling the methods. Second, it permits you to postpone exception handling to a method higher in the method call chain by declaring them in the method declaration but ignoring them in the method body.

If you want to explicitly generate an exception, use the throw construct as illustrated:

```
throw new IOException("Blocked by firewall");
throw new MalformedURLException(
        "Invalid protocol: telephone");
```

Using throw is more common with exceptions you define yourself. You can make your own exception classes by subclassing any of the existing exception types. Listing 8.29 gives an example of an exception type you might use when creating geometric objects that require nonnegative widths, heights, radii, and so forth. The class is demonstrated in Listing 8.30.

Listing 8.29 NegativeLengthException.java

```java
import java.io.*;

public class NegativeLengthException extends Exception {

  /** Test NegativeLengthException */

  public static void main(String[] args) {
    try {
      int lineLength = readLength();
      for(int i=0; i<lineLength; i++) {
        System.out.print("*");
      }
      System.out.println();
    } catch (NegativeLengthException nle) {
      System.out.println("NegativeLengthException: " +
                      nle.getMessage());
    }
  }

  public NegativeLengthException() {
    super("Negative dimensions not permitted.");
  }

  public NegativeLengthException(String message) {
    super(message);
  }
```

(continued)

Listing 8.29 `NegativeLengthException.java` *(continued)*

```java
    // readLength catches IOExceptions locally but lets the
    // calling method handle NegativeLengthExceptions.
    private static int readLength() throws NegativeLengthException {
      BufferedReader in = new BufferedReader(
                          new InputStreamReader(System.in));
      System.out.print("Enter length: ");
      System.out.flush();
      int len = 0;
      try {
        String line = in.readLine();
        len = Integer.parseInt(line);
        if (len < 0) {
          throw new NegativeLengthException();
        }
      } catch (IOException ioe) {
        System.out.println("Problem reading from keyboard");
      }
      return(len);
    }
}
```

Listing 8.30 Throwing `NegativeLengthExceptions`

```
> java NegativeLengthException
> Enter length: 4
****

> java NegativeLengthException
> Enter length: -345
NegativeLengthException: Negative dimensions not permitted.
```

Unchecked Exceptions

The exceptions discussed so far have been *checked exceptions*; exceptions that you are required to handle. Java also includes two classes of *unchecked exceptions*: `Error` and `RuntimeException`. You are permitted to handle these exceptions but are not required to, since the number of places from which they could be generated is too large. For instance, members of the `Error` class include `OutOfMemoryError` (e.g., array allocation or call to new failed because of insufficient memory) and `ClassFormatError` (e.g., a `.class` file in illegal format, perhaps because text mode instead of binary mode was used when the file was FTP'd).

The RuntimeException subclasses include ArithmeticException (e.g., an integer division-by-zero) and ArrayIndexOutOfBoundsException (e.g., you forgot to bound a loop at the array's length). A catch-all RuntimeException often extended in user code is IllegalArgumentException. This exception lets you create hooks in your code for the handling of unusual cases without requiring users to catch the exceptions.

8.13 Summary

This chapter briefly reviewed the fundamental syntax of Java programs: primitive and reference types, operators, the Math class, strings, arrays, vectors, and exceptions. Once you have assimilated this and the object-oriented programming coverage of Chapter 7, you are ready to focus on the more specific Java topics covered in the next chapters.

APPLETS AND BASIC GRAPHICS

Topics in This Chapter

- Creating *applets*: Java programs that are embedded in Web pages
- The applet life cycle
- Customizing applets through parameters embedded in HTML
- The Java Plug-In
- Creating graphical *applications*: Java programs that run independently of a Web page or browser
- Basic drawing, color, font, and clipping area operations
- Loading and drawing images
- Preloading images
- Controlling image loading with MediaTracker

Chapter 9

In this chapter we discuss the two basic types of graphical Java programs: applets and applications. For applets, we explain how to create them, how to associate them with Web pages, and how to supply customization parameters through the PARAM element. For applications, we discuss one common approach to creating windows, postponing alternatives until Chapter 13 (AWT Components). We cover the basic drawing operations that can be performed in applets and applications. However, for applications, Java2D graphics, presented in Chapter 10 (Java 2D: Graphics in Java 2), are preferred for basic drawing operations. Finally, we discuss methods for loading and displaying images in both applets and applications.

9.1 What Are Applets?

An applet is a particular type of Java program that is intended to be embedded in a Web page. When a user opens a Web page containing an applet, the applet runs *locally* (on the client machine that is running the Web browser), not *remotely* (on the system running the HTTP server). Consequently, security considerations are paramount, and applets are restricted from performing various operations that are allowed in general Java programs ("applications"). For instance, you might need to write a stand-alone program that deletes files, but you certainly don't want to let applets that come in over the Web delete your files. These restrictions are enforced by a SecurityManager object on the client system. In version 1.1 and later of the

Java Platform, classes can be digitally signed, and the user can ask the security manager to allow various restricted operations in classes signed by certain individuals or organizations. Technically, the precise restrictions placed upon applets depend on the `SecurityManager`. However, in Netscape and Internet Explorer, the default manager verifies that applets:

Do not read from the local (client) disk.

That is, they cannot read arbitrary files. Applets can, however, instruct the browser to display pages that are generally accessible on the Web, which might include some local files.

Do not write to the local (client) disk.

The browser may choose to cache certain files, including some loaded by applets, but this choice is not under direct control of the applet.

Do not open network connections other than to the server from which the applet was loaded.

This restriction prevents applets from browsing behind network firewalls.

Do not call local programs.

Ordinary Java applications can invoke locally installed programs (with the `exec` method of the `Runtime` class) as well as link to local C/C++ modules ("native" methods). These actions are prohibited in applets because there is no way to determine whether the operations these local programs perform are safe.

Cannot discover private information about the user.

Applets should not be able to discover the username of the person running them or specific system information such as current users, directory names or listings, system software, and so forth. However, applets *can* determine the name of the host they are on; this information is already reported to the HTTP server that delivered the applet.

9.2   Creating an Applet

Creating an applet involves two steps: making the Java class and making the associated HTML document. The Java class defines the actual behavior of the applet, and the HTML document associates the applet with a particular rectangular region of the Web page.

Template for Applets

Listing 9.1 shows the typical organization of an applet. It contains a section for declaring instance variables, an `init` method, and a `paint` method. The `init` method is automatically called by the browser when the applet is first created. Then, when the applet is ready to be drawn, `paint` is called. The `paint` method is automatically called again whenever the image has been obscured and is reexposed or when graphical components are added, or the method can be invoked programmatically. The default implementations of `init` and `paint` don't do anything; they are just provided as placeholders for the programmer to override. Although there are additional placeholders for user code (see Section 9.4, "The Applet Life Cycle"), this basic structure (declarations, `init`, `paint`) is a good starting point for most applets. Although the Java programming language, unlike C++, allows direct initialization of instance variables when they are declared in the body of the class, this initialization is not recommended for applets. Prior to `init`, the applet has not set up everything set up that it needs in order to initialize certain types of graphical objects. So, rather than trying to remember which variables can be directly initialized (strings) and which must be done in `init` (images), follow the good rule of simply declaring them in the main body of the applet and initializing them in `init`. Of course, variables that are only needed in `init` can be local to `init` rather than instance variables available to the whole class.

Listing 9.1   Java applet template

```
import java.applet.Applet;
import java.awt.*;

public class AppletTemplate extends Applet {

  // Variable declarations.

  public void init() {
    // Variable initializations, image loading, etc.
  }

  public void paint(Graphics g) {
    // Drawing operations.
  }
}
```

Template for HTML

Once an applet has been created and compiled, the resultant class file must be associated with a Web page. The `APPLET` element is used for this, as shown in Listing 9.2. This element is discussed further in Section 9.6, but for now note that `CODE` designates the name of the Java class file and that the two attributes, WIDTH and HEIGHT, are required. In addition, you need to use CODEBASE if the applet is being loaded from somewhere other than the place the associated HTML document resides. After the applet has been compiled and associated with a Web page, loading the Web page in a Java-enabled browser executes the applet. You sometimes name the HTML file with the same prefix as the Java file (e.g., AppletTemplate.html to correspond to AppletTemplate.class), but the name is arbitrary, and in fact, a single HTML document can load multiple applets.

Although the compiled file (*file*.class) for your applet must be available on the Web, the source code (*file*.java) need not be. If you put the source and class files in different locations, remember that *all* nonsystem class files used by your applet need to be WWW accessible and should be either in the same directory as the applet or in subdirectories corresponding to their package. If you move class files from one system to another by using FTP, be sure to use binary (raw) mode, not text mode.

Finally, some Java systems have the concept of a CLASSPATH that tells the system where to look for classes. If your system uses this feature, note that CLASSPATH settings apply only to local programs; a remote user accessing your applet won't know anything about your CLASSPATH. Also, since both Netscape and Internet Explorer grant extra privileges to class files that are listed in your CLASSPATH, you want to be sure your CLASSPATH is *not* set in the process that starts your browser. This practice prevents people who know your CLASSPATH from using your own classes to attack you.

Core Security

Make sure your CLASSPATH is not set when you start your browser.

Listing 9.2   HTML applet template

```
<!DOCTYPE HTML PUBLIC "-//W3C//DTD HTML 4.0 Transitional//EN">
<HTML>
<HEAD>
  <TITLE>A Template for Loading Applets</TITLE>
</HEAD>

<BODY>
<H1>A Template for Loading Applets</H1>
<P>
<APPLET CODE="AppletTemplate.class" WIDTH=120 HEIGHT=60>
  <B>Error! You must use a Java-enabled browser.</B>
</APPLET>

</BODY>
</HTML>
```

9.3   An Example Applet

Listing 9.3 presents an applet that follows the pattern shown in the previous section. The details of the various steps the applet performs are covered in later sections, but the basic approach is what is important here. The variable declaration section declares a variable of type Image. The init method sets the default color and font, loads an image file from the network and assigns it to the Image declared earlier, adds a label to the applet, then performs an informational printout. The paint method draws the image, placing its top 50 pixels from the top of the applet. Listing 9.4 shows the associated HTML document; the result in Internet Explorer 5.0 (Windows 2000) is shown in Figure 9–1.

Listing 9.3   JavaJump.java

```
import java.applet.Applet;
import java.awt.*;

/** An applet that draws an image. */

public class JavaJump extends Applet {
  private Image jumpingJava; // Instance var declarations here

  public void init() {         // Initializations here
    setBackground(Color.white);
    setFont(new Font("SansSerif", Font.BOLD, 18));
    jumpingJava = getImage(getDocumentBase(),
                        "images/Jumping-Java.gif");
    add(new Label("Great Jumping Java!"));
    System.out.println("Yow! I'm jiving with Java.");
  }

  public void paint(Graphics g) {  // Drawing here
    g.drawImage(jumpingJava, 0, 50, this);
  }
}
```

Listing 9.4 `JavaJump.html`

```html
<!DOCTYPE HTML PUBLIC "-//W3C//DTD HTML 4.0 Transitional//EN">
<HTML>
<HEAD>
  <TITLE>Jumping Java</TITLE>
</HEAD>
<BODY BGCOLOR="BLACK" TEXT="WHITE">
<H1>Jumping Java</H1>
<P>
<APPLET CODE="JavaJump.class" WIDTH=250 HEIGHT=335>
  <B>Sorry, this example requires Java.</B>
</APPLET>
</BODY>
</HTML>
```

Figure 9–1 Result of applet shown in Listing 9.3 and Listing 9.4.

Redrawing Automatically

In most applets, the main drawing is done in `paint`. If something changes that requires the drawing to change, you can call the `repaint` method, which calls `update`, which normally clears the screen and then calls `paint`. We'll give more details on `repaint` and `update` later, but the point is that they are called whenever the *programmer* wants the screen to be redrawn. The *system* may also want to redraw the screen, as is typical when part of the screen has been covered up by some other window and then reexposed. In the vast majority of cases, you don't care why `paint` is called; you do the same thing either way. However, when the system calls `paint`, it sets the clipping region of the `Graphics` object to be the part that was obscured. This means that in the unlikely case that `paint` draws something different every time it is called but `repaint` isn't invoked, the screen won't be redrawn correctly unless you adjust the clipping region (see Section 9.11, "Graphics Operations").

Reloading Applets During Development

In Netscape and Internet Explorer, the applet is automatically cached in memory. As a result, you can change the applet code and not see the changes reflected in the browser because the browser is using the previously cached applet version. To force loading of the new applet, use *Shift-Reload* (holding down the shift key when clicking the Reload button) in Netscape and use *Control-Reload* in Internet Explorer.

Getting Standard Output

For output in "production" applets, you normally create a text area or other GUI control to display results. We cover this approach at length in Chapter 13 (AWT Components). You can also send a single line of debugging results to the status line by using the applet's `showStatus` method. However, during development it is often convenient to print multiple lines of debugging output with `System.out.println`. When you print this way from an applet, where do you see the result? The answer depends on the browser being used.

Standard Output

In Netscape Navigator, the user can select Java Console from the Window menu, or in Netscape Communicator, the user can select Java Console from the Communicator menu, followed by the Tools menu, to get a pop-up window in which to see output. For example, Figure 9–2 shows the Java Console after the `JavaJump` example is run. You can enter the ? keystroke in the Java Console for a listing of available command options.

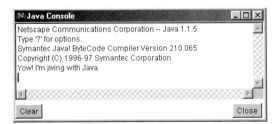

Figure 9-2   In Netscape, standard output is sent to a separate window: the Java Console.

In Internet Explorer 5, printing is a little more cumbersome to set up. First, from the Tools menu, select Internet Options, then choose the Advanced screen. There, under the Java VM category, select Java console enabled. Then, quit Internet Explorer, and restart. After restart, from the View menu, select Java Console to get a pop-up window for output. Entering the ? keystroke in the Java Console provides a listing of available command options. Note that the Java Console is enabled by default in Internet Explorer 4.

Standard Output in Appletviewer

In appletviewer on Windows and Unix platforms, the output is sent to the window that started appletviewer. On a Mac, a separate window pops up when output is sent to System.out.

9.4   The Applet Life Cycle

Applet is an unusual class since the browser automatically creates an instance of it and calls certain methods at certain times. The main method is never called by the browser. Instead, the following placeholder methods are called at various times. The methods are empty unless overridden by the author.

public void init()

This method is called after the applet instance is first created by the browser. In Netscape, init is not called again if the applet is stopped and restarted unless the applet has been "trimmed" (deleted from memory) by the browser. In Internet Explorer, init is called whenever the user returns to the page containing the applet.

public void start()

The start method is called after init is completed, but before the first invocation of paint. If the applet is stopped and restarted, start is called again each time. This makes start a good place to restart animation that gets paused when the user leaves the page. Netscape calls start and stop when the browser window is resized; Internet Explorer, appletviewer, and HotJava don't.

public void paint(Graphics g)

This is where user-level drawing is placed. The method is invoked by the browser after init and start have completed, and again whenever the browser thinks the screen needs to be redrawn, typically when part of the screen has been obscured and then reexposed. From another method, you can call repaint with no arguments to tell the browser's graphics thread to call paint at its first opportunity.

public void stop()

The browser calls stop when the user leaves the page containing the applet. The method can be used to halt animation that will be restarted by start. In Netscape, this method is also called when the browser window is resized.

public void destroy()

The destroy method is called when the applet is about to be permanently destroyed (e.g., when the browser is shut down or when it "trims" the applet from memory to keep the browser image size from growing too large). The method can be used for bookkeeping or to free up shared resources but is not used frequently. In Internet Explorer, destroy is called whenever the user leaves the page containing the applet.

Core Alert

In Internet Explorer, unlike in Navigator, init is called each time the user returns (in the same session) to a page containing a previously loaded applet, and destroy is called whenever the user leaves the page containing the applet.

9.5   Other Applet Methods

The built-in versions of the methods described in Section 9.4 don't actually *do* any-thing; they are simply placeholders for the user to override. `Applet` also contains a number of methods that perform common, useful tasks; the most frequently used ones are summarized below. `Applet` inherits from `Panel`, `Container`, and `Component`; full details of these classes are given in Chapter 13 (AWT Components).

public void add(Component c)
public void add(Component c, Object constraints)
public void add(String location, Component c)
public void add(PopupMenu menu)
These methods insert graphical components into the applet window. They are discussed in Chapter 13 (AWT Components) and Chapter 12 (Layout Managers).

public boolean contains(int x, int y)
public boolean contains(Point p)
The `contains` method determines if the specified location is contained inside the applet. That is, it returns `true` if and only if the *x*-coordinate is less than or equal to the applet's width and the *y*-coordinate is less than or equal to the applet's height.

public Image createImage(int width, int height)
public Image createImage(ImageProducer producer)
The `createImage` method is used to make an off-screen pixmap. Like `getImage`, `createImage` will fail if used prior to `init`. So, it should not be used to directly initialize instance variables.

public String getAppletInfo()
You can override this method to return a string describing the author, version, and other information about the applet.

public AudioClip getAudioClip(URL audioFile)
public AudioClip getAudioClip(URL base,
                                        String audioFilename)
These methods retrieve an audio or MIDI file from a remote location and assign it to an `AudioClip` object, which supports `play`, `loop`, and `stop` methods. The JDK 1.1 supports only `.au` file formats. In JDK 1.2, `.aiff`, and `.wav` audio file formats are also supported, along with MIDI Type 0, MIDI Type 1, and RMF song file formats.

public Color getBackground()
public void setBackground(Color bgColor)

These methods get and set the background color of the applet. Create colors by calling the `Color` constructor, as follows:

```
Color someColor = new Color(red, green, blue);
```

The red, green, and blue parameters should be integers from 0 to 255 or floats from 0.0 to 1.0. Colors can also be created with `Color.getHSBColor(hue, saturation, brightness)`, where the arguments are floats between 0.0 and 1.0. Alternatively, there are thirteen predefined colors: `Color.black`, `Color.blue`, `Color.cyan`, `Color.darkGray`, `Color.gray`, `Color.green`, `Color.lightGray`, `Color.magenta`, `Color.orange`, `Color.pink`, `Color.red`, `Color.white`, and `Color.yellow`.

A `SystemColor` class provides access to the desktop colors. This class lets you create applets that conform to the user's current color scheme. For instance, in paint you could call `g.setColor(SystemColor.windowText)` before doing `drawString`. Table 9.1 lists the options available.

Table 9.1 System Colors

Color (Static variables in SystemColor class)	Meaning
activeCaption	The background color for captions of active windows.
activeCaptionBorder	The border color for captions of active windows.
control	The background color for control objects ("widgets").
controlDkShadow	The dark shadow color used to give a 3D effect.
controlHighlight	The emphasis color.
controlLtHighlight	A lighter emphasis color.
controlShadow	The light shadow color used to give a 3D effect.
controlText	The text color.
desktop	The desktop background color.
inactiveCaption	The background color for captions of inactive windows.
inactiveCaptionBorder	The border color for captions of inactive windows.

(continued)

Table 9.1 System Colors (continued)

`inactiveCaptionText`	The text color for captions of inactive windows.
`info`	The background color for help text ("tool tips").
`infoText`	The text color for help text ("tool tips").
`menu`	The background color of deselected menu items. Selected menu items should use `textHighlight`.
`menuText`	The text color of deselected menu items. Selected menu items should use `textHighlightText`.
`scrollbar`	The background color for scrollbars.
`text`	The background color for text components.
`textHighlight`	The background color for highlighted text such as selected text in a textfield, selected menu items, etc.
`textHighlightText`	The text color for highlighted text.
`textInactiveText`	The text color for inactive components.
`textText`	The text color for text components.
`window`	The background color for windows.
`windowBorder`	The border color for windows.
`windowText`	The text color for windows.

The `SystemColor` class allows you to directly determine the desktop colors for setting the look of the applet to match the windowing system. However, if you create applets strictly based on Swing components, then you can easily present a particular platform "look and feel" by calling methods from the `UIManager` class. Available look and feels include Motif, Windows, Mac, and Java (Metal). See Chapter 14 (Basic Swing) for details on setting the look and feel of a Swing applet.

public URL getCodeBase()
public URL getDocumentBase()
These methods return the locations of the applet (`getCodeBase`) and the HTML document using the applet (`getDocumentBase`).

public Component getComponentAt(int x, int y)

The getComponentAt method returns the topmost component at the specified location. This will be the applet itself if no other component is at this location; null is returned if x and y are outside the applet.

public Cursor getCursor()
public void setCursor(Cursor cursor)

These methods get and set the cursor.

public Font getFont()
public void setFont(Font defaultFont)

These methods get and set the default font for the applet. Unless overridden explicitly, the default font is used for labels, buttons, textfields, and other such components; when strings are drawn, use the drawString method of Graphics. Fonts are created with the Font constructor, which takes a family, style, and size as follows:

```
String family = "Serif";
int style = Font.BOLD;
int size = 18;
Font font = new Font(family, style, size);
setFont(font);
```

In JDK 1.1, the font family can be Serif, SansSerif, Monospaced, Dialog, and DialogInput. The style should be one of Font.PLAIN, Font.BOLD, Font.ITALIC, or Font.BOLD|Font.ITALIC. The size must be an integer. In JDK 1.1, nonstandard fonts cannot be used even if they are locally installed. In JDK 1.2, any local font is available provided you call the getAvailableFontFamilyNames or getFonts method of Graphics-Environment first. See Section 10.5 (Using Local Fonts) for more details on font graphics.

public FontMetrics getFontMetrics(Font f)

This method returns an object that can be used to determine the size of strings (stringWidth) or individual characters (charWidth) in a given font.

public Color getForeground()
public Color setForeground(Color fgColor)

These methods get and set the default foreground color for the applet. See getBackground for a discussion of colors.

public Graphics getGraphics()

The getGraphics method returns the current graphics object for the applet. Use this method if you want to perform drawing operations from a method that is not directly called from paint. The paint method automatically has the graphics object.

public Image getImage(URL imageFile)
public Image getImage(URL base, String imageFilename)

These methods "register" a remote image file with an Image object. The Java platform does not actually load the image file until you try to draw it or ask the system to start loading it with prepareImage or with MediaTracker. For more details, see Section 9.12 (Drawing Images).

public Locale getLocale()
public void setLocale(Locale locale)

These methods get and retrieve the current locale for use in internationalized code.

public String getParameter(String parameterName)

This method retrieves the value of parameters set in the PARAM tag inside the APPLET element in the HTML document. For details, see Section 9.7 (Reading Applet Parameters).

public String[ ][ ] getParameterInfo()

This method supplies documentation on the parameters an applet recognizes. Each element in the top-level array should be an array containing the parameter name, its type, and a short description.

public Container getParent()

In general, getParent returns the enclosing window or null if there is none.

public Dimension getSize()

The getSize method retrieves a Dimension object describing the size of the applet. Dimension has width and height fields. Thus, to get the width of the applet, use getSize().width. Technically, applets also have a set-Size() method. However, in practice this method is ignored by most browsers other than appletviewer, and the sizes specified in the WIDTH and HEIGHT attributes of the APPLET element are used as the *permanent* dimensions.

public boolean isActive()

This method determines whether the applet is "active." Applets are inactive before start is called and after stop is called; otherwise, they are active.

public void play(URL audioFile)
public void play(URL base, String audioFilename)

These methods retrieve and play an audio file in `.au` format. The JDK 1.2 also supports `.aiff`, and `.wav` format, as well as MIDI Type 0, MIDI Type 1, and RMF song formats. See `getAudioClip`.

public void repaint()
public void repaint(long millisecondDelay)
public void repaint(int x, int y, int width, int height)
public void repaint(long msDelay, int x, int y, int width,
                   int height)

The `repaint` method asks the AWT update thread to call `update`, either immediately or after the specified number of milliseconds. In either case, control is returned immediately; the actual updating and painting are done in a separate thread. You can also ask the system to repaint only a portion of the screen. Doing so results in `update` and `paint` getting a `Graphics` object with the specified clipping region set.

public void showDocument(URL htmlDoc)
   [in class AppletContext]
public void showDocument(URL htmlDoc, String frameName)
   [in class AppletContext]

These methods ask the browser to retrieve and display a Web page. They are actually part of the `AppletContext` class, not `Applet`, but they are used from applets similarly to the other methods described here. To use them, you call `getAppletContext().showDocument(...)`, not just `show-Document(...)`. The `showDocument` method is ignored by appletviewer.

public void showStatus(String message)

The `showStatus` method displays a string in the status line at the bottom of the browser.

public void update(Graphics g)

This method is called by the AWT thread after `repaint` is called. The default implementation of `update` clears the screen, then calls `paint`. Animation and double buffering applications typically override `update` to simply call `paint`, omitting the screen-clearing step. This subject is discussed further in Chapter 16 (Concurrent Programming with Java Threads).

addComponentListener, addFocusListener, addKeyListener, andMouseListener, addMouseMotionListener

These public methods add listeners to the applet for handling of various events. Each addXxxListener method has a corresponding removeXxxListener method. They are discussed in Chapter 10 (Handling Mouse and Keyboard Events).

9.6   The HTML APPLET Element

HTML Element: `<APPLET CODE="..." WIDTH=xxx`
                              `HEIGHT=xxx ...>`
                    `... </APPLET>`

Attributes: CODE, WIDTH (required), HEIGHT (required), CODEBASE, ALT, ALIGN, HSPACE, VSPACE, NAME, OBJECT, ARCHIVE (nonstandard), MAYSCRIPT (nonstandard)

The APPLET element associates a class file with a Web page. The referenced class file must extend the Applet class. Either the CODE or OBJECT attribute, as well as the WIDTH and HEIGHT attributes are required in the APPLET tag.

CODE

CODE designates the filename of the Java class file to load and is required unless the OBJECT attribute is present. This is not an absolute URL; it is interpreted with respect to the current document's base directory unless CODEBASE is supplied. Although the class file must be Web accessible, the Java source file need not be.

Core Note

CODE cannot be used to give an absolute URL. Use CODEBASE if you want to load applets from someplace other than the current document's location.

WIDTH and HEIGHT

WIDTH and HEIGHT specify the area the applet will occupy. They can be specified in pixels or as a percentage of the browser window width. However, appletviewer cannot handle percentages because there is no preexisting window for the percentage to refer to. These attributes are required in all applets.

CODEBASE

This attribute designates the base URL. The entry in CODE is taken with respect to this directory. The default behavior is to use the directory from which the main HTML document originated.

ALT

Java-enabled browsers ignore markup between <APPLET ...> and </APPLET>, so alternative text for these browsers is normally placed there. The ALT attribute was intended for browsers that have Java disabled. The attribute is not widely supported. We recommend avoiding ALT.

ALIGN

This attribute specifies alignment options and has the same possible values (LEFT, RIGHT, TOP, BOTTOM, MIDDLE) and interpretation of values as the IMG element (see Section 3.4, "Embedded Images").

HSPACE

HSPACE specifies the empty space at the left and right of the applet (in pixels).

VSPACE

VSPACE specifies the empty space at the top and bottom of the applet (in pixels).

NAME

NAME gives a name to the applet. It is used in the Java programming language for interapplet communication and by JavaScript to reference an applet by name instead of using an index in the applet array. However, a bug in Netscape prevents recognition of applets that contain uppercase characters in their names. So, if you want two applets to talk to each other, use lowercase names.

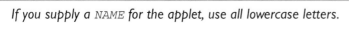

OBJECT

The OBJECT attribute can be used to supply a serialized applet that was saved with Java's object serialization facility.

ARCHIVE

ARCHIVE specifies an archive of class files to be preloaded. The archive should be in a Java ARchive (.jar) format, but Netscape 3.01 allows *uncompressed* Zip (.zip) archives. In addition to class files, you can also include images used by the applet in a JAR file. Often, the JAR filename is chosen to match the applet classname, but this approach is not required. For example, if the applet JavaMan1.class required the image Java-Man.gif, you could compress the two files into a JAR file named JavaMan.jar and specify the JAR file in the APPLET container, as in

```
<APPLET CODE="JavaMan1.class"
        ARCHIVE="JavaMan.jar"
        WIDTH=375 HEIGHT=370>
  <B>Sorry, you have a Java-challenged browser.</B>
</APPLET>
```

See Section 7.10 (Packages, Classpath, and JAR Archives) for information on creating JAR files.

MAYSCRIPT

Netscape and Internet Explorer use this attribute to determine if JavaScript is permitted to control the applet.

9.7   Reading Applet Parameters

HTML Element: `<PARAM NAME="..." VALUE="...">`
(No End Tag)
Attributes: NAME (required), VALUE (required)

An applet does not receive the String[] argument list that applications get in the main method. However, you can customize an applet by supplying information inside PARAM tags located between <APPLET ...> and </APPLET>. These parameters are declared as follows:

```
<PARAM NAME="Parameter Name" VALUE="Parameter Value">
```

The parameters are read from within an applet by getParameter ("Parameter Name"), which returns "Parameter Value" as a String, or null if the parameter is not found. Note that getParameter is case sensitive, but as with HTML in general, the PARAM, NAME, and VALUE element and attribute names themselves are case insensitive. Note also that strings should not be compared with ==, because == simply checks whether the two strings are the same object. Use the equals (case sensitive) or equalsIgnoreCase (case insensitive) method of String for this.

Although the return value of getParameter is always a String, you can convert it into an int by using the static parseInt method of the Integer class. Section 9.10 (Graphical Applications) gives an example of Integer.parseInt and lists methods to convert strings to bytes, shorts, longs, floats, and doubles.

Finally, be aware that PARAM names of WIDTH or HEIGHT override the WIDTH or HEIGHT values supplied in the APPLET tag itself and should be avoided.

Core Alert

Never use WIDTH or HEIGHT as PARAM names.

Reading Applet Parameters: An Example

Listing 9.5 gives a variation of the HelloWWW applet (Section 6.5) that allows the applet to be customized in the HTML document by a PARAM entry of the form

```
<PARAM NAME="BACKGROUND" VALUE="LIGHT">
```

or

```
<PARAM NAME="BACKGROUND" VALUE="DARK">
```

Note the check to see if the backgroundType is null, which would happen if the PARAM entry was missing or had a NAME other than "BACKGROUND" in all uppercase. If this test was not performed and the value was null, the backgroundType.equals(...) call would crash since null does not have an equals method (or any other method, for that matter). This could be avoided by

```
if ("LIGHT".equals(backgroundType))
```

instead of

```
if (backgroundType.equals("LIGHT"))
```

but many authors prefer to have an explicit test for null.

Core Approach

If you read applet parameters, be sure you handle the case when the parameter is not found.

Listing 9.6 shows an HTML document that loads the same applet three different times with different configuration parameters. Figure 9–3 shows the result in Netscape 4.08 on Windows 98.

Listing 9.5 HelloWWW2.java

```java
import java.applet.Applet;
import java.awt.*;

public class HelloWWW2 extends Applet {
  public void init() {
    setFont(new Font("SansSerif", Font.BOLD, 30));
    Color background = Color.gray;
    Color foreground = Color.darkGray;
    String backgroundType = getParameter("BACKGROUND");
    if (backgroundType != null) {
      if (backgroundType.equalsIgnoreCase("LIGHT")) {
        background = Color.white;
        foreground = Color.black;
      } else if (backgroundType.equalsIgnoreCase("DARK")) {
        background = Color.black;
        foreground = Color.white;
      }
    }
    setBackground(background);
    setForeground(foreground);
  }

  public void paint(Graphics g) {
    g.drawString("Hello, World Wide Web.", 5, 35);
  }
}
```

Listing 9.6 `HelloWWW2.html`

```
<!DOCTYPE HTML PUBLIC "-//W3C//DTD HTML 4.0 Transitional//EN">
<HTML>
<HEAD>
  <TITLE>Customizable HelloWWW Applet</TITLE>
</HEAD>
<BODY>
<H1>Customizable HelloWWW Applet</H1>
<P>
<APPLET CODE="HelloWWW2.class" WIDTH=400 HEIGHT=40>
  <PARAM NAME="BACKGROUND" VALUE="LIGHT">
  <B>Error! You must use a Java-enabled browser.</B>
</APPLET>
<P>
<APPLET CODE="HelloWWW2.class" WIDTH=400 HEIGHT=40>
  <PARAM NAME="BACKGROUND" VALUE="DARK">
  <B>Error! You must use a Java-enabled browser.</B>
</APPLET>
<P>
<APPLET CODE="HelloWWW2.class" WIDTH=400 HEIGHT=40>
  <B>Error! You must use a Java-enabled browser.</B>
</APPLET>
</BODY>
</HTML>
```

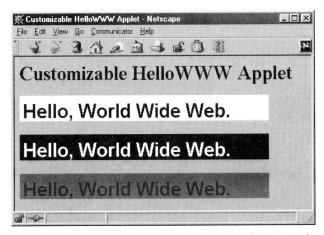

Figure 9–3 The PARAM element can be used in HTML documents to pass customizations parameters to applets.

9.8   HTML OBJECT Element

HTML Element: `<OBJECT CLASSID="..." ... > ...`
                    `</OBJECT>`
Attributes: CLASSID, CODETYPE, CODEBASE, STANDBY, WIDTH,
                  HEIGHT, NAME, ALIGN, HSPACE, VSPACE

Surprisingly, the HTML 4.0 specification deprecated the APPLET element in favor of the more universal element, OBJECT. Even though the OBJECT element can accommodate many types of objects, for example, ActiveX, Applet, QuickTime, many authors still prefer the simpler APPLET element in their HTML documents. Of course, the APPLET element forces a *Transitional* DOCTYPE declaration at the beginning of the HTML file, whereas the OBJECT element does not.

Technically, 32 attributes are defined for the OBJECT element in HTML 4.0, and browsers still support an additional 6 deprecated attributes for basic spacing and layout. Only those OBJECT attributes commonly used for an applet are presented here. The OBJECT element is fully described in Section 3.6 (Embedding Other Objects in Documents).

CLASSID

This specifies the URL. For applets, CLASSID is of the form
`java:Applet.class`.

CODETYPE

CODETYPE defines the content type of the object to download. For applets, the form is CODETYPE="application/java".

CODEBASE

The CODEBASE specifies the base URL of the object (applet).

STANDBY

This attribute provides a string to be displayed while the object is loading.

WIDTH, HEIGHT, NAME, ALIGN, HSPACE, and VSPACE

These attributes are used exactly the same way as they are for the APPLET element. See Section 9.6 (The HTML APPLET Element). Technically, ALIGN, HSPACE, and VSPACE are deprecated in HTML 4.0 in favor; see Chapter 5.

For specifying an applet with the OBJECT element, provide the CODETYPE to signify that the content type is Java and provide the CLASSID attribute to signify the URL of the class file. If the applet is located in a different directory from that of the HTML document, then add the CODEBASE attribute. An example applet using the OBJECT element is shown in Listing 9.7.

Listing 9.7   HelloWWWObject.html

```
<!DOCTYPE HTML PUBLIC "-//W3C//DTD HTML 4.0//EN">
<HTML>
<HEAD>
  <TITLE>A HelloWWW Object</TITLE>
</HEAD>

<BODY>
<H1>A HelloWWW Object</H1>

<OBJECT  CODETYPE="application/java"
         CLASSID="java:HelloWWW.class"
         CODEBASE="applets"
         WIDTH=400 HEIGHT=55>
  <PARAM NAME="codebase" value="applets">
  <PARAM NAME="code" value="HelloWWW.class">
  <PARAM NAME="BACKGROUND" VALUE="DARK">
  <B>Error! You must use a Java-enabled browser.</B>
</OBJECT>

</BODY>
</HTML>
```

Internet Explorer and appletviewer do not properly recognize the CODEBASE attribute if the class file is located in a different directory from that of the HTML file; thus, a common practice is to add a "codebase" PARAM element in the OBJECT declaration. In addition, appletviewer expects to see a CODE attribute to determine which class file to load. To resolve this minor discrepancy, simply add code as a named parameter in the OBJECT element whose value mirrors the Java class filename specified in the CLASSID attribute, for example,

```
<PARAM NAME="code" value="HelloWWW.class">
```

Core Approach

Add named code *and* codebase *parameter elements,*
< PARAM NAME=...> to the OBJECT *container for proper loading*
of the applet by both Internet Explorer and appletviewer.

9.9   The Java Plug-In

The Java Plug-In (at `http://java.sun.com/products/plugin/`), once installed, allows browsers to run the most current version of the Java Runtime Environment (JRE). This permits you to deliver applets designed with the latest version of the Java Platform that can run on either Netscape and Internet Explorer. Reliance on the vendors to include the latest Java release in their browser is no longer required. However, this capability comes at a price.

First, the Java 2 Plug-In is a hefty 5 Mbytes in size. Downloading the plug-in for your "state of the art" applet is not a viable solution for an *internet* client, especially one sitting on the other end of a V.90 (56.6K) or slower modem. However, in an *intranet* setting, the situation is different, and the Java Plug-In is a viable solution. Simply place the plug-in on a server located in the Local Area Network (LAN) for automatic downloading by *intranet* clients.

Core Approach

Avoid the Java Plug-In for Internet-based applets. The Java Plug-In is only suitable for intranet based-applets where the plug-in can easily be downloaded from a local server.

Second, the process to invoke the Java Plug-In is different on Internet Explorer than on Netscape. Internet Explorer requires the APPLET to be converted to an OBJECT element, whereas Netscape requires the APPLET to be converted to an EMBED element. Sun provides an HTML converter, located at `http://java.sun.com/products/plugin/1.3/features.html`, to automatically perform the HTML conversion of your applet.

The Java Plug-In HTML converter, shown in Figure 9–4, is simply a Java program, HTMLConverter, that provides multiple templates for targeting various platforms and browsers when converting applets in selected HTML files. Available conversion options in Version 1.3 of the Java Plug-In HTML Converter include:

- Standard (IE & Navigator) for Windows and Solaris only
- Extended (standard + all browsers/platforms)
- Internet Explorer for Windows and Solaris only
- Navigator for Windows only

Or, you can define your own template for converting the applet.

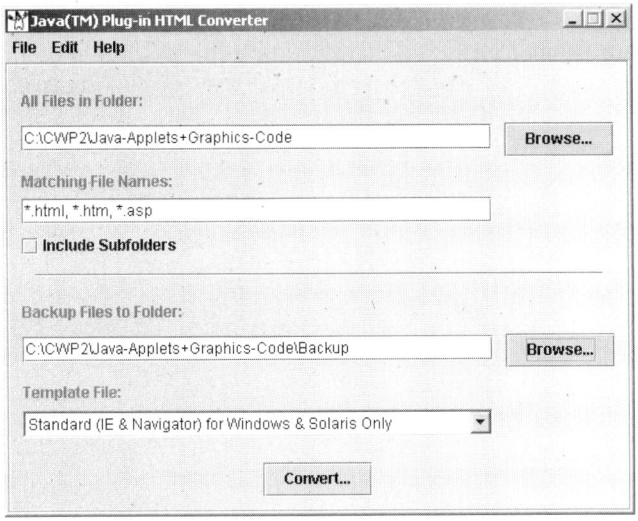

Figure 9–4   Java Plug-In HTML Converter, Version 1.3.

Based on the backup directory specified, the converter first creates a backup copy of the HTML file, then parses the document, converting each APPLET element to an OBJECT element, an EMBED element, or both, depending on the selected template and browser target. Listing 9.8 shows a typical APPLET prior to conversion by the Java Plug-In HTML Converter. The resultant APPLET container is shown in Listing 9.9 for a "Navigator for Windows Only" target, and in Listing 9.10 a "Internet Explorer for Windows & Solaris Only" target is shown.

Listing 9.8   Applet prior to conversion

```
<APPLET CODE="HelloWWW.class" CODEBASE="applets"
        WIDTH=400 HEIGHT=40>
  <PARAM NAME="BACKGROUND" VALUE="DARK">
  <B>Error! You must use a Java-enabled browser.</B>
</APPLET>
```

Listing 9.9   Applet conversion for "Navigator for Windows Only"

```
<EMBED type="application/x-java-applet;version=1.3"
   CODE = "HelloWWW.class" CODEBASE = "applets"
   WIDTH = 400 HEIGHT = 40
   BACKGROUND = "LIGHT"
   scriptable=false
   pluginspage="http://java.sun.com/products/plugin/1.3/
      plugin-install.html"
>
   <NOEMBED>
     <B>Error! You must use a Java-enabled browser.</B>
   </NOEMBED>
</EMBED>
```

Listing 9.10 Applet conversion for "Internet Explorer for Windows and Solaris Only"

```
<OBJECT classid="clsid:8AD9C840-044E-11D1-B3E9-00805F499D93"
   WIDTH = 400 HEIGHT = 40
   codebase="http://java.sun.com/products/plugin/1.3/
      jinstall-13-win32.cab#Version=1,3,0,0"
>
   <PARAM NAME = CODE VALUE = "HelloWWW.class" >
   <PARAM NAME = CODEBASE VALUE = "applets" >
   <PARAM NAME="type"
          VALUE="application/x-java-applet;version=1.3">
   <PARAM NAME="scriptable" VALUE="false">
   <PARAM NAME = "BACKGROUND" VALUE ="LIGHT">
   <B>Error! You must use a Java-enabled browser.</B>
</OBJECT>
```

Examination of the three listings shows that the HTML Converter adds a link pointing to the Java Plug-In for downloading if the plug-in is not already installed on the client browser. If the plug-in is not installed, the client is prompted to download the installation file. Typically, in an intranet setting, the required plug-in files are first downloaded from Sun and then placed on a server in the LAN where greater bandwidth is available. After the install point on the intranet is established for the plug-in, the link in the APPLET container is modified accordingly to point to the new location.

9.10 Graphical Applications

The previous examples used applets: Java programs that run within a Web browser. Local Java programs can use windows as well. Stand-alone graphical Java programs start with a Java JFrame, which is a heavyweight Swing component. Applications differ significantly from applets, in the sense that applets should be based on AWT components because most browsers do not fully support the new Swing components unless the Java Plug-In (covered in Section 9.9) is installed or Swing classes are supplied over the network.

On the other hand, Java applications run as a stand-alone instance of the Java Virtual Machine on the client workstation. Thus, you can assume that the client has a version of the JVM that does support Swing components, and in this regard, Swing components, which are truly platform-to-platform independent, should be used for all Java applications. Chapter 14 (Basic Swing) describes Swing components in much greater detail. For now, we only briefly discuss the topic. What is important throughout the remaining sections of this chapter are the graphical and image loading techniques presented.

The key steps in creating a JFrame for a Java application are to add a title through the class constructor, specify the width and height through setSize, and then pop up the frame by a call to setVisible. The following presents a basic template for creating an application frame,

```
public class MyFrame extends JFrame {
  JFrame frame;
  ...
  public static void main(String[] args) {
    frame = new MyFrame("title");
    ...
    frame.addWindowListener(new ExitListener());
    frame.setSize(width, height);
    frame.setVisible(true);
  }
}
```

One of the surprising things about frames is that the users cannot quit the (parent) frame unless you explicitly put in code to let them do so (child frames are closable). That's the purpose of adding the ExitListener object attached to the frame. The ExitListener class simply calls System.exit(0) on a window closing event. For example,

```
public class ExitListener extends WindowAdapter {
  public void windowClosing(WindowEvent event) {
    System.exit(0);
  }
}
```

Chapter 14 (Basic Swing) provides additional examples of creating Java applications. In Chapter 14, a utility class, `WindowUtilities`, provides numerous helper methods to simplify the task of creating windows. See Listing 14.1 and Listing 14.2 in Section 14.1 (Getting Started with Swing) for details.

9.11 Graphics Operations

In traditional applets and applications, the `paint` method is used to implement custom drawing. It takes a `Graphics` object as an argument; this object is used to draw onto the window. Methods outside `paint` can obtain the current `Graphics` object by calling `getGraphics`. Note that it is not reliable to simply call `getGraphics` once and store the `Graphics` object in an instance variable because subsequent invocations of `paint` get new versions. However, it *is* reliable to pass the `Graphics` object to other methods that draw and then return before `paint` returns.

Similarly, in newer *Swing* applets and applications, the `Graphics` object provides a means to perform *simple* drawing. In Swing, the `paintComponent` method, not `paint`, is used to perform basic drawing. The `paintComponent` method is only available in lightweight Swing components, which `JApplet` and `JFrame` are not. Thus, to perform drawing in Swing, a lightweight component, most often a `JPanel`, is always added to the `JApplet` or `JFrame`, and the drawing is performed in the lightweight component. Chapter 10 (Java 2D: Graphics in Java 2) and Chapter 14 (Basic Swing) provide more in-depth coverage of graphics drawing in applets and applications.

The drawing methods discussed next can be used in windows such as `Panel`, `Canvas`, `Frame`, and so forth, in addition to `Applet`. These other components are discussed in Chapter 13 (AWT Components). In addition, these drawing methods also work in lightweight Swing components, for example, a `JPanel`, but for drawing in Java 2, the use of Java 2D graphics is the recommended approach.

Java does not supply any method to determine the absolute location of an applet in the browser window, although you can discover the location of a frame. In any case, all coordinates in the following methods are relative, not absolute, and are interpreted with respect to (0,0) being the top-left corner of the window, with x increasing to the right and y increasing downward. As with many graphical systems, Java coordinates are considered to be between the screen pixels. Operations that draw the outline of figures draw the pixels down and to the right of the coordinates, and operations that fill a figure fill the interior of the coordinates. This means that drawing the outline of a rectangle will take one extra pixel on the bottom and right sides compared to filling the same rectangle.

The AWT `Graphics` object only supports simple drawing and does not support pen widths (line thicknesses) or fill patterns. However, the newer Java 2 Platform added the Java 2D API, a greatly improved graphics package based on the

Graphics2D object; Java 2D includes pen widths, stroke styles (dashed, dotted, etc.), fill patterns, antialiasing, much-improved font support, and much more. For additional information on Java 2D, see Chapter 10 or `http://java.sun.com/products/java-media/2D/`.

Core Approach

For simple drawing in applets, use the `Graphics` *object. For advanced, professional-quality graphics in applets, use the Java 2D* `Graphics2D` *object (which requires the Java Plug-In).*

The following subsections summarize the methods supported by `Graphics`.

Drawing Operations

public void clearRect(int left, int top, int width, int height)
The `clearRect` method draws a solid rectangle in the current background color.

**public void copyArea(int left, int top, int width, int height,
                        int deltaX, int deltaY)**
This method copies all pixels from the rectangle defined by (left, top, width, height) to (left+deltaX, top+deltaY, width, height).

public Graphics create()
public Graphics create(int left, int top, int width, int height)
This method creates a new graphics context. If a rectangle is specified, the context is translated to the designated location and its clipping region is set to the specified width and height.

**public void draw3DRect(int left, int top, int width, int height,
                         boolean raised)**
This method draws a 1-pixel-wide outline around the specified rectangle. If `raised` is `true`, then the left and top edges will be lighter, giving the appearance of the rectangle being above the surface of the window. If `raised` is `false`, then the rectangle is drawn with the top and left edges darker, giving the appearance of an indented rectangle. In most cases, it is a good idea to set the foreground color to be the same as the background color before calling this method, so that the shading calculation is based on the background.

public void fill3DRect(int left, int top, int width, int height, boolean raised)

This method makes a solid rectangle with a 3D outline.

public void drawArc(int left, int top, int width, int height, int startAngle, int deltaAngle)

This method draws a curve taken from a portion of the outside of an oval. The first four parameters specify the bounding rectangle for an oval. The angles specify what part of the oval will be drawn; 0 means east (3 o'clock), and angles go counterclockwise. Unlike the trigonometric functions in the Math class, angles are in degrees, not radians.

public void fillArc(int left, int top, int width, int height, int startAngle, int deltaAngle)

This method draws a solid "pie wedge" from an oval pie. See drawArc.

public void drawImage(Image image, int left, int top, ImageObserver observer)

This method draws an image in its original size. Create the image with the getImage method of Applet or Toolkit, but note that getImage operates asynchronously, so calls to drawImage immediately after getImage may draw blank images. Pass the applet or window (with this) as the argument for observer. See Section 9.12 for details on using images.

public void drawImage(Image image, int left, int top, int width, int height, ImageObserver observer)

This method draws an image scaled to fit in the rectangle defined by (left, top, width, height).

public void drawImage(Image image, int left, int top, Color bgColor, ImageObserver observer)
public void drawImage(Image image, int left, int top, int width, int height, Color bgColor, ImageObserver observer)

These methods are variations of the two previous methods for transparent images. The specified background color is used for transparent pixels.

public void drawLine(int x1, int y1, int x2, int y2)

This method draws a 1-pixel-thick line.

public void drawOval(int left, int top, int width, int height)
This method draws the outline of an oval. Arguments describe the rectangle that contains the oval. For example, `drawOval(75, 75, 50, 50)` specifies a circle of radius 50 centered at (100, 100).

public void fillOval(int left, int top, int width, int height)
This method draws a solid oval bounded by the specified rectangle.

public void drawPolygon(int[ ] xArray, int[ ] yArray,
**   int numPoints)**
public void drawPolygon(Polygon polygon)
These methods draw the outline of a polygon defined by the arrays or `Polygon` (a class that stores a series of points). The polygon is not closed by default. To make a closed polygon, specify the same location for the first and last points.

public void fillPolygon(int[ ] xArray, int[ ] yArray,
**   int numPoints)**
public void fillPolygon(Polygon polygon)
This method draws a solid polygon. The polygon is closed by default; a connection is automatically made between the first and last points.

public void drawRect(int left, int top, int width, int height)
This method draws the outline of a rectangle (1-pixel border) in the current color. See `draw3DRect` and `drawRoundRect` for variations on the theme.

public void fillRect(int left, int top, int width, int height)
This method draws a solid rectangle in the current color. The current AWT has no provision for setting fill patterns or images, so that filling would have to be reproduced manually. See also `fill3DRect` and `fillRoundRect`.

public void drawRoundRect(int left, int top, int width,
**   int height, int arcWidth,**
**   int arcHeight)**
This method draws the outline of a rectangle with rounded corners. The `arc-Width` and `arcHeight` parameters specify the amount of curve (in degrees) on the top/bottom and left/right sides. If either is zero, square corners are used.

public void drawString(String string, int left, int bottom)
This method draws a string in the current font and color with the *bottom*-left corner at the specified location. This is one of the few methods where the y coordinate refers to the bottom, not the top. There are also `drawChars` and `drawBytes` methods that take arrays of `char` or `byte`.

Colors and Fonts

public Color getColor()

This method returns the current Color. For more information on using custom and built-in colors, see the discussion of getBackground and setBackground in Section 9.5 (Other Applet Methods).

public void setColor(Color color)

This method sets the foreground color. When the Graphics object is created, the default drawing color is the foreground color of the window. Color changes made by calling setColor on the Graphics object do not change the default, so the next time paint or getGraphics is called, the new Graphics is reinitialized with the window defaults. You record permanent changes by calling the applet's or frame's setForeground method, but this call only affects drawing done with Graphics objects created *after* the call to setForeground.

public Font getFont()

This method returns the current Font. See the discussion of getFont and setFont in Section 9.5 (Other Applet Methods) for more information on fonts. Both Component (and thus Applet, which inherits from it) and Graphics have a getFontMetrics method that takes a Font as an argument. This FontMetrics object can then be used to find out the size of characters (charWidth) and strings (stringWidth) in that font.

public void setFont(Font font)

This method sets the font to be used by the drawString method. The font changes specified by the setFont method of the Graphics object do not persist to the next invocation of paint or to the next time getGraphics is called. Permanent font changes can be specified with the setFont method of the applet or other associated component.

Drawing Modes

public void setXORMode(Color color)

This method specifies that subsequent drawing operations will use XOR: the color of each pixel in the result will be determined by bitwise XORing the specified color with the color of the pixel at the location being drawn. Thus, a line drawn in XOR mode over a multicolor background will be in multiple colors. The resultant color at each pixel is unpredictable, since the XOR is done on the bits as they appear in the internal representation, which may vary from machine to machine. But drawing something using XOR twice in a row will return it to the original condition. This is useful for rubberbanding or other short-term erasable drawing done on top of some more complex drawing.

You should avoid using `Color.black` as the specified color, since it will be represented internally by all zeros on many (but not all) platforms, so the XOR results in the original color and your drawing will be invisible. Set the drawing mode back to normal with `setPaintMode()`.

public void setPaintMode()
This method sets the drawing mode back to normal (vs. XOR) mode. That is, drawing will use the normal foreground color only.

Coordinates and Clipping Rectangles

public void clipRect(int left, int top, int width, int height)
This method shrinks the clipping region to the intersection of the current clipping region and the specified rectangle.

public Rectangle getClipBounds()
This method returns the current clipping rectangle, which may be `null`.

public Shape getClip()
This method returns a `Shape` object describing the clipping region.

pubic void setClip(Shape clippingRegion)
This method designates a new clipping region.

public void translate(int deltaX, int deltaY)
This method moves the origin by the specified amount.

9.12 Drawing Images

Applets and applications written in the Java programming language can load and display static images in GIF or JPEG format, as well as GIF89A images (a.k.a. "animated GIF").

Image drawing is done in two steps. First, a remote or local image is registered by means of the getImage method of `Applet` or `Toolkit`. Second, the image is drawn on the screen with the drawImage method of `Graphics`. You can draw the image at its regular size or supply an explicit width and height. The key point to remember is that calls to getImage don't actually initiate image loading. Instead, Java technology doesn't start loading the image until it is needed.

Actual loading of the image is done in a background thread, and the image can be drawn incrementally while loading. Instead of waiting until you try to draw the image, you can specify that the image be loaded in advance by calling prepare-Image or using a MediaTracker object. The first approach (prepareImage) loads the image in the background, returning control to you immediately. This behavior is normally an advantage because processing can continue while the program might otherwise be waiting for a slow network connection. However, if draw-Image is called before the image is done loading, it just draws the portion that has arrived (possibly none) without giving any error messages. The paint method (or the paintComponent method in the case of lightweight Swing components) will get called once the image is done, so assuming drawImage is being invoked from paint, the image will eventually be drawn in its entirety. In the meantime, however, partial images may be drawn and the width and height of the image may be incorrect. If you want to be sure the image is finished before you do any drawing, you can use the second approach: the MediaTracker class.

Loading Applet Images from Relative URLs

The Applet class contains a getImage method that takes two arguments: a URL corresponding to a directory and a string corresponding to a filename relative to that URL. For the relative URLs, supply getCodeBase() (the applet's home directory) or getDocumentBase() (the Web page's home directory) for the URL argument. The getImage will not succeed until the applet's context is set up. This means that you should call getImage in init rather than trying to directly initialize the Image instance variable by:

```
private Image myImage = getImage(...); // fails
```

Core Warning

Trying to declare and initialize Image instance variables in the body of an applet will fail. Initialize them in init or a method that runs after init.

To actually draw the image, use the drawImage of the Graphics class. If you're using a method other than paint (which is automatically passed the current Graphics context), you can obtain the window's Graphics context by calling get-Graphics. There are two variations of drawImage:

```
drawImage(image, left, top, window)
```

and

```
drawImage(image, left, top, width, height, window)
```

The first uses the image's normal size; the second stretches the image to fit in the specified area. Technically, the last argument is an `ImageObserver`; in ordinary cases, you just use the current window (the applet in this case). So, for image drawing being performed in the paint method, `this` is almost always used as the last argument to `drawImage`. Listings 9.11 and 9.12 show an applet that loads images from the `images` subdirectory of the applet's home directory. The result is shown in Figure 9–5.

Listing 9.11 JavaMan1.java

```java
import java.applet.Applet;
import java.awt.*;

/** An applet that loads an image from a relative URL. */

public class JavaMan1 extends Applet {
  private Image javaMan;

  public void init() {
    javaMan = getImage(getCodeBase(),"images/Java-Man.gif");
  }

  public void paint(Graphics g) {
    g.drawImage(javaMan, 0, 0, this);
  }
}
```

Listing 9.12 JavaMan1.html

```html
<!DOCTYPE HTML PUBLIC "-//W3C//DTD HTML 4.0 Transitional//EN">
<HTML>
<HEAD>
  <TITLE>JavaMan1</TITLE>
</HEAD>
<BODY BGCOLOR="WHITE">
<H1>JavaMan1</H1>

<APPLET CODE="JavaMan1.class" WIDTH=370 HEIGHT=365>
  <B>Sorry, you have a Java-challenged browser.</B>
</APPLET>

</BODY>
</HTML>
```

Figure 9-5   The most common way to load images in applets is to use `getImage(getCodeBase(), path)`, or `getImage(getDocumentBase(), path)`.

Loading Applet Images from Absolute URLs

Using absolute URLs is a bit more cumbersome than using relative ones because making a `URL` object requires catching the exception that would result if the URL is in an illegal format. See Section 8.12 (Exceptions) for a review of handling exceptions. Furthermore, because the `SecurityManager` of most browsers only allows an applet to load images from the machine that served the applet, this approach is not particularly common. However, it is quite possible that you store images in a different location than that of the applets and their associated HTML documents, so using an absolute URL would be more convenient.

Listings 9.13 and 9.14 give an example applet and associated HTML document, with the result shown in Figure 9–6. Note the `try/catch` block around the URL constructor, and note, too, that the `java.net` package is imported: it contains the `URL` and `MalformedURLException` classes. Using this approach does not change the fact that the image loading is postponed until the image is needed, so the image might appear to flicker into view as progressively larger pieces are drawn. If this is a problem for your application, see the next sections on how to partially or completely preload the image.

Listing 9.13 JavaMan2.java

```java
import java.applet.Applet;
import java.awt.*;
import java.net.*;

/** An applet that loads an image from an absolute
 *  URL on the same machine that the applet came from.
 */

public class JavaMan2 extends Applet {
  private Image javaMan;

  public void init() {
    try {
      URL imageFile = new URL("http://www.corewebprogramming.com" +
                             "/images/Java-Man.gif");
      javaMan = getImage(imageFile);
    } catch(MalformedURLException mue) {
      showStatus("Bogus image URL.");
      System.out.println("Bogus URL");
    }
  }

  public void paint(Graphics g) {
    g.drawImage(javaMan, 0, 0, this);
  }
}
```

Listing 9.14 JavaMan2.html

```html
<!DOCTYPE HTML PUBLIC "-//W3C//DTD HTML 4.0 Transitional//EN">
<HTML>
<HEAD>
  <TITLE>JavaMan2</TITLE>
</HEAD>
<BODY BGCOLOR="WHITE">
<H1>JavaMan2</H1>

<APPLET CODE="JavaMan2.class" WIDTH=370 HEIGHT=365>
  <B>Sorry, you have a Java-challenged browser.</B>
</APPLET>

</BODY>
</HTML>
```

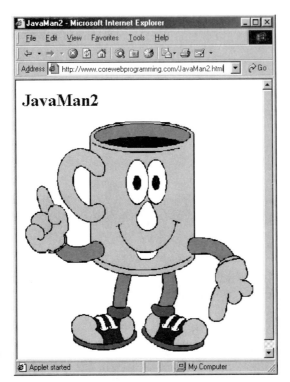

Figure 9–6 Applets can load images from absolute URLs, but security restrictions apply.

Loading Images in Applications

Graphical applications can load images from absolute URLs or from local files by using the getImage method of the Toolkit class. The concept of a relative URL is not completely applicable because applications are not normally associated with a Web page. Nevertheless, even though applications do not have a two-argument version of getImage as applets do, a URL object can be created from an existing URL and a filename. You can use this technique if, for instance, you want to load multiple images from the same directory. You can obtain the current Toolkit from any graphical object by calling getToolkit() or from an arbitrary object by calling Toolkit.getDefaultToolkit(). For instance, Listing 9.15 creates a simple JPanel and then draws an Image in the JPanel. Note the use of System.get-Property("user.dir") to make the filename relative to the directory containing the application. This use makes it easier to move directories around or to move the application from machine to machine. Figure 9–7 shows the result. The source code for WindowUtilities, which simply encapsulates the panel in a JFrame and attaches a WindowListener, is provided in Chapter 14 (Basic Swing).

Core Approach

Whenever possible, refer to local files by using pathnames relative to the application's directory.

Listing 9.15 JavaMan3.java

```
import java.awt.*;
import javax.swing.*;

/** An application that loads an image from a local file.
 *  Applets are not permitted to do this.
 */

class JavaMan3 extends JPanel {
  private Image javaMan;

  public JavaMan3() {
    String imageFile = System.getProperty("user.dir") +
                       "/images/Java-Man.gif";
    javaMan = getToolkit().getImage(imageFile);
    setBackground(Color.white);
  }

  public void paintComponent(Graphics g) {
    super.paintComponent(g);
    g.drawImage(javaMan, 0, 0, this);
  }

  public static void main(String[] args) {
    JPanel panel = new JavaMan3();
    WindowUtilities.setNativeLookAndFeel();
    WindowUtilities.openInJFrame(panel, 380, 390);
  }
}
```

Figure 9–7   Images can be loaded in applications through `getToolkit().getImage(arg)` or `Toolkit.getDefaultToolkit().getImage(arg)`. The `arg` can be a URL or local filename.

9.13 Preloading Images

In many cases, you'd like the system to start loading the images as soon as possible, rather than waiting until you try to draw them with `drawImage`. This is particularly true if the images will not be drawn until the user initiates some action such as clicking on a button or choosing a menu option. That way, if the user doesn't act right away, the image might arrive before action is taken. You can use the `prepareImage` method to start the image loading in a background process and immediately return control to you. There are two versions of `prepareImage`, one for each version of `drawImage`:

```
prepareImage(image, window)
```

and

```
prepareImage(image, width, height, window)
```

Each time you stretch the image, it counts as a new one, so be sure to call `prepareImage` once for each size at which you plan to draw. For example, Listing 9.16 shows an application that draws an image only when the user presses a button. The time from when the user presses the button to the time when the drawing is completed is printed in a textfield. If a `-preload` command-line argument is supplied, `prepareImage` is called. Figure 9–8 shows the result when `prepareImage` is not used, and Figure 9–9 shows what happens when the same image is loaded, -preload is specified, and the button is not clicked until several seconds have gone by. Of course, the time shown in Figure 9–8 could be much smaller or much larger, depending upon the speed of your network connection, but the fact remains that the time before the button is pressed is wasted unless you use prepareImage.

For now, don't worry about the details of Listing 9.16; we'll cover user interfaces at length in the upcoming chapters. Instead, concentrate on what goes on in the registerImage method, which is called from the Preload constructor.

Listing 9.16 Preload.java

```
import java.awt.*;
import java.awt.event.*;
import javax.swing.*;
import java.net.*;

/** A class that compares the time to draw an image preloaded
 *  (getImage, prepareImage, and drawImage) vs. regularly
 *  (getImage and drawImage).
 *  <P>
 *  The answer you get the regular way is dependent on the
 *  network speed and the size of the image, but if you assume
 *  you load the applet "long" (compared to the time the image
 *  loading requires) before pressing the button, the drawing
 *  time in the preloaded version depends only on the speed of
 *  the local machine.
 */

public class Preload extends JPanel implements ActionListener {

  private JTextField timeField;
  private long start = 0;
  private boolean draw = false;
  private JButton button;
  private Image plate;

  public Preload(String imageFile, boolean preload) {
    setLayout(new BorderLayout());
    button = new JButton("Display Image");
    button.setFont(new Font("SansSerif", Font.BOLD, 24));
    button.addActionListener(this);
    JPanel buttonPanel = new JPanel();
    buttonPanel.add(button);
    timeField = new JTextField(25);
    timeField.setEditable(false);
    timeField.setFont(new Font("SansSerif", Font.BOLD, 24));
    buttonPanel.add(timeField);
    add(buttonPanel, BorderLayout.SOUTH);
    registerImage(imageFile, preload);
```

(continued)

Listing 9.16 `Preload.java` *(continued)*

```java
  }

  /** No need to check which object caused this,
   *   since the button is the only possibility.
   */

  public void actionPerformed(ActionEvent event) {
    draw = true;
    start = System.currentTimeMillis();
    repaint();
  }

  // Do getImage, optionally starting the loading.

  private void registerImage(String imageFile, boolean preload) {
    try {
      plate = getToolkit().getImage(new URL(imageFile));
      if (preload) {
        prepareImage(plate, this);
      }
    } catch(MalformedURLException mue) {
      System.out.println("Bad URL: " + mue);
    }
  }

  /** If button has been clicked, draw image and
   *   show elapsed time. Otherwise, do nothing.
   */

  public void paintComponent(Graphics g) {
    super.paintComponent(g);
    if (draw) {
      g.drawImage(plate, 0, 0, this);
      showTime();
    }
  }

  // Show elapsed time in textfield.
  private void showTime() {
    timeField.setText("Elapsed Time: " + elapsedTime() +
                      " seconds.");
  }

  // Time in seconds since button was clicked.
```

(continued)

Listing 9.16 `Preload.java` *(continued)*

```java
private double elapsedTime() {
    double delta = (double)(System.currentTimeMillis() - start);
    return(delta/1000.0);
}

public static void main(String[] args) {
    JPanel preload;

    if (args.length == 0) {
        System.out.println("Must provide URL");
        System.exit(0);
    }
    if (args.length == 2 && args[1].equals("-preload")) {
        preload = new Preload(args[0], true);
    } else {
        preload = new Preload(args[0], false);
    }

    WindowUtilities.setNativeLookAndFeel();
    WindowUtilities.openInJFrame(preload, 1000, 750);
}
}
```

Figure 9–8 Results when no preload argument is supplied. If you use getImage and drawImage only, the image is not loaded over the network until the system tries to draw it.

Figure 9–9   Results when a preload argument is supplied. If you use prepareImage, the system starts loading the image immediately.

9.14 Controlling Image Loading: Waiting for Images and Checking Status

Even if you preload images, you often want to be sure that the images have finished loading before you perform certain tasks. For instance, because you cannot determine an image's width and height until the image has finished loading, programs that try to draw outlines around images must be careful how they go about it. As an example of a common but incorrect approach, consider Listings 9.17 and 9.18, which record the image's width and height in init, then draw a rectangle in paint based on these dimensions. Figure 9–10 shows the result in Internet Explorer 5 on a Windows 98 system; the rectangle is missing because the height is –1.

Listing 9.17 ImageBox.java

```java
import java.applet.Applet;
import java.awt.*;

/** A class that incorrectly tries to load an image and draw an
 *  outline around it. Don't try this at home.
 */

public class ImageBox extends Applet {
  private int imageWidth, imageHeight;
  private Image image;

  public void init() {
    String imageName = getParameter("IMAGE");
    if (imageName != null) {
      image = getImage(getDocumentBase(), imageName);
    } else {
      image = getImage(getDocumentBase(), "error.gif");
    }
    setBackground(Color.white);

    // The following is wrong, since the image won't be done
    // loading, and -1 will be returned.
    imageWidth = image.getWidth(this);
    imageHeight = image.getHeight(this);
  }

  public void paint(Graphics g) {
    g.drawImage(image, 0, 0, this);
    g.drawRect(0, 0, imageWidth, imageHeight);
  }
}
```

Listing 9.18 ImageBox.html

```html
<!DOCTYPE HTML PUBLIC "-//W3C//DTD HTML 4.0 Transitional//EN">
<HTML>
<HEAD>
  <TITLE>ImageBox</TITLE>
</HEAD>
<BODY>
<H1>ImageBox</H1>
<APPLET CODE="ImageBox.class" WIDTH=235 HEIGHT=135>
  <PARAM NAME="IMAGE" VALUE="images/surfing.gif">
  Sorry, you need a <B>real</B>browser.
</APPLET>
</BODY>
</HTML>
```

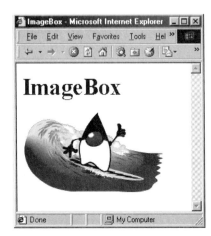

Figure 9-10 Trying to determine an image's size when you aren't sure it has finished loading can lead to bad results.

The solution to this problem is to use the `MediaTracker` class. This class lets you start to load one or more images, register them with a `MediaTracker` through `addImage`, then at some point explicitly wait by calling `waitForID` or `wait-ForAll` until all the images are loaded. `MediaTracker` also has various methods for checking whether the image file was not found or whether other errors occurred. These methods are summarized below.

MediaTracker

public void addImage(Image image, int id)
public void addImage(Image image, int id, int width, int height)

These methods register a normal or scaled image with a given ID. You can register one or more images with a particular ID, then either check the status of, or wait for, images with a given ID. You can also wait for all images; when you do so, the system tries to load the images with lower IDs first.

public boolean checkAll()
public boolean checkAll(boolean startLoading)

These methods return `true` if all the images registered with the `MediaTracker` have finished loading. They return `false` otherwise. If you supply `true` for the `startLoading` argument, the system will begin loading the images if it wasn't doing so already. Note that you should not normally put `CheckAll` inside a loop to wait until images are loaded. Instead, use `wait-ForAll`, which accomplishes the same goal without consuming nearly as much of the CPU resources.

public boolean checkID(int id)
public boolean checkID(int id, boolean startLoading)

These methods are similar to checkForAll, but they only report the status of images registered under a particular ID.

public Object[ ] getErrorsAny()
public Object[ ] getErrorsID(int id)

These methods return an array of images that have encountered an error while loading.

public boolean isErrorAny()
public boolean isErrorID(int id)

These methods return true if any image encountered an error while loading; false otherwise.

public void removeImage(Image image)
public void removeImage(Image image, int id)
public void removeImage(Image image, int id, int width,
                                        int height)

These methods let you "unregister" an image.

public int statusAll()
public int statusID(int id, boolean startLoading)

These methods return the bitwise inclusive OR of the status flags of all images being loaded. The status flag options are MediaTracker.LOADING, MediaTracker.ABORTED, MediaTracker.ERRORED, and MediaTracker.COMPLETE. Images that haven't started loading have zero for their status. If you supply true for the startLoading argument, the system will begin loading the images if it wasn't doing so already.

public void waitForAll()
public boolean waitForAll(long milliseconds)

These methods start loading any images that are not already loading; the methods do not return until all the images are loaded or the specified time has elapsed. The system starts loading images with lower IDs before those with higher ones. The methods throw an InterruptedException when done; you are required to catch it.

public void waitForID(int id)
public boolean waitForID(int id, long milliseconds)
These methods start loading any images registered under the specified ID that are not already loading; the methods do not return until all images are loaded or the specified time has elapsed. The methods throw an `InterruptedException` when done; you are required to catch it.

Listings 9.19 and 9.20 show a corrected version of the `ImageBox` applet that waits until the image is loaded before trying to determine its size. Figure 9–11 shows the result.

Listing 9.19 `BetterImageBox.java`

```
import java.applet.Applet;
import java.awt.*;

/** This version fixes the problems associated with ImageBox by
 *  using a MediaTracker to be sure the image is loaded before
 *  you try to get its dimensions.
 */

public class BetterImageBox extends Applet {
  private int imageWidth, imageHeight;
  private Image image;

  public void init() {
    String imageName = getParameter("IMAGE");
    if (imageName != null) {
      image = getImage(getDocumentBase(), imageName);
    } else {
      image = getImage(getDocumentBase(), "error.gif");
    }
    setBackground(Color.white);
    MediaTracker tracker = new MediaTracker(this);
    tracker.addImage(image, 0);
    try {
      tracker.waitForAll();
    } catch(InterruptedException ie) {}
    if (tracker.isErrorAny()) {
      System.out.println("Error while loading image");
    }
```

(continued)

Listing 9.19 `BetterImageBox.java` *(continued)*

```java
    // This is safe: image is fully loaded
    imageWidth = image.getWidth(this);
    imageHeight = image.getHeight(this);
  }

  public void paint(Graphics g) {
    g.drawImage(image, 0, 0, this);
    g.drawRect(0, 0, imageWidth, imageHeight);
  }
}
```

Listing 9.20 `BetterImageBox.html`

```html
<!DOCTYPE HTML PUBLIC "-//W3C//DTD HTML 4.0 Transitional//EN">
<HTML>
<HEAD>
  <TITLE>ImageBox</TITLE>
</HEAD>
<BODY>
<H1>ImageBox</H1>
<APPLET CODE="BetterImageBox.class" WIDTH=235 HEIGHT=135>
  <PARAM NAME="IMAGE" VALUE="images/surfing.gif">
  Sorry, you need a <B>real</B>browser.
</APPLET>
</BODY>
</HTML>
```

Figure 9–11 With `MediaTracker` you can wait until images are done loading.

Because waiting for images and checking for errors is the most common use of MediaTracker, it is convenient to combine these two tasks into a single method. Listing 9.21 defines a TrackerUtil class with two static methods: waitForImage and waitForImages. The waitForImage method can be used as follows:

```
someImage = getImage(...);
doSomeOtherStuff();
if (TrackerUtil.waitForImage(someImage, this))
  // someImage finished loading.
else
  // error loading someImage.
```

Similarly, the waitForImages method can be used as follows:

```
image1 = getImage(...);
image2 = getImage(...);
...
imageN = getImage(...);
doSomeOtherStuff();
Image[] images = { image1, image2, ... , imageN };
if (TrackerUtil.waitForImages(images, this))
  // all images finished loading.
else
  // error loading an image.
```

If you want more control over image loading than MediaTracker provides, you can override the imageUpdate method of the window. See the API for details.

Listing 9.21 TrackerUtil.java

```java
import java.awt.*;

/** A utility class that lets you load and wait for an image or
 *  images in one fell swoop. If you are loading multiple
 *  images, only use multiple calls to waitForImage if you
 *  <B>need</B> loading to be done serially. Otherwise, use
 *  waitForImages, which loads concurrently, which can be
 *  much faster.
 */

public class TrackerUtil {
  public static boolean waitForImage(Image image, Component c) {
    MediaTracker tracker = new MediaTracker(c);
    tracker.addImage(image, 0);
    try {
      tracker.waitForAll();
    } catch(InterruptedException ie) {}
    if (tracker.isErrorAny()) {
```

(continued)

Listing 9.21 `TrackerUtil.java` *(continued)*

```
          return(false);
      } else {
          return(true);
      }
  }

  public static boolean waitForImages(Image[] images,
                                      Component c) {
      MediaTracker tracker = new MediaTracker(c);
      for(int i=0; i<images.length; i++) {
          tracker.addImage(images[i], 0);
      }
      try {
          tracker.waitForAll();
      } catch(InterruptedException ie) {}
      if (tracker.isErrorAny()) {
          return(false);
      } else {
          return(true);
      }
  }
}
```

9.15 Summary

An applet is a type of graphical program that can be embedded in a Web page. Applets run on the client machine and consequently have various security restrictions. Applets are created by extending the `java.applet.Applet` class and are associated with a Web page through the `APPLET` element. Applets based on the newer Swing graphical components are possible; because browser support is lacking, Swing applets require installation of the Java Plug-In or require the Swing classes to be sent over the network, which is not a suitable approach for most Internet clients.

Graphical Java programs that will not be run in a Web browser are created by use of the Swing `JFrame` class. In the case of applets, drawing is typically performed in the `paint` method, whereas in the case of applications, drawing is performed in the `paintComponent` method of a lightweight Swing component, usually a `JPanel` is added to the `JFrame`. Both methods take a `Graphics` object as an argument; the `Graphics` class has a variety of basic drawing operations. But for professional-looking, advanced drawing techniques, including antialiasing, gradients, and textures, use the Java 2D API, which is the topic of the next chapter.

Lastly, another graphics operation of particular interest is `drawImage`, which can be used to draw GIF or JPEG images loaded earlier by the `getImage` method of `Applet` or `Toolkit`. Images loaded this way are loaded in a background thread and can be drawn in incremental pieces unless loading is explicitly controlled by use of a `MediaTracker`. For applets, any images referred to by an absolute or relative URL can only be loaded from the same server on which the class files are located.

JAVA 2D: GRAPHICS IN JAVA 2

Topics in This Chapter

- Drawing 2D shapes
- Tiling an image inside a shape
- Using local fonts
- Drawing with custom pen settings
- Changing the opaqueness of objects
- Translating and rotating coordinate systems

Chapter 10

nyone who has even lightly ventured into developing detailed graphical programs with the Abstract Windowing Toolkit (AWT) has quickly realized that the capabilities of the Graphics object are rather limited—not surprisingly, since Sun developed the AWT over a short period when moving Java from embedded applications to the World Wide Web. Shortcomings of the AWT include limited available fonts, lines drawn with a single-pixel width, shapes painted only in solid colors, and the inability to properly scale drawings prior to printing.

Java 2D is probably the second most significant addition to the Java 2 Platform, surpassed only by the Swing GUI components. The Java 2D API provides a robust package of drawing and imaging tools to develop elegant, professional, high-quality graphics. The following important Java 2D capabilities are covered in this chapter:

- Colors and patterns: graphics can be painted with color gradients and fill patterns.
- Transparent drawing: opaqueness of a shape is controlled through an alpha transparency value.
- Local fonts: all local fonts on the platform are available for drawing text.
- Explicit control of the drawing pen: thickness of lines, dashing patterns, and segment connection styles are available.
- Transformations of the coordinate system—translations, scaling, rotations, and shearing—are available.

These exciting capabilities come at a price—the Java 2D API is part of the Java Foundation Classes introduced in Java 2. Thus, unlike Swing, which can be added to the JDK 1.1, you cannot simply add Java 2D to the JDK 1.1. The Java Runtime Environment (JRE) for the Java 2 Platform is required for execution of 2D graphical applications, and a Java 2-capable browser or the Java Plug-In, covered in Section 9.9 (The Java Plug-In), is required for execution of 2D graphical applets. Complete documentation of the Java 2D API, along with additional developer information, is located at `http://java.sun.com/products/java-media/2D/`. Also, the JDK 1.3 includes a 2D demonstration program located in the installation directory: `root/jdk1.3/demo/jfc/Java2D/`. In addition, Java 2D also supports high-quality printing; this topic is covered in Chapter 15 (Advanced Swing).

10.1 Getting Started with Java 2D

In Java 2, the `paintComponent` method is supplied with a `Graphics2D` object, which contains a much richer set of drawing operations than the AWT `Graphics` object. However, to maintain compatibility with Swing as used in Java 1.1, the declared type of the `paintComponent` argument is `Graphics` (`Graphics2D` inherits from `Graphics`), so you must first cast the `Graphics` object to a `Graphics2D` object before drawing. Technically, in Java 2, all methods that receive a `Graphics` object (`paint`, `paintComponent`, `getGraphics`) actually receive a `Graphics2D` object.

The traditional approach for performing graphical drawing in Java 1.1 is reviewed in Listing 10.1. Here, every AWT `Component` defines a `paint` method that is passed a `Graphics` object (from the `update` method) on which to perform drawing. In contrast, Listing 10.2 illustrates the basic approach for drawing in Java 2D. All Swing components call `paintComponent` to perform drawing. Technically, you can use the `Graphics2D` object in the AWT `paint` method; however, the `Graphics2D` class is included only with the Java Foundations Classes, so the best course is to simply perform drawing on a Swing component, for example, a `JPanel`. Possible exceptions would include direct 2D drawing in the `paint` method of a `JFrame`, `JApplet`, or `JWindow`, since these are heavyweight Swing components without a `paintComponent` method.

Listing 10.1 Drawing graphics in Java 1.1

```
public void paint(Graphics g) {
  // Set pen parameters
  g.setColor(someColor);
  g.setFont(someLimitedFont);

  // Draw a shape
  g.drawString(...);
  g.drawLine(...)
  g.drawRect(...);      // outline
  g.fillRect(...);      // solid
  g.drawPolygon(...);   // outline
  g.fillPolygon(...);   // solid
  g.drawOval(...);      // outline
  g.fillOval(...);      // solid
  ...
}
```

Listing 10.2 Drawing graphics in the Java 2 Platform

```
public void paintComponent(Graphics g) {
  // Clear background if opaque
  super.paintComponent(g);
  // Cast Graphics to Graphics2D
  Graphics2D g2d = (Graphics2D)g;
  // Set pen parameters
  g2d.setPaint(fillColorOrPattern);
  g2d.setStroke(penThicknessOrPattern);
  g2d.setComposite(someAlphaComposite);
  g2d.setFont(anyFont);
  g2d.translate(...);
  g2d.rotate(...);
  g2d.scale(...);
  g2d.shear(...);
  g2d.setTransform(someAffineTransform);
  // Allocate a shape
  SomeShape s = new SomeShape(...);
  // Draw shape
  g2d.draw(s);  // outline
  g2d.fill(s);  // solid
}
```

The general approach for drawing in Java 2D is outlined as follows.

Cast the Graphics object to a Graphics2D object.

Always call the paintComponent method of the superclass first, because the default implementation of Swing components is to call the paint method of the associated ComponentUI; this approach maintains the component look and feel. In addition, the default paintComponent method clears the off-screen pixmap because Swing components implement double buffering. Next, cast the Graphics object to a Graphics2D object for Java 2D drawing.

```
public void paintComponent(Graphics g) {
  super.paintComponent(g);
  Graphics2D g2d = (Graphics2D)g;
  g2d.doSomeStuff(...);
  ...
}
```

Core Approach

When overriding the paintComponent *method of a Swing component, always call* super.paintComponent.

Modify drawing parameters (optional).

Drawing parameters are applied to the Graphics2D object, not to the Shape object. Changes to the graphics context (Graphics2D) apply to every subsequent drawing of a Shape.

```
g2d.setPaint(fillColorOrPattern);
g2d.setStroke(penThicknessOrPattern);
g2d.setComposite(someAlphaComposite);
g2d.setFont(someFont);
g2d.translate(...);
g2d.rotate(...);
g2d.scale(...);
g2d.shear(...);
g2d.setTransform(someAffineTransform);
```

Create a Shape object.

```
Rectangle2D.Double rect = ...;
Ellipse2D.Double ellipse = ...;
Polygon poly = ...;
GeneralPath path = ...;
// Satisfies Shape interface
SomeShapeYouDefined shape = ...;
```

Draw an outlined or filled version of the Shape.

Pass in the Shape object to either the draw or fill method of the
Graphics2D object. The graphic context (any paint, stroke, or transform
applied to the Graphics2D object) will define exactly how the shape is drawn
or filled.

```
g2d.draw(someShape);
g2d.fill(someShape);
```

The Graphics2D class extends the Graphics class and therefore inherits all the
familiar AWT graphic methods covered in Section 9.11 (Graphics Operations). The
Graphics2D class adds considerable functionality to drawing capabilities. Methods
that affect the appearance or transformation of a Shape are applied to the
Graphics2D object. Once the graphics context is set, all subsequent Shapes that
are drawn will undergo the same set of drawing rules. Keep in mind that the methods
that alter the coordinate system (rotate, translate, scale) are cumulative.

Useful Graphics2D Methods

The more common methods of the Graphics2D class are summarized below.

public void draw(Shape shape)

This method draws an outline of the shape, based on the current settings of
the Graphics2D context. By default, a shape is bound by a Rectangle with
the upper-left corner positioned at (0,0). To position a shape elsewhere, first
apply a transformation to the Graphics2D context: rotate, transform,
translate.

public boolean drawImage(BufferedImage image,
BufferedImageOp filter,
int left, int top)

This method draws the BufferedImage with the upper-left corner located at
(left, top). A filter can be applied to the image. See Section 10.3 (Paint
Styles) for details on using a BufferedImage.

public void drawString(String s, float left, float bottom)

The method draws a string in the bottom-left corner of the specified location,
where the location is specified in floating-point units. The Java 2D API does
not provide an overloaded drawString method that supports double arguments. Thus, the method call drawString(s, 2.0, 3.0) will not compile.
Correcting the error requires explicit statement of floating-point, literal arguments, as in drawString(s, 2.0f, 3.0f).

Java 2D supports fractional coordinates to permit proper scaling and transformations of the coordinate system. Java 2D objects live in the User Coordinate Space where the axes are defined by floating-point units. When the graphics are rendered on the screen or a printer, the User Coordinate Space is transformed to the Device Coordinate Space. The transformation maps 72 User Coordinate Space units to one physical inch on the output device. Thus, before the graphics are rendered on the physical device, fractional values are converted to their nearest integral values.

public void fill(Shape shape)

This method draws a solid version of the `shape`, based on the current settings of the `Graphics2D` context. See the `draw` method for details of positioning.

public void rotate(double theta)

This method applies a rotation of theta *radians* to the `Graphics2D` transformation. The point of rotation is about (x, y)=(0, 0). This rotation is *added* to any existing rotations of the `Graphics2D` context. See Section 10.7 (Coordinate Transformations).

public void rotate(double theta, double x, double y)

This method also applies a rotation of theta *radians* to the `Graphics2D` transformation. However, the point of rotation is about (x, y). See Section 10.7 (Coordinate Transformations) for details.

public void scale(double xscale, yscale)

This method applies a linear scaling to the x- and y-axis. Values greater than 1.0 expand the axis, and values less than 1.0 shrink the axis. A value of -1 for `xscale` results in a mirror image reflected across the x-axis. A `yscale` value of -1 results in a reflection about the y-axis.

public void setComposite(Composite rule)

This method specifies how the pixels of a new shape are combined with the existing background pixels. You can specify a custom composition `rule` or apply one of the predefined `AlphaComposite` rules: `AlphaComposite.Clear`, `AlphaComposite.DstIn`, `AlphaComposite.DstOut`, `AlphaComposite.DstOver`, `AlphaComposite.Src`, `AlphaComposite.SrcIn`, `AlphaComposite.SrcOut`, `AlphaComposite.ScrOver`.

To create a custom `AlphaComposite` rule, call `getInstance` as in

```
g2d.setComposite(AlphaComposite.SrcOver);
```

or

```
int type = AlphaComposite.SRC_OVER;
float alpha = 0.75f;
AlphaComposite rule =
    AlphaComposite.getInstance(type, alpha);
g2d.setComposite(rule);
```

The second approach permits you to set the alpha value associated with composite rule, which controls the transparency of the shape. By default, the transparency value is 1.0f (opaque). See Section 10.4 (Transparent Drawing) for details. Clarification of the mixing rules is given by T. Porter and T. Duff in "Compositing Digital Images," *SIGGRAPH* **84**, pp. 253–259.

public void setPaint(Paint paint)

This method sets the painting style of the Graphics2D context. Any style that implements the Paint interface is legal. Existing styles in the Java 2 Platform include a solid Color, a GradientPaint, and a TexturePaint.

public void setRenderingHints(Map hints)

This method allows you to control the quality of the 2D drawing. The AWT includes a RenderingHints class that implements the Map interface and provides a rich suite of predefined constants. Quality aspects that can be controlled include antialiasing of shape and text edges, dithering and color rendering on certain displays, interpolation between points in transformations, and fractional text positioning. Typically, antialiasing is turned on, and the image rendering is set to quality, not speed:

```
RenderingHints hints = new RenderingHints(
        RenderingHints.KEY_ANTIALIASING,
        RengeringHints.VALUE_ANTIALIAS_ON);
hints.add(new RenderingHints(
        RenderingHints.KEY_RENDERING,
        RenderingHints.VALUE_RENDER_QUALITY));
```

public void setStroke(Stroke pen)

The Graphics2D context determines how to draw the outline of a shape, based on the current Stroke. This method sets the drawing Stroke to the behavior defined by pen. A user-defined pen must implement the Stroke interface. The AWT includes a BasicStroke class to define the end styles of a line segment, to specify the joining styles of line segments, and to create dashing patterns. See Section 10.6 (Stroke Styles) for details.

public void transform(AffineTransform matrix)

This method applies the Affine transformation, matrix, to the existing transformation of the Graphics2D context. The Affine transformation can include both a translation and a rotation. See Section 10.7 (Coordinate Transformations).

public void translate(double x, double y)

This method translates the origin by (x, y) *units*. This translation is added to any prior translations of the Graphics2D context. The units passed to the drawing primitives initially represent 1/72nd of an inch, which on a monitor, amounts to one pixel. However, on a printer, one unit might map to 4 or 9 pixels (300 dpi or 600 dpi).

public void setPaintMode()

This method overrides the setPaintMode method of the Graphics object. This implementation also sets the drawing mode back to "normal" (vs. XOR) mode. However, when applied to a Graphics2D object, this method is equivalent to setComposite(AlphaComposite.SrcOver), which places the source shape on top of the destination (background) when drawn.

public void setXORMode(Color color)

This method overrides the setXORMode for the Graphics object. For a Graphics2D object, the setXORMode method defines a new compositing rule that is outside the eight predefined Porter-Duff alpha compositing rules (see Section 10.4). The XOR compositing rule does not account for transparency (alpha) values and is calculated by a bitwise XORing of the source color, destination color, and the passed-in XOR color. Using XOR twice in a row when you are drawing a shape will return the shape to the original color. The transparency (alpha) value is ignored under this mode, and the shape will always be opaque. In addition, antialiasing of shape edges is not supported under XOR mode.

10.2 Drawing Shapes

With the AWT, you generally drew a shape by calling the drawXxx or fillXxx method of the Graphics object. In Java 2D, you generally create a Shape object, then call either the draw or fill method of the Graphics2D object, supplying the Shape object as an argument. For example:

```
public void paintComponent(Graphics g) {
  super.paintComponent(g);
  Graphics2D g2d = (Graphics2D)g;
  // Assume x, y, and diameter are instance variables.
  Ellipse2D.Double circle =
    new Ellipse2D.double(x, y, diameter, diameter);
  g2d.fill(circle);
  ...
}
```

Most of the Shape classes define both a Shape.Double and a Shape.Float version of the class. Depending on the version of the class, the coordinate locations are stored as either double precision numbers (Shape.Double) or single precision numbers (Shape.Float). The idea is that single precision coordinates might be slightly faster to manipulate on some platforms. You can still call the familiar drawXxx methods of the Graphics class if you like; the Graphics2D object inherits from the Graphics object. This approach is necessary for drawString and drawImage and possibly is convenient for draw3DRect.

Shape Classes

Arguments to the Graphics2D draw and fill methods must implement the Shape interface. You can create your own shapes, of course, but you can also use major built-in classes: Arc2D, Area, CubicCurve2D, Ellipse2D, GeneralPath, Line2D, QuadCurve2D, Rectangle2D, and RoundRectangle2D. Each of these classes is contained in the java.awt.geom package. Each of these classes, except for Area, Polygon, and Rectangle, has float and double constructors.

The classes Polygon and Rectangle, holdovers from Java 1.1, also implement the Shape interface. These two shapes are covered in Section 9.11 (Graphics Operations).

The most common constructors for these Shapes follow.

public Arc2D.Float(float left, float top, float width, float height,
float startAngle, float deltaAngle,
int closure)
public Arc2D.Double(double left, double top, double width,
double height, double startAngle,
double deltaAngle, int closure)

These constructors create an arc by selecting a portion of a full ellipse whose bounding rectangle has an upper-left corner located at the (left, top). The vertex of the arc (ellipse) is located at the origin of the bounding rectangle. The reference for the start angle is the positive x-axis. Angles are specified in *degrees* and represent *arc* degrees, not true degrees. Arc angles are defined such that the 45 degree line runs from the ellipse center to the upper-right corner of the bounding rectangle. The arc closure is one of Arc2D.CHORD, Arc2D.OPEN, or Arc2D.PIE.

public Area(Shape shape)

This constructor creates an Area with the given Shape. Areas support geometrical operations, for example: add, subtract, intersect, and exclusiveOr.

public CubicCurve2D.Float(float xStart, float yStart,
float pX, float pY,
float qX, float qY,
float xEnd, float yEnd)
public CubicCurve2D.Double(double xStart, double yStart,
double pX, double pY,
double qX, double qY,
double xEnd, double yEnd)

These constructors create a `CubicCurve2D` shape representing a curve (spline) from (`xStart`, `yStart`) to (`xEnd`, `yEnd`). The curve has two control points (`pX`, `pY`) and (`qX`, `qY`) that impact the curvature of the line segment joining the two end points.

public Ellipse2D.Float(float left, float top, float width,
float height)
public Ellipse2D.Double(double left, double top,
double width, double height)

These constructors create an ellipse bounded by a rectangle of dimension `width` by `height`. The `Ellipse2D` class inherits from the `Rectangular-Shape` class and contains the same methods as common to `Rectangle2D` and `RoundRectangle2D`.

public GeneralPath()

A `GeneralPath` is an interesting class because you can define all the line segments to create a brand-new `Shape`. This class supports a handful of methods to add lines and Bézier (cubic) curves to the path: `closePath`, `curveTo`, `lineTo`, `moveTo`, and `quadTo`. Appending a path segment to a `General-Path` without first performing an initial `moveTo` generates an `IllegalPath-StateException`. An example of creating a `GeneralPath` follows:

```
GeneralPath path = new GeneralPath();
path.moveTo(100,100);
path.lineTo(300,205);
path.quadTo(205,250,340,300);
path.lineTo(340,350);
path.closePath();
```

public Line2D.Float(float xStart, float yStart, float xEnd,
float yEnd)
public Line2D.Double(double xStart, double yStart,
double xEnd, double yEnd)

These constructors create a `Line2D` shape representing a line segment from (`xStart`, `yStart`) to (`xEnd`, `yEnd`).

public Line2D.Float(Point p1, Point p2)
public Line2D.Double(Point p1, Point p2)

These constructors create a `Line2D` shape representing a line segment from `Point p1` to `Point p2`.

public QuadCurve2D.Float(float xStart, float yStart,
float pX, double pY,
float xEnd, float yEnd)
public QuadCurve2D.Double(double xStart, double yStart,
double pX, double pY,
double xEnd, double yEnd)

These constructors create a `Shape` representing a curve from (`xStart`, `yStart`) to (`xEnd`, `yEnd`). The point (`pX`, `pY`) represents a control point impacting the curvature of the line segment connecting the two end points.

public Rectangle2D.Float(float top, float left, float width,
float height)
public Rectangle2D.Double(double top, double left,
double width, double height)

These constructors create a `Rectangle2D` shape with the upper-left corner located at (`top`, `left`) and a dimension of `width` by `height`.

public RoundRectangle2D.Float(float top, float left,
float width, float height,
float arcX, float arcY)
public RoundRectangle2D.Double(double top, double left,
double width, double height,
double arcX, double arcY)

These two constructors create a `RectangleShape` with rounded corners. The upper-left corner of the rectangle is located at (`top`, `left`), and the dimension of the rectangle is `width` by `height`. The arguments `arcX` and `arcY` represent the distance from the rectangle corners (in the respective x direction and y direction) at which the rounded curve of the corners start.

An example of drawing a circle (`Ellispse2D` with equal width and height) and a rectangle (`Rectangle2D`) is presented in Listing 10.3. Here, the circle is filled completely, and an outline of the rectangle is drawn, both based on the default context settings of the `Graphics2D` object. Figure 10–1 shows the result. The method `getCircle` plays a role in other examples throughout this chapter. `ShapeExample` uses `WindowUtilities` in Listing 14.1 and `ExitListener` in Listing 14.2 to create a closable `JFrame` container for the drawing panel.

Most of the code examples throughout this chapter are presented as Java applications. To convert the examples to applets, follow the given template:

```
import java.awt.*;
import javax.swing.*;
public class YourApplet extends JApplet {
  public void init() {
    JPanel panel = new ChapterExample();
    panel.setBackground(Color.white);
    getContentPane().add(panel);
  }
}
```

The basic idea is to create a JApplet and add the chapter example, which is implemented as a JPanel, to the contentPane of the JApplet. Depending on the particular example you are converting, you may need to set the background color of the JPanel. Once the corresponding HTML file is created (with an applet of the same dimensions as the original JFrame), you can either use appletviewer or convert the HTML file to support the Java Plug-In. See Section 9.9 (The Java Plug-In) for details on converting the HTML file.

Listing 10.3 ShapeExample.java

```
import javax.swing.*;   // For JPanel, etc.
import java.awt.*;      // For Graphics, etc.
import java.awt.geom.*; // For Ellipse2D, etc.

/** An example of drawing/filling shapes with Java 2D in
 *  Java 1.2 and later.
 */

public class ShapeExample extends JPanel {
  private Ellipse2D.Double circle =
    new Ellipse2D.Double(10, 10, 350, 350);
  private Rectangle2D.Double square =
    new Rectangle2D.Double(10, 10, 350, 350);

  public void paintComponent(Graphics g) {
    clear(g);
    Graphics2D g2d = (Graphics2D)g;
    g2d.fill(circle);
    g2d.draw(square);
  }
```

(continued)

Listing 10.3 `ShapeExample.java` *(continued)*

```
  // super.paintComponent clears off screen pixmap,
  // since we're using double buffering by default.
  protected void clear(Graphics g) {
    super.paintComponent(g);
  }

  protected Ellipse2D.Double getCircle() {
    return(circle);
  }

public static void main(String[] args) {
    WindowUtilities.openInJFrame(new ShapeExample(), 380, 400);
  }
}
```

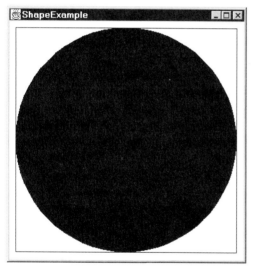

Figure 10–1 An ellipse (circle) drawn with a box outline in Java 2D.

10.3 Paint Styles

When you fill a `Shape`, the `Graphics2D` object uses the settings associated with the internal `Paint` attribute. The `Paint` setting can be a `Color` (solid color), a `GradientPaint` (gradient fill gradually combining two colors), a `TexturePaint` (tiled image), or a new version of `Paint` that you write yourself. Use `setPaint` and `get-`

Paint to change and retrieve the `Paint` settings. Note that `setPaint` and `get-Paint` supersede the `setColor` and `getColor` methods that were used in `Graphics`.

Paint Classes

Arguments to the `Graphics2D` `setPaint` method (and return values of `getPaint`) must implement the `Paint` interface. Here are the major built-in `Paint` classes.

Color

The `Color` class defines the same `Color` constants (`Color.red`, `Color.yellow`, etc.) as the AWT version but provides additional constructors to account for a transparency (alpha) value. A `Color` is represented by a 4-byte `int` value, where the three lowest bytes represent the red, green, and blue component, and the highest-order byte represents the alpha component. By default, colors are opaque with an alpha value of 255. A completely transparent color has an alpha value of 0. The common `Color` constructors are described below.

public Color(int red, int green, int blue)
public Color(float int, float green, float blue)

These two constructors create an opaque `Color` with the specified red, green, and blue components. The `int` values should range from 0 to 255, inclusive. The `float` values should range from 0.0f to 1.0f. Internally, each `float` value is converted to an `int` being multiplied by 255 and rounded up.

public Color(int red, int green, int blue, int alpha)
public Color(float red, float green, float blue, float alpha)

These two constructors create a `Color` object where the transparency value is specified by the `alpha` argument. See the preceding constructor for legal ranges for the `red`, `green`, `blue`, and `alpha` values.

Before drawing, you can also set the transparency (opaqueness) of a `Shape` by first creating an `AlphaComposite` object, then applying the `AlphaComposite` object to the `Graphics2D` context through the `setComposite` method. See Section 10.4 (Transparent Drawing) for details.

GradientPaint

A `GradientPaint` represents a smooth transition from one color to a second color. Two points establish a gradient line in the drawing, with one color located at one end point of the line and the second color located at other end point of the line. The color will smoothly transition along the gradient line, with parallel color bands extending orthogonally to the gradient line. Depending on the value of a boolean flag, the color pattern will repeat along the *extended* gradient line until the end of the shape is reached.

public GradientPaint(float xStart, float yStart, Color colorStart, float xEnd, float yEnd, Color colorEnd)

This constructor creates a `GradientPaint`, beginning with a color of `color-Start` at (`xStart, yStart`) and finishing with a color of `colorEnd` at (`xEnd, yEnd`). The gradient is nonrepeating (a single gradient cycle).

public GradientPaint(float xStart, float yStart, Color colorStart, float xEnd, float yEnd, Color colorEend, boolean repeat)

This constructor is the same as the preceding constructor, except that a boolean flag, `repeat`, can be set to produce a pattern that continues to repeat beyond the end point (cyclic).

TexturePaint

A `TexturePaint` is simply an image that is tiled across the shape. When creating a textured paint, you need to specify both the image on the tile and the tile size.

public TexturePaint(BufferedImage image, Rectangle2D tilesize)

The `TexturePaint` constructor maps a `BufferedImage` to a `Rectangle2D` and then tiles the rectangle. Creating a `BufferedImage` from a GIF or JPEG file is a pain. First, load an `Image` normally, get the size of the image, create a `BufferedImage` that sizes with `Buffered-Image.TYPE_INT_ARGB` as the image type, get the `BufferedImage`'s `Graphics` object through `createGraphics`, then draw the `Image` into the `BufferedImage` using `drawImage`.

Listing 10.4 is an example of applying a gradient fill prior to drawing a circle. The gradient begins with a red color (`Color.red`) located at (0, 0) and gradually changes to a yellow color (`Color.yellow`) located at (185, 185) near the center of the circle. The gradient fill pattern repeats across the remaining area of the circle, as shown in Figure 10–2.

Listing 10.4 `GradientPaintExample.java`

```java
import java.awt.*;

/** An example of applying a gradient fill to a circle. The
 *  color definition starts with red at (0,0), gradually
 *  changing to yellow at (175,175).
 */

public class GradientPaintExample extends ShapeExample {
  private GradientPaint gradient =
    new GradientPaint(0, 0, Color.red, 175, 175, Color.yellow,
                      true); // true means to repeat pattern

  public void paintComponent(Graphics g) {
    clear(g);
    Graphics2D g2d = (Graphics2D)g;
    drawGradientCircle(g2d);
  }

  protected void drawGradientCircle(Graphics2D g2d) {
    g2d.setPaint(gradient);
    g2d.fill(getCircle());
    g2d.setPaint(Color.black);
    g2d.draw(getCircle());
  }

  public static void main(String[] args) {
    WindowUtilities.openInJFrame(new GradientPaintExample(),
                                 380, 400);
  }
}
```

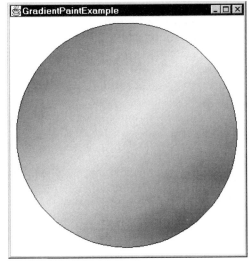

Figure 10–2 A circle drawn with a gradient fill in Java 2D.

Tiled Images as Fill Patterns

To use tiled images, you first create a `TexturePaint` object and pass the object to the `setPaint` method of `Graphics2D`, just as with solid colors and gradient fills. The `TexturePaint` constructor takes a `BufferedImage` and a `Rectangle2D` as arguments. The `BufferedImage` specifies what to draw, and the `Rectangle2D` specifies where the tiling starts. The rectangle also determines the size of the image that is drawn; the `BufferedImage` is scaled to the rectangle size before rendering. Creating a `BufferedImage` to hold a custom drawing is relatively straightforward: call the `BufferedImage` constructor with a width, a height, and a type of `BufferedImage.TYPE_INT_RGB`, then call `createGraphics` on the buffered image to get a `Graphics2D` with which to draw. For example,

```
int width =32;
int height=32;
BufferedImage bufferedImage =
  new BufferedImage(width, height
                     BufferedImage.TYPE_INT_RGB);
Graphics2D g2d = bufferedImage.createGraphics();
g2d.draw(someShape);
. . .
TexturePaint texture =
  new TexturePaint(bufferedImage,
                    new Rectangle(0, 0, width, height));
```

The `Graphics2D` object returned from `createGraphics` is bound to the `BufferedImage`. At that point, any drawing to the `Graphics2D` object is drawn to the `BufferedImage`. The texture "tile" in this example is a rectangle 32 pixels wide and 32 pixels high, where the drawing on the tile is what is contained in the buffered image.

Creating a `BufferedImage` from an image file is a bit harder. First, load an `Image` from an image file, then use `MediaTracker` to be sure that the image is loaded, then create an empty `BufferedImage` by using the `Image` width and height. Next, get the `Graphics2D` with `createGraphics`, then draw the `Image` onto the `BufferedImage`. This process has been wrapped up in the `getBufferedImage` method of the `ImageUtilities` class given in Listing 10.6.

An example of creating tiled images as fill patterns is shown in Listing 10.5. The result is presented in Figure 10–3. Two textures are created, one texture is an image of a blue drop, and the second texture is an image of Marty Hall contemplating another Java innovation while lounging in front of his vehicle. The first texture is applied before the large inverted triangle is drawn, and the second texture is applied before the centered rectangle is drawn. In the second case, the `Rectangle` is the same size as the `BufferedImage`, so the texture is tiled only once.

Listing 10.5 `TiledImages.java`

```java
import javax.swing.*;
import java.awt.*;
import java.awt.geom.*;
import java.awt.image.*;

/** An example of using TexturePaint to fill objects with tiled
 *  images. Uses the getBufferedImage method of ImageUtilities
 *  to load an Image from a file and turn that into a
 *  BufferedImage.
 */

public class TiledImages extends JPanel {
  private String dir = System.getProperty("user.dir");
  private String imageFile1 = dir + "/images/marty.jpg";
  private TexturePaint imagePaint1;
  private Rectangle imageRect;
  private String imageFile2 = dir + "/images/bluedrop.gif";
  private TexturePaint imagePaint2;
  private int[] xPoints = { 30, 700, 400 };
  private int[] yPoints = { 30, 30, 600 };
  private Polygon imageTriangle = new Polygon(xPoints, yPoints, 3);
  public TiledImages() {
    BufferedImage image =
      ImageUtilities.getBufferedImage(imageFile1, this);
    imageRect = new Rectangle(235, 70, image.getWidth(),
                                       image.getHeight());
    imagePaint1 = new TexturePaint(image, imageRect);
    image = ImageUtilities.getBufferedImage(imageFile2, this);
    imagePaint2 =
      new TexturePaint(image, new Rectangle(0, 0, 32, 32));
  }

  public void paintComponent(Graphics g) {
    super.paintComponent(g);
    Graphics2D g2d = (Graphics2D)g;
    g2d.setPaint(imagePaint2);
    g2d.fill(imageTriangle);
    g2d.setPaint(Color.blue);
    g2d.setStroke(new BasicStroke(5));
    g2d.draw(imageTriangle);
    g2d.setPaint(imagePaint1);
    g2d.fill(imageRect);
    g2d.setPaint(Color.black);
    g2d.draw(imageRect);
  }

  public static void main(String[] args) {
    WindowUtilities.openInJFrame(new TiledImages(), 750, 650);
  }
}
```

Listing 10.6 ImageUtilities.java

```java
import java.awt.*;
import java.awt.image.*;

/** A class that simplifies a few common image operations, in
 *  particular, creating a BufferedImage from an image file and
 *  using MediaTracker to wait until an image or several images
 *  are done loading.
 */

public class ImageUtilities {

  /** Create Image from a file, then turn that into a
   *  BufferedImage.
   */

  public static BufferedImage getBufferedImage(String imageFile,
                                               Component c) {
    Image image = c.getToolkit().getImage(imageFile);
    waitForImage(image, c);

    BufferedImage bufferedImage =
      new BufferedImage(image.getWidth(c), image.getHeight(c),
                        BufferedImage.TYPE_INT_RGB);
    Graphics2D g2d = bufferedImage.createGraphics();
    g2d.drawImage(image, 0, 0, c);
    return(bufferedImage);
  }

  /** Take an Image associated with a file, and wait until it is
   *  done loading (just a simple application of MediaTracker).
   *  If you are loading multiple images, don't use this
   *  consecutive times; instead, use the version that takes
   *  an array of images.
   */

  public static boolean waitForImage(Image image, Component c) {
    MediaTracker tracker = new MediaTracker(c);
    tracker.addImage(image, 0);
    try {
      tracker.waitForAll();
    } catch(InterruptedException ie) {}
    return(!tracker.isErrorAny());
  }
```

(continued)

Listing 10.6 `ImageUtilities.java` *(continued)*

```
/** Take some Images associated with files, and wait until they
 *   are done loading (just a simple application of
 *   MediaTracker).
 */

public static boolean waitForImages(Image[] images, Component c)
{
    MediaTracker tracker = new MediaTracker(c);
    for(int i=0; i<images.length; i++)
      tracker.addImage(images[i], 0);
    try {
      tracker.waitForAll();
    } catch(InterruptedException ie) {}
    return(!tracker.isErrorAny());
  }
}
```

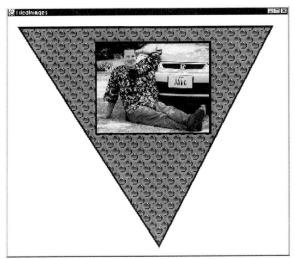

Figure 10–3 By creation of `TexturePaint` definition, images can be tiled across any shape.

10.4 Transparent Drawing

Java 2D permits you to assign transparency (alpha) values to drawing operations so that the underlying graphics partially shows through when you draw shapes or images. You set a transparency by creating an `AlphaComposite` object and then passing the `AlphaComposite` object to the `setComposite` method of the `Graphics2D` object. You create an `AlphaComposite` by calling Alpha-

`Composite.getInstance` with a mixing rule designator and a transparency (or "alpha") value. For example,

```
float alpha = 0.75f;
int type = AlphaComposite.SRC_OVER;
AlphaComposite composite =
    AlphaComposite.getInstance(type, alpha);
```

The `AlphaComposite` API provides eight built-in mixing rules, but the one normally used for drawing with transparency settings is `AlphaComposite.SRC_OVER`, a *source* over *destination* mixing rule that places the source (shape) over the destination (background). A complete definition of the mixing rule was provided by T. Porter and T. Duff in "Compositing Digital Images," *SIGGRAPH* **84**, pp. 253–259. Alpha values can range from 0.0f (completely transparent) to 1.0f (completely opaque).

Listing 10.7 demonstrates changing the transparency setting before drawing a red square that is partially overlapping a blue square. As shown in Figure 10–4, 11 opaque blue squares are drawn, equally spaced across the panel. Partially overlapping is a red square drawn with an initial alpha value of 0.0f at the far left. The red square is repeatedly drawn at new locations across the panel with alpha values that gradually increase by a step size of 0.1f until, finally, total opaqueness is reached at the far right with an alpha value of 1.0f.

Recall from Section 10.3 (Paint Styles) that the transparency (alpha) value of a color can be changed directly. Thus, for this example, the transparency of the red box could be directly set by a new color, as in:

```
private void drawSquares(Graphics2D g2d, float alpha) {
    g2d.setPaint(Color.blue);
    g2d.fill(blueSquare);
    Color color = new Color(1, 0, 0, alpha); //Red
    g2d.setPaint(color);
    g2d.fill(redSquare);
}
```

Here, the assumption is that the original compositing rule is `Alpha-Composite.SRC_OVER`, which is the default for the `Graphics2D` object. If the alpha value is set both through an `AlphaComposite` object and a `Color` object, the alpha values are multiplied to obtain the final transparency value.

Listing 10.7 `TransparencyExample.java`

```
import javax.swing.*;
import java.awt.*;
import java.awt.geom.*;

/** An illustration of the use of AlphaComposite to make
 *  partially transparent drawings.
 */
```

(continued)

Listing 10.7 `TransparencyExample.java` *(continued)*

```
public class TransparencyExample extends JPanel {
  private static int gap=10, width=60, offset=20,
                     deltaX=gap+width+offset;
  private Rectangle
    blueSquare = new Rectangle(gap+offset, gap+offset, width,
                               width),
    redSquare = new Rectangle(gap, gap, width, width);

  private AlphaComposite makeComposite(float alpha) {
    int type = AlphaComposite.SRC_OVER;
    return(AlphaComposite.getInstance(type, alpha));
  }

  private void drawSquares(Graphics2D g2d, float alpha) {
    Composite originalComposite = g2d.getComposite();
    g2d.setPaint(Color.blue);
    g2d.fill(blueSquare);
    g2d.setComposite(makeComposite(alpha));
    g2d.setPaint(Color.red);
    g2d.fill(redSquare);
    g2d.setComposite(originalComposite);
  }

  public void paintComponent(Graphics g) {
    super.paintComponent(g);
    Graphics2D g2d = (Graphics2D)g;
    for(int i=0; i<11; i++) {
      drawSquares(g2d, i*0.1F);
      g2d.translate(deltaX, 0);
    }
  }

  public static void main(String[] args) {
    String title = "Transparency example: alpha of the top " +
                   "(red) square ranges from 0.0 at the left " +
                   "to 1.0 at the right. Bottom (blue) square " +
                   "is opaque.";
    WindowUtilities.openInJFrame(new TransparencyExample(),
                                 11*deltaX + 2*gap,
                                 deltaX + 3*gap,
                                 title, Color.lightGray);
  }
}
```

Figure 10–4 Changing the transparency setting can allow the background image behind the shape to show through.

10.5 Using Local Fonts

In Java 2D you can use the same logical font names as in Java 1.1, namely, Serif (e.g., Times), SansSerif (e.g., Helvetica or Arial), Monospaced (e.g., Courier), Dialog, and DialogInput. However, you can also use arbitrary local fonts installed on the platform if you first look up the entire list, which may take a few seconds. Look up the fonts with the `getAvailableFontFamilyNames` or `getAllFonts` methods of `GraphicsEnvironment`. For example:

```
GraphicsEnvironment env =
    GraphicsEnvironment.getLocalGraphicsEnvironment();
```

Then, add

```
env.getAvailableFontFamilyNames();
```

or

```
env.getAllFonts();  // Much slower!
```

Despite a misleading description in the API, trying to use an available local font without first looking up the fonts, as above, gives the same result as asking for an unavailable font: a default font instead of the actual one.

Core Warning

Trying to use a local font without first looking up the fonts results in a default font being used instead of the actual one. You only need to incur this overhead the first time that you need to create a new Font *object.*

Note that `getAllFonts` returns an array of real `Font` objects that you can use like any other `Font` but is much slower. If all you need to do is tell Java to make all local fonts available, always use `getAvailableFontFamilyNames`.

The best approach is to loop down `getAvailableFontFamilyNames`, checking for the preferred font name and having several backup names to use if the first choice is not available. If you pass an unavailable family name to the `Font` constructor, a default font (SansSerif) is used. Listing 10.8 provides the basic code for listing all available fonts on the platform.

Listing 10.8 `ListFonts.java`

```java
import java.awt.*;

/** Lists the names of all available fonts. */

public class ListFonts {
  public static void main(String[] args) {
    GraphicsEnvironment env =
      GraphicsEnvironment.getLocalGraphicsEnvironment();
    String[] fontNames = env.getAvailableFontFamilyNames();
    System.out.println("Available Fonts:");
    for(int i=0; i<fontNames.length; i++)
      System.out.println("  " + fontNames[i]);
  }
}
```

Listing 10.9 gives a simple example of first looking up the available fonts on the system and then setting the style to Goudy Handtooled BT prior to drawing the String "Java 2D". The result is shown in Figure 10–5. On platforms without Goudy Handtooled BT, the text is drawn in the default font, SansSerif.

Listing 10.9 `FontExample.java`

```java
import java.awt.*;

/** An example of using local fonts to perform drawing in
 *  Java 2D.
 */

public class FontExample extends GradientPaintExample {
  public FontExample() {
    GraphicsEnvironment env =
      GraphicsEnvironment.getLocalGraphicsEnvironment();
    env.getAvailableFontFamilyNames();
    setFont(new Font("Goudy Handtooled BT", Font.PLAIN, 100));
  }

  protected void drawBigString(Graphics2D g2d) {
    g2d.setPaint(Color.black);
    g2d.drawString("Java 2D", 25, 215);
  }

  public void paintComponent(Graphics g) {
    clear(g);
```

(continued)

Listing 10.9 `FontExample.java` *(continued)*

```
    Graphics2D g2d = (Graphics2D)g;
    drawGradientCircle(g2d);
    drawBigString(g2d);
  }

  public static void main(String[] args) {
    WindowUtilities.openInJFrame(new FontExample(), 380, 400);
  }
}
```

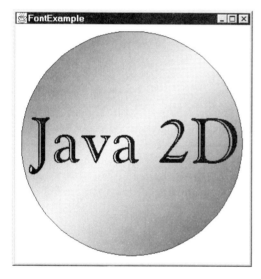

Figure 10–5 In Java 2D, writing text in any local font installed on the platform is possible.

10.6 Stroke Styles

In the AWT, the `drawXxx` methods of `Graphics` resulted in solid, 1-pixel-wide lines. Furthermore, drawing commands that consisted of multiple-line segments (e.g., `drawRect` and `drawPolygon`) had a predefined way of joining the line segments and terminating segments that did not join to others. Java 2D gives you much more flexibility. In addition to setting the pen color or pattern (through `setPaint`, as discussed in the previous section), with Java 2D you can set the pen thickness and dashing pattern and specify the way in which line segments end and are joined together. To control how lines are drawn, first create a `BasicStroke` object, then use the `setStroke` method to tell the `Graphics2D` object to use the `Basic-Stroke` object.

Stroke Attributes

Arguments to setStroke must implement the Stroke interface, and the Basic-Stroke class is the sole built-in class that implements Stroke. Here are the BasicStroke constructors.

public BasicStroke()

This constructor creates a BasicStroke with a pen width of 1.0, the default cap style of CAP_SQUARE, and the default join style of JOIN_MITER. See the following examples of pen widths and cap/join styles.

public BasicStroke(float penWidth)

This constructor creates a BasicStroke with the specified pen width and the default cap/join styles (CAP_SQUARE and JOIN_MITER).

public BasicStroke(float penWidth, int capStyle, int joinStyle)

This constructor creates a BasicStroke with the specified pen width, cap style, and join style. The cap style can be one of CAP_SQUARE (make a square cap that extends past the end point by half the pen width—the default), CAP_BUTT (cut off segment exactly at end point—use this one for dashed lines), or CAP_ROUND (make a circular cap centered on the end point, with a diameter of the pen width). The join style can be one of JOIN_MITER (extend outside edges of lines until they meet—the default), JOIN_BEVEL (connect outside corners of outlines with straight line), or JOIN_ROUND (round off corner with circle with diameter equal to the pen width).

public BasicStroke(float penWidth, int capStyle, int joinStyle, float miterLimit)

This constructor is the same as above, but you can limit how far up the line the miter join can proceed (default is 10.0). A miterLimit of 10.0 is a reasonable default, so you rarely need this constructor.

public BasicStroke(float penWidth, int capStyle, int joinStyle, float miterLimit, float[] dashPattern, float dashOffset)

This constructor lets you make dashed lines by specifying an array of opaque (entries at even array indices) and transparent (odd indices) segments. The offset, which is often 0.0, specifies where to start in the dashing pattern.

Two examples of controlling the pen attribute follow. The first example, Listing 10.10, sets the pen width to 8 pixels before drawing an outlined circle, and the second example, Listing 10.11, creates a dashed line. The dash pattern is

```
float[] dashPattern { 30, 10, 10, 10 };
```

where the values alternate between the dash length and the gap length. The result is an opaque dash for 30 units, a transparent dash for 10 units, another opaque dash for 10 units, and, finally, a transparent dash for the last 10 units. The pattern is repeated along the line segment. The results for the two examples are shown in Figure 10–6 and Figure 10–7, respectively.

Listing 10.10 `StrokeThicknessExample.java`

```java
import java.awt.*;

/** An example of controlling the Stroke (pen) widths when
 *  drawing.
 */

public class StrokeThicknessExample extends FontExample {
  public void paintComponent(Graphics g) {
    clear(g);
    Graphics2D g2d = (Graphics2D)g;
    drawGradientCircle(g2d);
    drawBigString(g2d);
    drawThickCircleOutline(g2d);
  }

  protected void drawThickCircleOutline(Graphics2D g2d) {
    g2d.setPaint(Color.blue);
    g2d.setStroke(new BasicStroke(8)); // 8-pixel wide pen
    g2d.draw(getCircle());
  }

  public static void main(String[] args) {
    WindowUtilities.openInJFrame(new StrokeThicknessExample(),
                                 380, 400);
  }
}
```

Figure 10–6 The outline of a circle drawn with a pen width of 8 pixels.

Listing 10.11 DashedStrokeExample.java

```java
import java.awt.*;

/** An example of creating a custom dashed line for drawing.
 */

public class DashedStrokeExample extends FontExample {
  public void paintComponent(Graphics g) {
    clear(g);
    Graphics2D g2d = (Graphics2D)g;
    drawGradientCircle(g2d);
    drawBigString(g2d);
    drawDashedCircleOutline(g2d);
  }

  protected void drawDashedCircleOutline(Graphics2D g2d) {
    g2d.setPaint(Color.blue);
    // 30-pixel line, 10-pixel gap, 10-pixel line, 10-pixel gap
    float[] dashPattern = { 30, 10, 10, 10 };
    g2d.setStroke(new BasicStroke(8, BasicStroke.CAP_BUTT,
                                  BasicStroke.JOIN_MITER, 10,
                                  dashPattern, 0));
    g2d.draw(getCircle());
  }

  public static void main(String[] args) {
    WindowUtilities.openInJFrame(new DashedStrokeExample(),
                                 380, 400);
  }
}
```

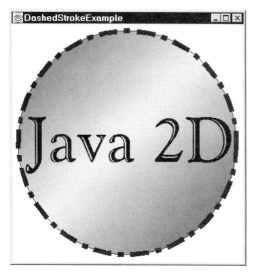

Figure 10–7 The outline of a circle drawn with a dashed line segment.

As a final example of pen styles, Listing 10.12 demonstrates the effect of different styles for *joining* line segments, and different styles for creating line end points (*cap* settings). Figure 10–8 clearly illustrates the differences of the three joining styles (JOIN_MITER, JOIN_BEVEL, and JOIN_ROUND), as well as the differences of the three cap styles (CAP_SQUARE, CAP_BUTT, and CAP_ROUND).

Listing 10.12 LineStyles.java

```java
import javax.swing.*;
import java.awt.*;
import java.awt.geom.*;

/** A demonstration of different controls when joining two line
 *  segments. The style of the line end point is controlled
 *  through the capStyle parameter.
 */

public class LineStyles extends JPanel {
  private GeneralPath path;
  private static int x = 30, deltaX = 150, y = 300,
                     deltaY = 250, thickness = 40;
  private Circle p1Large, p1Small, p2Large, p2Small,
                 p3Large, p3Small;
  private int compositeType = AlphaComposite.SRC_OVER;
```

(continued)

Listing 10.12 `LineStyles.java` *(continued)*

```
private AlphaComposite transparentComposite =
  AlphaComposite.getInstance(compositeType, 0.4F);
private int[] caps =
  { BasicStroke.CAP_SQUARE, BasicStroke.CAP_BUTT,
    BasicStroke.CAP_ROUND };
private String[] capNames =
  { "CAP_SQUARE", "CAP_BUTT", "CAP_ROUND" };
private int[] joins =
  { BasicStroke.JOIN_MITER, BasicStroke.JOIN_BEVEL,
    BasicStroke.JOIN_ROUND };
private String[] joinNames =
  { "JOIN_MITER", "JOIN_BEVEL", "JOIN_ROUND" };

public LineStyles() {
  path = new GeneralPath();
  path.moveTo(x, y);
  p1Large = new Circle(x, y, thickness/2);
  p1Small = new Circle(x, y, 2);
  path.lineTo(x + deltaX, y - deltaY);
  p2Large = new Circle(x + deltaX, y - deltaY, thickness/2);
  p2Small = new Circle(x + deltaX, y - deltaY, 2);
  path.lineTo(x + 2*deltaX, y);
  p3Large = new Circle(x + 2*deltaX, y, thickness/2);
  p3Small = new Circle(x + 2*deltaX, y, 2);
  setFont(new Font("SansSerif", Font.BOLD, 20));
}

public void paintComponent(Graphics g) {
  super.paintComponent(g);
  Graphics2D g2d = (Graphics2D)g;
  g2d.setColor(Color.lightGray);
  for(int i=0; i<caps.length; i++) {
    BasicStroke stroke =
      new BasicStroke(thickness, caps[i], joins[i]);
    g2d.setStroke(stroke);
    g2d.draw(path);
    labelEndPoints(g2d, capNames[i], joinNames[i]);
    g2d.translate(3*x + 2*deltaX, 0);
  }
}

// Draw translucent circles to illustrate actual end points.
// Include text labels for cap/join style.
private void labelEndPoints(Graphics2D g2d, String capLabel,
                            String joinLabel) {
```

(continued)

```
    Paint origPaint = g2d.getPaint();
    Composite origComposite = g2d.getComposite();
    g2d.setPaint(Color.black);
    g2d.setComposite(transparentComposite);
    g2d.fill(p1Large);
    g2d.fill(p2Large);
    g2d.fill(p3Large);
    g2d.setPaint(Color.yellow);
    g2d.setComposite(origComposite);
    g2d.fill(p1Small);
    g2d.fill(p2Small);
    g2d.fill(p3Small);
    g2d.setPaint(Color.black);
    g2d.drawString(capLabel, x + thickness - 5, y + 5);
    g2d.drawString(joinLabel, x + deltaX + thickness - 5,
                   y - deltaY);
    g2d.setPaint(origPaint);
  }

  public static void main(String[] args) {
    WindowUtilities.openInJFrame(new LineStyles(),
                                 9*x + 6*deltaX, y + 60);
  }
}

class Circle extends Ellipse2D.Double {
  public Circle(double centerX, double centerY, double radius) {
    super(centerX - radius, centerY - radius, 2.0*radius,
          2.0*radius);
  }
}
```

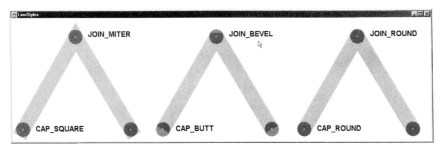

Figure 10–8 A demonstration of the different styles for joining line segments, and styles for ending a line segment.

10.7 Coordinate Transformations

Java 2D allows you to easily translate, rotate, scale, or shear the coordinate system. This capability is very convenient: moving the coordinate system is often much easier than calculating new coordinates for each of your points. Besides, for some data structures like ellipses and strings, the only way to create a rotated or stretched version is through a transformation. The meanings of translate, rotate, and scale are clear: to move, to spin, or to stretch/shrink evenly in the x and/or y direction. Shear means to stretch unevenly: an x shear moves points to the right, based on how far they are from the y-axis; a y shear moves points down, based on how far they are from the x-axis.

The easiest way to picture what is happening in a transformation is to imagine that the person doing the drawing has a picture frame that he lays down on top of a sheet of paper. The drawer always sits at the bottom of the frame. To apply a translation, you move the frame (also moving the drawer) and do the drawing in the new location. You then move the frame back to its original location, and what you now see is the final result. Similarly, for a rotation, you spin the frame (and the drawer), draw, then spin back to see the result. Similarly for scaling and shears: modify the frame without touching the underlying sheet of paper, draw, then reverse the process to see the final result.

An outside observer watching this process would see the frame move in the direction specified by the transformation but see the sheet of paper stay fixed. On the other hand, to the person doing the drawing, it would appear that the sheet of paper moved in the opposite way from that specified in the transformation but that he didn't move at all.

You can also perform complex transformations by directly manipulating the underlying arrays that control the transformations. This type of manipulation is a bit more complicated to envision than the basic translation, rotation, scaling, and shear transformations. The idea is that a new point (x_2, y_2) can be derived from an original point (x_1, y_1) as follows:

$$
\begin{bmatrix} x_2 \\ y_2 \\ 1 \end{bmatrix} = \begin{bmatrix} m_{00} & m_{01} & m_{02} \\ m_{10} & m_{11} & m_{12} \\ 0 & 0 & 1 \end{bmatrix} \begin{bmatrix} x_1 \\ y_1 \\ 1 \end{bmatrix} = \begin{bmatrix} m_{00}x_1 + m_{01}y_1 + m_{02} \\ m_{10}x_1 + m_{11}y_1 + m_{12} \\ 1 \end{bmatrix}
$$

Note that you can only supply six of the nine values in the transformation array (the m_{xx} values). The coefficients m_{02} and m_{12} provide x and y *translation* of the coordinate system. The other four transformation coefficients (m_{00}, m_{01}, m_{10}, m_{11}) provide *rotation* of the system. For the transformation to preserve orthogonality ("straightness" and "parallelness" of lines), the Jacobian (determinant) of the transformation matrix must equal 1. The bottom row is fixed at [0 0 1] to guarantee that the transformations does not rotate the shape out of the *x-y* plane (produce components along the *z*-axis). There are several ways to supply this array to the `Affine-Transform` constructor; see the `AffineTransform` API for details.

You use transformations in two basic ways—by creating an `AffineTransform` object or by calling basic transformation methods. In the first approach, you can create an `AffineTransform` object, set the parameters for the object, assign the `AffineTransform` to the `Graphics2D` object through `setTransform`, and then draw a `Shape`. In addition, you can use the `AffineTransform` object on a `Shape` to create a newly transformed `Shape` object. Simply call the `AffineTransform` method, `createTransformedShape`, to create a new transformed `Shape`. For complex transformations, creating an `AffineTransform` object is an excellent approach because you can explicitly define the transformation matrix.

Core Note

You can apply a transformation to a `Shape` *before drawing it. The* `AffineTransform` *method* `createTransformedShape` *creates a new* `Shape` *that has undergone the transformation defined by the* `AffineTransform` *object.*

In the second approach, you can call `translate`, `rotate`, `scale`, and `shear` directly on the `Graphics2D` object to perform basic transformations. The transformations applied to `Graphics2D` object are cumulative; each transform method is applied to the already transformed `Graphics2D` context. For example, calling `rotate(Math.PI/2)` followed by another call to `rotate(Math.PI/2)` is equivalent to `rotate(Math.PI)`. If you need to return to a previously existing transformation state, save the `Graphics2D` context by calling `getTransform` beforehand, perform your transformation operations, and then return to the original `Graphics2D` context by calling `setTransform`. For example,

```
// Save current graphics context.
AffineTransform transform = g2d.getTransform();
// Perform incremental transformations.
translate(...);
rotate(...);
...
// Return the graphics context to the original state.
g2d.setTransform(transform);
```

Listing 10.13 illustrates a beautiful example of continuously rotating the coordinate system while periodically writing the word "Java." The result is shown in Figure 10–9.

Listing 10.13 `RotationExample.java`

```java
import java.awt.*;

/** An example of translating and rotating the coordinate
 *  system before each drawing.
 */

public class RotationExample extends StrokeThicknessExample {
  private Color[] colors = { Color.white, Color.black };

  public void paintComponent(Graphics g) {
    clear(g);
    Graphics2D g2d = (Graphics2D)g;
    drawGradientCircle(g2d);
    drawThickCircleOutline(g2d);
    // Move the origin to the center of the circle.
    g2d.translate(185.0, 185.0);
    for (int i=0; i<16; i++) {
      // Rotate the coordinate system around current
      // origin, which is at the center of the circle.
      g2d.rotate(Math.PI/8.0);
      g2d.setPaint(colors[i%2]);
      g2d.drawString("Java", 0, 0);
    }
  }

  public static void main(String[] args) {
    WindowUtilities.openInJFrame(new RotationExample(), 380, 400);
  }
}
```

Figure 10–9 A example of translating
and rotating the coordinate system
before drawing text.

Shear Transformations

In a shear transformation, the coordinate system is stretched parallel to one axis. If you specify a nonzero x shear, then x values will be more and more shifted to the right the farther they are from the **y**-axis. For example, an x shear of 0.1 means that the x value will be shifted 10% of the distance the point is moved from the y-axis. A y shear is similar: points are shifted down in proportion to the distance they are from the **x**-axis. In addition, both the x- and y-axis can be sheared at the same time.

Probably the best way to visualize shear is in an example. The results for Listing 10.14 are shown in Figure 10–10. Here, the x shear is increased from a value of 0.0 for the first square to a value of +0.8 for the fifth square. The y values remain unaltered.

Listing 10.14 `ShearExample.java`

```java
import javax.swing.*;
import java.awt.*;
import java.awt.geom.*;

/** An example of shear transformations on a rectangle. */

public class ShearExample extends JPanel {
  private static int gap=10, width=100;
  private Rectangle rect = new Rectangle(gap, gap, 100, 100);

  public void paintComponent(Graphics g) {
    super.paintComponent(g);
    Graphics2D g2d = (Graphics2D)g;
    for (int i=0; i<5; i++) {
      g2d.setPaint(Color.red);
      g2d.fill(rect);
      // Each new square gets 0.2 more x shear.
      g2d.shear(0.2, 0.0);
      g2d.translate(2*gap + width, 0);
    }
  }

  public static void main(String[] args) {
    String title =
      "Shear: x shear ranges from 0.0 for the leftmost" +
      "'square' to 0.8 for the rightmost one.";
    WindowUtilities.openInJFrame(new ShearExample(),
                                 20*gap + 5*width,
                                 5*gap + width,
                                 title);
  }
}
```

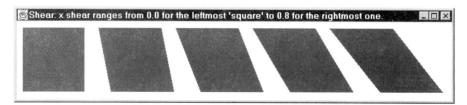

Figure 10–10 A positive x shear increases the shift in the x coordinate axis as y increases. Remember, the positive y-axis goes from the upper-left corner to the lower-left corner.

10.8 Other Capabilities of Java 2D

Since Java 2D already does a lot of calculations compared to the old AWT, by default, many of the optional features to improve performance are turned off. However, for crisper drawings, especially for rotated text, the optional features should be turned on.

The two most important settings are to turn on antialiasing (smooth jagged lines by blending colors) and to request the highest-quality graphics rendering. This approach is illustrated below:

```
RenderingHints renderHints =
  new RenderingHints(RenderingHints.KEY_ANTIALIASING,
                     RenderingHints.VALUE_ANTIALIAS_ON);
renderHints.put(RenderingHints.KEY_RENDERING,
                RenderingHints.VALUE_RENDER_QUALITY);
...

public void paintComponent(Graphics g) {
  super.paintComponent(g);
  Graphics2D g2d = (Graphics2D)g;
  g2d.setRenderingHints(renderHints);
  ...
}
```

Core Approach

For the highest-quality graphics, use RenderingHints *and turn antialiasing on,* VALUE_ANTIALIAS_ON, *and set the presentation for quality, not speed, with* VALUE_RENDER_QUALITY.

Thus far, we've only presented a small fraction of the power behind Java 2D. Once you've gained experience with the basics, you'll want to tackle advanced Java 2D techniques that allow you to:

- Create custom color mixing (implement Composite and CompositeContext interfaces).
- Perform bounds/hit testing (see contains and intersects methods of Shape).
- Create new fonts by transforming old ones (use Font.deriveFont).
- Draw multifont or multicolor strings (use the draw method of TextLayout).
- Draw outlines of fonts, or fill fonts with images or gradient colors (use the getOutline method of TextLayout).
- Perform low-level image processing and color model manipulation.
- Produce high-quality printing for Swing components. See Section 15.5 (Swing Component Printing) for details.

10.9 Summary

Java 2D enables the artistic imagination of any programmer to produce high-quality, professional graphics. Java 2D opens the door to numerous possibilities; you can

- Draw or fill any Shape. Simply call the Graphics2D's draw or fill methods with the shape as an argument.
- Take advantage of the setPaint method in the Graphics2D class to paint shapes in solid colors (Color), gradient fills (GradientPaint), or with tiled images (TexturePaint).
- Explore transparent shapes and change mixing rules for joining shapes. Numerous Porter-Duff mixing rules in the AlhpaComposite class define how shapes are combined with the background.
- Break the "one pixel wide" pen boundary and create a BasicStroke to control the width of the pen, create dashing patterns, and define how line segments are joined.
- Create an AffineTransform object and call setTransform on the Graphics2D object to translate, rotate, scale, and shear those shapes before drawing.
- Control the quality of image through the RenderingHints. In addition, the RenderingHints can control antialiasing of colors at shape boundaries for a smoother, more appealing presentation.

Remember that Java 2D is a part of the Java Foundation Classes and only available with the Java 2 platform. Swing, a robust set of lightweight components, is also a fundamental component of the Java Foundation Classes. Swing is covered in Chapter 14 (Basic Swing) and Chapter 15 (Advanced Swing).

Drawing fancy shapes, text, and images is nice, but for a complete user interface, you need to be able to react to actions taken by the user, create other types of windows, and insert user interface controls such as buttons, textfields, and the like. These topics are discussed in the next three chapters.

HANDLING MOUSE AND KEYBOARD EVENTS

Topics in This Chapter

- The general strategy for event handling
- Using a separate object to handle events
- Implementing an interface to handle events
- Using inner classes to handle events
- Understanding the standard event listeners
- Handling events with the `processXxxEvent` methods
- A spelling-correcting textfield
- An interactive whiteboard

Chapter 11

Certain user actions are classified as *events*. These include such actions as clicking a mouse button, typing a key, or moving a window. The interesting thing about event handling in Java is that you never actually check to see if events have occurred. Instead, you simply tell the system "If an event of the following type occurs in this window, tell such and such an object about it." Then, the system watches for the relevant events, notifying your listener object when it does. Handling events involves three basic steps:

1. **Determine what type of listener is of interest.**
   There are 11 standard AWT listener types, listed in Table 11.1 of Section 11.5 (The Standard Event Listeners). Browse through these options and choose the one that corresponds to the action that you want to monitor. For example, `KeyListener` corresponds to keystroke actions on the keyboard, `MouseListener` corresponds to mouse button actions, `FocusListener` corresponds to a GUI component getting or losing the keyboard focus, and so forth.

2. **Define a class of that type.**
   One way to accomplish this task is to directly implement the listener interface (`MouseListener`, `KeyListener`, `FocusListener`, etc.). You need to provide behavior for the methods that correspond to the specific subcategory of action that interests you. For example, if you are interested in handling mouse clicks, you need to use a `MouseListener`, but you still have to decide if you care about when the button is first pressed, when it is released, or both. Each action corre-

sponds to a different method in the `MouseListener` interface, as described in Section 11.5. As you will see shortly, if the interface includes more than one method, then you are also provided with an adapter class that provides a no-op implementation of each of the methods. This approach lets you override the method(s) of interest without bothering to implement the other methods. Adapters are described in detail in Sections 11.1, 11.3, and 11.4.

3. **Register an object of your listener class with the window.**
    Each listener of type *Something*`Listener` has a corresponding method called add*Something*`Listener` that is used to register it. For example, if you want mouse button events in window w to be handled by an instance of class `MyMouseListener`, you would use
    `w.addMouseListener(new MyMouseListener());`.

Within this general framework, there are four major variations in how you define the event handler class. You can define completely separate objects to be event listeners, designate an existing object that implements the listener interface, or use inner classes in two different ways. Sections 11.1 through 11.4 explain each of the four approaches.

11.1 Handling Events with a Separate Listener

Suppose you want to create an applet that, when the user clicks in it, prints the click location in the Java console. (Recall that you can bring up the Java console by means of the Communicator or Communicator/Tools menu in Netscape and by means of the View menu in Internet Explorer.) To accomplish this task, you would first look at the available listener types in Section 11.5 and determine that `MouseListener` is the listener type that corresponds to mouse button actions and that `MouseAdapter` is an implementation with empty versions of the `MouseListener` methods. Section 11.5 would also tell you that `mousePressed` is the method that is triggered when the button is first pressed, that the method takes an argument of type `MouseEvent`, and that the `MouseEvent` class has methods `getX` and `getY` that return the click location relative to the top-left corner of the window. So, you could define a listener like the one shown in Listing 11.1 and attach it to an applet as shown in Listing 11.2. Figure 11–1 shows the results. The tiny HTML file associated with the applet is available in the book's source code archive at http://www.coreweb-programming.com/.

Listing 11.1 `ClickListener.java`

```java
import java.awt.event.*;

/** The listener used by ClickReporter. */

public class ClickListener extends MouseAdapter {
  public void mousePressed(MouseEvent event) {
    System.out.println("Mouse pressed at (" +
                       event.getX() + "," +
                       event.getY() + ").");
  }
}
```

Listing 11.2 `ClickReporter.java`

```java
import java.applet.Applet;
import java.awt.*;

/** Prints a message saying where the user clicks.
 *  Uses an external listener.
 */

public class ClickReporter extends Applet {
  public void init() {
    setBackground(Color.yellow);
    addMouseListener(new ClickListener());
  }
}
```

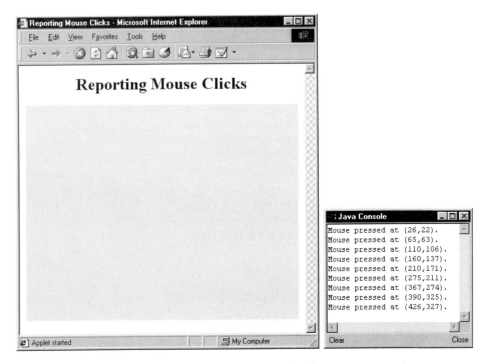

Figure 11–1 Results of the `ClickReporter` applet after a user opens the Java console and clicks several times while moving the mouse from the top-left corner toward the bottom right corner of the applet.

Drawing Circles

Now, instead of simply printing out the location of each click, suppose that you want to draw a circle wherever the user clicks the mouse. Obtaining a `Graphics` object in an applet when you are not in `paint` is easy: you just call `getGraphics`. The problem is that the event handler is not part of the `Applet` class and thus has no `getGraphics` method. The solution is to use the `getSource` method (defined for all event types) to obtain a reference to the window from which the event originated. This reference can be cast to type `Applet`, and then the `getGraphics` method can be called on it. Listings 11.3 and 11.4 give an example, with results shown in Figure 11–2.

Core Approach

Use `event.getSource()` *to obtain a reference to the window where* `event` *originated.*

Listing 11.3 `CircleListener.java`

```java
import java.applet.Applet;
import java.awt.*;
import java.awt.event.*;

/** The listener used by CircleDrawer1. Note call
 *  to getSource to obtain reference to the applet.
 */

public class CircleListener extends MouseAdapter {
  private int radius = 25;

  public void mousePressed(MouseEvent event) {
    Applet app = (Applet)event.getSource();
    Graphics g = app.getGraphics();
    g.fillOval(event.getX()-radius,
               event.getY()-radius,
               2*radius,
               2*radius);
  }
}
```

Listing 11.4 `CircleDrawer.java`

```java
import java.applet.Applet;
import java.awt.*;

/** Draw circles centered where the user clicks.
 *  Uses an external listener.
 */

public class CircleDrawer1 extends Applet {
  public void init() {
    setForeground(Color.blue);
    addMouseListener(new CircleListener());
  }
}
```

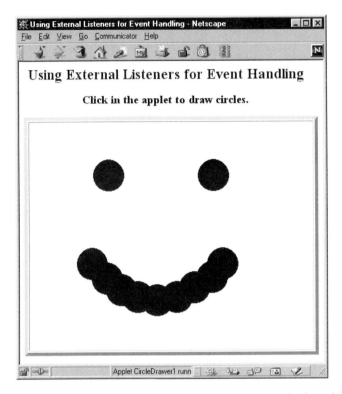

Figure 11-2 An external listener can call public methods in the window it is associated with by using the reference obtained by getSource.

11.2 Handling Events by Implementing a Listener Interface

In the previous example, the listener object was completely separate from the applet that used it. Although in some cases such a separation promotes object reuse, in this case the separation made it more difficult for the event listener to call the applet's methods. First of all, the event handler had to use the somewhat awkward approach of calling getSource and performing a typecast, just to obtain a reference to the applet. Second, this reference only enabled the listener to call public methods, not private or protected ones.

An alternative to this approach is for the applet to register itself as the mouse event listener. In order for this approach to comply with Java's strict typing rules, however, the applet has to declare that it implements the MouseListener interface. Implementing an interface can be viewed as a promise to the compiler that you will have certain methods. In this case, implementing the `MouseListener` interface is a promise that you will have the `mouseEntered`, `mouseExited`, `mousePressed`, `mouseReleased`, and `mouseClicked` methods, as described in Section 11.5 (The Standard Event Listeners).

Listing 11.5 shows an applet that follows this approach to obtain the same effect as in Figure 11–2. Notice that the `mousePressed` method is simplified, since it can call `getGraphics` directly because the `mousePressed` method is already part of the `Applet` class. However, the applet has to supply definitions for all five methods of `MouseListener` interface, even though it only cares about one of them.

Listing 11.5 `CircleDrawer2.java`

```java
import java.applet.Applet;
import java.awt.*;
import java.awt.event.*;

/** Draw circles centered where the user clicks.
 *  Attaches itself as a listener.
 */

public class CircleDrawer2 extends Applet
                           implements MouseListener {
  private int radius = 25;

  public void init() {
    setForeground(Color.blue);
    addMouseListener(this);
  }

  // Remaining methods are from the MouseListener interface.

  public void mouseEntered(MouseEvent event) {}
  public void mouseExited(MouseEvent event) {}
  public void mouseReleased(MouseEvent event) {}
  public void mouseClicked(MouseEvent event) {}

  public void mousePressed(MouseEvent event) {
    Graphics g = getGraphics();
    g.fillOval(event.getX()-radius,
               event.getY()-radius,
               2*radius,
               2*radius);
  }
}
```

11.3 Handling Events with Named Inner Classes

In the first circle-drawing applet, the separate event listener had to perform some minor contortions to call methods in the `Applet` class. That's because of the strict object-oriented nature of the Java programming language. In the second circle-drawing applet, the applet handled its own events, so needed nothing extra to call methods in the `Applet` class. However, to pass typing rules, that applet had to declare that it implemented the `MouseListener` interface, resulting in the necessity of implementing four methods in which the applet had no interest. *Inner classes* (or *nested classes*) provide the best of both worlds. Inner classes are simply classes whose definitions appear inside another class definition. They have full access to the code of the enclosing object, including private methods and fields. Here is an example:

```
public class Outer {
  private class Inner { ... }

  private Inner test = new Inner();
  ...
}
```

`Inner` can implement an interface or extend an arbitrary superclass, just like a regular class can. If you use the `this` reference within `Inner`, it refers to the inner class, but a reference to the outer class can be obtained by `Outer.this`. When compiled, each inner class generates a separate class file, even if the class is anonymous (see Section 11.4). In many cases, the file for the inner class will be a variation of the name of the file for the outer class (e.g., `Outer$Inner.class`). You usually don't care about the class file name, but if you move the class files to a location different from that of the source files, it is easy to overlook the files for the inner classes.

Core Warning

If you move the `.class` file of a class containing inner classes, don't forget to also move the `.class` files for the inner classes.

Listing 11.6 shows a variation of the `CircleDrawer` class that uses named inner classes. The inner class calls `getGraphics` directly without having to first call `event.getSource` to obtain a reference to the applet. The inner class extends `MouseAdapter` instead of implementing `MouseListener`, obviating the need for the empty implementations of `mouseEntered`, `mouseExited`, `mouseReleased`, and `mouseClicked` that appeared in the previous example (Section 11.2).

Listing 11.6 `CircleDrawer3.java`

```java
import java.applet.Applet;
import java.awt.*;
import java.awt.event.*;

/** Draw circles centered where the user clicks.
 *  Uses named inner classes.
 */

public class CircleDrawer3 extends Applet {
  public void init() {
    setForeground(Color.blue);
    addMouseListener(new CircleListener());
  }

  private class CircleListener extends MouseAdapter {
    private int radius = 25;

    public void mousePressed(MouseEvent event) {
      Graphics g = getGraphics();
      g.fillOval(event.getX()-radius,
                 event.getY()-radius,
                 2*radius,
                 2*radius);
    }
  }
}
```

11.4 Handling Events with Anonymous Inner Classes

In the previous example we defined a class within another class. Although the inner class definition appeared in an unusual location (inside another class), it still followed the same basic syntax rules as normal classes. In contrast, *anonymous* inner classes let you define and create a class within an expression. You never even name the class being defined. To define anonymous classes, you make what looks like a call to the constructor of the parent class, but you include the definition of the subclass right after the parentheses, as in the following two examples:

```java
Color someColor = pickColor();
add(new Panel() {
    public Color origColor = someColor;
    public void init() {
      setBackground(origColor);
```

```
        }
    });

KeyAdapter myAdapter =
    new KeyAdapter() {
        public void keyPressed(KeyEvent event) { ... }
    };
addKeyListener(myAdapter);
```

Listing 11.7 uses anonymous inner classes to implement the circle-drawing applet.
Although this version is slightly shorter than the one with named inner classes, it is
not clear that it is any simpler. Throughout the book, we will mostly use named inner
classes when performing event handling that calls for inner classes.

Listing 11.7 CircleDrawer4.java

```java
import java.applet.Applet;
import java.awt.*;
import java.awt.event.*;

/** Draw circles centered where the user clicks.
 *  Uses anonymous inner classes.
 */

public class CircleDrawer4 extends Applet {
    public void init() {
        setForeground(Color.blue);
        addMouseListener
            (new MouseAdapter() {
                private int radius = 25;

                public void mousePressed(MouseEvent event) {
                    Graphics g = getGraphics();
                    g.fillOval(event.getX()-radius,
                               event.getY()-radius,
                               2*radius,
                               2*radius);
                }
            });
    }
}
```

11.5 The Standard Event Listeners

Table 11.1 summarizes the 11 AWT event listeners. Each is described in more detail later in this section. The method to register a listener has the same name as the listener, prefixed by "add". For example, use `addMouseListener` to attach a `MouseListener`, `addComponentListener` to attach a `ComponentListener`, etc. For each `addXxxListener` there is a corresponding `removeXxxListener` method. In addition to the 11 AWT listener types, Swing defines some of its own. Many of these are discussed in the chapters on Swing. Note that all listener classes that contain more than one method have a corresponding adapter class that contains empty implementations of all the methods. Since you always implement at least one of the event handling methods (what good is an event "handler" that doesn't do anything?), there is no benefit to having an adapter for a class that contains only a single method.

Table 11.1 Event listeners

Listener	Adapter Class (If Any)	Registration Method
ActionListener		addActionListener
AdjustmentListener		addAdjustmentListener
ComponentListener	ComponentAdapter	addComponentListener
ContainerListener	ContainerAdapter	addContainerListener
FocusListener	FocusAdapter	addFocusListener
ItemListener		addItemListener
KeyListener	KeyAdapter	addKeyListener
MouseListener	MouseAdapter	addMouseListener
MouseMotionListener	MouseMotionAdapter	addMouseMotionListener
TextListener		addTextListener
WindowListener	WindowAdapter	addWindowListener

The listeners define methods that you can override to handle certain types of situations. Each of those methods takes a single argument that is a subclass of `AWTEvent`. `AWTEvent` contains four important methods: `consume` (delete the event), `isConsumed` (a `boolean` designating whether the event has already been consumed by another listener on the same source), `getID` (an `int` representing the event type), and `getSource` (the `Object` that the event came from).

ActionListener

This interface defines a single method:

```
public void actionPerformed(ActionEvent event)
```

Because there is only a single method, no adapter class is provided. This listener applies to buttons, list items, menu items, and textfields only, and `actionPerformed` is invoked when the user clicks on the button, presses ENTER in the textfield, and so forth. In addition to the standard methods of `AWTEvent`, `ActionEvent` has two additional methods: `getActionCommand` (return the `command` field of the source as a `String`) and `getModifiers` (return an `int` with SHIFT, CONTROL and other modifier flags set). The `getActionCommand` method returns the "command string" of the source—for buttons, this string defaults to the button label but can be defined separately to simplify processing of buttons whose labels change depending on the language in use. However, in most cases the most important thing is the `getSource` method, which specifies the particular component that generated the event.

AdjustmentListener

This interface defines a single method:

```
public void adjustmentValueChanged(AdjustmentEvent event)
```

Because there is only a single method, no adapter class is provided. This listener applies only to scrollbars, and `adjustmentValueChanged` is invoked when the scrollbar is moved. `AdjustmentEvent` has several new methods in addition to the standard `AWTEvent` methods. In particular, `getAdjustable` returns the source scrollbar; `getAdjustmentType` returns one of the static constants `UNIT_DECREMENT`, `UNIT_INCREMENT`, `BLOCK_DECREMENT`, `BLOCK_INCREMENT`, or `TRACK`; and `getValue` returns the current setting.

ComponentListener

This interface defines four methods:

```
public void componentResized(ComponentEvent event)
public void componentMoved(ComponentEvent event)
public void componentShown(ComponentEvent event)
public void componentHidden(ComponentEvent event)
```

The Java API provides a class called `ComponentAdapter` that has empty implementations of each of these four methods. Implementing this class allows you to override one method without bothering to implement the others. These methods are called when a component is resized, moved, made visible, or hidden, respectively. The `getComponent` method of `ComponentEvent` returns the originating `Component`. Using it is easier than calling `getSource` and casting the result to a `Component`.

ContainerListener

This interface defines two methods:

```
public void componentAdded(ContainerEvent event)
public void componentRemoved(ContainerEvent event)
```

The `ContainerAdapter` class provides empty implementations of both of these methods. A `ContainerListener` is invoked when components are added to or removed from a `Container`. The `ContainerEvent` class defines `getContainer` and `getChild` for accessing the window and its associated component.

FocusListener

This interface defines two methods:

```
public void focusGained(FocusEvent event)
public void focusLost(FocusEvent event)
```

`FocusAdapter` provides empty versions of these methods. The `FocusEvent` class has a boolean `isTemporary` method that determines whether the focus change was temporary or permanent.

ItemListener

This interface defines a single method:

```
public void itemStateChanged(ItemEvent event)
```

No adapter is provided. This listener applies to `Checkbox`, `CheckboxMenuItem`, `Choice`, and `List` and is invoked when an item is changed. The `ItemEvent` class defines three methods: `getItemSelectable` (the source object), `getItem` (the item selected), and `getStateChange` (an int that is either `ItemEvent.SELECTED` or `ItemEvent.DESELECTED`).

KeyListener

This interface defines three methods:

```
public void keyPressed(KeyEvent event)
public void keyReleased(KeyEvent event)
public void keyTyped(KeyEvent event)
```

The KeyAdapter class provides empty versions of these methods so that you can override one or more without implementing all three. This listener is invoked when a key is typed while the component has the input focus. Ordinary windows such as Panel or Canvas have to explicitly request the focus (by requestFocus) to get key events. The keyPressed and keyReleased methods are used to catch lower-level actions, where SHIFT, CONTROL, and so forth, are sent separately from the key they modify. Use consume in key-Pressed if you want to prevent a component from seeing the keystroke. This lets you restrict textfields to certain formats, for instance. If you are only interested in printable characters, override keyTyped instead.

The KeyEvent class defines a variety of methods and constants. Two methods of particular importance are getKeyChar and setKeyChar. The first returns the character typed, and the second can be used to replace the character with a different one. This behavior lets you do things like map tabs and newlines to spaces, convert lowercase to uppercase, and so forth. There are also getModifiers and setModifiers methods that let you retrieve and/or replace the modifier keys, and a boolean isActionKey method that differentiates function and arrow keys from normal keys. You can also use one of four related methods inherited from InputEvent: isAltDown, isControlDown, isMetaDown, and isShiftDown. Rather than acting on characters with getKeyChar, you can retrieve an integer with getKeyCode, then pass that to getKeyText to find the associated string. This is useful in internationalized code. There is a corresponding setKeyCode as well. Finally, you can obtain the Component receiving the event through get-Component, and the time the key was pressed through getWhen.

MouseListener

This interface defines five methods:

```
public void mouseEntered(MouseEvent event)
public void mouseExited(MouseEvent event)
public void mousePressed(MouseEvent event)
public void mouseReleased(MouseEvent event)
public void mouseClicked(MouseEvent event)
```

The mouseEntered and mouseExited methods correspond to the event of the mouse entering or exiting the window or component that is using the listener. Note that mouseExited will be called when the mouse enters a component that is on top of the current one, not just when mouse leaves the outside boundaries of the window. For example, suppose you put a button in an applet and move the mouse from outside the applet onto the button and then back outside the applet. The applet will first receive a mouseEntered event (when the mouse pointer enters the boundaries of the applet), then a mouseExited event (when the mouse moves over top of the button), then a second mouse-

`Entered` event (when the mouse leaves the button and is back over the main part of the applet), and then a second `mouseExited` event (when the mouse leaves the boundaries of the applet). Note that the x and y locations reported by `mouseExited` can be outside the applet boundaries; note, too, that Netscape often gives nonsensical values for the x and y positions of `mouseExited`.

The `mousePressed` method corresponds to the event of the mouse button first being pressed, `mouseReleased` corresponds to the mouse button release, and `mouseClicked` corresponds to mouse button release after it was pressed in the current location. So, for example, if you press and release the mouse without moving it, `mousePressed`, `mouseReleased`, and `mouse-Clicked` all get triggered (in that order). If, however, you press the mouse, drag it, and then release it, `mousePressed` and `mouseReleased` still get triggered, but `mouseClicked` doesn't.

You can use the `MouseAdapter` class if you want to override some but not all of these methods. If you consume the event in `mousePressed`, the associated graphical component will not see the mouse click. You can call `getModifiers` to determine which button was clicked. Java runs on systems that use a 1-button mouse (MacOS), a 2-button mouse (Windows), or a 3-button mouse (Unix), so Java doesn't have separate events for selections with the primary mouse button, the secondary button, and so on. However, on a multiple-button system, `event.getModifiers()` will be equal to `MouseEvent.Button2_MASK` for a middle click and equal to `Mouse-Event.Button3_MASK` for a right (secondary button) click. Note that the right button corresponds to `Button3_MASK` even on a 2-button mouse. To allow for multiple modifiers, you generally just check that the flag is set. So, rather than checking if

```
(event.getModifiers() == event.ALT_MASK)
```
you would check

```
((event.getModifiers() & event.ALT_MASK) != 0)
```

The `getClickCount` method lets you differentiate single clicks from multi-clicks. The determination of what constitutes a double click versus what should be interpreted as two consecutive single clicks is made by the operating system (often based on user settings), not by Java. Note that for a double click, `mousePressed` will be invoked *twice*, first with `event.getClickCount` equal to 1, then with `event.getClickCount` equal to 2. This is a standard procedure so that the system doesn't have to wait for the multiclick time to expire before reporting the first click, but it catches many first-time users off guard. The `getX`, `getY`, and `getPoint` methods determine the location of the click. The `isPopupTrigger` method is used to determine whether the user pressed the platform-specific key that requests a `PopupMenu`. Like

KeyEvent, MouseEvent inherits from InputEvent, getting isAltDown, isControlDown, isMetaDown, isShiftDown, getComponent, and getWhen methods.

MouseMotionListener

This interface defines two methods:

```
public void mouseMoved(MouseEvent event)
public void mouseDragged(MouseEvent event)
```

MouseMotionAdapter provides empty versions of these two methods. A MouseMotionListener is invoked when the mouse is moved. The MouseEvent class is described in the previous MouseListener section.

TextListener

This interface defines a single method:

```
public void textValueChanged(TextEvent event)
```

There is no associated adapter. This listener applies only to TextArea, TextField, and any custom subclasses of TextComponent. The textValueChanged method is invoked when text changes, regardless of whether this is from user action or from the program (e.g., using setText or append).

WindowListener

This final interface defines seven methods:

```
public void windowOpened(WindowEvent event)
public void windowClosing(WindowEvent event)
public void windowClosed(WindowEvent event)
public void windowIconified(WindowEvent event)
public void windowDeiconified(WindowEvent event)
public void windowActivated(WindowEvent event)
public void windowDeactivated(WindowEvent event)
```

If you are only concerned with one or two of these methods, you can extend a WindowAdapter class, which comes with empty versions of all seven methods. The windowOpened method is called when a window is first opened; windowClosing is called when the user tries to quit the window; windowClosed is called when the window actually is closed; windowIconified and windowDeiconified are called when the window is minimized and restored; and windowActivated and windowDeactivated are called when the window is brought to the front and either buried, minimized, or otherwise deactivated. The getWindow method of WindowEvent returns the Window being acted upon.

11.6 Behind the Scenes: Low-Level Event Processing

When a component receives an event, that event gets passed to a method called processXxxEvent, where Xxx is Mouse (i.e., the method is called process-MouseEvent), Key, Focus, Action, and so forth. For a summary, see Table 11.2 at the end of this section. The processXxxEvent method passes the event on to each of the attached listeners. In most cases, you just want to add listeners and don't care about the behind-the-scenes method. Occasionally, however, you may want to use these methods directly. For example, if you want to perform the same action for each of the possible mouse events, it is shorter to use processMouseEvent than to override all five methods of the MouseListener interface. If you override these methods, however, you almost always want to call super.processXxxEvent from within the body of processXxxEvent because processXxxEvent calls any attached listeners. If you forget to make the call to super.processXxxEvent and later come back and add some listeners to your component, the listeners will be ignored. You usually call the superclass version at the end of your method, but if you want the listeners to be activated before your code, you can call super.process-XxxEvent first.

Core Approach

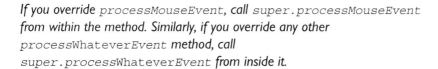

If you override processMouseEvent, *call* super.processMouseEvent *from within the method. Similarly, if you override any other* processWhateverEvent *method, call* super.processWhateverEvent *from inside it.*

For efficiency, the system does not send events to the processXxxEvent methods unless you ask it to. The way to instruct it to send events is to call enableEvents, using a mask in the AWTEvent class corresponding to the type of event. For instance, to enable the reporting of mouse button events to process-MouseEvent, use

```
enableEvents(AWTEvent.MOUSE_EVENT_MASK);
```

Similarly, for key events use

```
enableEvents(AWTEvent.KEY_EVENT_MASK);
```

and for focus events use

```
enableEvents(AWTEvent.FOCUS_EVENT_MASK);
```

To enable multiple events within a single call, use the bitwise OR of the masks. For example:

```
enableEvents(AWTEvent.MOUSE_EVENT_MASK |
             AWTEvent.KEY_EVENT_MASK |
             AWTEvent.FOCUS_EVENT_MASK);
```

In general, the process*Xxx*Event methods take an argument of type *Xxx*-Event. For instance, processMouseEvent gets a MouseEvent, process-KeyEvent gets a KeyEvent, processFocusEvent gets a FocusEvent, processItemEvent gets an ItemEvent, processActionEvent gets an ActionEvent, and so forth. There is one exception however: processMouse-MotionEvent does not have its own event type but instead shares MouseEvent with processMouseEvent. Also, there is a disableEvents method corresponding to enableEvents; it is used to undo inherited settings. Finally, note that AWTEvent is in the java.awt package, and MouseEvent and the other specific event types are in java.awt.event. So, you need to import both packages.

For example, Listing 11.8 shows an applet that reports mouse enter, mouse exit, and mouse press/release/click events from processMouseEvent and reports mouse move and drag events from processMouseMotionEvent. Figure 11–3 shows a typical result.

Listing 11.8 MouseReporter.java

```java
import java.applet.Applet;
import java.awt.*;
import java.awt.event.*;

/** Prints nondetailed reports of mouse events.
 *  Uses the low-level processXxxEvent methods instead
 *  of the usual event listeners.
 */

public class MouseReporter extends Applet {
  public void init() {
    setBackground(Color.blue); // So you can see applet in page
    enableEvents(AWTEvent.MOUSE_EVENT_MASK |
            AWTEvent.MOUSE_MOTION_EVENT_MASK);
  }
```

(continued)

Listing 11.8 `MouseReporter.java` *(continued)*

```
public void processMouseEvent(MouseEvent event) {
  System.out.println("Mouse enter/exit or click at (" +
                     event.getX() + "," +
                     event.getY() + ").");
  // In case there are MouseListeners attached:
  super.processMouseEvent(event);
}

public void processMouseMotionEvent(MouseEvent event) {
  System.out.println("Mouse move/drag at (" +
                     event.getX() + "," +
                     event.getY() + ").");
  // In case there are MouseMotionListeners attached:
  super.processMouseMotionEvent(event);
}
}
```

Figure 11–3 Result of `MouseReporter` applet after mouse enters the top-left corner of the applet and the button is pressed once.

Table 11.2 summarizes the low-level event-processing methods.

Table 11.2 Low-level event-processing methods

Low-Level Event Method	Corresponding Event Type	Mask for enableEvents (Static var in AWTEvent)
processActionEvent	ActionEvent	ACTION_EVENT_MASK
processAdjustmentEvent	AdjustmentEvent	ADJUSTMENT_EVENT_MASK
processComponentEvent	ComponentEvent	COMPONENT_EVENT_MASK
processContainerEvent	ContainerEvent	CONTAINER_EVENT_MASK
processFocusEvent	FocusEvent	FOCUS_EVENT_MASK
processItemEvent	ItemEvent	ITEM_EVENT_MASK
processKeyEvent	KeyEvent	KEY_EVENT_MASK
processMouseEvent	MouseEvent	MOUSE_EVENT_MASK
processMouseMotionEvent	MouseEvent	MOUSE_MOTION_EVENT_MASK
processTextEvent	TextEvent	TEXT_EVENT_MASK
processWindowEvent	WindowEvent	WINDOW_EVENT_MASK

11.7 A Spelling-Correcting Textfield

Listing 11.9 shows a spelling-correcting textfield that lets the user enter the name of a good programming language. The textfield monitors three types of events: key events (when a printable character is typed while the textfield has the keyboard focus), focus events (when the textfield obtains the keyboard focus), and action events (when ENTER is pressed while the textfield has the focus). When it detects a printable character (through the keyTyped method of the KeyAdapter class), it compares the string entered so far to a dictionary of good programming languages and replaces the string entered with the most closely matching substring from its dictionary. When it detects ENTER (through the actionPerformed method of the ActionListener interface), the text is filled in with the complete name of a good programming language whose name most closely matches the text entered so far. Finally, when the textfield detects that it has just received the keyboard focus (through the focusGained method of the FocusAdapter class), it repeatedly but briefly flashes a hint. Listing 11.10 presents an applet that uses this textfield, and Figure 11–4 shows a typical result.

Listing 11.9 LanguageField.java

```java
import java.awt.*;
import java.awt.event.*;

/** A spelling-correcting TextField for entering
 *  a language name.
 */

public class LanguageField extends TextField {
  private String[] substrings =
    { "", "J", "Ja", "Jav", "Java" };

  public LanguageField() {
    addKeyListener(new SpellingCorrector());
    addActionListener(new WordCompleter());
    addFocusListener(new SubliminalAdvertiser());
  }

  // Put caret at end of field.

  private void setCaret() {
    setCaretPosition(5);
  }

  // Listener to monitor/correct spelling as user types.

  private class SpellingCorrector extends KeyAdapter {
    public void keyTyped(KeyEvent event) {
      setLanguage();
      setCaret();
    }

    // Enter partial name of good programming language that
    // most closely matches what they've typed so far.

    private void setLanguage() {
      int length = getText().length();
      if (length <= 4) {
        setText(substrings[length]);
      } else {
        setText("Java");
      }
      setCaret();
    }
  }
```

(continued)

Listing 11.9 LanguageField.java *(continued)*

```java
// Listener to replace current partial name with
// most closely matching name of good language.

private class WordCompleter implements ActionListener {

  // When they press RETURN, fill in the right answer.

  public void actionPerformed(ActionEvent event) {
    setText("Java");
    setCaret();
  }
}

// Listener to give the user a hint.

private class SubliminalAdvertiser extends FocusAdapter {
  public void focusGained(FocusEvent event) {
    String text = getText();
    for(int i=0; i<10; i++) {
      setText("Hint: Java");
      setText(text);
    }
  }
}
}
```

Listing 11.10 JavaTextField.java

```java
import java.applet.Applet;
import java.awt.*;

/** Lets the user enter the name of <B>any</B>
 *  good programming language. Or does it?
 */

public class JavaTextField extends Applet {
  public void init() {
    setFont(new Font("Serif", Font.BOLD, 14));
    setLayout(new GridLayout(2, 1));
    add(new Label("Enter a Good Programming Language",
                  Label.CENTER));
    LanguageField langField = new LanguageField();
    Font langFont = new Font("SansSerif", Font.BOLD, 18);
    langField.setFont(langFont);
    add(langField);
  }
}
```

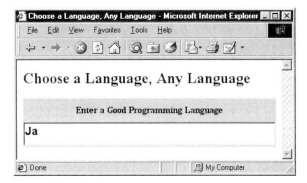

Figure 11–4 `JavaTextField` after user entered "C#" (an obvious typo).

11.8 A Whiteboard Class

Listing 11.11 shows an applet that lets the user create freehand drawings. The idea is to record the initial *x* and *y* position when the user presses the mouse and then to draw line segments from the previous position to the current position as the user drags the mouse. For example, Figure 11–5 shows a map to the Kossiakoff Center at the Johns Hopkins University Applied Physics Lab, and indicates where to park once there.

Listing 11.11 `SimpleWhiteboard.java`

```java
import java.applet.Applet;
import java.awt.*;
import java.awt.event.*;

/** An applet that lets you perform freehand drawing. */

public class SimpleWhiteboard extends Applet {
  protected int lastX=0, lastY=0;

  public void init() {
    setBackground(Color.white);
    setForeground(Color.blue);
    addMouseListener(new PositionRecorder());
    addMouseMotionListener(new LineDrawer());
  }
```

(continued)

Listing 11.11 `SimpleWhiteboard.java` *(continued)*

```java
protected void record(int x, int y) {
  lastX = x;
  lastY = y;
}

// Record position that mouse entered window or
// where user pressed mouse button.

private class PositionRecorder extends MouseAdapter {
  public void mouseEntered(MouseEvent event) {
    requestFocus(); // Plan ahead for typing
    record(event.getX(), event.getY());
  }

  public void mousePressed(MouseEvent event) {
    record(event.getX(), event.getY());
  }
}

// As user drags mouse, connect subsequent positions
// with short line segments.

private class LineDrawer extends MouseMotionAdapter {
  public void mouseDragged(MouseEvent event) {
    int x = event.getX();
    int y = event.getY();
    Graphics g = getGraphics();
    g.drawLine(lastX, lastY, x, y);
    record(x, y);
  }
}
}
```

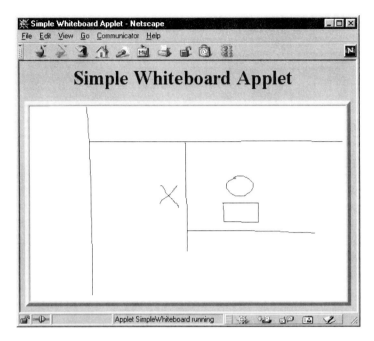

Figure 11–5 A simple whiteboard; drawing is performed when the mouse is dragged.

A Better Whiteboard

Now, although Figure 11–5 gave an absolutely clear map, it must be admitted that some people have trouble interpreting true art. So, we next add the ability to annotate the drawings with typed text (see Listing 11.12). Whenever a key is typed, the keyTyped method converts the key (an int in this case) to a String, draws the String at the current location, then shifts the current location to the right, depending on the width of the String in the current font. Figure 11–6 shows the result.

Listing 11.12 `Whiteboard.java`

```
import java.applet.Applet;
import java.awt.*;
import java.awt.event.*;

/** A better whiteboard that lets you enter
 *   text in addition to freehand drawing.
 */
```

(continued)

Listing 11.12 `Whiteboard.java` *(continued)*

```
public class Whiteboard extends SimpleWhiteboard {
  protected FontMetrics fm;

  public void init() {
    super.init();
    Font font = new Font("Serif", Font.BOLD, 20);
    setFont(font);
    fm = getFontMetrics(font);
    addKeyListener(new CharDrawer());
  }

  private class CharDrawer extends KeyAdapter {
    // When user types a printable character,
    // draw it and shift position rightwards.

    public void keyTyped(KeyEvent event) {
      String s = String.valueOf(event.getKeyChar());
      getGraphics().drawString(s, lastX, lastY);
      record(lastX + fm.stringWidth(s), lastY);
    }
  }
}
```

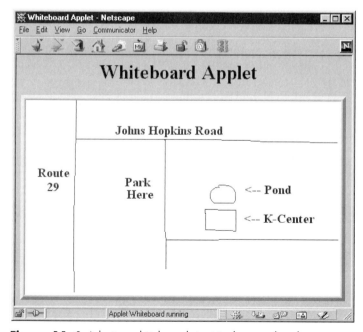

Figure 11-6 A better whiteboard; text is drawn when keys are typed.

11.9 Summary

The whiteboard presented in Section 11.8 is not too bad for such a small amount of code, but it is lacking in several ways. First, there are no options for choosing colors or fonts or for specifying the type of drawing operation (freehand, straight lines, circles, rectangles, and so forth). In Chapter 13 (AWT Components), we cover combo boxes, pull-down menus, and other GUI widgets needed to create such an interface. Second, because drawing is done directly to the window, it is transient. If another window is moved over the browser and then removed, the drawing is lost. In Chapter 16 (Concurrent Programming with Java Threads), we discuss several techniques for overcoming this problem, the most general of which is *double buffering*, a technique for drawing into off-screen images. Finally, for whiteboards to be most useful they should be shareable. We discuss methods for making a server that would permit this in Chapter 17 (Network Programming).

LAYOUT
MANAGERS

Topics in This Chapter

- How layout managers simplify interface design
- The FlowLayout manager
- The BorderLayout manager
- The GridLayout manager
- The CardLayout manager
- The GridBagLayout manager
- The BoxLayout manager
- Hand-positioning components
- Strategies for using layout managers effectively

Chapter 12

W hen a `Container` is created in the Java programming language, the container automatically gets an associated helper object known as a *layout manager* to give sizes and positions to the components inside it. The layout manager is intended to free the programmer from the burden of positioning each component pixel-by-pixel when the components may be different sizes on different platforms, when the main windows may be interactively resized or customized based on parameters in the HTML file, or when the design changes several times during development.

Although this idea is a good one, in practice the built-in layout managers are good for basic layouts but not flexible enough for many complex arrangements. However, by using nested containers, each of which has its own layout manager, you can achieve relatively complex layouts even with the simplest layout managers. Besides, you can always turn the layout manager off if you'd rather do things by hand. You can also design your own layout manager to fit your specific requirements or favored look.

To use a layout manager, you first associate a manager with the container by using `setLayout` (or by simply accepting the window's default), then insert components into the window with `add`. In an applet, setting the layout manager is usually performed in `init`. In an application, the layout manager is usually set in the constructor.

In this chapter, we first cover the five AWT layout managers: `FlowLayout`, `BorderLayout`, `GridLayout`, `CardLayout`, and `GridBagLayout` and then cover the new Swing layout manager, `BoxLayout`. We then discuss turning off the layout manager and tips for using layout managers effectively.

12.1 The FlowLayout Manager

The FlowLayout manager resizes components to their preferred (natural) size, then arranges them in rows in the window. The first component is placed in the leftmost position in the top row, the second component next, and so on until the next component would not fit in the current row, in which case the process is repeated in the next row for the remaining components. By default, each row is centered and five pixels are left between components in a row and between rows. The constructor options described later in this section let you make left-aligned or right-aligned rows and let you change the spacing between components. FlowLayout is the default layout manager for a Panel, JPanel, and Applet.

Listing 12.1 shows an example that places five buttons in a window that is wide enough to hold only four. As Figure 12–1 shows, the group containing the first four is centered on the top row of the applet, and the last button is centered in a row directly underneath. Note that because FlowLayout is the default layout manager for Applet, there is no need for an explicit setLayout call. For containers using other layout managers, you would use setLayout(new FlowLayout()) to stipulate that FlowLayout be used.

Listing 12.1 FlowTest.java

```java
import java.applet.Applet;
import java.awt.*;

/** FlowLayout puts components in rows. */

public class FlowTest extends Applet {
  public void init() {
    for(int i=1; i<6; i++) {
      add(new Button("Button " + i));
    }
  }
}
```

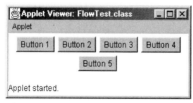

Figure 12–1 FlowLayout puts components in rows, moving to a new row only when the component won't fit in the current row.

FlowLayout Constructor Options

public FlowLayout()

This constructor builds a `FlowLayout` layout manager that centers each row and keeps five pixels between entries in a row and between rows.

public FlowLayout(int alignment)

This constructor builds a `FlowLayout` with left-aligned, right-aligned, or centered rows, depending on the value of the alignment argument (`FlowLayout.LEFT`, `FlowLayout.RIGHT`, or `FlowLayout.CENTER`). The horizontal and vertical gap is five pixels.

public FlowLayout(int alignment, int hGap, int vGap)

This constructor builds a `FlowLayout` that uses the specified alignment, keeps `hGap` pixels between entries in a row, and reserves `vGap` pixels between rows.

Other FlowLayout Methods

The following methods are available:

public int getAlignment()
public void setAlignment(int alignment)

These methods let you look up or modify the row alignment. As in the constructor, the alignment can be `FlowLayout.LEFT`, `FlowLayout.RIGHT`, or `FlowLayout.CENTER`.

public int getHgap()
public void setHgap(int hGap)

These methods let you look up or change the empty space kept between entries in a row. The default is 5.

public int getVgap()
public void setVgap(int vGap)

These methods let you look up or change the amount of empty space between rows. The default is 5.

The default `FlowLayout` instance used by panels is stored in a `static` (shared) variable in the `Panel` class. However, you have to exercise caution to avoid unintended side effects. Although the shared `FlowLayout` is stored in a `final` variable, that only means that the *reference* is constant; the reference cannot be redirected to refer to a new object. A final reference to an object does not mean that the *fields* of the object are unmodifiable. In this regard, the Java programming language has the equivalent of C++'s const pointers, but not the equivalent of const objects. For instance, if you want to change the horizontal gap in a Panel, you should do so with

```
Panel p = new Panel();
p.setLayout(new FlowLayout(FlowLayout.CENTER,10,5));
```

not

```
Panel p = new Panel();
FlowLayout layout = (FlowLayout)p.getLayout();
layout.setHgap(10);
```

You might think that the latter is more efficient because a new FlowLayout instance is not allocated, but the consequences of this fact mean that changes to the shared FlowLayout instance can affect other panels. Any other panel using the default layout manager will now have a horizontal gap of 10.

12.2 The BorderLayout Manager

BorderLayout divides the window into five sections: NORTH, SOUTH, EAST, WEST, and CENTER. You add a component to a region by using a version of the add method that takes two arguments instead of the normal one. The first argument is the component, and the second argument is a string naming the region that should hold the component, as follows:

```
add(buttonForTop, BorderLayout.NORTH);
add(scrollbarForRightSide, BorderLayout.EAST);
add(panelForRemainingSpace, BorderLayout.CENTER);
```

The role of the layout manager is to provide sizes and positions for the components. Components added to NORTH or SOUTH are resized to their preferred height, with a width equal to the Container, and then placed at the top or bottom of the window. Components added to EAST or WEST are resized to take the full height of the Container (minus any space taken by NORTH and SOUTH) and to be their preferred widths. A component in the CENTER region is expanded to take whatever space is remaining. The BorderLayout constructor also allows specification of the gaps between the areas; the default is 0. BorderLayout is the default layout manager for Frame, Dialog, and Window and for the content pane of JApplet, JFrame, JDialog, and JWindow.

Listing 12.2 shows an applet that uses BorderLayout and that places a button in each of the five regions. As Figure 12–2 shows, these buttons are stretched according to the size of the window, rather than remaining their preferred size as when FlowLayout is used.

Listing 12.2 `BorderTest.java`

```java
import java.applet.Applet;
import java.awt.*;

/** An example of BorderLayout. */

public class BorderTest extends Applet {
  public void init() {
    setLayout(new BorderLayout());
    add(new Button("Button 1"), BorderLayout.NORTH);
    add(new Button("Button 2"), BorderLayout.SOUTH);
    add(new Button("Button 3"), BorderLayout.EAST);
    add(new Button("Button 4"), BorderLayout.WEST);
    add(new Button("Button 5"), BorderLayout.CENTER);
  }
}
```

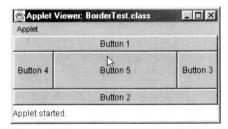

Figure 12–2 `BorderLayout` divides the window into five regions.

The single most likely error you will make when first using `BorderLayout` is forgetting to use:

```java
add(component, BorderLayout.REGION);
```

and instead doing the more familiar but incorrect

```java
add(component);
```

If you don't specify a region, the component is added to the CENTER region. Since entries in the CENTER occupy all available space, only the topmost component (last one added) is displayed. No warning is given when compiling or running.

Core Warning

If you forget to specify a region when adding a component to a window that uses `BorderLayout`, *the component is added to the* CENTER *region.*

Also remember that you should have at most one component per region when using BorderLayout. Otherwise, the top component will obscure the one underneath. If you want several components in a region, group them in a Panel and then put the Panel in the desired region.

Core Approach

Add at most one component to each region of a BorderLayout. To have multiple components in a region, group them in a Panel or other Container.

BorderLayout Constructor Options

public BorderLayout()

This constructor builds a BorderLayout object with regions that touch each other.

public BorderLayout(int hGap, int vGap)

This constructor builds a BorderLayout object that reserves hGap empty pixels between the WEST and CENTER regions and between CENTER and EAST. The constructor also keeps vGap blank pixels between the NORTH and CENTER regions and between CENTER and SOUTH.

Other BorderLayout Methods

You should be careful not to use setHgap or setVgap on the return value of getLayout when applied to a Frame or Dialog that has no explicit layout manager set, since the change will affect other containers that use BorderLayout by default. The same recommendation is also true for the contentPane of a JFrame, JApplet, JWindow, and JDialog.

public int getHgap()
public void setHgap(int hGap)

These methods look up and specify the empty space between horizontally adjacent regions.

public int getVgap()
public void setVgap(int vGap)

These methods look up and specify the empty space between vertically adjacent regions.

public float getLayoutAlignmentX(Container c)
public float getLayoutAlignmentY(Container c)

These methods tell you how the `Container` should be aligned. For more details, see `getAlignmentX` and `getAlignmentY` in Section 13.2 (The Component Class).

12.3 The GridLayout Manager

The `GridLayout` manager divides the window into equal-sized rectangles based upon the number of rows and columns specified. Items are placed into the cells left to right, top to bottom, based upon the order in which they are added. Each component is resized to fit into its grid cell without regard to its current or preferred size. A constructor option lets you specify the gaps between the rows and columns.

Listing 12.3 presents an applet divided into two rows and three columns, with a button placed into each cell. Figure 12–3 shows the result.

Listing 12.3 `GridTest.java`

```java
import java.applet.Applet;
import java.awt.*;

/** An example of GridLayout. */

public class GridTest extends Applet {
  public void init() {
    setLayout(new GridLayout(2,3)); // 2 rows, 3 cols
    add(new Button("Button One"));
    add(new Button("Button Two"));
    add(new Button("Button Three"));
    add(new Button("Button Four"));
    add(new Button("Button Five"));
    add(new Button("Button Six"));
  }
}
```

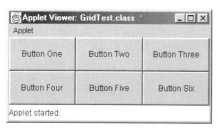

Figure 12–3 `GridLayout` divides the window into equal-sized rectangles.

GridLayout Constructor Options

public GridLayout()

This constructor creates a single row with one column allocated per component.

public GridLayout(int rows, int cols)

This constructor creates a GridLayout object that divides the window into the specified number of rows and columns, with each grid cell flush against the neighboring cell. Either rows or cols (but not both) can be 0. If you specify 0 for the number of rows, the Java platform will try to set the number of rows so that each column has approximately the same number of elements. Similarly, if you specify 0 for the column count, the Java platform will try to choose the number of columns so that each row gets approximately an even number of components. To illustrate this, Listing 12.4 places 11 buttons in a window that specifies zero columns, taking the number of rows as a command-line argument. See Listing 14.1 for WindowUtilities.java.

Listing 12.4 ElevenButtons.java

```java
import java.awt.*;
import javax.swing.*;

/** This illustrates the effect of specifying 0 for the number
 *  of columns. The number of rows is read from the command line
 *  (default 2), and the column number is chosen by the system
 *  to get as even a layout as possible.
 */

public class ElevenButtons extends JPanel {
  public ElevenButtons(int numRows) {
    setLayout(new GridLayout(numRows, 0));
    for(int i=0; i<11; i++) {
      add(new JButton("Button " + i));
    }
  }

  public static void main(String[] args) {
    int numRows = 2;
    if (args.length > 0) {
      numRows = Integer.parseInt(args[0]);
    }
    String title = "11 Buttons using GridLayout(" +
                   numRows + ",0).";
    WindowUtilities.setNativeLookAndFeel();
    WindowUtilities.openInJFrame(new ElevenButtons(numRows),
                                 550, 200, title);
  }
}
```

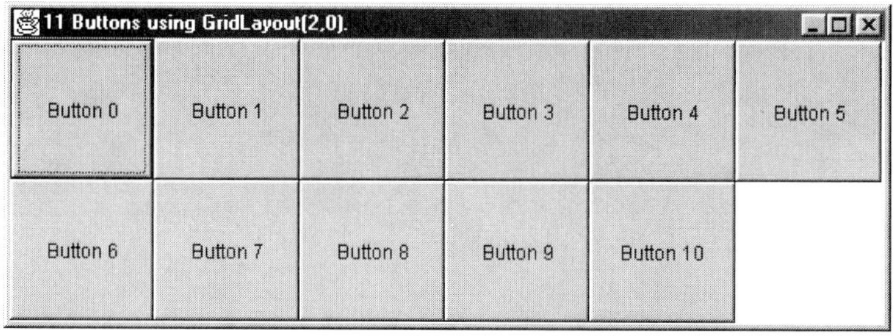

Figure 12–4 When specifying two rows and zero columns, the Java platform chooses 6 columns for an 11-component window.

public GridLayout(int rows, int cols, int hGap, int vGap)

This constructor divides the window into the specified number of rows and columns, leaving hGap and vGap empty pixels between columns and rows. Either the row count or the column count can be 0, but not both. A value of 0 is interpreted as "any number," as illustrated with the description of the previous constructor.

Other GridLayout Methods

public int getRows()
public void setRows(int rows)

These methods let you look up and modify the number of rows.

public int getColumns()
public void setColumns(int cols)

These methods let you read and change the number of columns.

public int getHgap()
public void setHgap(int hGap)

These methods report and specify the empty space between columns.

public int getVgap()
public void setVgap(int vGap)

These methods report and specify the empty space between rows.

12.4 The CardLayout Manager

The CardLayout manager stacks components on top of each other, displaying one at a time. To use this layout manager, you create a CardLayout instance, telling the window to use the manager but also saving the reference in a variable:

```
Panel cardPanel;
CardLayout layout;

...

layout = new CardLayout();
cardPanel.setLayout(layout);
```

Don't forget to save a reference to the layout manager; you'll need the reference later. You then associate a name with each component you add to the window, as below:

```
cardPanel.add(component1, "Card 1");
cardPanel.add(component2, "Card 2");

...
```

The first component added is shown by default. You tell the layout manager to display a particular component in a number of ways: for example, by specifying the name with a call to show or by calling first, last, previous, or next. In all cases, the Container using the layout manager must be supplied as an argument, as follows:

```
layout.show(cardPanel, "Card 1");
layout.first(cardPanel);
layout.next(cardPanel);
```

By way of example, consider Listing 12.5. It places a Panel, using CardLayout, in the right-hand region of the window and a column of buttons in the left-hand region. The Panel contains four versions of a CardPanel (Listing 12.6), which is a Panel that holds a Label and an ImageLabel (you can find the source code for ImageLabel.java at http://www.corewebprogramming.com/) showing a picture of a playing card. Depending on which button is selected, a different card is shown. Figure 12–5 shows one of the four possible configurations.

Listing 12.5 `CardDemo.java`

```java
import java.applet.Applet;
import java.awt.*;
import java.awt.event.*;

/** An example of CardLayout. The right side of the window holds
 *  a Panel that uses CardLayout to control four possible
 *  subpanels (each of which is a CardPanel that shows a
 *  picture of a playing card). The buttons on the left side of
 *  the window manipulate the "cards" in this layout by
 *  calling methods in the right-hand panel's layout manager.
 */

public class CardDemo extends Applet implements ActionListener {
  private Button first, last, previous, next;
  private String[] cardLabels = { "Jack","Queen","King","Ace" };
  private CardPanel[] cardPanels = new CardPanel[4];
  private CardLayout layout;
  private Panel cardDisplayPanel;

  public void init() {
    setBackground(Color.white);
    setLayout(new BorderLayout());
    addButtonPanel();
    addCardDisplayPanel();
  }

  private void addButtonPanel() {
    Panel buttonPanel = new Panel();
    buttonPanel.setLayout(new GridLayout(9, 1));
    Font buttonFont = new Font("SansSerif", Font.BOLD, 18);
    buttonPanel.setFont(buttonFont);
    for(int i=0; i<cardLabels.length; i++) {
      Button button = new Button(cardLabels[i]);
      button.addActionListener(this);
      buttonPanel.add(button);
    }
    first = new Button("First");
    first.addActionListener(this);
    last = new Button("Last");
    last.addActionListener(this);
    previous = new Button("Previous");
    previous.addActionListener(this);
    next = new Button("Next");
    next.addActionListener(this);
    buttonPanel.add(new Label("------------", Label.CENTER));
```

(continued)

Listing 12.5 CardDemo.java *(continued)*

```java
      buttonPanel.add(first);
      buttonPanel.add(last);
      buttonPanel.add(previous);
      buttonPanel.add(next);
      add(buttonPanel, BorderLayout.WEST);
  }
  private void addCardDisplayPanel() {
    cardDisplayPanel = new Panel();
    layout = new CardLayout();
    cardDisplayPanel.setLayout(layout);
    String cardName;
    for(int i=0; i<cardLabels.length; i++) {
      cardName = cardLabels[i];
      cardPanels[i] =
        new CardPanel(cardName, getCodeBase(),
                      "images/" + cardName + ".gif");
      cardDisplayPanel.add(cardPanels[i], cardName);
    }
    add(cardDisplayPanel, BorderLayout.CENTER);
  }

  public void actionPerformed(ActionEvent event) {
    Button source = (Button)event.getSource();
    if (source == first)
      layout.first(cardDisplayPanel);
    else if (source == last)
      layout.last(cardDisplayPanel);
    else if (source == previous)
      layout.previous(cardDisplayPanel);
    else if (source == next)
      layout.next(cardDisplayPanel);
    else
      layout.show(cardDisplayPanel, source.getLabel());
    return;
  }
}
```

Listing 12.6 `CardPanel.java`

```java
import java.awt.*;
import java.net.*;

/** A Panel that displays a playing card. This window does
 *  <B>not</B> use CardLayout. Rather, instances of CardPanel
 *  are contained in another window used in the CardDemo
 *  example. It is this enclosing window that uses CardLayout
 *  to manipulate which CardPanel it shows.
 */

public class CardPanel extends Panel {
  private Label name;
  private ImageLabel picture;

  public CardPanel(String cardName,
                   URL directory, String imageFile) {
    setLayout(new BorderLayout());
    name = new Label(cardName, Label.CENTER);
    name.setFont(new Font("SanSerif", Font.BOLD, 50));
    add(name, BorderLayout.NORTH);
    picture = new ImageLabel(directory, imageFile);
    Panel picturePanel = new Panel();
    picturePanel.add(picture);
    add(picturePanel, BorderLayout.CENTER);
    setSize(getPreferredSize());
  }

  public Label getLabel() {
    return(name);
  }

  public ImageLabel getImageLabel() {
    return(picture);
  }
}
```

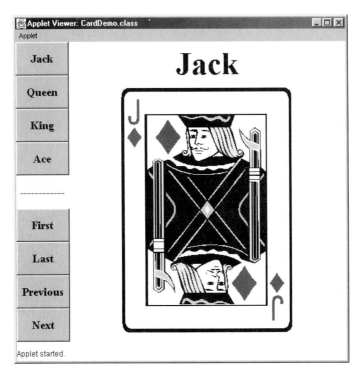

Figure 12-5 CardLayout stacks components above each other.

CardLayout Constructor Options

public CardLayout()

This constructor creates a CardLayout instance that places components in the top-left corner of the window.

public CardLayout(int sideMargins, int topMargins)

This constructor creates a CardLayout object that reserves the specified number of empty pixels on the sides and top/bottom of the window.

Other CardLayout Methods

The following methods are available in the CardLayout class. Note that the Container argument refers to the window that is using the CardLayout, not to the card (Component) itself.

public void show(Container c, String cardName)

This method displays the card that was given the specified name when added to the `Container`.

public void first(Container c)
public void last(Container c)

These methods display the card that was added first and last, respectively.

public void previous(Container c)
public void next(Container c)

These methods display the previous or next card in the sequence. Unless you use a version of `add` that lets you specify a position in the component array, the sequence is arranged in the order in which components were added.

public int getHgap()
public void setHgap(int hGap)

These methods report and specify the empty space reserved at the left and right sides. The names `getSideMargins` and `setSideMargins` might have been clearer in this case, but these names were chosen for consistency with other layout managers.

public int getVgap()
public void setVgap(int vGap)

These methods report and specify the empty space reserved at the top and bottom of the window. The names `getTopMargins` and `setTopMargins` might have been clearer in this case, but these names were chosen for consistency with other layout managers.

public float getLayoutAlignmentX(Container c)
public float getLayoutAlignmentY(Container c)

These methods tell you how the `Container` should be aligned. For more details, see `getAlignmentX` and `getAlignmentY` in Section 13.2 (The Component Class).

12.5 GridBagLayout

The `GridBagLayout` manager is about three times more flexible than any of the other standard layout managers. Unfortunately, `GridBagLayout` is also about *nine* times harder to use. The basic idea is that you chop up the window into grids, then you specify for each component which cell to start and end in. You can also specify how objects stretch when there is extra room and alignment within cells.

The basic steps to using `GridBagLayout` are:

Set the layout, saving a reference to it.

```
GridBagLayout layout = new GridBagLayout();
setLayout(layout);
```

Allocate a GridBagConstraints object.

```
GridBagConstraints constraints =
    new GridBagConstraints();
```

Set up the GridBagConstraints for component 1.

```
constraints.gridx = x1;
constraints.gridy = y1;
constraints.gridwidth = width1;
constraints.gridheight = height1;
...
```

Add the first component to the window, including constraints.

```
add(component1, constraints);
```

Repeat the last two steps for each remaining component.

The GridBagConstraints Object

In addition to setting the layout in the `Container`, you also need to allocate a `GridBagConstraints` object and specify the constraints for laying out each `Component`. Next, add the `Component` to the `Container` by the `add` method, passing in the `GridBagConstraints` object to control layout of the `Component`. Once you add the `Component` to the `Container`, you can reset the `GridBagConstraints` values, so allocating one `GridBagConstraints` object for each `Component` is not necessary. The `GridBagConstraints` class has many fields, most of which need to be set for every added `Component`. The available fields are described below.

public int gridx
public int gridy
These variables specify the top-left corner of the `Component`.

public int gridwidth
public int gridheight
These variables determine the number of columns and rows the `Component` occupies. Note that you do not specify the total number of rows or columns in the layout; the `GridBagLayout` determines this number automatically. In fact, you can set `gridwidth` and `gridheight` to `GridBagConstraints.RELATIVE`

and then add the components left to right, top to bottom, and let the layout manager try to figure out the widths and heights. If you use this approach, use the value `GridBagConstraints.REMAINDER` for the *last* entry in a row or column. The default value is 1.

public int anchor

If the `fill` field is set to `GridBagConstraints.NONE`, then the anchor field determines where the element gets placed. Use `GridBag-Constraints.CENTER` to center the component, or `GridBag-Constraints.NORTH`, `GridBagConstraints.NORTHEAST`, `GridBagConstraints.EAST`, `GridBagConstraints.SOUTHEAST`, `GridBagConstraints.SOUTH`, `GridBagConstraints.SOUTHWEST`, `GridBagConstraints.WEST`, or `GridBagConstraints.NORTHWEST` to position one side or corner in the allocated box.

public int fill

The size of the row or column is determined by the widest/tallest element contained in the row or column. The `fill` field specifies what to do to an element that is smaller than this size. `GridBagConstraints.NONE` (the default) means not to expand the element at all, `GridBagConstraints.HORIZONTAL` means to expand horizontally but not vertically, `GridBagConstraints.VERTICAL` means to expand vertically but not horizontally, and `GridBag-Constraints.BOTH` means to expand the element horizontally and vertically.

public Insets insets

You can use this field to supply an `Insets` object that specifies margins to go on all four sides of the component. The `Insets` class has a single constructor that allows you to specify the four margins around the component:

```
public Insets(int top, int left, int bottom, int right)
```

public int ipadx
public int ipady

These values specify internal padding to add to the component's minimum size. The new size will be the old size plus twice the padding.

public double weightx
public double weighty

These fields determine how much the `Component` will "stretch" in the x or y direction if space is left over after sizing each column based on the widest object and each row based on the tallest. Specifying 0.0 means that the `Component` will stay at its preferred size. Specifying 100.0 means that the `Component` will share extra space equally with other objects that have a weight of 100.0 specified. Values in between result in prorating.

Example

As an example, consider the an application show in Figure 12–6. The layout contains two input fields (`JTextArea` and `JTextfield`), and three buttons. In the schematic, grid placement of each component is illustrated by a shaded oval, and the cells in which a component can stretch are indicated by a dashed outline. For this design, as the window size increases, the text area should also increase to fill any remaining space. Similarly, the textfield should expand if the width of the window increases. The buttons should remain their original size as the window size changes. Because of the complexity of this layout, a `GridBagLayout` manager is a reasonable choice for controlling the layout of the components.

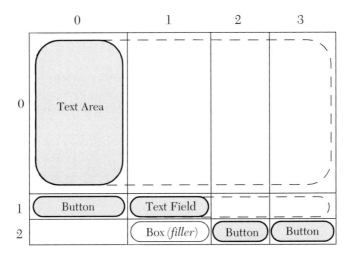

Figure 12–6 Schematic of `GridBagLayout` showing placement of components and the direction components can expand (stretch).

Listing 12.7 shows the code for setting up the components and constraints for the layout manager. For each component, the `GridBagConstraints` are first set, and then the component is added to the `GridBagLayout` panel. In many cases, the `GridBagContraints` instance variables are calculated relative to the previous assignment. In other cases, the instance variables carry over from the previous component assignment and are not reassigned. Behind the scenes, the `GridBagLayout` manager clones a copy of the `GridBagConstraints` and stores the copy in a private `Hashtable`, where the `Component` is the key. Thus, each `Component` always has an associated unique `GridBagContraints` object.

Other than `GridBagLayout`, no other *standard* layout manager will achieve this effect. However, before you leap to the conclusion that `GridBagLayout` is appropriate for this job, let us preview the advice of Section 12.8 (Effective Use of Layout

Managers)—consider using multiple nested layouts instead of one huge layout. In fact, in Section 12.8 you'll see how this exact layout can be achieved more easily by use of nested containers. For more information on the Swing components used in this example, see Chapter 14 (Basic Swing).

As in this example, using a *single* layout manager may require the addition of *fillers* (invisible lightweight components) to produce the desired layout. Consider the Box added to coordinate ($x=1$, $y=2$). The Box is simply a placeholder such that column 1 has at least one component present with a fixed width. Without the invisible Box, column 1 would collapse to a width of 0, because the textfield is stretchable and does not have a fixed horizontal width. The remaining space would be divided equally between columns 2 and 3. As a consequence, the placement of the Ok and Exit buttons would be undesirable, as shown in Figure 12–8. As discussed in Section 12.8 (Effective Use of Layout Managers), you can avoid the need for fillers by mixing or using nested containers.

Listing 12.7 `GridBagTest.java`

```java
import java.awt.*;
import java.awt.event.*;
import java.util.*;
import javax.swing.*;
import javax.swing.border.*;

/** An example demonstrating a GridBagLayout GUI with
 *  input text area and multiple buttons.
 */

public class GridBagTest extends JPanel {
    private JTextArea textArea;
    private JButton bSaveAs, bOk, bExit;
    private JTextField fileField;
    private GridBagConstraints c;

    public GridBagTest() {
        setLayout(new GridBagLayout());
        setBorder(BorderFactory.createEtchedBorder());

        textArea = new JTextArea(12,40);  // 12 rows, 40 cols
        bSaveAs = new JButton("Save As");
        fileField = new JTextField("C:\\Document.txt");
        bOk = new JButton("OK");
        bExit = new JButton("Exit");
```

(continued)

Listing 12.7 GridBagTest.java *(continued)*

```
c = new GridBagConstraints();

// Text Area.
c.gridx      = 0;
c.gridy      = 0;
c.gridwidth  = GridBagConstraints.REMAINDER;
c.gridheight = 1;
c.weightx    = 1.0;
c.weighty    = 1.0;
c.fill       = GridBagConstraints.BOTH;
c.insets     = new Insets(2,2,2,2); //t,l,b,r
add(textArea,c);

// Save As Button.
c.gridx      = 0;
c.gridy      = 1;
c.gridwidth  = 1;
c.gridheight = 1;
c.weightx    = 0.0;
c.weighty    = 0.0;
c.fill       = GridBagConstraints.VERTICAL;
add(bSaveAs,c);

// Filename Input (Textfield).
c.gridx      = 1;
c.gridwidth  = GridBagConstraints.REMAINDER;
c.gridheight = 1;
c.weightx    = 1.0;
c.weighty    = 0.0;
c.fill       = GridBagConstraints.BOTH;
add(fileField,c);

// OK Button.
c.gridx      = 2;
c.gridy++;
c.gridwidth  = 1;
c.gridheight = 1;
c.weightx    = 0.0;
c.weighty    = 0.0;
c.fill       = GridBagConstraints.NONE;
add(bOk,c);
```

(continued)

Listing 12.7 `GridBagTest.java` *(continued)*

```
    // Exit Button.
    c.gridx      = 3;
    c.gridwidth  = 1;
    c.gridheight = 1;
    c.weightx    = 0.0;
    c.weighty    = 0.0;
    c.fill       = GridBagConstraints.NONE;
    add(bExit,c);

    // Filler so Column 1 has nonzero width.
    Component filler = Box.createRigidArea(new Dimension(1,1));
    c.gridx      = 1;
    c.weightx    = 1.0;
    add(filler,c);
  }

  public static void main(String[] args) {
    WindowUtilities.setNativeLookAndFeel();
    JFrame frame = new JFrame("GrigBagLayout Test");
    frame.setContentPane(new GridBagTest());
    frame.addWindowListener(new ExitListener());
    frame.pack();
    frame.setVisible(true);
  }
}
```

Figure 12–7 Using `GridBagConstraints` gives you more control, but at a significant cost in code complexity.

Figure 12–8 Using GridBagLayout without the Box as a filler in column 1.

GridBagLayout Constructor Options

public GridBagLayout()
GridBagLayout has only one constructor. Options are provided through the GridBagConstraints object.

Other GridBagLayout Methods

The following are common methods of GridBagLayout.

public GridBagConstraints getConstraints(Component c)
This method returns a copy of the GridBagConstraints object used to set up the specified component.

public float getLayoutAlignmentX(Container c)
public float getLayoutAlignmentY(Container c)
These methods tell you how the Container is to be aligned. For more details, see getAlignmentX and getAlignmentY in Section 13.2 (The Component Class).

public int[ ][ ] getLayoutDimensions()
This method returns an array containing the dimensions of each row and column in the window.

public Point getLayoutOrigin()
This method returns the location of the top-left corner of the GridBagLayout relative to its containing window.

public double[ ][ ] getLayoutWeights

This method retrieves the `weightx` and `weighty` values.

**public void setConstraints(Component component,
GridBagConstraints constraints)**

This method registers the specified constraints with the given component; the method is rarely used because the preferred approach is to simply apply the constraints when adding a `Component` to a `Container`. For example, use

```
container.add(component, constraints)
```

instead of

```
container.add(component);
layout.setConstraints(constraints);
```

12.6 The BoxLayout Manager

`BoxLayout` is a new layout manager introduced in the Swing package. It supports arranging components either in a horizontal row (`BoxLayout.X_AXIS`) or in a vertical column (`BoxLayout.Y_AXIS`). The `BoxLayout` managers lays out the components in the same order in which they were added to the `Container`, left to right for a horizontal layout, and top to bottom for a vertical layout. Resizing the container does not cause the components to relocate.

`BoxLayout` first attempts to arrange the components at their preferred widths (vertical layout) or preferred heights (horizontal layout). For a vertical layout, if all the components are not the same width, `BoxLayout` then attempts to expand all the components to the width of the component with the largest preferred width. If expanding a component is not possible (restricted maximum size), then `BoxLayout` aligns that component horizontally in the container, according to the *x* alignment of the component.

Similarly for a horizontal layout, `BoxLayout` first attempts to arrange the components at their preferred heights. If all the components are not the same height, then `BoxLayout` attempts to expand all the components to the height of the highest component. If expanding the height of a component is not possible, then `BoxLayout` aligns that component vertically in the container, according to the *y* alignment of the component.

Every lightweight Swing component that inherits from `JComponent` can define an alignment value from 0.0f to 1.0f, where 0.0 represents positioning the component closest to the axis origin in the container, and 1.0 represents positioning the component farthest from the axis origin in the container. The `Component` class predefines five alignment values: `Component.LEFT_ALIGNMENT` (0.0), `Component.CENTER_ALIGNMENT` (0.5), `Component.RIGHT_ALIGNMENT` (1.0),

Component.TOP_ALIGNMENT (0.0), and Component.BOTTOM_ALIGNMENT (1.0). Depending on the BoxLayout orientation, the alignment of each JComponent can be set through the two following methods, where Xxx represents the relative position:

```
jcomponent.setAlignmentX(Component.Xxx_ALIGNMENT);
jcomponent.setAlignmentY(Component.Xxx_ALIGNMENT);
```

Most of the Swing components have a default x-axis alignment of center (Component.CENTER_ALIGNMENT). JButton, JComboBox, JLabel, and JMenu don't follow this general rule. These components have x-axis alignment of left (Component.LEFT_ALIGNMENT).

A simple example of a vertical BoxLayout (BoxLayout.Y_AXIS) is shown in Listing 12.8. The layout contains a label at the top with a default left alignment and three buttons that, when individually selected, will call a method to accordingly change the alignment of all three buttons and then revalidate the Container. The left default alignment of the label does not change.

Listing 12.8 BoxLayoutTest.java

```java
import java.awt.*;
import java.awt.event.*;
import javax.swing.*;

/** An example of BoxLayout. */

public class BoxLayoutTest extends JPanel
                           implements ActionListener{
  BoxLayout layout;
  JButton topButton, middleButton, bottomButton;

  public BoxLayoutTest() {
    layout = new BoxLayout(this, BoxLayout.Y_AXIS);
    setLayout(layout);

    JLabel label = new JLabel("BoxLayout Demo");

    topButton = new JButton("Left Alignment");
    middleButton = new JButton("Center Alignment");
    bottomButton = new JButton("Right Alignment");
    topButton.addActionListener(this);
    middleButton.addActionListener(this);
    bottomButton.addActionListener(this);
```

(continued)

Listing 12.8 `BoxLayoutTest.java` *(continued)*

```
      add(label);
      add(topButton);
      add(middleButton);
      add(bottomButton);
      setBackground(Color.white);
   }

   public void actionPerformed(ActionEvent event) {
      if (event.getSource() == topButton) {
        refresh(Component.LEFT_ALIGNMENT);
      } else if (event.getSource() == middleButton) {
        refresh(Component.CENTER_ALIGNMENT);
      } else if (event.getSource() == bottomButton) {
        refresh(Component.RIGHT_ALIGNMENT);
      }
   }

   private void refresh(float alignment){
     topButton.setAlignmentX(alignment);
     middleButton.setAlignmentX(alignment);
     bottomButton.setAlignmentX(alignment);
     revalidate();
     System.out.println("x: "+layout.getLayoutAlignmentX(this));
   }

   public static void main(String[] args) {
     WindowUtilities.setNativeLookAndFeel();
     WindowUtilities.openInJFrame(new BoxLayoutTest(), 300, 135,
                            "BoxLayoutTest");
   }
}
```

Figure 12–9(a) and 12–9(b) show the BoxLayout after the Left Alignment button and Right Alignment button, respectively, are selected. This example illustrates the problem when the components have differing alignment values.

In Figure 12–9(a), all the components have a left alignment and are correctly aligned to the *x*-axis origin. But in Figure 12–9(b), the three buttons have a *right* alignment, while the label maintains the original *left* alignment. As shown, if the components have different alignment values, the alignment of the components is no longer simply relative to the container but also relative to the other components in the container. In this situation, the alignment value (0.0–1.0) represents the portion of the component that is to the left of a common "component" axis (the component is always in contact with the component axis). Thus, 0% of the label (alignment 0.0) is to the left of the component axis, and 100% of the buttons (alignment 1.0) are to the left of the component axis. The location of the component axis relative to the container is based on a prorated calculation of the individual component alignments and widths. In this latter case, the component axis alignment (or simply, the alignment of the `Container`) is 0.581. To avoid the unexpected alignment in Figure 12–9(b), we recommend that you always set the alignment value for each component, and if appropriate, use the same alignment value for all the components in your `BoxLayout` design.

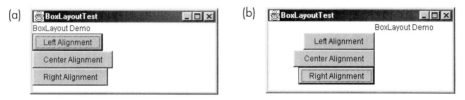

Figure 12–9   (a) `BoxLayout` where all components have a 0.0 (left) alignment. (b) `BoxLayout` where the label has a 0.0 alignment and the buttons have a 1.0 (right) alignment.

For a vertical `BoxLayout`, the default behavior is to size the width of all components to the width of the widest component. However, if a component has an unbounded maximum width, for example, `Integer.MAX_VALUE`, then that component will always be as wide as the `Container`. An unusual circumstance is where all the components have an unbounded width, but at least one of them has a *strict* left (0.0) or right (1.0) alignment. For this situation, the width of the components with a strict alignment will always be *less* than the width of the `Container`, while the other components will be as wide as the `Container`. In practice, nearly all components report the same maximum size as the preferred size and do not have an unbounded width, so this behavior of `BoxLayout` goes unnoticed. You can change the maximum size of a `Component` through

```
component.setMaximumSize(new Dimension(width, height));
```

A similar analogy holds for component heights in a horizontal layout.

BoxLayout Constructor Options

The `BoxLayout` manager has only one constructor.

public BoxLayout(Container container, int axis)

The first parameter in the `BoxLayout` constructor is a reference to the `Container` that the `BoxLayout` is managing. The `Container` is referenced internally as a private variable and checked when calling other `BoxLayout` methods. Thus, each `BoxLayout` manager can only be assigned to one

Container. The axis parameter specifies the direction of the layout, either BoxLayout.X_AXIS for a left-to-right (horizontal) layout or BoxLayout.Y_AXIS for a top-to-bottom (vertical) layout.

Core Alert

Unlike the other standard layout managers, the BoxLayout *manager cannot be shared with more than one* Container.

Other BoxLayout Methods

The following are the most common methods of the BoxLayout class.

public Dimension preferredLayoutSize(Container container)
public Dimension minimumLayoutSize(Container container)
public Dimension maximumLayoutSize(Container container)
These methods, respectively, return the preferred, minimum, and maximum Dimension necessary to lay out the Container, given the contained components.

public float getLayoutAlignmentX(Container container)
public float getLayoutAlignmentY(Container container)
These methods return the desired overall *x*- or *y*-axis alignment, respectively, for the Container (which is a Component), relative to *other* components in the window. The overall alignment of the Container is based on the required alignment of each internal Component in the Container. The alignment can range from 0.0f to 1.0f, inclusively. See Section 13.2 (The Component Class) for additional details on alignment.

public void layoutContainer(Container container)
This method positions and sizes all the components in the Container by calling setBounds on each Component.

public void invalidateLayout(container container)
This method discards any cached information for laying out the components.

Note that Swing also provides a Box container that uses a BoxLayout manager. In the Box constructor you can specify the axis orientation as BoxLayout.X_AXIS for a horizontal layout or BoxLayout.Y_AXIS for a vertical layout. The Box class also provides multiple static methods for creating invisible filler components. See Section 12.8 (Effective Use of Layout Managers) for details.

12.7 Turning Off the Layout Manager

Layout managers are supposed to make your life easier. If you find they're getting in the way, just turn them off. This action is no sin, although with a little experience you'll find that you want to do this less often than you might think at first. If the layout is set to `null`, then components can be (in fact, *must* be) sized and positioned by hand, with either `setSize(width, height)` and `setLocation(left, top)` or `setBounds(left, top, width, height)`. Applets are not resizable, but for `Frame` and `JFrame` you could override `setSize` and `setBounds` to call `super.setSize` and `super.setBounds`, respectively, and reposition the components.

Although this technique sounds tedious, if the window with the layout manager turned off contains only a few components (possibly other windows with non-`null` layout managers), this approach is quite tractable. Listing 12.9 gives an example, with the result shown in Figure 12–10. As we'll see in Section 12.8 (Effective Use of Layout Managers), using nested containers and basing dimensions on the current window size rather than on absolute pixels makes this approach significantly more flexible while requiring very little extra work.

Listing 12.9 `NullTest.java`

```java
import java.applet.Applet;
import java.awt.*;

/** Layout managers are intended to help you, but there
 *  is no law saying you <B>have</B> to use them.
 *  Set the layout to null to turn them off.
 */

public class NullTest extends Applet {
  public void init() {
    setLayout(null);
    Button b1 = new Button("Button 1");
    Button b2 = new Button("Button 2");
    Button b3 = new Button("Button 3");
    Button b4 = new Button("Button 4");
    Button b5 = new Button("Button 5");
    b1.setBounds(0, 0, 150, 50);
    b2.setBounds(150, 0, 75, 50);
    b3.setBounds(225, 0, 75, 50);
```

(continued)

Listing 12.9 `NullTest.java` *(continued)*

```
    b4.setBounds(25, 60, 100, 40);
    b5.setBounds(175, 60, 100, 40);
    add(b1);
    add(b2);
    add(b3);
    add(b4);
    add(b5);
  }
}
```

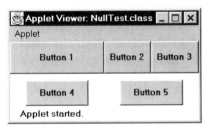

Figure 12-10 You can position elements by hand if you set the layout manager to `null`.

12.8 Effective Use of Layout Managers

The idea of a layout manager is a good one. In principle, a layout manager relieves the developer of the requirement to specify the sizes and positions of each and every component and simplifies the development of many interfaces. In practice, however, many developers feel that the layout managers are hindering them more than helping them. Although some layout managers such as `GridBagLayout` require more effort than they should, a few basic strategies for harnessing the power of layout managers will significantly simplify the UI layout process.

Use nested containers.

No law states that you have to use a single layout manager for everything. Divide and conquer!

Turn off the layout manager for some containers.

In a pinch, don't be afraid to position a few things by hand.

Use a custom layout manager.

Don't like the standard layout managers? Write your own.

Adjust the empty space around components.

If your layout is almost perfect except for some empty space, there are a few small tweaks you can use to fix up those last details.

Use Nested Containers

Rather than struggling to fit your design into a single layout, try dividing the design into rectangular sections. Let each section be a panel with a separate layout manager. In Section 12.5 (GridBagLayout), we showed you a layout incorporating various input fields and buttons. The original layout was performed with a single GridBag-Layout manager, but as Listing 12.10 shows, you could do the layout more easily by creating separate panels for the various regions and applying a different layout manager to each panel.

A schematic of the nested container layout is shown in Figure 12–11. The key idea when nesting different layouts is to remember how the different standard layout managers respect the preferred size of the contained components. Specifically,

- FlowLayout—Respects the preferred size of the components.
- GridLayout—Does not respect the preferred size of the components.
- BorderLayout—North and South respect the preferred height, East and West respect the preferred width, Center respects neither the width nor height of the component.

Based on these behaviors, the nested layout shown in Figure 12–11 falls out naturally. The text area should expand both horizontally and vertically to fill all remaining space; thus, the *preferred* width and height need not be respected. The button components at the bottom should maintain a fixed height, and the textfield should be allowed to expand horizontally. Thus, a BorderLayout manager is a natural choice for the first Container, where the EAST, NORTH, and WEST locations are empty.

The bottom area geometrically break up into two rows, so, a JPanel with a new GridLayout manager defining two rows and one column is added to the SOUTH location. To handle the input field and multiple buttons, a JPanel is added to each row of the GridLayout. Each JPanel is assigned a new layout manager to better control positioning of the components. To determine the best layout manager for each panel, examine the requirements of the contained components. The preferred size of the Save As JButton should be respected, whereas the input field, JText-Field, should expand horizontally with the window. Again, a BorderLayout is appropriate, where the NORTH, EAST, and SOUTH locations are empty. Lastly, the Ok JButton and Exit JButton should stay their preferred size but always be located in the far-right location of the JPanel. The default layout manager of a JPanel, FlowLayout, respects the size of all components but, by default, centers the components. All that is needed is to reassign the FlowLayout manager with a component alignment of FlowLayout.RIGHT. Ta da! Of course, other nested container layouts are possible, but this example clearly shows that a nested container approach significantly simplifies the code compared to that for a single GridBagLayout manager, as in Listing 12.7. The final result is shown in Figure 12–12.

Text Area

Button Text Field

Button Button

━━━━ BorderLayout
──── FlowLayout
──── GridLayout

Figure 12–11 Schematic of nested containers showing placement of components and implied panels. The layout manager for each panel is indicated by the key.

Listing 12.10 NestedLayout.java

```
import java.awt.*;
import java.awt.event.*;
import java.util.*;
import javax.swing.*;
import javax.swing.border.*;
import javax.swing.event.*;
```

(continued)

Listing 12.10 `NestedLayout.java` *(continued)*

```java
/** An example demonstrating the use of nested containers
 *  to lay out the components. See GridBagTest.java for
 *  implementation by a single layout manager, GridBagLayout.
 */

public class NestedLayout extends JPanel {

  private JTextArea textArea;
  private JButton bSaveAs, bOk, bExit;
  private JTextField fileField;

  public NestedLayout() {

    setLayout(new BorderLayout(2,2));
    setBorder(BorderFactory.createEtchedBorder());

    textArea = new JTextArea(12,40);  // 12 rows, 40 cols
    bSaveAs = new JButton("Save As");
    fileField = new JTextField("C:\\Document.txt");
    bOk = new JButton("OK");
    bExit = new JButton("Exit");

    add(textArea,BorderLayout.CENTER);

    // Set up buttons and textfield in bottom panel.
    JPanel bottomPanel = new JPanel();
    bottomPanel.setLayout(new GridLayout(2,1));

    JPanel subPanel1 = new JPanel();
    JPanel subPanel2 = new JPanel();
    subPanel1.setLayout(new BorderLayout());
    subPanel2.setLayout(new FlowLayout(FlowLayout.RIGHT,2,2));

    subPanel1.add(bSaveAs,BorderLayout.WEST);
    subPanel1.add(fileField,BorderLayout.CENTER);
    subPanel2.add(bOk);
    subPanel2.add(bExit);

    bottomPanel.add(subPanel1);
    bottomPanel.add(subPanel2);

    add(bottomPanel,BorderLayout.SOUTH);
  }
```

(continued)

Listing 12.10 `NestedLayout.java` *(continued)*

```java
  public static void main(String[] args) {
    WindowUtilities.setNativeLookAndFeel();
    JFrame frame = new JFrame("Nested Containers");
    frame.setContentPane(new NestedLayout());
    frame.addWindowListener(new ExitListener());
    frame.pack();
    frame.setVisible(true);
  }
}
```

Figure 12–12 Nested containers generally simplify complex layouts.

Turn Off the Layout Manager for Some Containers

Positioning components individually is not always particularly difficult, especially if combined with the use of nested windows. For instance, suppose that you wanted to arrange an applet with a column of buttons down the left side, with the remainder of the space reserved for drawing space (with a `Label` as a title). Further suppose that you wanted the button column to take up exactly 40% of the width of the applet, rather than a width independent of the `Container` size (enough space for the widest button). You can implement the design by allocating two `Panels` but positioning them by using `setBounds` after turning off the layout manager for the overall applet. Because each `Panel` still has a layout manager, components inside of them do *not* need to be positioned manually.

Listing 12.11 `ButtonCol.java`

```java
import java.applet.Applet;
import java.awt.*;

/** An example of a layout performed manually. The top-level
 *  panels are positioned by hand, after you determine the size
 *  of the applet. Since applets can't be resized in most
 *  browsers, setting the size once when the applet is created
 *  is sufficient.
 */

public class ButtonCol extends Applet {
  public void init() {
    setLayout(null);
    int width1 = getSize().width*4/10,
        width2 = getSize().width - width1,
        height = getSize().height;
    Panel buttonPanel = new Panel();
    buttonPanel.setBounds(0, 0, width1, height);
    buttonPanel.setLayout(new GridLayout(6, 1));
    buttonPanel.add(new Label("Buttons", Label.CENTER));
    buttonPanel.add(new Button("Button One"));
    buttonPanel.add(new Button("Button Two"));
    buttonPanel.add(new Button("Button Three"));
    buttonPanel.add(new Button("Button Four"));
    buttonPanel.add(new Button("Button Five"));
    add(buttonPanel);
    Panel everythingElse = new Panel();
    everythingElse.setBounds(width1+1, 0, width2, height);
    everythingElse.add(new Label("Everything Else"));
    add(everythingElse);
  }
}
```

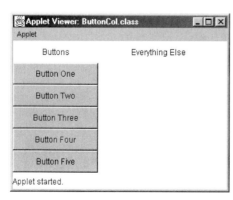

Figure 12–13 Manually position top-level windows, not individual components.

Adjust the Empty Space Around Components

Change the space allocated by the layout manager.

All the standard AWT layout managers except for GridBagLayout have a constructor option that lets you specify the amount of space that will be reserved between components. With GridBagLayout, you can specify this option by using the insets or ipadx and ipady fields of the GridBag-Constraints object.

Override insets in the Container.

Insets are designed to be empty margins around the inside of a Container. All built-in layout managers respect them, as should any custom layout managers. Insets allows for borders around components. Unfortunately, however, a Container does not provide a way to change its insets. So, a subclass of Container (probably a Panel subclass) must be created to override the getInsets method.

Use a Canvas or a Box as an invisible spacer.

For AWT layouts, use a Canvas that does not draw or handle mouse events as an "empty" component for spacing. A Canvas works as an invisible spacer in windows using FlowLayout, GridLayout, GridBagLayout, BoxLayout or in the noncenter region of a window using BorderLayout.

For Swing layouts, add a Box as an invisible spacer to improve positioning of components. The Box class provides three types of spacers:

- Rigid area—A two-dimensional invisible component (Box.createRigidArea) with a fixed width and height.
- Strut—A one-dimensional invisible component that can be either a *horizontal* strut with fixed width and (Box.CreateHorizontalStrut) zero height, or a *vertical* strut with zero width and (Box.CreateHorizontalStrut) fixed height.
- Glue—A one- (Box.createHorizontalGlue, Box.createVerticalGlue) or two-dimensional (Box.createGlue) invisible component that will expand to fill all remaining space.

Listing 12.12 illustrates the use of a rigid area, a horizontal strut, and horizontal glue. Four separate JPanels (default FlowLayout manager) are created, each containing a left and right button. As shown in Figure 12–14, the first panel incorporates an invisible rigid area (20 × 75 pixels) between the two buttons. The second panel incorporates a horizontal strut, 60 pixels wide with no height, to separate the buttons. The third panel attempts to use a Box component as glue to fill in the space between the buttons, but fails, because FlowLayout does not respect the *maximum* size of the Box. BoxLayout is the only manager that respects the desired maximum size of a component. The fourth panel, using a `BoxLayout`, shows the correct effect of horizontal glue.

Core Alert

Only apply "glue" to layout managers that respect the maximum size of a `Component`. The use of a glue component is correctly supported in `BoxLayout`.

Listing 12.12 `InvisibleComponentTest.java`

```java
import java.awt.*;
import javax.swing.*;
import javax.swing.border.*;

public class InvisibleComponentTest extends JPanel {
  Component spacer;

  public InvisibleComponentTest() {
    setLayout(new BoxLayout(this, BoxLayout.Y_AXIS));

    // Place a rigid invisible component 25 pixels wide and
    // 75 pixels tall between the two buttons
    JPanel p1= new JPanel();
    spacer = Box.createRigidArea(new Dimension(20,75));
    setUpPanel(p1, "Rigid Area - 20x75 pixels", spacer);

    // Separate two buttons by a 60-pixel horizontal strut
    JPanel p2= new JPanel();
    spacer = Box.createHorizontalStrut(60);
    setUpPanel(p2, "Horizontal Strut - 60 pixels", spacer);

    // Horizontal glue in FlowLayout - not useful
    JPanel p3= new JPanel();
    spacer = Box.createHorizontalGlue();
    setUpPanel(p3, "Horizontal Glue - FlowLayout", spacer);

    // Add glue to fill all remaining horizontal space between
    // the two buttons. Glue not supported by default FlowLayout
    // of JPanel.  Change layout of JPanel to BoxLayout.
    JPanel p4= new JPanel();
    p4.setLayout(new BoxLayout(p4,BoxLayout.X_AXIS));
```

(continued)

Listing 12.12 `InvisibleComponentTest.java` *(continued)*

```
    spacer = Box.createHorizontalGlue();
    setUpPanel(p4, "Horizontal Glue - BoxLayout", spacer);

    add(p1);
    add(p2);
    add(p3);
    add(p4);
  }

  // Helper to set the border and add components
  private void setUpPanel(JPanel p, String title,
                          Component spacer) {
    p.setBorder(BorderFactory.createTitledBorder(
                    BorderFactory.createEtchedBorder(),title,
                    TitledBorder.TOP,TitledBorder.CENTER));
    p.setBackground(Color.white);
    p.add(new JButton("Left"));
    p.add(spacer);
    p.add(new JButton("Right"));
  }

  public static void main(String[] args) {
    String title = "Using Invisible Components";
    WindowUtilities.setNativeLookAndFeel();
    WindowUtilities.openInJFrame(new InvisibleComponentTest(),
                                 350, 325, title);
  }
}
```

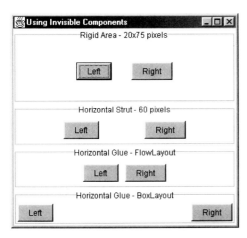

Figure 12–14 An invisible Box can improve the layout of the components.

Box Utility Methods

The `Box` class provides the following `static` methods for creating invisible components:

> **public static Component createRigidArea(Dimension size)**
> This method creates an invisible `Component` that maintains a fixed `Dimension` (width and height).

> **public static Component createHorizontalStrut(int width)**
> **public static Component createVerticalStrut(int height)**
> The first method creates an invisible `Component` of fixed width and zero height. The second method creates an invisible `Component` of fixed height and zero width.

> **public static Component createHorizontalGlue()**
> **public static Component createVerticalGlue()**
> **public static Component createGlue()**
> The first two methods create an invisible glue `Component` that can expand horizontally or vertically, respectively, to fill all remaining space. The third method creates a `Component` that can expand in both directions. A `Box` object achieves the glue effect by expressing a maximum size of `Short.MAX_VALUE`. If more than one glue component is present in a `BoxLayout`, the remaining space is divided equally between the glue components.

12.9 Summary

Layout managers help you position components in the window. They are particularly helpful when you resize the window, add components, or move the program among operating systems. There are five traditional layout managers: `FlowLayout`, `BorderLayout`, `GridLayout`, `CardLayout`, and `GridBagLayout`. In Java 2, the `BoxLayout` manager was added for additional flexibility. If you don't like any of those, you can always turn off the layout manager, but clever use of nested containers often makes turn-off unnecessary.

Okay, so you've got windows galore. You're a layout manager pro. But putting something *in* the windows would be nice. Read on: Chapter 13 covers buttons, check boxes, radio buttons, scrollbars, and other GUI controls.

AWT
COMPONENTS

Topics in This Chapter

- The Component class
- Creating lightweight components
- The major types of windows, including Panel, Applet, Frame, and Dialog
- Closing a Frame from a browser Applet
- Putting menus in Frames
- Creating scrollable windows
- Using object serialization to save components to disk and reload them
- Processing events in GUI controls
- The major types of controls including labels, buttons, check boxes, list boxes, and textfields

Chapter 13

The Abstract Window Toolkit (AWT), introduced in the first release of Java, provides basic window and control components for creating GUI programs. Since the release of the Java 2 Platform, the AWT components are now superseded by the newer Swing components (covered in Chapter 14, "Basic Swing," and Chapter 15, "Advanced Swing"). However, the only popular browser that currently supports Swing is Netscape 6; Swing is unsupported in earlier versions of Netscape and Internet Explorer without installation of the Java Plug-In (see Section 9.9), or including the required Swing classes in a JAR file for downloading along with the applet. So, if you are delivering Java content to customers over the Internet in Web pages, the best solution is to use the AWT components. In this chapter, we present the major types of windows and controls available in the AWT and discuss how to handle user events in the GUI controls. The Java 1.1 AWT API is supported by Netscape 4.06 and later, and Internet Explorer 4.0 and later.

The AWT has eight major types of windows for user interfaces: `Canvas`, `Panel`, `Applet`, `ScrollPane`, `Frame`, `Dialog`, `FileDialog`, and `Window`. Some windows (such as `Panel` and `ScrollPane`) are borderless and can only be placed in other windows; others (such as `Frame` and `Dialog`) have borders and title bars and can pop up anywhere on the screen. An `Applet` is the starting point for Web-embedded applets and remains the main driving force for still using the AWT components. A `Frame` is the base window for graphical applications. However, for most stand-alone graphical applications you would use the Swing components. Nonetheless, the AWT `Frame` still has an important role, since a `Frame` can be opened from an applet, creating a multiple-window user interface from a browser.

In the following sections, we describe each of the eight window types, summarizing their major purposes, their standard layout manager, the steps required to create and use them, and an example of their use. Separate sections are devoted to the Component and Container classes, the bases on which the windows are built.

After presenting the basic window types, we review the general approach for processing events in your program and then cover the major GUI controls (or "widgets") available in the AWT: buttons, check boxes, radio buttons, list boxes, textfields, labels, scollbars, and pop-up menus. All these GUI control components (as well as the major windowing components) can receive mouse and keyboard events; however, many of components use custom events for user input. For example, a List receives ItemSelectionEvents, and a Scrollbar receives AdjustmentEvents. For each major GUI control, we summarize the use of the component and the method of processing events.

GUI controls have their own graphical representation that you should not attempt to tamper directly with; the paint method is not used at all. Instead, the GUI controls adopt the look and feel of the operating system on which they are running (through a native "peer"), leaving interfaces that allow the user to change only certain aspects of their appearance. This feature is a two-edged sword. On the one hand, it lets you easily adapt to multiple platforms and saves you from the myriad details that implementing GUI controls yourself would require. On the other hand, you have only limited control over these graphical objects. For instance, you can always change the labels of buttons, but you can never change their shape, border thickness, or the means for clicking them.

Technically, you can create a custom AWT component that inherits directly from the Component class and that is lightweight and has no associated native window-system peer. For a custom component, you can override the paint method to create your own borders and colors. We present an example of a lightweight canvas to create a circle whose borders are transparent.

13.1 The Canvas Class

A Canvas is the simplest window and cannot contain any other GUI controls. Furthermore, you must place a canvas inside an existing window because a canvas cannot stand alone. As such, a Canvas does not have a layout manager. A canvas has two major roles:

1. **Drawing area.** Suppose that you have a complicated GUI and want to create a custom graph or image. Rather than directly drawing into the underlying window, you may find it more convenient to insert a separate Canvas on which to perform the drawing. Note, however, that the Canvas should draw *itself* by overriding the paint method.

2. **Custom component.** The Canvas is also the starting place for many custom components, for instance, an image label or image button.

Both approaches require you to subclass Canvas, so specialized extensions to the Canvas class are more common than direct instances of Canvas. Due to interaction of the default update and paint methods in a Canvas, looking up the Graphics object (i.e., getGraphics) of the Canvas for drawing into by an external class is not very reliable. Instead, the external routines should set some data that the Canvas knows about and then invoke the repaint method of the Canvas when drawing is required.

Core Approach

Windows that need to draw should override paint *to draw themselves. Don't try to get the* Graphics *object of another window and draw into it.*

Creating and Using a Canvas

The basic steps for creating and using a Canvas are shown below:

```
Canvas canvas = new Canvas();  // Create the canvas.
canvas.setSize(width, height); // Resize the canvas.
add(canvas); // Add the canvas to a Container.
// Or, for other layout managers,
add(canvas, region);
```

By default, the size of a Canvas is 0 pixels by 0 pixels, so if you forget to set the size of the canvas, then your Canvas won't show up. A few exceptions to this rule exist, such as when you put a Canvas into the Center region of a BorderLayout; see Chapter 12 (Layout Managers).

Core Alert

Don't forget to give a size to your Canvas.

Example: A Circle Component

Listing 13.1 gives an example of a simple custom component—one that draws a circle on the canvas. Use of a canvas does not require any modifications to the paint method of the window using it. Instead, you simply add the canvas to a window (Listing 13.2) and let Java take care the rest. The canvas is automatically redrawn whenever the window is covered and reexposed, or positioned by the layout managers if the enclosing window uses one. The result is shown in Figure 13–1. In this example, we let the `Applet` decide where to place the circles. In Chapter 12 (Layout Managers), we show you how to position the components by using different layout managers.

Listing 13.1 `Circle.java`

```
import java.awt.*;

/** A Circle component built using a Canvas. */

public class Circle extends Canvas {
  private int width, height;

  public Circle(Color foreground, int radius) {
    setForeground(foreground);
    width = 2*radius;
    height = 2*radius;
    setSize(width, height);
  }

  public void paint(Graphics g) {
    g.fillOval(0, 0, width, height);
  }

  public void setCenter(int x, int y) {
    setLocation(x - width/2, y - height/2);
  }
}
```

Listing 13.2 `CircleTest.java`

```
import java.awt.*;
import java.applet.Applet;

/** Insert three circles into an Applet using FlowLayout. */

public class CircleTest extends Applet {
  public void init() {
    setBackground(Color.lightGray);
    add(new Circle(Color.white, 30));
    add(new Circle(Color.gray, 40));
    add(new Circle(Color.black, 50));
  }
}
```

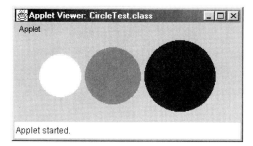

Figure 13–1 A Canvas can be used to create a new type of graphical component.

In the AWT, *all* graphical components are rectangular and opaque. This means that the circles cannot overlap or even be arbitrarily close together without interfering with each other. To illustrate this behavior, Listing 13.3 creates multiple circles aligned diagonally in the window. As can be seen in Figure 13–2, the corners of the underlying Canvas block part of the neighboring circles. When using an event handler for a circle, you would need to filter out mouse clicks that fall outside the area of the circle and explicitly pass them to the enclosing window.

Core Note

In the AWT, all windows and graphical components are rectangular and opaque.

Listing 13.3 CircleTest2.java

```
import java.awt.*;
import java.applet.Applet;

/** Position circles down the diagonal so that their borders
 *  just touch. Illustrates that AWT components are
 *  rectangular and opaque.
 */

public class CircleTest2 extends Applet {
  public void init() {
    setBackground(Color.lightGray);
    setLayout(null); // Turn off layout manager.
```

(continued)

Listing 13.3 `CircleTest2.java` *(continued)*

```
    Circle circle;
    int radius = getSize().width/6;
    int deltaX = round(2.0 * (double)radius / Math.sqrt(2.0));
    for (int x=radius; x<6*radius; x=x+deltaX) {
      circle = new Circle(Color.black, radius);
      add(circle);
      circle.setCenter(x, x);
    }
  }

  private int round(double num) {
    return((int)Math.round(num));
  }
}
```

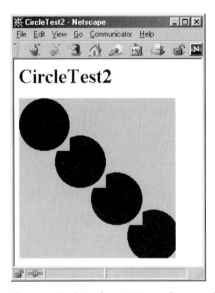

Figure 13-2 In the AWT, windows and GUI controls are rectangular and opaque.

13.2 The Component Class

All windows and GUI controls in the AWT inherit from the Component class. Below, we summarize the more common methods in the class.

public void add(PopupMenu menu)
public void remove(MenuComponent menu)

The `add` method associates a `PopupMenu` with the component. The menu won't pop up automatically; use `show` in the `PopupMenu` class to display the menu. The `remove` method removes the menu from the component.

public void addNotify()
public void removeNotify()

The `addNotify` method creates the "peer" (native window system object) associated with the component. If the component peer needs to exist before some action is performed, then call this method (or `setVisible`). For custom components, be sure to call `super.addNotify` to ensure that the peer is created. The `removeNotify` method destroys the native resource (peer). The method names are a bit unintuitive; the `addNotify` and `removeNotify` methods probably should have been called `createPeer` and `destroyPeer`.

public void addXxxListener(XxxListener listener)
public void removeXxxListener(XxxListener listener)

These two methods add and remove event listeners, where *Xxx* is one of the following listeners: `Component`, `Focus`, `InputMethod` (Java 2), `Key`, `Mouse`, `MouseMotion`, `PropertyChange` (Java 2). See Section 11.5 (The Standard Event Listeners) for more information.

public boolean contains(int x, int y)
public boolean contains(Point p)

These methods determine whether the specified location is inside the component.

protected final void disableEvents(long eventsToDisable)
protected final void enableEvents(long eventsToEnable)

These methods turn off and on the specified events for the component, respectively. See the `AWTEvent` class for input event types (masks).

public final void dispatchEvent(AWTEvent event)

This is a low-level event handling method for dispatching events to the component.

protected void firePropertyChange(String propertyName,
Object oldValue,
Object newValue) [Java 2]

The firePropertyChange method places a PropertyChangeEvent on
the event dispatch queue. The event is dispatched to any registered
PropertyChangeListeners.

public float getAlignmentX()
public float getAlignmentY()

These methods can be overridden to provide alignment information,
where a value of 0.0f should be interpreted to align the side closest to
the x or y axis (i.e., left and top, respectively), 0.5f should be interpreted to
align the centers, and 1.0f to align the side farthest from the axis (i.e., right and
bottom). The default value for both is 0.5f. The Component class defines five
associated constants: TOP_ALIGNMENT (0.0f), CENTER_ALIGNMENT (0.5f),
BOTTOM_ALIGNMENT (1.0f), LEFT_ALIGNMENT (0.0f), and
RIGHT_ALIGNMENT (1.0f).

public Color getBackground()
public void setBackground(Color bgColor)

These two methods return and set the background color of the component,
respectively.

public Rectangle getBounds()
public void setBounds(int x, int y, int width, int height)
public void setBounds(Rectangle boundingRectangle)

The getBounds method returns a Rectangle object describing the outside
edges of the component. A Rectangle is a nongraphical data structure with x,
y, width, and height fields. The remaining two methods change both the
size and location of a component. You can replace the combination of
setSize and setLocation with setBounds.

public Component getComponentAt(int x, int y)
public Component getComponentAt(Point p)

These methods return the topmost component at the specified location. The
component itself is returned if there is no nested component at the location;
null is returned for coordinates outside the component.

public Cursor getCursor()
public void setCursor(Cursor cursor)

The getCursor method returns the current cursor. Use setCursor in any
Component to set the cursor display. To obtain a Cursor object, call

`Cursor.getPredefinedCursor(type)`, where *type* is one of the constants defined in the `Cursor` class: `CROSSHAIR_CURSOR`, `DEFAULT_CURSOR`, `E_RESIZE_CURSOR`, `HAND_CURSOR`, `MOVE_CURSOR`, `N_RESIZE_CURSOR`, `NE_RESIZE_CURSOR`, `NW_RESIZE_CURSOR`, `S_RESIZE_CURSOR`, `SE_RESIZE_CURSOR`, `SW_RESIZE_CURSOR`, `TEXT_CURSOR`, `W_RESIZE_CURSOR`, or `WAIT_CURSOR`.

public Font getFont()
public void setFont(Font f)

The `getFont` method returns the current font, either from a `setFont` call or inherited from the enclosing window. The `Graphics` object used in `paint` and `update` also inherits the component font.

public FontMetrics getFontMetrics(Font f)

Given a `Font`, `getFontMetrics` returns a `FontMetrics` object. Use this object to find the width and height of characters or strings in the specified font.

public Color getForeground()
public void setForeground(Color fgColor)

These two methods return and set the foreground color of the component. The foreground color is inherited by the `Graphics` object of the component.

public Graphics getGraphics()

This method returns a `Graphics` object that can be used to draw onto the component. The `Graphics` object is initialized with the component's font and foreground and background colors.

public Point getLocation()
public void setLocation(int x, int y)
public void setLocation(Point p)

The `getLocation` method returns a `Point` object (with x and y fields) describing, *in the enclosing window's coordinate system*, the top-left corner of the window. See `getLocationOnScreen` for retrieving the absolute coordinates. The `setLocation` methods move the top-left corner of the component to the specified position in the enclosing window's coordinate system. If the parent window is using one of the standard layout managers, then setting the location can be undone by the layout manager.

public Point getLocationOnScreen()

This method returns the absolute location of the component's top-left corner. For applets, however, you cannot obtain the absolute location of the component on the screen.

public Dimension getMinimumSize()
public Dimension getMaximumSize()
public Dimension getPreferredSize()

These methods return a `Dimension` object (with `x`, `y`, `width`, and `height` fields) describing the smallest, largest, or preferred size of the component. Layout managers use these values and should not resize components beyond these bounds if possible.

public Container getParent()

This method returns the enclosing window (`null` in the case of a `Frame` or a `Component` not yet associated with a window).

public Dimension getSize()
public void setSize(int width, int height)
public void setSize(Dimension d)

The `getSize` method returns the current size of the component as a `Dimension` object. A `Dimension` has `width` and `height` fields. The `setSize` methods change the width and height of the component by calling `setBounds` with the specified width and height and the current top-left corner location.

public Toolkit getToolkit()

This method returns the `Toolkit`, which is used to load images (`getImage`), find the available fonts (`getFontList`), look up the screen size (`getScreenSize`), resolution (`getScreenResolution`), and so forth.

public void invalidate()
public void validate()

The `invalidate` method sets an internal flag, indicating that the component and all nested components are no longer valid and should be laid out again before painting. The `validate` method works in coordination with the `Container` class to update the layout of the component and all nested components.

public boolean isEnabled()

The `isEnabled` method determines whether a component is enabled. See `setEnabled`.

public boolean isFocusTraversable()

The `isFocusTraversable` method determines whether the component will receive the input focus when the user uses Tab or Shift-Tab. If not, the component can still explicitly request the focus with `requestFocus`.

public boolean isShowing()
public boolean isVisible()

The isShowing method determines whether the component is visible and that the window holding it is showing. The isVisible method determines whether the component is currently visible. Even if the isVisible method returns true, the component won't appear if the containing window is not visible.

public boolean isValid()

The isValid method determines whether the component is valid. See validate and invalidate.

public void list()
public void list(PrintStream stream)
public void list(PrintStream stream, int indentation)
public void list(PrintWriter writer)
public void list(PrintWriter writer, int indentation)

These methods print information about the component and subcomponents, traversing the tree in depth-first order and printing nested components indented relative to their parents. These methods are useful during development, since calling list on the top-level window (i.e., the Applet or Frame) gives information on every component in the application.

Core Approach

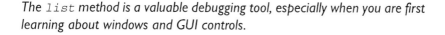

The list method is a valuable debugging tool, especially when you are first learning about windows and GUI controls.

public void paint(Graphics g)

The paint method is called whenever the user calls repaint or when the component is obscured and reexposed. Override this method to perform graphics operations in a component. If paint is called because part of the component has been covered, the clipping region of the Graphics object is set to that area.

public void paintAll(Graphics g)

This method paints the component and any nested components.

public boolean prepareImage(Image image,
                        ImageObserver observer)
public boolean prepareImage(Image image, int width,
                        int height,
                        ImageObserver observer)

These methods start the loading of the image data for the associated `Image`. They are used to preload images with `Graphics.drawImage` before you draw with them. For more information on loading images, see Section 9.12 (Drawing Images). Note that scaled images are treated as new images, so if you are going to draw an image at a size other than the default, you have to call `prepareImage` with that size. A value of `true` is returned if all the image data is already available; otherwise, `false`.

public void print(Graphics g)
public void printAll(Graphics g)

These methods print the component if the `Graphics` object implements the `PrintGraphics` interface. The default implementations do nothing but call `paint` and `paintAll`.

public void processXxxEvent(XxxEvent event)

This method processes the associated enabled, low-level events (see `enableEvents`). The type of event, *Xxx*, is any of the following: `Component`, `Focus`, `InputMethod` (Java 2) `Key`, `Mouse`, or `MouseMotion`. For more information on events, see Chapter 11 (Handling Mouse and Keyboard Events).

public void repaint()
public void repaint(int x, int y, int width, int height)
public void repaint(long milliseconds)
public void repaint(long milliseconds, int x, int y, int width, int height)

These methods ask the AWT thread to asynchronously call `update` as soon as possible (or after the specified number of milliseconds). This action places a `PaintEvent` on the event queue. Upon reaching the front of the queue, `PaintEvent` is dispatched to `update`, which normally results in the screen being cleared, followed by a call to the `paint` method. If a rectangular region is specified, it is used for the clipping region of the `Graphics` object in `update` and `paint`.

public void requestFocus()

This method is called when the component is to receive the input focus. For instance, you could use `requestFocus` so that clicking on a certain `Button` results in a given `TextField` receiving the focus.

public void setEnabled(boolean enabledFlag)

The `setEnabled` method enables (`true`) or disables (`false`) an AWT component. On most operating systems, disabling a GUI control such as a button results in the component being grayed out.

public void setVisible(boolean visibleFlag)

The `setVisible` method makes an AWT component visible (`true`) or invisible (`false`).

public void transferFocus()

This method passes the input focus to the next component in the Tab order. The tabbing order of AWT components is determined by order in which the components were added to the window.

public void update(Graphics g)

This method is called by the AWT event dispatch thread after the user calls `repaint`. The default implementation clears the screen and then calls `paint(g)`, but it is common to override `update` to simply call `paint`. This approach is particularly common when you are drawing into an off-screen pixmap. For more details on offscreen drawing, see the discussion on double buffering in Chapter 16 (Concurrent Programming with Java Threads).

13.3 Lightweight Components in Java 1.1

Java 1.1 introduced "lightweight" components that inherit directly from `Component` and have no associated native window-system "peer." Any region not directly drawn in the `paint` method will let the underlying component show through. For instance, Listing 13.4 shows a `BetterCircle` class that uses this approach. The code is similar to the version that used `Canvas` (Listing 13.1), with the exception that here we have to override `getPreferredSize` and `getMinimumSize` to do what `Canvas` already does: simply report its current size. In general, these two methods should be used to calculate the optimum and minimum sizes for the component. Listing 13.5 shows `BetterCircle` used in the same way as `Circle` was used in Section 13.1. As Figure 13-3 shows, the overlapping corners no longer cut into the underlying circle.

If you use lightweight components in a Container that has a custom paint method, this paint method *must* call super.paint or the lightweight components will not be drawn.

Listing 13.4 BetterCircle.java

```java
import java.awt.*;

/** An improved variation of the Circle class that uses Java 1.1
 *  lightweight components instead of Canvas.
 */

public class BetterCircle extends Component {
  private Dimension preferredDimension;
  private int width, height;

  public BetterCircle(Color foreground, int radius) {
    setForeground(foreground);
    width = 2*radius;
    height = 2*radius;
    preferredDimension = new Dimension(width, height);
    setSize(preferredDimension);
  }

  public void paint(Graphics g) {
    g.setColor(getForeground());
    g.fillOval(0, 0, width, height);
  }

  public void setCenter(int x, int y) {
    setLocation(x - width/2, y - height/2);
  }

  /** Report the original size as the preferred size.
   *  That way, the BetterCircle doesn't get
   *  shrunk by layout managers.
   */

  public Dimension getPreferredSize() {
    return(preferredDimension);
  }

  /** Report same thing for minimum size as
   *  preferred size.
   */

  public Dimension getMinimumSize() {
    return(preferredDimension);
  }
}
```

Listing 13.5 `BetterCircleTest.java`

```java
import java.awt.*;
import java.applet.Applet;

/** Position circles down the diagonal so that their borders
 *  just touch. Illustrates that Java 1.1 lightweight
 *  components can be partially transparent.
 */

public class BetterCircleTest extends Applet {
  public void init() {
    setBackground(Color.lightGray);
    setLayout(null);
    BetterCircle circle;
    int radius = getSize().width/6;
    int deltaX = round(2.0 * (double)radius / Math.sqrt(2.0));
    for (int x=radius; x<6*radius; x=x+deltaX) {
      circle = new BetterCircle(Color.black, radius);
      add(circle);
      circle.setCenter(x, x);
    }
  }

  private int round(double num) {
    return((int)Math.round(num));
  }
}
```

Figure 13–3 In Java 1.1, lightweight components can be transparent.

The ability to create components that are lightweight permits development of controls that truly appear the same across all platforms. This capability is so beneficial that nearly all Swing components are lightweight and do not rely on peer components for drawing. See Section 14.1 (Getting Started with Swing) for a discussion of lightweight Swing components.

13.4 The Panel Class

A `Panel` is a borderless window that can contain GUI controls and nested windows. Like `Canvas`, a `Panel` is not a stand-alone window, and you need to place the `Panel` in an existing window. A `Panel` has two major purposes:

1. Grouping or organizing other components. For complex GUI layouts, you may want to break the display into rectangular regions, embedding each in a `Panel`. Each `Panel` is then in charge of laying out the components it contains, and the top-level layout simply has to put the panels in the proper positions.

2. Creating a custom component that requires embedded components.

Default LayoutManager: FlowLayout

Windows that can hold other components (i.e., `Containers`) use a `Layout-Manager` to help them arrange their components. Components can have different sizes depending on the operating system; therefore, layout managers automatically help to position the components when the window size changes or when components are added and removed from the window

The `FlowLayout` layout manager respects the preferred size of the components and places them in rows, left to right, centered horizontally and vertically. Furthermore, a `Panel`'s *own* preferred size is calculated to be just barely large enough to enclose the components that it contains. This means that if you put a `Panel` into some other window that is using `FlowLayout`, the `Panel` may shrink or stretch. In fact, if you put an *empty* `Panel` into a `Container` that is using `FlowLayout`, your `Panel` is shrunk to a width and height of zero and will not show up at all.

Core Warning

If you put an empty `Panel` *into a* `Container` *that is using* `FlowLayout`, *your* `Panel` *will disappear.*

Creating and Using a Panel

In the following sections, we illustrate the basic steps for creating and using a `Panel`. Since the preferred size of a `Panel` is determined by the size of the contained components, a `Panel` is usually not given an explicit size before being added to a `Container`. The general approach for creating a panel is shown below.

```
// Create the Panel.
Panel panel = new Panel();
// Add components to the Panel.
panel.add(someComponent);
panel.add(someOtherComponent);
// Add the panel to a container. If FlowLayout,
container.add(panel);
// Or if a BorderLayout,
container.add(panel, region);
```

Example: Using a Panel for Grouping

Here's an example of using a `Panel` to group buttons. In the first example (Listing 13.6), eight buttons are added to an `Applet` that is wide enough to hold five buttons side by side. So, the first six buttons are placed in the first row, with the final two buttons placed in the second row (Figure 13–4). However, this is not the best layout, since the first four buttons are related to one topic and the second four buttons are related to another topic. The second example (Listing 13.7) shows a way to group the buttons by placing each set of buttons in a different panel. Figure 13–5 shows the result.

Listing 13.6 `ButtonTest1.java`

```
import java.applet.Applet;
import java.awt.*;

/** Eight ungrouped buttons in an Applet using FlowLayout. */

public class ButtonTest1 extends Applet {
  public void init() {
    String[] labelPrefixes = { "Start", "Stop", "Pause",
                               "Resume" };
    for (int i=0; i<4; i++) {
      add(new Button(labelPrefixes[i] + " Thread1"));
    }
    for (int i=0; i<4; i++) {
      add(new Button(labelPrefixes[i] + " Thread2"));
    }
  }
}
```

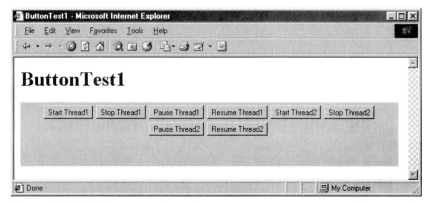

Figure 13–4 Without nested panels, as many components as can fit are packed into each row.

Listing 13.7 `ButtonTest2.java`

```java
import java.applet.Applet;
import java.awt.*;

/** Eight buttons: four each in two panels. */

public class ButtonTest2 extends Applet {
  public void init() {
    String[] labelPrefixes = { "Start", "Stop", "Pause",
                               "Resume" };
    Panel p1 = new Panel();
    for (int i=0; i<4; i++) {
      p1.add(new Button(labelPrefixes[i] + " Thread1"));
    }
    Panel p2 = new Panel();
    for (int i=0; i<4; i++) {
      p2.add(new Button(labelPrefixes[i] + " Thread2"));
    }
    add(p1);
    add(p2);
  }
}
```

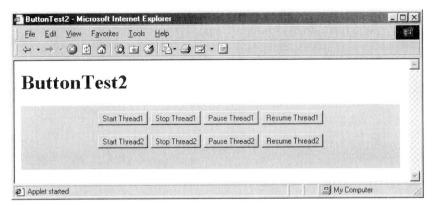

Figure 13–5 Use nested panels to group components together.

13.5 The Container Class

In Section 13.4 we looked at `Panel`—Java's basic window used to hold other components. Windows that can hold other components are part of the `Container` class. Being `Components` themselves, `Containers` inherit all the methods presented in Section 13.2 (The Component Class). The `Container` class has the following additional methods.

public Component add(Component c)
public Component add(Component c, Object constraints)
The first method simply inserts the component in the last position in the component array and is used with all standard layout managers. The one exception is `BorderLayout`, where you must specify a region `BorderLayout.NORTH`, `BorderLayout.SOUTH`, `BorderLayout.EAST`, `BorderLayout.WEST`, or `BorderLayout.CENTER`. In addition to these two `add` methods, the class also provides methods in which you can specify the index in the `Container`'s component array to place the new component. See the `java.awt.Container` API for details.

public void addContainerListener(ContainerListener listener)
public void removeContainerListener(ContainerListener listener)
These two methods add and remove a container listener from the `Container`, respectively. Whenever a component is added to or removed from the `Container`, a `ContainerEvent` is created and later processed by the container listener.

public int getComponentCount()

This method returns the number of components contained in the container. Components are counted even if they are not visible (see the `isVisible` method of `Component`).

public Component getComponent(int position)

The `getComponent` method returns the Nth element contained in the container (window), where 0 corresponds to the first component added. An `ArrayIndexOutOfBoundsException` is thrown if you supply an N greater than or equal to the value of `getComponentCount`.

public Component[ ] getComponents()

This method returns an array of the components contained in the container (window). The array might have zero length but will not be `null`.

public LayoutManager getLayout()

This method returns the layout manager instance used by the container, or `null` if there is no layout manager.

public Insets getInsets()

This method returns an `Insets` object (`top`, `bottom`, `left`, and `right` fields) describing the margins of the window. The standard layout managers do not draw into these margins. No corresponding `setInsets` method is available; you have to override `getInsets` to return a different value than the default (determined by the peer windows) or retrieve the `Insets` object and modify its `public` fields.

public boolean isAncestorOf(Component possibleSubComponent)

This method determines whether the specified component is contained *anywhere* in the containment hierarchy of the window.

public void paint(Graphics g)
public void print(Graphics g)

These methods are inherited from `Component`. However, there is an important difference in how they are used in containers. If your window contains any lightweight components and you override `paint` or `print`, you must call `super.paint` or `super.print` to make sure the components are drawn properly. Since you never know whether a lightweight component will be added later, it's a good idea to always call the corresponding supermethods at the end of `paint` or `print`.

public void processContainerEvent(ContainerEvent event)
If container events are enabled, this method can monitor them. See Section 11.5 (The Standard Event Listeners) for more information.

public void remove(int Component)
public void remove(int position)
The remove method takes a specified component out of the window. You can also remove the Nth component in the window's component array; a 0 corresponds to the first component added; getComponentCount()-1 corresponds to the last component.

public void setLayout(LayoutManager manager)
This method changes the layout manager. For instance, you could change BorderLayout to FlowLayout for a Frame or tell an Applet to use FlowLayout with a horizontal and vertical gap of 10 pixels instead of 5.

13.6 The Applet Class

An Applet is most commonly used for Java programs embedded in Web pages. Technically, you could use an Applet in a Java application, but a better approach is to simply use a Panel instead, since an Applet inherits from Panel. The layout manager for an Applet is unchanged from the parent Panel class—FlowLayout. For more details on using an Applet, see Chapter 9 (Applets and Basic Graphics).

13.7 The ScrollPane Class

A ScrollPane is a borderless window used to contain something too large to show all at once. In essence, a scroll pane is a window without borders and without a LayoutManager. A ScrollPane can contain only a *single* component. However, this one component could be a Panel containing many other components.

Creating and Using a ScrollPane

Although several options are available for controlling a scroll pane programmatically, the most common use is to simply place a large Component or Container in the ScrollPane and let the user perform the scrolling through scrollbars. When creating a ScrollPane, you can specify three possible behaviors for the scrollbars:

SCROLLBARS_ALWAYS,   SCROLLBARS_AS_NEEDED,   SCROLLBARS_NEVER.   A
ScrollPane created through the default constructor uses scrollbars only when they
are needed. Below is the basic approach for creating and using a ScrollBar.

```
// Create the scroll pane, indicating the presence
// of scrollbars.
ScrollPane pane =
  new ScrollPane(ScrollPane.SCROLLBARS_ALWAYS);
// Size the scroll pane and add to the container.
pane.setSize(width, height);
add(pane);
```

Example: ScrollPane with 100-Button Panel

Listing 13.8 shows a simple ScrollPane containing a 100-button Panel. Figure
13–6 shows the result after the horizontal scrollbar is moved to the right. The example makes use of the CloseableFrame class shown in Listing 13.11, which provides
support for letting the user close the frame. See Section 13.8 (The Frame Class) for
details.

Listing 13.8 ScrollPaneTest.java

```java
import java.applet.Applet;
import java.awt.*;

/** Places a Panel holding 100 buttons in a ScrollPane that is
 *  too small to hold it.
 */

public class ScrollPaneTest extends Applet {
  public void init() {
    setLayout(new BorderLayout());
    ScrollPane pane = new ScrollPane();
    Panel bigPanel = new Panel();
    bigPanel.setLayout(new GridLayout(10, 10));
    for(int i=0; i<100; i++) {
      bigPanel.add(new Button("Button " + i));
    }
    pane.add(bigPanel);
    add(pane, BorderLayout.CENTER);
  }
}
```

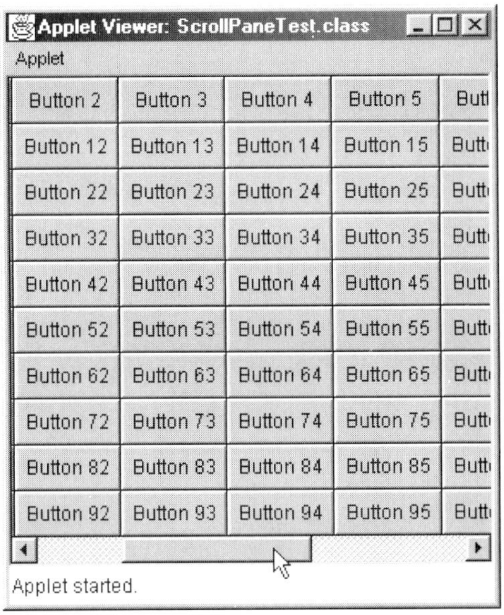

Figure 13–6 A ScrollPane can be scrolled to reveal any part of the enclosed Component that is beyond the bounds of the window.

13.8 The Frame Class

A Frame is the starting point for graphical applications and for pop-up windows in applets. Most often, a Frame is used to create a stand-alone window. A Frame has a title, menu bar, border, cursor, and icon image. Furthermore, a Frame is a container and can contain other GUI components.

Default LayoutManager: BorderLayout

The BorderLayout manager divides the screen into five regions: NORTH, SOUTH, EAST, WEST, and CENTER. Each region can contain at most one component, and you specify the region when adding the component to the window (e.g., add(component, BorderLayout.NORTH)). A component placed in the NORTH or SOUTH region is placed at the top or bottom of the frame, shrunk to its preferred height (see the preferredSize method of Component), and stretched to the full width of the frame, minus any margins (see the getInsets method of Container). Components placed in the EAST or WEST region are placed at the right or left sides, shrunk to their preferred widths, and stretched to the full frame height, minus any margins and space for NORTH and SOUTH. The CENTER region gets whatever is left. If you are already familiar with applets but not frames, the thing you will probably find most confusing is the layout manager. To switch the layout manager to the more familiar FlowLayout, use setLayout. For more details, see the discussion of BorderLayout in Chapter 12 (Layout Managers).

Creating and Using a Frame

When creating a Frame, you have two general design choices: explicitly defining the size of the Frame through setSize or letting the size of the Frame be determined by the size of the Components that the Frame is holding. Below, we illustrate both approaches.

To create a Frame with a fixed size:

```
// Create the Frame.
Frame frame = new Frame(titleString);
// Add any components to the Frame.
frame.add(somePanel, BorderLayout.CENTER);
frame.add(otherPanel, BorderLayout.NORTH);
...
// Set the Frame size. The location will be
// in the upper-left corner of the screen.
frame.setSize(width, height);
// Or ... specify both the size and position.
frame.setBounds(left, top, width, height);
// Pop up the Frame.
frame.setVisible(true);
```

One of the most common errors people make when first starting out with Frames is forgetting to specify a region in which to add the component. If you simply call frame.add(someComponent), the component is placed in the CENTER region. Subsequent calls to frame.add(someOtherComponent) simply replace the existing component in the CENTER region with the new component.

To create a Frame whose size is determined by the size of the components it is holding:

```
// Create the Frame.
Frame frame = new Frame(titleString);
// Position the Frame (optional).
frame.setLocation(left, top);
// Add any components to the Frame.
frame.add(somePanel, BorderLayout.CENTER);
...
// Stretch the Frame.
frame.pack();
// Pop up the Frame.
frame.setVisible(true);
```

By calling the `pack` method, you create the peer `Frame` component (see `add-Notify` in the `Component` class) and the layout manager lays out all the components in the container. The size for the internal window of the `Frame` is no larger than necessary to hold the components.

If you prefer that the user not be able to resize the `Frame`, then call `set-Resizeable(false)`. Furthermore, if you would like to determine the size of the screen before you position the `Frame`, then you can call `getScreenSize` from the frame's toolkit, `getToolKit`. For example, the following would center the frame on the screen.

```
Toolkit toolkit = frame.getToolkit();
Dimension scrnSize = toolkit.getScreenSize();
Dimension frameSize = frame.getSize();
frame.setLocation((scrnSize.width-frameSize.width)/2,
                  (scrnSize.height-frameSize.height)/2);
```

Note that you can pop up frames from applets, but the frames are generally annotated with some marking like "Unsigned Java Applet Window" (Netscape; see Figure 13–7) or "Warning: Applet Window" (Internet Explorer). The warning prevents applets from popping up in official-looking windows that say "Reestablishing lost network connection. Please enter username and password below," then reporting the password found to the applet's author.

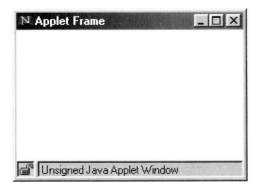

Figure 13–7 Frames started by applets typically have warning labels at the bottom.

Frame Examples

Following, we present two examples for creating a `Frame`. In the first example, Listing 13.9, all the steps for creating the frame are performed in the `main` method of the class. Specifically, a `Frame` object (or an object that inherits from `Frame`) is first instantiated and then assigned to a reference variable. At that point, any changes (setting the frame size, adding components) are performed in the `main` method through the reference variable. This approach is best suited to simple applications or to situations in which the main GUI interaction is provided through another component, most often a `Panel`, added to the frame.

Listing 13.9 `FrameExample1.java`

```
import java.awt.*;

public class FrameExample1 {
  public static void main(String[] args) {
    Frame f = new Frame("Frame Example 1");
    f.setSize(400, 300);
    f.setVisible(true);
  }
}
```

In the second example, Listing 13.10, the steps for building the frame are performed in the class constructor. For this approach, the class inherits from a `Frame` object and provides an entry point, `main`, for instantiating an instance of itself. The frame properties are then established in the constructor when the object is created. This approach is more common, because it more easily lends itself to good object-oriented design principles and easily supports inheritance for further customization.   Often, programmers use this approach to create child frames in a multi-frame application, because the constructor provides an entry point for adding a new frame to the parent window and the `main` method provides an entry point for unit testing.

Listing 13.10 `FrameExample2.java`

```
import java.awt.*;

public class FrameExample2 extends Frame {
  public static void main(String[] args) {
    new FrameExample2();
  }

  public FrameExample2() {
    super("Frame Example 2");
    setSize(400, 300);
    setVisible(true);
  }
}
```

A Closeable Frame

By default, a `Frame` ignores all events, including window-destroy events. So, for the window to properly close, you either need to enable the low-level window events or attach a `WindowListener` to the `Frame`. Listing 13.11 shows a `CloseableFrame` that calls `System.exit` when the user tries to quit the frame. This class is used as the starting point for graphical applications throughout much of the rest of this chapter. Frames that are popped up from existing windows (e.g., from applets or other frames) should call dispose, not System.exit, when the user tries to close them. Also, since the title bar is part of the Frame, any drawing performed in the top several pixels of the frame will be covered up. So, to draw reliably in frames, you should either read the getInsets values to determine where to start the drawing or add a Container (e.g., Panel) to the CENTER of the frame and perform the drawing in the panel.

Listing 13.11 CloseableFrame.java

```
import java.awt.*;
import java.awt.event.*;

/** A Frame that you can actually quit. Used as the starting
 *  point for most Java 1.1 graphical applications.
 */

public class CloseableFrame extends Frame {
  public CloseableFrame(String title) {
    super(title);
    enableEvents(AWTEvent.WINDOW_EVENT_MASK);
  }

  /** Since we are doing something permanent, we need
   *  to call super.processWindowEvent <B>first</B>.
   */

  public void processWindowEvent(WindowEvent event) {
    super.processWindowEvent(event); // Handle listeners.
    if (event.getID() == WindowEvent.WINDOW_CLOSING) {
      // If the frame is used in an applet, use dispose().
      System.exit(0);
    }
  }
}
```

Menus

Frames let you add menu bars that contain one or more menus. To use menus, first create a MenuBar, then create one or more Menu objects. You can add a String (a label), another Menu (a cascading choice), or a CheckboxMenuItem (a choice with a check box) to a Menu. Once you have your menus, place them in the MenuBar by using the MenuBar's add method (to put them left to right) or setHelpMenu method (to put a menu at the far-right corner). Finally, put the MenuBar in the Frame through the Frame's setMenuBar method. To handle events, attach an

ActionListener to each Menu and call event.getActionCommand to determine which menu item was selected by the user. Listing 13.12 gives an example that
creates a menu of color choices and sets the background color of the Frame whenever a choice is selected. Figure 13–8 shows the result.

Listing 13.12 ColorMenu.java

```java
import java.awt.*;
import java.awt.event.*;

/** Illustrates the insertion of menu entries in Frame
 *  menu bars.
 */

public class ColorMenu extends CloseableFrame
                       implements ActionListener {

  private String[] colorNames =
    { "Black", "White", "Light Gray", "Medium Gray",
      "Dark Gray" };
  private Color[] colorValues =
    { Color.black, Color.white, Color.lightGray,
      Color.gray, Color.darkGray };

  public ColorMenu() {
    super("ColorMenu");
    MenuBar bar = new MenuBar();
    Menu colorMenu = new Menu("Colors");
    for(int i=0; i<2; i++) {
      colorMenu.add(colorNames[i]);
    }
    Menu grayMenu = new Menu("Gray");
    for(int i=2; i<colorNames.length; i++) {
      grayMenu.add(colorNames[i]);
    }
    colorMenu.add(grayMenu);
    bar.add(colorMenu);
    setMenuBar(bar);
    colorMenu.addActionListener(this);
    grayMenu.addActionListener(this);

    setBackground(Color.lightGray);
    setSize(400, 200);
    setVisible(true);
  }
```

(continued)

Listing 13.12 `ColorMenu.java` *(continued)*

```
/** Catch menu events in the containing Frame. */

public void actionPerformed(ActionEvent event) {
   setBackground(colorNamed(event.getActionCommand()));
   repaint();
}

private Color colorNamed(String colorName) {
  for(int i=0; i<colorNames.length; i++) {
    if(colorNames[i].equals(colorName)) {
      return(colorValues[i]);
    }
  }
  return(Color.white);
}

public static void main(String[] args) {
  new ColorMenu();
}

}
```

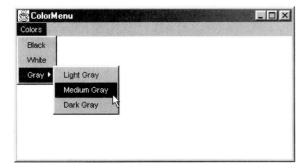

Figure 13–8 Frames can contain menu bars.

Other Useful Frame Methods

Following is a quick overview of the methods available in the Frame class. All of the
Component and Container methods are available as well, of course.

public void dispose()

This method destroys the Frame's peer (actual native window) and all nested components. Since you cannot call System.exit from applets, a frame launched from an applet should call dispose on a WINDOW_DESTROY event.

Core Approach

To close a Frame *launched from an* Applet, *use* dispose *instead of* System.exit.

public Image getIconImage()
public void setIconImage(Image icon)

These methods let you retrieve or change the image that will be used when the Frame is iconified. The return value of getIconImage is null if you haven't explicitly called setIconImage.

public MenuBar getMenuBar()
public void setMenuBar(MenuBar menuBar)
public void remove(MenuComponent menuBar)

These methods let you retrieve or change the menu bar, as illustrated earlier in this section.

public String getTitle()
public void setTitle(String title)

These methods let you retrieve or change the label in the Frame's title bar.

public boolean isResizable()
public void setResizable(boolean resizeFlag)

By default, users can interactively stretch or shrink frames you create. Call setResizable(false) to suppress this ability; isResizable reports the current setting.

public void pack()

The pack method resizes the Frame according to the preferred sizes of the components it contains.

public void toBack()
public void toFront()

These methods move the Frame to the back or front of the display (i.e., behind or on top of any overlapping windows).

13.9 Serializing Windows

Java 1.1 introduced an extremely useful capability: *serialization*. This capability lets you save the state of Java objects to disk or to send them over the network. In particular, with a single command (`writeObject`), you can save the state of a frame or other window, including all subwindows, sizes, locations, colors, and GUI controls. The only restriction is that any objects the window references must be serializable if you want them to be saved with the window. All AWT components are already serializable, and making other objects serializable is a trivial matter of having the class implement the `Serializable` interface. This interface does not declare any methods, so you can implement it by simply tacking "`implements Serializable`" onto the class definition. If you have a field you don't want to bother saving, you can declare it `transient`. The frame can be reconstituted later with a single command (`readObject`).

Writing a Window to Disk

A standard approach to saving a window is as follows, assuming your code imports `java.io.*`:

```
try {
  FileOutputStream fileOut =
    new FileOutputStream("SaveFilename");
  ObjectOutputStream out =
    new ObjectOutputStream(fileOut);
  out.writeObject(someWindow);
  out.flush();
  out.close();
} catch(IOException ioe) {
  System.out.println("Error saving window: " + ioe);
}
```

If you are concerned about disk space, you can interpose a `GZIPOutputStream` (in `java.util.zip`) between the `FileOutputStream` and the `ObjectOutputStream`, but serialized windows are relatively compact even without compression.

Reading a Window from Disk

Reading the window back in is equally easy:

```
try {
  File saveFile = new File("SaveFilename");
  FileInputStream fileIn =
    new FileInputStream(saveFile);
  ObjectInputStream in =
    new ObjectInputStream(fileIn);
```

```
    someWindow = (WindowType)in.readObject();
    doSomethingWith(someWindow); // E.g. setVisible.
  } catch(IOException ioe) {
    System.out.println("Error reading file: " + ioe);
  } catch(ClassNotFoundException cnfe) {
    System.out.println("No such class: " + cnfe);
  }
```

If the window was compressed when saved, you should put a GZIPInputStream between the FileInputStream and the ObjectInputStream.

Example: A Saveable Frame

Listing 13.13 creates a Frame that lets you draw circles by clicking the mouse. After drawing circles, moving the Frame around, and stretching it interactively, you can press Save to store the result on disk. Next time you run the same program, the saved version is automatically loaded: circles, buttons, location, size, and all. Figure 13–9 shows the result after a user adds some circles, quits, and restarts in a later session. The SavedFrame class makes use of two helper classes. CirclePanel is shown in Listing 13.14; it is simply a Panel with a MouseListener that adds circles wherever the mouse is clicked. The circles themselves are instances of the BetterCircle class, shown earlier in Listing 13.4.

Listing 13.13 SavedFrame.java

```
import java.awt.*;
import java.awt.event.*;
import java.io.*;

/** A Frame that lets you draw circles with mouse clicks
 *  and then save the Frame and all circles to disk.
 */

public class SavedFrame extends CloseableFrame
                        implements ActionListener {

  /** If a saved version exists, use it. Otherwise create a
   *  new one.
   */

  public static void main(String[] args) {
    SavedFrame frame;
    File serializeFile = new File(serializeFilename);
    if (serializeFile.exists()) {
      try {
```

(continued)

Listing 13.13 SavedFrame.java *(continued)*

```
      FileInputStream fileIn =
        new FileInputStream(serializeFile);
      ObjectInputStream in = new ObjectInputStream(fileIn);
      frame = (SavedFrame)in.readObject();
      frame.setVisible(true);
    } catch(IOException ioe) {
      System.out.println("Error reading file: " + ioe);
    } catch(ClassNotFoundException cnfe) {
      System.out.println("No such class: " + cnfe);
    }
  } else {
    frame = new SavedFrame();
  }
}

private static String serializeFilename ="SavedFrame.ser";
private CirclePanel circlePanel;
private Button clearButton, saveButton;

/** Build a frame with CirclePanel and buttons. */

public SavedFrame() {
  super("SavedFrame");
  setBackground(Color.white);
  setFont(new Font("Serif", Font.BOLD, 18));
  circlePanel = new CirclePanel();
  add("Center", circlePanel);
  Panel buttonPanel = new Panel();
  buttonPanel.setBackground(Color.lightGray);
  clearButton = new Button("Clear");
  saveButton = new Button("Save");
  buttonPanel.add(clearButton);
  buttonPanel.add(saveButton);
  add(buttonPanel, BorderLayout.SOUTH);
  clearButton.addActionListener(this);
  saveButton.addActionListener(this);
  setSize(300, 300);
  setVisible(true);
}

/** If "Clear" clicked, delete all existing circles. If "Save"
 *  clicked, save existing frame configuration (size,
 *  location, circles, etc.) to disk.
 */
```

(continued)

Listing 13.13 `SavedFrame.java` (continued)

```java
    public void actionPerformed(ActionEvent event) {
      if (event.getSource() == clearButton) {
        circlePanel.removeAll();
        circlePanel.repaint();
      } else if (event.getSource() == saveButton) {
        try {
          FileOutputStream fileOut =
            new FileOutputStream("SavedFrame.ser");
          ObjectOutputStream out =
            new ObjectOutputStream(fileOut);
          out.writeObject(this);
          out.flush();
          out.close();
        } catch(IOException ioe) {
          System.out.println("Error saving frame: " + ioe);
        }
      }
    }
  }
```

Listing 13.14 `CirclePanel.java`

```java
import java.awt.*;
import java.awt.event.*;
import java.io.*;

/** A Panel that draws circles centered wherever the user clicks
 *  the mouse. <B>Uses a null layout manager.</B>.
 */

public class CirclePanel extends Panel {
  class ClickAdapter extends MouseAdapter
                      implements Serializable {
    public void mouseClicked(MouseEvent event) {
      BetterCircle circle = new BetterCircle(Color.black, 25);
      add(circle);
      circle.setCenter(event.getX(), event.getY());
      invalidate();
      validate();
    }
  }

  public CirclePanel() {
    setLayout(null);
    addMouseListener(new ClickAdapter());
  }
}
```

Figure 13–9 Serialization lets you save the complete frame configuration to disk. The saved version is automatically used in later sessions.

13.10 The Dialog Class

A `Dialog` is a stripped-down `Frame`, useful for applications that don't need all of the capabilities of a `Frame`. A `Dialog` has two major roles:

1. A modal dialog that freezes interaction with other AWT components until it is closed. A modal dialog is used in situations that require the user to respond before other processing can continue.
2. A simplified frame (no cursor, menu, icon image). A nonmodal dialog is used in a similar manner to its use in a `Frame` but requires fewer resources and is faster to pop up.

A `Dialog` also has a `BorderLayout` manager that divides the screen into five regions: `NORTH`, `SOUTH`, `EAST`, `WEST`, and `CENTER`. See the discussion of `BorderLayout` in Chapter 12 (Layout Managers).

Creating and Using a Dialog

Using a `Dialog` is similar to using a `Frame` except that the constructor takes two additional arguments: the parent `Frame` and a `boolean` specifying whether or not the dialog is modal, as shown below.

```
Dialog dialog =
  new Dialog(parentFrame, titleString, false);
Dialog modalDialog =
  new Dialog(parentFrame, titleString, true);
```

To use dialog boxes from applets, you need to find the parent frame by using getFrame method described in Section 13.8 (The Frame Class). Modal dialogs will freeze all mouse/keyboard interaction with other Java components and suspend the calling thread.

Example: A Quit Confirmation Dialog

Listing 13.15 presents a dialog box with two buttons, asking you if you really want to quit. Clicking the Yes button quits the entire application; clicking the No button closes the dialog box itself but leaves the rest of the application alone. Listing 13.16 associates this dialog with the WINDOW_DESTROY event so that the dialog box pops up when the user tries to quit the window. Figure 13–10 shows the result.

Listing 13.15 `Confirm.java`

```
import java.awt.*;
import java.awt.event.*;

/** A modal dialog box with two buttons: Yes and No.
 *  Clicking Yes exits Java. Clicking No exits the
 *  dialog. Used for confirmed quits from frames.
 */

class Confirm extends Dialog implements ActionListener {
  private Button yes, no;

  public Confirm(Frame parent) {
    super(parent, "Confirmation", true);
    setLayout(new FlowLayout());
    add(new Label("Really quit?"));
    yes = new Button("Yes");
    yes.addActionListener(this);
    no  = new Button("No");
    no.addActionListener(this);
    add(yes);
    add(no);
    pack();
    setVisible(true);
  }

  public void actionPerformed(ActionEvent event) {
    if (event.getSource() == yes) {
      System.exit(0);
    } else {
      dispose();
    }
  }
}
```

Listing 13.16 `ConfirmTest.java`

```java
import java.awt.*;
import java.awt.event.*;

/** A Frame that uses the Confirm dialog to verify that
 *  users really want to quit.
 */

public class ConfirmTest extends Frame {
  public static void main(String[] args) {
    new ConfirmTest();
  }

  public ConfirmTest() {
    super("Confirming QUIT");
    setSize(200, 200);
    addWindowListener(new ConfirmListener());
    setVisible(true);
  }

  public ConfirmTest(String title) {
    super(title);
  }

  private class ConfirmListener extends WindowAdapter {
    public void windowClosing(WindowEvent event) {
      new Confirm(ConfirmTest.this);
    }
  }
}
```

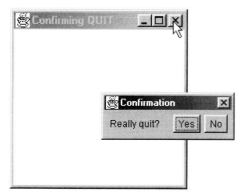

Figure 13–10 Modal dialogs freeze interaction with all other Java components.

13.11 The FileDialog Class

A FileDialog is a type of modal dialog that is used to load or save files. Use File-Dialog with applications; normal applets cannot access the local disk. Although a FileDialog is technically a Container, it cannot hold any other components and has no layout manager. Here are the basic steps for creating and using a File-Dialog.

```
// Make the FileDialog.
FileDialog fileLoader =
  new FileDialog(frame, title, FileDialog.LOAD);
FileDialog fileSaver =
  new FileDialog(frame, title, FileDialog.SAVE);
// Set a default file or file type.
fileLoader.setFile("*.txt");
// Pop up the FileDialog.
fileLoader.show();
// Look up the filename chosen.
String filename = fileLoader.getFile();
```

Example: Displaying Files in a TextArea

Listing 13.17 shows a Frame that is mostly filled with a large TextArea but that also contains one button at the bottom (see Figure 13–11). When the button is pressed, a FileDialog is displayed (also shown in Figure 13–11) to let the user choose a file-name. Once that filename is chosen, a FileInputStream is opened and the file contents are placed in the TextArea (Figure 13–12).

Listing 13.17 DisplayFile.java

```
import java.awt.*;
import java.awt.event.*;
import java.io.*;

/** Uses a FileDialog to choose the file to display. */

public class DisplayFile extends CloseableFrame
                         implements ActionListener {

  public static void main(String[] args) {
    new DisplayFile();
  }
```

(continued)

Listing 13.17 `DisplayFile.java` *(continued)*

```java
  private Button loadButton;
  private TextArea fileArea;
  private FileDialog loader;

  public DisplayFile() {
    super("Using FileDialog");
    loadButton = new Button("Display File");
    loadButton.addActionListener(this);
    Panel buttonPanel = new Panel();
    buttonPanel.add(loadButton);
    add(buttonPanel, BorderLayout.SOUTH);
    fileArea = new TextArea();
    add("Center", fileArea);
    loader = new FileDialog(this, "Browse", FileDialog.LOAD);
    // Default file extension: .java.
    loader.setFile("*.java");
    setSize(350, 450);
    setVisible(true);
  }

  /** When the button is clicked, a file dialog is opened. When
   * the file dialog is closed, load the file it referenced.
   */

  public void actionPerformed(ActionEvent event) {
      loader.show();
      displayFile(loader.getFile());
  }

  public void displayFile(String filename) {
    try {
      File file = new File(filename);
      FileInputStream in = new FileInputStream(file);
      int fileLength = (int)file.length();
      byte[] fileContents = new byte[fileLength];
      in.read(fileContents);
      String fileContentsString = new String(fileContents);
      fileArea.setText(fileContentsString);
    } catch(IOException ioe) {
      fileArea.setText("IOError: " + ioe);
    }
  }
}
```

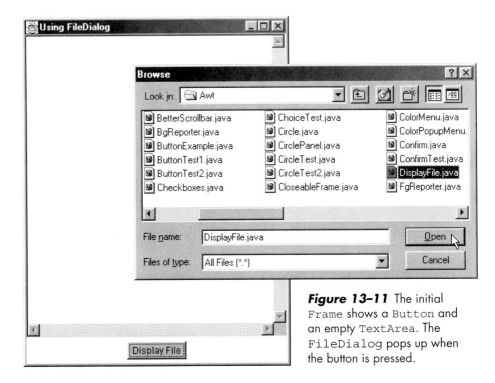

Figure 13–11 The initial `Frame` shows a `Button` and an empty `TextArea`. The `FileDialog` pops up when the button is pressed.

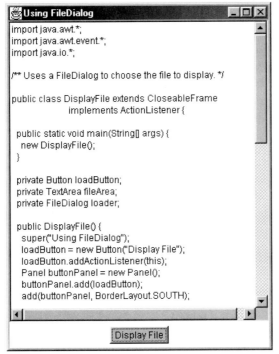

Figure 13–12 After the user chooses a file, it is displayed in the `TextArea`.

13.12 The Window Class

Window is the underlying class that Frame is built upon. A Window is used less frequently than the other window types and mainly serves to create pop-up windows with no border or title bar.

Default LayoutManager: BorderLayout

This layout manager divides the screen into five regions: NORTH, SOUTH, EAST, WEST, and CENTER. See the discussion of BorderLayout in Chapter 12 (Layout Managers).

Creating and Using a Window

When creating a Window, you can explicitly state the size of the Window through setSize or let the size of the Window be determined by the Components that the Window is holding. We show both approaches below.

To create a Window with a fixed size:

```
// Create the Window.
Window window = new Window(parentFrame);
// Add any components to the Window.
window.add(somePanel, BorderLayout.CENTER);
...
// Define the size of the Window.
window.setSize(width, height);
// Or specify both the size and position.
size.setBounds(left, top, width, height);
// Pop up the Window.
window.setVisible(true);
```

To create a Window whose size is determined by the size of the components it is holding:

```
// Create the Window.
Window window = new Window(parentFrame);
// Position the Window (optional).
window.setLocation(left, top);
// Add any components to the Window.
winddow.add(somePanel, BorderLayout.CENTER);
...
// Stretch the Window.
window.pack();
// Pop up the Frame.
window.setVisible(true);
```

Remember that a `Window` has a `BorderLayout` manager; when adding a component to a `Window`, you should specify the region to place the component. Simply calling `window.add(someComponent)` places the component in the `CENTER` region of the `BorderLayout`. Any subsequent calls to `add(someOther-Component)` simply replace the existing component located in the `CENTER` region with the new component.

13.13 Handling Events in GUI Controls

In this section we present the general approach for handling events in GUI controls. Depending on the graphical control, different events are generated. For example, a `Button` generates `ActionEvents` and a `Checkbox` generates `ItemEvents`. As presented in Chapter 10 (Handling Mouse and Keyboard Events), you can use either high-level or low-level event processing to handle events. The two levels of event processing are briefly reviewed below.

- **High-level event processing.** Process the event by attaching a listener to the component, using `addXxxListener`, where *Xxx* corresponds to the type of event the component can generate. Then, handle the event in the appropriate method defined by the listener. See Section 11.1 (Handling Events with a Separate Listener) for details.
- **Low-level event processing.** Process the event by first enabling the low-level event, using `enableEvents` with the appropriate `AWTEvent` mask. Then, handle the event in the component by using `processXxxEvent`, where *Xxx* corresponds to the type of event the component can generate. See Section 11.6 (Behind the Scenes: Low-Level Event Processing) for details.

Depending on the component, each defines a specialized event type that is a subclass of the more general `AWTEvent` class. Specifically, `ActionEvents` are generated by `Button`, `List`, `MenuItem`, and `TextField` and are handled through `addActionListener` or in `processActionEvent`. Item selection events (`ItemEvent`) are generated by `Checkbox`, `CheckboxMenuItem`, `Choice`, and `List` and are handled through `addItemListener` or in `processItemEvent`. Textfields and text areas generate both keyboard events (`KeyEvent`) and text events (`TextEvent`); they are handled with `addKeyListener` or `addTextListener` or in `processKeyEvent` and `processTextEvent`, respectively. Scrollbars generate adjustment events (`AdjustmentEvent`); they are handled with `addAdjustment-Listener` or in `processAdjustmentEvent`. Furthermore, the mouse and keyboard events (`MouseEvent`, `KeyEvent`) discussed in Chapter 11 are also delivered to all components except `MenuItem` and `CheckboxMenuItem`.

Two basic designs are available to handle high-level events through listeners: let each component process its own events, or handle the events in a centralized location such as an external component. Here, we describe these two approaches for handling `ActionEvents`. Processing of other events is handled in a similar manner.

Figure 13–13 presents a frame with three buttons that result in resizing of the frame when pressed by the user. Except for the frame title, the following two examples, decentralized event processing and centralized event processing, result in an identical interface and in identical behavior.

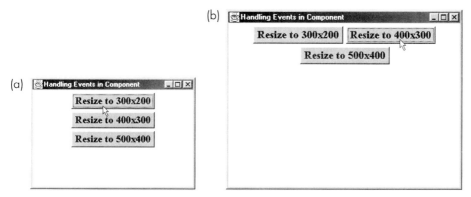

Figure 13–13 Frame after (a) the first button and (b) the second button are pressed.

Decentralized Event Processing

In decentralized event processing, each component is given its own event handling methods; the component itself assumes complete responsibility for processing its own events. Users of the component are unaware of how the events are processed internally. This approach favors the object-oriented approach of encapsulation and modularity. However, information about the container class holding the component is not directly available, and the component will need to be relatively independent of application that it is in. As an example of decentralized event processing, consider that you need a GUI control to handle `ActionEvents`. You would first create an object that implements the `ActionListener` interface and then define a method called `actionPerformed` that takes an `ActionEvent` as an argument. Next, you associate the event handling method with the object itself through the `addActionListener` method. In this manner, the object will handle only its `ActionEvents`.

Listings 13.18 and 13.19 show a decentralized event handler. Here, a customized `Button` implements the `ActionListener` interface and provides an `action-Performed` method for handling its own `ActionEvents`. The button itself is identified in the constructor to process the `ActionEvents` in the statement `addActionListener(this)`. When the user presses the button, the size of the parent container is set to a new width and height. Then, through the `invalidate` and `validate` methods, the parent container is requested to lay out its components again and subsequently redisplay itself. Remember to import `java.awt.event.*`; that's where all the event types are defined.

Listing 13.18 `ActionExample1.java`

```java
import java.awt.*;

public class ActionExample1 extends CloseableFrame {
  public static void main(String[] args) {
    new ActionExample1();
  }

  public ActionExample1() {
    super("Handling Events in Component");
    setLayout(new FlowLayout());
    setFont(new Font("Serif", Font.BOLD, 18));
    add(new SetSizeButton(300, 200));
    add(new SetSizeButton(400, 300));
    add(new SetSizeButton(500, 400));
    setSize(400, 300);
    setVisible(true);
  }
}
```

Listing 13.19 `SetSizeButton.java`

```java
import java.awt.*;
import java.awt.event.*;

public class SetSizeButton extends Button
                            implements ActionListener {
  private int width, height;
  private Container parent;

  public SetSizeButton(int width, int height) {
    super("Resize to " + width + "x" + height);
    this.width = width;
    this.height = height;
    parent = getParent();
    addActionListener(this);
  }

  public void actionPerformed(ActionEvent event) {
    parent.setSize(width, height);
    parent.invalidate();
    parent.validate();
  }
}
```

Centralized Event Processing

The second way to process GUI events is centralized event processing, where the events for multiple components are sent to a single ActionListener object. The disadvantage of this approach is that the single listener must first determine the source component from which the event originated before determining what processing to perform. However, from inside the actionPerformed method you can immediately access fields and methods in the ActionListener object, which, in most designs, is the container holding the components. Modularity and encapsulation are sacrificed for ease in accessing information in a common object.

Listing 13.20 gives an example of centralized event processing. In this particular case, the listener object for the three buttons is the window itself. Regardless of which button originates the ActionEvent, the event handling is processed by the single actionPerformed method in the external container. This approach suffers from the need to look up the source button from the ActionEvent object, but it simplifies common access to the private updateLayout method to resize the window.

Although it is sometimes convenient to handle events in the window itself, a variation to this approach is to assign a separate inner class (implementing the Action-Listener interface) to each button for event processing. The advantage is that the window's inner classes have direct access to all data fields and methods in the window itself, but because a separate ActionListener is assigned to each button, determination of the event source is no longer needed. See Section 11.3 (Handling Events with Named Inner Classes) for more details on using inner classes for event handling.

Listing 13.20 ActionExample2.java

```java
import java.awt.*;
import java.awt.event.*;

public class ActionExample2 extends CloseableFrame
                            implements ActionListener {
  public static void main(String[] args) {
    new ActionExample2();
  }

  private Button button1, button2, button3;

  public ActionExample2() {
    super("Handling Events in Other Object");
    setLayout(new FlowLayout());
    setFont(new Font("Serif", Font.BOLD, 18));
    button1 = new Button("Resize to 300x200");
    button2 = new Button("Resize to 400x300");
```

(continued)

Listing 13.20 `ActionExample2.java` *(continued)*

```
    button3 = new Button("Resize to 500x400");
    button1.addActionListener(this);
    button2.addActionListener(this);
    button3.addActionListener(this);
    add(button1);
    add(button2);
    add(button3);
    setSize(400, 300);
    setVisible(true);
  }

  public void actionPerformed(ActionEvent event) {
    if (event.getSource() == button1) {
      updateLayout(300, 200);
    } else if (event.getSource() == button2) {
      updateLayout(400, 300);
    } else if (event.getSource() == button3) {
      updateLayout(500, 400);
    }
  }

  private void updateLayout(int width, int height) {
    setSize(width, height);
    invalidate();
    validate();
  }
}
```

13.14 The Button Class

The Button class creates push buttons with text labels. The Java programming language doesn't have a built-in class that supports buttons with images. The most common usage for a button is to simply create one with a specified label, drop it in a window, then watch for action events when the button is pressed. For instance, to create and add a button to the current window, you would perform the following two steps.

```
    Button button = new Button("...");
    add(button);
```

Constructors

The Button class has two constructors.

public Button()
public Button(String buttonLabel)

The first constructor creates a button with no label. You can use setLabel to add a label to the button later. The width reported by preferredSize is greater than zero even when no label is present because the border requires some space. The second constructor creates a button with the specified label. The preferredSize (used by layout managers like FlowLayout and BorderLayout) of the button is based on the height and width of the label based on the current font, plus some additional border space that varies depending on the window operating system.

Example: Applet with Three Buttons

Listing 13.21 shows an applet that contains three buttons. In this particular case, because we don't ever do anything with the buttons, there is no need to assign the Button objects to separate instance variables; simply do add(new Button(...)). However, you will want access to the buttons when you attach a behavior to them, so you might as well plan ahead and store the button references somewhere that will be accessible in other methods. Figure 13–14 shows the result of Listing 13.21 in Netscape 4.7 on Windows 98.

Listing 13.21 Buttons.java

```java
import java.applet.Applet;
import java.awt.*;

public class Buttons extends Applet {
  private Button button1, button2, button3;

  public void init() {
    button1 = new Button("Button One");
    button2 = new Button("Button Two");
    button3 = new Button("Button Three");
    add(button1);
    add(button2);
    add(button3);
  }
}
```

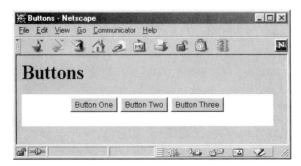

Figure 13-14 Java buttons on Windows 98.

Other Button Methods

Following are the five most common methods in the Button class.

public String getLabel()

The getLabel method retrieves the current label.

public void setLabel(String newLabel)

The setLabel method changes the button's label. If the button is already displayed, changing the label does not automatically resize the button. So, the containing window should be invalidated and validated to force a fresh layout and resize the button with the new label, as below:

```
someButton.setLabel("A New Label");
someButton.getParent().invalidate();
someButton.getParent().validate();
```

public void addActionListener(ActionListener listener)
public void removeActionListener(ActionListener listener)

These methods add and remove listeners (objects) that process Action-Events. See the following subsection for a discussion on their use.

public void processActionEvent(ActionEvent event)

This is a low-level, event-processing routine you use when you want a button to handle its own events. If you use this method, don't forget to enable events first with enableEvents and to call super.processActionEvent from within the body of the method. See the following section for examples.

Also, as with every `Component` (Section 13.2), buttons have `getForeground`, `setForeground`, `getBackground`, `setBackground`, `getFont`, `setFont`, and a variety of other inherited methods.

Handling Button Events

Precisely how Java determines that a button has been activated depends on the operating system. However, activation occurs typically either when the user clicks and releases the mouse on a button or when the user enters a carriage return while the button has the input focus.

Like other action events, button events can be handled in one of two ways. To handle events in the `Button` object itself, first enable `ActionEvents` through

```
enableEvents(AWTEvent.ACTION_EVENT_MASK);
```

Next, override `processActionEvent` to perform the specific behavior you want. You should call `super.processActionEvent` in the body so that if any other listeners are attached to your button, they will still be invoked. Following is an abstract example; for specifics, see `SetSizeButton` (Listing 13.19).

```
public void processActionEvent(ActionEvent event) {
  takeSomeAction(...);
  super.processActionEvent(event); // Handle listeners.
}
```

That's the first possible approach: processing events directly in the `Button`. The next option is to attach one or more `ActionListeners` to the button. For this approach, create an object that implements the `ActionListener` interface, then associate the listener with the button through `addActionListener`. You would place the code for the action to take when the button is selected in the `actionPerformed` method of the listener.

In Listing 13.20, the window itself was the `ActionListener`, but you can provide a listener in a variety of ways. For instance, Listing 13.22 creates three buttons, each with one to three different `ActionListeners` attached. It associates an `FgReporter` (Listing 13.23) with the first button, an `FgReporter` and a `BgReporter` (Listing 13.24) with the second, and an `FgReporter`, a `BgReporter`, and a `SizeReporter` (Listing 13.25) with the third. Each of these reporters is an `ActionListener` that simply prints some information about the component that was the source of the action. Figure 13–15 shows the result; the output after the user clicks on the three buttons once each is shown in Listing 13.26.

Listing 13.22 `ButtonExample.java`

```java
import java.awt.*;
import java.awt.event.*;

public class ButtonExample extends CloseableFrame {
  public static void main(String[] args) {
    new ButtonExample();
  }

  public ButtonExample() {
    super("Using ActionListeners");
    setLayout(new FlowLayout());
    Button b1 = new Button("Button 1");
    Button b2 = new Button("Button 2");
    Button b3 = new Button("Button 3");
    b1.setBackground(Color.lightGray);
    b2.setBackground(Color.gray);
    b3.setBackground(Color.darkGray);
    FgReporter fgReporter = new FgReporter();
    BgReporter bgReporter = new BgReporter();
    SizeReporter sizeReporter = new SizeReporter();
    b1.addActionListener(fgReporter);
    b2.addActionListener(fgReporter);
    b2.addActionListener(bgReporter);
    b3.addActionListener(fgReporter);
    b3.addActionListener(bgReporter);
    b3.addActionListener(sizeReporter);
    add(b1);
    add(b2);
    add(b3);
    setSize(350, 100);
    setVisible(true);
  }
}
```

Listing 13.23 `FgReporter.java`

```java
import java.awt.event.*;
import java.awt.*;

public class FgReporter implements ActionListener {
  public void actionPerformed(ActionEvent event) {
    Component c = (Component)event.getSource();
    System.out.println("Foreground: " + c.getForeground());
  }
}
```

Listing 13.24 `BgReporter.java`

```java
import java.awt.event.*;
import java.awt.*;

public class BgReporter implements ActionListener {
  public void actionPerformed(ActionEvent event) {
    Component c = (Component)event.getSource();
    System.out.println("Background: " + c.getBackground());
  }
}
```

Listing 13.25 `SizeReporter.java`

```java
import java.awt.event.*;
import java.awt.*;

public class SizeReporter implements ActionListener {
  public void actionPerformed(ActionEvent event) {
    Component c = (Component)event.getSource();
    Dimension d = c.getSize();
    System.out.println("Size: " + d.width + "x" + d.height);
  }
}
```

Figure 13–15 You can attach more than one `ActionListener` to a component.

Listing 13.26 ButtonExample output after user presses Button 1, Button 2, and Button 3, once each in that order.

```
Foreground: java.awt.Color[r=0,g=0,b=0]
Foreground: java.awt.Color[r=0,g=0,b=0]
Background: java.awt.Color[r=128,g=128,b=128]
Foreground: java.awt.Color[r=0,g=0,b=0]
Background: java.awt.Color[r=64,g=64,b=64]
Size: 59x23
```

Because AWT buttons do not have built-in support for displaying images, we provide an `ImageButton` class, based on a `Canvas`, to support button images. See the on-line archive at `http://www.corewebprogramming.com/` for the `ImageButton` class.

13.15 The Checkbox Class

This section describes check boxes (toggle buttons) that operate independently of other check boxes. In the next section, we'll show you how to put check boxes into a group so that they operate like radio buttons (where pressing one raises the previous selection). Most commonly, you would use the `Checkbox` class to create a check box with a specified label and then drop it into a window. You can watch for `Item-SelectionEvents` or simply wait until you need the value and then look it up with `getState`. The necessary steps to create a check box and place it in a nested window are:

```
Checkbox cb = new Checkbox("...");
somePanel.add(cb);
```

Constructors

These three constructors apply to check boxes that operate independently of each other. The following section introduces two other constructors that are used with radio buttons.

public Checkbox()
public Checkbox(String checkboxLabel)
public Checkbox(String checkboxLabel, boolean state)
  The first constructor creates an initially unchecked check box with no label. The second constructor creates a check box with the specified label. The check box is initially unchecked; see `setState` for changing the value. The last constructor creates a check box with the specified label, with a checked (`true`) or unchecked (`false`) state depending on the boolean value provided.

Example: Checked Checkboxes

Listing 13.27 creates twelve check boxes, placing them in a two-column layout with the even-numbered ones initially checked. Figure 13–16 shows the result on Windows 98.

Listing 13.27 `Checkboxes.java`

```java
import java.awt.*;

public class Checkboxes extends CloseableFrame {
  public static void main(String[] args) {
    new Checkboxes();
  }

  public Checkboxes() {
    super("Checkboxes");
    setFont(new Font("SansSerif", Font.BOLD, 18));
    setLayout(new GridLayout(0, 2));
    Checkbox box;
    for(int i=0; i<12; i++) {
      box = new Checkbox("Checkbox " + i);
      if (i%2 == 0) {
        box.setState(true);
      }
      add(box);
    }
    pack();
    setVisible(true);
  }
}
```

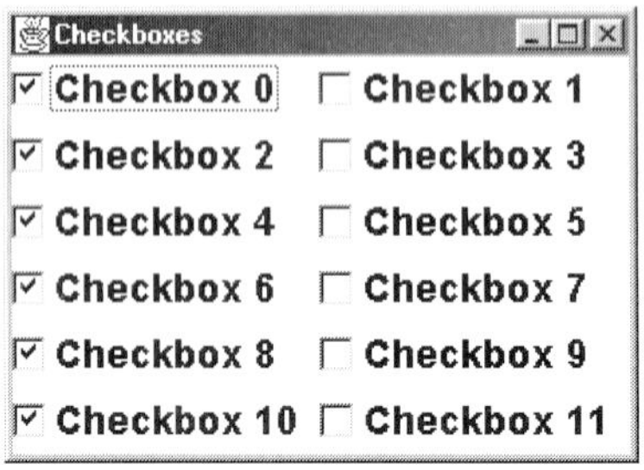

Figure 13–16 Check boxes in Java on Windows 98.

Other Checkbox Methods

Below are eight commonly used `Checkbox` methods.

public boolean getState()
public void setState(boolean checkedState)
The `getState` method determines if the check box is checked (`true`) or unchecked (`false`). The `setState` method sets the check box to be checked or unchecked.

public String getLabel()
public void setLabel(String newLabel)
The `getLabel` method retrieves the current label. The `setLabel` method changes the label. As with buttons, if the check box is already displayed, changing the label does not automatically resize the check box in its `Container`. So, the containing window should be invalidated and validated to force a new layout, as illustrated here:

```
someCheckbox.setLabel("A New Label");
someCheckbox.getParent().invalidate();
someCheckbox.getParent().validate();
```

public void addItemListener(ItemListener listener)
public void removeItemListener(ItemListener listener)
These methods associate or unassociate `ItemListeners` with the check box. They are discussed further in the following subsection.

public void processItemEvent(ItemEvent event)
This is a lower-level, event-processing method. If you use this method, enable events first and call `super.processItemEvent` from within the method. See the following subsection for details.

public Object[ ] getSelectedObjects()

> This method returns an array containing a single item: either the check box label (if the check box is checked) or `null` (if unchecked).

Like the other GUI controls, `Checkbox` inherits all of the `Component` methods listed in Section 13.2.

Handling Checkbox Events

Check boxes do not generate `ActionEvents`. They generate `ItemSelection-Events` instead. To handle events in the check box itself, you first enable events:

```
enableEvents(AWTEvent.ITEM_EVENT_MASK);
```

Next, you override `processItemEvent`, which takes an `ItemEvent` as an argument. You should call `super.processItemEvent` in the body of `process-ItemEvent` in case any `ItemListeners` are attached. The `ItemEvent` class has two useful methods above and beyond those in the `AWTEvent` class: `getItem-Selectable` and `getStateChange`. The first of these returns the check box as an `ItemSelectable` (an interface `Checkbox` implements); the second returns either `ItemEvent.SELECTED` or `ItemEvent.DESELECTED`.

To process events in another object, attach an `ItemListener` to the check box through `addItemListener`. An `ItemListener` *must* implement the `itemStateChanged` method, which takes an `ItemEvent` as an argument.

13.16 Check Box Groups (Radio Buttons)

If you combine check boxes into a `CheckboxGroup`, you get versions with a different graphical look where only one can be selected at any one time. Selecting a new entry results in the previously selected entry becoming unselected. Just as with radio button input forms in HTML (see Chapter 1, "HTML Forms"), there is no requirement that all the check boxes in a given group be placed near each other. However, you typically want the check boxes grouped together, so place them in a `Panel` or choose an appropriate layout manager for the container. The most common usage is to first create the `CheckboxGroup` object, then to create the check boxes that belong to the group. In the check box constructor, you can also specify whether the check box is initially checked. This approach is summarized as follows:

```
CheckboxGroup cbGroup = new CheckboxGroup();
Checkbox cb1 = new Checkbox("...", cbGroup, true);
add(cb1);
Checkbox cb2 = new Checkbox("...", cbGroup, false);
add(cb2);
...
```

Constructors

In this section we list the constructors for CheckboxGroup and Checkbox.

CheckboxGroup

public CheckboxGroup()
This constructor creates a nongraphical object used as a "tag" to group check boxes together into a set of radio buttons. Check boxes that are associated with a tag will look and act like radio buttons rather than like normal check boxes. Only one check box associated with a particular tag can be selected at any given time.

Checkbox

public Checkbox(String label, CheckboxGroup group,
boolean state)
public Checkbox(String label, boolean state,
CheckboxGroup group)
The first constructor creates a radio button associated with the specified group, with the given label and initial state. If you specify an initial state of true for more than one Checkbox in a group, the last one is shown as selected. The second constructor has the same effect but takes the final two arguments in the opposite order.

Example: Check Boxes vs. Radio Buttons

Listing 13.28 presents an applet that illustrates the difference between normal check boxes and those made into radio buttons through a CheckboxGroup. The left column shows radio buttons; the right shows regular check boxes. Figure 13–17 shows the result on Windows 98.

Listing 13.28 CheckboxGroups.java

```java
import java.applet.Applet;
import java.awt.*;

public class CheckboxGroups extends Applet {
  public void init() {
    setLayout(new GridLayout(4, 2));
    setBackground(Color.lightGray);
    setFont(new Font("Serif", Font.BOLD, 16));
    add(new Label("Flavor", Label.CENTER));
    add(new Label("Toppings", Label.CENTER));
    CheckboxGroup flavorGroup = new CheckboxGroup();
    add(new Checkbox("Vanilla", flavorGroup, true));
    add(new Checkbox("Colored Sprinkles"));
    add(new Checkbox("Chocolate", flavorGroup, false));
    add(new Checkbox("Cashews"));
    add(new Checkbox("Strawberry", flavorGroup, false));
    add(new Checkbox("Kiwi"));
  }
}
```

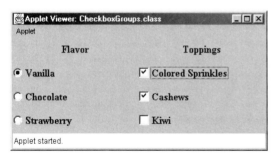

Figure 13–17 Radio buttons (left) vs. regular check boxes (right) on Windows 98.

Other CheckboxGroup and Checkbox Methods

Next, we list the most useful methods in the CheckboxGroup and Checkbox class.

CheckboxGroup

public Checkbox getSelectedCheckbox()

This method returns the radio button (Checkbox) that is currently selected. A null value is returned if none is checked.

public void setSelectedCheckbox(Checkbox boxToSelect)

This method sets the radio button that is currently selected. If you specify a radio button that is not part of the current group, the method call is ignored. Supplying `null` as an argument results in all radio buttons in the group becoming unselected.

Checkbox

In addition to the general methods described in Section 13.15 (The Checkbox Class), `Checkbox` has the following two methods specific to `CheckboxGroups`.

public CheckboxGroup getCheckboxGroup()

This method determines the group in which the radio button is associated.

public void setCheckboxGroup(CheckboxGroup newGroup)

This method registers the check box with a new group.

Handling CheckboxGroup Events

Putting check boxes into a `CheckboxGroup` does not change the basic way in which events are handled, so you should refer to Section 13.15 (The Checkbox Class) for details. However, one small variation does exist. As with ungrouped check boxes, it is common to ignore the events when they occur and simply look up the state when it is needed. Rather than cycling through the various check boxes in a group and checking `getState` on each, it is easier to call the `getSelectedCheckbox` method of the associated `CheckboxGroup`, which returns a reference to the currently selected `Checkbox`.

13.17 Choice Menus

`Choice` entries produce pull-down menus with a single selection showing but with other options displayed when the user clicks with the mouse. These GUI controls are sometimes known as "combo boxes," "drop-down list boxes," or "option menus," depending on the operating/windowing system you are using. Unlike buttons and check boxes, the entire `Choice` is not created with the constructor. Instead, a two-step process is required. The first step builds an empty menu, and the second adds elements to the menu with `add`. Creating a `Choice` menu and adding the menu to a panel is illustrated as follows:

```
Choice choice = new Choice();
choice.addItem("...");
choice.addItem("...");
...
somePanel.add(choice);
```

Constructor

The Choice class has only a single, default constructor.

public Choice()

This constructor creates an empty combo box. Menu entries are not added in the constructor, but in a separate step through add.

Example: Simple Choices

Listing 13.29 creates a simple Choice with three entries. Figure 13–18 shows the results in appletviewer on Windows 98.

Listing 13.29 ChoiceTest.java

```
import java.applet.Applet;
import java.awt.*;

public class ChoiceTest extends Applet {
  private Choice choice;

  public void init() {
    setFont(new Font("SansSerif", Font.BOLD, 36));
    choice = new Choice();
    choice.addItem("Choice 1");
    choice.addItem("Choice 2");
    choice.addItem("Choice 3");
    add(choice);
  }
}
```

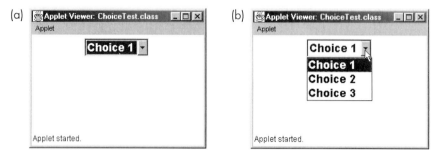

Figure 13-18 A Choice menu on Windows 98: (a) unselected, and (b) selected.

Other Choice Methods

Available Choice methods are listed below.

public void addItem(String menuItem)
public void add(String menuItem)

A Choice menu is built in two steps. First, an empty menu is created by the empty constructor. Second, entries are added to the menu through addItem or by add. By default, the first item added is the one initially displayed, but you can override this behavior by using select. To remove entries once they are added, use remove or removeAll.

public void addItemListener(ItemListener listener)
public void removeItemListener(ItemListener listener)

These methods let you attach/detach an ItemListener to process selection events.

public int getItemCount()

This method returns the number of entries in the Choice.

public String getItem(int itemIndex)

This method returns the label of the item at the specified index.

public int getSelectedIndex()

This method returns the index of the item that is currently selected. A – 1 value is returned if the Choice has no entries.

public String getSelectedItem()

This method returns the label of the currently selected item.

public Object[ ] getSelectedObjects()

This method returns an array containing either the selected entry or `null` if no entry is selected.

public void insert(String menuItem, int itemIndex)

The `insert` method adds an entry to the specified location in the list. This method is in contrast to `add` or `addItem`, which adds to the end of the list only.

public void processItemEvent(ItemEvent event)

You can override this lower-level, event-processing method if you want to have the `Choice` handle its own events.

public void remove(String menuItem)
public void remove(int itemIndex)
public void removeAll()

These methods remove entries from the combo box.

public void select(int itemIndex)
public void select(String itemLabel)

The first method selects the item at the specified index. Recall that the Java programming language uses zero-based indexing. The second method selects the first item with the specified label. No action is taken if no such label exists.

As usual, recall that the color, font, size, visibility, etc., methods of `Component` (Section 13.2) are inherited.

Handling Choice Events

Events are handled in a manner very similar to event handling of check boxes—you override `processItemEvent` or use `addItemListener` to attach an external listener. The main difference is that with check boxes you have only two possible values (selected or deselected). With choice menus, you can have an arbitrary number of options. So, after determining that the check box was acted upon, you have to next decide which entry was chosen. Listing 13.30 gives an expanded version of the `ChoiceTest` class shown earlier. Here, the event-processing model prints out which entry was selected. Also, as with check boxes, it is quite common to ignore the selection event when it occurs and simply determine which item is selected through `get-SelectedItem` or `getSelectedIndex` when it is needed.

Listing 13.30 ChoiceTest2.java

```java
import java.applet.Applet;
import java.awt.*;
import java.awt.event.*;

public class ChoiceTest2 extends Applet
                         implements ItemListener {
  private Choice choice;

  public void init() {
    setFont(new Font("SansSerif", Font.BOLD, 36));
    choice = new Choice();
    choice.addItem("Choice 1");
    choice.addItem("Choice 2");
    choice.addItem("Choice 3");
    choice.addItemListener(this);
    add(choice);
  }

  public void itemStateChanged(ItemEvent event) {
    Choice choice = (Choice)event.getSource();
    String selection = choice.getSelectedItem();
    if (selection.equals("Choice 1")) {
      doChoice1Action();
    } else if (selection.equals("Choice 2")) {
      doChoice2Action();
    } else if (selection.equals("Choice 3")) {
      doChoice3Action();
    }
  }

  private void doChoice1Action() {
    System.out.println("Choice 1 Action");
  }

  private void doChoice2Action() {
    System.out.println("Choice 2 Action");
  }

  private void doChoice3Action() {
    System.out.println("Choice 3 Action");
  }
}
```

13.18 List Boxes

List boxes present scrolling lists from which the user can select an item (single-selectable lists) or several items (multiple-selectable lists). As with `Choice` menus, you first create an empty list, then add items to it through `add`, as below:

```
List list = new List();
list.addItem("...");
list.addItem("...");
...
add(list);
```

Constructors

The `List` class has three constructors.

> **public List()**
> **public List(int rows)**
> **public List(int rows, boolean multiSelectable)**
> The first constructor creates a single-selectable list box with a platform-dependent number of rows and a platform-dependent width. The second constructor creates a single-selectable list box with the specified number of rows and a platform-dependent width.
>
> The last constructor creates a list box with the specified number of visible rows. The number of rows specified affects the height of the `List` box, not the maximum number of possible entries. If more are added, a scrollbar is automatically created. The second argument determines if the `List` is multiple-selectable. As with `Choice` menus, an empty `List` is created, then items are added to it with `addItem` or `add`. The preferred width is set to a platform-dependent value and is typically *not* directly related to the width of the widest entry. Of course, you can always resize the width explicitly if your layout manager permits doing so.

Example: Single and Multiple List Selections

Listing 13.31 creates two lists. The first allows a single selection only, and the second permits multiple selections. Figure 13–19 shows the results on Windows 98.

Listing 13.31 `Lists.java`

```java
import java.awt.*;

public class Lists extends CloseableFrame {
  public static void main(String[] args) {
    new Lists();
  }

  public Lists() {
    super("Lists");
    setLayout(new FlowLayout());
    setBackground(Color.lightGray);
    setFont(new Font("SansSerif", Font.BOLD, 18));
    List list1 = new List(3, false);
    list1.add("Vanilla");
    list1.add("Chocolate");
    list1.add("Strawberry");
    add(list1);
    List list2 = new List(3, true);
    list2.add("Colored Sprinkles");
    list2.add("Cashews");
    list2.add("Kiwi");
    add(list2);
    pack();
    setVisible(true);
  }
}
```

Figure 13–19 List boxes can allow single or multiple selections. This example shows both kinds on Windows 98.

Other List Methods

Below, we summarize 28 methods available in the List class.

public void add(String itemLabel)
public void add(String itemLabel, int itemIndex)
The first method adds an item with the specified label to the end of the list box. The second method adds an item with the specified label at the specified position in the list box and all items at that index or later get moved down.

public void addActionListener(ActionListener listener)
public void addItemListener(ItemListener listener)
public void removeActionListener(ActionListener listener)
public void removeItemListener(ItemListener listener)
These methods let you attach or detach an ActionListener or an Item-Listener. Item events are generated whenever you select or deselect an entry. Action events occur only when you double-click an entry or press Return while an entry is selected. These methods apply only to single-selectable list boxes.

public boolean isMultipleMode()
This method determines whether the list is multiple selectable (true) or single selectable (false).

public void removeAll()
This method removes all items from the list.

public int getItemCount()
This method returns the number of items in the list.

public void remove(String menuItem)
public void remove(int itemIndex)
These methods remove entries from the list.

public void deselect(int itemIndex)
If the item at the specified index is selected, this method deselects it. Otherwise, it does nothing.

public String getItem(int itemIndex)
public String[] getItems()
The first method returns the label at the specified location. The second method returns an array of the labels, in order.

public int getRows()

This method returns the number of rows (visible height) of the list box, which does not change during the life of the list box. This method is in contrast to `getItemCount`, which returns the number of items in the list; that number can change over time and be less than or greater than the number of rows. A vertical scrollbar is automatically added if the number of items is greater than the number of rows.

public int getSelectedIndex()
public int[] getSelectedIndexes()

For a single-selectable list, the first method returns the index of the selected item. A value of –1 is returned if nothing is selected or if the list permits multiple selections. The second method returns an array of the indices of all selected items. It works for single- or multiple-selectable lists. If no items are selected, a zero-length (but non-`null`) array is returned.

public String getSelectedItem()
public String[ ] getSelectedItems()

For a single-selectable list, the first method returns the label of the selected item. It returns `null` if nothing is selected or if the list permits multiple selections. The second method returns an array of all selected items. It works for single- or multiple-selectable lists. If no items are selected, a zero-length (but non-`null`) array is returned.

public Object[ ] getSelectedObjects()

This method returns an array of the selected labels. A `null` is returned if nothing is selected.

public int getVisibleIndex()

This method returns the index of the most recent item made visible through `makeVisible`. Zero is returned if `makeVisible` has never been called.

public boolean isIndexSelected(int itemIndex)

This method determines if the item at the specified index is currently selected.

public void makeVisible(int itemIndex)

If necessary, this method scrolls the list to make the item at the given index visible.

public void processItemEvent(ItemEvent event)
public void processActionEvent(ActionEvent event)

You can override these lower-level, event-processing methods if you want to have the `List` handle its own events. Item events are generated every time an entry is selected or deselected. `ActionEvents` are generated when you double-click on an entry in a single-selectable list box or press Enter while an entry is selected.

public void replaceItem(String newItemLabel, int itemIndex)

This method overwrites the item at the specified index.

public void select(int itemIndex)

This method selects the item at the current index. If the list does not permit multiple selections, then the previously selected item, if any, is also deselected. Note that unlike a `Choice`, a `List` does not have a `select` method that lets you supply the label to be selected; you must supply the index.

public void setMultipleMode(boolean multipleSelectable)

This method permits (`true`) or prohibits (`false`) the list from allowing multiple selections.

As a subclass of `Component` (Section 13.2), `List` has access to all `Component` methods.

Handling List Events

Lists are interesting in that they generate two main kinds of events. `Item-SelectionEvents` are generated whenever an item is selected or deselected by the user. Calling `select` from the program does not generate selection events. `ActionEvents` apply only to single-selectable list boxes and are generated when the user *double*-clicks on an entry or presses Return while an entry is selected. A `List` also receives all mouse, keyboard, or focus events that occur over it.

If you want the `List` to handle its own events, you can enable `AWTEvent.ITEM_EVENT_MASK` and `AWTEvent. ACTION_EVENT_MASK`, then overrides `processItemEvent` and `processActionEvent` to handle item selection and action events. In general, however, it is more flexible to pass the events to an external object to process. You do this by registering an `ItemListener` through `addItemListener`, and an `ActionListener` through `addActionListener`. Listing 13.32 shows an example of the second approach, using the helper classes of Listings 13.33 (an `ItemListener`) and 13.34 (an `ActionListener`). Figure 13–20 shows the result.

Listing 13.32 ListEvents.java

```java
import java.awt.*;
import java.awt.event.*;

/** A class to demonstrate list selection/deselection
 *  and action events.
 */

public class ListEvents extends CloseableFrame {
  public static void main(String[] args) {
    new ListEvents();
  }

  protected List languageList;
  private TextField selectionField, actionField;
  private String selection = "[NONE]", action;

  /** Build a Frame with list of language choices
   *  and two textfields to show the last selected
   *  and last activated items from this list.
   */
  public ListEvents() {
    super("List Events");
    setFont(new Font("Serif", Font.BOLD, 16));
    add(makeLanguagePanel(), BorderLayout.WEST);
    add(makeReportPanel(), BorderLayout.CENTER);
    pack();
    setVisible(true);
  }

  // Create Panel containing List with language choices.
  // Constructor puts this at left side of Frame.

  private Panel makeLanguagePanel() {
    Panel languagePanel = new Panel();
    languagePanel.setLayout(new BorderLayout());
    languagePanel.add(new Label("Choose Language"),
                  BorderLayout.NORTH);
```

(continued)

Listing 13.32 `ListEvents.java` (*continued*)

```java
    languageList = new List(3);
    String[] languages =
      { "Ada", "C", "C++", "Common Lisp", "Eiffel",
        "Forth", "Fortran", "Java", "Pascal",
        "Perl", "Scheme", "Smalltalk" };
    for(int i=0; i<languages.length; i++) {
      languageList.add(languages[i]);
    }
    showJava();
    languagePanel.add("Center", languageList);
    return(languagePanel);
  }

  // Creates Panel with two labels and two textfields.
  // The first will show the last selection in List; the
  // second, the last item activated. The constructor puts
  // this Panel at the right of Frame.

  private Panel makeReportPanel() {
    Panel reportPanel = new Panel();
    reportPanel.setLayout(new GridLayout(4, 1));
    reportPanel.add(new Label("Last Selection:"));
    selectionField = new TextField();
    SelectionReporter selectionReporter =
      new SelectionReporter(selectionField);
    languageList.addItemListener(selectionReporter);
    reportPanel.add(selectionField);
    reportPanel.add(new Label("Last Action:"));
    actionField = new TextField();
    ActionReporter actionReporter =
      new ActionReporter(actionField);
    languageList.addActionListener(actionReporter);
    reportPanel.add(actionField);
    return(reportPanel);
  }

  /** Select and show "Java". */

  protected void showJava() {
    languageList.select(7);
    languageList.makeVisible(7);
  }
}
```

Listing 13.33 `SelectionReporter.java`

```java
import java.awt.*;
import java.awt.event.*;

/** Whenever an item is selected, it is displayed
 *  in the textfield that was supplied to the
 *  SelectionReporter constructor.
 */

public class SelectionReporter implements ItemListener {
  private TextField selectionField;

  public SelectionReporter(TextField selectionField) {
    this.selectionField = selectionField;
  }

  public void itemStateChanged(ItemEvent event) {
    if (event.getStateChange() == event.SELECTED) {
      List source = (List)event.getSource();
      selectionField.setText(source.getSelectedItem());
    } else
      selectionField.setText("");
  }
}
```

Listing 13.34 `ActionReporter.java`

```java
import java.awt.*;
import java.awt.event.*;

/** Whenever an item is activated, it is displayed
 *  in the textfield that was supplied to the
 *  ActionReporter constructor.
 */

public class ActionReporter implements ActionListener {
  private TextField actionField;

  public ActionReporter(TextField actionField) {
    this.actionField = actionField;
  }

  public void actionPerformed(ActionEvent event) {
    List source = (List)event.getSource();
    actionField.setText(source.getSelectedItem());
  }
}
```

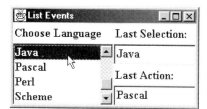

Figure 13–20 Result after user double-clicks "Pascal," then single-clicks "Java."

Lists can generate mouse, keyboard, and focus events. To demonstrate this, Listing 13.35 shows a variation of the previous example where typing any of the letters in "Java" (upper or lower case) results in the "Java" entry being selected and made visible. Note the use of an inner class to achieve this result. Instead of a separate KeyAdapter class being created, a nested version is made. Besides being more convenient in such a short class, this approach lets the showJava method of ListEvents remain protected.

Listing 13.35 ListEvents2.java

```java
import java.awt.event.*;

public class ListEvents2 extends ListEvents {
  public static void main(String[] args) {
    new ListEvents2();
  }

  /** Extends ListEvents with the twist that
   *  typing any of the letters of "JAVA" or "java"
   *  over the language list will result in "Java"
   *  being selected
   */

  public ListEvents2() {
    super();
    // Create a KeyAdapter and attach it to languageList.
    // Since this is an inner class, it has access
    // to nonpublic data (such as the ListEvent's
    // protected showJava method).
    KeyAdapter javaChooser = new KeyAdapter() {
      public void keyPressed(KeyEvent event) {
        int key = event.getKeyChar();
        if ("JAVAjava".indexOf(key) != -1) {
          showJava();
        }
      }
    };
    languageList.addKeyListener(javaChooser);
  }
}
```

13.19 The TextField Class

Textfields create boxed areas to display or read a single line of text. See `TextArea` (Section 13.20) for a component that can display multiple lines. Java textfields do not permit mixed fonts or colors within a single textfield. If a textfield is being used for input, you typically allocate it (perhaps with a default entry or size) by specifying everything in the constructor, as follows:

```
TextField lastNameField = new TextField(15);
add(lastNameField);
TextField langField = new TextField("Java");
add(langField);
```

Textfields used only for display are similar but require a call to `setEditable` to turn off input capability. Also, the value is often filled in through a separate step, since it might not be available when the textfield is first created. Here's the idea:

```
TextField temperatureField = new TextField(4);
temperatureField.setEditable(false);
statusPanel.add(temperatureField);
...
temperatureString = simulationTemperature("F");
temperatureField.setText(temperatureString);
```

Constructors

The `TextField` class has four constructors.

public TextField()
public TextField(int numChars)
public TextField(String initialString)
public TextField(String initialString, int numChars)

The first constructor creates an empty textfield with a platform-dependent width (often one character). The second constructor creates an empty textfield that is the specified number of characters wide. Note that if a proportional-spaced font is being used, the definition of "the space required for *N* characters" is ambiguous. So the *average* character width is used. The third constructor creates a textfield filled with an initial string. It will be just wide enough to hold the string. The last constructor creates a textfield of the specified width, filled with an initial string. As before, the width is based on the *average* width of characters in the font the textfield is using.

Example: Creating TextFields

Listing 13.36 creates a TextField with each of the four constructors. The result is shown in Figure 13–21.

Listing 13.36 TextFields.java

```
import java.applet.Applet;
import java.awt.*;

/** A TextField from each of the four constructors */

public class TextFields extends Applet {
  public void init() {
    add(new TextField());
    add(new TextField(30));
    add(new TextField("Initial String"));
    add(new TextField("Initial", 30));
  }
}
```

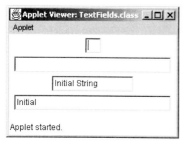

Figure 13–21 A TextField from each of the four constructors.

Other TextField Methods

A TextField is a subclass of TextComponent. The following two subsections list the methods of TextComponent and TextField. Some of the most commonly used methods are getText and setText (for retrieving and specifying TextField contents), setEditable (for allowing or disallowing user input), getColumns and setColumns (for looking up and setting the TextField width), and setEcho-Char (for specifying that "*" or some other character be displayed when text is entered, as for password fields).

TextComponent Methods

public void addTextListener(TextListener listener)
public void removeTextListener(TextListener listener)

These methods let you add or remove a `TextListener` for processing text events. Recall that `Component` (Section 13.2) already supplies `addKey-Listener` and `removeKeyListener` methods, but text events occur whenever the text value changes, even if the change is programmatic (i.e., through `setText`). A `TextListener` needs to implement a single method: `textValueChanged`. This method takes a `TextEvent` as an argument. To get the component's string from this event, use `getSource` to find the source object, cast the result to a `TextComponent`, and do `getText` on that.

public int getCaretPosition()
public void setCaretPosition(int index)

The first method lets you look up the position of the text insertion caret. The second method sets the position of the text insertion caret.

public String getSelectedText()

This method returns the selected text. If no text is currently selected, a zero-length (but non-`null`) string is returned.

public int getSelectionEnd()
public void setSelectionEnd(int startIndex)

The first method returns the index of the first character *after* the end of the selected text. Zero is returned if no text is selected. The second method sets the index of the first character *after* the end of the selected text.

public int getSelectionStart()
public void setSelectionStart(int endIndex)

The first method returns the index of the first character of any selected text. Zero is returned if no text is selected. The second method sets the index of the first character of selected text.

public String getText()
public void setText(String newText)

The `getText` method returns the text, if any, in the textfield. If there is no text, a zero-length (but non-`null`) string is returned. The `setText` method replaces any text with the supplied string. An input value of `null` is the same as `" "`.

public boolean isEditable()
public void setEditable(boolean editableStatus)
The `isEditable` method determines whether the textfield allows user input (`true`) or whether it is just for display (`false`). The `setEditable` method permits (`true`) or prohibits (`false`) the user from typing into the textfield.

public void processTextEvent(TextEvent event)
This lower-level, event-processing method can be overridden to handle text events. See `addTextListener` for more details. You can also handle individual keyboard events, since `processKeyEvent` is inherited from the `Component` class (Section 13.2). Don't forget to enable text events, call `super.processTextEvent` from within the method, and import `java.awt.event.*`.

public void select(int startIndex, int endIndex)
This method selects the text starting at `startIndex`, up through but *not* including `endIndex`. Selected text is highlighted on most operating systems. If the ending index is longer than the length of the text, the entire text is selected.

public void selectAll()
This method selects all the text.

TextField Methods

In addition to the `TextComponent` methods, the following methods are available:

public void addActionListener(ActionListener listener)
public void removeActionListener(ActionListener listener)
`ActionEvents` are generated when the user presses Return while the textfield has the focus. These methods let you attach or remove an `Action-Listener` to process these events. In many cases, `addTextListener` and `removeTextListener` (inherited from `TextComponent`) or `addKeyListener` and `removeKeyListener` (inherited from `Component`) are of more interest.

public boolean echoCharIsSet()
This method determines whether an echo character has been specified. See `setEchoCharacter`.

public int getColumns()
This method tells you the number of columns in the textfield. If you are using a proportional font, this method does not guarantee that this number of charac-

ters will really fit in the textfield, however, because the value is based on the *average* width of characters in the current font.

public char getEchoChar()
public void setEchoChar(char echoChar)

The getEchoChar method returns the current echo character. This value is only meaningful if echoCharIsSet is true. The setEchoChar specifies a character to display for each character the user types in. The actual text entered is still available from getText. The "*" character is often used for implementing fields that gather passwords or other sensitive data.

public void processActionEvent(ActionEvent event)

Action events are generated when the user presses Return while the textfield has the focus. If you want the textfield to process its own events, you first enable AWTEvent.ACTION_EVENT_MASK, then override this method. Be sure to call super.processActionEvent in case any listeners are attached. Also, see addActionListener.

public void setColumns(int cols)

The setColumns method lets you specify the width of the Textfield directly. Note that the width is in terms of the *average* width of characters in the textfield's font.

Because TextField is a subclass of Component, it has access to all Component methods. See Section 13.2 (The Component Class).

Handling TextField Events

Four event types are of interest: focus events, keyboard events, text events, and action events. Focus events happen when the textfield acquires or loses the input focus, keyboard and text events when the user presses a key while the textfield has the focus, and action events when the user presses Return while the textfield has the focus. The difference between keyboard events and text events is that text events are generated even when someone calls setText programmatically; keyboard events are not. As usual, you have the choice of handling events in the component itself by using the lower-level processXxxEvent methods or of attaching an external listener to process them. See Section 11.6 (Behind the Scenes: Low-Level Event Processing) for an example of low-level event handling and TextFields.

13.20 The TextArea Class

A `TextArea` is similar to a `TextField`, except that it can have multiple lines and does not generate action events. Here are some typical examples:

```
TextArea inputArea = new TextArea(4, 15);
add(inputArea);
TextArea resultsArea = new TextArea("No Results Yet", 2, 10);
resultsArea.setEditable(false);
add(resultsArea);
```

Constructors

The following five `TextArea` constructors are available:

public TextArea()
This constructor creates an empty text area with a platform-dependent number of rows and columns and both vertical and horizontal scrollbars. The default size may be very large, so use this constructor with caution if you're not using a layout manager that will size the text area for you.

public TextArea(int rows, int cols)
This constructor creates an empty text area with the specified number of rows and columns. The column value is based on the average width of characters in whatever font the `TextArea` is using. Vertical and horizontal scrollbars are included.

public TextArea(String initialString)
This constructor creates an initialized text area with a platform-dependent size and both types of scrollbars. The initial string can contain explicit line breaks (\n) to force it to span multiple lines.

public TextArea(String initialString, int rows, int cols)
This constructor creates an initialized text area with the specified size and both types of scrollbars.

public TextArea(String initialString, int rows, int cols, int scrollbarType)
This constructor creates an initialized text area with the specified size. If the scrollbar type is `TextArea.SCROLLBARS_BOTH`, the result is the same as with the previous constructor. If `TextArea.SCROLLBARS_VERTICAL_ONLY` is specified, then the text area will have vertical but not horizontal scrollbars,

and words will wrap to the next line if the user enters text that would otherwise extend past the right side of the text area. If `TextArea.SCROLLBARS_HORIZONTAL_ONLY` is supplied, then the text area will have horizontal but not vertical scrollbars. Finally, if you specify `TextArea.SCROLLBARS_NEITHER`, no scrollbars will be included. Again, text will wrap as it is entered.

Example: Empty and Filled Text Areas

Listing 13.37 creates two text areas: an empty one and another filled with three initial lines. Figure 13–22 shows the result on Windows 98.

Listing 13.37 `TextAreas.java`

```
import java.applet.Applet;
import java.awt.*;

public class TextAreas extends Applet {
  public void init() {
    setBackground(Color.lightGray);
    add(new TextArea(3, 10));
    add(new TextArea("Some\nInitial\nText", 3, 10));
  }
}
```

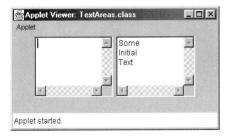

Figure 13–22 Text areas on Windows 98.

Other TextArea Methods

`TextArea` inherits `getText`, `setText`, `setEditable`, `select` and all of the other methods of `TextComponent` described in Section 13.19 (The TextField Class). In addition, `TextArea` supports the following methods:

public void append(String additionalText)

This method adds the specified text to the end of the text area.

public int getColumns()

This method returns the number of columns in the text area.

public int getRows()

This method returns the number of rows used to create the text area.

public void insert(String additionalText, int index)

These methods insert the specified text at the given index. Any text at that location or later is moved down.

public void replaceRange(String replacement, int startIndex,
int endIndex)

This method replaces the text starting at `startIndex`, up through but *not* including `endIndex`, with the specified string. The replacement string need not be the same length as the text being replaced.

As a subclass of `Component` (Section 13.2), `TextArea` has access to all `Component` methods.

Handling TextArea Events

Keyboard, text, and focus events are handled in exactly the same manner as with textfields. Text areas do not generate `ActionEvents`.

13.21 The Label Class

Labels are simple textual displays. It is often more convenient to use a `Label` than to draw text with the `drawString` method of `Graphics` because labels are redisplayed automatically and can be moved around by layout managers. You can just create one with designated text and drop it in a window, as follows:

```
Label label = new Label("...");
add(label);
```

Frequently, however, you may use the label to describe some other object and want to be sure the label is aligned with it. So, you may want to use the label with a layout manager other than `FlowLayout`. Changing the label font or alignment is common as well. For instance, the following might be used to make a title on a panel:

```
Panel resultsPanel = new Panel();
resultsPanel.setLayout(new BorderLayout());
Label title = new Label("Results", Label.CENTER);
title.setFont(new Font("SansSerif", Font.BOLD, 18));
resultsPanel.add(title, BorderLayout.NORTH);
TextArea resultsArea = new TextArea();
resultsPanel.add(resultsArea, BorderLayout.CENTER);
```

Constructors

The Label class has only three constructors.

public Label()
public Label(String labelString)
public Label(String labelString, int alignment)

The first constructor simply creates a blank label. You can specify the text later with setText. The second constructor creates a label displaying the specified string. The last constructor creates a label with the specified alignment. The alignment is one of Label.LEFT (default), Label.RIGHT, and Label.CENTER. The alignment is not particularly important if the label is used in a window that is using FlowLayout or in the East or West regions of a BorderLayout. The preferred width of a Label is only a little bit bigger than the text it contains, and there's not much aligning left to be done. However, alignment is quite important if you resize a Label by hand or use one in a GridLayout, GridBagLayout, or the NORTH or SOUTH regions of a BorderLayout. In such a case, the width of the Label might be much larger than the text it contains, and you need to specify where to place the text in that area.

Example: Four Different Labels

Listing 13.38 creates four labels with various fonts and alignment options. Figure 13–23 shows the result.

Listing 13.38 `Labels.java`

```java
import java.applet.Applet;
import java.awt.*;

public class Labels extends Applet {
  public void init() {
    setLayout(new GridLayout(4,1));
    Label label1, label2, label3, label4;
    label1 = new Label("Label 1");
    label2 = new Label("Label 2", Label.LEFT);
    label3 = new Label("Label 3", Label.RIGHT);
    label4 = new Label("Label 4", Label.CENTER);
    Font bigFont = new Font("SanSerif", Font.BOLD, 25);
    label2.setFont(bigFont);
    label3.setFont(bigFont);
    label4.setFont(bigFont);
    add(label1);
    add(label2);
    add(label3);
    add(label4);
  }
}
```

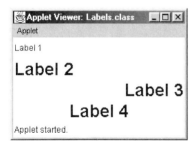

Figure 13–23 Labels can have different fonts and can be left-aligned, right-aligned, or centered.

Other Label Methods

The Label class has seven methods. We summarize the most important four below.

public int getAlignment()
public void setAlignment(int alignment)

The first method returns the current alignment, which will be one of Label.LEFT, Label.RIGHT, or Label.CENTER. The second method sets the text alignment.

public String getText()
public void setText(String newLabel)

The getText method returns the text of the label. If none has been set, a zero-length (but non-null) string is returned. The setText method changes the label's text. If the label is already displayed, changing the text does not automatically resize it in its Container. So, the containing window should be invalidated and validated to force a new layout, as follows.

```
someLabel.setText("A Different Label");
someLabel.getParent().invalidate();
someLabel.getParent().validate();
```

As a Component subclass, Label inherits all the color, font, and resizing methods of Component (Section 13.2).

Handling Label Events

For labels, the normal mouse and keyboard events are generated, but there are no selection or action events. Listing 13.39 shows a frame that inserts two "reversible" labels (Listing 13.40): labels with attached mouse listeners that switch the foreground and background colors when the mouse enters the label and switch back when the mouse leaves. Figures 13–24 and 13–25 show the original result and the result after the mouse is moved over the second ReversibleLabel, respectively.

Listing 13.39 ReverseLabels.java

```
import java.awt.*;

public class ReverseLabels extends CloseableFrame {
  public static void main(String[] args) {
    new ReverseLabels();
  }

  public ReverseLabels() {
    super("Reversible Labels");
    setLayout(new FlowLayout());
    setBackground(Color.lightGray);
    setFont(new Font("Serif", Font.BOLD, 18));
    ReversibleLabel label1 =
      new ReversibleLabel("Black on White",
                          Color.white, Color.black);
    add(label1);
    ReversibleLabel label2 =
      new ReversibleLabel("White on Black",
                          Color.black, Color.white);
    add(label2);
    pack();
    setVisible(true);
  }
}
```

Listing 13.40 `ReversibleLabel.java`

```java
import java.awt.*;
import java.awt.event.*;

/** A Label that reverses its background and
 *  foreground colors when the mouse is over it.
 */

public class ReversibleLabel extends Label {
  public ReversibleLabel(String text,
                         Color bgColor, Color fgColor) {
    super(text);
    MouseAdapter reverser = new MouseAdapter() {
      public void mouseEntered(MouseEvent event) {
        reverseColors();
      }

      public void mouseExited(MouseEvent event) {
        reverseColors(); // or mouseEntered(event);
      }
    };
    addMouseListener(reverser);
    setText(text);
    setBackground(bgColor);
    setForeground(fgColor);
  }

  protected void reverseColors() {
    Color fg = getForeground();
    Color bg = getBackground();
    setForeground(bg);
    setBackground(fg);
  }
}
```

Figure 13-24 `ReverseLabels`: original appearance.

Figure 13–25 ReverseLabels: after the mouse is moved over right label.

13.22 Scrollbars and Sliders

The AWT uses the same basic component for scrollbars (used to scroll windows) and sliders (used to interactively select values): the Scrollbar class. The "preferred" size and shape of a Scrollbar is not generally usable, so scrollbars are not usually placed in a window that uses FlowLayout. Instead, they are typically placed in the east or south sections of a BorderLayout, used in a GridLayout, or resized by hand.

Unfortunately, scrollbars are not implemented in the same manner on all Java systems and are painful to use directly. The preferred alternative is to use TextAreas and ScrollPanes, unless you want sliders. If you are developing a Swing applet or application, the JSlider class (Section 14.7) is a significant improvement over the AWT Scrollbar for implementing sliders.

Constructors

Following are the Scrollbar constructors:

public Scrollbar()
This constructor creates a vertical scrollbar. The bubble (or thumb–part that actually moves) size defaults to 10% of the trough length. The internal minimum and maximum values (see below) are set to zero.

public Scrollbar(int orientation)
This constructor creates a horizontal or vertical scrollbar. The orientation can be either Scrollbar.HORIZONTAL or Scrollbar.VERTICAL. The bubble (thumb) size defaults to 10% of the trough length. The internal minimum and maximum values (see below) are set to zero.

public Scrollbar(int orientation, int initialValue,
                   int bubbleSize, int min, int max)
This constructor is the one you use when you want to make a slider for interactively selecting values. It creates a horizontal or vertical slider or scrollbar with a customized bubble (or thumb—the part that actually moves) thickness and a specific internal range of values. The bubble thickness is in terms of the scrollbar's range of values, not in pixels, so that if max minus min was 5, a bubble size

of 1 would specify 20% of the trough length. Note, however, that some operating systems (some versions of MacOS, in particular) do not support varying sizes for scrollbar thumbs.

Also, the value corresponds to the location of the *left* (horizontal sliders) or *top* (vertical sliders) edge of the bubble, not its center. For a horizontal scrollbar, rather the maximum corresponding to the highest value the left side of the slider can reach, it corresponds to the highest value the right side of the slider can reach, and similarly for vertical scrollbars. This means that the actual values that can be set to range from the minimum value to the bubble size *less* than the maximum value. For example, the following statement makes a scrollbar that can range only from 0 to 45, with the initial value at 25 and a bubble size of 5:

```java
new Scrollbar(Scrollbar.HORIZONTAL, 25, 5, 0, 50);
```

Core Warning

To get a scrollbar with a thumb size of t that can range in value from min to max, you have to create it with a maximum value of max+t.

Example: Variety of Sliders

Listing 13.41 creates a variety of horizontal and vertical sliders (scrollbars for selecting values). The values range from 0 to 100 with an initial value of 50 and various bubble thicknesses. Figure 13–26 shows the result on Windows 98.

Listing 13.41 `Scrollbars.java`

```java
import java.applet.Applet;
import java.awt.*;

public class Scrollbars extends Applet {
  public void init() {
    int i;
    setLayout(new GridLayout(1, 2));
    Panel left = new Panel(), right = new Panel();
    left.setLayout(new GridLayout(10, 1));
    for(i=5; i<55; i=i+5) {
      left.add(new Scrollbar(Scrollbar.HORIZONTAL, 50, i, 0, 100));
    }
    right.setLayout(new GridLayout(1, 10));
    for(i=5; i<55; i=i+5) {
      right.add(new Scrollbar(Scrollbar.VERTICAL, 50, i, 0, 100));
    }
    add(left);
    add(right);
  }
}
```

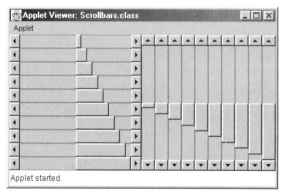

Figure 13–26 Scrollbars with varying bubble sizes but constant ranges and initial values, shown on Windows 98.

Other Scrollbar Methods

The following `Scrollbar` methods are available.

public void addAdjustmentListener(AdjustmentListener listener)
public void removeAdjustmentListener(AdjustmentListener listener)

These methods add and remove an `AdjustmentListener` to the scrollbar, used to monitor user adjustments to the scrollbar. An `AdjustmentListener` needs to implement `adjustmentValueChanged`, which takes an `AdjustmentEvent` as an argument. The `AdjustmentEvent` class contains a `getAdjustmentType` method that returns one of `Adjustment-Event.UNIT_INCREMENT` (the right or down arrow was clicked), `AdjustmentEvent.UNIT_DECREMENT` (the left or up arrow was clicked), `AdjustmentEvent.BLOCK_INCREMENT` (the trough to the right of or below the bubble was clicked), `AdjustmentEvent.BLOCK_DECREMENT` (the trough to the left of or above the bubble was clicked), or `AdjustmentEvent.TRACK` (the bubble was dragged).

public int getUnitIncrement()
public void setUnitIncrement(int increment)

The `getUnitIncrement` method is intended to return the amount that the value will be adjusted when the arrows at either end of the scrollbar are pressed. It is usually 1 if the user has not specified anything different with `setUnitIncrement`. Unfortunately, however, some implementations ignore this method. For instance, the line increment value has no effect on Solaris in

JDK 1.1. For many applications you can remedy this situation. See Listing 13.42 for an example. The `setUnitIncrement` method changes the amount the scrollbar will move when the user clicks on the arrows but is not supported on all platforms.

public int getMaximum()
public void setMaximum(int maxValue)

The `getMaximum` method returns the scrollbar's maximum possible value. This value is the `getVisibleAmount` *more* than the largest possible select-able value. The `setMaximum` method changes the maximum possible value.

public int getMinimum()
public void setMinimum(int minValue)

These two methods return and set the scrollbar's minimum possible value, respectively.

public int getOrientation()
public void setOrientation(int orientation)

These methods return and set the orientation of the scrollbar. Legal values are `Scrollbar.HORIZONTAL` or `Scrollbar.VERTICAL`.

public int getBlockIncrement()
public void setBlockIncrement(int increment)

These methods return and set how much the value will change when the user clicks inside the trough above or below the scrollbar bubble. The default is platform dependent; common defaults are 10 (Windows 98) or the bubble size (Solaris).

public int getValue()
public void setValue(int value)
public void setValues(int value, int bubbleSize, int min, int max)

These methods return and set the current value of the scrollbar. Specifying a value below the minimum value does not cause an error; the minimum value is simply stored. Specifying a value above the maximum minus the thumb size does not cause an error either. Instead, the scrollbar takes on the maximum minus the thumb size. The last method changes several parameters in one fell swoop.

public int getVisibleAmount()

This method returns the size of the bubble (thumb), represented in terms of the units used for the scrollbar range, not in terms of pixels.

public void processAdjustmentEvent(AdjustmentEvent event)

If you want to have a scrollbar handle its own events, you first enable adjustment events as follows:

```
enableEvents(AWTEvent.ADJUSTMENT_EVENT_MASK);
```

Next, you override `processAdjustmentEvent`, which takes an `AdjustmentEvent` as an argument. Remember to call `super.process-AdjustmentEvent` in case there are listeners on the scrollbar. See the following subsection for an example.

As a subclass of `Component`, the `setForeground` and `setBackground` methods are available, but `setForeground` is not generally supported. On Windows 95/NT, `setBackground` sets the color of the scrollbar trough. On Solaris, it sets the color of the bubble and the arrows. Many MacOS implementations do not support scrollbar colors.

Handling Scrollbar Events

To process scrolling events, you can either use `processAdjustmentEvent` or attach an `AdjustmentListener`. If you override `processAdjustmentEvent`, you can let a scrollbar handle its own events. If you attach an `Adjustment-Listener`, an external object can handle the events. In either case, note that the `AdjustmentEvent` class has two methods of particular import: `getValue` and `getAdjustmentType`. The first returns an `int` giving the scrollbar's current value, and the second returns one of `AdjustmentEvent.UNIT_INCREMENT`, `AdjustmentEvent.UNIT_DECREMENT`, `AdjustmentEvent.BLOCK_INCREMENT`, `AdjustmentEvent.BLOCK_DECREMENT`, or `AdjustmentEvent.TRACK`. For instance, Listing 13.42 shows how you could use `processAdjustmentEvent` to make a scrollbar that honors the unit increment and block increment values, regardless of whether the underlying implementation already honors those values. Note, however, that this approach only works if all scrollbar adjustment is done by the user. Calling `setValue` will not properly update the `lastValue` variable, but there is no way around this since you cannot tell the difference between a system-generated `setValue` call (when the scrollbar is adjusted) and a user-generated one.

Note that the Swing API defines a `JSlider` class (Section 14.7) that provides significant improvements over the AWT `Scrollbar` and functions the same on all platforms. However, Swing components are not supported by all browsers and may require that the client install the Java Plug-In (Section 9.9).

Listing 13.42 `BetterScrollbar.java`

```java
import java.awt.*;
import java.awt.event.*;

/** The beginnings of a better scrollbar. This one
 *  adjusts for the fact that many implementations
 *  ignore the line or page increment. Created to
 *  demonstrate low-level scrollbar events.
 */

public class BetterScrollbar extends Scrollbar {
  private int lastValue;

  public BetterScrollbar(int orientation,
                         int initialValue,
                         int bubbleSize,
                         int min,
                         int max) {
    super(orientation, initialValue, bubbleSize, min, max);
    enableEvents(AWTEvent.ADJUSTMENT_EVENT_MASK);
    lastValue = initialValue;
  }

  /** Watch the events, adjusting by unit increment
   *  or block increment if appropriate.
   */

  public void processAdjustmentEvent(AdjustmentEvent e) {
    int type = e.getAdjustmentType();
    switch(type) {
      case AdjustmentEvent.UNIT_INCREMENT:
        setValue(lastValue + getUnitIncrement());
        break;
      case AdjustmentEvent.UNIT_DECREMENT:
        setValue(lastValue - getUnitIncrement());
        break;
      case AdjustmentEvent.BLOCK_INCREMENT:
        setValue(lastValue + getBlockIncrement());
        break;
      case AdjustmentEvent.BLOCK_DECREMENT:
        setValue(lastValue - getBlockIncrement());
        break;
    }
    lastValue = getValue();
    super.processAdjustmentEvent(e);
  }
}
```

See the archive at http://www.corewebprogramming.com/ for a custom Slider class that combines both horizontal Scrollbar and TextField as a single GUI component.

13.23 Pop-up Menus

Pop-up menus are remarkably simple to use: allocate a PopupMenu, add some MenuItems to it, then watch for the pop-up trigger in a Component by checking mouse events with isPopupTrigger. When the trigger is received, call show to display the menu. When the menu is shown, an ActionEvent is triggered for a selected menu item.

Constructors

The two PopupMenu constructors are:

public PopupMenu()
public PopupMenu(String title)
The first constructor creates an untitled pop-up menu. The second constructor creates a pop-up menu with the specified title. However, most current Windows 95/98/NT implementations do not display the title.

Example: Applet Pop-up Menu

Listing 13.43 creates a pop-up menu in an applet. It then watches the mouse events until one occurs that is a pop-up trigger (whatever mouse action normally displays menus in the current operating system), in which case the menu is displayed. By implementing the ActionListener interface and adding itself as a listener on each item in the menu, the applet calls its own actionPerformed method when items are selected. Figure 13–27 shows the result on Windows 95.

Listing 13.43 ColorPopupMenu.java

```
import java.applet.Applet;
import java.awt.*;
import java.awt.event.*;

/** Simple demo of pop-up menus. */
```

(continued)

Listing 13.43 `ColorPopupMenu.java` *(continued)*

```java
public class ColorPopupMenu extends Applet
                            implements ActionListener {
  private String[] colorNames =
    { "White", "Light Gray", "Gray", "Dark Gray", "Black" };
  private Color[] colors =
    { Color.white, Color.lightGray, Color.gray,
      Color.darkGray, Color.black };
  private PopupMenu menu;

  /** Create PopupMenu and add MenuItems. */

  public void init() {
    setBackground(Color.gray);
    menu = new PopupMenu("Background Color");
    enableEvents(AWTEvent.MOUSE_EVENT_MASK);
    MenuItem colorName;
    for(int i=0; i<colorNames.length; i++) {
      colorName = new MenuItem(colorNames[i]);
      menu.add(colorName);
      colorName.addActionListener(this);
      menu.addSeparator();
    }
    add(menu);
  }

  /** Don't use a MouseListener, since in Win95/98/NT
   *  you have to check isPopupTrigger in
   *  mouseReleased, but do it in mousePressed in
   *  Solaris (boo!).
   */
  public void processMouseEvent(MouseEvent event) {
    if (event.isPopupTrigger()) {
      menu.show(event.getComponent(), event.getX(),
                event.getY());
    }
    super.processMouseEvent(event);
  }

  public void actionPerformed(ActionEvent event) {
    setBackground(colorNamed(event.getActionCommand()));
    repaint();
  }
```

(continued)

Listing 13.43 `ColorPopupMenu.java` *(continued)*

```
private Color colorNamed(String colorName) {
  for(int i=0; i<colorNames.length; i++) {
    if(colorNames[i].equals(colorName)) {
      return(colors[i]);
    }
  }
  return(Color.white);
}
}
```

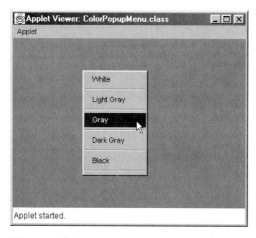

Figure 13–27 Pop-up menus on Windows 98 are displayed without titles.

Other PopupMenu Methods

The only method directly in the `PopupMenu` class is `show`, which displays the menu. Selected methods from the ancestor classes `Menu` and `MenuItem` are listed here as well.

public void add(MenuItem item)
public void add(String label)

These methods add an entry to the menu. Rather than adding a string directly, you usually do better to turn it into a `MenuItem` first through `new Menu-Item(label)`. This approach lets you add an `ActionListener` on the label.

public void addActionListener(ActionListener listener)

This method is normally applied to `MenuItems` within the pop-up menu and lets you add a listener to take action when the item is selected. Note that the label is available in the `ActionEvent` class through `getActionCommand()`.

public void addSeparator()

This method adds a nonselectable horizontal line to the menu. In Figure 13–27, there is a separator after every entry.

public void setShortcut(MenuShortcut shortcut)
public MenuShortcut getShortcut()
public void deleteShortcut()

In JDK 1.1 and later, you can create portable shortcuts (keyboard shortcuts associated with menu items). Simply create a `MenuShortcut` through

```
MenuShortcut shortcut = new MenuShortcut(int key);
```

Next, add the shortcut to a `MenuItem` through `setShortcut`. The `getShortcut` and `deleteShortcut` methods retrieve and delete the shortcut associated with a menu item.

public void show(Component c, int x, int y)

This method displays the pop-up menu at the specified location relative to the top-left corner of the component.

Strictly speaking, `PopupMenu` is a `Component`. However, you should not rely on custom colors or fonts being supported.

Handling PopupMenu Events

With pop-up menus you have two types of events you need to worry about. The first is the mouse click that brings up the menu in the first place. The second is the event that occurs when an entry is actually selected.

Rather than requiring programmers to remember what types of mouse clicks are supposed to initiate pop-up menus on different platforms, the Java programming language provides a convenient method in the `MouseEvent` class: `isPopupTrigger`. However, since some operating systems invoke the menu when the mouse is first pressed (e.g., Solaris) but others when it is released (e.g., Windows 98 and Windows NT), you probably want to watch mouse events in `processMouseEvent` rather than in a `MouseListener`. If you do use a `MouseListener`, be sure to check *both* `mousePressed` and `mouseReleased`. So, the process of popping up the menu would go something like this:

```
PopupMenu menu = new PopupMenu("[Title]");
...
```

```
enableEvents(AWTEvent.MOUSE_EVENT_MASK);
...
public void processMouseEvent(MouseEvent event) {
  if (event.isPopupTrigger())
    menu.show(event.getComponent(),
              event.getX(), event.getY());
  super.processMouseEvent(event);
}
```

To process the selections, add an `ActionListener` to each as it is created, as follows:

```
MenuItem item = new MenuItem("[Label]");
menu.add(item);
item.addActionListener(someListener);
```

Recall that an `ActionListener` needs to implement the `actionPerformed` method, which takes an `ActionEvent` as an argument. The `getActionCommand` method of `ActionEvent` returns the label of the `MenuItem`.

13.24 Summary

The AWT offers eight major types of windows that the developer can use for user interfaces: `Canvas`, `Panel`, `Applet`, `ScrollPane`, `Frame`, `Dialog`, `File-Dialog`, and `Window`. This chapter explains the differences among these and described the basics of their use. The major GUI controls available in Java are `Button`, `Checkbox` (which can create regular check boxes or radio buttons), `Choice`, `List`, `TextField`, `TextArea`, `Label`, `Scrollbar` (used for scrolling and for selecting values), and `PopupMenu`. To use built-in or custom GUI components, you need to know two things: how to create them with the look you want and how to process the events that occur when the user interacts with them. In most cases, the main look is specified in the interface element's constructor, but some elements (`Choice`, `List`, `PopupMenu`) are created empty, then filled later. Action events are perhaps the most important type of event that applies to GUI elements, but item selection events, keyboard events, text events, and scrolling events are important as well.

You should now be familiar with all the components available in the AWT for developing GUI programs. Most likely you will only use the AWT components for development of applets, since the newer Swing components, available in the Java 2 Platform, are more suitable for developing stand-alone GUI applications. The advantage of creating AWT `Applets` for browsers is that your program will run in most versions of Netscape and Internet Explorer; the Java 1.1 AWT API is supported in Netscape 4.06 and later and Internet Explorer 4.0 and later.

BASIC SWING

Topics in This Chapter

- Building Swing applets and applications
- Changing the GUI look and feel
- Adding custom borders to components
- Creating text and image buttons
- Using HTML in labels and buttons
- Selecting colors with JColorChooser
- Sending dialog alerts for user input
- Adding child frames to applications
- Building custom toolbars
- Implementing a Web browser in Swing

Chapter 14

Many programmers consider the Swing components to be the single most significant improvement and change in the Java platform for development of graphical user interfaces. Swing adds the small touches (icons in dialog boxes, tool-tips, borders) that distinguish a commercial-quality GUI from an amateurish one.

The Swing components are standard in the Java 2 Platform and go far beyond the simple components found in the AWT. The benefits of Swing include:

- A significantly increased set of built-in controls including image buttons, tabbed panes, sliders, toolbars, color choosers, text areas that can display HTML or RTF, lists, trees, and tables.
- Increased customization of components, including border styles, text alignments, and basic drawing features. In addition, an image can be added to almost any control.
- A pluggable "look and feel" that can be changed at runtime. If desired, you can design your own look and feel.
- Many miscellaneous new features, for example, built-in double buffering, tool-tips, dockable toolbars, keyboard accelerators, and custom cursors.

Complete coverage of the entire Swing library is beyond the scope of this book. We discuss the basic usage most often employed in applications. For more in-depth treatment on the topic, please see *Core Java Foundation Classes* or *Core Swing: Advanced Programming*, both by Kim Topley.

14.1 Getting Started with Swing

Swing is standard in the Java 2 Platform but can be added to JDK 1.1 as a separate package. The JDK 1.1 version of Swing is downloadable from `http://java.sun.com/products/jfc/download.html`. You can also use Swing in an applet, but unless you are using Netscape 6, you will need to install the Java Plug-In (covered in Section 9.9).

Differences Between Swing and the AWT

The following subsections summarize the basic differences between Swing and the AWT.

Naming Convention

All Swing component names begin with a capital `J` and follow the format `JXxx`, where the `Xxx` represents a common component name, for example, `JFrame`, `JPanel`, `JApplet`, `JDialog`, `JButton`. All the AWT components have an almost equivalent Swing component. Nearly all the Swing components inherit directly from `JComponent`, which provides support for the pluggable look and feel, custom borders, and tool-tips.

Lightweight Components

Most Swing components are lightweight: formed by drawing in the underlying window using Java code rather than relying on native peer code to perform the drawing. The four Swing lightweight exceptions are `JFrame`, `JApplet`, `JWindow`, and `JDialog`. As the graphics in the off-screen buffer must be eventually drawn to the screen, these four *heavyweight* Swing components form a bridge to the corresponding AWT peers to perform the drawing.

Use of the paintComponent Method for Drawing

For Swing, custom drawing is performed in `paintComponent`, not `paint`. The default implementation of `paintComponent` is to invoke the user interface (UI) delegate to control the look and feel of the component. In addition, the UI delegate is responsible for erasing the off-screen buffer before drawing. Thus, you should always call the superclass `paintComponent` method before performing any drawing to guarantee that the off-screen buffer is cleared and that the component's look and feel is maintained. Thus, each `paintComponent` method should begin as follows:

```
public void paintComponent(Graphics g){
  super.paintComponent(g);
  // Drawing on the Swing component ...
  ...
}
```

Core Approach

In Swing, perform drawing in `paintComponent`, *not* `paint`. *Always call*
`super.paintComponent` before performing custom drawing.

Use of the Content Pane for Adding Components

Instead of adding components directly to a JFrame or JApplet, you add the components to the "content pane," for example,

```
Container content = getContentPane();
content.add(new JButton("Welcome"));
content.add(new JLabel("JavaOne"));
```

Adding a component *directly* to a JFrame or JApplet produces an error. The content pane is simply a Container with a layout manager of BorderLayout. Thus, both a JFrame and a JApplet in Swing have the same layout manager, unlike the case with an AWT Frame (BorderLayout) and Applet (FlowLayout). If you want to replace the content pane with a different container, call setContentPane.

Core Approach

Add components to the content pane of a `JFrame` *or* `JApplet`.

Double Buffering

By default, a JPanel is double buffered. See Section 16.7 (Multithreaded Graphics and Double Buffering) for a detailed explanation of double buffering. In Swing, a single off-screen buffer, large enough to accommodate the size of the screen, is maintained by the RepaintManager. When the paint method is executed, the basic behavior is to obtain the off-screen buffer from the RepaintManager, call paintComponent for custom drawing into the buffer, and then, copy the buffer to the screen. Any drawing to a JPanel through paintComponent is drawn into the off-screen buffer; however, if you perform "out of paint method" drawing using panel.getGraphics(), then drawing is performed directly on screen and is not double buffered.

Any components placed in a double buffered container are also automatically double buffered. Since the content pane of a `JFrame` and a `JApplet` is a double buffered `Container`, all Java Swing applications are automatically double buffered.

Model-View-Controller Architecture

Lightweight Swing components are designed around a model-view-controller (MVC) architecture, shown in Figure 14–1. Conceptually, the *model* is a data structure that provides accessor methods for accessing the data. The data structure could be as simple as a couple of state variables (pressed, enabled) for a button, or as complicated as an `ArrayList` of input fields for a table. The *view* is the visual presentation of the data in the model. The *controller* is the event handler.

Each lightweight Swing component has an associated user interface (UI) delegate that inherits from `ComponentUI` and controls the look (view) and feel (listeners) of the component. When the component is instantiated, the `UIManager` returns the correct Swing UI (`LabelUI`, `TableUI`, `TreeUI`, etc.) based on the selected look and feel (Windows, Motif, Java) of the program. The UI delegate is responsible for reporting the minimum, maximum, and preferred size of the component, painting the component, and handling component events.

The beauty of the MVC architecture is that a single data model can be assigned to more than one Swing component, thereby allowing more than one view of the data. Consider a data series displayed in a table and a corresponding display of the data in a histogram chart; both views of the data reference the same data model. If the user adds a new data value to the model, both views are dynamically updated after a corresponding change event is fired from the model. The use of multiple views for complicated data is common in advanced Swing components like `JTree` and `JTable`, covered in Chapter 15 (Advanced Swing).

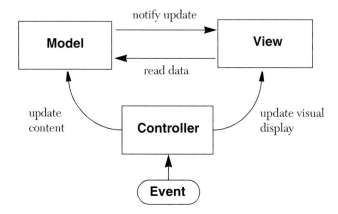

Figure 14–1 Schematic of a Model-View-Controller (MVC).

New Look and Feel as Default

The MVC architecture permits a pluggable look and feel of the Swing components. In Swing, the graphical user interface can have the look of a Windows, Motif, MacOS, or Java (formerly called Metal) environment. The `UIManager` class allows you to set the look and feel of the graphical user interface before any Swing components are created. When you create a component, the `UIManager` returns the *correct* UI delegate (responsible for painting the component with the selected look and feel) to the component. Thus, you should set the look and feel before creating new lightweight components. The following list summarizes additional key points about Swing look and feel:

- The default cross-platform look and feel is "Java" (or "Metal"), a custom look and feel somewhat similar to the Windows look.

- The Motif look is available on all platforms. However, Windows and Mac looks are only available on their native platforms. Technically, you can easily work around this restriction, but distributing applications that do this is currently illegal.

- The look and feel can be changed at runtime. After you set the new look and feel, calling `SwingUtilties.updateComponentTreeUI` will hand off a new UI delegate to each component. For example,

```
try {
   UIManager.setLookAndFeel(
         "javax.swing.motif.MotifLookAndFeel");
} catch(Exception e) {
   System.out.println("LAF Error: " + e);
}
SwingUtilties.updateComponentTreeUI(
              getContentPane());
```

  This capability sounds cool, but it is rarely used in real life. The normal place to set the look and feel is in the constructor (or `main`) of the top-level `JFrame`, or in `init` of the `JApplet`.

- The look and feel can be set to the *native* windows look for the operating system. Call the `getSystemLookAndFeelClassName` method of `UIManager`, and pass the result to `UIManager.setLookAndFeel`. Since `setLookAndFeel` throws an exception, a direct approach is a bit inconvenient, and you might want to create a `static` method called `setNativeLookAndFeel` in a utility class.

Listing 14.1 presents a utility class, `WindowUtilities`, that provides static methods to set the look and feel to native, Java (Metal), and Motif, respectively. Since most users expect the native look and may be unfamiliar with the Java look (which is the default when installing the JRE), you can consider calling `setNative-LookAndFeel` at the beginning of Swing programs to obtain the native look and feel.

In addition, `WindowUtilities` provides static methods for displaying containers in a `JFrame`. The various `openInJFrame` methods are used throughout the chapter as a convenience to display a `JPanel` in a `JFrame`. The frames take advantage of the `ExitListener` class to exit the application when closing the frame.

Listing 14.1 `WindowUtilities.java`

```
import javax.swing.*;
import java.awt.*;    // For Color and Container classes.

/** A few utilities that simplify using windows in Swing. */

public class WindowUtilities {

  /** Tell system to use native look and feel, as in previous
   *  releases. Metal (Java) LAF is the default otherwise.
   */

  public static void setNativeLookAndFeel() {
    try {
     UIManager.setLookAndFeel(
       UIManager.getSystemLookAndFeelClassName());
    } catch(Exception e) {
      System.out.println("Error setting native LAF: " + e);
    }
  }

  public static void setJavaLookAndFeel() {
    try {
     UIManager.setLookAndFeel(
       UIManager.getCrossPlatformLookAndFeelClassName());
    } catch(Exception e) {
      System.out.println("Error setting Java LAF: " + e);
    }
  }
```

(continued)

Listing 14.1 `WindowUtilities.java` *(continued)*

```
public static void setMotifLookAndFeel() {
  try {
    UIManager.setLookAndFeel(
      "com.sun.java.swing.plaf.motif.MotifLookAndFeel");
  } catch(Exception e) {
    System.out.println("Error setting Motif LAF: " + e);
  }
}

/** A simplified way to see a JPanel or other Container. Pops
 *  up a JFrame with specified Container as the content pane.
 */

public static JFrame openInJFrame(Container content,
                                  int width,
                                  int height,
                                  String title,
                                  Color bgColor) {
  JFrame frame = new JFrame(title);
  frame.setBackground(bgColor);
  content.setBackground(bgColor);
  frame.setSize(width, height);
  frame.setContentPane(content);
  frame.addWindowListener(new ExitListener());
  frame.setVisible(true);
  return(frame);
}

/** Uses Color.white as the background color. */

public static JFrame openInJFrame(Container content,
                                  int width,
                                  int height,
                                  String title) {
  return(openInJFrame(content, width, height,
                      title, Color.white));
}

/** Uses Color.white as the background color, and the
 *  name of the Container's class as the JFrame title.
 */

public static JFrame openInJFrame(Container content,
                                  int width,
                                  int height) {
  return(openInJFrame(content, width, height,
                      content.getClass().getName(),
                      Color.white));
}
}
```

Listing 14.2 `ExitListener.java`

```java
import java.awt.*;
import java.awt.event.*;

/** A listener that you attach to the top-level JFrame of
 *  your application, so that quitting the frame exits the
 *  application.
 */
public class ExitListener extends WindowAdapter {
  public void windowClosing(WindowEvent event) {
    System.exit(0);
  }
}
```

Included in the Java 2 JDK is an excellent applet demonstrating the various components available in Swing. The SwingSet2 demonstration applet is located in the `root/jdk1.3/demo/jfc/SwingSet2` install directory. Figures 14–2 through 14–4 illustrate the Windows, Motif, and Java look and feel of Swing, respectively.

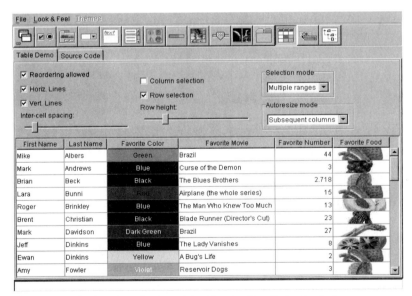

Figure 14–2 Windows look and feel for the Sun SwingSet2 demo.

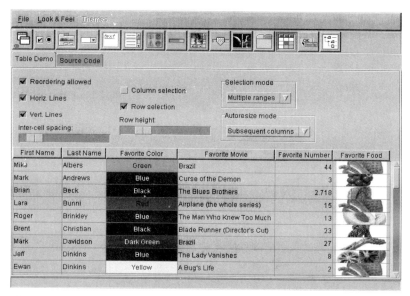

Figure 14–3 Motif look and feel for the Sun SwingSet2 demo.

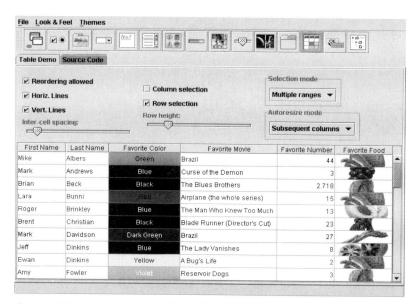

Figure 14–4 Java (Metal) look and feel for the Sun SwingSet2 demo.

Don't Mix AWT and Swing Components

The z-ordering always places AWT components on top. In the Java platform, z-ordering determines the order in which components in the same container are displayed. The first component added to a container has the highest z-order; the last component added to a container has the lowest z-order. Components with a higher z-order are displayed on top of components with a lower z-order. Consequently, the windowing container always has the lowest z-order and is displayed underneath all other heavyweight components. Lightweight Swing components are always drawn in the heavyweight windowing container in which they reside, and therefore Swing components have the same z-order as their container. As a result, AWT components will always be drawn on top of any Swing components. This behavior is problematic and can catch you in many unexpected ways. For example, consider an AWT `Button` in a Swing application that also includes a drop-down menu. Depending on the placement of the AWT `Button`, when the drop-down menu is selected, the `Button` can cover the drop-down menu list. The best advice is to always stick with AWT or move completely to Swing.

Before we present the various Swing components, you should note that the `javax.swing.SwingConstants` class defines numerous constants for positioning components. The available constants are `LEFT`, `CENTER`, `RIGHT`, `TOP`, `BOTTOM`, `NORTH`, `EAST`, `SOUTH`, `WEST`, `NORTH_EAST`, `NORTH_WEST`, `SOUTH_EAST`, `SOUTH_WEST`, `HORIZONTAL`, `VERTICAL`, `LEADING`, and `TRAILING`. The last two constants specifically identify the leading or trailing side of the component according to the locale's reading order (i.e., left-to-right and right-to-left languages).

14.2 The JApplet Component

`JApplet` is the Swing equivalent of an AWT `Applet`. The major limitation of a `JApplet` is that the only major browser that supports the Java 2 Platform is Netscape 6. However, you can add Swing to Java 1.1 in other browsers, but for the greatest Swing capabilities, we recommend the Swing version in Java 2. In order to run the Swing applet in a browser, you may need to install the Java 2 Plug-In as described in Section 9.9 (note that Netscape 6 supports JDK 1.3). As the Java Plug-In download is over 5 Mbytes, the use of Swing applets on the Internet is not common; use Swing only for an intranet environment where the plug-in can be located on a local server for downloading.

A `JApplet` is a heavyweight Swing component and inherits directly from `Applet` instead of inheriting from `JComponent` as with the lightweight Swing components. Therefore, the `JApplet` class inherits the familiar methods of `init`, `start`, `stop`, and `destroy`. As a Swing applet though, it exhibits some major differences exist. For instance,

- A JApplet contains a content pane in which to add components. Changing other properties like the layout manager, background color, etc., also applies to the content pane. Access the content pane through getContentPane.

- The default layout manager is BorderLayout (as with Frame and JFrame), not FlowLayout (as with Applet). BorderLayout is really the layout manager of the content pane.

- The default look and feel is Java (Metal), so you have to explicitly switch the look and feel if you want the native look.

- Drawing is done in paintComponent, not paint. You don't draw directly in a JApplet, however. Instead you add a JPanel to the content pane, override the paintComponent method of the added JPanel, and perform all drawing in the JPanel.

- Double buffering is turned on by default.

Core Note

The default layout manager of a JApplet *is* BorderLayout, *not* FlowLayout *as in an* Applet.

Listing 14.3 provides a simple example showing the steps required to create what you would have in the AWT if you had a simple applet whose init method did nothing but drop three buttons into the window. In the Swing version, to achieve the same positioning of the buttons, the LayoutManager changed to FlowLayout. The result in Netscape 6 is shown in Figure 14–5.

Listing 14.3 JAppletExample.java

```
import java.awt.*;
import javax.swing.*;

/** Tiny example showing the main differences in using
 *  JApplet instead of Applet: using the content pane,
 *  getting Java (Metal) look and feel by default, and
 *  having BorderLayout be the default instead of FlowLayout.
 */
```

(continued)

Listing 14.3 `JAppletExample.java` *(continued)*

```java
public class JAppletExample extends JApplet {
  public void init() {
    WindowUtilities.setNativeLookAndFeel();
    Container content = getContentPane();
    content.setBackground(Color.white);
    content.setLayout(new FlowLayout());
    content.add(new JButton("Button 1"));
    content.add(new JButton("Button 2"));
    content.add(new JButton("Button 3"));
  }
}
```

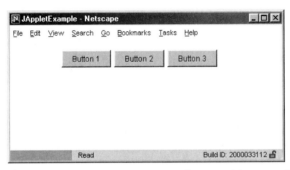

Figure 14–5 Swing `JButtons` shown in Netscape 6 on Windows 98.

14.3 The JFrame Component

The `JFrame` is the Swing equivalent of the AWT `Frame` and, as in the AWT, the `JFrame` is a starting point for graphical applications. Similar to `JApplet`, a `JFrame` is a *heavyweight* Swing component and does not inherit from `JComponent`. `JFrame` inherits directly from `Frame`. The main differences between a `JFrame` and an AWT `Frame` are these:

- Components are added to the content pane, not directly to the frame. Changing the layout manager, background color, etc., also applies to the content pane. Access the content pane through `getContentPane`.
- `JFrames` close automatically when you click on the Close button (unlike AWT `Frames`). However, closing the last `JFrame` does not result in your program exiting the Java application. So, your "main" `JFrame` still needs a `WindowListener` to call `System.exit`. Or,

alternatively, if using JDK 1.3, you can call `setDefault-CloseOpertion(EXIT_ON_CLOSE)`. This latter case permits the JFrame to close; however, you won't be able to complete any house cleaning as you might in the `WindowListener`.

- The default look and feel is Java (Metal), so you have to explicitly switch the look and feel if you want the native look.

Core Note

Child Swing frames automatically close when you click the Close button; however, the parent frame still requires a `WindowListener` to invoke `System.exit`.

Listing 14.4 shows the steps required to imitate what you would get in the AWT if you popped up a simple `Frame`, set the layout manager to `FlowLayout`, and dropped three buttons into the frame. The complete listings for `WindowUtilities.java` and `ExitListener.java`, required by this application, are provided in Section 14.1 (Getting Started with Swing) and can be downloaded from the on-line archive at `http://www.corewebprogramming.com/`. The result is shown in Figure 14–6.

Listing 14.4 `JFrameExample.java`

```java
import java.awt.*;
import javax.swing.*;

/** Tiny example showing the main difference in using
 *  JFrame instead of Frame: using the content pane
 *  and getting the Java (Metal) look and feel by default
 *  instead of the native look and feel.
 */

public class JFrameExample {
  public static void main(String[] args) {
    WindowUtilities.setNativeLookAndFeel();
    JFrame f = new JFrame("This is a test");
    f.setSize(400, 150);
    Container content = f.getContentPane();
    content.setBackground(Color.white);
    content.setLayout(new FlowLayout());
    content.add(new JButton("Button 1"));
    content.add(new JButton("Button 2"));
    content.add(new JButton("Button 3"));
    f.addWindowListener(new ExitListener());
    f.setVisible(true);
  }
}
```

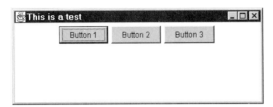

Figure 14–6 A Swing `JFrame` containing three buttons.

14.4 The JLabel Component

In many cases, `JLabel` is used exactly like `Label`: as a way to display text. However, a `JLabel` has three major features that a `Label` does not. A `JLabel` can display an image instead of or in addition to the text, can have borders, and can use HTML content to format the label. These three major features are discussed next.

New Features: Images, Borders, and HTML Content

The first new feature of a `JLabel` is image display, which you use usually by supplying an `ImageIcon` either to the constructor or through a call to `setIcon`. The use of icons in `JLabel` is just like the use in `JButton`; see Section 14.5 (The JButton Component) for additional details and code examples. For an example, however, see the third `JLabel` in Listing 14.5. Note that even though `JLabels` and `JButtons` have significant common functionality, they are not related through inheritance.

The second new feature for labels is label borders. The use of borders is covered in Section 14.6 (The JPanel Component). For a quick preview, however, see the example in Listing 14.5 that uses titled borders.

The third new feature, and the one that we are focusing on here, is label formatting with HTML. The idea is that if the string for the label begins with `<html>`, then the string is interpreted as HTML rather than taken as literal characters. The ability to interpret HTML allows you to create multiline labels, labels with mixed colors and fonts, and various other fancy effects. This capability to render HTML also applies to `JButton`. Although nice, this feature also has several significant limitations:

- HTML labels only work in JDK 1.2.2 or later, or in Swing 1.1.1 or later. Since the Java platform provides no programmatic way to test if this capability is supported, using HTML labels can cause significant portability problems.

- In JDK 1.2 the label string must begin with `<html>`, not `<HTML>`. Case-insensitive HTML tags are supported in JDK 1.3.
- In JDK 1.2, if you would like to include an image in the label, you must supply an `ImageIcon` to the `JLabel` constructor or use `setIcon`; the HTML label cannot have an `IMG` tag. In JDK 1.3, embedded images are supported in the HTML, but the technique required to embed an image is beyond the scope of this book.
- `JLabel` fonts are ignored if HTML is used. If you use HTML, all font control must be performed by HTML. For example, one would think that the following would result in large, bold Serif text, but the code actually results in small, bold Sans Serif text instead:

```
JLabel label =
  new JLabel("<html>Bold Text</html>");
label.setFont(new Font("Serif",Font.BOLD,36));
...
```

- You must use `<P>`, not `<BR>`, to force a line break. The `<BR>` tag is ignored, and `<P>` in a `JLabel` or `JButton` works like `<BR>` does in "real" HTML, starting a new line but not leaving a blank line in between.
- Other HTML support is spotty. Be sure to test each HTML construct you use. Permitting the user to enter HTML text at runtime is asking for trouble.

JLabel Constructors

The `JLabel` class has six constructors. The four most common constructors are listed below:

public JLabel()
public JLabel(String label)
public JLabel(Icon image)
public JLabel(String label, Icon image, int hAlignment)

The `JLabel` constructors permit direct creation of an empty label, a text label, and an image label. The last constructor creates a label with both an image and an icon. In the last constructor, you must also specify the desired horizontal alignment of the text-icon pair relative to the label itself. Legal values are LEFT, CENTER, RIGHT, LEADING, or TRAILING.

Useful JLabel Methods

The following paragraphs list the more common methods of the JLabel class. All property value methods have corresponding get methods.

public void setHorizontalAlignment(int alignment)
public void setVerticalAlignment(int alignment)

These methods set the horizontal and vertical alignment of the text-icon pair, respectively, relative to the label itself. The legal alignments are defined in javax.swing.SwingConstraints and include LEFT, CENTER, RIGHT, LEADING, and TRAILING for horizontal alignment, and TOP, CENTER, and BOTTOM for vertical alignment.

public void setHorizontalTextPosition(int alignment)
public void setVerticalTextPosition(int alignment)

These methods set the horizontal and vertical position of the text, relative to label's image, if present. The legal values are the same as those for setting the text-icon pair alignment.

public void setIcon(Icon image)
public void setDisabledIcon(Icon image)

These two methods specify the image for the JLabel when enabled and disabled, respectively. A JLabel is disabled through setEnabled(false).

public void setText(String label)
public void setFont(Font font)

The first method sets the text to display in the label. The text can include HTML tags if enclosed in <html> ... </html>. The second method sets the font style of the label.

Examples of the new JLabel features are given in Listing 14.5, with the result shown in Figure 14–7. The first and second labels use simple HTML text to control the text colors and to set the text font, respectively. The last label incorporates both an image and HTML containing an unordered list, <UL>. All three labels incorporate a titled border (see Section 14.6, "The JPanel Component," for border styles).

Listing 14.5 `JLabels.java`

```java
import java.awt.*;
import javax.swing.*;

/** Simple example illustrating the use of JLabel, especially
 *  the ability to use HTML text (Swing 1.1.1 and Java 1.2.2 and
 *  later only!).
 */

public class JLabels extends JFrame {
  public static void main(String[] args) {
    new JLabels();
  }

  public JLabels() {
    super("Using HTML in JLabels");
    WindowUtilities.setNativeLookAndFeel();
    addWindowListener(new ExitListener());
    Container content = getContentPane();
    Font font = new Font("Serif", Font.PLAIN, 30);
    content.setFont(font);
    String labelText =
      "<html><FONT COLOR=WHITE>WHITE</FONT> and " +
      "<FONT COLOR=GRAY>GRAY</FONT> Text</html>";
    JLabel coloredLabel =
      new JLabel(labelText, JLabel.CENTER);
    coloredLabel.setBorder
      (BorderFactory.createTitledBorder("Mixed Colors"));
    content.add(coloredLabel, BorderLayout.NORTH);
    labelText =
      "<html><B>Bold</B> and <I>Italic</I> Text</html>";
    JLabel boldLabel =
      new JLabel(labelText, JLabel.CENTER);
    boldLabel.setBorder
      (BorderFactory.createTitledBorder("Mixed Fonts"));
    content.add(boldLabel, BorderLayout.CENTER);
    labelText =
      "<html>The Applied Physics Laboratory is a division " +
      "of the Johns Hopkins University." +
      "<P>" +
      "Major JHU divisions include:" +
      "<UL>" +
```

(continued)

Listing 14.5 `JLabels.java` *(continued)*

```
        "   <LI>The Applied Physics Laboratory" +
        "   <LI>The Krieger School of Arts and Sciences" +
        "   <LI>The Whiting School of Engineering" +
        "   <LI>The School of Medicine" +
        "   <LI>The School of Public Health" +
        "   <LI>The School of Nursing" +
        "   <LI>The Peabody Institute" +
        "   <LI>The Nitze School of Advanced International Studies" +
        "</UL>" +
        "</html>";
      JLabel fancyLabel =
      new JLabel(labelText,
                 new ImageIcon("images/JHUAPL.gif"),
                 JLabel.CENTER);
    fancyLabel.setBorder
      (BorderFactory.createTitledBorder("Fancy HTML"));
    content.add(fancyLabel, BorderLayout.SOUTH);
    pack();
    setVisible(true);
  }
}
```

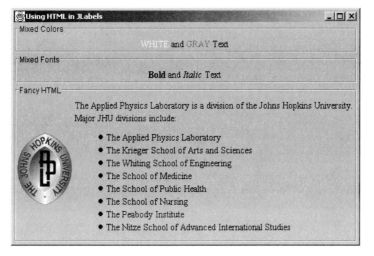

Figure 14–7 Swing components provide HTML text support for captions.

14.5 The JButton Component

Simple uses of JButton are similar to those for the AWT Button. You create a JButton with a String as a label and then drop the button into a window. Events are normally handled just as with a Button: you attach an ActionListener through the addActionListener method.

New Features: Icons, Alignment, and Mnemonics

The most obvious new feature is the ability to associate images with buttons. Many Swing controls allow the inclusion of icons. Swing introduced a utility class called ImageIcon that lets you easily specify an image file (JPEG or GIF, including animated GIF) for the icon. The simplest way to associate an image with a JButton is to pass the ImageIcon to the constructor, either in place of the text or in addition to the text. JButton actually defines seven associated images:

1. The main image (use setIcon to specify the main image if not supplied in the constructor).
2. The image to use when the button is pressed (setPressedIcon).
3. The image to use when the mouse is over the button (setRollover-Icon, but first you need to call setRolloverEnabled(true)).
4. The image to use when the button is disabled (setDisabledIcon).
5. The image to use when the button is selected and enabled (setSelectedIcon).
6. The image to use when the button is selected but disabled (setDisabledSelectedIcon).
7. The image to use when the mouse is over the button while selected (setRolloverSelectedIcon).

The images—setSelectedIcon, setRolloverSelectedIcon, and setDisabledSelectedIcon—for a selected button, are supported in JDK 1.3. but not in JDK 1.2 You can only select a button programmatically by calling setSelected(true). Selecting a button does not trigger an ActionEvent. If you are not creating a custom, selectable button to maintain state, you might choose instead a standard JToggleButton (not covered; see on-line API for javax.swing.JToggleButton) that is selectable either programmatically or by the user.

You can also change the alignment of the text, icon, or text-icon pair in the button through setHorizontalAlignment and setVerticalAlignment (only valid if button is larger than the preferred size), and you can change the position of the text relative to the icon through setHorizontalTextPosition and setVerticalTextPosition). The pixel gap between the text and icon is controlled through setIconTextGap.

You can also easily set keyboard mnemonics through setMnemonic. Doing so results in the specified character being underlined on the button and also results in ALT-char activating the button.

HTML in Button Labels

In JDK 1.2.2 and Swing 1.1.1 (and later), Sun added the ability to use HTML to describe the text in JButtons and JLabels. Now you can easily have multiline text in buttons, mixed fonts and colors, and other fancy features in your buttons. Examples of HTML text in labels are given in Section 14.4 (The JLabel Component).

JButton Constructors

The JButton class has five constructors:

> **public JButton()**
> **public JButton(String label)**
> **public JButton(Icon image)**
> **public JButton(String label, Icon image)**
> **public JButton(Action action)**
>
> The first four constructors create an empty JButton, a JButton with a text label, a JButton with an image label, and a JButton with both a text and an image label, respectively. The fifth constructor, new in JDK 1.3, accepts an Action object to share state information (icon, label, for example) with other components.

Useful JButton (AbstractButton) Methods

The JButton class defines very few methods itself. However, JButton does implement a robust number of abstract methods from the AbstractButton class. The more common methods are listed below. Properties with set methods have corresponding get methods but are not listed.

> **public void setAction(Action action)**
> **public Action getAction()**
>
> These two methods, new in JDK 1.3, set and get the Action object for the button. Action objects can define the text and icon to use for the button, as well as define an actionPerformed method. Actions permit you to share state and event handling among multiple components that interact with the user, for example, a button in a panel and a button in a toolbar.

public void setHorizontalAlignment(int alignment)
public void setVerticalAlignment(int alignment)
These methods set the horizontal and vertical alignment of the icon-text pair, respectively, relative to the button itself. The legal alignments values are the same as defined for `JLabel`.

public void setHorizontalTextPosition(int alignment)
public void setVerticalTextPosition(int alignment)
These methods set and get the horizontal and vertical position of the text, respectively, relative to button's image. The legal values are the same as those for setting the icon-text alignment for a `JLabel`.

public void setText(String label)
public void setFont(Font font)
The first method defines the text to display on the button, and the second method defines the font style of the text on the button. The text can include HMTL tags if enclosed in `<html>` ... `</html>`.

public void setIcon(Icon image)
public void setPressedIcon(Icon image)
public void setRolloverIcon(Icon image)
public void setDisabledIcon(Icon image)
The first method sets the image on the `JButton`. The next three methods set the image displayed when the button is pressed, when the mouse goes over the button, and when the button is disabled, respectively. A `JButton` can be disabled through `setEnabled(false)`.

public void setEnabled(boolean state)
The `setEnable` method enables (`true`) or disables (`false`) the button. By default, a button is enabled.

public void setMargin(Insets margins)
This method specifies the margins between the button content and the button boundaries. For example,

```
JButton button = new JButton("Continue");
button.setMargin(new Insets(10,5,10,5));
```

sets a 10-pixel margin above and below the button text, and a 5-pixel margin to the left and right of the text.

Listing 14.6 illustrates the basic three basic types of buttons: a text button, an image button, and a combination button comprising both text and an image. The result is shown in Figure 14–5.

Listing 14.6 JButtons.java

```
import java.awt.*;
import javax.swing.*;

/** Simple example illustrating the use of JButton, especially
 *  the new constructors that permit you to add an image.
 */

public class JButtons extends JFrame {
  public static void main(String[] args) {
    new JButtons();
  }

  public JButtons() {
    super("Using JButton");
    WindowUtilities.setNativeLookAndFeel();
    addWindowListener(new ExitListener());
    Container content = getContentPane();
    content.setBackground(Color.white);
    content.setLayout(new FlowLayout());
    JButton button1 = new JButton("Java");
    content.add(button1);
    ImageIcon cup = new ImageIcon("images/cup.gif");
    JButton button2 = new JButton(cup);
    content.add(button2);
    JButton button3 = new JButton("Java", cup);
    content.add(button3);
    JButton button4 = new JButton("Java", cup);
    button4.setHorizontalTextPosition(SwingConstants.LEFT);
    content.add(button4);
    pack();
    setVisible(true);
  }
}
```

Figure 14–8 Swing JButtons support both text and images.

14.6 The JPanel Component

In the simplest case, you use a JPanel exactly the same as you would a Panel: Allocate the panel, drop components into the panel, and then add the JPanel to a Container. However, JPanel also acts as a replacement for Canvas (there is no JCanvas). When using JPanel as a drawing area in lieu of a Canvas, you need to follow two additional steps. First, you should set the preferred size with setPreferredSize (recall that the preferred size of a Canvas is just its current size, whereas a Panel and JPanel determine their preferred size from the components they contain). Second, you should use paintComponent, not paint, for drawing. And since double buffering is turned on by default, the first thing you normally do in paintComponent is clear the off-screen bitmap through super.paintComponent, as in

```
public void paintComponent(Graphics g) {
  super.paintComponent(g);
  . . .
}
```

Note that if you are using Swing in Java 2, you can cast the Graphics object to a Graphics2D object and do all sorts of new stuff added in the Java 2D package; see Chapter 10 (Java 2D: Graphics in Java 2).

JPanel Constructors

JPanel has four constructors, as listed below. As a convenience, JPanel lets you supply the LayoutManager to the constructor in addition to specifying the manager later through setLayout. Virtually all JPanel methods are inherited from JComponent and not discussed (see the JComponent API for available methods).

public JPanel()
public JPanel(LayoutManager manager)
public JPanel(boolean isDoubleBuffered)
public JPanel(LayoutManager manager,
           boolean isDoubleBuffered)

The first constructor creates a JPanel with a default layout manager of FlowLayout and double buffering turned on. The remaining three constructors allow you to explicitly specify the layout manager and the double buffering property.

New Feature: Borders

Aside from double buffering, the most obvious new feature of JPanel is the ability to assign borders. Actually, borders are available for every JComponent, and most of the Swing components install their own border. JPanel is about the only case where it makes real sense to install your own border. Swing gives you seven basic border types: titled, etched, beveled (regular plus a "softer" version), line, matte, compound, and empty. You can also create your own border, of course. You assign a Border through the setBorder method, and you create the Border either by calling constructors directly or, more often, by using one of the convenience factory methods in BorderFactory. For example:

```
JPanel p = new JPanel();
p.setBorder(BorderFactory.createTitledBorder("Java"));
```

The factory methods reuse existing Border objects whenever possible. Thus, to save resources, you should check for the available BorderFactory methods before creating a new Border object.

Core Approach

Whenever possible use one of the BorderFactory createXxxBorder *methods to create a* Border *object.*

Useful BorderFactory Methods

The BorderFactory class provides 23 static methods for creating different styles of Borders. The Border class is found in the javax.swing.border package. Also found in the border package is the AbstractBorder class, which is a base class implementing Border, from which EmptyBorder, TitledBorder, LineBorder, EtchedBorder, BevelBorder, SoftBevelBorder, MatteBorder, and CompoundBorder are derived. Of the 23 available factory methods, the most common are listed below. All methods are declared public static.

Border createEmptyBorder(int top, int left, int bottom, int right)
This factory method creates an EmptyBorder object that simply adds space (margins) around the component.

Border createLineBorder(Color color)
Border createLineBorder(Color color, int thickness)
These two factory methods create a colored LineBorder. By default, the border is one pixel wide. In the second constructor, you can explicitly state the border thickness in pixels. The LineBorder class also provides two static methods for creating a 1-pixel-wide black- or gray-lined border: createBlackLineBorder and createGrayLineBorder.

TitledBorder createTitledBorder(String title)
TitledBorder createTitledBorder(Border border, String title)

These two factory methods create a `TitledBorder` with the title located in the default position (`TOP`) at the left of the border's top line. By default, the border is an etched line unless you explicitly provide a border style as in the second constructor. `BorderFactory` provides additional factory methods to position the title. The `TitledBorder` class provides `setTitlePosition` and `setTitleJustification` methods also. The position of title is relative to the top and bottom border line: `ABOVE_TOP`, `TOP`, `BELOW_TOP`, and `ABOVE_BOTTOM`, `BOTTOM`, `BELOW_BOTTOM`. The title justification can be `LEFT`, `CENTER`, or `RIGHT`. You can also set the color and font of the title through `setTitleColor` and `setTitleFont` or by selecting other `BorderFactory` factory methods.

Border createEtchedBorder()
Border createEtchedBorder(Color highlight, Color shadow)

The first factory method creates a `LOWERED` `EtchedBorder` that has a 2-pixel-wide lowered groove. The groove is drawn in two colors to provide a three-dimensional effect. By default, the highlight color is slightly lighter than the background color and the shadow color is slightly darker than the background color. The second factory method allows you to explicitly specify the highlight and shadow colors. For a raised border, you must create an `Etched-Border` object directly, passing in an argument of `RAISED` for the etch type.

In addition to the methods listed above, `BorderFactory` provides other static methods for creating empty, line, titled, and etched borders. Furthermore, the `BorderFactory` class provide methods for creating a beveled border (`createBevel-Border`), a raised or lowered bevel border (`createRaisedBevelBorder`, `createLoweredBevelBorder`), a matte border that paints a solid color or an `Icon` around the border (`createMatteBorder`), and a compound border made up of two borders (`createCompoundBorder`).

Listing 14.7 creates a simple `JPanel` with a blue custom `LineBorder` two pixels wide. Before setting the border, we set the `JPanel`'s preferred size to a `Dimension` of 400 pixels wide by 0 pixels high. The height of the `JPanel` is irrelevant, since the `JPanel` is placed in the `WEST` location of the `JFrame` `BorderLayout`. In addition, this example creates three panels with different button choices (see Listing 14.8). Each choice panel has a `TitledBorder`. The result is shown in Figure 14–9.

Listing 14.7 `JPanels.java`

```java
import java.awt.*;
import javax.swing.*;

/** Simple example illustrating the use of JPanels, especially
 *  the ability to add Borders.
 */

public class JPanels extends JFrame {
  public static void main(String[] args) {
    new JPanels();
  }

  public JPanels() {
    super("Using JPanels with Borders");
    WindowUtilities.setNativeLookAndFeel();
    addWindowListener(new ExitListener());
    Container content = getContentPane();
    content.setBackground(Color.lightGray);
    JPanel controlArea = new JPanel(new GridLayout(3, 1));
    String[] colors = { "Red", "Green", "Blue",
                        "Black", "White", "Gray" };
    controlArea.add(new SixChoicePanel("Color", colors));
    String[] thicknesses = { "1", "2", "3", "4", "5", "6" };
    controlArea.add(new SixChoicePanel("Line Thickness",
                                       thicknesses));
    String[] fontSizes = { "10", "12", "14", "18", "24", "36" };
    controlArea.add(new SixChoicePanel("Font Size",
                                       fontSizes));
    content.add(controlArea, BorderLayout.EAST);
    JPanel drawingArea = new JPanel();
    // Preferred height is irrelevant, since using WEST region.
    drawingArea.setPreferredSize(new Dimension(400, 0));
    drawingArea.setBorder
            (BorderFactory.createLineBorder (Color.blue, 2));
    drawingArea.setBackground(Color.white);
    content.add(drawingArea, BorderLayout.WEST);
    pack();
    setVisible(true);
  }
}
```

Listing 14.8 `SixChoicePanel.java`

```java
import java.awt.*;
import javax.swing.*;

/** A JPanel that displays six JRadioButtons. */

public class SixChoicePanel extends JPanel {
  public SixChoicePanel(String title, String[] buttonLabels) {
    super(new GridLayout(3, 2));
    setBackground(Color.lightGray);
    setBorder(BorderFactory.createTitledBorder(title));
    ButtonGroup group = new ButtonGroup();
    JRadioButton option;
    int halfLength = buttonLabels.length/2; // Assumes even length
    for(int i=0; i<halfLength; i++) {
      option = new JRadioButton(buttonLabels[i]);
      group.add(option);
      add(option);
      option = new JRadioButton(buttonLabels[i+halfLength]);
      group.add(option);
      add(option);
    }
  }
}
```

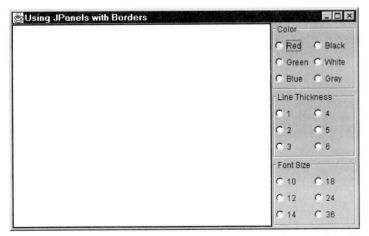

Figure 14–9 `JPanels` provide an added touch of custom borders.

14.7 The JSlider Component

In the AWT, the `Scrollbar` class did double duty as a control for interactively selecting numeric values and as a widget used to control scrolling. This double duty resulted in poor-looking sliders. Swing gives you a "real" slider: `JSlider`. You create a `JSlider` in a manner similar to creating a `Scrollbar`: the zero-argument constructor creates a horizontal slider with a range from 0 to 100 and an initial value of 50. You can also supply the orientation (through `JSlider.HORIZONTAL` or `JSlider.VERTICAL`), the range, and initial value to the constructor. You handle events by attaching a `ChangeListener`. The `JSlider` `stateChanged` method normally calls `getValue` to look up the current `JSlider` value.

New Features: Tick Marks and Labels

Swing sliders can have major and minor tick marks. Turn tick marks on through `setPaintTicks(true)`, and then specify the tick spacing with `set-MajorTickSpacing` and `setMinorTickSpacing`. If you want to limit users to selecting values only at the tick marks, call `setSnapToTicks(true)`. Turn on drawing of labels at major tick marks through `setPaintLabels(true)`. You can also specify arbitrary labels (including `ImageIcons` or other components) by creating a `Dictionary` with `Integers` as keys and `Components` as values and then associating the `Dictionary` with the slider through `setLabelTable`.

Other `JSlider` capabilities include borders (as with all `JComponents`), sliders that go from high to low instead of low to high (`setInverted(true)`), and the ability to determine when the mouse is in the middle of a drag (when `getValueIs-Adjusting()` returns `true`) so that you can postpone action until the drag finishes.

JSlider Constructors

The `JSlider` class has five constructors:

> **public JSlider()**
> **public JSlider(int orientation)**
> **public JSlider(int min, int max)**
> **public JSlider(int min, int max, int initialValue)**
> **public JSlider(int orientation, int min, int max,**
>   **int initialValue)**

The first constructor creates a `JSlider` with a minimum and maximum value of 0 and 100, respectively. The initial value is 50. The second constructor creates a `JSlider` with the same values as the no-argument constructor; however, you can specify the orientation as either HORIZONTAL or VERTICAL. The remaining three constructors allow you to specify different minimum, maximum, and initial values, as well as orientation.

Useful JSlider Methods

JSlider defines 43 methods, of which only the 11 most popular are listed. All set methods have corresponding get methods.

public void setMinimum(int min)
public void setMaximum(int max)
public void setValue(int initialValue)
public void setOrientation(int orientation)

These methods allow you to set minimum, maximum, and initial slider value, as well as the orientation of the slider. The orientation can be HORIZONTAL or VERTICAL.

public void setPaintTicks(boolean paint)
public void setMinorTickSpacing(int stepSize)
public void setMajorTickSpacing(int stepSize)

By default, a JSlider does not display tick marks until you call setPaintTicks(true) and set the minor or major (or both) tick spacing by calling setMinorTickSpacing or setMajorTickSpacing.

Core Note

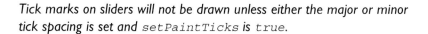

Tick marks on sliders will not be drawn unless either the major or minor tick spacing is set and `setPaintTicks` *is* `true`.

public void setSnapToTicks(boolean snap)

Setting setSnapToTicks(true) forces the slider cursor to align with a tick mark; a value of false (default) allows positioning of the slider cursor from the minimum to maximum values inclusive.

public void setInverted(boolean inverted)

The setInverted method reverses the maximum and minimum end points of the slider.

public void setPaintLabels(boolean paint)
public void setLabelTable(Dictionary labels)

The first method turns on or off the display of slider labels, which can be either `Strings` or `Icons`. However, labels are not actually drawn unless the tick spacing is also set. The `JSlider` can automatically generate numerical labels, or you can define custom labels through `setLabelTable` by supplying a `Hashtable` where each key-data pair is represented by an `Integer` value and a `JComponent` (typically, a `JLabel`).

Core Note

Labels will not be drawn unless either the major or minor tick spacing is set and `setPaintLabels` *is* `true`.

Listing 14.9 provides an example of three sliders, one without tick marks, one with tick marks, and one with tick marks and labels. Figure 14–10 shows the result for a Windows, Motif, and Java look and feel.

Listing 14.9 `JSliders.java`

```java
import java.awt.*;
import javax.swing.*;

/** Simple example illustrating the use of JSliders, especially
 *  the ability to specify tick marks and labels.
 */

public class JSliders extends JFrame {
  public static void main(String[] args) {
    new JSliders();
  }

  public JSliders() {
    super("Using JSlider");
    WindowUtilities.setNativeLookAndFeel();
    addWindowListener(new ExitListener());
    Container content = getContentPane();
    content.setBackground(Color.white);

    JSlider slider1 = new JSlider();
    slider1.setBorder(BorderFactory.createTitledBorder
                      ("JSlider without Tick Marks"));
```

(continued)

Listing 14.9 `JSliders.java` *(continued)*

```java
    content.add(slider1, BorderLayout.NORTH);

    JSlider slider2 = new JSlider();
    slider2.setBorder(BorderFactory.createTitledBorder
                        ("JSlider with Tick Marks"));
    slider2.setMajorTickSpacing(20);
    slider2.setMinorTickSpacing(5);
    slider2.setPaintTicks(true);
    content.add(slider2, BorderLayout.CENTER);

    JSlider slider3 = new JSlider();
    slider3.setBorder(BorderFactory.createTitledBorder
                        ("JSlider with Tick Marks & Labels"));
    slider3.setMajorTickSpacing(20);
    slider3.setMinorTickSpacing(5);
    slider3.setPaintTicks(true);
    slider3.setPaintLabels(true);
    content.add(slider3, BorderLayout.SOUTH);

    pack();
    setVisible(true);
  }
}
```

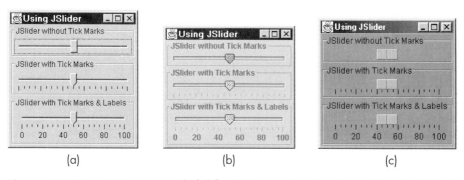

Figure 14–10 `JSliders` provide full flexibility to add tick marks and labels: (a) look and feel for Windows, (b) Java (Metal), and (c) Motif.

14.8 The JColorChooser Component

JColorChooser is a component that is new to Swing; the AWT has no equivalent. JColorChooser lets the user interactively select a Color. The default behavior is to present a dialog box containing a tabbed pane by which the user chooses the color through swatches, HSB (hue, saturation, brightness) values, or RGB values.

The simplest use is to call JColorChooser.showDialog, supplying parent Component as the first argument, the title as the second argument, and the initial color selection as the third argument, for example,

```
JColorChooser.showDialog
    (parent, "Select Background", getBackground());
```

The dialog presents an OK, Cancel, and Reset button as shown in Figure 14–11 on page 597. If the user selects OK, the return value is the Color chosen. If the user cancels the dialog, either by pressing the Esc key, selecting the Cancel button, or closing the dialog, then the return value is null.

You can also allocate a JColorChooser through a constructor. This approach is common if you want to display the color chooser somewhere other than in a pop-up dialog or if you are likely to display the color chooser many times. In the latter case, pass the JColorChooser instance to JColorChooser.createDialog, as in

```
JColorChooser chooser = new JColorChooser();
JDialog dialog = new JColorChooser.createDialog(
        this,            // parent component
        "Select Color",  // title
        true,            // open as modal
        chooser,         // color chooser for dialog
        okListener,      // handle selecting color
        exitListener);   // handle cancel selection
```

The okListener and exitListener should implement ActionListener to capture the event of the user selecting a color and canceling the color chooser, respectively. A call to dialog.setVisible(true) displays the dialog containing the color chooser. Creating a JColorChooser and binding it to a JDialog produces significant performance benefits since showDialog creates a new instance of a JColorChooser each time.

Constructors

The two most common `JColorChooser` constructors are:

public JColorChooser()
public JColorChooser(Color initialColor)
The first constructor creates a `JColorChooser` with an initial color selection of `Color.white`. The second constructor permits you to explicitly specify the initial selection color.

Useful JColorChooser Methods

The following paragraphs list the six most common methods of the `JColorChooser` class.

public static Color showDialog(Component parent,
String title,
Color initialColor)
This `static` method creates a modal dialog containing a *new* `JColorChooser` with the specified title and initial color selection. The `JColorChooser` is immediately displayed with the Swatch color tab. Either the selected `Color` is returned or, if the user selects Cancel, `null` is returned.

public static JDialog createDialog(Component parent,
String title,
boolean modal,
JColorChooser chooser,
ActionListener okListener
ActionListener cancelListener)
This `static` method creates a customized `JDialog` holding the passed-in `JColorChooser`. The dialog can be modal or nonmodal. When creating the dialog, you must specify the two `ActionListeners` that will handle the user selecting OK and Cancel, respectively. After creating the dialog, you can set the color and display the dialog through `setColor` and `setVisible`, as in

```
JColorChooser chooser = new JColorChooser();
JDialog dialog = new JColorChooser.createDialog(...);
chooser.setColor(someColor);
dialog.setVisible(true);
```

In the okListener, determine the selected color from getColor, for example,

```
class okListener implements ActionListener {
  public void actionPerformed(ActionEvent e)) {
    Color color = chooser.getColor();
    ...
    repaint();
  }
}
```

public Color getColor()
public void setColor(Color color)
public void setColor(int red, int green, int blue)
public void setColor(int color)

The first method returns the selected Color. The remaining three methods set the selected color of the JColorChooser. In the second setColor method, the RGB int values must range from 0-255 inclusive. In the third setColor method, the int represents four packed color bytes. See the Color class on page 372 for details.

The simple example in Listing 14.10 creates a small JFrame with a button that pops up a JColorChooser. Upon selection of a color, the background of the JFrame content pane is set to the color selected. Figure 14-11 show the Swatch tab of the JColorChooser.

Listing 14.10 JColorChooserTest.java

```
import java.awt.*;
import java.awt.event.*;
import javax.swing.*;

/** Simple example illustrating the use of JColorChooser. */

public class JColorChooserTest extends JFrame
                               implements ActionListener {
  public static void main(String[] args) {
    new JColorChooserTest();
  }

  public JColorChooserTest() {
    super("Using JColorChooser");
    WindowUtilities.setNativeLookAndFeel();
    addWindowListener(new ExitListener());
```

(continued)

Listing 14.10 `JColorChooserTest.java` *(continued)*

```
  Container content = getContentPane();
  content.setBackground(Color.white);
  content.setLayout(new FlowLayout());
  JButton colorButton
    = new JButton("Choose Background Color");
  colorButton.addActionListener(this);
  content.add(colorButton);
  setSize(300, 100);
  setVisible(true);
}

public void actionPerformed(ActionEvent e) {
  // Args are parent component, title, initial color.
  Color bgColor
    = JColorChooser.showDialog(this,
                                "Choose Background Color",
                                getBackground());
  if (bgColor != null)
    getContentPane().setBackground(bgColor);
  }
}
```

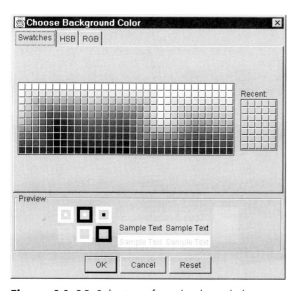

Figure 14–11 Selection of a color through the `JColorChooser` swatch tabbed pane.

14.9 Internal Frames

Many commercial Windows products such as Microsoft PowerPoint, Corel Draw, Borland JBuilder, and Allaire HomeSite are Multiple Document Interface (MDI) applications. This means that the program has one large "desktop" pane that holds all other windows. The other windows can be iconified (minimized) and moved around within this desktop pane, but not moved outside the pane. Furthermore, minimizing the desktop pane hides all the contained windows as well.

Swing introduced MDI support by means of two main classes. The first class, JDesktopPane, serves as a holder for the other windows. The second class, JInternalFrame, acts mostly like a JFrame, except that a JInternalFrame is constrained to stay inside the JDesktopPane. Using the JInternalFrame constructor with just a title results in an internal frame that is not resizable, closable, maximizable, or minimizable (i.e., iconifiable). However, JInternalFrame provides a five-argument constructor that accepts boolean values for each of these properties (in the order mentioned above). Internal frames also have two useful methods for controlling the z-order: moveToFront and moveToBack.

JInternalFrame Constructors

The JInternalFrame actually has six constructors to specify the initial behavior of the frame. The simplest two constructors, along with a fully specified constructor, are listed below:

> **public JInternalFrame()**
> **public JInternalFrame(String title)**
> **public JInternalFrame(String title,**
> **boolean resizable,**
> **boolean closeable,**
> **boolean maximizable,**
> **boolean iconifiable)**

By default, an internal frame does not support the ability to resize, close, maximize, and iconify. Thus, the first two constructors create frames that the user can only move about on the desktop pane. The last constructor allows you to explicitly control the frame functionality.

Useful JInternalFrame Methods

The JInternalFrame class provides many methods similar to those found in JFrame. The most common ones are summarized below.

public void setCloseable(boolean closeable)
public void setIconifiable(boolean iconifiable)
public void setMaximizable(boolean maximizable)
public void setResizable(boolean resizable)
These four methods allow you to programmatically set the behavior of the internal frame. Each method has a corresponding `isXxx` method instead of a `getXxx` method to query the state behavior of the frame. Each `set` method can throw a `PropertyVetoException`.

public String getTitle()
public void setTitle(String title)
These two methods allow you to set and retrieve the title of the internal frame, respectively.

public void moveToBack()
public void moveToFront()
These two methods position the z-order of the internal frame relative to the other internal frames in the desktop pane.

public void show()
public void dispose()
The `show` method makes the internal frame visible on the screen. If the frame is already visible, then the frame is moved to the front. Before showing the frame, you must call `setBounds` (or `setLocation` and `setSize`) to position and establish the size of the frame. The `JLayeredPane` holding the internal frames has a `null` layout manager. Thus, you are responsible for sizing and positioning the frame before displaying it. The second method, `dispose`, sets the visibility of the frame to `false` and, if not closed, fires an `INTERNAL_FRAME_CLOSED` event.

Core Note

Internal frames will not appear (`show`) on the desktop pane unless the bounds of the frame are explicitly specified.

public void setFrameIcon(Icon image)
This method sets the icon that is displayed in the upper-left corner of the internal frame.

public void addInternalFrameListener(
InternalFrameListener listener)
public void removeInternalFrameListener(
InternalFrameListener listener)

JInternalFrames generate InternalFrameEvents equivalent to
WindowEvents. The InternalFrameListener class defines seven abstract
methods to handle internal frame events:

- internalFrameActivated
- internalFrameClosed
- internalFrameClosing
- internalFrameDeactivated
- internalFrameDeiconified
- internalFrameIconified
- internalFrameOpened

Either attach or remove a listener implementing these event methods through
addInternalFrameListener or removeInternalFrameListener,
respectively.

The JDesktopPane class provides two methods to obtain the JInternal-
Frames contained in the desktop: getAllFrames, which returns an array of all
visible and iconized internal frames, and getAllFramesInLayer(layer), which
returns all internal frames at the specified layer in the JDesktopPane.

The following example in Listing 14.11 creates five empty internal frames inside a
desktop pane, which in turn resides inside a JFrame. Note that in JDK 1.2 the
default visibility for a JInternalFrame is true. However, in JDK 1.3, the default
visibility is false and you must call setVisible(true) to display the frame. The
screen capture in Figure 14–12 (a) shows the result with all frames open, and Figure
14–12 (b) shows the result with two of the frames minimized.

Core Note

In JDK 1.2, the default visibility of an internal frame is true, *whereas in
JDK 1.3, the default visibility of an internal frame is* false.

Listing 14.11 JInternalFrames.java

```java
import java.awt.*;
import java.awt.event.*;
import javax.swing.*;

/** Simple example illustrating the use of internal frames. */

public class JInternalFrames extends JFrame {
  public static void main(String[] args) {
    new JInternalFrames();
  }

  public JInternalFrames() {
    super("Multiple Document Interface");
    WindowUtilities.setNativeLookAndFeel();
    addWindowListener(new ExitListener());
    Container content = getContentPane();
    content.setBackground(Color.white);
    JDesktopPane desktop = new JDesktopPane();
    desktop.setBackground(Color.white);
    content.add(desktop, BorderLayout.CENTER);
    setSize(450, 400);
    for(int i=0; i<5; i++) {
      JInternalFrame frame
        = new JInternalFrame(("Internal Frame " + i),
                             true, true, true, true);
      frame.setLocation(i*50+10, i*50+10);
      frame.setSize(200, 150);
      frame.setBackground(Color.white);
      frame.setVisible(true);
      desktop.add(frame);
      frame.moveToFront();
    }
    setVisible(true);
  }
}
```

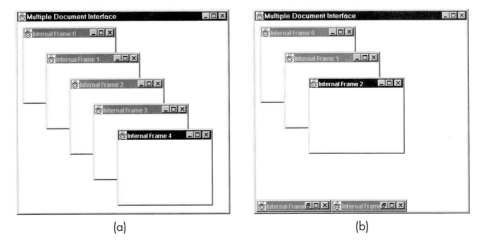

(a)   (b)

Figure 14–12 Swing JFrames support internal child frames: (a) all internal frames open, and (b) two internal frames minimized.

14.10 The JOptionPane Component

Static methods in the JOptionPane class let you easily create modal dialogs to show messages (JOptionPane.showMessageDialog), to ask for confirmation (JOptionPane.showConfirmDialog), to let the user enter text or to choose among predefined options (JOptionPane.showInputDialog), or to choose among a variety of buttons (JOptionPane.showOptionDialog). Each of these methods either returns an int specifying which button was pressed or returns a String specifying the option selected.

Useful JOptionPane Methods

JOptionPane is a robust class defining 26 constants, 7 constructors, and 59 methods. We only present five static methods for creating messages and input dialogs. All five methods define the same first three arguments for specifying the *parent* component of the dialog, the *message* to display in the dialog, and the *title* of the dialog window. Table 14.1 lists several helpful class constants typically used for arguments to JOptionPane methods.

Table 14.1 `JOptionPane` defined constants	
Message Icon Type	PLAIN_MESSAGE INFORMATION_MESSAGE QUESTION_MESSAGE (default) WARNING_MESSAGE ERROR_MESSAGE
Confirm Dialog Type	DEFAULT_OPTION OK_CANCEL_OPTION YES_NO_OPTION YES_NO_CANCEL_OPTION (default)
Confirm Dialog Return Type	YES_OPTION NO_OPTION CANCEL_OPTION CLOSED_OPTION

public static void showMesssageDialog(Component parent,
                                   Object message,
                                   String title,
                                   int iconType)

This method creates a simple *modal* dialog displaying an icon, a message, and an OK button. Since the purpose of this dialog is to simply present the user a message while blocking the main thread of execution, this method returns no response value. Alongside the text message, the dialog can display one of four message icons based on the `iconType` value defined in Table 14.1. Example message dialogs are shown in Figure 14–13.

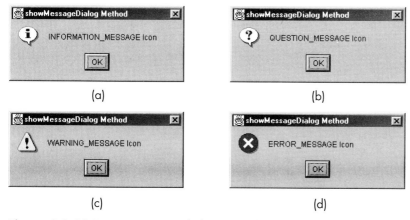

(a)   (b)

(c)   (d)

Figure 14–13 Various message dialogs (Windows look and feel) with selected message icons: (a) information, (b) question, (c) warning, and (d) error.

Specifying PLAIN_MESSAGE results in no displayed icon. Typically, the message argument is a String. However, the message can be any Object; a JComponent message is displayed as the component itself, an Icon message is displayed wrapped in a JLabel, and any other Object type is converted to a String through toString before displaying.

public static int showConfirmDialog(Component parent,
Object message,
String title,
int optionType,
int iconType)

The showConfirmDialog method creates a modal dialog where the user response is returned as an int mapping to one of the confirm dialog return types defined in Table 14.1 (YES_OPTION, NO_OPTION, CANCEL_OPTION, and CLOSE_OPTION). The optionType (legal option types are summarized in Table 14.1) determines which buttons are displayed, as shown in Figure 14–14.

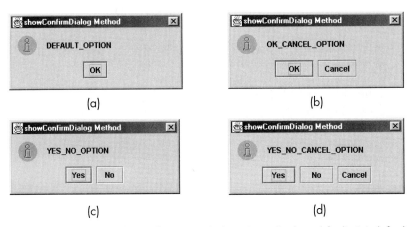

Figure 14–14 Various confirmation dialogs (Java look and feel): (a) default, (b) OK/Cancel, (c) Yes/No, and (d) Yes/No/Cancel.

The following example code creates a confirmation dialog and processes the user response.

```
int response = JOptionPane.showConfirmDialog
                (parentComponent,
                 "Do you like Java?",
                 "Confirm Dialog Example",
                 JOptionPane.YES_NO_OPTION,
```

```
                        JOptionPane.QUESTION_MESSAGE);
    if (response == JOptionPane.YES_OPTION) {
      // Do something for Yes option.
    } else if (response == JOptionPane.NO_OPTION) {
      // Do something for No options.
    } else {
      // Do something else.
    }
```

The `iconType` defines the icon displayed along with the message. See Table 14.1 for legal values.

public static String showInputDialog(Component parent, Object message, String title, int iconType)

The `showInputDialog` method creates a modal dialog with an icon, textfield for user input, OK button, and Cancel button, as shown in Figure 14–15. Input dialogs always present an OK and Cancel button. Selecting OK returns the `String` in the textfield; otherwise, `null` is returned when Cancel is selected. The icon displayed alongside the message is determined by `iconType`. See Table 14.1 for legal `iconType` values.

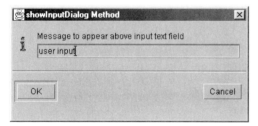

Figure 14–15 `JOptionPane` input dialog (Motif look and feel).

public static Object showInputDialog(Component parent, Object message, String title, int iconType, Icon icon, Object[] selections Object initialSelection)

This `showInputDialog` method provides additional flexibility by allowing you to specify an array of objects (`selections`) to present to the user for selection. The selection values are displayed as `Strings`, so the corresponding objects must provide a `toString` method. If the array contains fewer than 20 items, a combo box is presented (as shown in Figure 14–16); otherwise, a list is presented to the user. The `initialSelection` for the array is required. Selecting OK returns the `toString` value of the selected object; otherwise, a `null` string is returned when Cancel is selected. The icon displayed alongside the message is determined by the `iconType` parameter as defined in Table 14.1. Alternatively, you can specify a custom icon to display next to the dialog message (instead of the standard message icons) by supplying the `icon` argument.

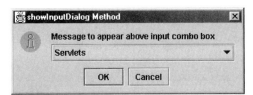

Figure 14–16 `JOptionPane` input dialog where input is a combo box (Java look and feel).

public static Object showOptionDialog(Component parent,
                                                       Object message,
                                                       String title,
                                                       int iconType,
                                                       Icon image,
                                                       Object[] selections
                                                       Object initialSelection)

The `showOptionDialog` allows you to customize the dialog buttons (as shown in Figure 14–17) instead of going with the traditional OK and Cancel buttons. Typically, the `selections` array defines an array of `JButtons`, and the `initialSelection` specifies which `JButton` should receive initial focus. Any `String` object specified in the selection array is internally converted to a `JButton`. For example, the following is valid for defining the selection array:

```
Object[] selections = { "OK,
                        "Cancel";
                        new JButton("End Program") };
```

Note that any `JComponent` is also allowed in the selection array. However, the traditional use is to simply display a button. The icon displayed alongside the message is determined by the `iconType`. See Table 14.1 for legal `iconType` values. If you prefer, you can specify a custom icon to display next to the dialog message by supplying an `icon` argument.

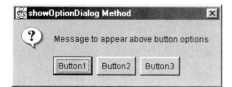

Figure 14–17 JOptionPane option dialog where the options are an array of buttons (Windows look and feel).

Don't underestimate the flexibility and power of showOptionDialog and showConfirmDialog for capturing user input. Both of these methods accept an Object for the message, not just a String. You could easily populate a JPanel with check boxes or radio buttons and pass in the JPanel as the message argument for the dialog window to display.

All the dialog figures in this section were created from JOptionPane-Examples.java. The source code for this program can be downloaded from the on-line archive at http://www.corewebprogramming.com/.

14.11 The JToolBar Component

Swing provides a nice new component not available in the AWT: JToolBar. In the most basic use, JToolBar is little more than a JPanel acting as a container to hold small buttons. However, the main distinction is that JToolBar is dockable (or float-able), meaning that a JToolBar can be dragged out of the original window and kept as a stand-alone window. A JToolBar can also be dragged back into the window or, if originally located at the top, can even be moved to the side of the window.

To build a JToolBar, you simply call the empty constructor (for a horizontal tool-bar) or pass in JToolBar.VERTICAL. You typically place a horizontal toolbar in the NORTH or SOUTH region of a container that uses BorderLayout, and a vertical tool-bar in the EAST or WEST region.

Core Approach

Place a horizontal toolbar in the NORTH or SOUTH location of a container by using BorderLayout. Similarly, place a vertical toolbar in the EAST or WEST location of a container by using BorderLayout.

The only complexity arising from JToolBar comes from the buttons placed inside. You could just drop normal JButtons into the toolbar or call add on an Action (a special subclass of ActionListener that includes information on labels and icons), which automatically creates a JButton. But the problem in both cases is that a graphical button for a toolbar differs from a normal JButton in two ways:

1. A toolbar button should be very small, whereas JButton maintains relatively large margins. Solution: call setMargin with an Insets object with all margin values zero (or at least small).
2. A JButton puts text labels to the right of the icon, but in toolbars we usually place the label below the icon. Solution: call setVerticalTextPosition(BOTTOM) and setHorizontalTextPosition(CENTER).

An example of a floating JToolBar, following this technique, is shown in Figure 14–18.

Figure 14-18 A floating JToolBar built with JButtons having zero Insets.

Since setting the insets margins to zero and placing the button text at the bottom of the icon is a common task for virtually all buttons, Listing 14.12 provides a small class that extends JButton to implement these modifications.

Listing 14.12 ToolBarButton.java

```
import java.awt.*;
import javax.swing.*;

/** Part of a small example showing basic use of JToolBar.
 *  The point here is that dropping a regular JButton in a
 *  JToolBar (or adding an Action) in JDK 1.2 doesn't give
 *  you what you want -- namely, a small button just enclosing
 *  the icon, and with text labels (if any) below the icon,
 *  not to the right of it. In JDK 1.3, if you add an Action
 *  to the toolbar, the Action label is no longer displayed.
 */
```

(continued)

Listing 14.12 `ToolBarButton.java` *(continued)*

```
public class ToolBarButton extends JButton {
  private static final Insets margins =
    new Insets(0, 0, 0, 0);

  public ToolBarButton(Icon icon) {
    super(icon);
    setMargin(margins);
    setVerticalTextPosition(BOTTOM);
    setHorizontalTextPosition(CENTER);
  }

  public ToolBarButton(String imageFile) {
    this(new ImageIcon(imageFile));
  }

  public ToolBarButton(String imageFile, String text) {
    this(new ImageIcon(imageFile));
    setText(text);
  }
}
```

JToolBar Constructors

`JToolBar` only has two constructors:

public JToolBar()
public JToolBar(int orientation)
The first constructor creates a `JToolBar` with a default horizontal orientation. The second constructor lets you specify an orientation of `HORIZONTAL` or `VERTICAL`.

Useful JToolBar Methods

`JToolBar` defines 23 methods. Only the five most common methods are covered below.

public JButton add(Action action)

This method creates a button capable of handling user interaction and then adds the button to the toolbar. The `Action` class is simply an interface extending `ActionListener` (which defines an `actionPerformed` method for handling an `ActionEvent`). The typical approach is to pass in an object that inherits from the concrete `AbstractAction` class (which implements the methods in the `Action` interface). `AbstractAction` allocates `Icon` and `String` instance variables for storing the button image and text. This concept is best illustrated in an example.

```
public class MyApplet extends JApplet{
  public void init{
    JToolBar toolbar = new JToolBar();
    toolbar.add(new PrintAction());
    getContentPane().add(toolbar,
                         BorderLayout.WEST);
    ...
  }
  ...
}
// "Button" for toolbar to handle event
class PrintAction extends AbstractAction {
  public PrintAction() {
    super("Print",new ImageIcon("print.gif"));
  }
  public void actionPerformed(ActionEvent evt) {
   System.out.println("Print button selected.");
    ...
  }
}
```

Alternatively, you could attach an `ActionListener` to a `JButton` and then add the button to the toolbar by calling `add(someButton)`, remembering that `container.add(...)` is in the `JToolBar` inheritance hierarchy.

In JDK 1.2, when an `Action` is added to a toolbar, the label is shown along with the icon. In JDK 1.3, only the `Action` icon is shown—the `Action` label is not displayed. This is the preferred behavior, as toolbars usually have tool-tips, not labels.

Core Note

In JDK 1.2, both the label and icon are displayed for an `Action` *added to a toolbar. In JDK 1.3, only the icon is shown for an* `Action` *added to the toolbar.*

Also, note that if you consult the JDK 1.3 API, the recommendation is to no longer add an `Action` to a toolbar, but to bind the `Action` to a button and then add the button to the toolbar, as in

```
JToolBar toolbar = new JToolBar();
JButton button = new JButton();
button.setAction(new PrintAction());
toolbar.add(button);
```

However, both the button label and icon are displayed in the toolbar for this case.

public void addSeparator()
public void addSeparator(Dimension size)

These two methods add a separator (blank space) between toolbar buttons. The default separator size is determined by the current look and feel. Alternatively, you can specify the width and height of the spacer by passing in a `Dimension` object.

public void setFloatable(boolean float)
public void setOrientation(int orientation)

These two methods set the floating and orientation (`JToolBar.HORIZONTAL`, `JToolBar.VERTICAL`) property of the toolbar. Both methods have corresponding `getXxx` accessors for the retrieving these property values.

The example in Listing 14.13 and Listing 14.14 creates a simple `JFrame` with a `JToolBar` at the top. The toolbar is intended to look somewhat like a toolbar that might come with a simple Web browser. Text labels are initially turned off but can be toggled on or off by the use of a `JCheckBox`. Each `JButton` has an added tool-tip. Figure 14–19 illustrates the toolbar docked in the horizontal position, vertical position, floating independently, and with labels. Closing a floating toolbar returns the toolbar to the initial docked position.

Listing 14.13 `ToolBarExample.java`

```java
import java.awt.*;
import javax.swing.*;
import java.awt.event.*;

/** Small example showing basic use of JToolBar. */

public class JToolBarExample extends JFrame
                             implements ItemListener {
  private BrowserToolBar toolbar;
  private JCheckBox labelBox;

  public static void main(String[] args) {
    new JToolBarExample();
  }

  public JToolBarExample() {
    super("JToolBar Example");
    WindowUtilities.setNativeLookAndFeel();
    addWindowListener(new ExitListener());
    Container content = getContentPane();
    content.setBackground(Color.white);

    JPanel panel = new JPanel(new BorderLayout());
    labelBox = new JCheckBox("Show Text Labels?");
    labelBox.setHorizontalAlignment(SwingConstants.CENTER);
    labelBox.addItemListener(this);
    panel.add(new JTextArea(10,30), BorderLayout.CENTER);
    panel.add(labelBox, BorderLayout.SOUTH);

    toolbar = new BrowserToolBar();
    content.add(toolbar, BorderLayout.NORTH);
    content.add(panel, BorderLayout.CENTER);

    pack();
    setVisible(true);
  }

  public void itemStateChanged(ItemEvent event) {
    toolbar.setTextLabels(labelBox.isSelected());
    pack();
  }
}
```

Listing 14.14 BrowserToolBar.java

```
import java.awt.*;
import javax.swing.*;

/** Part of a small example showing basic use of JToolBar.
 *  Creates a small dockable toolbar that is supposed to look
 *  vaguely like one that might come with a Web browser.
 *  Makes use of ToolBarButton, a small extension of JButton
 *  that shrinks the margins around the icon and puts text
 *  label, if any, below the icon.
 */

public class BrowserToolBar extends JToolBar {
  public BrowserToolBar() {
    String[] imageFiles =
      { "Left.gif", "Right.gif", "RotCCUp.gif",
        "TrafficRed.gif", "Home.gif", "Print.gif", "Help.gif" };
    String[] toolbarLabels =
      { "Back", "Forward", "Reload", "Stop",
        "Home", "Print", "Help" };
    Insets margins = new Insets(0, 0, 0, 0);
    for(int i=0; i<toolbarLabels.length; i++) {
      ToolBarButton button =
        new ToolBarButton("images/" + imageFiles[i]);
      button.setToolTipText(toolbarLabels[i]);
      button.setMargin(margins);
      add(button);
    }
  }

  public void setTextLabels(boolean labelsAreEnabled) {
    Component c;
    int i = 0;
    while((c = getComponentAtIndex(i++)) != null) {
      ToolBarButton button = (ToolBarButton)c;
      if (labelsAreEnabled) {
        button.setText(button.getToolTipText());
      } else {
        button.setText(null);
      }
    }
  }
}
```

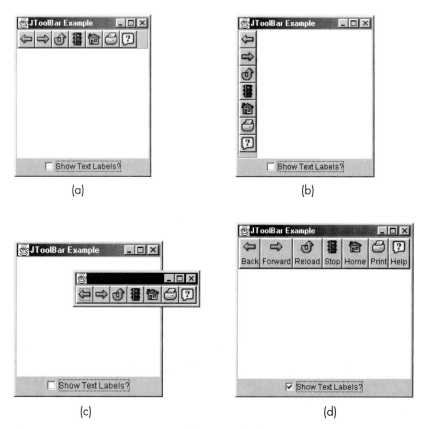

Figure 14–19 A `JToolBar` (a) horizontally docked, (b) vertically docked, (c) floating, and (d) labeled.

14.12 The JEditorPane Component

`JEditorPane` is sort of a fancy text area that can display text derived from different file formats. The built-in version supports HTML and RTF (Rich Text Format) only, but you can build "editor kits" to handle special-purpose applications. In principle, you choose the type of document you want to display by calling `setContentType`, and you specify a custom editor kit through `setEditorKit`. Note that unless you extend the `JEditorPane` class, the only legal choices are `text/html`, `text/plain`, (which is also what you get if you supply an unknown type), and `text/rtf`.

In practice, however, JEditorPane is almost always used for displaying HTML. If you have plain text, you might as well use JTextField. RTF support is currently somewhat primitive. You put content into the JEditorPane in one of four ways.

1. The most common way to build a JEditorPane is through the constructor, where you supply either a URL object or a String corresponding to a URL (which, in applications, could be a file URL to read off the local disk). Note that the constructor accepting a URL throws an IOException, so the call needs to be placed inside a try/catch block.

2. You can use setPage on a JEditorPane instance that was created through the empty constructor. The setPage method also takes either a URL object or a String and also throws an IOException. This approach is generally used when the content is determined at runtime by some user action.

3. You can use setText on a JEditorPane instance, supplying a String that is the actual content.

4. On occasion, you can use read, supplying an InputStream and an HTMLDocument object.

In principle, a JEditorPane can be editable, but in practice, editing tends to look pretty poor, so a JEditorPane is most often used simply to display HTML. Beforehand, you would call setEditable(false) on the editor pane. In addition, as with all Swing components, you enable scrolling by dropping the editor pane in a JScrollPane. The following illustrates the most common way to use JEditorPane:

```
String url = "http://host/path/file.html";
try {
  JEditorPane htmlPane = new JEditorPane(url);
  htmlPane.setEditable(false);
  someWindow.add(new JScrollPane(htmlPane));
} catch(IOException ioe) {
  System.err.println("Error displaying " + url);
}
```

Following Hypertext Links

In most cases, you use a noneditable JEditorPane to display HTML text. In such a case, you can detect when the user selects a link, you can determine which link was selected, and you can replace the contents of the JEditorPane with the document at the specified URL (by using setPage). To follow hyperlinks, attach a HyperlinkListener (notice that the method name is HyperlinkListener, not HyperLinkListener) through addHyperlinkListener, and implement the hyperlinkUpdate method to catch the events. Once you receive the event, look up the specific event type through `getEventType` and compare the event to `HyperlinkEvent.EventType.ACTIVATED`. This last point was not needed in early releases of Swing, but as of Java 1.2, if you neglect the step, then the link will be followed whenever the mouse simply moves over the link. Here is an example.

```java
public class SomeWindow extends JFrame
                        implements HyperlinkListener {
  private JEditorPane htmlPane;

  ...

  public void hyperlinkUpdate(HyperlinkEvent event) {
    if (event.getEventType() ==
                HyperlinkEvent.EventType.ACTIVATED) {
      try {
        htmlPane.setPage(event.getURL());
      } catch(IOException ioe) {
        // Some warning to user
      }
    }
  }
}
```

JEditorPane Constructors

JEditorPane provides four constructors:

> **public JEditorPane()**
> **public JEditorPane(String url)**
> **public JEditorPane(URL url)**
> **public JEditorPane(String mimeType, String document)**
> By default, the JEditorPane treats the document as plain text. By providing a URL, either as a String or URL object, you install the HTML editor kit and load the page associated with the URL. Both the second and third constructor can throw an IOException. The last constructor allows you to specify the MIME type (text/plain, text/html, or text/rtf) and the document.

Useful JEditorPane Methods

The following paragraphs list the more common JEditorPane methods. All property values have corresponding get and set methods.

public String getContentType()
public void setContentType(String mimeType)

These two methods get and set the MIME type, respectively. The supported MIME types are `text/plain`, `text/html`, and `text/rtf`.

public String getText()
public void setText(String document)

These two methods either retrieve or set the document in the `JEditorPane`. The text is interpreted according to the editor kit for the MIME type.

public void replaceSelection(String newText)

This thread-safe (blocking) method replaces the selected document content with the new text. Passing in `null` removes the selected text. If no text is highlighted, then the text is inserted at the cursor caret point. Replacing text is only allowed if the document is editable, `setEditable(true)`.

public URL getPage()
public void setPage(String page)
public void setPage(URL url)

The first method, `getPage`, returns the URL of the displayed document. The next two methods define and retrieve the document page for the `JEditor-Pane`. The content type is inferred from the URL and, further, allows registration of the appropriate editor. An absolute URL is required. Both methods can throw an `IOException` and require a `try/catch` block.

public synchronized void addHyperlinkListener(
HyperlinkListener listener)
public synchronized void removeHyperlinkListener(
HyperlinkListener listener)

These two methods add and remove the `HyperlinkListener` that is invoked when a hyperlink is selected, respectively. If `setEditable` is `true`, then hyperlinks are not followed.

public void read(InputStream in, Object description)

This method reads the input stream into the `JEditorPane` document. If the description of the document is of type `HTMLDocument` and the `HTMLEditor-Kit` is registered, then the stream is read by the `HTMLEditorKit`; otherwise, the stream is read by the superclass (`JTextComponent`) as plain text.

Implementing a Simple Web Browser

By adding a simple URL text field to a JEditorPane that can display HTML and follow links, you have a simple but functioning Web browser. Listing 14.15 and Listing 14.16 provide the code to create a simple Web browser capable of following hyperlinks. The initial page loaded is http://www.corewebprogramming.com/. Figure 14–20 shows the result after we loaded the Milton S. Eisenhower Research and Technology Development Center Web page at http://www.jhuapl.edu/rc/.

Listing 14.15 Browser.java

```
import javax.swing.*;
import javax.swing.event.*;
import java.awt.*;
import java.awt.event.*;
import java.net.*;
import java.io.*;

/** Very simplistic "Web browser" using Swing. Supply a URL on
 *  the command line to see it initially and to set the
 *  destination of the "home" button.
 */

public class Browser extends JFrame implements HyperlinkListener,
                                               ActionListener {
  public static void main(String[] args) {
    if (args.length == 0)
      new Browser("http://www.corewebprogramming.com/");
    else
      new Browser(args[0]);
  }

  private JIconButton homeButton;
  private JTextField urlField;
  private JEditorPane htmlPane;
  private String initialURL;

  public Browser(String initialURL) {
    super("Simple Swing Browser");
    this.initialURL = initialURL;
    addWindowListener(new ExitListener());
    WindowUtilities.setNativeLookAndFeel();
```

(continued)

Listing 14.15 Browser.java *(continued)*

```java
    JPanel topPanel = new JPanel();
    topPanel.setBackground(Color.lightGray);
    homeButton = new JIconButton("home.gif");
    homeButton.addActionListener(this);
    JLabel urlLabel = new JLabel("URL:");
    urlField = new JTextField(30);
    urlField.setText(initialURL);
    urlField.addActionListener(this);
    topPanel.add(homeButton);
    topPanel.add(urlLabel);
    topPanel.add(urlField);
    getContentPane().add(topPanel, BorderLayout.NORTH);

    try {
      htmlPane = new JEditorPane(initialURL);
      htmlPane.setEditable(false);
      htmlPane.addHyperlinkListener(this);
      JScrollPane scrollPane = new JScrollPane(htmlPane);
      getContentPane().add(scrollPane, BorderLayout.CENTER);
    } catch(IOException ioe) {
      warnUser("Can't build HTML pane for " + initialURL
               + ": " + ioe);
    }

    Dimension screenSize = getToolkit().getScreenSize();
    int width = screenSize.width * 8 / 10;
    int height = screenSize.height * 8 / 10;
    setBounds(width/8, height/8, width, height);
    setVisible(true);
  }

  public void actionPerformed(ActionEvent event) {
    String url;
    if (event.getSource() == urlField) {
      url = urlField.getText();
    } else { // Clicked "home" button instead of entering URL.
      url = initialURL;
    }
    try {
      htmlPane.setPage(new URL(url));
      urlField.setText(url);
    } catch(IOException ioe) {
      warnUser("Can't follow link to " + url + ": " + ioe);
    }
  }
```

(continued)

Listing 14.15 `Browser.java` *(continued)*

```java
  public void hyperlinkUpdate(HyperlinkEvent event) {
    if (event.getEventType() ==
        HyperlinkEvent.EventType.ACTIVATED) {
      try {
        htmlPane.setPage(event.getURL());
        urlField.setText(event.getURL().toExternalForm());
      } catch(IOException ioe) {
        warnUser("Can't follow link to "
                + event.getURL().toExternalForm() + ": " + ioe);
      }
    }
  }

  private void warnUser(String message) {
    JOptionPane.showMessageDialog(this, message, "Error",
                                  JOptionPane.ERROR_MESSAGE);
  }
}
```

Listing 14.16 `JIconButton.java`

```java
import javax.swing.*;

/** A regular JButton created with an ImageIcon and with borders
 *  and content areas turned off.
 */

public class JIconButton extends JButton {
  public JIconButton(String file) {
    super(new ImageIcon(file));
    setContentAreaFilled(false);
    setBorderPainted(false);
    setFocusPainted(false);
  }
}
```

Figure 14–20 A simple browser created with Swing components. `JEditorPane` provides support for displaying HTML.

HTML Support and JavaHelp

Although HTML support is getting better, `JEditorPane` still only supports a subset of the HTML 4.0 standard. Many constructs cannot be displayed properly, and worse yet, many standard constructs crash the `JEditorPane`, generating long and ugly error messages. So, although writing a simple browser is fun, it is risky in a real application to accept HTML input that you haven't tested previously. So perhaps the single best use of `JEditorPane` is to display noneditable HTML that you have written (and tested!) for on-line help to your application. The use of `JEditorPane` to display on-line help is such a good idea that Sun has provided a small package called `JavaHelp` that assists by creating an outline (displayed in a `JTree`), generating an index, and so forth. See the `http://java.sun.com/projects/javahelp/` home page for more details.

14.13 Other Simple Swing Components

Finally, we'll very briefly mention a couple of other simple Swing components that map to AWT equivalents: JCheckBox, JRadioButton, JTextField, and JText-Area. In addition, we'll briefly cover JFileChooser for opening a dialog to select files. For additional information on these topics, please see *Core Java Foundation Classes* by Kim Topley.

The JCheckBox Component

JCheckBox is similar to Checkbox (but note the capital B in JCheckBox). You can attach either an ActionListener or an ItemListener to monitor events. If you use an ActionListener, you'll want to call isSelected to distinguish a selection from a deselection. If you use an ItemListener, the ItemEvent itself has information regarding the selection state: call getStateChange and compare the result to ItemEvent.SELECTED or ItemEvent.DESELECTED. Unless you are sure that the background color of the JCheckBox matches the background color of the Container, you should call setContentAreaFilled(false). In addition, you can supply an icon to replace the normal checkable square (through setIcon), but if you do, be sure to also supply an icon to display when the check box is selected (setSelectedIcon). Listing 14.17 demonstrates creating check boxes and processing ItemListener and ActionListener events to obtain the state of the check box. The result of JCheckBoxTest.java is shown in Figure 14–21.

Listing 14.17 JCheckBoxTest.java

```
import javax.swing.*;
import java.awt.event.*;

public class JCheckBoxTest extends JPanel
                       implements ItemListener,
                                      ActionListener{
  JCheckBox checkBox1, checkBox2;

  public JCheckBoxTest() {
    checkBox1 = new JCheckBox("Java Servlets");
    checkBox2 = new JCheckBox("JavaServer Pages");
    checkBox1.setContentAreaFilled(false);
    checkBox2.setContentAreaFilled(false);
```

(continued)

Listing 14.17 `JCheckBoxTest.java` *(continued)*

```
    checkBox1.addItemListener(this);
    checkBox2.addActionListener(this);

    add(checkBox1);
    add(checkBox2);
  }

  public void actionPerformed(ActionEvent event) {
    System.out.println("JavaServer Pages selected: " +
                       checkBox2.isSelected());
  }

  public void itemStateChanged(ItemEvent event) {
    JCheckBox checkbox = (JCheckBox)event.getItem();

    if (event.getStateChange() == ItemEvent.SELECTED) {
      System.out.println(checkbox.getText() + " selected.");
    } else {
      System.out.println(checkbox.getText() + " deselected.");
    }
  }

  public static void main(String[] args) {
    JPanel panel = new JCheckBoxTest();
    WindowUtilities.setNativeLookAndFeel();
    WindowUtilities.openInJFrame(panel, 300, 75);
  }
}
```

Figure 14–21 A standard `JCheckBox`.

The JRadioButton Component

A `JRadioButton` is somewhat similar to a `Checkbox` inside a `CheckboxGroup` (see Section 13.16, "Check Box Groups (Radio Buttons)"). The approach is to create several `JRadioButtons` and add them to a `ButtonGroup`. All radio buttons added to the `ButtonGroup` are logically grouped together. As with `JCheckBox`, you can attach either an `ActionListener` or an `ItemListener` to process events. However, only the radio button that is clicked will receive an `ActionEvent`, and both the one clicked and the one that becomes deselected receive an `ItemEvent`. Unless you are sure that the background color of the `JRadioButton` matches the back-

ground color of the Container, you should call setContentAreaF-
illed(false). As with JCheckBox, you can supply an icon to replace the normal
button look (through setIcon), but if you do, also supply an icon to be displayed
when the radio button is selected (setSelectedIcon). An example of three radio
buttons is provided in Listing 14.18, with the results shown in Figure 14–22.

Listing 14.18 JRadioButtonTest.java

```java
import javax.swing.JRadioButton;
import javax.swing.ButtonGroup;
import java.awt.*;
import java.awt.event.*;
import javax.swing.*;

public class JRadioButtonTest extends JPanel
                              implements ItemListener {

  public JRadioButtonTest() {

    String[] labels = {"Java Swing","Java Servlets",
                       "JavaServer Pages"};
    JRadioButton[] buttons = new JRadioButton[3];
    ButtonGroup group = new  ButtonGroup();

    for(int i=0; i<buttons.length; i++) {
      buttons[i] = new JRadioButton(labels[i]);
      buttons[i].setContentAreaFilled(false);
      buttons[i].addItemListener(this);
      group.add(buttons[i]);
      add(buttons[i]);
    }
  }

  public void itemStateChanged(ItemEvent event) {
    JRadioButton radiobutton = (JRadioButton)event.getItem();

    if (event.getStateChange() == ItemEvent.SELECTED) {
      System.out.println(radiobutton.getText() + " selected.");
    } else {
      System.out.println(radiobutton.getText() + " deselected.");
    }
  }

  public static void main(String[] args) {
    JPanel panel = new JRadioButtonTest();
    WindowUtilities.setNativeLookAndFeel();
    WindowUtilities.openInJFrame(panel, 400, 75);
  }
}
```

Figure 14–22 A logical group of JRadioButtons.

The JTextField Component

The basic use of the JTextField parallels almost exactly the AWT TextField: specify the initial text, width, and alignment in the constructor. Alternatively, after creating a JTextField with the no argument constructor, you can use setText, setColumns, and setHorizontalAlignment. Legal alignment values are JTextField.LEFT, JTextField.CENTER, and JTextField.RIGHT. To retrieve the entered text, call getText. Capture ActionEvents on Enter and Document-Events on regular keys. Note that JTextField does not do double duty as a password field; use JPasswordField instead.

The JTextArea Component

JTextArea is similar to the AWT TextArea, but two things are different. First, unlike the case in TextArea, scrolling is not a built-in behavior. Instead, as with other Swing components, you control the scrolling behavior by wrapping the component in a JScrollPane. Second, JTextArea is only for simple text, but Swing also provides JTextPane and JEditorPane, which support much more complex options. In particular, JEditorPane, discussed in Section 14.12 (The JEditorPane Component), can display HTML and RTF text.

The JFileChooser Component

The JFileChooser control, shown in Figure 14–23, lets users interactively select a file by browsing directories. Normal use involves allocating a JFileChooser by passing in a String for the directory to the constructor (pass in "." to indicate the current directory). You can optionally specify a default file (setSelectedFile) and limit the file types displayed by writing and attaching a FileFilter. You can set the dialog title through setDialogTitle, and you can display the file chooser by calling showOpenDialog or showSaveDialog, (passing in the parent Frame). FileChooser returns an int value. If the int matches JFile-Chooser.APPROVE_OPTION, then the user selected a file and did not choose Cancel. Call getSelectedFile to retrieve the selected file. For example,

```
JFileChooser chooser = new JFileChooser(".");
int result = chooser.showOpenDialog(parent);
File file = chooser.getSelectedFile();
```

```
if (file != null &&
        result == JFileChooser.APPROVE_OPTION) {
    // Do something
}
```

To permit the user to select multiple files, call `setMultiSelection-Enabled(true)` before opening the dialog, and use `getSelectedFiles` to retrieve the response and store it in a `File` array.

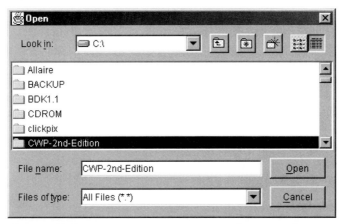

Figure 14–23 `JFileChooser` interactively permits the user to select one or multiple files.

Lastly, note that all `JComponents` can have a custom `Border` by calling `setBorder`, as covered in Section 14.6 (The JPanel Component), and can display custom tool-tips when the mouse pauses over the component (see `setToolTipText`).

14.14 Summary

This chapter introduced many of the standard Swing components that map to the familiar AWT components, including `JLabel`, `JButton`, `JSlider`, `JPanel`, `JApplet`, and `JFrame`, plus some new components like `JColorChooser`, `JOptionPane`, and `JInternalFrame` not seen in the AWT. Except for the windowing components, Swing components are all lightweight and drawn completely to memory through Java code. Instead of adding components to windows directly, you add components to the content pane. The content pane in `JFrame` and `JApplet` is simply a `JPanel` that by default implements double buffering. `JFrame` and `JApplet` now default to the same layout manager, `BorderLayout`.

As seen, Swing components are very rich and exciting, adding the capability for a selectable look and feel, custom borders, and tool-tips. Buttons can now include images instead of just text and can even display HTML. Sliders are reversible and can have image labels for the tick marks. The modal `JOptionPane` can present nearly any `JComponent` for the user to select a choice or enter a response, from text input, to a combo list, to check boxes, to custom buttons. Selecting a color is as simple as displaying a `JColorChooser`.

In this chapter, we've only scratched the surface of the Swing API. The next chapter examines more advanced components, for instance, `JList`, `JTree`, and `JTable`. These advanced components are slightly more complicated because they are built around data models and custom cell renderers. Once mastered, though, these advanced Swing components will allow you to create powerful and professional user interfaces for your Java programs.

ADVANCED SWING

Topics in This Chapter

- Using custom data models and renderers
- Adding and removing choices from a JList
- Displaying custom components in a JList
- Creating dynamic JTree displays
- Customizing icons in a JTree display
- Creating a scrollable JTable
- Editing cells in a JTable
- Printing Swing components
- Updating Swing components in a thread-safe manner

Chapter 15

I n this chapter, we focus on three advanced components available in Swing for building robust graphical user interfaces: JList, JTree, and JTable. A Swing list is similar to the familiar AWT List (Section 13.18, "List Boxes"); however, instead of just displaying a list of strings, a JList can also display icons. The JTree and JTable have no counterpart in the AWT package. A JTree displays data in a hierarchical structure. A common example of a tree display is the directory and file browser available in many software products. A table is equally familiar in graphical user interfaces. A JTable allows you to present data in a two-dimensional grid of table cells.

All three components are governed by the Model-View-Controller (MVC) architecture presented in Chapter 14 (Basic Swing), and the data for each component is stored in a data model. Multiple components may share the same data model. Once a change is made to the data through a listener (controller), an event is fired to update the display (view) of the component.

Because of their complexity, all three components provide default data models with built-in methods for modifying the data and firing change events. The default data models for a list, tree, and table all render their data as JLabels. We show you how to get around this limitation, that is, how to create custom data models and cell renderers to display other objects in these components. By defining your own custom cell renderer, you can display any simple Swing component in your user control, for example, an image in a tree or a check box in a table cell.

In this chapter we also cover two advanced techniques: printing Swing components and updating a Swing component in a thread-safe manner. With the Graphics2D class (see Chapter 10, "Java 2D: Graphics in Java 2"), first introduced in JDK 1.2, you can properly scale components to produce high-quality graphics on printers. We show you how to open up printer dialogs to enable users to select print options and how to write a general-purpose method to print any Swing component.

Painting of components has changed significantly in Swing as compared to AWT components. Swing components have separate borders and UI delegates to display the component in the proper look and feel (LAF). See Chapter 14 (Basic Swing), for information on UI delegates and component look and feel. Changing the state of a Swing component must always be performed in the event dispatch thread. To ensure a thread-safe GUI design, we show you how to properly access a Swing component from a user-defined thread. And, we demonstrate how to update the component from within the `run` method of a `Runnable` object and how to place the object on the event queue for execution in the event dispatch thread.

The Swing components and topics covered in this chapter apply to the Java 2 Platform. If you use these advanced components in an applet, you must either provide the Swing classes in a JAR file or install the Java Plug-In on the client machine. See Section 9.9 (The Java Plug-In) for details.

15.1 Using Custom Data Models and Renderers

With almost any Swing component, you can separate the underlying data structure from the GUI control that renders and displays the data. Often you can use an array to hold the data, as is the case with lists, trees, and tables. As a convenience, Swing lets you define and use your own data structures directly in these advanced GUI controls. You simply need to implement an interface that tells the Swing component how to access and display the data. The advantage here is that you don't have to copy the data into the control, but simply tell the GUI control how to access it.

Swing has a few simple defaults for displaying values in a `JList`, `JTree`, and `JTable`. For example, in a `JList`, values that are `Strings` or `Icons` are drawn directly, whereas other `Objects` are converted to strings through their `toString` method and then displayed in a `JLabel`. In addition, Swing also lets you define arbitrary mappings (custom views) between values and display components, thus permitting display of each element in the `JList` as a custom component. To correctly display the custom list data, you must build a "cell renderer" that accepts a reference to the `JList`, the value of the entry, and a few state parameters (for example, whether or not the value is currently selected). Based on this input, the cell renderer returns the appropriate `JComponent` to display in the list.

The next section illustrates different approaches for using models and renderers to display data in a `JList`. Models and renderers for `JTree` and `JTable` are covered in later sections.

15.2 JList

A JList presents a list of choices for selection. Either a single item or multiple items can be selected. In the following subsections, we present four approaches for creating a JList. The first approach creates a fixed set of choices by simply passing data directly to the JList. The second approach takes advantage of the default list model to support changeable choices. The third approach demonstrates a custom list model (data structure) for holding the list items. Finally, the fourth approach uses a custom renderer to build a custom JComponent for each item in the list.

JList with a Fixed Set of Choices

The simplest way to create a JList is to supply an array of strings to the JList constructor. Unlike an AWT List, a JList does not support direct addition or removal of elements once the JList is created. To create a dynamic list, you must use a ListModel, as discussed later in this section. But the approach of supplying an array of strings is easier for the common case of just displaying a fixed set of choices. This approach is demonstrated as follows:

```
String[] options = { "Option 1", ... , "Option N" };
JList optionList = new JList(options);
```

You can set the number of visible rows through the setVisibleRowCount method. However, if the list contains more items than the number of visible rows, then this approach is not useful unless the JList has scrollbars. As in all of Swing, you support scrollbars by dropping the component in a JScrollPane, as in

```
optionList.setVisibleRowCount(4);
JScrollPane optionPane = new JScrollPane(optionList);
someContainer.add(optionPane);
```

A JList generates ListSelectionEvents, so to handle selection events you attach a ListSelectionListener, which uses the valueChanged method. Be aware that a single click generates three events: one for the deselection of the originally selected entry, one for notification that the selection is moving, and one for the selection of the new entry. In the first two cases, the ListSelectionEvent's getValueIsAdjusting method returns true, so if you only care about the final selection, you would typically check that the return value is false. Of course, you can also totally ignore events and later look up which item (getSelectedValue) or index (getSelectedIndex) is currently selected. If the JList supports multiple selections, you use setSelectionMode to specify one of the ListSelection- Model constants: SINGLE_SELECTION, SINGLE_INTERVAL_SELECTION, or MULTIPLE_INTERVAL_SELECTION. Then, you use getSelectedValues and getSelectedIndices to get an array of the selections. For example,

```
public class SomeClass {
  private JList optionList;
  ...
  public void someMethod() {
    ...
    MyListListener listener = new MyListListener();
    optionList.addListSelectionListener(listener);
  }
  ...
  private class MyListListener
              implements ListSelectionListener {
    public void valueChanged(ListSelectionEvent event) {
      // Only concerned with the selection of the
      // new entry. Check to see if getValueIsAdjusting
      // returns false.
      if (!event.getValueIsAdjusting()) {
        String selection =
          optionList.getSelectedValue();
        doSomethingWith(selection);
      }
    }
  }
}
```

In the attached listener, the `ListSelectionEvent` is first checked to see if `getValueIsAdjusting` returns `false`. This approach effectively ignores the other two events that can occur when different items are selected in a list.

Core Approach

A single click in a list can generate three `ListSelectionEvent`s. If you are only concerned with the selection of a list entry, then check to see that event object returns `false` for `getValueIsAdjusting`.

JList Constructors

The `JList` class defines four constructors:

public JList()
public JList(Object[] data)
public JList(Vector data)
public JList(ListModel model)

The first constructor produces an empty `JList` with no data. The second and third constructors accept an array and a `Vector`, respectively. The fourth constructor accepts a `ListModel`, which defines methods for determining the size of the list and retrieving values from the list.

Useful JList Methods

The JList class defines over 60 methods. The 13 most common methods are summarized below.

public void clearSelection()

This method clears the selection of any items in the list.

public ListModel getModel()
public void setModel(ListModel model)

These two methods return and set the data model containing the items to display, respectively.

public int getSelectedIndex()
public int[] getSelectedIndices()

The getSelectedIndex method returns the index of the first selected item in the list. The getSelectedIndices method returns an array containing indices of all selected items.

public Object getSelectedValue()
public Object[] getSelectedValues()

The first method returns the first selected item in the list. The second method returns an array of all items selected.

public int getSelectionMode()
public setSelectionMode(int mode)

These two methods set and return the list selection mode, respectively. Legal values are ListSelectionModel.SINGLE_SELECTION, List-SelectionModel.SINGLE_INTERVAL_SELECTION, and ListSelectionModel.MULTIPLE_INTERVAL_SELECTION.

public boolean getValueIsAdjusting()

A ListSelectionEvent can occur in three different situations: one that deselects the originally selected entry, one that indicates the selection is moving (mouse drag), and one that selects the new entry (occurs when the mouse is released). The getValueIsAdjusting method returns true in the first two cases and false in the last case (when the final item is selected and the mouse is released).

public int getVisibleRowCount()
public void setVisibleRowCount(int rows)

These two methods return and set the number of visible rows in the list, respectively.

public boolean isSelectedIndex(int index)

The `isSelectedIndex` method returns `true` if the item in the list at the indicated `index` is selected; otherwise, it returns `false`.

Listing 15.1 constructs a simple `JList` to hold an array of strings and places the `JList` into a scrollable pane. A listener attached to the `JList` displays the item selected by the user in a textfield, as shown in Figure 15–1. Listings for the `Window-Utilities` and `ExitListener` helper classes are given in Section 14.1 (Getting Started with Swing). This code, like all code presented in the book, is available on-line at `http://www.corewebprogramming.com/`.

Listing 15.1 `JListSimpleExample.java`

```java
import java.awt.*;
import javax.swing.*;
import javax.swing.event.*;
import javax.swing.border.*;

/** Simple JList example illustrating
 *  <UL>
 *    <LI>Creating a JList, which we do by passing values
 *        directly to the JList constructor, rather than
 *        using a ListModel, and
 *    <LI>Attaching a listener to determine when values change.
 *  </UL>
 */

public class JListSimpleExample extends JFrame {
  public static void main(String[] args) {
    new JListSimpleExample();
  }

  private JList sampleJList;
  private JTextField valueField;
```

(continued)

Listing 15.1 `JListSimpleExample.java` *(continued)*

```java
public JListSimpleExample() {
  super("Creating a Simple JList");
  WindowUtilities.setNativeLookAndFeel();
  addWindowListener(new ExitListener());
  Container content = getContentPane();

  // Create the JList, set the number of visible rows, add a
  // listener, and put it in a JScrollPane.
  String[] entries = { "Entry 1", "Entry 2", "Entry 3",
                       "Entry 4", "Entry 5", "Entry 6" };
  sampleJList = new JList(entries);
  sampleJList.setVisibleRowCount(4);
  sampleJList.addListSelectionListener(new ValueReporter());
  JScrollPane listPane = new JScrollPane(sampleJList);
  Font displayFont = new Font("Serif", Font.BOLD, 18);
  sampleJList.setFont(displayFont);

  JPanel listPanel = new JPanel();
  listPanel.setBackground(Color.white);
  Border listPanelBorder =
    BorderFactory.createTitledBorder("Sample JList");
  listPanel.setBorder(listPanelBorder);
  listPanel.add(listPane);
  content.add(listPanel, BorderLayout.CENTER);
  JLabel valueLabel = new JLabel("Last Selection:");
  valueLabel.setFont(displayFont);
  valueField = new JTextField("None", 7);
  valueField.setFont(displayFont);
  valueField.setEditable(false);
  JPanel valuePanel = new JPanel();
  valuePanel.setBackground(Color.white);
  Border valuePanelBorder =
    BorderFactory.createTitledBorder("JList Selection");
  valuePanel.setBorder(valuePanelBorder);
  valuePanel.add(valueLabel);
  valuePanel.add(valueField);
  content.add(valuePanel, BorderLayout.SOUTH);
  pack();
  setVisible(true);
}
```

(continued)

Listing 15.1 `JListSimpleExample.java` *(continued)*

```java
private class ValueReporter implements ListSelectionListener {

    /** You get three events in many cases -- one for the
     *  deselection of the originally selected entry, one
     *  indicating the selection is moving, and one for the
     *  selection of the new entry. In the first two cases,
     *  getValueIsAdjusting returns true; thus, the test below
     *  when only the third case is of interest.
     */

    public void valueChanged(ListSelectionEvent event) {
        if (!event.getValueIsAdjusting()) {
            Object value = sampleJList.getSelectedValue();
            if (value != null) {
                valueField.setText(value.toString());
            }
        }
    }
}
```

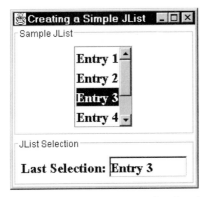

Figure 15–1 A `JList` with a fixed set of choices.

JLists with Changeable Choices

To create a `JList` in which the choices are changeable, first create a `Default-ListModel` by using the default constructor. This `DefaultListModel` implements the same methods as does `java.util.Vector`, so you can manipulate the data as you would a `Vector`. Then, pass the list model to the `JList` constructor. Afterwards, any changes to the items in the `DefaultListModel` are reflected in the `JList`.

At runtime you can add entries and remove entries in a JList by calling the same methods on the DefaultListModel as you would on a Vector. For example,

```
String choices = { "Choice 1", ... , "Choice N"};
DefaultListModel sampleModel = new DefaultListModel();
for(int i=0; i<choices.length; i++) {
  sampleModel.addElement(choices[i]);
}
JList optionList = new JList(sampleModel);
```

Use addElement to insert an entry at the end of the list, and remove(index) to delete an entry at a specified index in the list. Note that changing entries in the list model can change the preferred size of the JList, which, depending on the layout manager in use, might require you to revalidate the window containing the JList to update the presentation.

In Listing 15.2, instead of a String array being supplied in the JList constructor, we first create an instance of DefaultListModel and add entries. Then, we supply the populated list model in the JList constructor. We add a JButton to the example with an attached ActionListener implemented by the class ItemAdder. When the user selects the button, the listener's actionPerformed method adds a new entry to the list model and then revalidates the panel containing the JList. The result is shown in Figure 15–2.

Listing 15.2 DefaultListModelExample.java

```
import java.awt.*;
import java.awt.event.*;
import javax.swing.*;
import javax.swing.border.*;

/** JList example illustrating
 *   <UL>
 *     <LI>The creation of a JList by creating a DefaultListModel,
 *         adding the values there, then passing that to the
 *         JList constructor.
 *     <LI>Adding new values at runtime, the key thing that
 *         DefaultListModel lets you do that you can't do with
 *         a JList where you supply values directly.
 *   </UL>
 */

public class DefaultListModelExample extends JFrame {
  public static void main(String[] args) {
    new DefaultListModelExample();
  }
```

(continued)

Listing 15.2 `DefaultListModelExample.java` *(continued)*

```java
JList sampleJList;
private DefaultListModel sampleModel;

public DefaultListModelExample() {
  super("Creating a Simple JList");
  WindowUtilities.setNativeLookAndFeel();
  addWindowListener(new ExitListener());
  Container content = getContentPane();

  String[] entries = { "Entry 1", "Entry 2", "Entry 3",
                       "Entry 4", "Entry 5", "Entry 6" };
  sampleModel = new DefaultListModel();
  for(int i=0; i<entries.length; i++) {
    sampleModel.addElement(entries[i]);
  }
  sampleJList = new JList(sampleModel);
  sampleJList.setVisibleRowCount(4);
  Font displayFont = new Font("Serif", Font.BOLD, 18);
  sampleJList.setFont(displayFont);
  JScrollPane listPane = new JScrollPane(sampleJList);

  JPanel listPanel = new JPanel();
  listPanel.setBackground(Color.white);
  Border listPanelBorder =
    BorderFactory.createTitledBorder("Sample JList");
  listPanel.setBorder(listPanelBorder);
  listPanel.add(listPane);
  content.add(listPanel, BorderLayout.CENTER);
  JButton addButton =
    new JButton("Add Entry to Bottom of JList");
  addButton.setFont(displayFont);
  addButton.addActionListener(new ItemAdder());
  JPanel buttonPanel = new JPanel();
  buttonPanel.setBackground(Color.white);
  Border buttonPanelBorder =
    BorderFactory.createTitledBorder("Adding Entries");
  buttonPanel.setBorder(buttonPanelBorder);
  buttonPanel.add(addButton);
  content.add(buttonPanel, BorderLayout.SOUTH);
  pack();
  setVisible(true);
}
```

(continued)

Listing 15.2 `DefaultListModelExample.java` *(continued)*

```java
  private class ItemAdder implements ActionListener {

    /** Add an entry to the ListModel whenever the user
     *  presses the button. Note that since the new entries
     *  may be wider than the old ones (e.g., "Entry 10" vs.
     *  "Entry 9"), you need to rerun the layout manager.
     *  You need to do this <I>before</I> trying to scroll
     *  to make the index visible.
     */

    public void actionPerformed(ActionEvent event) {
      int index = sampleModel.getSize();
      sampleModel.addElement("Entry " + (index+1));
      ((JComponent)getContentPane()).revalidate();
      sampleJList.setSelectedIndex(index);
      sampleJList.ensureIndexIsVisible(index);
    }
  }
}
```

Figure 15–2 With a `JList`, choices can be added and deleted through the associated `DefaultListModel`.

JList with Custom Data Model

Instead of predetermining the data structure that holds the list elements, Swing lets you use your own data structure as long as you provide information on how to determine the number of elements in the data structure and how to read an element in the data structure. For use in a `JList`, any user-defined data structure must provide implementation of the four methods of the `ListModel` interface described below.

ListModel Interface

public Object getElementAt(int index)
Given an `index`, this method returns the corresponding data element.

public int getSize()

This method returns the number of entries in the list.

public void addListDataListener(ListDataListener listener)

This method adds to the model a listener that is notified when an item is selected or deselected.

public void removeListDataListener(ListDataListener listener)

This method removes the specified listener from the list model.

In Listing 15.3, we demonstrate the use of a custom list model. This example is based on a collection of JavaLocation objects that describe cities or regions named "Java." Rather than copying from the collection when the list requires an item, we simply define in Listing 15.4 a small helper class JavaLocationModel, that implements the ListModel interface and provides the specific methods to extract data from the collection. We then supply our custom list model to the JList constructor JListCustomModel (Listing 15.3).

The collection is stored in JavaLocationCollection, Listing 15.5. Listing 15.6 is the underlying data structure for the example. It contains each JavaLocation object, which in turn contains information on a city or region named Java, including the country in which the city is located, the country flag, and any neighboring landmark cities.

The result for this example is shown in Figure 15–3.

Listing 15.3 JListCustomModel.java

```java
import java.awt.*;
import javax.swing.*;

/** Simple JList example illustrating the use of a custom
 *  ListModel (JavaLocationListModel).
 */

public class JListCustomModel extends JFrame {
  public static void main(String[] args) {
    new JListCustomModel();
  }

  public JListCustomModel() {
    super("JList with a Custom Data Model");
    WindowUtilities.setNativeLookAndFeel();
    addWindowListener(new ExitListener());
    Container content = getContentPane();
```

(continued)

Listing 15.3 `JListCustomModel.java` *(continued)*

```
    JavaLocationCollection collection =
      new JavaLocationCollection();
    JavaLocationListModel listModel =
      new JavaLocationListModel(collection);
    JList sampleJList = new JList(listModel);
    Font displayFont = new Font("Serif", Font.BOLD, 18);
    sampleJList.setFont(displayFont);
    content.add(sampleJList);

    pack();
    setVisible(true);
  }
}
```

Listing 15.4 `JavaLocationListModel.java`

```
import javax.swing.*;
import javax.swing.event.*;

/** A simple illustration of writing your own ListModel.
 *  Note that if you wanted the user to be able to add and
 *  remove data elements at runtime, you should start with
 *  AbstractListModel and handle the event reporting part.
 */

public class JavaLocationListModel implements ListModel {
  private JavaLocationCollection collection;

  public JavaLocationListModel(JavaLocationCollection collec-
tion) {
    this.collection = collection;
  }

  public Object getElementAt(int index) {
    return(collection.getLocations()[index]);
  }

  public int getSize() {
    return(collection.getLocations().length);
  }

  public void addListDataListener(ListDataListener l) {}

  public void removeListDataListener(ListDataListener l) {}
}
```

Listing 15.5 `JavaLocationCollection.java`

```java
/** A simple collection that stores multiple JavaLocation
 *  objects in an array and determines the number of
 *  unique countries represented in the data.
 */

public class JavaLocationCollection {
  private static JavaLocation[] defaultLocations =
    { new JavaLocation("Belgium",
                       "near Liege",
                       "flags/belgium.gif"),
      new JavaLocation("Brazil",
                       "near Salvador",
                       "flags/brazil.gif"),
      new JavaLocation("Colombia",
                       "near Bogota",
                       "flags/colombia.gif"),
      new JavaLocation("Indonesia",
                       "main island",
                       "flags/indonesia.gif"),
      new JavaLocation("Jamaica",
                       "near Spanish Town",
                       "flags/jamaica.gif"),
      new JavaLocation("Mozambique",
                       "near Sofala",
                       "flags/mozambique.gif"),
      new JavaLocation("Philippines",
                       "near Quezon City",
                       "flags/philippines.gif"),
      new JavaLocation("Sao Tome",
                       "near Santa Cruz",
                       "flags/saotome.gif"),
      new JavaLocation("Spain",
                       "near Viana de Bolo",
                       "flags/spain.gif"),
      new JavaLocation("Suriname",
                       "near Paramibo",
                       "flags/suriname.gif"),
      new JavaLocation("United States",
                       "near Montgomery, Alabama",
                       "flags/usa.gif"),
      new JavaLocation("United States",
                       "near Needles, California",
                       "flags/usa.gif"),
```

(continued)

Listing 15.5 JavaLocationCollection.java *(continued)*

```java
      new JavaLocation("United States",
                       "near Dallas, Texas",
                       "flags/usa.gif")
  };

private JavaLocation[] locations;
private int numCountries;

public JavaLocationCollection(JavaLocation[] locations) {
  this.locations = locations;
  this.numCountries = countCountries(locations);
}

public JavaLocationCollection() {
  this(defaultLocations);
}

public JavaLocation[] getLocations() {
  return(locations);
}

public int getNumCountries() {
  return(numCountries);
}

// Count the number of unique countries in the data.
// Assumes the list is sorted by country name
private int countCountries(JavaLocation[] locations) {
  int n = 0;
  String currentCountry, previousCountry = "None";
  for(int i=0;i<locations.length;i++) {
    currentCountry = locations[i].getCountry();
    if (!previousCountry.equals(currentCountry)) {
      n++;
    }
    currentCountry = previousCountry;
  }
  return(n);
}
}
```

Listing 15.6 JavaLocation.java

```
/** Simple data structure with three properties: country,
 *  comment, and flagFile. All are strings, and they are
 *  intended to represent a country that has a city or
 *  province named "Java," a comment about a more
 *  specific location within the country, and a path
 *  specifying an image file containing the country's flag.
 *  Used in examples illustrating custom models and cell
 *  renderers for JLists.
 */

public class JavaLocation {
  private String country, comment, flagFile;

  public JavaLocation(String country, String comment,
                      String flagFile) {
    setCountry(country);
    setComment(comment);
    setFlagFile(flagFile);
  }

  /** String representation used in printouts and in JLists */

  public String toString() {
    return("Java, " + getCountry() + " (" + getComment() + ").");
  }

  /** Return country containing city or province named "Java." */

  public String getCountry() {
    return(country);
  }

  /** Specify country containing city or province named "Java." */

  public void setCountry(String country) {
    this.country = country;
  }

  /** Return comment about city or province named "Java."
   *  Usually of the form "near such and such a city."
   */

  public String getComment() {
    return(comment);
  }
```

(continued)

Listing 15.6 `JavaLocation.java` *(continued)*

```java
  /** Specify comment about city or province named "Java". */

  public void setComment(String comment) {
    this.comment = comment;
  }

  /** Return path to image file of country flag. */

  public String getFlagFile() {
    return(flagFile);
  }

  /** Specify path to image file of country flag. */

  public void setFlagFile(String flagFile) {
    this.flagFile = flagFile;
  }
}
```

Figure 15–3 With a custom `ListModel`, a `JList` can display data that is stored in a custom data structure.

JList with Custom Renderer

Instead of predetermining how the JList will draw the list elements, Swing lets you specify what graphical component to use for the various entries. Normally, Swing uses a JLabel to display the string representation of the list entry. If the entry is an Icon, that Icon is displayed in the JLabel. However, a string and an image cannot be presented in a JList entry at the same time unless a custom cell renderer that builds the special label (see Listing 15.8) is written. A custom cell renderer must implement the ListCellRenderer interface and return the desired component to display in the JList.

ListCellRenderer Interface

The only method in the ListCellRenderer interface is getListCell-RendererComponent:

public Component getListCellRendererComponent(JList list, Object value, int index, boolean isSelected, boolean cellHasFocus)

The getListCellRendererComponent method examines the object to render (value) and returns a component to render in the JList. In this approach, the JList is passed in as an argument so that the visual properties of the component match the properties of the list, for instance, the list foreground and background color. The remaining parameters in this method define the index of the cell in the list, state whether the cell is selected, and indicate whether the cell currently has focus.

As a convenience, the Java 2 Platform provides a DefaultListCellRenderer class that implements the ListCellRenderer interface. The default behavior for DefaultListCellRenderer is to return a JLabel.

In the following example we build upon the previous list example (Figure 15–3) that contains a custom data model of geographic areas named Java. We improve upon this example by adding a custom cell renderer to display both the country flag and name of each city. To build the custom renderer, in Listing 15.8 we define the class JavaLocationRenderer that implements the ListCellRenderer interface and provides a getListCellRendererComponent method to construct a *customized* JLabel component based on the JavaLocation data. This custom cell renderer is bound to the JList through the setCellRenderer method in Listing 15.7.

Listing 15.7 `JListCustomRenderer.java`

```java
import java.awt.*;
import javax.swing.*;

/** Simple JList example illustrating the use of a custom
 *  cell renderer (JavaLocationRenderer).
 */

public class JListCustomRenderer extends JFrame {
  public static void main(String[] args) {
    new JListCustomRenderer();
  }

  public JListCustomRenderer() {
    super("JList with a Custom Cell Renderer");
    WindowUtilities.setNativeLookAndFeel();
    addWindowListener(new ExitListener());
    Container content = getContentPane();

    JavaLocationCollection collection =
      new JavaLocationCollection();
    JavaLocationListModel listModel =
      new JavaLocationListModel(collection);
    JList sampleJList = new JList(listModel);
    sampleJList.setCellRenderer(new JavaLocationRenderer());
    Font displayFont = new Font("Serif", Font.BOLD, 18);
    sampleJList.setFont(displayFont);
    content.add(sampleJList);

    pack();
    setVisible(true);
  }
}
```

Rather than trying to explicitly determine how to color the component in the JList when the component is selected, has focus, and so forth, it is often easier to extend `DefaultListCellRenderer` (which implements `ListCellRenderer`) and modify the returned `JLabel`, which already has the colors set appropriately. For example, in Listing 15.8 the default `JLabel` is returned from the call to `super.getListCellRenderer`, and an `Icon` is added to the `JLabel`, maintaining the existing text, foreground color, and background color. Note that `getListCell-RendererComponent` is called every time the users click on a list entry, so for performance, you should cache any internal components that are generated to build the custom component. In this example, every time a list entry changes, the cell renderer needs an `ImageIcon` object to display the flag in the `JLabel`. To improve performance, a hash table that associates `ImageIcons` with `JavaLocations` is maintained. So, if the cell renderer has seen the `JavaLocation` before, we retrieve the previously created `ImageIcon` instead of generating a new `ImageIcon` object. The result for this improved `JList` with a custom cell renderer is shown in Figure 15–4.

Listing 15.8 `JavaLocationRenderer.java`

```
import javax.swing.*;
import java.awt.*;
import java.util.*;

/** Simple custom cell renderer. The idea here is to augment
 *  the default renderer instead of building one from scratch.
 *  The advantage of this approach is that you don't have to
 *  handle the highlighting of the selected entries yourself,
 *  plus values that aren't of the new type you want to draw can
 *  be handled automatically. The disadvantage is that you are
 *  limited to a variation of a JLabel, which is what the default
 *  renderer returns.
 *  <P>
 *  Note that this method can get called lots and lots of times
 *  as you click on entries. We don't want to keep generating
 *  new ImageIcon objects, so we make a Hashtable that associates
 *  previously displayed values with icons, reusing icons for
 *  entries that have been displayed already.
 *  <P>
 *  Note that in the first release of JDK 1.2, the default
 *  renderer  has a bug: the renderer doesn't clear out icons for
 *  later entries. So if you mix plain strings and ImageIcons in
 *  your JList, the plain strings still get an icon. The
 *  call below clears the old icon when the value is not a
 *  JavaLocation.
 */

public class JavaLocationRenderer extends
                              DefaultListCellRenderer {
  private Hashtable iconTable = new Hashtable();

  public Component getListCellRendererComponent(JList list,
                                      Object value,
                                      int index,
                                      boolean isSelected,
                                      boolean hasFocus) {
    // First build the label containing the text, then
    // later add the image.
```

(continued)

Listing 15.8 `JavaLocationRenderer.java` *(continued)*

```
  JLabel label =
    (JLabel)super.getListCellRendererComponent(list,
                                                value,
                                                index,
                                                isSelected,
                                                hasFocus);
  if (value instanceof JavaLocation) {
    JavaLocation location = (JavaLocation)value;
    ImageIcon icon = (ImageIcon)iconTable.get(value);
    if (icon == null) {
      icon = new ImageIcon(location.getFlagFile());
      iconTable.put(value, icon);
    }
    label.setIcon(icon);
  } else {
    // Clear old icon; needed in 1st release of JDK 1.2.
    label.setIcon(null);
  }
  return(label);
  }
}
```

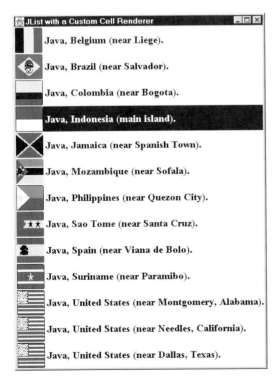

Figure 15–4 In a `JList`, the elements are not limited to just `String` entries but can be custom Swing components.

15.3 JTree

A JTree can display data elements (nodes) in a hierarchical structure. In this section, we illustrate the basic use a of JTree, show how to respond to node selection events, provide an example of a custom tree model (a tree that builds children on the fly), and show how to replace the icons that appear at the tree nodes with custom ones.

Simple JTree

The simplest and most common way to use a JTree is to create objects of type DefaultMutableTreeNode to act as the nodes of the tree. Nodes that have no children are displayed as leaves; nodes that have children are displayed as folders. You can associate any object with a node by supplying a value, known as the "user object," to the DefaultMutableTreeNode constructor. Node labels are represented by Strings; thus, before displaying the user object, you first call the toString method and display the resultant String.

Once you have created some nodes, you can hook them together in a tree structure through parentNode.add(childNode). Finally, you pass the root node to the JTree constructor. Note that since a tree display can change size when user input so dictates (expanding and collapsing nodes), you usually place a tree inside a JScrollPane. For example, here is a very simple tree:

```
DefaultMutableTreeNode root =
  new DefaultMutableTreeNode("Root");
DefaultMutableTreeNode child1 =
  new DefaultMutableTreeNode("Child 1");
root.add(child1);
DefaultMutableTreeNode child2 =
  new DefaultMutableTreeNode("Child 2");
root.add(child2);
JTree tree = new JTree(root);
someWindow.add(new JScrollPane(tree));
```

For complicated trees, linking all the nodes together by hand is tedious. So, you may want to first create a simple treelike data structure, then build nodes and hook them together automatically from that data structure.

DefaultMutableTreeNode Constructors

The `DefaultMutableTreeNode` class has three constructors:

public DefaultMutableTreeNode()
public DefaultMutableTreeNode(Object data)
public DefaultMutableTreeNode(Object data,
                                       boolean allowChildren)

All of these constructors create a basic tree node. The first constructor creates a node with no data; the second constructor lets you specify the data for the node. The third constructor allows you to explicitly specify whether the node can have children; by default, a tree node can have children.

Useful DefaultMutableTreeNode Methods

The `DefaultMutableTreeNode` class defines 50 methods to modify the node's parent and children nodes and to determine the relative location of the node in the tree hierarchy. Nine of the most common methods are listed below.

public void add(MutableTreeNode child)
public void remove(MutableTreeNode child)
These two methods add or remove a child node, respectively.

public Enumeration children()
The `children` method returns an `Enumeration` of the immediate children of the current node. If the node has no children, then `null` is returned.

public int getChildCount()
The `getChildCount` method returns the number of immediate children of the node.

public TreeNode getParent()
public TreeNode getRoot()
The `getParent` method returns the parent of the current node or `null` if the node has no parent. The `getRoot` method returns the root node of the tree containing the current node.

public boolean isLeaf()
public boolean isRoot()
These two methods determine if the node is a leaf node or a root node.

public void removeAllChildren()

This method removes all the children from the node.

In Listing 15.9, the data for the tree is initially defined in a nested data structure represented by arrays. As the tree is built, each array element is assigned to a tree node through the `processHierarchy` method. If the array element is itself another array (`instanceof Object[]`), then `processHierarchy` is recursively called to build the subtree. In Figure 15–5(a), the initial tree is shown, and in Figure 15–5(b), the tree is shown with the folders expanded.

Listing 15.9 `SimpleTree.java`

```
import java.awt.*;
import javax.swing.*;
import javax.swing.tree.*;

/** Example tree built out of DefaultMutableTreeNodes. */

public class SimpleTree extends JFrame {
  public static void main(String[] args) {
    new SimpleTree();
  }

  public SimpleTree() {
    super("Creating a Simple JTree");
    WindowUtilities.setNativeLookAndFeel();
    addWindowListener(new ExitListener());
    Container content = getContentPane();
    Object[] hierarchy =
      { "javax.swing",
        "javax.swing.border",
        "javax.swing.colorchooser",
        "javax.swing.event",
        "javax.swing.filechooser",
        new Object[] { "javax.swing.plaf",
                       "javax.swing.plaf.basic",
                       "javax.swing.plaf.metal",
                       "javax.swing.plaf.multi" },
        "javax.swing.table",
        new Object[] { "javax.swing.text",
                       new Object[] { "javax.swing.text.html",
                                      "javax.swing.text.html.parser" },
                       "javax.swing.text.rtf" },
        "javax.swing.tree",
        "javax.swing.undo" };
```

(continued)

Listing 15.9 `SimpleTree.java` *(continued)*

```java
    DefaultMutableTreeNode root = processHierarchy(hierarchy);
    JTree tree = new JTree(root);
    content.add(new JScrollPane(tree), BorderLayout.CENTER);
    setSize(275, 300);
    setVisible(true);
  }

  /** Small routine that will make a node out of the first entry
   *  in the array, then make nodes out of subsequent entries
   *  and make them child nodes of the first one. The process
   *  is repeated recursively for entries that are arrays.
   */

  private DefaultMutableTreeNode processHierarchy(
                                      Object[] hierarchy) {
    DefaultMutableTreeNode node =
      new DefaultMutableTreeNode(hierarchy[0]);
    DefaultMutableTreeNode child;
    for(int i=1; i<hierarchy.length; i++) {
      Object nodeSpecifier = hierarchy[i];
      if (nodeSpecifier instanceof Object[]) { //Node with children
        child = processHierarchy((Object[])nodeSpecifier);
      } else {
        child = new DefaultMutableTreeNode(nodeSpecifier); //Leaf
      }
      node.add(child);
    }
    return(node);
  }
}
```

(a) 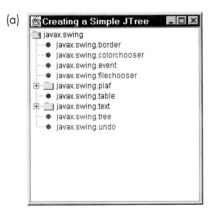   (b)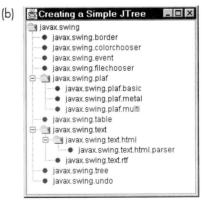

Figure 15–5 A `JTree` (a) before the folders are expanded and (b) after expansion of the nodes.

Before showing you how to dynamically modify the tree through JTree events, we first summarize the JTree constructors and methods.

JTree Constructors

The JTree class provides seven different constructors. The two most common constructors are listed below. The less common constructors allow you to supply the tree information in a Vector or Hashtable. Note that JTree also has a no-argument constructor, but in this case, the tree is automatically populated with a sample data set defined by Sun—useful only for initial testing.

> **public JTree(TreeNode root)**
> **public JTree(TreeModel model)**
> The first constructor creates a tree rooted at the specified node. The second constructor creates a tree according to the data in the specified tree model.

Useful JTree Methods

The JTree class is quite robust, defining over 110 methods. Many of these methods are for editing and working with selected branches of the tree, along with methods for firing TreeExpansionEvents. Instead of covering this huge list of methods, we refer you to the javax.swing.JTree API.

JTree Event Handling

To handle selection events, attach a TreeSelectionListener to the JTree. The TreeSelectionListener interface requires implementation of a single method: valueChanged. Once a TreeSelectionEvent occurs, you can determine the selected node through tree.getLastSelectedPathComponent and then cast the returned object to your node type (usually DefaultMutableTreeNode). The actual data contained in the node is extracted through getUserObject. However, if all you want is the node label, you can just call toString on the result of tree.getLastSelectedPathComponent.

In Listing 15.10 a simple tree is created where each child node has three children. A TreeSelectionListener is attached to the tree. When the user selects a node, the corresponding node's toString value is displayed in a text field below the tree, as shown in Figure 15–6(a) and (b).

Listing 15.10 `SelectableTree.java`

```java
import java.awt.*;
import javax.swing.*;
import javax.swing.tree.*;
import javax.swing.event.*;

/** JTree that reports selections by placing their string values
 *  in a JTextField.
 */

public class SelectableTree extends JFrame
                            implements TreeSelectionListener {
  public static void main(String[] args) {
    new SelectableTree();
  }

  private JTree tree;
  private JTextField currentSelectionField;

  public SelectableTree() {
    super("JTree Selections");
    WindowUtilities.setNativeLookAndFeel();
    addWindowListener(new ExitListener());
    Container content = getContentPane();
    DefaultMutableTreeNode root =
      new DefaultMutableTreeNode("Root");
    DefaultMutableTreeNode child;
    DefaultMutableTreeNode grandChild;
    for(int childIndex=1; childIndex<4; childIndex++) {
      child = new DefaultMutableTreeNode("Child " + childIndex);
      root.add(child);
      for(int grandChildIndex=1; grandChildIndex<4;
          grandChildIndex++) {
        grandChild =
          new DefaultMutableTreeNode("Grandchild " + childIndex +
                                     "." + grandChildIndex);
        child.add(grandChild);
      }
    }
    tree = new JTree(root);
    tree.addTreeSelectionListener(this);
    content.add(new JScrollPane(tree), BorderLayout.CENTER);
    currentSelectionField =
      new JTextField("Current Selection: NONE");
    content.add(currentSelectionField, BorderLayout.SOUTH);
    setSize(250, 275);
```

(continued)

Listing 15.10 `SelectableTree.java` *(continued)*

```
      setVisible(true);
   }

   public void valueChanged(TreeSelectionEvent event) {
      Object selection = tree.getLastSelectedPathComponent();
      if (selection != null) {
         currentSelectionField.setText
            ("Current Selection: " + selection.toString());
      }
   }
}
```

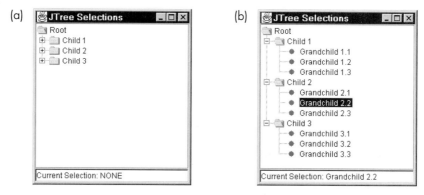

Figure 15–6 A selectable `JTree` (a) in an initial state and (b) after selection of a child node.

A `TreeExpansionEvent` occurs whenever a node in a tree is expanded or collapsed. You can handle `TreeExpansionEvents` by attaching a `TreeExpansion-Listener` to the `JTree`. The expansion listener defines two methods, `treeExpanded` and `treeCollapsed`, that are called when a node is expanded or collapsed, respectively. The `TreeExpansionEvent` has a single method, `getPath`, which returns a `Path` from the root node to the source node producing the event. Use `getLastPathComponent` to obtain the source node from the `Path`.

Custom Models and Dynamic Trees

A `JTree` uses a `TreeModel` to obtain the data from the underlying data structure. As with a `JList`, you can replace the model altogether, specifying how to extract data from a custom data structure. See Section 15.2 (JList) for an example of this general approach.

Technically, the `TreeModel` just keeps track of the root node in the tree and defines support methods for accessing node children and handling listeners. The nodes in a tree are interconnected in a linked manner. Thus, the common approach to create a custom tree is to leave the class implementing the `TreeModel` interface unchanged and, instead, create a custom `TreeNode`. The easiest approach is to inherit from `DefaultMutableTreeNode`, which provides the basic structure for a parent node and multiple children nodes.

Next, we define some of the useful `DefaultMutableTreeNode` methods and then show an example of how you might inherit from `DefaultMutableTreeNode` to create a custom tree node.

Useful DefaultMutableTreeNode Methods

The `DefaultMutableTreeNode` class defines over 50 methods for accessing related nodes in a general tree. References to the child nodes are stored in a `Vector` internal to the class. We summarize the more common methods below.

public void add(MutableTreeNode child)
public void remove(MutableTreeNode child)
These two methods add and remove a child node, respectively. The child is added to the end of the internal vector structure referring to the children.

public void insert(MutableTreeNode child, int index)
public void remove(int index)
The first method inserts a new child at the specified vector index, shifting up by one position all siblings in the vector with a higher or equal index. The greatest allowable index value is determined by the size of the internal vector; use `getChildCount` to determine the vector size and corresponding maximum index value. The second method removes the child at the specified index. If the index is outside the range of the vector, an `ArrayIndexOutOfBounds-Exception` is thrown.

public Enumeration children()
This method returns an `Enumeration` of the children of the current node.

public TreeNode getChildAt(int index)
public int getIndex(TreeNode child)
The `getChildAt` method returns the child node defined at the given index. An `ArrayIndexOutOfBoundsException` is thrown if the index value is outside the range of the internal vector storing the references to the children. Similarly, `getIndex` returns either the corresponding index of the child or -1 if the child is not a child of the current node.

public int getChildCount()

The `getChildCount` method returns the number of children of the node.

public TreeNode getParent()

This method returns the parent of the current node or `null` if the node has no parent.

public TreeNode[] getPath()

The `getPath` method returns an array of tree nodes representing the path from the root node to the current node.

public TreeNode getRoot()

This method returns the root node of the tree.

public boolean isLeaf()
public boolean isRoot()

The first method, `isLeaf`, returns `true` if the node is a leaf (no children); otherwise, it returns `false`. Similarly, the second method, `isRoot`, returns `true` if the node is the root of the tree; otherwise it returns `false`.

You might want to build a tree dynamically as user input is received, for example, to expand a folder—a common case. So, you would want to inherit from `Default-MutableTreeNode` to create a custom node so that you don't have to explicitly lay out each node in the tree beforehand. In that case, you would provide an algorithm that describes the children of a given node but actually generates children only for those instances when the user expands the folder.

In Listing 15.11, the tree represents a "numbered outline," where each node describes a separate part in the outline. The root is 1, the first-level children are 1.1, 1.2, 1.3, etc., the second-level children are 1.1.1, 1.1.2, etc., and so forth. The children are built dynamically, and the actual number of children of each node is determined by a command-line argument to the program.

The key to building a `JTree` dynamically is to ensure that `getChildCount` is called before any of the children are actually retrieved. Thus, you must define a flag indicating whether the children were built earlier. The approach is to simply wait until `getChildCount` is called, and then, if the flag is `false`, build the children and add them to the node. To keep the tree from trying to count the children (and subsequently build their nodes) to determine which nodes are leaf nodes, override `isLeaf` to always return `false`. This approach is shown in `OutlineNode`, Listing 15.12, which builds the children nodes dynamically. The result is shown in Figure 15–7.

Listing 15.11 `DynamicTree.java`

```java
import java.awt.*;
import javax.swing.*;

/** Example tree that builds child nodes on the fly.
 *  See OutlineNode for details.
 */

public class DynamicTree extends JFrame {
  public static void main(String[] args) {
    int n = 5; // Number of children to give each node.
    if (args.length > 0) {
      try {
        n = Integer.parseInt(args[0]);
      } catch(NumberFormatException nfe) {
        System.out.println(
          "Can't parse number; using default of " + n);
      }
    }
    new DynamicTree(n);
  }

  public DynamicTree(int n) {
    super("Creating a Dynamic JTree");
    WindowUtilities.setNativeLookAndFeel();
    addWindowListener(new ExitListener());
    Container content = getContentPane();
    JTree tree = new JTree(new OutlineNode(1, n));
    content.add(new JScrollPane(tree), BorderLayout.CENTER);
    setSize(300, 475);
    setVisible(true);
  }
}
```

Listing 15.12 `OutlineNode.java`

```java
import java.awt.*;
import javax.swing.*;
import javax.swing.tree.*;

/** Simple TreeNode that builds children on the fly.
 *  The key idea is that getChildCount is always called before
 *  any actual children are requested. That way, getChildCount
 *  builds the children if they don't already exist.
```

(continued)

Listing 15.12 `OutlineNode.java` *(continued)*

```
 *    <P>
 *    In this case, it just builds an "outline" tree. I.e.,
 *    if the root is current node is "x", the children are
 *    "x.0", "x.1", "x.2", and "x.3".
 *    <P>
 */

public class OutlineNode extends DefaultMutableTreeNode {
  private boolean areChildrenDefined = false;
  private int outlineNum;
  private int numChildren;

  public OutlineNode(int outlineNum, int numChildren) {
    this.outlineNum = outlineNum;
    this.numChildren = numChildren;
  }

  public boolean isLeaf() {
    return(false);
  }

  public int getChildCount() {
    if (!areChildrenDefined) {
      defineChildNodes();
    }
    return(super.getChildCount());
  }

  private void defineChildNodes() {
    // You must set the flag before defining children if you
    // use "add" for the new children. Otherwise, you get an
    // infinite recursive loop since add results in a call
    // to getChildCount. However, you could use "insert" in such
    // a case.
    areChildrenDefined = true;
    for(int i=0; i<numChildren; i++) {
      add(new OutlineNode(i+1, numChildren));
    }
  }

  public String toString() {
    TreeNode parent = getParent();
    if (parent == null) {
      return(String.valueOf(outlineNum));
    } else {
      return(parent.toString() + "." + outlineNum);
    }
  }
}
```

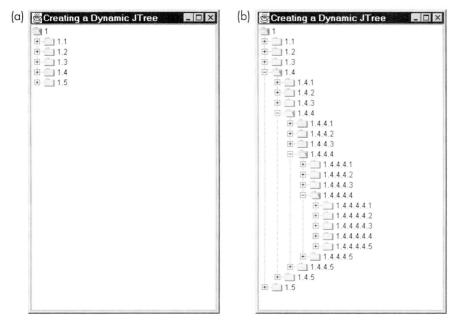

Figure 15–7 A custom `TreeNode` permits dynamic growth of the tree: (a) an initial tree, (b) nodes dynamically generated after user expands a node.

Icon Replacement at the Tree Nodes

A common enhancement to a default `JTree` is to simply change the three icons displayed for an unexpanded internal node (i.e., nonleaf), an expanded internal node, and a leaf node. To replace the `ImageIcons` displayed by the `JTree`, simply create an instance of `DefaultTreeCellRenderer` and then call `setOpenIcon`, `setClosedIcon`, and `setLeafIcon` either with the `Icon` of interest (usually an `ImageIcon` made from a small image file) or `null` to just turn off the node icons. Then, associate this cell renderer with the tree through `setCellRenderer`.

In Listing 15.13, three separate trees are created: in the first tree, the default node icons are displayed; in the second tree, the node icons are set to `null`; and not displayed; and in the third tree, the nodes are represented by custom icons. The three trees are shown in Figure 15–8.

Listing 15.13 `CustomIcons.java`

```java
import java.awt.*;
import java.awt.event.*;
import javax.swing.*;
import javax.swing.tree.*;

/** JTree with missing or custom icons at the tree nodes. */

public class CustomIcons extends JFrame {
  public static void main(String[] args) {
    new CustomIcons();
  }

  private Icon customOpenIcon =
          new ImageIcon("images/Circle_1.gif");
  private Icon customClosedIcon =
          new ImageIcon("images/Circle_2.gif");
  private Icon customLeafIcon =
          new ImageIcon("images/Circle_3.gif");

  public CustomIcons() {
    super("JTree Selections");
    WindowUtilities.setNativeLookAndFeel();
    addWindowListener(new ExitListener());
    Container content = getContentPane();
    content.setLayout(new FlowLayout());
    DefaultMutableTreeNode root =
      new DefaultMutableTreeNode("Root");
    DefaultMutableTreeNode child;
    DefaultMutableTreeNode grandChild;
    for(int childIndex=1; childIndex<4; childIndex++) {
      child = new DefaultMutableTreeNode("Child " + childIndex);
      root.add(child);
      for(int grandChildIndex=1; grandChildIndex<4;
                                 grandChildIndex++) {
        grandChild =
          new DefaultMutableTreeNode("Grandchild " +
                                     childIndex +
                                     "." + grandChildIndex);
        child.add(grandChild);
      }
    }
```

(continued)

Listing 15.13 `CustomIcons.java` *(continued)*

```
    JTree tree1 = new JTree(root);
    tree1.expandRow(1); // Expand children to illustrate leaf icons.
    JScrollPane pane1 = new JScrollPane(tree1);
    pane1.setBorder(
            BorderFactory.createTitledBorder("Standard Icons"));
    content.add(pane1);

    JTree tree2 = new JTree(root);
    // Expand children to illustrate leaf icons.
    tree2.expandRow(2);
    DefaultTreeCellRenderer renderer2 =
                              new DefaultTreeCellRenderer();
    renderer2.setOpenIcon(null);
    renderer2.setClosedIcon(null);
    renderer2.setLeafIcon(null);
    tree2.setCellRenderer(renderer2);
    JScrollPane pane2 = new JScrollPane(tree2);
    pane2.setBorder(
            BorderFactory.createTitledBorder("No Icons"));
    content.add(pane2);

    JTree tree3 = new JTree(root);
    // Expand children to illustrate leaf icons.
    tree3.expandRow(3);
    DefaultTreeCellRenderer renderer3 =
                              new DefaultTreeCellRenderer();
    renderer3.setOpenIcon(customOpenIcon);
    renderer3.setClosedIcon(customClosedIcon);
    renderer3.setLeafIcon(customLeafIcon);
    tree3.setCellRenderer(renderer3);
    JScrollPane pane3 = new JScrollPane(tree3);
    pane3.setBorder(
            BorderFactory.createTitledBorder("Custom Icons"));
    content.add(pane3);

    pack();
    setVisible(true);
  }
}
```

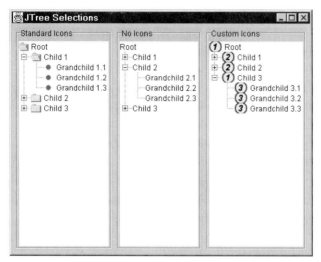

Figure 15–8 An example of customizing the node icons in a JTree.

15.4 JTable

A JTable provides a way to display rows and columns of data in a two-dimensional display. It is by far the most complex component available in the Swing API. A JTable is actually based upon three separate models: a table model, a column model, and a list selection model. The table model maintains the data in the table cells, the column model controls addition and removal of columns in the table, and the list selection model is responsible for the selection of rows in the table (selection of columns is controlled by the column model).

Because of the complexity of a JTable, each of the three table models has a default implementation in the javax.swing.table package. In this section, we examine the default and custom table models. For detailed coverage of column models and selection models, see *Core Java Foundation Classes* by Kim Topley.

Simple JTable

The simplest way to create a JTable is to supply the constructor with a two-dimensional array of strings for the table cells and a one-dimensional array of strings for the column names. For example, the following code creates a simple table with N columns and M rows,

```
String[][] data = { { "Cell (1,1)", ..., "Cell (1,N)" },
               ...
              { "Cell (M,1)", ..., "Cell (M,N)" } };
String[] columnNames = { "Column 1", ..., "Column N" };
JTable table = new JTable(data, columnNames);
```

Supplying an Object array for the column names and cell data is also legal because a JTable renders each object as a JLabel based upon the object's toString method.

Like a JList and a JTree, a table is most often placed inside a scroll pane. Without a scroll pane, the column labels are not displayed. The preferred size of the scroll pane is determined by the viewport size of the table, which, by default, is 450 x 400 pixels. You can change the default size of the viewport by providing a Dimension object to the table's setPreferredScrollableViewportSize method.

Core Note

The column labels for a JTable *are not displayed unless the table is placed in a* JScrollPane.

JTable Constructors

The JTable class defines seven constructors. In general, if data for the tables cells is not provided, then the cells are populated with null values. If not specified, column labels follow standard spreadsheet conventions (A, B, C, ..., AA, BB, CC, ...). We outline the five most common JTable constructors below. In all but the last constructor, the table is implemented with a DefaultTableModel, Default-ColumnModel, and DefaultListSelectionModel.

public JTable()
This constructor creates an empty table with an internal DefaultTable-Model, DefaultColumnModel, and DefaultListSelectionModel. Use addRow and addColumn to populate the table. By default, every cell in the table is editable.

public JTable(int rows, int columns)
This constructor is identical to the default class constructor except that the DefaultTableModel contains the specified number of rows and columns (each cell value is null).

public JTable(Object[][] data, Object[] columnNames)
This constructor lets you specify the table data and column names. Usually, the data and column names are strings and are rendered as JLabels when displayed. The use of toString is the default rendering for the table data; if a data type does not have a defined renderer to display the information, the toString method is called and the result is displayed in a JLabel. Note that you can take advantage of other cell renderers to display Boolean, Image-Icon, and Number objects in the table cells as described later in this section.

public JTable(Vector data, Vector columnNames)

This constructor allows you to define the table data and column names in `Vectors`. Each element of the data vector should itself be a `Vector` of `Objects` representing a single row in the table.

public JTable(TableModel model)

This constructor creates a `JTable` with cells and columns defined by the `TableModel` argument. Most often, the table model is based either on `AbstractTableModel` or `DefaultTableModel`, both of which fire `TableModelEvents`. The table also contains a `DefaultColumnModel` and `DefaultListSelectionModel`.

Useful JTable Methods

`JTable` defines over 125 methods, but many of these methods are mirrored by one of the three models from which a `JTable` is built: the `TableModel`, `TableColumnModel`, and `ListSelectionModel`. In fact, a reference to each of these three models is defined as a `protected` field member in the `JTable` class, and many of the class methods simply call the matching method in the corresponding model. We describe only a few of the methods below.

public TableModel getModel()
public void setModel(TableModel tableModel)

These two methods return and set the `TableModel`, respectively. The `TableModel` contains the data that is displayed in the `JTable` cells.

public TableColumnModel getColumnModel()
public setColumnModel(TableColumnModel columnModel)

These two methods retrieve or set the `TableColumnModel` for the table, respectively. By default, the table column model is automatically created. If your table design requires you to programmatically move your columns, you should write own custom column model. The `TableColumnModel` also controls selection of a single or multiple columns. For details, see the `javax.swing.table` API.

public ListSelectionModel getSelectionModel()
public void setSelectionModel(
ListSelectionModel selectionModel)

The `getListSelectionModel` method returns the table selection model, and the `setListSelectionModel` method sets the table selection model. The `ListSelectionModel` is used by both `JTable` and `JList` (see Section 15.2 for `JList`) and supports single selection, single-interval selection, and multiple-interval selection of cells. Whenever the user changes the selected rows, a `ListSelectionEvent` is placed on the event queue and later dispatched to the table's `valueChanged` method. Use `getSelectedRow` or `getSelectedRows` to determine which rows the user selected. Also, note that a `TableColumnModel` can support a `ListSelectionModel` for selecting columns. See the `javax.swing` API for additional information on the `ListSelectionModel`.

public int getRowHeight()
public void setRowHeight(int height)
public int getRowHeight(int row)
public void setRowHeight(int row, int height)

The first two methods return or set the row height in pixels. The default row height is 16 pixels. In JDK 1.3, methods were added to return or set the row height for an individual row.

public int getRowMargin()
public void setRowMargin(int margin)

The `getRowMargin` and `setRowMargin` methods return or set the pixel width (margin) between table rows. The default margin is one pixel. The column margin is specified in the `TableColumnModel` by `setColumnMargin`.

public void setShowGrid(boolean show)
public boolean getShowHorizontalLines()
public void setShowHorizontalLines(boolean show)
public boolean getShowVerticalLines()
public void setShowVerticalLines(boolean show)

The `setShowGrid` method turns off or on the display of the horizontal and vertical grid lines in the table. The color of the lines is determined by the installed UI delegate. The remaining four methods allow you to set and get the display status for the horizontal and vertical lines in the table.

Listing 15.14 creates a simple `JTable` with 4 columns and 15 rows. The height of each row is determined by the default font size of the text, and the width of each column is determined by equal division of viewport width among the four columns. The result for this simple `JTable` is shown in Figure 15–9.

Listing 15.14 JTableSimpleExample.java

```java
import java.awt.*;
import javax.swing.*;

/** Simple JTable example that uses a String array for the
 *  table header and table data.
 */

public class JTableSimpleExample extends JFrame {
  public static void main(String[] args) {
    new JTableSimpleExample();
  }

  private final int COLUMNS = 4;
  private final int ROWS = 15;
  private JTable sampleJTable;

  public JTableSimpleExample() {
    super("Creating a Simple JTable");
    WindowUtilities.setNativeLookAndFeel();
    addWindowListener(new ExitListener());
    Container content = getContentPane();

    String[]   columnNames = buildColumnNames(COLUMNS);
    String[][] tableCells = buildTableCells(ROWS, COLUMNS);

    sampleJTable = new JTable(tableCells, columnNames);
    JScrollPane tablePane = new JScrollPane(sampleJTable);
    content.add(tablePane, BorderLayout.CENTER);
    setSize(450,150);
    setVisible(true);
  }

  private String[] buildColumnNames(int columns) {
    String[] header = new String[columns];
    for(int i=0; i<columns; i++) {
      header[i] = "Column " + i;
    }
    return(header);
  }
  private String[][] buildTableCells(int rows, int columns) {
    String[][] cells = new String[rows][columns];
    for(int i=0; i<rows ; i++) {
      for(int j=0; j<columns; j++ ) {
        cells[i][j] = "Row " + i + ", Col " + j;
      }
    }
    return(cells);
  }
}
```

Simple JTable				
Column 0	Column 1	Column 2	Column 3	
Row 0, Col 0	Row 0, Col 1	Row 0, Col 2	Row 0, Col 3	▲
Row 1, Col 0	Row 1, Col 1	Row 1, Col 2	Row 1, Col 3	
Row 2, Col 0	Row 2, Col 1	Row 2, Col 2	Row 2, Col 3	
Row 3, Col 0	Row 3, Col 1	Row 3, Col 2	Row 3, Col 3	
Row 4, Col 0	Row 4, Col 1	Row 4, Col 2	Row 4, Col 3	
Row 5, Col 0	Row 5, Col 1	Row 5, Col 2	Row 5, Col 3	
Row 6, Col 0	Row 6, Col 1	Row 6, Col 2	Row 6, Col 3	
Row 7, Col 0	Row 7, Col 1	Row 7, Col 2	Row 7, Col 3	
Row 8, Col 0	Row 8, Col 1	Row 8, Col 2	Row 8, Col 3	▼

Figure 15–9 A simple JTable placed in a scrollable viewport.

Table Data Models

When a table is displayed, the data is mapped from the data model (data structure) to the cells in the JTable. To display the data correctly, the data model must implement the TableModel interface. The interface defines methods for determining the number of row and columns in the model, for changing data values in the model, and for adding or removing event listeners to the model. In practice, most programmers don't implement the TableModel interface directly but start with Abstract-TableModel, which inherits from TableModel and adds management of event listeners and methods for firing TableModelEvents. To use AbstractTableModel you must provide concrete methods for

- public int getRowCount()
- public int getColumnCount()
- public Object getValueAt(int row, int column)

The underlying structure of your data model will determine your implementation of these three methods.

The AbstractTableModel class also provides a concrete implementation of the setValueAt method to support noneditable data structures. Because setValueAt does not modify the data, the isCellEditable method always returns false.

As a convenience, the Swing API also includes a DefaultTableModel that directly inherits from AbstractTableModel and provides implementation of all the abstract methods in the superclass. DefaultTableModel is a vector-based data structure; the model is a Vector of rows, where each row is a Vector of data cells. To accommodate the internal data structure, arrays or vectors passed into the DefaultTableModel constructor are reformatted into the underlying vector model. For very large tables you may observe a performance hit when the DefaultTableModel object is first initialized with the data. The DefaultTable-Model always returns true for isCellEditable; therefore, by default the user is able to select any cell in the table and modify the contents.

Core Note

In the `AbstractTableModel` *class,* `isCellEditable` *always returns* `false`; *whereas in* `DefaultTableModel`, *the method always returns* `true`.

DefaultTableModel Constructors

The `DefaultTableModel` class defines six constructors. The three most common constructors are described below.

public DefaultTableModel(Object[][] data, Object[] columnNames)

This constructor creates a `DefaultTableModel` where the tables cells are defined by the two-dimensional array `data` and the names for the columns are provided by the one-dimensional array `columnNames`. Often, the cell data and column names are represented by `String`s but may be other objects (images, check boxes) if the proper cell renderers are installed. We discuss "Table Cell Renderers" later in this section.

public DefaultTableModel(Vector data, Vector columnNames)

This constructor accepts the table cell data in a `Vector`, where each element in the vector represents a row within the table and each row is represented by a vector of cells. The column names for the table are defined in the `columnNames` vector.

public DefaultTableModel(Vector columnNames, int numRows)

This constructor create a table model with the given column names and number of rows. Each row in the table is a vector equal in size to the number of columns. The data for the rows is initially set to `null`.

Useful DefaultTableModel Methods

`DefaultTableModel` supports methods to add or remove rows and columns to or from the data model, as well as to change cell values. The most common methods are summarized below:

public void addColumn(Object columnName)
public void addColumn(Object columnName,
                       Object[] columnData)
public void addColumn(Object columnName,
                       Vector columnData)

The first method adds a column with the given name to the table model. The corresponding row cells are filled with null values. The second and third methods also add a column to the table model, but you can also specify the data for the column either as an array or vector.

public void addRow(Object[] rowData)
public void addRow(Vector rowData)
public void insertRow(int row, Object[] rowData)
public void insertRow(int row, Vector rowData)

The first two addRow methods add a row to the data model, specified either as an array or vector. The row is appended *after* the last row in the data model. The third and fourth methods specify the row in the data model in which to insert the data. If rowData is null, the row is populated with null values. If you specify a row outside the range of the internal table model vector, an ArrayIndexOutOfBoundsException is thrown.

public void removeRow(int row)

The removeRow method removes the specified row from the table model. If the row value is less than zero or greater than the number of rows in the model, an ArrayIndexOutOfBoundsException is thrown.

public int getColumnCount()
public int getRowCount()

These two methods return the number of columns and rows in the table model, respectively.

public String getColumnName(int column)

This method returns the toString description of the specified column. If the column name is null, then a letter (following spreadsheet naming conventions, A, B, C, ..., AA, BB, ...) is returned. If the column value is less than zero or greater than or equal to the number of columns in the model, then an ArrayIndexOutOfBoundsException is thrown.

public Object getValueAt(int row, int column)
public setValueAt(Object value, int row, int column)

These two methods return and set the cell value at the specified row and column, respectively. After changing the cell value, the setValueAt method fires a TableModelEvent to update the display. An ArrayIndexOutOf-BoundsException is thrown if the row or column is outside the valid range of the table model.

public boolean isCellEditable(int row, int column)

For the DefaultTableModel, the isCellEditable method returns true regardless of the row and column value; every cell in a DefaultTableModel is editable.

Listing 15.15 provides an example of using the DefaultTableModel. The table contents are derived from the JavaLocationCollection presented earlier in Listing 15.5. Each JavaLocation object defines the following information for each region named Java: the country in which the region is located, the country flag (GIF file), and a comment describing any neighboring landmark cities. In this example, the DefaultTableModel is initially empty; later, the columns are added as needed to the model by a call to addColumn. After the columns are added to the table model, each row is subsequently added to the table model by a call to getRowData to build a vector from the JavaLocation information, followed by a call to addRow to add the new row to the table. In addition to the city and country, the table includes a column for the country flag (ImageIcon) and a column containing a boolean field to indicate whether the user has visited the city.

The result of Listing 15.15 is shown in Figure 15–10. Notice that each cell contains the String representation of the corresponding object. In the next section we explain how to take advantage of built-in cell renderers to display the ImageIcon as an image and Boolean as a check box in the table.

Listing 15.15 DefaultTableExample.java

```java
import java.util.Vector;
import javax.swing.*;
import javax.swing.table.*;

/** JTable that uses the DefaultTableModel, which permits
 *  adding rows and columns programmatically.
 */

public class DefaultTableExample extends JTable {

  private String[] columnNames =
    { "Flag", "City", "Country", "Comment", "Visited" };

  public DefaultTableExample() {
    this(new DefaultTableModel());
  }
```

(continued)

Listing 15.15 `DefaultTableExample.java` *(continued)*

```
  public DefaultTableExample(DefaultTableModel model) {
    super(model);

    JavaLocationCollection collection =
      new JavaLocationCollection();
    JavaLocation[] locations = collection.getLocations();

    // Set up the column labels and data for the table model.
    int i;
    for(i=0; i<columnNames.length; i++ ) {
      model.addColumn(columnNames[i]);
    }
    for(i=0; i<locations.length; i++) {
      model.addRow(getRowData(locations[i]));
    }
  }

  private Vector getRowData(JavaLocation location) {
    Vector vector = new Vector();
    vector.add(new ImageIcon(location.getFlagFile()));
    vector.add("Java");
    vector.add(location.getCountry());
    vector.add(location.getComment());
    vector.add(new Boolean(false));
    return(vector);
  }

  public static void main(String[] args) {
    WindowUtilities.setNativeLookAndFeel();
    WindowUtilities.openInJFrame(
       new JScrollPane(new DefaultTableExample()), 600, 150,
                       "Using a DefaultTableModel");
  }
}
```

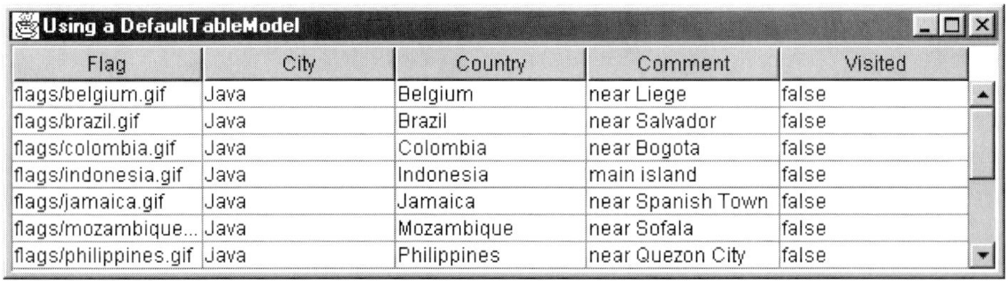

Flag	City	Country	Comment	Visited
flags/belgium.gif	Java	Belgium	near Liege	false
flags/brazil.gif	Java	Brazil	near Salvador	false
flags/colombia.gif	Java	Colombia	near Bogota	false
flags/indonesia.gif	Java	Indonesia	main island	false
flags/jamaica.gif	Java	Jamaica	near Spanish Town	false
flags/mozambique...	Java	Mozambique	near Sofala	false
flags/philippines.gif	Java	Philippines	near Quezon City	false

Figure 15–10 A table built with the `DefaultTableModel`.

Table Cell Renderers

Typically, the table renders an object in a table by using a JLabel. However, for certain classes of objects, the Java 2 Platform provides additional cell renderers to display the object in a more appropriate format. Specifically, default table cell renderers are already defined for the following class types:

- Boolean—Displayed by a JCheckBox.
- Date—Displayed by a JLabel after the date is formatted with the DateFormat class.
- ImageIcon—Displayed as an image by a JLabel.
- Number—Displayed by a JLabel after the number is formatted with the NumberFormat class.
- Object—Displayed by a JLabel after a call to the toString method.

To take advantage of the default cell renderers, you must override the getColumnClass method in DefaultTableModel to provide explicit class information about the type of objects contained in each column. By default, getColumnClass returns Object.class, which always results in the object being rendered as a JLabel.

The standard approach for enabling the default cell renderers is to create a custom table model that inherits from DefaultTableModel and then to override getColumnClass to return the true underlying class of the objects. For example,

```
public Class getColumnClass(int column) {
  return (getValueAt(0, column).getClass());
}
```

This method returns the class of object in the first cell of the specified column. Here, the assumption is that all objects in the column are of the same class, or at least, the objects have a common superclass that getColumnClass can return. In addition, a renderer for this common superclass needs to be installed in the table.

In Listing 15.16, CustomTableExample inherits from the previous example, DefaultTableExample, and defines a new constructor to instantiate an instance of CustomTableModel (Listing 15.17) as the data model for the table. Here, CustomTableModel inherits from DefaultTableModel and overrides getColumnClass to take advantage of the default cell renderers. In addition, CustomTableModel overrides isCellEditable to restrict the user to modification of data only in the Comment and Visited columns. The result is shown in Figure 15–11.

To improve the table layout, explicitly set the pixel width of each column by using setMinWidth, setMaxWidth, or setPreferredWidth. By default, the preferred width of a column is 75 pixels and the minimum width is 15 pixels. To set the column width, use

```
TableColumn column = table.getColumn(columnName);
column.setPreferredWidth(numPixels);
```

Because of a Swing bug in some JDK releases, after setting the column sizes, you must call

```
table.sizeColumnsToFit(JTable.AUTO_RESIZE_OFF);
```

to lay out the columns correctly to the viewport. TableColumn also defines a set-Width method; however, the column width does not persist when the table is subsequently resized.

Listing 15.16 CustomTableExample.java

```java
import javax.swing.*;
import javax.swing.table.*;

/** JTable that uses a CustomTableModel to correctly render
 *  the table cells that contain images and boolean values.
 */

public class CustomTableExample extends DefaultTableExample {

  public CustomTableExample() {
    super(new CustomTableModel());
    setCellSizes();
  }

  private void setCellSizes() {
    setRowHeight(50);
    getColumn("Flag").setMaxWidth(55);
    getColumn("City").setPreferredWidth(60);
    getColumn("Country").setMinWidth(80);
    getColumn("Comment").setMinWidth(150);
    // Call to resize columns in viewport (bug).
    sizeColumnsToFit(JTable.AUTO_RESIZE_OFF);
  }

  public static void main(String[] args) {
    WindowUtilities.setNativeLookAndFeel();
    WindowUtilities.openInJFrame(
      new JScrollPane(new CustomTableExample()), 525, 255,
                      "Using a CustomTableModel");
  }
}
```

Listing 15.17 CustomTableModel.java

```
import javax.swing.table.*;

/** A custom DefaultTableModel that returns the class
 *  type for the default cell renderers to use. The user is
 *  restricted to editing only the Comment and Visited columns.
 */

public class CustomTableModel extends DefaultTableModel {

  public Class getColumnClass(int column) {
    return(getValueAt(0, column).getClass());
  }

  // Only permit edit of "Comment" and "Visited" columns.
  public boolean isCellEditable(int row, int column) {
    return(column==3 || column==4);
  }
}
```

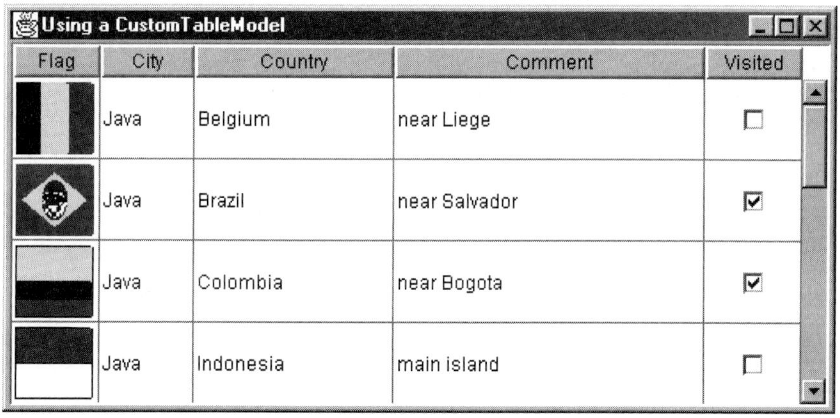

Figure 15-11 A table with cell renderers to display images and check boxes. The column widths are explicitly set to override default values.

Table Event Handling

Table events are not directly handled by listeners attached to the JTable. Instead, events are handled by listeners attached to one or more of the three available models in a table: TableModel, TableColumnModel, and ListSelectionModel. To handle changes to cell values, attach a TableModelListener to the table's

TableModel. The TableModelListener defines a single method, tableChanged, which receives a TableModelEvent when the data in the table is modified (observed when the user presses the Enter key or the cell loses focus). From the TableModelEvent you can call getColumn and getFirstRow or getLastRow to determine which table cell caused the event. Remember that a DefaultTableModel always returns true for isCellEditable, so unless you use default or custom cell editors, every cell in the table is editable and the default cell editor treats the cell as text that is rendered as a JLabel.

When the user presses the Enter key or moves to a different table cell, a TableModelEvent is fired. To handle this event, attach a TableModelListener to the TableModel, as below.

```
tablemodel.addTableModelListener(
  new TableModelListner() {
    public void tableChanged(TableModelEvent event) {
      int row = event.getFirstRow();
      int column = event.getColumn();
      ...
    }
  });
```

Once you know which cell caused the event, you can retrieve the data through getValueAt(row, column) and, similarly, set the data in a table cell through setValueAt(row, column). The getValueAt method returns an Object, so you may need to cast the object to the appropriate subclass type. The data changes are actually made to the structure of the underlying data model. So, to update the JTable display, you must fire a TableModelEvent that refreshes the display.

The AbstractTableModel class, from which TableModel inherits, provides seven helper methods for firing events. The two most commonly used methods are fireTableCellUpdated(row, column), which updates an individual cell, and fireTableDataChanged(), which updates the whole table.

The Java 2 Platform also defines TableColumnModelEvents for changes to the TableColumnModel, and ListSelectionEvents for changes to the List-SelectionModel.

Listing 15.18 creates a table from which the user can enter the number of books to purchase. The class imports the javax.swing.event package and attaches an event listener to the table model. When the user changes the number of desired books, the attached TableModelListener receives the TableModelEvent and a new total cost is calculated for the purchase. Once the calculation is completed and the data model updated, a TableModelEvent is fired to update the display. Figure 15–12 shows the results.

Much of the code in the event handler is for converting the data from Strings to numerical values and back again. If you are unfamiliar with the DecimalFormat class, see the java.text.DecimalFormat API.

Listing 15.18 `JTableEvents.java`

```java
import java.awt.*;
import java.text.DecimalFormat;
import javax.swing.*;
import javax.swing.event.*;
import javax.swing.table.*;

/** A JTable that responds to TableModelEvents and
 *  updates other cells in the table, based on user input.
 */

public class JTableEvents extends JFrame {
  private final int COL_COST    = 1;
  private final int COL_QTY     = 2;
  private final int COL_TOTAL   = 3;
  private final int ROW_LAST    = 5;
  private DecimalFormat df = new DecimalFormat("$####.##");
  private JTable sampleJTable;
  private DefaultTableModel tableModel;

  public static void main(String[] args) {
    new JTableEvents();
  }

  public JTableEvents() {
    super("Using TableEvents");
    WindowUtilities.setNativeLookAndFeel();
    addWindowListener(new ExitListener());
    Container content = getContentPane();

    String[] columnNames = { "Book", "Cost", "Qty", "Total" };

    final Object[][] data = {
      {"Core Web Programming", "$ 0.99", "0", "$0.00"},
      {"Core Servlets and JavaServer Pages",
                              "$34.39", "0", "$0.00"},
      {"Core Swing",          "$39.99", "0", "$0.00"},
      {"Core Java, Volume I", "$31.49", "0", "$0.00"},
      {"Core Java, Volume II", "$34.39", "0", "$0.00"},
      {null, null,                "Grand:", "$0.00"} };
    tableModel = new DefaultTableModel(data, columnNames);
    tableModel.addTableModelListener(
      new TableModelListener() {
        int row, col;
        int quantity;
        float cost, subTotal, grandTotal;
```

(continued)

Listing 15.18 `JTableEvents.java` *(continued)*

```java
      public void tableChanged(TableModelEvent event) {
        row = event.getFirstRow();
        col = event.getColumn();
        // Only update table if a new book quantity entered.
        if (col == COL_QTY) {
          try {
            cost = getFormattedCellValue(row, COL_COST);
            quantity = (int)getFormattedCellValue(row, COL_QTY);
            subTotal = quantity * cost;

            // Update row total.
            tableModel.setValueAt(df.format(subTotal),
                                  row, COL_TOTAL);
            // Update grand total.
            grandTotal =0;
            for(int row=0; row<data.length-1; row++) {
             grandTotal += getFormattedCellValue(row, COL_TOTAL);
            }
            tableModel.setValueAt(df.format(grandTotal),
                                  ROW_LAST,COL_TOTAL);
            tableModel.fireTableDataChanged();
          } catch (NumberFormatException nfe) {
              // Send error message to user.
              JOptionPane.showMessageDialog(
                          JTableEvents.this,
                          "Illegal value entered!");
          }
        }
      }

      private float getFormattedCellValue(int row, int col) {
        String value = (String)tableModel.getValueAt(row, col);
        return(Float.parseFloat(value.replace('$',' ')));
      }
    });

    sampleJTable = new JTable(tableModel);
    setColumnAlignment(sampleJTable.getColumnModel());
    JScrollPane tablePane = new JScrollPane(sampleJTable);

    content.add(tablePane, BorderLayout.CENTER);
    setSize(460,150);
    setVisible(true);
  }
```

(continued)

Listing 15.18 `JTableEvents.java` *(continued)*

```
// Right-align all but the first column.
private void setColumnAlignment(TableColumnModel tcm) {
  TableColumn column;
  DefaultTableCellRenderer renderer =
    new DefaultTableCellRenderer();
  for(int i=1; i<tcm.getColumnCount(); i++) {
    column = tcm.getColumn(i);
    renderer.setHorizontalAlignment(SwingConstants.RIGHT);
    column.setCellRenderer(renderer);
  }
}
}
```

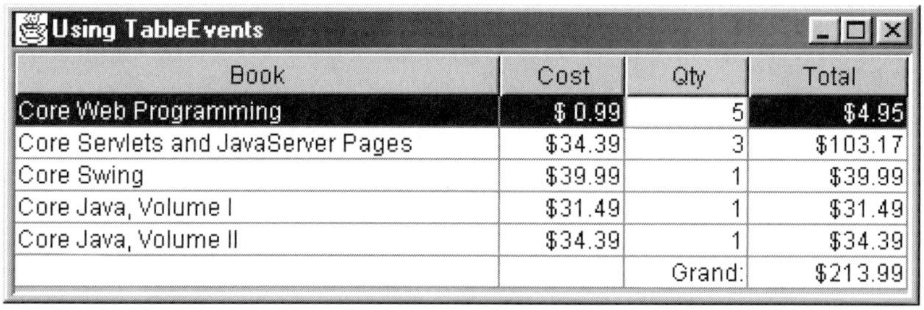

Figure 15-12 A table that calculates the grand total cost for a purchase order.

15.5 Swing Component Printing

The Java 2 Platform supports high-quality printing through classes in the `java.awt.print` package. This section describes how to use this printing package to print Swing components. In a sense, printing is little more than painting the component on the `Graphics2D` object and rendering the graphics on the printer. When printing in JDK 1.2, you must first globally turn off double buffering before painting the component. In JDK 1.3, the printing model changed and a `print` method was added to the `JComponent` class to automatically take care of double buffering. In the following sections, we look at the basics of printing and explain the importance of disabling double buffering before printing in JDK 1.2. Then, we illustrate the approach to printing in JDK 1.3.

Printing Basics

Two steps are required to print: setting up the print job and rendering graphics on the printer.

Setting Up the Print Job

Setting up a print job is always done in the same manner: get a `PrinterJob` object, pass a `Printable` object to the `setPrintable` method, call `printDialog` to open an operating-system-specific print dialog, and finally, call `print` on the `PrinterJob`. Figure 15–13 shows a representative print dialog on Windows 98. The user can select Cancel from the print dialog, so you should check the return value from `printDialog` before calling `print`.

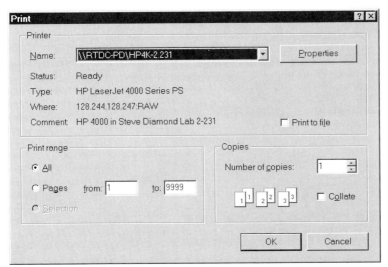

Figure 15–13 A typical display after `printDialog` is called.

The typical code for setting up a print job is:

```
PrinterJob printJob = PrinterJob.getPrinterJob();
printJob.setPrintable(this);
if (printJob.printDialog())
  try {
    printJob.print();
  } catch(PrinterException pe) {
      System.out.println("Error printing: " + pe);
}
```

Rendering Graphics on the Printer

The `Printable` that is passed to `setPrintable` must implement the `print` method that describes how to send the drawing to the printer. The print method accepts three arguments: the `Graphics` object, the `PageFormat`, and the `pageIndex`. `PrinterJob` calls the print method to render the graphics object according to the specified page format, where `pageIndex` specifies which page (in the document) to print. `PrinterJob` initially calls `print` with a `pageIndex` of 0. You should return `PAGE_EXISTS` if you have printed that page. Return `NO_SUCH_PAGE` to indicate that no pages are left.

In general, the first step is to decide what to do for different pages of your print job, since Java repeatedly calls `print` with higher and higher page indexes until `print` returns `NO_SUCH_PAGE`. In the specific case of printing the GUI interface, however, you basically print a single page document—the image on the screen. So, you return `PAGE_EXISTS` for index 0 and `NO_SUCH_PAGE` otherwise.

The second step is to start the drawing. For Swing components, your drawing should be a high-resolution version of what the component looks like on the screen. To create this drawing, cast the `Graphics` object to `Graphics2D`, scale the resolution of the object to that of the printer, and call the component's `paint` method with the scaled `Graphics2D` object. For more details on the `Graphics2D` object, see Chapter 10 (Java 2D: Graphics in Java 2).

The general approach for performing the print task is shown below.

```
public int print(Graphics g,
                 PageFormat pageFormat,
                 int pageIndex) {
  if (pageIndex > 0) {
    return(NO_SUCH_PAGE);
  } else {
    Graphics2D g2d = (Graphics2D)g;
    g2d.translate(pageFormat.getImageableX(),
                  pageFormat.getImageableY());

    // In JDK 1.2 you need to turn off double
    // buffering before painting the component,
    // and then turn double buffering back on.
    // In JDK 1.3 you would replace these three
    // lines with componentToBePainted.print(g2d).
    setDoubleBufferEnabled(false);
    componentToBePrinted.paint(g2d);
    setDoubleBufferEnabled(true);

    return(PAGE_EXISTS);
  }
}
```

The `getImageableX` and `getImageableY` methods return the upper-left coordinate of the page's printable image, which is based on the printer, paper size, and page orientation selected in Printer dialog window.

The Role of Double Buffering

With Swing, almost all components have double buffering turned on by default. In general, double buffering is a great boon, making for a convenient and efficient `paintComponent` method. However, in the specific case of printing in JDK 1.2, double buffering can be a huge problem. First, since component printing relies on scaling the coordinate system and then simply calling the component's `paint` method, if double buffering is enabled, then printing amounts to little more than scaling up the buffer (off-screen image). Scaling the off-screen image simply results in ugly low-resolution printing. Second, sending huge buffers to the printer produces large spooler files that take a very long time to print.

Consequently, you need to make sure double buffering is turned off before you print the Swing component. If you have only a single `JPanel` or other `JComponent`, you can call `setDoubleBuffered(false)` on the component before calling the `paint` method and then call `setDoubleBuffered(true)` afterward. However, this approach suffers from the flaw that if you later nest another container inside the component, the nested container has double buffering turned on by default and you're right back where you started. A better approach is to globally turn off double buffering through

```
RepaintManager currentManager =
   RepaintManager.currentManager(theComponent);
currentManager.setDoubleBufferingEnabled(false);
```

and then to reenable double buffering after calling `paint` through the `setDoubleBufferingEnabled(true)`. Although this approach will completely fix the problem with low-resolution printouts, if the components have large, complex filled backgrounds, you can still get big spool files and slow printing. In JDK 1.3, this step is automatically performed during the printing process and you no longer need to turn double buffering off and then on again.

Core Note

In JDK 1.2 printing you need to globally turn double buffering off before painting the component and then turn double buffering back on.

A General-Purpose Component-Printing Routine

The role of the `print` method when printing Swing components is to do nothing more than scale the `Graphics` object, turn off double buffering, and then call `paint`. Nothing in the API requires that the `print` method be placed in the component that is to be printed. Furthermore, requiring printable components to directly implement the `Printable` interface and define a `print` method produces cumbersome code and prevents you from printing components that were not originally planned for in the design. A better approach is to put the `print` method in an arbitrary object and tell that object which component's `paint` method to call when printing. This approach permits you to build a generic `printComponent` method to which you simply pass the component you want printed.

Core Approach

Instead of modifying the code for each Swing component you would like printed, simply provide a helper class that implements the `Printable` *interface.*

Listing 15.19 provides a utility class, `PrintUtilities`, for printing Swing components. Simply pass the component to the `PrintUtilities.printComponent` method. Listing 15.20 is an example of using the print utilities in JDK 1.2.

Listing 15.19 `PrintUtilities.java`

```
import java.awt.*;
import javax.swing.*;
import java.awt.print.*;

/** A simple utility class that lets you very simply print
 *  an arbitrary component in JDK 1.2. Just pass the
 *  component to PrintUtilities.printComponent. The
 *  component you want to print doesn't need a print method
 *  and doesn't have to implement any interface or do
 *  anything special at all.
 *  <P>
```

(continued)

Listing 15.19 `PrintUtilities.java` *(continued)*

```
*   If you are going to be printing many times, it is marginally
*   more efficient to first do the following:
*   <PRE>
*     PrintUtilities printHelper =
*       new PrintUtilities(theComponent);
*   </PRE>
*   then later do printHelper.print(). But this is a very tiny
*   difference, so in most cases just do the simpler
*   PrintUtilities.printComponent(componentToBePrinted).
*/

public class PrintUtilities implements Printable {
  protected Component componentToBePrinted;

  public static void printComponent(Component c) {
    new PrintUtilities(c).print();
  }

  public PrintUtilities(Component componentToBePrinted) {
    this.componentToBePrinted = componentToBePrinted;
  }

  public void print() {
    PrinterJob printJob = PrinterJob.getPrinterJob();
    printJob.setPrintable(this);
    if (printJob.printDialog())
      try {
        printJob.print();
      } catch(PrinterException pe) {
        System.out.println("Error printing: " + pe);
      }
  }

  // General print routine for JDK 1.2. Use PrintUtilities2
  // for printing in JDK 1.3.
  public int print(Graphics g, PageFormat pageFormat,
                   int pageIndex) {
    if (pageIndex > 0) {
      return(NO_SUCH_PAGE);
    } else {
      Graphics2D g2d = (Graphics2D)g;
      g2d.translate(pageFormat.getImageableX(),
                    pageFormat.getImageableY());
```

(continued)

Listing 15.19 `PrintUtilities.java` *(continued)*

```
      disableDoubleBuffering(componentToBePrinted);
      componentToBePrinted.paint(g2d);
      enableDoubleBuffering(componentToBePrinted);
      return(PAGE_EXISTS);
    }
  }

  /** The speed and quality of printing suffers dramatically if
   *  any of the containers have double buffering turned on,
   *  so this turns it off globally.  This step is only
   *  required in JDK 1.2.
   */

  public static void disableDoubleBuffering(Component c) {
    RepaintManager currentManager =
                     RepaintManager.currentManager(c);
    currentManager.setDoubleBufferingEnabled(false);
  }

  /** Reenables double buffering globally. This step is only
   *  required in JDK 1.2.
   */

  public static void enableDoubleBuffering(Component c) {
    RepaintManager currentManager =
                     RepaintManager.currentManager(c);
    currentManager.setDoubleBufferingEnabled(true);
  }
}
```

Listing 15.20 adds print capabilities to a `JFrame` by including a button that simply calls `PrintUtilities.printComponent` when selected. The frame includes a `DrawingPanel`, Listing 15.21, with a custom `paintComponent` method to draw the text "Java 2D" in a shadow effect, as shown in Figure 15–14. See Chapter 10 (Java 2D: Graphics in Java 2) for information about performing transformations and drawing on the `Graphics2D` object.

Listing 15.20 `PrintExample.java`

```
import java.awt.*;
import javax.swing.*;
import java.awt.event.*;
import java.awt.print.*;

/** An example of a printable window in Java 1.2. The key point
 *  here is that <B>any</B> component is printable in Java 1.2.
 *  However, you have to be careful to turn off double buffering
 *  globally (not just for the top-level window).
 *  See the PrintUtilities class for the printComponent method
 *  that lets you print an arbitrary component with a single
 *  function call.
 */

public class PrintExample extends JFrame
                          implements ActionListener {
  public static void main(String[] args) {
    new PrintExample();
  }

  public PrintExample() {
    super("Printing Swing Components in JDK 1.2");
    WindowUtilities.setNativeLookAndFeel();
    addWindowListener(new ExitListener());
    Container content = getContentPane();
    JButton printButton = new JButton("Print");
    printButton.addActionListener(this);
    JPanel buttonPanel = new JPanel();
    buttonPanel.setBackground(Color.white);
    buttonPanel.add(printButton);
    content.add(buttonPanel, BorderLayout.SOUTH);
    DrawingPanel drawingPanel = new DrawingPanel();
    content.add(drawingPanel, BorderLayout.CENTER);
    pack();
    setVisible(true);
  }

  public void actionPerformed(ActionEvent event) {
    PrintUtilities.printComponent(this);
  }
}
```

Listing 15.21 `DrawingPanel.java`

```java
import java.awt.*;
import javax.swing.*;
import java.awt.geom.*;

/** A window with a custom paintComponent method.
 *  Illustrates that you can make a general-purpose method
 *  that can print any component, regardless of whether
 *  that component performs custom drawing.
 *  See the PrintUtilities class for the printComponent method
 *  that lets you print an arbitrary component with a single
 *  function call.
 */

public class DrawingPanel extends JPanel {
  private int fontSize = 90;
  private String message = "Java 2D";
  private int messageWidth;

  public DrawingPanel() {
    setBackground(Color.white);
    Font font = new Font("Serif", Font.PLAIN, fontSize);
    setFont(font);
    FontMetrics metrics = getFontMetrics(font);
    messageWidth = metrics.stringWidth(message);
    int width = messageWidth*5/3;
    int height = fontSize*3;
    setPreferredSize(new Dimension(width, height));
  }

  /** Draws a black string with a tall angled "shadow"
   *  of the string behind it.
   */

  public void paintComponent(Graphics g) {
    super.paintComponent(g);
    Graphics2D g2d = (Graphics2D)g;
    int x = messageWidth/10;
    int y = fontSize*5/2;
    g2d.translate(x, y);
    g2d.setPaint(Color.lightGray);
    AffineTransform origTransform = g2d.getTransform();
    g2d.shear(-0.95, 0);
    g2d.scale(1, 3);
    g2d.drawString(message, 0, 0);
    g2d.setTransform(origTransform);
    g2d.setPaint(Color.black);
    g2d.drawString(message, 0, 0);
  }
}
```

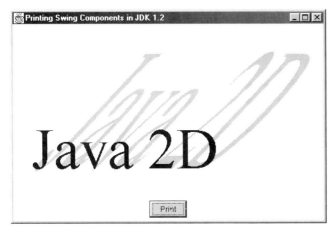

Figure 15-14 Selecting the `JButton` invokes the print service to send the `Graphics2D` object to the printer.

Printing in JDK 1.3

The burden of disabling and enabling double buffering during the printing process in JDK 1.2 was lifted in JDK 1.3. Now, `JComponent` provides its own `print` method to facilitate printing. The `print` method simply sets an internal boolean flag, `IS_PRINTING`, to `true` and calls `paint`. The `paint` method in `JComponent` was rewritten to check the flag and, if set to disable double buffering before calling three internal `protected` methods (`printComponent`, `printBorder`, and `print-Children`) to print the components.

Now, when printing in JDK 1.3, use

```
componentToBePrinted.print(g2d);
```

instead of

```
setDoubleBufferEnabled(false);
componentToBePrinted.paint(g2d);
setDoubleBufferEnabled(true);
```

to facilitate printing.

Core Approach

For printing in JDK 1.3, call the component's `print(Graphics2d g2d)` method. Disabling and enabling double buffering during the print process is no longer required.

In Listing 15.22 we provide a new utility, `PrintUtilities2`, for printing in JDK 1.3. This class inherits from `PrintUtilities` (Listing 15.19) and overrides the `print` method to call the component's `print` method instead of the component's `paint` method. To use this class for printing, call

```
PrintUtilities2.printComponent(componentToBePrinted);
```

where `componentToBePrinted` is the Swing component to print.

Listing 15.22 `PrintUtilities2.java`

```java
import java.awt.*;
import javax.swing.*;
import java.awt.print.*;

/** A simple utility class for printing an arbitrary
 *  component in JDK 1.3. The class relies on the
 *  fact that in JDK 1.3 the JComponent class overrides
 *  print (in Container) to automatically set a flag
 *  that disables double buffering before the component
 *  is painted. If the printing flag is set, paint calls
 *  printComponent, printBorder, and printChildren.
 *
 *  To print a component, just pass the component to
 *  PrintUtilities2.printComponent(componentToBePrinted).
 */

public class PrintUtilities2 extends PrintUtilities {

  public static void printComponent(Component c) {
    new PrintUtilities2(c).print();
  }

  public PrintUtilities2(Component componentToBePrinted) {
    super(componentToBePrinted);
  }

  // General print routine for JDK 1.3. Use PrintUtilities1
  // for printing in JDK 1.2.
  public int print(Graphics g, PageFormat pageFormat,
                   int pageIndex) {
    if (pageIndex > 0) {
      return(NO_SUCH_PAGE);
    } else {
      Graphics2D g2d = (Graphics2D)g;
      g2d.translate(pageFormat.getImageableX(),
                    pageFormat.getImageableY());
      componentToBePrinted.print(g2d);
      return(PAGE_EXISTS);
    }
  }
}
```

15.6 Swing Threads

Swing follows the familiar AWT event model and uses a single-threaded design for updating components. Recall from Chapter 10 (Handling Mouse and Keyboard Events) that painting of components and handling of listeners are both processed in a single event dispatch thread. As a consequence of the event model, two general rules apply for robust GUI design:

1. If tasks in the event handling method require considerable CPU time, then execute these time-intensive tasks in a separate thread. Freeing the event dispatch thread to process other queued events yields a more responsive user interface.
2. Make changes to the state of a realized (visible) Swing component only within the event dispatch thread and not within a user-defined thread.

If you do not follow these design rules when modifying a Swing component, your GUI could be unresponsive to user interaction or race conditions could occur for the state of a component.

To illustrate potential design problems, we consider a simple application that transfers a file from a client machine to a remote server. Suppose that the GUI design includes a Start button to initiate the file transfer and a label that shows the status of the file transfer (i.e., "Transferring *filename* ..."). An initial, albeit poor, design for the `actionPerformed` method of the Start button is shown below:

```
// Poorly designed event handler for Start button.
public void actionPerformed(ActionEvent event){

  // Change to label is ok here because it is executed
  // on the event dispatch thread.
  label.setText("Transferring " + filename);

  // Transfer file to server - time intensive.
  transferFile(filename);

  // Ok to change label here also, executed on
  // event dispatch thread.
  label.setText("Transfer completed.");
}
```

Here, changing the text on the label is perfectly legal because the `setText` method is executed within the event dispatch thread. However, the results are not what one might expect. Each call to `setText` places a `PropertyChangeEvent` on the event queue, and only *after* the file is transferred and the `actionPerformed` method is completed are the change events dispatched from the queue. The initial update to the label does not occur until *after* the file is transferred. The second change to the label immediately occurs and the user never sees the "Transferring ..." label message. Furthermore, because the file transfer is executing in the event dispatch thread, user interaction with any other components in the user interface is effectively blocked until the current actionPerformed method completes. This is definitely not the desired behavior!

One possible solution to the dilemma is to perform the file transfer and final label update in a separate user thread and free the event dispatch thread to process the queued events. Once the thread completes the file transfer, the thread can communicate the completion to the JLabel. Consider the improved actionPerformed method,

```
// Improved event handler. Time-intensive task is
// moved to a separate thread.
public void actionPerformed(ActionEvent event) {
  // Change to label is ok here since it is executed
  // on the event thread.
  label.setText("Transferring " + filename);

  // Transferring the file is time intensive, so the
  // task is performed in a separate thread to permit
  // processing of other events on the event queue.
  Thread t = new FileTransfer(filename, label);
  t.start();
}
```

and supporting threaded class, FileTransfer,

```
// Improperly designed thread class - update
// of Swing component is not thread safe.
public class FileTransfer extends Thread {
  private String filename;
  private JLabel = label;

  public FileTransfer(String filename, JLabel label) {
    this.filename = filename;
    this.label = label;
  }

  public void run() {
    // Transfer file to server. Lengthy process.
    doTransfer(...);

    // Update of label is not ok. Update is not
    // executed on the event dispatch thread.
    label.setText("Transfer complete.");
  }
}
```

This design certainly frees up the event dispatch thread to handle other events on the queue. However, because the `FileTransfer` thread directly modifies the state of the `JLabel`, the second design rule is violated—update Swing components only in the event dispatch thread. If you don't follow this rule, then a race condition could occur when the event dispatch thread is relying on one value for the label and the user-defined thread changes the label to a different value. Depending on the scheduling of the threads on the CPU, two different outcomes could be observed for multiple runs of the program.

To resolve this problem, Swing provides two methods, `invokeLater` and `invokeAndWait`, to place a Runnable object on the event queue for updating Swing components. Once the Runnable object is dispatched from the front of the event queue, the object's `run` method is executed in the event dispatch thread. The idea here is to place the label update in the `run` method of the Runnable object. An example of creating a Runnable object is illustrated shortly. For more information on multithreading and Runnable objects, see Chapter 16 (Concurrent Programming with Java Threads).

Core Approach

To properly access Swing components from a thread other than the event dispatch thread, place the code in a `Runnable` object and then use one of the static `SwingUtilities` methods, `invokeLater` or `invokeAndWait`, to place the `Runnable` object on the event queue.

SwingUtilities Methods

The `SwingUtilities` class provides two methods to queue a `Runnable` object on the event dispatch thread. Changes to a Swing component from a user thread should be wrapped (placed) in the `run` method of the `Runnable` object.

public static void invokeLater(Runnable object)
The `invokeLater` method places the `Runnable` object on the event queue and immediately returns. Once the runnable object reaches the front of the event queue, the object's `run` method is executed on the event dispatch thread. You can call `invokeLater` from within the event dispatch thread and any user thread.

public static void invokeAndWait(Runnable object)
      throws InterruptedException, InvocationTargetException
The `invokeAndWait` method places the `Runnable` object on the event queue and blocks (waits) until the object's `run` method completes execution.

Use this method when the Swing component must be updated before the thread proceeds to the next operation or when information from the component must be first retrieved before the thread proceeds. You cannot call invokeAndWait from the event dispatch thread because doing so produces as a deadlock condition. Use isEventDispatchThread to determine if the current thread is the event dispatch thread. The possibly thrown InvocationTargetException is located in the java.lang.reflect package.

Next, we illustrate the general approach for creating a Runnable object to update a Swing component on the event dispatch thread. Consider the situation described earlier where a file is transferred to a remote server and a label is updated on the user interface to indicate the status of the file transfer. As shown earlier, transferring the file in the event dispatch thread cripples the responsiveness of the event handler. Moving the task to a user-defined thread and modifying the Swing label from a user-defined thread violates the fundamental design rule of only modifying Swing components during execution in the event dispatch thread. Failure to follow this rule could produce a race condition. Below we provide our final design for the actionPerformed method and FileTransfer class. In this final design, we update the label in a thread-safe manner.

```
// Correctly designed event handler. Time-intensive
// task is moved to a separate thread and modification
// of the Swing component from the thread is performed
// in a Runnable object placed on the event queue.

public void actionPerformed(ActionEvent event) {

    // Time-intensive task is moved to a separate thread.
    Thread t = new FileTransfer(filename, label);
    t.start();
  }
}
```

In the FileTransfer constructor, a reference to the JLabel is provided so that the Runnable object can update the label. Two Runnable objects are created, one to update the label before the file transfer and one to update the label after the file transfer. Here, each Runnable object is actually defined as an anonymous class. See Chapter 10 (Handling Mouse and Keyboard Events) for further examples on creating and using anonymous classes.

```
// Final version of FileTransfer. Modification of the
// label is thread safe.
public class FileTransfer extends Thread {
  private String filename;
  private JLabel label;

  public FileTransfer(String filename, JLabel label) {
    this.filename = filename;
    this.label = label;
  }
```

```
public void run() {

  try {
    // Place the runnable object to update the label
    // on the event queue. The invokeAndWait method
    // will block until the label is updated.
    SwingUtilities.invokeAndWait(
      new Runnable() {
        public void run() {
          label.setText("Transferring " + filename);
        }
      });
  } catch(InvocationTargetException ite) {
  } catch(InterruptedException ie) { }

  // Transfer file to server. Lengthy process.
  doTransfer(...);

  // Perform the final update to the label from
  // within the runnable object. Use invokeLater;
  // blocking is not necessary.
  SwingUtilities.invokeLater(
    new Runnable() {
      public void run() {
        label.setText("Transfer completed");
      }
    });
  }
}
```

In this design we use invokeAndWait to place the first Runnable object on the event queue, ensuring that the label is updated to "Transferring *file*" before we proceed with the actual file transfer. After the file transfer is completed, another Runnable object is created and placed on the event queue by invokeLater. Here, we are not so concerned that the label is updated before we proceed. Eventually, the object will reach the front of the event queue and the run method will execute, changing the label to "Transfer completed."

As we've shown, you need to pay special attention to updating Swing components from threads other than the event dispatch thread. The need to move tasks to separate threads actually occurs quite often, for example, when querying databases, communicating with remote objects by means of RMI, accessing Web servers, and transferring files. Always remember that if you modify a component from a user-defined thread, use either invokeLater or invokeAndWait to change the component.

15.7 Summary

Now you have the skillset to create outstanding graphical user interfaces with the advanced Swing components. In this chapter, we've only shown you the basic functions of each component. You'll need to spend time developing your own Swing interfaces to appreciate the full capabilities of these advanced components.

A `JList`, `JTree`, and `JTable` all have default models for accessing and modifying their data (as well as firing change events), so you can get started right away or you can write your own custom models to interact with the data and visual presentation directly. Technically, you can display almost any Swing component in a list, tree, or table, but you must provide a custom cell renderer to display the component correctly.

Once you've created a Swing interface, printing the component simply requires you to provide the class with a `print` method. But the `print` method is not required to be in the components class, so it's often useful to write a separate utility class to handle the printing. Finally, if you modify a Swing component, you must do so in a thread-safe manner. Swing provides both `invokeAndWait` and `invoke-Later` to ensure that modification of the component is executed in the event dispatch thread.

CONCURRENT PROGRAMMING WITH JAVA THREADS

Topics in This Chapter

- Starting threads by using separate thread objects
- Starting threads within an existing object
- Solving common thread problems
- Synchronizing access to shared resources
- Methods in the Thread class
- Exploring alternative approaches to multithreaded graphics
- Implementing double buffering
- Animating images
- Controlling timers

Chapter 16

The Java programming language has one of the most powerful and usable concurrent programming packages of any modern programming language: the `Thread` class. Threads are sometimes known as "lightweight processes": processes that share the heap but have their own stack. Threads provide three distinct advantages.

Efficiency

Performing some tasks is quicker in a multithreaded manner. For instance, consider the task of downloading and analyzing five text files from various URLs. Suppose that it took 12 seconds to establish the network connection and 1 second to download the file once the connection was open. Doing this serially would take $5 \times 13 = 65$ seconds. But if done in separate threads, the waiting could be done in parallel, and the total time might take about $12 + 5 = 17$ seconds. In fact, the efficiency benefits of this type of approach are so great that the Java platform *automatically* downloads images in separate threads. For more information, see Section 9.12 (Drawing Images).

Convenience

Some tasks are simpler to visualize and implement when various pieces are considered separately. For instance, consider a clock display or an image animation; in each case, a separate thread is responsible for controlling the display updates.

New Capabilities

Finally, some tasks simply cannot be done without multiprocessing. For instance, an HTTP server needs to listen on a given network port for a connection. When the server obtains one, the connection is passed to a different process that actually handles the request. If the server didn't do this, the original port would be tied up until the request was finished and only very light loads could be supported; the server would be unusable for real-life applications. In fact, in Chapter 17 (Network Programming) we'll present code for a simple multithreaded HTTP server that is based on the socket techniques discussed in Chapter 17 and the threading techniques explained here.

However, a word of caution is in order. Threads in the Java programming language are more convenient than threads or "heavyweight" processes in other languages (e.g., `fork` in C). Threads add significant capability in some situations. Nevertheless, testing and debugging a program where multiple things are going on at once is much harder than debugging a program where only one thing is happening at a time. So, carefully weigh the pros and cons of using threads before considering them, and be prepared for extra development and debugging time when you do, especially until you gain experience.

16.1 Starting Threads

The Java implementation provides two convenient mechanisms for thread programming: (1) making a separate subclass of the `Thread` class that contains the code that will be run, and (2) using a `Thread` instance to call back to code in an ordinary object.

Mechanism 1: Put Behavior in a Separate Thread Object

The first way to run threads in the Java platform is to make a separate subclass of `Thread`, put the actions to be performed in the `run` method of the subclass, create an instance of the subclass, and call that instance's `start` method. This technique is illustrated in Listings 16.1 and 16.2.

Listing 16.1 `DriverClass.java`

```java
public class DriverClass extends SomeClass {
  ...
  public void startAThread() {
    // Create a Thread object.
    ThreadClass thread = new ThreadClass();
    // Start it in a separate process.
    thread.start();
    ...
  }
}
```

Listing 16.2 `ThreadClass.java`

```java
public class ThreadClass extends Thread {
  public void run() {
    // Thread behavior here.
  }
}
```

If a class extends `Thread`, then the class will inherit a `start` method that calls the `run` method in a separate thread of execution. The author of the class is responsible for implementing `run`, and the thread dies when `run` ends. So, even though you put your code in `run`, you call `start`, not `run`. If you call `run` directly, the code will be executed in the current thread, just like a normal method. Data that is to be local to that thread is normally kept in local variables of `run` or in private instance variables of that object. Outside data is only accessible to the thread if the data (or a reference to the data) is passed to the thread's constructor or if publicly available static variables or methods are used.

Core Warning

Never call a thread's `run` *method directly. Doing so does* ***not*** *start a separate thread of execution.*

For example, Listing 16.3 gives a `Counter` class that counts from 0 to *N* with random pauses in between. The driver class (Listing 16.4) can create and start multiple instances of `Counter`, resulting in interleaved execution (Listing 16.5).

Listing 16.3 `Counter.java`

```java
/** A subclass of Thread that counts up to a specified
 *  limit with random pauses in between each count.
 */

public class Counter extends Thread {
  private static int totalNum = 0;
  private int currentNum, loopLimit;

  public Counter(int loopLimit) {
    this.loopLimit = loopLimit;
    currentNum = totalNum++;
  }

  private void pause(double seconds) {
    try { Thread.sleep(Math.round(1000.0*seconds)); }
    catch(InterruptedException ie) {}
  }

  /** When run finishes, the thread exits. */

  public void run() {
    for(int i=0; i<loopLimit; i++) {
      System.out.println("Counter " + currentNum + ": " + i);
      pause(Math.random()); // Sleep for up to 1 second
    }
  }
}
```

Listing 16.4 `CounterTest.java`

```java
/** Try out a few instances of the Counter class. */

public class CounterTest {
  public static void main(String[] args) {
    Counter c1 = new Counter(5);
    Counter c2 = new Counter(5);
    Counter c3 = new Counter(5);
    c1.start();
    c2.start();
    c3.start();
  }
}
```

Listing 16.5 `CounterTest` **Output**

```
Counter 0: 0
Counter 1: 0
Counter 2: 0
Counter 1: 1
Counter 2: 1
Counter 1: 2
Counter 0: 1
Counter 0: 2
Counter 1: 3
Counter 2: 2
Counter 0: 3
Counter 1: 4
Counter 0: 4
Counter 2: 3
Counter 2: 4
```

Mechanism 2: Put Behavior in the Driver Class, Which Must Implement Runnable

The second way to perform multithreaded computation is to implement the Runnable interface, construct an instance of Thread passing the current class (i.e., the Runnable) as an argument, and call that Thread's start method. You put the actions you want executed in the run method of the main class; the thread's run method is ignored. This means that run has full access to all variables and methods of the class containing the run method. The actual run method executed (either the run method in the Thread class or the run method in the class implementing Runnable) is determined by the object passed to the thread constructor. If a Runnable is supplied, the thread's start method will use the Runnable's run method instead of its own. Declaring that you implement Runnable serves as a guarantee to the thread that you have a public run method. Listing 16.6 shows an outline of this approach.

Listing 16.6 `ThreadedClass.java`

```java
public class ThreadedClass extends AnyClass implements Runnable {
  public void run() {
    // Thread behavior here.
  }

  public void startThread() {
    Thread t = new Thread(this);
    t.start(); // Calls back to the run method in "this."
  }
  ...
}
```

You can invoke multiple threads of the class implementing the `Runnable` interface. In this case, each thread concurrently executes the *same* `run` method. Furthermore, each invocation of `run` owns a separate copy of the local variables, but you must carefully control access to any class variables, since they are shared among all thread instances of the class. Contention for common data is discussed in Section 16.2 (Race Conditions). If you want to access the thread instance to get private per-thread data, use `Thread.currentThread()`.

Listing 16.7 gives an example of this process. Note that the driver class (Listing 16.8) does not call `start` on the instantiated `Counter2`'s objects because `Counter2` is not a `Thread` and thus does not necessarily have a `start` method. The result (Listing 16.9) is substantially the same as with the original `Counter`.

Listing 16.7 `Counter2.java`

```java
/** A Runnable that counts up to a specified
 *  limit with random pauses in between each count.
 */

public class Counter2 implements Runnable {
  private static int totalNum = 0;
  private int currentNum, loopLimit;

  public Counter2(int loopLimit) {
    this.loopLimit = loopLimit;
    currentNum = totalNum++;
    Thread t = new Thread(this);
    t.start();
  }

  private void pause(double seconds) {
    try { Thread.sleep(Math.round(1000.0*seconds)); }
    catch(InterruptedException ie) {}
  }

  public void run() {
    for(int i=0; i<loopLimit; i++) {
      System.out.println("Counter " + currentNum + ": " + i);
      pause(Math.random()); // Sleep for up to 1 second.
    }
  }
}
```

Listing 16.8 `Counter2Test.java`

```java
/** Try out a few instances of the Counter2 class. */

public class Counter2Test {
  public static void main(String[] args) {
    Counter2 c1 = new Counter2(5);
    Counter2 c2 = new Counter2(5);
    Counter2 c3 = new Counter2(5);
  }
}
```

Listing 16.9 `Counter2Test` **Output**

```
Counter 0: 0
Counter 1: 0
Counter 2: 0
Counter 1: 1
Counter 1: 2
Counter 0: 1
Counter 1: 3
Counter 2: 1
Counter 0: 2
Counter 0: 3
Counter 1: 4
Counter 2: 2
Counter 2: 3
Counter 0: 4
Counter 2: 4
```

In this particular instance, this approach probably seems more cumbersome than making a separate subclass of `Thread`. However, because the Java programming language does not have multiple inheritance, if your class already is a subclass of something else (say, `Applet`), then your class cannot also be a subclass of `Thread`. In such a case, if the thread needs access to the instance variables and methods of the main class, this approach works well, whereas the previous approach (a separate `Thread` subclass) requires some extra work to give the `Thread` subclass access to the applet's variables and methods (perhaps by passing along a reference to the `Applet`). When you are doing this from an `Applet`, the applet's `start` method is usually the place to create and start the threads.

16.2 Race Conditions

A class that implements `Runnable` could start more than one thread per instance. However, all of the threads started from that object will be looking at the *same* instance of that object. Per-thread data can be in local variables of `run`, but take care when accessing class instance variables or data in other classes because multiple threads can access the same variables concurrently. For instance, Listing 16.10 shows an *incorrect* counter applet. Before reading further, take a look at the `run` method and see if you can see what is wrong.

Listing 16.10 `BuggyCounterApplet.java`

```java
import java.applet.Applet;
import java.awt.*;

/** Emulates the Counter and Counter2 classes, but this time
 *  from an applet that invokes multiple versions of its own run
 *  method. This version is likely to work correctly
 *  <B>except</B> when  an important customer is visiting.
 */

public class BuggyCounterApplet extends Applet
                                  implements Runnable{
  private int totalNum = 0;
  private int loopLimit = 5;

  // Start method of applet, not the start method of the thread.
  // The applet start method is called by the browser after init is
  // called.
  public void start() {
    Thread t;
    for(int i=0; i<3; i++) {
      t = new Thread(this);
      t.start();
    }
  }

  private void pause(double seconds) {
    try { Thread.sleep(Math.round(1000.0*seconds)); }
    catch(InterruptedException ie) {}
  }
```

(continued)

Listing 16.10 BuggyCounterApplet.java *(continued)*

```java
  public void run() {
    int currentNum = totalNum;
    System.out.println("Setting currentNum to " + currentNum);
    totalNum = totalNum + 1;
    for(int i=0; i<loopLimit; i++) {
      System.out.println("Counter " + currentNum + ": " + i);
      pause(Math.random());
    }
  }
}
```

Listing 16.11 Usual BuggyCounterApplet **Output**

```
> appletviewer BuggyCounterApplet.html
Setting currentNum to 0
Counter 0: 0
Setting currentNum to 1
Counter 1: 0
Setting currentNum to 2
Counter 2: 0
Counter 2: 1
Counter 1: 1
Counter 0: 1
Counter 2: 2
Counter 0: 2
Counter 1: 2
Counter 1: 3
Counter 0: 3
Counter 2: 3
Counter 1: 4
Counter 2: 4
Counter 0: 4
```

In the vast majority of cases, the output is correct as in Listing 16.11, and the temptation would be to assume that the class is indeed correct and to leave the class as it stands. In fact, however, the class suffers from the flawed assumption that no new thread will be created and read totalNum between the time the previous thread reads totalNum and increments the value. That is, the operation of this code depends on the previous thread "winning the race" to the increment operation. This assumption is unsafe, and, in fact, a small percent of the time the already activated thread will lose the race, as shown in Listing 16.12, obtained after running the same applet over and over *many* times.

Listing 16.12 Occasional `BuggyCounterApplet` **Output**

```
> appletviewer BuggyCounterApplet.html
Setting currentNum to 0
Counter 0: 0
Setting currentNum to 1
Setting currentNum to 1
Counter 0: 1
Counter 1: 0
Counter 1: 0
Counter 0: 2
Counter 0: 3
Counter 1: 1
Counter 0: 4
Counter 1: 1
Counter 1: 2
Counter 1: 3
Counter 1: 2
Counter 1: 3
Counter 1: 4
Counter 1: 4
```

Now, one obvious "solution" is to perform the updating of the thread number in a single step, as follows, rather than first reading the value, then incrementing the value a couple of lines later.

```
public void run() {
    int currentNum = totalNum++;
    System.out.println("Setting currentNum to " +
                        currentNum);
    for(int i=0; i<loopLimit; i++) {
        System.out.println("Counter " + currentNum +
                            ": " + i);
        pause(Math.random());
    }
}
```

Although the idea of performing the update in a single step is a good one, the Java Virtual Machine does not guarantee that this code really *will* be done in a single step. Sure, the program statement is a single line of Java source code, but who knows what goes on behind the scenes? The most likely scenario is that this approach simply shortens the race so the error occurs less frequently. Less frequent errors are *worse*, not better, because they are more likely to survive unnoticed until some critical moment. Fortunately, the Java programming language has a construct (`synchronized`) that lets you guarantee that a thread can complete a designated series of operations before another thread gets to execute any of the same operations. This concept is so important that we devote the entire next section to the topic.

16.3 Synchronization

Synchronization is a way to arbitrate contention for shared resources. When you synchronize a section of code, a "lock" (or "monitor") is set when the first thread enters that section of code. Unless the thread explicitly gives up the lock, no other thread can enter that section of code until the first one exits. In fact, synchronization can be even stronger than just locking a single section of code. A synchronized block has an Object as a tag, and once a thread enters a synchronized section of code, no other thread can enter *any* other section of code that is locked with the same tag.

Synchronizing a Section of Code

The way to protect a section of code that accesses shared resources is to place the code inside a synchronized block, as follows:

```
synchronized(someObject) {
  code
}
```

The synchronization statement tells the system to block other threads from entering this section of code when the section is already in use. Once a thread enters the enclosed code, no other thread will be allowed to enter until the first thread exits or voluntarily gives up the lock through wait. Note that this lock does *not* mean that the designated code is executed uninterrupted; the thread scheduler can suspend a thread in the middle of the synchronized section to let another thread run. The key point is that the other thread will be executing a *different* section of code.

Also note that you lock sections of *code*, not *objects*. Every object has an associated flag that can be used as a monitor to control a synchronization lock. Using someObject as a label on the lock in no way "locks" someObject; the synchronized statement simply sets the flag. Other threads can still access the object, and race conditions are still possible if a different section of code accesses the same resources as those inside the synchronized block. However, you are permitted to use the same label on more than one block of code. Thus, once a thread enters a block that is synchronized on someObject, no other section of code that is also synchronized on someObject can run until either the first thread exits the synchronized section or the section of code explicitly gives up the lock. In fact, a single thread is allowed to hold the same lock multiple times, as when one synchronized block calls another block that is synchronized with the same lock.

Core Note

The synchronized *construct locks sections of code, not objects.*

Synchronizing an Entire Method

If you want to synchronize all of the code in a method, the Java programming language provides a shorthand method using the `synchronized` keyword, as follows:

```
public synchronized void someMethod() {
  body
}
```

This declaration tells the system to perform `someMethod` in a synchronized manner, using the current object instance (i.e., `this`) as the lock label. That is, once a thread starts executing `someMethod`, no other thread can enter the method or any other section of code that is synchronized on the current object (`this`) until the current thread exits from `someMethod` or gives up the lock explicitly with `wait`. Thus, the following are equivalent.

```
public synchronized void someMethod() {
  body
}

public void someMethod() {
  synchronized(this) {
    body
  }
}
```

Now, after all the dire warnings about race conditions, programmers are sometimes tempted to synchronize everything in sight. Unfortunately, this can have performance penalties and can result in coarser-grained threading. For an extreme case, consider what would happen if you marked the `run` method as `synchronized`: you'd be forcing your code to run completely serially!

A `static` method that specifies `synchronized` has the same effect as one whose body is synchronized on the class object. The `synchronized` modifier of a method is *not* inherited, so if `someMethod` is overridden in a subclass, the method is no longer synchronized unless the `synchronized` keyword is repeated.

Core Warning

Overridden methods in subclasses do not inherit the `synchronized` *declaration.*

Common Synchronization Bug

When extending the `Thread` class, a common bug is to synchronize on `this` when sharing data across multiple instances of the threaded class. Consider the following example, where `SomeThreadedClass` contains a `static` object, `someShared-`

`Object`, that has classwide visibility and is shared by all instances of the class. To avoid race conditions between each thread and to preserve data integrity of the shared object, the method, `doSomeOperation`, is synchronized. Does this block the other threads from entering the same method and modifying the shared data?

```
public class SomeThreadedClass extends Thread {
  private static RandomClass someSharedObject;
  ...
  public synchronized void doSomeOperation() {
    accessSomeSharedObject();
  }
  ...
  public void run() {
    while(someCondition) {
      doSomeOperation();    // Accesses shared data.
      doSomeOtherOperation();// No shared data.
    }
  }
}
```

Remember that a `synchronized` method declaration is equivalent to

```
synchronized(this){
  ...
}
```

But if there are multiple instances of `SomeThreadedClass`, then there are multiple *different* `this` references. For this situation, each `this` reference is unique and not an appropriate lock to protect the shared data. Correcting the bug is simply a matter of selecting an appropriate lock object.

Synchronize on the Shared Data

One solution is to synchronize on the shared data object. Again, the internal data fields of the object are not "locked" and can be modified. The object is just a label (acting as a tag), telling all other threads looking at the same label (tag) whether or not they can enter the block of code.

```
public void doSomeOperation() {
  synchronized(someSharedObject) {
    accessSomeSharedObject();
  }
}
```

Synchronize on the Class Object

Another solution is to synchronize on the `class` object. Java uses a unique `Class` object to represent information about each class. The syntax is as follows:

```
public void doSomeOperation() {
  synchronized(SomeThreadedClass.class) {
    accessSomeSharedObject();
  }
}
```

Note that if you synchronize a `static` method, the lock is the corresponding `Class` object, not `this`.

Synchronize on an Arbitrary Object

The last solution is to simply create a new, arbitrary, shared (`static`) object in `SomeThreadedClass` to function as the lock monitor. Specifically,

```
public class SomeThreadedClass extends Thread {
  private static Object lockObject = new Object();
  ...

  public void doSomeOperation() {
    synchronized(lockObject) {
      accessSomeSharedObject();
    }
  }
  ...
}
```

This last approach allows you to select an appropriate name for the lock to simplify code maintenance. In addition, if the class has multiple shared objects requiring synchronization in different methods, then creating a new lock object is probably the easiest to implement.

The synchronization problem that occurs with multiple `this` references is not a concern for a class that implements the `Runnable` interface. In this situation, all the associated threads are executing in the *same* `run` method of the class. Each thread has the same `this`. To avoid race conditions with the shared data, synchronization on `this` (either explicitly in a synchronized block or implicitly by means of the synchronized keyword) is perfectly appropriate.

16.4 Creating a Multithreaded Method

Occasionally, you will realize, after the fact, that some of the code that you wrote just begs to be threaded. Often this occurs because the program moved from a single-user environment to a multiuser environment. Here, processing each user serially is no longer acceptable. Or, another possibility is that your program invokes a computation-intensive method, leaving the user to simply wait until the process has completed before continuing. Not pretty.

In many cases, you can create a new class that runs the designated task in the background without modifying the original class at all. Conceptually, the idea is to inherit from the original class, make the class `Runnable`, and override the original method to produce the threaded behavior and invoke the original method located in the superclass. For this approach to work, the following two restrictions should hold:

- The method performs a task only; no side effects are produced on other variables.
- The method does not return data; the method simply returns `void`.

For the first requirement, the understanding is that the method does not modify other variables (either in the class or outside the class) that might be required by a subsequent thread requiring the data; otherwise, a race condition may be produced. The second requirement is also necessary because the calling program would otherwise simply wait for the return result anyway. If these two conditions do not hold, then most likely the original class will require modification to prevent race conditions. Real examples where this approach is common include sending messages to a log file, processing clients on an HTTP (Web) server, and handling mail through an SMTP server.

To illustrate this approach, assume that the class, `SomeClass`, contains a method, `foo`, with a single parameter argument, `randomArg`, and that `foo` produces no side effects on other variables or objects. The basic template for threading the `foo` method without modifying the original class is:

```
public class ThreadedSomeClass extends SomeClass
                           implements Runnable {
  //foo returns void, since no side effects are allowed.
  public void foo(RandomClass randomArg) {
    MyThread t = new MyThread(this, randomArg);
    t.start();
  }

  public void run() {
    MyThread t = (MyThread)Thread.currentThread();
    RandomClass randomArg =
              (RandomClass)t.getValueSavedEarlier();
    super.foo(randomArg);
  }
}
```

Wrapping a thread around the `foo` method (`super.foo`) permits `foo` to return immediately while the task continues to run in the background.

The basic template for MyThread is:

```java
public class MyThread extends Thread {
  private Object data;
  public MyThread(Runnable runnable, Object data) {
    super(runnable);
    this.data = data;
  }
  public Object getValueSavedEarlier() {
    return data;
  }
}
```

The foo method argument, randomArg, is passed to the constructor of MyThread and saved as a *local* copy inside MyThread to avoid the possibility of a race condition. Saving a local copy of randomArg inside foo doesn't prevent the race condition because randomArg might be modified between the time that the thread is started and the time that the same thread is able to call super.foo in run. Synchronization in foo does not solve the problem either because program execution immediately jumps to another method. Once the thread is running, the data saved earlier in MyThread is retrieved and the original foo, located in the superclass, is then called.

The template for MyThread made one subtle assumption: that a "new" RandomClass object is passed into foo each time, or RandomClass is an immutable class (instance variables cannot change), for example, String, Integer, Float, Double, etc. MyThread only saves a *reference* to the randomArg object; any changes to instance variables of randomArg are also seen by data. Thus, if foo doesn't pass in a new RandomClass object each time, then object cloning in MyThread is required to truly preserve a local copy, as in

```java
this.data = data.clone();
```

The clone method in RandomClass should perform *deep* cloning (copying of all internal objects—primitive instance variables are always copied by default).

An example of creating a background process from an originally nonthreaded class method is shown in Listing 16.13 and Listing 16.14. The nonthreaded class, RSAKey, provides a method, calculateKey, to calculate an RSA public-private key pair, where the minimum number of digits for the public key is passed in as a parameter. The calculated RSA pair, along with the modulus, N, is printed to System.out. The source for Primes.java can be downloaded from the on-line archive at http://corewebprogramming.com/.

Listing 16.13 RSAKey.java

```java
import java.math.BigInteger;

/** Calculate RSA public key pairs with a minimum number of
 *   required digits.
 */

public class RSAKey {
  private static final BigInteger ONE = new BigInteger("1");

  // Determine the encryption and decryption key.
  // To encrypt an integer M, compute R = M^e mod N.
  // To decrypt the encrypted integer R, compute M = R^d mod N,
  // where e is the public key and d is the private key.
  // For a discussion of the algorithm see section 7.4.3 of
  // Weiss's Data Structures and Problem Solving with Java.

  public void computeKey(String strNumDigits) {
    BigInteger p, q, n, m, encrypt, decrypt;
    int numDigits = Integer.parseInt(strNumDigits);
    if (numDigits%2==1) {
      numDigits++;
    }
    do {
      p = Primes.nextPrime(Primes.random(numDigits/2));
      q = Primes.nextPrime(Primes.random(numDigits/2));

      n = p.multiply(q);
      m = (p.subtract(ONE)).multiply(q.subtract(ONE));

      // Find encryption key, relatively prime to m.
      encrypt = Primes.nextPrime(Primes.random(numDigits));
      while (!encrypt.gcd(m).equals(ONE)) {
        encrypt = Primes.nextPrime(encrypt);
      }
      // Decrypt key is multiplicative inverse of encrypt mod m.
      decrypt = encrypt.modInverse(m);
    // Ensure public and private key have size numDigits.
    }while ((decrypt.toString().length() != numDigits) ||
            (encrypt.toString().length() != numDigits) ||
            (n.toString().length() != numDigits));
    System.out.println("\nN       => " + n);
    System.out.println("public  => " + encrypt);
    System.out.println("private => " + decrypt);
  }
}
```

Listing 16.14 ThreadedRSAKey.java

```java
import java.io.*;

/** An example of creating a background process for an
 *  originally nonthreaded, class method. Normally,
 *  the program flow will wait until computeKey is finished.
 */

public class ThreadedRSAKey extends RSAKey implements Runnable {

  // Store strNumDigits into the thread to prevent race
  // conditions.
  public void computeKey(String strNumDigits) {
    RSAThread t = new RSAThread(this, strNumDigits);
    t.start();
  }

  // Retrieve the stored strNumDigits and call the original
  // method.  Processing is now done in the background.
  public void run() {
    RSAThread t = (RSAThread)Thread.currentThread();
    String strNumDigits = t.getStrDigits();
    super.computeKey(strNumDigits);
  }

  public static void main(String[] args){
    ThreadedRSAKey key = new ThreadedRSAKey();
    for (int i=0; i<args.length ; i++) {
        key.computeKey(args[i]);
    }
  }
}

class RSAThread extends Thread {
   protected String strNumDigits;

   public RSAThread(Runnable rsaObject, String strNumDigits) {
      super(rsaObject);
      this.strNumDigits = strNumDigits;
   }

   public String getStrDigits() {
     return(strNumDigits);
   }
}
```

Finding very large prime numbers is an extremely CPU-intensive process, so a natural extension is to thread the calculateKey method as a background process instead of waiting for the results to finish before performing another task. The class, ThreadedRSAKey, provides a threaded version of calculateKey, saving a local copy of the argument in an instance of RSAThread. An example of the output from the ThreadedRSAKey application is shown in Listing 16.15. As shown, calculation of the key pair with 5 digits (first command-line argument) is completed before the key pair with 25 digits (second command-line argument).

Prior to October 2000, the RSA algorithm was protected under United States Patent No. 4,405,829. Commercial use of the algorithm to encode and decode data without a license is now permitted.

Listing 16.15 ThreadedRSAKey Output

```
>java ThreadedRSAKey 50 8

N        => 22318033
public   => 99371593
private  => 13439917

N        => 8058780597283442598051643118448241601994149946039
public   => 8214567321079385034667082232491070474311391748417
private  => 5473857675407953015796790835919772340167728388913
```

An additional example of creating a multithreaded method in an originally non-threaded class is given in Section 17.8 (Example: A Simple HTTP Server). Here, a simple HTTP server handles client connections serially. After the handle-Connection method is threaded, the number of clients that can make a connection to the HTTP server in a fixed time interval is limited by how fast a Socket object is obtained and how quickly a new thread can be launched.

16.5 Thread Methods

The following subsections summarize the constructors, constants, and methods in the Thread class. Included also are the wait, notify, and notifyAll methods (which really belong to Object, not just to Thread).

Constructors

public Thread()

Using this constructor on the original `Thread` class is not very useful because once started, the thread will call its own `run` method, which is empty. However, a zero-argument constructor is commonly used for thread *subclasses* that have overridden the `run` method. Calling `new Thread()` is equivalent to calling `new Thread(null, null, "Thread-N")`, where *N* is automatically chosen by the system.

public Thread(Runnable target)

When you create a thread with a `Runnable` as a target, the target's `run` method will be used when `start` is called. This constructor is equivalent to `Thread(null, target, "Thread-N")`.

public Thread(ThreadGroup group, Runnable target)

This method creates a thread with the specified target (whose `run` method will be used), placing the thread in the designated `ThreadGroup` as long as that group's `checkAccess` method permits this action. A `ThreadGroup` is a collection of threads that can be operated on as a set; see Section 16.6 for details. In fact, *all* threads belong to a `ThreadGroup`; if one is not specified, then `ThreadGroup` of the thread creating the new thread is used. This constructor is equivalent to `Thread(group, target, "Thread-N")`.

public Thread(String name)

When threads are created, they are automatically given a name of the form `"Thread-N"` if a name is not specified. This constructor lets you supply your own name. Thread names can be retrieved with the `getName` method. This constructor is equivalent to `Thread(null, null, name)`, meaning that the calling thread's `ThreadGroup` will be used and the new thread's own `run` method will be called when the thread is started.

public Thread(ThreadGroup group, String name)

This constructor creates a thread in the given group with the specified name. The thread's own `run` method will be used when the thread is started. This constructor is equivalent to `Thread(group, null, name)`.

public Thread(Runnable target, String name)

This constructor creates a thread with the specified target and name. The target's `run` method will be used when the thread is started; this constructor is equivalent to `Thread(null, target, name)`.

public Thread(ThreadGroup group, Runnable target, String name)

This constructor creates a thread with the given group, target, and name. If the group is not `null`, the new thread is placed in the specified group unless the group's `checkAccess` method throws a `SecurityException`. If the group is `null`, the calling thread's group is used. If the target is not `null`, the passed-in thread's `run` method is used when started; if the target is `null`, the thread's own `run` is used.

Constants

public final int MAX_PRIORITY

This priority is the highest assignable priority of a thread.

public final int MIN_PRIORITY

This priority is the lowest assignable priority of a thread.

public final int NORM_PRIORITY

This priority given to the first user thread. Subsequent threads are automatically given the priority of their creating thread.

Typical implementations of the JVM define `MAX_PRIORITY` equal to 10, `NORM_PRIORITY` equal to 5, and `MIN_PRIORITY` equal to 1. However, be advised that the priority of a Java thread may map differently to the thread priorities supported by the underlying operating system. For instance, the Solaris Operating Environment supports 2^{31} priority levels, whereas Windows NT supports only 7 user priority levels. Thus, the 10 Java priority levels will map differently on the two operating systems. In fact, on Windows NT, two Java thread priorities can map to a single OS thread priority. If your program design is strongly dependent on thread priorities, thoroughly test your implementation before production release.

Methods

public static int activeCount()

This method returns the number of active threads in the thread's `Thread-Group` (and all subgroups).

public void checkAccess()

This method determines if the currently running thread has permission to modify the thread. The `checkAccess` method is used in applets and other applications that implement a `SecurityManager`.

public static native Thread currentThread()

This method returns a reference to the currently executing thread. Note that this is a `static` method and can be called by arbitrary methods, not just from within a `Thread` object.

public void destroy()

This method kills the thread without performing any cleanup operations. If the thread locked any locks, they remain locked. As of JDK 1.2, this method is not implemented.

public static void dumpStack()

This method prints a stack trace to `System.err`.

public static int enumerate(Thread[ ] groupThreads)

This method finds all active threads in the `ThreadGroup` belonging to the *currently executing* thread (not a particular specified thread), placing the references in the designated array. Use `activeCount` to determine the size of the array needed.

public ClassLoader getContextClassLoader() [Java 2]

This method returns the `ClassLoader` used by the thread to load resources and other classes. Unless explicitly assigned through `setContext-ClassLoader`, the `ClassLoader` for the thread is the same as the `Class-Loader` for the parent thread.

public final String getName()

This method gives the thread's name.

public final int getPriority()

This method gives the thread's priority. See `setPriority` for a discussion of the way Java schedules threads of different priorities.

public final ThreadGroup getThreadGroup()

This method returns the `ThreadGroup` to which the thread belongs. All threads belong to a group; if none is specified in the `Thread` constructor, the calling thread's group is used.

public void interrupt()

This method can force two possible outcomes. First, if the thread is executing the `join`, `sleep`, or `wait` methods, then the corresponding method will throw an `InterruptedException`. Second, the method sets a flag in the thread that can be detected by `isInterrupted`. In that case, the thread is responsible for checking the status of the interrupted flag and taking action if required. Calling `interrupted` resets the flag; calling `isInterrupted` does not reset the flag.

public static boolean interrupted()

This static method checks whether the *currently executing* thread is interrupted (i.e., has its interrupted flag set through `interrupt`) and clears the flag. This method differs from `isInterrupted`, which only checks whether the *specified* thread is interrupted.

public final native boolean isAlive()

This method returns `true` for running or suspended threads, `false` for threads that have completed the `run` method. A thread calling `isAlive` on itself is not too useful, since if you can call *any* method, then you are obviously alive. The method is used by external methods to check the liveness of thread references they hold.

public final boolean isDaemon()

This method determines whether the thread is a daemon thread. A Java program will exit when the only active threads remaining are daemon threads. A thread initially has the same status as the creating thread, but this can be changed with `setDaemon`. The garbage collector is an example of a daemon thread.

public boolean isInterrupted()

This method checks whether the thread's interrupt flag has been set and does so without modifying the status of the flag. You can reset the flag by calling `interrupted` from within the `run` method of the flagged thread.

public final void join() throws InterruptedException
public final synchronized join(long milliseconds)
throws InterruptedException
public final synchronized join(long milliseconds,
int nanoseconds)
throws InterruptedException

This method suspends the calling thread until either the specified timeout has elapsed or the thread on which `join` was called has terminated (i.e., would return `false` for `isAlive`). For those not familiar with the terminology of "thread joining," naming this method `sleepUntilDead` would have been clearer. This method provides a convenient way to wait until one thread has finished before starting another, but without polling or consuming too many CPU cycles. A thread should never try to join itself; the thread would simply wait forever (a bit boring, don't you think?). For more complex conditions, use wait and notify instead.

public final native void notify()
public final native void notifyAll()
Like wait, the notify and notifyAll method are really methods of Object, not just of Thread. The first method (notify) wakes up a single thread, and the second method (notifyAll) wakes all threads that are waiting for the specified object's lock. Only code that holds an object's lock (i.e., is inside a block of code synchronized on the object) can send a notify or notifyAll request; the thread or threads being notified will not actually be restarted until the process issuing the notify request gives up the lock. See the discussion of wait for more details.

public void run()
In this method the user places the actions to be performed. When run finishes, the thread exits. The method creating the thread should not call run directly on the thread object; the method should instead call start on the thread object.

public void setContextClassLoader(ClassLoader loader) [Java 2]
This method sets the ClassLoader for the thread. The ClassLoader defines the manner in which the Java Virtual Machine loads classes and resources used by the thread. If a SecurityManager prevents the assignment of a different ClassLoader, then a SecurityException is thrown. If not explicitly assigned, the ClassLoader for the thread assumes the same loader as for the parent thread.

public final void setDaemon(boolean becomeDaemon)
This method sets the daemon status of the thread. A thread initially has the same status as that of the creating thread, but this status can be changed with setDaemon. A Java program will exit when the only active threads remaining are daemon threads.

public final void setName(String threadName)
This method changes the name of the thread.

public final void setPriority(int threadPriority)
This method changes the thread's priority; higher-priority threads are supposed to be executed in favor of lower-priority ones. Legal values range from Thread.MIN_PRIORITY to Thread.MAX_PRIORITY. A thread's default pri-

ority is the same as the creating thread. The priority cannot be set higher than the MAX_PRIORITY of the thread's thread group. Be careful because starvation can occur: almost all current implementations use a completely preemptive scheduler where lower-priority threads will *never* be executed unless the higher-priority threads terminate, sleep, or wait for I/O.

public static native void sleep(long milliseconds)
 throws InterruptedException
public static native void sleep(long milliseconds,
                              int nanoseconds)
 throws InterruptedException

This method does a nonbusy wait for at least the specified amount of time unless the thread is interrupted. Since sleep is a static method, sleep is used by nonthreaded applications as well.

Core Approach

You can use Thread.sleep *from any method, not just in threads.*

public synchronized native void start()

This method is called to initialize the thread and then call run. If the thread is created with a null target (see the constructors earlier in this section), then start calls its own run method. But if some Runnable is supplied, then start calls the run method of that Runnable.

Note that applets also have a start method that is called after init is finished and before the first call to paint. Don't confuse the applet's start method with the start method of threads, although the applet's start method is a convenient place for applets to initiate threads.

public final void wait() throws InterruptedException
public final void wait(long milliseconds)
 throws InterruptedException
public final void wait(long milliseconds, int nanoseconds)
 throws InterruptedException

These methods give up the lock and suspend the current thread. The thread is restarted by notify or notifyAll. This method is actually a member of Object, not just of Thread, but can only be called from within a synchronized method or block of code. For example,

```
public synchronized void someMethod() {
  doSomePreliminaries();
  while (!someContinueCondition()) {
    try {
      // Give up the lock and suspend ourselves.
      // We'll rely on somebody else to wake us up,
      // but will check someContinueCondition before
      // proceeding, just in case we get woken up
      // for the wrong reason.
      wait();
    } catch(InterruptedException ie) {}
  }
  continueOperations();
}
```

You call `wait` on the object that is used to set up (tag) the synchronized block, so if the synchronization object is not the current object (`this`), simply call `wait` on the synchronizing object explicitly, as in the following example.

```
public void someOtherMethod() {
  doSomeUnsynchronizedStuff();
  synchronized(someObject) {
    doSomePreliminaries();
    while (!someContinueCondition()) {
      try {
        someObject.wait();
      } catch(InterruptedException ie) {}
    }
    continueOperations();
  }
  doSomeMoreUnsynchronizedStuff();
}
```

See Listing 16.16 for an example of using `wait` and `notify`.

public static native void yield()

If two threads of the same priority are running and neither thread sleeps or waits for I/O, they may or may not alternate execution. Using `yield` gives up execution to any other process of the same priority that is waiting and is a good practice to ensure that time-slicing takes place. Although leaving the details of time-slicing to the implementation definitely seems appropriate, in our opinion, not requiring that threads be time-sliced is a significant drawback in an otherwise excellent thread specification. Fortunately, virtually all Java 2 implementations perform time-slicing properly.

Stopping a Thread

In the original Java thread model, a `stop` method was included to terminate a live thread. This method was immediately deprecated in the next release of the Java platform since termination of a thread by `stop` immediately released all associated locks, potentially placing these locks in an inconsistent state for the remaining threads; housecleaning was not performed. The correct approach for terminating a thread is to set a flag that causes the `run` method to complete. For example,

```
class ThreadExample implements Runnable {
  private boolean running;
  public ThreadExample()
     Thread thread = new Thread(this);
     thread.start();
  }
  public void run(){
    running = true;
    while (running) {
    ...
    }
  }
  public void setRunning(boolean running) {
    this.running = running;
  }
}
```

Setting the flag `running` to `false` anywhere in the program will terminate the `while` loop the next time the thread is granted CPU time and the loop test is performed. This approach works well for a single thread executing in the `run` method or if all threads executing in the `run` method should be terminated through the same single flag.

For classes that inherit from `Thread`, each instance of the class contains a separate `run` method. The best approach for this situation is to add a public method to the class for setting an internal flag to terminate the `run` method. Consider the template shown in Listing 16.16 (originally written by Scott Oaks and published in *Java Report*, Vol. 2, No. 11, 1997, p. 87). The class provides a public method, `setState`, to change the thread state to `STOP`, `RUN`, or `WAIT`. In the `run` method of the class, the state of the thread is continuously polled, and when the state is changed to `STOP` (either through the object itself or through another object invoking the public `set-State` method), the `while` loop terminates and the instance of the thread dies. In addition, the thread can conveniently be placed in a waiting state (`WAIT`), where the thread will remain until interrupted, `thread.interrupt()`, or the state is set to `RUN`. Each instance of a thread from the class can be controlled individually through this technique.

Listing 16.16 `StoppableThread.java`

```java
/** A template to control the state of a thread through setting
 *  an internal flag.
 */

public class StoppableThread extends Thread {

   public static final int STOP    = 0;
   public static final int RUN     = 1;
   public static final int WAIT    = 2;
   private int state = RUN;

  /** Public method to permit setting a flag to stop or
   *  suspend the thread.  The state is monitored through the
   *  corresponding checkState method.
   */

   public synchronized void setState(int state) {
      this.state = state;
      if (state==RUN) {
         notify();
      }
   }

  /** Returns the desired state of the thread (RUN, STOP, WAIT).
   *  Normally, you may want to change the state or perform some
   *  other task if an InterruptedException occurs.
   */

   private synchronized int checkState() {
      while (state==WAIT) {
        try {
          wait();
        } catch (InterruptedException e) { }
      }
      return state;
   }

  /** An example of thread that will continue to run until
   *  the creating object tells the thread to STOP.
   */

   public void run() {
      while (checkState()!=STOP) {
         ...
      }
   }
}
```

Stopping Threads in an Applet

Applets have a `stop` method that is called whenever the Web page is exited or, in the case of Netscape, when the browser is resized. Depending on the browser, threads are not automatically stopped when transferring to another Web page, so you should normally put code in the applet's `stop` method to set flags to terminate all active threads.

Core Approach

If you make a multithreaded applet, you should halt the threads in the applet's `stop` *method, restarting them in the applet's* `start` *method.*

16.6 Thread Groups

The `ThreadGroup` class provides a convenient mechanism for controlling sets of threads. A `ThreadGroup` can contain other thread groups in addition to threads, letting you arrange groups hierarchically. The constructors and methods for the `ThreadGroup` class are summarized in the following subsections.

Constructors

public ThreadGroup(String groupName)

This constructor creates a named `ThreadGroup` that belongs to the same group as the thread that called the constructor.

public ThreadGroup(ThreadGroup parent, String groupName)

This constructor creates a named `ThreadGroup` that belongs to the specified parent group.

Methods

public synchronized int activeCount()

This method gives the number of active threads directly or indirectly in the thread group as of the time the method call was initiated.

public synchronized int activeGroupCount()

This method gives the number of active thread groups in the group as of the time the method call was initiated.

public final void checkAccess()

This method determines whether the calling thread is allowed to modify the group. The `checkAccess` method is used by applets and applications with a custom `SecurityManager`.

public final synchronized void destroy()

If the group contains no threads, the group (and any empty subgroups) is destroyed and removed from the parent group. The method throws an `IllegalThreadStateException` if the group contains any threads when this method is called.

public int enumerate(Thread[ ] threads)
public int enumerate(Thread[ ] threads, boolean recurse)
public int enumerate(ThreadGroup[ ] groups)
public int enumerate(ThreadGroup[ ] groups, boolean recurse)

These methods copy the references of active threads or thread groups into the specified array. If the `recurse` flag is `true`, the method recursively descends child groups.

public final int getMaxPriority()

This method returns the maximum priority that can be assigned to any thread in the group. See `setMaxPriority` for setting the value.

public final String getName()

This method returns the name of the group.

public final ThreadGroup getParent()

This method returns the parent group. The first group created in the system will have a `null` parent.

public final void interrupt()

This method invokes the `interrupt` method of each thread in the group and all subgroups if permitted by the security manager.

public final boolean isDaemon()

This methods tells you whether the group is a daemon group. Daemon groups are automatically destroyed when they are empty.

public final boolean isDestroyed()

This method determines whether the thread group is destroyed. A daemon group is automatically destroyed if the last thread is no longer running or the last subgroup is destroyed. Adding a `Thread` or `ThreadGroup` to a destroyed thread group is not permitted.

public synchronized void list()

This method prints all the threads and subgroups in the group to `System.out` and is a useful debugging tool.

public final boolean parentOf(ThreadGroup descendant)

This method determines whether the group is an ancestor (not necessarily the direct parent) of the specified descendant group.

public final void setDaemon(boolean becomeDaemon)

A group automatically gets the daemon status of the parent group; this method can change that initial status. A daemon group is automatically destroyed when the group becomes empty.

public final synchronized void setMaxPriority(int max)

This method gives the maximum priority that any thread in the group can be explicitly given by `setPriority`. Threads in the thread group with higher priorities remain unchanged. The threads can still inherit a higher priority from their creating thread, however.

public void uncaughtException(Thread thread, Throwable error)

When a thread throws an exception that is not caught, execution flow is transferred to the `uncaughtException` method first. The default behavior is to print a stack trace.

16.7 Multithreaded Graphics and Double Buffering

One common application of threads is to develop dynamic graphics. Various standard approaches are available, each of which has various advantages and disadvantages.

- **Redraw Everything in paint.** This approach is simple and easy, but if things change quickly, drawing everything in `paint` is slow and can result in a flickering display.

- **Implement the Dynamic Part as a Separate Component.** This approach is relatively easy and eliminates the flickering problem but requires a `null` layout manager and can be quite slow.
- **Have Routines Other Than paint Draw Directly.** This approach is easy, efficient, and flicker free but results in "transient" drawing that is lost the next time the screen is redrawn.
- **Override update and Have paint Do Incremental Updating.** This approach eliminates the flicker and improves efficiency somewhat but requires the graphics to be nonoverlapping.
- **Use Double Buffering.** This approach is the most efficient option and has no problem with overlapping graphics. However, double buffering is more complex than other approaches and requires additional memory resources.

Redraw Everything in paint

A common technique in graphical Java programs is to have processes set parameters that describe the appearance of the window, rather than drawing the graphics themselves. The various routines call `repaint` to schedule a call to `paint`, and `paint` does the necessary drawing based on the parameters that have been set. The `repaint` method actually calls `update`, which clears the screen and then calls `paint` with the appropriate `Graphics` object. The `paint` method also is called automatically after the applet is initialized, whenever part of the applet is obscured and reexposed and when certain other resizing or layout events occur. A rectangular region can also be supplied when the `repaint` method is called to determine the clipping region given to the `Graphics` object used in `update` and `paint`. However, determining the proper area is difficult, and the entire region, not just some particular graphical items, is still redrawn.

For instance, suppose you are developing a user interface for a naval simulation system and you need to animate the icons that represent the ships. A background thread (or threads) could be updating the positions, then periodically invoking `repaint`. The `paint` method simply loops over all the simulation objects, drawing them in their current positions, as shown in the simplified example of Listing 16.17.

Listing 16.17 ShipSimulation.java

```
import java.applet.Applet;
import java.awt.*;

public class ShipSimulation extends Applet implements Runnable {
  ...
    public void run() {
    Ship s;
    for(int i=0; i<ships.length; i++) {
      s = ships[i];
      s.move(); // Update location.
    }
    repaint();
  }

  ...

  public void paint(Graphics g) {
    Ship s;
    for(int i=0; i<ships.length; i++) {
      s = ships[i];
      g.draw(s); // Draw at current location.
    }
  }
}
```

Alternatively, you might only initiate changes to the interface at user request but still redraw everything each time. For example, suppose that you want to draw some sort of image wherever the user clicks the mouse. Listing 16.18 shows a solution using the "store and redraw" approach, with a sample result shown in Figure 16–1. Here, when the user clicks the mouse, a new SimpleCircle object is created and added to the data structure. The repaint method is immediately called and completely redraws each SimpleCircle in the data structure on the applet.

Listing 16.18 `DrawCircles.java`

```java
import java.applet.Applet;
import java.awt.*;
import java.awt.event.*;
import java.util.Vector;

/** An applet that draws a small circle where you click.*/

public class DrawCircles extends Applet {

  private Vector circles;

  /** When you click the mouse, create a SimpleCircle,
   *  put it in the Vector, and tell the system
   *  to repaint (which calls update, which clears
   *  the screen and calls paint).
   */

  private class CircleDrawer extends MouseAdapter {
    public void mousePressed(MouseEvent event) {
      circles.addElement(
          new SimpleCircle(event.getX(),event.getY(),25));
      repaint();
    }
  }

  public void init() {
    circles = new Vector();
    addMouseListener(new CircleDrawer());
    setBackground(Color.white);
  }

  /** This loops down the available SimpleCircle objects,
   *  drawing each one.
   */

  public void paint(Graphics g) {
    SimpleCircle circle;
    for(int i=0; i<circles.size(); i++) {
      circle = (SimpleCircle)circles.elementAt(i);
      circle.draw(g);
    }
  }
}
```

Listing 16.19 presents the `SimpleCircle` class used in `DrawCircles`.

Listing 16.19 `SimpleCircle.java`

```java
import java.awt.*;

/** A class to store an x, y, and radius, plus a draw method.
 */

public class SimpleCircle {
  private int x, y, radius;

  public SimpleCircle(int x, int y, int radius) {
    setX(x);
    setY(y);
    setRadius(radius);
  }

  /** Given a Graphics, draw the SimpleCircle
   *   centered around its current position.
   */

  public void draw(Graphics g) {
    g.fillOval(x - radius, y - radius,
               radius * 2, radius * 2);
  }

  public int getX() { return(x); }

  public void setX(int x) { this.x = x; }

  public int getY() { return(y); }

  public void setY(int y) { this.y = y; }

  public int getRadius() { return(radius); }

  public void setRadius(int radius) {
    this.radius = radius;
  }
}
```

Pros and Cons

This approach is quite simple and was well suited to the circle-drawing application. However, the approach is poorly suited to applications that have complicated, time-consuming graphics (because all or part of the window gets redrawn each time) or for ones that have frequent changes (because of the flicker caused by the clearing of the screen).

Implement the Dynamic Part as a Separate Component

Components know how to update themselves, so the Container that uses a Component need not explicitly draw it. For instance, in the simulation example above, the ships could be implemented as custom subclasses of Canvas and placed in a window with a null layout manager. To update the positions, the main simulation process could simply call move on the components. Similarly, drawing triggered by user events is a simple matter of creating a Component, setting its x and y locations, and adding the component to the current Container. An example of drawing circles this way is shown in Section 13.9 (Serializing Windows).

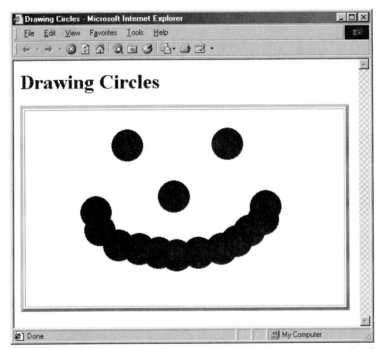

Figure 16–1 By storing results in a permanent data structure and redrawing the whole structure every time paint is invoked, you cause the drawing to persist even after the window is covered up and reexposed.

Pros and Cons

In some situations, this approach is easier than doing things explicitly in paint because the movement can be controlled directly by the Component, with few changes required in the code for the Container. However, this approach suffers from problems with overlapping components and also suffers from poor speed performance and memory usage. Creating a separate `Canvas` for each drawing is expensive, and moving the component involves more than just redrawing.

Have Routines Other Than paint Draw Directly

In some cases, you don't want to bother to call `paint` *at all*, but you want to do drawing directly. You can do the drawing by getting the `Graphics` object, using `getGraphics`, setting the drawing mode to use XOR, then directly calling the `drawXxx` methods of the `Graphics` object. You can erase the original drawing by drawing in the same location a second time, at least as long as multiple drawing does not overlap. To illustrate this technique, Listing 16.20 creates a simple `Applet` that lets the user create and stretch "rubberband" rectangles. Figure 16–2 shows a typical result.

Listing 16.20 `Rubberband.java`

```java
import java.applet.Applet;
import java.awt.*;
import java.awt.event.*;

/** Draw "rubberband" rectangles when the user drags
 *  the mouse.
 */

public class Rubberband extends Applet {
  private int startX, startY, lastX, lastY;

  public void init() {
    addMouseListener(new RectRecorder());
    addMouseMotionListener(new RectDrawer());
    setBackground(Color.white);
  }

  /** Draw the rectangle, adjusting the x, y, w, h
   *  to correctly accommodate for the opposite corner of the
   *  rubberband box relative to the start position.
   */

  private void drawRectangle(Graphics g, int startX, int startY,
                             int stopX, int stopY ) {
    int x, y, w, h;
    x = Math.min(startX, stopX);
    y = Math.min(startY, stopY);
    w = Math.abs(startX - stopX);
    h = Math.abs(startY - stopY);
    g.drawRect(x, y, w, h);
  }
```

(continued)

Listing 16.20 Rubberband.java *(continued)*

```java
private class RectRecorder extends MouseAdapter {

  /** When the user presses the mouse, record the
   *  location of the top-left corner of rectangle.
   */

  public void mousePressed(MouseEvent event) {
    startX = event.getX();
    startY = event.getY();
    lastX = startX;
    lastY = startY;
  }

  /** Erase the last rectangle when the user releases
   *  the mouse.
   */

  public void mouseReleased(MouseEvent event) {
    Graphics g = getGraphics();
    g.setXORMode(Color.lightGray);
    drawRectangle(g, startX, startY, lastX, lastY);
  }
}

private class RectDrawer extends MouseMotionAdapter {

  /** This draws a rubberband rectangle, from the location
   *  where the mouse was first clicked to the location
   *  where the mouse is dragged.
   */

  public void mouseDragged(MouseEvent event) {
    int x = event.getX();
    int y = event.getY();

    Graphics g = getGraphics();
    g.setXORMode(Color.lightGray);
    drawRectangle(g, startX, startY, lastX, lastY);
    drawRectangle(g, startX, startY, x, y);

    lastX = x;
    lastY = y;
  }
}
}
```

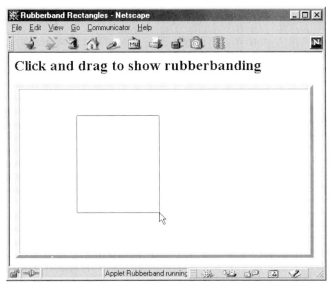

Figure 16–2 Direct drawing from threads or event handlers is easy to implement and is very fast but gives transient results.

Pros and Cons

This approach (direct drawing instead of setting variables that `paint` will use) is appropriate for temporary drawing; direct drawing is simple and efficient. However, if `paint` is ever triggered, this drawing will be lost. So, this approach is not appropriate for permanent drawing.

Override update and Have paint Do Incremental Updating

Suppose that some graphical objects need to be moved around on the screen. Suppose further that the objects never overlap one another. In such a case, rather than clearing the screen and completely redrawing the new situation, you could use the `paint` method to erase the object at its old location (say, by drawing a solid rectangle in the background color) and then redraw the object at the new location, saving the time required to redraw the rest of the window. The `paint` method could be triggered from some mouse or keyboard event or by a background thread calling the applet's `repaint` method. For this technique to work without flickering, however, you must define a new version of `update` that does not clear the screen before calling `paint`.

```
public void update(Graphics g) {
  paint(g);
}
```

Also, because `paint` runs from the same foreground thread that watches for mouse and keyboard events, keeping the time spent in `paint` as short as possible is important to prevent the system from being unresponsive to buttons, scrollbars, and the like.

Core Approach

Minimize the amount of time spent in `paint` because event handling executes in the same thread.

To illustrate this approach, Listing 16.21 shows an applet that lets you create any number of small circles that bounce around in the window. As can be seen in Figure 16–3, the incremental drawing works well everywhere except where the circles overlap, where erasing one circle can accidentally erase part of another circle.

Listing 16.21 `Bounce.java`

```java
import java.applet.Applet;
import java.awt.*;
import java.awt.event.*;
import java.util.Vector;

/** Bounce circles around on the screen. Doesn't use double
 *  buffering, so has problems with overlapping circles.
 *  Overrides update to avoid flicker problems.
 */

public class Bounce extends Applet implements Runnable,
                                              ActionListener {
  private Vector circles;
  private int width, height;
  private Button startButton, stopButton;
  private Thread animationThread = null;

  public void init() {
    setBackground(Color.white);
    width = getSize().width;
    height = getSize().height;
    circles = new Vector();
```

(continued)

Listing 16.21 Bounce.java *(continued)*

```
    startButton = new Button("Start a circle");
    startButton.addActionListener(this);
    add(startButton);
    stopButton = new Button("Stop all circles");
    stopButton.addActionListener(this);
    add(stopButton);
  }

  /** When the "start" button is pressed, start the animation
   *  thread if it is not already started. Either way, add a
   *  circle to the Vector of circles that are being bounced.
   *  <P>
   *  When the "stop" button is pressed, stop the thread and
   *  clear the Vector of circles.
   */

  public void actionPerformed(ActionEvent event) {
    if (event.getSource() == startButton) {
      if (circles.size() == 0) {
        // Erase any circles from previous run.
        getGraphics().clearRect(0, 0, getSize().width,
                                      getSize().height);
        animationThread = new Thread(this);
        animationThread.start();
      }
      int radius = 25;
      int x = radius + randomInt(width - 2 * radius);
      int y = radius + randomInt(height - 2 * radius);
      int deltaX = 1 + randomInt(10);
      int deltaY = 1 + randomInt(10);
      circles.addElement(new MovingCircle(x, y, radius, deltaX,
                                          deltaY));
    } else if (event.getSource() == stopButton) {
      if (animationThread != null) {
        animationThread = null;
        circles.removeAllElements();
      }
    }
    repaint();
  }

  /** Each time around the loop, call paint and then take a
   *  short pause. The paint method will move the circles and
   *  draw them.
   */
```

(continued)

Listing 16.21 `Bounce.java` *(continued)*

```java
public void run() {
  Thread myThread = Thread.currentThread();
  // Really while animationThread not null
  while(animationThread==myThread) {
    repaint();
    pause(100);
  }
}

/** Skip the usual screen-clearing step of update so that
 *  there is no flicker between each drawing step.
 */

public void update(Graphics g) {
  paint(g);
}

/** Erase each circle's old position, move it, then draw it
 *  in new location.
 */

public void paint(Graphics g) {
  MovingCircle circle;
  for(int i=0; i<circles.size(); i++) {
    circle = (MovingCircle)circles.elementAt(i);
    g.setColor(getBackground());
    circle.draw(g);  // Old position.
    circle.move(width, height);
    g.setColor(getForeground());
    circle.draw(g);  // New position.
  }
}

// Returns an int from 0 to max (inclusive),
// yielding max + 1 possible values.

private int randomInt(int max) {
  double x =
    Math.floor((double)(max + 1) * Math.random());
  return((int)(Math.round(x)));
}

// Sleep for the specified amount of time.

private void pause(int milliseconds) {
  try {
    Thread.sleep((long)milliseconds);
  } catch(InterruptedException ie) {}
}
}
```

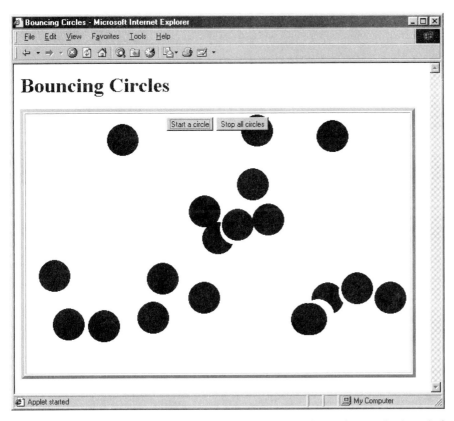

Figure 16–3 Incremental updating from `paint` can be flicker free and relatively fast, but it does not easily handle overlapping items.

The `Bounce` class makes use of `MovingCircle`, a class that encapsulates the movement of the circle as well as the position and size, which are inherited from `SimpleCircle`. `MovingCircle` is shown in Listing 16.22.

Listing 16.22 `MovingCircle.java`

```
/** An extension of SimpleCircle that can be moved around
 *  according to deltaX and deltaY values. Movement will
 *  continue in a given direction until the edge of the circle
 *  reaches a wall, when it will "bounce" and move in the other
 *  direction.
 */
```

(continued)

Listing 16.22 MovingCircle.java *(continued)*

```java
public class MovingCircle extends SimpleCircle {
  private int deltaX, deltaY;

  public MovingCircle(int x, int y, int radius, int deltaX,
                      int deltaY) {
    super(x, y, radius);
    this.deltaX = deltaX;
    this.deltaY = deltaY;
  }

  public void move(int windowWidth, int windowHeight) {
    setX(getX() + getDeltaX());
    setY(getY() + getDeltaY());
    bounce(windowWidth, windowHeight);
  }

  private void bounce(int windowWidth, int windowHeight) {
    int x = getX(), y = getY(), radius = getRadius(),
        deltaX = getDeltaX(), deltaY = getDeltaY();
    if ((x - radius < 0) && (deltaX < 0)) {
      setDeltaX(-deltaX);
    } else if ((x + radius > windowWidth) && (deltaX > 0)) {
      setDeltaX(-deltaX);
    }
    if ((y -radius < 0) && (deltaY < 0)) {
      setDeltaY(-deltaY);
    } else if((y + radius > windowHeight) && (deltaY > 0)) {
      setDeltaY(-deltaY);
    }
  }

  public int getDeltaX() {
    return(deltaX);
  }

  public void setDeltaX(int deltaX) {
    this.deltaX = deltaX;
  }

  public int getDeltaY() {
    return(deltaY);
  }

  public void setDeltaY(int deltaY) {
    this.deltaY = deltaY;
  }
}
```

Pros and Cons

This approach takes a bit more effort than previous ones and requires that your objects be nonoverlapping. However, incremental updating lets you implement "permanent" drawing more quickly than redrawing everything every time.

Use Double Buffering

Consider a scenario that involves many different moving objects or overlapping objects. Drawing several different objects individually is expensive, and, if the objects overlap, reliably erasing them in their old positions is difficult. In such a situation, double buffering is often employed. In this approach, an off-screen image (pixmap) is created, and all of the drawing operations are done into this image. The actual "drawing" of the window consists of a single step: draw the image on the screen. As before, the `update` method is overridden to avoid clearing of the screen. Even though the image replaces the applet graphics each time something is drawn to the image, the default implementation of `update` would still clear the applet in the background color before drawing the image.

Double buffering is automatically built into Swing components. However, for AWT components, double buffering must be provided by the programmer. Although different variations are available for double buffering, the basic approach involves five steps.

1. **Override update to simply call `paint`.** This step prevents the flicker that would normally occur each time `update` clears the screen before calling `paint`.

2. **Allocate an `Image` by using `createImage`.** Since this image uses native window-system support, the allocation cannot be done until a window actually appears. For instance, you should call `createImage` in an applet from `init` (or later), not in the direct initialization of an instance variable. For an application, you should wait until after the initial frame has been displayed (e.g., by `setVisible`) before calling `createImage`. However, calling `createImage` for a component that has no peer results in the return of `null`. Normally, the peer is created when the component is first displayed. Or, you can call `add-Notify` to force creation of the peer prior to `setVisible`.

Core Warning

Calling `createImage` from a component that is not visible results in `null`.

3. **Look up the `Graphics` object by using `getGraphics`.** Unlike the case with windows, where you need to look up the `Graphics` context each time you draw, with images you can reliably get the `Graphics` object associated with the image once, store the object in a reference, and reuse the same reference thereafter.

4. **For each step, clear the image and redraw all objects.** This step will be dramatically faster than drawing onto a visible window. In Swing, you achieve this result by calling `super.paintComponent`.

5. **Draw the off-screen image onto the window.** Use `drawImage` for this step.

Listing 16.23 shows a concrete implementation of this approach. `Double-BufferBounce` changes the previous `Bounce` applet to use double buffering, resulting in improved performance and eliminating the problems with overlapping circles. Figure 16–4 shows the result.

Listing 16.23 `DoubleBufferBounce.java`

```java
import java.applet.Applet;
import java.awt.*;
import java.awt.event.*;
import java.util.Vector;

/** Bounce circles around on the screen, using double buffering
 *  for speed and to avoid problems with overlapping circles.
 *  Overrides update to avoid flicker problems.
 */

public class DoubleBufferBounce extends Applet implements
                                    Runnable, ActionListener {
  private Vector circles;
  private int width, height;
  private Image offScreenImage;
  private Graphics offScreenGraphics;
  private Button startButton, stopButton;
  private Thread animationThread = null;

  public void init() {
    setBackground(Color.white);
    width = getSize().width;
    height = getSize().height;
    offScreenImage = createImage(width, height);
    offScreenGraphics = offScreenImage.getGraphics();
```

(continued)

Listing 16.23 `DoubleBufferBounce.java` *(continued)*

```java
    // Automatic in some systems, not in others.
    offScreenGraphics.setColor(Color.black);
    circles = new Vector();
    startButton = new Button("Start a circle");
    startButton.addActionListener(this);
    add(startButton);
    stopButton = new Button("Stop all circles");
    stopButton.addActionListener(this);
    add(stopButton);
  }

  /** When the "start" button is pressed, start the animation
   *  thread if it is not already started. Either way, add a
   *  circle to the Vector of circles that are being bounced.
   *  <P>
   *  When the "stop" button is pressed, stop the thread and
   *  clear the Vector of circles.
   */

  public void actionPerformed(ActionEvent event) {
    if (event.getSource() == startButton) {
      if (circles.size() == 0) {
        animationThread = new Thread(this);
        animationThread.start();
      }
      int radius = 25;
      int x = radius + randomInt(width - 2 * radius);
      int y = radius + randomInt(height - 2 * radius);
      int deltaX = 1 + randomInt(10);
      int deltaY = 1 + randomInt(10);
      circles.addElement(new MovingCircle(x, y, radius, deltaX,
                                          deltaY));
      repaint();
    } else if (event.getSource() == stopButton) {
      if (animationThread != null) {
        animationThread = null;
        circles.removeAllElements();
      }
    }
  }

  /** Each time around the loop, move each circle based on its
   *  current position and deltaX/deltaY values. These values
   *  reverse when the circles reach the edge of the window.
   */
```

(continued)

Listing 16.23 `DoubleBufferBounce.java` *(continued)*

```java
public void run() {
  MovingCircle circle;
  Thread myThread = Thread.currentThread();
  // Really while animationThread not null.
  while(animationThread==myThread) {
    for(int j=0; j<circles.size(); j++) {
      circle = (MovingCircle)circles.elementAt(j);
      circle.move(width, height);
    }
    repaint();
    pause(100);
  }
}

/** Skip the usual screen-clearing step of update so that
 *  there is no flicker between each drawing step.
 */

public void update(Graphics g) {
  paint(g);
}

/** Clear the off-screen pixmap, draw each circle onto it, then
 *  draw that pixmap onto the applet window.
 */

public void paint(Graphics g) {
  offScreenGraphics.clearRect(0, 0, width, height);
  MovingCircle circle;
  for(int i=0; i<circles.size(); i++) {
    circle = (MovingCircle)circles.elementAt(i);
    circle.draw(offScreenGraphics);
  }
  g.drawImage(offScreenImage, 0, 0, this);
}

// Returns an int from 0 to max (inclusive), yielding max + 1
// possible values.

private int randomInt(int max) {
  double x = Math.floor((double)(max + 1) * Math.random());
  return((int)(Math.round(x)));
}

// Sleep for the specified amount of time.

private void pause(int milliseconds) {
  try {
    Thread.sleep((long)milliseconds);
  } catch(InterruptedException ie) {}
}
}
```

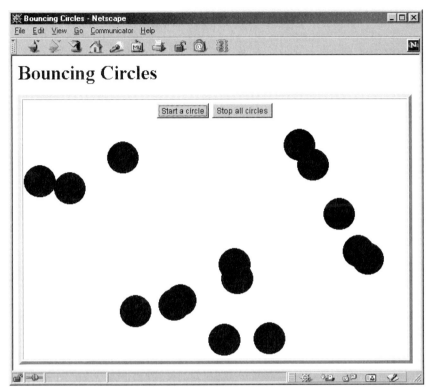

Figure 16–4 Double buffering allows fast, flicker-free updating of possibly overlapping images, but at the cost of some complexity and additional memory usage.

Pros and Cons

Drawing into an off-screen image and then drawing that image once to the screen is much faster than drawing directly to the screen. Double buffering allows fast, flicker-free updating even when no reliable way to erase the old graphics is available. However, double buffering is more complex than most of the previously discussed options and requires extra memory for the off-screen image.

Don't underestimate the beauty and strength of double buffering. Granted, additional programing is required to achieve double buffering in the AWT model. However, once you move to Swing components (covered in Chapter 14, Basic Swing), everything you've learned about double buffering becomes commonplace, because double buffering is built right into the Swing model. What a plus!

16.8 Animating Images

An exciting application for threads is animation of images. Many Web pages contain animated GIF files (GIF89A) that cycle through a sequence of images. Typically, these animated GIF files are created with graphical packages like Adobe PhotoShop and Quark, which permit selection of a sequence of equal-sized images to combine into a single GIF file. When loaded into a browser, each subimage in the GIF sequence is presented to the user in a time-sliced fashion. The Java programming language provides better control over animated GIF89A files because the sequence of images can be explicitly controlled, as can the timing interval between image updates. The basic concept for creating animated images is as follows:

- Read the sequence of images into an `Image` array.
- Define an index variable to sequence through the `Image` array.
- Start a thread to continuously cycle through a sequence of index values, calling `repaint` and `sleep` after each change of the index value.
- In `paint` (AWT) or `paintComponent` (Swing), draw the indexed image to the `Graphics` or `Graphics2D` object.

The order in which the images are presented to the user is controlled by the index sequence, and the delay between image updates is controlled by the sleeping interval of the thread (as well as by the OS). See Section 9.12 (Drawing Images) for additional information on loading and drawing images.

An example of creating an animated image is shown in Listing 16.24. In this applet, each `Duke` object represents a unique thread cycling an index through an array of 15 images. One thread cycles through the index values in increasing order (`tumbleDirection` of `1`), while the other thread cycles through the index values in decreasing order (`tumbleDirection` of `-1`). For each thread to have knowledge of the `repaint` method in the applet, a reference to the parent `Applet` is passed in to the `Duke` constructor. Whenever an index value is changed in either thread, redrawing of the applet is requested by a call to `repaint`. The `paint` method queries each thread for the corresponding image index value and then draws the correct Duke^{TM} image stored in the array to the `Graphics` object.

Additionally, the `Duke` class provides a public `setState` method so that the thread can be courteously started and stopped when the HTML file is loaded and removed from the browser. The result for this applet is shown in Figure 16–5. An excellent enhancement to this animation would be to preload the images before any drawing is performed. See Section 9.13 (Preloading Images) and Section 9.14 (Controlling Image Loading: Waiting for Images and Checking Status) for additional details.

Listing 16.24 ImageAnimation.java

```java
import java.applet.Applet;
import java.awt.*;

public class ImageAnimation extends Applet {

/** Sequence through an array of 15 images to perform the
 *  animation. A separate Thread controls each tumbling Duke.
 *  The Applet's stop method calls a public service of the
 *  Duke class to terminate the thread. Override update to
 *  avoid flicker problems.
 */

  private static final int NUMDUKES  = 2;
  private Duke[] dukes;
  private int i;

  public void init() {
    dukes = new Duke[NUMDUKES];
    setBackground(Color.white);
  }


  /** Start each thread, specifying a direction to sequence
   *  through the array of images.
   */

  public void start() {
    int tumbleDirection;
    for (int i=0; i<NUMDUKES ; i++) {
      tumbleDirection = (i%2==0) ? 1 :-1;
      dukes[i] = new Duke(tumbleDirection, this);
      dukes[i].start();
    }
  }


  /** Skip the usual screen-clearing step of update so that
   *  there is no flicker between each drawing step.
   */

  public void update(Graphics g) {
    paint(g);
  }
```

(continued)

Listing 16.24 `ImageAnimation.java` *(continued)*

```java
public void paint(Graphics g) {
  for (i=0 ; i<NUMDUKES ; i++) {
    if (dukes[i] != null) {
      g.drawImage(Duke.images[dukes[i].getIndex()],
                  200*i, 0, this);
    }
  }
}


/** When the Applet's stop method is called, use the public
 *  service, setState, of the Duke class to set a flag and
 *  terminate the run method of the thread.
 */

public void stop() {
  for (int i=0; i<NUMDUKES ; i++) {
    if (dukes[i] != null) {
      dukes[i].setState(Duke.STOP);
    }
  }
}
}
```

Listing 16.25 `Duke.java`

```java
import java.applet.Applet;
import java.awt.*;

/** Duke is a Thread that has knowledge of the parent applet
 *  (highly coupled) and thus can call the parent's repaint
 *  method. Duke is mainly responsible for changing an index
 *  value into an image array.
 */

public class Duke extends Thread {
  public static final int STOP = 0;
  public static final int RUN  = 1;
  public static final int WAIT = 2;
```

(continued)

Listing 16.25 `Duke.java` *(continued)*

```java
public static Image[] images;
private static final int NUMIMAGES = 15;
private static Object lock = new Object();
private int state = RUN;
private int tumbleDirection;
private int index = 0;
private Applet parent;

public Duke(int tumbleDirection, Applet parent) {
  this.tumbleDirection = tumbleDirection;
  this.parent = parent;
  synchronized(lock) {
    if (images==null) {  // If not previously loaded.
      images = new Image[ NUMIMAGES ];
      for (int i=0; i<NUMIMAGES; i++) {
        images[i] = parent.getImage( parent.getCodeBase(),
                                     "images/T" + i + ".gif");
      }
    }
  }
}

/** Return current index into image array.  */

public int getIndex() { return index; }

/** Public method to permit setting a flag to stop or
 *  suspend the thread. State is monitored through
 *  corresponding checkState method.
 */

public synchronized void setState(int state) {
  this.state = state;
  if (state==RUN) {
    notify();
  }
}

/** Returns the desired state (RUN, STOP, WAIT) of the
 *  thread. If the thread is to be suspended, then the
 *  thread method wait is continuously called until the
 *  state is changed through the public method setState.
 */
```

(continued)

Listing 16.25 Duke.java *(continued)*

```java
  private synchronized int checkState() {
    while (state==WAIT) {
      try {
        wait();
      } catch (InterruptedException e) {}
    }
    return state;
  }

  /** The variable index (into image array) is incremented
   *  once each time through the while loop, calls repaint,
   *  and pauses for a moment. Each time through the loop the
   *  state (flag) of the thread is checked.
   */

  public void run() {
    while (checkState()!=STOP) {
      index += tumbleDirection;
      if (index < 0) {
        index = NUMIMAGES - 1;
      }
      if (index >= NUMIMAGES) {
        index = 0;
      }

      parent.repaint();

      try {
        Thread.sleep(100);
      } catch (InterruptedException e) {
        break;    // Break while loop.
      }
    }
  }
}
```

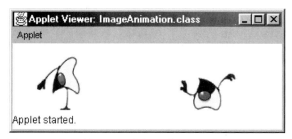

Figure 16–5 The use of threads to perform animation of Duke. [Duke™ is a registered trademark of Sun Microsystems, Inc. Images used with permission. All rights reserved.]

Interestingly, Java does support GIF89A files. Simply load the GIF file into an `Image` object and then draw the image in `paint` as normally would be done. Behind the scenes, Java sets up a *separate* Animator thread which continuously calls `repaint` and adjusts for the subimage embedded in the GIF89A file when `paint` is called. Ok, so you've placed an animated GIF (GIF89A) file in your applet and the user goes to a different HTML page. How do you gracefully stop the thread that is controlling the animation? What flag would you set and for which `run` method? Good question. In Internet Explorer, the Animator thread is automatically terminated when the user goes to a new Web page. Sadly though, in Netscape the browser must be closed to terminate the Animator thread.

16.9 Timers

Timers are useful for numerous tasks, including image animation, starting and stopping simulations, and timing out secure network connections. The previous section (Animating Images) illustrated the capability of animating images by creating a user-defined thread that periodically invokes a specified action and then goes to sleep. To simplify this common and useful task, a robust `Timer` class, `javax.swing.Timer`, was added to the Swing package. A `Timer` can run for a single cycle or be set to ring periodically.

Creating a Swing `Timer` is as simple as instantiating a `Timer` object, specifying the period in milliseconds that the `Timer` should fire an `ActionEvent` and specifying a listener that should receive the event. Once the timer is created, activate the timer by calling the `start` method, as in:

```
Timer timer = new Timer(period, listener);
timer.start();
```

By default, a `Timer` creates a thread that periodically fires an `ActionEvent` event every `period` milliseconds to *all* attached listeners (see `addActionListener`). Alternatively, the `Timer` can be defined to only fire one event, using `setRepeats(false)`, and then stop. However, unlike a normal `Thread` that once stopped, cannot be restarted, calling `restart` on a `Timer` begins the timing sequence over again.

When the `Timer` fires, an event object is sent to the event queue. Depending on how many events are already in the queue and how heavily the system is tasked, multiple `Timer` events can be queued before the first event is processed. By default, `Timer` events are coalesced. That is, if an earlier event is already in the queue, then the next trigger will not add a new event object into the queue. If *every* trigger event does indeed require processing, set coalescing to `false` with `setCoalese(false)`. By turning on logging, `setLogTimers(true)`, you send a print message to the standard output each time a `Timer` fires an `ActionEvent`, thus providing an easy means for determining when the timers are firing. The `setLogTimers` method is a `static` method; thus, *all* active timers in the program will generate a log message.

The application of a `Timer` to control image animation is shown in Listing 16.26 and Listing 16.27. Here, the use of timers *greatly* simplifies the animation, since *explicit* creation and control of `Thread` objects is no longer required. In this example, the applet creates two separate `TimedDuke` objects, each with an internal `Timer`. The triggering period for each timer is different. As more than one `TimedDuke` object is instantiated, the synchronization block in the constructor of `TimedDuke` (along with the `loaded` flag) prevents the potential race condition of loading the images twice. Once the `MediaTracker` acknowledges loading of the animation images into the array, each timer is started by the applet. When a timer fires, the `actionPerformed` method is eventually called on the appropriate `TimedDuke` object, which in turn increments an internal index into the image array and then calls `repaint` on the applet. Support methods permit the applet to start and stop the timers when the user transfers to a new HTML page and returns.

Listing 16.26 `TimedAnimation.java`

```
import java.awt.*;
import javax.swing.*;

/** An example of performing animation through Swing timers.
 *   Two timed Dukes are created with different timer periods.
 */

public class TimedAnimation extends JApplet {
  private static final int NUMDUKES = 2;
  private TimedDuke[] dukes;
  private int i, index;

  public void init() {
    dukes = new TimedDuke[NUMDUKES];
    setBackground(Color.white);
    dukes[0] = new TimedDuke( 1, 100, this);
    dukes[1] = new TimedDuke(-1, 500, this);

  }

  //   Start each Duke timer.
```

(continued)

Listing 16.26 `TimedAnimation.java` *(continued)*

```java
public void start() {
  for (int i=0; i<NUMDUKES ; i++) {
    dukes[i].startTimer();
  }
}

public void paint(Graphics g) {
  for (i=0 ; i<NUMDUKES ; i++) {
    if (dukes[i] != null) {
      index = dukes[i].getIndex();
      g.drawImage(TimedDuke.images[index], 200*i, 0, this);
    }
  }
}

// Stop each Duke timer.

public void stop() {
  for (int i=0; i<NUMDUKES ; i++) {
    dukes[i].stopTimer();
  }
}
}
```

Listing 16.27 `TimedDuke.java`

```java
import java.applet.Applet;
import java.awt.*;
import java.awt.event.*;
import javax.swing.*;

/** Duke facilitates animation by creating an internal timer.
 *  When the timer fires, an actionPerformed event is
 *  triggered, which in turn calls repaint on the parent
 *  Applet.
 */

public class TimedDuke implements ActionListener {
  private static final int NUMIMAGES = 15;
  private static boolean loaded = false;
  private static Object lock = new Object();
```

(continued)

Listing 16.27 `TimedDuke.java` *(continued)*

```java
private int tumbleDirection;
private int msec;
private int index = 0;
private Applet parent;
private Timer timer;
public static Image[] images = new Image[NUMIMAGES];

public TimedDuke(int tumbleDirection, int msec,
                                    Applet parent) {
  this.tumbleDirection = tumbleDirection;
  this.msec = msec;
  this.parent = parent;

  synchronized (lock) {
    if (!loaded) {
      MediaTracker tracker = new MediaTracker(parent);
      for (int i=0; i<NUMIMAGES; i++) {
        images[i] = parent.getImage(parent.getCodeBase(),
                                    "images/T" + i + ".gif");
        tracker.addImage(images[i],0);
      }
      try {
        tracker.waitForAll();
      } catch (InterruptedException ie) {}
      if (!tracker.isErrorAny()) {
        loaded = true;
      }
    }
  }

  timer = new Timer(msec, this);
}

// Return current index into image array.

public int getIndex() { return index; }

// Receives timer firing event.  Increments the index into
// image array and forces repainting of the new image.

public void actionPerformed(ActionEvent event) {
  index += tumbleDirection;
  if (index < 0){
    index = NUMIMAGES - 1;
  }
```

(continued)

> **Listing 16.27** `TimedDuke.java` *(continued)*

```
    if (index >= NUMIMAGES) {
      index = 0;
    }
    parent.repaint();
  }

  // Public service to start the timer.
  public void startTimer() {
    timer.start();
  }

  // Public service to stop the timer.
  public void stopTimer() {
    timer.stop();
  }
}
```

Constructor

The `Timer` class has only one constructor:

public Timer(int period, ActionListener listener)

The `Timer` class has a single constructor that sets the timing period and listener to receive the timing event. By default, the timer will fire (ring) an `ActionEvent` event every `period` milliseconds. The fired event is delivered to all registered listeners.

Other Timer Methods

public void addActionListener(ActionListener listener)

This method registers an `ActionListener` with the `Timer`. Each queued `ActionEvent` is delivered to the `actionPerformed` method of each registered listener.

public boolean isRunning()

This method returns `true` if the timer is actively executing; otherwise, returns `false`.

public void removeActionListener(ActionListener listener)

This method removes the `ActionListener` from the list of listeners registered with the `Timer`.

public void restart()

This method cancels any undelivered events and immediately starts the timer again from an initial starting point.

public void setCoalesce(boolean flag)

The `setCoalesce` method turns on (`true`) or off (`false`) `ActionEvent` coalescing. By default, if an `ActionEvent` from the timer is already waiting in the event queue for processing, the timer will not create a new `ActionEvent` at the next firing interval. Turning coalescing off forces queueing and processing of all the timer events.

public void setDelay(int period)

This method permits changing the timing event `period` to a new value. The new period is applied immediately.

public void setInitialDelay(int delay)

The `setInitialDelay` method applies an initial offset of `delay` milliseconds until the first firing (ringing) of the timer. Setting the initial delay has no effect once the timer is started.

public static void setLogTimers(boolean flag)

This `static` method enables or disables logging of event triggers for *all* timers. The event is recorded to `System.out` in the form:
`Timer ringing: TimedDuke@3f345a.`

public void setRepeats(boolen repeat)

This method sets the timer to ring once (`false`) or to ring periodically (`true`). Periodic ringing is the default.

public void start()

The `start` method begins the initial timing sequence of the `Timer`. If the timer had been halted by `stop`, the timing begins from the point at which the timer was stopped; the elapsed time is not set to 0.

public void stop()

The `stop` method halts the timing sequence; no further `ActionEvents` are generated from the `Timer`.

16.10 Summary

Threads can be used for a variety of applications. In some cases, using threads makes software design simpler by letting you separate various pieces of work into independent chunks rather than coordinating them in a central routine. In other cases, threads can improve efficiency by letting you continue processing while a routine is waiting for user input or a network connection.

However, threaded programs tend to be more difficult to understand and debug, and improper synchronization can lead to inconsistent results. So use threads with some caution.

A particular difficulty arises when threads are used for animation or when graphics change dynamically based on user interaction. A variety of potential solutions are possible, but one of the most generally applicable ones is double buffering, where graphics operations are performed in an off-screen pixmap which is then drawn to the screen.

Concurrent processing can be particularly beneficial in network programming. The next chapter discusses a variety of issues concerning that topic, including how servers should be made multithreaded.

NETWORK
PROGRAMMING

Topics in This Chapter

- Implementing a generic network client
- Processing strings with StringTokenizer
- Validating e-mail addresses with a network client
- Retrieving files from an HTTP server
- Retrieving Web documents by using the URL class
- Implementing a generic network server
- Creating a simple HTTP server
- Converting a single-threaded server to a multithreaded server
- Invoking distributed objects with RMI

Chapter 17

Network programming involves two distinct pieces: a *client* and a *server*. A *client* is the program that connects to a system to request services. A *server* is a program that runs on a machine listening on a designated part of the network (a "port"), waiting for other programs to connect. When the client requests the connection, the server fulfills the request and provides some service to the connecting program. Servers often provide services to more than one connecting program, either one after the other or to several concurrently. If the distinction between who is requesting the service and who is providing the server seems blurry, just remember that the server starts first and doesn't need to know who will be connecting, whereas the client starts second and has to specify a particular host to talk to.

Core Note

Remember that the security manager of most browsers prohibits applets from making network connections to machines other than the one from which they are loaded.

In this chapter, you'll see how to directly implement clients and servers by using network "sockets." Although this is the lowest-level type of network programming in the Java platform, if you've used sockets in other languages, you may be surprised at how simple they are to use in Java technology. The URL class helps hide the details of network programming by providing methods for opening connections and binding input/output streams with sockets. In addition to sockets, which can communicate with general-purpose programs in arbitrary languages, Java provides two higher-level packages for communicating with specific types of systems: Remote Method Invocation (RMI) and database connectivity (JDBC). The RMI package lets you easily access methods in remote Java objects and transfer serializable objects across network connections. RMI is covered in Section 17.9. JDBC lets you easily send SQL statements to remote databases. Java Database Connectivity is covered in Chapter 22.

17.1 Implementing a Client

The client is the program that initiates a network connection. Implementing a client consists of five basic steps:

1. Create a `Socket` object.
2. Create an output stream that can be used to send information to the `Socket`.
3. Create an input stream to read the response from the server.
4. Do I/O with input and output streams.
5. Close the `Socket` when done.

Each of these steps is described in the sections that follow. Note that most of the methods described in these sections throw an `IOException` and need to be wrapped in a `try/catch` block.

Create a `Socket` object.

A `Socket` is the Java object corresponding to a network connection. A client connects to an existing server that is listening on a numbered network port for a connection. The standard way of making a socket is to supply a hostname or IP address and port as follows:

```
Socket client = new Socket("hostname", portNumber);
```

or

```
Socket client = new Socket("IP address", portNumber);
```

If you are already familiar with network programming, note that this approach creates a connection-oriented socket. The Java programming language also supports connectionless (UDP) sockets through the `DatagramSocket` class.

Create an output stream that can be used to send information to the `Socket`.

The Java programming language does not have separate methods to send data to files, sockets, and standard output. Instead, Java starts with different underlying objects, then layers standard output streams on top of them. So, any variety of `OutputStream` available for files is also available for sockets. A common one is `PrintWriter`. This stream lets you use `print` and `println` on the socket in exactly the same way as you would print to the screen. The `PrintWriter` constructor takes a generic `OutputStream` as an argument, which you can obtain from the `Socket` by means of `getOutputStream`. In addition, you should specify `true` in the constructor to force autoflush. Normally, the contents written to the stream will remain in a buffer until the buffer becomes completely full. Once the buffer is full, the contents are flushed out the stream. Autoflush guarantees that the buffer is flushed after every `println`, instead of waiting for the buffer to fill. Here's an example:

```
PrintWriter out =
  new PrintWriter(client.getOutputStream(), true);
```

You can also use an `ObjectOutputStream` to send complex Java objects over the network to be reassembled at the other end. An `ObjectOutputStream` connected to the network is used in exactly the same way as one connected to a file; simply use `writeObject` to send a serializable object and all referenced serializable objects. The server on the other end would use an `ObjectInputStream`'s `readObject` method to reassemble the sent object. Note that all AWT components are automatically serializable, and making other objects serializable is a simple matter of declaring that they implement the `Serializable` interface. See Section 13.9 (Serializing Windows) for more details and an example. Also see Section 17.9 (RMI: Remote Method Invocation) for a high-level interface that uses serialization to let you distribute Java objects across networks.

Create an input stream to read the response from the server.

Once you send data to the server, you will want to read the server's response. Again, there is no socket-specific way of doing this; you use a standard input stream layered on top of the socket. The most common one is an `InputStreamReader`, for handling character-based data. Here is a sample:

```
InputStreamReader in =
  new InputStreamReader(client.getInputStream());
```

Although this approach is the simplest, in most cases a better approach is to wrap the socket's generic `InputStream` inside a `BufferedReader`. This approach causes the system to read the data in blocks behind the scenes, rather than reading the underlying stream every time the user performs a read. This approach usually results in significantly improved performance at the cost of a small increase in memory usage (the buffer size, which defaults to 512 bytes). Here's the idea:

```
BufferedReader in =
  new BufferedReader
    (new InputStreamReader(client.getInputStream()));
```

Core Performance Tip

If you are going to read from a socket multiple times, a buffered input stream can speed things up considerably.

In a few cases, you might want to send data to a server but not read anything back. You could imagine a simple e-mail client working this way. In that case, you can skip this step. In other cases, you might want to read data without sending anything first. For instance, you might connect to a network "clock" to read the time. In such a case, you would skip the output stream and just follow this step. In most cases, however, you will want to both send and receive data, so you will follow both steps. Also, if the server is sending complex objects and is written in the Java programming language, you will want to open an `ObjectInputStream` and use `readObject` to receive data.

Do I/O with input and output streams.

A `PrintStream` has `print` and `println` methods that let you send a single primitive value, a `String`, or a string representation of an `Object` over the network. If you send an `Object`, the object is converted to a `String` by calling the `toString` method of the class. Most likely you are already familiar with these methods, since `System.out` is in fact an instance of `PrintStream`. `PrintStream` also inherits some simple `write` methods from `OutputStream`. These methods let you send binary data by sending an individual byte or an array of bytes.

`PrintWriter` is similar to `PrintStream` and has the same `print` and `println` methods. The main difference is that you can create print writers for different Unicode character sets, and you can't do that with `PrintStream`.

`BufferedReader` has two particularly useful methods: `read` and `readLine`. The `read` method returns a single `char` (as an `int`); `readLine` reads a whole line and returns a `String`. Both of these methods are *blocking*; they do not return until data is available. Because `readLine` will wait until receiving a carriage return or an `EOF` (the server closed the connection), `readLine` should be used only when you are sure the server will close the socket when done transmitting or when you know the number of lines that will be sent by the server. The `readLine` method returns `null` upon receiving an `EOF`.

Close the `Socket` when done.

When you are done, close the socket with the `close` method:

```
client.close();
```

This method closes the associated input and output streams as well.

Example: A Generic Network Client

Listing 17.1 illustrates the approach outlined in the preceding section. Processing starts with the `connect` method, which initiates the connection, then passes the socket to `handleConnection` to do the actual communication. This version of `handleConnection` simply reports who made the connection, sends a single line to the server ("`Generic Network Client`"), reads and prints a single response line, and exits. Real clients would override `handleConnection` to implement their desired behavior but could leave `connect` unchanged.

Listing 17.1 `NetworkClient.java`

```java
import java.net.*;
import java.io.*;

/** A starting point for network clients. You'll need to
 *  override handleConnection, but in many cases connect can
 *  remain unchanged. It uses SocketUtil to simplify the
 *  creation of the PrintWriter and BufferedReader.
 */

public class NetworkClient {
  protected String host;
  protected int port;

  /** Register host and port. The connection won't
   *  actually be established until you call
   *  connect.
   */

  public NetworkClient(String host, int port) {
    this.host = host;
    this.port = port;
  }

  /** Establishes the connection, then passes the socket
   *  to handleConnection.
   */
```

(continued)

Listing 17.1 `NetworkClient.java` *(continued)*

```java
  public void connect() {
    try {
      Socket client = new Socket(host, port);
      handleConnection(client);
    } catch(UnknownHostException uhe) {
      System.out.println("Unknown host: " + host);
      uhe.printStackTrace();
    } catch(IOException ioe) {
      System.out.println("IOException: " + ioe);
      ioe.printStackTrace();
    }
  }

  /** This is the method you will override when
   *  making a network client for your task.
   *  The default version sends a single line
   *  ("Generic Network Client") to the server,
   *  reads one line of response, prints it, then exits.
   */

  protected void handleConnection(Socket client)
    throws IOException {
    PrintWriter out = SocketUtil.getWriter(client);
    BufferedReader in = SocketUtil.getReader(client);
    out.println("Generic Network Client");
    System.out.println
      ("Generic Network Client:\n" +
       "Made connection to " + host +
       " and got '" + in.readLine() + "' in response");
    client.close();
  }

  /** The hostname of the server we're contacting. */

  public String getHost() {
    return(host);
  }

  /** The port connection will be made on. */

  public int getPort() {
    return(port);
  }
}
```

The `SocketUtil` class is just a simple interface to the `BufferedReader` and `PrintWriter` constructors and is given in Listing 17.2.

Listing 17.2 `SocketUtil.java`

```java
import java.net.*;
import java.io.*;

/** A shorthand way to create BufferedReaders and
 *  PrintWriters associated with a Socket.
 */

public class SocketUtil {
  /** Make a BufferedReader to get incoming data. */

  public static BufferedReader getReader(Socket s)
      throws IOException {
    return(new BufferedReader(
      new InputStreamReader(s.getInputStream())));
  }

  /** Make a PrintWriter to send outgoing data.
   *  This PrintWriter will automatically flush stream
   *  when println is called.
   */

  public static PrintWriter getWriter(Socket s)
      throws IOException {
    // Second argument of true means autoflush.
    return(new PrintWriter(s.getOutputStream(), true));
  }
}
```

Finally, the `NetworkClientTest` class, shown in Listing 17.3, provides a way to use the `NetworkClient` class with any hostname and any port.

Listing 17.3 `NetworkClientTest.java`

```java
/** Make simple connection to host and port specified. */

public class NetworkClientTest {
  public static void main(String[] args) {
    String host = "localhost";
    int port = 8088;
    if (args.length > 0) {
      host = args[0];
    }
```

(continued)

Listing 17.3 `NetworkClientTest.java` *(continued)*

```
    if (args.length > 1) {
      port = Integer.parseInt(args[1]);
    }
    NetworkClient nwClient = new NetworkClient(host, port);
    nwClient.connect();
  }
}
```

Output: Connecting to an FTP Server

Let's use the test program in Listing 17.3 to connect to Netscape's public FTP server, which listens on port 21. Assume > is the DOS or Unix prompt.

```
> java NetworkClientTest ftp.netscape.com 21

Generic Network Client:

Made connection to ftp.netscape.com and got '220 ftp26 FTP server
(UNIX(r) System V Release 4.0) ready.' in response
```

17.2 Parsing Strings by Using StringTokenizer

A common task when doing network programming is to break a large string down into various constituents. A developer could accomplish this task by using low-level `String` methods such as `indexOf` and `substring` to return substrings bounded by certain delimiters. However, the Java platform has a built-in class to simplify this process: the `StringTokenizer` class. This class isn't specific to network programming (the class is located in `java.util`, not `java.net`), but because string processing tends to be a large part of client-server programming, we discuss it here.

The StringTokenizer Class

The idea is that you build a tokenizer from an initial string, then retrieve tokens one at a time with `nextToken`, either based on a set of delimiters defined when the tokenizer was created or as an optional argument to `nextToken`. You can also see how many tokens are remaining (`countTokens`) or simply test whether the number of tokens remaining is nonzero (`hasMoreTokens`). The most common methods are summarized below.

Constructors

public StringTokenizer(String input)
This constructor builds a tokenizer from the input string, using white space (space, tab, newline, return) as the set of delimiters. The delimiters will not be included as part of the tokens returned.

public StringTokenizer(String input, String delimiters)
This constructor creates a tokenizer from the input string, using the specified delimiters. The delimiters will not be included as part of the tokens returned.

public StringTokenizer(String input, String delimiters, boolean includeDelimiters)
This constructor builds a tokenizer from the input string using the specified delimiters. The delimiters *will* be included as part of the tokens returned if the third argument is `true`.

Methods

public String nextToken()
This method returns the next token. The method throws a `NoSuch-ElementException` if no characters remain or only delimiter characters remain.

public String nextToken(String delimiters)
This method changes the set of delimiters, then returns the next token. The `nextToken` method throws a `NoSuchElementException` if no characters remain or only delimiter characters remain.

public int countTokens()
This method returns the number of tokens remaining, based on the current set of delimiters.

public boolean hasMoreTokens()
This method determines whether any tokens remain, based on the current set of delimiters. Most applications should either check for tokens before calling `nextToken` or catch a `NoSuchElementException` when calling `nextToken`. Note that `hasMoreTokens` has the side effect of advancing the internal counter, which yields unexpected results when doing the rare but possible sequence of checking `hasMoreTokens` with one delimiter set, then calling `nextToken` with another delimiter set.

Example: Interactive Tokenizer

A good way to get a feel for how StringTokenizer works is to try a bunch of test cases. Listing 17.4 gives a simple class that lets you enter an input string and a set of delimiters on the command line and prints the resultant tokens one to a line.

Listing 17.4 TokTest.java

```
import java.util.StringTokenizer;

/** Prints the tokens resulting from treating the first
 *  command-line argument as the string to be tokenized
 *  and the second as the delimiter set.
 */

public class TokTest {
  public static void main(String[] args) {
    if (args.length == 2) {
      String input = args[0], delimiters = args[1];
      StringTokenizer tok =
        new StringTokenizer(input, delimiters);
      while (tok.hasMoreTokens()) {
        System.out.println(tok.nextToken());
      }
    } else {
      System.out.println
        ("Usage: java TokTest string delimeters");
    }
  }
}
```

Here is TokTest in action:

```
> java TokTest http://www.microsoft.com/~gates/ :/.
http
www
microsoft
com
~gates
> java TokTest "if (tok.hasMoreTokens()) {" "(){. "
if
tok
hasMoreTokens
```

17.3 Example: A Client to Verify E-Mail Addresses

One of the best ways to get comfortable with a network protocol is to open a telnet connection to the port a server is on and try out commands interactively. For example, consider connecting directly to a mail server to verify the correctness of potential e-mail addresses. To connect to the mail server, we need to know that SMTP (Simple Mail Transfer Protocol) servers generally listen on port 25, send one or more lines of data after receiving a connection, accept commands of the form `expn username` to expand usernames, and accept `quit` as the command to terminate the connection. Commands are case insensitive. For instance, Listing 17.5 shows an interaction with the mail server at `apl.jhu.edu`.

Listing 17.5 Talking to a Mail Server

```
> telnet apl.jhu.edu 25
Trying 128.220.101.100...
Connected to aplcenMP.apl.jhu.edu.
Escape character is '^]'.
220 aplcenMP.apl.jhu.edu ESMTP Sendmail 8.9.3/8.9.1; Sat, 10 Feb
2001 12:05:42
500 (EST)
expn hall
250 Marty Hall <hall@aplcenMP.apl.jhu.edu>
expn root
250-Tom Vellani <vellani@aplcenMP.apl.jhu.edu>
250 Gary Gafke <gary@aplcenMP.apl.jhu.edu>
quit
221 aplcenMP.apl.jhu.edu closing connection
Connection closed by foreign host.
```

For a network client to verify an e-mail address, the program needs to break up the address into username and hostname sections, connect to port 25 of the host, read the initial connection message, send an `expn` on the username, read and print the result, then send a `quit`. The response from the SMTP server may not consist of only a single line. Because `readLine` blocks if the connection is still open but no line of data has been sent, we cannot call `readLine` more than once. So, rather than using `readLine` at all, we use `read` to populate a byte array *large* enough to hold the likely response, record how many bytes were read, then use `write` to print out that number of bytes. This process is shown in Listing 17.6, with Listing 17.7 showing the helper class that breaks an e-mail address into separate username and hostname components.

Listing 17.6 AddressVerifier.java

```java
import java.net.*;
import java.io.*;

/** Given an e-mail address of the form user@host,
 *  connect to port 25 of the host and issue an
 *  'expn' request for the user. Print the results.
 */

public class AddressVerifier extends NetworkClient {
  private String username;

  public static void main(String[] args) {
    if (args.length != 1) {
      usage();
    }
    MailAddress address = new MailAddress(args[0]);
    AddressVerifier verifier
      = new AddressVerifier(address.getUsername(),
                            address.getHostname(), 25);
    verifier.connect();
  }

  public AddressVerifier(String username, String hostname,
                         int port) {
    super(hostname, port);
    this.username = username;
  }

  /** NetworkClient, the parent class, automatically establishes
   *  the connection and then passes the Socket to
   *  handleConnection. This method does all the real work
   *  of talking to the mail server.
   */

  // You can't use readLine, because it blocks. Blocking I/O
  // by readLine is only appropriate when you know how many
  // lines to read. Note that mail servers send a varying
  // number of lines when you first connect or send no line
  // closing the connection (as HTTP servers do), yielding
  // null for readLine. Also, we'll assume that 1000 bytes
  // is more than enough to handle any server welcome
  // message and the actual EXPN response.
```

(continued)

Listing 17.6 `AddressVerifier.java` *(continued)*

```java
  protected void handleConnection(Socket client) {
    try {
      PrintWriter out = SocketUtil.getWriter(client);
      InputStream in = client.getInputStream();
      byte[] response = new byte[1000];
      // Clear out mail server's welcome message.
      in.read(response);
      out.println("EXPN " + username);
      // Read the response to the EXPN command.
      int numBytes = in.read(response);
      // The 0 means to use normal ASCII encoding.
      System.out.write(response, 0, numBytes);
      out.println("QUIT");
      client.close();
    } catch(IOException ioe) {
      System.out.println("Couldn't make connection: " + ioe);
    }
  }

  /** If the wrong arguments, thn warn user. */

  public static void usage() {
    System.out.println ("You must supply an email address " +
        "of the form 'username@hostname'.");
    System.exit(-1);
  }
}
```

Listing 17.7 `MailAddress.java`

```java
import java.util.*;

/** Takes a string of the form "user@host" and
 *  separates it into the "user" and "host" parts.
 */

public class MailAddress {
  private String username, hostname;

  public MailAddress(String emailAddress) {
    StringTokenizer tokenizer
      = new StringTokenizer(emailAddress, "@");
```

(continued)

Listing 17.7 `MailAddress.java` (continued)

```
      this.username = getArg(tokenizer);
      this.hostname = getArg(tokenizer);
   }

   private static String getArg(StringTokenizer tok) {
     try { return(tok.nextToken()); }
     catch (NoSuchElementException nsee) {
       System.out.println("Illegal email address");
       System.exit(-1);
       return(null);
     }
   }

   public String getUsername() {
     return(username);
   }

   public String getHostname() {
     return(hostname);
   }
}
```

Finally, here is an example of the address verifier in action, looking for the addresses of the main originators of the WWW and the Java platform.

```
> java AddressVerifier tbl@w3.org
250 <timbl@hq.lcs.mit.edu>
> java AddressVerifier timbl@hq.lcs.mit.edu
250 Tim Berners-Lee <timbl>
> java AddressVerifier gosling@mail.javasoft.com
550 gosling... User unknown
```

17.4 Example: A Network Client That Retrieves URLs

Retrieving a document through HTTP is remarkably simple. You open a connection to the HTTP port of the machine hosting the page, send the string GET followed by the address of the document, followed by the string HTTP/1.0, followed by a blank line (at least one blank space is required between GET and address, and between address and HTTP). You then read the result one line at a time. Reading a line at a time was not safe with the mail client of Section 17.3 because the server sent an indeterminate number of lines but kept the connection open. Here, however, a readLine is safe because the server closes the connection when done, yielding null as the return value of readLine.

Although quite simple, even this approach is slightly harder than necessary, because the Java programming language has built-in classes (URL and URL-Connection) that simplify the process even further. These classes are demonstrated in Section 17.5, but connecting to a HTTP server "by hand" is a useful exercise to prepare yourself for dealing with protocols that don't have built-in helping methods as well as to gain familiarity with the HTTP protocol. Listing 17.8 shows a telnet connection to the www.corewebprogramming.com HTTP server running on port 80.

Listing 17.8 Retrieving an HTML document directly through telnet

```
Unix> telnet www.corewebprogramming.com 80
Trying 216.248.197.112...
Connected to www.corewebprogramming.com.
Escape character is '^]'.
GET / HTTP/1.0

HTTP/1.1 200 OK
Date: Sat, 10 Feb 2001 18:04:17 GMT
Server: Apache/1.3.3 (Unix) PHP/3.0.11 FrontPage/4.0.4.3
Connection: close
Content-Type: text/html

<!DOCTYPE HTML PUBLIC "-//W3C//DTD HTML 4.0 Transitional//EN">
<HTML>
...
</HTML>
Connection closed by foreign host.
```

In this telnet session, the document was retrieved through a GET request. In other cases, you may only want to receive the HTTP headers associated with the document. For instance, a link validator is an important class of network program that verifies that the links in a specified Web page point to "live" documents. Writing such a program in the Java programming language is relatively straightforward, but to limit load on your servers, you probably want the program to use HEAD instead of GET (see Section 19.7, "The Client Request: HTTP Request Headers"). Java has no helping class for simply sending a HEAD request, but only a trivial change in the following code is needed to perform this request.

A Class to Retrieve a Given URI from a Given Host

Listing 17.9 presents a class that retrieves a file given the host, port, and URI (the filename part of the URL) as separate arguments. The application uses the

NetworkClient shown earlier in Listing 17.1 to send a single GET line to the specified host and port, then reads the result a line at a time, printing each line to the standard output.

Listing 17.9 `UriRetriever.java`

```java
import java.net.*;
import java.io.*;

/** Retrieve a URL given the host, port, and file as three
 *  separate command-line arguments. A later class
 *  (UrlRetriever) supports a single URL instead.
 */

public class UriRetriever extends NetworkClient {
  private String uri;

  public static void main(String[] args) {
    UriRetriever uriClient
      = new UriRetriever(args[0], Integer.parseInt(args[1]),
                         args[2]);
    uriClient.connect();
  }

  public UriRetriever(String host, int port, String uri) {
    super(host, port);
    this.uri = uri;
  }

  /** Send one GET line, then read the results one line at a
   *  time, printing each to standard output.
   */

  // It is safe to use blocking IO (readLine), since
  // HTTP servers close connection when done, resulting
  // in a null value for readLine.

  protected void handleConnection(Socket uriSocket)
      throws IOException {
    PrintWriter out = SocketUtil.getWriter(uriSocket);
    BufferedReader in = SocketUtil.getReader(uriSocket);
    out.println("GET " + uri + " HTTP/1.0\n");
    String line;
    while ((line = in.readLine()) != null) {
      System.out.println("> " + line);
    }
  }
}
```

A Class to Retrieve a Given URL

The previous program requires the user to pass the hostname, port, and URI as three separate command-line arguments. Listing 17.10 improves on this program by building a front end that parses a whole URL, using `StringTokenizer` (Section 17.2), then passes the appropriate pieces to the `UriRetriever`.

Listing 17.10 `UrlRetriever.java`

```java
import java.util.*;

/** This parses the input to get a host, port, and file, then
 *  passes these three values to the UriRetriever class to
 *  grab the URL from the Web.
 */

public class UrlRetriever {
  public static void main(String[] args) {
    checkUsage(args);
    StringTokenizer tok = new StringTokenizer(args[0]);
    String protocol = tok.nextToken(":");
    checkProtocol(protocol);
    String host = tok.nextToken(":/");
    String uri;
    int port = 80;
    try {
      uri = tok.nextToken("");
      if (uri.charAt(0) == ':') {
        tok = new StringTokenizer(uri);
        port = Integer.parseInt(tok.nextToken(":/"));
        uri = tok.nextToken("");
      }
    } catch(NoSuchElementException nsee) {
      uri = "/";
    }
    UriRetriever uriClient = new UriRetriever(host, port, uri);
    uriClient.connect();
  }

  /** Warn user if the URL was forgotten. */
```

(continued)

Listing 17.10 `UrlRetriever.java` *(continued)*

```java
  private static void checkUsage(String[] args) {
    if (args.length != 1) {
      System.out.println("Usage: UrlRetriever <URL>");
      System.exit(-1);
    }
  }

  /** Tell user that this can only handle HTTP. */

  private static void checkProtocol(String protocol) {
    if (!protocol.equals("http")) {
      System.out.println("Don't understand protocol " + protocol);
      System.exit(-1);
    }
  }
}
```

UrlRetriever Output

No explicit port number:

```
Prompt> java UrlRetriever
http://www.microsoft.com/netscape-beats-ie.html
> HTTP/1.1 404 Object Not Found
> Server: Microsoft-IIS/5.0
> Date: Fri, 31 Mar 2000 18:22:11 GMT
> Content-Length: 3243
> Content-Type: text/html
>
> <!DOCTYPE HTML PUBLIC "-//W3C//DTD HTML 3.2 Final//EN">
> <html dir=ltr>Explicit port number:
```

Explicit port number:

```
Prompt> java UrlRetriever
http://home.netscape.com:80/ie-beats-netscape.html
> HTTP/1.1 404 Not found
> Server: Netscape-Enterprise/3.6
> Date: Fri, 04 Feb 2000 21:52:29 GMT
> Content-type: text/html
> Connection: close
>
> <TITLE>Not Found</TITLE><H1>Not Found</H1> The requested
object does not exist on this server. The link you followed is
either outdated, inaccurate, or the server has been
instructed not to let you have it.
```

Hey! We just wrote a browser. OK, not quite, seeing as there is still the small matter of formatting the result. Still, not bad for about four pages of code. But we can do even better. In the next section, we'll reduce the code to two pages through the use of the built-in URL class. In Section 17.6 (WebClient: Talking to Web Servers Interactively) we'll add a simple user interface that lets you do HTTP requests interactively and view the raw HTML results. Also note that in Section 14.12 (The JEditorPane Component) we showed you how to use a JEditorPane to create a real browser that formats the HTML and lets the user follow the hypertext links.

DILBERT© UFS. Reprinted with permission.

17.5 The URL Class

The URL class provides simple access to URLs. The class automatically parses a string for you, letting you retrieve the protocol (e.g., http), host (e.g., java.sun.com), port (e.g., 80), and filename (e.g., /reports/earnings.html) separately. The URL class also provides an easy-to-use interface for reading remote files.

Reading from a URL

Although writing a client to explicitly connect to an HTTP server and retrieve a URL was quite simple, this task is so common that the Java programming language provides a helper class: java.net.URL. We saw this class when we looked at applets (see Section 9.5, "Other Applet Methods"): a URL object of this type that needed to be passed to getAppletContext().showDocument. However, the URL class can also be used to parse a string representing a URL and read the contents. An example of parsing a URL is shown in Listing 17.11.

Listing 17.11 `UrlRetriever2.java`

```java
import java.net.*;
import java.io.*;

/** Read a remote file using the standard URL class
 *  instead of connecting explicitly to the HTTP server.
 */

public class UrlRetriever2 {
  public static void main(String[] args) {
    checkUsage(args);
    try {
      URL url = new URL(args[0]);
      BufferedReader in = new BufferedReader(
        new InputStreamReader(url.openStream()));
      String line;
      while ((line = in.readLine()) != null) {
        System.out.println("> " + line);
      }
      in.close();
    } catch(MalformedURLException mue) { // URL constructor
        System.out.println(args[0] + "is an invalid URL: " + mue);
    } catch(IOException ioe) { // Stream constructors
      System.out.println("IOException: " + ioe);
    }
  }

  private static void checkUsage(String[] args) {
    if (args.length != 1) {
      System.out.println("Usage: UrlRetriever2 <URL>");
      System.exit(-1);
    }
  }
}
```

Here is the `UrlRetriever2` in action:

```
Prompt> java UrlRetriever2 http://www.whitehouse.gov/
> <HTML>
> <HEAD>
> <TITLE>Welcome To The White House</TITLE>
> </HEAD>
> ... Remainder of HTML document omitted ...
> </HTML>
```

This implementation just prints out the resultant document, not the HTTP response lines included in the original "raw" `UrlRetriever` class. However, another Java class called `URLConnection` will supply this information. Create a `URLConnection` object by calling the `openConnection` method of an existing

URL, then use methods such as `getContentType` and `getLastModified` to retrieve the response header information. See the on-line API for `java.net.URL-Connection` for more details.

Other Useful Methods of the URL Class

The most valuable use of a URL object is to use the constructor to parse a string representation and then to use `openStream` to provide an `InputStream` for reading. However, the class is useful in a number of other ways, as outlined in the following sections.

public URL(String absoluteSpec)
public URL(URL base, String relativeSpec)
public URL(String protocol, String host, String file)
public URL(String protocol, String host, int port, String file)
These four constructors build a URL in different ways. All throw a `MalformedURLException`.

public String getFile()
This method returns the filename (URI) part of the URL. See the output following Listing 17.12.

public String getHost()
This method returns the hostname part of the URL. See the output following Listing 17.12.

public int getPort()
This method returns the port if one was explicitly specified. If not, it returns –1 (*not* 80). See the output following Listing 17.12.

public String getProtocol()
This method returns the protocol part of the URL (i.e., `http`). See the output following Listing 17.12.

public String getRef()
The `getRef` method returns the "reference" (i.e., section heading) part of the URL. See the output following Listing 17.12.

public final InputStream openStream()
This method returns the input stream that can be used for reading, as used in the `UrlRetriever2` class. The method can also throw an `IOException`.

public URLConnection openConnection()

This method yields a URLConnection that can be used to retrieve header lines and (for POST requests) to supply data to the HTTP server. The POST method is discussed in Chapter 19 (Server-Side Java: Servlets).

public String toExternalForm()

This method gives the string representation of the URL, useful for printouts. This method is identical to toString.

Listing 17.12 gives an example of some of these methods.

Listing 17.12 UrlTest.java

```java
import java.net.*;

/** Read a URL from the command line, then print
 *  the various components.
 */

public class UrlTest {
  public static void main(String[] args) {
    if (args.length == 1) {
      try {
        URL url = new URL(args[0]);
        System.out.println
          ("URL: " + url.toExternalForm() + "\n" +
           "  File:      " + url.getFile() + "\n" +
           "  Host:      " + url.getHost() + "\n" +
           "  Port:      " + url.getPort() + "\n" +
           "  Protocol:  " + url.getProtocol() + "\n" +
           "  Reference: " + url.getRef());
      } catch(MalformedURLException mue) {
        System.out.println("Bad URL.");
      }
    } else
      System.out.println("Usage: UrlTest <URL>");
  }
}
```

Here's UrlTest in action:

```
> java UrlTest http://www.irs.gov/mission/#squeeze-them-dry
URL: http://www.irs.gov/mission/#squeeze-them-dry
  File:      /mission/
  Host:      www.irs.gov
  Port:      -1
  Protocol:  http
  Reference: squeeze-them-dry
```

17.6 WebClient: Talking to Web Servers Interactively

In Section 17.4 (Example: A Network Client That Retrieves URLs) and Section 17.5 (The URL Class) we illustrated how easy it is to connect to a Web server and request a document. The programs presented accept a URL from the command line and display the retrieved page to the output stream. In this section, we present WebClient, a simple graphical interface to HTTP servers. This program, Listing 17.13, accepts an HTTP request line and request headers from the user. When the user presses Submit Request, the request and headers are sent to the server, followed by a blank line. The response is displayed in a scrolling text area. Downloading is performed in a separate thread so that the user can interrupt the download of long documents.

The HttpClient class, Listing 17.14, does the real network communication. It simply sends the designated request line and request headers to the Web server, then reads, one at a time, the lines that come back, placing them into a JTextArea until either the server closes or the HttpClient is interrupted by means of the isInterrupted flag.

The LabeledTextField class, Listing 17.15, is a simple combination of a JTextField and a JLabel and is used in the upper panel of WebClient for user input. The Interruptible class, Listing 17.16, is a simple interface used to identify classes that have an isInterrupted method. Interruptible is used by HttpClient to poll WebClient to see if the user has interrupted the program.

As always, the source code can be downloaded from the on-line archive at http://www.corewebprogramming.com/, and there are no restrictions on use of the code.

A representative conversation with www.coreservlets.com is shown in Figure 17–1. Here, only a GET request was sent to the server, without any additional HTTP request headers. For more information on HTTP request headers, see Section 19.7 (The Client Request: HTTP Request Headers), and for HTTP response headers, see Section 19.8 (The Server Response: HTTP Response Headers).

Listing 17.13 WebClient.java

```
import java.awt.*; // For BorderLayout, GridLayout, Font, Color.
import java.awt.event.*;
import java.util.*;
import javax.swing.*;
```

(continued)

Listing 17.13 `WebClient.java` *(continued)*

```java
/** A graphical client that lets you interactively connect to
 *  Web servers and send custom request lines and
 *  request headers.
 */

public class WebClient extends JPanel
    implements Runnable, Interruptible, ActionListener {
  public static void main(String[] args) {
    WindowUtilities.setNativeLookAndFeel();
    WindowUtilities.openInJFrame(new WebClient(), 600, 700,
                                 "Web Client",
                                 SystemColor.control);
  }

  private LabeledTextField hostField, portField,
          requestLineField;
  private JTextArea requestHeadersArea, resultArea;
  private String host, requestLine;
  private int port;
  private String[] requestHeaders = new String[30];
  private JButton submitButton, interruptButton;
  private boolean isInterrupted = false;

  public WebClient() {
    setLayout(new BorderLayout(5, 30));
    int fontSize = 14;
    Font labelFont =
      new Font("Serif", Font.BOLD, fontSize);
    Font headingFont =
      new Font("SansSerif", Font.BOLD, fontSize+4);
    Font textFont =
      new Font("Monospaced", Font.BOLD, fontSize-2);
    JPanel inputPanel = new JPanel();
    inputPanel.setLayout(new BorderLayout());
    JPanel labelPanel = new JPanel();
    labelPanel.setLayout(new GridLayout(4,1));
    hostField = new LabeledTextField("Host:", labelFont,
                                     30, textFont);
    portField = new LabeledTextField("Port:", labelFont,
                                     "80", 5, textFont);
    // Use HTTP 1.0 for compatibility with the most servers.
    // If you switch this to 1.1, you *must* supply a
    // Host: request header.
```

(continued)

Listing 17.13 `WebClient.java` *(continued)*

```
requestLineField =
  new LabeledTextField("Request Line:", labelFont,
                       "GET / HTTP/1.0", 50, textFont);
labelPanel.add(hostField);
labelPanel.add(portField);
labelPanel.add(requestLineField);
JLabel requestHeadersLabel =
  new JLabel("Request Headers:");
requestHeadersLabel.setFont(labelFont);
labelPanel.add(requestHeadersLabel);
inputPanel.add(labelPanel, BorderLayout.NORTH);
requestHeadersArea = new JTextArea(5, 80);
requestHeadersArea.setFont(textFont);
JScrollPane headerScrollArea =
  new JScrollPane(requestHeadersArea);
inputPanel.add(headerScrollArea, BorderLayout.CENTER);
JPanel buttonPanel = new JPanel();
submitButton = new JButton("Submit Request");
submitButton.addActionListener(this);
submitButton.setFont(labelFont);
buttonPanel.add(submitButton);
inputPanel.add(buttonPanel, BorderLayout.SOUTH);
add(inputPanel, BorderLayout.NORTH);
JPanel resultPanel = new JPanel();
resultPanel.setLayout(new BorderLayout());
JLabel resultLabel =
  new JLabel("Results", JLabel.CENTER);
resultLabel.setFont(headingFont);
resultPanel.add(resultLabel, BorderLayout.NORTH);
resultArea = new JTextArea();
resultArea.setFont(textFont);
JScrollPane resultScrollArea =
  new JScrollPane(resultArea);
resultPanel.add(resultScrollArea, BorderLayout.CENTER);
JPanel interruptPanel = new JPanel();
interruptButton = new JButton("Interrupt Download");
interruptButton.addActionListener(this);
interruptButton.setFont(labelFont);
interruptPanel.add(interruptButton);
resultPanel.add(interruptPanel, BorderLayout.SOUTH);
add(resultPanel, BorderLayout.CENTER);
}
```

(continued)

Listing 17.13 `WebClient.java` *(continued)*

```java
public void actionPerformed(ActionEvent event) {
  if (event.getSource() == submitButton) {
    Thread downloader = new Thread(this);
    downloader.start();
  } else if (event.getSource() == interruptButton) {
    isInterrupted = true;
  }
}

public void run() {
  isInterrupted = false;
  if (hasLegalArgs())
    new HttpClient(host, port, requestLine,
   requestHeaders, resultArea, this);
}

public boolean isInterrupted() {
  return(isInterrupted);
}

private boolean hasLegalArgs() {
  host = hostField.getTextField().getText();
  if (host.length() == 0) {
    report("Missing hostname");
    return(false);
  }
  String portString =
    portField.getTextField().getText();
  if (portString.length() == 0) {
    report("Missing port number");
    return(false);
  }
  try {
    port = Integer.parseInt(portString);
  } catch(NumberFormatException nfe) {
    report("Illegal port number: " + portString);
    return(false);
  }
  requestLine =
    requestLineField.getTextField().getText();
  if (requestLine.length() == 0) {
    report("Missing request line");
    return(false);
  }
  getRequestHeaders();
  return(true);
}
```

(continued)

Listing 17.13 `WebClient.java` *(continued)*

```java
  private void report(String s) {
    resultArea.setText(s);
  }

  private void getRequestHeaders() {
    for(int i=0; i<requestHeaders.length; i++) {
      requestHeaders[i] = null;
    }
    int headerNum = 0;
    String header =
      requestHeadersArea.getText();
    StringTokenizer tok =
      new StringTokenizer(header, "\r\n");
    while (tok.hasMoreTokens()) {
      requestHeaders[headerNum++] = tok.nextToken();
    }
  }
}
```

Listing 17.14 `HttpClient.java`

```java
import java.net.*;
import java.io.*;
import javax.swing.*;

/** The underlying network client used by WebClient. */

public class HttpClient extends NetworkClient {
  private String requestLine;
  private String[] requestHeaders;
  private JTextArea outputArea;
  private Interruptible app;

  public HttpClient(String host, int port,
                    String requestLine, String[] requestHeaders,
                    JTextArea outputArea, Interruptible app) {
    super(host, port);
    this.requestLine = requestLine;
    this.requestHeaders = requestHeaders;
    this.outputArea = outputArea;
    this.app = app;
```

(continued)

Listing 17.14 `HttpClient.java` *(continued)*

```java
    if (checkHost(host)) {
      connect();
    }
  }

  protected void handleConnection(Socket uriSocket)
      throws IOException {
    try {
      PrintWriter out = SocketUtil.getWriter(uriSocket);
      BufferedReader in = SocketUtil.getReader(uriSocket);
      outputArea.setText("");
      out.println(requestLine);
      for(int i=0; i<requestHeaders.length; i++) {
        if (requestHeaders[i] == null) {
          break;
        } else {
          out.println(requestHeaders[i]);
        }
      }
      out.println();
      String line;
      while ((line = in.readLine()) != null &&
             !app.isInterrupted()) {
        outputArea.append(line + "\n");
      }
      if (app.isInterrupted()) {
        outputArea.append("---- Download Interrupted ----");
      }
    } catch(Exception e) {
      outputArea.setText("Error: " + e);
    }
  }

  private boolean checkHost(String host) {
    try {
      InetAddress.getByName(host);
      return(true);
    } catch(UnknownHostException uhe) {
      outputArea.setText("Bogus host: " + host);
      return(false);
    }
  }
}
```

Listing 17.15 LabeledTextField.java

```
import java.awt.*; // For FlowLayout, Font.
import javax.swing.*;

/** A TextField with an associated Label. */

public class LabeledTextField extends JPanel {
  private JLabel label;
  private JTextField textField;

  public LabeledTextField(String labelString,
                          Font labelFont,
                          int textFieldSize,
                          Font textFont) {
    setLayout(new FlowLayout(FlowLayout.LEFT));
    label = new JLabel(labelString, JLabel.RIGHT);
    if (labelFont != null) {
      label.setFont(labelFont);
    }
    add(label);
    textField = new JTextField(textFieldSize);
    if (textFont != null) {
      textField.setFont(textFont);
    }
    add(textField);
  }

  public LabeledTextField(String labelString,
                          String textFieldString) {
    this(labelString, null, textFieldString,
         textFieldString.length(), null);
  }

  public LabeledTextField(String labelString,
                          int textFieldSize) {
    this(labelString, null, textFieldSize, null);
  }

  public LabeledTextField(String labelString,
                          Font labelFont,
                          String textFieldString,
                          int textFieldSize,
                          Font textFont) {
```

(continued)

Listing 17.15 `LabeledTextField.java` *(continued)*

```java
    this(labelString, labelFont,
        textFieldSize, textFont);
    textField.setText(textFieldString);
  }

  /** The Label at the left side of the LabeledTextField.
   *  To manipulate the Label, do:
   *  <PRE>
   *    LabeledTextField ltf = new LabeledTextField(...);
   *    ltf.getLabel().someLabelMethod(...);
   *  </PRE>
   */

  public JLabel getLabel() {
    return(label);
  }

  /** The TextField at the right side of the
   *  LabeledTextField.
   */

  public JTextField getTextField() {
    return(textField);
  }
}
```

Listing 17.16 `Interruptible.java`

```java
/** An interface for classes that can be polled to see
 *  if they've been interrupted. Used by HttpClient
 *  and WebClient to allow the user to interrupt a network
 *  download.
 */

public interface Interruptible {
  public boolean isInterrupted();
}
```

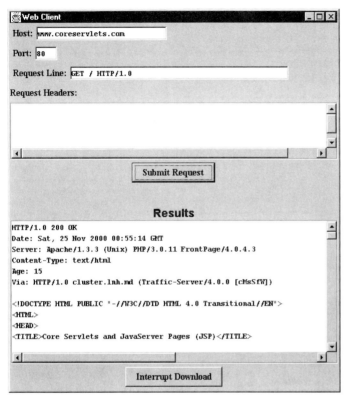

Figure 17-1 A conversation with www.coreservlets.com shows a typical request and response.

17.7 Implementing a Server

The server is the program that starts first and waits for incoming connections. Implementing a server consists of six basic steps:

1. Create a `ServerSocket` object.
2. Create a `Socket` object from the `ServerSocket`.
3. Create an input stream to read input from the client.
4. Create an output stream that can be used to send information back to the client.
5. Do I/O with input and output streams.
6. Close the `Socket` when done.

Each of these steps is described in more detail in the following sections. As with the client, note that most of the methods described throw an `IOException`, so they need to be wrapped inside a `try/catch` block in an actual implementation.

Create a `ServerSocket` object.

With a client socket, you actively go out and connect to a particular system. With a server, however, you passively sit and wait for someone to come to you. So, creation requires only a port number, not a host, as follows:

```
ServerSocket listenSocket =
  new ServerSocket(portNumber);
```

On Unix, if you are a nonprivileged user, this port number *must* be greater than 1023 (lower numbers are reserved) and *should* be greater than 5000 (numbers from 1024 to 5000 are more likely to already be in use). In addition, you should check /etc/services to make sure your selected port doesn't conflict with other services running on the same port number. If you try to listen on a socket that is already in use, an `IOException` will be thrown.

Create a `Socket` object from the `ServerSocket`.

Many servers allow multiple connections, continuing to accept connections until some termination condition is reached. The `ServerSocket accept` method blocks until a connection is established, then returns a normal `Socket` object. Here is the basic idea:

```
while(someCondition) {
  Socket server = listenSocket.accept();
  doSomethingWith(server);
}
```

If you want to allow multiple simultaneous connections to the socket, you should pass this socket to a separate thread to create the input/output streams. In the next section, we give an example of creating a separate thread for each connection.

Create an input stream to read input from the client.

Once you have a `Socket`, you can use the socket in the same way as with the client code shown in Section 17.1. The example here shows the creation of an input stream before an output stream, assuming that most servers will read data before transmitting a reply. You can switch the order of this step and the next if you send data before reading, and even omit this step if your server only transmits information.

As was also discussed in the client section, a `BufferedReader` is more efficient to use underneath the `InputStreamReader`, as follows:

```
BufferedReader in =
  new BufferedReader
   (new InputStreamReader(server.getInputStream()));
```

Java also lets you use ObjectInputStream to receive complex objects from another Java program. An ObjectInputStream connected to the network is used in exactly the same way as one connected to a file; simply use read-Object and cast the result to the appropriate type. See Section 13.9 (Serializing Windows) for more details and an example. Also see Section 17.9 (RMI: Remote Method Invocation) for a high-level interface that uses serialization to let you distribute Java objects across networks.

Create an output stream that can be used to send information back to the client.

You can use a generic OutputStream if you want to send binary data. If you want to use the familiar print and println commands, create a PrintWriter. Here is an example of creating a PrintWriter:

```
PrintWriter out =
  new PrintWriter(server.getOutputStream());
```

In Java, you can use an ObjectOutputStream if the client is written in the Java programming language and is expecting complex Java objects.

Do I/O with input and output streams.

The BufferedReader, DataInputStream, and PrintWriter classes can be used in the same ways as discussed in the client section earlier in this chapter. BufferedReader provides read and readLine methods for reading characters or strings. DataInputStream has readByte and readFully methods for reading a single byte or a byte array. Use print and println for sending high-level data through a PrintWriter; use write to send a byte or byte array.

Close the Socket when done.

When finished, close the socket:

```
server.close();
```

This method closes the associated input and output streams but does *not* terminate any loop that listens for additional incoming connections.

Example: A Generic Network Server

Listing 17.17 gives a sample implementation of the approach outlined at the beginning of Section 17.7. Processing starts with the listen method, which waits until receiving a connection, then passes the socket to handleConnection to do the actual communication. Real servers might have handleConnection operate in a separate thread to allow multiple simultaneous connections, but even if not, they would override the method to provide the server with the desired behavior. The generic version of handleConnection simply reports the hostname of the system that made the connection, shows the first line of input received from the client, sends a single line to the client ("Generic Network Server"), then closes the connection.

Listing 17.17 NetworkServer.java

```java
import java.net.*;
import java.io.*;

/** A starting point for network servers. You'll need to
 *  override handleConnection, but in many cases listen can
 *  remain unchanged. NetworkServer uses SocketUtil to simplify
 *  the creation of the PrintWriter and BufferedReader.
 */

public class NetworkServer {
  private int port, maxConnections;

  /** Build a server on specified port. It will continue to
   *  accept connections, passing each to handleConnection until
   *  an explicit exit command is sent (e.g., System.exit) or
   *  the maximum number of connections is reached. Specify
   *  0 for maxConnections if you want the server to run
   *  indefinitely.
   */

  public NetworkServer(int port, int maxConnections) {
    setPort(port);
    setMaxConnections(maxConnections);
  }

  /** Monitor a port for connections. Each time one is
   *  established, pass resulting Socket to handleConnection.
   */

  public void listen() {
    int i=0;
    try {
      ServerSocket listener = new ServerSocket(port);
      Socket server;
      while((i++ < maxConnections) || (maxConnections == 0)) {
        server = listener.accept();
        handleConnection(server);
      }
```

(continued)

Listing 17.17 NetworkServer.java *(continued)*

```java
    } catch (IOException ioe) {
      System.out.println("IOException: " + ioe);
      ioe.printStackTrace();
    }
  }

  /** This is the method that provides the behavior to the
   *  server, since it determines what is done with the
   *  resulting socket. <B>Override this method in servers
   *  you write.</B>
   *  <P>
   *  This generic version simply reports the host that made
   *  the connection, shows the first line the client sent,
   *  and sends a single line in response.
   */

  protected void handleConnection(Socket server)
      throws IOException{
    BufferedReader in = SocketUtil.getReader(server);
    PrintWriter out = SocketUtil.getWriter(server);
    System.out.println
      ("Generic Network Server: got connection from " +
       server.getInetAddress().getHostName() + "\n" +
       "with first line '" + in.readLine() + "'");
    out.println("Generic Network Server");
    server.close();
  }

  /** Gets the max connections server will handle before
   *  exiting. A value of 0 indicates that server should run
   *  until explicitly killed.
   */

  public int getMaxConnections() {
    return(maxConnections);
  }

  /** Sets max connections. A value of 0 indicates that server
   *  should run indefinitely (until explicitly killed).
   */

  public void setMaxConnections(int maxConnections) {
    this.maxConnections = maxConnections;
  }
```

(continued)

Listing 17.17 `NetworkServer.java` *(continued)*

```java
/** Gets port on which server is listening. */

public int getPort() {
  return(port);
}

/** Sets port. <B>You can only do before "connect" is
 *  called.</B> That usually happens in the constructor.
 */

protected void setPort(int port) {
  this.port = port;
}
}
```

Finally, the `NetworkServerTest` class provides a way to invoke the `Network-Server` class on a specified port, shown in Listing 17.18.

Listing 17.18 `NetworkServerTest.java`

```java
public class NetworkServerTest {
public static void main(String[] args) {
    int port = 8088;
    if (args.length > 0) {
      port = Integer.parseInt(args[0]);
    }
    NetworkServer nwServer = new NetworkServer(port, 1);
    nwServer.listen();
  }
}
```

Output: Accepting a Connection from a WWW Browser

Suppose the test program in Listing 17.18 is started on port 8088 of `system1.com`:

```
system1> java NetworkServerTest
```

Then, a standard Web browser (Netscape in this case) on `system2.com` requests `http://system1.com:8088/foo/:`, yielding the following back on `system1.com`:

```
Generic Network Server:
got connection from system2.com
with first line 'GET /foo/ HTTP/1.0'
```

Connecting NetworkClient and NetworkServer

OK, we showed the `NetworkClient` and `NetworkServer` classes tested separately, with the client talking to a standard FTP server and the server talking to a standard Web browser. However, we can also connect them to each other. No changes in the source code are required; simply specify the appropriate hostnames and port. The test server is started on port 6001 of `system1.com`, then the client is started on `system2.com`, yielding the following results:

Time t_0, system1:

```
system1> java NetworkServerTest 6001
```

Time t_1, system2:

```
system2> java NetworkClientTest system1.com 6001
```

Time t_2, system1:

```
Generic Network Server:
got connection from system2.com
with first line 'Generic Network Client'
```

Time t_3, system2:

```
Generic Network Client:
Made connection to system1.com and got 'Generic Network
Server' in response
```

17.8 Example: A Simple HTTP Server

In Listing 17.19 we adapt the `NetworkServer` class to act as an HTTP server. Rather than returning files, however, we have the server simply echo back the received input by storing all of the input lines, then transmit back an HTML file that shows the sent line. Although writing programs that output HTML seems odd, in Chapter 19 (Server-Side Java: Servlets) and Chapter 24 (JavaScript: Adding Dynamic Content to Web Pages) you'll see that this is actually common practice. Furthermore, having a program that can act as an HTTP server but returns a Web page showing the received input is a useful debugging tool when you are working with HTTP clients and servlet or JSP programming. You'll see this class used many times in the HTTP and servlet chapters.

Listing 17.19 EchoServer.java

```java
import java.net.*;
import java.io.*;
import java.util.StringTokenizer;

/** A simple HTTP server that generates a Web page showing all
 *  of the data that it received from the Web client (usually
 *  a browser). To use this server, start it on the system of
 *  your choice, supplying a port number if you want something
 *  other than port 8088. Call this system server.com. Next,
 *  start a Web browser on the same or a different system, and
 *  connect to http://server.com:8088/whatever. The resultant
 *  Web page will show the data that your browser sent. For
 *  debugging in servlet or CGI programming, specify
 *  http://server.com:8088/whatever as the ACTION of your HTML
 *  form. You can send GET or POST data; either way, the
 *  resultant page will show what your browser sent.
 */

public class EchoServer extends NetworkServer {
  protected int maxRequestLines = 50;
  protected String serverName = "EchoServer";

  /** Supply a port number as a command-line
   *  argument. Otherwise, use port 8088.
   */

  public static void main(String[] args) {
    int port = 8088;
    if (args.length > 0) {
      try {
        port = Integer.parseInt(args[0]);
      } catch(NumberFormatException nfe) {}
    }
    new EchoServer(port, 0);
  }

  public EchoServer(int port, int maxConnections) {
    super(port, maxConnections);
    listen();
  }
```

(continued)

Listing 17.19 EchoServer.java *(continued)*

```java
/** Overrides the NetworkServer handleConnection method to
 *  read each line of data received, save it into an array
 *  of strings, then send it back embedded inside a PRE
 *  element in an HTML page.
 */

public void handleConnection(Socket server)
    throws IOException{
  System.out.println
      (serverName + ": got connection from " +
       server.getInetAddress().getHostName());
  BufferedReader in = SocketUtil.getReader(server);
  PrintWriter out = SocketUtil.getWriter(server);
  String[] inputLines = new String[maxRequestLines];
  int i;
  for (i=0; i<maxRequestLines; i++) {
    inputLines[i] = in.readLine();
    if (inputLines[i] == null) // Client closed connection.
      break;
    if (inputLines[i].length() == 0) { // Blank line.
      if (usingPost(inputLines)) {
        readPostData(inputLines, i, in);
        i = i + 2;
      }
      break;
    }
  }
  printHeader(out);
  for (int j=0; j<i; j++) {
    out.println(inputLines[j]);
  }
  printTrailer(out);
  server.close();
}

// Send standard HTTP response and top of a standard Web page.
// Use HTTP 1.0 for compatibility with all clients.

private void printHeader(PrintWriter out) {
  out.println
      ("HTTP/1.0 200 OK\r\n" +
       "Server: " + serverName + "\r\n" +
       "Content-Type: text/html\r\n" +
       "\r\n" +
```

(continued)

Listing 17.19 EchoServer.java *(continued)*

```java
    "<HTML>\n" +
    "<!DOCTYPE HTML PUBLIC " +
      "\"-//W3C//DTD HTML 4.0 Transitional//EN\">\n" +
    "<HEAD>\n" +
    "  <TITLE>" + serverName + " Results</TITLE>\n" +
    "</HEAD>\n" +
    "\n" +
    "<BODY BGCOLOR=\"#FDF5E6\">\n" +
    "<H1 ALIGN=\"CENTER\">" + serverName +
      " Results</H1>\n" +
    "Here is the request line and request headers\n" +
    "sent by your browser:\n" +
    "<PRE>");
}

// Print bottom of a standard Web page.

private void printTrailer(PrintWriter out) {
  out.println
    ("</PRE>\n" +
    "</BODY>\n" +
    "</HTML>\n");
}

// Normal Web page requests use GET, so this server can simply
// read a line at a time. However, HTML forms can also use
// POST, in which case we have to determine the number of POST
// bytes that are sent so we know how much extra data to read
// after the standard HTTP headers.

private boolean usingPost(String[] inputs) {
  return(inputs[0].toUpperCase().startsWith("POST"));
}

private void readPostData(String[] inputs, int i,
                          BufferedReader in)
    throws IOException {
  int contentLength = contentLength(inputs);
  char[] postData = new char[contentLength];
  in.read(postData, 0, contentLength);
  inputs[++i] = new String(postData, 0, contentLength);
}
```

(continued)

Listing 17.19 EchoServer.java *(continued)*

```
// Given a line that starts with Content-Length,
// this returns the integer value specified.

private int contentLength(String[] inputs) {
  String input;
  for (int i=0; i<inputs.length; i++) {
    if (inputs[i].length() == 0)
      break;
    input = inputs[i].toUpperCase();
    if (input.startsWith("CONTENT-LENGTH"))
      return(getLength(input));
  }
  return(0);
}

private int getLength(String length) {
  StringTokenizer tok = new StringTokenizer(length);
  tok.nextToken();
  return(Integer.parseInt(tok.nextToken()));
}
}
```

Figure 17–2 shows the EchoServer in action, displaying the header lines sent by Netscape 4.7 on Windows 98.

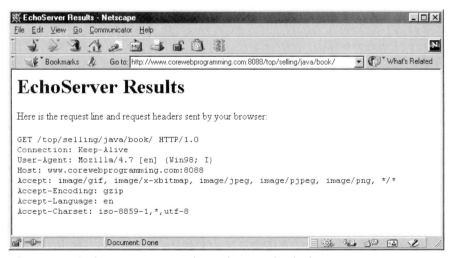

Figure 17–2 The EchoServer shows data sent by the browser.

ThreadedEchoServer: Adding Multithreading

The problem with the EchoServer is that the service can only accept one connection at a time. If, for instance, it takes 0.001 seconds to establish a connection but 0.01 seconds for the client to transmit the request and 0.01 seconds for the server to return the results, then the entire process takes about 0.02 seconds, and the server can only handle about 50 connections per second. By doing the socket processing in a separate thread, establishing the connection becomes the rate-limiting step, and the server could handle about 1,000 connections per second with these example times.

Listing 17.20 shows how to convert the EchoServer into a multithreaded version. Section 16.4 (Creating a Multithreaded Method) discusses in detail the process for converting a single-threaded method to a multithreaded method. The basic idea is that the new version's handleConnection starts up a thread, which calls back to the original handleConnection. The problem is how to get the Socket object from handleConnection to run, because placing the Socket object in an instance variable would subject it to race conditions. So, a Connection class, which is simply a Thread with a place to store the Socket object, is used.

Listing 17.20 ThreadedEchoServer.java

```java
import java.net.*;
import java.io.*;

/** A multithreaded variation of EchoServer. */

public class ThreadedEchoServer extends EchoServer
                                implements Runnable {
  public static void main(String[] args) {
    int port = 8088;
    if (args.length > 0) {
      try {
        port = Integer.parseInt(args[0]);
      } catch(NumberFormatException nfe) {}
    }
    ThreadedEchoServer echoServer =
      new ThreadedEchoServer(port, 0);
    echoServer.serverName = "Threaded EchoServer";
  }

  public ThreadedEchoServer(int port, int connections) {
    super(port, connections);
  }
```

(continued)

Listing 17.20 `ThreadedEchoServer.java` *(continued)*

```java
/** The new version of handleConnection starts a thread. This
 *  new thread will call back to the <I>old</I> version of
 *  handleConnection, resulting in the same server behavior
 *  in a multithreaded version. The thread stores the Socket
 *  instance since run doesn't take any arguments, and since
 *  storing the socket in an instance variable risks having
 *  it overwritten if the next thread starts before the run
 *  method gets a chance to copy the socket reference.
 */

public void handleConnection(Socket server) {
  Connection connectionThread = new Connection(this, server);
  connectionThread.start();
}

public void run() {
  Connection currentThread =
    (Connection)Thread.currentThread();
  try {
    super.handleConnection(currentThread.getSocket());
  } catch(IOException ioe) {
    System.out.println("IOException: " + ioe);
    ioe.printStackTrace();
  }
}
}

/** This is just a Thread with a field to store a Socket object.
 *  Used as a thread-safe means to pass the Socket from
 *  handleConnection to run.
 */

class Connection extends Thread {
  private Socket serverSocket;

  public Connection(Runnable serverObject,
                    Socket serverSocket) {
    super(serverObject);
    this.serverSocket = serverSocket;
  }

  public Socket getSocket() {
    return serverSocket;
  }
}
```

This server gives the same results as the EchoServer but allows multiple simultaneous connections.

17.9 RMI: Remote Method Invocation

Java directly supports distributing run-time objects across multiple computers through Remote Method Invocation (RMI). This distributed-objects package simplifies communication among Java applications on multiple machines. If you are already familiar with the Common Object Request Broker Architecture, think of RMI as a simpler but less powerful variation of CORBA that only works with Java systems. If you don't know anything about CORBA, think of RMI as an object-oriented version of remote procedure calls (RPC).

The idea is that the client requests an object from the server, using a simple high-level request. Once the client has the object, the client invokes the object's methods as though the object were a normal local object. Behind the scenes, however, the requests are routed to the server, where methods in the "real" object are invoked and the results returned. The beauty of the process is that neither the client nor the server has to do anything explicit with input streams, output streams, or sockets. The values that are sent back and forth can be complex Java objects (including windows and other graphical components), but no parsing is required at either end. The conversion of the object is handled by the Java serialization facility.

Now, RMI seems so convenient that you might wonder why anyone would implement sockets "by hand." First of all, RMI only works among Java systems, so RMI cannot be used for an HTTP client, an HTTP server, an e-mail client, or other applications where the other end will not necessarily be using Java. Second, even for Java-to-Java applications, RMI requires some common code to be installed on both the client and the server. This approach is in contrast to sockets, where random programs can talk to each other as long as they both understand the types of commands that should be sent. Finally, RMI is a bit more taxing on the server than regular sockets because RMI requires two versions of the Java Virtual Machine to be running (one to broker requests for objects, the other to provide the actual object implementation).

Following, we summarize the steps necessary to build an RMI application. Afterward, we present four RMI examples:

1. A simple RMI example that returns a message string from a remote object.
2. A realistic example that performs numerical integration through a remote object.

3. Extension of the numerical integration to an enterprise configuration showing how to set up a security policy file and HTTP server for downloading of RMI files.
4. An RMI applet that connects to a remote object.

Steps to Build an RMI Application

To use RMI, you need to do two things: build four classes and execute five compilation steps. We briefly describe the classes and the steps here. In the next subsections, we build the classes—simple and more advanced—and show the command-line commands that execute the steps, along with the output, if any, of the commands.

The Four Required Classes

To use RMI, you will need to build four main classes:

1. **An interface for the remote object.** This interface will be used by both the client and the server.
2. **The RMI client.** This client will look up the object on the remote server, cast the object to the type of the interface from Step 1, then use the object like a local object. Note that as long as a "live" reference to the remote object is present, the network connection will be maintained. The connection will be automatically closed when the remote object is garbage-collected on the client.
3. **The object implementation.** This object must implement the interface of Step 1 and will be used by the server.
4. **The RMI server.** This class will create an instance of the object from Step 3 and register the object with a particular URL.

Compiling and Running the System

Once you have the basic four classes, five further steps are required to actually use the application.

1. **Compile client and server.** This step automatically compiles the remote object interface and implementation.
2. **Generate the client stub and the server skeleton.** The client stub and server skeleton support the method calls and provide parameter marshalling (device-independent coding and serialization for transmission across a byte stream). Use the `rmic` compiler on the remote object implementation for this step.
   The client system will need the client class, the interface class, and the client stub class. If the client is an applet, these three classes must be available from the applet's home machine.

The server system will need the server class, the remote object interface and implementation, and the server skeleton class. Note that Java 2 no longer requires the skeleton class normally placed on the server. If both the server and client are running the Java 2 Platform, then use the `-v1.2` switch for the `rmic` compiler.

3. **Start the RMI registry.** This step needs to be done only once, not for each remote object. The current version of RMI requires this registry to be running on the same system as the server.

4. **Start the server.** This step must be done on the same machine as the registry of Step 3.

5. **Start the client.** This step can be on an arbitrary machine.

A Simple Example

Here's a simple example to illustrate the process. The remote object simply returns a message string. See the next subsection for a more realistic example.

A Simple Example of the Four Required Classes

1. The interface for the remote object.

The interface should extend `java.rmi.Remote`, and all the methods should throw `java.rmi.RemoteException`. Listing 17.21 shows an example.

Listing 17.21 `Rem.java`

```java
import java.rmi.*;

/** The RMI client will use this interface directly. The RMI
 *  server will make a real remote object that implements this,
 *  then register an instance of it with some URL.
 */

public interface Rem extends Remote {
  public String getMessage() throws RemoteException;
}
```

2. The RMI client.

This class should look up the object from the appropriate host, using `Naming.lookup`, cast the object to the appropriate type, then use the object like a local object. Unlike the case in CORBA, RMI clients must know the host that is providing the remote services. The URL can be specified by `rmi://host/path` or `rmi://host:port/path`. If the port is omitted,

1099 is used. This process can throw three possible exceptions: `Remote-Exception`, `NotBoundException`, and `MalformedURLException`. You are required to catch all three. You should import `java.rmi.*` for `Remote-Exception`, `Naming`, and `NotBoundException`. You should import `java.net.*` for `MalformedURLException`. In addition, many clients will pass `Serializable` objects to the remote object, so importing `java.io.*` is a good habit, even though it is not required in this particular case. Listing 17.22 shows an example.

Listing 17.22 `RemClient.java`

```java
import java.rmi.*; // For Naming, RemoteException, etc.
import java.net.*; // For MalformedURLException
import java.io.*;  // For Serializable interface

/** Get a Rem object from the specified remote host.
 *  Use its methods as though it were a local object.
 */

public class RemClient {
  public static void main(String[] args) {
    try {
      String host =
        (args.length > 0) ? args[0] : "localhost";
      // Get the remote object and store it in remObject:
      Rem remObject =
        (Rem)Naming.lookup("rmi://" + host + "/Rem");
      // Call methods in remObject:
      System.out.println(remObject.getMessage());
    } catch(RemoteException re) {
      System.out.println("RemoteException: " + re);
    } catch(NotBoundException nbe) {
      System.out.println("NotBoundException: " + nbe);
    } catch(MalformedURLException mfe) {
      System.out.println("MalformedURLException: " + mfe);
    }
  }
}
```

3. The remote object implementation.

This class must extend `UnicastRemoteObject` and implement the remote object interface defined earlier. The constructor should throw `Remote-Exception`. Listing 17.23 shows an example.

Listing 17.23 `RemImpl.java`

```java
import java.rmi.*;
import java.rmi.server.UnicastRemoteObject;

/** This is the actual implementation of Rem that the RMI
 *  server uses. The server builds an instance of this, then
 *  registers it with a URL. The client accesses the URL and
 *  binds the result to a Rem (not a RemImpl; it doesn't
 *  have this).
 */

public class RemImpl extends UnicastRemoteObject
                        implements Rem {
  public RemImpl() throws RemoteException {}

  public String getMessage() throws RemoteException {
    return("Here is a remote message.");
  }
}
```

---

4. The RMI server.

The server's job is to build an object and register the object with a particular URL. Use `Naming.rebind` (replace any previous bindings) or `Naming.bind` (throw `AlreadyBoundException` if a previous binding exists) to register the object. (The term "bind" is used differently than in the CORBA world; here, bind means "register" and is performed by the server, not the client.) You are required to catch `RemoteException` and `MalformedURLException`. Listing 17.24 shows an example.

Listing 17.24 `RemServer.java`

```java
import java.rmi.*;
import java.net.*;

/** The server creates a RemImpl (which implements the Rem
 *  interface), then registers it with the URL Rem, where
 *  clients can access it.
 */

public class RemServer {
  public static void main(String[] args) {
    try {
```

(continued)

Listing 17.24 `RemServer.java` *(continued)*

```
      RemImpl localObject = new RemImpl();
      Naming.rebind("rmi:///Rem", localObject);
    } catch(RemoteException re) {
      System.out.println("RemoteException: " + re);
    } catch(MalformedURLException mfe) {
      System.out.println("MalformedURLException: " + mfe);
    }
  }
}
```

Compiling and Running the System for the Simple Example

As outlined earlier in this section, compiling and running the system requires five steps.

For this example, you must start the RMI registry, the server (`RemServer`), and the client (`RemClient`) in the same host directory. If the client and server are started from different directories, then the RMI protocol requires a `Security-Manager` on the client to load the stub files. Configuration of RMI to run the client and server on different hosts (or different directories) is explained later.

Core Note

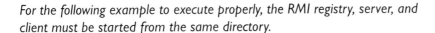

For the following example to execute properly, the RMI registry, server, and client must be started from the same directory.

1. Compile the client and the server.

The following command automatically compiles the `Rem` interface.

    Prompt> **javac RemClient.java**

The following command automatically compiles the `RemImpl` object implementation.

    Prompt> **javac RemServer.java**

2. Generate the client Stub and server Skeleton.

The following command builds `RemImpl_Stub.class` and `RemImpl_Skeleton.class`.

    Prompt> **rmic RemImpl**

or

    Prompt> **rmic -v1.2 RemImpl** (for Java 2 Platform)

The client requires `Rem.class`, `RemClient.class`, and
`RemImpl_Stub.class`. The server requires `Rem.class`, `RemImpl.class`,
`RemServer.class`, and `RemImpl_Skeleton.class`.

For the Java 2 platform, the `RemImpl_Skeleton.class` is no longer
required. To generate only the stub file required for the Java 2 Platform, add
the `-v1.2` switch in the RMI compiler command. This switch generates a stub
file consistent with the RMI 1.2 stub protocol used by the Java 2 Platform. By
default, `rmic` creates stubs and skeletons compatible with both the RMI 1.2
stub protocol and the earlier RMI 1.1 stub protocol used in JDK 1.1.

Core Note

If the client and server are both running the Java 2 Platform, use `rmic`
`-v1.2` *to compile the interface. Using the* `-v1.2` *switch does not generate
the unnecessary skeleton file.*

3. Start the RMI registry.

Start the registry as follows.

```
Prompt> rmiregistry
```

On Unix systems, you would probably add `&` to put the registry process in the
background. On Windows, you would probably precede the command with
`start`, as in `start rmiregistry`. You can also specify a port number; if
omitted, port 1099 is used.

4. Start the server.

Start the server as follows.

```
Server> java RemServer
```

Again, on Unix systems, you would probably add `&` to put the process in the
background. On Windows, you would probably precede the command with
`start`, as in `start java RemServer`.

5. Start the client.

Issue the following command.

```
Prompt> java RemClient
Here is a remote message.
```

A Realistic Example: A Server for Numeric Integration

Listing 17.25 shows a class that provides two methods. The first method, sum, calculates

$$\sum_{x=start}^{stop} f(x)$$

The definition of $f(x)$ is provided by an Evaluatable object (Listing 17.26). The second method, integrate, uses the midpoint rule (Figure 17–3) to approximate the integral

$$\int_{start}^{stop} f(x)\,dx$$

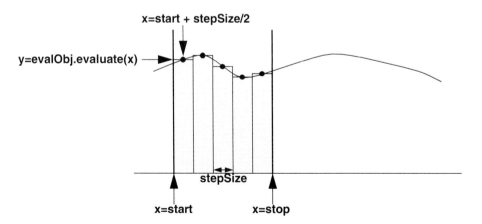

Figure 17–3 The integrate method approximates the area under the curve by adding up the area of many small rectangles that have width stepSize and whose length $y = f(x)$ is evaluated at the midpoint of each width.

Listing 17.25 `Integral.java`

```java
/** A class to calculate summations and numeric integrals. The
 *  integral is calculated according to the midpoint rule.
 */

public class Integral {
  /** Returns the sum of f(x) from x=start to x=stop, where the
   *  function f is defined by the evaluate method of the
   *  Evaluatable object.
   */

  public static double sum(double start, double stop,
                           double stepSize,
                           Evaluatable evalObj) {
    double sum = 0.0, current = start;
    while (current <= stop) {
      sum += evalObj.evaluate(current);
      current += stepSize;
    }
    return(sum);
  }

  /** Returns an approximation of the integral of f(x) from
   *  start to stop, using the midpoint rule. The function f is
   *  defined by the evaluate method of the Evaluatable object.
   */

  public static double integrate(double start, double stop,
                                 int numSteps,
                                 Evaluatable evalObj) {
    double stepSize = (stop - start) / (double)numSteps;
    start = start + stepSize / 2.0;
    return(stepSize * sum(start, stop, stepSize, evalObj));
  }
}
```

Listing 17.26 `Evaluatable.java`

```java
/** An interface for evaluating functions y = f(x) at a specific
 *  value. Both x and y are double-precision floating-point
 *  numbers.
 */

public interface Evaluatable {
  public double evaluate(double value);
}
```

Now suppose that you have a powerful workstation that has very fast floating-point capabilities and a variety of slower PCs that need to run an interface that makes use of numerical integration. A natural approach is to make the workstation the integration server. RMI makes this solution very simple.

A Realistic Example of the Four Required Classes

In this section we provide listings for the four classed required to establish a workstation and integration server.

1. The RemoteIntegral interface.

Listing 17.27 shows the interface that will be shared by the client and server.

Listing 17.27 `RemoteIntegral.java`

```java
import java.rmi.*;

/** Interface for remote numeric integration object. */

public interface RemoteIntegral extends Remote {

  public double sum(double start, double stop, double stepSize,
                  Evaluatable evalObj)
    throws RemoteException;

  public double integrate(double start, double stop,
                          int numSteps, Evaluatable evalObj)
    throws RemoteException;
}
```

---

2. The RemoteIntegral client.

Listing 17.28 shows the RMI client. It obtains a `RemoteIntegral` from the specified host, then uses it to approximate a variety of integrals. Note that the `Evaluatable` instances (`Sin`, `Cos`, `Quadratic`) implement `Serializable` in addition to `Evaluatable` so that these objects can be transmitted over the network. The `Sin`, `Cos`, and `Quadratic` classes are shown in Listing 17.29, 17.30, and 17.31, respectively. The `toString` method in each of the three classes is used later in the RMI Applet example.

Listing 17.28 `RemoteIntegralClient.java`

```java
import java.rmi.*;
import java.net.*;
import java.io.*;

/** This class calculates a variety of numerical integration
 *  values, printing the results of successively more accurate
 *  approximations. The actual computation is performed on a
 *  remote machine whose hostname is specified as a command-
 *  line argument.
 */

public class RemoteIntegralClient {
  public static void main(String[] args) {
    try {
      String host = (args.length > 0) ? args[0] : "localhost";
      RemoteIntegral remoteIntegral =
        (RemoteIntegral)Naming.lookup("rmi://" + host +
                                  "/RemoteIntegral");
      for(int steps=10; steps<=10000; steps*=10) {
        System.out.println
          ("Approximated with " + steps + " steps:" +
           "\n  Integral from 0 to pi of sin(x)=" +
           remoteIntegral.integrate(0.0, Math.PI,
                                  steps, new Sin()) +
           "\n  Integral from pi/2 to pi of cos(x)=" +
           remoteIntegral.integrate(Math.PI/2.0, Math.PI,
                                  steps, new Cos()) +
           "\n  Integral from 0 to 5 of x^2=" +
           remoteIntegral.integrate(0.0, 5.0, steps,
                                  new Quadratic()));
      }
      System.out.println
        ("'Correct' answer using Math library:" +
         "\n  Integral from 0 to pi of sin(x)=" +
         (-Math.cos(Math.PI) - -Math.cos(0.0)) +
         "\n  Integral from pi/2 to pi of cos(x)=" +
         (Math.sin(Math.PI) - Math.sin(Math.PI/2.0)) +
         "\n  Integral from 0 to 5 of x^2=" +
         (Math.pow(5.0, 3.0) / 3.0));
    } catch(RemoteException re) {
      System.out.println("RemoteException: " + re);
    } catch(NotBoundException nbe) {
      System.out.println("NotBoundException: " + nbe);
    } catch(MalformedURLException mfe) {
      System.out.println("MalformedURLException: " + mfe);
    }
  }
}
```

Listing 17.29 `Sin.java`

```java
import java.io.Serializable;

/** An evaluatable version of sin(x). */

class Sin implements Evaluatable, Serializable {
  public double evaluate(double val) {
    return(Math.sin(val));
  }

  public String toString() {
    return("Sin");
  }
}
```

Listing 17.30 `Cos.java`

```java
import java.io.Serializable;

/** An evaluatable version of cos(x). */

class Cos implements Evaluatable, Serializable {
  public double evaluate(double val) {
    return(Math.cos(val));
  }

  public String toString() {
    return("Cosine");
  }
}
```

Listing 17.31 `Quadratic.java`

```java
import java.io.Serializable;

/** An evaluatable version of x^2. */

class Quadratic implements Evaluatable, Serializable {
  public double evaluate(double val) {
    return(val * val);
  }

  public String toString() {
    return("Quadratic");
  }
}
```

---

3. The RemoteIntegral implementation.

Listing 17.32 shows the implementation of the `RemoteIntegral` interface. It simply uses methods in the `Integral` class.

Listing 17.32 `RemoteIntegralImpl.java`

```java
import java.rmi.*;
import java.rmi.server.UnicastRemoteObject;

/** The actual implementation of the RemoteIntegral interface.
 */

public class RemoteIntegralImpl extends UnicastRemoteObject
                                implements RemoteIntegral {

  /** Constructor must throw RemoteException. */

  public RemoteIntegralImpl() throws RemoteException {}

  /** Returns the sum of f(x) from x=start to x=stop, where the
   *  function f is defined by the evaluate method of the
   *  Evaluatable object.
   */

  public double sum(double start, double stop, double stepSize,
                    Evaluatable evalObj) {
    return(Integral.sum(start, stop, stepSize, evalObj));
  }

  /** Returns an approximation of the integral of f(x) from
   *  start to stop, using the midpoint rule. The function f is
   *  defined by the evaluate method of the Evaluatable object.
   *  @see #sum
   */

  public double integrate(double start, double stop, int numSteps,
                          Evaluatable evalObj) {
    return(Integral.integrate(start, stop, numSteps, evalObj));
  }
}
```

---

4. The RemoteIntegral server.

Listing 17.33 shows the server that creates a `RemoteIntegralImpl` object and registers the object with the URL `RemoteIntegral` on the local system.

Listing 17.33 `RemoteIntegralServer.java`

```java
import java.rmi.*;
import java.net.*;

/** Creates a RemoteIntegralImpl object and registers it under
 *  the name 'RemoteIntegral' so that remote clients can connect
 *  to it for numeric integration results. The idea is to place
 *  this server on a workstation with very fast floating-point
 *  capabilities, while slower interfaces can run on smaller
 *  computers but still use the integration routines.
 */

public class RemoteIntegralServer {
  public static void main(String[] args) {
    try {
      RemoteIntegralImpl integral =  new RemoteIntegralImpl();
      Naming.rebind("rmi:///RemoteIntegral", integral);
    } catch(RemoteException re) {
      System.out.println("RemoteException: " + re);
    } catch(MalformedURLException mfe) {
      System.out.println("MalformedURLException: " + mfe);
    }
  }
}
```

Compiling and Running the System for the Realistic Example

For this example, you must start the RMI registry, the server (`Remote-IntegralServer`), and the client (`RemoteIntegralClient`) in the same host directory. If the client and server are started from different directories, then the RMI protocol requires a `SecurityManager` on the client to load the stub files. Configuration of RMI to run the client and server on different hosts (or different directories) is explained following this example.

Core Note

For the following example to execute properly, the RMI registry, server, and client must be started from the same directory.

1. Compile the client and server.

At the prompt, enter these commands:

```
Prompt> javac RemoteIntegralClient.java
Prompt> javac RemoteIntegralServer.java
```

2. Generate the client Stub and server Skeleton.

At the prompt, enter this command.

```
Prompt> rmic -v1.2 RemoteIntegralImpl
```

The classes required by the client are: `RemoteIntegral.class`, `RemoteIntegralClient.class`. and `RemoteIntegralImpl_Stub.class`. The classes required by the server are: `RemoteIntegral.class`, `RemoteIntegralImpl.class`, and `RemoteIntegralServer.class`. If the server and client are both running JDK 1.1, use the `-v1.1` switch to produce the RMI 1.1 skeleton stub, `RemoteIntegralImpl_Skeleton`, required by the server.

3. Start the RMI registry.

The following command starts the RMI registry:

```
Prompt> rmiregistry
```

4. Start the Server.

At the prompt, enter this command:

```
Prompt> java RemoteIntegralServer
```

5. Start the client.

At the prompt, enter this command to obtain the output listed below:

```
Prompt> java RemoteIntegralClient
Approximated with 10 steps:
  Integral from 0 to pi of sin(x)=2.0082484079079745
  Integral from pi/2 to pi of cos(x)=-1.0010288241427086
  Integral from 0 to 5 of x^2=41.5625
Approximated with 100 steps:
  Integral from 0 to pi of sin(x)=2.0000822490709877
  Integral from pi/2 to pi of cos(x)=-1.000010280911902
  Integral from 0 to 5 of x^2=41.665624999999906
Approximated with 1000 steps:
  Integral from 0 to pi of sin(x)=2.0000008224672983
  Integral from pi/2 to pi of cos(x)=-1.000000102808351
  Integral from 0 to 5 of x^2=41.666656249998724
Approximated with 10000 steps:
  Integral from 0 to pi of sin(x)=2.00000000822436
  Integral from pi/2 to pi of cos(x)=-1.0000000010278831
  Integral from 0 to 5 of x^2=41.666666562504055
```

```
'Correct' answer using Math library:
  Integral from 0 to pi of sin(x)=2.0
  Integral from pi/2 to pi of cos(x)=-0.9999999999999999
  Integral from 0 to 5 of x^2=41.666666666666664
```

The actual integral value are:

$$\int_0^\pi \sin x \; dx \; = \; 2$$

$$\int_{\pi/2}^\pi \cos x \; dx \; = \; -1$$

$$\int_0^5 x^2 dx \; = \; 41\frac{2}{3}$$

As the number of steps increases, the numerical integration approaches the actual value. The benefit of RMI is that you can off-load the integration to a more powerful server.

Enterprise RMI Configuration

In the previous examples, the RMI registry, server, and client, were all assumed to be running on the same host. Certainly, this configuration does not take advantage of the distributed capabilities of RMI. However, once the server and client are running on different hosts, Java 2 requires that the client and server have an installed security manager to load the RMI classes remotely; by default, the required RMI classes can only be loaded from the local host. Furthermore, the RMI registry and server must be started on the same host. The `rmiregistry` only permits registration of remote objects from the local host.

In addition to a security manager, changes in the default security policies are required to allow the client to open connections to remote hosts. Following, we show you the steps to use RMI in an enterprise environment where the server and client are located on different machines.

To load classes remotely, the client must install an `RMISecurityManager`

```
System.setSecurityManager(new RMISecurityManager());
```

as shown in the modified client, `RemoteIntegralClient2` (Listing 17.34).

Core Note

In an enterprise configuration, the `rmiregistry` *and server must be started on the same host; otherwise, an* `AccessException` *is thrown. Additionally, the client must provide a policy file and set an* `RMISecurityManager` *to remotely load the stub files.*

Listing 17.34 `RemoteIntegralClient2.java`

```java
import java.rmi.*;
import java.net.*;
import java.io.*;

/** This class is a Java 2 version of RemoteIntegralClient
 *  that imposes a SecurityManager to allow the client to
 *  connect to a remote machine for loading stub files and
 *  performing numerical integration through a remote
 *  object.
 */

public class RemoteIntegralClient2 {
  public static void main(String[] args) {
    try {
      System.setSecurityManager(new RMISecurityManager());
      String host =
        (args.length > 0) ? args[0] : "localhost";
      RemoteIntegral remoteIntegral =
        (RemoteIntegral)Naming.lookup("rmi://" + host +
                                    "/RemoteIntegral");
      for(int steps=10; steps<=10000; steps*=10) {
        System.out.println
          ("Approximated with " + steps + " steps:" +
          "\n  Integral from 0 to pi of sin(x)=" +
          remoteIntegral.integrate(0.0, Math.PI,
                                  steps, new Sin()) +
          "\n  Integral from pi/2 to pi of cos(x)=" +
          remoteIntegral.integrate(Math.PI/2.0, Math.PI,
                                  steps, new Cos()) +
          "\n  Integral from 0 to 5 of x^2=" +
          remoteIntegral.integrate(0.0, 5.0, steps,
                                  new Quadratic()));
      }
      System.out.println
        ("'Correct' answer using Math library:" +
        "\n  Integral from 0 to pi of sin(x)=" +
        (-Math.cos(Math.PI) - -Math.cos(0.0)) +
        "\n  Integral from pi/2 to pi of cos(x)=" +
        (Math.sin(Math.PI) - Math.sin(Math.PI/2.0)) +
        "\n  Integral from 0 to 5 of x^2=" +
        (Math.pow(5.0, 3.0) / 3.0));
    } catch(RemoteException re) {
      System.out.println("RemoteException: " + re);
```

(continued)

Listing 17.34 `RemoteIntegralClient2.java` *(continued)*

```
    } catch(NotBoundException nbe) {
      System.out.println("NotBoundException: " + nbe);
    } catch(MalformedURLException mfe) {
      System.out.println("MalformedURLException: " + mfe);
    }
  }
}
```

In Java 2, in addition to imposing a security manager, the client requires a policy file to specify permission for dynamic loading of remote classes. Basically, you need to state in which host and ports the client can open a socket connection. Listing 17.35 illustrates the client permissions to connect to the `rmiregistry` and server running on *rmihost* and to an HTTP server, *webhost*, to load the stub files.

By default the `rmiregistry` listens on port 1099. When the client looks up the remote object, it first connects to the `rmiregistry` on port 1099. Afterward, the client communicates directly to the remote server on the port at which the server is listening. Note that when the server is started and registers the remote object, the source port used to communicate with the RMI registry and client is randomly selected from an available port in the range 1024–65535 on the host. As a consequence, to allow connection to the rmihost, permission is required over the complete range of possible ports, 1024–65535, not just port 1099. Also, the stub classes are often placed on an HTTP server, so the policy file should also grant permission for the client to connect to the webhost.

Listing 17.35 Policy file for client, `rmiclient.policy`

```
grant {
  // rmihost - RMI registry and the server
  // webhost - HTTP server for stub classes
  permission java.net.SocketPermission
    "rmihost:1024-65535", "connect";
  permission java.net.SocketPermission
    "webhost:80", "connect";
};
```

You can specify the security policy file through a command-line argument when executing the client, as in

```
java -Djava.security.policy=rmiclient.policy RemoteIntegralClient2
```

Or, you can add the permission statements to the `java.policy` file used by the Java Virtual Machine and avoid the command-line argument. For JDK 1.3, the `java.policy` file is located in the directory `/root/jdk1.3/lib/security/`.

When starting the server that registers the remote object, you also need to specify the codebase location (HTTP server) to load the stub files. As with the policy file, you can specify the codebase on the command line through the system property, `java.rmi.server.codebase`, as in

```
java -Djava.rmi.server.codebase=http://webhost:port/directory/
    RemoteIntegralServer
```

The `java.rmi.server.codebase` property tells the server that any stub files required by the client or the RMI registry should be loaded from the HTTP server at `http://webhost:port/directory/`. The port parameter is required only if the HTTP server is not running on standard port 80.

Compiling and Running the System for an Enterprise RMI Configuration

1. Compile the client and server.

At the prompt, enter these commands:

```
Prompt> javac RemoteIntegralClient2.java
Prompt> javac RemoteIntegralServer.java
```

2. Generate the client Stub and server Skeleton.

At the prompt, enter this command.

```
Prompt> rmic -v1.2 RemoteIntegralImpl
```

3. Place the appropriate files on the correct machines.

Table 17.1 summarizes the locations to place the class files. The client requires `RemoteIntegralClient2` and all other instantiated or referenced classes, including `RemoteIntegral`, `Sin`, `Cos`, and `Quadratic`. As the later three classes inherit from `Evaluatable`, that class is also needed on the client machine; `Evaluatable` is not downloaded from the server. Also, the client needs the policy file, `rmipolicy.client`.

The server that instantiates and registers the remote object requires `RemoteIntegralServer`, and when it creates the remote object, the server requires `RemoteIntegralImpl`, `RemoteIntegral` (inherited class), and `Evaluatable`; these last three classes are not downloaded from the codebase directory (HTTP server). The class `Integral` is required on the server, since the static methods, `Integer.sum` and `Integer.evaluate`, are called in `RemoteIntegralImpl`. The server also requires `RemoteIntegralImpl_Stub` when registering the remote object. Finally, `Sin`, `Cos`, and `Quadratic` are required on the server; these classes override the `evaulate` method defined in the interface `Evaluatable` and are later required through dynamic binding in `Integral` when `evaluate` is called. These class definitions are not sent from the client.

The HTTP server requires the stub file, `RemoteIntegralImpl_Stub`, for downloading to the client. In addition, you must place any `Remote-IntegralImpl` dependencies, `RemoteIntegral` and `Evaluatable`, on the HTTP server for use when the remote object is registered; the `rmiregistry` does not receive these files from the server instantiating the remote object.

Table 17.1 Required location for class files

Client	*Server*	*HTTP Server*
RemoteIntegralClient2	RemoteIntegralServer	RemoteIntegralImpl_Stub
RemoteIntegral	RemoteIntegralImpl	RemoteIntegral
Evaluatable	RemoteIntegralImpl_Stub	Evaluatable
Sin	RemoteIntegral	
Cos	Integral	
Quadratic	Evaluatable	
	Sin	
	Cos	
	Quadratic	

4. Start the HTTP server.

Place `RemoteIntegral_Stub.class`, `RemoteIntegeral.class`, and `Evaluatable.class` on an HTTP server and verify that you can access the files through a browser.

5. Start the RMI registry.

Start the RMI registry:

```
Server> /somedirectory/rmiregistry
```

When you start the `rmiregistry`, make sure that none of the class files are in the directory in which you started the registry or available through the classpath.

Core Warning

The client and server may not be able to load the stub files from the correct location if the RMI registry is able to locate the files through the classpath. Always start the `rmiregistry`, without a set classpath, in a different directory than that of the server.

6. Start the server.

At the prompt, enter this command:

```
Server> java -Djava.rmi.server.codebase=http://webhost/rmi/
            RemoteIntegralServer
```

assuming that the stub files are placed on the HTTP server, webhost, and in the rmi subdirectory. Note that the server must be started on the same host as the rmiregistry, but not from within the same directory. If an exception is thrown when starting the server, correct the source of the problem, and restart the RMI registry before attempting to restart the server.

Core Note

The rmiregistry *and server need to run on the same host or an* AccessException *is received by the server.*

7. Start the client.

At the prompt, enter the following command (where rmihost is the host in which you started the rmiregistry and server) to obtain the output listed below:

```
Client> java -Djava.security.policy=rmiclient.policy
            RemoteIntegralClient2 rmihost
```

```
Approximated with 10 steps:
  Integral from 0 to pi of sin(x)=2.0082484079079745
  Integral from pi/2 to pi of cos(x)=-1.0010288241427086
  Integral from 0 to 5 of x^2=41.5625
Approximated with 100 steps:
  Integral from 0 to pi of sin(x)=2.0000822490709877
  Integral from pi/2 to pi of cos(x)=-1.000010280911902
  Integral from 0 to 5 of x^2=41.665624999999906
Approximated with 1000 steps:
  Integral from 0 to pi of sin(x)=2.0000008224672983
  Integral from pi/2 to pi of cos(x)=-1.000000102808351
  Integral from 0 to 5 of x^2=41.666656249998724
Approximated with 10000 steps:
  Integral from 0 to pi of sin(x)=2.00000000822436
  Integral from pi/2 to pi of cos(x)=-1.0000000010278831
  Integral from 0 to 5 of x^2=41.666666562504055
'Correct' answer using Math library:
  Integral from 0 to pi of sin(x)=2.0
  Integral from pi/2 to pi of cos(x)=-0.9999999999999999
  Integral from 0 to 5 of x^2=41.666666666666664
```

RMI Applet Example

Compared to writing an application communicating with a remote object through RMI, writing an applet that communicates through RMI is greatly simplified because the applet already invokes a security manager for loading remote files; an applet using RMI does not require a RMISecurityManager. In contrast though, an applet cannot open network connections other than to the server from which the applet was loaded. Therefore, the RMI registry, the server registering the remote object, and the HTTP server from which the applet and stub files are loaded *must* be the same host.

When posting the applet on an HTTP server, be sure to place all the client files in the same directory as the applet class file. Or, alternatively, you can place a single JAR file in the applet directory and specify the JAR file through the ARCHIVE attribute in the APPLET tag. See Section 7.10 (Packages, Classpath, and JAR Archives) for details on creating JAR files.

Listing 17.36 presents an applet client that communicates to a remote object through RMI. Since the RMI registry and server are located on the same host in which the applet was loaded, the host for the RMI URL is determined by a call to getCodeBase().getHost(). The results are shown in Figure 17–4 in Netscape 6.

Listing 17.36 RemoteIntegralApplet.java

```
import java.awt.*;
import java.awt.event.*;
import java.rmi.*;
import java.net.*;
import java.io.*;
import javax.swing.*;

/** This class is an applet version of RemoteIntegralClient
 *  that connects to a remote machine for performing
 *  numerical integration in a sine, cosine, or quadratic
 *  equation. As an Applet imposes its own security
 *  manager, a RMISecurityManager is not needed to load
 *  the stub classes.
 */

public class RemoteIntegralApplet extends JApplet
                                  implements ActionListener {
  private Evaluatable[] shapes;
  private RemoteIntegral remoteIntegral;
  private JLabel result;
  private JTextField startInput, stopInput, stepInput;
  private JComboBox combo;
```

(continued)

Listing 17.36 RemoteIntegralApplet.java *(continued)*

```
public void init() {
  String host = getCodeBase().getHost();
  try {
    remoteIntegral =
      (RemoteIntegral)Naming.lookup("rmi://" + host +
                                    "/RemoteIntegral");
  } catch(RemoteException re) {
    reportError("RemoteException: " + re);
  } catch(NotBoundException nbe) {
    reportError("NotBoundException: " + nbe);
  } catch(MalformedURLException mfe) {
    reportError("MalformedURLException: " + mfe);
  }

  Container context = getContentPane();
  // Set up combo box.
  shapes = new Evaluatable[]{ new Sin(),
                              new Cos(),
                              new Quadratic() };
  combo = new JComboBox(shapes);
  context.add(combo, BorderLayout.NORTH);

  // Input area.
  startInput = new JTextField();
  stopInput = new JTextField();
  stepInput = new JTextField();
  result = new JLabel();
  JPanel labelPanel = new JPanel(new GridLayout(4,1));
  labelPanel.add(new JLabel("Start:"));
  labelPanel.add(new JLabel("Stop:"));
  labelPanel.add(new JLabel("Steps:"));
  labelPanel.add(new JLabel("Result:  "));
  context.add(labelPanel, BorderLayout.WEST);
  JPanel inputPanel = new JPanel(new GridLayout(4,1));
  inputPanel.add(startInput);
  inputPanel.add(stopInput);
  inputPanel.add(stepInput);
  inputPanel.add(result);
  context.add(inputPanel, BorderLayout.CENTER);
```

(continued)

Listing 17.36 `RemoteIntegralApplet.java` *(continued)*

```
    // Set up button.
    JPanel buttonPanel = new JPanel(new FlowLayout());
    JButton submit = new JButton("Submit");
    submit.addActionListener(this);
    buttonPanel.add(submit);
    context.add(buttonPanel, BorderLayout.SOUTH);
  }

  public void actionPerformed(ActionEvent event) {
    try {
      int steps = Integer.parseInt(stepInput.getText());
      double start = Double.parseDouble(startInput.getText());
      double stop = Double.parseDouble(stopInput.getText());
      showStatus("Calculating ...");
      Evaluatable shape = (Evaluatable)combo.getSelectedItem();
      double area = remoteIntegral.integrate(start, stop,
                                             steps, shape);
      result.setText(Double.toString(area));
      showStatus("");
    } catch(NumberFormatException nfe) {
      reportError("Bad input: " + nfe);
    } catch(RemoteException re) {
      reportError("RemoteException: " + re);
    }
  }

  private void reportError(String message) {
    System.out.println(message);
    showStatus(message);
  }
}
```

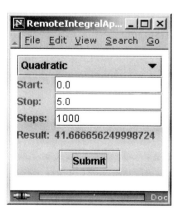

Figure 17–4 Applet that communicates to a remote object through RMI in Netscape 6.

Aside from Netscape 6, earlier versions of Netscape and all versions of Internet Explorer do not support Java 2 and the RMI 1.2 stub protocol without having the Java Plug-In installed (see Section 9.9, "The Java Plug-In"). Even worse, Internet Explorer does not support the RMI 1.1 stub protocol without having the RMI add-on installed. The RMI add-on is available at `ftp://ftp/microsoft.com/developr/msdn/unsup-ed/`. The RMI 1.1 stub protocol is supported in Netscape 4.06 and later.

17.10 Summary

Java sockets let you create network clients or servers that can communicate with general-purpose network programs written in any language. The process of building a client is straightforward: open a socket, create input and output streams from the socket, use these streams for communication, then close the socket. A server is similar but waits for an incoming connection before the socket can be created. Both types of systems frequently need to parse input they receive, and a `StringTokenizer` is a convenient tool for this. RMI is a powerful and convenient alternative when distributing processing among Java-only systems.

In the next part of the book we focus on server-side programming. First, we cover HTML forms as front ends to servlets or other server-side programs such as CGI scripts. These forms provide simple and reliable user interface controls to collect data from the user and transmit it to the servlet. Following that, we cover Java servlets, which run on a Web server, acting as a middle layer between a request coming from a Web browser or other HTTP client and databases or applications on the HTTP server. Next, we cover JavaServer Pages (JSP) technology to enable you to mix regular, static HTML with dynamically generated content from servlets. In addition, we show you how to write applet front ends to send data to HTTP servers through firewalls by means of HTTP tunneling. Also, we present the JDBC API, which allows to you send SQL queries to databases; and finally, we examine the Java API for XML parsing to process XML files.

SERVER-SIDE PROGRAMMING

HTML FORMS

Chapter 18

U p to this point, our discussion has focused on desktop Java (applications) and client-side Java (applets). Another very important use of Java is for middleware on a Web server. The two main technologies for Java middleware, servlets and JavaServer Pages, are discussed in Chapters 19 and 20. However, before you can understand how to process data on the server, you need to be able to collect and transmit data to those server-side programs.

This chapter discusses the use of HTML forms as front ends to servlets or other server-side programs such as CGI scripts. These forms provide simple and reliable user interface controls to collect data from the user and to transmit it to the servlet.

18.1 How HTML Forms Transmit Data

HTML forms let you create a variety of user interface controls to collect input on a Web page. Each of the controls typically has a name and a value; the name is specified in the HTML, and the value comes either from the HTML or from user input. The entire form is associated with the URL of a program that will process the data. When the user submits the form (usually by pressing a button), the names and values of the controls are sent to the designated URL as a string of the form

```
Name1=Value1&Name2=Value2...NameN=ValueN
```

This string can be sent to the designated program in one of two ways. The first, which uses the HTTP GET method, appends the string to the end of the specified URL, after a question mark. The second way data can be sent is by the HTTP POST method. Here, the POST request line, the HTTP request headers, and a blank line are first sent to the server, then the data string is sent on the following line.

For example, Listing 18.1 (HTML code) and Figure 18–1 (typical result) show a simple form with two textfields. The HTML elements that make up this form are discussed in detail in the rest of this chapter, but for now note a couple of things. First, observe that one textfield has a name of firstName and the other has a name of lastName. Second, note that the GUI controls are considered text-level (inline) elements, so you need to use explicit HTML formatting to make sure that the controls appear next to the text describing them. Finally, notice that the FORM element designates http://localhost:8088/SomeProgram as the URL to which the data will be sent.

Listing 18.1 GetForm.html

```
<!DOCTYPE HTML PUBLIC "-//W3C//DTD HTML 4.0 Transitional//EN">
<HTML>
<HEAD>
  <TITLE>A Sample Form Using GET</TITLE>
</HEAD>

<BODY BGCOLOR="#FDF5E6">
<H2 ALIGN="CENTER">A Sample Form Using GET</H2>

<FORM ACTION="http://localhost:8088/SomeProgram">
  <CENTER>
  First name:
  <INPUT TYPE="TEXT" NAME="firstName" VALUE="Joe"><BR>
  Last name:
  <INPUT TYPE="TEXT" NAME="lastName" VALUE="Hacker"><P>
  <INPUT TYPE="SUBMIT"> <!-- Press this button to submit form -->
  </CENTER>
</FORM>

</BODY>
</HTML>
```

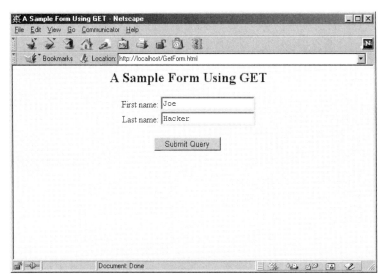

Figure 18–1 Initial result of `GetForm.html`.

Before submitting the form, we start a server program called `EchoServer` on port 8088 of the local machine. `EchoServer`, shown in Section 17.8 (Example: A Simple HTTP Server), is a mini "Web server" used for debugging. No matter what URL is specified and what data is sent to it, `EchoServer` merely returns a Web page showing all the HTTP information sent by the browser. As shown in Figure 18–2, when the form is submitted with `Joe` in the first textfield and `Hacker` in the second, the browser simply requests the URL `http://localhost:8088/Some-Program?firstName=Joe&lastName=Hacker`. Listing 18.2 (HTML code) and Figure 18–3 (typical result) show a variation that uses `POST` instead of `GET`. As shown in Figure 18–4, submitting the form with textfield values of `Joe` and `Hacker` results in the line `firstName=Joe&lastName=Hacker` being sent to the server on a separate line after the HTTP request headers and a blank line.

That's the general idea behind HTML forms: GUI controls gather data from the user, each control has a name and a value, and a string containing all the name/value pairs is sent to the server when the form is submitted. Extracting the names and values on the server is covered in Section 19.6 (The Client Request: Form Data). The remainder of this chapter covers options in setting up forms and the various GUI controls you can put in them.

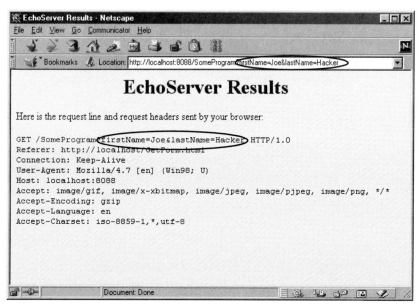

Figure 18–2 HTTP request sent by Netscape 4.7 when submitting GetForm.html.

Listing 18.2 PostForm.html

```html
<!DOCTYPE HTML PUBLIC "-//W3C//DTD HTML 4.0 Transitional//EN">
<HTML>
<HEAD>
  <TITLE>A Sample Form Using POST</TITLE>
</HEAD>

<BODY BGCOLOR="#FDF5E6">
<H2 ALIGN="CENTER">A Sample Form Using POST</H2>

<FORM ACTION="http://localhost:8088/SomeProgram"
      METHOD="POST">
  <CENTER>
  First name:
  <INPUT TYPE="TEXT" NAME="firstName" VALUE="Joe"><BR>
  Last name:
  <INPUT TYPE="TEXT" NAME="lastName" VALUE="Hacker"><P>
  <INPUT TYPE="SUBMIT">
  </CENTER>
</FORM>

</BODY>
</HTML>
```

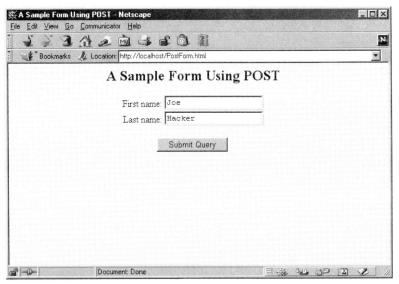

Figure 18–3 Initial result of `PostForm.html`.

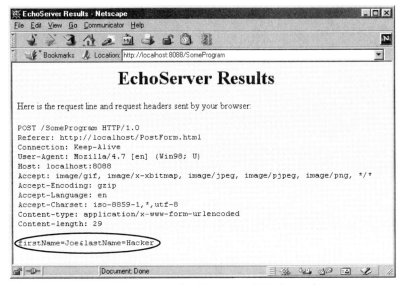

Figure 18–4 HTTP request sent by Netscape 4.7 when submitting `PostForm.html`.

18.2 The **FORM** Element

HTML forms allow you to create a set of data input elements associated with a particular URL. Each of these elements is typically given a name and has a value based on the original HTML or user input. When the form is submitted, the names and values of all active elements are collected into a string with and equal sign (=) between each name and value and with an ampersand (&) between each name/value pair. This string is then transmitted to the URL designated by the FORM element. The string is either appended to the URL after a question mark or sent on a separate line after the HTTP request headers and a blank line, depending on whether GET or POST is used as the submission method. This section covers the FORM element itself, used primarily to designate the URL and to choose the submission method. The following sections cover the various user interface controls that can be used within forms.

HTML Element: `<FORM ACTION="URL" ...> ... </FORM>`
Attributes: ACTION (required), METHOD, ENCTYPE, TARGET, ONSUBMIT, ONRESET, ACCEPT, ACCEPT-CHARSET

The FORM element creates an area for data input elements and designates the URL to which any collected data will be transmitted. For example:

```
<FORM ACTION="http://some.isp.com/servlet/SomeServlet">
  FORM input elements and regular HTML
</FORM>
```

The rest of this section explains the attributes that apply to the FORM element: ACTION, METHOD, ENCTYPE, TARGET, ONSUBMIT, ONRESET, ACCEPT, and ACCEPT-CHARSET. Note that we are not discussing attributes like STYLE, CLASS, and LANG that apply to general HTML elements, but only those that are specific to the FORM element.

ACTION

The ACTION attribute specifies the URL of the servlet or CGI program that will process the FORM data (e.g., http://cgi.whitehouse.gov/bin/schedule-fund-raiser) or an email address which the FORM data will be sent (e.g., mailto:audit@irs.gov). Some ISPs do not allow ordinary users to create servlets or CGI programs, or they charge extra for this privilege. In such a case, sending the data by email is a convenient option when you create pages that need to collect data but not return results (e.g., accepting orders for products). You must use the POST method (see METHOD in the following subsection) when using a mailto URL.

METHOD

The METHOD attribute specifies how the data will be transmitted to the HTTP server. When GET is used, the data is appended to the end of the designated URL after a question mark. For an example, see Section 18.1 (How HTML Forms Transmit Data). GET is the default and is also the method that is used when a browser requests a normal URL. When POST is used, the data is sent on a separate line.

The advantages of using the GET method are twofold: the method is simple; and with server-side programs that use GET, users can access those programs for testing and debugging without creating a form, simply by using a URL with the proper data appended. On the other hand, owing to URL size restrictions on some browsers, GET requests have limits on the amount of data that can be appended, whereas POST requests do not. Another disadvantage of GET is that most browsers show the URL, including the attached data string, in an address field at the top of the browser. This display makes GET inappropriate for sending sensitive data if your computer is in a relatively public place.

ENCTYPE

This attribute specifies the way in which the data will be encoded before being transmitted. The default is application/x-www-form-urlencoded, which means that the client converts each space into a plus sign (+) and every other nonalphanumeric character into a percent sign (%) followed by the two hexadecimal digits representing that character (e.g., in ASCII or ISO Latin-1). Those transformations are in addition to placing an equal sign (=) between entry names and values and an ampersand (&) between entries.

For example, Figure 18–5 shows a version of the GetForm.html page (Listing 18.1) where "Marty (Java Hacker?)" is entered for the first name. As can be seen in Figure 18–6, this entry gets sent as "Marty+%28Java+Hacker%3F%29". That's because spaces become plus signs, 28 is the ASCII value (in hex) for a left parenthesis, 3F is the ASCII value of a question mark, and 29 is a right parenthesis.

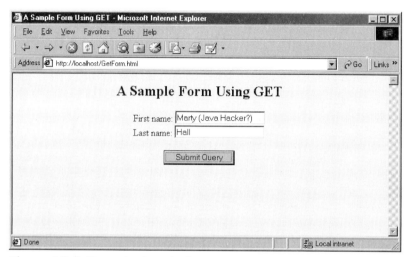

Figure 18–5 Customized result of `GetForm.html`.

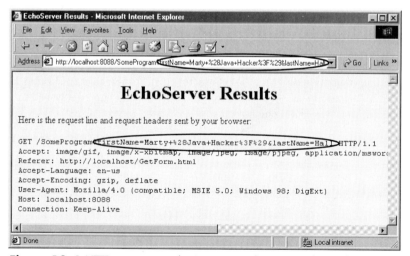

Figure 18–6 HTTP request sent by Internet Explorer 5.0 when submitting `GetForm.html` with the data shown in Figure 18–5.

Most recent browsers support an additional ENCTYPE of multipart/
form-data. This encoding transmits each of the fields as separate parts of a
MIME-compatible document and automatically uses POST to submit them.
This encoding sometimes makes it easier for the server-side program to handle
complex data and is required when file upload controls are used to send entire
documents (see Section 18.7). For example, Listing 18.3 shows a form that differs from GetForm.html (Listing 18.1) only in that

```
<FORM ACTION="http://localhost:8088/SomeProgram">
```

has been changed to

```
<FORM ACTION="http://localhost:8088/SomeProgram"
      ENCTYPE="multipart/form-data">
```

Figures 18–7 and 18–8 show the results.

Listing 18.3 MultipartForm.html

```
<!DOCTYPE HTML PUBLIC "-//W3C//DTD HTML 4.0 Transitional//EN">
<HTML>
<HEAD>
  <TITLE>Using ENCTYPE="multipart/form-data"</TITLE>
</HEAD>

<BODY BGCOLOR="#FDF5E6">
<H2 ALIGN="CENTER">Using ENCTYPE="multipart/form-data"</H2>

<FORM ACTION="http://localhost:8088/SomeProgram"
      ENCTYPE="multipart/form-data">
  <CENTER>
  First name:
  <INPUT TYPE="TEXT" NAME="firstName" VALUE="Joe"><BR>
  Last name:
  <INPUT TYPE="TEXT" NAME="lastName" VALUE="Hacker"><P>
  <INPUT TYPE="SUBMIT">
  </CENTER>
</FORM>

</BODY>
</HTML>
```

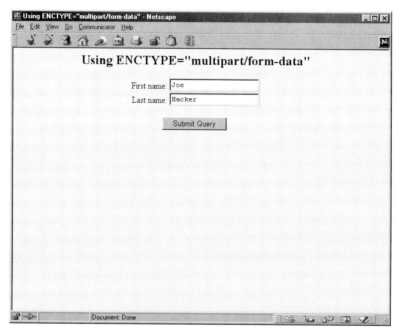

Figure 18–7 Initial result of `MultipartForm.html`.

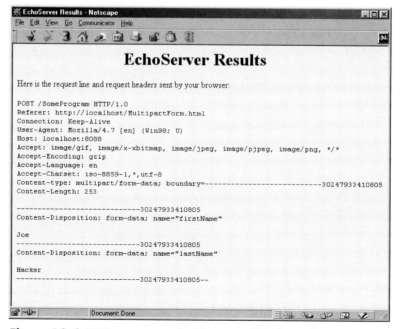

Figure 18–8 HTTP request sent by Netscape 4.7 when submitting
`MultipartForm.html`.

TARGET

The TARGET attribute is used by frame-capable browsers to determine which frame cell should be used to display the results of the servlet or other program handling the form submission. The default is to display the results in whatever frame contains the form being submitted.

ONSUBMIT and ONRESET

These attributes are used by JavaScript to attach code that should be evaluated when the form is submitted or reset. For ONSUBMIT, if the expression evaluates to false, the form is not submitted. This case lets you invoke JavaScript code on the client to check the format of the form field values before they are submitted, prompting the user for missing or illegal entries.

ACCEPT and ACCEPT-CHARSET

These attributes are new in HTML 4.0 and specify the MIME types (ACCEPT) and character encodings (ACCEPT-CHARSET) that must be accepted by the servlet or other program processing the form data. The MIME types listed in ACCEPT could also be used by the client to limit the file types that are displayed to the user for file upload elements.

18.3 Text Controls

HTML supports three types of text-input elements: textfields, password fields, and text areas. Each is given a name, and the value is taken from the content of the control. The name and value are sent to the server when the form is submitted, which is typically done by means of a submit button (see Section 18.4).

Textfields

HTML Element: `<INPUT TYPE="TEXT" NAME="..." ...>`
                   (No End Tag)

Attributes: NAME (required), VALUE, SIZE, MAXLENGTH, DISABLED, READONLY, ONCHANGE, ONSELECT, ONFOCUS, ONBLUR, ONKEYDOWN, ONKEYPRESS, ONKEYUP

This element creates a single-line input field where the user can enter text, as illustrated earlier in Listings 18.1, 18.2, and 18.3. For multiline fields, see TEXTAREA in the following subsection. TEXT is the default TYPE in INPUT forms, although it is recommended that TEXT be supplied explicitly. You should remember that the normal browser word wrapping applies inside FORM elements, so be careful to make sure the browser will not separate the descriptive text from the associated textfield.

Core Approach

Use explicit HTML constructs to group textfields with their descriptive text.

Some browsers submit the form when the user presses Enter when the cursor is in a textfield, but you should not depend on this behavior since it is not standard. For instance, Netscape submits the form when the user types a carriage return only if the current form has a single textfield, regardless of the number of forms on the page. Internet Explorer submits the form on Enter only when the page holds only a single form, regardless of the number of textfields in the form. Mosaic submits the form on Enter only when the cursor is in the last textfield on the entire page.

Core Warning

Don't rely on the browser submitting the form when the user presses Enter when in a textfield. Always include a button or image map that submits the form explicitly.

The following subsections describe the attributes that apply specifically to text-fields. Attributes that apply to general HTML elements (e.g., STYLE, CLASS, ID) are not discussed. The TABINDEX attribute, which applies to *all* form elements, is discussed in Section 18.11 (Tab Order Control).

NAME

The NAME attribute identifies the textfield when the form is submitted. In standard HTML the attribute is required. Because data is always sent to the server in the form of name/value pairs, no data is sent from form controls that have no NAME.

VALUE

A VALUE attribute, if supplied, specifies the *initial* contents of the textfield. When the form is submitted, the *current* contents are sent; these can reflect user input. If the textfield is empty when the form is submitted, the form data simply consists of the name and an equal sign (e.g., other-data&**text-fieldname**=&other-data).

SIZE

This attribute specifies the width of the textfield, based on the average character width of the font being used. If text beyond this size is entered, the textfield scrolls to accommodate it. This overflow could occur if the user enters more characters than the SIZE or enters SIZE number of wide characters (e.g., capital W) when a proportional-width font is being used. Netscape automatically uses a proportional font in textfields. Internet Explorer, unfortunately, does not, and you cannot change the font by embedding the INPUT element in a FONT or CODE element.

MAXLENGTH

MAXLENGTH gives the maximum number of *allowable* characters. This number is in contrast to the number of *visible* characters, which is specified by SIZE.

DISABLED, READONLY

These attributes let you completely disable a textfield or make it read-only. A disabled textfield cannot be edited, receive the input focus, be tabbed to, or be part of a form submission. A read-only textfield cannot be edited but can receive the input focus, be tabbed to, and be part of a form submission. Although these attributes are officially part of HTML 4.0, they are not supported by Netscape 4.x.

ONCHANGE, ONSELECT, ONFOCUS, ONBLUR, ONKEYDOWN, ONKEYPRESS, and ONKEYUP

These attributes are used only by browsers that support JavaScript. They specify the action to take when the mouse leaves the textfield after a change has occurred, when the user selects text in the textfield, when the textfield gets the input focus, when it loses the input focus, and when individual keys are pressed.

Password Fields

HTML Element: `<INPUT TYPE="PASSWORD" NAME="..." ...>`
        (No End Tag)

Attributes: NAME (required), VALUE, SIZE, MAXLENGTH, DISABLED, READONLY, ONCHANGE, ONSELECT, ONFOCUS, ONBLUR, ONKEYDOWN, ONKEYPRESS, ONKEYUP

Password fields are created and used just like textfields, except that when the user enters text, the input is not echoed, but instead some obscuring character, usually an asterisk, is displayed (see Figure 18–9). Obscured input is useful for collecting data such as credit card numbers or passwords that the user would not want shown to people who may be near his computer. The regular, unobscured text is transmitted as the value of the field when the form is submitted. Since GET data is appended to the URL after a question mark, you will want to use the POST method when using a password field so that a bystander cannot read the unobscured password from the URL display at the top of the browser.

Core Approach

To protect the user's privacy, always use POST when creating forms with password fields.

NAME, VALUE, SIZE, MAXLENGTH, DISABLED, READ-ONLY, ONCHANGE, ONSELECT, ONFOCUS, ONBLUR, ONKEYDOWN, ONKEYPRESS, and ONKEYUP

Attributes for password fields are used in exactly the same manner as with text-fields.

Enter Password: `******`

Figure 18–9 A password field created by means of `<INPUT TYPE="PASSWORD" ...>`.

Text Areas

HTML Element: `<TEXTAREA NAME="..."`
`                 ROWS=xxx COLS=yyy> ...`
`        </TEXTAREA>`

Attributes: NAME (required), ROWS (required), COLS (required), WRAP (nonstandard), DISABLED, READONLY, ONCHANGE, ONSELECT, ONFOCUS, ONBLUR, ONKEYDOWN, ONKEYPRESS, ONKEYUP

The TEXTAREA element creates a multiline text area; see Figure 18–10. There is no VALUE attribute; instead, text between the start and end tags is used as the initial content of the text area. The initial text between `<TEXTAREA ...>` and `</TEXT-AREA>` is treated similarly to text inside the now-obsolete XMP element. That is, white space in this initial text is maintained and HTML markup between the start and end tags is taken literally, except for character entities such as `&lt;`, `&copy;`, and so forth, which are interpreted normally. Unless a custom `ENCTYPE` is used in the form (see Section 18.2, "The FORM Element"), characters, including those generated from character entities, are URL-encoded before being transmitted. That is, spaces become plus signs and other nonalphanumeric characters become %*XX*, where *XX* is the numeric value of the character in hex.

NAME

This attribute specifies the name that will be sent to the server.

ROWS

`ROWS` specifies the number of visible lines of text. If more lines of text are entered, a vertical scrollbar will be added to the text area.

COLS

`COLS` specifies the visible width of the text area, based on the average width of characters in the font being used. If the text on a single line contains more characters than the specified width allows, the result is browser dependent. In Netscape, horizontal scrollbars are added (but see the `WRAP` attribute, described next, to change this behavior). In Internet Explorer, the word wraps around to the next line.

WRAP

The Netscape-specific `WRAP` attribute specifies what to do with lines that are longer than the size specified by `COLS`. A value of `OFF` disables word wrap and is the default. The user can still enter explicit line breaks in such a case. A value of `HARD` causes words to wrap in the text area *and* the associated line breaks to be transmitted when the form is submitted. Finally, a value of `SOFT` causes the words to wrap in the text area but no extra line breaks to be transmitted when the form is submitted.

DISABLED, READONLY

These attributes let you completely disable a text area or make it read-only. A disabled text area cannot be edited, receive the input focus, be tabbed to, or be part of a form submission. A read-only text area cannot be edited but can receive the input focus, be tabbed to, and be part of a form submission. The status of these attributes can be changed dynamically with JavaScript. Although officially part of HTML 4.0, these attributes are not supported by Netscape 4.x.

ONCHANGE, ONSELECT, ONFOCUS, ONBLUR, ONKEYDOWN, ONKEYPRESS, and ONKEYUP

These attributes apply only to browsers that support JavaScript; they specify code to be executed when certain conditions arise. `ONCHANGE` handles the situation when the input focus leaves the text area after it has changed, ONSELECT describes what to do when text in the text area is selected by the user, ONFOCUS and ONBLUR specify what to do when the text area acquires or loses the input focus, and the remaining attributes determine what to do when individual keys are typed.

The following example creates a text area with 5 visible rows that can hold about 30 characters per row. The result is shown in Figure 18–10.

```
<CENTER>
<P>
Enter some HTML:<BR>
<TEXTAREA NAME="HTML" ROWS=5 COLS=30>
Delete this text and replace
with some HTML to validate.
</TEXTAREA>
<CENTER>
```

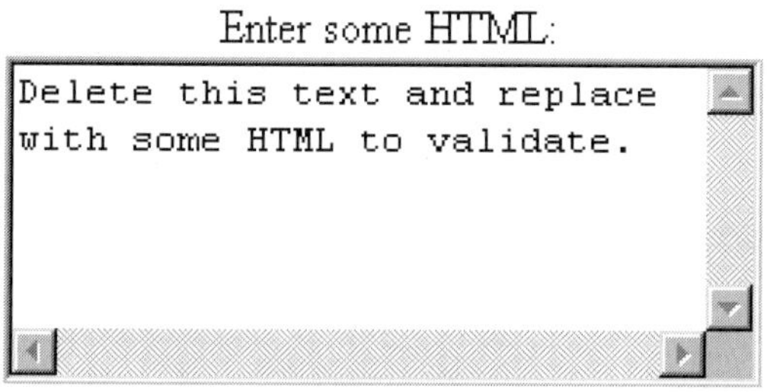

Enter some HTML:

```
Delete this text and replace
with some HTML to validate.
```

Figure 18–10 A text area.

18.4 Push Buttons

Push buttons are used for two main purposes in HTML forms: to submit forms and to reset the controls to the values specified in the original HTML document. Browsers that use JavaScript can also use buttons for a third purpose: to trigger arbitrary JavaScript code.

Traditionally, buttons have been created by the INPUT element used with a TYPE attribute of SUBMIT, RESET, or BUTTON. In HTML 4.0, the BUTTON element was introduced but is currently supported only by Internet Explorer. This new element lets you create buttons with multiline labels, images, font changes, and the like, so is preferred if you are sure your users will all be using browsers that support it (e.g., in a corporate intranet). Since the element is not supported by Netscape, at least as of Netscape version 4.7, for now you should reserve BUTTON for intranets that use Internet Explorer exclusively.

Core Warning

Netscape does not support the BUTTON element.

Submit Buttons

HTML Element: `<INPUT TYPE="SUBMIT" ...>` (No End Tag)
Attributes: NAME, VALUE, DISABLED, ONCLICK, ONDBLCLICK,
            ONFOCUS, ONBLUR

When a submit button is clicked, the form is sent to the servlet or other server-side program designated by the ACTION parameter of the FORM. Although the action can be triggered other ways, such as the user clicking on an image map, most forms have at least one submit button. Submit buttons, like other form controls, adopt the look and feel of the client operating system, so will look slightly different on different platforms. Figure 18–11 shows a submit button on Windows 98, created by

```
<INPUT TYPE="SUBMIT">
```

    Submit Query

Figure 18–11 A submit button with the default label.

NAME and VALUE
Most input elements have a name and an associated value. When the form is submitted, the names and values of active elements are concatenated to form the data string. If a submit button is used simply to initiate the submission of the form, its name can be omitted. In that case, the name does not contribute to the data string that is sent. If a name *is* supplied, then only the name and value of the button that was actually clicked are sent. The label is used as the value that is transmitted.

Supplying an explicit VALUE will change the default label. For instance, the following code snippet creates a textfield and two submit buttons, shown in Figure 18–12. If, for example, the first button is selected, the data string sent to the server would be `Item=256MB+SIMM&Add=Add+Item+to+Cart`.

```
<CENTER>
Item:
<INPUT TYPE="TEXT" NAME="Item" VALUE="256MB SIMM"><BR>
<INPUT TYPE="SUBMIT" NAME="Add"
       VALUE="Add Item to Cart">
<INPUT TYPE="SUBMIT" NAME="Delete"
       VALUE="Delete Item from Cart">
</CENTER>
```

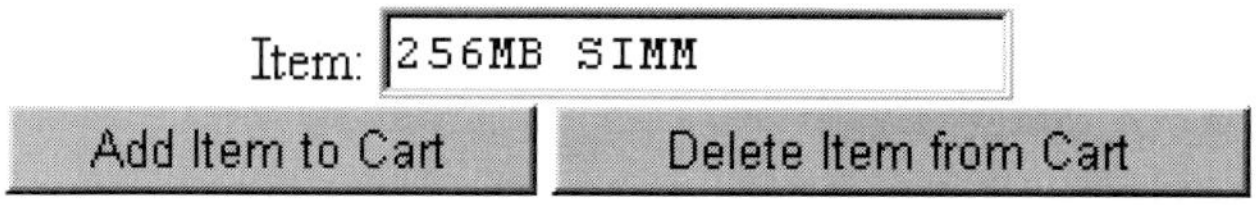

Item: 256MB SIMM

Add Item to Cart   Delete Item from Cart

Figure 18–12 Submit buttons with user-defined labels.

DISABLED

This attribute lets you completely disable a button. A disabled button cannot receive the input focus, be tabbed to, or be part of a form submission. The status of this attribute can be changed dynamically through the use of JavaScript. Although officially part of HTML 4.0, DISABLED is not supported by Netscape 4.x.

ONCLICK, ONDBLCLICK, ONFOCUS, and ONBLUR

These nonstandard attributes are used by JavaScript-capable browsers to associate JavaScript code with the button. The ONCLICK and ONDBLCLICK code is executed when the button is pressed, the ONFOCUS code when the button gets the input focus, and the ONBLUR code when the button loses the focus. If the code attached to a button returns false, the submission of the form is suppressed. HTML attributes are not case sensitive, and these attributes are traditionally called onClick, onDblClick, onFocus, and onBlur by JavaScript programmers.

HTML Element: `<BUTTON TYPE="SUBMIT" ...>`
`HTML Markup`
`</BUTTON>`
Attributes: NAME, VALUE, DISABLED, ONCLICK, ONDBLCLICK, ONFOCUS, ONBLUR

This alternative way of creating submit buttons, supported only by Internet Explorer, lets you use arbitrary HTML markup for the content of the button. This element lets you have multiline button labels, button labels with font changes, image buttons, and so forth. Listing 18.4 gives a few examples, with results shown in Figure 18–13.

NAME, VALUE, DISABLED, ONCLICK, ONDBLCLICK, ONFOCUS, and ONBLUR

These attributes are used in the same way as with
`<INPUT TYPE="SUBMIT" ...>`.

Listing 18.4 `ButtonElement.html`

```
<!DOCTYPE HTML PUBLIC "-//W3C//DTD HTML 4.0 Transitional//EN">
<HTML>
<HEAD>
  <TITLE>The BUTTON Element</TITLE>
</HEAD>
<BODY BGCOLOR="WHITE">
<H2 ALIGN="CENTER">The BUTTON Element</H2>

<FORM ACTION="http://localhost:8088/SomeProgram">
<CENTER>
<BUTTON TYPE="SUBMIT">Single-line Label</BUTTON>
  
<BUTTON TYPE="SUBMIT">Multi-line<BR>label</BUTTON>
<P>
<BUTTON TYPE="SUBMIT">
<B>Label</B> with <I>font</I> changes.
</BUTTON>
<P>
<BUTTON TYPE="SUBMIT">
<IMG SRC="images/Java-Logo.gif" WIDTH=110 HEIGHT=101
     ALIGN="LEFT" ALT="Java Cup Logo">
Label<BR>with image
</BUTTON>
</CENTER>
</FORM>

</BODY>
</HTML>
```

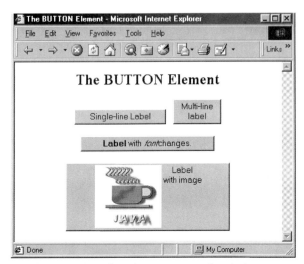

Figure 18-13 Submit buttons created with the BUTTON element.

Reset Buttons

HTML Element: <INPUT TYPE="RESET" ...> (No End Tag)

Attributes: VALUE, NAME, DISABLED, ONCLICK, ONDBLCLICK, ONFOCUS, ONBLUR

Reset buttons serve to reset the values of all items in the FORM to those specified in the original VALUE parameters. Their value is never transmitted as part of the form's contents.

VALUE

The VALUE attribute specifies the button label; "Reset" is the default.

NAME

Because reset buttons do not contribute to the data string transmitted when the form is submitted, they are not named in standard HTML. However, Java-Script permits a NAME attribute to be used to simplify reference to the element.

DISABLED

This attribute lets you completely disable a button. A disabled button cannot receive the input focus, be tabbed to, or be part of a form submission. The status of this attribute can be changed dynamically with JavaScript. Although officially part of HTML 4.0, DISABLED is not supported by Netscape 4.x.

ONCLICK, ONDBLCLICK, ONFOCUS, and ONBLUR

These nonstandard attributes are used by JavaScript-capable browsers to associate JavaScript code with the button. The `ONCLICK` and `ONDBLCLICK` code is executed when the button is pressed, the `ONFOCUS` code when the button gets the input focus, and the `ONBLUR` code when it loses the focus. HTML attributes are not case sensitive, and these attributes are traditionally called `onClick`, `onDblClick`, `onFocus`, and `onBlur` by JavaScript programmers.

HTML Element: `<BUTTON TYPE="RESET" ...>`
　　　　　　　　　　`HTML Markup`
　　　　　　　　　　`</BUTTON>`

Attributes:　`VALUE, NAME, DISABLED, ONCLICK, ONDBLCLICK, ONFOCUS, ONBLUR`

This alternative way of creating reset buttons, supported only by Internet Explorer, lets you use arbitrary HTML markup for the content of the button. All attributes are used identically to those in `<INPUT TYPE="RESET" ...>`.

JavaScript Buttons

HTML Element: `<INPUT TYPE="BUTTON" ...>` **(No End Tag)**

Attributes:　`NAME, VALUE, DISABLED, ONCLICK, ONDBLCLICK, ONFOCUS, ONBLUR`

The `BUTTON` element is recognized only by browsers that support JavaScript. It creates a button with the same visual appearance as a `SUBMIT` or `RESET` button and allows the author to attach JavaScript code to the `ONCLICK`, `ONDBLCLICK`, `ONFOCUS`, or `ONBLUR` attributes. The name/value pair associated with a JavaScript button is not transmitted as part of the data when the form is submitted. Arbitrary code can be associated with the button, but one of the most common uses is to verify that all input elements are in the proper format before the form is submitted to the server. For instance, the following would create a button where the user-defined `validateForm` function would be called whenever the button is activated.

```
<INPUT TYPE="BUTTON" VALUE="Check Values"
       onClick="validateForm()">
```

HTML Element: `<BUTTON TYPE="BUTTON"  ...>`
                 `HTML Markup`
                 `</BUTTON>`

Attributes: NAME, VALUE, DISABLED, ONCLICK, ONDBLCLICK,
                 ONFOCUS, ONBLUR

This alternative way of creating JavaScript buttons, supported only by Internet Explorer, lets you use arbitrary HTML markup for the content of the button. All attributes are used identically to those in `<INPUT TYPE="BUTTON"  ...>`.

18.5 Check Boxes and Radio Buttons

Check boxes and radio buttons are useful controls for allowing the user to select among a set of predefined choices. While each individual check box can be selected or deselected individually, radio buttons can be grouped so that only a single member of the group can be selected at a time.

Check Boxes

HTML Element: `<INPUT TYPE="CHECKBOX" NAME="..."  ...>`
                 (No End Tag)

Attributes: NAME (required), VALUE, CHECKED, DISABLED, READONLY,
                 ONCLICK, ONFOCUS, ONBLUR

This input element creates a check box whose name/value pair is transmitted *only* if the check box is checked when the form is submitted. For instance, the following code results in the check box shown in Figure 18–14.

```
<P>
<INPUT TYPE="CHECKBOX" NAME="noEmail" CHECKED>
Check here if you do <I>not</I> want to
get our email newsletter
```

☑ Check here if you do *not* want to get our email newsletter

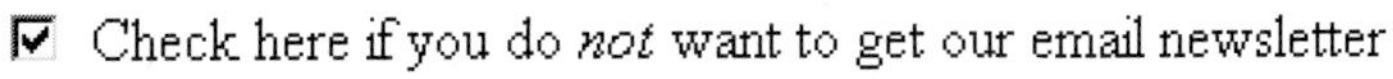

Figure 18–14 An HTML check box.

Note that the descriptive text associated with the check box is normal HTML; developers should take care to guarantee that it appears next to the check box. Thus, the `<P>` in the preceding example ensures that the check box isn't part of the previous paragraph.

Core Approach

Paragraphs inside a FORM are filled and wrapped just like regular paragraphs. So, be sure to insert explicit HTML markup to keep input elements with the text that describes them.

NAME

This attribute supplies the name that is sent to the server. It is required for standard HTML check boxes but optional when used with JavaScript.

VALUE

The VALUE attribute is optional and defaults to on. Recall that the name and value are only sent to the server if the check box is checked when the form is submitted. For instance, in the preceding example, noEmail=on would be added to the data string since the box is checked, but nothing would be added if the box was unchecked. As a result, servlets or CGI programs often check only for the existence of the check box name, ignoring its value.

CHECKED

If the CHECKED attribute is supplied, then the check box is initially checked when the associated Web page is loaded. Otherwise, it is initially unchecked.

DISABLED, READONLY

These attributes let you completely disable a check box or make it read-only. Although officially part of HTML 4.0, these attributes are not supported by Netscape 4.x.

ONCLICK, ONFOCUS, and ONBLUR

These attributes supply JavaScript code to be executed when the button is clicked, receives the input focus, and loses the focus, respectively.

Radio Buttons

HTML Element: `<INPUT TYPE="RADIO" NAME="..."`
`VALUE="..." ...>` **(No End Tag)**
Attributes: NAME (required), VALUE (required), CHECKED, DISABLED, READONLY, ONCLICK, ONFOCUS, ONBLUR

Radio buttons differ from check boxes in that only a single radio button in a given group can be selected at any one time. You indicate a group of radio buttons by providing all of them with the same NAME. Only one button in a group can be depressed at a time; selecting a new button when one is already selected results in the previous choice becoming deselected. The value of the one selected is sent when the form is submitted. Although radio buttons technically need not appear near each other, this proximity is almost always recommended.

An example of a radio button group follows. Because input elements are wrapped as part of normal paragraphs, a DL list is used to make sure that the buttons appear under each other in the resultant page and are indented from the heading above them. Figure 18–15 shows the result. In this case, creditCard=java would get sent as part of the form data when the form is submitted.

```
<DL>
  <DT>Credit Card:
  <DD><INPUT TYPE="RADIO" NAME="creditCard" VALUE="visa">
      Visa
  <DD><INPUT TYPE="RADIO" NAME="creditCard" VALUE="mastercard">
      Master Card
  <DD><INPUT TYPE="RADIO" NAME="creditCard"
            VALUE="java" CHECKED>
      Java Smart Card
  <DD><INPUT TYPE="RADIO" NAME="creditCard" VALUE="amex">
      American Express
  <DD><INPUT TYPE="RADIO" NAME="creditCard" VALUE="discover">
      Discover
</DL>
```

Credit Card:

- ○ Visa
- ○ Master Card
- ◉ Java Smart Card
- ○ American Express
- ○ Discover

Figure 18–15 Radio buttons in HTML.

NAME

Unlike the NAME attribute of most input elements, this NAME is shared by multiple elements. All radio buttons associated with the same name are grouped logically so that no more than one can be selected at any given time. Note that attribute values are case sensitive, so the following would result in two radio buttons that are *not* logically connected.

```
<INPUT TYPE="RADIO" NAME="Foo" VALUE="Value1">
<INPUT TYPE="RADIO" NAME="FOO" VALUE="Value2">
```

Core Warning

Be sure the NAME of each radio button in a logical group matches exactly.

VALUE

The VALUE attribute supplies the value that gets transmitted with the NAME when the form is submitted. It doesn't affect the appearance of the radio button. Instead, normal text and HTML markup are placed around the radio button, just as with check boxes.

CHECKED

If the CHECKED attribute is supplied, then the radio button is initially checked when the associated Web page is loaded. Otherwise, it is initially unchecked.

DISABLED, READONLY

These attributes let you completely disable a radio button or make it read-only. Although these attributes are officially part of HTML 4.0, they are not supported by Netscape 4.x.

ONCLICK, ONFOCUS, and ONBLUR

These attributes supply JavaScript code to be executed when the button is clicked, receives the input focus, and loses the focus, respectively.

18.6 Combo Boxes and List Boxes

A SELECT element presents a set of options to the user. If only a single entry can be selected and no visible size has been specified, the options are presented in a combo box (drop-down menu); list boxes are used when multiple selections are permitted or a specific visible size has been specified. The choices themselves are specified by OPTION entries embedded in the SELECT element. The typical format is as follows:

```
<SELECT NAME="Name" ...>
  <OPTION VALUE="Value1">Choice 1 Text
  <OPTION VALUE="Value2">Choice 2 Text
  ...
  <OPTION VALUE="ValueN">Choice N Text
</SELECT>
```

The HTML 4.0 specification suggests the use of OPTGROUP (with a single attribute of LABEL) to enclose OPTION elements to create cascading menus, but neither Netscape nor Internet Explorer supports this element.

HTML Element: `<SELECT NAME="..." ...> ... </SELECT>`
Attributes: NAME (required), SIZE, MULTIPLE, DISABLED, ONCLICK, ONFOCUS, ONBLUR, ONCHANGE

SELECT creates a combo box or list box for selecting among choices. You specify each choice with an OPTION element enclosed between `<SELECT ...>` and `</SELECT>`.

NAME
NAME identifies the form to the servlet or CGI program.

SIZE
SIZE gives the number of visible rows. If SIZE is used, the SELECT menu is usually represented as a list box instead of a combo box. A combo box is the normal representation when neither SIZE nor MULTIPLE is supplied.

MULTIPLE
The MULTIPLE attribute specifies that multiple entries can be selected simultaneously. If MULTIPLE is omitted, only a single selection is permitted.

DISABLED
This attribute let you completely disable a combo box. Although officially part of HTML 4.0, it is not supported by Netscape 4.x.

ONCLICK, ONFOCUS, ONBLUR, and ONCHANGE
These nonstandard attributes are supported by browsers that understand JavaScript. They indicate code to be executed when the entry is clicked on, gains the input focus, loses the input focus, and loses the focus after having been changed, respectively.

HTML Element: `<OPTION ...>` (End Tag Optional)
Attributes: SELECTED, VALUE, DISABLED

Only valid inside a SELECT element, this element specifies the menu choices.

SELECTED
If present, SELECTED specifies that the particular menu item shown is selected when the page is first loaded.

VALUE
VALUE gives the value to be transmitted with the NAME of the SELECT menu if the current option is selected. This is *not* the text that is displayed to the user; that text is specified separately, listed after the OPTION tag.

DISABLED

This attribute lets you completely disable an entry in a combo box. Although officially part of HTML 4.0, it is not supported by Netscape 4.x.

The following example creates a menu of programming language choices. Because only a single selection is allowed and no visible SIZE is specified, the menu is displayed as a combo box. Figures 18–16 and 18–17 show the initial appearance and the appearance after the user activates the menu by clicking on it. If the entry Java is active when the form is submitted, then language=java is sent to the server-side program. Notice that it is the VALUE attribute, not the descriptive text, that is transmitted.

```
Favorite language:
<SELECT NAME="language">
    <OPTION VALUE="c">C
    <OPTION VALUE="c++">C++
    <OPTION VALUE="java" SELECTED>Java
    <OPTION VALUE="lisp">Lisp
    <OPTION VALUE="perl">Perl
    <OPTION VALUE="smalltalk">Smalltalk
</SELECT>
```

Favorite language: | Java ▼ |

Figure 18–16 A SELECT element displayed as a combo box (drop-down menu).

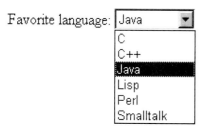

Figure 18–17 Choosing options from a SELECT menu.

The second example shows a SELECT element rendered as a list box. If more than one entry is active when the form is submitted, then more than one value is sent, listed as separate entries (repeating the NAME). For instance, in the example shown in Figure 18–18, language=java&language=perl is added to the data being sent to the server. Multiple entries that share the same name is the reason servlet authors need be familiar with the `getParameterValues` method of `HttpServlet-Request` in addition to the more common `getParameter` method. See Section 19.6 (The Client Request: Form Data) for details.

```
Languages you know:<BR>
<SELECT NAME="language" MULTIPLE>
  <OPTION VALUE="c">C
  <OPTION VALUE="c++">C++
  <OPTION VALUE="java" SELECTED>Java
  <OPTION VALUE="lisp">Lisp
  <OPTION VALUE="perl" SELECTED>Perl
  <OPTION VALUE="smalltalk">Smalltalk
</SELECT>
```

Figure 18–18 A `SELECT` element that specifies `MULTIPLE` or `SIZE` results in a list box.

18.7 File Upload Controls

HTML Element: `<INPUT TYPE="FILE" ...>` **(No End Tag)**

Attributes: NAME (required), VALUE (ignored), SIZE, MAXLENGTH, ACCEPT, DISABLED, READONLY, ONCHANGE, ONSELECT, ONFOCUS, ONBLUR (nonstandard)

This element results in a filename textfield next to a Browse button. Users can enter a path directly in the textfield or click on the button to open a file selection dialog that lets them interactively choose the path to a file. When the form is submitted, the *contents* of the file are transmitted as long as an ENCTYPE of multipart/form-data was specified in the initial FORM declaration. This element provides a convenient way to make user-support pages, where the user sends a description of the problem along with any associated data or configuration files.

Core Tip

Always specify `ENCTYPE="multipart/form-data"` *in forms with file upload controls.*

NAME

The `NAME` attribute identifies the textfield when the form is submitted.

VALUE

For security reasons, this attribute is ignored. Only the end user can specify a filename.

SIZE and MAXLENGTH

The `SIZE` and `MAXLENGTH` attributes are used the same way as in textfields, specifying the number of visible and maximum allowable characters, respectively.

ACCEPT

The `ACCEPT` attribute is a comma-separated list of **MIME** types intended to restrict the available filenames. However, very few browsers support this attribute.

DISABLED, READONLY

These attributes let you completely disable an upload control or make it read-only. Although officially part of HTML 4.0, these attributes are not supported by Netscape 4.x.

ONCHANGE, ONSELECT, ONFOCUS, and ONBLUR

These attributes are used by browsers that support JavaScript to specify the action to take when the mouse leaves the textfield after a change has occurred, when the user selects text in the textfield, when the textfield gets the input focus, and when it loses the input focus, respectively.

For example, the following code creates a file upload control. Figure 18–19 shows the initial result, and Figure 18–20 shows a typical pop-up window that results when the Browse button is activated.

```
<FORM ACTION="http://localhost:8088/SomeProgram"
      ENCTYPE="multipart/form-data">
Enter data file below:<BR>
<INPUT TYPE="FILE" NAME="fileName">
</FORM>
```

Enter data file below:

Figure 18-19 Initial look of a file upload control.

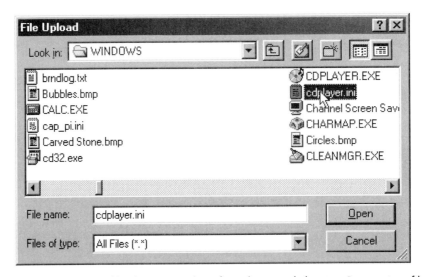

Figure 18-20 A file chooser resulting from the user clicking on Browse in a file upload control.

18.8 Server-Side Image Maps

In HTML, an element called MAP lets you associate URLs with various regions of an image; then, when the image is clicked in one of the designated regions, the browser loads the appropriate URL. This form of mapping is known as a *client-side image map*, since the determination of which URL to contact is made on the client and no server-side program is involved. HTML also supports *server-side image maps* that can be used within HTML forms. With such maps, an image is drawn, and when the user clicks on it, the coordinates of the click are sent to a server-side program.

Client-side image maps are simpler and more efficient than server-side ones; use them when all you want to do is associate a fixed set of URLs with some predefined image regions. However, server-side image maps are appropriate if the URL needs to be computed (e.g., for weather maps), the regions change frequently, or other form data needs to be included with the request. This section discusses two approaches to server-side image maps.

IMAGE—Standard Server-Side Image Maps

The usual way to create server-side image maps is by means of an `<INPUT TYPE="IMAGE" ...>` element inside a form.

HTML Element: `<INPUT TYPE="IMAGE" ...>` (No End Tag)
Attributes: `NAME` (required), `SRC`, `ALIGN`, `DISABLED`

This element displays an image that, when clicked, sends the form to the servlet or other server-side program specified by the enclosing form's `ACTION`. The name itself is not sent; instead, *name*`.x=`*xpos* and *name*`.y=`*ypos* are transmitted, where *xpos* and *ypos* are the coordinates of the mouse click relative to the upper-left corner of the image.

NAME
The `NAME` attribute identifies the textfield when the form is submitted.

SRC
`SRC` designates the URL of the associated image.

ALIGN
The `ALIGN` attribute has the same options (`TOP`, `MIDDLE`, `BOTTOM`, `LEFT`, `RIGHT`) and default (`BOTTOM`) as the `ALIGN` attribute of the `IMG` element and is used in the same way.

DISABLED
This attribute lets you completely disable an image map. Although the attribute is officially part of HTML 4.0, it is not supported by Netscape 4.x.

Listing 18.5 shows a simple example which the form's `ACTION` specifies the `EchoServer` developed in Section 17.8 (Example: A Simple HTTP Server). Figures 18–21 and 18–22 show the results before and after the image is clicked.

Listing 18.5 `ImageMap.html`

```
<!DOCTYPE HTML PUBLIC "-//W3C//DTD HTML 4.0 Transitional//EN">
<HTML>
<HEAD>
  <TITLE>The IMAGE Input Control</TITLE>
</HEAD>

<BODY>
<H1 ALIGN="CENTER">The IMAGE Input Control</H1>
Which island is Java? Click and see if you are correct.

<FORM ACTION="http://localhost:8088/GeographyTester">
  <INPUT TYPE="IMAGE" NAME="map" SRC="images/indonesia.gif">
</FORM>

Of course, image maps can be implemented <B>in</B>
Java as well. :-)

</BODY>
</HTML>
```

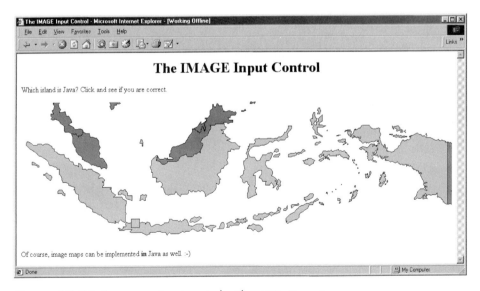

Figure 18–21 An `IMAGE` input control with `NAME="map"`.

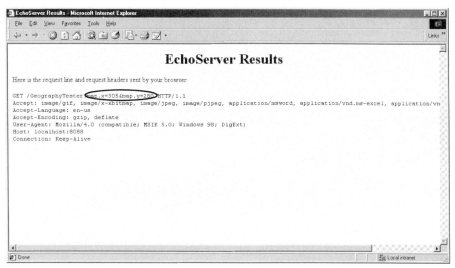

Figure 18–22 Clicking on the image at (305, 280) submits the form and adds `map.x=305&map.y=280` to the form data.

ISMAP—Alternative Server-Side Image Maps

ISMAP is an optional attribute of the IMG element and can be used similarly to the `<INPUT TYPE="IMAGE" ...>` FORM entry. ISMAP is not actually a FORM element at all but can still be used for simple connections to servlets or CGI programs. If an image with ISMAP is inside a hypertext link, then clicking on the image results in the coordinates of the click being sent to the specified URL. Coordinates are separated by commas and are specified in pixels relative to the top-left corner of the image.

For instance, Listing 18.6 embeds an image that uses the ISMAP attribute inside a hypertext link to `http://localhost:8088/ChipTester`, which is answered by the mini HTTP server developed in Section 17.8. Figure 18–23 shows the initial result, which is identical to what would have been shown had the ISMAP attribute been omitted. However, when the mouse button is pressed 271 pixels to the right and 184 pixels below the top-left corner of the image, the browser requests the URL `http://localhost:8088/ChipTester?271,184` (as shown in Figure 18–24).

If a server-side image map is used simply to select among a static set of destination URLs, then a client-side MAP element is a much better option because the server doesn't have to be contacted just to decide which URL applies. If the image map is intended to be mixed with other input elements, then the IMAGE input type is preferred instead. However, for a stand-alone image map where the URL associated with a region changes frequently or requires calculation, an image with ISMAP is a reasonable choice.

Listing 18.6 `IsMap.html`

```html
<!DOCTYPE HTML PUBLIC "-//W3C//DTD HTML 4.0 Transitional//EN">
<HTML>
<HEAD>
  <TITLE>The ISMAP Attribute</TITLE>
</HEAD>

<BODY>

<H1 ALIGN="CENTER">The ISMAP Attribute</H1>
<H2>Select a pin:</H2>
<A HREF="http://localhost:8088/ChipTester">
<IMG SRC="images/chip.gif" WIDTH=495 HEIGHT=200 ALT="Chip"
     BORDER=0 ISMAP></A>

</BODY>
</HTML>
```

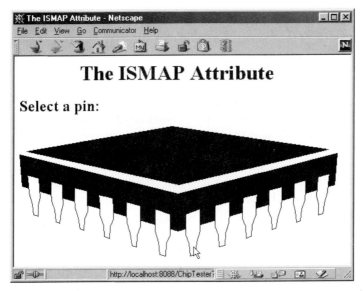

Figure 18–23 Setting the `ISMAP` attribute of an `IMG` element inside a hypertext link changes what happens when the image is selected.

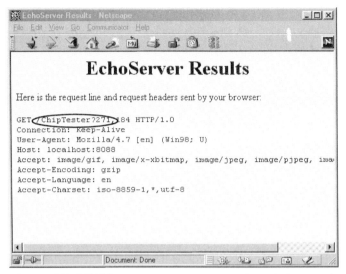

Figure 18–24 When an ISMAP image is selected, the coordinates of the selection are transmitted with the URL.

18.9 Hidden Fields

Hidden fields do not affect the appearance of the page that is presented to the user. Instead, they store fixed names and values that are sent unchanged to the server, regardless of user input. Hidden fields are typically used for three purposes.

First, they are one method of tracking users as they move around within a site. Servlet authors typically rely on the servlet session tracking API (Section 19.12) rather than attempting to implement session tracking at this low level.

Second, hidden fields provide predefined input to a server-side program when a variety of static HTML pages act as front ends to the same program on the server. For example, an on-line store might pay commissions to people who refer customers to their site. In this scenario, the referring page could let visitors search the store's catalog by means of a form but would embed a hidden field listing its referral ID.

Third, hidden fields store contextual information in pages that are dynamically generated. For example, an on-line store might use hidden fields to store the current user's customer ID or the current discount rate.

HTML Element: `<INPUT TYPE="HIDDEN" NAME="..."` `VALUE="...">` (No End Tag)

Attributes: `NAME` (required), `VALUE`

This element stores a name and a value, but no graphical element is created in the browser. The name/value pair is added to the form data when the form is submitted. For instance, with the following example, `itemID=hall001` will always be sent with the form data.

```
<INPUT TYPE="HIDDEN" NAME="itemID" VALUE="hall001">
```

Note that the term "hidden" does not mean that the field cannot be discovered by the user, since it is clearly visible in the HTML source. Because there is no reliable way to "hide" the HTML that generates a page, authors are cautioned not to use hidden fields to embed passwords or other sensitive information.

18.10 Grouping Controls

HTML 4.0 defines the `FIELDSET` element, with an associated `LEGEND`, that visually groups controls within a form. This capability is quite useful but is supported only by Internet Explorer. It is likely that Netscape version 6 will add support for this element. In the meantime, you should reserve use of this element to intranet applications where all your users are using Internet Explorer.

Core Warning

As of version 4.7, Netscape does not support the `FIELDSET` element.

HTML Element: `<FIELDSET>` ... `</FIELDSET>`

Attributes: None

This element is used as a container to enclose controls and, optionally, a `LEGEND` element. It has no attributes beyond the universal ones for style sheets, language, and so forth. Listing 18.7 gives an example, with the result shown in Figure 18–25.

Listing 18.7 `Fieldset.html`

```html
<!DOCTYPE HTML PUBLIC "-//W3C//DTD HTML 4.0 Transitional//EN">
<HTML>
<HEAD>
  <TITLE>Grouping Controls in Internet Explorer</TITLE>
</HEAD>

<BODY BGCOLOR="#FDF5E6">
<H2 ALIGN="CENTER">Grouping Controls in Internet Explorer</H2>

<FORM ACTION="http://localhost:8088/SomeProgram">

<FIELDSET>
<LEGEND>Group One</LEGEND>
Field 1A: <INPUT TYPE="TEXT" NAME="field1A" VALUE="Field A"><BR>
Field 1B: <INPUT TYPE="TEXT" NAME="field1B" VALUE="Field B"><BR>
Field 1C: <INPUT TYPE="TEXT" NAME="field1C" VALUE="Field C"><BR>
</FIELDSET>

<FIELDSET>
<LEGEND ALIGN="RIGHT">Group Two</LEGEND>
Field 2A: <INPUT TYPE="TEXT" NAME="field2A" VALUE="Field A"><BR>
Field 2B: <INPUT TYPE="TEXT" NAME="field2B" VALUE="Field B"><BR>
Field 2C: <INPUT TYPE="TEXT" NAME="field2C" VALUE="Field C"><BR>
</FIELDSET>

</FORM>

</BODY>
</HTML>
```

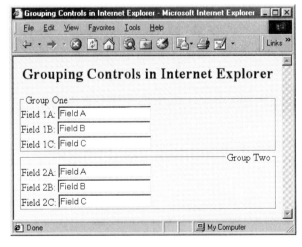

Figure 18–25 The
`FIELDSET` element lets you
visually group related controls.

HTML Element: `<LEGEND> ... </LEGEND>`
Attributes: `ALIGN`

This element, legal only within an enclosing `FIELDSET`, places a label on the etched border that is drawn around the group of controls.

ALIGN

This attribute controls the position of the label. Legal values are `TOP` (the default), `BOTTOM`, `LEFT`, and `RIGHT`. In Figure 18–25, the first group has the default legend alignment, and the second group stipulates `ALIGN="RIGHT"`. In HTML, style sheets are often a better way to control element alignment, since they permit a single change to be propagated to multiple places.

18.11 Tab Order Control

HTML 4.0 defines a `TABINDEX` attribute that can be used in any of the visual HTML elements. Its value is an integer, and it controls the order in which elements receive the input focus when the TAB key is pressed. Unfortunately, however, it is supported only by Internet Explorer. Nevertheless, you can use `TABINDEX` even for pages that will be viewed by multiple browsers, as long as the designated tabbing order is a convenience to the user, not a necessity for proper operation of the page. Listing 18.8 gives an example, with the results shown in Figure 18–26.

Core Warning

As of version 4.7, Netscape does not support the `TABINDEX` attribute.

Listing 18.8 `Tabindex.html`

```
<!DOCTYPE HTML PUBLIC "-//W3C//DTD HTML 4.0 Transitional//EN">
<HTML>
<HEAD>
  <TITLE>Controlling TAB Order</TITLE>
</HEAD>

<BODY BGCOLOR="#FDF5E6">
<H2 ALIGN="CENTER">Controlling TAB Order</H2>
```

(continued)

Listing 18.8 `Tabindex.html` *(continued)*

```
<FORM ACTION="http://localhost:8088/SomeProgram">
Field 1 (first tab selection):
<INPUT TYPE="TEXT" NAME="field1" TABINDEX=1><BR>
Field 2 (third tab selection):
<INPUT TYPE="TEXT" NAME="field2" TABINDEX=3><BR>
Field 3 (second tab selection):
<INPUT TYPE="TEXT" NAME="field3" TABINDEX=2><BR>
</FORM>

</BODY>
</HTML>
```

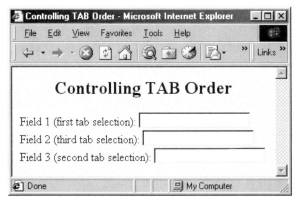

Figure 18–26 In Internet Explorer, repeatedly pressing the TAB key cycles the input focus among the first, third, and second textfields, in that order (as dictated by TABINDEX). In Netscape, the input focus would cycle among the first, second, and third fields, in that order (based on the order in which the elements appear on the page).

18.12 Summary

HTML forms generally consist of two main parts: a FORM element that designates the URL that processes the data and INPUT elements that gather the data. The INPUT elements have a NAME specified in HTML and a value either specified in HTML or supplied by the end user. The name/value pairs are sent to the server either attached to the end of the main URL (with GET requests) or on a separate line (with POST requests).

Gathering data is all well and good. But *processing* data is the really interesting part. That's the subject of the next two chapters.

SERVER-SIDE JAVA: SERVLETS

Topics in This Chapter

- The advantages of servlets over competing technologies
- Free servlet and JSP engines
- The basic servlet structure and life cycle
- Servlet initialization parameters
- Access to form data
- HTTP 1.1 request headers, response headers, and status codes
- The servlet equivalent of the standard CGI variables
- Compression of pages generated by servlets
- Cookies in servlets
- Session tracking

Chapter 19

Servlets are Java technology's answer to Common Gateway Interface (CGI) programming. They are programs that run on a Web server, acting as a middle layer between a request coming from a Web browser or other HTTP client and databases or applications on the HTTP server. Their job is to:

1. **Read any data sent by the user.**
   This data is usually entered in a form on a Web page but could also come from an applet or a custom HTTP client program.
2. **Look up any other information about the request that is embedded in the HTTP request.**
   This information includes details about browser capabilities, cookies, the host name of the requesting client, and so forth.
3. **Generate the results.**
   This process may require talking to a database, executing an RMI or CORBA call, invoking a legacy application, or computing the response directly.
4. **Format the results inside a document.**
   In most cases, this involves embedding the information inside an HTML document.
5. **Set the appropriate HTTP response parameters.**
   This means telling the browser what type of document is being returned (e.g., HTML), setting cookies and caching parameters, and other such tasks.

6. **Send the document back to the client.**
   This document can be sent in text format (HTML), binary format (GIF images), or even in a compressed format like gzip that is layered on top of some other underlying format.

Many client requests can be satisfied by prebuilt documents, and the server would handle these requests without invoking servlets. In many cases, however, a static result is not sufficient, and a page needs to be generated for each request. There are a number of reasons why Web pages need to be built on-the-fly like this:

- **The Web page is based on data submitted by the user.**
  For instance, the results page from search engines and order-confirmation pages at on-line stores are specific to particular user requests.
- **The Web page is derived from data that changes frequently.**
  For example, a weather report or news headlines site might build the pages dynamically, perhaps returning a previously built page if it is still up to date.
- **The Web page uses information from corporate databases or other server-side sources.**
  For example, an e-commerce site could use a servlet to build a Web page that lists the current price and availability of each sale item.

In principle, servlets are not restricted to Web or application servers that handle HTTP requests but can be used for other types of servers as well. For example, servlets could be embedded in FTP or mail servers to extend their functionality. In practice, however, this use of servlets has not caught on, and we'll only be discussing HTTP servlets.

19.1 The Advantages of Servlets Over "Traditional" CGI

Java servlets are more efficient, easier to use, more powerful, more portable, safer, and cheaper than traditional CGI and many alternative CGI-like technologies.

Efficient

With traditional CGI, a new process is started for each HTTP request. If the CGI program itself is relatively short, the overhead of starting the process can dominate the execution time. With servlets, the Java Virtual Machine stays running and handles each request with a lightweight Java thread, not a heavyweight operating system process. Similarly, in traditional CGI, if there are N simultaneous requests to the same CGI program, the code for the CGI program is loaded into memory N times. With servlets, however, there would be N threads but only a single copy of the servlet class. Finally, when a CGI program finishes handling a request, the program terminates. This approach makes it difficult to cache computations, keep database connections open, and perform other optimizations that rely on persistent data. Servlets, however, remain in memory even after they complete a response, so it is straightforward to store arbitrarily complex data between client requests.

Convenient

Servlets have an extensive infrastructure for automatically parsing and decoding HTML form data, reading and setting HTTP headers, handling cookies, tracking sessions, and many other such high-level utilities. Besides, you already know the Java programming language. Why learn Perl too? You're already convinced that Java technology makes for more reliable and reusable code than does C++. Why go back to C++ for server-side programming?

Powerful

Servlets support several capabilities that are difficult or impossible to accomplish with regular CGI. Servlets can talk directly to the Web server, whereas regular CGI programs cannot, at least not without using a server-specific API. Communicating with the Web server makes it easier to translate relative URLs into concrete path names, for instance. Multiple servlets can also share data, making it easy to implement database connection pooling and similar resource-sharing optimizations. Servlets can also maintain information from request to request, simplifying techniques like session tracking and caching of previous computations.

Portable

Servlets are written in the Java programming language and follow a standard API. Consequently, servlets written for, say, iPlanet Enterprise Server can run virtually unchanged on Apache, Microsoft Internet Information Server (IIS), IBM WebSphere, or StarNine WebStar. In fact, servlets are supported directly or by a plug-in on virtually *every* major Web server. They are now part of the Java 2 Platform, Enterprise Edition (J2EE; see `http://java.sun.com/j2ee/`), so industry support for servlets is becoming even more pervasive.

Secure

One of the main sources of vulnerabilities in traditional CGI programs stems from the fact that they are often executed by general-purpose operating system shells. So, the CGI programmer must be careful to filter out characters such as backquotes and semicolons that are treated specially by the shell. Implementing this precaution is harder than one might think, and weaknesses stemming from this problem are constantly being uncovered in widely used CGI libraries.

A second source of problems is the fact that some CGI programs are processed by languages that do not automatically check array or string bounds. For example, in C and C++ it is perfectly legal to allocate a 100-element array then write into the 999th "element," which is really some random part of program memory. So, programmers who forget to perform this check open up their system to deliberate or accidental buffer overflow attacks. Servlets suffer from neither of these problems. Even if a servlet executes a remote system call to invoke a program on the local operating system, it does not use a shell to do so. And, of course, array bounds checking and other memory protection features are a central part of the Java programming language.

Inexpensive

A number of free or very inexpensive Web servers are available that are good for personal use or low-volume Web sites. However, with the major exception of Apache, which is free, most commercial-quality Web servers are relatively expensive. Nevertheless, once you have a Web server, no matter its cost, adding servlet support to it (if it doesn't come preconfigured to support servlets) costs very little extra. This is in contrast to many of the other CGI alternatives, which require a significant initial investment to purchase a proprietary package.

19.2 Server Installation and Setup

Before you can get started, you have to download the servlet software you need and configure your system to take advantage of it. Here's an outline of the steps involved. Please note, however, that although your servlet code will follow a standard API, there is no standard for downloading and configuring Web or application servers. Thus, unlike most sections of this book, the methods described here vary significantly from server to server, and the examples in this section should be taken only as representative samples. Check your server's documentation for authoritative instructions.

Obtain Servlet and JSP Software

Your first step is to download software that implements the Java Servlet 2.1 or 2.2 and JavaServer Pages 1.0 or 1.1 specifications. If you are using an up-to-date Web or application server, there is a good chance that it already has everything you need. Check your server documentation or see the latest list of servers that support servlets at `http://java.sun.com/products/servlet/industry.html`. Although you'll eventually want to deploy in a commercial-quality server, it is useful to have a free system that you can install on your desktop machine for development and testing. Here are some of the most popular options:

- **Apache Tomcat.**
  Tomcat is the official reference implementation of the servlet 2.2 and JSP 1.1 specifications. It can be used as a small stand-alone server for testing servlets and JSP pages or can be integrated into the Apache Web server. It runs on almost any operating system that supports the Java 2 platform. For details, see `http://jakarta.apache.org/tomcat/`.
- **Allaire JRun.**
  JRun is a servlet 2.2 and JSP 1.1 engine that can be plugged into Netscape Enterprise or FastTrack servers, IIS, Microsoft Personal Web Server, Apache, O'Reilly's WebSite, or StarNine WebStar. It is free for desktop development, but not for deployment. For details, see `http://www.allaire.com/products/jrun/`.
- **Unify eWave ServletExec.**
  ServletExec is a servlet 2.2 and JSP 1.1 engine that can be plugged into most popular Web servers for Solaris, Windows, MacOS, HP-UX, and Linux. You can download and use it for free, but some of the advanced features and administration utilities are disabled until you purchase a license. For details, see `http://www.servletexec.com/`.
- **LiteWebServer (LWS) from Gefion Software.**
  LWS is a small free Web server derived from Tomcat. It supports servlets version 2.2 and JSP 1.1. Gefion also has a free plug-in called WAICoolRunner that adds servlet 2.2 and JSP 1.1 support to Netscape FastTrack and Enterprise servers. For details, see `http://www.gefionsoftware.com/`.
- **Caucho's Resin.**
  Resin is a fast servlet 2.2 and JSP 1.1 engine that also supports load balancing. It is free for development and non-commercial deployment purposes. For details, see `http://www.caucho.com/products/resin/`.
- **JavaServer Web Development Kit (JSWDK).**
  The JSWDK is the official reference implementation of the servlet 2.1 and JSP 1.0 specifications. It is used as a small stand-alone server for

testing servlets and JSP pages before they are deployed to a full
Web server that supports these technologies. For details, see
`http://java.sun.com/products/servlet/download.html`.

Bookmark or Install the Servlet and JSP API Documentation

Just as no serious programmer should develop general-purpose Java applications
without access to the JDK 1.1 or 1.3 API documentation, no serious programmer
should develop servlets or JSP pages without access to the API for classes in the
`javax.servlet` packages. Here is a summary of where to find the API:

- `http://java.sun.com/products/jsp/download.html`
  This site lets you download either the 2.1/1.0 API or the 2.2/1.1 API to
  your local system. You may have to download the entire reference
  implementation and then extract the documentation.

- `http://java.sun.com/products/servlet/2.2/javadoc/`
  This site lets you browse the servlet 2.2 and JSP 1.1 API on-line.

- `http://www.java.sun.com/j2ee/j2sdkee/techdocs/api/`
  This address lets you browse the complete API for the Java 2
  Platform, Enterprise Edition (J2EE), which includes the servlet 2.2
  and JSP 1.1 packages.

Identify the Classes to the Java Compiler

Once you've obtained the necessary software, you need to tell the Java compiler
(`javac`) where to find the servlet and JSP class files when it compiles your servlets.
Check the documentation of your particular system for definitive details, but the
necessary class files are usually in the `lib` subdirectory of the server's installation
directory, with the servlet classes in `servlet.jar` and the JSP classes in `jsp.jar`,
`jspengine.jar`, or `jasper.jar`. There are a couple of different ways to tell
`javac` about these classes, the easiest of which is to put the JAR files in your
CLASSPATH. If you've never dealt with the CLASSPATH before, it is the variable that
specifies where `javac` looks for classes when compiling. If the variable is unspecified, `javac` looks in the current directory and the standard system libraries. If you
set CLASSPATH yourself, be sure to include ".", signifying the current directory. See
Section 7.10 (Packages, Classpath, and JAR Archives) for details.

Package Your Classes

As you'll see in the next sections, you probably want to put your servlets into packages to avoid name conflicts with servlets other people write for the same Web or application server. In that case, you may find it convenient to add the top-level directory of your package hierarchy to the CLASSPATH as well.

Configure the Server

Before you start the server, you may want to designate parameters like the port on which the server listens, the directories in which it looks for HTML files, and so forth. This process is server specific, and for commercial-quality Web servers should be clearly documented in the installation notes.

DOS Memory Setting

If you start Tomcat or the JSWDK server from Windows 95 or 98, you probably have to modify the amount of memory DOS allocates for environment variables. To do this, start a fresh DOS window, click on the MS-DOS icon in the top-left corner of the window, and select Properties. From there, choose the Memory tab, go to the Initial Environment setting, and change the value from Auto to 2816. This configuration only needs to be done once.

Compile and Install Your Servlets

Once you've properly set your CLASSPATH, as described earlier in this section, just use javac ServletName.java to compile a servlet. The resultant class file needs to go in a location that the server knows to check during execution. As you might expect, this location varies from server to server. Check your server's documentation for details. Following is a quick summary of the locations used by the latest releases of Tomcat and the JSWDK. In both cases, assume install_dir is the server's main installation directory.

Tomcat 3

- **install_dir/webapps/ROOT/WEB-INF/classes**
  Standard location for servlet classes. Note that all servers that support servlets 2.2 and JSP 1.1 will have a an installation directory that looks like .../WEB-INF/classes. For example, the default location for Allaire JRun is *install_dir*/servers/default/default-app/WEB-INF/classes.
- **install_dir/lib**
  Location for JAR files containing classes.

- **install_dir/webapps/ROOT**
  Location for HTML files, images, and JSP pages. Again, the pattern is similar for other 2.2-compatible servers. For example, Allaire JRun uses *install_dir*/servers/default/default-app/ for HTML, JSP, and image files in its default Web application.

The JSWDK 1.0.1

- **install_dir/webpages/WEB-INF/servlets**
  Standard location for servlet classes.
- **install_dir/lib**
  Location for JAR files containing classes.
- **install_dir/webpages**
  Location for HTML files, images, and JSP pages.

Invoke Your Servlets

Most servers let you register names for servlets, so a servlet can be invoked by http://*host*/*any-path*/*any-file*. The process for doing this is server-specific; check your server's documentation for details. However, there is a common default way to invoke servlets: use a URL of the form http://*host*/servlet/ *ServletName*. Note that the URL refers to servlet, singular, even if the real directory containing the servlet code is called servlets, plural, or has an unrelated name like classes or lib.

There are two variations of this default URL. First, since servlets are typically placed in packages to avoid name conflicts with other servlets, the package name must appear in the URL. You would use a URL of the form http://*host*/servlet/ *packageName.ServletName* in such a case. Second, many modern Web servers let you define multiple separate *Web applications*—collections of servlets and JSP files (and associated images, HTML documents, etc.). In such a case, the default URL for accessing servlets would be of the form http://*host*/*webApplicationPath*/ servlet/*packageName.ServletName*. Again, most Web servers let you define custom URL-to-servlet mappings, regardless of whether packages or Web applications are being used.

19.3 Basic Servlet Structure

Listing 19.1 outlines a basic servlet that handles GET requests. GET requests, for those unfamiliar with HTTP, are the usual type of browser requests for Web pages. A browser generates this request when the user enters a URL on the address line, follows a link from a Web page, or submits an HTML form that either does not specify a METHOD or specifies METHOD="GET". Servlets can also very easily handle POST requests, which are generated when someone submits an HTML form that specifies METHOD="POST". For details on using HTML forms, see Chapter 18.

Listing 19.1 `ServletTemplate.java`

```java
import java.io.*;
import javax.servlet.*;
import javax.servlet.http.*;

public class ServletTemplate extends HttpServlet {
  public void doGet(HttpServletRequest request,
                    HttpServletResponse response)
    throws ServletException, IOException {

    // Use "request" to read incoming HTTP headers
    // (e.g., cookies) and query data from HTML forms.

    // Use "response" to specify the HTTP response status
    // code and headers (e.g. the content type, cookies).

    PrintWriter out = response.getWriter();
    // Use "out" to send content to browser.
  }
}
```

To be a servlet, a class should extend HttpServlet and override doGet or doPost, depending on whether the data is being sent by GET or by POST. If you want a servlet to take the same action for both GET and POST requests, simply have doGet call doPost, or vice versa.

Both of these methods take two arguments: an HttpServletRequest and an HttpServletResponse. The HttpServletRequest has methods by which you can find out about incoming information such as form (query) data, HTTP request headers, and the client's hostname. The HttpServletResponse lets you specify outgoing information such as HTTP status codes (200, 404, etc.) and response headers (Content-Type, Set-Cookie, etc.). Most importantly, it lets you obtain a PrintWriter with which you send the document content back to the client. For simple servlets, most of the effort is spent in println statements that generate the desired page. Form data, HTTP request headers, HTTP responses, and cookies are all discussed in the following sections.

Since doGet and doPost throw two exceptions, you are required to include them in the declaration. Finally, you must import classes in java.io (for PrintWriter, etc.), javax.servlet (for HttpServlet, etc.), and javax.servlet.http (for HttpServletRequest and HttpServletResponse).

A Servlet That Generates Plain Text

Listing 19.2 shows a simple servlet that outputs plain text, with the output shown in Figure 19–1. Listing 19.3 shows the more usual case where HTML is generated. However, before we move, it is worth spending some time going through the process of installing, compiling, and running this simple servlet.

First, be sure that your server is set up properly and that your CLASSPATH refers to the JAR file containing the javax.servlet classes, as described in Section 19.2 (Server Installation and Setup). Second, type javac HelloWorld.java (or click "build" in your IDE). Third, move HelloWorld.class to the directory that your server uses to store servlets (usually *install_dir*/.../WEB-INF/classes). Alternatively, you can use the -D option of javac to automatically place the .class files in the appropriate location. Finally, invoke your servlet. This last step involves either the default URL of http://*host*/servlet/*ServletName* or a custom URL defined in a server-specific manner. Figure 19–1 shows the servlet being accessed by means of the default URL, with the server running on the local machine.

Listing 19.2 HelloWorld.java

```java
import java.io.*;
import javax.servlet.*;
import javax.servlet.http.*;

public class HelloWorld extends HttpServlet {
  public void doGet(HttpServletRequest request,
                    HttpServletResponse response)
      throws ServletException, IOException {
    PrintWriter out = response.getWriter();
    out.println("Hello World");
  }
}
```

Figure 19–1 Result of Listing 19.2 (HelloWorld.java).

A Servlet That Generates HTML

Most servlets generate HTML, not plain text as in the previous example. To build HTML, you need two additional steps:

1. Tell the browser that you're sending back HTML.
2. Modify the `println` statements to build a legal Web page.

You accomplish the first step by setting the HTTP `Content-Type` response header. In general, headers are set by the `setHeader` method of `HttpServlet-Response`, but setting the content type is such a common task that there is also a special `setContentType` method just for this purpose. The way to designate HTML is with a type of `text/html`, so the code would look like this:

```
response.setContentType("text/html");
```

Although HTML is the most common type of document servlets create, it is not unusual to create other document types. For example, it is quite common to use servlets to generate GIF images (content type `image/gif`) and Excel spreadsheets (content type `application/vnd.ms-excel`).

Don't be concerned if you are not yet familiar with HTTP response headers; they are discussed in Section 19.10. Note that you need to set response headers *before* actually returning any of the content with the `PrintWriter`. That's because an HTTP response consists of the status line, one or more headers, a blank line, and the actual document, *in that order*. The headers can appear in any order, and servlets buffer the headers and send them all at once, so it is legal to set the status code (part of the first line returned) even after setting headers. But servlets do not necessarily buffer the document itself, since users might want to see partial results for long pages. In version 2.1 of the servlet specification, the `PrintWriter` output is not buffered at all, so the first time you use the `PrintWriter`, it is too late to go back and set headers. In version 2.2, servlet engines are permitted to partially buffer the output, but the size of the buffer is left unspecified. You can use the `getBufferSize` method of `HttpServletResponse` to determine the size or use `setBufferSize` to specify it. In version 2.2 with buffering enabled, you can set headers until the buffer fills up and is actually sent to the client. If you aren't sure if the buffer has been sent, you can use the `isCommitted` method to check.

Core Approach

*Always set the content type **before** transmitting the actual document.*

The second step in writing a servlet that builds an HTML document is to have your `println` statements output HTML, not plain text. The structure of HTML documents is discussed in Part 1 of this book. Listing 19.3 gives an example servlet that is placed in the cwp package; Figure 19–2 shows the result. Remember that, to use packages, you need to place your code in a directory corresponding to the package name and your CLASSPATH needs to refer to the top-level directory (i.e., the one containing your package-specific directory, cwp in this case).

Listing 19.3 HelloWWW.java

```
package cwp;

import java.io.*;
import javax.servlet.*;
import javax.servlet.http.*;

public class HelloWWW extends HttpServlet {
  public void doGet(HttpServletRequest request,
                    HttpServletResponse response)
    throws ServletException, IOException {
    response.setContentType("text/html");
    PrintWriter out = response.getWriter();
    String docType =
      "<!DOCTYPE HTML PUBLIC \"-//W3C//DTD HTML 4.0 " +
      "Transitional//EN\">\n";
    out.println(docType +
              "<HTML>\n" +
              "<HEAD><TITLE>Hello WWW</TITLE></HEAD>\n" +
              "<BODY>\n" +
              "<H1>Hello WWW</H1>\n" +
              "</BODY></HTML>");
  }
}
```

Figure 19–2 Result of Listing 19.3 (HelloWWW.java).

Simple HTML-Building Utilities

As you know from Part I of the book, an HTML document is structured as follows:

```
<!DOCTYPE ...>
<HTML>
<HEAD><TITLE>...</TITLE>...</HEAD>
<BODY ...>...</BODY>
</HTML>
```

When using servlets to build the HTML, you might be tempted to omit part of this structure, especially the DOCTYPE line, noting that virtually all major browsers ignore it even though the HTML 3.2 and 4.0 specifications require it. We strongly discourage this practice. The advantage of the DOCTYPE line is that it tells HTML validators which version of HTML you are using, so they know which specification to check your document against. These validators are valuable debugging services, helping you catch HTML syntax errors that your browser guesses well on but that other browsers will have trouble displaying. The two most popular on-line validators are the ones from the World Wide Web Consortium (http://validator.w3.org/) and from the Web Design Group (http://www.htmlhelp.com/tools/validator/). They let you submit a URL, then they retrieve the page, check the syntax against the formal HTML specification, and report any errors to you. Since a servlet that generates HTML looks like a regular Web page to visitors, it can be validated in the normal manner unless it requires POST data to return its result. Remember that GET data is attached to the URL, so you can send the validators a URL that includes GET data.

Core Approach

Use an HTML validator to check the syntax of pages that your servlets generate.

Admittedly, it is a bit cumbersome to generate HTML with println statements, especially long tedious lines like the DOCTYPE declaration. Some people address this problem by writing detailed HTML generation utilities in Java, then use them throughout their servlets. We're skeptical of the utility of such an extensive library. First and foremost, the inconvenience of generating HTML programmatically is one of the main problems addressed by JavaServer Pages (discussed in the next chapter). Second, HTML generation routines can be cumbersome and tend not to support the full range of HTML attributes (CLASS and ID for style sheets, JavaScript event handlers, table cell background colors, and so forth). Despite the questionable value of a full-blown HTML generation library, if you find you're repeating the same constructs many times, you might as well create a simple utility file that simplifies those constructs. For standard servlets, there are two parts of the Web page (DOCTYPE and HEAD) that are unlikely to change and thus could benefit from being incorporated into a simple utility file. These are shown in Listing 19.4, with Listing 19.5 showing a variation of `HelloWWW` that makes use of this utility. We'll add a few more utilities throughout the chapter.

Listing 19.4 `ServletUtilities.java`

```
package cwp;

/** Some simple time savers. Note that most are static methods. */

public class ServletUtilities {
  public static final String DOCTYPE =
    "<!DOCTYPE HTML PUBLIC \"-//W3C//DTD HTML 4.0 " +
    "Transitional//EN\">";

  public static String headWithTitle(String title) {
    return(DOCTYPE + "\n" +
           "<HTML>\n" +
           "<HEAD><TITLE>" + title + "</TITLE></HEAD>\n");
  }

  // Rest of ServletUtilities omitted
}
```

Listing 19.5 `SimplerHelloWWW.java`

```
package cwp;

import java.io.*;
import javax.servlet.*;
import javax.servlet.http.*;

/** Simple servlet that generates HTML. This variation of
 *  HelloWWW uses the ServletUtilities utility class
 *  to generate the DOCTYPE, HEAD, and TITLE.
 */

public class SimplerHelloWWW extends HttpServlet {
  public void doGet(HttpServletRequest request,
                    HttpServletResponse response)
      throws ServletException, IOException {
    response.setContentType("text/html");
    PrintWriter out = response.getWriter();
    out.println(ServletUtilities.headWithTitle("Hello WWW") +
                "<BODY>\n" +
                "<H1>Hello WWW</H1>\n" +
                "</BODY></HTML>");
  }
}
```

19.4 The Servlet Life Cycle

Earlier in this chapter, we vaguely referred to the fact that only a single instance of a servlet gets created, with each user request resulting in a new thread that is handed off to doGet or doPost as appropriate. We'll now be more specific about how servlets are created and destroyed, and how and when the various methods are invoked. We give a quick summary here, then elaborate in the following subsections.

When the servlet is first created, its init method is invoked, so that is where you put one-time setup code. After this, each user request results in a thread that calls the service method of the previously created instance. Multiple concurrent requests normally result in multiple threads calling service simultaneously, although your servlet can implement a special interface (SingleThreadModel) that stipulates that only a single thread is permitted to run at any one time. The service method then calls doGet, doPost, or another doXxx method, depending on the type of HTTP request it received. Finally, when the server decides to unload a servlet, it first calls the servlet's destroy method.

The init Method

The init method is called when the servlet is first created and is *not* called again for each user request. So, it is used for one-time initializations, just as with the init method of applets. The servlet can be created when a user first invokes a URL corresponding to the servlet or when the server is first started, depending on how you have registered the servlet with the Web server. The servlet will be created for the first user request if it is not explicitly registered but is instead just placed in one of the standard server directories. See the discussion of Section 19.2 (Server Installation and Setup) for details on these directories.

The init method definition looks like this:

```
public void init() throws ServletException {
  // Initialization code...
}
```

One of the most common tasks that init performs is reading server-specific initialization parameters. For example, the servlet might need to know about database settings, password files, server-specific performance parameters, hit count files, or serialized cookie data from previous requests. To accomplish this task, you obtain a ServletConfig object by means of getServletConfig, then call getInitParameter on the result. Here is an example:

```
public void init() throws ServletException {
  ServletConfig config = getServletConfig();
  String param1 = config.getInitParameter("SomeParameter");
}
```

Notice two things about this code. First, the init method uses getServlet-Config to obtain a reference to the ServletConfig object. Second, Servlet-Config has a getInitParameter method with which you can look up initialization parameters associated with the servlet. Just as with the getParameter method used in the init method of applets, both the input (the parameter name) and the output (the parameter value) are strings. For an example of the use of initialization parameters, see Section 19.5 (An Example Using Initialization Parameters). Note that although you *look up* parameters in a portable manner, you *set* them in a server-specific way. For example, with Tomcat and servers compliant with servlets 2.2, you embed servlet properties in a file called web.xml; with the JSWDK, you use servlets.properties; and with the Java Web Server, you set the properties interactively with the administration console.

The service Method

Each time the server receives a request for a servlet, the server spawns a new thread and calls service. The service method checks the HTTP request type (GET, POST, PUT, DELETE, etc.) and calls doGet, doPost, doPut, doDelete, etc., as appropriate. Now, if you have a servlet that needs to handle both POST and GET requests identically, you may be tempted to override service directly, rather than implementing both doGet and doPost. This is not a good idea. Instead, just have doPost call doGet (or vice versa), as below.

```
public void doGet(HttpServletRequest request,
                  HttpServletResponse response)
   throws ServletException, IOException {
  // Servlet Code
}

public void doPost(HttpServletRequest request,
                   HttpServletResponse response)
   throws ServletException, IOException {
  doGet(request, response);
}
```

Although this approach takes a couple of extra lines of code, it has several advantages over directly overriding service. First, you can later add support for other HTTP request methods by adding doPut, doTrace, etc., perhaps in a subclass. Overriding service directly precludes this possibility. Second, you can add support for modification dates by adding a getLastModified method. Since getLast-Modified is invoked by the default service method, overriding service eliminates this option. Finally, you get automatic support for HEAD, OPTION, and TRACE requests.

Core Tip

If your servlet needs to handle both GET *and* POST *identically, have your* doPost *method call* doGet, *or vice versa. Don't override* service.

The doGet, doPost, and doXxx Methods

These methods contain the real meat of your servlet. Ninety-nine percent of the time, you only care about GET or POST requests, so you override doGet and/or doPost. However, if you want to, you can also override doDelete for DELETE requests, doPut for PUT, doOptions for OPTIONS, and doTrace for TRACE. Recall, however, that you have automatic support for OPTIONS and TRACE. Note that there is no doHead method. That's because the system automatically uses the status line and header settings of doGet to answer HEAD requests.

The SingleThreadModel Interface

Normally, the system makes a single instance of your servlet and then creates a new thread for each user request, with multiple simultaneous threads running if a new request comes in while a previous request is still executing. This means that your doGet and doPost methods must be careful to synchronize access to fields and other shared data, since multiple threads may access the data simultaneously. If you want to prevent this multithreaded access, you can have your servlet implement the SingleThreadModel interface, as below.

```
public class YourServlet extends HttpServlet
                     implements SingleThreadModel {
    ...
}
```

If you implement this interface, the system guarantees that there is never more than one request thread accessing a single instance of your servlet. It does so either by queuing up all the requests and passing them one at a time to a single servlet instance or by creating a pool of multiple instances, each of which handles one request at a time. This means that you don't have to worry about simultaneous access to regular fields (instance variables) of the servlet. You *do*, however, still have to synchronize access to class variables (static fields) or shared data stored outside the servlet.

Synchronous access to your servlets can significantly hurt performance (latency) if your servlet is accessed frequently. So think twice before using the SingleThread-Model approach.

The destroy Method

The server may decide to remove a previously loaded servlet instance, perhaps because it is explicitly asked to do so by the server administrator, or perhaps because the servlet is idle for a long time. Before it does, however, it calls the servlet's destroy method. This method gives your servlet a chance to close database connections, halt background threads, write cookie lists or hit counts to disk, and perform other such cleanup activities. Be aware, however, that it is possible for the Web server to crash. So, don't count on destroy as the only mechanism for saving state to disk. Activities like hit counting or accumulating lists of cookie values that indicate special access should also proactively write their state to disk periodically.

19.5 An Example Using Initialization Parameters

Listing 19.6 shows a servlet that, when initialized, reads the message and repeats initialization parameters. Figure 19–3 shows the result when message is Shibboleth, repeats is 5, and the servlet is registered under the name ShowMsg. Listing 19.7 shows the XML configuration file used with Tomcat 3 to obtain the result of Figure 19–3, and Listing 19.8 shows the configuration file used with the JSWDK. Servers compliant with the 2.2 servlet specification use the same file format (web.xml) as Tomcat, albeit sometimes with a graphical user interface to generate it.

It is a good idea to minimize the number of separate initialization entries that have to be specified. Doing so will limit the work you need to do when moving servlets that use init parameters from one server to another. If you need to read a large amount of data, we recommend that the init parameter itself merely give the location of a parameter file and that the real data go in that file.

Core Approach

For complex initializations, store the data in a separate file and use the init parameters to give the location of that file.

Listing 19.6 ShowMessage.java

```java
package cwp;

import java.io.*;
import javax.servlet.*;
import javax.servlet.http.*;

/** Example using servlet initialization. Here, the message
 *  to print and the number of times the message should be
 *  repeated is taken from the init parameters.
 */

public class ShowMessage extends HttpServlet {
  private String message;
  private String defaultMessage = "No message.";
  private int repeats = 1;

  public void init() throws ServletException {
    ServletConfig config = getServletConfig();
    message = config.getInitParameter("message");
    if (message == null) {
      message = defaultMessage;
    }
    try {
      String repeatString = config.getInitParameter("repeats");
      repeats = Integer.parseInt(repeatString);
    } catch(NumberFormatException nfe) {
      // NumberFormatException handles case where repeatString
      // is null *and* case where it is in an illegal format.
    }
  }

  public void doGet(HttpServletRequest request,
                    HttpServletResponse response)
      throws ServletException, IOException {
    response.setContentType("text/html");
    PrintWriter out = response.getWriter();
    String title = "The ShowMessage Servlet";
    out.println(ServletUtilities.headWithTitle(title) +
                "<BODY BGCOLOR=\"#FDF5E6\">\n" +
                "<H1 ALIGN=\"CENTER\">" + title + "</H1>");
    for(int i=0; i<repeats; i++) {
      out.println("<B>" + message + "</B><BR>");
    }
    out.println("</BODY></HTML>");
  }
}
```

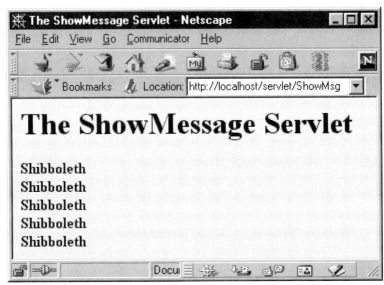

Figure 19–3 The `ShowMessage` servlet, registered under the name `ShowMsg` and supplied with server-specific initialization parameters.

Listing 19.7 `web.xml` (for Tomcat 3)

```xml
<?xml version="1.0" encoding="ISO-8859-1"?>

<!DOCTYPE web-app PUBLIC
    "-//Sun Microsystems, Inc.//DTD Web Application 2.2//EN"
    "http://java.sun.com/j2ee/dtds/web-app_2.2.dtd">

<web-app>
  <servlet>
    <servlet-name>ShowMsg</servlet-name>
    <servlet-class>cwp.ShowMessage</servlet-class>
    <init-param>
      <param-name>message</param-name>
      <param-value>Shibboleth</param-value>
    </init-param>
    <init-param>
      <param-name>repeats</param-name>
      <param-value>5</param-value>
    </init-param>
  </servlet>
</web-app>
```

Listing 19.8 `servlets.properties` (for the JSWDK 1.0.1)

```
# servlets.properties used with the JSWDK

# Register servlet via servletName.code=servletClassFile
# You access it via http://host/examples/servlet/servletName
ShowMsg.code=cwp.ShowMessage

# Set init params via
#    servletName.initparams=param1=val1,param2=val2,...
ShowMsg.initparams=message=Shibboleth,repeats=5

# Standard setting
jsp.code=com.sun.jsp.runtime.JspServlet

# Set this to keep servlet source code built from JSP
jsp.initparams=keepgenerated=true
```

19.6 The Client Request: Form Data

One of the main motivations for building Web pages dynamically is to base the result upon query data submitted by the user. This section shows you how to access that data.

If you've ever used a search engine, visited an on-line bookstore, tracked stocks on the Web, or asked a Web-based site for quotes on plane tickets, you've probably seen funny-looking URLs like `http://host/path?user=Marty+Hall&origin=bwi&dest=lax`. The part after the question mark (i.e., `user=Marty+Hall&origin=bwi&dest=lax`) is known as *form data* (or *query data*) and is the most common way to get information from a Web page to a server-side program. Form data can be attached to the end of the URL after a question mark (as above) for `GET` requests, or sent to the server on a separate line for `POST` requests. If you're not familiar with HTML forms, see Chapter 18 (HTML Forms) for details on how to build forms that collect and transmit data of this sort.

Reading Form Data from CGI Programs

Extracting the needed information from form data is traditionally one of the most tedious parts of CGI programming. First of all, you have to read the data one way for `GET` requests (in traditional CGI, this is usually through the `QUERY_STRING` environment variable) and a different way for `POST` requests (by reading the standard input in traditional CGI). Second, you have to chop the pairs at the ampersands, then separate the parameter names (left of the equal signs) from the parameter values (right of the equal signs). Third, you have to URL-decode the values. Alphanumeric characters are sent unchanged, but spaces are converted to plus signs and other characters are converted to %XX where XX is the ASCII (or ISO Latin-1) value of the character, in hex.

Reading Form Data from Servlets

One of the nice features of servlets is that all the form parsing is handled automatically. You simply call the `getParameter` method of the `HttpServletRequest`, supplying the case-sensitive parameter name as an argument. You use `get-Parameter` exactly the same way when the data is sent by GET as you do when it is sent by POST. The servlet knows which request method was used and automatically does the right thing behind the scenes. The return value is a `String` corresponding to the URL-decoded value of the first occurrence of that parameter name. An empty `String` is returned if the parameter exists but has no value, and `null` is returned if there was no such parameter. If the parameter could potentially have more than one value, you should call `getParameterValues` (which returns an array of strings) instead of `getParameter` (which returns a single string). The return value of `get-ParameterValues` is `null` for nonexistent parameter names and is a one-element array when the parameter has only a single value.

Parameter names are case sensitive, so, for example, `request.get-Parameter("Param1")` and `request.getParameter("param1")` are *not* interchangeable.

Core Warning

The values supplied to `getParameter` *and* `getParameterValues` *are case sensitive.*

Finally, although most real servlets look for a specific set of parameter names, for debugging purposes it is sometimes useful to get a full list. Use `getParameter-Names` to get this list in the form of an `Enumeration`, each entry of which can be cast to a `String` and used in a `getParameter` or `getParameterValues` call. Just note that the `HttpServletRequest` API does not specify the order in which the names appear within that `Enumeration`.

Example: Reading Three Explicit Parameters

Listing 19.9 presents a simple servlet called `ThreeParams` that reads form data parameters named `param1`, `param2`, and `param3` and places their values in a bulleted list. Listing 19.10 shows an HTML form that collects user input and sends it to this servlet. By use of an ACTION URL that begins with a slash (e.g., /servlet/cwp.ThreeParams), the form can be installed anywhere on the system running the servlet; there need not be any particular association between the directory containing the form and the servlet installation directory. On engines compatible with servlets 2.2, HTML files (and images and JSP pages) go in the directory above the one containing the WEB-INF directory. For example, the default Tomcat location is *install_dir*/webapps/ROOT and the default JRun location is *install_dir*/servers/default/default-app. Older servers have no standard location (e.g., the JSWDK uses *install_dir*/webpages). Also note that the ThreeParams servlet reads the query data after it starts generating the page. Although you are required to specify *response* settings before beginning to generate the content, there is no requirement that you read the *request* parameters at any particular time.

Figures 19–4 and 19–5 show the result of the HTML front end and the servlet, respectively.

Listing 19.9 ThreeParams.java

```
package cwp;

import java.io.*;
import javax.servlet.*;
import javax.servlet.http.*;

public class ThreeParams extends HttpServlet {
  public void doGet(HttpServletRequest request,
                    HttpServletResponse response)
      throws ServletException, IOException {
    response.setContentType("text/html");
    PrintWriter out = response.getWriter();
    String title = "Reading Three Request Parameters";
    out.println(ServletUtilities.headWithTitle(title) +
                "<BODY BGCOLOR=\"#FDF5E6\">\n" +
                "<H1 ALIGN=\"CENTER\">" + title + "</H1>\n" +
                "<UL>\n" +
                "  <LI><B>param1</B>: "
                + request.getParameter("param1") + "\n" +
                "  <LI><B>param2</B>: "
                + request.getParameter("param2") + "\n" +
                "  <LI><B>param3</B>: "
                + request.getParameter("param3") + "\n" +
                "</UL>\n" +
                "</BODY></HTML>");
  }
}
```

Listing 19.10 `ThreeParamsForm.html`

```
<!DOCTYPE HTML PUBLIC "-//W3C//DTD HTML 4.0 Transitional//EN">
<HTML>
<HEAD>
  <TITLE>Collecting Three Parameters</TITLE>
</HEAD>
<BODY BGCOLOR="#FDF5E6">
<H1 ALIGN="CENTER">Collecting Three Parameters</H1>

<FORM ACTION="/servlet/cwp.ThreeParams">
  First Parameter:   <INPUT TYPE="TEXT" NAME="param1"><BR>
  Second Parameter:  <INPUT TYPE="TEXT" NAME="param2"><BR>
  Third Parameter:   <INPUT TYPE="TEXT" NAME="param3"><BR>
  <CENTER><INPUT TYPE="SUBMIT"></CENTER>
</FORM>

</BODY>
</HTML>
```

If you're accustomed to the traditional CGI approach where you read POST data through the standard input, you should note that you can do the same thing with servlets by calling `getReader` or `getInputStream` on the `HttpServlet-Request` and then using that stream to obtain the raw input. This is a bad idea for regular parameters; `getParameter` is simpler and yields results that are parsed and URL-decoded. However, reading the raw input might be of use for uploaded files or POST data being sent by custom clients. Note, however, that if you read the POST data in this manner, it might no longer be found by `getParameter`.

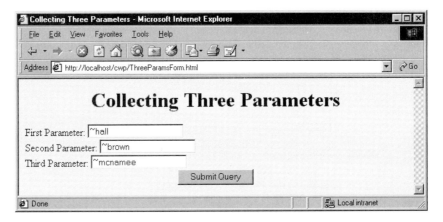

Figure 19–4 HTML front end resulting from `ThreeParamsForm.html`.

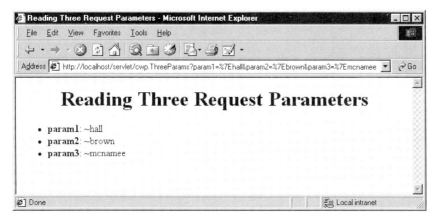

Figure 19–5 Output of `ThreeParams` servlet.

Filtering Query Data

In the previous example, we read the `param1`, `param2`, and `param3` request parameters and inserted them verbatim into the page being generated. This is not necessarily safe, since the request parameters might contain HTML characters such as "<" that could disrupt the rest of the page processing, causing some of the subsequent tags to be interpreted incorrectly. A safer approach is to filter out the HTML-specific characters before inserting the values into the page. Listing 19.11 shows a static `filter` method that accomplishes this task.

Listing 19.11 `ServletUtilities.java`

```
package cwp;

import javax.servlet.*;
import javax.servlet.http.*;

public class ServletUtilities {
// Other parts of ServletUtilities shown elsewhere.

/** Given a string, this method replaces all occurrences of
 *   '<' with '&lt;', all occurrences of '>' with
 *   '&gt;', and (to handle cases that occur inside attribute
 *   values), all occurrences of double quotes with
 *   '&quot;' and all occurrences of '&' with '&amp;'.
 *   Without such filtering, an arbitrary string
 *   could not safely be inserted in a Web page.
 */
```

(continued)

Listing 19.11 `ServletUtilities.java` *(continued)*

```java
public static String filter(String input) {
  StringBuffer filtered = new StringBuffer(input.length());
  char c;
  for(int i=0; i<input.length(); i++) {
    c = input.charAt(i);
    if (c == '<') {
      filtered.append("&lt;");
    } else if (c == '>') {
      filtered.append("&gt;");
    } else if (c == '"') {
      filtered.append("&quot;");
    } else if (c == '&') {
      filtered.append("&amp;");
    } else {
      filtered.append(c);
    }
  }
  return(filtered.toString());
}
}
```

19.7 The Client Request: HTTP Request Headers

One of the keys to creating effective servlets is understanding how to manipulate the HyperText Transfer Protocol (HTTP). Getting a thorough grasp of this protocol is not an esoteric, theoretical concept, but rather a practical issue that can have an immediate impact on the performance and usability of your servlets. This section discusses the HTTP information that is sent from the browser to the server in the form of request headers. It explains the most important HTTP 1.1 request headers, summarizing how and why they would be used in a servlet. The section also includes two detailed examples: listing all request headers sent by the browser and reducing download time by encoding the Web page with gzip when appropriate.

Note that HTTP request headers are distinct from the form (query) data discussed in the previous section. Form data results directly from user input and is sent as part of the URL for GET requests and on a separate line for POST requests. Request headers, on the other hand, are indirectly set by the browser and are sent immediately following the initial GET or POST request line. For instance, the following example shows an HTTP request that might result from a user submitting a book-search request to a servlet at `http://www.somebookstore.com/servlet/Search`. The request includes the headers Accept, Accept-Encoding, Connection, Cookie, Host, Referer, and User-Agent, all of which might be important to the operation of the servlet, but none of which can be derived from the form data or deduced automatically: the servlet needs to explicitly read the request headers to make use of this information.

```
GET /servlet/Search?keywords=servlets+jsp HTTP/1.1
Accept: image/gif, image/jpg, */*
Accept-Encoding: gzip
Connection: Keep-Alive
Cookie: userID=id456578
Host: www.somebookstore.com
Referer: http://www.somebookstore.com/findbooks.html
User-Agent: Mozilla/4.7 [en] (Win98; U)
```

Reading Request Headers from Servlets

Reading headers is straightforward; just call the getHeader method of HttpServletRequest, which returns a String if the specified header was supplied on this request, null otherwise. Header names are not case sensitive. So, for example, request.getHeader("Connection") and request.getHeader ("connection") are interchangeable.

Although getHeader is the general-purpose way to read incoming headers, a few headers are so commonly used that they have special access methods in Http-ServletRequest. Following is a summary.

- **getCookies**
  The getCookies method returns the contents of the Cookie header, parsed and stored in an array of Cookie objects. This method is discussed in more detail in Section 19.11 (Cookies).
- **getAuthType and getRemoteUser**
  The getAuthType and getRemoteUser methods break the Authorization header into its component pieces.
- **getContentLength**
  The getContentLength method returns the value of the Content-Length header (as an int).
- **getContentType**
  The getContentType method returns the value of the Content-Type header (as a String).
- **getDateHeader and getIntHeader**
  The getDateHeader and getIntHeader methods read the specified headers and then convert them to Date and int values, respectively.

- `getHeaderNames`

  Rather than looking up one particular header, you can use the `getHeaderNames` method to get an `Enumeration` of all header names received on this particular request. This capability is illustrated in Listing 19.12.

- `getHeaders`

  In most cases, each header name appears only once in the request. Occasionally, however, a header can appear multiple times, with each occurrence listing a separate value. `Accept-Language` is one such example. With servlets version 2.2, you can use `getHeaders` to obtain an `Enumeration` of the values of all occurrences of the header.

Finally, in addition to looking up the request headers, you can get information on the main request line itself, also by means of methods in `HttpServletRequest`. Here is a summary of the three main methods:

- `getMethod`

  The `getMethod` method returns the main request method (normally `GET` or `POST`, but things like `HEAD`, `PUT`, and `DELETE` are possible).

- `getRequestURI`

  The `getRequestURI` method returns the part of the URL that comes after the host and port but before the form data. For example, for a URL of `http://randomhost.com/servlet/search.BookSearch`, `getRequestURI` would return `/servlet/search.BookSearch`.

- `getProtocol`

  The `getProtocol` method returns the third part of the request line, which is generally `HTTP/1.0` or `HTTP/1.1`. Servlets should usually check `getProtocol` before specifying *response* headers (Section 19.10) that are specific to HTTP 1.1.

Example: Making a Table of All Request Headers

Listing 19.12 shows a servlet that simply creates a table of all the headers it receives, along with their associated values. It also prints out the three components of the main request line (method, URI, and protocol). Figures 19–6 and 19–7 show typical results with Netscape and Internet Explorer.

Listing 19.12 ShowRequestHeaders.java

```java
package cwp;

import java.io.*;
import javax.servlet.*;
import javax.servlet.http.*;
import java.util.*;

/** Shows all the request headers sent on this request. */

public class ShowRequestHeaders extends HttpServlet {
  public void doGet(HttpServletRequest request,
                    HttpServletResponse response)
      throws ServletException, IOException {
    response.setContentType("text/html");
    PrintWriter out = response.getWriter();
    String title = "Servlet Example: Showing Request Headers";
    out.println(ServletUtilities.headWithTitle(title) +
                "<BODY BGCOLOR=\"#FDF5E6\">\n" +
                "<H1 ALIGN=\"CENTER\">" + title + "</H1>\n" +
                "<B>Request Method: </B>" +
                request.getMethod() + "<BR>\n" +
                "<B>Request URI: </B>" +
                request.getRequestURI() + "<BR>\n" +
                "<B>Request Protocol: </B>" +
                request.getProtocol() + "<BR><BR>\n" +
                "<TABLE BORDER=1 ALIGN=\"CENTER\">\n" +
                "<TR BGCOLOR=\"#FFAD00\">\n" +
                "<TH>Header Name<TH>Header Value");
    Enumeration headerNames = request.getHeaderNames();
    while(headerNames.hasMoreElements()) {
      String headerName = (String)headerNames.nextElement();
      out.println("<TR><TD>" + headerName);
      out.println("    <TD>" + request.getHeader(headerName));
    }
    out.println("</TABLE>\n</BODY></HTML>");
  }

  /** Let the same servlet handle both GET and POST. */

  public void doPost(HttpServletRequest request,
                     HttpServletResponse response)
      throws ServletException, IOException {
    doGet(request, response);
  }
}
```

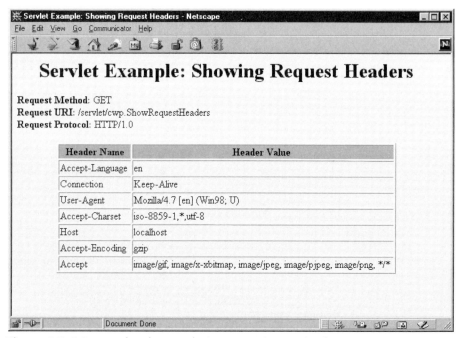

Figure 19–6 Request headers sent by Netscape 4.7 on Windows 98.

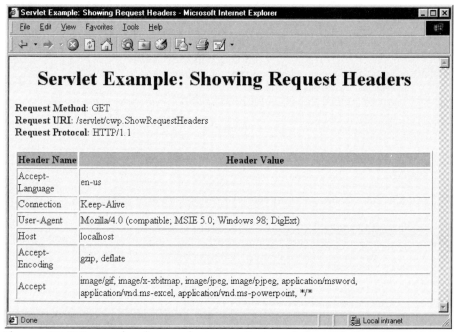

Figure 19–7 Request headers sent by Internet Explorer 5.0 on Windows 98.

HTTP 1.1 Request Headers

Access to the request headers permits servlets to perform a number of optimizations and to provide a number of features not otherwise possible. This subsection summarizes the headers most often used by servlets. Note that HTTP 1.1 supports a superset of the headers permitted in HTTP 1.0. For additional details on these and other headers, see the HTTP 1.1 specification, given in RFC 2616. The official RFCs are archived in a number of places; your best bet is to start at `http://www.rfc-editor.org/` to get a current list of the archive sites.

Accept

This header specifies the MIME types that the browser or other clients can handle. A servlet that can return a resource in more than one format can examine the `Accept` header to decide which format to use. For example, images in PNG format have some compression advantages over those in GIF, but only a few browsers support PNG. If you had images in both formats, a servlet could call `request.getHeader("Accept")`, check for `image/png`, and if it finds a match, use *xxx*.`png` filenames in all the `IMG` elements it generates. Otherwise, it would just use *xxx*.`gif`.

See Table 19.1 in Section 19.10 (The Server Response: HTTP Response Headers) for the names and meanings of the common MIME types.

Accept-Charset

This header indicates the character sets (e.g., ISO-8859-1) the browser can use.

Accept-Encoding

This header designates the types of encodings that the client knows how to handle. If the server receives this header, it is free to encode the page by using the format specified (usually to reduce transmission time), sending the `Content-Encoding` response header to indicate that it has done so. This encoding type is completely distinct from the MIME type of the actual document (as specified in the `Content-Type` response header), since this encoding is reversed *before* the browser decides what to do with the content. On the other hand, using an encoding the browser doesn't understand results in totally incomprehensible pages. Consequently, it is critical that you explicitly check the `Accept-Encoding` header before using any type of content encoding. Values of `gzip` or `compress` are the two standard possibilities.

Compressing pages before returning them is a valuable service because the decoding time is likely to be small compared to the savings in transmission time. See the following subsection for an example where compression reduces download times by a factor of 10.

Accept-Language

This header specifies the client's preferred languages in case the servlet can produce results in more than one language. The value of the header should be one of the standard language codes such as en, en-us, da, etc. See RFC 1766 for details.

Authorization

This header is used by clients to identify themselves when accessing password-protected Web pages.

Connection

This header tells whether or not the client can handle persistent HTTP connections. These let the client or other browser retrieve multiple files (e.g., an HTML file and several associated images) with a single socket connection, saving the overhead of negotiating several independent connections. With an HTTP 1.1 request, persistent connections are the default, and the client must specify a value of close for this header to use old-style connections. In HTTP 1.0, a value of Keep-Alive means that persistent connections should be used.

Each HTTP request results in a new invocation of a servlet, regardless of whether the request is a separate connection. That is, the server invokes the servlet only after the server has already read the HTTP request. This means that servlets need help from the server to handle persistent connections. Consequently, the servlet's job is just to make it *possible* for the server to use persistent connections, which the server does by sending a Content-Length response header.

Content-Length

This header is only applicable to POST requests and gives the size of the POST data in bytes. Rather than calling request.getIntHeader("Content-Length"), you can simply use request.getContentLength(). However, since servlets take care of reading the form data for you (see Section 19.6, "The Client Request: Form Data"), you rarely use this header explicitly.

Cookie

This header is used to return cookies to servers that previously sent them to the browser. For details, see Section 19.11 (Cookies). Technically, Cookie is not part of HTTP 1.1. It was originally a Netscape extension but is now widely supported, including support by both Netscape and Internet Explorer.

Host

Browsers and other clients are *required* to specify this header, which indicates the host and port as given in the original URL. Due to request forwarding and machines that have multiple hostnames, it is quite possible that the server could not otherwise determine this information. This header is not new in HTTP 1.1, but in HTTP 1.0 it was optional, not required.

If-Modified-Since

This header indicates that the client wants the page only if it has been changed after the specified date. The server sends a 302 (Not Modified) header if no newer result is available. This option is useful because it lets browsers cache documents and reload them over the network only when they've changed. However, servlets don't need to deal directly with this header. Instead, they should just implement the `getLastModified` method to have the system handle modification dates automatically.

If-Unmodified-Since

This header is the reverse of `If-Modified-Since`; it indicates that the operation should succeed only if the document is older than the specified date. Typically, `If-Modified-Since` is used for `GET` requests ("give me the document only if it is newer than my cached version"), whereas `If-Unmodified-Since` is used for `PUT` requests ("update this document only if nobody else has changed it since I generated it").

Referer

This header indicates the URL of the referring Web page. For example, if you are at Web page 1 and click on a link to Web page 2, the URL of Web page 1 is included in the `Referer` header when the browser requests Web page 2. All major browsers set this header, so it is a useful way of tracking where requests came from. This capability is helpful for tracking advertisers who refer people to your site, for slightly changing content depending on the referring site, or simply for keeping track of where your traffic comes from. In the last case, most people simply rely on Web server log files, since the `Referer` is typically recorded there. Although the `Referer` header is useful, don't rely too heavily on it since it can easily be spoofed by a custom client. Finally, note that this header is `Referer`, not the expected `Referrer`, due to a spelling mistake by one of the original HTTP authors.

User-Agent

This header identifies the browser or other client making the request and can be used to return different content to different types of browsers. Be wary of this usage, however; relying on a hard-coded list of browser versions and associated features can make for unreliable and hard-to-modify servlet code.

Whenever possible, use something specific in the HTTP headers instead. For example, instead of trying to remember which browsers support gzip on which platforms, simply check the `Accept-Encoding` header.

Most Internet Explorer versions list a "Mozilla" (Netscape) version first in their `User-Agent` line, with the real browser version listed parenthetically. This is done for compatibility with JavaScript, where the `User-Agent` header is sometimes used to determine which JavaScript features are supported. Also note that this header can be easily spoofed, a fact that calls into question the reliability of sites that use this header to "show" market penetration of various browser versions. Hmm, millions of dollars in marketing money riding on statistics that could be skewed by a custom client written in less than an hour, and we should take those numbers as accurate ones?

Sending Compressed Web Pages

Several recent browsers know how to handle gzipped content, automatically uncompressing documents that are marked with the `Content-Encoding` header and then treating the result as though it were the original document. Sending such compressed content can be a real time saver, since the time required to compress the document on the server and then uncompress it on the client is typically dwarfed by the savings in download time, especially when dialup connections are used.

Browsers that support content encoding include most versions of Netscape for Unix, Netscape 4.7 and later for Windows, and most versions of Internet Explorer for Windows. Earlier Netscape versions on Windows and Internet Explorer on non-Windows platforms generally do not support gzip compression. Fortunately, browsers that support this feature indicate that they do so by setting the `Accept-Encoding` request header. Listing 19.13 and Figure 19–8 show a servlet that checks this header, sending a compressed Web page to clients that support gzip encoding and sending a regular Web page to those that don't. The result showed a *tenfold* speedup for the compressed page when a dialup connection was used. In repeated tests with Netscape 4.7 and Internet Explorer 5.0 on a 28.8K modem connection, the compressed page averaged less than 5 seconds to completely download, whereas the uncompressed page consistently took more than 50 seconds.

Core Tip

Gzip compression can dramatically reduce the download time of long text pages.

Implementing compression is straightforward since the gzip format is built in to the Java programming languages through classes in `java.util.zip`. The servlet first checks the `Accept-Encoding` header to see if it contains an entry for gzip. If so, it uses a `GZIPOutputStream` to generate the page, specifying `gzip` as the value of the `Content-Encoding` header. You must explicitly call `close` when using a `GZIPOutputStream`. If gzip is not supported, the servlet uses the normal `PrintWriter` to send the page. To make it easy to compare compressed and uncompressed times with the same browser, we also added a feature whereby compression could be suppressed by including `?encoding=none` at the end of the URL.

Listing 19.13 `EncodedPage.java`

```java
package cwp;

import java.io.*;
import javax.servlet.*;
import javax.servlet.http.*;
import java.util.zip.*;

/** Example showing benefits of gzipping pages to browsers
 *  that can handle gzip.
 */

public class EncodedPage extends HttpServlet {
  public void doGet(HttpServletRequest request,
                    HttpServletResponse response)
      throws ServletException, IOException {
    response.setContentType("text/html");
    String encodings = request.getHeader("Accept-Encoding");
    String encodeFlag = request.getParameter("encoding");
    PrintWriter out;
    String title;
    if ((encodings != null) &&
        (encodings.indexOf("gzip") != -1) &&
        !"none".equals(encodeFlag)) {
      title = "Page Encoded with GZip";
      OutputStream out1 = response.getOutputStream();
      out = new PrintWriter(new GZIPOutputStream(out1), false);
      response.setHeader("Content-Encoding", "gzip");
    } else {
      title = "Unencoded Page";
      out = response.getWriter();
    }
```

(continued)

> **Listing 19.13** EncodedPage.java *(continued)*

```
    out.println(ServletUtilities.headWithTitle(title) +
                "<BODY BGCOLOR=\"#FDF5E6\">\n" +
                "<H1 ALIGN=\"CENTER\">" + title + "</H1>\n");
    String line = "Blah, blah, blah, blah, blah. " +
                  "Yadda, yadda, yadda, yadda.";
    for(int i=0; i<10000; i++) {
      out.println(line);
    }
    out.println("</BODY></HTML>");
    out.close();
  }
}
```

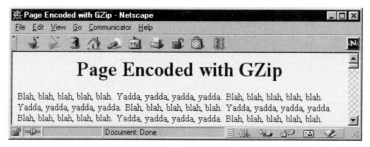

Figure 19–8 Since the Windows version of Netscape 4.7 supports gzip (see Figure 19–6), this page was sent gzipped over the network and reconstituted by the browser, resulting in a large saving in download time.

19.8 The Servlet Equivalent of the Standard CGI Variables

If you come to servlets with a background in traditional Common Gateway Interface (CGI) programming, you are probably used to the idea of "CGI variables." These are a somewhat eclectic collection of information about the current request. Some are based on the HTTP request line and headers (e.g., form data), others are derived from the socket itself (e.g., the name and IP address of the requesting host), and still others are taken from server installation parameters (e.g., the mapping of URLs to actual paths).

Although it probably makes more sense to think of different sources of data (request data, server information, etc.) as distinct, experienced CGI programmers may find it useful to see the servlet equivalent of each of the CGI variables. If you don't have a background in traditional CGI, first, count your blessings; servlets are easier to use, more flexible and more efficient than standard CGI. Second, just skim this section, noting the parts not directly related to the incoming HTTP request. In particular, observe that you can use `getServletContext().getRealPath` to map a URI (here, URI refers to the part of the URL that comes after the host and port) to an actual path and that you can use `request.getRemoteHost()` and `request.getRemoteAddress()` to get the name and IP address of the client.

AUTH_TYPE

If an `Authorization` header was supplied, this variable gives the scheme specified (`basic` or `digest`). Access it with `request.getAuthType()`.

CONTENT_LENGTH

For `POST` requests only, this variable stores the number of bytes of data sent, as given by the `Content-Length` request header. Technically, since the `CONTENT_LENGTH` CGI variable is a string, the servlet equivalent is `String.valueOf(request.getContentLength())` or `request.get-Header("Content-Length")`. You'll probably want to just call `request.getContentLength()`, which returns an `int`.

CONTENT_TYPE

`CONTENT_TYPE` designates the MIME type of attached data, if specified. See Table 19.1 in Section 19.10 (The Server Response: HTTP Response Headers) for the names and meanings of the common MIME types. Access `CONTENT_TYPE` with `request.getContentType()`.

DOCUMENT_ROOT

The `DOCUMENT_ROOT` variable specifies the real directory corresponding to the URL `http://host/`. Access it with `getServletContext().get-RealPath("/")`. In older servlet specifications, you accessed this variable with `request.getRealPath("/")`; however, the older access method is no longer supported. Also, you can use `getServletContext().getRealPath` to map an arbitrary URI (i.e., URL suffix that comes after the hostname and port) to an actual path on the local machine.

HTTP_XXX_YYY

Variables of the form `HTTP_HEADER_NAME` were how CGI programs obtained access to arbitrary HTTP request headers. The `Cookie` header became `HTTP_COOKIE`, User-Agent became `HTTP_USER_AGENT`, Referer became `HTTP_REFERER`, and so forth. Servlets should just use `request.getHeader` or one of the shortcut methods described in Section 19.7 (The Client Request: HTTP Request Headers).

PATH_INFO

This variable supplies any path information attached to the URL after the address of the servlet but before the query data. For example, with `http://host/servlet/cwp.SomeServlet/foo/bar?baz=quux`, the path information is `/foo/bar`. Since servlets, unlike standard CGI programs, can talk directly to the server, they don't need to treat path information specially. Path information could be sent as part of the regular form data and then translated by `getServletContext().getRealPath`. Access the value of `PATH_INFO` by using `request.getPathInfo()`.

PATH_TRANSLATED

`PATH_TRANSLATED` gives the path information mapped to a real path on the server. Again, with servlets there is no need to have a special case for path information, since a servlet can call `getServletContext().getReal-Path()` to translate partial URLs into real paths. This translation is not possible with standard CGI because the CGI program runs entirely separately from the server. Access this variable by means of `request.getPath-Translated()`.

QUERY_STRING

For `GET` requests, this variable gives the attached data as a single string with values still URL-encoded. You rarely want the raw data in servlets; instead, use `request.getParameter` to access individual parameters, as described in Section 19.7 (The Client Request: HTTP Request Headers). However, if you do want the raw data, you can get it with `request.getQueryString()`.

REMOTE_ADDR

This variable designates the IP address of the client that made the request, as a `String` (e.g., `"198.137.241.30"`). Access it by calling `request.get-RemoteAddr()`.

REMOTE_HOST

`REMOTE_HOST` indicates the fully qualified domain name (e.g., `whitehouse.gov`) of the client that made the request. The IP address is returned if the domain name cannot be determined. You can access this variable with `request.getRemoteHost()`.

REMOTE_USER

If an `Authorization` header was supplied and decoded by the server itself, the `REMOTE_USER` variable gives the user part, which is useful for session tracking in protected sites. Access it with `request.getRemoteUser()`.

REQUEST_METHOD

This variable stipulates the HTTP request type, which is usually GET or POST but is occasionally HEAD, PUT, DELETE, OPTIONS, or TRACE. Servlets rarely need to look up REQUEST_METHOD explicitly, since each of the request types is typically handled by a different servlet method (doGet, doPost, etc.). An exception is HEAD, which is handled automatically by the service method returning whatever headers and status codes the doGet method would use. Access this variable by means of request.getMethod().

SCRIPT_NAME

This variable specifies the path to the servlet, relative to the server's root directory. It can be accessed through request.getServletPath().

SERVER_NAME

SERVER_NAME gives the host name of the server machine. It can be accessed by means of request.getServerName().

SERVER_PORT

This variable stores the port the server is listening on. Technically, the servlet equivalent is String.valueOf(request.getServerPort()), which returns a String. You'll usually just want request.getServerPort(), which returns an int.

SERVER_PROTOCOL

The SERVER_PROTOCOL variable indicates the protocol name and version used in the request line (e.g., HTTP/1.0 or HTTP/1.1). Access it by calling request.getProtocol().

SERVER_SOFTWARE

This variable gives identifying information about the Web server. Access it with getServletContext().getServerInfo().

19.9 The Server Response: HTTP Status Codes

When a Web server responds to a request from a browser or other Web client, the response typically consists of a status line, some response headers, a blank line, and the document. Here is a minimal example:

```
HTTP/1.1 200 OK
Content-Type: text/plain
```

```
Hello World
```

The status line consists of the HTTP version (HTTP/1.1 in the example above), a status code (an integer; 200 in the example), and a very short message corresponding to the status code (OK in the example). In most cases, all of the headers are optional except for Content-Type, which specifies the MIME type of the document that follows. Although most responses contain a document, some don't. For example, responses to HEAD requests should never include a document, and a variety of status codes essentially indicate failure and either don't include a document or include only a short error message document.

Servlets can perform a variety of important tasks by manipulating the status line and the response headers. For example, they can forward the user to other sites; indicate that the attached document is an image, Adobe Acrobat file, or HTML file; tell the user that a password is required to access the document; and so forth. This section discusses the most important status codes and what can be accomplished with them; the following section discusses the response headers.

Specifying Status Codes

As just described, the HTTP response status line consists of an HTTP version, a status code, and an associated message. Since the message is directly associated with the status code and the HTTP version is determined by the server, all a servlet needs to do is to set the status code. The way to do this is by the setStatus method of HttpServletResponse. If your response includes a special status code *and* a document, be sure to call setStatus *before* actually returning any of the content with the PrintWriter. That's because an HTTP response consists of the status line, one or more headers, a blank line, and the actual document, *in that order.* As discussed in Section 19.3 (Basic Servlet Structure), servlets do not necessarily buffer the document (version 2.1 servlets never do so), so you have to either set the status code before first using the PrintWriter or carefully check that the buffer hasn't been flushed and content actually sent to the browser.

Core Approach

Set status codes **before** sending any document content to the client.

The setStatus method takes an int (the status code) as an argument, but instead of using explicit numbers, for clarity and reliability use the constants defined in HttpServletResponse. The name of each constant is derived from the standard HTTP 1.1 message for each constant, all upper case with a prefix of

SC (for *Status Code*) and spaces changed to underscores. Thus, since the message for 404 is "Not Found," the equivalent constant in HttpServletResponse is SC_NOT_FOUND. In version 2.1 of the servlet specification, there are three exceptions. The constant for code 302 is derived from the HTTP 1.0 message (Moved Temporarily), not the HTTP 1.1 message (Found), and the constants for codes 307 (Temporary Redirect) and 416 (Requested Range Not Satisfiable) are missing altogether. Version 2.2 added the constant for 416, but the inconsistencies for 307 and 302 remain.

Although the general method of setting status codes is simply to call response.setStatus(int), there are two common cases where a shortcut method in HttpServletResponse is provided. Just be aware that both of these methods throw IOException, whereas setStatus doesn't.

- **public void sendError(int code, String message)**
  The sendError method sends a status code (usually 404) along with a short message that is automatically formatted inside an HTML document and sent to the client.
- **public void sendRedirect(String url)**
  The sendRedirect method generates a 302 response along with a Location header giving the URL of the new document. With servlets version 2.1, this must be an absolute URL. In version 2.2, either an absolute or a relative URL is permitted; the system automatically translates relative URLs into absolute ones before putting them in the Location header.

Setting a status code does not necessarily mean that you don't need to return a document. For example, although most servers automatically generate a small "File Not Found" message for 404 responses, a servlet might want to customize this response. Again, remember that if you do send output, you have to call setStatus or sendError *first*.

HTTP 1.1 Status Codes

In this subsection we describe the most important status codes available for use in servlets talking to HTTP 1.1 clients, along with the standard message associated with each code. A good understanding of these codes can dramatically increase the capabilities of your servlets, so you should at least skim the descriptions to see what options are at your disposal. You can come back for details when you are ready to make use of some of the capabilities.

The complete HTTP 1.1 specification is given in RFC 2616, which you can access on-line by going to http://www.rfc-editor.org/ and following the links to the latest RFC archive sites. Codes that are new in HTTP 1.1 are noted, since some browsers support only HTTP 1.0. You should only send the new codes to clients that support HTTP 1.1, as verified by checking request.getRequestProtocol.

The rest of this section describes the specific status codes available in HTTP 1.1. These codes fall into five general categories:

- **100–199**
  Codes in the 100s are informational, indicating that the client should respond with some other action.
- **200–299**
  Values in the 200s signify that the request was successful.
- **300–399**
  Values in the 300s are used for files that have moved and usually include a `Location` header indicating the new address.
- **400–499**
  Values in the 400s indicate an error by the client.
- **500–599**
  Codes in the 500s signify an error by the server.

The constants in `HttpServletResponse` that represent the various codes are derived from the standard messages associated with the codes. In servlets, you usually refer to status codes only by means of these constants. For example, you would use `response.setStatus(response.SC_NO_CONTENT)` rather than `response.setStatus(204)`, since the latter is unclear to readers and is prone to typographical errors. However, you should note that servers are allowed to vary the messages slightly, and clients pay attention only to the numeric value. So, for example, you might see a server return a status line of `HTTP/1.1 200 Document Follows` instead of `HTTP/1.1 200 OK`.

100 (Continue)

If the server receives an `Expect` request header with a value of `100-continue`, it means that the client is asking if it can send an attached document in a follow-up request. In such a case, the server should either respond with status 100 (`SC_CONTINUE`) to tell the client to go ahead or use 417 (`Expectation Failed`) to tell the browser it won't accept the document. This status code is new in HTTP 1.1.

200 (OK)

A value of 200 (`SC_OK`) means that everything is fine. The document follows for `GET` and `POST` requests. This status is the default for servlets; if you don't use `setStatus`, you'll get 200.

201 (Created)

A status code of 201 (`SC_CREATED`) signifies that the server created a new document in response to the request; the `Location` header should give its URL.

202 (Accepted)

A value of 202 (SC_ACCEPTED) tells the client that the request is being acted upon, but processing is not yet complete.

204 (No Content)

A status code of 204 (SC_NO_CONTENT) stipulates that the browser should continue to display the previous document because no new document is available. This behavior is useful if the user periodically reloads a page by pressing the Reload button, and you can determine that the previous page is already up-to-date.

205 (Reset Content)

A value of 205 (SC_RESET_CONTENT) means that there is no new document, but the browser should reset the document view. This status code is used to force browsers to clear form fields. It is new in HTTP 1.1.

301 (Moved Permanently)

The 301 (SC_MOVED_PERMANENTLY) status indicates that the requested document is elsewhere; the new URL for the document is given in the Location response header. Browsers should automatically follow the link to the new URL.

302 (Found)

This value is similar to 301, except that in principle the URL given by the Location header should be interpreted as a temporary replacement, not a permanent one. In practice, most browsers treat 301 and 302 identically. Note: in HTTP 1.0, the message was Moved Temporarily instead of Found, and the constant in HttpServletResponse is SC_MOVED_TEMPORARILY, not the expected SC_FOUND.

Core Note

The constant representing 302 is SC_MOVED_TEMPORARILY, not SC_FOUND.

Status code 302 is useful because browsers automatically follow the reference to the new URL given in the Location response header. It is so useful, in fact, that there is a special method for it, sendRedirect. Using response.sendRedirect(url) has a couple of advantages over using response.setStatus(response.SC_MOVED_TEMPORARILY) and response.setHeader("Location", url). First, it is shorter and easier.

Second, with `sendRedirect`, the servlet automatically builds a page containing the link to show to older browsers that don't automatically follow redirects. Finally, with version 2.2 of servlets (the version in J2EE), `sendRedirect` can handle relative URLs, automatically translating them into absolute ones.

Technically, browsers are only supposed to automatically follow the redirection if the original request was `GET`. For details, see the discussion of the 307 status code.

303 (See Other)

The 303 (`SC_SEE_OTHER`) status is similar to 301 and 302, except that if the original request was `POST`, the new document (given in the `Location` header) should be retrieved with `GET`. This code is new in HTTP 1.1.

304 (Not Modified)

When a client has a cached document, it can perform a conditional request by supplying an `If-Modified-Since` header to indicate that it only wants the document if it has been changed since the specified date. A value of 304 (`SC_NOT_MODIFIED`) means that the cached version is up-to-date and the client should use it. Otherwise, the server should return the requested document with the normal (200) status code. Servlets normally should not set this status code directly. Instead, they should implement the `getLastModified` method and let the default `service` method handle conditional requests based upon this modification date.

307 (Temporary Redirect)

The rules for how a browser should handle a 307 status are identical to those for 302. The 307 value was added to HTTP 1.1 since many browsers erroneously follow the redirection on a 302 response even if the original message is a `POST`. Browsers are supposed to follow the redirection of a `POST` request only when they receive a 303 response status. This new status is intended to be unambiguously clear: follow redirected `GET` *and* `POST` requests in the case of 303 responses; follow redirected `GET` but *not* `POST` requests in the case of 307 responses. Note: For some reason there is no constant in `HttpServlet-Response` corresponding to this status code, so you have to use 307 explicitly. This status code is new in HTTP 1.1.

400 (Bad Request)

A 400 (`SC_BAD_REQUEST`) status indicates bad syntax in the client request.

401 (Unauthorized)

A value of 401 (`SC_UNAUTHORIZED`) signifies that the client tried to access a password-protected page without proper identifying information in the `Authorization` header. The response must include a `WWW-Authenticate` header.

403 (Forbidden)

A status code of 403 (`SC_FORBIDDEN`) means that the server refuses to supply the resource, regardless of authorization. This status is often the result of bad file or directory permissions on the server.

404 (Not Found)

The infamous 404 (`SC_NOT_FOUND`) status tells the client that no resource could be found at that address. This value is the standard "no such page" response. It is such a common and useful response that there is a special method for it in the `HttpServletResponse` class: `send-Error("message")`. The advantage of `sendError` over `setStatus` is that, with `sendError`, the server automatically generates an error page showing the error message. Unfortunately, however, the default behavior of Internet Explorer 5 is to ignore the error page you send back and to display its own, even though doing so contradicts the HTTP specification. To turn off this setting, you can go to the Tools menu, select Internet Options, choose the Advanced tab, and make sure "Show friendly HTTP error messages" box is not checked. Unfortunately, however, few users are aware of this setting, so this "feature" prevents most users of Internet Explorer version 5 from seeing any informative messages you return. Other major browsers and version 4 of Internet Explorer properly display server-generated error pages.

Core Warning

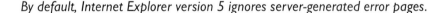

By default, Internet Explorer version 5 ignores server-generated error pages.

405 (Method Not Allowed)

A 405 (`SC_METHOD_NOT_ALLOWED`) value indicates that the request method (`GET`, `POST`, `HEAD`, `PUT`, `DELETE`, etc.) was not allowed for this particular resource. This status code is new in HTTP 1.1.

410 (Gone)

A value of 410 (`SC_GONE`) tells the client that the requested document is gone and no forwarding address is known. Status 410 differs from 404 in that the document is known to be permanently gone, not just unavailable for unknown reasons, as with 404. This status code is new in HTTP 1.1.

411 (Length Required)

A status of 411 (SC_LENGTH_REQUIRED) signifies that the server cannot process the request (presumably a POST request with an attached document) unless the client sends a Content-Length header indicating the amount of data being sent to the server. This value is new in HTTP 1.1.

413 (Request Entity Too Large)

A status code of 413 (SC_REQUEST_ENTITY_TOO_LARGE) tells the client that the requested document is bigger than the server wants to handle. If the server thinks it can handle the request later, it should include a Retry-After response header. This value is new in HTTP 1.1.

414 (Request URI Too Long)

The 414 (SC_REQUEST_URI_TOO_LONG) status is used when the URI is too long. In this context, "URI" means the part of the URL that came after the host and port in the URL. For example, in http://www.y2k-disaster.com: 8080/we/look/silly/now/, the URI is /we/look/silly/now/. This status code is new in HTTP 1.1.

415 (Unsupported Media Type)

A value of 415 (SC_UNSUPPORTED_MEDIA_TYPE) means that the request had an attached document of a type the server doesn't know how to handle. This status code is new in HTTP 1.1.

417 (Expectation Failed)

If the server receives an Expect request header with a value of 100-continue, it means that the client is asking if it can send an attached document in a follow-up request. In such a case, the server should either respond with this status (417) to tell the browser it won't accept the document or use 100 (SC_CONTINUE) to tell the client to go ahead. This status code is new in HTTP 1.1.

500 (Internal Server Error)

500 (SC_INTERNAL_SERVER_ERROR) is the generic "server is confused" status code. It often results from CGI programs or (heaven forbid!) servlets that crash or return improperly formatted headers.

501 (Not Implemented)

The 501 (`SC_NOT_IMPLEMENTED`) status notifies the client that the server doesn't support the functionality to fulfill the request. It is used, for example, when the client issues a command like `PUT` that the server doesn't support.

503 (Service Unavailable)

A status code of 503 (`SC_SERVICE_UNAVAILABLE`) signifies that the server cannot respond because of maintenance or overloading. For example, a servlet might return this header if some thread or database connection pool is currently full. The server can supply a `Retry-After` header to tell the client when to try again.

505 (HTTP Version Not Supported)

The 505 (`SC_HTTP_VERSION_NOT_SUPPORTED`) code means that the server doesn't support the version of HTTP named in the request line. This status code is new in HTTP 1.1.

A Front End to Various Search Engines

Listing 19.14 presents an example that makes use of the two most common status codes other than 200 (OK): 302 (Found) and 404 (Not Found). The 302 code is set by the shorthand `sendRedirect` method of `HttpServletResponse`, and 404 is specified by `sendError`.

In this application, an HTML form (see Figure 19–9 and the source code in Listing 19.16) first displays a page that lets the user choose a search string, the number of results to show per page, and the search engine to use. When the form is submitted, the servlet extracts those three parameters, constructs a URL with the parameters embedded in a way appropriate to the search engine selected (see the `SearchSpec` class of Listing 19.15), and redirects the user to that URL (see Figure 19–10). If the user fails to choose a search engine or specify search terms, an error page informs the client of this fact (but see warning under the 404 status code in the previous subsection).

Listing 19.14 `SearchEngines.java`

```
package cwp;

import java.io.*;
import javax.servlet.*;
import javax.servlet.http.*;
import java.net.*;
```

(continued)

Listing 19.14 `SearchEngines.java` *(continued)*

```
/** Servlet that takes a search string, number of results per
 *  page, and a search engine name, sending the query to
 *  that search engine. Illustrates manipulating
 *  the response status line. It sends a 302 response
 *  (via sendRedirect) if it gets a known search engine,
 *  and sends a 404 response (via sendError) otherwise.
 */

public class SearchEngines extends HttpServlet {
  public void doGet(HttpServletRequest request,
                    HttpServletResponse response)
      throws ServletException, IOException {
    String searchString = request.getParameter("searchString");
    if ((searchString == null) ||
        (searchString.length() == 0)) {
      reportProblem(response, "Missing search string.");
      return;
    }
    // The URLEncoder changes spaces to "+" signs and other
    // non-alphanumeric characters to "%XY", where XY is the
    // hex value of the ASCII (or ISO Latin-1) character.
    // Browsers always URL-encode form values, so the
    // getParameter method decodes automatically. But since
    // we're just passing this on to another server, we need to
    // re-encode it.
    searchString = URLEncoder.encode(searchString);
    String numResults = request.getParameter("numResults");
    if ((numResults == null) ||
        (numResults.equals("0")) ||
        (numResults.length() == 0)) {
      numResults = "10";
    }
    String searchEngine =
      request.getParameter("searchEngine");
    if (searchEngine == null) {
      reportProblem(response, "Missing search engine name.");
      return;
    }
    SearchSpec[] commonSpecs = SearchSpec.getCommonSpecs();
    for(int i=0; i<commonSpecs.length; i++) {
      SearchSpec searchSpec = commonSpecs[i];
      if (searchSpec.getName().equals(searchEngine)) {
        String url =
          searchSpec.makeURL(searchString, numResults);
```

(continued)

Listing 19.14 `SearchEngines.java` *(continued)*

```java
        response.sendRedirect(url);
        return;
      }
    }
    reportProblem(response, "Unrecognized search engine.");
  }

  private void reportProblem(HttpServletResponse response,
                             String message)
      throws IOException {
    response.sendError(response.SC_NOT_FOUND,
                       "<H2>" + message + "</H2>");
  }

  public void doPost(HttpServletRequest request,
                     HttpServletResponse response)
      throws ServletException, IOException {
    doGet(request, response);
  }
}
```

Listing 19.15 `SearchSpec.java`

```java
package cwp;

/** Small class that encapsulates how to construct a
 *  search string for a particular search engine.
 */

public class SearchSpec {
  private String name, baseURL, numResultsSuffix;

  private static SearchSpec[] commonSpecs =
    { new SearchSpec("google",
                     "http://www.google.com/search?q=",
                     "&num="),
      new SearchSpec("infoseek",
                     "http://infoseek.go.com/Titles?qt=",
                     "&nh="),
      new SearchSpec("lycos",
                     "http://lycospro.lycos.com/cgi-bin/" +
                        "pursuit?query=",
                     "&maxhits="),
```

(continued)

Listing 19.15 `SearchSpec.java`

```java
      new SearchSpec("hotbot",
                     "http://www.hotbot.com/?MT=",
                     "&DC=")
   };

  public SearchSpec(String name,
                    String baseURL,
                    String numResultsSuffix) {
    this.name = name;
    this.baseURL = baseURL;
    this.numResultsSuffix = numResultsSuffix;
  }

  public String makeURL(String searchString,
                        String numResults) {
    return(baseURL + searchString +
           numResultsSuffix + numResults);
  }

  public String getName() {
    return(name);
  }

  public static SearchSpec[] getCommonSpecs() {
    return(commonSpecs);
  }
}
```

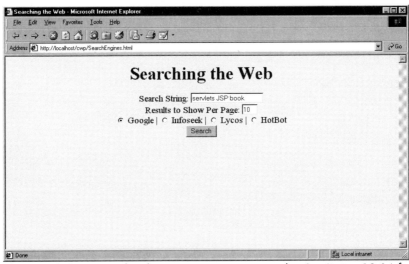

Figure 19–9 Front end to the `SearchEngines` servlet. See Listing 19.16 for the HTML source code.

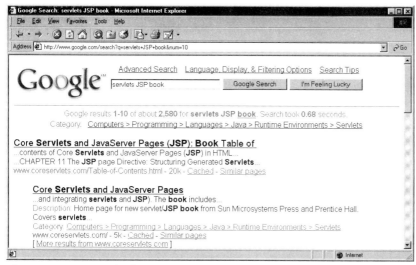

Figure 19-10 Result of the SearchEngines servlet when the form of Figure 19-9 is submitted.

Listing 19.16 SearchEngines.html

```
<!DOCTYPE HTML PUBLIC "-//W3C//DTD HTML 4.0 Transitional//EN">
<HTML>
<HEAD>
  <TITLE>Searching the Web</TITLE>
</HEAD>

<BODY BGCOLOR="#FDF5E6">
<H1 ALIGN="CENTER">Searching the Web</H1>

<FORM ACTION="/servlet/cwp.SearchEngines">
  <CENTER>
    Search String:
    <INPUT TYPE="TEXT" NAME="searchString"><BR>
    Results to Show Per Page:
    <INPUT TYPE="TEXT" NAME="numResults"
                      VALUE=10 SIZE=3><BR>
    <INPUT TYPE="RADIO" NAME="searchEngine"
                      VALUE="google">
    Google |
    <INPUT TYPE="RADIO" NAME="searchEngine"
                      VALUE="infoseek">
```

(continued)

Listing 19.16 `SearchEngines.html` *(continued)*

```
      Infoseek |
      <INPUT TYPE="RADIO"  NAME="searchEngine"
                           VALUE="lycos">
      Lycos |
      <INPUT TYPE="RADIO"  NAME="searchEngine"
                           VALUE="hotbot">
      HotBot
      <BR>
      <INPUT TYPE="SUBMIT" VALUE="Search">
    </CENTER>
  </FORM>

  </BODY>
  </HTML>
```

19.10 The Server Response: HTTP Response Headers

As discussed in the previous section, a response from a Web server normally consists of a status line, one or more response headers, a blank line, and the document. To get the most out of your servlets, you need to know how to use the status line and response headers effectively, not just how to generate the document.

Setting the HTTP response headers often goes hand in hand with setting the status codes in the status line, as discussed in the previous section. For example, all the "document moved" status codes (300 through 307) have an accompanying `Location` header, and a 401 (`Unauthorized`) code always includes an accompanying `WWW-Authenticate` header. However, specifying headers can also play a useful role even when no unusual status code is set. Response headers can be used to specify cookies, to supply the page modification date (for client-side caching), to instruct the browser to reload the page after a designated interval, to give the file size so that persistent HTTP connections can be used, to designate the type of document being generated, and to perform many other tasks.

Setting Response Headers from Servlets

The most general way to specify headers is to use the `setHeader` method of `HttpServletResponse`. This method takes two strings: the header name and the header value. As with setting status codes, you must specify headers *before* returning the actual document.

In addition to the general-purpose `setHeader` method, `HttpServlet-Response` also has two specialized methods to set headers that contain dates and integers:

- **`setDateHeader(String header, long milliseconds)`**
  This method saves you the trouble of translating a Java date in milliseconds since 1970 (as returned by `System.currentTimeMillis`, `Date.getTime`, or `Calendar.getTimeInMillis`) into a GMT time string.

- **`setIntHeader(String header, int headerValue)`**
  This method spares you the minor inconvenience of converting an `int` to a `String` before inserting it into a header.

HTTP allows multiple occurrences of the same header name, and you sometimes want to add a new header rather than replace any existing header with the same name. For example, it is quite common to have multiple `Accept` and `Set-Cookie` headers that specify different supported MIME types and different cookies, respectively. With servlets version 2.1, `setHeader`, `setDateHeader` and `setInt-Header`, always *add* new headers, so there is no way to "unset" headers that were set earlier (e.g., by an inherited method). With servlets version 2.2, `setHeader`, `set-DateHeader`, and `setIntHeader` *replace* any existing headers of the same name, whereas `addHeader`, `addDateHeader`, and `addIntHeader` add a header regardless of whether a header of that name already exists. If it matters to you whether a specific header has already been set, use `containsHeader` to check.

Finally, `HttpServletResponse` also supplies a number of convenience methods for specifying common headers. These methods are summarized as follows.

- **`setContentType`**
  This method sets the `Content-Type` header and is used by the majority of servlets.

- **`setContentLength`**
  This method sets the `Content-Length` header, which is useful if the browser supports persistent (keep-alive) HTTP connections.

- **`addCookie`**
  This method inserts a cookie into the `Set-Cookie` header. There is no corresponding `setCookie` method, since it is normal to have multiple `Set-Cookie` lines. See Section 19.11 (Cookies) for a discussion of cookies.

- **`sendRedirect`**
  As discussed in the previous section, the `sendRedirect` method sets the `Location` header as well as setting the status code to 302. See Listing 19.14 for an example.

HTTP 1.1 Response Headers

Following is a summary of the most useful HTTP 1.1 response headers. A good understanding of these headers can increase the effectiveness of your servlets, so you should at least skim the descriptions to see what options are at your disposal. You can come back for details when you are ready to use the capabilities.

These headers are a superset of those permitted in HTTP 1.0. For additional details on these headers, see the HTTP 1.1 specification, given in RFC 2616. The official RFCs are on-line in various places; your best bet is to start at `http://www.rfc-editor.org/` to get a current list of the archive sites. Header names are not case sensitive but are traditionally written with the first letter of each word capitalized.

Be cautious in writing servlets whose behavior depends on response headers that are only available in HTTP 1.1, especially if your servlet needs to run on the WWW "at large," rather than on an intranet—many older browsers support only HTTP 1.0. It is best to explicitly check the HTTP version with `request.getRequest-Protocol` before using new headers.

Allow

The `Allow` header specifies the request methods (`GET`, `POST`, etc.) that the server supports. It is required for 405 (`Method Not Allowed`) responses. The default `service` method of servlets automatically generates this header for `OPTIONS` requests.

Cache-Control

This useful header tells the browser or other client the circumstances in which the response document can safely be cached. It has the following possible values:

- `public`: Document is cacheable, even if normal rules (e.g., for password-protected pages) indicate that it shouldn't be.
- `private`: Document is for a single user and can only be stored in private (nonshared) caches.
- `no-cache`: Document should never be cached (i.e., used to satisfy a later request). The server can also specify "`no-cache="header1,header2,...,headerN"`" to indicate the headers that should be omitted if a cached response is later used. Browsers normally do not cache documents that were retrieved by requests that include form data. However, if a servlet generates different content for different requests even when the requests contain no form data, it is critical to tell the browser not to cache the response. Since older browsers use the `Pragma` header for this purpose, the typical servlet approach is to set *both* headers, as in the following example.

```
response.setHeader("Cache-Control", "no-cache");
response.setHeader("Pragma", "no-cache");
```

- no-store: Document should never be cached and should not even be stored in a temporary location on disk. This header is intended to prevent inadvertent copies of sensitive information.
- must-revalidate: Client must revalidate document with original server (not just intermediate proxies) each time it is used.
- proxy-revalidate: This is the same as must-revalidate, except that it applies only to shared caches.
- max-age=*xxx*: Document should be considered stale after *xxx* seconds. This is a convenient alternative to the Expires header but only works with HTTP 1.1 clients. If both max-age and Expires are present in the response, the max-age value takes precedence.
- s-max-age=*xxx*: Shared caches should consider the document stale after *xxx* seconds.

The Cache-Control header is new in HTTP 1.1.

Connection

A value of close for this response header instructs the browser not to use persistent HTTP connections. Technically, persistent connections are the default when the client supports HTTP 1.1 and does *not* specify a "Connection: close" request header (or when an HTTP 1.0 client specifies "Connection: keep-alive"). However, since persistent connections require a Content-Length response header, there is no reason for a servlet to explicitly use the Connection header. Just omit the Content-Length header if you aren't using persistent connections.

Content-Encoding

This header indicates the way in which the page was encoded during transmission. The browser should reverse the encoding before deciding what to do with the document. Compressing the document with gzip can result in huge savings in transmission time; for an example, see Section 19.7 (The Client Request: HTTP Request Headers).

Content-Language

The Content-Language header signifies the language in which the document is written. The value of the header should be one of the standard language codes such as en, en-us, da, etc. See RFC 1766 for details (you can access RFCs on-line at one of the archive sites listed at http://www.rfc-editor.org/).

Content-Length

This header indicates the number of bytes in the response. This information is needed only if the browser is using a persistent (keep-alive) HTTP connection. See the `Connection` header for determining when the browser supports persistent connections. If you want your servlet to take advantage of persistent connections when the browser supports it, your servlet should write the document into a `ByteArrayOutputStream`, look up its size when done, put that into the `Content-Length` field with `response.setContentLength`, then send the content by `byteArrayStream.writeTo(response.getOutputStream())`.

Content-Type

The `Content-Type` header gives the MIME (Multipurpose Internet Mail Extension) type of the response document. Setting this header is so common that there is a special method in `HttpServletResponse` for it: `setContentType`. MIME types are of the form `maintype/subtype` for officially registered types, and of the form `maintype/x-subtype` for unregistered types. The default MIME type for servlets is `text/plain`, but servlets usually explicitly specify `text/html`. They can, however, specify other types instead.

Table 19.1 lists some the most common MIME types used by servlets.

For more detail, many of the common MIME types are listed in RFC 1521 and RFC 1522 (again, see `http://www.rfc-editor.org/` for a list of RFC archive sites). However, new MIME types are registered all the time, so a dynamic list is a better place to look. The officially registered types are listed at `http://www.isi.edu/in-notes/iana/assignments/media-types/media-types`. For common unregistered types, `http://www.ltsw.se/knbase/internet/mime.htp` is a good source.

Table 19.1 Common MIME Types

Type	*Meaning*
application/msword	Microsoft Word document
application/octet-stream	Unrecognized or binary data
application/pdf	Acrobat (.pdf) file
application/postscript	PostScript file
application/vnd.lotus-notes	Lotus Notes file

(continued)

Table 19.1 Common MIME Types *(continued)*

application/vnd.ms-excel	Excel spreadsheet
application/vnd.ms-powerpoint	PowerPoint presentation
application/x-gzip	Gzip archive
application/x-java-archive	JAR file
application/x-java-serialized-object	Serialized Java object
application/x-java-vm	Java bytecode (.class) file
application/zip	Zip archive
audio/basic	Sound file in .au or .snd format
audio/x-aiff	AIFF sound file
audio/x-wav	Microsoft Windows sound file
audio/midi	MIDI sound file
text/css	HTML cascading style sheet
text/html	HTML document
text/plain	Plain text
image/gif	GIF image
image/jpeg	JPEG image
image/png	PNG image
image/tiff	TIFF image
image/x-xbitmap	X Windows bitmap image
video/mpeg	MPEG video clip
video/quicktime	QuickTime video clip

Expires

This header stipulates the time at which the content should be considered out-of-date and thus no longer be cached. A servlet might use this for a document that changes relatively frequently, to prevent the browser from displaying a stale cached value. For example, the following would instruct the browser not to cache the document for longer than 10 minutes.

```
long currentTime = System.currentTimeMillis();
long tenMinutes = 10*60*1000; // In milliseconds
response.setDateHeader("Expires",
                       currentTime + tenMinutes);
```

Also see the max-age value of the Cache-Control header.

Last-Modified

This very useful header indicates when the document was last changed. The client can then cache the document and supply a date by an If-Modified-Since request header in later requests. This request is treated as a conditional GET, with the document being returned only if the Last-Modified date is later than the one specified for If-Modified-Since. Otherwise, a 304 (Not Modified) status line is returned, and the client uses the cached document. If you set this header explicitly, use the setDateHeader method to save yourself the bother of formatting GMT date strings. However, in most cases you simply implement the getLastModified method and let the standard service method handle If-Modified-Since requests.

Location

This header, which should be included with all responses that have a status code in the 300s, notifies the browser of the document address. The browser automatically reconnects to this location and retrieves the new document. This header is usually set indirectly, along with a 302 status code, by the sendRedirect method of HttpServletResponse. An example is given in the previous section.

Pragma

Supplying this header with a value of no-cache instructs HTTP 1.0 clients not to cache the document. However, support for this header was inconsistent with HTTP 1.0 browsers. In HTTP 1.1, "Cache-Control: no-cache" is a more reliable replacement.

Refresh

This header indicates how soon (in seconds) the browser should ask for an updated page. For example, to tell the browser to ask for a new copy in 30 seconds, you would specify a value of 30 with

```
response.setIntHeader("Refresh", 30)
```

Note that Refresh does not stipulate continual updates; it just specifies when the *next* update should be. So, you have to continue to supply Refresh in all subsequent responses, and sending a 204 (No Content) status code stops the browser from reloading further. For an example, see the following subsection.

Instead of having the browser just reload the current page, you can specify the page to load. You do this by supplying a semicolon and a URL after the refresh time. For example, to tell the browser to go to http://host/path after 5 seconds, you would do the following.

```
response.setHeader("Refresh", "5; URL=http://host/path/")
```

This setting is useful for "splash screens," where an introductory image or message is displayed briefly before the real page is loaded.

Note that this header is commonly set indirectly by putting

```
<META HTTP-EQUIV="Refresh"
      CONTENT="5; URL=http://host/path/">
```

in the HEAD section of the HTML page, rather than as an explicit header from the server. That usage came about because automatic reloading or forwarding is something often desired by authors of static HTML pages. For servlets, however, setting the header directly is easier and clearer.

This header is not officially part of HTTP 1.1 but is an extension supported by both Netscape and Internet Explorer.

Retry-After

This header can be used in conjunction with a 503 (Service Unavailable) response to tell the client how soon it can repeat its request.

Set-Cookie

The Set-Cookie header specifies a cookie associated with the page. Each cookie requires a separate Set-Cookie header. Servlets should not use response.setHeader("Set-Cookie", ...) but instead should use the special-purpose addCookie method of HttpServletResponse. For details, see Section 19.11 (Cookies). Technically, Set-Cookie is not part of HTTP 1.1. It was originally a Netscape extension but is now widely supported, including support in both Netscape and Internet Explorer.

WWW-Authenticate

This header is always included with a 401 (Unauthorized) status code. It tells the browser what authorization type and realm the client should supply in its Authorization header. Frequently, servlets let password-protected Web pages be handled by the Web server's specialized mechanisms (e.g., .htaccess or declarative security in J2EE servers) rather than handling them directly.

Persistent Servlet State and Auto-Reloading Pages

Here is an example that lets you ask for a list of some large, randomly chosen prime numbers. This computation may take some time for very large numbers (e.g., 150 digits), so the servlet immediately returns initial results but then keeps calculating, using a low-priority thread so that it won't degrade Web server performance. If the calculations are not complete, the servlet uses the Refresh header to instruct the browser to ask for a new page in a few seconds.

In addition to illustrating the value of HTTP response headers, this example shows two other valuable servlet capabilities. First, it shows that the same servlet can handle multiple simultaneous connections, each with its own thread. So, while one thread is finishing a calculation for one client, another client can connect and still see partial results.

Second, this example shows how easy it is for servlets to maintain state between requests, something that is cumbersome to implement in traditional CGI and many CGI alternatives. Only a single instance of the servlet is created, and each request simply results in a new thread calling the servlet's service method (which calls doGet or doPost). So, shared data simply has to be placed in a regular instance variable (field) of the servlet. Thus, the servlet can access the appropriate ongoing calculation when the browser reloads the page and can keep a list of the N most recently requested results, returning them immediately if a new request specifies the same parameters as a recent one. Of course, the normal rules that require authors to synchronize multithreaded access to shared data still apply to servlets. Servlets can also store persistent data in the ServletContext object that is available through the getServletContext method. ServletContext has setAttribute and getAttribute methods that let you store arbitrary data associated with specified keys. The difference between storing data in instance variables and storing it in the ServletContext is that the ServletContext is shared by all servlets in the servlet engine (or in the Web application, if your server supports such a capability).

Listing 19.17 shows the main servlet class. First, it receives a request that specifies two parameters: numPrimes and numDigits. These values are normally collected from the user and sent to the servlet by means of a simple HTML form. Listing 19.18 shows the source code and Figure 19–11 shows the result. Next, these parameters are converted to integers by means of a simple utility that uses Integer.parseInt (see Listing 19.21). These values are then matched by the findPrimeList method to a Vector of recent or ongoing calculations to see if there is a previous computation corresponding to the same two values. If so, that previous value (of type PrimeList) is used; otherwise, a new PrimeList is created and stored in the ongoing-calculations Vector, potentially displacing the oldest previous list. Next, that PrimeList is checked to determine if it has finished finding all of its primes. If not, the client is sent a Refresh header to tell it to come back in five seconds for updated results. Either way, a list of the current values is returned to the client. Figure 19–12 shows intermediate results; Figure 19–13 shows the final result.

Listings 19.19 (PrimeList.java) and 19.20 (Primes.java) present auxiliary code used by the servlet. PrimeList.java handles the background thread for the creation of a list of primes for a specific set of values. Primes.java contains the low-level algorithms for choosing a random number of a specified length and then finding a prime at or above that value. It uses built-in methods in the BigInteger class for determining if the number is prime.

Listing 19.17 PrimeNumbers.java

```java
package cwp;

import java.io.*;
import javax.servlet.*;
import javax.servlet.http.*;
import java.util.*;

/** Servlet that processes a request to generate n
 *   prime numbers, each with at least m digits.
 *   It performs the calculations in a low-priority background
 *   thread, returning only the results it has found so far.
 *   If these results are not complete, it sends a Refresh
 *   header instructing the browser to ask for new results a
 *   little while later. It also maintains a list of a
 *   small number of previously calculated prime lists
 *   to return immediately to anyone who supplies the
 *   same n and m as a recent completed computation.
 */

public class PrimeNumbers extends HttpServlet {
  private Vector primeListVector = new Vector();
  private int maxPrimeLists = 30;

  public void doGet(HttpServletRequest request,
                    HttpServletResponse response)
      throws ServletException, IOException {
    int numPrimes =
      ServletUtilities.getIntParameter(request,
                                       "numPrimes", 50);
    int numDigits =
      ServletUtilities.getIntParameter(request,
                                       "numDigits", 120);
    PrimeList primeList =
      findPrimeList(primeListVector, numPrimes, numDigits);
```

(continued)

Listing 19.17 `PrimeNumbers.java` *(continued)*

```java
  if (primeList == null) {
    primeList = new PrimeList(numPrimes, numDigits, true);
    // Multiple servlet request threads share the instance
    // variables (fields) of PrimeNumbers. So
    // synchronize all access to servlet fields.
    synchronized(primeListVector) {
      if (primeListVector.size() >= maxPrimeLists)
        primeListVector.removeElementAt(0);
      primeListVector.addElement(primeList);
    }
  }
  Vector currentPrimes = primeList.getPrimes();
  int numCurrentPrimes = currentPrimes.size();
  int numPrimesRemaining = (numPrimes - numCurrentPrimes);
  boolean isLastResult = (numPrimesRemaining == 0);
  if (!isLastResult) {
    response.setHeader("Refresh", "5");
  }
  response.setContentType("text/html");
  PrintWriter out = response.getWriter();
  String title = "Some " + numDigits + "-Digit Prime Numbers";
  out.println(ServletUtilities.headWithTitle(title) +
              "<BODY BGCOLOR=\"#FDF5E6\">\n" +
              "<H2 ALIGN=CENTER>" + title + "</H2>\n" +
              "<H3>Primes found with " + numDigits +
              " or more digits: " + numCurrentPrimes +
              ".</H3>");
  if (isLastResult)
    out.println("<B>Done searching.</B>");
  else
    out.println("<B>Still looking for " + numPrimesRemaining +
                " more<BLINK>...</BLINK></B>");
  out.println("<OL>");
  for(int i=0; i<numCurrentPrimes; i++) {
    out.println("  <LI>" + currentPrimes.elementAt(i));
  }
  out.println("</OL>");
  out.println("</BODY></HTML>");
}

public void doPost(HttpServletRequest request,
                   HttpServletResponse response)
    throws ServletException, IOException {
  doGet(request, response);
}
```

(continued)

Listing 19.17 `PrimeNumbers.java` *(continued)*

```java
// See if there is an existing ongoing or completed
// calculation with the same number of primes and number
// of digits per prime. If so, return those results instead
// of starting a new background thread. Keep this list
// small so that the Web server doesn't use too much memory.
// Synchronize access to the list since there may be
// multiple simultaneous requests.

private PrimeList findPrimeList(Vector primeListVector,
                                int numPrimes,
                                int numDigits) {
  synchronized(primeListVector) {
    for(int i=0; i<primeListVector.size(); i++) {
      PrimeList primes =
        (PrimeList)primeListVector.elementAt(i);
      if ((numPrimes == primes.numPrimes()) &&
          (numDigits == primes.numDigits()))
        return(primes);
    }
    return(null);
  }
}
}
```

Listing 19.18 `PrimeNumbers.html`

```html
<!DOCTYPE HTML PUBLIC "-//W3C//DTD HTML 4.0 Transitional//EN">
<HTML>
<HEAD>
  <TITLE>Finding Large Prime Numbers</TITLE>
</HEAD>

<BODY BGCOLOR="#FDF5E6">
<H2 ALIGN="CENTER">Finding Large Prime Numbers</H2>
<BR><BR>
<CENTER>
<FORM ACTION="/servlet/cwp.PrimeNumbers">
  <B>Number of primes to calculate:</B>
  <INPUT TYPE="TEXT" NAME="numPrimes" VALUE=25 SIZE=4><BR>
  <B>Number of digits:</B>
  <INPUT TYPE="TEXT" NAME="numDigits" VALUE=150 SIZE=3><BR>
  <INPUT TYPE="SUBMIT" VALUE="Start Calculating">
</FORM>
</CENTER>
</BODY>
</HTML>
```

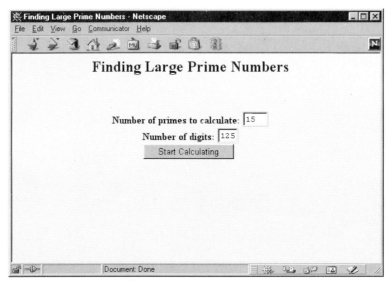

Figure 19-11 Result of `PrimeNumbers.html`, used as a front end to the `PrimeNumbers` servlet.

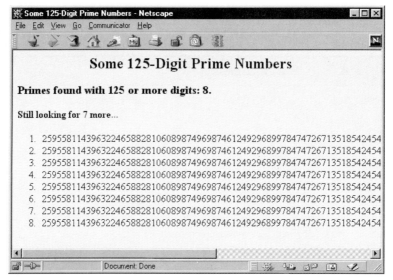

Figure 19-12 Intermediate result of a request to the `PrimeNumbers` servlet. This result can be obtained when the browser reloads automatically or when a different client independently enters the same parameters as those from an ongoing or recent request. Either way, the browser will automatically reload the page to get updated results.

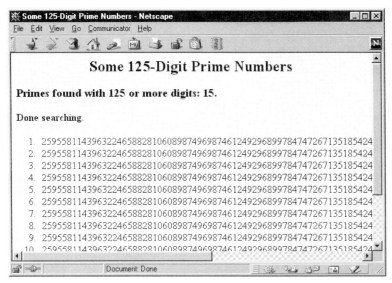

Figure 19–13 Final result of a request to the `PrimeNumbers` servlet. This result can be obtained when the browser reloads automatically or when a different client independently enters the same parameters as those from an ongoing or recent request. The browser will stop updating the page at this point.

Listing 19.19 `PrimeList.java`

```java
package cwp;

import java.util.*;
import java.math.BigInteger;

/** Creates a Vector of large prime numbers, usually in
 *  a low-priority background thread. Provides a few small
 *  thread-safe access methods.
 */

public class PrimeList implements Runnable {
  private Vector primesFound;
  private int numPrimes, numDigits;

  /** Finds numPrimes prime numbers, each of which is
   *  numDigits long or longer. You can set it to only
   *  return when done, or have it return immediately,
   *  and you can later poll it to see how far it
   *  has gotten.
   */
```

(continued)

Listing 19.19 PrimeList.java *(continued)*

```java
public PrimeList(int numPrimes, int numDigits,
                 boolean runInBackground) {
  // Using Vector instead of ArrayList
  // to support JDK 1.1 servlet engines
  primesFound = new Vector(numPrimes);
  this.numPrimes = numPrimes;
  this.numDigits = numDigits;
  if (runInBackground) {
    Thread t = new Thread(this);
    // Use low priority so you don't slow down server.
    t.setPriority(Thread.MIN_PRIORITY);
    t.start();
  } else {
    run();
  }
}

public void run() {
  BigInteger start = Primes.random(numDigits);
  for(int i=0; i<numPrimes; i++) {
    start = Primes.nextPrime(start);
    synchronized(this) {
      primesFound.addElement(start);
    }
  }
}

public synchronized boolean isDone() {
  return(primesFound.size() == numPrimes);
}

public synchronized Vector getPrimes() {
  if (isDone())
    return(primesFound);
  else
    return((Vector)primesFound.clone());
}

public int numDigits() {
  return(numDigits);
}

public int numPrimes() {
  return(numPrimes);
}
public synchronized int numCalculatedPrimes() {
  return(primesFound.size());
}
}
```

Listing 19.20 `Primes.java`

```java
package cwp;

import java.math.BigInteger;

/** A few utilities to generate a large random BigInteger,
 *  and find the next prime number above a given BigInteger.
 */

public class Primes {
  // Note that BigInteger.ZERO was new in JDK 1.2, and 1.1
  // code is being used to support the most servlet engines.
  private static final BigInteger ZERO = new BigInteger("0");
  private static final BigInteger ONE = new BigInteger("1");
  private static final BigInteger TWO = new BigInteger("2");

  // Likelihood of false prime is less than 1/2^ERR_VAL
  // Assumedly BigInteger uses the Miller-Rabin test or
  // equivalent, and thus is NOT fooled by Carmichael numbers.
  // See section 33.8 of Cormen et al. Introduction to
  // Algorithms for details.
  private static final int ERR_VAL = 100;

  public static BigInteger nextPrime(BigInteger start) {
    if (isEven(start))
      start = start.add(ONE);
    else
      start = start.add(TWO);
    if (start.isProbablePrime(ERR_VAL))
      return(start);
    else
      return(nextPrime(start));
  }

  private static boolean isEven(BigInteger n) {
    return(n.mod(TWO).equals(ZERO));
  }

  private static StringBuffer[] digits =
    { new StringBuffer("0"), new StringBuffer("1"),
      new StringBuffer("2"), new StringBuffer("3"),
      new StringBuffer("4"), new StringBuffer("5"),
      new StringBuffer("6"), new StringBuffer("7"),
      new StringBuffer("8"), new StringBuffer("9") };
```

(continued)

Listing 19.20 `Primes.java` *(continued)*

```java
private static StringBuffer randomDigit() {
  int index = (int)Math.floor(Math.random() * 10);
  return(digits[index]);
}

public static BigInteger random(int numDigits) {
  StringBuffer s = new StringBuffer("");
  for(int i=0; i<numDigits; i++) {
    s.append(randomDigit());
  }
  return(new BigInteger(s.toString()));
}

/** Simple command-line program to test. Enter number
 *  of digits, and it picks a random number of that
 *  length and then prints the first 50 prime numbers
 *  above that.
 */

public static void main(String[] args) {
  int numDigits;
  if (args.length > 0)
    numDigits = Integer.parseInt(args[0]);
  else
    numDigits = 150;
  BigInteger start = random(numDigits);
  for(int i=0; i<50; i++) {
    start = nextPrime(start);
    System.out.println("Prime " + i + " = " + start);
  }
}
}
```

Listing 19.21 `ServletUtilities.java`

```java
package cwp;

import javax.servlet.*;
import javax.servlet.http.*;

public class ServletUtilities {
  // Other methods shown earlier

  /** Read a parameter with the specified name, convert it
   *  to an int, and return it. Return the designated default
   *  value if the parameter doesn't exist or if it is an
   *  illegal integer format.
   */

  public static int getIntParameter(HttpServletRequest request,
                                    String paramName,
                                    int defaultValue) {
    String paramString = request.getParameter(paramName);
    int paramValue;
    try {
      paramValue = Integer.parseInt(paramString);
    } catch(NumberFormatException nfe) { // null or bad format
      paramValue = defaultValue;
    }
    return(paramValue);
  }
}
```

19.11 Cookies

Cookies are small bits of textual information that a Web server sends to a browser and that the browser returns unchanged when later visiting the same Web site or domain. By letting the server read information it sent the client previously, the site can provide visitors with a number of conveniences such as presenting the site the way the visitor previously customized it or letting identifiable visitors in without their having to enter a password. Most browsers avoid caching documents associated with cookies, so the site can return different content each time.

This section discusses how to explicitly set and read cookies from within servlets, and the next section shows how to use the servlet session tracking API (which can use cookies behind the scenes) to keep track of users as they move around to different pages within your site.

Benefits of Cookies

There are four typical ways in which cookies can add value to your site.

Identifying a User During an E-commerce Session

Many on-line stores use a "shopping cart" metaphor in which the user selects an item, adds it to his shopping cart, then continues shopping. Since the HTTP connection is usually closed after each page is sent, when the user selects a new item to add to the cart, how does the store know that it is the same user who put the previous item in the cart? Persistent (keep-alive) HTTP connections do not solve this problem, since persistent connections generally apply only to requests made very close together in time, as when a browser asks for the images associated with a Web page. Besides, many servers and browsers lack support for persistent connections. Cookies, however, *can* solve this problem. In fact, this capability is so useful that servlets have an API specifically for session tracking, and servlet authors don't need to manipulate cookies directly to take advantage of it. Session tracking is discussed in Section 19.12.

Avoiding Username and Password

Many large sites require you to register to use their services, but it is inconvenient to remember and enter the username and password each time you visit. Cookies are a good alternative for low-security sites. When a user registers, a cookie containing a unique user ID is sent to him. When the client reconnects at a later date, the user ID is returned, the server looks it up, determines it belongs to a registered user, and permits access without an explicit username and password. The site may also remember the user's address, credit card number, and so forth, thus simplifying later transactions.

Customizing a Site

Many "portal" sites let you customize the look of the main page. They might let you pick which weather report you want to see, what stock and sports results you care about, how search results should be displayed, and so forth. Since it would be inconvenient for you to have to set up your page each time you visit their site, they use cookies to remember what you wanted. For simple settings, this customization could be accomplished by storing the page settings directly in the cookies. For more complex customization, however, the site just sends the client a unique identifier and keeps a server-side database that associates identifiers with page settings.

Focusing Advertising

Most advertiser-funded Web sites charge their advertisers much more for displaying "directed" ads than "random" ads. Advertisers are generally willing to pay much more to have their ads shown to people that are known to have some interest in the general product category. For example, if you go to a search engine and do a search on "Java Servlets," the search site can charge an advertiser much more for showing you an ad for a servlet development environment than for an ad for an on-line travel agent specializing in Indonesia. On the other hand, if the search had been for "Java Hotels," the situation would be reversed. Without cookies, the sites have to show a random ad when you first arrive and haven't yet performed a search, as well as when you search on something that doesn't match any ad categories.

Some Problems with Cookies

Providing convenience to the user and added value to the site owner is the purpose behind cookies. And despite much misinformation, cookies are not a serious security threat. Cookies are never interpreted or executed in any way and thus cannot be used to insert viruses or attack your system. Furthermore, since browsers generally only accept 20 cookies per site and 300 cookies total and since each cookie can be limited to 4 kilobytes, cookies cannot be used to fill up someone's disk or launch other denial-of-service attacks.

However, even though cookies don't present a serious *security* threat, they can present a significant threat to *privacy*. First, some people don't like the fact that search engines can remember that they're the user who usually does searches on certain topics. For example, they might search for job openings or sensitive health data and don't want some banner ad tipping off their coworkers next time they do a search. Even worse, two sites can share data on a user by each loading small images off the same third-party site, where that third party uses cookies and shares the data with both original sites. (Netscape, however, provides a nice feature that lets you refuse cookies from sites other than that to which you connected, but without disabling cookies altogether.) This trick of associating cookies with images can even be exploited via e-mail if you use an HTML-enabled e-mail reader that "supports" cookies and is associated with a browser. Thus, people could send you e-mail that loads images, attach cookies to those images, then identify you (e-mail address and all) if you subsequently visit their Web site. Boo.

A second privacy problem occurs when sites rely on cookies for overly sensitive data. For example, some of the big on-line bookstores use cookies to remember users and let you order without reentering much of your personal information. This is not a particular problem since they don't actually display the full credit card number and only let you send books to an address that was specified when you *did* enter the credit card in full or use the username and password. As a result, someone using your computer (or stealing your cookie file) could do no more harm than sending a big book order to your address, where the order could be refused. However, other companies might not be so careful, and an attacker who gained access to someone's computer or cookie file could get on-line access to valuable personal information. Even worse, incompetent sites might embed credit card or other sensitive information directly in the cookies themselves, rather than using innocuous identifiers that are only linked to real users on the server. This is dangerous, since most users don't view leaving their computer unattended in their office as being tantamount to leaving their credit card sitting on their desk.

The point of this discussion is twofold. First, due to real and perceived privacy problems, some users turn off cookies. So, even when you use cookies to give added value to a site, your site shouldn't *depend* on them. Second, as the author of servlets that use cookies, you should be careful not to use cookies for particularly sensitive information, since this would open users up to risks if somebody accessed their computer or cookie files.

The Servlet Cookie API

To send cookies to the client, a servlet should create one or more cookies with designated names and values with new Cookie(name, value), set any optional attributes with cookie.set*Xxx* (readable later by cookie.get*Xxx*), and insert the cookies into the response headers with response.addCookie(cookie). To read incoming cookies, a servlet should call request.getCookies, which returns an array of Cookie objects corresponding to the cookies the browser has associated with your site (this is a zero-length but non-null array if there are no cookies in the request). In most cases, the servlet loops down this array until it finds the one whose name (getName) matches the name it had in mind, then calls getValue on that Cookie to see the value associated with that name. Each of these topics is discussed in more detail in the following sections.

Creating Cookies

You create a cookie by calling the Cookie constructor, which takes two strings: the cookie name and the cookie value. Neither the name nor the value should contain white space or any of the following characters:

```
[ ] ( ) = , " / ? @ : ;
```

Placing Cookies in the Response Headers

The cookie is inserted into a Set-Cookie HTTP response header by means of the addCookie method of HttpServletResponse. The method is called addCookie, not setCookie, because any previously specified Set-Cookie headers are left alone and a new header is set. Here's an example:

```
Cookie userCookie = new Cookie("user", "uid1234");
userCookie.setMaxAge(60*60*24*365); // 1 year
response.addCookie(userCookie);
```

Reading Cookies from the Client

To send cookies *to* the client, you create a `Cookie`, then use `addCookie` to send a `Set-Cookie` HTTP response header. To read the cookies that come back *from* the client, you call `getCookies` on the `HttpServletRequest`. This call returns an array of `Cookie` objects corresponding to the values that came in on the `Cookie` HTTP request header. If the request contains no cookies, `getCookies` returns `null`. Once you have this array, you typically loop down it, calling `getName` on each `Cookie` until you find one matching the name you have in mind. You then call `getValue` on the matching `Cookie` and finish with some processing specific to the resultant value. This is such a common process that, at the end of this section, we present two utilities that simplify retrieving a cookie or cookie value that matches a designated cookie name.

Cookie Attributes

Before adding the cookie to the outgoing headers, you can set various characteristics of the cookie by using one of the following set*Xxx* methods, where *Xxx* is the name of the attribute you want to specify. Each set*Xxx* method has a corresponding get*Xxx* method to retrieve the attribute value. Except for name and value, the cookie attributes apply only to *outgoing* cookies from the server to the client; they aren't set on cookies that come *from* the browser to the server.

public String getComment()
public void setComment(String comment)
These methods look up or specify a comment associated with the cookie. With version 0 cookies (see the upcoming entry on `getVersion` and `set-Version`), the comment is used purely for informational purposes on the server; it is not sent to the client.

public String getDomain()
public void setDomain(String domainPattern)
These methods get or set the domain to which the cookie applies. Normally, the browser only returns cookies to the same hostname that sent them. You can use `setDomain` method to instruct the browser to return them to other hosts within the same domain. To prevent servers from setting cookies that apply to hosts outside their domain, the domain specified is required to start with a dot (e.g., `.prenhall.com`), and must contain two dots for noncountry domains like `.com`, `.edu`, and `.gov`; and three dots for country domains like `.co.uk` and `.edu.es`. For instance, cookies sent from a servlet at

`bali.vacations.com` would not normally get sent by the browser to pages at `mexico.vacations.com`. If the site wanted this to happen, the servlets could specify `cookie.setDomain(".vacations.com")`.

public int getMaxAge()
public void setMaxAge(int lifetime)

These methods tell how much time (in seconds) should elapse before the cookie expires. A negative value, which is the default, indicates that the cookie will last only for the current session (i.e., until the user quits the browser) and will not be stored on disk. See the `LongLivedCookie` class (Listing 19.25), which defines a subclass of `Cookie` with a maximum age automatically set one year in the future. Specifying a value of 0 instructs the browser to delete the cookie.

public String getName()
public void setName(String cookieName)

This pair of methods gets or sets the name of the cookie. The name and the value are the two pieces you virtually *always* care about. However, since the name is supplied to the `Cookie` constructor, you rarely need to call `setName`. On the other hand, `getName` is used on almost every cookie received on the server. Since the `getCookies` method of `HttpServletRequest` returns an array of `Cookie` objects, it is common to loop down this array, calling `get-Name` until you have a particular name, then to check the value with `getValue`. For an encapsulation of this process, see the `getCookieValue` method shown in Listing 19.24.

public String getPath()
public void setPath(String path)

These methods get or set the path to which the cookie applies. If you don't specify a path, the browser returns the cookie only to URLs in or below the directory containing the page that sent the cookie. For example, if the server sent the cookie from `http://ecommerce.site.com/toys/ specials.html`, the browser would send the cookie back when connecting to `http://ecommerce.site.com/toys/bikes/beginners.html`, but not to `http://ecommerce.site.com/cds/classical.html`. The `setPath` method can specify something more general. For example, `someCookie.set-Path("/")` specifies that *all* pages on the server should receive the cookie. The path specified must include the current page; that is, you may specify a more general path than the default, but not a more specific one. So, for example, a servlet at `http://host/store/cust-service/request` could specify a path of `/store/` (since `/store/` includes `/store/cust-service/`) but not a path of `/store/cust-service/returns/` (since this directory does not include `/store/cust-service/`).

public boolean getSecure()
public void setSecure(boolean secureFlag)

This pair of methods gets or sets the boolean value indicating whether the cookie should only be sent over encrypted (i.e., SSL) connections. The default is `false`; the cookie should apply to all connections.

public String getValue()
public void setValue(String cookieValue)

The `getValue` method looks up the value associated with the cookie; the `setValue` method specifies it. Again, the name and the value are the two parts of a cookie that you almost *always* care about, although in a few cases, a name is used as a boolean flag and its value is ignored (i.e., the existence of a cookie with the designated name is all that matters).

public int getVersion()
public void setVersion(int version)

These methods get and set the cookie protocol version the cookie complies with. Version 0, the default, follows the original Netscape specification (`http://www.netscape.com/newsref/std/cookie_spec.html`). Version 1, not yet widely supported, adheres to RFC 2109 (retrieve RFCs from the archive sites listed at `http://www.rfc-editor.org/`).

Examples of Setting and Reading Cookies

Listing 19.22 and Figure 19–14 show the `SetCookies` servlet, a servlet that sets six cookies. Three have the default expiration date, meaning that they should apply only until the user next restarts the browser. The other three use `setMaxAge` to stipulate that they should apply for the next hour, regardless of whether the user restarts the browser or reboots the computer to initiate a new browsing session.

Listing 19.23 shows a servlet that creates a table of all the cookies sent to it in the request. Figure 19–15 shows this servlet immediately after the `SetCookies` servlet is visited. Figure 19–16 shows it after `SetCookies` is visited and the browser is then closed and restarted.

Listing 19.22 `SetCookies.java`

```java
package cwp;

import java.io.*;
import javax.servlet.*;
import javax.servlet.http.*;

/** Sets six cookies: three that apply only to the current
 *  session (regardless of how long that session lasts)
 *  and three that persist for an hour (regardless of
 *  whether the browser is restarted).
 */

public class SetCookies extends HttpServlet {
  public void doGet(HttpServletRequest request,
                    HttpServletResponse response)
      throws ServletException, IOException {
    for(int i=0; i<3; i++) {
      // Default maxAge is -1, indicating cookie
      // applies only to current browsing session.
      Cookie cookie = new Cookie("Session-Cookie-" + i,
                                 "Cookie-Value-S" + i);
      response.addCookie(cookie);
      cookie = new Cookie("Persistent-Cookie-" + i,
                          "Cookie-Value-P" + i);
      // Cookie is valid for an hour, regardless of whether
      // user quits browser, reboots computer, or whatever.
      cookie.setMaxAge(3600);
      response.addCookie(cookie);
    }
    response.setContentType("text/html");
    PrintWriter out = response.getWriter();
    String title = "Setting Cookies";
    out.println
      (ServletUtilities.headWithTitle(title) +
       "<BODY BGCOLOR=\"#FDF5E6\">\n" +
       "<H1 ALIGN=\"CENTER\">" + title + "</H1>\n" +
       "There are six cookies associated with this page.\n" +
       "To see them, visit the\n" +
       "<A HREF=\"/servlet/cwp.ShowCookies\">\n" +
       "<CODE>ShowCookies</CODE> servlet</A>.\n" +
       "<P>\n" +
       "Three of the cookies are associated only with the\n" +
       "current session, while three are persistent.\n" +
       "Quit the browser, restart, and return to the\n" +
       "<CODE>ShowCookies</CODE> servlet to verify that\n" +
       "the three long-lived ones persist across sessions.\n" +
       "</BODY></HTML>");
  }
}
```

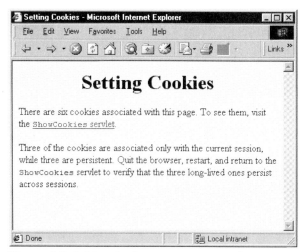

Figure 19–14 Result of `SetCookies` servlet.

Listing 19.23 `ShowCookies.java`

```java
package cwp;

import java.io.*;
import javax.servlet.*;
import javax.servlet.http.*;

/** Creates a table of the cookies associated with
 *  the current page.
 */

public class ShowCookies extends HttpServlet {
  public void doGet(HttpServletRequest request,
                    HttpServletResponse response)
      throws ServletException, IOException {
    response.setContentType("text/html");
    PrintWriter out = response.getWriter();
    String title = "Active Cookies";
    out.println(ServletUtilities.headWithTitle(title) +
                "<BODY BGCOLOR=\"#FDF5E6\">\n" +
                "<H1 ALIGN=\"CENTER\">" + title + "</H1>\n" +
                "<TABLE BORDER=1 ALIGN=\"CENTER\">\n" +
                "<TR BGCOLOR=\"#FFAD00\">\n" +
                "  <TH>Cookie Name\n" +
                "  <TH>Cookie Value");
```

(continued)

Listing 19.23 ShowCookies.java *(continued)*

```
    Cookie[] cookies = request.getCookies();
    if (cookies != null) {
      Cookie cookie;
      for(int i=0; i<cookies.length; i++) {
        cookie = cookies[i];
        out.println("<TR>\n" +
                    "  <TD>" + cookie.getName() + "\n" +
                    "  <TD>" + cookie.getValue());
      }
    }
    out.println("</TABLE></BODY></HTML>");
  }
}
```

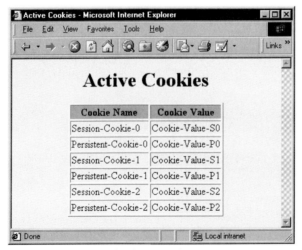

Figure 19–15 Result of visiting the ShowCookies servlet within an hour of visiting SetCookies in the same browser session.

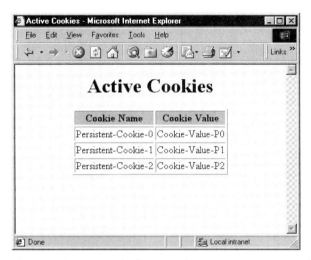

Figure 19-16 Result of visiting the `ShowCookies` servlet within an hour of visiting `SetCookies` in a different browser session.

Basic Cookie Utilities

This section presents some simple but useful utilities for dealing with cookies.

Finding Cookies with Specified Names

Listing 19.24 shows a section of `ServletUtilities.java` that simplifies the retrieval of a cookie or cookie value, given a cookie name. The `getCookieValue` method loops through the array of available `Cookie` objects, returning the value of any `Cookie` whose name matches the input. If there is no match, the designated default value is returned. So, for example, our typical approach for dealing with cookies is as follows:

```
Cookie[] cookies = request.getCookies();
String color =
  ServletUtilities.getCookieValue(cookies, "color", "black");
String font =
  ServletUtilities.getCookieValue(cookies, "font", "Arial");
```

The `getCookie` method also loops through the array comparing names but returns the actual `Cookie` object instead of just the value. That method is for cases when you want to do something with the `Cookie` other than just read its value.

Listing 19.24 ServletUtilities.java

```java
package cwp;

import javax.servlet.*;
import javax.servlet.http.*;

public class ServletUtilities {
  // Other methods in this class shown earlier.

/** Given an array of Cookies, a name, and a default value,
  *  this method tries to find the value of the cookie with
  *  the given name. If there is no cookie matching the name
  *  in the array, then the default value is returned instead.
  */

  public static String getCookieValue(Cookie[] cookies,
                                      String cookieName,
                                      String defaultValue) {
    if (cookies != null) {
      for(int i=0; i<cookies.length; i++) {
        Cookie cookie = cookies[i];
        if (cookieName.equals(cookie.getName()))
          return(cookie.getValue());
      }
    }
    return(defaultValue);
  }

  /** Given an array of cookies and a name, this method tries
    *  to find and return the cookie from the array that has
    *  the given name. If there is no cookie matching the name
    *  in the array, null is returned.
    */

  public static Cookie getCookie(Cookie[] cookies,
                                 String cookieName) {
    if (cookies != null) {
      for(int i=0; i<cookies.length; i++) {
        Cookie cookie = cookies[i];
        if (cookieName.equals(cookie.getName()))
          return(cookie);
      }
    }
    return(null);
  }
}
```

Creating Long-Lived Cookies

Listing 19.25 shows a small class that you can use instead of Cookie if you want your cookie to automatically persist for a year when the client quits the browser.

Listing 19.25 LongLivedCookie.java

```
package cwp;

import javax.servlet.http.*;

/** Cookie that persists 1 year. Default Cookie doesn't
 *  persist past current session.
 */

public class LongLivedCookie extends Cookie {
  public static final int SECONDS_PER_YEAR = 60*60*24*365;

  public LongLivedCookie(String name, String value) {
    super(name, value);
    setMaxAge(SECONDS_PER_YEAR);
  }
}
```

19.12 Session Tracking

This section shows you how to use the servlet session tracking API to keep track of visitors as they move around at your site.

The Need for Session Tracking

HTTP is a "stateless" protocol: each time a client retrieves a Web page, it opens a separate connection to the Web server, and the server does not automatically maintain contextual information about a client. Even with servers that support persistent (keep-alive) HTTP connections and keep a socket open for multiple client requests that occur close together in time, there is no built-in support for maintaining contextual information. This lack of context causes a number of difficulties. For example, when clients at an on-line store add an item to their shopping carts, how does the server know what's already in the carts? Similarly, when clients decide to proceed to checkout, how can the server determine which previously created shopping carts are theirs?

There are three typical solutions to this problem: cookies, URL-rewriting, and hidden form fields. The following subsections quickly summarize what would be required if you had to implement session tracking yourself (without using the built-in session tracking API) by each of the three ways.

Cookies

You can use HTTP cookies to store information about a shopping session, and each subsequent connection can look up the current session and then extract information about that session from some location on the server machine. For example, a servlet could do something like the following:

```
String sessionID = makeUniqueString();
Hashtable sessionInfo = new Hashtable();
Hashtable globalTable = findTableStoringSessions();
globalTable.put(sessionID, sessionInfo);
Cookie sessionCookie = new Cookie("JSESSIONID", sessionID);
sessionCookie.setPath("/");
response.addCookie(sessionCookie);
```

Then, in later requests the server could use the `globalTable` hash table to associate a session ID from the `JSESSIONID` cookie with the `sessionInfo` hash table of data associated with that particular session. This is an excellent solution and is the most widely used approach for session handling. Still, it is nice that servlets have a higher-level API that handles all this plus the following tedious tasks:

- Extracting the cookie that stores the session identifier from the other cookies (there may be many cookies, after all)
- Setting an appropriate expiration time for the cookie
- Associating the hash tables with each request
- Generating the unique session identifiers

URL-Rewriting

With this approach, the client appends some extra data on the end of each URL that identifies the session, and the server associates that identifier with data it has stored about that session. For example, with `http://host/path/file.html;jsessionid=1234`, the session information is attached as `jsessionid=1234`. This is also an excellent solution and even has the advantage that it works when browsers don't support cookies or when the user has disabled them. However, it has most of the same problems as cookies, namely, that the server-side program has a lot of straightforward but tedious processing to do. In addition, you have to be very careful that every URL that references your site and is returned to the user (even by indirect means like `Location` fields in server redirects) has the extra information appended. And, if the user leaves the session and comes back via a bookmark or link, the session information can be lost.

Hidden Form Fields

HTML forms can have an entry that looks like the following:

```
<INPUT TYPE="HIDDEN" NAME="session" VALUE="...">
```

This entry means that, when the form is submitted, the specified name and value are included in the GET or POST data. This hidden field can be used to store information about the session but has the major disadvantage that it only works if every page is dynamically generated.

Session Tracking in Servlets

Servlets provide an outstanding technical solution: the HttpSession API. This high-level interface is built on top of cookies or URL-rewriting. In fact, some servers use cookies if the browser supports them but automatically revert to URL-rewriting when cookies are unsupported or explicitly disabled. But, the servlet author doesn't need to bother with many of the details, doesn't have to explicitly manipulate cookies or information appended to the URL, and is automatically given a convenient place to store arbitrary objects that are associated with each session.

The Session Tracking API

Using sessions in servlets is straightforward and involves looking up the session object associated with the current request, creating a new session object when necessary, looking up information associated with a session, storing information in a session, and discarding completed or abandoned sessions. Finally, if you return any URLs to the clients that reference your site and URL-rewriting is being used, you need to attach the session information to the URLs.

Looking Up the HttpSession Object Associated with the Current Request

You look up the HttpSession object by calling the getSession method of HttpServletRequest. Behind the scenes, the system extracts a user ID from a cookie or attached URL data, then uses that as a key into a table of previously created HttpSession objects. But this is all done transparently to the programmer: you just call getSession. If getSession returns null, this means that the user is not already participating in a session, so you can create a new session. Creating a new session in this case is so commonly done that there is an option to automatically create a new session if one doesn't already exist. Just pass true to getSession. Thus, your first step usually looks like this:

```
HttpSession session = request.getSession(true);
```

If you care whether the session existed previously or is newly created, you can use isNew to check.

Looking Up Information Associated with a Session

HttpSession objects live on the server; they're just automatically associated with the client by a behind-the-scenes mechanism like cookies or URL-rewriting. These session objects have a built-in data structure that lets you store any number of keys and associated values. In version 2.1 and earlier of the servlet API, you use session.getValue("attribute") to look up a previously stored value. The return type is Object, so you have to do a typecast to whatever more specific type of data was associated with that attribute name in the session. The return value is null if there is no such attribute, so you need to check for null before calling methods on objects associated with sessions.

In version 2.2 of the servlet API, getValue is deprecated in favor of get-Attribute because of the better naming match with setAttribute (in version 2.1, the match for getValue is putValue, not setValue).

Here's a representative example, assuming ShoppingCart is some class you've defined to store information on items being purchased.

```
HttpSession session = request.getSession(true);
ShoppingCart cart =
  (ShoppingCart)session.getAttribute("shoppingCart");
if (cart == null) { // No cart already in session
  cart = new ShoppingCart();
  session.setAttribute("shoppingCart", cart);
}
doSomethingWith(cart);
```

In most cases, you have a specific attribute name in mind and want to find the value (if any) already associated with that name. However, you can also discover all the attribute names in a given session by calling getValueNames, which returns an array of strings. This method is your only option for finding attribute names in version 2.1, but in servlet engines supporting version 2.2 of the servlet specification, you can use getAttributeNames. That method is more consistent in that it returns an Enumeration, just like the getHeaderNames and getParameterNames methods of HttpServletRequest.

Although the data that was explicitly associated with a session is the part you care most about, some other pieces of information are sometimes useful as well. Here is a summary of the methods available in the HttpSession class.

public Object getValue(String name)
public Object getAttribute(String name)

These methods extract a previously stored value from a session object. They return `null` if no value is associated with the given name. Use `getValue` in version 2.1 of the servlet API. Version 2.2 supports both methods, but `getAttribute` is preferred and `getValue` is deprecated.

public void putValue(String name, Object value)
public void setAttribute(String name, Object value)

These methods associate a value with a name. Use `putValue` with version 2.1 servlets and either `setAttribute` (preferred) or `putValue` (deprecated) with version 2.2 servlets. If the object supplied to `putValue` or `setAttribute` implements the `HttpSessionBindingListener` interface, the object's `valueBound` method is called after it is stored in the session. Similarly, if the previous value implements `HttpSessionBindingListener`, its `valueUnbound` method is called.

public void removeValue(String name)
public void removeAttribute(String name)

These methods remove any values associated with the designated name. If the value being removed implements `HttpSessionBindingListener`, its `valueUnbound` method is called. With version 2.1 servlets, use `removeValue`. In version 2.2, `removeAttribute` is preferred, but `removeValue` is still supported (albeit deprecated) for backward compatibility.

public String[] getValueNames()
public Enumeration getAttributeNames()

These methods return the names of all attributes in the session. Use `getValueNames` in version 2.1 of the servlet specification. In version 2.2, `getValueNames` is supported but deprecated; use `getAttributeNames` instead.

public String getId()

This method returns the unique identifier generated for each session. It is useful for debugging or logging.

public boolean isNew()

This method returns `true` if the client (browser) has never seen the session, usually because it was just created rather than being referenced by an incoming client request. It returns `false` for preexisting sessions.

public long getCreationTime()

This method returns the time in milliseconds since midnight, January 1, 1970 (GMT) at which the session was first built. To get a value useful for printing, pass the value to the `Date` constructor or the `setTimeInMillis` method of `GregorianCalendar`.

public long getLastAccessedTime()

This method returns the time in milliseconds since midnight, January 1, 1970 (GMT) at which the session was last sent from the client.

public int getMaxInactiveInterval()
public void setMaxInactiveInterval(int seconds)

These methods get or set the amount of time, in seconds, that a session should go without access before being automatically invalidated. A negative value indicates that the session should never time out. Note that the timeout is maintained on the server and is *not* the same as the cookie expiration date, which is sent to the client.

public void invalidate()

This method invalidates the session and unbinds all objects associated with it.

Associating Information with a Session

As discussed in the previous section, you *read* information associated with a session by using `getValue` (in version 2.1 of the servlet specification) or `getAttribute` (in version 2.2). To *specify* information in version 2.1 servlets, you use `putValue`, supplying a key and a value. Use `setAttribute` in version 2.2. This is a more consistent name because it uses the `get`/`set` notation of the JavaBeans API. To let your values perform side effects when they are stored in a session, simply have the object you are associating with the session implement the `HttpSessionBinding-Listener` interface. Now, every time `putValue` or `setAttribute` is called on one of those objects, its `valueBound` method is called immediately afterward.

Be aware that `putValue` and `setAttribute` replace any previous values; if you want to remove a value without supplying a replacement, use `removeValue` in version 2.1 and `removeAttribute` in version 2.2. These methods trigger the `value-Unbound` method of any values that implement `HttpSessionBindingListener`. Sometimes, you just want to replace previous values; see the `referringPage` entry in the example below for an example. Other times, you want to retrieve a previous value and augment it; for an example, see the `previousItems` entry below. This example assumes a `ShoppingCart` class with an `addItem` method to store items being ordered, and a `Catalog` class with a static `getItem` method that returns an item, given an item identifier.

```
HttpSession session = request.getSession(true);
session.setAttribute("referringPage",
                    request.getHeader("Referer"));
ShoppingCart cart =
  (ShoppingCart)session.getAttribute("previousItems");
if (cart == null) { // No cart already in session
  cart = new ShoppingCart();
  session.setAttribute("previousItems", cart);
}
String itemID = request.getParameter("itemID");
if (itemID != null) {
  cart.addItem(Catalog.getItem(itemID));
}
```

Terminating Sessions

Sessions automatically become inactive when the amount of time between client accesses exceeds the interval specified by getMaxInactiveInterval. When this happens, any objects bound to the HttpSession object automatically get unbound. Then, your attached objects are automatically notified if they implement the HttpSessionBindingListener interface.

Rather than waiting for sessions to time out, you can explicitly deactivate a session with the session's invalidate method.

Encoding URLs Sent to the Client

If you are using URL-rewriting for session tracking and you send a URL that references your site to the client, you need to explicitly add on the session data. Since some servlet and JSP engines automatically switch to URL-rewriting when cookies aren't supported by the client, you should routinely encode *all* URLs that reference your site. There are two possible places where you might use URLs that refer to your own site. The first is where the URLs are embedded in the Web page that the servlet generates. These URLs should be passed through the encodeURL method of Http-ServletResponse. The method determines if URL-rewriting is currently in use and appends the session information only if necessary. The URL is returned unchanged otherwise.

Here's an example:

```
String originalURL = someRelativeOrAbsoluteURL;
String encodedURL = response.encodeURL(originalURL);
out.println("<A HREF=\"" + encodedURL + "\">...</A>");
```

The second place you might use a URL that refers to your own site is in a send-Redirect call (i.e., placed into the Location response header). In this second situation, different rules determine whether session information needs to be attached, so you cannot use encodeURL. Fortunately, HttpServletResponse supplies an encodeRedirectURL method to handle that case. Here's an example:

```
String originalURL = someURL; // Relative URL OK in version 2.2
String encodedURL = response.encodeRedirectURL(originalURL);
response.sendRedirect(encodedURL);
```

Since you often don't know if your servlet will later become part of a series of pages that use session tracking, it is good practice with servlets to plan ahead and encode URLs that reference their site.

Core Approach

Plan ahead: pass URLs that refer to your own site through `response.encodeURL` *or* `response.encodeRedirectURL`, *regardless of whether your servlet is using session tracking.*

A Servlet Showing Per-Client Access Counts

Listing 19.26 presents a simple servlet that shows basic information about the client's session. When the client connects, the servlet uses `request.getSession(true)` to either retrieve the existing session or, if there was no session, to create a new one. The servlet then looks for an attribute of type `Integer` called `accessCount`. If it cannot find such an attribute, it uses 0 as the number of previous accesses. This value is then incremented and associated with the session by `putValue`. Finally, the servlet prints a small HTML table showing information about the session. Figures 19–17 and 19–18 show the servlet on the initial visit and after the page was reloaded several times.

Listing 19.26 `ShowSession.java`

```
package cwp;

import java.io.*;
import javax.servlet.*;
import javax.servlet.http.*;
import java.net.*;
import java.util.*;

/** Simple example of session tracking. */

public class ShowSession extends HttpServlet {
  public void doGet(HttpServletRequest request,
                    HttpServletResponse response)
      throws ServletException, IOException {
    response.setContentType("text/html");
    PrintWriter out = response.getWriter();
```

(continued)

Listing 19.26 ShowSession.java *(continued)*

```
String title = "Session Tracking Example";
HttpSession session = request.getSession(true);
String heading;
Integer accessCount =
  (Integer)session.getAttribute("accessCount");
if (accessCount == null) {
  accessCount = new Integer(0);
  heading = "Welcome, Newcomer";
} else {
  heading = "Welcome Back";
  accessCount = new Integer(accessCount.intValue() + 1);
}
// Use setAttribute instead of putValue in version 2.2.
session.setAttribute("accessCount", accessCount);

out.println(ServletUtilities.headWithTitle(title) +
            "<BODY BGCOLOR=\"#FDF5E6\">\n" +
            "<H1 ALIGN=\"CENTER\">" + heading + "</H1>\n" +
            "<H2>Information on Your Session:</H2>\n" +
            "<TABLE BORDER=1 ALIGN=\"CENTER\">\n" +
            "<TR BGCOLOR=\"#FFAD00\">\n" +
            "  <TH>Info Type<TH>Value\n" +
            "<TR>\n" +
            "  <TD>ID\n" +
            "  <TD>" + session.getId() + "\n" +
            "<TR>\n" +
            "  <TD>Creation Time\n" +
            "  <TD>" +
            new Date(session.getCreationTime()) + "\n" +
            "<TR>\n" +
            "  <TD>Time of Last Access\n" +
            "  <TD>" +
            new Date(session.getLastAccessedTime()) + "\n" +
            "<TR>\n" +
            "  <TD>Number of Previous Accesses\n" +
            "  <TD>" + accessCount + "\n" +
            "</TABLE>\n" +
            "</BODY></HTML>");

}

/** Handle GET and POST requests identically. */

public void doPost(HttpServletRequest request,
                   HttpServletResponse response)
    throws ServletException, IOException {
  doGet(request, response);
}
}
```

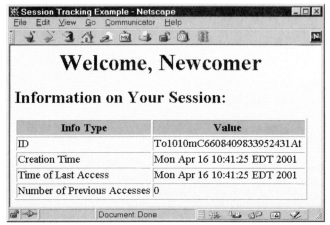

Figure 19–17 First visit by client to ShowSession servlet.

Figure 19–18 Eleventh visit to ShowSession servlet. Access count is independent of number of visits by other clients.

19.13 Summary

Servlets are efficient, convenient, powerful, portable, secure, and inexpensive alternatives to CGI and other server-side programming technologies. Despite their many benefits, they have one major drawback: generating HTML. Using println statements to build large sections of mostly static HTML is tedious, awkward, and hard to maintain. Besides, it mixes the code that generates the data with the code that presents it, making it hard to put different team members on different parts of the same project. That's where JavaServer Pages (JSP) comes in. Read on!

JAVASERVER PAGES

Topics in This Chapter

- The benefits of JSP
- JSP expressions, scriptlets, and declarations
- Controlling the structure of the servlet that results from a JSP page
- Including files and applets in JSP documents
- Using JavaBeans with JSP
- Creating custom JSP tag libraries
- Combining servlets and JSP: the Model View Controller (Model 2) architecture

Chapter 20

20.1 JSP Overview

JavaServer Pages (JSP) technology enables you to mix regular, static HTML with dynamically generated content from servlets. You simply write the regular HTML in the normal manner, using familiar Web-page-building tools. You then enclose the code for the dynamic parts in special tags, most of which start with `<%` and end with `%>`. For example, here is a section of a JSP page that results in "Thanks for ordering *Core Web Programming*" for a URL of *http://host/OrderConfirmation.jsp?title=Core+Web+Programming*:

```
Thanks for ordering <I><%= request.getParameter("title") %></I>
```

Separating the static HTML from the dynamic content provides a number of benefits over servlets alone, and the approach used in JavaServer Pages offers several advantages over competing technologies such as ASP, PHP, or ColdFusion. Section 20.2 gives some details on these advantages, but they basically boil down to two facts: that JSP is widely supported and thus doesn't lock you into a particular operating system or Web server and that JSP gives you full access to Java servlet technology for the dynamic part, rather than requiring you to use an unfamiliar and weaker special-purpose language.

The process of making JavaServer Pages accessible on the Web is much simpler than that for servlets. Assuming you have a Web server that supports JSP, you give your file a `.jsp` extension and simply install it in any of the designated JSP locations (which, on many servers, is any place you could put a normal Web page): no compiling, no packages, and no user CLASSPATH settings. However, although your *personal* environment doesn't need any special settings, the *server* still has to be set up with access to the servlet and JSP class files and the Java compiler. For details, see your server's documentation or Section 19.2 (Server Installation and Setup).

Although what you write often looks more like a regular HTML file than a servlet, behind the scenes the JSP page is automatically converted to a normal servlet, with the static HTML simply being printed to the output stream associated with the servlet. This translation is normally done the first time the page is requested. To ensure that the first real user doesn't get a momentary delay when the JSP page is translated into a servlet and compiled, developers can simply request the page themselves after first installing it.

One warning about the automatic translation process is in order. If you make an error in the dynamic portion of your JSP page, the system may not be able to properly translate it into a servlet. If your page has such a fatal translation-time error, the server will present an HTML error page describing the problem to the client. Internet Explorer 5, however, typically replaces server-generated error messages with a canned page that it considers friendlier. You will need to turn off this "feature" when debugging JSP pages. To do so with Internet Explorer 5, go to the Tools menu, select Internet Options, choose the Advanced tab, and make sure "Show friendly HTTP error messages" box is not checked.

Core Approach

When debugging JSP pages, be sure to turn off Internet Explorer's "friendly" HTTP error messages.

Aside from the regular HTML, there are three main types of JSP constructs that you embed in a page: *scripting elements*, *directives*, and *actions*. Scripting elements let you specify Java code that will become part of the resultant servlet, directives let you control the overall structure of the servlet, and actions let you specify existing components that should be used and otherwise control the behavior of the JSP engine. To simplify the scripting elements, you have access to a number of predefined variables, such as request in the code snippet just shown.

This chapter covers versions 1.0 and 1.1 of the JavaServer Pages specification. JSP changed dramatically from version 0.92 to version 1.0, and although these changes are very much for the better, you should note that newer JSP pages are almost totally incompatible with the early 0.92 JSP engines and that older JSP pages are equally incompatible with 1.0 JSP engines. The changes from version 1.0 to 1.1 are much less dramatic: the main additions in version 1.1 are the ability to portably define new tags and the use of the servlet 2.2 specification for the underlying servlets. JSP 1.1 pages that do not use custom tags or explicitly call 2.2-specific statements are compatible with JSP 1.0 engines; JSP 1.0 pages are totally upward compatible with JSP 1.1 engines.

20.2 Advantages of JSP

JSP has a number of advantages over many of its alternatives. Here are a few of them.

Versus Active Server Pages (ASP) or ColdFusion

ASP is a competing technology from Microsoft. The advantages of JSP are twofold. First, the dynamic part is written in Java, not VBScript or another ASP-specific language, so it is more powerful and better suited to complex applications that require reusable components. Second, JSP is portable to other operating systems and Web servers; you aren't locked into Windows NT/2000 and IIS. You could make the same argument when comparing JSP to ColdFusion; with JSP you can use Java for the "real code" and are not tied to a particular server product.

Versus PHP

PHP is a free, open-source HTML-embedded scripting language that is somewhat similar to both ASP and JSP. One advantage of JSP is that the dynamic part is written in Java, which already has an extensive API for networking, database access, distributed objects, and the like, whereas PHP requires learning an entirely new, less widely used language. A second advantage is that JSP is much more widely supported by tool and server vendors than is PHP.

Versus Pure Servlets

JSP doesn't provide any capabilities that couldn't, in principle, be accomplished with a servlet. In fact, JSP documents are automatically translated into servlets behind the scenes. But it is more convenient to write (and to modify!) regular HTML than to have a zillion `println` statements that generate the HTML. Plus, by separating the presentation from the content, you can put different people on different tasks: your Web page design experts can build the HTML using familiar tools and leave places for your servlet programmers to insert the dynamic content.

Does this mean that you can just learn JSP and forget about servlets? By no means! JSP developers need to know servlets for four reasons:

1. JSP pages get translated into servlets. You can't understand how JSP works without understanding servlets.
2. JSP consists of static HTML, special-purpose JSP tags, and Java code. What kind of Java code? Servlet code!

3. Some tasks are better accomplished by servlets than by JSP. JSP is good at generating pages that consist of large sections of fairly well structured HTML or other character data. Servlets are better for generating binary data, building pages with highly variable structure, and performing tasks (such as redirection) that involve little or no output.

4. Some tasks are better accomplished by a *combination* of servlets and JSP than by *either* servlets or JSP alone. See Section 20.8 (Integrating Servlets and JSP) for details.

Versus Server-Side Includes (SSI)

SSI is a widely supported technology for inserting externally defined pieces into a static Web page. JSP is better because you have a richer set of tools for building that external piece and have more options regarding the stage of the HTTP response at which the piece actually gets inserted. Besides, SSI is really intended only for simple inclusions, not for "real" programs that use form data, make database connections, and the like.

Versus JavaScript

JavaScript, which is completely distinct from the Java programming language, is normally used to generate HTML dynamically on the *client*, building parts of the Web page as the browser loads the document. This is a useful capability and does not normally overlap with the capabilities of JSP (which runs only on the server). Although JavaScript can also be used on the server, most notably on Netscape, IIS, and Broad-Vision, Java is more powerful, flexible, reliable, and portable.

20.3 JSP Scripting Elements

JSP scripting elements let you insert code into the servlet that will be generated from the JSP page. There are three forms:

1. *Expressions* of the form `<%= expression %>`, which are evaluated and inserted into the servlet's output
2. *Scriptlets* of the form `<% code %>`, which are inserted into the servlet's _jspService method (called by service)
3. *Declarations* of the form `<%! code %>`, which are inserted into the body of the servlet class, outside of any existing methods

Each of these scripting elements is described in more detail in the following sections.

In many cases, a large percentage of your JSP page just consists of static HTML, known as *template text*. In almost all respects, this HTML looks just like normal HTML, follows all the same syntax rules, and is simply "passed through" to the client by the servlet created to handle the page. Not only does the HTML look normal, it can be created by whatever tools you already are using for building Web pages. For example, we used Allaire's HomeSite for most of the JSP pages in this book.

There are two minor exceptions to the "template text is passed straight through" rule. First, if you want to have <% in the output, you need to put <\% in the template text. Second, if you want a comment to appear in the JSP page but not in the resultant document, use

```
<%-- JSP Comment --%>
```

HTML comments of the form

```
<!-- HTML Comment -->
```

are passed through to the resultant HTML normally.

Expressions

A JSP expression is used to insert values directly into the output. It has the following form:

```
<%= Java Expression %>
```

The expression is evaluated, converted to a string, and inserted in the page. That is, this evaluation is performed at run time (when the page is requested) and thus has full access to information about the request. For example, the following shows the date/time that the page was requested:

```
Current time: <%= new java.util.Date() %>
```

It would result in code in the `_jspService` method (called by `service` in servlets that result from JSP pages) similar to the following.

```
out.print("Current time: ");
out.println(new Java.util.Date());
```

Predefined Variables

To simplify these expressions, you can use a number of predefined variables. These implicit objects are discussed in more detail later in this section, but for the purpose of expressions, the most important ones are:

- **request**, the `HttpServletRequest`
- **response**, the `HttpServletResponse`
- **session**, the `HttpSession` associated with the request (unless disabled with the `session` attribute of the `page` directive—see Section 20.4)

- **out**, the PrintWriter (a buffered version called JspWriter) used to send output to the client

Here is an example:

```
Your hostname: <%= request.getRemoteHost() %>
```

XML Syntax for Expressions

On some servers, XML authors can use the following alternative syntax for JSP expressions:

```
<jsp:expression>Java Expression</jsp:expression>
```

However, in JSP 1.1 and earlier, servers are not required to support this alternative syntax, and in practice few do. In JSP 1.2, servers are required to support this syntax as long as authors don't mix the XML version and the ASP-like version (<%= ... %>) in the same page. Note that XML elements, unlike HTML ones, are case sensitive, so be sure to use jsp:expression in lower case.

Installing JSP Pages

Servlets require you to set your CLASSPATH, use packages to avoid name conflicts, install the class files in servlet-specific locations, and use special-purpose URLs. Not so with JSP pages. JSP pages can be placed in the same directories as normal HTML pages, images, and style sheets; they can also be accessed through URLs of the same form as those HTML pages, images, and style sheets. Here are a few examples of installation locations and associated URLs:

- **Tomcat default installation directory**
  install_dir\webapps\ROOT
  install_dir\webapps\ROOT\anyDir
- **Tomcat URL**
  http://host/filename.jsp
  http://host/anyDir/filename.jsp
- **JRun installation directory**
  install_dir\servers\default\default-app
  install_dir\servers\default\default-app\anyDir
- **JRun URL**
  http://host/filename.jsp
  http://host/anyDir/filename.jsp

Note that, although JSP pages *themselves* need no special installation directories, any Java classes called *from* JSP pages still need to go in the standard locations used by servlet classes (e.g., .../WEB-INF/classes).

Example: JSP Expressions

Listing 20.1 gives an example JSP page and Figure 20–1 shows the result. With Tomcat we installed the page in *install_dir*\webapps\ROOT\cwp\ Expressions.jsp and used a URL of http://*host*/cwp/Expressions.jsp. Notice that we included META tags and a style sheet link in the HEAD section of the HTML page. It is good practice to include these elements, but there are two reasons why they are often omitted from pages generated by normal servlets. First, with serv- lets, it is tedious to generate the required println statements. With JSP, however, the format is simpler and you can make use of the code reuse options in your usual HTML building tool. Second, servlets cannot use the simplest form of relative URLs (ones that refer to files in the same directory as the current page) since the servlet directories are not mapped to URLs in the same manner as are URLs for normal Web pages. JSP pages, on the other hand, are installed in the normal Web page hier- archy on the server, and relative URLs are resolved properly. Thus, style sheets and JSP pages can be kept together in the same directory. The source code for the style sheet, like all code shown or referenced in the book, can be downloaded from http://www.corewebprogramming.com/.

Listing 20.1 Expressions.jsp

```
<!DOCTYPE HTML PUBLIC "-//W3C//DTD HTML 4.0 Transitional//EN">
<HTML>
<HEAD>
<TITLE>JSP Expressions</TITLE>
<META NAME="keywords"
      CONTENT="JSP,expressions,JavaServer,Pages,servlets">
<META NAME="description"
      CONTENT="A quick example of JSP expressions.">
<LINK REL=STYLESHEET
      HREF="JSP-Styles.css"
      TYPE="text/css">
</HEAD>
<BODY>
<H2>JSP Expressions</H2>
<UL>
  <LI>Current time: <%= new java.util.Date() %>
  <LI>Your hostname: <%= request.getRemoteHost() %>
  <LI>Your session ID: <%= session.getId() %>
  <LI>The <CODE>testParam</CODE> form parameter:
      <%= request.getParameter("testParam") %>
</UL>
</BODY>
</HTML>
```

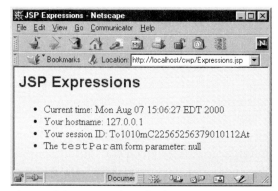

Figure 20–1 Typical result of Expressions.jsp.

Scriptlets

If you want to do something more complex than insert a simple expression, JSP scriptlets let you insert arbitrary code into the servlet's _jspService method (which is called by service). Scriptlets have the following form:

```
<% Java Code %>
```

Scriptlets have access to the same automatically defined variables as expressions (request, response, session, out, etc.). So, for example, if you want output to appear in the resultant page, you would use the out variable, as in the following example.

```
<%
String queryData = request.getQueryString();
out.println("Attached GET data: " + queryData);
%>
```

In this particular instance, you could have accomplished the same effect more easily by using the following JSP expression:

```
Attached GET data: <%= request.getQueryString() %>
```

In general, however, scriptlets can perform a number of tasks that cannot be accomplished with expressions alone. These tasks include setting response headers and status codes, invoking side effects such as writing to the server log or updating a database, or executing code that contains loops, conditionals, or other complex constructs. For instance, the following snippet specifies that the current page is sent to the client as plain text, not as HTML (which is the default).

```
<% response.setContentType("text/plain"); %>
```

It is important to note that you can set response headers or status codes at various places within a JSP page, even though this capability appears to violate the rule that this type of response data needs to be specified before any document content is sent to the client. Setting headers and status codes is permitted because servlets that result from JSP pages use a special variety of `Writer` (of type `JspWriter`) that partially buffers the document. This buffering behavior can be changed, however; see Section 20.4 for a discussion of the `buffer` and `autoflush` attributes of the `page` directive.

As an example of executing code that is too complex for a JSP expression, Listing 20.2 presents a JSP page that uses the `bgColor` request parameter to set the background color of the page. Some results are shown in Figures 20–2 and 20–3.

Listing 20.2 `BGColor.jsp`

```
<!DOCTYPE HTML PUBLIC "-//W3C//DTD HTML 4.0 Transitional//EN">
<HTML>
<HEAD>
  <TITLE>Color Testing</TITLE>
</HEAD>
<%
String bgColor = request.getParameter("bgColor");
boolean hasExplicitColor = true;
if (bgColor == null) {
  hasExplicitColor = false;
  bgColor = "WHITE";
}
%>
<BODY BGCOLOR="<%= bgColor %>">
<H2 ALIGN="CENTER">Color Testing</H2>
<%
if (hasExplicitColor) {
  out.println("You supplied an explicit background color of " +
              bgColor + ".");
} else {
  out.println("Using default background color of WHITE. " +
              "Supply the bgColor request attribute to try " +
              "a standard color or RRGGBB value, or to see " +
              "if your browser supports X11 color names.");
}
%>
</BODY>
</HTML>
```

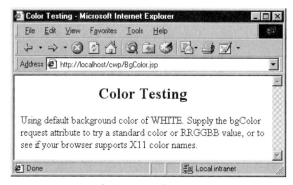

Figure 20–2 Default result of `BGColor.jsp`.

Figure 20–3 Result of `BGColor.jsp` when accessed with a `bgColor` parameter having the RGB value `C0C0C0`.

Using Scriptlets to Make Parts of the JSP File Conditional

Another use of scriptlets is to conditionally include standard HTML and JSP constructs. The key to this approach is the fact that code inside a scriptlet gets inserted into the resultant servlet's `_jspService` method (called by `service`) *exactly* as written and that any static HTML (template text) before or after a scriptlet gets converted to `print` statements. This means that scriptlets need not contain complete Java statements and that blocks left open can affect the static HTML or JSP outside of the scriptlets. For example, consider the following JSP fragment containing mixed template text and scriptlets.

```
<% if (Math.random() < 0.5) { %>
Have a <B>nice</B> day!
<% } else { %>
Have a <B>lousy</B> day!
<% } %>
```

When converted to a servlet by the JSP engine, this fragment will result in something similar to the following.

```
if (Math.random() < 0.5) {
  out.println("Have a <B>nice</B> day!");
} else {
  out.println("Have a <B>lousy</B> day!");
}
```

Special Scriptlet Syntax

There are two special constructs you should take note of. First, if you want to use the characters `%>` inside a scriptlet, enter `%\>` instead. Second, the XML equivalent of `<% Java Code %>` is

```
<jsp:scriptlet>Java Code</jsp:scriptlet>
```

The two forms are treated identically by some JSP engines, but `jsp:scriptlet` is not required to be supported until JSP 1.2.

Declarations

A JSP declaration lets you define methods or fields that get inserted into the main body of the servlet class (*outside* of the `_jspService` method that is called by `service` to process the request). A declaration has the following form:

```
<%! Java Code %>
```

Since declarations do not generate any output, they are normally used in conjunction with JSP expressions or scriptlets. The declarations define methods or fields that are later used by expressions or scriptlets. One caution is warranted however: do not use JSP declarations to override the standard servlet lifecycle methods (`service`, `doGet`, `init`, etc.). The servlet into which the JSP page gets translated already makes use of these methods. There is no need for declarations to gain access to `service`, `doGet`, or `doPost`, since calls to `service` are automatically dispatched to `_jspService`, which is where code resulting from expressions and scriptlets gets put. However, for initialization and cleanup, you can use `jspInit` and `jsp-Destroy`—the standard `init` and `destroy` methods are guaranteed to call these two methods when in servlets that come from JSP.

Core Note

For initialization and cleanup in JSP pages, use JSP declarations to override `jspInit` and/or `jspDestroy`.

For example, here is a JSP fragment that prints the number of times the current page has been requested since the server was booted (or the servlet class was changed and reloaded). Recall that multiple client requests to the same servlet result only in multiple threads calling the `service` method of a single servlet instance. They do *not* result in the creation of multiple servlet instances except possibly when the servlet implements `SingleThreadModel`. For a discussion of `Single-ThreadModel`, see the `isThreadSafe` attribute of the `page` directive (Section 20.4) and Section 19.4 (The Servlet Life Cycle). Thus, instance variables (fields) of a servlet are shared by multiple requests and `accessCount` does not have to be declared `static` below.

```
<%! private int accessCount = 0; %>
Accesses to page since server reboot:
<%= ++accessCount %>
```

Listing 20.3 shows the full JSP page; Figure 20–4 shows a representative result.

Listing 20.3 `AccessCounts.jsp`

```
<!DOCTYPE HTML PUBLIC "-//W3C//DTD HTML 4.0 Transitional//EN">
<HTML>
<HEAD>
<TITLE>JSP Declarations</TITLE>
<META NAME="keywords"
      CONTENT="JSP,declarations,JavaServer,Pages,servlets">
<META NAME="description"
      CONTENT="A quick example of JSP declarations.">
<LINK REL=STYLESHEET
      HREF="JSP-Styles.css"
      TYPE="text/css">
</HEAD>
<BODY>
<H1>JSP Declarations</H1>
<%! private int accessCount = 0; %>
<H2>Accesses to page since server reboot:
<%= ++accessCount %></H2>
</BODY>
</HTML>
```

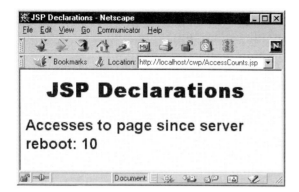

Figure 20–4 Visiting `AccessCounts.jsp` after it has been requested nine previous times by the same or different clients.

Special Declaration Syntax

As with scriptlets, if you want to use the characters `%>`, enter `%\>` instead. Finally, note that the XML equivalent of `<%!` *Java Code* `%>` is

```
<jsp:declaration>Java Code</jsp:declaration>
```

Predefined Variables

To simplify code in JSP expressions and scriptlets, you are supplied with eight automatically defined variables, sometimes called *implicit objects*. Since JSP declarations result in code that appears outside of the `_jspService` method, these variables are not accessible in declarations. The available variables are `request`, `response`, `out`, `session`, `application`, `config`, `pageContext`, and `page`. Details for each are given below.

request

This variable is the `HttpServletRequest` associated with the request; it gives you access to the request parameters, the request type (e.g., `GET` or `POST`), and the incoming HTTP headers (e.g., cookies).

response

This variable is the `HttpServletResponse` associated with the response to the client. Note that since the output stream (see out) is normally buffered, it is legal to set HTTP status codes and response headers in JSP pages, even though the setting of headers or status codes is not permitted in servlets once any output has been sent to the client.

out

This variable is the `PrintWriter` used to send output to the client. However, to make the `response` object useful, this is a buffered version of `Print-Writer` called `JspWriter`. You can adjust the buffer size through use of the `buffer` attribute of the `page` directive. The `out` variable is used almost exclusively in scriptlets, since JSP expressions are automatically placed in the output stream and thus rarely need to refer to `out` explicitly.

session

This variable is the `HttpSession` object associated with the request. Recall that sessions are created automatically, so this variable is bound even if there is no incoming session reference. The one exception is if you use the `session` attribute of the `page` directive to turn sessions off. In that case, attempts to reference the `session` variable cause errors at the time the JSP page is translated into a servlet.

application

This variable is the `ServletContext` as obtained by `getServletContext`. Servlets and JSP pages can store persistent data in the `ServletContext` object rather than in instance variables. `ServletContext` has `set-Attribute` and `getAttribute` methods that let you store arbitrary data associated with specified keys. The difference between storing data in instance variables and storing it in the `ServletContext` is that the `Servlet-Context` is shared by all servlets in the servlet engine (or in the Web application).

config

This variable is the `ServletConfig` object for this page.

pageContext

JSP introduced a new class called `PageContext` to give a single point of access to many of the page attributes and to provide a convenient place to store shared data. The `pageContext` variable stores the value of the `Page-Context` object associated with the current page.

page

This variable is simply a synonym for `this` and is not very useful. It was created as a placeholder for the time when the scripting language could be something other than Java.

20.4 The JSP page Directive

A JSP *directive* affects the overall structure of the servlet that results from the JSP page. The following templates show the two possible forms for directives. Single quotes can be substituted for the double quotes around the attribute values, but the quotation marks cannot be omitted altogether. To obtain quote marks within an attribute value, precede them with a back slash, using \' for ' and \" for ".

```
<%@ directive attribute="value" %>

<%@ directive attribute1="value1"
              attribute2="value2"
              ...
              attributeN="valueN" %>
```

In JSP, there are three types of directives: `page`, `include`, and `taglib`. The `page` directive lets you control the structure of the servlet by importing classes, customizing the servlet superclass, setting the content type, and the like. A `page` directive can be placed anywhere within the document; its use is the topic of this section. The second directive, `include`, lets you insert a file into the servlet class at the time the JSP file is translated into a servlet. An `include` directive should be placed in the document at the point at which you want the file to be inserted; it is discussed in Section 20.5. JSP 1.1 introduces a third directive, `taglib`, which can be used to define custom markup tags; it is discussed in Section 20.7.

The `page` directive lets you define one or more of the following case-sensitive attributes: `import`, `contentType`, `isThreadSafe`, `session`, `buffer`, `autoflush`, `extends`, `info`, `errorPage`, `isErrorPage`, and `language`. These attributes are explained in the following subsections.

The import Attribute

The `import` attribute of the `page` directive lets you specify the packages that should be imported by the servlet into which the JSP page gets translated. If you don't explicitly specify any classes to import, the servlet imports `java.lang.*`, `javax.servlet.*`, `javax.servlet.jsp.*`, `javax.servlet.http.*`, and possibly some number of server-specific entries. Never write JSP code that relies on any server-specific classes being imported automatically. Use of the `import` attribute takes one of the following two forms:

```
<%@ page import="package.class" %>
<%@ page import="package.class1,...,package.classN" %>
```

For example, the following directive signifies that all classes in the `java.util` package should be available to use without explicit package identifiers.

```
<%@ page import="java.util.*" %>
```

The `import` attribute is the only `page` attribute that is allowed to appear multiple times within the same document. Although `page` directives can appear anywhere within the document, it is traditional to place `import` statements either near the top of the document or just before the first place that the referenced package is used.

Note that some servers have different rules about where to put different types of class files. For example, the Java Web Server 2.0 lets you put the actual servlet classes in the `servlets` directory but requires you to put classes used by servlets or JSP pages in the `classes` directory. The JSWDK and Tomcat have no such restrictions; check your server's documentation for definitive guidance.

For example, Listing 20.4 presents a page that uses two classes not in the standard JSP import list: `java.util.Date`, and `cwp.ServletUtilities` (see Listing 19.21). To simplify references to these classes, the JSP page uses

```
<%@ page import="java.util.*,cwp.*" %>
```

Figures 20–5 and 20–6 show some typical results.

Listing 20.4 `ImportAttribute.jsp`

```
<!DOCTYPE HTML PUBLIC "-//W3C//DTD HTML 4.0 Transitional//EN">
<HTML>
<HEAD>
<TITLE>The import Attribute</TITLE>
<LINK REL=STYLESHEET
      HREF="JSP-Styles.css"
      TYPE="text/css">
</HEAD>
<BODY>
<H2>The import Attribute</H2>
<%-- JSP page directive --%>
<%@ page import="java.util.*,cwp.*" %>
<%-- JSP Declaration --%>
<%!
private String randomID() {
  int num = (int)(Math.random()*10000000.0);
  return("id" + num);
}
private final String NO_VALUE = "<I>No Value</I>";
%>
<%-- JSP Scriptlet --%>
<%
Cookie[] cookies = request.getCookies();
String oldID =
  ServletUtilities.getCookieValue(cookies, "userID", NO_VALUE);
if (oldID.equals(NO_VALUE)) {
```

(continued)

Listing 20.4 `ImportAttribute.jsp` *(continued)*

```
    String newID = randomID();
    Cookie cookie = new Cookie("userID", newID);
    response.addCookie(cookie);
}
%>
<%-- JSP Expressions --%>
This page was accessed on <%= new Date() %> with a userID
cookie of <%= oldID %>.

</BODY>
</HTML>
```

Figure 20–5 `ImportAttribute.jsp` when first accessed.

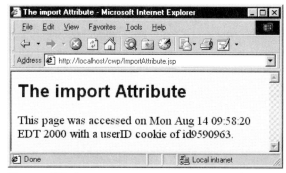

Figure 20–6 `ImportAttribute.jsp` when accessed
in a subsequent request.

The contentType Attribute

The contentType attribute sets the Content-Type response header, indicating the MIME type of the document being sent to the client. For more information on MIME types, see Table 19.1 (Common MIME Types) in Section 19.10 (The Server Response: HTTP Response Headers).

Use of the contentType attribute takes one of the following two forms:

```
<%@ page contentType="MIME-Type" %>
<%@ page contentType="MIME-Type; charset=Character-Set" %>
```

For example, the directive

```
<%@ page contentType="application/vnd.ms-excel" %>
```

has the same effect as the scriptlet

```
<% response.setContentType("application/vnd.ms-excel"); %>
```

Unlike regular servlets, where the default MIME type is text/plain, the default for JSP pages is text/html (with a default character set of ISO-8859-1).

Listing 20.5 shows a JSP page that generates tab-separated Excel output. Figure 20–7 shows the result in Internet Explorer on a system that has Microsoft Office installed.

Listing 20.5 `Excel.jsp`

```
First     Last       Email Address
Marty     Hall       hall@corewebprogramming.com
Larry     Brown      brown@corewebprogramming.com
Bill      Gates      gates@sun.com
Larry     Ellison    ellison@microsoft.com
<%@ page contentType="application/vnd.ms-excel" %>
<%-- There are tabs, not spaces, between columns. --%>
```

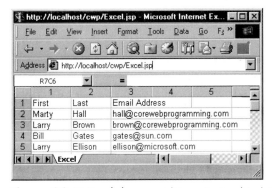

Figure 20–7 Excel document (`Excel.jsp`) in Internet Explorer.

The isThreadSafe Attribute

The isThreadSafe attribute controls whether or not the servlet that results from the JSP page will implement the SingleThreadModel interface. Use of the isThreadSafe attribute takes one of the following two forms:

```
<%@ page isThreadSafe="true" %> <%-- Default --%>
<%@ page isThreadSafe="false" %>
```

With normal servlets, simultaneous user requests result in multiple threads concurrently accessing the service method of the same servlet instance. This behavior assumes that the servlet is *thread safe*; that is, that the servlet synchronizes access to data in its fields so that inconsistent values will not result from an unexpected ordering of thread execution. In some cases (such as page access counts), you may not care if two visitors occasionally get the same value, but in other cases (such as user IDs), identical values can spell disaster. For example, the following snippet is not thread safe since a thread could be preempted after reading idNum but before updating it, yielding two users with the same user ID.

```
<%! private int idNum = 0; %>
<%
String userID = "userID" + idNum;
out.println("Your ID is " + userID + ".");
idNum = idNum + 1;
%>
```

The code should have used a synchronized block. This construct is written

```
synchronized(someObject) { ... }
```

and means that once a thread enters the block of code, no other thread can enter the same block (or any other block marked with the same object reference) until the first thread exits. So, the previous snippet should have been written in the following manner.

```
<%! private int idNum = 0; %>
<%
synchronized(this) {
  String userID = "userID" + idNum;
  out.println("Your ID is " + userID + ".");
  idNum = idNum + 1;
}
%>
```

That's the normal servlet behavior: multiple simultaneous requests are dispatched to multiple threads concurrently accessing the same servlet instance. However, if a servlet implements the SingleThreadModel interface, the system guarantees that there will not be simultaneous access to the same servlet instance. The system can satisfy this guarantee either by queuing up all requests and passing them to the same servlet instance or by creating a pool of instances, each of which handles a single request at a time.

You use `<%@ page isThreadSafe="false" %>` to indicate that your code is *not* thread safe and thus that the resulting servlet should implement `Single-ThreadModel`. The default value is `true`, which means that the system assumes you made your code thread safe and it can consequently use the higher-performance approach of multiple simultaneous threads accessing a single servlet instance.

The session Attribute

The `session` attribute controls whether or not the page participates in HTTP sessions. Use of this attribute takes one of the following two forms:

```
<%@ page session="true" %> <%-- Default --%>
<%@ page session="false" %>
```

A value of `true` (the default) indicates that the predefined variable `session` (of type `HttpSession`) should be bound to the existing session if one exists; otherwise, a new session should be created and bound to `session`. A value of `false` means that no sessions will be used automatically and attempts to access the variable `session` will result in errors at the time the JSP page is translated into a servlet. Turning off session tracking may save significant amounts of server memory on high traffic sites. Just remember that sessions are *user-specific*, not *page-specific*. Thus, it doesn't do any good to turn off session tracking for one page unless you also turn it off for related pages that are likely to be visited in the same client session.

The buffer Attribute

The `buffer` attribute specifies the size of the buffer used by the `out` variable, which is of type `JspWriter` (a subclass of `PrintWriter`). Use of this attribute takes one of two forms:

```
<%@ page buffer="sizekb" %>
<%@ page buffer="none" %>
```

Servers can use a larger buffer than you specify, but not a smaller one. For example, `<%@ page buffer="32kb" %>` means the document content should be buffered and not sent to the client until at least 32 kilobytes have been accumulated or the page is completed. The default buffer size is server specific, but must be at least 8 kilobytes. Be cautious about turning off buffering; doing so requires JSP entries that set headers or status codes to appear at the top of the file, before any HTML content.

The autoflush Attribute

The `autoflush` attribute controls whether the output buffer should be automatically flushed when it is full or whether an exception should be raised when the buffer overflows. Use of this attribute takes one of the following two forms:

```
<%@ page autoflush="true" %> <%-- Default --%>
<%@ page autoflush="false" %>
```

A value of `false` is illegal when `buffer="none"` is also used.

The extends Attribute

The `extends` attribute designates the superclass of the servlet that will be generated for the JSP page and takes the following form:

```
<%@ page extends="package.class" %>
```

Use this attribute with extreme caution since the server will almost certainly be using a custom superclass already.

The info Attribute

The `info` attribute defines a string that can be retrieved from the servlet by means of the `getServletInfo` method. Use of `info` takes the following form:

```
<%@ page info="Some Message" %>
```

The errorPage Attribute

The `errorPage` attribute specifies a JSP page that should process any exceptions (i.e., something of type `Throwable`) thrown but not caught in the current page. It is used as follows:

```
<%@ page errorPage="Relative URL" %>
```

The exception thrown will be automatically available to the designated error page by means of the `exception` variable.

The isErrorPage Attribute

The `isErrorPage` attribute indicates whether or not the current page can act as the error page for another JSP page. Use of `isErrorPage` takes one of the following two forms:

```
<%@ page isErrorPage="true" %>
<%@ page isErrorPage="false" %> <%-- Default --%>
```

The language Attribute

At some point, the `language` attribute is intended to specify the underlying programming language being used, as below.

```
<%@ page language="cobol" %>
```

For now, don't bother with this attribute since `java` is both the default and the only legal choice.

XML Syntax for Directives

Some servers permit you to use an alternative XML-compatible syntax for directives. These constructs take the following form:

```
<jsp:directive.directiveType attribute="value" />
```

For example, the XML equivalent of

```
<%@ page import="java.util.*" %>
```

is

```
<jsp:directive.page import="java.util.*" />
```

20.5 Including Files and Applets in JSP Documents

JSP has three main capabilities for including external pieces into a JSP document.

1. **The include directive.** The construct lets you insert JSP code into the main page before that main page is translated into a servlet. The included code can contain JSP constructs such as field definitions and content-type settings *that affect the main page as a whole*. This capability is discussed in the first following subsection.

2. **The jsp:include action.** Although reusing chunks of JSP code is a powerful capability, most times you would rather sacrifice a small amount of power for the convenience of being able to change the included documents without updating the main JSP page. The jsp:include action lets you include the output of a page at request time. Note that jsp:include only lets you include the *result* of the secondary page, not the code itself as with the include directive. Consequently, the secondary page cannot use any JSP constructs that affect the main page as a whole. Use of jsp:include is discussed in the second subsection.

3. **The jsp:plugin action.** Although this chapter is primarily about server-side Java, client-side Java in the form of Web-embedded applets continues to play a role, especially within corporate intranets. The jsp:plugin element is used to insert applets that use the Java Plug-In into JSP pages. This capability is discussed in the third subsection.

The include Directive: Including Files at Page Translation Time

You use the `include` directive to include a file in the main JSP document at the time the document is translated into a servlet (which is typically the first time it is accessed). The syntax is as follows:

```
<%@ include file="Relative URL" %>
```

There are two ramifications of the fact that the included file is inserted at page translation time, not at request time as with `jsp:include` (see the next subsection).

First, the included file is permitted to contain JSP code such as response header settings and field definitions that affect the main page. For example, suppose `snippet.jsp` contained the following code:

```
<%! int accessCount = 0; %>
```

In such a case, you could do the following:

```
<%@ include file="snippet.jsp" %> <%-- Defines accessCount --%>
<%= accessCount++ %>                <%-- Uses accessCount --%>
```

Second, if the included file changes, all the JSP files that use it need to be updated. Unfortunately, although servers are *allowed* to support a mechanism for detecting when an included file has changed (and then recompiling the servlet), they are not *required* to do so. In practice, few servers support this capability. JSP 1.1 lets you supply a `jsp_precompile` request parameter to instruct the JSP engine to translate the JSP page into a servlet. However, this fails in JSP 1.0. So, the simplest and most portable approach is to update the modification date of the JSP page. Some operating systems have commands that update the modification date without your actually editing the file (e.g., the Unix `touch` command), but a simple portable alternative is to include a JSP comment in the top-level page. Update the comment whenever the included file changes. For example, you might put the modification date of the included file in the comment, as below.

```
<%-- Navbar.jsp modified 3/1/00 --%>
<%@ include file="Navbar.jsp" %>
```

Core Warning

If you change an included JSP file, you must update the modification dates of all JSP files that use it.

For example, Listing 20.6 shows a page fragment that gives corporate contact information and some per-page access statistics appropriate to be included at the bottom of multiple pages within a site. Listing 20.7 shows a page that makes use of it, and Figure 20–8 shows the result.

Listing 20.6 `ContactSection.jsp`

```
<%@ page import="java.util.Date" %>
<%-- The following become fields in each servlet that
     results from a JSP page that includes this file. --%>
<%!
private int accessCount = 0;
private Date accessDate = new Date();
private String accessHost = "<I>No previous access</I>";
%>
<P>
<HR>
This page &copy; 2001
<A HREF="http//www.my-company.com/">my-company.com</A>.
This page has been accessed <%= ++accessCount %>
times since server reboot. It was last accessed from
<%= accessHost %> at <%= accessDate %>.
<% accessHost = request.getRemoteHost(); %>
<% accessDate = new Date(); %>
```

Listing 20.7 `SomeRandomPage.jsp`

```
<!DOCTYPE HTML PUBLIC "-//W3C//DTD HTML 4.0 Transitional//EN">
<HTML>
<HEAD>
<TITLE>Some Random Page</TITLE>
<META NAME="author" CONTENT="J. Random Hacker">
<META NAME="keywords"
      CONTENT="foo,bar,baz,quux">
<META NAME="description"
      CONTENT="Some random Web page.">
<LINK REL=STYLESHEET
      HREF="JSP-Styles.css"
      TYPE="text/css">
</HEAD>
<BODY>
<TABLE BORDER=5 ALIGN="CENTER">
  <TR><TH CLASS="TITLE">
      Some Random Page</TABLE>
<P>
Information about our products and services.
<P>
Blah, blah, blah.
<P>
Yadda, yadda, yadda.
<%@ include file="ContactSection.jsp" %>
</BODY>
</HTML>
```

Figure 20–8 Ninth access to `SomeRandomPage.jsp`.

XML Syntax for the include Directive

The XML-compatible equivalent of

```
<%@ include file="..." %>
```

is

```
<jsp:directive.include file="..." />
```

Including Files at Request Time

The `include` directive (see the previous subsection) lets you include actual JSP code into multiple different pages. Including the code itself is sometimes a useful capability, but the `include` directive requires you to update the modification date of the page whenever the included file changes. This is a significant inconvenience. The `jsp:include` action includes the output of a secondary page at the time the main page is requested. Thus, `jsp:include` does not require you to update the main file when an included file changes. On the other hand, the page has already been translated into a servlet by request time, so the included pages cannot contain JSP that affects the main page as a whole. This is a minor restriction, and `jsp:include` is almost always preferred.

Core Approach

For file inclusion, use `jsp:include` *whenever possible. Reserve the* `include` *directive for cases when the included file defines fields or methods that the main page uses or when the included file sets response headers of the main page.*

Although the *output* of the included files cannot contain JSP, they can be the result of resources that use JSP to *create* the output. That is, the URL that refers to the included resource is interpreted in the normal manner by the server and thus can be a servlet or JSP page. This is precisely the behavior of the `include` method of the `RequestDispatcher` class, which is what servlets use if they want to do this type of file inclusion.

The `jsp:include` element has two required attributes, as shown in the sample below: page (a relative URL referencing the file to be included) and `flush` (which can be omitted in JSP 1.1, and *must* have the value `true` if present).

```
<jsp:include page="Relative URL" flush="true" />
```

As an example, consider the simple news summary page shown in Listing 20.8. Page developers can change the news items in the files `Item1.html` through `Item3.html` (Listings 20.9 through 20.11) without having to update the main news page. Figure 20–9 shows the result.

Listing 20.8 `WhatsNew.jsp`

```
<!DOCTYPE HTML PUBLIC "-//W3C//DTD HTML 4.0 Transitional//EN">
<HTML>
<HEAD>
<TITLE>What's New at JspNews.com</TITLE>
<LINK REL=STYLESHEET
      HREF="JSP-Styles.css"
      TYPE="text/css">
</HEAD>
<BODY>
<TABLE BORDER=5 ALIGN="CENTER">
  <TR><TH CLASS="TITLE">
      What's New at JspNews.com</TABLE>
<P>
Here is a summary of our three most recent news stories:
<OL>
  <LI><jsp:include page="news/Item1.html" flush="true" />
  <LI><jsp:include page="news/Item2.html" flush="true" />
  <LI><jsp:include page="news/Item3.html" flush="true" />
</OL>
</BODY>
</HTML>
```

Listing 20.9 `Item1.html`

```
<B>Bill Gates acts humble.</B> In a startling and unexpected
development, Microsoft big wig Bill Gates put on an open act of
humility yesterday.
<A HREF="http://www.microsoft.com/Never.html">More details...</A>
```

Listing 20.10 `Item2.html`

```
<B>Scott McNealy acts serious.</B> In an unexpected twist,
wisecracking Sun head Scott McNealy was sober and subdued at
yesterday's meeting.
<A HREF="http://www.sun.com/Imposter.html">More details...</A>
```

Listing 20.11 `Item3.html`

```
<B>Larry Ellison acts conciliatory.</B> Catching his competitors
off guard yesterday, Oracle prez Larry Ellison referred to his
rivals in friendly and respectful terms.
<A HREF="http://www.oracle.com/Mistake.html">More details...</A>
```

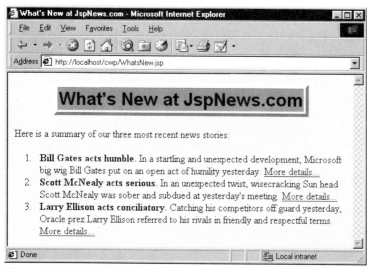

Figure 20–9 Including files at request time makes it easier to update the individual files.

Including Applets for the Java Plug-In

With JSP, you don't need any special syntax to include ordinary applets: just use the normal HTML APPLET tag. However, except for intranets that use Netscape 6 exclusively, these applets must use JDK 1.1 or JDK 1.02 since neither Netscape 4.x nor Internet Explorer 5.x supports the Java 2 platform (i.e., JDK 1.2 or 1.3). This lack of support imposes several restrictions on applets:

- In order to use Swing, you must send the Swing files over the network. This process is time consuming and fails in Internet Explorer 3 and Netscape 3.x and 4.01-4.05 (which only support JDK 1.02), since Swing depends on JDK 1.1.
- You cannot use Java 2D.
- You cannot use the Java 2 collections package.
- Your code runs more slowly, since most compilers for the Java 2 platform are significantly improved over their 1.1 predecessors.

To address these problems, Sun developed a browser plug-in for Netscape and Internet Explorer that lets you use the Java 2 platform in a variety of browsers. This plug-in is available at http://java.sun.com/products/plugin/ and also comes bundled with JDK 1.2.2 and later. Since the plug-in is quite large (several megabytes), it is not reasonable to expect users on the WWW at large to download and install it just to run your applets. On the other hand, it is a reasonable alternative for fast corporate intranets, especially since applets can automatically prompt browsers that lack the plug-in to download it.

Unfortunately, however, the normal APPLET tag will not work with the plug-in, since browsers are specifically designed to use only their built-in virtual machine when they see APPLET. Instead, you have to use a long and messy OBJECT tag for Internet Explorer and an equally long EMBED tag for Netscape. Furthermore, since you typically don't know which browser type will be accessing your page, you have to either include both OBJECT and EMBED (placing the EMBED within the COMMENT section of OBJECT) or identify the browser type at the time of the request and conditionally build the right tag. This process is straightforward but tedious and time consuming.

The jsp:plugin element instructs the server to build a tag appropriate for applets that use the plug-in. Servers are permitted some leeway in exactly how they implement this support, but most simply include both OBJECT and EMBED.

The jsp:plugin Element

The simplest way to use jsp:plugin is to supply four attributes: type, code, width, and height. You supply a value of applet for the type attribute and use the other three attributes in exactly the same way as with the APPLET element, with two exceptions: the attribute names are case sensitive, and single or double quotes are always required around the attribute values. So, for example, you could replace

```
<APPLET CODE="MyApplet.class"
        WIDTH=475 HEIGHT=350>
</APPLET>
```

with

```
<jsp:plugin type="applet"
            code="MyApplet.class"
            width="475" height="350">
</jsp:plugin>
```

The jsp:plugin element has a number of other optional attributes. Most, but not all, parallel attributes of the APPLET element. Here is a full list.

- **type**
  For applets, this attribute should have a value of applet. However, the Java Plug-In also permits you to embed JavaBeans elements in Web pages. Use a value of bean in such a case.
- **code**
  This attribute is used identically to the CODE attribute of APPLET, specifying the top-level applet class file that extends Applet or JApplet.
- **width**
  This attribute is used identically to the WIDTH attribute of APPLET, specifying the width in pixels to be reserved for the applet.
- **height**
  This attribute is used identically to the HEIGHT attribute of APPLET, specifying the height in pixels to be reserved for the applet.
- **codebase**
  This attribute is used identically to the CODEBASE attribute of APPLET, specifying the base directory for the applets. The code attribute is interpreted relative to this directory. As with the APPLET element, if you omit this attribute, the directory of the current page is used as the default. In the case of JSP, this default location is the directory where the original JSP file resided, not the system-specific location of the servlet that results from the JSP file.
- **align**
  This attribute is used identically to the ALIGN attribute of APPLET and IMG, specifying the alignment of the applet within the Web page. Legal values are left, right, top, bottom, and middle.
- **hspace**
  This attribute is used identically to the HSPACE attribute of APPLET, specifying empty space in pixels reserved on the left and right of the applet.

- **vspace**
  This attribute is used identically to the VSPACE attribute of APPLET, specifying empty space in pixels reserved on the top and bottom of the applet.
- **archive**
  This attribute is used identically to the ARCHIVE attribute of APPLET, specifying a JAR file from which classes and images should be loaded.
- **name**
  This attribute is used identically to the NAME attribute of APPLET, specifying a name to use for inter-applet communication or for identifying the applet to scripting languages like JavaScript.
- **title**
  This attribute is used identically to the very rarely used TITLE attribute of APPLET (and virtually all other HTML elements in HTML 4.0), specifying a title that could be used for a tool-tip or for indexing.
- **jreversion**
  This attribute identifies the version of the Java Runtime Environment (JRE) that is required. The default is 1.1.
- **iepluginurl**
  This attribute designates a URL from which the plug-in for Internet Explorer can be downloaded. Users who don't already have the plug-in installed will be prompted to download it from this location. The default value will direct the user to the Sun site, but for intranet use you might want to direct the user to a local copy.
- **nspluginurl**
  This attribute designates a URL from which the plug-in for Netscape can be downloaded. The default value will direct the user to the Sun site, but for intranet use you might want to direct the user to a local copy.

The jsp:param and jsp:params Elements

The jsp:param element is used with jsp:plugin in a manner similar to the way that PARAM is used with APPLET, specifying a name and value that are accessed from within the applet by getParameter. There are two main differences, however. First, since jsp:param follows XML syntax, attribute names must be lower case, attribute values must be enclosed in single or double quotes, and the element must end with />, not just >. Second, all jsp:param entries must be enclosed within a jsp:param**s** element.

So, for example, you would replace

```
<APPLET CODE="MyApplet.class"
        WIDTH=475 HEIGHT=350>
  <PARAM NAME="PARAM1" VALUE="VALUE1">
  <PARAM NAME="PARAM2" VALUE="VALUE2">
</APPLET>
```

with

```
<jsp:plugin type="applet"
            code="MyApplet.class"
            width="475" height="350">
  <jsp:params>
    <jsp:param name="PARAM1" value="VALUE1" />
    <jsp:param name="PARAM2" value="VALUE2" />
  </jsp:params>
</jsp:plugin>
```

The jsp:fallback Element

The jsp:fallback element provides alternative text to browsers that do not support OBJECT or EMBED. You use this element in almost the same way as you would use alternative text placed within an APPLET element. So, for example, you would replace

```
<APPLET CODE="MyApplet.class"
        WIDTH=475 HEIGHT=350>
  <B>Error: this example requires Java.</B>
</APPLET>
```

with

```
<jsp:plugin type="applet"
            code="MyApplet.class"
            width="475" height="350">
  <jsp:fallback>
    <B>Error: this example requires Java.</B>
  </jsp:fallback>
</jsp:plugin>
```

A jsp:plugin Example

Listing 20.12 shows a JSP page that uses the jsp:plugin element to generate an entry for the Java 2 Plug-In. Listings 20.13 through 20.15 show the code for the applet itself (which uses Swing and Java 2D), and Figure 20–10 shows the result.

Listing 20.12 `PluginApplet.jsp`

```
<!DOCTYPE HTML PUBLIC "-//W3C//DTD HTML 4.0 Transitional//EN">
<HTML>
<HEAD>
<TITLE>Using jsp:plugin</TITLE>
<LINK REL=STYLESHEET
      HREF="JSP-Styles.css"
      TYPE="text/css">
</HEAD>
<BODY>
<TABLE BORDER=5 ALIGN="CENTER">
  <TR><TH CLASS="TITLE">
      Using jsp:plugin</TABLE>
<P>
<CENTER>
<jsp:plugin type="applet"
            code="PluginApplet.class"
            width="370" height="420">
</jsp:plugin>
</CENTER>
</BODY>
</HTML>
```

Listing 20.13 `PluginApplet.java`

```
import javax.swing.*;

/** An applet that uses Swing and Java 2D and thus requires
 *  the Java Plug-In.
 */

public class PluginApplet extends JApplet {
  public void init() {
    WindowUtilities.setNativeLookAndFeel();
    setContentPane(new TextPanel());
  }
}
```

Listing 20.14 `TextPanel.java`

```java
import java.awt.*;
import java.awt.event.*;
import javax.swing.*;

/** JPanel that places a panel with text drawn at various angles
 *  in the top part of the window and a JComboBox containing
 *  font choices in the bottom part.
 */

public class TextPanel extends JPanel
                       implements ActionListener {
  private JComboBox fontBox;
  private DrawingPanel drawingPanel;

  public TextPanel() {
    GraphicsEnvironment env =
      GraphicsEnvironment.getLocalGraphicsEnvironment();
    String[] fontNames = env.getAvailableFontFamilyNames();
    fontBox = new JComboBox(fontNames);
    setLayout(new BorderLayout());
    JPanel fontPanel = new JPanel();
    fontPanel.add(new JLabel("Font:"));
    fontPanel.add(fontBox);
    JButton drawButton = new JButton("Draw");
    drawButton.addActionListener(this);
    fontPanel.add(drawButton);
    add(fontPanel, BorderLayout.SOUTH);
    drawingPanel = new DrawingPanel();
    fontBox.setSelectedItem("Serif");
    drawingPanel.setFontName("Serif");
    add(drawingPanel, BorderLayout.CENTER);
  }

  public void actionPerformed(ActionEvent e) {
    drawingPanel.setFontName((String)fontBox.getSelectedItem());
    drawingPanel.repaint();
  }
}
```

Listing 20.15 DrawingPanel.java

```java
import java.awt.*;
import java.awt.geom.*;
import javax.swing.*;

/** A window with text drawn at an angle. The font is
 *  set by means of the setFontName method.
 */

class DrawingPanel extends JPanel {
  private Ellipse2D.Double circle =
    new Ellipse2D.Double(10, 10, 350, 350);
  private GradientPaint gradient =
    new GradientPaint(0, 0, Color.red, 180, 180, Color.yellow,
                      true); // true means to repeat pattern
  private Color[] colors = { Color.white, Color.black };

  public void paintComponent(Graphics g) {
    super.paintComponent(g);
    Graphics2D g2d = (Graphics2D)g;
    g2d.setPaint(gradient);
    g2d.fill(circle);
    g2d.translate(185, 185);
    for (int i=0; i<16; i++) {
      g2d.rotate(Math.PI/8.0);
      g2d.setPaint(colors[i%2]);
      g2d.drawString("jsp:plugin", 0, 0);
    }
  }

  public void setFontName(String fontName) {
    setFont(new Font(fontName, Font.BOLD, 35));
  }
}
```

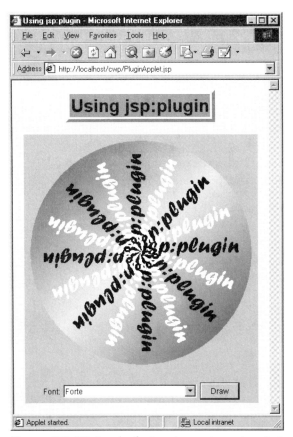

Figure 20–10 Result of `PluginApplet.jsp` in Internet Explorer when the Java 2 Plug-In is installed.

20.6 Using JavaBeans with JSP

The JavaBeans API provides a standard format for Java classes. Visual manipulation tools and other programs can automatically discover information about classes that follow this format and can then create and manipulate the classes without the user having to explicitly write any code.

Full coverage of JavaBeans is beyond the scope of this book. If you want details, pick up one of the many books on the subject or see the documentation and tutorials at `http://java.sun.com/beans/docs/`. For the purposes of this chapter, all you need to know about beans are three simple points:

1. **A bean class must have a zero-argument (empty) constructor.**
    You can satisfy this requirement either by explicitly defining such a
    constructor or by omitting all constructors, which results in an empty
    constructor being created automatically. The empty constructor will
    be called when JSP elements create beans.

2. **A bean class should have no public instance variables (fields).**
    We hope you already follow this practice and use accessor methods
    instead of allowing direct access to the instance variables. Use of
    accessor methods lets you do three things: (1) impose constraints on
    variable values (e.g., have the `setSpeed` method of your `Car` class
    disallow negative speeds); (2) change your internal data structures
    without changing the class interface (e.g., change from English units
    to metric units internally, but still have `getSpeedInMPH` and
    `getSpeedInKPH` methods); (3) perform side effects automatically
    when values change (e.g., update the user interface when
    `setPosition` is called).

3. **Persistent values should be accessed through methods called**
    get*Xxx* and set*Xxx*. For example, if your `Car` class stores the current
    number of passengers, you might have methods named `getNum-`
    `Passengers` (which takes no arguments and returns an `int`) and
    `setNumPassengers` (which takes an `int` and has a `void` return
    type). In such a case, the `Car` class is said to have a *property* named
    `numPassengers` (notice the lowercase n in the property name, but
    the uppercase N in the method names). If the class has a `get`*Xxx*
    method but no corresponding `set`*Xxx*, the class is said to have a
    read-only property named *xxx*.

    The one exception to this naming convention is with boolean proper-
    ties: they use a method called `is`*Xxx* to look up their values. So, for
    example, your `Car` class might have methods called `isLeased` (which
    takes no arguments and returns a `boolean`) and `setLeased` (which
    takes a `boolean` and has a `void` return type), and would be said to
    have a `boolean` property named `leased` (again, notice the lowercase
    leading letter in the property name).

    Although you can use JSP scriptlets or expressions to access arbitrary
    methods of a class, standard JSP actions for accessing beans can only
    make use of methods that use the `get`*Xxx*/`set`*Xxx* or `is`*Xxx*/`set`*Xxx*
    design pattern.

Basic Bean Use

The `jsp:useBean` action lets you load a bean to be used in the JSP page. Beans provide a very useful capability because they let you exploit the reusability of Java classes without sacrificing the convenience that JSP adds over servlets alone.

The simplest syntax for specifying that a bean should be used is:

```
<jsp:useBean id="name" class="package.Class" />
```

This usually means "instantiate an object of the class specified by `Class`, and bind it to a variable with the name specified by `id`." The bean class definition should be in the server's class path (generally, in the same directories where servlets can be installed), *not* in the directory that contains the JSP file. So, for example, the JSP action

```
<jsp:useBean id="book1" class="cwp.Book" />
```

can normally be thought of as equivalent to the scriptlet

```
<% cwp.Book book1 = new cwp.Book(); %>
```

Although it is convenient to think of `jsp:useBean` as being equivalent to building an object, `jsp:useBean` has additional options that make it more powerful. As we'll see later, you can specify a `scope` attribute that makes the bean associated with more than just the current page. If beans can be shared, it is useful to obtain references to existing beans, so the `jsp:useBean` action specifies that a new object is instantiated only if there is no existing one with the same `id` and `scope`.

Rather than using the `class` attribute, you are permitted to use `beanName` instead. The difference is that `beanName` can refer either to a class or to a file containing a serialized bean object. The value of the `beanName` attribute is passed to the `instantiate` method of `java.beans.Bean`.

In most cases, you want the local variable to have the same type as the object being created. In a few cases, however, you might want the variable to be declared to have a type that is a superclass of the actual bean type or is an interface that the bean implements. Use the `type` attribute to control this, as in the following example:

```
<jsp:useBean id="thread1" class="MyClass" type="Runnable" />
```

This use results in code similar to the following being inserted into the `_jspService` method:

```
Runnable thread1 = new MyClass();
```

Note that since `jsp:useBean` uses XML syntax, the format differs in three ways from HTML syntax: the attribute names are case sensitive, either single or double quotes can be used (but one or the other *must* be used), and the end of the tag is marked with `/>`, not just `>`. The first two syntactic differences apply to all JSP elements that look like `jsp:xxx`. The third difference applies unless the element is a container with a separate start and end tag.

There are also a few character sequences that require special handling in order to appear inside attribute values. To get ' within an attribute value, use \'. Similarly, to get ", use \"; to get \ use \\; to get %>, use %\>; and to get <%, use <\%.

Accessing Bean Properties

Once you have a bean, you can access its properties with jsp:getProperty, which takes a name attribute that should match the id given in jsp:useBean and a property attribute that names the property of interest. Alternatively, you could use a JSP expression and explicitly call a method on the object that has the variable name specified with the id attribute. For example, assuming that the Book class has a String property called title and that you've created an instance called book1 by using the jsp:useBean example just given, you could insert the value of the title property into the JSP page in either of the following two ways:

```
<jsp:getProperty name="book1" property="title" />
<%= book1.getTitle() %>
```

The first approach is preferable in this case, since the syntax is more accessible to Web page designers who are not familiar with the Java programming language. However, direct access to the variable is useful when you are using loops, conditional statements, and methods not represented as properties.

If you are not familiar with the concept of bean properties, the standard interpretation of the statement "this bean has a property of type T called foo" is "this class has a method called getFoo that returns something of type T and has another method called setFoo that takes a T as an argument and stores it for later access by getFoo."

Setting Bean Properties: Simple Case

To modify bean properties, you normally use jsp:setProperty. This action has several different forms, but with the simplest form you just supply three attributes: name (which should match the id given by jsp:useBean), property (the name of the property to change), and value (the new value). Later in this section we will present some alternate forms of jsp:setProperty that let you automatically associate a property with a request parameter. That section also explains how to supply values that are computed at request time (rather than fixed strings) and discusses the type conversion conventions that let you supply string values for parameters that expect numbers, characters, or boolean values.

An alternative to using the jsp:setProperty action is to use a scriptlet that explicitly calls methods on the bean object. For example, given the book1 object shown earlier in this section, you could use either of the following two forms to modify the title property:

```
<jsp:setProperty name="book1"
                 property="title"
```

```
                    value="Core Web Programming" />
   <% book1.setTitle("Core Web Programming"); %>
```

Using jsp:setProperty has the advantage that it is more accessible to the non-programmer, but direct access to the object lets you perform more complex operations such as setting the value conditionally or calling methods other than get*Xx* or set*Xx* on the object.

Example: StringBean

Listing 20.16 presents a simple class called StringBean that is in the cwp package. Because the class has no public instance variables (fields) and has a zero-argument constructor since it doesn't declare any explicit constructors, it satisfies the basic criteria for being a bean. Since StringBean has a method called getMessage that returns a String and another method called setMessage that takes a String as an argument, in beans terminology the class is said to have a String parameter called message.

Listing 20.17 shows a JSP file that uses the StringBean class. First, an instance of StringBean is created with the jsp:useBean action as follows:

```
<jsp:useBean id="stringBean" class="cwp.StringBean" />
```

After this, the message property can be inserted into the page in either of the following two ways:

```
<jsp:getProperty name="stringBean" property="message" />
<%= stringBean.getMessage() %>
```

The message property can be modified in either of the following two ways:

```
<jsp:setProperty name="stringBean"
                 property="message"
                 value="some message" />
<% stringBean.setMessage("some message"); %>
```

Figure 20–11 shows the result.

Listing 20.16 StringBean.java

```java
package cwp;

/** A simple bean that has a single String property
 *  called message.
 */

public class StringBean {
  private String message = "No message specified";
```

(continued)

Listing 20.16 `StringBean.java` *(continued)*

```java
  public String getMessage() {
    return(message);
  }

  public void setMessage(String message) {
    this.message = message;
  }
}
```

Listing 20.17 `StringBean.jsp`

```html
<!DOCTYPE HTML PUBLIC "-//W3C//DTD HTML 4.0 Transitional//EN">
<HTML>
<HEAD>
<TITLE>Using JavaBeans with JSP</TITLE>
<LINK REL=STYLESHEET
      HREF="JSP-Styles.css"
      TYPE="text/css">
</HEAD>
<BODY>
<TABLE BORDER=5 ALIGN="CENTER">
  <TR><TH CLASS="TITLE">
      Using JavaBeans with JSP</TABLE>
<jsp:useBean id="stringBean" class="cwp.StringBean" />
<OL>
<LI>Initial value (getProperty):
    <I><jsp:getProperty name="stringBean"
                        property="message" /></I>
<LI>Initial value (JSP expression):
    <I><%= stringBean.getMessage() %></I>
<LI><jsp:setProperty name="stringBean"
                     property="message"
                     value="Best string bean: Fortex" />
    Value after setting property with setProperty:
    <I><jsp:getProperty name="stringBean"
                        property="message" /></I>
<LI><% stringBean.setMessage("My favorite: Kentucky Wonder"); %>
    Value after setting property with scriptlet:
    <I><%= stringBean.getMessage() %></I>
</OL>
</BODY>
</HTML>
```

Figure 20–11 Result of `StringBean.jsp`.

Setting Bean Properties

You normally use `jsp:setProperty` to set bean properties. The simplest form of this action takes three attributes: `name` (which should match the `id` given by `jsp:useBean`), `property` (the name of the property to change), and `value` (the new value).

For example, the `SaleEntry` class shown in Listing 20.18 has an `itemID` property (a `String`), a `numItems` property (an `int`), a `discountCode` property (a `double`), and two read-only properties `itemCost` and `totalCost` (each of type `double`). Listing 20.19 shows a JSP file that builds an instance of the `SaleEntry` class by means of:

```
<jsp:useBean id="entry" class="cwp.SaleEntry" />
```

The results are shown in Figure 20–12.

Once the bean is instantiated, using an input parameter to set the `itemID` is straightforward, as shown below:

```
<jsp:setProperty
    name="entry"
    property="itemID"
    value='<%= request.getParameter("itemID") %>' />
```

Notice that we used a JSP expression for the `value` parameter. Most JSP attribute values have to be fixed strings, but the `value` and `name` attributes of `jsp:setProperty` are permitted to be request-time expressions. If the expression uses double quotes internally, recall that single quotes can be used instead of double quotes around attribute values and that `\ '` and `\ "` can be used to represent single or double quotes within an attribute value.

Listing 20.18 `SaleEntry.java`

```java
package cwp;

/** Simple bean to illustrate the various forms
 *  of jsp:setProperty.
 */

public class SaleEntry {
  private String itemID = "unknown";
  private double discountCode = 1.0;
  private int numItems = 0;

  public String getItemID() {
    return(itemID);
  }

  public void setItemID(String itemID) {
    if (itemID != null) {
      this.itemID = itemID;
    } else {
      this.itemID = "unknown";
    }
  }

  public double getDiscountCode() {
    return(discountCode);
  }

  public void setDiscountCode(double discountCode) {
    this.discountCode = discountCode;
  }

  public int getNumItems() {
    return(numItems);
  }

  public void setNumItems(int numItems) {
    this.numItems = numItems;
  }
```

(continued)

Listing 20.18 `SaleEntry.java` *(continued)*

```java
  // In real life, replace this with database lookup.

  public double getItemCost() {
    double cost;
    if (itemID.equals("a1234")) {
      cost = 12.99*getDiscountCode();
    } else {
      cost = -9999;
    }
    return(roundToPennies(cost));
  }

  private double roundToPennies(double cost) {
    return(Math.floor(cost*100)/100.0);
  }

  public double getTotalCost() {
    return(getItemCost() * getNumItems());
  }
}
```

Listing 20.19 `SaleEntry1.jsp`

```jsp
<!DOCTYPE HTML PUBLIC "-//W3C//DTD HTML 4.0 Transitional//EN">
<HTML>
<HEAD>
<TITLE>Using jsp:setProperty</TITLE>
<LINK REL=STYLESHEET
      HREF="JSP-Styles.css"
      TYPE="text/css">
</HEAD>
<BODY>
<TABLE BORDER=5 ALIGN="CENTER">
  <TR><TH CLASS="TITLE">
      Using jsp:setProperty</TABLE>
<jsp:useBean id="entry" class="cwp.SaleEntry" />
<jsp:setProperty
    name="entry"
    property="itemID"
    value='<%= request.getParameter("itemID") %>' />
<%
int numItemsOrdered = 1;
try {
  numItemsOrdered =
    Integer.parseInt(request.getParameter("numItems"));
```

(continued)

Listing 20.19 `SaleEntry1.jsp` *(continued)*

```
} catch(NumberFormatException nfe) {}
%>
<jsp:setProperty
    name="entry"
    property="numItems"
    value="<%= numItemsOrdered %>" />
<%
double discountCode = 1.0;
try {
  String discountString =
    request.getParameter("discountCode");
  // Double.parseDouble not available in JDK 1.1.
  discountCode =
    Double.valueOf(discountString).doubleValue();
} catch(NumberFormatException nfe) {}
%>
<jsp:setProperty
    name="entry"
    property="discountCode"
    value="<%= discountCode %>" />
<BR>
<TABLE ALIGN="CENTER" BORDER=1>
<TR CLASS="COLORED">
  <TH>Item ID<TH>Unit Price<TH>Number Ordered<TH>Total Price
<TR ALIGN="RIGHT">
  <TD><jsp:getProperty name="entry" property="itemID" />
  <TD>$<jsp:getProperty name="entry" property="itemCost" />
  <TD><jsp:getProperty name="entry" property="numItems" />
  <TD>$<jsp:getProperty name="entry" property="totalCost" />
</TABLE>
</BODY>
</HTML>
```

Figure 20–12 Result of `SaleEntry1.jsp`.

Associating Individual Properties with Input Parameters

Setting the `itemID` property is easy since its value is a `String`. Setting the `numItems` and `discountCode` properties is a bit more problematic since their values must be numbers and `getParameter` returns a `String`. Here is the somewhat cumbersome code required to set `numItems`:

```
<%
int numItemsOrdered = 1;
try {
  numItemsOrdered =
    Integer.parseInt(request.getParameter("numItems"));
} catch(NumberFormatException nfe) {}
%>
<jsp:setProperty
    name="entry"
    property="numItems"
    value="<%= numItemsOrdered %>" />
```

Fortunately, JSP has a nice solution to this problem. It lets you associate a property with a request parameter and automatically perform type conversion from strings to numbers, characters, and boolean values. Instead of using the `value` attribute, you use `param` to name an input parameter. The value of this parameter is automatically used as the value of the property, and simple type conversions are performed automatically. If the specified input parameter is missing from the request, no action is taken (the system does not pass `null` to the associated property). So, for example, setting the `numItems` property can be simplified to:

```
<jsp:setProperty
    name="entry"
    property="numItems"
    param="numItems" />
```

Listing 20.20 shows the entire JSP page reworked in this manner.

Listing 20.20 `SaleEntry2.jsp`

```
. . .
<jsp:useBean id="entry" class="cwp.SaleEntry" />
<jsp:setProperty
    name="entry"
    property="itemID"
    param="itemID" />
<jsp:setProperty
    name="entry"
    property="numItems"
    param="numItems" />
<jsp:setProperty
    name="entry"
    property="discountCode"
    param="discountCode" />
. . .
```

Automatic Type Conversions

When bean properties are associated with input parameters, the system automatically performs simple type conversions for properties that expect primitive types (byte, int, double, etc.) or the corresponding wrapper types (Byte, Integer, Double, etc.). One warning is in order, however: both JSWDK 1.0.1 and the Java Web Server 2.0 have a bug that causes them to crash at page translation time for pages that try to perform automatic type conversions for properties that expect `double` values. Tomcat and most recent servers work as expected.

Associating All Properties with Input Parameters

Associating a property with an input parameter saves you the bother of performing conversions for many of the simple built-in types. JSP lets you take the process one step further by associating *all* properties with identically named input parameters. All you have to do is to supply `"*"` for the `property` parameter. So, for example, all three of the `jsp:setProperty` statements of Listing 20.20 can be replaced by the following simple line. Listing 20.21 shows the complete page.

```
<jsp:setProperty name="entry" property="*" />
```

Although this approach is simple, four small warnings are in order. First, as with individually associated properties, no action is taken when an input parameter is missing. In particular, the system does not supply `null` as the property value. Second, the JSWDK and the Java Web Server both fail for conversions to properties that expect `double` values. Third, automatic type conversion does not guard against illegal values as effectively as does manual type conversion. So, you might consider error pages when using automatic type conversion. Fourth, since both property names and input parameters are case sensitive, the property name and input parameter must match exactly.

Listing 20.21 `SaleEntry3.jsp`

```
...
<jsp:useBean id="entry" class="cwp.SaleEntry" />
<jsp:setProperty name="entry" property="*" />
...
```

Sharing Beans

Up to this point, we have treated the objects that were created with `jsp:useBean` as though they were simply bound to local variables in the `_jspService` method (which is called by the `service` method of the servlet that is generated from the page). Although the beans are indeed bound to local variables, that is not the only behavior. They are also stored in one of four different locations, depending on the value of the optional `scope` attribute of `jsp:useBean`. The `scope` attribute has the following possible values:

- **page**
  This is the default value. It indicates that, in addition to being bound to a local variable, the bean object should be placed in the `PageContext` object for the duration of the current request. Storing the object there means that servlet code can access it by calling `getAttribute` on the predefined `pageContext` variable.

- **application**
  This very useful value means that, in addition to being bound to a local variable, the bean will be stored in the shared `ServletContext` available through the predefined `application` variable or by a call to `getServletContext()`. The `ServletContext` is shared by all servlets in the same Web application (or all servlets in the same server or servlet engine if no explicit Web applications are defined). Values in the `ServletContext` can be retrieved by the `getAttribute` method. This sharing has a couple of ramifications.

  First, it provides a simple mechanism for multiple servlets and JSP pages to access the same object. See the following subsection (Conditional Bean Creation) for details and an example.

  Second, it lets a servlet *create* a bean that will be used in JSP pages, not just *access* one that was previously created. This approach lets a servlet handle complex user requests by setting up beans, storing them in the `ServletContext`, then forwarding the request to one of several possible JSP pages to present results appropriate to the request data. For details on this approach, see Section 20.8 (Integrating Servlets and JSP).

- **session**
  This value means that, in addition to being bound to a local variable, the bean will be stored in the `HttpSession` object associated with the current request, where it can be retrieved with `getAttribute`.

- **request**
  This value signifies that, in addition to being bound to a local variable, the bean object should be placed in the `ServletRequest` object for the duration of the current request, where it is available by means of the `getAttribute` method. Storing values in the request object is common when using the MVC (Model 2) architecture. For details, see Section 20.8 (Integrating Servlets and JSP)

Conditional Bean Creation

To make bean sharing more convenient, there are two situations where bean-related elements are evaluated conditionally.

First, a `jsp:useBean` element results in a new bean being instantiated only if no bean with the same `id` and `scope` can be found. If a bean with the same `id` and scope *is* found, the preexisting bean is simply bound to the variable referenced by `id`. A typecast is performed if the preexisting bean is of a more specific type than the bean being declared, and a `ClassCastException` results if this typecast is illegal.

Second, instead of

```
<jsp:useBean ... />
```

you can use

```
<jsp:useBean ...>statements</jsp:useBean>
```

The point of using the second form is that the statements between the `jsp:use-Bean` start and end tags are executed *only* if a new bean is created, *not* if an existing bean is used. This conditional execution is convenient for setting initial bean properties for beans that are shared by multiple pages. Since you don't know which page will be accessed first, you don't know which page should contain the initialization code. No problem: they can all contain the code, but only the page first accessed actually executes it. For example, Listing 20.22 shows a simple bean that can be used to record cumulative access counts to any of a set of related pages. It also stores the name of the first page that was accessed. Since there is no way to predict which page in a set will be accessed first, each page that uses the shared counter has statements like the following:

```
<jsp:useBean id="counter"
             class="cwp.AccessCountBean"
             scope="application">
  <jsp:setProperty name="counter"
                   property="firstPage"
                   value="Current Page Name" />
</jsp:useBean>

Collectively, the pages using the counter have been accessed
<jsp:getProperty name="counter" property="accessCount" />
times.
```

Listing 20.23 shows the first of three pages that use this approach. The source code archive at http://www.corewebprogramming.com/ contains the other two nearly identical pages. Figure 20–13 shows a typical result.

Listing 20.22 AccessCountBean.java

```
package cwp;

/** Simple bean to illustrate sharing beans through
 *  use of the scope attribute of jsp:useBean.
 */

public class AccessCountBean {
  private String firstPage;
  private int accessCount = 1;

  public String getFirstPage() {
    return(firstPage);
  }

  public void setFirstPage(String firstPage) {
    this.firstPage = firstPage;
  }

  public int getAccessCount() {
    return(accessCount++);
  }
}
```

Listing 20.23 `SharedCounts1.jsp`

```
<!DOCTYPE HTML PUBLIC "-//W3C//DTD HTML 4.0 Transitional//EN">
<HTML>
<HEAD>
<TITLE>Shared Access Counts: Page 1</TITLE>
<LINK REL=STYLESHEET
      HREF="JSP-Styles.css"
      TYPE="text/css">
</HEAD>
<BODY>
<TABLE BORDER=5 ALIGN="CENTER">
  <TR><TH CLASS="TITLE">
      Shared Access Counts: Page 1</TABLE>
<P>
<jsp:useBean id="counter"
             class="cwp.AccessCountBean"
             scope="application">
  <jsp:setProperty name="counter"
                   property="firstPage"
                   value="SharedCounts1.jsp" />
</jsp:useBean>
Of SharedCounts1.jsp (this page),
<A HREF="SharedCounts2.jsp">SharedCounts2.jsp</A>, and
<A HREF="SharedCounts3.jsp">SharedCounts3.jsp</A>,
<jsp:getProperty name="counter" property="firstPage" />
was the first page accessed.
<P>
Collectively, the three pages have been accessed
<jsp:getProperty name="counter" property="accessCount" />
times.
</BODY>
</HTML>
```

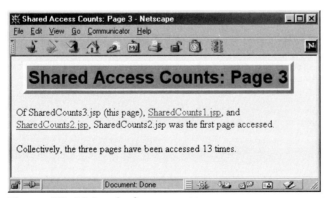

Figure 20–13 Result of a user visiting `SharedCounts3.jsp`. The first page visited by any user was `SharedCounts2.jsp`. `SharedCounts1.jsp`, `SharedCounts2.jsp`, and `SharedCounts3.jsp` were collectively visited a total of twelve times after the server was last started but prior to the visit shown in this figure.

20.7 Defining Custom JSP Tags

JSP 1.1 introduced an extremely valuable new capability: the ability to create your own JSP tags. You define how a tag, its attributes, and its body are interpreted, then group your tags into collections called *tag libraries* that can be used in any number of JSP files. The ability to define tag libraries in this way permits Java developers to boil down complex server-side behaviors into simple and easy-to-use elements that content developers can easily incorporate into their JSP pages.

Custom tags accomplish some of the same goals as beans that are accessed with `jsp:useBean` (see Section 20.6)—encapsulating complex behaviors into simple and accessible forms. There are several differences, however. First, beans cannot manipulate JSP content; custom tags can. Second, complex operations can be reduced to a significantly simpler form with custom tags than with beans. Third, custom tags require quite a bit more work to set up than do beans. Fourth, beans are often defined in one servlet and then used in a different servlet or JSP page (see the following section on integrating servlets and JSP), whereas custom tags usually define more self-contained behavior. Finally, custom tags are available only in JSP 1.1, but beans can be used in both JSP 1.0 and 1.1.

The Components That Make Up a Tag Library

To use custom JSP tags, you need to define three separate components: the tag handler class that defines the tag's behavior, the tag library descriptor file that maps the XML element names to the tag implementations, and the JSP file that uses the tag library. The rest of this subsection gives an overview of each of these components, and the following subsections give details on how to build these components for various styles of tags.

The Tag Handler Class

When defining a new tag, your first task is to define a Java class that tells the system what to do when it sees the tag. This class must implement the `javax.servlet.jsp.tagext.Tag` interface. This is usually accomplished by extending the `TagSupport` or `BodyTagSupport` class. Listing 20.24 is an example of a simple tag that just inserts "`Custom tag example (cwp.tags.ExampleTag)`" into the JSP page wherever the corresponding tag is used. Don't worry about understanding the exact behavior of this class; that will be made clear in the next subsection. For now, just note that it is in the `cwp.tags` class and is called `ExampleTag`. Thus, with Tomcat 3, the class file would be in *install_dir*/webapps/ROOT/WEB-INF/classes/cwp/tags/ExampleTag.class.

Listing 20.24 `ExampleTag.java`

```
package cwp.tags;

import javax.servlet.jsp.*;
import javax.servlet.jsp.tagext.*;
import java.io.*;

/** Very simple JSP tag that just inserts a string
 *  ("Custom tag example...") into the output.
 *  The actual name of the tag is not defined here;
 *  that is given by the Tag Library Descriptor (TLD)
 *  file that is referenced by the taglib directive
 *  in the JSP file.
 */

public class ExampleTag extends TagSupport {
  public int doStartTag() {
    try {
      JspWriter out = pageContext.getOut();
      out.print("Custom tag example " +
                "(cwp.tags.ExampleTag)");
    } catch(IOException ioe) {
      System.out.println("Error in ExampleTag: " + ioe);
    }
    return(SKIP_BODY);
  }
}
```

The Tag Library Descriptor File

Once you have defined a tag handler, your next task is to identify the class to the server and to associate it with a particular XML tag name. This task is accomplished by means of a tag library descriptor file (in XML format) like the one shown in Listing 20.25. This file contains some fixed information, an arbitrary short name for your library, a short description, and a series of tag descriptions. The nonbold part of the listing is the same in virtually all tag library descriptors and can be copied verbatim from the source code archive at `http://www.corewebprogramming.com/` or from the Tomcat 3 standard examples (*install_dir*/webapps/examples/ WEB-INF/jsp).

The format of tag descriptions is described in later sections. For now, just note that the `tag` element defines the main name of the tag (really tag suffix, as will be seen shortly) and identifies the class that handles the tag. Since the tag handler class is in the `cwp.tags` package, the fully qualified class name of `cwp.tags.ExampleTag` is used. Note that this is a class name, not a URL or relative path name. The class can be installed anywhere on the server that beans or other supporting classes can be put. With Tomcat 3, the standard base location is *install_dir*/webapps/ROOT/WEB-INF/classes, so ExampleTag would be in install_dir/webapps/ROOT/WEB-INF/classes/cwp/tags. Although it is always a good idea to put your servlet classes in packages, a surprising feature of Tomcat 3.1 is that tag handlers are *required* to be in packages.

Listing 20.25 `cwp-taglib.tld`

```
<?xml version="1.0" encoding="ISO-8859-1" ?>
<!DOCTYPE taglib
  PUBLIC "-//Sun Microsystems, Inc.//DTD JSP Tag Library 1.1//EN"
  "http://java.sun.com/j2ee/dtds/web-jsptaglibrary_1_1.dtd">

<taglib>
  <tlibversion>1.0</tlibversion>
  <jspversion>1.1</jspversion>
  <shortname>cwp</shortname>
  <info>
    A tag library from Core Web Programming Java 2 Edition,
    http://www.corewebprogramming.com/.
  </info>
  <tag>
    <name>example</name>
    <tagclass>cwp.tags.ExampleTag</tagclass>
    <info>Simplest example: inserts one line of output</info>
  </tag>
</taglib>
```

The JSP File

Once you have a tag handler implementation and a tag library description, you are ready to write a JSP file that makes use of the tag. Listing 20.26 gives an example. Somewhere before the first use of your tag, you need to use the `taglib` directive. This directive has the following form:

```
<%@ taglib uri="..." prefix="..." %>
```

The required `uri` attribute can be either an absolute or relative URL referring to a tag library descriptor file like the one shown in Listing 20.25.

The `prefix` attribute, also required, specifies a prefix that will be used in front of whatever tag name the tag library descriptor defined. For example, if the TLD file defines a tag named `tag1` and the `prefix` attribute has a value of `test`, the actual tag name would be `test:tag1`. This tag could be used in either of the following two ways, depending on whether it is defined to be a container that makes use of the tag body:

```
<test:tag1>Arbitrary JSP</test:tag1>
```

or just

```
<test:tag1 />
```

To illustrate, the descriptor file of Listing 20.25 is called `cwp-taglib.tld`, and resides in the same directory as the JSP file shown in Listing 20.26. Thus, the `taglib` directive in the JSP file uses a simple relative URL giving just the filename, as shown below.

```
<%@ taglib uri="cwp-taglib.tld" prefix="cwp" %>
```

Furthermore, since the `prefix` attribute is `cwp` (for *Core Web Programming*), the rest of the JSP page uses `cwp:example` to refer to the `example` tag defined in the descriptor file. Figure 20–14 shows the result.

Listing 20.26 `SimpleExample.jsp`

```
<!DOCTYPE HTML PUBLIC "-//W3C//DTD HTML 4.0 Transitional//EN">
<HTML>
<HEAD>
<%@ taglib uri="cwp-taglib.tld" prefix="cwp" %>
<TITLE><cwp:example /></TITLE>
<LINK REL=STYLESHEET
      HREF="JSP-Styles.css"
      TYPE="text/css">
</HEAD>
<BODY>
<H1><cwp:example /></H1>
<cwp:example />
</BODY>
</HTML>
```

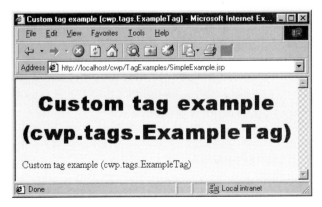

Figure 20–14 Result of `SimpleExample.jsp`.

Defining a Basic Tag

This subsection gives details on defining simple tags without attributes or tag bodies; the tags are thus of the form `<prefix:tagname />`.

A Basic Tag: Tag Handler Class

Tags that either have no body or that merely include the body verbatim should extend the `TagSupport` class. This is a built-in class in the `javax.servlet.jsp.tagext` package that implements the `Tag` interface and contains much of the standard functionality basic tags need. Because of other classes you will use, your tag should normally import classes in the `javax.servlet.jsp` and `java.io` packages as well. So, most tag implementations contain the following `import` statements after the package declaration:

```
import javax.servlet.jsp.*;
import javax.servlet.jsp.tagext.*;
import java.io.*;
```

We recommend that you download an example from `http://www.coreweb-programming.com/` and use it as the starting point for your own implementations.

For a tag without attributes or body, all you need to do is override the `doStart-Tag` method, which defines code that gets called *at request time* where the element's start tag is found. To generate output, the method should obtain the `JspWriter` (the specialized `PrintWriter` available in JSP pages through use of the predefined `out` variable) from the `pageContext` field by means of `getOut`. In addition to the `getOut` method, the `pageContext` field (of type `PageContext`) has methods for obtaining other data structures associated with the request. The most important ones are `getRequest`, `getResponse`, `getServletContext`, and `getSession`.

Since the `print` method of `JspWriter` throws `IOException`, the `print` statements should be inside a `try/catch` block. To report other types of errors to the client, you can declare that your `doStartTag` method throws a `JspException` and then throw one when the error occurs.

If your tag does not have a body, your `doStartTag` should return the `SKIP_BODY` constant. This instructs the system to ignore any content between the tag's start and end tags. As we will see shortly, `SKIP_BODY` is sometimes useful even when there is a tag body (e.g., if you sometimes include it and other times omit it), but the simple tag we're developing here will be used as a stand-alone tag (`<prefix:tagname />`) and thus does not have body content.

Listing 20.27 shows a tag implementation that uses this approach to generate a random 50-digit prime through use of the `Primes` class shown in the previous chapter.

Listing 20.27 `SimplePrimeTag.java`

```
package cwp.tags;

import javax.servlet.jsp.*;
import javax.servlet.jsp.tagext.*;
import java.io.*;
import java.math.*;
import cwp.*;

/** Generates a prime of approximately 50 digits. */

public class SimplePrimeTag extends TagSupport {
  protected int len = 50;

  public int doStartTag() {
    try {
      JspWriter out = pageContext.getOut();
      BigInteger prime = Primes.nextPrime(Primes.random(len));
      out.print(prime);
    } catch(IOException ioe) {
      System.out.println("Error generating prime: " + ioe);
    }
    return(SKIP_BODY);
  }
}
```

A Basic Tag: Tag Library Descriptor File

The general format of a descriptor file is almost always the same: it should contain an XML version identifier followed by a DOCTYPE declaration followed by a `taglib` container element. To get started, just download a sample from `http://www.corewebprogramming.com/`. The important part to understand is what goes *in* the `taglib` element: the `tag` element. For tags without attributes, the `tag` element should contain four elements between `<tag>` and `</tag>`:

1. **name**, whose body defines the base tag name to which the prefix of the `taglib` directive will be attached. In this case, we use
   `<name>simplePrime</name>`
   to assign a base tag name of `simplePrime`.

2. **tagclass**, which gives the fully qualified class name of the tag handler. In this case, we use
   `<tagclass>cwp.tags.SimplePrimeTag</tagclass>`

3. **info**, which gives a short description. Here, we use
   `<info>Outputs a random 50-digit prime.</info>`

4. **bodycontent**, which can be omitted, but if present should have the value `empty` for tags without bodies. Tags with normal bodies that might be interpreted as normal JSP use a value of `JSP`, and the rare tags whose handlers completely process the body themselves use a value of `tagdependent`. For the `SimplePrimeTag` discussed here, we would use `empty` as below:

```
<bodycontent>empty</bodycontent>
```

Unfortunately, however, Tomcat 3.1 does not support the body-content element, and TLD files that contain it will not work. Tomcat 3.2, JRun, and most other servers support `bodycontent` properly.

Core Warning

Do not use the `bodycontent` element with Tomcat 3.1.

Listing 20.28 shows the relevant part of the TLD file.

Listing 20.28 `cwp-taglib.tld` **(Excerpt)**

```
<tag>
   <name>simplePrime</name>
   <tagclass>cwp.tags.SimplePrimeTag</tagclass>
   <info>Outputs a random 50-digit prime.</info>
</tag>
```

A Basic Tag: JSP File

JSP documents that make use of custom tags need to use the `taglib` directive, supplying a `uri` attribute that gives the location of the tag library descriptor file and a `prefix` attribute that specifies a short string that will be attached (along with a colon) to the main tag name. Listing 20.29 shows a JSP document that uses

```
<%@ taglib uri="cwp-taglib.tld" prefix="cwp" %>
```

to use the TLD file just shown in Listing 20.28 with a prefix of `cwp`. Since the base tag name is `simplePrime`, the full tag used is

```
<cwp:simplePrime />
```

Figure 20–15 shows the result.

Listing 20.29 `SimplePrimeExample.jsp`

```
<!DOCTYPE HTML PUBLIC "-//W3C//DTD HTML 4.0 Transitional//EN">
<HTML>
<HEAD>
<TITLE>Some 50-Digit Primes</TITLE>
<LINK REL=STYLESHEET
      HREF="JSP-Styles.css"
      TYPE="text/css">
</HEAD>
<BODY>
<H1>Some 50-Digit Primes</H1>
<%@ taglib uri="cwp-taglib.tld" prefix="cwp" %>
<UL>
  <LI><cwp:simplePrime />
  <LI><cwp:simplePrime />
  <LI><cwp:simplePrime />
  <LI><cwp:simplePrime />
</UL>
</BODY>
</HTML>
```

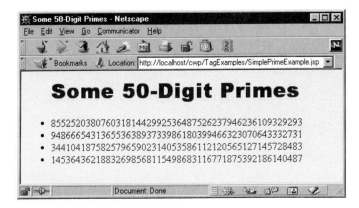

Figure 20–15 Result of `SimplePrimeExample.jsp`.

Assigning Attributes to Tags

Allowing tags like

```
<prefix:name attribute1="value1" attribute2="value2" ... />
```

adds significant flexibility to your tag library. This subsection explains how to add attribute support to your tags.

Tag Attributes: Tag Handler Class

Providing support for attributes is straightforward. Use of an attribute called `attribute1` simply results in a call to a method called `setAttribute1` in your class that extends `TagSupport` (or that otherwise implements the `Tag` interface). The attribute value is supplied to the method as a `String`. Consequently, adding support for an attribute named `attribute1` is merely a matter of implementing the following method:

```
public void setAttribute1(String value1) {
  doSomethingWith(value1);
}
```

Note that an attribute of `attributeName` (lowercase a) corresponds to a method called `setAttributeName` (uppercase A).

One of the most common things to do in the attribute handler is to simply store the attribute in a field that will later be used by `doStartTag` or a similar method. For example, the following is a section of a tag implementation that adds support for the `message` attribute.

```
private String message = "Default Message";

public void setMessage(String message) {
  this.message = message;
}
```

If the tag handler will be accessed from other classes, it is a good idea to provide a `getAttributeName` method in addition to the `setAttributeName` method. Only `setAttributeName` is required, however.

Listing 20.30 shows a subclass of `SimplePrimeTag` that adds support for the `length` attribute. When such an attribute is supplied, it results in a call to `setLength`, which converts the input `String` to an `int` and stores it in the `len` field already used by the `doStartTag` method in the parent class.

Listing 20.30 `PrimeTag.java`

```
package cwp.tags;

import javax.servlet.jsp.*;
import javax.servlet.jsp.tagext.*;
import java.io.*;
```

(continued)

> **Listing 20.30** `PrimeTag.java` *(continued)*

```
/** Generates an N-digit random prime (default N = 50).
 *  Extends SimplePrimeTag, adding a length attribute
 *  to set the size of the prime. The doStartTag
 *  method of the parent class uses the len field
 *  to determine the approximate length of the prime.
 */

public class PrimeTag extends SimplePrimeTag {
  public void setLength(String length) {
    try {
      len = Integer.parseInt(length);
    } catch(NumberFormatException nfe) {
      len = 50;
    }
  }
}
```

Tag Attributes: Tag Library Descriptor File

Tag attributes must be declared inside the `tag` element by means of an `attribute` element. The `attribute` element has three nested elements that can appear between `<attribute>` and `</attribute>`.

1. **name**, a required element that defines the case-sensitive attribute name. In this case, we use
    `<name>length</name>`

2. **required**, a required element that stipulates whether the attribute must always be supplied (`true`) or is optional (`false`). In this case, to indicate that `length` is optional, we use
    `<required>false</required>`
    If you omit the attribute, no call is made to the `setAttributeName` method. So, be sure to give default values to the fields that the method sets.

3. **rtexprvalue**, an optional attribute that indicates whether the attribute value can be a JSP expression like `<%= expression %>` (`true`) or whether it must be a fixed string (`false`). The default value is `false`, so this element is usually omitted except when you want to allow attributes to have values determined at request time.

Listing 20.31 shows the relevant `tag` element within the tag library descriptor file. In addition to supplying an `attribute` element to describe the `length` attribute, the `tag` element also contains the standard name (prime), `tagclass` (`cwp.tags.PrimeTag`), and `info` (short description) elements.

Listing 20.31 `cwp-taglib.tld` (Excerpt)

```
<tag>
  <name>prime</name>
  <tagclass>cwp.tags.PrimeTag</tagclass>
  <info>Outputs a random N-digit prime.</info>
  <attribute>
    <name>length</name>
    <required>false</required>
  </attribute>
</tag>
```

Tag Attributes: JSP File

Listing 20.32 shows a JSP document that uses the `taglib` directive to load the tag library descriptor file and to specify a prefix of `cwp`. Since the `prime` tag is defined to permit a `length` attribute, Listing 20.32 uses

```
<cwp:prime length="xxx" />
```

Remember that custom tags follow XML syntax, which requires attribute values to be enclosed in either single or double quotes. Also, since the `length` attribute is not required, it is permissible to just use

```
<cwp:prime />
```

The tag handler is responsible for using a reasonable default value in such a case. Figure 20–16 shows the result of Listing 20.32.

Listing 20.32 `PrimeExample.jsp`

```
<!DOCTYPE HTML PUBLIC "-//W3C//DTD HTML 4.0 Transitional//EN">
<HTML>
<HEAD>
<TITLE>Some N-Digit Primes</TITLE>
<LINK REL=STYLESHEET
      HREF="JSP-Styles.css"
      TYPE="text/css">
</HEAD>
<BODY>
<H1>Some N-Digit Primes</H1>
<%@ taglib uri="cwp-taglib.tld" prefix="cwp" %>
<UL>
  <LI>20-digit: <cwp:prime length="20" />
  <LI>40-digit: <cwp:prime length="40" />
  <LI>80-digit: <cwp:prime length="80" />
  <LI>Default (50-digit): <cwp:prime />
</UL>
</BODY>
</HTML>
```

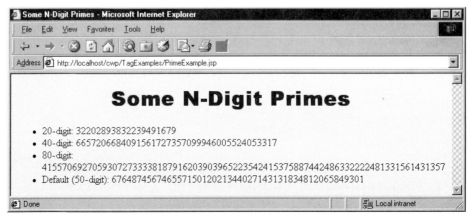

Figure 20–16 Result of `PrimeExample.jsp`.

Including the Tag Body

Up to this point, all of the custom tags you have seen ignore the tag body and thus are used as stand-alone tags of the form

```
<prefix:tagname />
```

In this section, we see how to define tags that use their body content and are thus used in the following manner:

```
<prefix:tagname>body</prefix:tagname>
```

Tag Bodies: Tag Handler Class

In the previous examples, the tag handlers defined a `doStartTag` method that returned `SKIP_BODY`. To instruct the system to make use of the body that occurs between the new element's start and end tags, your `doStartTag` method should return `EVAL_BODY_INCLUDE` instead. The body content can contain JSP scripting elements, directives, and actions, just like the rest of the page. The JSP constructs are translated into servlet code at page translation time, and that code is invoked at request time.

If you make use of a tag body, then you might want to take some action *after* the body as well as before it. Use the `doEndTag` method to specify this action. In almost all cases, you want to continue with the rest of the page after finishing with your tag, so the `doEndTag` method should return `EVAL_PAGE`. If you want to abort the processing of the rest of the page, you can return `SKIP_PAGE` instead.

Listing 20.33 defines a tag for a heading element that is more flexible than the standard HTML `H1` through `H6` elements. This new element allows a precise font size, a list of preferred font names (the first entry that is available on the client system will be used), a foreground color, a background color, a border, and an alignment

(LEFT, CENTER, RIGHT). Only the alignment capability is available with the H1 through H6 elements. The heading is implemented through use of a one-cell table enclosing a SPAN element that has embedded style sheet attributes. The doStart-Tag method generates the TABLE and SPAN start tags, then returns EVAL_BODY_INCLUDE to instruct the system to include the tag body. The doEnd-Tag method generates the </SPAN> and </TABLE> tags, then returns EVAL_PAGE to continue with normal page processing. Various setAttributeName methods are used to handle the attributes like bgColor and fontSize.

Listing 20.33 HeadingTag.java

```java
package cwp.tags;

import javax.servlet.jsp.*;
import javax.servlet.jsp.tagext.*;
import java.io.*;

/** Generates an HTML heading with the specified background
 *  color, foreground color, alignment, font, and font size.
 *  You can also turn on a border around it, which normally
 *  just barely encloses the heading, but which can also
 *  stretch wider. All attributes except the background
 *  color are optional.
 */

public class HeadingTag extends TagSupport {
  private String bgColor; // The one required attribute
  private String color = null;
  private String align="CENTER";
  private String fontSize="36";
  private String fontList="Arial, Helvetica, sans-serif";
  private String border="0";
  private String width=null;

  public void setBgColor(String bgColor) {
    this.bgColor = bgColor;
  }

  public void setColor(String color) {
    this.color = color;
  }

  public void setAlign(String align) {
    this.align = align;
  }
```

(continued)

Listing 20.33 `HeadingTag.java` *(continued)*

```java
  public void setFontSize(String fontSize) {
    this.fontSize = fontSize;
  }

  public void setFontList(String fontList) {
    this.fontList = fontList;
  }

  public void setBorder(String border) {
    this.border = border;
  }

  public void setWidth(String width) {
    this.width = width;
  }

  public int doStartTag() {
    try {
      JspWriter out = pageContext.getOut();
      out.print("<TABLE BORDER=" + border +
                " BGCOLOR=\"" + bgColor + "\"" +
                " ALIGN=\"" + align + "\"");
      if (width != null) {
        out.print(" WIDTH=\"" + width + "\"");
      }
      out.print("><TR><TH>");
      out.print("<SPAN STYLE=\"" +
                "font-size: " + fontSize + "px; " +
                "font-family: " + fontList + "; ");
      if (color != null) {
        out.println("color: " + color + ";");
      }
      out.print("\"> "); // End of <SPAN ...>
    } catch(IOException ioe) {
      System.out.println("Error in HeadingTag: " + ioe);
    }
    return(EVAL_BODY_INCLUDE); // Include tag body
  }
  public int doEndTag() {
    try {
      JspWriter out = pageContext.getOut();
      out.print("</SPAN></TABLE>");
    } catch(IOException ioe) {
      System.out.println("Error in HeadingTag: " + ioe);
    }
    return(EVAL_PAGE); // Continue with rest of JSP page
  }
}
```

Tag Bodies: Tag Library Descriptor File

There is only one new feature in the use of the `tag` element for tags that use body content: the `bodycontent` element should contain the value `JSP` as below.

```
<bodycontent>JSP</bodycontent>
```

Remember, however, that Tomcat 3.1 does not support `bodycontent`, and since `bodycontent` is intended primarily as a hint to development environments, we will omit it in our examples. The name, `tagclass`, `info`, and `attribute` elements are used in the same manner as described previously. Listing 20.34 gives the relevant part of the code.

Listing 20.34 `cwp-taglib.tld` **(Excerpt)**

```
<tag>
  <name>heading</name>
  <tagclass>cwp.tags.HeadingTag</tagclass>
  <info>Outputs a 1-cell table used as a heading.</info>
  <attribute>
    <name>bgColor</name>
    <required>true</required>  <!-- bgColor is required -->
  </attribute>
  <attribute>
    <name>color</name>
    <required>false</required>
  </attribute>
  <attribute>
    <name>align</name>
    <required>false</required>
  </attribute>
  <attribute>
    <name>fontSize</name>
    <required>false</required>
  </attribute>
  <attribute>
    <name>fontList</name>
    <required>false</required>
  </attribute>
  <attribute>
    <name>border</name>
    <required>false</required>
  </attribute>
  <attribute>
    <name>width</name>
    <required>false</required>
  </attribute>
</tag>
```

Tag Bodies: JSP File

Listing 20.35 shows a document that uses the heading tag just defined. Since the bgColor attribute was defined to be required, all uses of the tag include it. Figure 20–17 shows the result.

Listing 20.35 HeadingExample.jsp

```
<!DOCTYPE HTML PUBLIC "-//W3C//DTD HTML 4.0 Transitional//EN">
<HTML>
<HEAD>
<TITLE>Some Tag-Generated Headings</TITLE>
</HEAD>
<BODY>
<%@ taglib uri="cwp-taglib.tld" prefix="cwp" %>
<cwp:heading bgColor="#C0C0C0">
Default Heading
</cwp:heading>
<P>
<cwp:heading bgColor="BLACK" color="WHITE">
White on Black Heading
</cwp:heading>
<P>
<cwp:heading bgColor="#EF8429" fontSize="60" border="5">
Large Bordered Heading
</cwp:heading>
<P>
<cwp:heading bgColor="CYAN" width="100%">
Heading with Full-Width Background
</cwp:heading>
<P>
<cwp:heading bgColor="CYAN" fontSize="60"
             fontList="Brush Script MT, Times, serif">
Heading with Non-Standard Font
</cwp:heading>
</BODY>
</HTML>
```

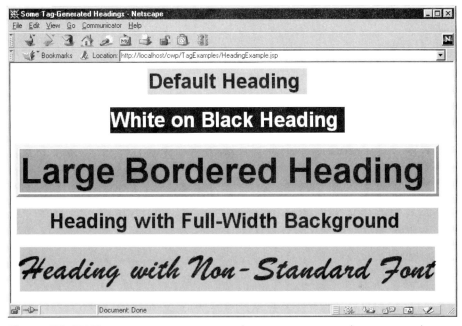

Figure 20–17 The custom `cwp:heading` element gives you much more control over heading format than do the standard `H1` through `H6` elements in HTML.

Optionally Including the Tag Body

Most tags either *never* make use of body content or *always* do so. This section shows you how to use request time information to decide whether or not to include the tag body. Although the body can contain JSP that is interpreted at page translation time, the result of that translation is servlet code that can be invoked or ignored at request time.

Optional Body Inclusion: Tag Handler Class

Optionally including the tag body is a trivial exercise: just return `EVAL_BODY_INCLUDE` or `SKIP_BODY` depending on the value of some request time expression. The important thing to know is how to discover that request time information, since `doStartTag` does not have `HttpServletRequest` and `HttpServletResponse` arguments as do `service`, `_jspService`, `doGet`, and `doPost`. The solution to this dilemma is to use `getRequest` to obtain the `HttpServletRequest` from the automatically defined `pageContext` field of `TagSupport`. Strictly speaking, the return type of `getRequest` is `ServletRequest`, so you have to do a typecast to `HttpServletRequest` if you want to call a method that is not inherited from `ServletRequest`. However, in this case we just use `getParameter`, so no typecast is required.

Listing 20.36 defines a tag that ignores its body unless a request time `debug` parameter is supplied. Such a tag provides a useful capability whereby you embed debugging information directly in the JSP page during development but activate it only when a problem occurs.

Listing 20.36 `DebugTag.java`

```java
package cwp.tags;

import javax.servlet.jsp.*;
import javax.servlet.jsp.tagext.*;
import java.io.*;
import javax.servlet.*;

/** A tag that includes the body content only if
 *  the "debug" request parameter is set.
 */

public class DebugTag extends TagSupport {
  public int doStartTag() {
    ServletRequest request = pageContext.getRequest();
    String debugFlag = request.getParameter("debug");
    if ((debugFlag != null) &&
        (!debugFlag.equalsIgnoreCase("false"))) {
      return(EVAL_BODY_INCLUDE);
    } else {
      return(SKIP_BODY);
    }
  }
}
```

Optional Body Inclusion: Tag Library Descriptor File

If your tag *ever* makes use of its body, you should provide the value `JSP` inside the `bodycontent` element (if you use `bodycontent` at all). Other than that, all the elements within `tag` are used in the same way as described previously. Listing 20.37 shows the entries needed for `DebugTag`.

Listing 20.37 `cwp-taglib.tld` **(Excerpt)**

```
<tag>
  <name>debug</name>
  <tagclass>cwp.tags.DebugTag</tagclass>
  <info>Includes body only if debug param is set.</info>
</tag>
```

Optional Body Inclusion: JSP File

Listing 20.38 shows a page that encloses debugging information between `<cwp:debug>` and `</cwp:debug>`. Figures 20–18 and 20–19 show the normal result and the result when a request time debug parameter is supplied, respectively.

Listing 20.38 `DebugExample.jsp`

```
<!DOCTYPE HTML PUBLIC "-//W3C//DTD HTML 4.0 Transitional//EN">
<HTML>
<HEAD>
<TITLE>Using the Debug Tag</TITLE>
<LINK REL=STYLESHEET
      HREF="JSP-Styles.css"
      TYPE="text/css">
</HEAD>
<BODY>
<H1>Using the Debug Tag</H1>
<%@ taglib uri="cwp-taglib.tld" prefix="cwp" %>
Top of regular page. Blah, blah, blah. Yadda, yadda, yadda.
<P>
<cwp:debug>
<B>Debug:</B>
<UL>
  <LI>Current time: <%= new java.util.Date() %>
  <LI>Requesting hostname: <%= request.getRemoteHost() %>
  <LI>Session ID: <%= session.getId() %>
</UL>
</cwp:debug>
<P>
Bottom of regular page. Blah, blah, blah. Yadda, yadda, yadda.
</BODY>
</HTML>
```

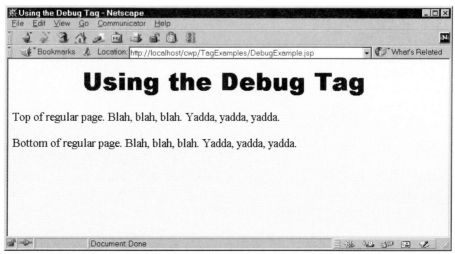

Figure 20–18 The body of the cwp:debug element is normally ignored.

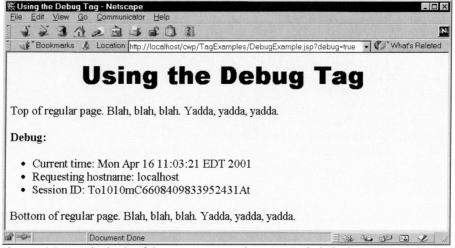

Figure 20–19 The body of the cwp:debug element is included when a debug request parameter is supplied.

Manipulating the Tag Body

The cwp:prime element ignored any body content, the cwp:heading element used body content, and the cwp:debug element ignored or used it depending on a request time parameter. The common thread among these elements is that the tag body was never modified; it was either ignored or included verbatim (after JSP translation). This section shows you how to process the tag body.

Manipulating Body: Tag Handler Class

Up to this point, all of the tag handlers have extended the `TagSupport` class. This is a good standard starting point, as it implements the required `Tag` interface and performs a number of useful setup operations like storing the `PageContext` reference in the `pageContext` field. However, `TagSupport` is not powerful enough for tag implementations that need to manipulate their body content, and `BodyTag-Support` should be used instead.

`BodyTagSupport` extends `TagSupport`, so the `doStartTag` and `doEndTag` methods are used in the same way as before. The two important new methods defined by `BodyTagSupport` are:

1. **doAfterBody**, a method that you should override to handle the manipulation of the tag body. This method should normally return `SKIP_BODY` when it is done, indicating that no further body processing should be performed.
2. **getBodyContent**, a method that returns an object of type `Body-Content` that encapsulates information about the tag body.

The `BodyContent` class has three important methods:

1. **getEnclosingWriter**, a method that returns the `JspWriter` being used by `doStartTag` and `doEndTag`.
2. **getReader**, a method that returns a `Reader` that can read the tag's body.
3. **getString**, a method that returns a `String` containing the entire tag body.

The `ServletUtilities` class (see Listing 19.11) contains a static `filter` method that takes a string and replaces <, >, ", and & with <, >, ", and &, respectively. This method is useful when servlets output strings that might contain characters that would interfere with the HTML structure of the page in which the strings are embedded. Listing 20.39 shows a tag implementation that gives this filtering functionality to a custom JSP tag.

Listing 20.39 `FilterTag.java`

```
package cwp.tags;

import javax.servlet.jsp.*;
import javax.servlet.jsp.tagext.*;
import java.io.*;
import cwp.*;
```

(continued)

Listing 20.39 `FilterTag.java` *(continued)*

```
/** A tag that replaces <, >, ", and & with their HTML
 *  character entities (&lt;, &gt;, &quot;, and &amp;).
 *  After filtering, arbitrary strings can be placed
 *  in either the page body or in HTML attributes.
 */

public class FilterTag extends BodyTagSupport {
  public int doAfterBody() {
    BodyContent body = getBodyContent();
    String filteredBody =
      ServletUtilities.filter(body.getString());
    try {
      JspWriter out = body.getEnclosingWriter();
      out.print(filteredBody);
    } catch(IOException ioe) {
      System.out.println("Error in FilterTag: " + ioe);
    }
    // SKIP_BODY means we're done. If we wanted to evaluate
    // and handle the body again, we'd return EVAL_BODY_TAG.
    return(SKIP_BODY);
  }
}
```

Manipulating Body: Tag Library Descriptor File

Tags that manipulate their body content should use the `bodycontent` element the same way as tags that simply include it verbatim; they should supply a value of JSP. Again, however, remember that Tomcat 3.1 does not properly support body-content, and omitting `bodycontent` is perfectly acceptable on any server. Other than that, nothing new is required in the descriptor file, as you can see by examining Listing 20.40, which shows the relevant portion of the TLD file.

Listing 20.40 `cwp-taglib.tld` **(Excerpt)**

```
<tag>
  <name>filter</name>
  <tagclass>cwp.tags.FilterTag</tagclass>
  <info>Replaces HTML-specific characters in body.</info>
</tag>
```

Manipulating Body: JSP File

Listing 20.41 shows a page that uses a table to show some sample HTML and its result. Creating this table would be tedious in regular HTML since the table cell that shows the original HTML would have to change all the < and > characters to < and >. Doing so is particularly onerous during development when the sample HTML is frequently changing. Use of the <cwp:filter> tag greatly simplifies the process, as Listing 20.41 illustrates. Figure 20–20 shows the result.

Listing 20.41 `FilterExample.jsp`

```
<!DOCTYPE HTML PUBLIC "-//W3C//DTD HTML 4.0 Transitional//EN">
<HTML>
<HEAD>
<TITLE>HTML Logical Character Styles</TITLE>
<LINK REL=STYLESHEET
      HREF="JSP-Styles.css"
      TYPE="text/css">
</HEAD>
<BODY>
<H1>HTML Logical Character Styles</H1>
Physical character styles (B, I, etc.) are rendered consistently
in different browsers. Logical character styles, however,
may be rendered differently by different browsers.
Here's how your browser
(<%= request.getHeader("User-Agent") %>)
renders the HTML 4.0 logical character styles:
<P>
<%@ taglib uri="cwp-taglib.tld" prefix="cwp" %>
<TABLE BORDER=1 ALIGN="CENTER">
<TR CLASS="COLORED"><TH>Example<TH>Result
<TR>
<TD><PRE><cwp:filter>
<EM>Some emphasized text.</EM><BR>
<STRONG>Some strongly emphasized text.</STRONG><BR>
<CODE>Some code.</CODE><BR>
<SAMP>Some sample text.</SAMP><BR>
<KBD>Some keyboard text.</KBD><BR>
<DFN>A term being defined.</DFN><BR>
<VAR>A variable.</VAR><BR>
<CITE>A citation or reference.</CITE><BR>
</cwp:filter></PRE>
<TD>
<EM>Some emphasized text.</EM><BR>
```

(continued)

Listing 20.41 `FilterExample.jsp` *(continued)*

```
<STRONG>Some strongly emphasized text.</STRONG><BR>
<CODE>Some code.</CODE><BR>
<SAMP>Some sample text.</SAMP><BR>
<KBD>Some keyboard text.</KBD><BR>
<DFN>A term being defined.</DFN><BR>
<VAR>A variable.</VAR><BR>
<CITE>A citation or reference.</CITE>
</TABLE>
</BODY>
</HTML>
```

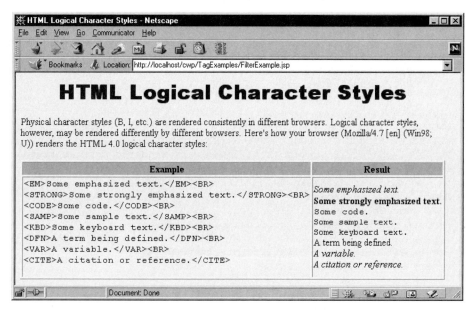

Figure 20–20 The `cwp:filter` element lets you insert text without worrying about it containing special HTML characters.

Including or Manipulating the Tag Body Multiple Times

Rather than just including or processing the body of the tag a single time, you sometimes want to do so more than once. The ability to support multiple body inclusion lets you define a variety of iteration tags that repeat JSP fragments a variable number of times, repeat them until a certain condition occurs, and so forth. This subsection shows you how to build such tags.

The Tag Handler Class

Tags that process the body content multiple times should start by extending BodyTagSupport and implementing doStartTag, doEndTag, and, most importantly, doAfterBody as before. The difference lies in the return value of doAfterBody. If this method returns EVAL_BODY_TAG, the tag body is evaluated again, resulting in a new call to doAfterBody. This process continues until doAfterBody returns SKIP_BODY.

Listing 20.42 defines a tag that repeats the body content the number of times specified by the reps attribute. Since the body content can contain JSP (which is converted into servlet code at page translation time but is invoked at request time), each repetition does not necessarily result in the same output to the client.

Listing 20.42 RepeatTag.java

```
package cwp.tags;

import javax.servlet.jsp.*;
import javax.servlet.jsp.tagext.*;
import java.io.*;

/** A tag that repeats the body the specified
 *  number of times.
 */

public class RepeatTag extends BodyTagSupport {
  private int reps;

  public void setReps(String repeats) {
    try {
      reps = Integer.parseInt(repeats);
    } catch(NumberFormatException nfe) {
      reps = 1;
    }
  }

  public int doAfterBody() {
    if (reps-- >= 1) {
      BodyContent body = getBodyContent();
      try {
        JspWriter out = body.getEnclosingWriter();
        out.println(body.getString());
        body.clearBody(); // Clear for next evaluation
```

(continued)

Listing 20.42 `RepeatTag.java` *(continued)*

```
      } catch(IOException ioe) {
        System.out.println("Error in RepeatTag: " + ioe);
      }
      return(EVAL_BODY_TAG);
    } else {
      return(SKIP_BODY);
    }
  }
}
```

The Tag Library Descriptor File

Listing 20.43 shows the relevant section of the TLD file that gives the name `cwp:repeat` to the tag just defined. To accommodate request time values in the reps attribute, the file uses an `rtexprvalue` element (enclosing a value of `true`) within the `attribute` element.

Listing 20.43 `cwp-taglib.tld` **(Excerpt)**

```
<tag>
  <name>repeat</name>
  <tagclass>cwp.tags.RepeatTag</tagclass>
  <info>Repeats body the specified number of times.</info>
  <attribute>
    <name>reps</name>
    <required>true</required>
    <!-- rtexprvalue indicates whether attribute
         can be a JSP expression. -->
    <rtexprvalue>true</rtexprvalue>
  </attribute>
</tag>
```

The JSP File

Listing 20.44 shows a JSP document that creates a numbered list of prime numbers. The number of primes in the list is taken from the request time `repeats` parameter. Figure 20–21 shows one possible result.

Listing 20.44 RepeatExample.jsp

```
<!DOCTYPE HTML PUBLIC "-//W3C//DTD HTML 4.0 Transitional//EN">
<HTML>
<HEAD>
<TITLE>Some 40-Digit Primes</TITLE>
<LINK REL=STYLESHEET
      HREF="JSP-Styles.css"
      TYPE="text/css">
</HEAD>
<BODY>
<H1>Some 40-Digit Primes</H1>
Each entry in the following list is the first prime number
higher than a randomly selected 40-digit number.
<%@ taglib uri="cwp-taglib.tld" prefix="cwp" %>
<OL>
<!-- Repeats N times. A null reps value means repeat once. -->
<cwp:repeat reps='<%= request.getParameter("repeats") %>'>
  <LI><cwp:prime length="40" />
</cwp:repeat>
</OL>
</BODY>
</HTML>
```

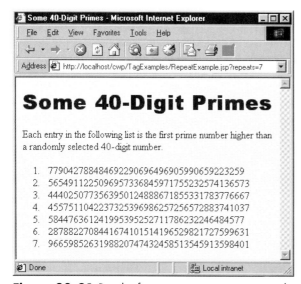

Figure 20–21 Result of RepeatExample.jsp when accessed with a repeats parameter of 20.

Using Nested Tags

Although Listing 20.44 places the cwp:prime element within the cwp:repeat element, the two elements are independent of each other. The first generates a prime number regardless of where it is used, and the second repeats the enclosed content regardless of whether that content uses a cwp:prime element.

Some tags, however, depend on a particular nesting. For example, in standard HTML, the TD and TH elements can only appear within TR, which in turn can only appear within TABLE. The color and alignment settings of TABLE are inherited by TR, and the values of TR affect how TD and TH behave. So, the nested elements cannot act in isolation even when nested properly. Similarly, the tag library descriptor file makes use of a number of elements like taglib, tag, attribute, and required where a strict nesting hierarchy is imposed.

This subsection shows you how to define tags that depend on a particular nesting order and where the behavior of certain tags depends on values supplied by earlier ones.

The Tag Handler Classes

Class definitions for nested tags can extend *either* TagSupport or BodyTagSupport, depending on whether they need to manipulate their body content (these extend BodyTagSupport) or, more commonly, just ignore it or include it verbatim (these extend TagSupport).

There are two key new approaches for nested tags, however. First, nested tags can use findAncestorWithClass to find the tag in which they are nested. This method takes a reference to the current class (e.g., this) and the Class object of the enclosing class (e.g., EnclosingTag.class) as arguments. If no enclosing class is found, the method in the nested class can throw a JspTagException that reports the problem. Second, if one tag wants to store data that a later tag will use, it can place that data in the instance of the enclosing tag. The definition of the enclosing tag should provide methods for storing and accessing this data.

Suppose that we want to define a set of tags that would be used like this:

```
<cwp:if>
  <cwp:condition><%= someExpression %></cwp:condition>
  <cwp:then>JSP to include if condition is true</cwp:then>
  <cwp:else>JSP to include if condition is false</cwp:else>
</cwp:if>
```

To accomplish this task, the first step is to define an IfTag class to handle the cwp:if tag. This handler should have methods to specify and check whether the condition is true or false (setCondition and getCondition) as well as methods to designate and check whether the condition has ever been explicitly set (setHasCondition and getHasCondition), since we want to disallow cwp:if tags that contain no cwp:condition entry. Listing 20.45 shows the code for IfTag.

The second step is to define a tag handler for `cwp:condition`. This class, called `IfConditionTag`, defines a `doStartTag` method that merely checks whether the tag appears within `IfTag`. It returns `EVAL_BODY_TAG` if so and throws an exception if not. The handler's `doAfterBody` method looks up the body content (`getBody-Content`), converts it to a `String` (`getString`), and compares that to `"true"`. This approach means that an explicit value of `true` can be substituted for a JSP expression like `<%= expression %>` if, during initial page development, you want to temporarily designate that the `then` portion should always be used. Using a comparison to `"true"` also means that *any* other value will be considered false. Once this comparison is performed, the result is stored in the enclosing tag by means of the `setCondition` method of `IfTag`. The code for `IfConditionTag` is shown in Listing 20.46.

The third step is to define a class to handle the `cwp:then` tag. The `doStartTag` method of this class verifies that it is inside `IfTag` and also checks that an explicit condition has been set (i.e., that the `IfConditionTag` has already appeared within the `IfTag`). The `doAfterBody` method checks for the condition in the `IfTag` class, and, if it is true, looks up the body content and prints it. Listing 20.47 shows the code.

The final step in defining tag handlers is to define a class for `cwp:else`. This class is very similar to the one to handle the `then` part of the tag, except that this handler only prints the tag body from `doAfterBody` if the condition from the surrounding `IfTag` is false. The code is shown in Listing 20.48.

Listing 20.45 `IfTag.java`

```java
package cwp.tags;

import javax.servlet.jsp.*;
import javax.servlet.jsp.tagext.*;
import java.io.*;
import javax.servlet.*;

/** A tag that acts like an if/then/else. */

public class IfTag extends TagSupport {
  private boolean condition;
  private boolean hasCondition = false;

  public void setCondition(boolean condition) {
    this.condition = condition;
    hasCondition = true;
  }

  public boolean getCondition() {
    return(condition);
  }
```

(continued)

Listing 20.45 IfTag.java *(continued)*

```java
  public void setHasCondition(boolean flag) {
    this.hasCondition = flag;
  }

  /** Has the condition field been explicitly set? */

  public boolean hasCondition() {
    return(hasCondition);
  }

  public int doStartTag() {
    return(EVAL_BODY_INCLUDE);
  }
}
```

Listing 20.46 IfConditionTag.java

```java
package cwp.tags;

import javax.servlet.jsp.*;
import javax.servlet.jsp.tagext.*;
import java.io.*;
import javax.servlet.*;

/** The condition part of an if tag. */

public class IfConditionTag extends BodyTagSupport {
  public int doStartTag() throws JspTagException {
    IfTag parent =
      (IfTag)findAncestorWithClass(this, IfTag.class);
    if (parent == null) {
      throw new JspTagException("condition not inside if");
    }
    return(EVAL_BODY_TAG);
  }
  public int doAfterBody() {
    IfTag parent =
      (IfTag)findAncestorWithClass(this, IfTag.class);
    String bodyString = getBodyContent().getString();
    if (bodyString.trim().equals("true")) {
      parent.setCondition(true);
    } else {
      parent.setCondition(false);
    }
    return(SKIP_BODY);
  }
}
```

Listing 20.47 IfThenTag.java

```
package cwp.tags;

import javax.servlet.jsp.*;
import javax.servlet.jsp.tagext.*;
import java.io.*;
import javax.servlet.*;

/** The then part of an if tag. */

public class IfThenTag extends BodyTagSupport {
  public int doStartTag() throws JspTagException {
    IfTag parent =
      (IfTag)findAncestorWithClass(this, IfTag.class);
    if (parent == null) {
      throw new JspTagException("then not inside if");
    } else if (!parent.hasCondition()) {
      String warning =
        "condition tag must come before then tag";
      throw new JspTagException(warning);
    }
    return(EVAL_BODY_TAG);
  }

  public int doAfterBody() {
    IfTag parent =
      (IfTag)findAncestorWithClass(this, IfTag.class);
    if (parent.getCondition()) {
      try {
        BodyContent body = getBodyContent();
        JspWriter out = body.getEnclosingWriter();
        out.print(body.getString());
      } catch(IOException ioe) {
        System.out.println("Error in IfThenTag: " + ioe);
      }
    }
    return(SKIP_BODY);
  }
}
```

Listing 20.48 `IfElseTag.java`

```java
package cwp.tags;

import javax.servlet.jsp.*;
import javax.servlet.jsp.tagext.*;
import java.io.*;
import javax.servlet.*;

/** The else part of an if tag. */

public class IfElseTag extends BodyTagSupport {
  public int doStartTag() throws JspTagException {
    IfTag parent =
      (IfTag)findAncestorWithClass(this, IfTag.class);
    if (parent == null) {
      throw new JspTagException("else not inside if");
    } else if (!parent.hasCondition()) {
      String warning =
        "condition tag must come before else tag";
      throw new JspTagException(warning);
    }
    return(EVAL_BODY_TAG);
  }

  public int doAfterBody() {
    IfTag parent =
      (IfTag)findAncestorWithClass(this, IfTag.class);
    if (!parent.getCondition()) {
      try {
        BodyContent body = getBodyContent();
        JspWriter out = body.getEnclosingWriter();
        out.print(body.getString());
      } catch(IOException ioe) {
        System.out.println("Error in IfElseTag: " + ioe);
      }
    }
    return(SKIP_BODY);
  }
}
```

The Tag Library Descriptor File

Even though there is an explicit required nesting structure for the tags just defined, the tags must be declared separately in the TLD file. This means that nesting validation is performed only at request time, not at page translation time. In principle, you could instruct the system to do some validation at page translation time by using a `TagExtraInfo` class. This class has a `getVariableInfo` method that you can use to check that attributes exist and where they are used. Once you have defined a subclass of TagExtraInfo, you associate it with your tag in the tag library descriptor file by means of the teiclass element, which is used just like tagclass. In practice, however, TagExtraInfo is a bit cumbersome to use.

Listing 20.49 `cwp-taglib.tld` **(Excerpt)**

```
<tag>
  <name>if</name>
  <tagclass>cwp.tags.IfTag</tagclass>
  <info>if/condition/then/else tag.</info>
</tag>
<tag>
  <name>condition</name>
  <tagclass>cwp.tags.IfConditionTag</tagclass>
  <info>condition part of if/condition/then/else tag.</info>
</tag>
<tag>
  <name>then</name>
  <tagclass>cwp.tags.IfThenTag</tagclass>
  <info>then part of if/condition/then/else tag.</info>
</tag>
<tag>
  <name>else</name>
  <tagclass>cwp.tags.IfElseTag</tagclass>
  <info>else part of if/condition/then/else tag.</info>
</tag>
```

The JSP File

Listing 20.50 shows a page that uses the cwp:if tag three different ways. In the first instance, a value of true is hardcoded for the condition. In the second instance, a parameter from the HTTP request is used for the condition, and in the third case, a random number is generated and compared to a fixed cutoff. Figure 20–22 shows a typical result.

Listing 20.50 `IfExample.jsp`

```
<!DOCTYPE HTML PUBLIC "-//W3C//DTD HTML 4.0 Transitional//EN">
<HTML>
<HEAD>
<TITLE>If Tag Example</TITLE>
<LINK REL=STYLESHEET
      HREF="JSP-Styles.css"
      TYPE="text/css">
```

(continued)

Listing 20.50 `IfExample.jsp` *(continued)*

```
</HEAD>
<BODY>
<H1>If Tag Example</H1>
<%@ taglib uri="cwp-taglib.tld" prefix="cwp" %>
<cwp:if>
  <cwp:condition>true</cwp:condition>
  <cwp:then>Condition is true</cwp:then>
  <cwp:else>Condition is false</cwp:else>
</cwp:if>
<P>
<cwp:if>
  <cwp:condition><%= request.isSecure() %></cwp:condition>
  <cwp:then>Request is using SSL (https)</cwp:then>
  <cwp:else>Request is not using SSL</cwp:else>
</cwp:if>
<P>
Some coin tosses:<BR>
<cwp:repeat reps="10">
  <cwp:if>
    <cwp:condition><%= Math.random() < 0.5 %></cwp:condition>
    <cwp:then><B>Heads</B><BR></cwp:then>
    <cwp:else><B>Tails</B><BR></cwp:else>
  </cwp:if>
</cwp:repeat>
</BODY>
</HTML>
```

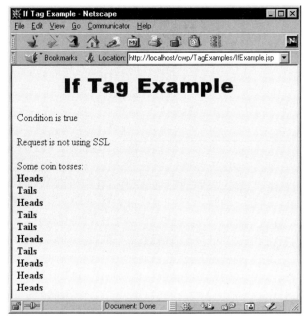

Figure 20–22
Result of `IfExample.jsp`.

20.8 Integrating Servlets and JSP

Servlets are great when your application requires a lot of real programming to accomplish its task. As you've seen in the previous chapter, servlets can manipulate HTTP status codes and headers, use cookies, track sessions, save information between requests, compress pages, access databases, generate GIF images on-the-fly, and perform many other tasks flexibly and efficiently. But, generating HTML with servlets can be tedious and can yield a result that is hard to modify. That's where JSP comes in; it lets you separate much of the presentation from the dynamic content. That way, you can write the HTML in the normal manner, even using HTML-specific tools and putting your Web content developers to work on your JSP documents. JSP expressions, scriptlets, and declarations let you insert simple Java code into the servlet that results from the JSP page, and directives let you control the overall layout of the page. For more complex requirements, you can wrap up Java code inside beans or define your own JSP tags.

Great. We have everything we need, right? Well, no, not quite. The assumption behind a JSP document is that it provides a *single* overall presentation. What if you want to give totally different results depending on the data that you receive? Beans and custom tags, although extremely powerful and flexible, don't overcome the limitation that the JSP page defines a relatively fixed top-level page appearance. The solution is to use *both* servlets and JavaServer Pages. If you have a complicated application that may require several substantially different presentations, a servlet can handle the initial request, partially process the data, set up beans, and then forward the results to one of a number of different JSP pages, depending on the circumstances. This approach is known as the *model view controller architecture* or *model 2* approach to JSP. For code that supports a formalization of this approach, see the Apache Struts Framework at `http://jakarta.apache.org/struts/`.

Forwarding Requests

The key to letting servlets forward requests or include external content is to use a `RequestDispatcher`. You obtain a `RequestDispatcher` by calling the `get-RequestDispatcher` method of `ServletContext`, supplying a URL relative to the server root. For example, to obtain a `RequestDispatcher` associated with `http://yourhost/presentations/presentation1.jsp`, you would do the following:

```
String url = "/presentations/presentation1.jsp";
RequestDispatcher dispatcher =
  getServletContext().getRequestDispatcher(url);
```

Once you have a `RequestDispatcher`, you use `forward` to completely transfer control to the associated URL and you use `include` to output the associated URL's content. In both cases, you supply the `HttpServletRequest` and `HttpServlet-`

Response as arguments. Both methods throw `ServletException` and `IOException`. For example, Listing 20.51 shows a portion of a servlet that forwards the request to one of three different JSP pages, depending on the value of the `operation` parameter. To avoid repeating the `getRequestDispatcher` call, we use a utility method called `gotoPage` that takes the URL, the `HttpServlet-Request`, and the `HttpServletResponse`; gets a `RequestDispatcher`; and then calls `forward` on it.

Listing 20.51 Request Forwarding Example

```
public void doGet(HttpServletRequest request,
                  HttpServletResponse response)
    throws ServletException, IOException {
  String operation = request.getParameter("operation");
  if (operation == null) {
    operation = "unknown";
  }
  if (operation.equals("operation1")) {
    gotoPage("/operations/presentation1.jsp",
             request, response);
  } else if (operation.equals("operation2")) {
    gotoPage("/operations/presentation2.jsp",
             request, response);
  } else {
    gotoPage("/operations/unknownRequestHandler.jsp",
             request, response);
  }
}

private void gotoPage(String address,
                      HttpServletRequest request,
                      HttpServletResponse response)
    throws ServletException, IOException {
  RequestDispatcher dispatcher =
    getServletContext().getRequestDispatcher(address);
  dispatcher.forward(request, response);
}
```

Using Static Resources

In most cases, you forward requests to a JSP page or another servlet. In some cases, however, you might want to send the request to a static HTML page. In an e-commerce site, for example, requests that indicate that the user does not have a valid account name might be forwarded to an account application page that uses HTML forms to gather the requisite information. With GET requests, forwarding requests to a static HTML page is perfectly legal and requires no special syntax; just supply the address of the HTML page as the argument to `getRequest-Dispatcher`. However, since forwarded requests use the same request method as the original request, POST requests cannot be forwarded to normal HTML pages. The solution to this problem is to simply rename the HTML page to have a `.jsp` extension. Renaming `somefile.html` to `somefile.jsp` does not change its output for GET requests, but `somefile.html` cannot handle POST requests, whereas `somefile.jsp` gives an identical response for both GET and POST.

Supplying Information to the Destination Pages

There are three main places for the servlet to store the data that the JSP pages will use: in the `HttpServletRequest`, in the `HttpSession`, and in the `Servlet-Context`. These storage locations correspond to the three non-default values of the scope attribute `jsp:useBean`: `request`, `session`, and `application`.

1. **Storing data that servlet looked up and that JSP page will use only in this request.** The servlet would create and store data as follows:

   ```
   SomeClass value = new SomeClass(...);
   request.setAttribute("key", value);
   ```

   Then, the servlet would forward to a JSP page that uses the following to retrieve the data:

   ```
   <jsp:useBean id="key" class="SomeClass"
                scope="request" />
   ```

2. **Storing data that servlet looked up and that JSP page will use in this request and in later requests from *same* client.** The servlet would create and store data as follows:

   ```
   SomeClass value = new SomeClass(...);
   HttpSession session = request.getSession(true);
   session.setAttribute("key", value);
   ```

   Then, the servlet would forward to a JSP page that uses the following to retrieve the data:

   ```
   <jsp:useBean id="key" class="SomeClass"
                scope="session" />
   ```

3. **Storing data that servlet looked up and that JSP page will use in this request and in later requests from *any* client.** The servlet would create and store data as follows:

   ```
   SomeClass value = new SomeClass(...);
   getServletContext().setAttribute("key", value);
   ```

   Then, the servlet would forward to a JSP page that uses the following to retrieve the data:

   ```
   <jsp:useBean id="key" class="SomeClass"
                scope="application" />
   ```

Interpreting Relative URLs in the Destination Page

Although a servlet can forward the request to arbitrary locations on the same server, the process is quite different from that of using the `sendRedirect` method of `HttpServletResponse`. First, `sendRedirect` requires the client to reconnect to the new resource, whereas the `forward` method of `RequestDispatcher` is handled completely on the server. Second, `sendRedirect` does not automatically preserve all of the request data; `forward` does. Third, `sendRedirect` results in a different final URL, whereas with `forward`, the URL of the original servlet is maintained.

This final point means that, if the destination page uses relative URLs for images or style sheets, it needs to make them relative to the server root, not to the destination page's actual location. For example, consider the following style sheet entry:

```
<LINK REL=STYLESHEET
      HREF="my-styles.css"
      TYPE="text/css">
```

If the JSP page containing this entry is accessed by means of a forwarded request, `my-styles.css` will be interpreted relative to the URL of the *originating* servlet, not relative to the JSP page itself, almost certainly resulting in an error. The solution is to give the full server path to the style sheet file, as follows:

```
<LINK REL=STYLESHEET
      HREF="/path/my-styles.css"
      TYPE="text/css">
```

The same approach is required for addresses used in `<IMG SRC=...>` and `<A HREF=...>`.

Alternative Means of Getting a RequestDispatcher

In servers that support version 2.2 of the servlet specification, there are two additional ways of obtaining a `RequestDispatcher` besides the `getRequest-Dispatcher` method of `ServletContext`.

First, since most servers let you register explicit names for servlets or JSP pages, it makes sense to access them by name rather than by path. Use the `getNamed-Dispatcher` method of `ServletContext` for this task.

Second, you might want to access a resource by a path relative to the current servlet's location, rather than relative to the server root. This approach is not common when servlets are accessed in the standard manner (`http://host/servlet/ServletName`), because JSP files would not be accessible by means of `http://host/servlet/...` since that URL is reserved especially for servlets. However, it is common to register servlets under another path, and in such a case you can use the `getRequestDispatcher` method of `HttpServletRequest` rather than the one from `ServletContext`. For example, if the originating servlet is at `http://host/travel/TopLevel`,

```
getServletContext().getRequestDispatcher("/travel/cruises.jsp")
```

could be replaced by

```
request.getRequestDispatcher("cruises.jsp");
```

Example: An On-Line Travel Agent

Consider the case of an on-line travel agent that has a quick-search page, as shown in Figure 20–23 and Listing 20.52. Users need to enter their e-mail address and password to associate the request with their previously established customer account. Each request also includes a trip origin, trip destination, start date, and end date. However, the action that will result will vary substantially based upon the action requested. For example, pressing the "Book Flights" button should show a list of available flights on the dates specified, ordered by price (see Figure 20–24). The user's real name, frequent flyer information, and credit card number should be used to generate the page. On the other hand, selecting "Edit Account" should show any previously entered customer information, letting the user modify values or add entries. Likewise, the actions resulting from choosing "Rent Cars" or "Find Hotels" will share much of the same customer data but will have a totally different presentation.

To accomplish the desired behavior, the front end (Listing 20.52) submits the request to the top-level travel servlet shown in Listing 20.53. This servlet looks up the customer information (see `http://www.corewebprogramming.com` for the actual code used, but this would be replaced by a database lookup in real life), puts it in the `HttpSession` object associating the value (of type `cwp.TravelCustomer`) with the name `customer`, and then forwards the request to a different JSP page corresponding to each of the possible actions. The destination page (see Listing 20.54 and the result in Figure 20–24) looks up the customer information by means of

```
<jsp:useBean id="customer"
             class="cwp.TravelCustomer"
             scope="session" />
```

then uses `jsp:getProperty` to insert customer information into various parts of the page.

You should pay careful attention to the `TravelCustomer` class (shown partially in Listing 20.55; available in full at `www.corewebprogramming.com`). In particular, note that the class spends a considerable amount of effort making the customer information accessible as plain strings or even HTML-formatted strings through simple properties. Every task that requires any substantial amount of programming is spun off into the bean, rather than being performed in the JSP page itself. This is typical of servlet/JSP integration—the use of JSP does not *entirely* obviate the need to format data as strings or HTML in Java code. Significant up-front effort to make the data conveniently available to JSP more than pays for itself when multiple JSP pages access the same type of data.

Figure 20–23 Front end to travel servlet (see Listing 20.52).

Listing 20.52 /travel/quick-search.html (Excerpt)

```
<!DOCTYPE HTML PUBLIC "-//W3C//DTD HTML 4.0 Transitional//EN">
<HTML>
<HEAD>
  <TITLE>Online Travel Quick Search</TITLE>
  <LINK REL=STYLESHEET
        HREF="travel-styles.css"
        TYPE="text/css">
</HEAD>
<BODY>
<BR>
<H1>Online Travel Quick Search</H1>
<FORM ACTION="/servlet/cwp.Travel" METHOD="POST">
<CENTER>
Email address: <INPUT TYPE="TEXT" NAME="emailAddress"><BR>
Password: <INPUT TYPE="PASSWORD" NAME="password" SIZE=10><BR>
...
<TABLE CELLSPACING=1>
<TR>
  <TH> <IMG SRC="airplane.gif" WIDTH=100 HEIGHT=29
                ALIGN="TOP" ALT="Book Flight"> 
  ...
<TR>
  <TH><SMALL>
      <INPUT TYPE="SUBMIT" NAME="flights" VALUE="Book Flight">
      </SMALL>
  ...
</TABLE>
</CENTER>
</FORM>
...
</BODY>
</HTML>
```

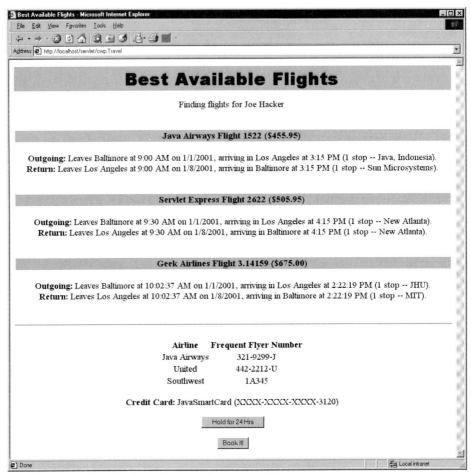

Figure 20–24 Result of travel servlet (Listing 20.53) dispatching request to `BookFlights.jsp` (Listing 20.54).

Listing 20.53 `Travel.java`

```java
package cwp;

import java.io.*;
import javax.servlet.*;
import javax.servlet.http.*;

/** Top-level travel-processing servlet. This servlet sets up
 *  the customer data as a bean, then forwards the request
 *  to the airline booking page, the rental car reservation
 *  page, the hotel page, the existing account modification
 *  page, or the new account page.
 */

public class Travel extends HttpServlet {
  private TravelCustomer[] travelData;

  public void init() {
    travelData = TravelData.getTravelData();
  }

  /** Since password is being sent, use POST only. */

  public void doPost(HttpServletRequest request,
                     HttpServletResponse response)
      throws ServletException, IOException {
    String emailAddress = request.getParameter("emailAddress");
    String password = request.getParameter("password");
    TravelCustomer customer =
      TravelCustomer.findCustomer(emailAddress, travelData);
    if ((customer == null) || (password == null) ||
        (!password.equals(customer.getPassword()))) {
      gotoPage("/travel/accounts.jsp", request, response);
    }
    // The methods that use the following parameters will
    // check for missing or malformed values.
    customer.setStartDate(request.getParameter("startDate"));
    customer.setEndDate(request.getParameter("endDate"));
    customer.setOrigin(request.getParameter("origin"));
    customer.setDestination(request.getParameter
                              ("destination"));
    HttpSession session = request.getSession(true);
    session.setAttribute("customer", customer);
```

(continued)

Listing 20.53 `Travel.java` *(continued)*

```java
    if (request.getParameter("flights") != null) {
      gotoPage("/travel/BookFlights.jsp",
               request, response);
    } else if (request.getParameter("cars") != null) {
      gotoPage("/travel/RentCars.jsp",
               request, response);
    } else if (request.getParameter("hotels") != null) {
      gotoPage("/travel/FindHotels.jsp",
               request, response);
    } else if (request.getParameter("cars") != null) {
      gotoPage("/travel/EditAccounts.jsp",
               request, response);
    } else {
      gotoPage("/travel/IllegalRequest.jsp",
               request, response);
    }
  }

  private void gotoPage(String address,
                        HttpServletRequest request,
                        HttpServletResponse response)
      throws ServletException, IOException {
    RequestDispatcher dispatcher =
      getServletContext().getRequestDispatcher(address);
    dispatcher.forward(request, response);
  }
}
```

Listing 20.54 `BookFlights.jsp`

```html
<!DOCTYPE HTML PUBLIC "-//W3C//DTD HTML 4.0 Transitional//EN">
<HTML>
<HEAD>
  <TITLE>Best Available Flights</TITLE>
  <LINK REL=STYLESHEET
        HREF="/travel/travel-styles.css"
        TYPE="text/css">
</HEAD>
<BODY>
<H1>Best Available Flights</H1>
<CENTER>
<jsp:useBean id="customer"
             class="cwp.TravelCustomer"
             scope="session" />
Finding flights for
<jsp:getProperty name="customer" property="fullName" />
<P>
<jsp:getProperty name="customer" property="flights" />
<P><BR><HR><BR>
<FORM ACTION="/servlet/BookFlight">
<jsp:getProperty name="customer"
                 property="frequentFlyerTable" />
<P>
<B>Credit Card:</B>
<jsp:getProperty name="customer" property="creditCard" />
<P>
<INPUT TYPE="SUBMIT" NAME="holdButton" VALUE="Hold for 24 Hrs">
<P>
<INPUT TYPE="SUBMIT" NAME="bookItButton" VALUE="Book It!">
</FORM>
</CENTER>
</BODY>
</HTML>
```

Listing 20.55 `TravelCustomer.java` **(Excerpt)**

```
package cwp;

import java.util.*;
import java.text.*;

/** Describes a travel services customer. Implemented
 *  as a bean with some methods that return data in HTML
 *  format, suitable for access from JSP.
 */

public class TravelCustomer {
  private String emailAddress, password, firstName, lastName;
  private String creditCardName, creditCardNumber;
  private String phoneNumber, homeAddress;
  private String startDate, endDate;
  private String origin, destination;
  private FrequentFlyerInfo[] frequentFlyerData;
  private RentalCarInfo[] rentalCarData;
  private HotelInfo[] hotelData;

  public TravelCustomer(String emailAddress,
                        String password,
                        String firstName,
                        String lastName,
                        String creditCardName,
                        String creditCardNumber,
                        String phoneNumber,
                        String homeAddress,
                        FrequentFlyerInfo[] frequentFlyerData,
                        RentalCarInfo[] rentalCarData,
                        HotelInfo[] hotelData) {
    setEmailAddress(emailAddress);
    setPassword(password);
    setFirstName(firstName);
    setLastName(lastName);
    setCreditCardName(creditCardName);
    setCreditCardNumber(creditCardNumber);
    setPhoneNumber(phoneNumber);
    setHomeAddress(homeAddress);
    setStartDate(startDate);
    setEndDate(endDate);
    setFrequentFlyerData(frequentFlyerData);
    setRentalCarData(rentalCarData);
    setHotelData(hotelData);
  }
```

(continued)

Listing 20.55 `TravelCustomer.java` **(Excerpt)** *(continued)*

```java
public String getEmailAddress() {
  return(emailAddress);
}

public void setEmailAddress(String emailAddress) {
  this.emailAddress = emailAddress;
}
...
public String getCreditCard() {
  String cardName = getCreditCardName();
  String cardNum = getCreditCardNumber();
  cardNum = cardNum.substring(cardNum.length() - 4);
  return(cardName + " (XXXX-XXXX-XXXX-" + cardNum + ")");
}
...
private String getFlightDescription(String airline,
                                    String flightNum,
                                    String price,
                                    String stop1,
                                    String stop2,
                                    String time1,
                                    String time2,
                                    String flightOrigin,
                                    String flightDestination,
                                    String flightStartDate,
                                    String flightEndDate) {
  String flight =
    "<P><BR>\n" +
    "<TABLE WIDTH=\"100%\"><TR><TH CLASS=\"COLORED\">\n" +
    "<B>" + airline + " Flight " + flightNum +
    " ($" + price + ")</B></TABLE><BR>\n" +
    "<B>Outgoing:</B> Leaves " + flightOrigin +
    " at " + time1 + " AM on " + flightStartDate +
    ", arriving in " + flightDestination +
    " at " + time2 + " PM (1 stop -- " + stop1 + ").\n" +
    "<BR>\n" +
    "<B>Return:</B> Leaves " + flightDestination +
    " at " + time1 + " AM on " + flightEndDate +
    ", arriving in " + flightOrigin +
    " at " + time2 + " PM (1 stop -- " + stop2 + ").\n";
  return(flight);
}
...
}
```

Forwarding Requests From JSP Pages

The most common request-forwarding scenario is that the request first comes to a servlet and the servlet forwards the request to a JSP page. The reason a servlet usually handles the original request is that checking request parameters and setting up beans requires a lot of programming, and it is more convenient to do this programming in a servlet than in a JSP document. The reason that the destination page is usually a JSP document is that JSP simplifies the process of creating the HTML content.

However, just because this is the *usual* approach doesn't mean that it is the *only* way of doing things. It is certainly possible for the destination page to be a servlet. Similarly, it is quite possible for a JSP page to forward requests elsewhere. For example, a request might go to a JSP page that normally presents results of a certain type and that forwards the request elsewhere only when it receives unexpected values.

Sending requests to servlets instead of JSP pages requires no changes whatsoever in the use of the `RequestDispatcher`. However, there is special syntactic support for forwarding requests from JSP pages. In JSP, the `jsp:forward` action is simpler and easier to use than wrapping up `RequestDispatcher` code in a scriptlet. This action takes the following form:

```
<jsp:forward page="Relative URL" />
```

The `page` attribute is allowed to contain JSP expressions so that the destination can be computed at request time. For example, the following sends about half the visitors to `http://host/examples/page1.jsp` and the others to `http://host/examples/page2.jsp`.

```
<% String destination;
   if (Math.random() > 0.5) {
     destination = "/examples/page1.jsp";
   } else {
     destination = "/examples/page2.jsp";
   }
%>
<jsp:forward page="<%= destination %>" />
```

20.9 Summary

In principle, everything that can be accomplished with JSP can be accomplished with servlets alone. In practice, JSP makes the generation of HTML content easier and more reliable. In doing so, JSP encourages a separation between the Java code that generates the content and the HTML code that presents it, thus permitting the use of standard HTML development tools, a division of labor on large projects, and the ability to change either the content or the presentation without altering the other piece.

As a result, few real sites use servlets alone. That does not, however, mean that they use JSP entirely in lieu of servlets. Instead, complex sites typically combine servlets and JSP, using servlets for some pages, JSP for others, and a combination for the remainder.

In this chapter we gave you the basic building blocks of JSP and showed you how to control both the specific dynamic content that is invoked and the high-level structure of the servlet that results from each JSP page. We also showed what tools are needed to make complex pages maintainable by non-Java programmers: beans and custom tags. Finally, we showed you how to put all those pieces together in integrated servlet/JSP applications.

Whew. Give yourself a rest, then go buy an answering machine to screen all those calls that will soon be arriving from eager potential employers.

USING APPLETS AS FRONT ENDS TO SERVER-SIDE PROGRAMS

Topics in This Chapter

- Sending GET data and having the browser display the results
- Sending GET data and processing the results within the applet (HTTP tunneling)
- Using object serialization to exchange high-level data structures between applets and servlets
- Sending POST data and processing the results within the applet (HTTP tunneling)
- Bypassing the HTTP server altogether

Chapter 21

HTML forms, discussed in Chapter 18, provide a simple but limited way of collecting user input and transmitting it to a servlet or CGI program. Occasionally, however, a more sophisticated user interface is required. Applets give you more control over the size, color, and font of the GUI controls; provide more built-in capability (sliders, line drawing, pop-up windows, and the like); let you track mouse and keyboard events; support the development of custom input forms (dials, thermometers, draggable icons, and so forth); and let you send a single user submission to multiple server-side programs. This extra capability comes at a cost, however, as it tends to require more effort to develop an interface with the Java programming language than it does with HTML forms, particularly if the interface contains a lot of formatted text. So, the choice between HTML forms and applets depends upon the application.

With HTML forms, GET and POST requests are handled almost exactly the same way. All the input elements are identical; only the METHOD attribute of the FORM element needs to change. With applets, however, there are three distinct approaches. In the first approach, covered in Section 21.1, the applet imitates a GET-based HTML form, with GET data being transmitted and the resultant page being displayed by the browser. Section 21.2 (A Multisystem Search Engine Front End) gives an example. In the second approach, covered in Section 21.3, the applet sends GET data to a servlet and then processes the results itself. Section 21.4 (A Query Viewer That Uses Object Serialization and HTTP Tunneling) gives an example. In the third approach, covered in Section 21.5, the applet sends POST data to a servlet and then processes the results itself. Section 21.6 (An Applet That Sends POST Data) gives an example. Finally, Section 21.7 serves as a reminder that an applet can bypass the HTTP server altogether and talk directly to a custom server program running on the applet's home machine.

This chapter assumes that you already have some familiarity with basic applets (see Chapter 9) and focuses on the techniques to allow applets to communicate with server-side programs.

21.1 Sending Data with GET and Displaying the Resultant Page

The `showDocument` method instructs the browser to display a particular URL. You can transmit GET data to a servlet or CGI program by appending it to the program's URL after a question mark (?). Thus, to send GET data from an applet, you simply need to append the data to the string from which the URL is built, then create the URL object and call `showDocument` in the normal manner. A basic template for doing this in applets follows. Assume that `baseURL` is a string representing the URL of the server-side program and that `someData` is the information to be sent with the request.

```
try {
  URL programURL = new URL(baseURL + "?" + someData);
  getAppletContext().showDocument(programURL);
} catch(MalformedURLException mue) { ... }
```

When data is sent by a browser, it is *URL encoded*, which means that spaces are converted to plus signs (+) and nonalphanumeric characters are changed into a percent sign (%) followed by the two hex digits representing that character, as discussed in Section 18.2 (The FORM Element). The preceding example assumes that `someData` has already been encoded properly and fails if this assumption is wrong. JDK 1.1 and later have a `URLEncoder` class with a static `encode` method that can perform this encoding. So, if an applet is contacting a server-side program that normally receives GET data from HTML forms, the applet needs to encode the value of each entry, but not the equal sign (=) between each entry name and its value or the ampersand (&) between each name/value pair. Therefore, you cannot simply call `URLEncoder.encode(someData)` but instead need to selectively encode the value parts of each name/value pair. This encoding could be accomplished as follows:

```
String someData =
  name1 + "=" + URLEncoder.encode(val1) + "&" +
  name2 + "=" + URLEncoder.encode(val2) + "&" +
  ...
  nameN + "=" + URLEncoder.encode(valN);
```

```
try {
  URL programURL = new URL(baseURL + "?" + someData);
  getAppletContext().showDocument(programURL);
} catch(MalformedURLException mue) { ... }
```

The following section gives a full-fledged example.

21.2 A Multisystem Search Engine Front End

Listing 21.1 shows an applet that creates a textfield to gather user input. When the user submits the data, the applet URL-encodes the textfield value and generates three distinct URLs with embedded GET data: one each for the Google, Infoseek, and Lycos search engines. The applet then uses showDocument to instruct the browser to display the results of those URLs in three different frame cells. HTML forms cannot be used for this application since a form can submit its data to only a single URL. Listing 21.2 shows the SearchSpec class used by the applet to generate the specific URLs needed to redirect requests to various search engines. The SearchSpec class can also be used by servlets, as discussed in Chapter 19. The applet results are shown in Figures 21–1 and 21–2.

Listing 21.3 shows the top-level HTML document, and Listing 21.4 shows the HTML used for the frame cell actually containing the applet. If you are curious about the three tiny HTML files used for the initial contents of the bottom three frame cells shown in Figure 21–1, please refer to this book's Web site (http://www.corewebprogramming.com/).

Listing 21.1 SearchApplet.java

```
import java.applet.Applet;
import java.awt.*;
import java.awt.event.*;
import java.net.*;

/** An applet that reads a value from a TextField,
 *  then uses it to build three distinct URLs with embedded
 *  GET data: one each for Google, Infoseek, and Lycos.
 *  The browser is directed to retrieve each of these
 *  URLs, displaying them in side-by-side frame cells.
 *  Note that standard HTML forms cannot automatically
 *  perform multiple submissions in this manner.
 */
```

(continued)

Listing 21.1 SearchApplet.java *(continued)*

```java
public class SearchApplet extends Applet
                          implements ActionListener {
  private TextField queryField;
  private Button submitButton;

  public void init() {
    setBackground(Color.white);
    setFont(new Font("Serif", Font.BOLD, 18));
    add(new Label("Search String:"));
    queryField = new TextField(40);
    queryField.addActionListener(this);
    add(queryField);
    submitButton = new Button("Send to Search Engines");
    submitButton.addActionListener(this);
    add(submitButton);
  }

  /** Submit data when button is pressed <B>or</B>
   *  user presses Return in the TextField.
   */

  public void actionPerformed(ActionEvent event) {
    String query = URLEncoder.encode(queryField.getText());
    SearchSpec[] commonSpecs = SearchSpec.getCommonSpecs();
    // Omitting HotBot (last entry), as they use JavaScript to
    // pop result to top-level frame. Thus the length-1 below.
    for(int i=0; i<commonSpecs.length-1; i++) {
      try {
        SearchSpec spec = commonSpecs[i];
        // The SearchSpec class builds URLs of the
        // form needed by some common search engines.
        URL searchURL = new URL(spec.makeURL(query, "10"));
        String frameName = "results" + i;
        getAppletContext().showDocument(searchURL, frameName);
      } catch(MalformedURLException mue) {}
    }
  }
}
```

Listing 21.2 `SearchSpec.java`

```java
/** Small class that encapsulates how to construct a
 *  search string for a particular search engine.
 */

public class SearchSpec {
  private String name, baseURL, numResultsSuffix;

  private static SearchSpec[] commonSpecs =
    { new SearchSpec("google",
                     "http://www.google.com/search?q=",
                     "&num="),
      new SearchSpec("infoseek",
                     "http://infoseek.go.com/Titles?qt=",
                     "&nh="),
      new SearchSpec("lycos",
                     "http://lycospro.lycos.com/cgi-bin/" +
                         "pursuit?query=",
                     "&maxhits="),
      new SearchSpec("hotbot",
                     "http://www.hotbot.com/?MT=",
                     "&DC=")
    };

  public SearchSpec(String name,
                    String baseURL,
                    String numResultsSuffix) {
    this.name = name;
    this.baseURL = baseURL;
    this.numResultsSuffix = numResultsSuffix;
  }

  public String makeURL(String searchString,
                        String numResults) {
    return(baseURL + searchString +
           numResultsSuffix + numResults);
  }

  public String getName() {
    return(name);
  }

  public static SearchSpec[] getCommonSpecs() {
    return(commonSpecs);
  }
}
```

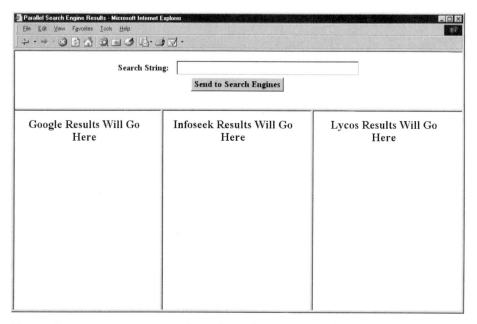

Figure 21-1 `SearchApplet` allows the user to enter a single search string for multiple search engines.

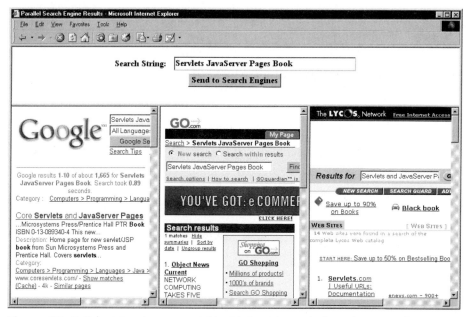

Figure 21-2 Submitting the query yields side-by-side results from three search engines.

Listing 21.3 `ParallelSearches.html`

```
<!DOCTYPE HTML PUBLIC "-//W3C//DTD HTML 4.0 Frameset//EN">
<HTML>
<HEAD>
  <TITLE>Parallel Search Engine Results</TITLE>
</HEAD>

<FRAMESET ROWS="120,*">
  <FRAME SRC="SearchAppletFrame.html" SCROLLING="NO">
  <FRAMESET COLS="*,*,*">
    <FRAME SRC="GoogleResultsFrame.html" NAME="results0">
    <FRAME SRC="InfoseekResultsFrame.html" NAME="results1">
    <FRAME SRC="LycosResultsFrame.html" NAME="results2">
  </FRAMESET>
</FRAMESET>
```

Listing 21.4 `SearchAppletFrame.html`

```
<!DOCTYPE HTML PUBLIC "-//W3C//DTD HTML 4.0 Transitional//EN">
<HTML>
<HEAD>
  <TITLE>Search Applet Frame</TITLE>
</HEAD>

<BODY BGCOLOR="WHITE">
<CENTER>
<APPLET CODE="SearchApplet.class" WIDTH=600 HEIGHT=100>
  <B>This example requires a Java-enabled browser.</B>
</APPLET>
</CENTER>
</BODY>
</HTML>
```

21.3 Using GET and Processing the Results Directly (HTTP Tunneling)

In the previous example, an applet instructs the browser to display the output of a server-side program in a particular frame. Using the browser to display results is a reasonable approach when you are working with existing services, since most CGI programs are already set up to return HTML documents. However, if you are developing *both* the client and the server sides of the process, it seems a bit wasteful to always send back an entire HTML document. In some cases, it would be nice to simply return data to an applet that is already running. The applet could then present the data in a graph or some other custom display. This approach is sometimes known as *HTTP tunneling* since a custom communication protocol is embedded within the HTTP packets: proxies, encryption, server redirection, connections through firewalls, and all.

There are two main variations to this approach. Both make use of the URL-Connection class to open an input stream from a URL. The difference lies in the type of stream they use. The first option is to use a BufferedInputStream or some other low-level stream that lets you read binary or ASCII data from an arbitrary server-side program. That approach is covered in the first subsection. The second option is to use an ObjectInputStream to directly read high-level data structures. That approach, covered in the second subsection, is available only when the server-side program is also written in the Java programming language.

Reading Binary or ASCII Data

An applet can read the content sent by the server by first creating a URL-Connection derived from the URL of the server-side program and then attaching a BufferedInputStream to it. Seven main steps are required to implement this approach on the client, as described below. We are omitting the server-side code since the client code described here works with arbitrary server-side programs or static Web pages.

Note that many of the stream operations throw an IOException, so the following statements need to be enclosed in a try/catch block.

1. **Create a URL object referring to applet's home host.** You can pass an absolute URL string to the URL constructor (e.g., "http://host/path"), but since browser security restrictions prohibit connections from applets to machines other than the home server, it makes more sense to build a URL based upon the hostname from which the applet was loaded.

    ```
    URL currentPage = getCodeBase();
    String protocol = currentPage.getProtocol();
    String host = currentPage.getHost();
    int port = currentPage.getPort();
    String urlSuffix = "/servlet/SomeServlet";
    URL dataURL = new URL(protocol, host, port, urlSuffix);
    ```

2. **Create a URLConnection object.** The openConnection method of URL returns a URLConnection object. This object will be used to obtain streams with which to communicate.

    ```
    URLConnection connection = dataURL.openConnection();
    ```

3. **Instruct the browser not to cache the URL data.** The first thing you do with the URLConnection object is to specify that the browser not cache it. This approach guarantees that you get a fresh result each time.

   ```
   connection.setUseCaches(false);
   ```

4. **Set any desired HTTP headers.** If you want to set HTTP request headers (see Section 19.7), you can use setRequestProperty to do so.

   ```
   connection.setRequestProperty("header", "value");
   ```

5. **Create an input stream.** There are a variety of appropriate streams; a common one is BufferedReader. The connection to the Web server is established when you create the input stream.

   ```
   BufferedReader in =
     new BufferedReader(new InputStreamReader(
                         connection.getInputStream()));
   ```

6. **Read each line of the document.** The HTTP specification stipulates that the server closes the connection when it is done. When the connection is closed, readLine returns null. So, simply read until you get null.

   ```
   String line;
   while ((line = in.readLine()) != null) {
     doSomethingWith(line);
   }
   ```

7. **Close the input stream.**

   ```
   in.close();
   ```

Reading Serialized Data Structures

The approach shown in the previous subsection makes good sense when your applet is talking to an arbitrary server-side program or reading the content of static Web pages. However, when an applet talks to a servlet, you can do even better. Rather than sending binary or ASCII data, the servlet can transmit arbitrary data structures by using the Java serialization mechanism. The applet can read this data in a single step by using readObject; no long and tedious parsing is required. The steps required to implement HTTP tunneling are summarized below.

The Client Side

An applet needs to perform the following seven steps to read serialized data structures sent by a servlet. Only Steps 5 and 6 differ from what is required to read ASCII data. These steps are slightly simplified by the omission of the try/catch blocks.

1. **Create a URL object referring to the applet's home host.** As before, since the URL must refer to the host from which the applet was loaded, it makes the most sense to specify a URL suffix and construct the rest of the URL automatically.

   ```
   URL currentPage = getCodeBase();
   String protocol = currentPage.getProtocol();
   String host = currentPage.getHost();
   int port = currentPage.getPort();
   String urlSuffix = "/servlet/SomeServlet";
   URL dataURL = new URL(protocol, host, port, urlSuffix);
   ```

2. **Create a URLConnection object.** The openConnection method of URL returns a URLConnection object. This object will be used to obtain streams with which to communicate.

   ```
   URLConnection connection = dataURL.openConnection();
   ```

3. **Instruct the browser not to cache the URL data.** The first thing you do with the URLConnection object is to specify that the browser not cache it. This approach guarantees you get a fresh result each time.

   ```
   connection.setUseCaches(false);
   ```

4. **Set any desired HTTP headers.** If you want to set HTTP request headers (see Section 19.7), you can use setRequestProperty to do so.

   ```
   connection.setRequestProperty("header", "value");
   ```

5. **Create an ObjectInputStream.** The constructor for this class simply takes the raw input stream from the URLConnection. The connection to the Web server is established when you create the input stream.

   ```
   ObjectInputStream in =
     new ObjectInputStream(connection.getInputStream());
   ```

6. **Read the data structure with readObject.** The return type of readObject is Object, so you need to make a typecast to whatever more specific type the server actually sent.

   ```
   SomeClass value = (SomeClass)in.readObject();
   doSomethingWith(value);
   ```

7. **Close the input stream.**

   ```
   in.close();
   ```

The Server Side

A servlet needs to perform the following four steps to send serialized data structures to an applet. Assume that request and response are the HttpServletRequest and HttpServletResponse objects supplied to the doGet and doPost methods. Again, these steps are simplified slightly by the omission of the required try/catch blocks.

1. **Specify that binary content is being sent.** Designate
    `application/x-java-serialized-object` as the MIME type of
    the response. This is the standard MIME type for objects encoded with
    an ObjectOutputStream, although in practice, since the applet (not the
    browser) is reading the result, the MIME type is not very important. See
    the discussion of Content-Type in Section 19.10 (The Server Response:
    HTTP Response Headers) for more information on MIME types.

    ```
    String contentType =
      "application/x-java-serialized-object";
    response.setContentType(contentType);
    ```

2. **Create an `ObjectOutputStream`.**

    ```
    ObjectOutputStream out =
      new ObjectOutputStream(response.getOutputStream());
    ```

3. **Write the data structure by using `writeObject`.** Most built-in
    data structures can be sent with `writeObject`. Classes *you* write,
    however, must implement the `Serializable` interface. This is a
    simple requirement, however, since `Serializable` defines no
    methods. Simply declare that your class implements it.

    ```
    SomeClass value = new SomeClass(...);
    out.writeObject(value);
    ```

4. **Flush the stream to be sure all content has been sent to the client.**

    ```
    out.flush();
    ```

The following section gives an example of this HTTP tunneling approach.

21.4 A Query Viewer That Uses Object Serialization and HTTP Tunneling

Many people are curious about what types of queries are sent to the major search
engines. This is partly idle curiosity ("Is it really true that 64 percent of the queries at
AltaVista are from employers looking for programmers that know Java technology?")
and partly so that HTML authors can arrange their page content to fit the types of queries normally submitted, hoping to improve their site's ranking with the search engines.

This section presents an applet/servlet combination that displays the fictitious
`super-search-engine.com` "live," continually updating sample queries to visitors that load their query viewer page. Listing 21.5 shows the main applet, which
makes use of an auxiliary class (Listing 21.6) to retrieve the queries in a background
thread. Once the user initiates the process, the applet places a sample query in a
scrolling text area every half-second, as shown in Figure 21–3. Finally, Listing 21.7

shows the servlet that generates the queries on the server. It generates a random sampling of actual recent user queries and sends 50 of them to the client for each request. Servlet details are explained in Chapter 19.

If you download the applet and servlet source code from `http://www.corewebprogramming.com/` and try this application yourself, be aware that it will only work when you load the top-level HTML page by using HTTP (i.e., by using a URL of the form `http://...` to request the page from a Web server). Loading the applet directly off your disk fails—the applet connects back to its home site to contact the servlet. Besides, `URLConnection` fails for non-HTTP applets in general.

Listing 21.5 `ShowQueries.java`

```java
import java.applet.Applet;
import java.awt.*;
import java.awt.event.*;
import java.net.*;

/** Applet reads arrays of strings packaged inside
 *  a QueryCollection and places them in a scrolling
 *  TextArea. The QueryCollection obtains the strings
 *  by means of a serialized object input stream.
 */

public class ShowQueries extends Applet
                         implements ActionListener, Runnable {
  private TextArea queryArea;
  private Button startButton, stopButton, clearButton;
  private QueryCollection currentQueries;
  private QueryCollection nextQueries;
  private boolean isRunning = false;
  private String address =
    "/servlet/cwp.QueryGenerator";
  private URL currentPage;

  public void init() {
    setBackground(Color.white);
    setLayout(new BorderLayout());
    queryArea = new TextArea();
    queryArea.setFont(new Font("Serif", Font.PLAIN, 14));
    add(queryArea, BorderLayout.CENTER);
    Panel buttonPanel = new Panel();
    Font buttonFont = new Font("SansSerif", Font.BOLD, 16);
    startButton = new Button("Start");
    startButton.setFont(buttonFont);
```

(continued)

Listing 21.5 ShowQueries.java *(continued)*

```java
    startButton.addActionListener(this);
    buttonPanel.add(startButton);
    stopButton = new Button("Stop");
    stopButton.setFont(buttonFont);
    stopButton.addActionListener(this);
    buttonPanel.add(stopButton);
    clearButton = new Button("Clear TextArea");
    clearButton.setFont(buttonFont);
    clearButton.addActionListener(this);
    buttonPanel.add(clearButton);
    add(buttonPanel, BorderLayout.SOUTH);
    currentPage = getCodeBase();
    // Request a set of sample queries. They
    // are loaded in a background thread, and
    // the applet checks to see if they have finished
    // loading before trying to extract the strings.
    currentQueries = new QueryCollection(address, currentPage);
    nextQueries = new QueryCollection(address, currentPage);
  }

  /** If you press the "Start" button, the system
   *  starts a background thread that displays
   *  the queries in the TextArea. Pressing "Stop"
   *  halts the process, and "Clear" empties the
   *  TextArea.
   */

  public void actionPerformed(ActionEvent event) {
    if (event.getSource() == startButton) {
      if (!isRunning) {
        Thread queryDisplayer = new Thread(this);
        isRunning = true;
        queryArea.setText("");
        queryDisplayer.start();
        showStatus("Started display thread...");
      } else {
        showStatus("Display thread already running...");
      }
    } else if (event.getSource() == stopButton) {
      isRunning = false;
      showStatus("Stopped display thread...");
    } else if (event.getSource() == clearButton) {
      queryArea.setText("");
    }
  }
```

(continued)

Listing 21.5 `ShowQueries.java` *(continued)*

```java
/** The background thread takes the currentQueries
 *  object and every half-second places one of the queries
 *  the object holds into the bottom of the TextArea. When
 *  all of the queries have been shown, the thread copies
 *  the value of the nextQueries object into
 *  currentQueries, sends a new request to the server
 *  in order to repopulate nextQueries, and repeats
 *  the process.
 */

public void run() {
  while(isRunning) {
    showQueries(currentQueries);
    currentQueries = nextQueries;
    nextQueries = new QueryCollection(address, currentPage);
  }
}

private void showQueries(QueryCollection queryEntry) {
  // If a request has been sent to server but the result
  // isn't back yet, poll every second. This should
  // happen rarely but is possible with a slow network
  // connection or an overloaded server.
  while(!queryEntry.isDone()) {
    showStatus("Waiting for data from server...");
    pause(1);
  }
  showStatus("Received data from server...");
  String[] queries = queryEntry.getQueries();
  String linefeed = "\n";
  // Put a string into TextArea every half-second.
  for(int i=0; i<queries.length; i++) {
    if (!isRunning) {
      return;
    }
    queryArea.append(queries[i]);
    queryArea.append(linefeed);
    pause(0.5);
  }
}

public void pause(double seconds) {
  try {
    Thread.sleep((long)(seconds*1000));
  } catch(InterruptedException ie) {}
}
}
```

Listing 21.6 `QueryCollection.java`

```java
import java.net.*;
import java.io.*;

/** When this class is built, it returns a value
 *  immediately, but this value returns false for isDone
 *  and null for getQueries. Meanwhile, it starts a Thread
 *  to request an array of query strings from the server,
 *  reading them in one fell swoop by means of an
 *  ObjectInputStream. Once they've all arrived, they
 *  are placed in the location getQueries returns,
 *  and the isDone flag is switched to true.
 *  Used by the ShowQueries applet.
 */

public class QueryCollection implements Runnable {
  private String[] queries;
  private String[] tempQueries;
  private boolean isDone = false;
  private URL dataURL;

  public QueryCollection(String urlSuffix, URL currentPage) {
    try {
      // Only the URL suffix need be supplied, since
      // the rest of the URL is derived from the current page.
      String protocol = currentPage.getProtocol();
      String host = currentPage.getHost();
      int port = currentPage.getPort();
      dataURL = new URL(protocol, host, port, urlSuffix);
      Thread queryRetriever = new Thread(this);
      queryRetriever.start();
    } catch(MalformedURLException mfe) {
      isDone = true;
    }
  }

  public void run() {
    try {
      tempQueries = retrieveQueries();
      queries = tempQueries;
    } catch(IOException ioe) {
      tempQueries = null;
      queries = null;
    }
    isDone = true;
  }
```

(continued)

Listing 21.6 `QueryCollection.java` *(continued)*

```java
  public String[] getQueries() {
    return(queries);
  }

  public boolean isDone() {
    return(isDone);
  }

  private String[] retrieveQueries() throws IOException {
    URLConnection connection = dataURL.openConnection();
    // Make sure browser doesn't cache this URL, since
    // I want different queries for each request.
    connection.setUseCaches(false);
    // Use ObjectInputStream so I can read a String[]
    // all at once.
    ObjectInputStream in =
      new ObjectInputStream(connection.getInputStream());
    try {
      // The return type of readObject is Object, so
      // I need a typecast to the actual type.
      String[] queryStrings = (String[])in.readObject();
      return(queryStrings);
    } catch(ClassNotFoundException cnfe) {
      return(null);
    }
  }
}
```

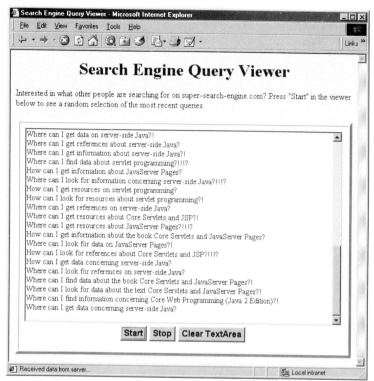

Figure 21-3 The ShowQueries applet in action.

Listing 21.7 QueryGenerator.java

```java
package cwp;

import java.io.*;
import javax.servlet.*;
import javax.servlet.http.*;

/** Servlet that generates an array of strings and
 *  sends them via an ObjectOutputStream to applet
 *  or other Java client.
 */
```

(continued)

Listing 21.7 QueryGenerator.java *(continued)*

```java
public class QueryGenerator extends HttpServlet {
  public void doGet(HttpServletRequest request,
                    HttpServletResponse response)
     throws ServletException, IOException {
    boolean useNumbering = true;
    String useNumberingFlag =
      request.getParameter("useNumbering");
    if ((useNumberingFlag == null) ||
        useNumberingFlag.equals("false")) {
      useNumbering = false;
    }
    String contentType =
      "application/x-java-serialized-object";
    response.setContentType(contentType);
    ObjectOutputStream out =
      new ObjectOutputStream(response.getOutputStream());
    String[] queries = getQueries(useNumbering);
    // If you send a nonstandard data structure, be
    // sure it is defined with "implements Serializable".
    out.writeObject(queries);
    out.flush();
  }

  public void doPost(HttpServletRequest request,
                     HttpServletResponse response)
     throws ServletException, IOException {
    doGet(request, response);
  }

  private String[] getQueries(boolean useNumbering) {
    String[] queries = new String[50];
    for(int i=0; i<queries.length; i++) {
      queries[i] = randomQuery();
      if (useNumbering) {
        queries[i] = "" + (i+1) + ": " + queries[i];
      }
    }
    return(queries);
  }

  // The real, honest-to-goodness queries people have sent :-)
```

(continued)

Listing 21.7 `QueryGenerator.java` *(continued)*

```java
  private String randomQuery() {
    String[] locations = { "Where ", "How " };
    String[] actions =
      { "can I look for ", "can I find ", "can I get " };
    String[] sources =
      { "information ", "resources ", "data ", "references " };
    String[] prepositions = { "on ", "about ", "concerning " };
    String[] subjects =
      { "the book Core Servlets and JavaServer Pages",
        "the text Core Servlets and JavaServer Pages",
        "Core Servlets and JavaServer Pages",
        "Core Servlets and JSP",
        "the book Core Web Programming (Java 2 Edition)",
        "Core Web Programming (Java 2 Edition)",
        "servlet programming", "JavaServer Pages", "JSP",
        "Java alternatives to CGI", "server-side Java" };
    String[] endings = { "?", "?", "?", "?!", "?!!!?" };
    String[][] sentenceTemplates =
      { locations, actions, sources,
        prepositions, subjects, endings };
    String query = "";
    for(int i=0; i<sentenceTemplates.length; i++) {
      query = query + randomEntry(sentenceTemplates[i]);
    }
    return(query);
  }

  private String randomEntry(String[] strings) {
    int index = (int)(Math.random()*strings.length);
    return(strings[index]);
  }
}
```

21.5 Using POST and Processing the Results Directly (HTTP Tunneling)

With GET data, an applet has two options for the results of a submission: tell the browser to display the results (construct a URL object and call get-AppletContext().showDocument) or process the results itself (construct a URL object, get a URLConnection, open an input stream, and read the results). These two options are discussed in Sections 21.1 and 21.3, respectively. With POST data, however, only the second option is available since the URL constructor has no method to let you associate POST data with it. Sending POST data has some of the same advantages and disadvantages as when applets send GET data. The two main disadvantages are that the server-side program must be on the host from which the applet was loaded, and that the applet is required to display all the results itself: it cannot pass HTML to the browser in a portable manner. On the plus side, the server-side program can be simpler (not needing to wrap the results in HTML) and the applet can update its display without requiring the page to be reloaded. Furthermore, applets that communicate by using POST can use serialized data streams to send data *to* a servlet, in addition to reading serialized data *from* a servlet. This is quite an advantage, since serialized data simplifies communication and HTTP tunneling lets you piggyback on existing connections through firewalls even when direct socket connections are prohibited. Applets using GET can read serialized data (see Section 21.4) but are unable to send it since it is not legal to append arbitrary binary data to URLs.

Thirteen steps are required for the applet to send POST data to the server and read the results, as shown below. Although there are many required steps, each step is relatively simple. The code is slightly simplified by the omission of try/catch blocks around the statements.

1. **Create a URL object referring to the applet's home host.** As before, since the URL must refer to the host the applet came from, it makes the most sense to specify a URL suffix and construct the rest of the URL automatically.

   ```
   URL currentPage = getCodeBase();
   String protocol = currentPage.getProtocol();
   String host = currentPage.getHost();
   int port = currentPage.getPort();
   String urlSuffix = "/servlet/SomeServlet";
   URL dataURL =
       new URL(protocol, host, port, urlSuffix);
   ```

2. **Create a URLConnection object.** This object will be used to obtain input and output streams that connect to the server.

   ```
   URLConnection connection = dataURL.openConnection();
   ```

3. **Instruct the browser not to cache the results.**

   ```
   connection.setUseCaches(false);
   ```

4. **Tell the system to permit you to send data, not just read it.**

   ```
   connection.setDoOutput(true);
   ```

5. **Create a ByteArrayOutputStream to buffer the data that will be sent to the server.** The purpose of the ByteArrayOutput-Stream here is to determine the size of the output so that the applet can set the Content-Length header, a required part of POST requests. The ByteArrayOutputStream constructor specifies an

initial buffer size, but this value is not critical since the buffer will grow automatically if necessary.

```
ByteArrayOutputStream byteStream =
  new ByteArrayOutputStream(512);
```

6. **Attach an output stream to the `ByteArrayOutputStream`.**
   Use a `PrintWriter` to send normal form data. To send serialized data structures, use an `ObjectOutputStream` instead.

   ```
   PrintWriter out = new PrintWriter(byteStream, true);
   ```

7. **Put the data into the buffer.** For form data, use `print`. For high-level serialized objects, use `writeObject`.

   ```
   String val1 = URLEncoder.encode(someVal1);
   String val2 = URLEncoder.encode(someVal2);
   String data = "param1=" + val1 +
                 "&param2=" + val2; // Note '&'
   out.print(data);  // Note print, not println
   out.flush(); // Necessary since no println used
   ```

8. **Set the `Content-Length` header.** This header is required for POST data, even though it is unused with GET requests.

   ```
   connection.setRequestProperty
     ("Content-Length", String.valueOf(byteStream.size()));
   ```

9. **Set the `Content-Type` header.** Netscape uses `multi-part/form-data` by default, but regular form data requires a setting of `application/x-www-form-urlencoded`, which is the default with Internet Explorer. So, for portability you should set this value explicitly when sending regular form data. The value is irrelevant when you are sending serialized data.

   ```
   connection.setRequestProperty
     ("Content-Type", "application/x-www-form-urlencoded");
   ```

10. **Send the real data.**

    ```
    byteStream.writeTo(connection.getOutputStream());
    ```

11. **Open an input stream.** You typically use a `BufferedReader` for ASCII or binary data and an `ObjectInputStream` for serialized Java objects.

    ```
    BufferedReader in =
      new BufferedReader(new InputStreamReader
                         (connection.getInputStream()));
    ```

12. **Read the result.**
    The specific details depend on what type of data the server sends. Here is an example that does something with each line sent by the server:

    ```
    String line;
    while((line = in.readLine()) != null) {
    ```

```
      doSomethingWith(line);
    }
```

13. **Pat yourself on the back.** Yes, the procedure for handling POST is long and tedious. Fortunately, it is a relatively rote process. Besides, you can always download an example from www.coreweb-programming.com and use it as a starting point.

The next section gives an example of an applet that performs these steps.

21.6 An Applet That Sends POST Data

Listing 21.8 presents an applet that follows the approach outlined in the previous section. The applet uses a URLConnection and an attached ByteArray-OutputStream to send POST data to a URL the user specifies. The applet also makes use of the LabeledTextField class, available for download from http://www.corewebprogramming.com/.

Figure 21–4 shows the results of submitting the data to the ShowParameters servlet, a small servlet that builds a Web page illustrating all of the query parameters sent to it; see Section 19.6 (The Client Request: Form Data).

Listing 21.8 SendPost.java

```
import java.applet.Applet;
import java.awt.*;
import java.awt.event.*;
import java.net.*;
import java.io.*;

/** Applet that reads firstName, lastName, and
 *  emailAddress parameters and sends them via
 *  POST to the host, port, and URI specified.
 */

public class SendPost extends Applet
                    implements ActionListener {
  private LabeledTextField firstNameField, lastNameField,
                           emailAddressField, hostField,
                           portField, uriField;
  private Button sendButton;
  private TextArea resultsArea;
  URL currentPage;
```

(continued)

Listing 21.8 `SendPost.java` *(continued)*

```
public void init() {
  setBackground(Color.white);
  setLayout(new BorderLayout());
  Panel inputPanel = new Panel();
  inputPanel.setLayout(new GridLayout(9, 1));
  inputPanel.setFont(new Font("Serif", Font.BOLD, 14));
  firstNameField =
    new LabeledTextField("First Name:", 15);
  inputPanel.add(firstNameField);
  lastNameField =
    new LabeledTextField("Last Name:", 15);
  inputPanel.add(lastNameField);
  emailAddressField =
    new LabeledTextField("Email Address:", 30);
  inputPanel.add(emailAddressField);
  Canvas separator1 = new Canvas();
  inputPanel.add(separator1);
  hostField =
    new LabeledTextField("Host:", 15);

  // Applets loaded over the network can only connect
  // to the server from which they were loaded.
  hostField.getTextField().setEditable(false);

  currentPage = getCodeBase();
  // getHost returns empty string for applets from local disk.
  String host = currentPage.getHost();
  String resultsMessage = "Results will be shown here...";
  if (host.length() == 0) {
    resultsMessage = "Error: you must load this applet\n" +
                     "from a real Web server via HTTP,\n" +
                     "not from the local disk using\n" +
                     "a 'file:' URL. It is fine,\n" +
                     "however, if the Web server is\n" +
                     "running on your local system.";
    setEnabled(false);
  }
  hostField.getTextField().setText(host);
  inputPanel.add(hostField);
  portField =
    new LabeledTextField("Port (-1 means default):", 4);
  String portString = String.valueOf(currentPage.getPort());
  portField.getTextField().setText(portString);
  inputPanel.add(portField);
```

(continued)

Listing 21.8 SendPost.java *(continued)*

```java
        uriField =
          new LabeledTextField("URI:", 40);
        String defaultURI = "/servlet/cwp.ShowParameters";
        uriField.getTextField().setText(defaultURI);
        inputPanel.add(uriField);
        Canvas separator2 = new Canvas();
        inputPanel.add(separator2);
        sendButton = new Button("Submit Data");
        sendButton.addActionListener(this);
        Panel buttonPanel = new Panel();
        buttonPanel.add(sendButton);
        inputPanel.add(buttonPanel);
        add(inputPanel, BorderLayout.NORTH);
        resultsArea = new TextArea();
        resultsArea.setFont(new Font("Monospaced", Font.PLAIN, 14));
        resultsArea.setText(resultsMessage);
        add(resultsArea, BorderLayout.CENTER);
    }

    public void actionPerformed(ActionEvent event) {
        try {
            String protocol = currentPage.getProtocol();
            String host = hostField.getTextField().getText();
            String portString = portField.getTextField().getText();
            int port;
            try {
                port = Integer.parseInt(portString);
            } catch(NumberFormatException nfe) {
                port = -1; // I.e., default port of 80
            }
            String uri = uriField.getTextField().getText();
            URL dataURL = new URL(protocol, host, port, uri);
            URLConnection connection = dataURL.openConnection();

            // Make sure browser doesn't cache this URL.
            connection.setUseCaches(false);

            // Tell browser to allow me to send data to server.
            connection.setDoOutput(true);

            ByteArrayOutputStream byteStream =
              new ByteArrayOutputStream(512); // Grows if necessary
            // Stream that writes into buffer
            PrintWriter out = new PrintWriter(byteStream, true);
```

(continued)

Listing 21.8 `SendPost.java` *(continued)*

```java
String postData =
  "firstName=" + encodedValue(firstNameField) +
  "&lastName=" + encodedValue(lastNameField) +
  "&emailAddress=" + encodedValue(emailAddressField);

// Write POST data into local buffer
out.print(postData);
out.flush(); // Flush since above used print, not println

// POST requests are required to have Content-Length
String lengthString =
  String.valueOf(byteStream.size());
connection.setRequestProperty
  ("Content-Length", lengthString);

// Netscape sets the Content-Type to multipart/form-data
// by default. So, if you want to send regular form data,
// you need to set it to
// application/x-www-form-urlencoded, which is the
// default for Internet Explorer. If you send
// serialized POST data with an ObjectOutputStream,
// the Content-Type is irrelevant, so you could
// omit this step.
connection.setRequestProperty
  ("Content-Type", "application/x-www-form-urlencoded");

// Write POST data to real output stream
byteStream.writeTo(connection.getOutputStream());

BufferedReader in =
  new BufferedReader(new InputStreamReader
                    (connection.getInputStream()));
String line;
String linefeed = "\n";
resultsArea.setText("");
while((line = in.readLine()) != null) {
  resultsArea.append(line);
  resultsArea.append(linefeed);
}
} catch(IOException ioe) {
  // Print debug info in Java Console
  System.out.println("IOException: " + ioe);
}
}
```

(continued)

Listing 21.8 `SendPost.java` *(continued)*

```
// LabeledTextField is really a Panel with a Label and
// TextField inside it. This extracts the TextField part,
// gets the text inside it, URL-encodes it, and
// returns the result.

private String encodedValue(LabeledTextField field) {
  String rawValue = field.getTextField().getText();
  return(URLEncoder.encode(rawValue));
}
}
```

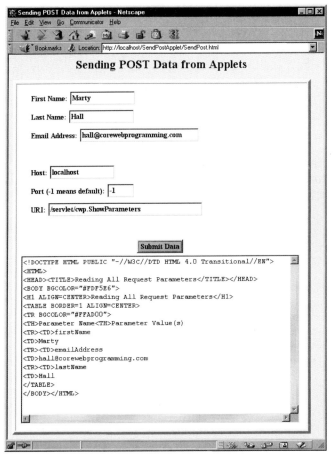

Figure 21–4 Result of using `SendPost` to send `POST` data to the `ShowParameters` servlet.

21.7 Bypassing the HTTP Server

Although applets can only open network connections to the same machine they were loaded from, they need not necessarily connect on the same *port* (e.g., 80, the HTTP port). So, applets are permitted to use raw sockets, JDBC, or RMI to communicate with custom clients running on the server host.

Applets do these operations in exactly the same manner as do normal Java programs, so you can use whatever approaches to socket, JDBC, and RMI programming you are already familiar with, provided that the network server is on the same host as the Web server that delivered the applet.

21.8 Summary

HTML forms provide the simplest and most common front end to server-side programs. Applets, however, provide richer user interfaces, support continuously updating displays, and simplify the transmission of large complex data structures. The general rule of thumb is to use HTML forms whenever possible. But it is nice to be able to fall back to applets when HTML forms are too limiting.

JDBC

Chapter 22

J DBC provides a standard library for accessing relational databases. Using the JDBC API, you can access a wide variety of different SQL databases with exactly the same Java syntax. However, it is important to note that, although JDBC standardizes the mechanism for connecting to databases, the syntax for sending queries and committing transactions, and the data structure representing the result, it does *not* attempt to standardize the SQL syntax. So, you can use any SQL extensions your database vendor supports. Since most queries follow standard SQL syntax, using JDBC lets you change database hosts, ports, and even database vendors with minimal changes in your code.

DILBERT © UFS. Reprinted with permission.

Officially, JDBC is not an acronym and thus does not stand for anything. Unofficially, "Java Database Connectivity" is commonly used as the long form of the name. Although a complete tutorial on database programming is beyond the scope of this chapter, we'll cover the basics of using JDBC here, assuming you are already familiar with SQL. For more details on JDBC, see `http://java.sun.com/products/jdbc/`, the on-line API for `java.sql`, or the JDBC tutorial at `http://java.sun.com/docs/books/tutorial/jdbc/`. If you don't already have access to a database, you might find mySQL a good choice for practice. It is free for any purpose on non-Microsoft operating systems as well as free for educational or research use on Windows. For details, see `http://www.mysql.com/`.

22.1 Basic Steps in Using JDBC

There are seven standard steps in querying databases:

1. Load the JDBC driver.
2. Define the connection URL.
3. Establish the connection.
4. Create a statement object.
5. Execute a query or update.
6. Process the results.
7. Close the connection.

Here are some details of the process.

Load the Driver

The driver is the piece of software that knows how to talk to the actual database server. To load the driver, all you need to do is load the appropriate class; a `static` block in the class itself automatically makes a driver instance and registers it with the JDBC driver manager. To make your code as flexible as possible, it is best to avoid hard-coding the reference to the class name.

These requirements bring up two interesting questions. First, how do you load a class without making an instance of it? Second, how can you refer to a class whose name isn't known when the code is compiled? The answer to both questions is: use `Class.forName`. This method takes a string representing a fully qualified class name (i.e., one that includes package names) and loads the corresponding class. This call could throw a `ClassNotFoundException`, so should be inside a `try/catch` block. Here is an example:

```
try {
  Class.forName("connect.microsoft.MicrosoftDriver");
  Class.forName("oracle.jdbc.driver.OracleDriver");
  Class.forName("com.sybase.jdbc.SybDriver");
} catch(ClassNotFoundException cnfe) {
  System.err.println("Error loading driver: " + cnfe);
}
```

One of the beauties of the JDBC approach is that the database server requires no changes whatsoever. Instead, the JDBC driver (which is on the client) translates calls written in the Java programming language into the specific format required by the server. This approach means that you have to obtain a JDBC driver specific to the database you are using; you will need to check its documentation for the fully qualified class name to use. Most database vendors supply free JDBC drivers for their databases, but there are many third-party vendors of drivers for older databases. For an up-to-date list, see `http://industry.java.sun.com/products/jdbc/drivers`. Many of these driver vendors supply free trial versions (usually with an expiration date or with some limitations on the number of simultaneous connections), so it is easy to learn JDBC without paying for a driver.

In principle, you can use `Class.forName` for any class in your `CLASSPATH`. In practice, however, most JDBC driver vendors distribute their drivers inside JAR files. So, be sure to include the path to the JAR file in your `CLASSPATH` setting. For example, most recent servlet and JSP engines automatically add JAR files that are in the `lib` directory to their `CLASSPATH`. So, if your server-side programs are using JDBC, the JAR files containing the drivers should go in the server's `lib` directory.

Define the Connection URL

Once you have loaded the JDBC driver, you need to specify the location of the database server. URLs referring to databases use the `jdbc:` protocol and have the server host, port, and database name (or reference) embedded within the URL. The exact format will be defined in the documentation that comes with the particular driver, but here are two representative examples:

```
String host = "dbhost.yourcompany.com";
String dbName = "someName";
int port = 1234;
String oracleURL = "jdbc:oracle:thin:@" + host +
                   ":" + port + ":" + dbName;
String sybaseURL = "jdbc:sybase:Tds:" + host   +
                   ":" + port + ":" + "?SERVICENAME=" + dbName;
```

JDBC is most often used from servlets or regular desktop applications but is also sometimes employed from applets. If you use JDBC from an applet, remember that, to prevent hostile applets from browsing behind corporate firewalls, browsers prevent applets from making network connections anywhere except to the server from which they were loaded. Consequently, for JDBC to be used from applets, either the database server needs to reside on the same machine as the HTTP server or you need to use a proxy server that reroutes database requests to the actual server.

Establish the Connection

To make the actual network connection, pass the URL, the database username, and the password to the getConnection method of the DriverManager class, as illustrated in the following example. Note that getConnection throws an SQL-Exception, so you need to use a try/catch block. We are omitting this block from the following example since the methods in the following steps throw the same exception, and thus you typically use a single try/catch block for all of them.

```
String username = "jay_debesee";
String password = "secret";
Connection connection =
  DriverManager.getConnection(oracleURL, username, password);
```

An optional part of this step is to look up information about the database by using the getMetaData method of Connection. This method returns a DatabaseMetaData object that has methods to let you discover the name and version of the database itself (getDatabaseProductName, getDatabaseProduct-Version) or of the JDBC driver (getDriverName, getDriverVersion). Here is an example:

```
DatabaseMetaData dbMetaData = connection.getMetaData();
String productName =
  dbMetaData.getDatabaseProductName();
System.out.println("Database: " + productName);
String productVersion =
  dbMetaData.getDatabaseProductVersion();
System.out.println("Version: " + productVersion);
```

Other useful methods in the Connection class include prepareStatement (create a PreparedStatement; discussed in Section 22.6), prepareCall (create a CallableStatement), rollback (undo statements since last commit), commit (finalize operations since last commit), close (terminate connection), and isClosed (has the connection either timed out or been explicitly closed?).

Create a Statement

A Statement object is used to send queries and commands to the database and is created from the Connection as follows:

```
Statement statement = connection.createStatement();
```

Execute a Query

Once you have a `Statement` object, you can use it to send SQL queries by using the `executeQuery` method, which returns an object of type `ResultSet`. Here is an example:

```
String query = "SELECT col1, col2, col3 FROM sometable";
ResultSet resultSet = statement.executeQuery(query);
```

To modify the database, use `executeUpdate` instead of `executeQuery` and supply a string that uses `UPDATE`, `INSERT`, or `DELETE`. Other useful methods in the `Statement` class include `execute` (execute an arbitrary command) and `set-QueryTimeout` (set a maximum delay to wait for results). You can also create parameterized queries where values are supplied to a precompiled fixed-format query. See Section 22.6 for details.

Process the Results

The simplest way to handle the results is to process them one row at a time, using the `ResultSet`'s next method to move through the table a row at a time. Within a row, `ResultSet` provides various get*Xxx* methods that take a column index or column name as an argument and return the result as a variety of different data types. For instance, use `getInt` if the value should be an integer, `getString` for a `String`, and so on for most other data types. If you just want to display the results, you can use `getString` regardless of the actual column type. However, if you use the version that takes a column index, note that columns are indexed starting at 1 (following the SQL convention), not at 0 as with arrays, vectors, and most other data structures in the Java programming language.

Core Warning

The first column in a `ResultSet` row has index 1, not 0.

Here is an example that prints the values of the first three columns in all rows of a `ResultSet`.

```
while(resultSet.next()) {
  System.out.println(results.getString(1) + " " +
                     results.getString(2) + " " +
                     results.getString(3));
}
```

In addition to the get*Xxx* and next methods, other useful methods in the `ResultSet` class include `findColumn` (get the index of the named column), `get-MetaData` (retrieve information about the `ResultSet` in a `ResultSetMetaData` object), and wasNull (was the last getXxx result SQL NULL? Alternatively, for strings you can simply compare the return value to null).

The getMetaData method is particularly useful. Given only a ResultSet, you have to know about the name, number, and type of the columns to be able to process the table properly. For most fixed-format queries, this is a reasonable expectation. For ad hoc queries, however, it is useful to be able to dynamically discover high-level information about the result. That is the role of the ResultSetMetaData class: it lets you determine the number, names, and types of the columns in the ResultSet. Useful ResultSetMetaData methods include getColumnCount (the number of columns), getColumnName (a column name, indexed starting at 1), getColumn-Type (an int to compare against entries in java.sql.Types), isReadOnly (is entry a read-only value?), isSearchable (can it be used in a WHERE clause?), isNullable (is a null value permitted?), and several other methods that give details on the type and precision of the column. ResultSetMetaData does *not* include the number of rows, however; the only way to determine that is to repeatedly call next on the ResultSet until it returns false.

Close the Connection

To close the connection explicitly, you would do:

```
connection.close();
```

You should postpone this step if you expect to perform additional database operations, since the overhead of opening a connection is usually large.

22.2 Basic JDBC Example

Listing 22.3 presents a simple class called FruitTest that follows the seven steps outlined in the previous section to show a simple table called fruits. It uses the command-line arguments to determine the host, port, database name, and driver type to use, as shown in Listings 22.1 and 22.2. Rather than putting the driver name and the logic for generating an appropriately formatted database URL directly in this class, these two tasks are spun off to a separate class called DriverUtilities, shown in Listing 22.4. This separation minimizes the places that changes have to be made when different drivers are used.

This example does not depend on the way in which the database table was actually created, only on its resultant format. So, for example, an interactive database tool could have been used. In fact, however, JDBC was also used to create the tables, as shown in Listing 22.5. For now, just skim quickly over this listing—it makes use of utilities not discussed until the next section.

Also, a quick reminder to those who are not familiar with packages. Since Fruit-Test is in the cwp package, it resides in a subdirectory called cwp. Before compiling the file, we set our CLASSPATH to include the directory *containing* the cwp directory (the JAR file containing the JDBC drivers should be in the CLASSPATH also, of course). With this setup, we compile simply by doing "javac FruitTest.java" from within the cwp subdirectory. But to run FruitTest, we need to refer to the full package name with "java **cwp.**FruitTest ...".

Listing 22.1 FruitTest result (connecting to Oracle on Solaris)

```
Prompt> java cwp.FruitTest dbhost1.apl.jhu.edu PTE
        hall xxxx oracle
Database: Oracle
Version: Oracle7 Server Release 7.2.3.0.0 - Production Release
PL/SQL Release 2.2.3.0.0 - Production

Comparing Apples and Oranges
=============================
```

QUARTER	APPLES	APPLESALES	ORANGES	ORANGESALES	TOPSELLER
1	32248	$3547.28	18459	$3138.03	Maria
2	35009	$3850.99	18722	$3182.74	Bob
3	39393	$4333.23	18999	$3229.83	Joe
4	42001	$4620.11	19333	$3286.61	Maria

Listing 22.2 FruitTest result (connecting to Sybase on NT)

```
Prompt> java cwp.FruitTest dbhost2.apl.jhu.edu 605741
        hall xxxx sybase
Database: Adaptive Server Anywhere
Version: 6.0.2.2188

Comparing Apples and Oranges
=============================
```

quarter	apples	applesales	oranges	orangesales	topseller
1	32248	$3547.28	18459	$3138.03	Maria
2	35009	$3850.99	18722	$3182.74	Bob
3	39393	$4333.23	18999	$3229.83	Joe
4	42001	$4620.11	19333	$3286.61	Maria

Listing 22.3 `FruitTest.java`

```java
package cwp;

import java.sql.*;

/** A JDBC example that connects to either an Oracle or
 *  a Sybase database and prints out the values of
 *  predetermined columns in the "fruits" table.
 */

public class FruitTest {

  /** Reads the hostname, database name, username, password,
   *  and vendor identifier from the command line. It
   *  uses the vendor identifier to determine which
   *  driver to load and how to format the URL. The
   *  driver, URL, username, host, and password are then
   *  passed to the showFruitTable method.
   */

  public static void main(String[] args) {
    if (args.length < 5) {
      printUsage();
      return;
    }
    String vendorName = args[4];
    int vendor = DriverUtilities.getVendor(vendorName);
    if (vendor == DriverUtilities.UNKNOWN) {
      printUsage();
      return;
    }
    String driver = DriverUtilities.getDriver(vendor);
    String host = args[0];
    String dbName = args[1];
    String url = DriverUtilities.makeURL(host, dbName, vendor);
    String username = args[2];
    String password = args[3];
    showFruitTable(driver, url, username, password);
  }
```

(continued)

Listing 22.3 `FruitTest.java` *(continued)*

```
/** Get the table and print all the values. */

public static void showFruitTable(String driver,
                                  String url,
                                  String username,
                                  String password) {
  try {
    // Load database driver if not already loaded.
    Class.forName(driver);
    // Establish network connection to database.
    Connection connection =
      DriverManager.getConnection(url, username, password);
    // Look up info about the database as a whole.
    DatabaseMetaData dbMetaData = connection.getMetaData();
    String productName =
      dbMetaData.getDatabaseProductName();
    System.out.println("Database: " + productName);
    String productVersion =
      dbMetaData.getDatabaseProductVersion();
    System.out.println("Version: " + productVersion + "\n");
    System.out.println("Comparing Apples and Oranges\n" +
                       "============================");
    Statement statement = connection.createStatement();
    String query = "SELECT * FROM fruits";
    // Send query to database and store results.
    ResultSet resultSet = statement.executeQuery(query);
    // Look up information about a particular table.
    ResultSetMetaData resultsMetaData =
      resultSet.getMetaData();
    int columnCount = resultsMetaData.getColumnCount();
    // Column index starts at 1 (a la SQL) not 0 (a la Java).
    for(int i=1; i<columnCount+1; i++) {
      System.out.print(resultsMetaData.getColumnName(i) +
                       "   ");
    }
    System.out.println();
    // Print results.
    while(resultSet.next()) {
      // Quarter
      System.out.print("   " + resultSet.getInt(1));
      // Number of Apples
      System.out.print("    " + resultSet.getInt(2));
      // Apple Sales
      System.out.print("   $" + resultSet.getFloat(3));
```

(continued)

Listing 22.3 `FruitTest.java` *(continued)*

```java
        // Number of Oranges
        System.out.print("     " + resultSet.getInt(4));
        // Orange Sales
        System.out.print("     $" + resultSet.getFloat(5));
        // Top Salesman
        System.out.println("        " + resultSet.getString(6));
      }
    } catch(ClassNotFoundException cnfe) {
      System.err.println("Error loading driver: " + cnfe);
    } catch(SQLException sqle) {
      System.err.println("Error connecting: " + sqle);
    }
  }

  private static void printUsage() {
    System.out.println("Usage: FruitTest host dbName " +
                       "username password oracle|sybase.");
  }
}
```

Listing 22.4 `DriverUtilities.java`

```java
package cwp;

/** Some simple utilities for building Oracle and Sybase
 *  JDBC connections. This is <I>not</I> general-purpose
 *  code -- it is specific to my local setup.
 */

public class DriverUtilities {
  public static final int ORACLE = 1;
  public static final int SYBASE = 2;
  public static final int UNKNOWN = -1;

  /** Build a URL in the format needed by the
   *  Oracle and Sybase drivers we are using.
   */

  public static String makeURL(String host, String dbName,
                               int vendor) {
    if (vendor == ORACLE) {
      return("jdbc:oracle:thin:@" + host + ":1521:" + dbName);
    } else if (vendor == SYBASE) {
```

(continued)

Listing 22.4 `DriverUtilities.java` *(continued)*

```java
      return("jdbc:sybase:Tds:" + host  + ":1521" +
             "?SERVICENAME=" + dbName);
    } else {
      return(null);
    }
  }

  /** Get the fully qualified name of a driver. */

  public static String getDriver(int vendor) {
    if (vendor == ORACLE) {
      return("oracle.jdbc.driver.OracleDriver");
    } else if (vendor == SYBASE) {
      return("com.sybase.jdbc.SybDriver");
    } else {
      return(null);
    }
  }

  /** Map name to int value. */

  public static int getVendor(String vendorName) {
    if (vendorName.equalsIgnoreCase("oracle")) {
      return(ORACLE);
    } else if (vendorName.equalsIgnoreCase("sybase")) {
      return(SYBASE);
    } else {
      return(UNKNOWN);
    }
  }
}
```

Listing 22.5 `FruitCreation.java`

```java
package cwp;

import java.sql.*;

/** Creates a simple table named "fruits" in either
 *  an Oracle or a Sybase database.
 */
```

(continued)

Listing 22.5 FruitCreation.java *(continued)*

```java
public class FruitCreation {
  public static void main(String[] args) {
    if (args.length < 5) {
      printUsage();
      return;
    }
    String vendorName = args[4];
    int vendor = DriverUtilities.getVendor(vendorName);
    if (vendor == DriverUtilities.UNKNOWN) {
      printUsage();
      return;
    }
    String driver = DriverUtilities.getDriver(vendor);
    String host = args[0];
    String dbName = args[1];
    String url =
      DriverUtilities.makeURL(host, dbName, vendor);
    String username = args[2];
    String password = args[3];
    String format =
      "(quarter int, " +
      "apples int, applesales float, " +
      "oranges int, orangesales float, " +
      "topseller varchar(16))";
    String[] rows =
    { "(1, 32248, 3547.28, 18459, 3138.03, 'Maria')",
      "(2, 35009, 3850.99, 18722, 3182.74, 'Bob')",
      "(3, 39393, 4333.23, 18999, 3229.83, 'Joe')",
      "(4, 42001, 4620.11, 19333, 3286.61, 'Maria')" };
    Connection connection =
      DatabaseUtilities.createTable(driver, url,
                                    username, password,
                                    "fruits", format, rows,
                                    false);
    // Test to verify table was created properly. Reuse
    // old connection for efficiency.
    DatabaseUtilities.printTable(connection, "fruits",
                                 11, true);
  }

  private static void printUsage() {
    System.out.println("Usage: FruitCreation host dbName " +
                       "username password oracle|sybase.");
  }
}
```

22.3 Some JDBC Utilities

In many applications, you don't need to process query results a row at a time. For example, in servlets and JSP pages, it is common to simply format the database results (treating all values as strings) and present them to the user in an HTML table, in an Excel spreadsheet, or distributed throughout the page. In such a case, it simplifies processing to have methods that retrieve and store an entire ResultSet for later display.

This section presents two classes that provide this basic functionality along with a few formatting, display, and table creation utilities. The core class is Database-Utilities, which implements static methods for four common tasks:

1. **getQueryResults**
   This method connects to a database, executes a query, retrieves all the rows as arrays of strings, and puts them inside a DBResults object (see Listing 22.7). This method also places the database product name, database version, the names of all the columns and the Connection object into the DBResults object. There are two versions of getQueryResults: one that makes a new connection and another that uses an existing connection.

2. **createTable**
   Given a table name, a string denoting the column formats, and an array of strings denoting the row values, this method connects to a database, removes any existing versions of the designated table, issues a CREATE TABLE command with the designated format, then sends a series of INSERT INTO commands for each of the rows. Again, there are two versions: one that makes a new connection and another that uses an existing connection.

3. **printTable**
   Given a table name, this method connects to the specified database, retrieves all the rows, and prints them on the standard output. It retrieves the results by turning the table name into a query of the form "SELECT * FROM tableName" and passing it to getQueryResults.

4. **printTableData**
   Given a DBResults object from a previous query, this method prints it on the standard output. This is the underlying method used by print-Table, but it is also useful for debugging arbitrary database results.

Listing 22.6 gives the main code, and Listing 22.7 presents the auxiliary DBResults class that stores the accumulated results and return them as arrays of strings (getRow) or wrapped up inside an HTML table (toHTMLTable). For example, the following two statements perform a database query, retrieve the results, and format them inside an HTML table that uses the column names as headings with a cyan background color.

```
DBResults results =
  DatabaseUtilities.getQueryResults(driver, url,
                                    username, password,
                                    query, true);
out.println(results.toHTMLTable("CYAN"));
```

Since an HTML table can do double duty as an Excel spreadsheet, the toHTML-Table method provides an extremely simple method for building tables or spreadsheets from database results.

Remember that the source code for DatabaseUtilities and DBResults, like all the source code in the book, can be downloaded from www.coreweb-programming.com and used or adapted without restriction.

Listing 22.6 DatabaseUtilities.java

```java
package cwp;

import java.sql.*;

public class DatabaseUtilities {

  /** Connect to database, execute specified query,
   *  and accumulate results into DBRresults object.
   *  If the database connection is left open (use the
   *  close argument to specify), you can retrieve the
   *  connection with DBResults.getConnection.
   */

  public static DBResults getQueryResults(String driver,
                                          String url,
                                          String username,
                                          String password,
                                          String query,
                                          boolean close) {
    try {
      Class.forName(driver);
      Connection connection =
        DriverManager.getConnection(url, username, password);
      return(getQueryResults(connection, query, close));
    } catch(ClassNotFoundException cnfe) {
      System.err.println("Error loading driver: " + cnfe);
      return(null);
    } catch(SQLException sqle) {
      System.err.println("Error connecting: " + sqle);
      return(null);
    }
  }
}
```

(continued)

Listing 22.6 DatabaseUtilities.java *(continued)*

```java
/** Retrieves results as in previous method but uses
 *  an existing connection instead of opening a new one.
 */

public static DBResults getQueryResults(Connection connection,
                                        String query,
                                        boolean close) {
  try {
    DatabaseMetaData dbMetaData = connection.getMetaData();
    String productName =
      dbMetaData.getDatabaseProductName();
    String productVersion =
      dbMetaData.getDatabaseProductVersion();
    Statement statement = connection.createStatement();
    ResultSet resultSet = statement.executeQuery(query);
    ResultSetMetaData resultsMetaData =
      resultSet.getMetaData();
    int columnCount = resultsMetaData.getColumnCount();
    String[] columnNames = new String[columnCount];
    // Column index starts at 1 (a la SQL) not 0 (a la Java).
    for(int i=1; i<columnCount+1; i++) {
      columnNames[i-1] =
        resultsMetaData.getColumnName(i).trim();
    }
    DBResults dbResults =
      new DBResults(connection, productName, productVersion,
                    columnCount, columnNames);
    while(resultSet.next()) {
      String[] row = new String[columnCount];
      // Again, ResultSet index starts at 1, not 0.
      for(int i=1; i<columnCount+1; i++) {
        String entry = resultSet.getString(i);
        if (entry != null) {
          entry = entry.trim();
        }
        row[i-1] = entry;
      }
      dbResults.addRow(row);
    }
    if (close) {
      connection.close();
    }
    return(dbResults);
```

(continued)

Listing 22.6 DatabaseUtilities.java *(continued)*

```java
    } catch(SQLException sqle) {
      System.err.println("Error connecting: " + sqle);
      return(null);
    }
}

/** Build a table with the specified format and rows. */

public static Connection createTable(String driver,
                                     String url,
                                     String username,
                                     String password,
                                     String tableName,
                                     String tableFormat,
                                     String[] tableRows,
                                     boolean close) {
  try {
    Class.forName(driver);
    Connection connection =
      DriverManager.getConnection(url, username, password);
    return(createTable(connection, username, password,
                       tableName, tableFormat,
                       tableRows, close));
  } catch(ClassNotFoundException cnfe) {
    System.err.println("Error loading driver: " + cnfe);
    return(null);
  } catch(SQLException sqle) {
    System.err.println("Error connecting: " + sqle);
    return(null);
  }
}

/** Like the previous method, but uses existing connection. */

public static Connection createTable(Connection connection,
                                     String username,
                                     String password,
                                     String tableName,
                                     String tableFormat,
                                     String[] tableRows,
                                     boolean close) {
  try {

    Statement statement = connection.createStatement();
    // Drop previous table if it exists, but don't get
    // error if it doesn't. Thus the separate try/catch here.
```

(continued)

Listing 22.6 `DatabaseUtilities.java` *(continued)*

```
    try {
      statement.execute("DROP TABLE " + tableName);
    } catch(SQLException sqle) {}
    String createCommand =
      "CREATE TABLE " + tableName + " " + tableFormat;
    statement.execute(createCommand);
    String insertPrefix =
      "INSERT INTO " + tableName + " VALUES";
    for(int i=0; i<tableRows.length; i++) {
      statement.execute(insertPrefix + tableRows[i]);
    }
    if (close) {
      connection.close();
      return(null);
    } else {
      return(connection);
    }
  } catch(SQLException sqle) {
    System.err.println("Error creating table: " + sqle);
    return(null);
  }
}

public static void printTable(String driver,
                             String url,
                             String username,
                             String password,
                             String tableName,
                             int entryWidth,
                             boolean close) {
  String query = "SELECT * FROM " + tableName;
  DBResults results =
    getQueryResults(driver, url, username,
                  password, query, close);
  printTableData(tableName, results, entryWidth, true);
}

/** Prints out all entries in a table. Each entry will
 *  be printed in a column that is entryWidth characters
 *  wide, so be sure to provide a value at least as big
 *  as the widest result.
 */
```

(continued)

Listing 22.6 `DatabaseUtilities.java` *(continued)*

```java
public static void printTable(Connection connection,
                              String tableName,
                              int entryWidth,
                              boolean close) {
  String query = "SELECT * FROM " + tableName;
  DBResults results =
    getQueryResults(connection, query, close);
  printTableData(tableName, results, entryWidth, true);
}

public static void printTableData(String tableName,
                                  DBResults results,
                                  int entryWidth,
                                  boolean printMetaData) {
  if (results == null) {
    return;
  }
  if (printMetaData) {
    System.out.println("Database: " +
                       results.getProductName());
    System.out.println("Version: " +
                       results.getProductVersion());
    System.out.println();
  }
  System.out.println(tableName + ":");
  String underline =
    padString("", tableName.length()+1, "=");
  System.out.println(underline);
  int columnCount = results.getColumnCount();
  String separator =
    makeSeparator(entryWidth, columnCount);
  System.out.println(separator);
  String row = makeRow(results.getColumnNames(), entryWidth);
  System.out.println(row);
  System.out.println(separator);
  int rowCount = results.getRowCount();
  for(int i=0; i<rowCount; i++) {
    row = makeRow(results.getRow(i), entryWidth);
    System.out.println(row);
  }
  System.out.println(separator);
}
```

(continued)

Listing 22.6 DatabaseUtilities.java *(continued)*

```
// A String of the form "|  xxx  |  xxx  |  xxx  |"

private static String makeRow(String[] entries,
                              int entryWidth) {
  String row = "|";
  for(int i=0; i<entries.length; i++) {
    row = row + padString(entries[i], entryWidth, " ");
    row = row + "  |";
  }
  return(row);
}

// A String of the form "+------+------+------+"

private static String makeSeparator(int entryWidth,
                                    int columnCount) {
  String entry = padString("", entryWidth+1, "-");
  String separator = "+";
  for(int i=0; i<columnCount; i++) {
    separator = separator + entry + "+";
  }
  return(separator);
}

private static String padString(String orig, int size,
                                String padChar) {
  if (orig == null) {
    orig = "<null>";
  }
  // Use StringBuffer, not just repeated String concatenation
  // to avoid creating too many temporary Strings.
  StringBuffer buffer = new StringBuffer("");
  int extraChars = size - orig.length();
  for(int i=0; i<extraChars; i++) {
    buffer.append(padChar);
  }
  buffer.append(orig);
  return(buffer.toString());
}
}
```

Listing 22.7 DBResults.java

```java
package cwp;

import java.sql.*;
import java.util.*;

/** Class to store completed results of a JDBC Query.
 *  Differs from a ResultSet in several ways:
 *  <UL>
 *    <LI>ResultSet doesn't necessarily have all the data;
 *        reconnection to database occurs as you ask for
 *        later rows.
 *    <LI>This class stores results as strings, in arrays.
 *    <LI>This class includes DatabaseMetaData (database product
 *        name and version) and ResultSetMetaData
 *        (the column names).
 *    <LI>This class has a toHTMLTable method that turns
 *        the results into a long string corresponding to
 *        an HTML table.
 *  </UL>
 */

public class DBResults {
  private Connection connection;
  private String productName;
  private String productVersion;
  private int columnCount;
  private String[] columnNames;
  private Vector queryResults;
  String[] rowData;

  public DBResults(Connection connection,
                   String productName,
                   String productVersion,
                   int columnCount,
                   String[] columnNames) {
    this.connection = connection;
    this.productName = productName;
    this.productVersion = productVersion;
    this.columnCount = columnCount;
    this.columnNames = columnNames;
    rowData = new String[columnCount];
    queryResults = new Vector();
  }
```

(continued)

Listing 22.7 DBResults.java *(continued)*

```
public Connection getConnection() {
  return(connection);
}

public String getProductName() {
  return(productName);
}

public String getProductVersion() {
  return(productVersion);
}

public int getColumnCount() {
  return(columnCount);
}

public String[] getColumnNames() {
  return(columnNames);
}

public int getRowCount() {
  return(queryResults.size());
}

public String[] getRow(int index) {
  return((String[])queryResults.elementAt(index));
}

public void addRow(String[] row) {
  queryResults.addElement(row);
}

/** Output the results as an HTML table, with
 *  the column names as headings and the rest of
 *  the results filling regular data cells.
 */

public String toHTMLTable(String headingColor) {
  StringBuffer buffer =
    new StringBuffer("<TABLE BORDER=1>\n");
  if (headingColor != null) {
    buffer.append("  <TR BGCOLOR=\"" + headingColor +
                  "\">\n    ");
```

(continued)

Listing 22.7 DBResults.java *(continued)*

```
    } else {
      buffer.append("  <TR>\n    ");
    }
    for(int col=0; col<getColumnCount(); col++) {
      buffer.append("<TH>" + columnNames[col]);
    }
    for(int row=0; row<getRowCount(); row++) {
      buffer.append("\n  <TR>\n    ");
      String[] rowData = getRow(row);
      for(int col=0; col<getColumnCount(); col++) {
        buffer.append("<TD>" + rowData[col]);
      }
    }
    buffer.append("\n</TABLE>");
    return(buffer.toString());
  }
}
```

22.4 Applying the Database Utilities

Now, let's see how the database utilities of Section 22.3 can simplify the retrieval and display of database results. Listing 22.8 presents a class that connects to the database specified on the command line and prints out all entries in the employees table. Listings 22.9 and 22.10 show the results when connecting to Oracle and Sybase databases, respectively. Listing 22.11 shows a similar class that performs the same database lookup but formats the results in an HTML table. Listing 22.12 shows the raw HTML result.

Listing 22.13 shows the JDBC code used to create the employees table.

Listing 22.8 EmployeeTest.java

```
package cwp;

import java.sql.*;

/** Connect to Oracle or Sybase and print "employees" table. */

public class EmployeeTest {
  public static void main(String[] args) {
    if (args.length < 5) {
      printUsage();
      return;
    }
    String vendorName = args[4];
    int vendor = DriverUtilities.getVendor(vendorName);
    if (vendor == DriverUtilities.UNKNOWN) {
      printUsage();
      return;
    }
    String driver = DriverUtilities.getDriver(vendor);
    String host = args[0];
    String dbName = args[1];
    String url =
      DriverUtilities.makeURL(host, dbName, vendor);
    String username = args[2];
    String password = args[3];
    DatabaseUtilities.printTable(driver, url,
                                 username, password,
                                 "employees", 12, true);
  }

  private static void printUsage() {
    System.out.println("Usage: EmployeeTest host dbName " +
                       "username password oracle|sybase.");
  }
}
```

Listing 22.9 `EmployeeTest` result (connecting to Oracle on Solaris)

```
Prompt> java cwp.EmployeeTest dbhost1.apl.jhu.edu PTE
        hall xxxx oracle
Database: Oracle
Version: Oracle7 Server Release 7.2.3.0.0 - Production Release
PL/SQL Release 2.2.3.0.0 - Production

employees:
==========
+-------------+-------------+-------------+-------------+-------------+
|          ID |   FIRSTNAME |    LASTNAME |    LANGUAGE |      SALARY |
+-------------+-------------+-------------+-------------+-------------+
|           1 |         Wye |       Tukay |       COBOL |       42500 |
|           2 |       Britt |        Tell |         C++ |       62000 |
|           3 |         Max |     Manager |        none |       15500 |
|           4 |       Polly |     Morphic |   Smalltalk |       51500 |
|           5 |       Frank |    Function | Common Lisp |       51500 |
|           6 |      Justin |Timecompiler |        Java |       98000 |
|           7 |         Sir |        Vlet |        Java |      114750 |
|           8 |         Jay |        Espy |        Java |      128500 |
+-------------+-------------+-------------+-------------+-------------+
```

Listing 22.10 `EmployeeTest` result (connecting to Sybase on NT)

```
Prompt> java cwp.EmployeeTest dbhost2.apl.jhu.edu 605741
        hall xxxx sybase
Database: Adaptive Server Anywhere
Version: 6.0.2.2188

employees:
==========
+-------------+-------------+-------------+-------------+-------------+
|          id |   firstname |    lastname |    language |      salary |
+-------------+-------------+-------------+-------------+-------------+
|           1 |         Wye |       Tukay |       COBOL |     42500.0 |
|           2 |       Britt |        Tell |         C++ |     62000.0 |
|           3 |         Max |     Manager |        none |     15500.0 |
|           4 |       Polly |     Morphic |   Smalltalk |     51500.0 |
|           5 |       Frank |    Function | Common Lisp |     51500.0 |
|           6 |      Justin |Timecompiler |        Java |     98000.0 |
|           7 |         Sir |        Vlet |        Java |    114750.0 |
|           8 |         Jay |        Espy |        Java |    128500.0 |
+-------------+-------------+-------------+-------------+-------------+
```

Listing 22.11 `EmployeeTest2.java`

```java
package cwp;

import java.sql.*;

/** Connect to Oracle or Sybase and print "employees" table
 *  as an HTML table.
 */

public class EmployeeTest2 {
  public static void main(String[] args) {
    if (args.length < 5) {
      printUsage();
      return;
    }
    String vendorName = args[4];
    int vendor = DriverUtilities.getVendor(vendorName);
    if (vendor == DriverUtilities.UNKNOWN) {
      printUsage();
      return;
    }
    String driver = DriverUtilities.getDriver(vendor);
    String host = args[0];
    String dbName = args[1];
    String url =
      DriverUtilities.makeURL(host, dbName, vendor);
    String username = args[2];
    String password = args[3];
    String query = "SELECT * FROM employees";
    DBResults results =
      DatabaseUtilities.getQueryResults(driver, url,
                                        username, password,
                                        query, true);
    System.out.println(results.toHTMLTable("CYAN"));
  }

  private static void printUsage() {
    System.out.println("Usage: EmployeeTest2 host dbName " +
                       "username password oracle|sybase.");
  }
}
```

Listing 22.12 `EmployeeTest2` **result (connecting to Sybase on NT)**

```
Prompt> java cwp.EmployeeTest2 dbhost2 605741
        hall xxxx sybase
<TABLE BORDER=1>
  <TR BGCOLOR="CYAN">
    <TH>id<TH>firstname<TH>lastname<TH>language<TH>salary
  <TR>
    <TD>1<TD>Wye<TD>Tukay<TD>COBOL<TD>42500.0
  <TR>
    <TD>2<TD>Britt<TD>Tell<TD>C++<TD>62000.0
  <TR>
    <TD>3<TD>Max<TD>Manager<TD>none<TD>15500.0
  <TR>
    <TD>4<TD>Polly<TD>Morphic<TD>Smalltalk<TD>51500.0
  <TR>
    <TD>5<TD>Frank<TD>Function<TD>Common Lisp<TD>51500.0
  <TR>
    <TD>6<TD>Justin<TD>Timecompiler<TD>Java<TD>98000.0
  <TR>
    <TD>7<TD>Sir<TD>Vlet<TD>Java<TD>114750.0
  <TR>
    <TD>8<TD>Jay<TD>Espy<TD>Java<TD>128500.0
</TABLE>
```

Listing 22.13 `EmployeeCreation.java`

```java
package cwp;

import java.sql.*;

/** Make a simple "employees" table using DatabaseUtilities. */

public class EmployeeCreation {
  public static Connection createEmployees(String driver,
                                           String url,
                                           String username,
                                           String password,
                                           boolean close) {
    String format =
      "(id int, firstname varchar(32), lastname varchar(32), " +
      "language varchar(16), salary float)";
```

(continued)

Listing 22.13 `EmployeeCreation.java` *(continued)*

```
      String[] employees =
        {"(1, 'Wye', 'Tukay', 'COBOL', 42500)",
         "(2, 'Britt', 'Tell',   'C++',   62000)",
         "(3, 'Max',   'Manager', 'none',  15500)",
         "(4, 'Polly', 'Morphic', 'Smalltalk', 51500)",
         "(5, 'Frank', 'Function', 'Common Lisp', 51500)",
         "(6, 'Justin', 'Timecompiler', 'Java', 98000)",
         "(7, 'Sir', 'Vlet', 'Java', 114750)",
         "(8, 'Jay', 'Espy', 'Java', 128500)" };
      return(DatabaseUtilities.createTable(driver, url,
                                           username, password,
                                           "employees",
                                           format, employees,
                                           close));
  }

  public static void main(String[] args) {
    if (args.length < 5) {
      printUsage();
      return;
    }
    String vendorName = args[4];
    int vendor = DriverUtilities.getVendor(vendorName);
    if (vendor == DriverUtilities.UNKNOWN) {
      printUsage();
      return;
    }
    String driver = DriverUtilities.getDriver(vendor);
    String host = args[0];
    String dbName = args[1];
    String url =
      DriverUtilities.makeURL(host, dbName, vendor);
    String username = args[2];
    String password = args[3];
    createEmployees(driver, url, username, password, true);
  }

  private static void printUsage() {
    System.out.println("Usage: EmployeeCreation host dbName " +
                       "username password oracle|sybase.");
  }
}
```

22.5 An Interactive Query Viewer

Up to this point, all the database results have been based upon queries that were known at the time the program was written. In many real applications, however, queries are derived from user input that is not known until run time. Sometimes the queries follow a fixed format even though certain values change. You should make use of prepared statements in such a case; see Section 22.6 for details. Other times, however, even the query format is variable. Fortunately, this situation presents no problem, since ResultSetMetaData can be used to determine the number, names, and types of columns in a ResultSet, as was discussed in Section 22.1 (Basic Steps in Using JDBC). In fact, the database utilities of Listing 22.6 store that metadata in the DBResults object that is returned from the showQueryData method. Access to this metadata makes it straightforward to implement an interactive graphical query viewer as shown in Figures 22–1 through 22–5. The code to accomplish this result is presented in the following subsection.

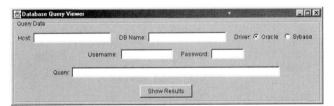

Figure 22–1 Initial appearance of the query viewer.

ID	FIRSTNAME	LASTNAME	LANGUAGE	SALARY
1	Wye	Tukay	COBOL	42500
2	Britt	Tell	C++	62000
3	Max	Manager	none	15500
4	Polly	Morphic	Smalltalk	51500
5	Frank	Function	Common Lisp	51500
6	Justin	Timecompiler	Java	98000
7	Sir	Vlet	Java	114750
8	Jay	Espy	Java	128500

Figure 22–2 Query viewer after a request for the complete employees table from an Oracle database.

Figure 22–3 Query viewer after a request for part of the `employees` table from an Oracle database.

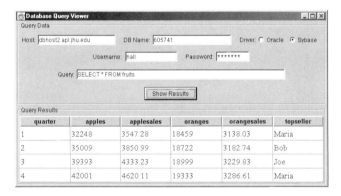

Figure 22–4 Query viewer after a request for the complete `fruits` table from a Sybase database.

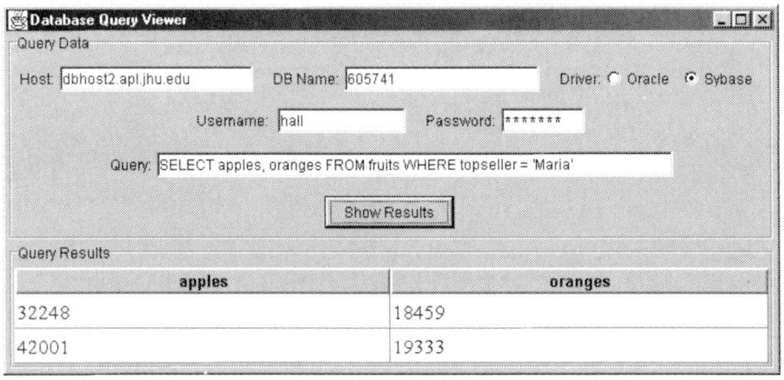

Figure 22–5 Query viewer after a request for part of the `fruits` table from a Sybase database.

Query Viewer Code

Building the display shown in Figures 22–1 through 22–5 is relatively straightforward. In fact, given the database utilities shown earlier, it takes substantially more code to build the user interface than it does to communicate with the database. The full code is shown in Listing 22.14, but we'll give a quick summary of the process that takes place when the user presses the Show Results button.

First, the system reads the host, port, database name, username, password, and driver type from the user interface elements shown. Next, it submits the query and stores the result, as below:

```
DBResults results =
  DatabaseUtilities.getQueryResults(driver, url,
                                    username, password,
                                    query, true);
```

Next, the system passes these results to a custom table model (see Listing 22.15). If you are not familiar with the Swing GUI library, note that a table model acts as the glue between a JTable and the actual data.

```
DBResultsTableModel model = new DBResultsTableModel(results);
JTable table = new JTable(model);
```

Finally, the system places this JTable in the bottom region of the JFrame and calls pack to tell the JFrame to resize itself to fit the table.

Listing 22.14 QueryViewer.java

```
package cwp;

import java.awt.*;
import java.awt.event.*;
import javax.swing.*;
import javax.swing.table.*;

/** An interactive database query viewer. Connects to
 *  the specified Oracle or Sybase database, executes a query,
 *  and presents the results in a JTable.
 */

public class QueryViewer extends JFrame
                         implements ActionListener{
  public static void main(String[] args) {
    new QueryViewer();
  }
```

(continued)

Listing 22.14 `QueryViewer.java` *(continued)*

```java
  private JTextField hostField, dbNameField,
                     queryField, usernameField;
  private JRadioButton oracleButton, sybaseButton;
  private JPasswordField passwordField;
  private JButton showResultsButton;
  private Container contentPane;
  private JPanel tablePanel;

  public QueryViewer () {
    super("Database Query Viewer");
    WindowUtilities.setNativeLookAndFeel();
    addWindowListener(new ExitListener());
    contentPane = getContentPane();
    contentPane.add(makeControlPanel(), BorderLayout.NORTH);
    pack();
    setVisible(true);
  }

  /** When the "Show Results" button is pressed or
   *  RETURN is hit while the query textfield has the
   *  keyboard focus, a database lookup is performed,
   *  the results are placed in a JTable, and the window
   *  is resized to accommodate the table.
   */

  public void actionPerformed(ActionEvent event) {
    String host = hostField.getText();
    String dbName = dbNameField.getText();
    String username = usernameField.getText();
    String password =
      String.valueOf(passwordField.getPassword());
    String query = queryField.getText();
    int vendor;
    if (oracleButton.isSelected()) {
      vendor = DriverUtilities.ORACLE;
    } else {
      vendor = DriverUtilities.SYBASE;
    }
    if (tablePanel != null) {
      contentPane.remove(tablePanel);
    }
    tablePanel = makeTablePanel(host, dbName, vendor,
                                username, password,
                                query);
    contentPane.add(tablePanel, BorderLayout.CENTER);
    pack();
  }
```

(continued)

Listing 22.14 `QueryViewer.java` *(continued)*

```java
// Executes a query and places the result in a
// JTable that is, in turn, inside a JPanel.

private JPanel makeTablePanel(String host,
                              String dbName,
                              int vendor,
                              String username,
                              String password,
                              String query) {
  String driver = DriverUtilities.getDriver(vendor);
  String url = DriverUtilities.makeURL(host, dbName, vendor);
  DBResults results =
    DatabaseUtilities.getQueryResults(driver, url,
                                      username, password,
                                      query, true);
  JPanel panel = new JPanel(new BorderLayout());
  if (results == null) {
    panel.add(makeErrorLabel());
    return(panel);
  }
  DBResultsTableModel model =
    new DBResultsTableModel(results);
  JTable table = new JTable(model);
  table.setFont(new Font("Serif", Font.PLAIN, 17));
  table.setRowHeight(28);
  JTableHeader header = table.getTableHeader();
  header.setFont(new Font("SansSerif", Font.BOLD, 13));
  panel.add(table, BorderLayout.CENTER);
  panel.add(header, BorderLayout.NORTH);
  panel.setBorder
    (BorderFactory.createTitledBorder("Query Results"));
  return(panel);
}

// The panel that contains the textfields, check boxes,
// and button.

private JPanel makeControlPanel() {
  JPanel panel = new JPanel(new GridLayout(0, 1));
  panel.add(makeHostPanel());
  panel.add(makeUsernamePanel());
  panel.add(makeQueryPanel());
  panel.add(makeButtonPanel());
  panel.setBorder
```

(continued)

Listing 22.14 `QueryViewer.java` *(continued)*

```
    (BorderFactory.createTitledBorder("Query Data"));
  return(panel);
}

// The panel that has the host and db name textfield and
// the driver radio buttons. Placed in control panel.

private JPanel makeHostPanel() {
  JPanel panel = new JPanel();
  panel.add(new JLabel("Host:"));
  hostField = new JTextField(15);
  panel.add(hostField);
  panel.add(new JLabel("    DB Name:"));
  dbNameField = new JTextField(15);
  panel.add(dbNameField);
  panel.add(new JLabel("    Driver:"));
  ButtonGroup vendorGroup = new ButtonGroup();
  oracleButton = new JRadioButton("Oracle", true);
  vendorGroup.add(oracleButton);
  panel.add(oracleButton);
  sybaseButton = new JRadioButton("Sybase");
  vendorGroup.add(sybaseButton);
  panel.add(sybaseButton);
  return(panel);
}

// The panel that has the username and password textfields.
// Placed in control panel.

private JPanel makeUsernamePanel() {
  JPanel panel = new JPanel();
  usernameField = new JTextField(10);
  passwordField = new JPasswordField(10);
  panel.add(new JLabel("Username: "));
  panel.add(usernameField);
  panel.add(new JLabel("    Password:"));
  panel.add(passwordField);
  return(panel);
}

// The panel that has textfield for entering queries.
// Placed in control panel.
```

(continued)

Listing 22.14 `QueryViewer.java` *(continued)*

```java
  private JPanel makeQueryPanel() {
    JPanel panel = new JPanel();
    queryField = new JTextField(40);
    queryField.addActionListener(this);
    panel.add(new JLabel("Query:"));
    panel.add(queryField);
    return(panel);
  }

  // The panel that has the "Show Results" button.
  // Placed in control panel.

  private JPanel makeButtonPanel() {
    JPanel panel = new JPanel();
    showResultsButton = new JButton("Show Results");
    showResultsButton.addActionListener(this);
    panel.add(showResultsButton);
    return(panel);
  }

  // Shows warning when bad query sent.

  private JLabel makeErrorLabel() {
    JLabel label = new JLabel("No Results", JLabel.CENTER);
    label.setFont(new Font("Serif", Font.BOLD, 36));
    return(label);
  }
}
```

Listing 22.15 `DBResultsTableModel.java`

```java
package cwp;

import javax.swing.table.*;

/** Simple class that tells a JTable how to extract
 *  relevant data from a DBResults object (which is
 *  used to store the results from a database query).
 */

public class DBResultsTableModel extends AbstractTableModel {
  private DBResults results;
```

(continued)

Listing 22.15 `DBResultsTableModel.java` *(continued)*

```java
  public DBResultsTableModel(DBResults results) {
    this.results = results;
  }

  public int getRowCount() {
    return(results.getRowCount());
  }

  public int getColumnCount() {
    return(results.getColumnCount());
  }

  public String getColumnName(int column) {
    return(results.getColumnNames()[column]);
  }

  public Object getValueAt(int row, int column) {
    return(results.getRow(row)[column]);
  }
}
```

22.6 Prepared Statements (Precompiled Queries)

If you are going to execute similar SQL statements multiple times, using "prepared" statements can be more efficient than executing a raw query each time. The idea is to create a parameterized statement in a standard form that is sent to the database for compilation before actually being used. You use a question mark to indicate the places where a value will be substituted into the statement. Each time you use the prepared statement, you simply replace some of the marked parameters, using a set*Xxx* call corresponding to the entry you want to set (using 1-based indexing) and the type of the parameter (e.g., `setInt`, `setString`). You then use `execute-Query` (if you want a `ResultSet` back) or `execute/executeUpdate` (for side effects) as with normal statements. For instance, if you were going to give raises to all the personnel in the `employees` database, you might do something like the following:

```java
Connection connection =
  DriverManager.getConnection(url, user, password);
String template =
  "UPDATE employees SET salary = ? WHERE id = ?";
PreparedStatement statement =
```

```
  connection.prepareStatement(template);
float[] newSalaries = getNewSalaries();
int[] employeeIDs = getIDs();
for(int i=0; i<employeeIDs.length; i++) {
  statement.setFloat(1, newSalaries[i]);
  statement.setInt(2, employeeIDs[i]);
  statement.execute();
}
```

The performance advantages of prepared statements can vary significantly, depending on how well the server supports precompiled queries and how efficiently the driver handles raw queries. For example, Listing 22.16 presents a class that sends 40 different queries to a database by means of prepared statements, then repeats the same 40 queries with regular statements. With a PC and a 28.8K modem connection to the Internet to talk to an Oracle database, prepared statements took only *half* the time of raw queries, averaging 17.5 seconds for the 40 queries as compared with an average of 35 seconds for the raw queries. When a fast LAN connection to the same Oracle database was used, prepared statements took only about 70 percent of the time required by raw queries, averaging 0.22 seconds for the 40 queries as compared with an average of 0.31 seconds for the regular statements. With the Sybase driver we used, prepared statement times were virtually identical to times for raw queries both with the modem connection and with the fast LAN connection. To get performance numbers for your setup, download `DriverUtilities.java` from `http://www.corewebprogramming.com/`, add information about your drivers to it, then run the `PreparedStatements` program yourself.

Listing 22.16 `PreparedStatements.java`

```
package cwp;

import java.sql.*;

/** An example to test the timing differences resulting
 *  from repeated raw queries vs. repeated calls to
 *  prepared statements. These results will vary dramatically
 *  among database servers and drivers.
 */

public class PreparedStatements {
  public static void main(String[] args) {
    if (args.length < 5) {
      printUsage();
      return;
    }
```

(continued)

Listing 22.16 `PreparedStatements.java` *(continued)*

```
  String vendorName = args[4];
  int vendor = DriverUtilities.getVendor(vendorName);
  if (vendor == DriverUtilities.UNKNOWN) {
    printUsage();
    return;
  }
  String driver = DriverUtilities.getDriver(vendor);
  String host = args[0];
  String dbName = args[1];
  String url =
    DriverUtilities.makeURL(host, dbName, vendor);
  String username = args[2];
  String password = args[3];
  // Use "print" only to confirm it works properly,
  // not when getting timing results.
  boolean print = false;
  if ((args.length > 5) && (args[5].equals("print"))) {
    print = true;
  }
  Connection connection =
    getConnection(driver, url, username, password);
  if (connection != null) {
    doPreparedStatements(connection, print);
    doRawQueries(connection, print);
  }
}

private static void doPreparedStatements(Connection conn,
                                         boolean print) {
  try {
    String queryFormat =
      "SELECT lastname FROM employees WHERE salary > ?";
    PreparedStatement statement =
      conn.prepareStatement(queryFormat);
    long startTime = System.currentTimeMillis();
    for(int i=0; i<40; i++) {
      statement.setFloat(1, i*5000);
      ResultSet results = statement.executeQuery();
      if (print) {
        showResults(results);
      }
    }
```

(continued)

Listing 22.16 `PreparedStatements.java` *(continued)*

```
    long stopTime = System.currentTimeMillis();
    double elapsedTime = (stopTime - startTime)/1000.0;
    System.out.println("Executing prepared statement " +
                       "40 times took " +
                       elapsedTime + " seconds.");
  } catch(SQLException sqle) {
    System.out.println("Error executing statement: " + sqle);
  }
}

public static void doRawQueries(Connection conn,
                                boolean print) {
  try {
    String queryFormat =
      "SELECT lastname FROM employees WHERE salary > ";
    Statement statement = conn.createStatement();
    long startTime = System.currentTimeMillis();
    for(int i=0; i<40; i++) {
      ResultSet results =
        statement.executeQuery(queryFormat + (i*5000));
      if (print) {
        showResults(results);
      }
    }
    long stopTime = System.currentTimeMillis();
    double elapsedTime = (stopTime - startTime)/1000.0;
    System.out.println("Executing raw query " +
                       "40 times took " +
                       elapsedTime + " seconds.");
  } catch(SQLException sqle) {
    System.out.println("Error executing query: " + sqle);
  }
}

private static void showResults(ResultSet results)
    throws SQLException {
  while(results.next()) {
    System.out.print(results.getString(1) + " ");
  }
  System.out.println();
}

private static Connection getConnection(String driver,
                                        String url,
                                        String username,
                                        String password) {
```

(continued)

Listing 22.16 `PreparedStatements.java` (continued)

```
    try {
      Class.forName(driver);
      Connection connection =
        DriverManager.getConnection(url, username, password);
      return(connection);
    } catch(ClassNotFoundException cnfe) {
      System.err.println("Error loading driver: " + cnfe);
      return(null);
    } catch(SQLException sqle) {
      System.err.println("Error connecting: " + sqle);
      return(null);
    }
  }

  private static void printUsage() {
    System.out.println("Usage: PreparedStatements host " +
                       "dbName username password " +
                       "oracle|sybase [print].");
  }
}
```

22.7 Summary

JDBC provides a standard way of accessing relational databases from programs written in the Java programming language. It lets you avoid vendor-specific code, thus simplifying the process of using multiple databases and switching from one database vendor to another.

Although JDBC standardizes the mechanism for connecting to the database and the data structure that represents the result, it does not standardize SQL syntax. This means that you can still use vendor-specific SQL commands if you want to; it also means that SQL queries and commands need to be built from raw strings rather than by means of SQL-related method calls.

JDBC can be used from desktop applications and applets, although with applets you are restricted to the case where the database server runs on the same host as the Web server. However, JDBC is most commonly used from server-side applications such as servlets and JSP. In fact, in many server-side applications, most of the real work is done in the database; servlets and JSP just provide a convenient middle tier for passing the data from the browser to the database and formatting the results that come back from the database.

XML PROCESSING WITH JAVA

Topics in This Chapter

- Representing an entire XML document using the Document Object Model (DOM) Level 2

- Using DOM to display the outline of an XML document in a JTree

- Responding to individual XML parsing events with the Simple API for XML Parsing (SAX) 2.0

- Printing the outline of an XML document using SAX

- Counting book orders using SAX

- Transforming XML using XSLT

- Invoking XSLT through custom JSP tags

- Hiding vendor-specific details with the Java API for XML Processing (JAXP)

Chapter 23

X ML is a "meta" markup language used to describe the structure of data. XML has taken the computer industry by storm since its inception and is now the markup language of choice for configuration files, data interchange, B2B transactions, and Java 2 Enterprise architectures. XML is even being used to represent calls to distributed objects through the Simple Object Access Protocol (SOAP), an XML application.

XML has numerous advantages including being easy to read, easy to parse, extensible, and widely adopted. In addition, you can define a grammar through a Document Type Definition (DTD) to enforce application-specific syntax. However, the greatest single advantage of XML is that the data can be easily processed by other applications; XML data is not in a proprietary format. In essence, XML has done for data what the Java language has done for programs:

Java = Portable Programs
XML = Portable Data

This chapter doesn't focus on how to *write* XML but rather how to *process* XML documents with Java. We show you how to use Java to process XML documents by using the Document Object Model (DOM), the Simple API for XML (SAX), and the Extensible Style sheet Language for Transformations (XSLT). If you are new to XML, here are some good starting points for additional information:

XML 1.0 Specification
`http://www.w3.org/TR/REC-xml`

Sun Page on XML and Java
`http://java.sun.com/xml/`

WWW Consortium's Home Page on XML
`http://www.w3.org/XML/`

Apache XML Project
`http://xml.apache.org/`

XML Resource Collection
`http://xml.coverpages.org/`

O'Reilly XML Resource Center
`http://www.xml.com/`

23.1 Parsing XML Documents with DOM Level 2

The Document Object Model (DOM) represents an entire XML document in a tree-like data structure that can be easily manipulated by a Java program. The advantages of DOM are that it is relatively simple to use and you can modify the data structure in addition to extracting data from it. However, the disadvantage is that DOM parses and stores the entire document, even if you only care about part of it. Section 23.3 (Parsing XML Documents with SAX 2.0) discusses an alternative approach appropriate for cases when you are dealing with very large XML documents but care about only small sections of them.

Installation and Setup

DOM is not a standard part of either Java 2 Standard Edition or the servlet and JSP APIs. So, your first step is to download the appropriate classes and configure them for use in your programs. Here is a summary of what is required.

1. **Download a DOM-compliant parser.** The parser provides the Java classes that follow the DOM Level 2 API as specified by the WWW Consortium. You can obtain a list of XML parsers in Java at `http://www.xml.com/pub/rg/Java_Parsers`.

We use the Apache Xerces-J parser in this book. See `http://xml.apache.org/xerces-j/`. This parser also comes with the complete DOM API in Javadoc format.

2. **Download the Java API for XML Processing (JAXP).** This API provides a small layer on top of DOM that lets you plug in different vendor's parsers without making any changes to your basic code. See `http://java.sun.com/xml/`.

3. **Set your `CLASSPATH` to include the DOM classes.** In the case of Apache Xerces, you need to include *xerces_install_dir*\ `xerces.jar`. For example, for desktop applications on Windows you would do

   ```
   set CLASSPATH=xerces_install_dir\xerces.jar;%CLASSPATH%
   ```

   If you wanted to use DOM from servlets and JSP, you would copy the appropriate JAR file to the server's `lib` directory (if supported), unpack the JAR file (using `jar -xvf`) into the server's `classes` directory, or explicitly change the server's `CLASSPATH`, usually by modifying the server start-up script.

4. **Set your `CLASSPATH` to include the JAXP classes.** These classes are in *jaxp_install_dir*/`jaxp.jar`. For example, on Unix/Linux and the C shell, you would do

   ```
   setenv CLASSPATH jaxp_install_dir/jaxp.jar:$CLASSPATH
   ```

   For use from servlets and JSP, see the preceding step.

5. **Bookmark the DOM Level 2 and JAXP APIs.** The official DOM specification can be found at `http://www.w3.org/TR/DOM-Level-2-Core/`, but the API in Javadoc format that comes with Apache Xerces is easier to read and also includes the JAXP and SAX (see Section 23.3) APIs.

6. **Print the JAXP specification for your reference.** Download it from `http://java.sun.com/xml/jaxp-1_1-spec.pdf`.

Parsing

With DOM processing, there are two high-level tasks: turning an XML document into a DOM data structure and looking through that data structure for the data that interests you. The following list summarizes the detailed steps needed to accomplish these tasks.

1. **Tell the system which parser you want to use.** This can be done in a number of ways: through the `javax.xml.parsers.Document-BuilderFactory` system property, through `jre_dir/lib/jaxp.properties`, through the J2EE Services API and the class specified in `META-INF/services/javax.xml.parsers.Document-`

`BuilderFactory`, or with a system-dependent default parser. The system property is the easiest method. For example, the following code permits users to specify the parser on the command line with the `-D` option to `java`, and uses the Apache Xerces parser otherwise.

```
public static void main(String[] args) {
  String jaxpPropertyName =
    "javax.xml.parsers.DocumentBuilderFactory";
  if (System.getProperty(jaxpPropertyName) == null) {
    String apacheXercesPropertyValue =
      "org.apache.xerces.jaxp.DocumentBuilderFactoryImpl";
    System.setProperty(jaxpPropertyName,
                       apacheXercesPropertyValue);
  }
  ...
}
```

2. **Create a JAXP document builder.** This is basically a wrapper around a specific XML parser.

```
DocumentBuilderFactory builderFactory =
  DocumentBuilderFactory.newInstance();
DocumentBuilder builder =
  builderFactory.newDocumentBuilder();
```

Note that you can use the `setNamespaceAware` and `setValidating` methods on the `DocumentBuilderFactory` to make the parser namespace aware and validating, respectively.

3. **Invoke the parser to create a Document representing an XML document.** You invoke the parser by calling the `parse` method of the document builder, supplying an input stream, URI (represented as a string), or `org.xml.sax.InputSource`. The `Document` class represents the parsed result in a tree structure.

```
Document document = builder.parse(someInputStream);
```

4. **Normalize the tree.** This means to combine textual nodes that were on multiple lines and to eliminate empty textual nodes.

```
document.getDocumentElement().normalize();
```

5. **Obtain the root node of the tree.** This returns an `Element`, which is a subclass of the more general `Node` class that represents an XML element.

```
Element rootElement = document.getDocumentElement();
```

6. **Examine various properties of the node.** These properties include the name of the element (`getNodeName`), the node type (`getNode-Type`; compare the return value to predefined constants in the `Node` class), the node value (`getNodeValue`; e.g., for text nodes the value is the string between the element's start and end tags), the attributes used by the element's start tag (`getAttributes`), and the child

nodes (getChildNodes; i.e., the elements contained between the current element's start and end tags). You can recursively examine each of the child nodes.

7. **Modify properties of the nodes.** Instead of just extracting data from an XML document, you can modify the document by adding child nodes (appendChild), removing child nodes (removeChild), and changing the node's value (setNodeValue). Unfortunately, however, DOM doesn't provide a standard method of writing out a DOM structure in textual format. So, you have to either do it yourself (printing out a "<", the node name, the attribute names and values with equal signs between them and quotes around the values, a ">", etc.) or use one of the many existing packages that generate text from a DOM element.

23.2 DOM Example: Representing an XML Document as a JTree

Listing 23.1 shows a class that represents the basic structure of an XML document as a JTree. Each element is represented as a node in the tree, with tree node being either the element name or the element name followed by a list of the attributes in parentheses. This class performs the following steps:

1. Parses and normalizes an XML document, then obtains the root element. These steps are performed exactly as described in steps one through five of the previous section.

2. Makes the root element into a JTree node. If the XML element has attributes (as given by node.getAttributes), the tree node is represented by a string composed of the element name (getNodeName) followed by the attributes and values in parentheses. If there are no attributes (getLength applied to the result of node.get-Attributes returns 0), then just the element name is used for the tree node label.

3. Looks up the child elements of the current element using getChild-Nodes, turns them into JTree nodes, and links those JTree nodes to the parent tree node.

4. Recursively applies step 3 to each of the child elements.

Listing 23.2 shows a class that creates the JTree just described and places it into a JFrame. Both the parser and the XML document can be specified by the user. The parser is specified when the user invokes the program with

```
java -Djavax.xml.parsers.DocumentBuilderFactory=xxx XMLFrame
```

If no parser is specified, the Apache Xerces parser is used. The XML document can be supplied on the command line, but if it is not given, a JFileChooser is used to interactively select the file of interest. The file extensions shown by the JFileChooser are limited to xml and tld (JSP tag library descriptors) through use of the ExtensionFileFilter class of Listing 23.3.

Figure 23–1 shows the initial file chooser used to select the perennials.xml file (Listing 23.4; see Listing 23.5 for the DTD). Figures 23–2 and 23–3 show the result in its unexpanded and partially expanded forms, respectively.

Note that because the XML file specifies a DTD, Xerces-J will attempt to parse the DTD even though no validation of the document is performed. If perennials.dtd is not available on-line, then you can place the DTD in a dtds subdirectory (below the directory containing XMLTree) and change the DOCTYPE in perennials.xml to

```
<!DOCTYPE perennials SYSTEM "dtds/perennials.dtd">
```

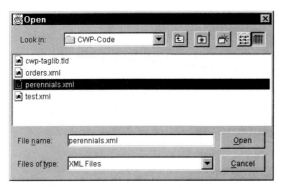

Figure 23–1 JFileChooser that uses ExtensionFileFilter (Listing 23.3) to interactively select an XML file.

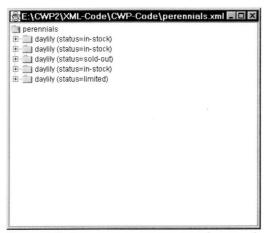

Figure 23–2 JTree representation of root node and top-level child elements of perennials.xml (Listing 23.4).

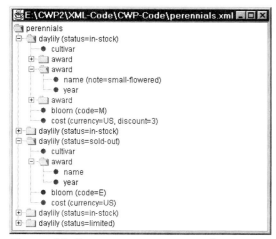

Figure 23–3 JTree representation of `perennials.xml` with several nodes expanded.

Listing 23.1 `XMLTree.java`

```java
import java.awt.*;
import javax.swing.*;
import javax.swing.tree.*;
import java.io.*;
import org.w3c.dom.*;
import javax.xml.parsers.*;

/** Given a filename or a name and an input stream,
 *  this class generates a JTree representing the
 *  XML structure contained in the file or stream.
 *  Parses with DOM then copies the tree structure
 *  (minus text and comment nodes).
 */

public class XMLTree extends JTree {
  public XMLTree(String filename) throws IOException {
    this(filename, new FileInputStream(new File(filename)));
  }

  public XMLTree(String filename, InputStream in) {
    super(makeRootNode(in));
  }
```

(continued)

Listing 23.1 XMLTree.java *(continued)*

```
// This method needs to be static so that it can be called
// from the call to the parent constructor (super), which
// occurs before the object is really built.

private static DefaultMutableTreeNode
                              makeRootNode(InputStream in) {
  try {
    // Use JAXP's DocumentBuilderFactory so that there
    // is no code here that is dependent on a particular
    // DOM parser. Use the system property
    // javax.xml.parsers.DocumentBuilderFactory (set either
    // from Java code or by using the -D option to "java").
    // or jre_dir/lib/jaxp.properties to specify this.
    DocumentBuilderFactory builderFactory =
      DocumentBuilderFactory.newInstance();
    DocumentBuilder builder =
      builderFactory.newDocumentBuilder();
    // Standard DOM code from hereon. The "parse"
    // method invokes the parser and returns a fully parsed
    // Document object. We'll then recursively descend the
    // tree and copy non-text nodes into JTree nodes.
    Document document = builder.parse(in);
    document.getDocumentElement().normalize();
    Element rootElement = document.getDocumentElement();
    DefaultMutableTreeNode rootTreeNode =
      buildTree(rootElement);
    return(rootTreeNode);
  } catch(Exception e) {
    String errorMessage =
      "Error making root node: " + e;
    System.err.println(errorMessage);
    e.printStackTrace();
    return(new DefaultMutableTreeNode(errorMessage));
  }
}

private static DefaultMutableTreeNode
                              buildTree(Element rootElement) {
  // Make a JTree node for the root, then make JTree
  // nodes for each child and add them to the root node.
  // The addChildren method is recursive.
  DefaultMutableTreeNode rootTreeNode =
    new DefaultMutableTreeNode(treeNodeLabel(rootElement));
  addChildren(rootTreeNode, rootElement);
  return(rootTreeNode);
}
```

(continued)

Listing 23.1 XMLTree.java *(continued)*

```
private static void addChildren
                    (DefaultMutableTreeNode parentTreeNode,
                    Node parentXMLElement) {
  // Recursive method that finds all the child elements
  // and adds them to the parent node. We have two types
  // of nodes here: the ones corresponding to the actual
  // XML structure and the entries of the graphical JTree.
  // The convention is that nodes corresponding to the
  // graphical JTree will have the word "tree" in the
  // variable name. Thus, "childElement" is the child XML
  // element whereas "childTreeNode" is the JTree element.
  // This method just copies the non-text and non-comment
  // nodes from the XML structure to the JTree structure.

  NodeList childElements =
    parentXMLElement.getChildNodes();
  for(int i=0; i<childElements.getLength(); i++) {
    Node childElement = childElements.item(i);
    if (!(childElement instanceof Text ||
          childElement instanceof Comment)) {
      DefaultMutableTreeNode childTreeNode =
        new DefaultMutableTreeNode
          (treeNodeLabel(childElement));
      parentTreeNode.add(childTreeNode);
      addChildren(childTreeNode, childElement);
    }
  }
}

// If the XML element has no attributes, the JTree node
// will just have the name of the XML element. If the
// XML element has attributes, the names and values of the
// attributes will be listed in parens after the XML
// element name. For example:
// XML Element: <blah>
// JTree Node:  blah
// XML Element: <blah foo="bar" baz="quux">
// JTree Node:  blah (foo=bar, baz=quux)

private static String treeNodeLabel(Node childElement) {
  NamedNodeMap elementAttributes =
    childElement.getAttributes();
  String treeNodeLabel = childElement.getNodeName();
```

(continued)

Listing 23.1 `XMLTree.java` *(continued)*

```java
      if (elementAttributes != null &&
          elementAttributes.getLength() > 0) {
        treeNodeLabel = treeNodeLabel + " (";
        int numAttributes = elementAttributes.getLength();
        for(int i=0; i<numAttributes; i++) {
          Node attribute = elementAttributes.item(i);
          if (i > 0) {
            treeNodeLabel = treeNodeLabel + ", ";
          }
          treeNodeLabel =
            treeNodeLabel + attribute.getNodeName() +
            "=" + attribute.getNodeValue();
        }
        treeNodeLabel = treeNodeLabel + ")";
      }
      return(treeNodeLabel);
    }
}
```

Listing 23.2 `XMLFrame.java`

```java
import java.awt.*;
import javax.swing.*;
import java.io.*;

/** Invokes an XML parser on an XML document and displays
 *  the document in a JTree. Both the parser and the
 *  document can be specified by the user. The parser
 *  is specified by invoking the program with
 *  java -Djavax.xml.parsers.DocumentBuilderFactory=xxx XMLFrame
 *  If no parser is specified, the Apache Xerces parser is used.
 *  The XML document can be supplied on the command
 *  line, but if it is not given, a JFileChooser is used
 *  to interactively select the file of interest.
 */

public class XMLFrame extends JFrame {
  public static void main(String[] args) {
    String jaxpPropertyName =
      "javax.xml.parsers.DocumentBuilderFactory";
```

(continued)

Listing 23.2 XMLFrame.java *(continued)*

```java
    // Pass the parser factory in on the command line with
    // -D to override the use of the Apache parser.
    if (System.getProperty(jaxpPropertyName) == null) {
      String apacheXercesPropertyValue =
        "org.apache.xerces.jaxp.DocumentBuilderFactoryImpl";
      System.setProperty(jaxpPropertyName,
                         apacheXercesPropertyValue);
    }
    String filename;
    if (args.length > 0) {
      filename = args[0];
    } else {
      String[] extensions = { "xml", "tld" };
      WindowUtilities.setNativeLookAndFeel();
      filename = ExtensionFileFilter.getFileName(".",
                                                 "XML Files",
                                                 extensions);
      if (filename == null) {
        filename = "test.xml";
      }
    }
    new XMLFrame(filename);
  }

  public XMLFrame(String filename) {
    try {
      WindowUtilities.setNativeLookAndFeel();
      JTree tree = new XMLTree(filename);
      JFrame frame = new JFrame(filename);
      frame.addWindowListener(new ExitListener());
      Container content = frame.getContentPane();
      content.add(new JScrollPane(tree));
      frame.pack();
      frame.setVisible(true);
    } catch(IOException ioe) {
      System.out.println("Error creating tree: " + ioe);
    }
  }
}
```

Listing 23.3 `ExtensionFileFilter.java`

```java
import java.io.File;
import java.util.*;
import javax.swing.*;
import javax.swing.filechooser.FileFilter;

/** A FileFilter that lets you specify which file extensions
 *  will be displayed. Also includes a static getFileName
 *  method that users can call to pop up a JFileChooser for
 *  a set of file extensions.
 *  <P>
 *  Adapted from Sun SwingSet demo.
 */

public class ExtensionFileFilter extends FileFilter {
  public static final int LOAD = 0;
  public static final int SAVE = 1;
  private String description;
  private boolean allowDirectories;
  private Hashtable extensionsTable = new Hashtable();
  private boolean allowAll = false;

  public ExtensionFileFilter(boolean allowDirectories) {
    this.allowDirectories = allowDirectories;
  }

  public ExtensionFileFilter() {
    this(true);
  }


  public static String getFileName(String initialDirectory,
                                   String description,
                                   String extension) {
    String[] extensions = new String[]{ extension };
    return(getFileName(initialDirectory, description,
                       extensions, LOAD));
  }

  public static String getFileName(String initialDirectory,
                                   String description,
                                   String extension,
                                   int mode) {
    String[] extensions = new String[]{ extension };
    return(getFileName(initialDirectory, description,
                       extensions, mode));
  }
```

(continued)

```java
public static String getFileName(String initialDirectory,
                                 String description,
                                 String[] extensions) {
  return(getFileName(initialDirectory, description,
                     extensions, LOAD));
}


/** Pops up a JFileChooser that lists files with the
 *  specified extensions. If the mode is SAVE, then the
 *  dialog will have a Save button; otherwise, the dialog
 *  will have an Open button. Returns a String corresponding
 *  to the file's pathname, or null if Cancel was selected.
 */

public static String getFileName(String initialDirectory,
                                 String description,
                                 String[] extensions,
                                 int mode) {
  ExtensionFileFilter filter = new ExtensionFileFilter();
  filter.setDescription(description);
  for(int i=0; i<extensions.length; i++) {
    String extension = extensions[i];
    filter.addExtension(extension, true);
  }
  JFileChooser chooser =
    new JFileChooser(initialDirectory);
  chooser.setFileFilter(filter);
  int selectVal = (mode==SAVE) ? chooser.showSaveDialog(null)
                               : chooser.showOpenDialog(null);
  if (selectVal == JFileChooser.APPROVE_OPTION) {
    String path = chooser.getSelectedFile().getAbsolutePath();
    return(path);
  } else {
    JOptionPane.showMessageDialog(null, "No file selected.");
    return(null);
  }
}

public void addExtension(String extension,
                         boolean caseInsensitive) {
  if (caseInsensitive) {
    extension = extension.toLowerCase();
  }
```

(continued)

Listing 23.3 `ExtensionFileFilter.java` *(continued)*

```java
    if (!extensionsTable.containsKey(extension)) {
      extensionsTable.put(extension,
                          new Boolean(caseInsensitive));
      if (extension.equals("*") ||
          extension.equals("*.*") ||
          extension.equals(".*")) {
        allowAll = true;
      }
    }
  }

  public boolean accept(File file) {
    if (file.isDirectory()) {
      return(allowDirectories);
    }
    if (allowAll) {
      return(true);
    }
    String name = file.getName();
    int dotIndex = name.lastIndexOf('.');
    if ((dotIndex == -1) || (dotIndex == name.length() - 1)) {
      return(false);
    }
    String extension = name.substring(dotIndex + 1);
    if (extensionsTable.containsKey(extension)) {
      return(true);
    }
    Enumeration keys = extensionsTable.keys();
    while(keys.hasMoreElements()) {
      String possibleExtension = (String)keys.nextElement();
      Boolean caseFlag =
        (Boolean)extensionsTable.get(possibleExtension);
      if ((caseFlag != null) &&
          (caseFlag.equals(Boolean.FALSE)) &&
          (possibleExtension.equalsIgnoreCase(extension))) {
        return(true);
      }
    }
    return(false);
  }

  public void setDescription(String description) {
    this.description = description;
  }
  public String getDescription() {
    return(description);
  }
}
```

Listing 23.4 `perennials.xml`

```
<?xml version="1.0" ?>
<!DOCTYPE perennials SYSTEM
  "http://archive.corewebprogramming.com/dtds/perennials.dtd">
<perennials>
  <daylily status="in-stock">
    <cultivar>Luxury Lace</cultivar>
    <award>
      <name>Stout Medal</name>
      <year>1965</year>
    </award>
    <award>
      <name note="small-flowered">Annie T. Giles</name>
      <year>1965</year>
    </award>
    <award>
      <name>Lenington All-American</name>
      <year>1970</year>
    </award>
    <bloom code="M">Midseason</bloom>
    <cost discount="3" currency="US">11.75</cost>
  </daylily>
  <daylily status="in-stock">
    <cultivar>Green Flutter</cultivar>
    <award>
      <name>Stout Medal</name>
      <year>1976</year>
    </award>
    <award>
      <name note="small-flowered">Annie T. Giles</name>
      <year>1970</year>
    </award>
    <bloom code="M">Midseason</bloom>
    <cost discount="3+" currency="US">7.50</cost>
  </daylily>
  <daylily status="sold-out">
    <cultivar>My Belle</cultivar>
    <award>
      <name>Stout Medal</name>
      <year>1984</year>
    </award>
    <bloom code="E">Early</bloom>
    <cost currency="US">12.00</cost>
  </daylily>
```

(continued)

Listing 23.4 `perennials.xml` *(continued)*

```xml
  <daylily status="in-stock">
    <cultivar>Stella De Oro</cultivar>
    <award>
      <name>Stout Medal</name>
      <year>1985</year>
    </award>
    <award>
      <name note="miniature">Donn Fishcer Memorial Cup</name>
      <year>1979</year>
    </award>
    <bloom code="E-L">Early to Late</bloom>
    <cost discount="10+" currency="US">5.00</cost>
  </daylily>
  <daylily status="limited">
    <cultivar>Brocaded Gown</cultivar>
    <award>
      <name>Stout Medal</name>
      <year>1989</year>
    </award>
    <bloom code="E">Early</bloom>
    <cost currency="US" discount="3+">14.50</cost>
  </daylily>
</perennials>
```

Listing 23.5 `perennials.dtd`

```
<?xml version="1.0" encoding="ISO-8859-1" ?>

<!ELEMENT perennials (daylily)*>

<!ELEMENT daylily (cultivar, award*, bloom, cost)+>
<!ATTLIST daylily
    status (in-stock | limited | sold-out) #REQUIRED>

<!ELEMENT cultivar (#PCDATA)>

<!ELEMENT award (name, year)>

<!ELEMENT name (#PCDATA)>
<!ATTLIST name
    note CDATA #IMPLIED>
```

(continued)

Listing 23.5 `perennials.dtd` *(continued)*

```
<!ELEMENT year (#PCDATA)>

<!ELEMENT bloom (#PCDATA)>
<!ATTLIST bloom
    code (E | EM | M | ML | L | E-L) #REQUIRED>

<!ELEMENT cost (#PCDATA)>
<!ATTLIST cost
    discount CDATA #IMPLIED>
<!ATTLIST cost
    currency (US | UK | CAN) "US">
```

23.3 Parsing XML Documents with SAX 2.0

DOM processing is relatively straightforward since the DOM classes do all the "real" parsing—you just have to look through the parsed result for the data you want. However, DOM can be quite wasteful if you only care about a small part of the document. For example, suppose that you want to extract the first word from an XML document representing an entire dictionary. DOM would require you to parse and store the entire XML document (which could be huge in this case). With SAX, you need only store the parts you care about and can stop parsing whenever you want. On the other hand, SAX is a bit more work. The idea is that the system tells you when certain parsing events such as finding a start tag (`<language rating="good">`), an end tag (`</language>`), or a tag body (e.g., `Java` between the aforementioned start and end tags). You have to decide what to do when these events occur. Are you a JSP programmer? Does this process sound familiar? It should—SAX processing is very similar to the way you go about defining custom JSP tag libraries (Section 20.7).

Installation and Setup

SAX is not a standard part of either Java 2 Standard Edition or the servlet and JSP APIs. So, your first step is to download the appropriate classes and configure them for use in your programs. Here is a summary of what is required.

1. **Download a SAX-compliant parser.** The parser provides the Java classes that follow the SAX 2 API as specified by the WWW Consortium. You can obtain a list of XML parsers in Java at `http://www.xml.com/pub/rg/Java_Parsers`. We use the Apache Xerces-J parser in this book. See `http://xml.apache.org/xerces-j/`. This parser comes with the complete SAX API in Javadoc format.

2. **Download the Java API for XML Processing (JAXP).** This API provides a small layer on top of SAX that lets you plug in different vendor's parsers without making any changes to your basic code. See `http://java.sun.com/xml/`.

3. **Set your `CLASSPATH` to include the SAX classes.** In the case of Apache Xerces, you need to include `xerces_install_dir\` `xerces.jar`. For example, on Windows you would do

   ```
   set CLASSPATH=xerces_install_dir\xerces.jar;%CLASSPATH%
   ```

   If you wanted to use DOM from servlets and JSP, you would copy the appropriate JAR file to the server's `lib` directory (if supported), unpack the JAR file (using `jar -xvf`) into the server's `classes` directory, or explicitly change the server's `CLASSPATH`, usually by modifying the server startup script.

4. **Set your `CLASSPATH` to include the JAXP classes.** These classes are in `jaxp_install_dir/jaxp.jar`. For example, on Unix/Linux and the C shell, you would do

   ```
   setenv CLASSPATH jaxp_install_dir/jaxp.jar:$CLASSPATH
   ```

   For use from servlets and JSP, see the preceding step.

5. **Bookmark the SAX 2 and JAXP APIs.** You can browse the official API at `http://www.megginson.com/SAX/Java/` `javadoc/`, but the API that comes with Apache Xerces is easier to use because it is on your local system and is integrated with the DOM and JAXP APIs. More information on SAX can be found at `http://www.megginson.com/SAX/`.

Parsing

With SAX processing, there are two high-level tasks: creating a content handler and invoking the parser with the designated content handler. The following list summarizes the detailed steps needed to accomplish these tasks.

1. **Tell the system which parser you want to use.** This can be done in a number of ways: through the `javax.xml.parsers.SAX-` `ParserFactory` system property, through `jre_dir/lib/` `jaxp.properties`, through the J2EE Services API and the class specified in `META-INF/services/javax.xml.parsers.SAX-` `ParserFactory`, or with a system-dependent default parser. The system property is the easiest method. For example, the following code permits users to specify the parser on the command line with the `-D` option to `java`, and uses the Apache Xerces parser otherwise.

   ```
   public static void main(String[] args) {
     String jaxpPropertyName =
       "javax.xml.parsers.SAXParserFactory";
     if (System.getProperty(jaxpPropertyName) == null) {
   ```

```
    String apacheXercesPropertyValue =
      "org.apache.xerces.jaxp.SAXParserFactoryImpl";
    System.setProperty(jaxpPropertyName,
                       apacheXercesPropertyValue);
  }
  ...
}
```

2. **Create a parser instance.** First make an instance of a parser factory, then use that to create a parser object.

```
SAXParserFactory factory = SAXParserFactory.newInstance();
SAXParser parser = factory.newSAXParser();
```

Note that you can use the setNamespaceAware and set-Validating methods on the SAXParserFactory to make the parser namespace aware and validating, respectively.

3. **Create a content handler to respond to parsing events.** This handler is typically a subclass of DefaultHandler. You override any or all of the following placeholders

   - **startDocument, endDocument**
     Use these methods to respond to the start and end of the document; they take no arguments.

   - **startElement, endElement**
     Use these methods to respond to the start and end tags of an element. The startElement method takes four arguments: the namespace URI (a String; empty if no namespace), the namespace or prefix (a String; empty if no namespace), the fully qualified element name (a String; i.e., "prefix:mainName" if there is a namespace; "mainName" otherwise), and an Attributes object representing the attributes of the start tag. The endElement method takes the same arguments except for the attributes (since end tags are not permitted attributes).

   - **characters, ignoreableWhitespace**
     Use these methods to respond to the tag body. They take three arguments: a char array, a start index, and an end index. A common approach is to turn the relevant part of the character array into a String by passing all three arguments to the String constructor. Non-whitespace data is always reported to the characters method. Whitespace is always reported to the ignoreable-Whitespace method a parser is run in validating mode, but can be reported to either method otherwise.

4. **Invoke the parser with the designated content handler.** You invoke the parser by calling the parse method, supplying an input stream, URI (represented as a string), or org.xml.sax.Input-Source along with the content handler.

```
parser.parse(filename, handler);
```

The content handler does the rest.

23.4 SAX Example 1: Printing the Outline of an XML Document

Listing 23.7 shows a content handler that responds to three parts of an XML document: start tags, end tags, and tag bodies. It overrides the `startElement`, `endElement`, and `characters` methods to accomplish this. The handler simply prints out the start element, end element, and first word of tag body, with two spaces of indentation for each nesting level. To accomplish this task, the content handler overrides the following three methods:

- **startElement**
  This method prints a message indicating that it found the start tag for the element name. Any attributes associated with the element are listed in parentheses. The method also puts spaces in front of the printout, as specified by the `indentation` variable (initially 0). Finally, it adds 2 to this variable.

- **endElement**
  This method subtracts 2 from the `indentation` variable and then prints a message indicating that it found the end tag for the element.

- **characters**
  This method prints the first word of the tag body, leaving the indentation level unchanged.

Listing 23.8 shows a program that lets the user specify a SAX-compliant parser and an XML file, then invokes the parser with the outline-printing content handler just described (and shown in Listing 23.7). Figure 23–4 shows the initial result, and Listing 23.6 shows the top part of the output when `orders.xml` (Listing 23.9) is selected.

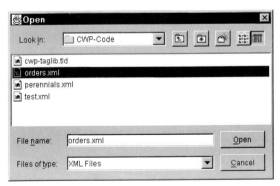

Figure 23–4 Interactively selecting the `orders.xml` file.

Listing 23.6 Partial output of `SAXPrinter` **applied to** `orders.xml`

```
Start tag: orders
  Start tag: order
    Start tag: count
      37
    End tag: count
    Start tag: price
      49.99
    End tag: price
    Start tag: book
      Start tag: isbn
        0130897930
      End tag: isbn
      Start tag: title
        Core...
      End tag: title
      Start tag: authors
        Start tag: author
          Marty...
        End tag: author
        Start tag: author
          Larry...
        End tag: author
      End tag: authors
    End tag: book
  End tag: order
  Start tag: order
    Start tag: count
      1
    End tag: count
    Start tag: price
      9.95
    End tag: price
    Start tag: yacht
      Start tag: manufacturer
        Luxury...
      End tag: manufacturer
      Start tag: model
        M-1
      End tag: model
      Start tag: standardFeatures (oars=plastic, lifeVests=none)
        false
      End tag: standardFeatures
    End tag: yacht
  End tag: order
  ... (Rest of results omitted)
End tag: orders
```

Listing 23.7 `PrintHandler.java`

```java
import org.xml.sax.*;
import org.xml.sax.helpers.*;
import java.util.StringTokenizer;

/** A SAX handler that prints out the start tags, end tags,
 *  and first word of tag body. Indents two spaces
 *  for each nesting level.
 */

public class PrintHandler extends DefaultHandler {
  private int indentation = 0;

  /** When you see a start tag, print it out and then
   *  increase indentation by two spaces. If the
   *  element has attributes, place them in parens
   *  after the element name.
   */

  public void startElement(String namespaceUri,
                           String localName,
                           String qualifiedName,
                           Attributes attributes)
      throws SAXException {
    indent(indentation);
    System.out.print("Start tag: " + qualifiedName);
    int numAttributes = attributes.getLength();
    // For <someTag> just print out "someTag". But for
    // <someTag att1="Val1" att2="Val2">, print out
    // "someTag (att1=Val1, att2=Val2).
    if (numAttributes > 0) {
      System.out.print(" (");
      for(int i=0; i<numAttributes; i++) {
        if (i>0) {
          System.out.print(", ");
        }
        System.out.print(attributes.getQName(i) + "=" +
                         attributes.getValue(i));
      }
      System.out.print(")");
    }
    System.out.println();
    indentation = indentation + 2;
  }
```

(continued)

Listing 23.7 `PrintHandler.java` *(continued)*

```java
/** When you see the end tag, print it out and decrease
 *  indentation level by 2.
 */

public void endElement(String namespaceUri,
                       String localName,
                       String qualifiedName)
    throws SAXException {
  indentation = indentation - 2;
  indent(indentation);
  System.out.println("End tag: " + qualifiedName);
}

/** Print out the first word of each tag body. */

public void characters(char[] chars,
                       int startIndex,
                       int endIndex) {
  String data = new String(chars, startIndex, endIndex);
  // Whitespace makes up default StringTokenizer delimeters
  StringTokenizer tok = new StringTokenizer(data);
  if (tok.hasMoreTokens()) {
    indent(indentation);
    System.out.print(tok.nextToken());
    if (tok.hasMoreTokens()) {
      System.out.println("...");
    } else {
      System.out.println();
    }
  }
}

private void indent(int indentation) {
  for(int i=0; i<indentation; i++) {
    System.out.print(" ");
  }
}
}
```

Listing 23.8 `SAXPrinter.java`

```java
import javax.xml.parsers.*;
import org.xml.sax.*;
import org.xml.sax.helpers.*;

/** A program that uses SAX to print out the start tags,
 *  end tags, and first word of tag body of an XML file.
 */

public class SAXPrinter {
  public static void main(String[] args) {
    String jaxpPropertyName =
      "javax.xml.parsers.SAXParserFactory";
    // Pass the parser factory in on the command line with
    // -D to override the use of the Apache parser.
    if (System.getProperty(jaxpPropertyName) == null) {
      String apacheXercesPropertyValue =
        "org.apache.xerces.jaxp.SAXParserFactoryImpl";
      System.setProperty(jaxpPropertyName,
                         apacheXercesPropertyValue);
    }
    String filename;
    if (args.length > 0) {
      filename = args[0];
    } else {
      String[] extensions = { "xml", "tld" };
      WindowUtilities.setNativeLookAndFeel();
      filename = ExtensionFileFilter.getFileName(".",
                                                "XML Files",
                                                extensions);

      if (filename == null) {
        filename = "test.xml";
      }
    }
    printOutline(filename);
    System.exit(0);
  }

  public static void printOutline(String filename) {
    DefaultHandler handler = new PrintHandler();
    SAXParserFactory factory = SAXParserFactory.newInstance();
    try {
      SAXParser parser = factory.newSAXParser();
      parser.parse(filename, handler);
    } catch(Exception e) {
      String errorMessage =
        "Error parsing " + filename + ": " + e;
      System.err.println(errorMessage);
      e.printStackTrace();
    }
  }
}
```

Listing 23.9 `orders.xml`

```xml
<?xml version="1.0" ?>
<orders>
  <order>
    <count>37</count>
    <price>49.99</price>
    <book>
      <isbn>0130897930</isbn>
      <title>Core Web Programming Second Edition</title>
      <authors>
        <author>Marty Hall</author>
        <author>Larry Brown</author>
      </authors>
    </book>
  </order>
  <order>
    <count>1</count>
    <price>9.95</price>
    <yacht>
      <manufacturer>Luxury Yachts, Inc.</manufacturer>
      <model>M-1</model>
      <standardFeatures oars="plastic"
                        lifeVests="none">
        false
      </standardFeatures>
    </yacht>
  </order>
  <order>
    <count>3</count>
    <price>22.22</price>
    <book>
      <isbn>B000059Z4H</isbn>
      <title>Harry Potter and the Order of the Phoenix</title>
      <authors>
        <author>J.K. Rowling</author>
      </authors>
    </book>
  </order>
  <order>
    <count>2</count>
    <price>10452689.01</price>
    <yacht>
      <manufacturer>We B Boats, Inc.</manufacturer>
      <model>236-A</model>
      <standardFeatures bowlingAlley="double"
                        tennisCourt="grass">
```

(continued)

Listing 23.9 `orders.xml` *(continued)*

```
        true
      </standardFeatures>
    </yacht>
  </order>
  <order>
    <count>13</count>
    <price>49.99</price>
    <book>
      <isbn>0130897930</isbn>
      <title>Core Web Programming Second Edition</title>
      <authors>
        <author>Marty Hall</author>
        <author>Larry Brown</author>
      </authors>
    </book>
  </order>
</orders>
```

23.5 SAX Example 2: Counting Book Orders

One of the advantages of SAX over DOM is that SAX does not require you to process and store the entire document; you can quickly skip over the parts that do not interest you. The following example looks for sections of an XML file that look like this:

```
<orders>
  ...
  <count>23</count>
  <book>
    <isbn>0130897930</isbn>
    ...
  </book>
  ...
</orders>
```

The idea is that the program will count up how many copies of *Core Web Programming Second Edition* (you *did* recognize that ISBN number, right?) are contained in a set of orders. Thus, it can skip over most elements. Since SAX, unlike DOM, does not store anything automatically, we need to take care of storing the pieces of data that are of interest. The one difficulty in that regard is that the isbn element comes after the count element. So, we need to record every count temporarily but only add the temporary value to the running total when the ISBN number matches. To accomplish this task, the content handler (Listing 23.10) overrides the following four methods:

- **startElement**
  This method checks whether the name of the element is either `count` or `isbn`. If so, it sets a flag that tells the `characters` method to be on the lookout.
- **endElement**
  This method checks whether the name of the element is either `count` or `isbn`. If so, it turns off the flag that the `characters` method watches.
- **characters**
  If the `count` flag is set, this method parses the tag body as an `int` and records the result in a temporary location. If the `isbn` flag is set, the method reads the tag body and compares it to the ISBN number of the second edition of *Core Web Programming*. If this comparison results in a match, then the temporary count is added to the running count.
- **endDocument**
  This method prints out the running count. If the number of copies is less than 250 (a real slacker!), it urges the user to buy more copies in the future.

The `CountBooks` class (Listing 23.11) invokes a user-speciﬁable parser on an XML ﬁle with `CountHandler` as the parser's content handler. Figure 23–5 shows the initial result and Figure 23–6 shows the ﬁnal result, after `orders.xml` (Listing 23.9) is used as input.

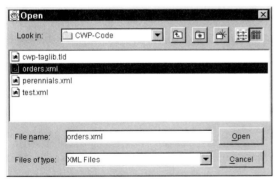

Figure 23–5 Interactively selecting the `orders.xml` file.

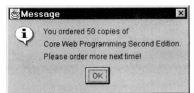

Figure 23–6 Result of running `CountBooks` on `orders.xml`.

Listing 23.10   `CountHandler.java`

```java
import org.xml.sax.*;
import org.xml.sax.helpers.*;
import java.util.StringTokenizer;
import javax.swing.*;

/** A SAX parser handler that keeps track of the number
 *  of copies of Core Web Programming ordered. Entries
 *  that look like this will be recorded:
 *  <XMP>
 *     ...
 *     <count>23</count>
 *     <book>
 *        <isbn>0130897930</isbn>
 *        ...
 *     </book>
 *  </XMP>
 *  All other entries will be ignored -- different books,
 *  orders for yachts, things that are not even orders, etc.
 */

public class CountHandler extends DefaultHandler {
  private boolean collectCount = false;
  private boolean collectISBN = false;
  private int currentCount = 0;
  private int totalCount = 0;

  /** If you start the "count" or "isbn" elements,
   *  set a flag so that the characters method can check
   *  the value of the tag body.
   */

  public void startElement(String namespaceUri,
                           String localName,
                           String qualifiedName,
                           Attributes attributes)
      throws SAXException {
    if (qualifiedName.equals("count")) {
      collectCount = true;
      currentCount = 0;
    } else if (qualifiedName.equals("isbn")) {
      collectISBN = true;
    }
  }
```

(continued)

Listing 23.10 `CountHandler.java` *(continued)*

```java
/** If you end the "count" or "isbn" elements,
 *  set a flag so that the characters method will no
 *  longer check the value of the tag body.
 */

public void endElement(String namespaceUri,
                       String localName,
                       String qualifiedName)
   throws SAXException {
  if (qualifiedName.equals("count")) {
    collectCount = false;
  } else if (qualifiedName.equals("isbn")) {
    collectISBN = false;
  }
}

/** Since the "count" entry comes before the "book"
 *  entry (which contains "isbn"), we have to temporarily
 *  record all counts we see. Later, if we find a
 *  matching "isbn" entry, we will record that temporary
 *  count.
 */

public void characters(char[] chars,
                       int startIndex,
                       int endIndex) {
  if (collectCount || collectISBN) {
    String dataString =
      new String(chars, startIndex, endIndex).trim();
    if (collectCount) {
      try {
        currentCount = Integer.parseInt(dataString);
      } catch(NumberFormatException nfe) {
        System.err.println("Ignoring malformed count: " +
                           dataString);
      }
    } else if (collectISBN) {
      if (dataString.equals("0130897930")) {
        totalCount = totalCount + currentCount;
      }
    }
  }
}
```

(continued)

Listing 23.10 `CountHandler.java` *(continued)*

```java
/** Report the total number of copies ordered.
 *  Gently chide underachievers.
 */

public void endDocument() throws SAXException {
  String message =
    "You ordered " + totalCount + " copies of \n" +
    "Core Web Programming Second Edition.\n";
  if (totalCount < 250) {
    message = message + "Please order more next time!";
  } else {
    message = message + "Thanks for your order.";
  }
  JOptionPane.showMessageDialog(null, message);
  }
}
```

Listing 23.11 `CountBooks.java`

```java
import javax.xml.parsers.*;
import org.xml.sax.*;
import org.xml.sax.helpers.*;

/** A program using SAX to keep track of the number
 *  of copies of Core Web Programming ordered. Entries
 *  that look like this will be recorded:<XMP>
 *
 *    ...
 *    <count>23</count>
 *    <book>
 *      <isbn>0130897930</isbn>
 *      ...
 *    </book>
 *
 *  </XMP>All other entries will be ignored -- different books,
 *  orders for yachts, things that are not even orders, etc.
 */

public class CountBooks {
  public static void main(String[] args) {
    String jaxpPropertyName =
      "javax.xml.parsers.SAXParserFactory";
```

(continued)

Listing 23.11 CountBooks.java *(continued)*

```java
      // Pass the parser factory in on the command line with
      // -D to override the use of the Apache parser.
      if (System.getProperty(jaxpPropertyName) == null) {
        String apacheXercesPropertyValue =
          "org.apache.xerces.jaxp.SAXParserFactoryImpl";
        System.setProperty(jaxpPropertyName,
                           apacheXercesPropertyValue);
      }
      String filename;
      if (args.length > 0) {
        filename = args[0];
      } else {
        String[] extensions = { "xml" };
        WindowUtilities.setNativeLookAndFeel();
        filename = ExtensionFileFilter.getFileName(".",
                                                   "XML Files",
                                                   extensions);

        if (filename == null) {
          filename = "orders.xml";
        }
      }
      countBooks(filename);
      System.exit(0);
    }

    private static void countBooks(String filename) {
      DefaultHandler handler = new CountHandler();
      SAXParserFactory factory = SAXParserFactory.newInstance();
      try {
        SAXParser parser = factory.newSAXParser();
        parser.parse(filename, handler);
      } catch(Exception e) {
        String errorMessage =
          "Error parsing " + filename + ": " + e;
        System.err.println(errorMessage);
        e.printStackTrace();
      }
    }
  }
```

23.6 Transforming XML with XSLT

XSLT is a language for transforming XML documents into HTML, XML, or other types of documents. When performing a transformation, an XSLT engine converts the XML document according to formatting rules and XPath addresses specified in an XML style sheet (XSL). The XPath information identifies the different parts of the XML document for processing, and the style sheet information identifies the layout of the output.

The benefit of XSLT is that you can define multiple style sheets for transforming a single XML document. For example, a database could return a query in an XML format, and depending on the client protocol, HTTP or WAP, a servlet could use different style sheets to convert the data into HTML or WML, respectively. As another example of an XSLT application, consider an e-commerce business order; the order could be sent to the supplier in an XML format and then processed by the recipient with XSLT, using different XSL documents to convert the original order into separate billing and shipping documents.

Specifications for XSLT, XSL, and XPath technologies are maintained by the WWW Consortium. These specifications are located at:

XSLT 1.0
> `http://www.w3.org/TR/xslt.html`

XSL 1.0
> `http://www.w3.org/TR/xsl/`

XPath 1.0
> `http://www.w3.org/TR/xpath.html`

Upcoming specifications are summarized at `http://www.w3.org/Style/XSL/`. In addition, an excellent XSLT resource site, sponsored by GoXML, is located at `http://www.xslt.com/`.

Installation and Setup

XSLT is not a standard part of either Java 2 Standard Edition or the servlet and JSP APIs. So, your first step is to download the appropriate classes and configure them for use in your programs. Here is a summary of what is required:

1. **Download an XSLT-compliant transformer.** The transformer provides the Java classes that follow the XSLT 1.0 specification as specified by the WWW Consortium. You can obtain a list of XSLT parsers at `http://www.w3.org/Style/XSL/` or

`http://www.xslt.com/xslt_tools_engines.htm`. We use
the Apache Xalan-J transformer in this book. See
`http://xml.apache.org/xalan-j/`.

2. **Set your CLASSPATH to include the DOM and SAX classes.** XSLT
   builds upon DOM and SAX for handling the document processing. In
   the case of Apache Xalan-J, you need to include `xerces.jar` in the
   `CLASSPATH`.   See Section 23.1 (Parsing XML Documents with DOM
   Level 2) and Section 23.3 (Parsing XML Documents with SAX 2.0) for
   configuration of Apache Xerces-J. Note that `xerces.jar` is included
   in the Xalan-J installation directory.

3. **Set your CLASSPATH to include the XSLT classes.** With Xalan,
   these classes are in `xalan_install_dir\xalan.jar`. For example, for desktop application on Windows, you would do

   ```
   set CLASSPATH=xalan_install_dir\xalan.jar;
       %CLASSPATH%
   ```

   On Unix/Linux and the C shell, you would do

   ```
   setenv CLASSPATH xalan_install_dir/xalan.jar:
          $CLASSPATH
   ```

   If you wanted to use XSLT from servlets and JSP, you would copy the
   appropriate DOM, SAX, and XSLT JAR files to the server's `lib` directory (if supported), unpack the JAR files (using `jar -xvf`) into the
   server's classes directory, or explicitly change the server's `CLASSPATH`,
   usually by modifying the server's startup script.

4. **Bookmark the XSL 1.0 and XPath 1.0 specifications.** The official
   documentation for these two specifications can be found at
   `http://www.w3.org/Style/XSL/`.

5. **Bookmark the XSLT specification.** The official XSLT specification
   can be found at `http://www.w3.org/TR/xslt.html`. The XSLT
   specification is implemented in Apache Xalan through the Transformation API for XML (TrAX). The complete TrAX API comes with
   Xalan-J in Javadoc format and is also available on-line at
   `http://xml.apache.org/xalan-j/apidocs/`.

Translating

With XSLT processing, there are two high-level tasks, establishing an XSL template
from which to build a transformer and invoking the transformer on the XML document. The following list summarizes the detailed steps needed to accomplish these
tasks.

1. **Tell the system which parser you want to use for transformations.** This can be done in a number of ways: through the
   `javax.xml.transform.TransformFactory` system property,

through the jre_dir/lib/jaxp.properties, through the J2EE Services API and the class specified in the META-INF/services/ javax.xml.transform.TransformFactory, or with a system-dependent default processor. As XSLT depends on DOM and SAX, you can tell the system which DOM and SAX parser to use for processing the document. See Section 23.1 and Section 23.3 for information on configuring DOM and SAX parsers. By default, Apache Xalan-J uses the Apache Xerces-J DOM and SAX parsers.

2. **Establish a factory in which to create transformers.** Before processing an XML document, you first need to establish a TransformerFactory. The factory allows you to create different transformers for different style sheet templates.

```
TransformerFactory factory =
  TransformerFactory.newInstance();
```

3. **Generate a transformer for a particular style sheet template.** For each style sheet you can generate a separate transformer to apply to multiple XML documents.

```
Source xsl = new StreamSource(xslStream);
Templates template = factory.newTemplates(xsl);
Transformer transformer = template.newTransformer();
```

Typically, the XSL source is a StreamSource object. You can easily convert an XSL document to a StreamSource through a File, Reader, InputStream, or URI (represented as a string) reference to the document.

4. **Invoke the transformer to process the source document.** You invoke the transformation by calling the transform method, supplying the XML source and a Result object to receive the transformed document.

```
Source xml = new StreamSource(xmlStream);
Result result = new StreamResult(outputStream);
tranformer.transform(xml, result);
```

Similar to the XSL source, the XML source is typically a StreamSource constructed from a File, Reader, InputStream, or URI. The transformed StreamResult can be a File, Writer, OutputStream or URI.

Listing 23.12 presents a class for preforming XSLT transformations of documents. The XML and XSL source documents can be either Readers or Files, and the resulting transformed document can be a Writer or File. The advantage of handling the documents as Readers and Writers is that they can remain in memory and can easily be processed as strings by a StringReader or CharArrayReader for the source documents and a StringWriter or CharArrayWriter for the result document. For example, a servlet could receive a database query as an XML character stream, process the input using XSLT, and deliver the result as an HTML document to a browser client. At no time do the XML document and transformed result need to reside on disk.

Listing 23.12 `XslTransformer.java`

```java
package cwp;

import javax.xml.transform.*;
import javax.xml.transform.stream.*;
import java.io.*;
import java.util.*;

/** Creates an XSLT transformer for processing an XML document.
 *  A new transformer, along with a style template are created
 *  for each document transformation. The XSLT, DOM, and
 *  SAX processors are based on system default parameters.
 */

public class XslTransformer {
  private TransformerFactory factory;

  public XslTransformer() {
    factory = TransformerFactory.newInstance();
  }

  /** Transform an XML and XSL document as <code>Reader</code>s,
   *  placing the resulting transformed document in a
   *  <code>Writer</code>. Convenient for handling an XML
   *  document as a String (<code>StringReader</code>) residing
   *  in memory, not on disk. The output document could easily be
   *  handled as a String (<code>StringWriter</code>) or as a
   *  <code>JSPWriter</code> in a JavaServer page.
   */

  public void process(Reader xmlFile, Reader xslFile,
                      Writer output)
             throws TransformerException {
    process(new StreamSource(xmlFile),
            new StreamSource(xslFile),
            new StreamResult(output));
  }

  /** Transform an XML and XSL document as <code>File</code>s,
   *  placing the resulting transformed document in a
   *  <code>Writer</code>. The output document could easily
   *  be handled as a String (<code>StringWriter</code>) or as
   *  a <code>JSPWriter</code> in a JavaServer page.
   */
```

(continued)

Listing 23.12 XslTransformer.java *(continued)*

```java
public void process(File xmlFile, File xslFile,
                    Writer output)
            throws TransformerException {
  process(new StreamSource(xmlFile),
          new StreamSource(xslFile),
          new StreamResult(output));
}

/** Transform an XML <code>File</code> based on an XSL
 *  <code>File</code>, placing the resulting transformed
 *  document in a <code>OutputStream</code>. Convenient for
 *  handling the result as a <code>FileOutputStream</code> or
 *  <code>ByteArrayOutputStream</code>.
 */

public void process(File xmlFile, File xslFile,
                    OutputStream out)
            throws TransformerException {
  process(new StreamSource(xmlFile),
          new StreamSource(xslFile),
          new StreamResult(out));
}

/** Transform an XML source using XSLT based on a new template
 *  for the source XSL document. The resulting transformed
 *  document is placed in the passed in <code>Result</code>
 *  object.
 */

public void process(Source xml, Source xsl, Result result)
            throws TransformerException {
  try {
    Templates template = factory.newTemplates(xsl);
    Transformer transformer = template.newTransformer();
    transformer.transform(xml, result);
  } catch(TransformerConfigurationException tce) {
    throw new TransformerException(
              tce.getMessageAndLocation());
  } catch (TransformerException te) {
    throw new TransformerException(
              te.getMessageAndLocation());
  }
}
}
```

23.7 XSLT Example I: XSLT Document Editor

Listing 23.13 shows a simple Swing document editor that presents three tabbed panes: one for an XML document, one for an XSL style sheet, and one for a resulting XSLT-transformed document. Both the XML and XSL document panes are editable, so after you load the XML and XSL files from disk you can edit the documents directly. Each tabbed pane contains a scrollable DocumentPane that inherits from a JEditorPane (see Listing 23.14). The XML and XSL panes are treated as plain text, and the XSLT pane is treated as HTML. If an XML file and XSL file are loaded, selecting the XSLT tab will invoke an XslTransformer (Listing 23.12) to process the XML file by using the style sheet, and present the results as HTML in the XSLT document pane.

Listing 23.13 XsltExample.java

```java
import javax.xml.transform.*;
import java.awt.*;
import java.awt.event.*;
import javax.swing.*;
import javax.swing.event.*;
import java.io.*;
import cwp.XslTransformer;

/** A document editor to process XML and XSL text using
 *  XSLT and presenting the results as HTML. Three tabbed panes
 *  are presented:  an editable text pane for the XML document,
 *  an editable text pane for the XSL style sheet, and a non-
 *  editable HTML pane for the HTML result. If an XML and XSL
 *  file are loaded, then selecting the XSLT tab will perform
 *  the transformation and present the results. If there is
 *  a problem processing the XML or XSL document, then a
 *  message box is popped up describing the problem.
 */

public class XsltExample extends JFrame
                         implements ChangeListener {
  private static final int XML  = 0;
  private static final int XSL  = 1;
  private static final int XSLT = 2;
  private static final String DEFAULT_TITLE = "XSLT Example";
```

(continued)

Listing 23.13 XsltExample.java *(continued)*

```java
private static final String[] tabTitles =
                                { "XML", "XSL", "XSLT" };
private static final String[] extensions =
                                { "xml", "xsl", "html" };
private Action openAction, saveAction, exitAction;
private JTabbedPane tabbedPane;
private DocumentPane[] documents;
private XslTransformer transformer;

public XsltExample() {
  super(DEFAULT_TITLE);
  transformer = new XslTransformer();
  WindowUtilities.setNativeLookAndFeel();
  Container content = getContentPane();
  content.setBackground(SystemColor.control);

  // Set up menus
  JMenuBar menubar = new JMenuBar();
  openAction = new OpenAction();
  saveAction = new SaveAction();
  exitAction = new ExitAction();
  JMenu fileMenu = new JMenu("File");
  fileMenu.add(openAction);
  fileMenu.add(saveAction);
  fileMenu.add(exitAction);
  menubar.add(fileMenu);
  setJMenuBar(menubar);

  // Set up tabbed panes
  tabbedPane = new JTabbedPane();
  documents = new DocumentPane[3];
  for(int i=0; i<3; i++) {
    documents[i] = new DocumentPane();
    JPanel panel = new JPanel();
    JScrollPane scrollPane = new JScrollPane(documents[i]);
    panel.add(scrollPane);
    tabbedPane.add(tabTitles[i], scrollPane);
  }
  documents[XSLT].setContentType(DocumentPane.HTML);
  // JEditorPane has a bug, whereas the setText method does
  // not properly recognize an HTML document that has a META
  // element containing a CONTENT-TYPE, unless the EditorKit
  // is first created through setPage. Xalan automatically
  // adds a META CONTENT-TYPE to the document. Thus,
  // preload a document containing a META CONTENT-TYPE.
```

(continued)

Listing 23.13 XsltExample.java *(continued)*

```java
    documents[XSLT].loadFile("XSLT-Instructions.html");
    documents[XSLT].setEditable(false);
    tabbedPane.addChangeListener(this);
    content.add(tabbedPane, BorderLayout.CENTER);

    setDefaultCloseOperation(JFrame.EXIT_ON_CLOSE);
    setSize(450, 350);
    setVisible(true);
  }

  /** Checks to see which tabbed pane was selected by the
   *  user. If the XML and XSL panes hold a document, then
   *  selecting the XSLT tab will perform the transformation.
   */

  public void stateChanged(ChangeEvent event) {
    int index = tabbedPane.getSelectedIndex();
    switch (index) {
      case XSLT: if (documents[XML].isLoaded() &&
                     documents[XSL].isLoaded()) {
                   doTransform();
                 }
      case XML:
      case XSL:  updateMenuAndTitle(index);
                 break;
      default:
    }
  }

  /** Retrieve the documents in the XML and XSL pages
   *  as text (String), pipe into a StringReader, and
   *  perform the XSLT transformation. If an exception
   *  occurs, present the problem in a message dialog.
   */

  private void doTransform() {
    StringWriter strWriter = new StringWriter();
    try {
      Reader xmlInput =
        new StringReader(documents[XML].getText());
      Reader xslInput =
        new StringReader(documents[XSL].getText());
      transformer = new XslTransformer();
      transformer.process(xmlInput, xslInput, strWriter);
```

(continued)

Listing 23.13 `XsltExample.java` *(continued)*

```java
    } catch(TransformerException te) {
      JOptionPane.showMessageDialog(this,
                  "Error: " + te.getMessage());
    }
    documents[XSLT].setText(strWriter.toString());
}

/** Update the title of the application to present
 *  the name of the file loaded into the selected
 *  tabbed pane. Also, update the menu options (Save,
 *  Load) based on which tab is selected.
 */

private void updateMenuAndTitle(int index) {
  if ((index > -1) && (index < documents.length)) {
    saveAction.setEnabled(documents[index].isLoaded());
    openAction.setEnabled(documents[index].isEditable());
    String title = DEFAULT_TITLE;
    String filename = documents[index].getFilename();
    if (filename.length() > 0) {
      title += " - [" + filename + "]";
    }
    setTitle(title);
  }
}

/** Open a file dialog to either load a new file to or save
 *  the existing file in the present document pane.
 */

private void updateDocument(int mode) {
  int index = tabbedPane.getSelectedIndex();
  String description = tabTitles[index] + " Files";
  String filename = ExtensionFileFilter.getFileName(".",
                                           description,
                                           extensions[index],
                                           mode);
  if (filename != null) {
    if (mode==ExtensionFileFilter.SAVE) {
      documents[index].saveFile(filename);
    } else {
      documents[index].loadFile(filename);
    }
    updateMenuAndTitle(index);
  }
}
```

(continued)

Listing 23.13 XsltExample.java *(continued)*

```java
  public static void main(String[] args) {
    new XsltExample();
  }

  // Open menu action to load a new file into a
  // document when selected.
  class OpenAction extends AbstractAction {
    public OpenAction() {
      super("Open ...");
    }
    public void actionPerformed(ActionEvent event) {
      updateDocument(ExtensionFileFilter.LOAD);
    }
  }

  // Save menu action to save the document in the
  // selected pane to a file.
  class SaveAction extends AbstractAction {
    public SaveAction() {
      super("Save");
      setEnabled(false);
    }
    public void actionPerformed(ActionEvent event) {
      updateDocument(ExtensionFileFilter.SAVE);
    }
  }

  // Exit menu action to close the application.
  class ExitAction extends AbstractAction {
    public ExitAction() {
      super("Exit");
    }
    public void actionPerformed(ActionEvent event) {
      System.exit(0);
    }
  }
}
```

Listing 23.14 DocumentPane.java

```java
import java.awt.*;
import java.awt.event.*;
import javax.swing.*;
import java.io.*;
import java.net.*;

/** A JEditorPane with support for loading and saving the
 *  document. The document should be one of two
 *  types: "text/plain" (default) or "text/html".
 */

public class DocumentPane extends JEditorPane {
  public static final String TEXT = "text/plain";
  public static final String HTML = "text/html";

  private boolean loaded = false;
  private String filename = "";

  /** Set the current page displayed in the editor pane,
   *  replacing the existing document.
   */

  public void setPage(URL url) {
    loaded = false;
    try {
      super.setPage(url);
      File file = new File(getPage().toString());
      setFilename(file.getName());
      loaded = true;
    } catch (IOException ioe) {
      System.err.println("Unable to set page: " + url);
    }
  }

  /** Set the text in the document page, replace the exiting
   *  document.
   */

  public void setText(String text) {
    super.setText(text);
    setFilename("");
    loaded = true;
  }
```

(continued)

Listing 23.14 DocumentPane.java *(continued)*

```java
/** Load a file into the editor pane.
 *
 * Note that the setPage method of JEditorPane checks the
 * URL of the currently loaded page against the URL of the
 * new page to laod.  If the two URLs are the same, then
 * the page is <b>not</b> reloaded.
 */

public void loadFile(String filename) {
  try {
    File file = new File(filename);
    setPage(file.toURL());
  } catch (IOException mue) {
    System.err.println("Unable to load file: " + filename);
  }
}

public void saveFile(String filename) {
  try {
    File file = new File(filename);
    FileWriter writer = new FileWriter(file);
    writer.write(getText());
    writer.close();
    setFilename(file.getName());
  } catch (IOException ioe) {
    System.err.println("Unable to save file: " + filename);
  }
}

/** Return the name of the file loaded into the editor pane. */

public String getFilename() {
  return(filename);
}

/** Set the filename of the document. */

public void setFilename(String filename) {
  this.filename = filename;
}

/** Return true if a document is loaded into the editor
 * page, either through <code>setPage</code> or
 * <code>setText</code>.
 */

public boolean isLoaded() {
  return(loaded);
}
}
```

The results for the XsltExample are shown in Figure 23–7 through Figure 23–9. Specifically, the result for the XML document pane with the loaded file, perennials.xml (Listing 23.4), is shown in Figure 23–7. The XSL document pane with the loaded file, perennials.xsl (Listing 23.15), is shown in Figure 23–8. Finally, the XSLT transformation of the XML document is presented in Figure 23–8. For this example, all daylilies awarded a Stout Medal are selected from the XML file and listed in an HTML TABLE. For each daylily matching the criteria, the year of hybridization, cultivar name, bloom season, and cost are presented in the table.

Note that for Apache Xalan-J to perform the XSLT transformation, the DTD, perennials.dtd, must be accessible on-line from http://archive.coreweb-programming.com/dtds/. If you would like to test this example locally, place the file, perennials.dtd, in a dtds subdirectory below the XML file, and change the DOCTYPE statement from

```
<!DOCTYPE perennials SYSTEM
   "http://archive.corewebprogramming.com/dtds/perennials.dtd">
```

to

```
<!DOCTYPE perennials SYSTEM "dtds/perennials.dtd">
```

Note that in the XSL file, if you include a doctype-public attribute for the xsl:output element, then Xalan will include a DOCTYPE statement for the first line of the output document.

Core Approach

Include a `doctype-public` attribute in the `xsl:output` element to produce a DOCTYPE statement in the transformed output.

Listing 23.15 perennials.xsl

```
<?xml version="1.0"?>
<xsl:stylesheet version="1.0"
  xmlns:xsl="http://www.w3.org/1999/XSL/Transform">
  <xsl:output method="html"
    doctype-public ="-//W3C//DTD HTML 4.0 Transitional//EN"/>

  <xsl:template match="/">
  <HTML>
  <HEAD>
```

(continued)

Listing 23.15 `perennials.xsl` *(continued)*

```
        <TITLE>Daylilies</TITLE>
      </HEAD>
      <BODY>
        <TABLE CELLPADDING="3">
          <CAPTION>Stout Medal Award</CAPTION>
          <TR>
            <TH>Year</TH>
            <TH>Cultivar</TH>
            <TH>Bloom Season</TH>
            <TH>Cost</TH>
          </TR>
          <!-- Select daylilies awarded a Stout Medal. -->
          <xsl:apply-templates
             select="/perennials/daylily[award/name='Stout Medal']"/>
          <TR>
            <TD COLSPAN="4" ALIGN="CENTER">
               E-early M-midseason L-late</TD>
          </TR>
        </TABLE>
      </BODY>
    </HTML>
    </xsl:template>

    <xsl:template match="daylily">
      <TR>
        <TD><xsl:value-of select="award/year"/></TD>
        <TD><xsl:value-of select="cultivar"/></TD>
        <!-- Select the bloom code. -->
        <TD ALIGN="CENTER"><xsl:value-of select="bloom/@code"/></TD>
        <TD ALIGN="RIGHT"><xsl:value-of select="cost"/></TD>
      </TR>
    </xsl:template>

</xsl:stylesheet>
```

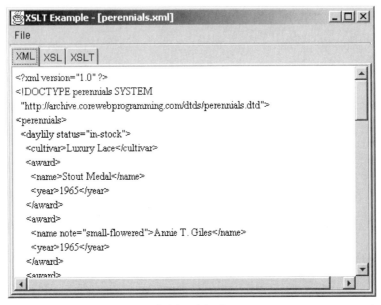

Figure 23–7 Presentation of XML tabbed pane in `XsltExample` with `perennials.xml` (Listing 23.4) loaded.

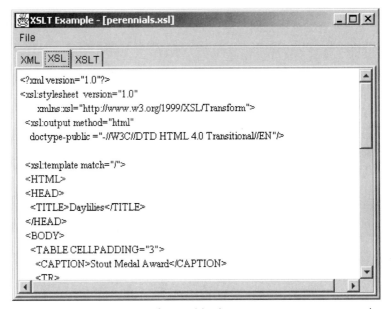

Figure 23–8 Presentation of XSL tabbed pane in `XsltExample` with `perennials.xsl` (Listing 23.15) loaded.

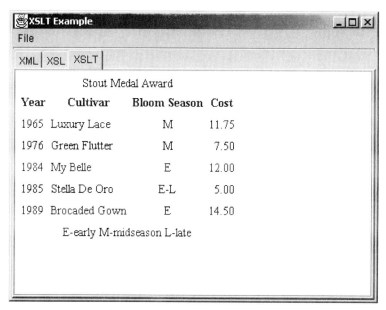

Stout Medal Award			
Year	Cultivar	Bloom Season	Cost
1965	Luxury Lace	M	11.75
1976	Green Flutter	M	7.50
1984	My Belle	E	12.00
1985	Stella De Oro	E-L	5.00
1989	Brocaded Gown	E	14.50
E-early M-midseason L-late			

Figure 23–9 Result of XSLT transformation of `perennials.xml` (Listing 23.4) and `perennials.xsl` (Listing 23.15).

23.8 XSLT Example 2: Custom JSP Tag

In this example, a custom JSP tag is used along with XSLT to output a listing of Stout Medal daylilies in an HTML table, formatted specifically for the client's browser type. Netscape 4.7 and earlier do not support the HTML 4.0 elements: THEAD, TBODY, and TFOOT. However, these three elements are supported by Internet Explorer 4.x and later (see Section 2.4, "Tables," for details on these elements). Thus, in this example, two separate style sheets are used to process the XML file, `perennials.xml` (Listing 23.4), and depending on which client browser accesses the JavaServer Page, `Daylilies.jsp` (Listing 23.18), the correct style sheet is applied. The first XSL document, `perennials-ie.xsl` (Listing 23.16) formats the daylilies in a table suitable for Internet Explorer by using THEAD, TBODY, and TFOOT elements, and the second XSL document, `perennials-ns.xsl` (Listing 23.17) formats the daylilies in a basic table suitable for Netscape.

The Tag Library Descriptor (TLD) for the custom JSP tag, `xsltransform`, used in `Daylilies.jsp`, is presented in `xsltransform.tld` (Listing 23.19). The tag class for this custom tag is `cwp.tags.XslTransformTag`. Three attributes are defined for the tag: `xml`, the source XML file (required), `xslie`, the XSL style sheet targeting Internet Explorer, and `xslns` (required), the XSL style sheet targeting Netscape. The `xslns` style sheet is required because this is the default style sheet applied if the client browser is not Internet Explorer. For additional information on custom tags, see Section 20.7 (Defining Custom JSP Tags).

The tag class, `XslTransformTag`, is shown in Listing 23.20. The `doStartTag` method builds the `File` objects for the XML and XSL document, where the XSL document applied for the style sheet is determined by the `User-Agent` header in the HTTP request. After the source files are determined, the XSLT transform is performed with `XslTransformer` (Listing 23.12) and the result is sent to the `Jsp-Writer`.

This example requires numerous files that must be located in the proper directories on the server to run correctly. In Figure 23–10, we illustrate where to place the files on a Tomcat server. If the DTD, `perennials.dtd`, is not accessible on-line from `http://www.corewebprogramming.com/dtds/`, then place the DTD file in a `dtds` subdirectory as illustrated and modify the `DOCTYPE` to

```
<!DOCTYPE perennials SYSTEM "dtds/perennials.dtd">
```

The result for Internet Explorer 5.0 on Windows 2000 is shown in Figure 23–11 and the result for Netscape 4.7 on Windows 98 is shown in Figure 23–12.

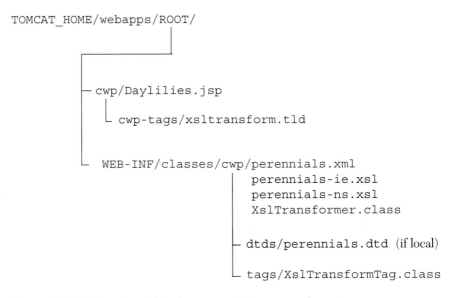

Figure 23–10 Location of files for custom JSP tag example on Tomcat.

Listing 23.16 `perennials-ie.xsl`

```xml
<?xml version="1.0"?>
<!-- Style sheet using THEAD, TBODY, and TFOOT elements. -->
<!-- Suitable for Internet Explorer 4.x and later.        -->
<xsl:stylesheet
    xmlns:xsl="http://www.w3.org/1999/XSL/Transform"
    version="1.0">
  <xsl:output method="html"/>
  <xsl:template match="/">
    <TABLE CELLPADDING="3" RULES="GROUPS" ALIGN="CENTER">
      <CAPTION>Stout Medal Award</CAPTION>
      <COLGROUP>
        <COL ALIGN="CENTER"/>
        <COL ALIGN="LEFT"/>
        <COL ALIGN="CENTER"/>
      </COLGROUP>
      <COLGROUP ALIGN="RIGHT"/>
      <THEAD>
        <TR>
          <TH>Year</TH>
          <TH>Cultivar</TH>
          <TH>Bloom Season</TH>
          <TH>Cost</TH>
        </TR>
      </THEAD>
      <TBODY>
        <!-- Select daylilies awarded Stout Medal. -->
        <xsl:apply-templates
          select="/perennials/daylily[award/name='Stout Medal']"/>
      </TBODY>
      <TFOOT>
        <TR>
          <TD COLSPAN="4">E-early M-midseason L-late</TD>
        </TR>
      </TFOOT>
    </TABLE>
  </xsl:template>
  <xsl:template match="daylily">
    <TR>
      <TD><xsl:value-of select="award/year"/></TD>
      <TD><xsl:value-of select="cultivar"/></TD>
      <!-- Select the bloom code. -->
      <TD><xsl:value-of select="bloom/@code"/></TD>
      <TD><xsl:value-of select="cost"/></TD>
    </TR>
  </xsl:template>
</xsl:stylesheet>
```

Listing 23.17 `perennials-ns.xsl`

```xml
<?xml version="1.0"?>
<!-- Style sheet using a basic TABLE elements.      -->
<!-- Suitable for Netscape.                          -->
<xsl:stylesheet version="1.0"
    xmlns:xsl="http://www.w3.org/1999/XSL/Transform">
  <xsl:output method="html"/>
  <xsl:template match="/">
    <TABLE CELLPADDING="3" BORDER="1" ALIGN="CENTER">
      <CAPTION>Stout Medal Award</CAPTION>
      <TR>
        <TH>Year</TH>
        <TH>Cultivar</TH>
        <TH>Bloom Season</TH>
        <TH>Cost</TH>
      </TR>
      <!-- Select daylilies awarded Stout Medal. -->
      <xsl:apply-templates
        select="/perennials/daylily[award/name='Stout Medal']"/>
      <TR>
        <TD COLSPAN="4" ALIGN="CENTER">
          E-early M-midseason L-late</TD>
      </TR>
    </TABLE>
  </xsl:template>
  <xsl:template match="daylily">
    <TR>
      <TD><xsl:value-of select="award/year"/></TD>
      <TD><xsl:value-of select="cultivar"/></TD>
      <!-- Select the bloom code. -->
      <TD ALIGN="CENTER"><xsl:value-of select="bloom/@code"/></TD>
      <TD ALIGN="RIGHT"><xsl:value-of select="cost"/></TD>
    </TR>
  </xsl:template>
</xsl:stylesheet>
```

Listing 23.18 `Daylilies.jsp`

```
<!DOCTYPE HTML PUBLIC "-//W3C//DTD HTML 4.0 Transitional//EN">
<html>
<head>
  <title>Daylilies</title>
</head>
<body>
<%@ taglib uri="cwp-tags/xsltransform.tld" prefix="cwp" %>

<H1 ALIGN="CENTER">Katie's Favorite Daylilies
<p>
<cwp:xsltransform xml='perennials.xml'
                  xslie='perennials-ie.xsl'
                  xslns='perennials-ns.xsl'
/>

</body>
</html>
```

Listing 23.19 `xsltransform.tld`

```
<?xml version="1.0" encoding="ISO-8859-1" ?>
<!DOCTYPE taglib
  PUBLIC "-//Sun Microsystems, Inc.//DTD JSP Tag Library 1.1//EN"
  "http://java.sun.com/j2ee/dtds/web-jsptaglibrary_1_1.dtd">

<taglib>
  <tlibversion>1.0</tlibversion>
  <jspversion>1.1</jspversion>
  <shortname>cwp</shortname>
  <urn></urn>
  <info>
    A tag library from Core Web Programming,
    http://www.corewebprogramming.com/.
  </info>

  <tag>
    <name>xsltransform</name>
    <tagclass>cwp.tags.XslTransformTag</tagclass>
    <info>Applies xslt transform based on browser type.</info>
    <attribute>
```

(continued)

Listing 23.19 `xsltransform.tld` *(continued)*

```
      <name>xml</name>
      <required>yes</required>
    </attribute>
    <attribute>
      <name>xslie</name>
      <required>false</required>
    </attribute>
    <attribute>
      <name>xslns</name>
      <required>true</required>
    </attribute>
  </tag>
</taglib>
```

Listing 23.20 `XslTransformTag.java`

```java
package cwp.tags;

import java.io.*;
import javax.servlet.*;
import javax.servlet.jsp.*;
import javax.servlet.http.*;
import javax.servlet.jsp.tagext.*;
import javax.xml.transform.*;
import cwp.XslTransformer;

/** A tag that translates an XML document to HTML using XSLT.
 *  Depending on the client browser type, either an XSL style
 *  targeting Internet Explorer or Netscape (default) is
 *  applied.
 */

public class XslTransformTag extends TagSupport {
  private static final String FS =
    System.getProperty("file.separator");
  private static final int IE = 1;
  private static final int NS = 2;
  private String xml, xslie, xslns;
  public void setXml(String xml) {
    this.xml = xml;
  }
```

(continued)

Listing 23.20 XslTransformTag.java *(continued)*

```java
public String getXml() {
  return(xml);
}

public void setXslie(String xslie) {
  this.xslie = xslie;
}

public String getXslie() {
  return(xslie);
}

public void setXslns(String xslns) {
  this.xslns = xslns;
}

public String getXslns() {
  return(xslns);
}

public int doStartTag() throws JspException {
  // Determine the path to XML and XSL source files.
  // The path of SERVLET_HOME/WEB-INF/classes/cwp/ is
  // assumed for the location of the source files.
  String FS = System.getProperty("file.separator");
  ServletContext context = pageContext.getServletContext();
  String path = context.getRealPath(FS) + "WEB-INF" + FS +
                "classes" + FS + "cwp" + FS;

  HttpServletRequest request =
    (HttpServletRequest)pageContext.getRequest();

  // Use either IE or NS style sheet depending on
  // browser type.
  File xslFile = null;
  if ((browserType(request) == IE) && (getXslie() != null)) {
    xslFile = new File(path + getXslie());
  } else {
    xslFile = new File(path + getXslns());
  }
  File xmlFile = new File(path + getXml());
  try {
    JspWriter out = pageContext.getOut();
    XslTransformer transformer = new XslTransformer();
    transformer.process(xmlFile, xslFile, out);
  }
```

(continued)

Listing 23.20 `XslTransformTag.java` *(continued)*

```java
    catch(TransformerException tx) {
      context.log("XslTransformTag: " + tx.getMessage());
    }
    return(SKIP_BODY);
  }

  // Determine the browser type based on the User-Agent
  // HTTP request header.
  private int browserType(HttpServletRequest request) {
    int type = NS;
    String userAgent = request.getHeader("User-Agent");
    if ((userAgent != null) &&
        (userAgent.indexOf("IE") >=0)) {
      type = IE;
    }
    return(type);
  }
}
```

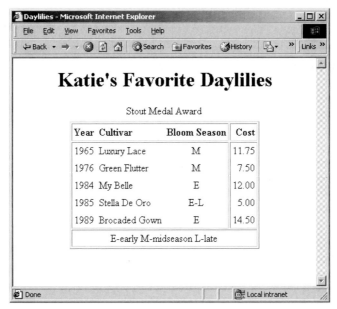

Figure 23–11 Transformation of `perennials.xml` through a custom JSP tag for Internet Explorer 5.0 on Windows 2000.

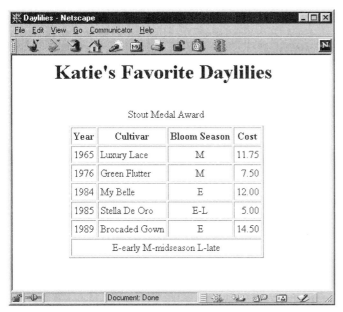

Figure 23–12 Transformation of `perennials.xml` through a custom JSP tag on Netscape 4.7 on Windows 98.

23.9 Summary

Wow! This wraps up the section on server-side programming. Now you know how to process XML documents by using DOM, SAX, and XSLT. You also know how to write servlets and JavaServer Pages, perform HTTP tunneling, and communicate with databases by using JDBC. No doubt you've already started to put these technologies to use in new and exciting Web applications. No doubt your boss is impressed (or are *you* the boss now?).

In the next section we move back to the client side and discuss JavaScript, an interpreted language that runs in the browser. JavaScript can be applied in a variety of ways to make Web pages more flexible and dynamic, but one of the major applications is to check the format of HTML form data *before* it is submitted to the server.

Part 4

JAVASCRIPT

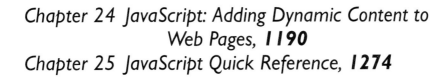

JAVASCRIPT: ADDING DYNAMIC CONTENT TO WEB PAGES

Topics in This Chapter

- Building HTML as the page is loaded
- Monitoring user events
- Building cross-platform scripts
- Mastering JavaScript syntax
- Using JavaScript to customize Web pages
- Using JavaScript to make pages more dynamic
- Using JavaScript to validate CGI forms
- Using JavaScript to manipulate HTTP cookies
- Using JavaScript to interact with and control frames
- Calling Java from JavaScript
- Accessing JavaScript from Java

Chapter 24

Despite the similarity in name, JavaScript is very different from Java. JavaScript is a scripting language that is embedded in Web pages and interpreted as the page is loaded. Java is a general-purpose programming language that can be used for desktop application, server-side programs, and applets that execute in a browser. JavaScript can discover a lot of information about the HTML document it is in and can manipulate a variety of HTML elements. Java, if used in a Web page at all, is relatively isolated from the Web page in which it is embedded. JavaScript has no graphics library, explicit threads, or networking. Java has robust graphics (AWT, Swing, Java 2D), an extensive threading library, and networking options that include sockets, RMI, and JDBC.

Currently, there are six versions of JavaScript, 1.0 through 1.5, with a seventh version, JavaScript 2.0, proposed by The Mozilla Organization (http://www.mozilla.org/). JavaScript 1.0 was originally developed by Netscape and released in Netscape Navigator 2.0. Afterwards, Netscape submitted JavaScript to the European Computer Manufacturers Association (ECMA) for standardization. Following that, the ECMA released the ECMAScript standard, ECMA-262, in June 1997. This standard is completely supported by JavaScript 1.1 in Navigator 3.0x. Netscape later departed from the ECMA standard and released JavaScript 1.2 in Navigator 4.0-4.05. In August 1998, the ECMA wrote a second edition of ECMA-262 to align with the corresponding ISO/IEC 16262 standard. The ECMAScript standard, second edition, is implemented as JavaScript 1.3 in Navigator 4.06 and later. Netscape also added significant changes to some of the object classes in JavaScript 1.3 and introduced floating-point constants like Infinity and NaN. The subsequent version, JavaScript 1.4, provides full support for handling exceptions. To incorporate exceptions and to better handle strings for internationalization in the standard, the ECMA released a third edition of EMCA-262 in December of 1999. The latest browser version from Netscape, Navigator 6, introduced JavaScript 1.5 for full compliance with the third edition of ECMAScript.

To complicate the issue, Microsoft defines its own implementation of the ECMA-Script standard, known as JScript. Since Microsoft provides other scripting platforms (Internet Information Server, Windows Scripting Host, and Visual Studio) that support various versions of JScript, we simply summarize which versions of JavaScript are supported by Internet Explorer. For the most part, JavaScript 1.1 is supported in Internet Explorer 3.0x. JavaScript 1.2 is fully supported in Internet Explorer 4.0x and complies also with EMCA-262, second edition. Internet Explorer 5.0x supports Java-Script 1.3 and most of JavaScript 1.4. Internet Explorer 5.5 fully supports the third edition of the EMCA-262 standard and is compatible with JavaScript 1.5.

JavaScript's core language has not changed significantly since version 1.2 and is supported by most popular browsers (Netscape 4 and Internet Explorer 4 and greater). In the following two chapters, we focus on the core language as found in JavaScript 1.2. We do not cover the Document Object Model (DOM) for implementing DHTML. For details on DOM and various scripting versions, we refer you to the following web sites.

ECMAScript Language Specification

```
http://www.ecma.ch/ecma1/STAND/ECMA-262.HTM
```

Netscape JavaScript Developer Central

```
http://developer.netscape.com/tech/javascript/
```

Microsoft JScript

```
http://msdn.microsoft.com/scripting/
```

The Mozilla Organization

```
http://www.mozilla.org/js/
```

Document Object Model

```
http://www.w3.org/DOM/
```

Two complete reference sources on JavaScript are *Pure JavaScript* by R. Allen Wyke, Jason D. Gilliam, and Charlton Ting (covers JavaScript 1.4), and *Dynamic HTML, The Definitive Reference* by Danny Goodman (covers JavaScript 1.2).

There are two basic ways to use JavaScript in your Web pages. The first is to build HTML dynamically as the Web page is loaded. The second is to monitor various user events and to take action when these events occur. These two syntactic styles are described in the first two sections, with the following section summarizing some other important syntax. These two styles can be combined in a variety of ways and are used for seven general classes of applications: customizing Web pages, making pages more dynamic, validating CGI forms, manipulating cookies, interacting with frames, calling Java from JavaScript, and accessing JavaScript from Java. The remaining sections of this chapter describe each of these application areas, providing two or three examples of each. The following chapter gives details of the standard JavaScript objects in JavaScript 1.2.

24.1 Generating HTML Dynamically

JavaScript code contained inside a SCRIPT element is executed as the page is loaded, with any output the code generates being inserted into the document at the place the SCRIPT occurred. Listing 24.1 outlines the basic format. Don't worry about all the syntactic details for now; we explain them at the end of this section. For now, just note the standard form.

Listing 24.1 Template for Generating HTML with JavaScript

```
...
<BODY>
Regular HTML

<SCRIPT TYPE="text/javascript">
<!--
Build HTML Here
// -->
</SCRIPT>

More Regular HTML
</BODY>
```

You can also use the SRC attribute of SCRIPT to load remote JavaScript code.

The simplest way to build HTML is to use document.write, which places a single string in the current document. Listing 24.2 gives an example, with the result shown in Figure 24–1.

Listing 24.2 `FirstScript.html`

```
<!DOCTYPE HTML PUBLIC "-//W3C//DTD HTML 4.0//EN">
<HTML>
<HEAD>
  <TITLE>First JavaScript Page</TITLE>
</HEAD>
<BODY>
<H1>First JavaScript Page</H1>

<SCRIPT TYPE="text/javascript">
<!--
document.write("<HR>");
document.write("Hello World Wide Web");
document.write("<HR>");
// -->
</SCRIPT>

</BODY>
</HTML>
```

Figure 24–1 The HR elements and the text in between them are generated by JavaScript.

Now, this script is not particularly useful because JavaScript did not contribute anything that couldn't have been done with static HTML. It is more common to use JavaScript to build different HTML in different circumstances. Listing 24.3 gives an example, with Figures 24–2 and 24–3 showing the results in Netscape Navigator and Microsoft Internet Explorer, respectively. Note the use of the `referringPage` helper function and the "+" string concatenation operator. Building one large string for each chunk of HTML often yields code that is easier to read than it would be with a separate `document.write` for each line of HTML. Also note that this script outputs a linefeed after each line of HTML, using `document.writeln` instead of `document.write` and adding \n to each line of text. This linefeed has no effect whatsoever on the resultant Web page. However, some browser versions show the script results when displaying the "source" of a page, and adding the extra newlines makes the result much easier to read. This technique is a very useful debugging tool. If your browser shows you the source in this manner, you can cut and paste the results into a file, then check the syntax of this result with a standard HTML validator (see Section 1.3, "Steps to Publish a Document on the Web"). Highly recommended!

Core Approach

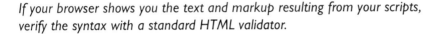

If your browser shows you the text and markup resulting from your scripts, verify the syntax with a standard HTML validator.

Listing 24.3 `ShowInfo.html`

```html
<!DOCTYPE HTML PUBLIC "-//W3C//DTD HTML 4.0 Transitional//EN">
<HTML>
<HEAD>
  <TITLE>Extracting Document Info with JavaScript</TITLE>
</HEAD>
<BODY BGCOLOR="WHITE">
<H1>Extracting Document Info with JavaScript</H1>
<HR>

<SCRIPT TYPE="text/javascript">
<!--

function referringPage() {
  if (document.referrer.length == 0) {
    return("<I>none</I>");
  } else {
    return(document.referrer);
  }
}
```

(continued)

Listing 24.3 `ShowInfo.html` *(continued)*

```
document.writeln
  ("Document Info:\n" +
   "<UL>\n" +
   "  <LI><B>URL:</B> " + document.location + "\n" +
   "  <LI><B>Modification Date:</B> " + "\n" +
   "        document.lastModified + "\n" +
   "  <LI><B>Title:</B> " + document.title + "\n" +
   "  <LI><B>Referring page:</B> " + referringPage() + "\n" +
   "</UL>");
document.writeln
  ("Browser Info:" + "\n" +
   "<UL>" + "\n" +
   "  <LI><B>Name:</B> " + navigator.appName + "\n" +
   "  <LI><B>Version:</B> " + navigator.appVersion + "\n" +
   "</UL>");

// -->
</SCRIPT>

<HR>
</BODY>
</HTML>
```

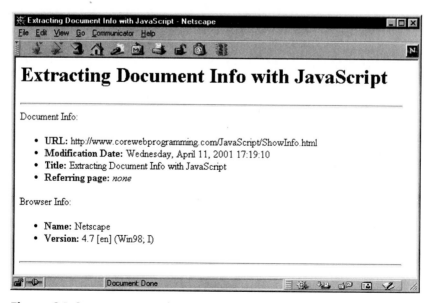

Figure 24–2 `ShowInfo` result in Netscape 4.7 on Windows 98.

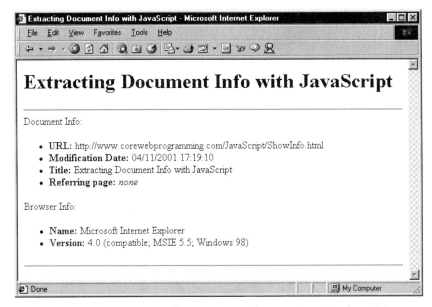

Figure 24–3 `ShowInfo` result in Internet Explorer 5.0 on Windows 98.

Compatibility with Multiple Browsers

Note that the JavaScript code is enclosed inside an HTML comment. This approach is not required but is a good standard practice. Older browsers that do not support JavaScript will automatically ignore the `<SCRIPT>` and `</SCRIPT>` tags but will still see text in between. Using the HTML comment will hide the script contents as well. This works because JavaScript treats both "`//`" and "`<!--`" as the beginning of a single-line comment. Now, this script-hiding strategy is not foolproof, because there are things inside the script that could fool older browsers if you are not careful to avoid them. For instance, in HTML 2.0, the official comment syntax is that comments must be inside pairs of "`--`", which in turn must be between "`<!`" and "`>`". Thus,

```
<!-- Foo -- -- Bar -->
```

is a legal comment, but

```
<!-- Foo -- Bar -->
```

is illegal. Consequently, both of the following are illegal comments in HTML 2.0.

```
<!--
var x = 3;
if (x-->2) // Illegal
  doOneThing();
else
  doAnotherThing();
// -->
```

```
<!--
var x = 3;
var y = x--; // Illegal
// -->
```

Surprisingly, JavaScript does not have a property corresponding to "the current language version," so you have to create your own, as in the following example.

```
<SCRIPT LANGUAGE="JavaScript">
<!--
languageVersion = "1.0";
// -->
</SCRIPT>

<SCRIPT LANGUAGE="JavaScript1.1">
<!--
languageVersion = "1.1";
// -->
</SCRIPT>

...

<SCRIPT LANGUAGE="JavaScript1.4">
<!--
languageVersion = "1.4";
// -->
</SCRIPT>

<SCRIPT LANGUAGE="JavaScript1.5">
<!--
languageVersion = "1.5";
// -->
</SCRIPT>
```

When performing this test do not include the attribute `TYPE="text/java-script"`. In most browsers, adding the `TYPE` attribute results in the script executing regardless of the true JavaScript version. Netscape 6 does not suffer from this problem.

24.2 Monitoring User Events

In addition to building HTML on-the-fly, JavaScript can attach expressions to various HTML elements to be triggered when certain user actions are performed. You can monitor events such as a user clicking on a button or hypertext link, loading or unloading (exiting) a page, moving the mouse on or off a link, giving or taking away the input focus from a `FORM` element, submitting a CGI form, and getting an error when an image is loaded. Listing 24.4 gives an example where the `dontClick` method is attached to a button by the onClick attribute. Figures 24–4 and 24–5 show the result. The BUTTON input element was added to HTML just for JavaScript, but this type of event handler can be attached to a variety of standard HTML elements. Note that dontClick was defined in the HEAD instead of the BODY. This practice is common for functions that don't directly generate HTML.

Listing 24.4 `DontClick.html`

```
<!DOCTYPE HTML PUBLIC "-//W3C//DTD HTML 4.0 Transitional//EN">
<HTML>
<HEAD>
  <TITLE>Simple JavaScript Button</TITLE>

<SCRIPT TYPE="text/javascript">
<!--
function dontClick() {
  alert("I told you not to click!");
}
// -->
</SCRIPT>

</HEAD>
<BODY BGCOLOR="WHITE">
<H1>Simple JavaScript Button</H1>

<FORM>
  <INPUT TYPE="BUTTON"
         VALUE="Don't Click Me"
         onClick="dontClick()">
</FORM>

</BODY>
</HTML>
```

Figure 24–4 The DontClick page before the button is pressed.

Microsoft Internet Explorer
I told you not to click!
OK

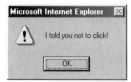

Figure 24–5 The result of clicking the button in the `DontClick` page.

24.3 Mastering JavaScript Syntax

The fundamental syntax of JavaScript looks a lot like Java or C. Most simple constructs will look familiar: `if`, "`? :`", `while`, `for`, `break`, and `continue` are used just as in the Java programming language. JavaScript 1.2 added a `switch` statement that looks very similar to Java's `switch`, with the exception that the `case` values need not be integers. The operators `+` (addition and string concatenation), `-`, `*`, `/`, `++`, `--`, `&&`, `||`, and so forth are virtually identical. Trailing semicolons are optional, but we use them throughout for the sake of familiarity. We outline several important features here; details are given in the next chapter (JavaScript Quick Reference).

Also note that Netscape provides a convenient interactive JavaScript input window (see Figure 24–6). To open the window, simply enter a URL of "`javascript:`" (nothing after the colon). Alternatively, you enter the complete expression for the URL, for example, "`javascript:Math.cos(Math.PI/4)*2`"; the result is displayed in the browser window. The second approach works both in Netscape and Internet Explorer.

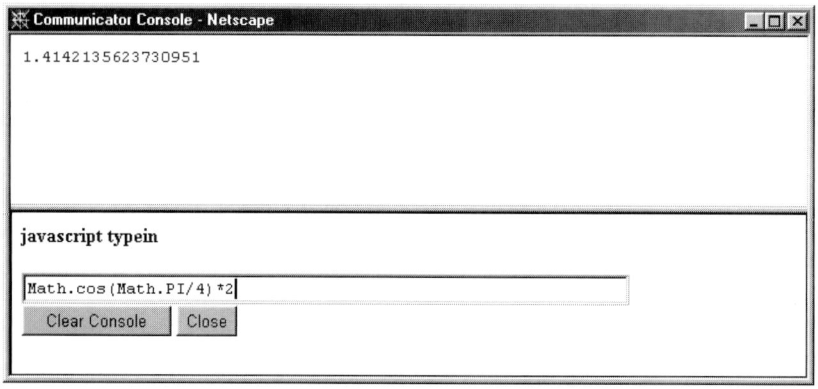
Communicator Console - Netscape
1.4142135623730951
javascript typein
Math.cos(Math.PI/4)*2
Clear Console
Close

Figure 24–6 Netscape provides an interactive JavaScript "listener."

Dynamic Typing

The most striking difference between Java and JavaScript is the lack of declared types in JavaScript. You don't declare types for local variables, instance variables (called "properties" in JavaScript lingo), or even return types for functions. A variable can even change type during its lifetime. So, for example, the following is perfectly legal.

```
var x = 5; // int
x = 5.5; // float
x = "five point five"; // String
```

Function Declarations

Functions are declared with the `function` reserved word. The return value is not declared, nor are the types of the arguments. Here are some examples.

```
function square(x) {
   return(x * x);
}

function factorial(n) {
   if (n <= 0) {
     return(1);
   } else {
     return(n * factorial(n - 1));
   }
}

function printHeading(message) {
   document.writeln("<H1>" + message + "</H1>");
}
```

Functions can be passed around and assigned to variables, as follows:

```
var fun = Math.sin;
alert("sin(pi/2)=" + fun(Math.PI/2));
```

Figure 24–7 shows the result.

Figure 24–7 JavaScript lets you assign a function to a new name.

You can also reassign existing functions. In fact, you can even override system functions, as in the following example, although you almost always want to avoid doing that in real applications.

```
Math.sin = Math.cos;  // Don't do this at home
alert("Yikes! sin(pi/2)=" + Math.sin(Math.PI/2));
```

Figure 24–8 shows the result.

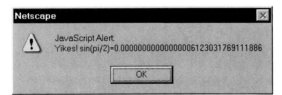

Figure 24–8 JavaScript even lets you reassign standard functions.

Objects and Classes

JavaScript's approach to object-oriented programming seems a bit haphazard compared to the strict and consistent approach of the Java programming language. Following are a few of the most unusual features.

Fields Can Be Added On-the-Fly

Adding a new property (field) is a simple matter of assigning a value to one. If the field doesn't already exist when you try to assign to it, JavaScript creates it automatically. For instance:

```
var test = new Object();
test.field1 = "Value 1"; // Create field1 property
test.field2 = 7; // Create field2 property
```

Although this approach simplifies the addition of new properties, it also makes it difficult to catch typos because misspelled property names will be happily accepted. Also, if you try to look up a property that doesn't exist, you will get the special undefined value. This value compares == to null.

You Can Use Literal Notation

You can create objects by using a shorthand "literal" notation of the form

```
{ field1:val1, field2:val2, ... , fieldN:valN }
```

For example, the following gives equivalent values to object1 and object2.

```
var object1 = new Object();
object1.x = 3;
object1.y = 4;
object1.z = 5;

var object2 = { x:3, y:4, z:5 };
```

The for/in Statement Iterates over Properties

JavaScript, unlike Java or C++, has a construct that lets you easily retrieve all of the fields of an object. The basic format is as follows:

```
for(fieldName in object) {
  doSomethingWith(fieldName);
}
```

Given a field name, you can access the field through `object["field"]` as well as through `object.field`. This feature is useful when you are iterating over fields in an object, as in Listing 24.5, which defines a general-purpose `makeObjectTable` function that will create an HTML table for a given object. Figure 24–9 gives the result in Internet Explorer 5.0.

Listing 24.5 `ForIn.html`

```
<!DOCTYPE HTML PUBLIC "-//W3C//DTD HTML 4.0 Transitional//EN">
<HTML>
<HEAD>
  <TITLE>For/In Loops</TITLE>

<SCRIPT TYPE="text/javascript">
<!--

function makeObjectTable(name, object) {
  document.writeln("<H2>" + name + "</H2>");
  document.writeln("<TABLE BORDER=1>\n" +
                   "  <TR><TH>Field<TH>Value");
  for(field in object) {
    document.writeln ("  <TR><TD>" + field +
                      "<TD>" + object[field]);
  }
  document.writeln("</TABLE>");
}
```

(continued)

Listing 24.5 `ForIn.html` *(continued)*

```
// -->
</SCRIPT>

</HEAD>
<BODY BGCOLOR="WHITE">
<H1>For/In Loops</H1>

<SCRIPT TYPE="text/javascript">
<!--

var test = new Object();
test.field1 = "Field One";
test.field2 = "Field Two";
test.field3 = "Field Three";
makeObjectTable("test", test);

// -->
</SCRIPT>

</BODY>
</HTML>
```

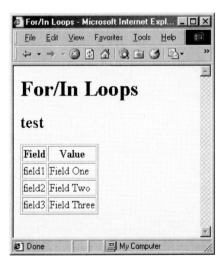

Figure 24–9 The `for/in` statement iterates over the properties of an object.

A Constructor Is Just a Function That Assigns to "this"

JavaScript does not have an exact equivalent to Java's class definition. The closest you can get is to define a function that assigns values to properties in the this reference. Calling that function with new binds this to a new Object. For example, following is a simple constructor for a Ship class.

```
function Ship(x, y, speed, direction) {
  this.x = x;
  this.y = y;
  this.speed = speed;
  this.direction = direction;
}
```

Given the previous definition of makeObjectTable, putting the following in a script in the BODY of a document yields the result shown in Figure 24–10.

```
var ship1 = new Ship(0, 0, 1, 90);
makeObjectTable("ship1", ship1);
```

Figure 24–10 Constructors are simply a shorthand way to define objects and assign properties.

Methods Are Function-Valued Properties

There is no special syntax for defining methods of objects. Instead, you simply assign a function to a property. For instance, here is a version of the Ship class that includes a move method.

```
function degreesToRadians(degrees) {
  return(degrees * Math.PI / 180.0);
}

function move() {
  var angle = degreesToRadians(this.direction);
  this.x = this.x + this.speed * Math.cos(angle);
  this.y = this.y + this.speed * Math.sin(angle);
}

function Ship(x, y, speed, direction) {
  this.x = x;
  this.y = y;
  this.speed = speed;
  this.direction = direction;
  this.move = move;
}
```

Note the use of `var` before the `angle` variable. This declaration is JavaScript's indication of a local variable. If you forget the declaration, JavaScript won't complain but will treat the variable as a property of the current window. In this case, like-named variables in different functions could conflict with each other. As a result, this behavior of undeclared local variables can lead to hard-to-diagnose problems, so a good standard practice is to always declare your variables.

Core Approach

Introduce all local variables with `var`.

Here is an example that uses the above functions, with the result shown in Figure 24–11.

```
var ship1 = new Ship(0, 0, 1, 90);
makeObjectTable("ship1 (originally)", ship1);
ship1.move();
makeObjectTable("ship1 (after move)", ship1);
```

The prototype Property

You can simplify the creation of methods and constant properties by use of the special `prototype` property. Once at least one object of a given class exists, assigning values to a field in the object stored in the `prototype` property of the class object (really the function object named for the class) gives a shared reference to this value to all members of the class that do not override it. For instance, here is a definition of `Ship` that adds a shared `maxSpeed` property intended to specify the highest speed at which _any_ `Ship` can travel.

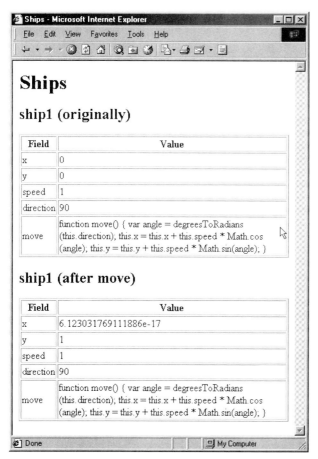

Figure 24–11 Methods are really a special type of property.

```
function Ship(x, y, speed, direction) {
  this.x = x;
  this.y = y;
  this.speed = speed;
  this.direction = direction;
}

new Ship(0, 0, 0, 0);
Ship.prototype.move = move;
Ship.prototype.maxSpeed = 50;
```

Arrays

For the most part, you can use arrays in JavaScript much like you use Java arrays. Here are a few examples of using the `Array` constructor to simplify the building of arrays.

```
var squares = new Array(5);
for(var i=0; i<squares.length; i++) {
  vals[i] = i * i;
}
// Or, in one fell swoop:
var squares = new Array(0, 1, 4, 9, 16);
var array1 = new Array("fee", "fie", "fo", "fum");
// Literal Array notation for creating an array.
var array2 = [ "fee", "fie", "fo", "fum" ];
```

Using arrays this way is probably the simplest use. Behind the scenes, however, JavaScript simply represents arrays as objects with numbered fields. You can access named fields by using either `object.field` or `object["field"]`, but you access numbered fields only by `object[fieldNumber]`. Here is an example, with Figure 24–12 showing the result.

```
var arrayObj = new Object();
arrayObj[0] = "Index zero";
arrayObj[10] = "Index ten";
arrayObj.field1 = "Field One";
arrayObj["field2"] = "Field Two";

makeObjectTable("arrayObj", arrayObj);
```

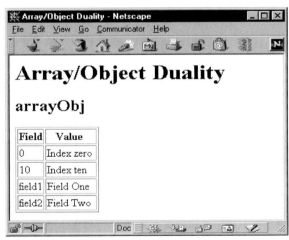

Figure 24–12 Arrays are really just objects with numbered fields.

In general, it is a good idea to avoid mixing array and object notation and to treat them as two separate varieties of object. Occasionally, however, it is convenient to mix the notations because the array notation is required when an existing string is to be used as a property name. For instance, the `makeObjectTable` (Listing 24.5) function relied upon this capability.

24.4 Using JavaScript to Customize Web Pages

Because JavaScript can determine several characteristics of the current browser and document, you can use it to build different Web pages in different circumstances. For instance, you might want to use certain Microsoft-specific features on Internet Explorer and Netscape-specific features on Netscape Navigator. Or omit certain background information if users came to your page from another one of your pages, as opposed to an outside page. Or use smaller images if the user has a small screen. Or use embedded objects only if the browser has a plug-in that supports them. Integration with Java (Section 24.9) will allow additional applications such as printing only a "Sorry, no Web page for you, buddy!" page to users who visit from spam-tolerant ISPs, or removing the prominent link to your resumé when people access your Web page from your company domain. Following are two examples. The first shows how to customize the page for the browser window size, and the second illustrates how to tell if certain plug-ins are available.

Adjusting to the Browser Window Size

Netscape 4.0 introduced the `window.innerWidth` and `window.innerHeight` properties, which let you determine the usable size of the current browser window. Listing 24.6 uses this value to shrink/stretch images to a fixed percentage of the window width and to adjust the size of a heading font accordingly. Figures 24–13 and 24–14 show the results in a large and a small browser window.

There are a couple of other stylistic notes to make about this example. First of all, notice that the function definitions are placed in the HEAD, even though they are used in the BODY. This is a standard practice that has three benefits. (1): It can make the actual script easier to read. (2): It allows a single function to be used multiple places. And (3): Because the HEAD is parsed before the BODY, JavaScript routines defined in the HEAD will be available even if the user interrupts the loading or clicks on an image or cross-reference before the page is done loading. This behavior is particularly valuable for event-handling functions.

Core Approach

Define JavaScript functions in the HEAD, *especially if they will be used in event handlers.*

Also note the use of single quotes instead of double quotes for strings in this example. JavaScript allows either, so using single quotes for document.writeln makes it easier to embed double quotes inside the string, as needed in this case for the "better berry" quotation.

Core Note

Either single or double quotes can be used for JavaScript strings. Double quotes can be embedded inside strings created with single quotes; single quotes can be used inside strings made with double quotes.

Listing 24.6 `Strawberries.html`

```
<!DOCTYPE HTML PUBLIC "-//W3C//DTD HTML 4.0 Transitional//EN">
<HTML>
<HEAD>
  <TITLE>Strawberries</TITLE>

<SCRIPT TYPE="text/javascript">
<!--
function image(url, width, height) {
 return('<IMG SRC="' + url + '"' +
          ' WIDTH=' + width +
          ' HEIGHT=' + height + '>');
}

function strawberry1(width) {
  return(image("Strawberry1.gif", width,
Math.round(width*1.323)));
}

function strawberry2(width) {
  return(image("Strawberry2.gif", width,
Math.round(width*1.155)));
}
// -->
```

(continued)

Listing 24.6 `Strawberries.html` *(continued)*

```
</SCRIPT>
</HEAD>
<BODY BGCOLOR="WHITE">

<HR>
<SCRIPT TYPE="text/javascript">
<!--
  var imageWidth = window.innerWidth/4;
  var fontSize = Math.min(7, Math.round(window.innerWidth/100));
}

document.writeln
  ('<TABLE>\n' +
  '  <TR><TD>' + strawberry1(imageWidth) + '\n' +
  '      <TH><FONT SIZE=' + fontSize + '>\n' +
  '          "Doubtless God <I>could</I> have made\n' +
  '          a better berry, but doubtless He\n' +
  '          never did."</FONT>\n' +
  '      <TD>'  + strawberry2(imageWidth) + '\n' +
  '</TABLE>');
// -->
</SCRIPT>
<HR>

Strawberries are my favorite garden crop; a fresh
strawberry picked five minutes ago makes the dry and
woody grocery store variety seem like a <B>totally</B>
different fruit. My favorite varieties are Surecrop
and Cardinal.

</BODY>
</HTML>
```

Figure 24–13 In a large browser, large images and fonts are used.

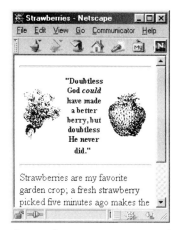

Figure 24–14 Even in a tiny browser window, the heading is still legible.

Determining Whether Plug-Ins Are Available

In Netscape (but not Internet Explorer), the `navigator.plugins` array contains information about the available browser plug-ins. Each element in this array is a `Plugin` object that has `name`, `description`, `filename`, and `length` properties and contains an array of `MimeType` objects. These properties give a short name to the plug-in, a textual description, the filename containing the plug-in, and the number of supported MIME types, respectively. Each `MimeType` object has properties `type` (MIME datatype such as "text/html"), `description` (descriptive text), `enabledPlugin` (the `Plugin` object supporting this type), and `suffixes` (a comma-separated list of file extensions associated with this type). An interesting aspect of JavaScript arrays is that you can reference them with a string "index" instead of an integer. In fact, as explained in Section 24.3 (Mastering JavaScript Syntax), arrays in JavaScript are really just objects with numbered fields. Anyhow, you can use this shortcut to determine if a plug-in is installed, as in the following snippet.

```
if (navigator.plugins["Cosmo Player 1.0"]) {
  document.write('<EMBED SRC="coolWorld.vrml" ...>"');
} else {
  document.write('This example requires VRML.');
}
```

Note that this code tells you whether a *particular* plug-in is available. If you are more concerned about whether a certain MIME type is supported *somehow* (directly, through a plug-in, or through an external application), you can check the `navigator.mimeTypes` property. For example,

```
if (navigator.mimeTypes["application/postscript"]) {
  addPostScriptLink();
}
```

For more information, see Section 25.19 (The MimeType Object).

Listing 24.7 uses this approach to build a table of available plug-ins and their supported MIME types. Figure 24–15 show the results in Netscape 4.7.

Listing 24.7 `Plugins.html`

```
<!DOCTYPE HTML PUBLIC "-//W3C//DTD HTML 4.0 Transitional//EN">
<HTML>
<HEAD>
  <TITLE>Plug-ins Supported</TITLE>

<SCRIPT TYPE="text/javascript">
<!--

function printRow(plugin) {
  document.write
    ("  <TR><TD>" + plugin.name + "\n" +
     "       <TD>" + plugin.description + "\n" +
     "       <TD>");
  document.write(plugin[0].type);
  for(var i=1; i<plugin.length; i++)
    document.writeln("<BR>" + plugin[i].type);
}

// -->
</SCRIPT>
</HEAD>
<BODY>
<H1>Plug-ins Supported</H1>

<SCRIPT TYPE="text/javascript">
<!--
if (navigator.appName == "Netscape") {
  document.writeln
    ("<TABLE BORDER=1>\n" +
     "  <TR><TH>Plug-in\n" +
     "       <TH>Description\n" +
     "       <TH>MIME Types Supported");
  for(var i=0; i<navigator.plugins.length; i++)
    printRow(navigator.plugins[i]);
  document.writeln
    ("\n</TABLE>");
}
// -->
</SCRIPT>

</BODY>
</HTML>
```

Figure 24–15 Partial list of plug-ins available in this version of Netscape 4.7.

24.5 Using JavaScript to Make Pages Dynamic

In most of the previous examples, parts of the document were built dynamically (when the page was loaded), but the resultant document was normal HTML. Java-Script can also be used to create elements that are dynamic. For instance, one common application is to create images that change when the user moves the mouse over them. This application can be used to implement toolbars with regions that "light up" to indicate hypertext links or custom buttons that show a grayed-out image when you press them. Alternatively, by using timers, JavaScript can animate images even without being triggered by user events. JavaScript can manipulate layers, scroll the document, and even move the browser window around on the screen.

Modifying Images Dynamically

In JavaScript, the document.images property contains an array of Image objects corresponding to each IMG element in the current document. To display a new image, simply set the SRC property of an existing image to a string representing a different image file. For instance, the following function changes the first image in a document.

```
function changeImage() {
  document.images[0].src = "images/new-image.gif";
}
```

This function could be invoked from an event handler (e.g., when the user clicks a button) or even executed automatically after a certain amount of time. Now, referring to images by number is not very flexible, because the addition of a new image in the middle of the document would require changing the references to all later images. Fortunately, JavaScript recognizes the NAME attribute of the IMG element. For example, if you provide a name for your image

```
<IMG SRC="cool-image.jpg" NAME="cool"
    WIDTH=75 HEIGHT=25>
```

then you could refer to an array element by name instead of number, as in

```
function improveImage() {
  document.images["cool"].src = "way-cool.jpg";
}
```

A Clickable Image Button

The concept of images that change when you click on them is implemented with a clickable image button. For example, following is a clickButton function that temporarily changes an image, switching it back to the original version after 1/10 of a second. To do this, it uses the setImage and setTimeout function. The first of these is defined as follows, where setTimeout is a built-in routine that takes a string designating a JavaScript expression and a time in milliseconds. It returns immediately but starts a background process that waits for the specified time, then executes the code specified by the string.

```
function setImage(name, image) {
  document.images[name].src = image;
}

function clickButton(name, grayImage) {
  var origImage = document.images[name].src;
  setImage(name, grayImage);
  var resetString =
    "setImage('" + name + "', '" + origImage + "')";
  setTimeout(resetString, 100);
}
```

To use this routine for a clickable image button, we need to do two more things: (1) attach the routine to a button or buttons, and (2) make sure that the images needed are already cached by the browser. The first step is straightforward: simply use the onClick attribute of the <A HREF...> element, as shown below.

```
<A HREF="location1.html"
    onClick="clickButton('Button1',
                         'images/Button1-Down.gif')">
```

```
<IMG SRC="images/Button1-Up.gif" NAME="Button1"
    WIDTH=150 HEIGHT=25></A>

<A HREF="location2.html"
  onClick="clickButton('Button2',
                       'images/Button2-Down.gif')">
<IMG SRC="images/Button2-Up.gif" NAME="Button2"
    WIDTH=150 HEIGHT=25></A>
```

Finally, before trying to display an image, you should make sure it is already loaded. This extra step will prevent long pauses when the button is pressed. You can do this step by creating an `Image` object (Section 25.12), then setting its `SRC` property. Oddly, this `Image` object never actually gets used; its only purpose is to force the browser to load (and cache) the image. Here is an example.

```
imageFiles = new Array("images/Button1-Up.gif",
                       "images/Button1-Down.gif",
                       "images/Button2-Up.gif",
                       "images/Button2-Down.gif");
imageObjects = new Array(imageFiles.length);

for(var i=0; i<imageFiles.length; i++) {
  imageObjects[i] = new Image(150, 25);
  imageObjects[i].src = imageFiles[i];
}
```

Listing 24.8 shows the whole process put together. If you are handling a lot of images, you can simplify the process by having a consistent naming scheme for the images; we give an example later in this section.

Listing 24.8 `ImageButton.html`

```
<!DOCTYPE HTML PUBLIC "-//W3C//DTD HTML 4.0 Transitional//EN">
<HTML>
<HEAD>
  <TITLE>JavaScript Image Buttons</TITLE>

<SCRIPT TYPE="text/javascript">
<!--

imageFiles = new Array("images/Button1-Up.gif",
                       "images/Button1-Down.gif",
                       "images/Button2-Up.gif",
                       "images/Button2-Down.gif");
imageObjects = new Array(imageFiles.length);
```

(continued)

Listing 24.8 `ImageButton.html` *(continued)*

```
for(var i=0; i<imageFiles.length; i++) {
  imageObjects[i] = new Image(150, 25);
  imageObjects[i].src = imageFiles[i];
}

function setImage(name, image) {
  document.images[name].src = image;
}

function clickButton(name, grayImage) {
  var origImage = document.images[name].src;
  setImage(name, grayImage);
  var resetString =
    "setImage('" + name + "', '" + origImage + "')";
  setTimeout(resetString, 100);
}

// -->
</SCRIPT>

</HEAD>
<BODY>
<H1>JavaScript Image Buttons</H1>

<A HREF="location1.html"
   onClick="clickButton('Button1', 'images/Button1-Down.gif')">
<IMG SRC="images/Button1-Up.gif" NAME="Button1"
    WIDTH=150 HEIGHT=25></A>

<A HREF="location2.html"
   onClick="clickButton('Button2', 'images/Button2-Down.gif')">
<IMG SRC="images/Button2-Up.gif" NAME="Button2"
    WIDTH=150 HEIGHT=25></A>

</BODY>
</HTML>
```

Highlighting Images Under the Mouse

An even more common application of the image modification process is to create a series of images that change as the user moves the mouse over them, using the hypertext link's onMouseOver to display the highlighted image and onMouseOut to change the image back. This approach can make toolbars more appealing by providing visual cues about which regions are clickable. However, when you are dealing with a large number of images, listing each explicitly when preloading them can be tedious. Listing 24.9 shows an approach that simplifies this process considerably:

using consistent names. The normal image and highlighted image are both derived from the NAME of the IMG element (see regularImageFile and negative-ImageFile), obviating the need to list the full filenames in the array of images to be preloaded or to pass the highlighted image name in the onMouseOver call. Toolbars of this type are most commonly used with frames. Listing 24.10 and Listing 24.11 show the rest of the frame structure; Figure 24–16 shows the results.

If you can't remember how to use frames, this would be a good time to review them (Chapter 4), because they are used quite frequently with JavaScript.

Listing 24.9 HighPeaksNavBar.html

```
<!DOCTYPE HTML PUBLIC "-//W3C//DTD HTML 4.0 Transitional//EN">
<HTML>
<HEAD>
  <TITLE>High Peaks Navigation Bar</TITLE>

<SCRIPT TYPE="text/javascript">
<!--

// Given "Foo", returns "images/Foo.gif".

function regularImageFile(imageName) {
  return("images/" + imageName + ".gif");
}

// Given "Bar", returns "images/Bar-Negative.gif".

function negativeImageFile(imageName) {
  return("images/" + imageName + "-Negative.gif");
}

// Cache image at specified index. E.g., given index 0,
// take imageNames[0] to get "Home". Then preload
// images/Home.gif and images/Home-Negative.gif.

function cacheImages(index) {
  regularImageObjects[index] = new Image(150, 25);
  regularImageObjects[index].src =
    regularImageFile(imageNames[index]);
  negativeImageObjects[index] = new Image(150, 25);
  negativeImageObjects[index].src =
    negativeImageFile(imageNames[index]);
}
```

(continued)

Listing 24.9 `HighPeaksNavBar.html` *(continued)*

```
imageNames = new Array("Home", "Tibet", "Nepal",
                       "Austria", "Switzerland");
regularImageObjects = new Array(imageNames.length);
negativeImageObjects = new Array(imageNames.length);

// Put images in cache for fast highlighting.
for(var i=0; i<imageNames.length; i++) {
  cacheImages(i);
}

// This is attached to onMouseOver -- change image
// under the mouse to negative (reverse video) version.

function highlight(imageName) {
  document.images[imageName].src =
    negativeImageFile(imageName);
}

// This is attached to onMouseOut -- return image to
// normal.

function unHighlight(imageName) {
  document.images[imageName].src = regularImageFile(imageName);
}

// -->
</SCRIPT>
</HEAD>

<BODY BGCOLOR="WHITE">

<TABLE BORDER=0 WIDTH=150 BGCOLOR="WHITE"
       CELLPADDING=0 CELLSPACING=0>
  <TR><TD><A HREF="Home.html"
           TARGET="Main"
           onMouseOver="highlight('Home')"
           onMouseOut="unHighlight('Home')">
         <IMG SRC="images/Home.gif"
             NAME="Home"
             WIDTH=150 HEIGHT=25 BORDER=0>
         </A>
  <TR><TD><A HREF="Tibet.html"
           TARGET="Main"
           onMouseOver="highlight('Tibet')"
           onMouseOut="unHighlight('Tibet')">
```

(continued)

Listing 24.9 `HighPeaksNavBar.html` *(continued)*

```
            <IMG SRC="images/Tibet.gif"
                NAME="Tibet"
                WIDTH=150 HEIGHT=25 BORDER=0>
            </A>
  <TR><TD><A HREF="Nepal.html"
            TARGET="Main"
            onMouseOver="highlight('Nepal')"
            onMouseOut="unHighlight('Nepal')">
          <IMG SRC="images/Nepal.gif"
                NAME="Nepal"
                WIDTH=150 HEIGHT=25 BORDER=0></A>
  <TR><TD><A HREF="Austria.html"
            TARGET="Main"
            onMouseOver="highlight('Austria')"
            onMouseOut="unHighlight('Austria')">
          <IMG SRC="images/Austria.gif"
                NAME="Austria"
                WIDTH=150 HEIGHT=25 BORDER=0></A>
  <TR><TD><A HREF="Switzerland.html"
            TARGET="Main"
            onMouseOver="highlight('Switzerland')"
            onMouseOut="unHighlight('Switzerland')">
          <IMG SRC="images/Switzerland.gif"
                NAME="Switzerland"
                WIDTH=150 HEIGHT=25 BORDER=0></A>
</TABLE>
</BODY>
</HTML>
```

Listing 24.10 `HighPeaks.html`

```
<!DOCTYPE HTML PUBLIC "-//W3C//DTD HTML 4.0 Frameset//EN">
<HTML>
<HEAD>
  <TITLE>High Peaks Travel Inc.</TITLE>
</HEAD>

<FRAMESET COLS="160,*" FRAMEBORDER=0 BORDER=0>
  <FRAME SRC="HighPeaksNavBar.html" SCROLLING="NO">
  <FRAME SRC="HighPeaksIntro.html" NAME="Main">

  <NOFRAMES>
    If you can't hack frames, how do you expect
    to handle the Himalayas? Get a real browser.
  </NOFRAMES>
</FRAMESET>

</HTML>
```

Listing 24.11 `HighPeaksIntro.html`

```
<!DOCTYPE HTML PUBLIC "-//W3C//DTD HTML 4.0 Transitional//EN">
<HTML>
<HEAD>
  <TITLE>High Peaks Travel Inc.</TITLE>
</HEAD>
<BODY BGCOLOR="WHITE">
<CENTER>
  <IMG SRC="images/peak2.gif" WIDTH=511 HEIGHT=128>
</CENTER>
<H1 ALIGN="CENTER">High Peaks Travel Inc.</H1>
<HR>

<IMG SRC="images/peak1.gif" WIDTH=170 HEIGHT=121 ALIGN="RIGHT">
Tired of the same old vacations in Cleveland?
Tour the high peaks with <B>High Peaks Travel</B>!
<P>
We have package deals for beginner, experienced, and expert
climbers, discount priced (*) for the budget-conscious
traveller.
<BR CLEAR="ALL">
<IMG SRC="images/peak.jpg" WIDTH=320 HEIGHT=240
     ALIGN="LEFT">
HPT is currently arranging trips to the following
exciting locations:
<UL>
  <LI><A HREF="Tibet.html">Tibet</A>
  <LI><A HREF="Nepal.html">Nepal</A>
  <LI><A HREF="Austria.html">Austria</A>
  <LI><A HREF="Switzerland.html">Switzerland</A>
</UL>
Sign up today!

<BR CLEAR="ALL">
<CENTER>
<FONT SIZE="-2">(*) No ropes or safety equipment provided
on discount tours. </FONT>
</CENTER>

</BODY>
</HTML>
```

Figure 24–16 Toolbar entries light up when you move the mouse over them.

Moving Layers

Netscape 4.0 introduced "layers." These are HTML regions that can overlap and be positioned arbitrarily; they are covered in Section 5.12 (Layers). JavaScript 1.2 lets you access layers through the document.layers array, each element of which is a Layer object with properties corresponding to the attributes of the LAYER element. A named layer can be accessed through document.layers["layer name"] rather than through an index or simply by use of document.layerName. Layers can be accessed this way no matter how they are defined in the HTML: by the LAYER element, by the ILAYER element, or through style sheets.

Listing 24.12 presents an example with two layers that are initially hidden (Figure 24–17). When a certain button is pressed, the first layer is made visible near the upper-left corner, then moves down over the top of the regular page to its final location, where it annotates an image (Figure 24–18). Clicking a second button hides the first layer and displays a second, which also drifts to its final location. The properties and methods of the Layer object are described in Section 25.15, but for this example, the properties of interest are visibility (show or hidden) and pageX (absolute location in window). The methods used are moveToAbsolute (position layer at absolute location) and moveBy (move layer relative to its previous position).

This example runs only in Netscape 4; LAYERS are not legal in the HTML 4.0 specification and are unsupported in Netscape 6. Furthermore, Internet Explorer uses a different document object model (DOM) to access and move the layers. We provide an on-line, cross-browser version of this example at http://www.corewebprogramming.com/. For detailed information on how to upgrade existing documents containing the LAYER element to Netscape 6 and Internet Explorer, see http://sites.netscape.net/ekrock/standards.html.

Listing 24.12 Camps.html

```
<!DOCTYPE HTML PUBLIC "-//W3C//DTD HTML 4.0 Transitional//EN">
<HTML>
<HEAD>
  <TITLE>Camps on K-3</TITLE>

<SCRIPT TYPE="text/javascript">
<!--

function hideCamps() {
  // Netscape 4 document model.
  document.layers["baseCamp"].visibility = "hidden";
  document.layers["highCamp"].visibility = "hidden";
  // Or document.baseCamp.visibility = "hidden";
}

function moveBaseCamp() {
  baseCamp.moveBy(1, 3);
  if (baseCamp.pageX < 130) {
    setTimeout("moveBaseCamp()", 10);
  }
}
```

(continued)

Listing 24.12 `Camps.html` *(continued)*

```
// Hide camps, position base camp near top-left corner,
// make it visible, then have it slowly drift down to
// final position.

function showBaseCamp() {
  hideCamps();
  baseCamp = document.layers["baseCamp"];
  baseCamp.moveToAbsolute(0, 20);
  baseCamp.visibility = "show";
  moveBaseCamp();
}

function moveHighCamp() {
  highCamp.moveBy(2, 1);
  if (highCamp.pageX < 110) {
    setTimeout("moveHighCamp()", 10);
  }
}

// Hide camps, position high camp near top-left corner,
// make it visible, then have it slowly drift down to
// final position.

function showHighCamp() {
  hideCamps();
  highCamp = document.layers["highCamp"];
  highCamp.moveToAbsolute(0, 65);
  highCamp.visibility = "show";
  moveHighCamp();
}

// -->
</SCRIPT>
</HEAD>
<BODY>

<IMG SRC="images/peak4.gif" WIDTH=511 HEIGHT=600 ALIGN="LEFT">
<H1>Camps on K-3</H1>
The High Peaks Tours trip to the summit:
```

(continued)

Listing 24.12 Camps.html *(continued)*

```
<UL>
  <LI>Day 1: Travel to Base Camp
  <LI>Day 2: Climb to High Camp
  <LI>Day 3: Ascend summit, return to High Camp
  <LI>Day 4: Descend to Base Camp
  <LI>Day 5: Return Home
</UL>
<BR CLEAR="ALL">

<!--           LAYER only supported Netscape 4           -->
<LAYER ID="highCamp" PAGEX=50 PAGEY=100 VISIBILITY="hidden">
  <TABLE>
    <TR><TH BGCOLOR="WHITE" WIDTH=50>
        <FONT SIZE="+2">High Camp</FONT>
        <TD><IMG SRC="images/Arrow-Right.gif">
  </TABLE>
</LAYER>

<!--           LAYER only supported Netscape 4           -->
<LAYER ID="baseCamp" PAGEX=50 PAGEY=100 VISIBILITY="hidden">
  <TABLE>
    <TR><TH BGCOLOR="WHITE" WIDTH=50>
        <FONT SIZE="+3">Base Camp</FONT>
        <TD><IMG SRC="images/Arrow-Right.gif">
  </TABLE>
</LAYER>

<FORM>
  <INPUT TYPE="Button" VALUE="Show Base Camp"
        onClick="showBaseCamp()">
  <INPUT TYPE="Button" VALUE="Show High Camp"
        onClick="showHighCamp()">
  <INPUT TYPE="Button" VALUE="Hide Camps"
        onClick="hideCamps()">
</FORM>

</BODY>
</HTML>
```

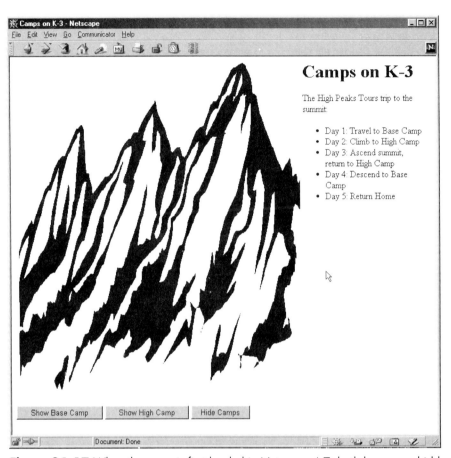

Figure 24-17 When the page is first loaded in Netscape 4.7, both layers are hidden.

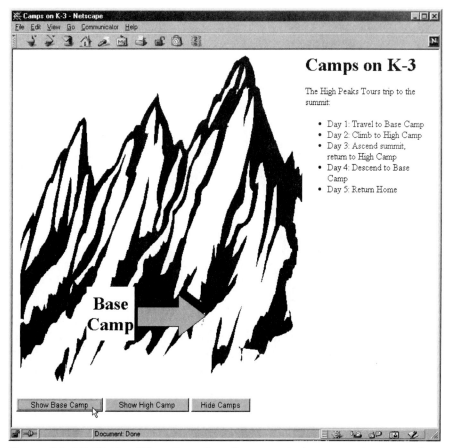

Figure 24–18 Clicking "Show Base Camp" turns on the base camp layer near the top-left corner of the page. It then drifts down to its final position.

24.6 Using JavaScript to Validate HTML Forms

Another important application of JavaScript is to check the format of form fields before the form is submitted to the server. Contacting the server can be expensive, especially over a slow connection, and simple tasks like checking that all required fields are filled out or making sure textfields that should contain numbers don't have strings should be performed on the client if at all possible. The `document.forms` property contains an array of `Form` entries contained in the document. As usual in

JavaScript, named entries can be accessed by name instead of by number; moreover, named forms are automatically inserted as properties in the document object, so any of the following formats would be legal to access forms.

```
var firstForm = document.forms[0];
// Assumes <FORM NAME="orders" ...>
var orderForm = document.forms["orders"];
// Assumes <FORM NAME="register" ...>
var registrationForm = document.register;
```

The Form object contains an elements property that holds an array of Element objects. You can retrieve form elements by number, by name from the array, or by the property name.

```
var firstElement = firstForm.elements[0];
// Assumes <INPUT ... NAME="quantity">
var quantityField = orderForm.elements["quantity"];
// Assumes <INPUT ... NAME="submitSchedule">
var submitButton = register.submitSchedule;
```

Different elements can be manipulated in different ways. Some generally important capabilities include the ability to execute code before a form is submitted (through the onSubmit attribute of FORM), look up and change form values (through the element's value property), to recognize when keyboard focus is gained or lost (through onFocus and onBlur), and to notice changed values automatically (through onChange). The following examples illustrate two major ways form entries are checked: individually (each time one changes) and en masse (only when the form is submitted). For more details, see the Element and Form objects (Sections 25.6 and 25.8).

Checking Values Individually

Listing 24.13 gives a simple input form containing a single textfield and a SUBMIT button. JavaScript is used in two ways. First, when the textfield gets the input focus, text describing the expected value is printed in the status line. The status line is reset when the textfield loses the focus. Second, if the user changes the textfield value to something illegal, a warning is issued when that user leaves the textfield. Then, the textfield value is reset (changing the value through JavaScript does *not* trigger onChange), and it is given the input focus for the user to enter a correction. Figure 24–19 shows the results.

Listing 24.13 `CheckText.html`

```html
<!DOCTYPE HTML PUBLIC "-//W3C//DTD HTML 4.0 Transitional//EN">
<HTML>
<HEAD>
  <TITLE>On-Line Training</TITLE>

<SCRIPT TYPE="text/javascript">
<!--

// Print a description of the legal text in the status line.

function describeLanguage() {
  status = "Enter an important Web language";
}

// Clear status line.

function clearStatus() {
  status = "";
}

// When the user changes and leaves textfield, check
// that a valid choice was entered. If not, alert
// user, clear field, and set focus back there.

function checkLanguage() {
  // or document.forms["langForm"].elements["langField"]
  var field = document.langForm.langField;
  var lang = field.value;
  var prefix = lang.substring(0, 4).toUpperCase();
  if (prefix != "JAVA") {
    alert("Sorry, '" + lang + "' is not valid.\n" +
          "Please try again.");
    field.value = "";  // Erase old value
    field.focus();     // Give keyboard focus
  }
}

// -->
</SCRIPT>
</HEAD>
<BODY BGCOLOR="WHITE">
<H1>On-Line Training</H1>
```

(continued)

Listing 24.13 `CheckText.html` *(continued)*

```
<FORM ACTION="cgi-bin/registerLanguage" NAME="langForm">
To see an introduction to any of our on-line training
courses, please enter the name of an important Web
programming language below.
<P>
<B>Language:</B>
<INPUT TYPE="TEXT" NAME="langField"
       onFocus="describeLanguage()"
       onBlur="clearStatus()"
       onChange="checkLanguage()">
<P>
<INPUT TYPE="SUBMIT" VALUE="Show It To Me">
</FORM>

</BODY>
</HTML>
```

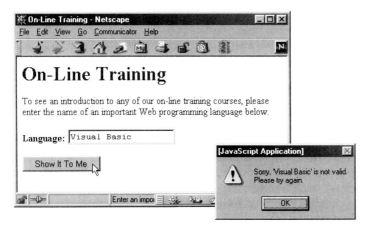

Figure 24–19 If the user enters an illegal value, a warning is printed when the keyboard focus leaves the textfield.

Checking Values When Form Is Submitted

Sometimes it is more convenient to check the entire form in one fell swoop. Some people feel that correcting the user after every mistake is too intrusive, since the user may enter values temporarily but correct them before submission. Other times, it is simply easier to check a bunch of values than to create a separate function for each of several dozen input elements. The key idea is that the function invoked by the FORM onSubmit attribute prevents submission of the form if the function returns false.

Checking numeric values is one of the most common validation tasks, but the value property of textfields and text areas is a string, not a number. Fortunately, JavaScript provides two built-in functions to assist in this validation: parseInt and parseFloat. These functions take a string as input and return either an integer or a floating-point number. In JavaScript 1.2, if no prefix of the string is a valid number, they return the special value NaN (not a number), which can be recognized with the built-in isNaN function (not by ==, because NaNs return false for all comparisons). Surprisingly, as mentioned in Section 24.1 (Generating HTML Dynamically), JavaScript does not have a property corresponding to "the current language version."

Listing 24.14 illustrates checking input for valid numbers, with the result in Internet Explorer 5.0 shown in Figure 24–20.

Listing 24.14 Numbers.html

```
<!DOCTYPE HTML PUBLIC "-//W3C//DTD HTML 4.0 Transitional//EN">
<HTML>
<HEAD>
  <TITLE>Testing Numbers</TITLE>

<SCRIPT TYPE="text/javascript">
<!--

function isInt(numString) {
    // It's an int if parseInt doesn't return NaN
    return(!isNaN(parseInt(numString)));
}

// -->
</SCRIPT>

</HEAD>
<BODY BGCOLOR="WHITE">

<SCRIPT TYPE="text/javascript">
<!--

function testInt(numString) {
  return("<TR><TD>" + numString +
         "<TD>" + parseInt(numString) +
         "<TD>" + isInt(numString) + "\n");
}
```

(continued)

Listing 24.14 `Numbers.html` *(continued)*

```
document.writeln
  ("<H1>Testing for Numbers in JavaScript 1.2+</H1>\n" +
   "<TABLE BORDER=5 CELLSPACING=5>\n" +
   "<TR><TH>Input<TH>Parsed Value<TH>Legal Integer?\n" +
   testInt("0") +
   testInt("10") +
   testInt("-10") +
   testInt("FF") +
   testInt("#FF") +
   testInt("123abc") +
   testInt("abc123") +
   "</TABLE>");

// -->
</SCRIPT>

</BODY>
</HTML>
```

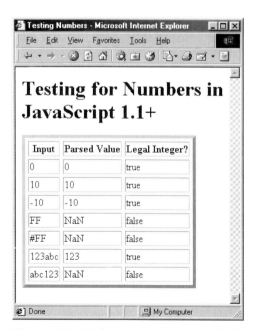

Figure 24–20 If the value is not preceded by a number, then the `parseInt` method returns NaN.

JavaScript versions earlier than 1.1 do not have an isNAN method. However, if a text-field value is supposed to be greater than zero, you can simplify the test considerably by relying on the fact that NaN returns false when compared to any other number. Here is a variation of isInt that uses this idea.

```
function isInt(string) {

  var val = parseInt(string);

  return(val > 0);

}
```

Listing 24.15 uses this approach to create a simple input form with three text-fields. The first and third should contain numbers, and the second should contain a string. Rather than correction of values as they are entered, the only action taken during data entry is to print a descriptive message whenever a textfield has the input focus. However, when the form is submitted, the checkRegistration function is invoked. This function verifies that the first and third entries are integers and that the second is neither an integer nor missing. Results are shown in Figures 24–21 and 24–22.

Listing 24.15 CheckSeveral.html

```
<!DOCTYPE HTML PUBLIC "-//W3C//DTD HTML 4.0 Transitional//EN">
<HTML>
<HEAD>
  <TITLE>Camp Registration</TITLE>

<SCRIPT TYPE="text/javascript">
<!--

function clearStatus() { status = ""; }

function promptAge() { status = "Age (no fractions)"; }

function promptRank() { status = "Rank Name"; }

function promptSerial() { status = "Serial Number"; }

// In JavaScript 1.1+, parseInt returns NaN (recognizable
// through isNaN() for nonintegers. But JavaScript 1.0
// returns 0 and doesn't have an isNaN routine. Since
// comparisons to NaN always fail, the > 0 test works on
// either version.
```

(continued)

Listing 24.15 CheckSeveral.html *(continued)*

```
function isInt(string) {
  var val = parseInt(string);
  return(val > 0);
}

// Four tests:
// 1) Age is an integer.
// 2) Rank is not an integer.
// 3) Rank is not missing.
// 4) Serial number is an integer.
// If any of the tests pass, submission is canceled.

function checkRegistration() {
  var ageField = document.registerForm.ageField;
  if (!isInt(ageField.value)) {
    alert("Age must be an integer.");
    return(false);
  }
  var rankField = document.registerForm.rankField;
  if (isInt(rankField.value)) {
    alert("Use rank name, not rank number.");
    return(false);
  }
  if (rankField.value == "") {
    alert("Missing rank.");
    return(false);
  }
  var serialField = document.registerForm.serialField;
  if (!isInt(serialField.value)) {
    alert("Serial number must be an integer.");
    return(false);
  }
  // Format looks OK. Submit form.
  return(true);
}

// -->
</SCRIPT>

</HEAD>
<BODY BGCOLOR="WHITE">
<H1>Camp Registration</H1>
```

(continued)

Listing 24.15 `CheckSeveral.html` *(continued)*

```
<FORM ACTION="cgi-bin/register"
      NAME="registerForm"
      onSubmit="return(checkRegistration())">
Age: <INPUT TYPE="TEXT" NAME="ageField"
            onFocus="promptAge()"
            onBlur="clearStatus()">
<BR>
Rank: <INPUT TYPE="TEXT" NAME="rankField"
            onFocus="promptRank()"
            onBlur="clearStatus()">
<BR>
Serial Number: <INPUT TYPE="TEXT" NAME="serialField"
                      onFocus="promptSerial()"
                      onBlur="clearStatus()">
<P>
<INPUT TYPE="SUBMIT" VALUE="Submit Registration">
</FORM>

</BODY>
</HTML>
```

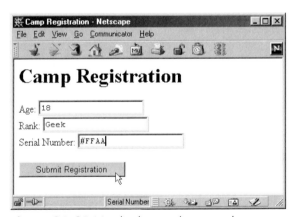

Figure 24–21 No checking is done as values are entered.

Figure 24–22 Wait! That *is* an integer! Sorry, Charlie, the page designer wasn't planning on hex input.

Also, be aware that in JavaScript 1.2, Netscape chooses *not* to perform type conversions on operands for the == and != operators. For example, consider the following two statements,

```
"123" == 123    // Evaluates to false. JavaScript 1.2 only!
"777" != 777    // Evaluates to true. JavaScript 1.2 only!
```

In all other versions of JavaScript, Netscape implements type conversion of the operands for these two operators. Internet Explorer performs type conversion for all JScript implementations of ECMAScript and does not suffer from this inconsistency found in JavaScript 1.2.

Core Note

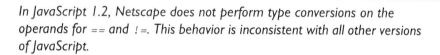

In JavaScript 1.2, Netscape does not perform type conversions on the operands for == and !=. This behavior is inconsistent with all other versions of JavaScript.

24.7 Using JavaScript to Store and Examine Cookies

A cookie is a small amount of textual information about a page that is stored by the browser on the client system. A cookie can also be manipulated entirely on the client through the use of the document.cookie property. This property behaves in a very unusual fashion. If you look up the value of document.cookie, you will get a *single* big string containing all the cookie values, as sent by the browser through the Cookie HTTP request header. For example, if the current page has three cookies name1, name2, and name3, the value of document.cookie would be something like

```
"name1=val1; name2=val2; name3=val3"
```

However, you do not assign values to document.cookie by using a single large string like this. Instead, you specify a single cookie at a time, using the same format as would be used in the Set-Cookie HTTP response header. See Section 19.11 (Cookies) for a complete description of the syntax, but here are a couple of examples.

```
document.cookie = "name1=val1";
document.cookie = "name2=val2; expires=" + someDate;
document.cookie = "name3=val3; path=/; domain=test.com";
```

Each time `document.cookie` is set, the cookie is stored by the browser. The cookies persist as long as the browser remains open, and if an expiration date is specified, the cookie is reloaded in a later session. This works in any version of Netscape, but it only works in Internet Explorer 5.0 and later.

Core Warning

Cookies are ignored by Internet Explorer 4.x and earlier when the page comes from a local file.

To illustrate the use of cookies, Listing 24.16 creates a simplified order form for "Widgets R Us" corporation. When the form is submitted, the first and last name and account number are stored in cookies. A user can store the name and number without submitting an order by clicking the Register Account button. When the page is visited later in the same or a different session, the cookie values are used to fill in the first three textfields automatically as a time-saving feature for the user.

There are two particular things you should pay attention to in this example. The first is that the function that fills the textfield values is invoked from the `onLoad` attribute of `BODY`. This guarantees that the page is done loading before the function is invoked, so there is no risk of trying to access textfields that do not yet exist. The second thing to note is the `cookieVal` function, which takes a cookie name (e.g., `"name2"`) and a cookie string (e.g., `"name1=val1;    name2=val2; name3=val3"`) and returns the value associated with the name (e.g., `"val2"`).

```
function cookieVal(cookieName, cookieString) {
  var startLoc = cookieString.indexOf(cookieName);
  if (startLoc == -1) {
    return("");  // No such cookie
  }
  var sepLoc = cookieString.indexOf("=", startLoc);
  var endLoc = cookieString.indexOf(";", startLoc);
  if (endLoc == -1) { // Last one has no ";"
    endLoc = cookieString.length;
  }
  return(cookieString.substring(sepLoc+1, endLoc));
}
```

This function uses two important methods of the `String` class: `indexOf` and `substring`. The first of these takes two strings as arguments and, if the first appears in the second, returns the location in the second string corresponding to the leftmost occurrence of the first string. There is also a `lastIndexOf` method that returns the starting index of the rightmost occurrence. In either case, −1 is returned if the second string does not contain the first. The `substring` method takes a start index and an end index and returns the string starting at the start index (inclusive) and going up to the end index (exclusive). The `cookieVal` function might have been a little simpler if the `split` method had been used; this method takes a string and returns an array derived from breaking the string at white space or at a user-specified delimiter. See Section 25.31 for a complete description of the `String` object.

This version of `cookieVal` does not distinguish between an empty value (e.g., the value corresponding to `"bar"` in `"foo=a; bar=; baz=c"`) and a missing cookie (e.g., the value corresponding to `"quux"` in `"foo=a; bar=; baz=c"`). If you want to differentiate these two cases, simply return `null` instead of the empty string from the line containing the "No such cookie" comment. In this case, however, returning an empty string either way simplifies the processing considerably.

Figures 24–23 and 24–24 show the before and after results in Internet Explorer 5.0. Cookies can be hard to debug. To see if any cookies are present for the currently loaded page, you can enter

```
javascript:alert(document.cookie)
```

in the browser URL.

Listing 24.16 `Widgets.html`

```
<!DOCTYPE HTML PUBLIC "-//W3C//DTD HTML 4.0 Transitional//EN">
<HTML>
<HEAD>
  <TITLE>Widgets "R" Us</TITLE>

<SCRIPT TYPE="text/javascript">
<!--

// Read last name, first name, and account number
// from textfields and store as cookies.

function storeCookies() {
  var expires = "; expires=Monday, 01-Dec-01 23:59:59 GMT";
  var first = document.widgetForm.firstField.value;
  var last = document.widgetForm.lastField.value;
  var account = document.widgetForm.accountField.value;
  document.cookie = "first=" + first + expires;
  document.cookie = "last=" + last + expires;
  document.cookie = "account=" + account + expires;
}

// Store cookies and give user confirmation.

function registerAccount() {
  storeCookies();
  alert("Registration Successful.");
}
```

(continued)

Listing 24.16 `Widgets.html` *(continued)*

```
// This does not distinguish an empty cookie from no cookie
// at all, since it doesn't matter here.

function cookieVal(cookieName, cookieString) {
  var startLoc = cookieString.indexOf(cookieName);
  if (startLoc == -1) {
    return("");   // No such cookie
  }
  var sepLoc = cookieString.indexOf("=", startLoc);
  var endLoc = cookieString.indexOf(";", startLoc);
  if (endLoc == -1) { // Last one has no ";"
    endLoc = cookieString.length;
  }
  return(cookieString.substring(sepLoc+1, endLoc));
}

// If cookie values for name or account exist,
// fill in textfields with them.

function presetValues() {
  var firstField = document.widgetForm.firstField;
  var lastField = document.widgetForm.lastField;
  var accountField = document.widgetForm.accountField;
  var cookies = document.cookie;
  firstField.value = cookieVal("first", cookies);
  lastField.value = cookieVal("last", cookies);
  accountField.value = cookieVal("account", cookies);
}

// -->
</SCRIPT>
</HEAD>
<BODY BGCOLOR="WHITE" onLoad="presetValues()">

<H1>Widgets "R" Us</H1>

<FORM ACTION="servlet/cwp.Widgets"
      NAME="widgetForm"
      onSubmit="storeCookies()">
First Name: <INPUT TYPE="TEXT" NAME="firstField">
<BR>
Last Name: <INPUT TYPE="TEXT" NAME="lastField">
<BR>
```

(continued)

Listing 24.16 `Widgets.html` *(continued)*

```
Account Number: <INPUT TYPE="TEXT" NAME="accountField">
<BR>
Widget Name: <INPUT TYPE="TEXT" NAME="widgetField">
<BR>
<INPUT TYPE="BUTTON" VALUE="Register Account"
       onClick="registerAccount()">
<INPUT TYPE="SUBMIT" VALUE="Submit Order">

</FORM>
</BODY>
</HTML>
```

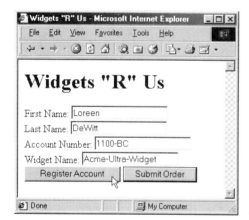

Figure 24–23 The initial page lets the user order widgets. The name and account number are stored when the order is submitted or if Register Account is pressed.

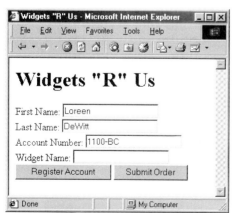

Figure 24–24 Even after Loreen quits and restarts the browser at a later time, the previous name and account number are automatically filled in.

24.8 Using JavaScript to Interact with Frames

JavaScript gives you a variety of tools for accessing and manipulating frames. The default `Window` object contains a `frames` property holding an array of frames (other `Window` objects) contained by the current window or frame. It also has `parent` and `top` properties referring to the directly enclosing frame or window and the top-level window, respectively. All of the properties of `Window` can be applied to any of these entries; see Section 25.35 (The Window Object) for details on the available properties. We show two examples here: having one frame direct another to display a particular URL and transferring the input focus to a frame when its contents change. Two additional examples were given in Chapter 4 (Frames). The first showed how you could update the contents of two frames at once, and the second showed how to use JavaScript to prevent your document from appearing as a frame in someone else's Web page. For details, see Section 4.5 (Solving Common Frame Problems).

Directing a Particular Frame to Display a URL

Because each of the frames specified by `frames`, `top`, and `bottom` has a `location` property that, when changed, redirects the window to a new URL, it is quite straightforward for JavaScript code in one frame to force other frames to show a particular URL. Once you have a reference to the parent frame of the one you want to change, you simply look up the frame in the `frames` array and set `location`. Here is an example.

```
someFrame.frames["frameName"].location = "url";
```

Alternatively, because the HTML Document Object Model automatically creates a property for each frame in a window, you could do:

```
someFrame.frames.frameName.location = "url";
```

The key point to changing the content in a frame is that you have to know enough about the frame structure to follow the `parent`, `top`, and `frames` links to the frame of interest. Alternatively, you can create new windows at run time and direct documents to be displayed there. Section 25.35 (The Window Object) gives several examples of this process.

Listing 24.17 creates a page that initially displays two frames: `GetURL.html` (Listing 24.18) and `DisplayURL.html` (Listing 24.19). The top frame contains a textfield for collecting a URL of interest. Entering a value and pressing the Show URL button instructs the other frame to display the specified URL. The process is amazingly simple. First, create a function to display the URL, as follows:

```
function showURL() {
  var url = document.urlForm.urlField.value;
  parent.displayFrame.location = url;
}
```

Next, attach this function to a button by using the onClick attribute, as in the following snippet.

```
<INPUT TYPE="BUTTON" VALUE="Show URL"
       onClick="showURL()">
```

That's all there is to it. Figures 24–25 and 24–26 show the results in Internet Explorer.

Listing 24.17 ShowURL.html

```
<!DOCTYPE HTML PUBLIC "-//W3C//DTD HTML 4.0 Frameset//EN">
<HTML>
<HEAD>
  <TITLE>Show a URL</TITLE>
</HEAD>

<FRAMESET ROWS="150, *">
  <FRAME SRC="GetURL.html" NAME="inputFrame">
  <FRAME SRC="DisplayURL.html" NAME="displayFrame">
</FRAMESET>

</HTML>
```

Listing 24.18 GetURL.html

```
<!DOCTYPE HTML PUBLIC "-//W3C//DTD HTML 4.0 Transitional//EN">
<HTML>
<HEAD>
  <TITLE>Choose a URL</TITLE>

<SCRIPT TYPE="text/javascript">
<!--

function showURL() {
  var url = document.urlForm.urlField.value;
  // or parent.frames["displayFrame"].location = url;
  parent.displayFrame.location = url;
}
```

(continued)

Listing 24.18 GetURL.html *(continued)*

```
function preloadUrl() {
  if (navigator.appName == "Netscape") {
    document.urlForm.urlField.value =
      "http://home.netscape.com/";
  } else {
    document.urlForm.urlField.value =
      "http://www.microsoft.com/";
  }
}

// -->
</SCRIPT>
</HEAD>

<BODY BGCOLOR="WHITE" onLoad="preloadUrl()">
<H1 ALIGN="CENTER">Choose a URL</H1>

<CENTER>
<FORM NAME="urlForm">
URL: <INPUT TYPE="TEXT" NAME="urlField" SIZE=35>
<INPUT TYPE="BUTTON" VALUE="Show URL"
      onClick="showURL()">
</FORM>
</CENTER>

</BODY>
</HTML>
```

Listing 24.19 DisplayURL.html

```
<!DOCTYPE HTML PUBLIC "-//W3C//DTD HTML 4.0 Transitional//EN">
<HTML>
<HEAD>
  <TITLE>Display URL</TITLE>
</HEAD>
<BODY BGCOLOR="WHITE">
<H2>Enter a URL in the textfield above. Press
"Show URL" to display it in this frame.</H2>

</BODY>
</HTML>
```

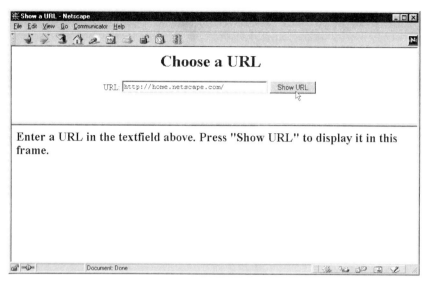

Figure 24–25 The textfield's initial value is set for Netscape, but arbitrary values can be entered.

Figure 24–26 Pressing Show URL instructs the bottom frame to show the URL entered in the textfield of the top frame. [© 2001 Netscape Communications Corp. Used with permission. All rights reserved.]

Giving a Frame the Input Focus

One of the surprising features of frames is that when you click on a hypertext link that directs the result to a particular frame, that frame does not automatically get the input focus. This can be annoying for a couple of reasons. First, it can give unintuitive results when printed. Suppose that a page is using a small borderless frame to act as a navigation bar. Now, you click in that toolbar to display a page of interest, then select Print. What do you get? A nice printout of the toolbar, that's what! Hardly what you were expecting. Second, it can decrease the value of keyboard shortcuts. Some users commonly use keyboard shortcuts to scroll in large documents. For instance, the up and down arrows cause scrolling on most systems, but only if the window has the input focus. So, if you use a hypertext link that sends a document to a frame, you have to click in that frame before using the keyboard shortcuts.

When JavaScript code is being used to display frames, the fix is trivial: just include a call to `focus`. For instance, here is an improved version of `showURL` that can be used in `GetURL.html` to give the bottom frame the input focus when a URL is sent there.

```
function showURL() {
  var url = document.urlForm.urlField.value;
  parent.displayFrame.location = url;
  // Give frame the input focus
  parent.displayFrame.focus();
}
```

Fixing the problem in regular HTML documents is a bit more tedious. It requires adding `onClick` handlers that call `focus` to each and every occurrence of A and AREA that includes a `TARGET`, and a similar `onSubmit` handler to each FORM that uses `TARGET`.

24.9 Accessing Java from JavaScript

Netscape 3.0 introduced a package called LiveConnect that allows JavaScript to talk to Java, and vice versa. This capability is very important because prior to the introduction of LiveConnect, applets were self-contained programs that had little knowledge of or interaction with the rest of the Web page that contained them. Now, applets can manipulate frames and windows, control images loaded from HTML, read and set values of form elements, read and store cookies, and all the other things that were previously restricted to JavaScript. This section discusses ways to use Java routines and control applets from within JavaScript. Section 24.10 explains the other side of the process: using JavaScript capabilities from within an applet. Here, we discuss three classes of applications.

- *Calling Java methods directly.* In particular, this section shows how to print debugging messages to the Java console.

- *Using applets to perform operations for JavaScript.* In particular, this section shows how a hidden applet can obtain the client hostname, information not otherwise available to JavaScript.
- *Controlling applets from JavaScript.* In particular, this section shows how LiveConnect allows user actions in the HTML part of the page to trigger actions in the applet.

Calling Java Methods Directly

JavaScript can access Java variables and methods simply by using the fully qualified name. For instance, using

```
java.lang.System.out.println("Hello Console");
```

will send the string "Hello Console" to the Java console. This is a useful debugging tool when you are developing JavaScript-enabled Web pages. You can also use new from within JavaScript to construct Java classes. For example, Listing 24.20 creates a simple page, using the getProperty method java.lang.System and an instance of the java.awt.Point class. Figure 24–27 shows the result.

Listing 24.20 `CallJava.html`

```
<!DOCTYPE HTML PUBLIC "-//W3C//DTD HTML 4.0//EN">
<HTML>
<HEAD>
  <TITLE>Calling Java</TITLE>
</HEAD>
<BODY>
<H1>Calling Java</H1>

<SCRIPT TYPE="text/javascript">
<!--

document.writeln
  ("This browser uses a virtual machine from " +
   java.lang.System.getProperty("java.vendor") + ".");
var pt = new java.awt.Point(3, 5);
pt.translate(7, 5);
document.writeln("<P>");
document.writeln("Translating (3,5) by (7,5) yields (" +
                pt.x + "," + pt.y + ").");

// -->
</SCRIPT>

</BODY>
</HTML>
```

Use of Java from JavaScript has two major limitations. First, you cannot perform any operation that would not be permitted in an applet, so you cannot use Java to open local files, call local programs, discover the user's login name, or execute any other such restricted operation. Second, and most significantly, JavaScript provides no mechanism for writing Java methods or creating subclasses. As a result, you will want to create an applet for all but the simplest uses of `java.lang.System.out.println` or a data structure like `java.util.StringTokenizer`.

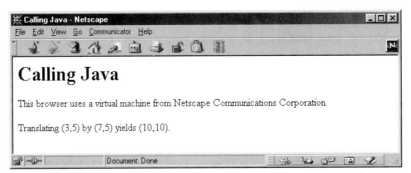

Figure 24–27 JavaScript can utilize Java even if the current page does not contain an applet.

Using Applets to Perform Operations for JavaScript

With its strong object-oriented framework and (on most platforms) Just In Time compiler, Java is better suited to writing complex data structures and performing long computations than is JavaScript. If JavaScript needs such things, a good alternative is to write them in Java, include them in a "hidden" applet, and call them from JavaScript. JavaScript can access applets either through the `document.applets` array or, if the applet is named, through `document.appletName`. Any public method of the applet can be called by JavaScript. For example, suppose that the applet `Acoustics` has a simple model for computing sound propagation through water and you want to create a Web page to demonstrate the model. You could include the applet in your page with

```
<APPLET CODE="Acoustics" WIDTH=10 HEIGHT=10
        NAME="acoustics">
</APPLET>
```

You could then call the public `getSignalExcess` method as follows:

```
function signalExcess(...) {
  return(document.acoustics.getSignalExcess(...));
}
```

To illustrate, Listing 24.21 creates a Web page with a hypertext link that takes visitors to one of two different resumés, depending on the domain of the client system. Since JavaScript doesn't have a way of determining the client hostname, the page uses a simple hidden applet (Figure 24–28, Listing 24.22) that uses `Inet-Address.getLocalHost` to determine this information. If the hostname is inside the author's own company network, the author displays a corporately-politically-correct resumé (Figure 24–29, Listing 24.23), while outside readers get a very different result (Figure 24–30, Listing 24.24) when clicking on the same link.

Listing 24.21 `Wonder-Widget.html`

```
<!DOCTYPE HTML PUBLIC "-//W3C//DTD HTML 4.0 Transitional//EN">
<HTML>
<HEAD>
  <TITLE>WonderWidget</TITLE>

<SCRIPT TYPE="text/javascript">
<!--

function contains(string, substring) {
  return(string.indexOf(substring) != -1);
}

function showResume() {
  if (contains(document.gethost.getHost(),
               "widgets-r-us.com")) {
    location = "ResumeLoyal.html";
  } else {
    location = "ResumeReal.html";
  }
  return(false);
}

// -->
</SCRIPT>

</HEAD>
<BODY BGCOLOR="WHITE">
<H1>WonderWidget</H1>

<APPLET CODE="GetHost" WIDTH=10 HEIGHT=10 NAME="gethost">
</APPLET>
```

(continued)

Listing 24.21 `Wonder-Widget.html` *(continued)*

```
Description:
<UL>
  <LI>Name: Wonder Widget
  <LI>Serial Number: 1544X
  <LI>Cost: $7.95 (plus 22.50 shipping and handling)
  <LI>Designer:
      <A HREF="ResumeLoyal.html" onClick="return(showResume())">
      J. Random Hacker</A>

</BODY>
</HTML>
```

Listing 24.22 `GetHost.java`

```java
import java.applet.Applet;
import java.awt.*;
import java.net.*;

public class GetHost extends Applet {
  private String host;

  public void init() {
    setBackground(Color.white);
    try {
      host = InetAddress.getLocalHost().toString();
    } catch(UnknownHostException uhe) {
      host = "Unknown Host";
    }
  }

  public String getHost() {
    return(host);
  }
}
```

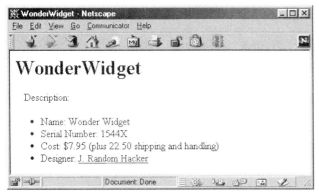

Figure 24–28 This page contains an applet, even though the applet doesn't contribute to the appearance of the page.

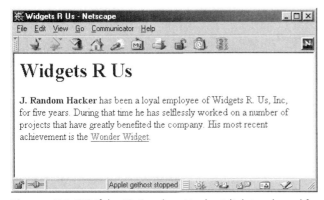

Figure 24–29 If the "J. Random Hacker" link is selected from within the widgets-r-us domain or from a browser that has JavaScript disabled, this first resumé is displayed.

Figure 24–30 If Java reports a "safe" hostname, a different resumé is displayed.

Listing 24.23 `ResumeLoyal.html`

```
<!DOCTYPE HTML PUBLIC "-//W3C//DTD HTML 4.0 Transitioanl//EN">
<HTML>
<HEAD>
  <TITLE>Widgets R Us</TITLE>
</HEAD>
<BODY BGCOLOR="WHITE">
<H1>Widgets R Us</H1>
<B>J. Random Hacker</B> has been a loyal employee of Widgets
R. Us, Inc, for five years. During that time he has
selflessly worked on a number of projects that have greatly
benefited the company. His most recent achievement is the
<A HREF="Wonder-Widget.html">Wonder Widget</A>.
</BODY>
</HTML>
```

Listing 24.24 `ResumeReal.html`

```
<!DOCTYPE HTML PUBLIC "-//W3C//DTD HTML 4.0 Transitional//EN">
<HTML>
<HEAD>
  <TITLE>J. Random Hacker</TITLE>
</HEAD>
<BODY BGCOLOR="WHITE">
<H1>J. Random Hacker</H1>
<H2>I'm looking for a job!</H2>
For the last five years, I've been underpaid and
underappreciated by Widgets R Us, Inc. Now I'm ready to take
my immense talents elsewhere. Who will open the bidding?
</BODY>
</HTML>
```

Controlling Applets from JavaScript

If an applet is designed with public methods to start it, stop it, customize its appearance, and control its behavior, the applet can be completely controlled from JavaScript. There are several reasons why you might want to do this in JavaScript instead of using GUI controls in Java. First, you might want to mix the controls with formatted text, something HTML excels at. For example, you might want to put controls into a table, and it is far easier to make nicely formatted tables in HTML than in Java. Second, you might want the applet actions to correspond to user events such as submitting a form, something Java could not detect by itself. Third, embedding controls in JavaScript lets you perform a consistent set of actions for *all* applets in a page. For example, Listing 24.25 gives a Web page that lets you control any number of "simulations" showing mold growth. You can insert any number of applets; the Start and Stop buttons apply to every applet on the page. The results are shown in Figures 24–31 and 24–32.

Listing 24.25 `MoldSimulation.html`

```
<!DOCTYPE HTML PUBLIC "-//W3C//DTD HTML 4.0 Transitional//EN">
<HTML>
<HEAD>
  <TITLE>Mold Propagation Simulation</TITLE>

<SCRIPT TYPE="text/javascript">
<!--

// Start simulation for all applets in document.

function startCircles() {
  for(var i=0; i<document.applets.length; i++) {
    document.applets[i].startCircles();
  }
}

// Stop simulation for all applets in document.

function stopCircles() {
  for(var i=0; i<document.applets.length; i++) {
    document.applets[i].stopCircles();
  }
}

// -->
</SCRIPT>
</HEAD>
<BODY BGCOLOR="#C0C0C0">
<H1>Mold Propagation Simulation</H1>

<APPLET CODE="RandomCircles.class" WIDTH=100 HEIGHT=75>
</APPLET>
<P>
<APPLET CODE="RandomCircles.class" WIDTH=300 HEIGHT=75>
</APPLET>
<P>
<APPLET CODE="RandomCircles.class" WIDTH=500 HEIGHT=75>
</APPLET>
```

(continued)

Listing 24.25 `MoldSimulation.html` *(continued)*

```
<FORM>
<INPUT TYPE="BUTTON" VALUE="Start Simulations"
       onClick="startCircles()">
<INPUT TYPE="BUTTON" VALUE="Stop Simulations"
       onClick="stopCircles()">
</FORM>

</BODY>
</HTML>
```

Listing 24.26 `RandomCircles.java`

```java
import java.applet.Applet;
import java.awt.*;

/** Draw random circles in a background thread.
 *  Needs an external event to start/stop drawing.
 */

public class RandomCircles extends Applet
                           implements Runnable {
  private boolean drawCircles = false;

  public void init() {
    setBackground(Color.white);
  }

  public void startCircles() {
    Thread t = new Thread(this);
    t.start();
  }

  public void run() {
    Color[] colors = { Color.lightGray, Color.gray,
                       Color.darkGray, Color.black };
    int colorIndex = 0;
    int x, y;
    int width = getSize().width;
    int height = getSize().height;

    Graphics g = getGraphics();
    drawCircles = true;
```

(continued)

Listing 24.26 RandomCircles.java *(continued)*

```
    while(drawCircles) {
      x = (int)Math.round(width * Math.random());
      y = (int)Math.round(height * Math.random());
      g.setColor(colors[colorIndex]);
      colorIndex = (colorIndex + 1) % colors.length;
      g.fillOval(x, y, 10, 10);
      pause(0.1);
    }
  }

  public void stopCircles() {
    drawCircles = false;
  }

  private void pause(double seconds) {
    try {
      Thread.sleep((int)(Math.round(seconds * 1000.0)));
    } catch(InterruptedException ie) {}
  }
}
```

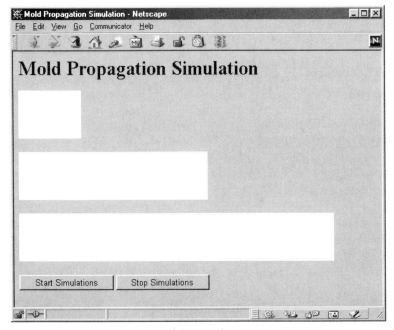

Figure 24–31 Initially, none of the simulations are running.

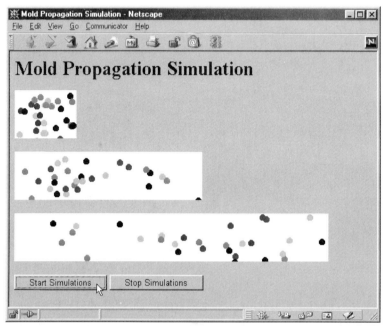

Figure 24–32 All three applet simulations can be controlled from a single HTML button. Adding additional applets does not require any changes to the Java or JavaScript code.

24.10 Accessing JavaScript from Java

Not only does LiveConnect let you call Java methods and control applets from JavaScript, but it also lets applets access JavaScript. The `netscape.java-script.JSObject` class lets you use Java syntax to access all JavaScript objects, read and set all available properties, and call any legal method. Furthermore, you can use the `eval` method to invoke arbitrary JavaScript code when doing so is easier than using Java syntax. This process involves seven steps, as follows:

1. Obtain and install the `JSObject` class.
2. Import the class in your applet.
3. From the applet, obtain a JavaScript reference to the current window.
4. Read the JavaScript properties of interest.
5. Set the JavaScript properties of interest.
6. Call the JavaScript methods of interest.
7. Give the applet permission to access its Web page.

Following are some details on these steps.

Obtain and install the JSObject class

The JSObject class is provided by Netscape 4, compressed in JAR file titled java40. The location of this file will vary among operating systems. On Windows 98, it should be in

```
NetscapeInstallPath\Program\Java\Classes\
```

Use Find from your Start menu if you have trouble finding the file. On Unix, this file will generally be in the Netscape installation directory. If you cannot find it, try the following:

```
Unix> cd /usr/local
Unix> find . -name java40 -print
```

Once you have this file, simply add it to the end of your CLASSPATH; the Java compiler knows how to look inside JAR files already. If you do this, be sure to unset CLASSPATH before trying to use appletviewer; it will not function properly otherwise. In fact, since both Netscape and Internet Explorer grant special privileges to classes that appear in the CLASSPATH, it is best to unset the CLASSPATH before starting any browser. If you prefer, you can decompress the JAR file from the command line, jar xf java40.jar, extract the JSObject.class file, and install it separately. You will *need* to do this if you develop and compile your code on a system that does not have Netscape installed. In addition, you should probably include the JSObject class file with your applets, since the client may be using a different browser vendor and version.

Import JSObject in your applet

At the top of your applet code, add the line:

```
import netscape.javascript.JSObject;
```

From the applet, obtain a JavaScript reference to the current window

Use the static getWindow method of JSObject to obtain a reference to the window containing the applet.

```
JSObject window =
   JSObject.getWindow(this); // this=applet
```

A complete list of the available methods in the JSObject class is given at the end of this section.

Read the JavaScript properties of interest

Use the getMember method to read properties of the main JavaScript window. Then, use getMember on the results to access properties of other JavaScript objects. For example,

```
JSObject document =
  (JSObject)window.getMember("document");
String cookies =
  (String)document.cookie;
JSObject someForm =
  (JSObject)document.getMember("someFormName");
JSObject someElement =
  (JSObject)someForm.getMember("someElementName");
```

You can also use `getSlot` with an index to access elements of an array.

Set the JavaScript properties of interest

Use the `setMember` method for this step. For example,

```
document.setMember("bgColor", "red");
someElement.setMember("value", "textfield value");
```

Note that the second argument to `setMember` must be a Java `Object`, so primitive objects must be converted to their corresponding wrapper type before being passed. Thus, an `int` named `intValue` must be turned into an `Integer` through `new Integer(intValue)` before being assigned to a property expecting an integer. An alternative is to construct a string corresponding to the assignment in JavaScript, then pass that string to `eval` (see below).

Call the JavaScript methods of interest

You call JavaScript methods either by using the `call` method or by constructing a JavaScript expression containing the method calls and passing it to `eval`. The `call` method takes the method name and an array of arguments; `eval` takes a single string. For instance,

```
String[] message = { "An alert message" };
window.call("alert", message);
window.eval("alert('An alert message')");
```

Give the applet permission to access its Web page

To prevent Web page authors from accidentally using applets that read or modify their pages (perhaps reporting results over the network), the Web page author must explicitly give the applet permission to access the page. Access is granted through the `MAYSCRIPT` attribute of the `APPLET` element. For example,

```
<APPLET CODE=... WIDTH=... HEIGHT=... MAYSCRIPT>
   ...
</APPLET>
```

Example: Matching Applet Background with Web Page

One of the problems with writing general-purpose applets is that they don't have access to the background color of the Web page that contains them, so they can't adapt their color to match. A common solution is to supply the background color as a PARAM entry, but this has the drawback that the color has to be repeated (once in the BODY tag, and again in the PARAM), risking inconsistency if one is updated without the other. With LiveConnect, the applet can read the background color from the Document object and set its color automatically. Listings 24.27 and 24.28 give an example.

Listing 24.27 `MatchColor.java`

```java
import java.applet.Applet;
import java.awt.*;
import netscape.javascript.JSObject;

public class MatchColor extends Applet {
  public void init() {
    JSObject window = JSObject.getWindow(this); // this=applet
    JSObject document = (JSObject)window.getMember("document");
    // E.g., "#ff0000" for red
    String pageColor = (String)document.getMember("bgColor");
    // E.g., parseInt("ff0000", 16) --> 16711680
    int bgColor =
          Integer.parseInt(pageColor.substring(1, 7), 16);
    setBackground(new Color(bgColor));
  }
}
```

Listing 24.28 `MatchColor.html`

```html
<!DOCTYPE HTML PUBLIC "-//W3C//DTD HTML 4.0 Transitional//EN">
<HTML>
<HEAD>
  <TITLE>MatchColor</TITLE>
</HEAD>
<BODY BGCOLOR="RED">
<H1>MatchColor</H1>
<APPLET CODE="MatchColor.class" WIDTH=300 HEIGHT=300 MAYSCRIPT>
</APPLET>
</BODY>
</HTML>
```

Example: An Applet That Controls HTML Form Values

For a more extensive example, Listing 24.29 creates a page that lets users select mountain climbing trips based upon two criteria: the altitude they want to attain and the budget they want to stay within. On any platform, users can enter these two values directly in the HTML form and submit them to get information on available options. Moving the cost slider changes the value displayed in the HTML form; moving the mouse up and down the mountain changes the value displayed in the altitude form. Figure 24–33 shows the result after the user drags the slider and moves the mouse partway up the mountain.

Listing 24.29 `Everest.html`

```
<!DOCTYPE HTML PUBLIC "-//W3C//DTD HTML 4.0 Transitional//EN">
<HTML>
<HEAD>
  <TITLE>Design Your Trek!</TITLE>
</HEAD>
<BODY>

<APPLET CODE="Everest.class" WIDTH=400 HEIGHT=600
        MAYSCRIPT ALIGN="LEFT">
</APPLET>

<H1 ALIGN="CENTER">Design Your Trek!</H1>
To see a listing of the treks that interest you, enter the
desired altitude (up to 29,000 feet) and the maximum cost you
think your budget can afford. Then choose "Show Treks" below.
We'll show a list of all planned High Peaks Travel expeditions
that are under that price and reach the desired altitude or
higher.
<P>
You can enter values directly in the textfields. Alternatively,
select a cost with the slider. Also, clicking the mouse on the
mountain peak will set the altitude.
<CENTER>
<FORM ACTION="servlet/trekOptions"  NAME="highPeaksForm">
<B>Desired Altitude:</B>
<INPUT TYPE="TEXT" NAME="altitudeField">
<BR>
<B>Maximum Cost:</B>
<INPUT TYPE="TEXT" NAME="costField">
<BR>
<INPUT TYPE="SUBMIT" VALUE="Show Treks">
</FORM>
</CENTER>
</BODY>
</HTML>
```

Listing 24.30 Everest.java

```java
import java.applet.Applet;
import java.awt.*;
import java.awt.event.*;
import netscape.javascript.JSObject;

/** An applet that draws a mountain image and displays
 *  a slider. Dragging the slider changes a textfield
 *  in the HTML file containing the applet. Moving the
 *  mouse over the image changes another textfield in the
 *  containing HTML file, using an altitude value
 *  where the bottom of the applet corresponds to 0
 *  and the top to 29000 feet. This requires
 *  an HTML file with a form named "highPeaksForm"
 *  containing two textfields: one named "costField"
 *  and one named "altitudeField". It also requires use
 *  of the MAYSCRIPT tag in the <APPLET ...> declaration.
 */

public class Everest extends Applet {
  private Image mountain;
  private JSObject window, document, highPeaksForm,
          costField, altitudeField;
  private int width, height;

  public void init() {
    setBackground(Color.lightGray);
    mountain = getImage(getCodeBase(), "images/peak5.gif");
    width = getSize().width;
    height = getSize().height;
    // Start image loading immediately.
    prepareImage(mountain, width, height, this);
    setLayout(new BorderLayout());
    Font sliderFont = new Font("Helvetica", Font.BOLD, 18);
    LabeledCostSlider costSlider =
      new LabeledCostSlider("Specify a maximum cost:",
                            sliderFont, 2000, 20000, 5000,
                            this);
    add(costSlider, BorderLayout.SOUTH);
    addMouseMotionListener(new MouseMotionAdapter() {
      // When user moves the mouse, scale the y value
      // from 29000 (top) to 0 (bottom) and send it
      // to external textfield through JavaScript.
```

(continued)

Listing 24.30 Everest.java *(continued)*

```java
        public void mouseMoved(MouseEvent event) {
          System.out.println("Mouse Move at : " + event.getY());
          setAltitudeField((height - event.getY()) * 29000 / height);
        }
      });

      // Get references to HTML textfields through JavaScript.
      window = JSObject.getWindow(this); // this=applet
      document = (JSObject)window.getMember("document");
      highPeaksForm =
        (JSObject)document.getMember("highPeaksForm");
      costField =
        (JSObject)highPeaksForm.getMember("costField");
      altitudeField =
        (JSObject)highPeaksForm.getMember("altitudeField");
      setCostField(5000);
      setAltitudeField(15000);
    }

    public void paint(Graphics g) {
      g.drawImage(mountain, 0, 0, width, height, this);
    }

    /** Change textfield through JavaScript. */

    public void setCostField(int val) {
      costField.setMember("value", String.valueOf(val));
    }

    /** Change textfield through JavaScript. */

    private void setAltitudeField(int val) {
      altitudeField.setMember("value", String.valueOf(val));
    }
  }
```

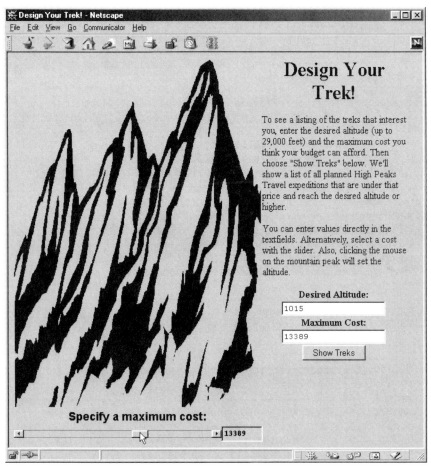

Figure 24–33 Moving the mouse over the image or dragging the slider changes the values in the HTML textfields.

The Everest applet makes use of a `LabeledCostSlider` (shown in the bottom-left region of Figure 24–33) to provide a custom slider with a text label above the slider. The `LabeledCostSlider` source is shown in Listing 24.31. The custom slider, `CostSlider` (Listing 24.32), extends `Slider`, Listing 24.33, and updates the value in the cost field whenever the thumbnail of the slider is adjusted. The `Slider` class combines a horizontal `Scrollbar` and a `TextField` (to the right of the scrollbar) grouped together by a `ScrollbarPanel`, Listing 24.34.

Listing 24.31 `LabeledCostSlider.java`

```java
import java.awt.*;

/** A CostSlider with a label centered above it. */

public class LabeledCostSlider extends Panel {
  public LabeledCostSlider(String labelString,
                           Font labelFont,
                           int minValue, int maxValue,
                           int initialValue,
                           Everest app) {
    setLayout(new BorderLayout());
    Label label = new Label(labelString, Label.CENTER);
    if (labelFont != null) {
      label.setFont(labelFont);
    }
    add(label, BorderLayout.NORTH);
    CostSlider slider = new CostSlider(minValue,
                                       maxValue,
                                       initialValue,
                                       app);
    add(slider, BorderLayout.CENTER);
  }
}
```

Listing 24.32 `CostSlider.java`

```java
/** A Slider that takes an Everest applet as an argument,
 *  calling back to its setCostField when the slider value
 *  changes.
 */

public class CostSlider extends Slider {
  private Everest app;

  public CostSlider(int minValue, int maxValue,
                    int initialValue, Everest app) {
    super(minValue, maxValue, initialValue);
    this.app = app;
  }

  public void doAction(int value) {
    app.setCostField(value);
  }
}
```

Listing 24.33 `Slider.java`

```java
import java.awt.*;
import java.awt.event.*;

/** A class that combines a horizontal Scrollbar and a TextField
 *  (to the right of the Scrollbar). The TextField shows the
 *  current scrollbar value, plus, if setEditable(true) is set,
 *  it can be used to change the value as well.
 */

public class Slider extends Panel implements ActionListener,
                                             AdjustmentListener {
  private Scrollbar scrollbar;
  private TextField textfield;
  private ScrollbarPanel scrollbarPanel;
  private int preferredWidth = 250;

  /** Construct a slider with the specified min, max and initial
   *  values. The "bubble" (thumb) size is set to 1/10th the
   *  scrollbar range.
   */

  public Slider(int minValue, int maxValue, int initialValue) {
    this(minValue, maxValue, initialValue,
         (maxValue - minValue)/10);
  }

  /** Construct a slider with the specified min, max,and initial
   *  values, plus the specified "bubble" (thumb) value. This
   *  bubbleSize should be specified in the units that min and
   *  max use, not in pixels. Thus, if min is 20 and max is 320,
   *  then a bubbleSize of 30 is 10% of the visible range.
   */

  public Slider(int minValue, int maxValue, int initialValue,
                int bubbleSize) {
    setLayout(new BorderLayout());
    maxValue = maxValue + bubbleSize;
    scrollbar = new Scrollbar(Scrollbar.HORIZONTAL,
                              initialValue, bubbleSize,
                              minValue, maxValue);
    scrollbar.addAdjustmentListener(this);
    scrollbarPanel = new ScrollbarPanel(6);
    scrollbarPanel.add(scrollbar, BorderLayout.CENTER);
    add(scrollbarPanel, BorderLayout.CENTER);
    textfield = new TextField(numDigits(maxValue) + 1);
```

(continued)

Listing 24.33 `Slider.java` *(continued)*

```java
    textfield.addActionListener(this);
    setFontSize(12);
    textfield.setEditable(false);
    setTextFieldValue();
    add(textfield, BorderLayout.EAST);
  }

  /** A placeholder to override for action to be taken when
   *  scrollbar changes.
   */

  public void doAction(int value) {
  }

  /** When textfield changes, sets the scrollbar */

  public void actionPerformed(ActionEvent event) {
    String value = textfield.getText();
    int oldValue = getValue();
    try {
      setValue(Integer.parseInt(value.trim()));
    } catch(NumberFormatException nfe) {
      setValue(oldValue);
    }
  }

  /** When scrollbar changes, sets the textfield */

  public void adjustmentValueChanged(AdjustmentEvent event) {
    setTextFieldValue();
    doAction(scrollbar.getValue());
  }

  /** Returns the Scrollbar part of the Slider. */

  public Scrollbar getScrollbar() {
    return(scrollbar);
  }

  /** Returns the TextField part of the Slider */

  public TextField getTextField() {
    return(textfield);
  }
```

(continued)

Listing 24.33 `Slider.java` *(continued)*

```
/** Changes the preferredSize to take a minimum width, since
 *  super-tiny scrollbars are hard to manipulate.
 */

public Dimension getPreferredSize() {
  Dimension d = super.getPreferredSize();
  d.height = textfield.getPreferredSize().height;
  d.width = Math.max(d.width, preferredWidth);
  return(d);
}

/** This just calls preferredSize */

public Dimension getMinimumSize() {
  return(getPreferredSize());
}

/** To keep scrollbars legible, a minimum width is set. This
 *  returns the current value (default is 150).
 */

public int getPreferredWidth() {
  return(preferredWidth);
}

/** To keep scrollbars legible, a minimum width is set. This
 *  sets the current value (default is 150).
 */

public void setPreferredWidth(int preferredWidth) {
  this.preferredWidth = preferredWidth;
}

/** This returns the current scrollbar value */

public int getValue() {
  return(scrollbar.getValue());
}

/** This assigns the scrollbar value. If it is below the
 *  minimum value or above the maximum, the value is set to
 *  the min and max value, respectively.
 */
```

(continued)

Listing 24.33 `Slider.java` *(continued)*

```java
public void setValue(int value) {
  scrollbar.setValue(value);
  setTextFieldValue();
}

/** Sometimes horizontal scrollbars look odd if they are very
 *  tall. So empty top/bottom margins can be set. This returns
 *  the margin setting. The default is four.
 */

public int getMargins() {
  return(scrollbarPanel.getMargins());
}

/** Sometimes horizontal scrollbars look odd if they are very
 *  tall. So empty top/bottom margins can be set. This sets
 *  the margin setting.
 */

public void setMargins(int margins) {
  scrollbarPanel.setMargins(margins);
}

/** Returns the current textfield string. In most cases this
 *  is just the same as a String version of getValue, except
 *  that there may be padded blank spaces at the left.
 */

public String getText() {
  return(textfield.getText());
}

/** This sets the TextField value directly. Use with extreme
 *  caution since it does not right-align or check whether
 *  value is numeric.
 */

public void setText(String text) {
  textfield.setText(text);
}

/** Returns the Font being used by the textfield.
 *  Courier bold 12 is the default.
 */
```

(continued)

Listing 24.33 Slider.java *(continued)*

```java
public Font getFont() {
  return(textfield.getFont());
}

/** Changes the Font being used by the textfield. */

public void setFont(Font textFieldFont) {
  textfield.setFont(textFieldFont);
}

/** The size of the current font */

public int getFontSize() {
  return(getFont().getSize());
}

/** Rather than setting the whole font, you can just set the
 *  size (Monospaced bold will be used for the family/face).
 */

public void setFontSize(int size) {
  setFont(new Font("Monospaced", Font.BOLD, size));
}

/** Determines if the textfield is editable. If it is, you can
 *  enter a number to change the scrollbar value. In such a
 *  case, entering a value outside the legal range results in
 *  the min or max legal value. A noninteger is ignored.
 */

public boolean isEditable() {
  return(textfield.isEditable());
}

/** Determines if you can enter values directly into the
 *  textfield to change the scrollbar.
 */

public void setEditable(boolean editable) {
  textfield.setEditable(editable);
}
```

(continued)

Listing 24.33 `Slider.java` *(continued)*

```java
  // Sets a right-aligned textfield number.

  private void setTextFieldValue() {
    int value = scrollbar.getValue();
    int digits = numDigits(scrollbar.getMaximum());
    String valueString = padString(value, digits);
    textfield.setText(valueString);
  }

  // Repeated String concatenation is expensive, but this is
  // only used to add a small amount of padding, so converting
  // to a StringBuffer would not pay off.

  private String padString(int value, int digits) {
    String result = String.valueOf(value);
    for(int i=result.length(); i<digits; i++) {
      result = " " + result;
    }
    return(result + " ");
  }

  // Determines the number of digits in a decimal number.

  private static final double LN10 = Math.log(10.0);

  private static int numDigits(int num) {
    return(1 + (int)Math.floor(Math.log((double)num)/LN10));
  }
}
```

Listing 24.34 `ScrollbarPanel.java`

```java
import java.awt.*;

/** A Panel with adjustable top/bottom insets value.
 *  Used to hold a Scrollbar in the Slider class
 */

public class ScrollbarPanel extends Panel {
  private Insets insets;
```

(continued)

Listing 24.34 `ScrollbarPanel.java` *(continued)*

```
  public ScrollbarPanel(int margins) {
    setLayout(new BorderLayout());
    setMargins(margins);
  }

  public Insets insets() {
    return(insets);
  }

  public int getMargins() {
    return(insets.top);
  }

  public void setMargins(int margins) {
    this.insets = new Insets(margins, 0, margins, 0);
  }
}
```

Methods in the JSObject Class

The following methods are available as part of JSObject. JSObject is final, so it cannot be subclassed.

public Object call(String methodName, Object[ ] args)
This method lets you call the JavaScript method of the specified name.

public Object eval(String javaScriptCode)
This method lets you evaluate an arbitrary JavaScript expression.

public Object getMember(String propertyName)
This method returns a property value. Cast the result to the appropriate type.

public Object getSlot(int arrayIndex)
This method returns an array value. Cast the result to the appropriate type.

public static JSObject getWindow(Applet applet)
This *static* method retrieves the JavaScript Window corresponding to the one holding the applet.

public void removeMember(String propertyName)
This method deletes a property.

public void setMember(String propertyName, Object value)
This method assigns a value to the specified property.

public void setSlot(int arrayIndex, Object value)
This method places a value in the specified location in the array.

24.11 Summary

This chapter introduced JavaScript and gave examples of the main ways in which JavaScript can be applied to do the following:

- Customize Web pages based on the situation
- Make pages more dynamic
- Validate HTML form input
- Manipulate cookies
- Control frames
- Integrate Java and JavaScript

This chapter did not, however, give a complete description of Window, Document, Navigator and other standard classes in JavaScript 1.2. The Quick Reference given in the next chapter provides a description of the constructors, properties, and methods for the JavaScript objects.

JAVASCRIPT QUICK REFERENCE

Topics in This Chapter

- Objects corresponding to the browser and its environment: Navigator, Plugin, Screen, and similar high-level objects

- Objects corresponding to HTML elements: Window, Document, Layer, Image, and similar objects directly associated with specific markup elements

- Objects corresponding to HTML forms and input elements: Form, Text, Button, Select, and similar objects used in CGI input forms

- Internal data structures: String, Array, Function, Math, Date, and similar utility libraries

- Regular expressions: RegExp

Chapter 25

The previous chapter introduced JavaScript and gave examples of its use. This chapter provides a quick description of the core and client-side JavaScript 1.2 constructors, properties, methods, and event handlers. JavaScript 1.2 is supported in all Netscape and Internet Explorer versions 4.0 and greater. For specifics on later versions of JavaScript, see `http://developer.netscape.com/docs/manuals/javascript.html`.

25.1 The Array Object

In the first version of JavaScript, an array was implemented as a JavaScript object containing multiple property settings. Later, in JavaScript 1.1, an array was implemented as a separate `Array` object.

Constructors

new Array()
This constructor builds a new zero-length array. Adding an element to a specified index automatically changes the length. For example,

```
var a = new Array();              // a.length = 0
a[12] = "foo";                    // a.length = 13
```

new Array(length)

This constructor builds an array with indices from 0 to length-1. All the values will initially be null.

Note that this constructor is not properly recognized in Netscape's implementation of JavaScript 1.2 (Internet Explorer is fine); in Netscape this constructor produces an array with a single element where the value of the element is the constructor parameter. This Netscape problem is resolved in JavaScript 1.3.

new Array(entry0, entry1, ... , entryN)

This constructor creates an array of length N containing the specified elements.

[entry0, entry1, ... , entryN]

This constructor lets you create arrays by using a "literal" notation. For example, the following two statements create equivalent arrays.

```
var a1 = new Array("foo", "bar", "baz");
var a2 = [ "foo", "bar", "baz" ];
```

Properties

length

This property gives the number of elements in the array. It is 1 greater than the index of the last element and is read/write. If you set length smaller, array elements beyond that point are lost. If you set length bigger, array elements beyond the old length have the special undefined value (which compares == to null).

Methods

concat(secondArray)

This method returns a new array it forms by concatenating the current array with the specified array.

join()
join(delimiterString)

The first method returns a single large string it makes by converting all the array elements to strings and then concatenating the results. The second method is similar except that it inserts the delimiter string between each element (but not at the beginning or end).

reverse()

This method changes the existing array so that the elements now appear in the opposite order. It does *not* create a new array.

slice(startIndex)
slice(startIndex, endIndex)

This method returns a new array formed by extracting the elements from startIndex (inclusive) to endIndex (exclusive).

sort()
sort(comparisonFunction)

The first, i.e., no argument, method puts the array in alphabetical order without creating a new array. The second method puts the array in the order specified by the comparison function. This function should take two array elements as arguments, returning a negative number if the arguments are in order (the first is "less" than the second), zero if they are in order and would also be if they are swapped (the first is "equal to" the second in sorting value), and a positive number if they are out of order (the second is "less" than the first). For example, here is a comparison function that takes two Car objects and compares their maxSpeed properties.

```
function slower(car1, car2) {     .
   return(car1.maxSpeed - car2.maxSpeed);
}
```

Listing 25.1 uses this approach to create an array of Car objects and then sorts the array based on their maxSpeed property. Figure 25–1 shows the result.

Listing 25.1 `Sort.html`

```
<!DOCTYPE HTML PUBLIC "-//W3C//DTD HTML 4.0//EN">
<HTML>
<HEAD>
  <TITLE>Sorting</TITLE>

<SCRIPT TYPE="text/javascript">
<!--

function makeObjectTable(name, object) {
  document.writeln("<H2>" + name + "</H2>");
  document.writeln("<TABLE BORDER=1>\n" +
                   "  <TR><TH>Field<TH>Value");
  for(field in object) {
    document.writeln("  <TR><TD>" + field + "<TD>" +
                     object[field]);
  }
  document.writeln("</TABLE>");
}
```

(continued)

Listing 25.1 `Sort.html` *(continued)*

```
// -->
</SCRIPT>
</HEAD>
<BODY>
<H1>Sorting</H1>

<SCRIPT TYPE="text/javascript">
<!--

function carString() {
  return("Car{" + this.maxSpeed + "}");
}

function Car(maxSpeed) {
  this.maxSpeed = maxSpeed;
  this.toString = carString;
}

function slower(car1, car2) {
  return(car1.maxSpeed - car2.maxSpeed);
}

var cars = new Array(new Car(10), new Car(20),
                     new Car(30), new Car(25),
                     new Car(15), new Car(5));
// -->
</SCRIPT>

<TABLE>
  <TR><TD>
      <SCRIPT TYPE="text/javascript">
          <!--
          makeObjectTable("Original Car Array", cars);
          // -->
          </SCRIPT>
      <TD><PRE>            </PRE>
      <TD><SCRIPT TYPE="text/javascript">
          <!--
          cars.sort(slower);
          makeObjectTable("Sorted Array (slow to fast)", cars);
          // -->
          </SCRIPT>
</TABLE>

</BODY>
</HTML>
```

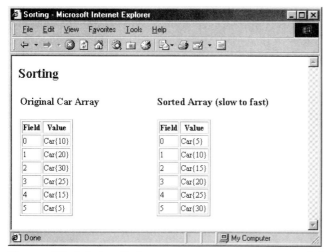

Figure 25-1 In JavaScript you can sort arrays with user-defined ordering functions.

Event Handlers

None.

25.2 The Button Object

The Button object corresponds to form elements created through `<INPUT TYPE="BUTTON" ...>`. Most of its characteristics are shared by elements created through `<INPUT TYPE="SUBMIT" ...>` and `<INPUT TYPE="RESET" ...>`.

However, SUBMIT and RESET buttons have more specific types: Submit and Reset, respectively. A Button is typically accessed either through the elements array of the corresponding Form or, if both the form and the button are named, through `document.formName.buttonName`.

Properties

form

This read-only property gives the Form object containing the button.

name

If the button used the NAME attribute, this read-only property retrieves it.

type
For pure Button objects, this property is always equal to button. For SUBMIT and RESET buttons, the type is submit and reset, respectively. All Element objects contain the type property, so it can be used to distinguish among the element types. The type property is read-only.

value
This read/write property gives the label of the button and, for SUBMIT buttons, is transmitted with the button name when the button is used to trigger form submission.

Methods

blur()
This method removes the keyboard focus from the button.

click()
This method acts as though the button was clicked, but it does not trigger the onClick handler. For SUBMIT and RESET buttons, you can use the form's submit and reset methods instead of click.

focus()
This method gives the keyboard focus to the button.

Event Handlers

onblur()
This method is called when the button loses the input focus; it is normally set through the onBlur attribute, as below.

```
<INPUT TYPE="BUTTON" ...
    onBlur="doSomeAction()">
```

onclick()
This method is called when the user clicks on the button, but not when the click method is called programmatically. It is normally set through the onClick attribute.

```
<INPUT TYPE="BUTTON" ...
    onClick="doSomeAction()">
```

If you return false from this method, then any additional action the button would trigger (i.e., submitting or resetting the form) is suppressed. For example,

```
<INPUT TYPE="RESET" ...
        onClick="return(maybeReset())">
```

The same effect can be achieved by the `onSubmit` and `onReset` handlers on the form containing the button.

ondblclick()

This method is called on the second click of a double click. The `onclick` handler, if any, will be called first. It is set by the `onDblClick` attribute. This method is not supported on the Macintosh or in Netscape 6.

onfocus()

This method is called when the button gains the input focus. It is normally set through the `onFocus` attribute.

25.3 The Checkbox Object

The `Checkbox` object corresponds to form elements created through `<INPUT TYPE="CHECKBOX" ...>`. A `Checkbox` is typically accessed either through the `elements` array of the corresponding `Form` or, if both the form and the check box are named, through `document.formName.checkboxName`.

Properties

checked

This `Boolean` property specifies whether the box is currently checked. It is read/write.

defaultChecked

This property is a `Boolean` specifying whether the box should be initially set. It is set through the `CHECKED` attribute and is read-only.

form

This read-only property refers to the `Form` object containing the checkbox.

name

This read-only property gives the name of the check box as given in the `NAME` attribute.

type

This property contains the string `checkbox`. Since all `Element` objects have this property, it can be used to differentiate among them when the `form.elements` array is looked at. This property is read-only.

value

This read/write property gives the value that is sent with the name to the CGI program if the form is submitted when the box is checked.

Methods

blur()

This method removes the keyboard focus from the check box.

click()

This method acts as though the check box was clicked, but it does not trigger the `onClick` handler.

focus()

This method gives the keyboard focus to the check box.

Event Handlers

onblur()

This method is called when the check box loses the input focus. It is normally set through the `onBlur` attribute, as below.

```
<INPUT TYPE="CHECKBOX" ...
      onBlur="doSomeAction()">
```

onclick()

This method is called when the user clicks on the check box, but not when the `click` method is called programmatically. It is usually specified through the `onClick` attribute of the input element.

onfocus()

This method is called when the check box gains the input focus. It is normally set through the `onFocus` attribute.

25.4 The Date Object

The Date object creates and manipulates dates and times.

Constructors

new Date()

This constructor creates a Date object for the current time.

new Date(year, month, day)

This constructor creates a Date object for midnight on the morning of the specified day.

new Date(year, month, day, hrs, mins, secs)

This constructor creates a Date object for the specified time.

new Date("month day, year hrs:mins:secs")

This constructor creates a Date object from the given string. The month should be the full name, not a number. For example,

```
var bDay = new Date("January 30, 1962 00:00:00");
```

new Date(millisecondsSinceEpoch)

This constructor creates a Date object for the time corresponding to the specified number of milliseconds after midnight (GMT) on January 1, 1970.

Properties

None.

Methods

Note that parseDate and UTC are not really methods of Date objects but instead act like static methods of the Date "class" (really constructor). They *must* be invoked as Date.parseDate and Date.UTC, respectively, never through an individual Date object. The other methods should be invoked through someDateObject.method(args).

getDate()
setDate(dayOfMonth)
These methods get and set the day of the month. The value is an integer from 1 to 31.

getDay()
This method returns the day of the week as an integer from 0 (Sunday) to 6 (Saturday).

getHours()
setHours(hours)
These methods get and set the hour of the day as an integer from 0 to 23.

getMinutes()
setMinutes(minutes)
The getMinutes method returns the number of minutes past the hour given in getHours. Similarly, the setMinutes sets the number of minutes past the hour, specified as an integer from 0 to 59.

getMonth()
setMonth(monthIndex)
These methods get and set the month of the year as an integer from 0 (January) to 11 (December).

getSeconds()
setSeconds(seconds)
These methods get and set the number of seconds past the minute given by getMinutes. The seconds value is an integer from 0 to 59.

getTime()
setTime(millisecondsSinceEpoch)
These methods get and set the number of milliseconds after midnight January 1, 1970, GMT.

getTimezoneOffset()
This method gives the difference in *minutes* between GMT and the local time.

getFullYear()
setFullYear(year)
The first method, getFullYear, returns the year of the Date object as a four-digit integer. The second method, setFullYear, sets the year to the Date object and returns the number of milliseconds since midnight January 1,

1970, GMT to the time specified in the `Date` object. Note that the `get-Year/setYear` methods introduced in JavaScript 1.0 are deprecated because the year was represented as a two-digit or a four-digit number, depending on the browser.

parse(dateString)

This method is not really a method of `Date` objects, but rather a method named `Date.parse`. It *must* be invoked that way, not on a `Date` object. It takes a string in any of a variety of formats as input and returns the corresponding number of milliseconds after midnight, January 1, 1970. It understands the standard IETF date formats used on the Internet (and generated by `toGMT-String`), so, for instance, the following generates "Wed Sep 03 11:30:00 1997" on systems on the U.S. East Coast, which is in EDT (minus 4 hours offset from GMT).

```
// US Pacific Time
var dateString = "Wed, 3 Sep 1997 08:30:00 -0700";
var d1 = new Date(Date.parse(dateString));
// US Eastern Time
document.writeln(d1.toLocaleString());
```

The `parse` method also understands strings of the form `"Month Day, Year"`, where the month is spelled out completely or the first three letters are used (upper or lower case). In the IETF format, you can also use U.S. time zone abbreviations (e.g., EDT) instead of numeric offsets.

toGMTString()

This method generates a string representing the date in GMT. It is formatted with IETF conventions; see `parse`.

toLocaleString()

This method generates a string representing the date in the local time zone. It is formatted with local conventions.

UTC(year, month, day)
UTC(year, month, day, hrs)
UTC(year, month, day, hrs, mins)
UTC(year, month, day, hrs, mins, secs)

Each method is not really a method of `Date` objects, but rather a method named `Date.UTC`. It *must* be invoked that way, not on a `Date` object. It assumes that the input parameters are in GMT (also called UTC—Universal Coordinated Time) and returns the number of milliseconds since midnight, Jan 1, 1970, GMT.

Event Handlers

None. `Date` does not correspond to an HTML element.

25.5 The Document Object

Each `Window` object contains a `document` property referring to the document contained in the window. The top-level document is obtained through `window.document` or, more commonly, simply by `document`.

Properties

alinkColor

This string specifies the color of activated links. It is initially set by the `ALINK` attribute of `BODY` and can only be modified by scripts that run in the `HEAD` of the document (which are parsed before the `BODY`). After that, it is read-only.

anchors

This property returns an array of `Anchor` objects, one for each occurrence of `<A NAME=...>` in the document.

applets

This is an array of `Applet` objects, one for each occurrence of `<APPLET ...>` in the document. If the `APPLET` tag includes a `MAYSCRIPT` attribute, you can call the applet's methods directly from JavaScript. See Section 24.9 (Accessing Java from JavaScript) for an example.

bgColor

This string specifies the background color of the document. It is initially set by the `BGCOLOR` attribute of `BODY` but is read/write (anytime, not just in the `HEAD`, as with other colors). For example,

```
document.bgColor = "red";
document.bgColor = "#00FF00"; // green
```

cookie

This string is the value of the cookie associated with the document. It is read/write; setting the value has the side effect of changing the cookie stored by the browser. For more details, see Section 24.7 (Using JavaScript to Store and Examine Cookies).

domain

This string specifies the Internet domain that the document came from. It is read-only. JavaScript provides no standard way to find the domain or hostname of the *client* system (the one currently viewing the page), but you can do this with a little help from Java. See Section 24.9 (Accessing Java from JavaScript).

embeds

This is an array of `JavaObject` objects corresponding to plug-in entries inside `EMBED` elements in the document. If the embedded object is not a Java-enabled plug-in, you cannot do anything with it, but if it is, you can call its public methods. Synonymous with the `plugins` array.

fgColor

This string specifies the foreground color of the document. It is initially set by the `TEXT` attribute of `BODY` and can only be modified by scripts that run in the `HEAD` of the document. After that, it is read-only.

forms

This is an array of `Form` objects, one for each occurrence of `<FORM ...>` in the document. See Section 25.8 for more on `Form`.

images

This is an array of `Image` objects, one for each occurrence of `<IMG ...>` in the document. See Section 24.5 (Using JavaScript to Make Pages Dynamic) for examples.

lastModified

This property gives the date of the most recent change to the document. Inserting this information near the top of the document is useful for readers who visit a page repeatedly, looking for new information. It is read-only.

linkColor

This string specifies the color of unvisited links. It is initially set through the `LINK` attribute of `BODY` and can only be modified by scripts that run in the `HEAD` of the document. After that, it is read-only.

links

This is an array of `Link` objects, one for each occurrence of `<A HREF...>` in the document.

location
This read-only property refers to the same Location object as window.location and contains the requested URL, which might have been redirected. The document.URL property contains the actual URL.

plugins
This property is a synonym for the embeds array. Note that the array contains objects of type JavaObject, not Plugin, and describes embedded plug-ins in the current document, not plug-ins available to the browser. Use navigator.plugins to get an array describing the available plug-ins.

referrer
This string, possibly empty, gives the URL of the document that contained the link to the current one. It is read-only.

title
This property gives the string specified through <TITLE>. It is read-only.

URL
This string gives the actual URL of the current document. It is read-only.

vlinkColor
This string specifies the color of visited hypertext links. It is initially set through the VLINK attribute of BODY and can only be modified by scripts that run in the HEAD of the document. After that, it is read-only.

Methods

close()
This method closes the output stream to the specified document, displaying any results that haven't already been displayed. It is used with open to build new documents.

getSelection()
This method gives the text, if any, contained in the selected area.

open()
open(mimeType)
open(mimeType, "replace")
This method creates a new document in the current window. The most common usage is simply to call open(), then use write and writeln to add the content. However, you can optionally specify a MIME type, as follows:

- `text/html`—for regular HTML; the default.
- `text/plain`—for ASCII text with newline characters to delimit lines.
- `image/gif`—for encoded bytes representing a GIF file.
- `image/jpg`—for encoded bytes representing a JPEG file.
- `image/x-bitmap`—for encoded bytes representing an X bitmap.
- *pluginName*—for loading into plug-ins. For instance, specify `x-world/vrml`. Future `write/writeln` calls go to the plug-in.

If `replace` is specified, the new document replaces the previous one in the history list. Otherwise, a new history entry is created.

write(arg1, arg2, ... , argN)
writeln(arg1, arg2, ... , argN)
These methods send output to the document, with or without a trailing newline character.

Event Handlers

Technically, `Document` has no event handlers; the `onLoad` and `onUnload` attributes of `BODY` set the `onload` and `onunload` event handlers of the `Window` object, not the `Document`.

25.6 The Element Object

The `Element` object corresponds to a form element and is contained in the `elements` array of the `Form` object. The `Form` objects are accessible through the `document.forms` array or, if named, by `document.formName`. Rather than treating elements of the elements array as `Element` objects, you are usually better off to treat them as `Button` objects, `Checkbox` objects, and so forth, based on their more specific types. In general, you should name objects and access them through their name.

Properties

The following only lists the more specific type of `Element` that uses these properties. See the sections describing those objects for details on the properties.

checked
This property is used by `Checkbox` and `Radio` objects.

defaultChecked
This property is used by `Checkbox` and `Radio` objects.

defaultValue
This property is used by `FileUpload`, `Password`, `Text`, and `Textarea` objects.

form
This property is used by all `Element` objects and refers to the HTML form containing the element.

length
This property is used only by `Select` objects.

name
This property is used by all `Element` objects and gives the value of the HTML `NAME` attribute.

options
This property is used only by `Select` objects.

selectedIndex
This property is used only by `Select` objects.

type
In JavaScript 1.1, this property is used by all `Element` objects and can be used to differentiate among element types. The value of this property is one of `button`, `checkbox`, `file`, `hidden`, `password`, `radio`, `reset`, `select-one`, `select-multiple`, `submit`, `text`, or `textarea`.

value
This property is used by all `Element` objects and gives the value that will be associated with the element's name when the form is submitted.

Methods

Again, the following lists only the more specific type of `Element` that uses these methods. See the sections describing those objects for more information on the methods.

blur()
This method is used by all `Element` types except `Hidden`.

click()

This method is used by `Button`, `Checkbox`, `Radio`, `Reset`, and `Submit` objects.

focus()

This method is used by all `Element` types except `Hidden`.

select()

This method is used by all elements that have textual values, namely, `FileUpload`, `Password`, `Text`, and `Textarea`.

Event Handlers

Again, the following only lists the more specific type of `Element` that uses these methods.

onblur()

This method is used by all `Element` types except `Hidden`.

onchange()

This method is used by `FileUpload`, `Password`, `Text`, `Textarea`, and `Select` objects.

onclick()

This method is used by `Button`, `Checkbox`, `Radio`, `Reset`, and `Submit` objects.

ondblclick

This method is used by `Button`, `Reset`, and `Submit`.

onfocus()

This method is used by all `Element` types except `Hidden`.

25.7 The FileUpload Object

The `FileUpload` object corresponds to form elements declared through `<INPUT TYPE="FILE" ...>`. Objects of this type are generally accessed through the `elements` array of the `Form` object.

Properties

form

This read-only property gives the `Form` object containing the element.

name

If the element used the `NAME` attribute, this property retrieves it. The property is read-only.

type

This read-only property is always equal to `file`. All `Element` objects contain this property, so it can be used to distinguish among the various types.

value

This property gives the string set in the `VALUE` attribute. It is read-only.

Methods

blur()

This method removes the keyboard focus from the element.

focus()

This method gives the keyboard focus to the element.

select()

This method selects the text in the element. Any user entry will replace the existing text.

Event Handlers

onblur()

This method is called when the element loses the input focus. It is normally set through the `onBlur` attribute, as follows:

```
<INPUT TYPE="FILE" ...
        onBlur="doSomeAction()">
```

onchange()

This method is called when the element loses the focus after its value has been changed. It is normally set through the `onChange` attribute.

onfocus()
This method, normally set through the onFocus attribute, is called when the element gains the input focus.

25.8 The Form Object

Form objects correspond to elements created with the HTML FORM element. They are normally accessed from the document.forms array or, if named, through document.formName.

Properties

action
This string specifies the URL to which the form should be submitted. It is read/write.

elements
This property is an array of Element objects corresponding to the input elements contained in the HTML form. See Section 25.6 for information on Element.

encoding
This string specifies the form's encoding method, as initially set by the ENCTYPE attribute. It is read/write.

method
This string is either get or post. It is initially set through the METHOD attribute but is read/write.

target
This string specifies the frame in which the form results should be displayed. It is initially set through the TARGET attribute but is read/write.

Methods

reset()
This method calls onreset and then, if the return value is not false, restores all input elements to the values originally specified in the document. The result is the same as if a RESET button was pressed.

submit()

This method submits the form *without* first calling `onsubmit`.

Event Handlers

onreset()

This method is called when the user presses a Reset button or the `reset` method is called. If `onReset` returns `false`, the form is not reset. It is normally specified through the `onReset` attribute, as follows:

```
<FORM ACTION="..." ...
      onReset="return(maybeReset())">
```

onsubmit()

This method is called when the user presses a Submit button. It is *not* automatically called by `submit`. If `onSubmit` returns `false`, the form is not submitted. It is normally specified through the `onSubmit` attribute, as follows:

```
<FORM ACTION="..." ...
      onSubmit="return(validateEntries())">
```

For an example, see Section 24.6 (Using JavaScript to Validate HTML Forms).

25.9 The Function Object

The `Function` object corresponds to a JavaScript function, not to any HTML element.

Constructor

new Function(arg0Name, ... , argNName, bodyString)

This constructor builds a new function. For instance, the following two forms have the same effect, but the second can be performed inside another routine at run time.

```
function square(x) { return(x * x); }
square = new Function("x", "return(x * x)");
```

Properties

arguments

From within the body of a function, this property gives an array of arguments used to call the function. Use this property to create variable-argument functions. For example, the following function adds any number of values together.

```
function sum() {
  var total = 0;
  for(var i=0; i<arguments.length; i++) {
    total = total + arguments[i];
  }
  return(total);
}
```

arity

This read-only property gives the number of declared arguments a function expects. This may be different from the number it is actually called with, which is given from within the body by the `length` property.

caller

From within the body of a function, this property gives the `Function` that called this one. The value is `null` if the function was called at the top level. It is read-only.

prototype

For constructors, this property defines properties that are shared by all objects of the specified type. For an example, see Section 24.3 (Mastering JavaScript Syntax).

Methods

None, other than those defined for every `Object`.

Event Handlers

None. `Function` does not correspond to an HTML element.

25.10 The Hidden Object

The HIDDEN object corresponds to elements created through <INPUT TYPE="HIDDEN" ...>. Objects of this type are usually accessed through the elements property of Form or, if both the form and the hidden element are named, through document.formName.elementName.

Properties

form
This read-only property refers to the Form object that holds this element.

name
This read-only property gives the name of the element, as specified by the NAME attribute.

type
This read-only property contains the value hidden.

value
This property gives the string that is sent along with the name when the form is submitted. It is read/write.

Methods

None.

Event Handlers

None.

25.11 The History Object

The HISTORY object corresponds to the current window or frame's list of previously visited URLs. It is accessible through the history property of Window, which can be accessed through window.history or just history.

Properties

current

In signed scripts you can read the URL of the current document. The property is a string and is read-only.

length

This read-only property gives the number of URLs contained in the history list.

next

This string specifies the URL of the next document in the history list. It is read-only and requires a signed script.

previous

This string specifies the URL of the next document in the history list. It is read-only and requires a signed script.

Methods

back()

This method instructs the browser to go back one entry in the history list.

forward()

This method instructs the browser to go forward one entry in the history list.

go(n)

This method instructs the browser to go *n* entries forward (if *n* is positive) or backward (if *n* is negative) in the history list.

Event Handlers

None. `History` does not correspond directly to an HTML element on the page.

25.12 The Image Object

The `Image` object corresponds to HTML elements inserted through `<IMG SRC="..." ...>`. An `Image` object is accessed through the `document.images` array or, if the image is named, through `document.imageName`. Manipulating images through JavaScript is an important capability; see Section 24.5 (Using Java-Script to Make Pages Dynamic) for examples.

Constructor

new Image(width, height)

This constructor allocates a new `Image` object of the specified size. The main purpose for an `Image` object is to then set its `src` property in order to preload images that are used later. In such an application, the `Image` object is never actually used after its `src` is set; the purpose is to get the *browser* to cache the image. See Section 24.5 (Using JavaScript to Make Pages Dynamic) for an example.

Properties

border

This property gives the size of the border around images that appear inside hypertext links. It is specified through the `BORDER` attribute of the `IMG` element. It is read-only.

complete

This is a `Boolean` that determines whether the image has finished loading. It is read-only.

height

This property gives the height of the image either as specified through the `HEIGHT` attribute (if present) or as it is in the actual image file. It is read-only.

hspace

This property gives the number of empty pixels on the left and right of the image as given in the `HSPACE` attribute. It is read-only.

lowsrc

Netscape (but not Internet Explorer) supports the nonstandard `LOWSRC` attribute in the `IMG` element, which gives an alternate image to show on low-resolution displays. This property gives that value (as a string). It is read/write.

name

This read-only property gives the name of the image as given by the `NAME` attribute.

src

This property gives a string representing the URL of the image file. It is read/write.

vspace

This read-only property gives the number of empty pixels on the top and bottom of the image as given in the VSPACE attribute.

width

This property gives the width of the image either as specified through the HEIGHT attribute (if present) or as it is in the actual image file. It is read-only.

Methods

None.

Event Handlers

onabort()

This method is called when the user halts image loading by pressing the Stop button or by clicking on a hypertext link to go to another page. It is normally specified through the onAbort attribute, as below.

```
<IMG SRC="..." ...
    onAbort="takeSomeAction()">
```

onerror()

This method is called when the image file cannot be found or is in illegal format. It is normally specified by the onError attribute, as follows:

```
<IMG SRC="..." ...
    onAbort="alert('Error loading image')">
```

Supplying a value of null suppresses error messages, as in this example.

```
<IMG SRC="..." ...
    onAbort="null">
```

onload()

This method is called when the browser *finishes* loading the image. Every time the src is changed, this method is called again. It is normally set through the onLoad attribute, as follows:

```
<IMG SRC="..." ...
    onLoad="startImageAnimation()">
```

In an example like this, the startImageAnimation would change the src to a new image (perhaps after a fixed pause), which, when done, would trigger startImageAnimation all over again.

25.13 The JavaObject Object

A JavaObject is a JavaScript representation of either a real Java object (an applet) or a plug-in from the document.embeds array that is treated as a Java object. This object has no predefined properties or methods, but you can use for/in to look at the specific properties of any particular JavaObject. This behavior, known as *reflection*, is also available in Java 1.1 and later.

25.14 The JavaPackage Object

Objects of the JavaPackage type are accessed through the java, netscape, sun, and Packages properties of Window. They are used to access Java objects; for instance, you can call java.lang.System.getProperty. For an example, see Section 24.9 (Accessing Java from JavaScript).

25.15 The Layer Object

Netscape 4.0 supports layered HTML: HTML in separate, possibly overlapping regions. Layers can be defined with the LAYER or ILAYER element or through cascading style sheets; see Section 5.12, (Layers). JavaScript can access and manipulate layers; see Section 24.5 (Using JavaScript to Make Pages Dynamic) for examples. However, note that in Netscape 6, to be compliant with the HTML 4.0 specification, LAYER and ILAYER elements are no longer supported.

Constructors

new Layer(width)
This constructor creates a new Layer object. You can specify its contents by setting the src property or by using the load method.

new Layer(width, parentLayer)
This constructor builds a layer that is a child of the one specified.

Properties

above
This read-only property specifies the layer above the current one.

background
This property specifies the image to use for the layer of the background. It is read/write. For example,

```
someLayer.background.src = "bricks.gif";
```

below
This property specifies the layer below the current one. It is read-only.

bgColor
Layers are normally transparent, but the `bgColor` property can make them opaque. It is read/write. For instance,

```
someLayer.bgColor = "blue";
anotherLayer.bgColor = "#FF00FF";
thirdLayer.bgColor = null; // transparent
```

clip
This property defines the clipping rectangle and is composed of `clip.top`, `clip.bottom`, `clip.left`, `clip.right`, `clip.width`, and `clip.height`. It is read/write.

document
Each layer contains its own `Document` object. This property references the document object and is read-only.

left
This property is the horizontal position of the layer with respect to the parent layer or, for floating layers, with respect to the natural document flow position. It is read/write.

name
This read-only property gives the layer name as specified through the `ID` or `NAME` attributes.

pageX
This property is the absolute horizontal position of the layer in the page. It is read/write.

pageY

This property is the absolute vertical position of the layer in the page. It is read/write.

parentLayer

This property returns the enclosing layer if there is one. Otherwise, it returns the enclosing `Window` object. It is read-only.

siblingAbove

Of the layers that share the same parent as the current one, this property refers to the layer directly above the current one. It is read-only.

siblingBelow

Of the layers that share the same parent as the current one, this property refers to the one directly below the current one. It is read-only.

src

This property gives a URL specifying the content of the layer. It is read/write.

top

This property is the vertical position of the layer with respect to the parent layer or, for floating layers, with respect to the natural document flow position. It is read/write.

visibility

This property determines the layer's visibility. Legal values are `show` (layer is visible), `hide` or `hidden` (layer is invisible), or `inherit` (use parent's visibility). It is read/write.

zIndex

This property specifies the stacking order relative to sibling layers. Lower numbers are underneath; higher numbers are on top. It is read/write.

Methods

load(sourceString, width)

This method changes the source of the layer while simultaneously changing its width. See the `src` property.

moveAbove(layer)

This method stacks the current layer above the one specified.

moveBelow(layer)

This method stacks the current layer below the one specified.

moveBy(dx, dy)

This method changes the layer's location by the specified number of pixels.

moveTo(x, y)

This method moves the layer so that its top-left corner is at the specified location in the containing layer or document. See the `left` and `top` properties.

moveToAbsolute(x, y)

This method moves the layer so that its top-left corner is at the specified location in the window. See the `pageX` and `pageY` properties.

resizeBy(dWidth, dHeight)

This method changes the layer's width and height by the specified number of pixels. See the `clip.width` and `clip.height` properties.

resizeTo(width, height)

This method changes the layer's width and height to the specified size in pixels. See the `clip.width` and `clip.height` properties.

Event Handlers

onblur()

This method is called when the layer loses the keyboard focus. It is specified through the `onBlur` attribute of `LAYER` or `ILAYER`. If the layer is created with style sheets, you set this behavior by directly assigning a function, as below.

```
function blurHandler() { ... }
someLayer.onblur = blurHandler;
```

onfocus()

This method is called when the layer gets the keyboard focus. It is normally specified by the `onFocus` attribute.

onload()

This method is called when the layer is loaded (which may be before it is displayed). The method is normally specified by the `onLoad` attribute.

onmouseout()
This method is called when the mouse moves off the layer. It is normally specified through the use of the onMouseOut attribute.

onmouseover()
This method is called when the mouse moves onto the layer. It is normally specified through the use of the onMouseOver attribute.

25.16 The Link Object

The Link object corresponds to a hypertext link created through <A HREF=...>. On non-Windows platforms, the AREA client-side image map element also results in Link objects. Links are normally accessed through the document.links array. You cannot name links through the NAME attribute, since using NAME inside an A element creates an anchor for internal hypertext links.

Properties

hash
This property gives the "section" part of the hypertext reference and includes the leading # (hash mark). It is read/write.

host
This property returns a string of the form hostname:port. It is read/write.

hostname
This property returns the hostname. It is read/write.

href
This property gives the complete URL. It is read/write.

pathname
This property gives the part of the URL that comes after the host and port. It is read/write.

port
This property is a *string* (not integer) specifying the port. It is read/write.

protocol

This property specifies the protocol. The colon is included as part of this property. It is read/write.

search

This property gives the search part (e.g., `"?x,y"` from an `ISMAP` entry) or query part (e.g., `"?x=1&y=2"` from a form submission) of the URL. It is read/write.

target

This property gives the name given as the value of the `TARGET` attribute. It is read/write. For instance, to redirect all hypertext links to a frame named `frame1`, you could do the following:

```
for(var i=0; i<document.links.length; i++) {
  document.links[i].target = "frame1";
}
```

Methods

None (other than the event handlers).

Event Handlers

onclick()

This method is called when the user clicks on the hypertext link. Returning `false` prevents the browser from following the link. It is normally specified through the `onClick` attribute, as follows:

```
<A HREF="..." ...
   onClick="return(maybeCancel())">
```

ondblclick()

This method is called on the second click of a double click. The `onclick` handler, if any, will be called first. It is set by the `onDblClick` attribute. This method is not supported on the Macintosh or in Netscape 6.

onmouseout()

This method is called when the user moves the mouse off the link. Combined with `onmouseover`, this provides a good method to highlight images under the mouse. For an example, see Section 24.5 (Using JavaScript to Make Pages Dynamic). It is normally specified by the `onMouseOut` attribute.

onmouseover()

This method is called when the user moves the mouse over a link. It is normally specified by using the onMouseOver attribute. If the method returns true, the browser does not display the associated URL in the status line. This behavior lets you use this method to display custom status-line messages.

25.17 The Location Object

The Location object corresponds to a window's current URL, as given in the window.location property.

Properties

hash

This property gives the "section" part of the hypertext reference and includes the leading # (hash mark). It is read/write.

host

This property returns a string of the form hostname:port. It is read/write.

hostname

This property returns the hostname. It is read/write.

href

This property gives the complete URL. It is read/write.

pathname

This property gives the part of the URL that came after the host and port. It is read/write.

port

This property is a *string* (not integer) specifying the port. It is read/write.

protocol

This property specifies the protocol. The colon is included as part of this property. It is read/write.

search

This property gives the search part (e.g., `"?x,y"` from an `ISMAP` entry) or query part (e.g., `"?x=1&y=2"` from a form submission) of the URL. It is read/write. You can use this property to implement self-processing "server"-side image maps or CGI forms by specifying the current document as the target URL and then checking `location.search` at the top of the document. See the `unescape` function, described in Section 25.31 (The String Object), for URL-decoding strings.

Methods

reload()
reload(true)

The first method reloads the document if the server reports it as having changed since last loaded. The second method always reloads the document.

replace(newURL)

This method replaces the current document with a new one (just like setting `location` to a new value), but without adding a new entry in the history list.

Event Handlers

None.

25.18 The Math Object

The `Math` object does not correspond to an HTML element but is used for basic arithmetic operations. It supports substantially the same methods as does the `java.lang.Math` class in Java. You never make a new `Math` object, but instead you access the properties and methods through `Math.propertyName` or `Math.methodName(...)`.

Properties

Using these constants is faster than recalculating them each time.

E

This is *e*, the base used for natural logarithms.

LN10
This is ln(10), that is, $\log_e(10)$.

LN2
This is ln(2), that is, $\log_e(2)$.

LOG10E
This is $\log_{10}(e)$.

LOG2E
This is lg(e), that is, $\log_2(e)$.

PI
This is π.

SQRT1_2
This is $\sqrt{1/2}$, that is, $1/\sqrt{2}$.

SQRT2
This is $\sqrt{2}$.

Methods

General-Purpose Methods

abs(num)
This method returns the absolute value of the specified number.

ceil(num)
This method returns the smallest integer greater than or equal to the specified number.

exp(num)
This method returns e^{num}.

floor(num)
This method returns the greatest integer less than or equal to num.

log(num)

This method returns the natural logarithm of the specified number. JavaScript does not provide a method to calculate logarithms using other common bases (e.g., 10 or 2), but following is a method that does this, using the relationship

$$\log_{b1}(n) = \frac{\log_{b2}(n)}{\log_{b2}(b1)}$$

```
function log(num, base) {
   return(Math.log(num) / Math.log(base));
}
```

max(num1, num2)

This method returns the larger of the two numbers.

min(num1, num2)

This method returns the smaller of the two numbers.

pow(base, exponent)

This method returns $base^{exponent}$.

random()

This method returns a random number from 0.0 (inclusive) to 1.0 (exclusive).

round(num)

This method rounds toward the nearest number, rounding up if *num* is of the form xxx.5.

sqrt(num)

This method returns the square root of *num*. Taking the square root of a negative number returns NaN.

Trigonometric Methods

All of these methods are in radians, not degrees. Convert degrees to radians with

```
function degreesToRadians(degrees) {
   return(degrees * Math.PI / 180);
}
```

acos(num)

This method returns the arc cosine of the specified value. The result is expressed *in radians*.

asin(num)

This method returns the arc sine of the specified number.

atan(num)

This method returns the arc tangent of the specified number.

atan2(y, x)

This method returns the θ part of the polar coordinate (r, θ) that corresponds to the Cartesian coordinate (x, y). This is the arc tangent of y/x that is in the range $-\pi$ to π.

cos(radians)

This method returns the cosine of the specified number, interpreted as a number in radians.

sin(radians)

This method returns the sine of the specified number.

tan(radians)

This method returns the tangent of the specified number.

Event Handlers

None. Math does not correspond to an HTML element.

25.19 The MimeType Object

The MimeType object describes a MIME type. The navigator.mimeTypes array lists all types supported by the browser, either directly by plug-ins or through external "helper" applications. For example, you could use code like the following to insert a link to an Adobe Acrobat file only if the current browser supports Acrobat; otherwise, you would use a plain text document.

```
document.writeln('For more information, see');
if (navigator.mimeTypes["application/pdf"] != null) {
  document.writeln
    ('<A HREF="manual.pdf">the widget manual</A>.');
} else {
  document.writeln
    ('<A HREF="manual.text">the widget manual</A>.');
}
```

For a list of common MIME types, see Table 19.1.

Properties

description
This read-only property gives a textual description of the type.

enabledPlugin
This property refers to the `Plugin` object that supports this MIME type if the plug-in is enabled. The property is `null` if no installed and enabled plug-in supports this type. It is read-only.

suffixes
This property gives a comma-separated list of the filename extensions that are assumed to be of this type. It is read-only.

type
This string is the type itself, e.g., `application/postscript`.

Methods

None.

Event Handlers

None. `MimeType` does not correspond directly to any HTML element.

25.20 The Navigator Object

The `Navigator` object provides information about the browser. It is available through the `navigator` property of `Window`; i.e., through `window.navigator` or simply `navigator`.

Properties

Following the property descriptions, Listing 25.2 shows a page that makes a table of several properties. Results are shown in Figures 25–2 and 25–3.

appCodeName
This property is intended to give the code name of the browser. Internet Explorer and Netscape use `Mozilla` for this property. It is read-only.

appName

This is the browser name, for example, Netscape or Microsoft Internet Explorer. It is read-only.

appVersion

This read-only property gives operating system and release number information.

language

This property gives the browser translation. For English versions, the property is en. It is read-only.

mimeTypes

This property is an array of MimeType objects supported by the browser either through plug-ins or helper applications. See Section 25.19 (The MimeType Object).

platform

This property gives the machine type for which the browser was compiled. For instance, on Windows 95, 98, and NT, the type is Win32. It is read-only.

plugins

This property is an array of Plugin objects supported by the browser. See Section 24.4 (Using JavaScript to Customize Web Pages) for an example of its use.

userAgent

This is the string sent by the browser to the server in the User-Agent HTTP request header. It is read-only.

Figures 25–2 and 25–3 show examples of some of these properties, based on a page generated from Listing 25.2.

Listing 25.2 Navigator.html

```
<!DOCTYPE HTML PUBLIC "-//W3C//DTD HTML 4.0 Transitional//EN">
<HTML>
<HEAD>
  <TITLE>The Navigator Object</TITLE>

<SCRIPT TYPE="text/javascript">
<!--
```

(continued)

Listing 25.2 `Navigator.html` *(continued)*

```
function makePropertyTable(name, object, propertyList) {
  document.writeln("<H2>" + name + "</H2>");
  document.writeln("<TABLE BORDER=1>\n" +
                   "  <TR><TH>Property<TH>Value");
  var propertyName;
  for(var i=0; i<propertyList.length; i++) {
    propertyName = propertyList[i];
    document.writeln("  <TR><TD>" + propertyName +
                     "<TD>" + object[propertyName]);
  }
  document.writeln("</TABLE>");
}

// -->
</SCRIPT>
</HEAD>

<BODY BGCOLOR="WHITE">

<SCRIPT TYPE="text/javascript">
<!--

var propNames = new Array("appCodeName", "appName",
                          "appVersion", "userAgent");
makePropertyTable("The Navigator Object", navigator, propNames);

// -->
</SCRIPT>

</BODY>
</HTML>
```

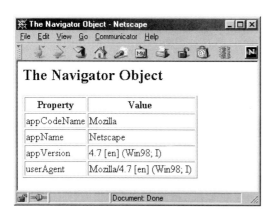

Figure 25–2 Navigator properties in Netscape 4.7 on Windows 98.

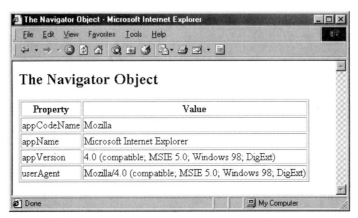

Figure 25-3 Navigator properties in Internet Explorer 5.0 on Windows 98.

Methods

javaEnabled()

This method returns `true` if the browser supports Java *and* currently has it enabled. The method returns `false` otherwise.

taintEnabled()

This method returns `true` if the browser has data tainting enabled, as when the user has set the `NS_ENABLE_TAINT` environment variable. That variable allows JavaScript on one page to discover privileged information about other pages. Netscape removed the capability to perform data tainting in JavaScript 1.2 and replaced it with signed scripts. For information on JavaScript security, see `http://developer.netscape.com/docs/manuals/js/client/jsguide/sec.htm`.

Event Handlers

None. `Navigator` does not correspond to an HTML element.

25.21 The Number Object

The `Number` object accesses information about numbers. You do not need to create an object of this type to access the properties; instead, you can access `Number.propertyName`. The main reason for making a `Number` object is to call `toString()`, which lets you specify a radix.

Constructor

new Number(value)

This constructs a `Number` object for the specified primitive value.

Properties

MAX_VALUE

This property specifies the largest number representable in JavaScript.

MIN_VALUE

This property specifies the smallest number representable in JavaScript.

NaN

This property is the special not-a-number value. Use the global `isNaN` function to compare to it, since all comparisons with `NaN` return `false`, including testing (`Number.NaN == Number.NaN`).

NEGATIVE_INFINITY

This property represents negative overflow values. For instance, `Number.MAX_VALUE` times –2 returns this value. This value times any number is this value. Any number divided by this value is 0, except that an infinite value divided by another infinite value is `NaN`.

POSITIVE_INFINITY

This property represents positive overflow values.

Methods

toString()

This method is the same as calling `toString(10)`.

toString(radix)

This method converts a number to a string in the specified radix. For example, Listing 25.3 creates a table of numbers in various radixes. Figure 25–4 shows the result in Netscape 4.7 on Windows 98.

Listing 25.3 `NumberToString.html`

```
<!DOCTYPE HTML PUBLIC "-//W3C//DTD HTML 4.0 Transitional//EN">
<HTML>
<HEAD>
  <TITLE>Converting Numbers to Strings</TITLE>

<SCRIPT TYPE="text/javascript">
<!--

function makeNumberTable(numberList, radixList) {
  document.write("<TABLE BORDER=1>\n<TR>");
  for(var i=0; i<radixList.length; i++) {
    document.write("<TH>Base " + radixList[i]);
  }
  var num;
  for(var i=0; i<numberList.length; i++) {
    document.write("\n<TR>");
    num = new Number(numberList[i]);
    for(var j=0; j<radixList.length; j++) {
      document.write("<TD>" + num.toString(radixList[j]));
    }
  }
  document.writeln("\n</TABLE>");
}

// -->
</SCRIPT>
</HEAD>

<BODY BGCOLOR="WHITE">
<H1>Converting Numbers to Strings</H1>

<SCRIPT TYPE="text/javascript">
<!--

var nums = new Array(0, 1, 2, 4, 5, 6, 7, 8, 9, 10, 15, 100,
                     512, 1000);
var radixes = new Array(10, 2, 8, 16);

makeNumberTable(nums, radixes);

// -->
</SCRIPT>

</BODY>
</HTML>
```

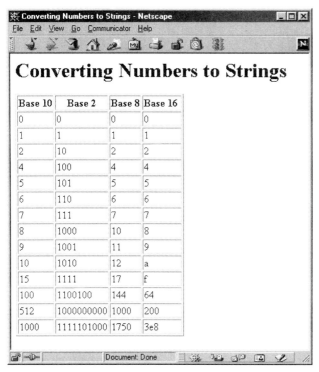

Figure 25–4 The Number object lets you print numbers in any radix.

valueOf()

This method returns the primitive number value associated with the Number.

Event Handlers

None. Number does not correspond to an HTML element.

25.22 The Object Object

Object is the object upon which all others are built. Properties and methods here are shared by *all* JavaScript objects.

Constructors

new Object()
This constructor builds a generic `Object`.

new Object(primitiveValue)
Depending on the argument type, this constructor creates a `Number`, `String`, `Boolean`, or `Function` "wrapper" object.

{prop1:val1, prop2:val2, ... , propN:valN}
You can also create objects by using "literal" notation.

Properties

constructor
This read-only property refers to the JavaScript function that created the object instance.

prototype
This property is not actually a property of `Object`, but rather of all constructor functions. It is mentioned here since it is used in a general-purpose way for all user-defined objects. See Section 24.3 (Mastering JavaScript Syntax) for more details.

Methods

assign(value)
This method is called when an object of the type you define appears on the left side of an assignment operation. In most cases, the version of `assign` that you build calls `new` and fills in fields appropriately.

eval(javaScriptCode)
This method takes an arbitrary string and evaluates the result.

toString()
This method generates a string for the object. You define this in your classes to get custom string representations.

valueOf()
This method returns the primitive value this `Object` represents if one is present. See the `Number` object (Section 25.21).

Event Handlers

None.

25.23 The Option Object

The Option object represents OPTION entries in a SELECT element. It is normally accessed through the options array of a Select object, which in turn is accessed through the elements array of a Form object.

Constructors

new Option()
new Option(text)
new Option(text, value)
new Option(text, value, defaultSelected)
new Option(text, value, defaultSelected, selected)

These constructors create a new Option object, which you can dynamically insert into a Select object by placing it on the end of the options array.

Properties

defaultSelected

This Boolean property determines whether the Option is selected by default. It is specified through the SELECTED attribute and is read-only.

index

This property gives the position of this Option within its Select object's options array. It is read-only.

selected

This property is a Boolean specifying whether or not the option is currently selected. It is read/write.

text

This property gives the text following the option in the SELECT element. It is read/write.

value

This property designates the value that is transmitted along with the `Select` object's name when the form is submitted. It is initially specified through the VALUE attribute and is read/write.

Methods

None.

Event Handlers

None. The `onblur`, `onfocus`, and `onchange` handlers are associated with the enclosing `Select` object, not with the `Option` object itself.

25.24 The Password Object

The `Password` object corresponds to HTML elements created through `<INPUT TYPE="PASSWORD" ...>`. Password objects are normally accessed through the `elements` array of the enclosing `Form` object or, if both it and the form are named, through `document.formName.passwordName`.

Properties

defaultValue

This read-only property is the initial value as given in the VALUE attribute.

form

This read-only property is the `Form` object containing the password field.

name

This read-only property is the value of the NAME attribute.

type

This read-only property contains the value `password`.

value

This property gives the plain-text value of the password field. On a Unix system, a string of asterisks shows you the number of characters the user entered, but not the actual value.

Methods

blur()

This method removes the keyboard focus from the element.

focus()

This method gives the keyboard focus to the element.

select()

This method highlights the text in the element. If the user types, the input replaces the existing text.

Event Handlers

onblur()

This method is called when the password field loses the input focus. It is normally specified by means of the onBlur attribute.

onchange()

This method is called when the password field loses the input focus after its value has changed. It is normally specified by means of the onChange attribute.

onfocus()

This method is called when the password field gets the input focus. It is normally specified by means of the onFocus attribute.

onkeydown()

This method is called when the user first presses any key in the password field. Returning false cancels the input of the character.

onkeypress()

When the user first presses a key, this method is called after onkeydown. It is also called repeatedly when the key is held down, while onkeydown is not. Returning false cancels the input of the character.

onkeyup()

This method is called when the user releases a key.

25.25 The Plugin Object

This section describes an installed plug-in, accessible through the `navigator.plugins` array. This array gives the plug-ins installed in the browser, not the objects in the current document that require plug-ins; for that information, see the `embeds` array of `Document`. `Plugin` is an unusual object in that it has normal properties and you can index it as an array (remember that JavaScript arrays are really just objects with number-valued property names). Each element of this array is a `MimeType` object. See Section 24.4 (Using JavaScript to Customize Web Pages) for an example of using `Plugin` and its associate `MimeType` objects.

Properties

description
This property is a textual description of the plug-in, provided by the plug-in vendor. It is read-only.

filename
This property gives the name of the file containing the code for the plug-in. It is read-only.

length
This property specifies the number of `MimeType` objects in the array.

name
This property gives a short name for the plug-in. You can use the name as an index into the `document.plugins` array.

Methods

None.

Event Handlers

None. A `Plugin` does not correspond to any HTML element.

25.26 The Radio Object

The Radio object corresponds to HTML input elements created inside a form through <INPUT TYPE="RADIO" ...>. Radio objects are normally accessed through the elements array of the enclosing Form object. If both the Radio object and the surrounding Form are named, you can access the Radio object through document.formName.radioName.

Properties

checked
This is a Boolean property specifying whether the radio button is currently checked. It is read/write.

defaultChecked
This is a Boolean specifying whether the radio button should be initially set. It is set through the CHECKED attribute and is read-only in JavaScript.

form
This read-only property refers to the Form object containing the radio button.

name
This property gives the name of the radio button as given in the NAME attribute. Remember that the whole point of radio buttons is that multiple entries share the same name but only one can be checked at any one time. The property is read-only.

type
This property contains the string radio. Since all Element objects have this property, it can be used to differentiate among them when the form.elements array is looked at. It is read-only.

value
This property gives the value that is sent with the name to the CGI program if the form is submitted when the radio button is checked. It is read/write.

Methods

blur()
This method removes the keyboard focus from the radio button.

click()

This method acts as though the radio button was clicked, but it does not trigger the onClick handler. Thus, calling this method is just like setting the checked property.

focus()

This method gives the keyboard focus to the radio button.

Event Handlers

onblur()

This method is called when the radio button loses the input focus. It is normally set through the onBlur attribute, as below.

```
<INPUT TYPE="RADIO" ...
       onBlur="doSomeAction()">
```

onclick()

This method is called when the user clicks the radio button, but not when the click method is called programmatically. It is usually specified through the onClick attribute of the input element.

onfocus()

This method is called when the radio button gains the input focus. It is normally set through the onFocus attribute.

25.27 The RegExp Object

Netscape 4.0 introduced the RegExp object to represent regular expressions and added support for it in the String object through the match, replace, search, and split methods.

Constructors

new RegExp("pattern")

This constructor builds a regular expression. A regular expression is a string containing some special characters that Java uses to check for occurrences of certain patterns in strings. These characters are listed in Table 25.1, but the most important three are +, which means "match one or more occurrences of the previous character"; *, which means "match zero or more occurrences of the previous character"; and ?, which means "match zero or one occurrence of the previous character." In the absence of these special characters, characters in the regular expression are matched exactly against some comparison string. For example, the following regular expression means "a 'z', followed by one or more 'a's, followed by a 'b', followed by zero or more 'c's, followed by zero or one 'd', followed by an 'e'."

```
var re = new RegExp("za+bc*d?e");
```

RegExp has a test method that reads a string and returns true if and only if it contains the regular expression. Given the above definition of re, all of the following would return true:

```
re.test("zabcde");
re.test("xxxxxzabcdexxxxx");
re.test("zaaaabcde");
re.test("zaaaabde");
re.test("zaaaabe");
re.test("XXzaabcccccdeYY");
```

new RegExp("pattern", "g")

This constructor builds a regular expression for global matches in a string. String has a match method that returns an array describing the matches against a particular string. If g is not specified, the first match is returned. With g, all matches are returned. For example, the first call to exec below returns an array containing abc, and the second returns an array containing abc and abbbbc.

```
var str = "abcabbbbcABCABBBBC";
var re1 = new RegExp("ab+c");
var re2 = new RegExp("ab+c", "g");
var result1 = str.match(re1);
var result2 = str.match(re2);
```

new RegExp("pattern", "i")

This constructor builds a regular expression for case-insensitive matches.

new RegExp("pattern", "gi")

This constructor builds a regular expression for global, case-insensitive matches. For example, the following builds an array containing abc, abbbbc, ABC, and ABBBBC.

```
var str = "abcabbbbcABCABBBBC";
var re = new RegExp("ab+c", "gi");
var result = str.match(re);
```

/pattern/

This notation is shorthand for new RegExp("pattern"). For example, the following two statements create equivalent regular expressions.

```
var re1 = /ab+c/;
var re2 = new RegExp("ab+c");
```

See further examples in Section 25.31 (The String Object).

/pattern/g

This notation is shorthand for `new RegExp("pattern", "g")`.

/pattern/i

This notation is shorthand for `new RegExp("pattern", "i")`.

/pattern/gi

This notation is shorthand for `new RegExp("pattern", "gi")`.

Properties

These are properties of the global `RegExp` object, not of individual regular expressions. Thus, they are always accessed through `RegExp.propertyName`. The short version of the property names (`$_`, `$*`, etc.) are taken from the Perl language.

input
$_

If a regular expression's `exec` or `test` methods are called with no associated string, the expression uses the value of this global property. When an event handler for a `Text`, `TextArea`, `Select`, or `Link` object is invoked, this property is automatically filled in with the associated text. This property is read/write.

lastMatch
$&

This property gives the last matched substring. It is filled in after `exec` is called and is read-only.

lastParen
$+

This property gives the value of the last parenthesized match. It is filled in after `exec` is called and is read-only.

leftContext
$`

This property gives the left part of the string, up to but not including the most recent match. It is filled in after `exec` is called and is read-only.

multiline
$*

This property is a `Boolean` determining if matching should occur across line breaks. Set this property before calling `exec`; the `Textarea` event handler automatically sets this property to `true`. It is read/write.

rightcontext
$'

This property gives the right part of the string, starting after the most recent match. It is filled in after `exec` is called and is read-only.

$1
$2
...
$9

These properties give the values of the first nine parenthesized matches. They are filled in after `exec` is called and are read-only.

Methods

These methods belong to individual regular expression objects, not to the global `RegExp` object.

compile(pattern, flags)

This method compiles a regular expression for faster execution.

exec(string)

This method searches the string for the regular expression, filling in the fields of the `RegExp` object as described under Properties. As a shorthand, you can use `someRegExp(string)` instead of `someRegExp.exec(string)`.

exec()

This method is the same as `exec(RegExp.input)`.

test(string)

This method simply determines whether the string contains at least one occurrence of the regular expression, returning `true` or `false`. Using `someRegExp.test(string)` is equivalent to using `string.search(someRegExp)`.

Event Handlers

None. `RegExp` does not correspond to an HTML element.

Special Patterns in Regular Expressions

The discussion of the `RegExp` constructors explained the purpose of the +, *, and ? characters. Table 25.1 gives a complete list of special characters and patterns. For clarity in the examples, we typically say something like "`/ab+c/` matches `abbbc`", but note that `/ab+c/` also matches `XXabbbc` and `XXabbbcYYYY`; i.e., the string only has to *contain* a match, not *be* a match.

Table 25.1 Special Regular Expression Patterns

Pattern	*Interpretation*
+	Match one or more occurrences of the previous character. For instance, `/ab+c/` will match `abc` and `abbbbbc`, but not `ac`.
*	Match zero or more occurrences of the previous character. For instance, `/ab*c/` will match `ac`, `abc`, and `abbbbbc`.
?	Match zero or one occurrence of the previous character. For instance, `/ab?c/` will match `ac` and `abc`, but not `abbbbbc`.
.	Match exactly one character. For instance, `/a.c/` matches `abc` or `aqc`, but not `ac` or `abbc`. A newline does *not* match ".".
\	Treat the next character literally if it is a special character; treat it specially otherwise. For instance, `/a\**b/` matches `ab`, `a*b`, and `a*****b`.
(pattern)	Match *pattern*, but also "remember" the match for access through the $*N* properties of `RegExp`.
p1|p2	Match either *p1* or *p2*. For instance `/foo|bar/` matches `football` and `barstool`.
{*n*}	Match exactly *n* occurrences of the previous character. For instance, `/ab{3}c/` matches `abbbc` but not `abbc` or `abbbbc`.
{*n,*}	Match at least *n* occurrences of the previous character. For instance, `/ab{3,}c/` matches `abbbc` and `abbbbc` but not `abbc`.

Table 25.1 Special Regular Expression Patterns *(continued)*

Pattern	*Interpretation*
{*n1,n2*}	Match at least *n1* but no more than *n2* occurrences of the previous character.
[$c_1c_2...c_n$]	Match any one of the enclosed characters. For instance, /a[pl]*e/ matches ae, apple, and allpe. You can use dashes to represent series: e.g., [a-z] for any lowercase character, [0-7] for any digit from 0 to 7, and so forth.
[^$c_1c_2...c_n$]	Match any one character that is not part of the designated set. For instance, /a[^pl]*e/ matches ae and aqqxxe but not apple or allpe.
\b, \B	Match a word boundary (\b) or any one nonword-boundary character (\B). For example, /a\bc/ matches "a c" but not "abc"; /a\Bc/ matches "abc" but not "a c".
\w, \W	Match any word (\w) or nonword (\W) character. \w is equivalent to [A-Za-z0-9_], and \W is like [^A-Za-z0-9_].
\d, \D	Match any digit (\d) or nondigit (\D). Equivalent to [0-9] or [^0-9], respectively.
\f, \n, \r, \t, \v	Match formfeed, linefeed, carriage return, tab, and vertical tab, respectively.
\s, \S	Match any white space (\s) or non-white-space character (\S). \s is equivalent to [\f\n\r\t\v], and \S is the same as [^\f\n\r\t\v].
/*xxx*/	Match the character represented by the ASCII code *xxx*.

25.28 The Reset Object

The Reset object corresponds to buttons created through <INPUT TYPE="RESET" ...> in an HTML form. Reset objects are normally accessed through the elements array of the enclosing Form object. If both the button and the form are named, they can also be accessed through document.formName.reset-ButtonName.

Properties

form

This property gives the Form object containing the button. It is read-only.

name

If the button used the NAME attribute, this property retrieves it. The property is read-only.

type

This property is always equal to reset. All Element objects contain this property, so it can be used to distinguish among the various types. It is read-only.

value

This property gives the label of the button. It is read/write.

Methods

blur()

This method removes the keyboard focus from the button.

click()

This method acts as though the button was clicked, but without triggering the onClick handler. You can use the form's reset method instead of click.

focus()

This method gives the keyboard focus to the button.

Event Handlers

onblur()

This method is called when the button loses the input focus. It is normally set through the onBlur attribute, as below.

```
<INPUT TYPE="RESET" ...
      onBlur="doSomeAction()">
```

onclick()

This method is called when the user clicks on the button, but not when the `click` method is called programmatically. It is normally set through the `onClick` attribute:

```
<INPUT TYPE="RESET" ...
        onClick="doSomeAction()">
```

If the method returns `false`, then the form is not actually reset. For example,

```
<INPUT TYPE="RESET" ...
        onClick="return(maybeReset())">
```

The same effect can be achieved by `onReset` handler on the form containing the button.

ondblclick()

This method is called on the second click of a double click. The `onclick` handler, if any, will be called first. It is set by the `onDblClick` attribute. It is not supported on the Macintosh or in Netscape 6.

onfocus()

This method is called when the button gains the input focus. It is normally set through the `onFocus` attribute.

25.29 The Screen Object

The `Screen` object, accessible through the global `screen` variable, contains information about the current screen's resolution and color.

Properties

availHeight

This read-only property gives the height of the screen (in pixels), minus space occupied by semipermanent user interface elements such as the Windows 98 task bar.

availWidth

This property gives the width of the screen (in pixels), minus space occupied by semipermanent user interface elements. It is read-only.

colorDepth

This property specifies the number of simultaneous colors that can be displayed. It is read-only.

height

This read-only property gives the height of the screen in pixels.

width

This read-only property gives the width of the screen in pixels.

pixelDepth

This property specifies the number of bits per pixel being used for color. It is read-only.

Methods

None.

Event Handlers

None. Screen does not correspond to an HTML element.

25.30 The Select Object

A Select object corresponds to an HTML element created through <SELECT ...>. It is normally accessed through the elements array of the enclosing Form. If the Form and Select objects both have names, you can also use document.formName.selectName.

Listing 25.4 shows a page that presents a pull-down menu of color choices. Choosing an entry changes the page's background color.

Listing 25.4 `SelectColor.html`

```
<!DOCTYPE HTML PUBLIC "-//W3C//DTD HTML 4.0 Transitional//EN">
<HTML>
<HEAD>
  <TITLE>Changing the Background Color</TITLE>
<SCRIPT TYPE="text/javascript">
<!--

function setBackgroundColor() {
  var selection = document.colorForm.colorSelection;
  document.bgColor =
    selection.options[selection.selectedIndex].value;
}

// -->
</SCRIPT>
</HEAD>
<BODY BGCOLOR="WHITE">
<H1>Changing the Background Color</H1>

<FORM NAME="colorForm">
<SELECT NAME="colorSelection"
        onChange="setBackgroundColor()">
  <OPTION VALUE="#FFFFFF" SELECTED>White
  <OPTION VALUE="#C0C0C0">Gray
  <OPTION VALUE="#FF0000">Red
  <OPTION VALUE="#00FF00">Green
  <OPTION VALUE="#0000FF">Blue
</SELECT>

</FORM>

</BODY>
</HTML>
```

Properties

form

This property refers to the `Form` object containing the selection element. It is read-only.

length

This property specifies the number of `Option` elements contained in the selection. It is the same as `options.length` and is read-only.

name

This property gives the name as specified through the `NAME` attribute. It is read-only.

options

This property is an array of `Option` objects contained in the selection. You are permitted to add `Option` objects to the end of this array.

selectedIndex

This property gives the index of the currently selected option. It will be `-1` if none is selected and will give the first selected index for `Select` elements that were created through `<SELECT ... MULTIPLE>`. It is read/write.

type

This property contains either `select-one` or `select-multiple`, depending on whether the `MULTIPLE` attribute was included. It is read-only.

Methods

blur()

This method removes the keyboard focus from the selection.

focus()

This method gives the keyboard focus to the selection.

Event Handlers

onblur()

This method is called when the selection loses the input focus. It is normally set through the `onBlur` attribute, as below.

```
<SELECT ... onBlur="doSomeAction()">
```

onchange()

This method is called when the selection loses the input focus after the selected option has changed. See Listing 25.4 for an example of its use.

onfocus()

This method is called when the selection gains the input focus. It is normally set through the `onFocus` attribute.

25.31 The String Object

String is an important datatype in JavaScript. It does not correspond directly to any particular HTML elements but is widely used.

Constructor

new String(value)
This constructor builds a new String.

Properties

length
This read-only property gives the number of characters in the string.

Methods

anchor(name)
This method returns a copy of the current string, embedded between `<A NAME="name">` and `</A>`. For example,

```
"Chapter One".anchor("Ch1")
```

evaluates to

```
'<A NAME="Ch1">Chapter One</A>'
```

big()
This method returns a copy of the string, embedded between `<BIG>` and `</BIG>`.

blink()
This method returns a copy of the string, embedded between `<BLINK>` and `</BLINK>`.

bold()
This method returns a copy of the string, embedded between `<B>` and `</B>`. For example,

```
"Wow".italics().bold()
```

evaluates to

```
"<B><I>Wow</I></B>"
```

charAt(index)

This method returns a one-character string taken from the character at the specified location. Strings, like most datatypes in JavaScript, are zero indexed.

charCodeAt()
charCodeAt(index)

The first method returns `charCodeAt(0)`. The second method returns the ISO Latin-1 number for the character at the designated location. The first 127 values correspond to ASCII values.

concat(suffixString)

This method concatenates two strings. The following two forms are equivalent.

```
var newString = string1.concat(string2);
var newString = string1 + string2;
```

escape(string)

The `escape` method is actually not a method of `String` but rather is a standard top-level function. However, because it is used for string manipulation, it is described here. It URL-encodes a string so that it can be attached to the query portion (`search` property) of a `Location` object. Note that this method replaces spaces with `%20`, not with `+`. For example, the following statement results in Figure 25-5.

```
alert(escape("Hello, world!"));
```

Figure 25-5 The `escape` method is used to URL-encode.

See unescape for URL decoding.

fixed()

This method returns a copy of the string, embedded between `<TT>` and `</TT>`.

fontcolor(colorName)

This method returns a copy of the string, embedded between `<FONT COLOR="colorName">` and `</FONT>`.

fontsize(size)
This method returns a copy of the string, embedded between
`<FONT SIZE=size>` and `</FONT>`.

fromCharCode(code0, code1, ... , codeN)
This method creates a string composed of the designated ISO Latin-1
characters. It is not actually a method of individual string objects, but rather of
the `String` constructor function itself. Thus, it is always called through
`String.fromCharCode(...)`. For example, the following assigns the string
`HELLO` to `helloString`.

```
var helloString =
  String.fromCharCode(72, 69, 76, 76, 79);
```

indexOf(substring)
indexOf(substring, startIndex)
If the specified substring is contained in the string, the first method returns the
beginning index of the first match. Otherwise, `-1` is returned. For example,
here is a `contains` predicate that returns `true` if and only if the second string
is contained somewhere in the first.

```
function contains(string, possibleSubstring) {
  return(string.substring(possibleSubstring) != -1);
}
```

In the second method, if the specified substring is contained somewhere
starting at or to the right of the specified starting point, the beginning index
(relative to the whole string, not with respect to the starting point) of the first
match is returned.

italics()
This method returns a copy of the string, embedded between `<I>` and `</I>`.

lastIndexOf(substring)
lastIndexOf(substring, startIndex)
If the specified substring is contained in the string, the first method returns the
beginning index of the last match. Otherwise, `-1` is returned. In the second
method, if the specified substring is contained somewhere starting at or to the
right of the specified starting point, then the beginning index of the last match
is returned.

link(url)
This method returns a copy of the string, embedded between
`<A HREF="url">` and `</A>`.

match(regExp)

This method returns an array showing the matches of the `RegExp` argument in the string. For example, the following builds an array `result` containing the strings abc, abbbbc, ABC, and ABBBBC.

```
var str = "abcabbbbcABCABBBBC";
var re = /ab+c/gi;
var result = str.match(re);
```

Since the `g` in `re` means "find all" and the `i` means "case insensitive match", this match is interpreted as saying "find all occurrences of an 'a' or 'A' followed by one or more 'b's and/or 'B's followed by a 'c' or 'C'." See the `RegExp` object (Section 25.27) for more details.

replace(regExp, replacementString)

This method returns a new string it formed by replacing the regular expression by the designated replacement string. All occurrences will be replaced if the regular expression includes the `g` (global) designation. For example, the following generates a `result` of `"We will use Java, Java, and Java"`.

```
var str = "We will use C, C++, and Java.";
var re = /C\+*/g;
var result = str.replace(re, "Java");
```

search(regExp)

This method is invoked just like the `match` method but simply returns `true` or `false` depending on whether there was at least one match. If all you care about is whether the string appears, this method is faster than `match`.

slice(startIndex, endIndex)

With a positive ending index, `slice` is just like `substring`. However, you can also supply a negative ending index, which is interpreted as an offset from the end of the string. Here are some examples.

```
var str = "0123456789";
var str2 = str.slice(1, 5);     //  "1234"
var str3 = str.substring(1, 5); //  "1234"
var str4 = str.slice(1, -2);    //  "1234567"
```

small()

This method returns a copy of the string, embedded between `<SMALL>` and `</SMALL>`.

split()

This method returns an array containing the string. Using `split` with a delimiter is much more useful.

split(delimChar)

This method returns an array formed by breaking the string at each occurrence of the delimiter character. For instance, the following creates a three-element array containing the strings foo, bar, and baz (in that order).

```
var test = "foo,bar,baz".split(",");
```

If you use a space as the argument, someString.split(" ") returns an array of the strings that were separated by *any* number of white space characters (spaces, tabs, newlines). This method is the inverse of the join method of Array.

split(regExp)

This variation splits on a regular expression. For example, the following creates a three-element array containing the strings foo, bar, and baz (in that order).

```
var str = "foo,bar,,,,,baz";
var re = /,+/;
var result = str.split(re);
```

split(separator, limit)

This method extracts at most limit entries from the string. The separator can be a delimiter character or a RegExp object.

strike()

This method returns a copy of the string, embedded between <STRIKE> and </STRIKE>.

sub()

This method returns a copy of the string, embedded between _{and}.

substr(startIndex, numChars)

This method returns the substring of the current string that starts at startIndex and is numChars long.

substring(startIndex, endIndex)

This method returns a new string taken from the characters from startIndex (inclusive) to endIndex (exclusive). For example, the following assigns "is" to the variable test.

```
var test = "this is a test".substring(5, 7);
```

sup()

This method returns a copy of the string, embedded between ^{and}.

toLowerCase()

This method returns a copy of the original string, converted to lower case.

toUpperCase()

This method returns a copy of the original string, converted to upper case.

unescape(string)

The unescape method is actually not a method of String but rather is a standard top-level function. However, since it is used for string manipulation, it is described here. It URL-decodes a string but has the unfortunate shortcoming that it does not map + to a space character.

Event Handlers

None. String does not correspond to an HTML element.

25.32 The Submit Object

The Submit object corresponds to buttons created through <INPUT TYPE="SUBMIT" ...> in an HTML form. Submit objects are normally accessed through the elements array of the enclosing Form object. If both the button and the form are named, they can also be accessed through document.formName.submitButtonName.

Properties

form

This read-only property gives the Form object containing the button.

name

If the button used the NAME attribute, this property retrieves it. The property is read-only.

type

This property is always equal to submit. All Element objects contain this property, so it can be used to distinguish among the various types. It is read-only.

value

This property gives the label of the button. It is read/write.

Methods

blur()

This method removes the keyboard focus from the button.

click()

This method acts as though the button was clicked, but it does not trigger the onClick handler. You can use the form's submit method instead of click.

focus()

This method gives the keyboard focus to the button.

Event Handlers

onblur()

This method is called when the button loses the input focus. It is normally set through the onBlur attribute, as below.

```
<INPUT TYPE="SUBMIT" ... onBlur="doSomeAction()">
```

onclick()

This method is called when the user clicks on the button, but not when the click method is called programmatically. It is normally set through the onClick attribute.

```
<INPUT TYPE="SUBMIT" ... onClick="doSomeAction()">
```

If the method returns false, then the form is not actually submitted. For example,

```
<INPUT TYPE="SUBMIT" ... onClick="return(maybeSubmit())">
```

The same effect can be achieved by the onSubmit handler on the form containing the button.

ondblclick()

This method is called on the second click of a double click. The onclick handler, if any, is called first. It is set by the onDblClick attribute. It is not supported on the Macintosh or in Netscape 6.

onfocus()

This method is called when the button gains the input focus. It is normally set through the onFocus attribute.

25.33 The Text Object

The Text object corresponds to HTML elements created through <INPUT TYPE="TEXT" ...>. Text objects are normally accessed through the elements array of the enclosing Form object or, if both it and the form are named, through document.formName.textfieldName.

Properties

defaultValue

This read-only property is the initial value as given in the VALUE attribute.

form

This read-only property is the Form object containing the password field.

name

This read-only property is the value of the NAME attribute.

type

This read-only property contains the value text.

value

This property gives the current text contained in the textfield. It is read/write.

Methods

blur()

This method removes the keyboard focus from the textfield.

focus()

This method gives the keyboard focus to the textfield.

select()

This method highlights the text in the element. If the user types, the input replaces the existing text.

Event Handlers

onblur()

This method is called when the textfield loses the input focus. It is normally specified by means of the `onBlur` attribute.

onchange()

This method is called when the textfield loses the input focus after its value has been changed by the user. It is *not* called each time the user presses a key. It is normally specified by means of the `onChange` attribute.

onfocus()

This method is called when the textfield gets the input focus. It is normally specified by means of the `onFocus` attribute.

onkeydown()

This method is called when the user first presses any key in the textfield. Returning `false` cancels the input of the character, so it can be used to restrict the type of text that can be placed in the field.

onkeypress()

When the user first presses a key, this method is called after `onkeydown`. It is also called repeatedly when the key is held down, whereas `onkeydown` is not. Returning `false` cancels the input of the character.

onkeyup()

This method is called when the user releases a key.

25.34 The Textarea Object

The `Textarea` object corresponds to HTML elements created through `<TEXT-AREA ...>` and `</TEXTAREA>`. `Textarea` objects are normally accessed through the `elements` array of the enclosing `Form` object or, if both it and the form are named, through `document.formName.textareaName`.

Properties

defaultValue
This property is the initial value as given by the text that appears between <TEXTAREA> and</TEXTAREA>. It is read-only.

form
This property is the Form object containing the text area. It is read-only.

name
This property is the value of the NAME attribute. It is read-only.

type
This read-only property contains the value textarea.

value
This property gives the current text contained in the text area. It is read/write; however, there is no way to determine the number of rows or columns used by the textfield, so it may be difficult to insert properly formatted text.

Methods

blur()
This method removes the keyboard focus from the text area.

focus()
This method gives the keyboard focus to the text area.

select()
This method highlights the text in the element. If the user types, the input replaces the existing text.

Event Handlers

onblur()
This method is called when the text area loses the input focus. It is normally specified by means of the onBlur attribute.

onchange()
This method is called when the text area loses the input focus after its value has been changed by the user. It is normally specified by means of the onChange attribute.

onfocus()
This method is called when the text area gets the input focus. It is normally specified by means of the onFocus attribute.

onkeydown()
This method is called when the user first presses any key in the text area. Returning false cancels the input of the character, so it can be used to restrict the type of text that can be placed in the field.

onkeypress()
When the user first presses a key, this method is called after onkeydown. It is also called repeatedly when the key is held down, whereas onkeydown is not. Returning false cancels the input of the character.

onkeyup()
This method is called when the user releases a key.

25.35 The Window Object

The window object describes a browser window or frame. The current window is available through the window reference, but you can omit that prefix when accessing its properties and methods. So, for instance, you can refer to the Document associated with the current window through window.document or simply by document. Similarly, to transfer the current window to a new page, you can set the window.location property or simply set location.

Properties

closed
This Boolean property specifies whether the window has been closed. It is read-only.

defaultStatus
This string specifies the default string that should appear in the status line. It is read/write.

document

This property refers to the Document object contained in the window. See Section 25.5 for details on Document. It is read-only.

frames

This array of Window objects refers to the entries contained in the frames of the current document.

history

This property gives the History object associated with the window. It is read-only.

innerHeight

This property gives the inner size of the browser window. It is read/write; changing it resizes the window.

innerWidth

This property gives the inner width of the browser window. See Section 24.4 (Using JavaScript to Customize Web Pages) for an example of its use. It is read/write; changing it resizes the window.

java

This property is a reference to the JavaPackage object that is the top of the java.* package hierarchy. For example, you can call java.lang.Math.random() to use Java's random number generator instead of JavaScript's or use java.lang.System.out.println to send output to the Java Console. It is read-only.

length

This read-only property is the same as frames.length.

location

This property refers to the Location object for this window, which is the *requested* URL. Due to redirection, this may be different from the *actual* URL. For that, see document.URL. This is a read/write variable; setting it changes the window to display a new document.

locationbar

Signed scripts in Netscape can set the visible property of locationbar to hide or show the location bar. Legal values are true (or 1) and false (or 0).

Math

This property is a reference to the `Math` object.

menubar

Signed scripts in Netscape can set the `visible` property of `menubar` to hide or show the menu bar. Legal values are `true` (or `1`) and `false` (or `0`).

name

When a window is created, you can specify a name. This property retrieves it. It is read/write.

navigator

This property is a reference to the `Navigator` object. It is read-only.

netscape

This property is a reference to the `JavaPackage` object corresponding to the `netscape.*` package. It is read-only.

opener

This property is a reference to the `Window` object, if any, that created this window. It is read/write.

outerHeight

This property gives the outside height of the browser window. It is read/write; changing it resizes the window. Windows smaller than 100 x 100 pixels can only be created from secure (signed) scripts.

outerWidth

This property gives the outside width of the browser window. It is read/write.

Packages

This property is a reference to the `JavaPackage` object that represents the top of the package hierarchy. It is read-only.

pageXOffset

This property gives the x offset of the page with respect to the window's content area. It is useful when you are deciding how much to scroll. It is read-only; use `scrollTo` or `scrollBy` to change it.

pageYOffset

This property gives the y offset of the page with respect to the window's content area. It is useful when you are deciding how much to scroll. It is read-only; use `scrollTo` or `scrollBy` to change it.

parent

This property gives the parent window or frame. For a top-level window `win`, `win.parent` is simply `win`. It is read-only.

personalbar

Signed scripts in Netscape can set the `visible` property of `personalbar` to hide or show the personal (directories) bar. Legal values are `true` (or `1`) and `false` (or `0`).

screen

This property is actually a global variable, not a property of `Window`. However, it is mentioned here since most seemingly global variables (`document`, `Math`, etc.) are really properties of the current window. See Section 25.29.

scrollbars

Signed scripts can set the `visible` property of `scrollbars` to hide or show scrollbars. Legal values are `true` (or `1`) and `false` (or `0`).

self

This property is a reference to the window itself and is synonymous with `window`. It is read-only.

status

This string represents the contents of the status bar. It is read/write. An ill-advised fad in the early JavaScript days was to put scrolling messages in the status bar through this property.

statusbar

Signed scripts can set the `visible` property of `personalbar` to hide or show the status bar. Legal values are `true` (or `1`) and `false` (or `0`).

sun

This property is a reference to the `JavaPackage` object that is the top of the `sun.*` package hierarchy. It is read-only.

tags

This property can be used by JavaScript style sheets to set style sheet properties. See Section 5.2 (Using External and Local Style Sheets) for an example.

toolbar

Signed scripts can set the `visible` property of `toolbar` to hide or show the Netscape toolbar. Legal values are `true` (or `1`) and `false` (or `0`).

top

This property refers to the top-level window containing the current one. It is the same as the current one if frames are not being used. It is read-only.

window

This property is a reference to the window itself and is synonymous with `self`. It is read-only.

Methods

alert(message)

This method displays a message in a pop-up dialog box.

back()

This method switches the window to the previous entry in the history list, as if the user clicked on the Back button.

blur()

This method removes the keyboard focus from the current window, usually by putting the window in the background.

captureEvents(eventType)

This method sets the window to capture all events of the specified type.

clearInterval(intervalID)

The `setInterval` method returns an ID. Supplying the ID to `clearInterval` kills the interval routine.

clearTimeout(timeoutID)

The `setTimeout` method returns an ID. Supplying the ID to `clearTimeout` kills the timeout routine.

close()

This method closes a window. You aren't supposed to be able to close windows that you didn't create, but there are some bugs that let you do this anyhow.

confirm(questionString)

This methods pops up a dialog box displaying your question. If the user presses OK, `true` is returned. Cancel results in `false` being returned. You can embed `\n` (newline) characters in the string to split the question across multiple lines.

enableExternalCapture()
disableExternalCapture()

Signed scripts can capture events in external pages. These two methods enable and disable this capability, respectively.

find()
find(searchString)
find(searchString, caseSensitivityFlag, backwardFlag)

The `find` method searches for strings in the current document. If you omit the search string, the Find dialog box pops up to let the user enter a string. Alternatively, you can supply a search string and optionally two boolean flags. These flags determine if a case-sensitive match should be used (`true` for the second parameter) or if the file should be searched from the end going backward (`true` for the third parameter). The methods return `true` if the string was found, `false` otherwise.

focus()

This method gives the specified window the keyboard focus. On most platforms, getting the focus brings the window to the front.

forward()

This method moves the window forward in the history list.

handleEvent(event)

If `captureEvents` has been set, then events of the specified type get passed to `handleEvent`.

home()

This method switches the window to the home document, as if the user clicked on the Home button.

moveBy(x, y)

This method moves the window on the screen by the specified number of pixels. In Netscape, moving the window off the screen requires a signed script, but even so, this method can easily be abused.

moveTo(x, y)

This method moves the window to an absolute location on the screen. In Netscape, moving the window off the screen requires a signed script, but even so, this method can easily be abused.

open(url, name)
open(url, name, features)
open(url, name, features, replaceFlag)

This method can be used to find an existing window or to open a new one. To avoid confusion with `document.open`, it is common practice to use `window.open(...)` instead of simply `open(...)`. Specifying an empty string for the URL opens a blank window. You can then write into it using that window's `document` property. The name can be used for other JavaScript methods or as the `TARGET` attribute in `A`, `BASE`, `AREA`, and `FORM` elements. The `replaceFlag` specifies whether the new window replaces the old entry in the history list (`true`) or whether a new entry should be created (`false`). The `features` string gives comma-separated *feature=value* entries (with *no* spaces!) and determines what browser features the window should include (all if `features` is omitted). Using *feature* is shorthand for *feature*=yes. If the `features` entry is omitted, *all* standard features are used, regardless of what the user has set in the preferences. Legal feature names are summarized in Table 25.2. Listing 25.5 (at the end of this section) gives a couple of examples of using `window.open`, with results shown in Figures 25–6 through 25–9. Also see the window-creation example in Section 24.10.

Core Warning

Feature lists should not have any blank spaces, or they will not be parsed properly.

Table 25.2 Features available in the open method

Feature	Legal Values	Meaning
alwaysLowered	yes/no	Should window always be below others? Available only with signed scripts.
alwaysRaised	yes/no	Should window always be above others? Available only with signed scripts.
dependent	yes/no	Is window a child of creating window? That is, should it close when parent window closes and be omitted from window's task bar?
directories	yes/no	Show the directory buttons ("What's Cool?", etc.)?
hotkeys	yes/no	Disable most hotkeys?
innerHeight	pixels	Sets the content area height. Unix users should note that .Xdefaults entries can override this value.
innerWidth	pixels	Sets the content area width. Unix users should note that .Xdefaults entries can override this value.
location	yes/no	Show the current location textfield?
menubar	yes/no	Show the menu bar?
outerHeight	pixels	Sets the outside window height.
outerWidth	pixels	Sets the outside window width.
resizable	yes/no	Let the user stretch the window?
screenX	pixels	Sets the location of the left side of the window.
screenY	pixels	Sets the location of the top side of the window.
scrollbars	yes/no	Use scrollbars if necessary?
status	yes/no	Show the status line at the bottom?
titlebar	yes/no	Include title bar? Disabling it requires a signed script.
toolbar	yes/no	Show the toolbar that contains back/forward/home/stop buttons?
z-lock	yes/no	Prevent window from being raised/lowered? Available only in signed scripts.

print()

This method prints the document as though by the Print button. Note that the method brings up a dialog box; there is (fortunately) no way to print documents without user confirmation.

prompt(message)
prompt(message, defaultText)

These methods pop up a dialog box with a simple textfield, returning the value entered when it is closed. You can supply the initial string as the second argument if desired.

releaseEvents(eventType)

This method tells JavaScript to stop capturing the specified event type.

resizeBy(x, y)

This method lets you change the size of the browser window by the specified amount.

resizeTo(x, y)

This method changes the *outer* width and height to the specified size.

routeEvent(event)

This method is used by `handleEvent` to send the event along the normal event-handling path.

scrollBy(x, y)

This method scrolls by the specified number of pixels.

scrollTo(x, y)

This method scrolls the document so that the upper-left corner of the window shows the specified location of the document.

setInterval(code, delay)

This method *repeatedly* executes a string representing code until the window is destroyed or `clearInterval` is called. See `setTimeout`.

setTimeout(code, delay)

Given a string specifying JavaScript code and a delay time in milliseconds, this method executes the code after the specified delay unless `clearTimeout` is called with the `setTimeout` return value in the meantime. Note that `setTimeout` *returns* immediately; it just doesn't *execute* the code until later.

stop()

This method stops the current document download, as if through the Stop button.

Event Handlers

onblur()

This is the method called when the window loses the keyboard focus. It is normally set through the `onBlur` attribute of `BODY` or `FRAMESET`, as in the following example.

```
<BODY onBlur="alert('We will miss you')">
...
</BLUR>
```

A more useful application might be to halt certain processing when the user leaves the window, restarting it through `onfocus`.

ondragdrop()

This Netscape method is called when a file or shortcut is dragged onto the Navigator window and released. If the method returns `false`, the normal action of loading the file is canceled. It is set by the `onDragDrop` attribute.

onerror()

This method is called when a JavaScript error occurs. This error handler has no associated HTML attribute, so you have to set it directly, as in the example below.

```
function reportError() {
  return(!confirm("An error occurred.\n" +
                  "Please report it to\n" +
                  "gates@microsoft.com.\n\n" +
                  "See more details?"));
}

onerror = reportError;
```

Returning `true` prevents the browser from also reporting the error, so in the preceding example, users only see the standard error report if they click OK in the confirmation dialog box. Setting the value of `onerror` to `null` suppresses error reporting altogether.

onfocus()

This method is called when the window gets the keyboard focus. It is normally set through the `onFocus` attribute of `BODY` or `FRAMESET`, as in the following example.

```
<FRAMESET ROWS=...
          onFocus="alert('Welcome back')">
...
</FRAMESET>
```

onload()

This method is called when the browser finishes loading the page. It is normally set through the `onLoad` attribute of `BODY` or `FRAMESET`. It is useful for recording that the document finished loading so that functions that depend on various pieces of the document will operate correctly.

onmove()

This method is called *after* the window is moved (either by the user or programmatically). It is set through the `onMove` attribute, as follows:

```
<BODY onMove="alert('Hey, move me back!')" ...>
...
</BODY>
```

onresize()

This method is called when the user or JavaScript code stretches or shrinks the window. It is normally set by the `onResize` attribute.

onunload()

This method is called when the user leaves the page. It is normally set through the `onUnload` attribute of `BODY` or `FRAMESET`.

An Example of the open Method

Listing 25.5 gives examples of several different features used in the `window.open` method. Figures 25–6 through 25–9 show the results.

Listing 25.5   `OpenWindows.html`

```html
<!DOCTYPE HTML PUBLIC "-//W3C//DTD HTML 4.0 Transitional//EN">
<HTML>
<HEAD>
  <TITLE>Opening Windows with JavaScript</TITLE>

<SCRIPT TYPE="text/javascript">
<!--
```

(continued)

Listing 25.5   `OpenWindows.html` *(continued)*

```
function openSmallWindow() {
  window.open("http://home.netscape.com/",
              "smallWindow",
              "width=375,height=125");
}

function openMediumWindow() {
  window.open("http://home.netscape.com/",
              "mediumWindow",
              "width=550,height=225," +
              "menubar,scrollbars,status,toolbar");
}

function openBigWindow() {
  window.open("http://home.netscape.com/",
              "bigWindow",
              "width=850,height=450," +
              "directories,location,menubar," +
              "scrollbars,status,toolbar");
}

// -->
</SCRIPT>
</HEAD>

<BODY>
<H1>Opening Windows with JavaScript</H1>

<FORM>
  <INPUT TYPE="BUTTON" VALUE="Open Small Window"
         onClick="openSmallWindow()">
  <INPUT TYPE="BUTTON" VALUE="Open Medium Window"
         onClick="openMediumWindow()">
  <INPUT TYPE="BUTTON" VALUE="Open Big Window"
         onClick="openBigWindow()">
</FORM>

</BODY>
</HTML>
```

Figure 25–6 `OpenWindows.html` before any buttons are clicked.

Figure 25–7 Using `window.open` with a width and height but no other features results in a bare-bones, undecorated browser window. [© 2001 Netscape Communications Corp. Used with permission. All rights reserved.]

Figure 25–8 This version creates a moderately decorated browser window. [© 2001 Netscape Communications Corp. Used with permission. All rights reserved.]

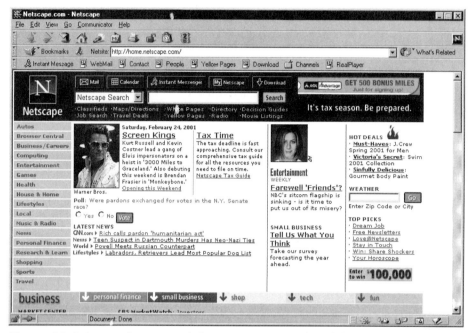

Figure 25–9 By specifying enough features, you can make a fully loaded browser window. [© 2001 Netscape Communications Corp. Used with permission. All rights reserved.]

25.36 Summary

Whew! You finished the book. Congratulations. We hope you are now comfortable with the basics of HTML, Java, Servlets, and JavaScript, so you can develop Web applications from beginning to end. Now you can go back and focus on specific areas that you skimmed earlier. You're familiar with standard HTML; maybe now you should go back and look at style sheets or layers. You have a handle on Java; maybe this is the time to try out threading, RMI, or JDBC. Perhaps you've used CGI but haven't seen what servlets can buy you. Or maybe you now want to see how Java-Script regular expressions can help you. But don't worry, you don't have to be an expert in everything; few people are. No matter where you choose to concentrate, a solid base will serve you well.

But before you move on, relax and take a day off. Oh, and tell your boss that we said you deserve a raise. Hmm, 20% ought to do it, don't you think?

Have fun!

Index

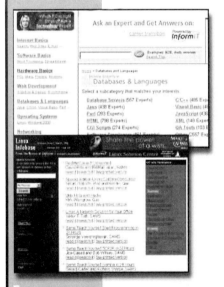

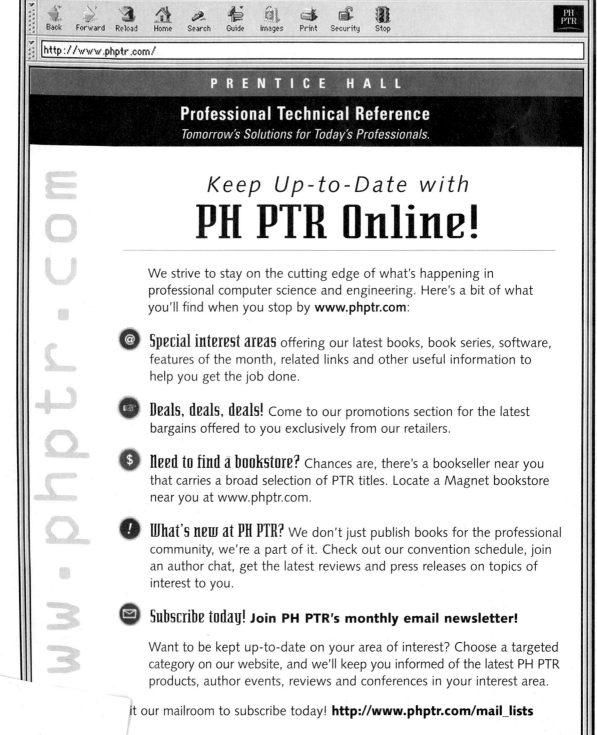